England

THE ROUGH GUIDE

written and researched by

**Robert Andrews, Jules Brown,
Phil Lee and Rob Humphreys**

THE ROUGH GUIDES

THE ROUGH GUIDES

 We set out to do something different when the first Rough Guide was published in 1982. Mark Ellingham, just out of university, was travelling in Greece. He brought along the popular guides of the day, but found they were all lacking in some way. They were either strong on ruins and museums but went on for pages without mentioning a beach or taverna. Or they were so conscious of the need to save money that they lost sight of Greece's cultural and historical significance. Also, none of the books told him anything about Greece's contemporary life – its politics, its culture, its people, and how they lived.

So with no job in prospect, Mark decided to write his own guidebook, one which aimed to provide practical information that was second to none, detailing the best beaches and the hottest clubs and restaurants, while also giving hard-hitting accounts of every sight, both famous and obscure, and providing up-to-the-minute information on contemporary culture. It was a guide that encouraged independent travellers to find the best of Greece, and was a great success, getting shortlisted for the Thomas Cook travel guide award, and encouraging Mark, along with three friends, to expand the series.

The Rough Guide list grew rapidly and the letters flooded in, indicating a much broader readership than had been anticipated, but one which uniformly appreciated the Rough Guide mix of practical detail and humour, irreverence and enthusiasm. Things haven't changed. The same four friends who began the series are still the caretakers of the Rough Guide mission today: to provide the most reliable, up-to-date and entertaining information to independent-minded travellers of all ages, on all budgets.

We now publish more than 150 titles and have offices in London and New York. The travel guides are written and researched by a dedicated team of more than 100 authors, based in Britain, Europe, the USA and Australia. We have also created a unique series of phrasebooks to accompany the travel series, along with an acclaimed series of music guides, and a best-selling pocket guide to the Internet and World Wide Web. We also publish comprehensive travel information on our Web site:

www.roughguides.com

HELP US UPDATE

We've gone to a lot of effort to ensure that the fourth edition of *The Rough Guide to England* is accurate and up-to-date. However, things change — places get "discovered", opening hours are notoriously fickle, restaurants and rooms raise prices or lower standards. If you feel we've got it wrong or left something out, we'd like to know, and if you can remember the address, the price, the time, the phone number, so much the better.

We'll credit all contributions, and send a copy of the next edition (or any other Rough Guide if you prefer) for the best letters. Please mark letters: "Rough Guide England Update" and send to:
Rough Guides, 62–70 Shorts Gardens, London WC2H 9AH, or Rough Guides, 375 Hudson St, New York NY 10014.
Or send email to: mail@roughguides.co.uk
Online updates about this book can be found on Rough Guides' Web site at www.roughguides.com

READERS' LETTERS

We would like to thank all the readers who have taken the time and trouble to write in with comments, suggestions and helpful advice. Thanks, especially, to: S.E. Anderton, Leanne Armstrong, L. Bramley, Graham Bryant, Tamara Edwards-Playne, Colin Hill, D. Hollaway, Professor Richard and Gaynor Hudson, John and Rachel Hyde, A. Johnston, B. Kowalski, Sharon McGrath, P.S. Metcalfe, Lily Neal, Dr Francis M. Russell, Ingrid van Sambeek and Marian Huisenan, Ray Smith, Monica S. Staaf, Paulette Staats, Margaret Steyer, Robert Sulley, A.D. Ridgewell, Dr R.J. Washington, Yvonne Wolff

CONTENTS

Introduction x

PART THREE CONTEXTS 911

LIST OF MAPS

MAP SYMBOLS

Motorway	Gorge	London Underground station
Major road	Waterfall	Metro station
Minor road	Cliffs	Motor racing circuit
Pedestrianised street (town maps)	Caves	Airport
Road with steep incline	Point of interest	Tourist information
Tunnel	Ruin	Post Office
Path	Museum	Hotel
Steps	Stately home	Restaurant
Wall	Public Gardens	Building
Railway	Battlefield	Market
Ferry route	Abbey (regional maps)	Church/cathedral
River	Castle	Built-up-area
National boundary	Church (regional maps)	Park
County boundary	Gate	National Park
Chapter boundary	Bridge	Forest
Mountain peak	Parking	Marshland

INTRODUCTION

Since the 1997 general election, and the rejection of the Conservative party after eighteen years in power, there's been a decidedly upbeat air about **England**. The election of the "New Labour" government has brought about some genuine changes of atmosphere. There's a lot of talk about the importance of "society", a concept much abused during the laissez-faire years of Thatcherism, and England is now being presented as a component part of Europe, whereas previously the attitude to the continent suggested that the Channel Tunnel was a bridgehead into enemy territory. But in several respects the new world isn't really that new. Many of the less appealing aspects of Conservatism – the under-investment in public services, the assumption that big business knows best – are still with us. And, conversely, many of the features that give England its buzz have not sprung into existence overnight – the celebration of "Cool Britannia" began some time before the arrival of Tony Blair. Indeed, the country has maintained its creative momentum consistently from the "Swinging Sixties" to the present day: the music scene is as vibrant as any in the world; the current crop of young artists has as high a profile as David Hockney ever had; all over Europe there are hi-tech and offbeat postmodern buildings that were born on the drawing boards of London; and when Jean-Paul Gaultier runs short of new ideas he comes to London's markets, outlets for Europe's riskiest street fashion.

However, you only have to scratch the surface and you'll find that England's notorious taste for nostalgia still persists. It's not altogether surprising that the English tend to dwell on former glories – as recently as 1950 London was the capital of the sixth wealthiest nation on the planet, but just three decades later it had slipped from the top twenty. History is constantly repackaged and recycled in England, whether in the form of TV costume dramas or industrial theme parks in which people enact the tasks that once supported their communities. The royal family, though dogged by bad press, continues to occupy a prominent place in the English self-image, a fact demonstrated by the extraordinary manner in which the death of Princess Diana was reported and mourned. The mythical tales of King Arthur and Camelot, the island race that spawned Shakespeare, Drake and Churchill, a golden rural past – these are the notions that lie at the heart of "Englishness", and monuments of the country's past are a major part of its attraction. There's a panoply of medieval and monumental towns; and the countryside yields all manner of delights, from walkers' trails around the hills and lakes, through prehistoric stone circles, to traditional rural villages and their pubs. Virtually every town bears a mark of former wealth and power, whether it be a magnificent Gothic cathedral financed from a monarch's treasury, a parish church funded by the tycoons of the medieval wool trade, or a triumphalist Victorian civic building, raised on the income of the British Empire. In the south of England you'll find old dockyards from which the navy patrolled the oceans, while up north there are mills that employed whole town populations. England's museums and galleries – several of them ranking among the world's finest – are full of treasures trawled from Europe and farther afield. And in their grandiose stuccoed terraces and wide esplanades the old resorts bear testimony to the heyday of the English holiday towns, when Brighton, Bath and diverse other towns were as fashionable and elegant as any European spa.

Contemporary England is at the same time a deeply conservative place and a richly multi-ethnic culture through which runs a strain of individualism that often verges on the anarchic. In essence, England's fascination lies in the tension between its inertia and its adventurousness. Which is the truer image of England at the end of the twentieth century: the record-breaking *Sensation* art show at the Royal Academy, with its dissected livestock and sexual mutants, or the ranks of Diana memorabilia in souvenir shops across the land?

Where to go

To get to grips with England, **London** is the place to start. Nowhere else in the country can match the scope and innovation of the metropolis, a colossal, frenetic city, perhaps not as immediately attractive as its European counterparts, but with so much variety that lack of cash is the only obstacle to a great time. It's here that you'll find England's best spread of nightlife, cultural events, museums, galleries, pubs and restaurants. Each of the other large cities, such as **Birmingham, Newcastle, Leeds, Manchester** and **Liverpool**, has its strengths, though to be honest these regional centres don't rank among the most alluring of destinations. For many people they come a long way behind ancient cities such as **Lincoln, York, Salisbury, Durham** and **Winchester**, to name just those with the most celebrated of England's cathedrals. Left adrift by the industrialization of the last century and spared the worst of postwar urban development, these cities remain small-scale and manageable, more hospitable than the big commercial and industrial centres. Most beguiling of all are the long-established **villages** of England, hundreds of which amount to nothing more than a pub, a shop, a gaggle of cottages and a farmhouse offering bed and breakfast – Devon, Cornwall, the Cotswolds and the Yorkshire Dales harbour some especially picturesque specimens, but every county can boast a decent showing of photogenic hamlets.

Evidence of England's pedigree is scattered between its settlements as well. Wherever you're based, you're never more than a few miles from a **ruined castle**, a majestic **country house**, a secluded chapel or a monastery, and in some parts of the country you'll come across the sites of civilizations that thrived here before England existed as a nation. In the southwest there are remnants of a **Celtic** culture that elsewhere was all but eradicated by the Romans, and from the south coast to the northern border you can find traces of **prehistoric** settlers – the most famous being the megalithic circles of Stonehenge and Avebury.

Then of course there's the English **countryside**, an extraordinarily diverse terrain from which Constable, Turner, Wordsworth, Emily Brontë and a host of other native luminaries took inspiration. Most dramatic and best known are the moors and uplands – **Exmoor, Dartmoor, Bodmin Moor**, the **North York Moors** and the **Lake District** – each of which, especially the Lakes, has its over-visited spots, though a brisk walk will usually take you out of the throng. Quieter areas are tucked away in every corner of England, from the lush vales of **Shropshire** near the border with Wales, to the flat waterlands of the eastern **Fens** and the chalk downland of **Sussex**. It's a similar story on the **coast**, where the finest sands and most rugged cliffs have long been discovered, and sizeable resorts have grown to exploit many of the choicest locations. But again, if it's peace you're after, you can find it by heading for the exposed strands of Northumbria, the pebbly flat horizons of East Anglia or the crumbling headlands of Dorset.

When to go

Considering the temperateness of the English **climate**, it's amazing how much mileage the locals get out of the subject – a two-day cold snap is discussed as if it were the onset of a new Ice Age, and a week in the upper 70s Fahrenheit starts rumours of drought. The fact is that English summers rarely get hot and the winters don't get very cold, and there's not a great deal of regional variation, as the chart shows. The average **summer temperature** in the landlocked Midlands is much the same as down on the southwest beaches, and within a degree or two of the average in the north. Summer rainfall is fairly even over all of England as well, though in general the south gets more **hours of sunshine** than the north. Differences between the regions are slightly more marked in **winter**, when the south tends to be appreciably milder and wetter than the north.

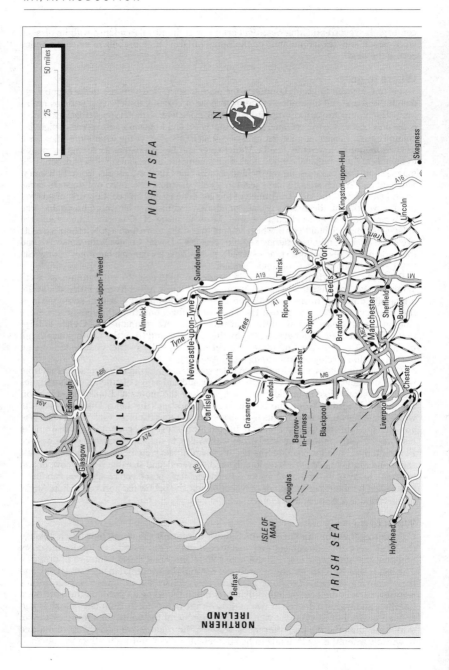

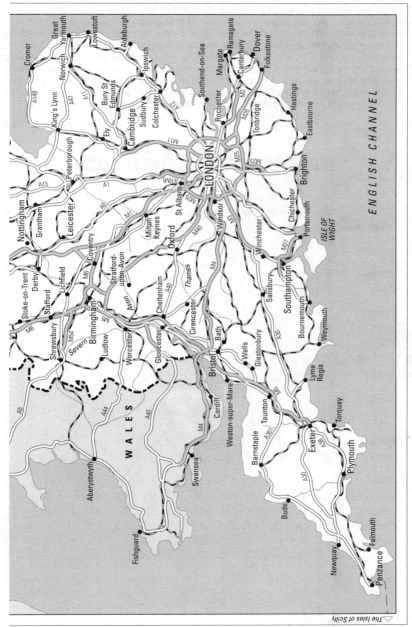

© Crown copyright

The bottom line is that it's impossible to say with any degree of certainty that the weather will be pleasant in any given month. May might be wet and grey one year and gloriously sunny the next, and the same goes for the autumnal months – November stands an equal chance of being crisp and clear or foggy and grim. Obviously, if you're planning to lie on a beach, or camp in the dry, you'll want to go between June and September – a period when you shouldn't go anywhere without booking your accommodation well in advance. Elsewhere, if you're balancing the likely fairness of the weather against the density of the crowds, the best time to get into the countryside or the towns would be between **April and early June** or in **September** or **October**.

AVERAGE TEMPERATURES AND RAINFALL

The figures below represent the average maximum temperatures in °F/°C; and the average monthly rainfall in inches/mm.

	Jan	Feb	Mar	Apr	May	Jun	Jul	Aug	Sept	Oct	Nov	Dec
Birmingham												
(°F)	42	43	48	54	60	66	68	68	63	55	48	44
(°C)	5	6	9	12	16	19	20	20	17	13	9	7
(inches)	3	2.1	2	2.1	2.5	2	2.7	2.7	2.4	2.7	3.3	2.6
(mm)	74	54	50	53	64	50	69	69	61	69	84	67
London												
(°F)	43	44	50	56	62	69	71	71	65	58	50	45
(°C)	6	7	10	13	17	20	22	21	19	15	10	7
(inches)	2.1	1.6	1.5	1.5	1.8	1.8	2.2	2.3	1.9	2.2	2.5	1.9
(mm)	54	40	37	37	46	45	57	59	49	57	64	48
Plymouth												
(°F)	47	47	50	54	59	64	66	67	64	58	52	49
(°C)	8	8	10	12	15	18	19	19	18	15	11	10
(inches)	3.9	2.9	2.7	2.1	2.5	2.1	2.8	3	3.1	3.6	4.5	4.3
(mm)	99	74	69	53	63	53	70	77	78	91	113	110
York												
(°F)	43	44	49	55	61	67	70	69	64	57	49	5
(°C)	6	7	10	13	16	19	21	20	18	14	10	7
(inches)	2.3	1.8	1.5	1.6	2	2	2.4	2.7	2.2	2.2	2.6	2
(mm)	59	46	37	41	50	50	62	68	55	55	65	50

PART ONE

THE

BASICS

BASICS

TRAVELLING FROM NORTH AMERICA

For visitors from the US and Canada, the range of options will always be greatest – and the fares will usually be lowest – flying into London, England's busiest gateway city. Two of London's airports – Heathrow and Gatwick – handle transatlantic flights, and in terms of convenience they are about equal. If you're planning to tour the north of England you might consider one of the growing number of direct flights into Manchester or Birmingham, or even Glasgow in Scotland. Birmingham airport is the one best equipped to get you on your way quickly, since it's directly linked to the rail network. It's also possible to connect from London to several other regional airports, such as Newcastle or the Isle of Man on one of Britain's domestic carriers.

Figure on six and a half hours' **flying time** from New York to any of the British airports (it's an hour extra coming the other way, due to headwinds). Most eastbound flights cross the Atlantic overnight, depositing you at your destination the next morning without much sleep, but if you can manage to stay awake until after dinner that night, you should be over the worst of the jet lag by the next morning. Some flights from the East Coast depart early in the morning, arriving late the same evening, but this lands you in London just as the city is shutting down – a recipe for a disorienting and expensive first night.

SHOPPING FOR TICKETS

Given the enormous volume of air traffic crossing the Atlantic, you should have no problem finding

a seat – the problem will be sifting through all the possibilities. Basic fares are kept very reasonable by intense competition, and discounts by bulk agents and periodic special offers by the airlines themselves can drive prices still lower. Any local **travel agent** should be able to access airlines' up-to-the-minute fares, although in practice they may not have time to research all the possibilities – you might want to call a few airlines directly or check their Web sites for further information (see p.4).

The cheapest tickets widely available from the airlines are **Apex** tickets, which carry certain restrictions: you have to book – and pay – at least 21 days before departure and spend at least 7 days abroad (maximum stay 3 months), and you tend to get penalized if you change your schedule. There are also winter **Super Apex** tickets, sometimes known as "Eurosavers" – slightly less expensive than an ordinary Apex, but limiting your stay to between 7 and 21 days. Some airlines also issue **Special Apex** tickets to those under 24, often extending the maximum stay to a year.

Whatever the airlines are offering, however, any number of specialist travel companies should be able to beat it. These are the outfits you'll see advertising in the Sunday newspaper travel sections, and they come in several forms. **Consolidators** buy up large blocks of tickets that airlines don't think they'll be able to sell at their published fares, and sell them at a discount. Many advertise fares on a one-way basis, enabling you to fly into one city and out from another without penalty. Besides being cheap, consolidators normally don't impose advance purchase requirements (although in busy times you'll want to book ahead just to be sure of getting a ticket), but they do often charge very stiff fees for date changes; note also that airlines generally won't alter tickets after they've gone to a consolidator, forcing you to make changes only through the consolidator. Also, these companies' margins are pretty small, so they make their money by dealing in volume – don't expect them to entertain lots of questions.

Discount agents also wheel and deal in blocks of tickets off-loaded by the airlines, but they typically tend to be most worthwhile to students and under-26s, who can often benefit from their special fares and deals. Agents also often

MAJOR AIRLINES IN NORTH AMERICA

Only direct routes are listed below; many other routeings are possible through these gateway cities.

Aer Lingus (☎1-800/223-6537, www.aerlingus.ie). Boston, Chicago, Los Angeles and New York to Dublin or Shannon with connections to many major British airports.

Air Canada (Canada call ☎1-800/555-1212 for local toll-free number; US ☎1-800/776-3000, www.aircanada.ca). Calgary, Halifax, Montreal, Ottawa, Toronto and Vancouver to London; Ottawa and Toronto to Manchester.

Air India (☎212/751-6200, www.airindia.com). Chicago and New York to London.

American Airlines (☎1-800/433-7300, www.aa.com). Chicago, Dallas/Fort Worth, Los Angeles, Miami, New York and Raleigh to London; Chicago to Birmingham and Manchester; Dallas/Forth Worth to Manchester.

British Airways (☎1-800/247-9297, www.british-airways.com). Atlanta, Baltimore, Boston, Charlotte, Chicago, Dallas/Fort Worth, Denver, Detroit, Houston, Los Angeles, Miami, Montreal, New York, Orlando, Philadelphia, Phoenix, Pittsburgh, San Diego, San Francisco, Seattle, Tampa, Toronto, Vancouver and Washington DC to London (with extensive connections on to other UK destinations); also Chicago, New York and Toronto to Birmingham and Manchester.

Canadian Airlines (Canada ☎1-800/665-1177; US ☎1-800/426-7000, www.cdnair.com). Calgary and Toronto to London.

Continental Airlines (☎1-800/231-0856, www.continental.com). Cleveland, Houston and Newark to London; Newark to Manchester.

Delta Airlines (☎1-800/241-4141, www.delta-air.com). Atlanta and Cincinnatti to London; Atlanta and New York to Manchester.

Kuwait Airways (☎1-800/458-9248, www.kuwait-airways.com). New York to London.

Northwest Airlines (☎1-800/447-4747, www.nwa. com). Detroit and Minneapolis to London.

TWA (☎1-800/221-2000, www.twa.com). St Louis to London.

United Airlines (☎1-800/538-2929, www.ual.com). Chicago, Los Angeles, Newark, New York, San Francisco and Washington DC to London (with many other onward connections possible through a co-operative agreement with British Midland).

Virgin Atlantic Airways (☎1-800/862-8621; www.virgin-atlantic.com). Boston, Chicago, Los Angeles, Miami, Newark, New York, Orlando, San Francisco and Washington DC to London.

offer a range of other travel-related services such as travel insurance, rail passes, youth and student ID cards, car rentals, tours and the like. Some agencies specialize in **charter flights**, which may be even cheaper than anything available on a scheduled flight, but again there's a trade-off: departure dates are fixed and withdrawal penalties are high. **Discount travel clubs** are another option for those who travel a lot – most charge an annual membership fee, which may be worth it for discounts on air tickets, car rental and the like.

Incidentally, don't automatically assume that tickets purchased through a travel specialist will be the least expensive on offer – once you get a quote, check with the airlines and you may turn up an even cheaper promotion. Be advised also that the pool of travel companies is swimming with sharks – exercise caution with any outfit that sounds shifty or impermanent, and never deal with a company that demands cash up front or refuses to accept payment by credit card.

Regardless of where you buy your ticket, the **fare** will depend on when you travel. Fares to Britain are highest from around early June to mid-September; they drop during the shoulder seasons, mid-September to early November and mid-April to early June; and you'll get the best deals during the low season, November through to April (excluding Christmas). The Christmas–New Year holiday period is a law unto itself – if you want to travel at this time, book at least two or three months ahead, and be prepared for fares even higher than those in summer.

A further possibility is to see if you can arrange a **courier flight**, although the hit-or-miss nature of these makes them most suitable for the single traveller who travels light and has a very flexible schedule. In return for shepherding a parcel through customs and possibly giving up your baggage allowance, you can expect to get a highly discounted ticket. A couple of courier outfits are listed in the box opposite; for more options, consult *A Simple Guide to Courier Travel* ($15.95; Carriage Group Publishing).

If England is only one stop on a longer journey, you might want to consider buying a **round-the-world** ticket (RTW). Some travel agents can sell you an "off-the-shelf" RTW ticket that will stop in about half a dozen cities, in which London is very easily included; others will have to assemble one for you, which can be tailored to your needs but is apt to be more expensive. Prices start at around $1400 ($1600 if travelling in summer) for a simple RTW ticket stopping in London.

Prices quoted in the sections below are based on the lowest typical Apex fares, exclusive of tax (which is around $60–85. Youth/student and consolidator tickets will usually be cheaper on high-volume routes, but not necessarily on the more obscure ones. Flying at weekends ordinarily adds $20–60.

FLIGHTS FROM THE US

Dozens of airlines fly from New York to London, and a few fly direct from other **East Coast** and Midwestern hubs. The best low-season fares from New York to London hover around $350 return. Low-season fares to London can also start as low as $360 from Boston, $390 from Washington DC or $430 from Chicago. Delta

DISCOUNT AGENTS, CONSOLIDATORS, TRAVEL CLUBS AND COURIER BROKERS

Air Brokers International, 323 Geary St, Suite 411, San Francisco, CA 94102 (☎1-800/883-3273, *www.airbrokers.com*). Consolidator.

Air Courier Association, 191 University Blvd, Suite 300, Denver, CO 80206 (☎303/278-8810, *www.aircourier.org*). Courier flight broker.

Airtech, 588 Broadway, Suite 204, New York, NY 10012 (☎1-800/575-TECH, *www.airtech.com*). Standby seat broker (mainly from northeastern US cities).

Council Travel, 205 E 42nd St, New York, NY 10017 (☎1-800/226-8624; *www.counciltravel.com*) and branches in many other US cities. Youth/student travel organization.

Educational Travel Center, 438 N Frances St, Madison, WI 53703 (☎1-800/747-5551 or 608/256-5551, *www.edtrav.com*). Student/youth discount agent.

Last Minute Travel Club, 100 Sylvan Rd, Suite 600, Woburn, MA 01801 (☎1-800/LAST-MIN, *www.vacationoutlet.com*). Travel club specializing in standby deals.

Moment's Notice, 7301 New Utrecht Ave, Brooklyn, NY 11204 (☎212/486-0500, *www.moments-notice.com*). Discount travel club.

New Frontiers/Nouvelles Frontières, 12 E 33rd St, New York, NY 10016 (☎1-800/366-6387, *www.nouvelles-frontieres.com*); 1001 Sherbrook East, Suite 720, Montreal, H2L 1L3 (☎514/526-8444, *www.nouvelles-frontieres.com*) and other branches in LA, San Francisco and Quebec City. French discount travel firm.

Now Voyager, 74 Varick St, Suite 307, New York, NY 10013 (☎212/431-1616, *www.nowvoyager-travel.com*). Courier flight broker and consolidator.

Preferred Traveler's Club, 4501 Forbes Blvd, Lanham, MD 20706 (☎1-800/444-9800, *www.emitravel.com*). Discount travel club.

STA Travel, 10 Downing St, New York, NY 10014 (☎1-800/781-4040 or 212/627-3111, *www.sta-travel.com*) and other branches in LA, San Francisco and Boston. Worldwide specialist in independent travel.

TFI Tours International, 34 W 32nd St, New York, NY 10001 (☎1-800/745-8000) and other offices in Las Vegas. Consolidator.

Travac, 989 6th Ave, New York, NY 10018 (☎1-800/872-8800 or 212/563-3303, *www.thetravel-site.com*). Consolidator and charter broker.

Travel Avenue, 10 S Riverside, Suite 1404, Chicago, IL 60606 (☎1-800/333-3335 or 312/876-6866, *www.travelavenue.com*). Discount travel agent.

Travel CUTS, 243 College St, Toronto, ON M5T 1P7 (Canada ☎1-800/667-2887; US 1-416/979-2406, *www.travelcuts.com*), and other branches all over Canada. Student/youth travel organization.

Travelers Advantage, 801 Royal Parkway, Suite 200, Nashville, TN 37214 (☎1-800/548-1116, *www.travelersadvantage.com*). Discount travel club; annual membership required ($59.95).

UniTravel, 11737 Administration, St Louis, MO 63146 (☎1-800/325-2222). Consolidator.

Worldtek Travel, 111 Water St, New Haven, CT 06511 (☎1-800/243-1723, *www.flightsforless.com*). Discount travel agency.

flies from Atlanta for as low as $400, Virgin from Miami or Orlando for $430, TWA from St Louis for $525 and Continental from Houston for about $460. For high-season fares, add $150–250.

Don't assume you'll have to change planes when flying from the **West Coast** – American, BA, United and Virgin all fly nonstop from Los Angeles, with low-season midweek fares starting at around $1700. From Seattle the price will be more in the region of $1800. High-season fares will be at least $200 higher. Travelling overnight on a Saturday can considerably reduce fares – Saturday-night flights out of LA can be as low as $500.

Several airlines fly **to Manchester** from some of the above cities, and American, Aer Lingus and BA fly **to Birmingham** (see box on p.4). Manchester and Birmingham are common rated with London, which means that the Apex fare should be the same. If you fly to London on a discounted ticket, expect to pay about $100 each way for an onward connection within England.

FLIGHTS FROM CANADA

In Canada, you'll get the best deal flying to London from the big gateway cities of **Toronto** and **Montreal**, where low season midweek fares start from around CDN$760 return; direct flights from Ottawa and Halifax will probably cost only slightly more. From Edmonton, Calgary and Vancouver, London flights start at CDN$960. If you're travelling in high-season, fares are likely to be about $200 higher.

Only Air Canada flies nonstop **to Manchester** (from Ottawa and Toronto), but you can pick up direct flights from many Canadian cities to Manchester, Birmingham and Newcastle (usually via London), often at no extra cost over the fare to London.

PACKAGES AND ORGANIZED TOURS

Although you'll want to see England at your own speed, you shouldn't dismiss the idea of a **package deal** out of hand. Many agents and airlines put together very flexible deals, sometimes

---

NORTH AMERICAN TOUR OPERATORS TO ENGLAND

Bargain Boating (☎1-800/637-0782, *www.bct-walk.com*). Specializes in canal trips.

BCT Scenic Walking (☎1-800/473-1210). Extensive line-up of walking trips of 8 to 16 days in the Cotswolds, Cornwall, Lake District and from coast to coast.

British Airways Holidays (☎1-800/247-9297, *www.british-airways.com*). Flight-inclusive vacations, customized itineraries.

BritRail Travel International (☎1-800/BRITRAIL, *www.raileurope.com*). Flexible, unescorted vacations of Britain and Europe.

British Travel International (☎1-800/327-6097, *www.britishtravel.com*). Agent for all independent arrangements: rail and bus passes, hotels and a comprehensive B&B and vacation-homes reservation service.

Dullien River and Canal Cruises (☎1-800/925-0444, *www.learninginc.com*). Canal boat rentals.

English Experience (☎1-800/892-9317, *www.english-experience.com*). Homestays with English families and small-group (12–15 people) guided tours.

English Lakeland Ramblers (☎1-800/724-8801, *www.ramblers.com*). Walking tours (usual-ly 7 or 8 days) in the Lake District and the Cotswolds.

Le Boat (☎1-800/922-0291, *www.leboat.com*). Specializes in canal trips and yacht charters.

Lynott Tours (☎1-800/221-2474 or 212-760-0101, *www.lynottours.com*). Special-interest tours, hotel and castle stays, self-drives, walking and cycling.

Mountain Travel/Sobek (☎1-800/227-2384, *www.mtsobek.com*). Hiking tours.

Select Travel Service (☎1-800/752-6787, *www.selecttravel.com*). Customized history, literature, theatre and horticulture tours.

Sterling Tours (☎1-800/727-4359, *www.ster-lingtours.com*). Offers a variety of independent itineraries and some packages.

Virgin Atlantic Vacations (☎1-800/862-8621, *www.virgin-atlantic.com*). Custom-made packages for independent travellers, including hotel, theatre and airfare deals.

Wilderness Travel (☎1-800/368-2794, *www.wildernesstravel.com*). Inn-to-inn hiking packages in the Cotswolds, through the Lake District and along the North Sea coast.

All these companies' tours can be booked through a travel agent at no extra cost.

amounting to nothing more restrictive than a flight plus accommodation and car or rail pass, and these can actually work out cheaper than the same arrangements made on arrival – especially car rental, which is expensive in Britain. A package can also be great for your peace of mind, if only to ensure a worry-free first week while you're finding your feet for a longer tour.

There are hundreds of **tour operators** specializing in travel to the British Isles. Most can do packages of the standard highlights, but of greater interest are the outfits that help you explore England's unique points: many organize walking or cycling trips through the countryside, boat trips along canals and any number of theme tours based around the country's literary heritage, history, pubs, gardens, theatre, golf – you name it. A few of the possibilities are listed in the box on p.6, and a travel agent will be able to point out others. For a full listing, contact the British Tourist Authority (see p.20).

Be sure to examine the fine print of any deal, and bear in mind that everything in brochures always sounds great. Choose only an operator that is a member of the United States Tour Operator Association (USTOA) or has been approved by the American Society of Travel Agents (ASTA).

TRAVELLING FROM AUSTRALIA AND NEW ZEALAND

Travel time between Australasia and England is over twenty hours and as long-haul flights can be very taxing you might want to consider taking advantage of a stopover and good night's sleep en route. The **route** from Australia and New Zealand to London is a highly competitive one, with flights via Southeast Asia generally being the cheapest option; the lowest fares are with Airtours or Britannia Airways, starting at A$1100/NZ$1600 during their charter season of November to March, but Garuda, Gulf Air, Korean Air and Japan Airlines (JAL) all offer good deals starting at A$1600/NZ$2000. More expensive, but worth it for the extras, such as fly-drive, accommodation packages and onward travel to other European destinations, are Malaysia Airlines, KLM, Thai Airways, Singapore Airlines, Qantas, British Airways and Air New Zealand, with fares starting at around A$1800/NZ$2275. Other options worth considering if you have plenty of time and a sense of adventure are flying to either Hong Kong or Beijing and then taking one of the Trans-Siberian rail connections to London, or a **round-the-world ticket** (RTW) if you intend to take in England as part of a wider trip. Most airlines can put together an RTW fare for as little as A$1850/NZ$2250 in low season, but for more flexible options, such as Qantas/British Airways' "Global Explorer" or the "Star Alliance" which includes Air New Zealand, United Airlines and Thai Airways, you can expect to pay from A$2400–2700/ NZ$3000–3300 in low season.

Fares are seasonally adjusted – low season is October to mid-November and mid-January to end-February; high season is mid-May to end-July and mid- to end-December; the rest of the year is classed as shoulder season. Tickets purchased direct from the airlines tend to be expensive; **travel agents** offer much better deals on fares and have the latest information on limited special deals and stopovers with some of the best discounts through Flight Centres and STA, who can also advise on visa regulations.

AIRLINES IN AUSTRALIA AND NEW ZEALAND

Air New Zealand (Australia ☎13/2476; New Zealand ☎09/357 3000; *www.airnz.com.au*). Daily flights to London from Brisbane, Melbourne and Sydney (code share with Ansett from other major cities in Australia) via Asia and from New Zealand via Los Angeles.

Air France (Australia ☎02/9244 2100, *www.air-france.fr*). Several flights a week to London from Australia via Johannesburg and Paris, and return via Paris and Bangkok, Hong Kong or Singapore. Code-share with Qantas.

Airtours/Britannia Airways (Australia ☎02/9247 4833). Several flights a month (Nov–March only) from Adelaide, Auckland, Brisbane, Perth and Sydney to London and once a week to Manchester via Singapore and Bahrain.

British Airways (Australia ☎02/8904 8800; New Zealand ☎09/356 8690; *www.british-airways.com/regional/australia*). Daily direct flights from Brisbane, Melbourne, Perth and Sydney. Code share with Qantas (part owners of the company) from other major cities to London via Los Angeles and Singapore and twice weekly via Harare or Johannesburg from Sydney; daily from Auckland via Los Angeles. Onward connections to other destinations in Britain.

Canadian Airlines (Australia ☎1300/655 767; New Zealand ☎09/309 0735; *www.cdnair.ca*). Several flights a week from Auckland, Melbourne and Sydney to London via Toronto or Vancouver.

Cathay Pacific (Australia ☎13/1747; New Zealand ☎09/379 0861; *www.au.cathaypacific.com*). Several flights a week from Brisbane, Auckland, Cairns, Melbourne, Perth and Sydney to London and Manchester via Hong Kong.

Garuda (Australia ☎1300/365 330; New Zealand ☎09/366 1855; *www/151.196.75.122/garuda*). Several flights weekly from Adelaide, Auckland, Brisbane, Cairns, Darwin, Melbourne, Perth and Sydney to London via Denpasar or Jakarta.

Gulf Air (Australia ☎02/9244 2199, *www.gulfair-co.com*). Several flights weekly from Sydney to London via Singapore and Bahrain or Abu Dhabi.

Japan Airlines (JAL) (Australia ☎02/9272 1111; New Zealand ☎09/379 9906; *www.jal.co.jp*). Daily flights from Brisbane, Cairns and Sydney to London via Osaka or Tokyo and several weekly from Auckland and Cairns, also via Osaka and Tokyo.

Code share with Air New Zealand.

KLM (Australia ☎02/9231 6333 or 1-800/505 747, *www.klm.com.au*). Twice weekly flights from Sydney to London via Singapore and Amsterdam.

Korean Air (Australia ☎02/9262 6000; New Zealand ☎09/307 3687; *www.koreanair.com*). Several flights a week via Seoul from Auckland, Brisbane and Sydney to London and once a week from Christchurch.

Malaysia Airlines (MAS) (Australia ☎13/2627; New Zealand ☎09/373 2741; *www.malaysiaairlines.com.my*). Several flights a week from Auckland, Melbourne, Perth and Sydney to London via Kuala Lumpur. With onward connections to the northwest.

Qantas (Australia ☎13/1313; New Zealand ☎09/357 8900 or 0800/808 767; *www.qantas.com.au*). Daily flights from Auckland, Christchurch, Wellington, Adelaide, Brisbane, Darwin, Melbourne, Perth and Sydney to London via Bangkok or Singapore.

South African Airways (SAS) (Australia ☎02/9223 4402, *www.saairways.com.au*). Flights from the eastern Australian cities to London via Perth and Johannesburg or Harare. Code-share with Qantas.

Singapore Airlines (Australia ☎13/1011; New Zealand ☎09/379 3209; *www.singaporeair.com.au*). Daily flights from Brisbane, Melbourne, Perth, Sydney, Auckland and Christchurch, and several weekly from Adelaide and Cairns to London and Manchester via Singapore.

Thai Airways (Australia ☎1300/651 960; New Zealand ☎09/377 3886; *www.thaiair.com*). Several flights a week from Brisbane, Melbourne, Perth, Sydney and Auckland to London via Bangkok.

United Airlines (Australia ☎13/1777; New Zealand ☎09/379 3800; *www.ual.com*). Daily flights from Melbourne, Sydney and Auckland to London and Manchester via Los Angeles and Chicago, New York or Washington.

Virgin Atlantic (Australia ☎02/9244 2747, *www.fly.virgin.com.au*). Daily flights from Sydney and several weekly from Melbourne to London via Kuala Lumpur. Code-share with Malaysia Airlines for the first leg.

DISCOUNT TRAVEL AGENTS

Anywhere Travel, 345 Anzac Parade, Kingsford, Sydney NSW 2032 (☎02/9663 0411, *anywhere@ozemail.com.au*).

Budget Travel, 16 Fort St, Auckland; plus branches around the city (☎09/366 0061 or 0800/808 040).

Destinations Unlimited, 3 Milford Rd, Auckland (☎09/373 4033).

Flight Centres, Australia: 82 Elizabeth St, Sydney NSW 2000; plus branches nationwide (☎13/1600, *www.flightcentre.com.au*). New Zealand: 205 Queen St, Auckland (☎09/309 6171); plus branches nationwide.

Status Travel, 22 Cavenagh St, Darwin NT 0800 (☎08/8941 1843).

STA Travel, Australia: 702 Harris St, Ultimo, Sydney NSW 2007; 256 Flinders St, Melbourne Vic 3000; plus branches nationwide (nearest branch ☎13/1776; fastfare telesales ☎1300/360 960; *www.statravel.com.au*). New Zealand: 10 High St, Auckland (☎09/309 0458; fastfare telesales ☎09/366 6673); plus branches nationwide.

Student Uni Travel, 92 Pitt St, Sydney NSW 2000 (☎02/9232 8444); plus branches in Brisbane, Cairns, Darwin, Melbourne and Perth.

Thomas Cook, Australia: 175 Pitt St, Sydney NSW 2000; 257 Collins St, Melbourne; plus branches nationwide (nearest branch ☎13/1771, telesales ☎1800/063 913, *www.thomascook.com.au*). New Zealand: 159 Queen St, Auckland (☎09/359 5200, *www.thomascook.com*).

Trailfinders, 8 Spring St, Sydney NSW 2000 (☎02/9247 7666, *www.trailfinders.com.au/ australia*).

Travel.com.au, 80 Clarence St, Sydney NSW 2000 (☎02/9290 1500, *www.travel.com.au*).

Usit Beyond, corner of Shortland St and Jean Batten Place, Auckland (☎09/379 4224, *www.usitbeyond.co.nz*); plus branches in Christchurch, Hamilton, Palmerston North and Wellington.

UK Flight Shop, 7 Macquarie Place, Sydney NSW 2000 (☎02/9247 7833, *www.ukflightshop.com.au*); plus branches in Melbourne and Perth.

SPECIALIST AGENTS

Adventure Specialists, 69 Liverpool St, Sydney NSW 2000 (☎02/9261 2927, *www.adventurespec.citysearch.com.au*). Offers a selection of walking and cycling holidays throughout England.

Adventure Travel Company, 164 Parnell Rd, Parnell, East Auckland (☎09/379 9755). New Zealand agents for Peregrine Adventures.

Adventure World, 73 Walker St, North Sydney NSW 2060 (☎02/9956 7766 or 1-800/221 931, *www.adventureworld.com.au*), plus branches in Adelaide, Brisbane, Melbourne and Perth. New Zealand: 101 Great South Rd, Remuera, Auckland (☎09/524 5118). Offering a wide variety of tours around England.

Best of Britain, 352a Military Rd, Cremorne, Sydney NSW 2090 (☎02/9909 1055). Arranges flights, accommodation, car and canal-boat rental and tours.

Explore Holidays, 55 Blaxland Rd, Ryde NSW 2112 (☎02/9857 6200). Arranges accommodation as well as rambling and other special-interest trips.

Peregrine Adventures, 258 Lonsdale St, Melbourne Vic 3000 (☎03/9663 8611, *www.peregrine.net.au*), plus offices in Adelaide, Brisbane, Perth and Sydney. Adventure travel company specializing in small-group walking and cycling tours, with travel between main points by minibus.

Sundowners, Suite 15, 600 Lonsdale St, Melbourne Vic 3000 (☎03/9600 1934 or 1800/337 089, *www.sundowners.com.au*). Russian and Trans-Siberian Railway specialists; escorted group tours and independent travel by train to London via Moscow.

Wiltrans/Maupintour, Level 10, 189 Kent St, Sydney (☎02/9225 0899). Fully escorted tours around England's historic homes and gardens, staying in upmarket accommodation.

YHA Travel Centre, 422 Kent St, Sydney NSW 2000 (☎02/9261 1111); 205 King St, Melbourne Vic 3000 (☎03/9670 9611, *www.yha.com.au*). New Zealand: corner of Shortland St and Jean Batten Place, Auckland (☎09/379 4224, *www.yha.co.nz*). Organizes budget accommodation throughout Britain for YHA members.

FLIGHTS FROM AUSTRALIA

Fares from **Australia**'s eastern cities are common rated while flights from Perth via Asia and Africa are $200–400 less, and via the Americas about $400 more. The cheapest **scheduled** flights are via Asia with Garuda, Gulf Air, Korean Air, JAL and Royal Brunei for around $1400–$1600 in low season and $1850 in high season; these usually involve a transfer in the carrier's hub city. For just a little more Virgin Atlantic–Malaysia Airlines can get you to London via Kuala Lumpur from around $1600–1800. In the mid-range are Cathay Pacific, Malaysia Airlines, Thai Airways and Singapore Airlines, all at around $1700–1900. British Airways and Qantas both quote **direct-flight** fares from $1850 in low season up to $3000 in high season. Many of the airlines also offer **free stopovers** in their hub cities and some, like British Airways, throw in free side-trips to other European cities or car rental in the UK on fly-drive packages.

Flights are pricier **via North America**, with United Airlines offering the cheapest deal via Los Angeles and either Chicago, New York or Washington for $1950–$2430 while Air New Zealand fly from Auckland via Los Angeles – and Canadian Airlines via Toronto or Vancouver – for around $1975–2450.

The lowest fares for routes **via Africa** are with Qantas and South African Airways who have a joint route via Johannesburg or Harare with a free stopover in Perth, starting at $2000.

Currently the best fare of all on offer is the Airtours/Britannia Airways **charter flight** to London and Manchester which runs several times a month between November and March via Singapore and Bahrain. Fares start at A$1100 in low season, A$1800 in high season.

FLIGHTS FROM NEW ZEALAND

The most direct route from **New Zealand** is **via North America**, with United Airlines offering the best value, stopping in Los Angeles and Chicago for $2270 low season and $3170 in high season, while Air New Zealand have a similar deal for around $2350/$3000. British Airways are a bit more expensive starting at $2780/$3200, but this does include onward connections to other destinations in Britain.

Garuda, JAL, Korean Air and Thai Airways fly to London **via Asia** with either a transfer or stopover in their home city for around $2150; for a little more money and comfort Qantas fly via Sydney and Bangkok from $2450.

The cheapest fare is Airtours or Britannia Airways' **charter flight** from Auckland to London and Manchester that runs several times a month from November to March; fares are from $1620 low season, $1850 shoulder season and $2110 high season.

TRAVELLING FROM IRELAND AND THE CONTINENT

Stiff competition on routes between Ireland and England has kept the cost of flights relatively low, with airlines offering return tickets **from Dublin** at off-peak periods for as little as IR£44, though these will need to be booked well in advance. Ryanair (☎01/609 7800, *www.ryanair.ie*) fly to eleven destinations in England from Cork, Kerry and Knock, and are generally the cheapest, with their best deals being to London Stansted; booking a week ahead brings the price of a return ticket to IR£70. Aer Lingus (☎01/886 3333) offer a greater choice of departure points, with fares from IR£87 if your journey includes a Saturday

night, and British Airways (☎1800/626747) often give good discounts on their published fares from Dublin. Flying **from Belfast**, however, your best bet is Easyjet (☎0870/600 0000, *www.easyjet.com*) whose cheapest return flight to Luton Airport costs £48. British Midland (☎0870/607 0555, *www.britishmidland.com*) flies to Heathrow from £67 and BA (☎0345/222111, *www.british-airways.com*) also cover this route, with open returns at a published fare of £283 – though booking through a travel agent will undercut this – and special off-peak deals from £89 if you travel mid-week and your journey includes a Saturday.

Flying cuts out a long overland and ferry journey, but if you're keeping costs to a minimum, then take the **coach**. Eurolines (☎01232/333000, 01/836 6111 or 0990/143219, *www.eurolines.com*) runs a service from Belfast (from £49 return) and Dublin (from IR£34) via Birmingham to London, with connections throughout Ireland. Considering the distances involved, these fares are great value; the downside is that the trip, with an overnight ferry crossing to Holyhead, takes around ten hours from Belfast, twelve hours from Dublin and up to fourteen hours from elsewhere. Travelling to England from the Republic **by train** is marginally less uncomfortable, but if you're starting from

FERRY COMPANIES IN BRITAIN, IRELAND & EUROPE

Brittany Ferries UK ☎0990/360360; France ☎02.31.36.36.36; Spain ☎42 22 00 00; *www.brittany-ferries.com*

Condor UK ☎01305/761551; France ☎02.99.20.03.00; *www.condorferries.co.uk*

Fjord Line UK ☎0191/296 1313; Norway ☎55/548600.

DFDS Scandinavian Seaways UK ☎0990/333000; Holland ☎0255/03456; Sweden ☎031/650650; Germany ☎040/389 0371; Denmark ☎79.17.79.17; *www.scansea.com*

Hoverspeed/Seacat UK ☎08705/240241; France ☎3.21.46.14.14; *www.hoverspeed.co.uk*

Irish Ferries UK ☎08705/171717; Ireland ☎01/638 3333; *www.irishferries.ie*

Isle of Man Steam Packet UK ☎08705/523523; *www.steam-packet.com*

P&O European Ferries UK ☎0870/242 4999; France ☎08.03.01.30.13; *www.poef.com*

P&O North Sea Ferries UK ☎01482/377177; Holland ☎0181/255555; Belgium ☎050.54.34.30; *www.ponsf.com*

P&O Portsmouth UK ☎0870/242 4999; *www.poportsmouth.com*

P&O ☎0870/600 600; France ☎08.02.01.00.20; *www.posl.com*

Sea France ☎0990/711711; *www.seafrance.com*

Stena Line UK & Ireland ☎0990/707070; Holland ☎017/438 9333; *www.posl.com*

Swansea Cork Ferries UK ☎01792/456116; Ireland ☎021/271166; *www.swansea-cork.ie*

FERRY CONNECTIONS

	Company	Frequency	Duration
From Belgium			
Ostend–Dover	Hoverspeed (SeaCat)	4–7 daily	2hr
Zeebrugge–Hull	P & O North Sea Ferries	1 daily	14hr 45min
From Denmark			
Esbjerg–Harwich	Scandinavian/Stena	3–4 weekly	18hr
From France			
Boulogne–Folkestone	Hoverspeed SeaCat	April–Sept, 4 daily	55min
Caen–Portsmouth	Brittany	Jan–mid-Nov, 2–3 daily	6hr
Calais–Dover	P&O Stena	30–35 daily	75 min
Calais–Dover	Hoverspeed (Hovercraft/SeaCat)	6–20 daily	35min/50min
Cherbourg–Poole	Brittany	Jan–mid-Nov, 1–2 daily	4hr 15min
Cherbourg–Portsmouth	P&O	1–5 daily	3hr–5hr
Dieppe–Newhaven	P&O Stena	2 daily	4hr
Dieppe–Newhaven	Hoverspeed (Super SeaCat)	April–Sept 3 daily	2 hr
St Malo–Poole (via Jersey)	Condor	May–Oct, 1 daily	5hr 40min
St Malo–Weymouth (via Jersey)	Condor	May–Oct, I daily	5hr
St Malo–Portsmouth	Brittany	Jan–mid-Nov, 1–7 weekly	8hr 45min
Le Havre–Portsmouth	P&O	2–3 daily	6hr–8hr
Roscoff–Plymouth	Brittany	Jan–mid-Nov, 1–3 daily	6hr
From Germany			
Hamburg–Harwich	Scandinavian	3–4 weekly	19hr
Hamburg–Newcastle	Scandinavian	May–Sept, 2 weekly	22hr
From Holland			
Amsterdam–Newcastle	Scandinavian	2–7 weekly	14hr
Hook of Holland–Harwich	Stena (Catamaran)	2 daily	3hr 40min
Rotterdam–Hull	North Sea	1 daily	15hr 30min
From Ireland			
Cork–Swansea	Swansea–Cork Ferries	4–6 weekly, mid-March–Nov	10hr
Dun Laoghaire–Holyhead	Stena (Catamaran)	4–5 daily	99min
Dublin–Holyhead	Stena/Irish Ferries	2–6 daily	1hr 50min/3hr 15min
Dublin–Liverpool	Isle of Man Steam Packet (SuperSeaCat)	March–Sept, 1–2 daily	3hr 45min
Rosslare–Fishguard	Stena	2 daily	3hr 30min
Rosslare–Fishguard	Stena Sea Lynx	2–6 daily	1hr 5min
Rosslare–Pembroke	Irish Ferries	2 daily	4hr
From Norway			
Stavanger/Bergen –Newcastle	Fjord Line	4–6 weekly	20–27hr
Kristiansand	Scandinavian	2 weekly	18hr
From Spain			
Bilbao–Portsmouth	P&O	2 weekly	29hr–40hr
Santander–Plymouth	Brittany	March–mid-Nov 1–2 weekly	24hr
From Sweden			
Gothenburg–Newcastle	Scandanavian	Feb–Dec 2 weekly	26hr

the south or west the best ferry crossings are the more expensive Cork–Swansea or Rosslare–Fishguard/Rosslare–Pembroke routes, which can bring the train fare to around the same as a flight. For more information, contact British and European Rail (☎01/703 4095). Driving is the other option, although the cost of taking your car on the ferry can make this an expensive alternative if you're travelling alone and can't split the fare. A full rundown of the ferry routes between Ireland and England appears in the box opposite; fares fluctuate wildly depending on the time of year and the day of the week you travel, and also the length of your car, but expect to pay IR£118–280 for a small vehicle and up to five adults between Dublin and Holyhead, or IR£90–185 on the Cork–Swansea route.

Drivers **from Europe** also have the option of using **Eurotunnel**, (☎0990/353535, *www. eurotunnel.com*) crossing underneath the Channel on freight trains which carry coaches, cars and motorbikes. The service runs every 15 minutes at peak periods and takes 35 minutes to get between the loading terminals at Folkestone and Calais. You can just turn up, but booking is advised, especially at weekends; tickets are fully flexible. A five-day return for a car and passengers travelling off-peak costs £159, £195 in peak season. Travelling between 10pm and 6am brings the price down to £139.

For foot passengers there are frequent through trains between Paris, Brussels, Lille and London run by **Eurostar** (☎0990/186186, *www.eurostar.co.uk*). The least expensive return fare (which must be booked three days in advance and include a Saturday night) is £89 from Paris, £79 from Brussels and £69 from Lille. Full fares with no restrictions are £249 from Paris and Brussels and £190 from Lille. Youth

tickets (for under-26s) have no restrictions attached and cost £79 from Paris, £69 from Brussels and £65 from Lille. Eurostar also offers frequent promotional fares. Eurail and Britrail pass holders qualify for a Passholder return which allows unrestricted journeys for £79 from Paris, £69 from Brussels and £65 from Lille.

Tariffs on the **ferries** are bewilderingly complex: prices vary with the month, day or even hour at certain times of the year, not to mention how long you're staying and the size of your car. Another thing to bear in mind is that some kind of sleeping accommodation is often obligatory on the longer crossings if made at night, pushing the price way above the basic rate. As an indication of cost, two people driving in a small car from Calais, Boulogne, Dieppe or Ostend to one of the English Channel ports could expect to pay around £80–95 (the return fares are usually just twice the price); for a foot passenger the single fare is £24. The Gothenburg–Newcastle route, one of the longest crossings, costs over £175 at the least expensive time of the year rising to £400 in high season for a car and up to five passengers, with prices from £54 for a foot passenger. All current crossings, including foot-passenger, hovercraft and catamaran services, are listed in the box opposite.

You can, of course, also catch **buses** from a long list of European countries to England. Given the low cost of air fares from many cities, however, you'd have to be a masochist to want to travel by bus from, say, Athens – a journey of two nights and three days that actually costs more than the price of a three-and-a-half-hour flight to London. Eurolines is Britain's largest international coach company, with departures to London from 48 European cities, including Amsterdam, Brussels, Frankfurt, Hamburg, Madrid, Paris and Rome.

VISAS, WORK PERMITS, CUSTOMS AND TAX

Citizens of all the countries of Europe – other than Albania, Romania, Bulgaria and the republics of the former Soviet Union (with the exception of the Baltic States) – can enter Britain with just a passport, generally for up to three months. US, Canadian, Australian and New Zealand citizens can enter the country for up to six months with just a passport. All other nationalities require a visa, obtainable from the British Consular office in the country of application.

For stays of longer than six months, **US**, **Canadian**, **Australian** and **New Zealand** citizens should apply to the British Embassy or High Commission (see box opposite). If you want to extend your visa, you should write, before the expiry date given on the endorsement in your passport, to: The UnderSecretary of State, Home Office, Immigration and Nationality Dept, Lunar House, Wellesley Road, Croydon CR9 2BY (☎0181/686 0688), enclosing your passport or National Identity Card and form IS120 (if these were your entry documents).

WORK PERMITS

Unless you're a resident of an EU country, you need a permit to work legally in the UK, although without the backing of an established employer or company this can be very difficult to obtain. Persons aged between 17 and 27 may, however, apply for a Working Holiday-Maker Entry Certificate, which entitles you to a two-year stay in the UK, during which time you are permitted to undertake work of a casual nature (ie, not in a

profession, or as a sportsperson or entertainer). The certificates are only available abroad, from British embassies and consulates, and when you apply you must be able to convince the officer you have a valid return or onward ticket, and the means to support yourself while you're in Britain without having to claim state benefits of any kind. Note, too, that the certificates are valid from the date of entry into Britain – you won't be able to recoup time spent out of the country in the two-year period of validity.

In **North America**, full-time college students can get temporary work or study permits through BUNAC, PO Box 49, South Britain, CT 06487 (☎203/264-0901). Permits are valid for up to six months and cost $225; send an application form, college verification form and two passport photos to the above address; allow two to three weeks for processing of the application.

Other visitors entitled to work in Britain are **Commonwealth citizens** with a parent or grandparent who was born in the UK. If you fall into this category, you can apply for a Certificate of Entitlement to the Right of Abode. If you're unsure about whether or not you may be eligible for one of these, contact your nearest British Mission (embassy or consulate), or the Foreign and Commonwealth Office in London (☎0171/270 1500 or 238 4633).

The kind of work you can expect to find in England as a visitor is generally unskilled **employment** in hotels, restaurants, cleaning companies and on farms. Working conditions may not be up to much, and as a casual employee you can be fired at short notice. Pay is poor, too (£3–4 per hour), and will bring in barely enough to survive. So unless you're desperate, try to save at home before travelling. With **voluntary work**, the choice of jobs improves considerably, ranging from farm camps to placements with service organizations. Scores of useful addresses are featured in a guide called *Working Holidays* (£9.99), published by the Central Bureau for Educational Visits and Exchanges (CBEVE), 10 Spring Gardens, London SW1A 2BN. *Summer Jobs in Britain* by David Woodworth (£8.99) gives comprehensive information on paid seasonal work in the UK.

If you're between 17 and 27, you might also consider **working as an au pair**. This enables you to live for a maximum of two years with an

English-speaking family. In return for your accommodation, food and a small amount of pocket money (say £40 per week), you'll be expected to help around the house and to look after the children for a maximum of five hours each day. The easiest way to find au pair work is through a licensed agency. The Federation of Recruitment and Employment Services (FRES), 36–38 Mortimer St, London W1N 7RB (☎0800/320558, *www.fres.co.uk*) will send you a list of reputable agents (ie, those that are vetted annually by the government) for £3.75.

CUSTOMS

Since the inauguration of the EU Single Market, travellers coming into Britain directly from another EU country do not have to make a declaration to Customs at their place of entry. In other words, you can bring almost as much French wine or German beer across the Channel as you like. The guidance levels are 90 litres of wine and 110 of beer, which should suffice for anyone's requirements – any more than this, and you'll have to provide proof that it's for personal use only. If you're travelling to or from a non-EU country, you can still buy duty-free goods, but within the EU, this perk no longer exists. The duty-free allowances are as follows:

Tobacco: 200 cigarettes; or 100 cigarillos; or 50 cigars; or 250 grams of loose tobacco.

• **Alcohol**: 2 litres of still wine plus 1 litre of drink over 22 percent alcohol, or 2 litres of alcoholic drinks not over 22 percent.

• **Perfumes**: 60ml of perfume plus 250ml of toilet water.

Plus other goods to the value of £145.

There are **import restrictions** on a variety of articles and substances, from firearms to furs derived from endangered species, none of which should bother the average tourist. However, if you need any clarification on British import regulations, contact HM Customs and Excise, Dorset House, Stamford St, London, SE1 9PY (☎0171/202 4227). You are not allowed to bring **pets** into Britain.

Most goods in Britain, with the chief exceptions of books and food, are subject to **Value Added Tax** (VAT), which increases the cost of an item by 17.5 percent (included in the marked price of goods). Visitors from non-EU countries can save a lot of money through the **Retail Export Scheme**, that allows a refund of VAT on goods to be taken out of the country. (Savings will usually be minimal for EU nationals because of the rates at which the goods will be taxed upon import to the home country.) Note that not all shops participate in this scheme (those doing so will display a sign to this effect) and that you cannot reclaim VAT charged on hotel bills or other services.

BRITISH EMBASSIES AND HIGH COMMISSIONS ABROAD

Australia British High Commission, Commonwealth Ave, Yarralumla, Canberra, ACT 2600 (☎1902/941 555, *www.uk.emb.gov.au*).

Canada British High Commission, 80 Elgin St, Ottawa, ON K1P 5K7 (☎613/237-1530, *www.biscanada.org*).

Ireland 29 Merrion Rd, Dublin 4 (☎01/205 3700).

New Zealand British High Commission, 44 Hill St, Wellington (☎04/495 0889, *www.brithighcomm.org.nz*).

USA 3100 Massachusetts Ave, NW, Washington, DC 20008 (☎202/462-1340, *www.britain-info.org*).

OVERSEAS EMBASSIES AND HIGH COMMISSIONS IN ENGLAND

American Embassy, 5 Upper Grosvenor St, London W1X 9PG (☎0171/499 9000, *www.usembassy.org.uk*).

Australian High Commission, Australia House, The Strand, London WC2B 42A (☎0171/379 4334, *www.australia.org.uk*).

Canadian High Commission, 1 Grosvenor Square, London W1X 0AB (☎0171/258 6600, *www.canada.org.uk*).

Irish Embassy, 17 Grosvenor Place, London SW1X 7HR (☎0171/235 2171, *www.irlgov.ie*).

New Zealand High Commission, New Zealand House, 80 Haymarket, London SW1Y 4TQ (☎0171/930 8422, *www.newzealandhc.org*).

MONEY, BANKS AND COSTS

The easiest and safest way to carry your money is in travellers' cheques, available for a small commission (normally one percent) from any major bank. The most commonly accepted travellers' cheques are American Express, followed by Visa and Thomas Cook – most cheques issued by banks will be one of these three brands. You'll usually pay commission again when you cash each cheque, normally another one percent or so, or a flat rate – though no commission is payable on Amex cheques exchanged at Amex branches. Keep a record of the cheques as you cash them, and you can get the value of all uncashed cheques refunded immediately if you lose them.

You'll find that most hotels, shops and restaurants in England accept the major **credit cards** – MasterCard, Visa, American Express and Diners Club – although they're less useful in the most rural areas, and smaller establishments all over the country, such as B&B accommodation, will often accept cash only. Your card will also enable you to get cash advances from certain ATMs (known as cashpoints in England) – call the issuing bank or credit company to get a list of locations. In addition, you may be able to make withdrawals using your **ATM cash card** – your bank's international banking department should be able to advise on this. Make sure you have a personal identification number (PIN) that's designed to work overseas. Every sizeable town in England has a branch of at least one of the big four high-street **banks**: Barclays, Lloyds TSB, HSBC and National

Westminster. Basic opening hours are Mon–Fri 9.30am–4.30pm, though many branches in larger towns open at 9am, close at 5.30pm and also remain open until 3 or 4pm on Saturdays.

Banks or the larger post offices are the best places to change money and cheques. Outside banking and office hours you're best advised to go to a **bureau de change**; these are to be found in most city centres, often at train stations or airports. Try to avoid changing money or cheques in hotels, where the rates are normally the poorest on offer.

If, as a foreign visitor, you run out of money or there is some kind of emergency, the quickest way to get **money sent out** is to contact your bank at home and have them wire the cash to the nearest bank. You can do the same thing through Thomas Cook or American Express if there is a branch nearby. Americans, Canadians and Australians can have cash sent out through Western Union (☎1-800/325 6000) or American Express MoneyGram (☎1-800/543 4080). Both companies' fees depend on the destination and the amount being transferred, but, as an example, wiring $1000 to England will cost around $75. The funds should be available for collection at Western Union's or Amex's local office within minutes of being sent.

There are no exchange controls in Britain, so you can bring in as much cash as you like and change travellers' cheques up to any amount.

CURRENCY

The British **pound sterling** (£) is a decimal currency, divided into 100 pence (p). Coins come in denominations of 1p, 2p, 5p, 10p, 20p, 50p and £1, £2 and £5. Notes come in denominations of £5, £10, £20 and £50; shopkeepers will carefully scrutinize any £20 or £50 notes, as forgeries are widespread, and you'd be well advised to do the same. The quickest test is to hold the note up to the light to make sure there's a thin wire filament running from top to bottom; this is by no means foolproof, but it will catch most fakes. Very occasionally you may receive Scottish banknotes from £1 upwards: they're legal tender throughout Britain, but you may want to get rid of them sooner rather than later as some unworldly traders south of the border may be unwilling to accept them.

Britain remains sceptical about the **euro**, and despite moves in other EU countries, it's unlikely to become currency in this country until well after the next election, if then.

COSTS

England is an expensive place to visit. The minimum expenditure, if you're camping, or hostelling, using public transport, buying picnic food and eating in pubs and cafes, would be in the region of £25–35 a day. Couples staying at budget B&Bs, eating at unpretentious restaurants and visiting a fair number of tourist attractions are looking at around £40–50 each per day, and if you're renting a car, staying in comfortable B&Bs or hotels and eating well, budget on at least £80 each per day. Single travellers should budget on spending around 60 percent of what a couple would spend (single rooms cost more than half a double), and on any visit to London, work on the basis that you'll need an extra £15 per day to get much pleasure out of the place. For more detail on the cost of accommodation, transport and eating, see the relevant sections below.

TIPPING

There are no fixed rules for tipping in England. If you think you've received good service, particularly in restaurants or cafés, you may want to leave a tip of ten percent of the total bill (unless service has already been included). It is not normal, however, to leave tips in pubs, although bar staff are sometimes offered drinks, which they may accept in the form of money (the assumption is they'll spend this on a drink after closing time). **Taxi drivers**, on the other hand, will expect tips on longer journeys – expect to add about ten percent to the fare. The other occasion when you'll be expected to tip is in **upmarket hotels** where, in common with most other countries, porters, bell boys and table waiters rely on being tipped to bump up their often dismal wages.

YOUTH AND STUDENT DISCOUNTS

Various official and quasi-official youth/student ID cards are widely available and most will pay for themselves in savings pretty soon. Full-time students over the age of sixteen are eligible for the **International Student ID Card** (ISIC), which entitles the bearer to special fares on local transport, and discounts at museums, theatres and other attractions; for Americans and Canadians there's also a health benefit (see p.18). The card costs $20 for Americans, CDN$15 for Canadians, A$15 for Australians, NZ$17 for New Zealanders, £5 in the UK, and is available from branches of Council Travel, STA and Travel CUTS around the world (see pp.5 & 9).

You only have to be 25 or younger to qualify for the **Go-25 Card**, which costs the same as the ISIC and carries the same benefits. It can be purchased through Council Travel in the US, Hostelling International in Canada and STA in Australia (see pp.5 & 9).

STA also sells its own ID card that's good for some discounts, as do various other travel organizations. A university photo ID might open some doors, too.

INSURANCE, HEALTH AND EMERGENCIES

Wherever you're travelling from, it's a very good idea to have some kind of travel insurance. The amount of cover you get varies according to the premium you pay, but a standard policy should always cover the cost of cancellation and curtailment of flights, medical expenses, travel delay, accident, missed departures, lost baggage, lost passport, personal liability and legal expenses. **In the UK**, low-cost policies start at around £13 per month, and it is usually worth shopping around: try Columbus Travel Insurance (☎0171/375 0011), Worldwide (☎01892/833338), Endsleigh Insurance (☎0171/436 4451) or Marcus Hearne & Co Ltd (☎0171/739 3444). Note that some insurance companies refuse to cover **travellers over 65**, or have upper-limits of 69 or 74 years of age, and most that do provide insurance charge hefty premiums; the best policies, with no upper age

limit, are offered by Age Concern (☎01883/346 964).

Whatever your policy, and regardless of who you buy it from, if you have anything stolen, get a copy of the police report of the incident, as this is essential to substantiate your claim.

In the **US** and **Canada** you should carefully check the insurance policies you already have before taking out a new one. You may discover that you're covered already for medical and other losses while abroad. Canadians especially are usually covered by their provincial health plans. Holders of an official student/teacher/youth card, such as ISIC (see p.17), are entitled (outside the USA) to be reimbursed for accident coverage and hospital in-patient benefits, with up to $3000 in emergency medical coverage and $100 a day for up to 60 days in hospital, plus a 24-hour hotline to call in the event of a medical, legal or financial emergency. Students may also find their health coverage extends during vacations, and many bank and charge accounts include some form of travel cover; insurance is also sometimes included if you pay for your trip with a credit card. Premiums vary, so shop around. The best deals are usually to be had through student/youth travel agencies – ISIS now offers STA Travel Insurance for travellers under the age of 60. Coverage is worldwide and comes in packages covering 7 days ($35), 15 days ($55), 1 month ($115), 45 days ($155), 2 months ($180), and 1 year ($730) – add an extra $35–50 for each additional month on longer stays. If you're planning to

TRAVEL INSURANCE COMPANIES IN NORTH AMERICA

Access America US ☎1-800/284-8300; Canada ☎1-800/654-1908.
Carefree Travel Insurance US & Canada ☎1-800/323-3149.
Desjardins Travel Insurance Canada ☎1-800/463-7830).
International Student Insurance Service (ISIS) – sells STA Travel Insurance. US & Canada ☎1-800/777- 0112.

Travel Assistance International US & Canada ☎1-800/821-2828.
Travel Guard US ☎1-800/826-1300; Canada ☎715/345-0505.
Travel Insurance Services US ☎1-800/937-1387.

TRAVEL INSURANCE COMPANIES IN AUSTRALASIA

Ready Plan Australia ☎03/9791 5077 or 1300/555 017; New Zealand ☎09/300 5333.

Cover More Level Australia ☎02/9202 8000 or 1800/251 881; New Zealand ☎09/377 5958.

do any dangerous sports, be sure to ask whether these activities are covered: some policies add a hefty surcharge.

Note that most North American travel policies apply only to items lost, stolen or damaged while in the custody of an identifiable, responsible third party – hotel porter, airline, luggage consignment, etc – and very few insurers will arrange on-the-spot payments in the event of a major expense or loss; you will usually be reimbursed only after going home.

Travel insurance policies in **Australia** and **New Zealand** tend to be put together by the airlines and travel agent groups, which are all fairly similar in terms of coverage and price – but if you plan to indulge in high-risk activities such as mountaineering, bungee jumping or scuba diving, check the policy carefully to make sure you'll be covered. A typical policy for the UK covering medical bills, lost baggage and personal liability will cost around A$140/NZ$160 for 2 weeks, A$190/NZ$210 for 1 month, A$300/NZ$330 for 2 months. The companies listed in the box opposite offer some of the widest cover available which can be arranged through most travel agents.

MEDICAL MATTERS

No vaccinations are required for entry into Britain. Citizens of all EU countries and those with a reciprocal health care agreement with this country are entitled to free medical treatment at National Health Service hospitals. If you don't fall into either of these categories, you will be charged for all medical services, in which case **health insurance** is strongly advised.

Pharmacists (known as chemists in England) can dispense only a limited range of drugs without a doctor's prescription. Most pharmacies are open standard shop hours, though in large towns some may stay open as late as 10pm – local newspapers carry lists of late-opening pharmacies. Doctor's surgeries tend to be open from about 9am to noon and then for a couple of hours in the evenings; outside **surgery hours**, you can turn up at the casualty department of the local hospital for complaints that require immediate attention. In an **emergency**, call for an ambulance on ☎999.

POLICE

Although the traditional image of the friendly British "Bobby" has become increasingly tarnished by stories of corruption, racism and crooked dealings, the **police** continue to be approachable and helpful. If you're lost in a major town, asking a police officer is generally the quickest way to pinpoint your destination – alternatively, you could ask a **traffic warden**, a species of law-enforcer much maligned in car-loving England. Most traffic wardens are distinguishable by their flat caps with a yellow band (though uniforms do vary), and by the fact that they are generally armed with a hand-set for dispensing parking-fine tickets; police officers on street duty wear a distinctive domed hat with a silver tip, and are generally armed with just a truncheon.

As with any country, the major towns of England have their dangerous spots, but these tend to be inner-city housing estates where no tourist has any reason to be. The chief risk on England's streets is pickpocketing, and there are some virtuoso villains at work in London, especially on the big shopping streets and on the Underground. Carry only as much money as you need, and keep all bags and pockets fastened. Should you have anything stolen or be involved in some incident that requires reporting, go to the local police station; the ☎999 number should only be used in emergencies.

EMERGENCIES

For Police, Fire Brigade, Ambulance and, in certain areas, Mountain Rescue or Coastguard, dial ☎999.

INFORMATION AND MAPS

If you want to do a bit of research before arriving in England, you could contact the British Tourist Authority (BTA) in your country – the addresses are given in the box below. The BTA will send you a wealth of free literature, some of it just rose-tinted advertising copy, but much of it extremely useful – especially the maps, city guides and event calendars. If you want more hard facts on a particular area, you should approach the regional tourist offices in England, which are also listed in the box below. Some are extremely helpful, others give the impression of being harassed to breaking point by years of understaffing, but all of them will have a few leaflets worth scanning before you set out.

BRITISH TOURIST AUTHORITY HEAD OFFICES

Australia: Level UK, The Gateway, 1 Macquarie Place, Circular Quay, Sydney NSW 2000 (☎02/9377 4400).

Canada: 111 Avenue Rd, Suite 450, Toronto, ON M5R 3J8 (☎1-800/ VISIT UK or 905-405-1840, *www.visitbritain.com/ca*).

Ireland: BTA, 18–19 College Green, Dublin 2 (☎01/670 8100).

New Zealand: Floor 17, Fay Richwhite Building, 151 Queen Street, Auckland (☎09/303 1446).

US: 551 5th Ave, Suite 701, New York, NY 10176 (☎1-800/ GO-2-BRITAIN or 212-986-2200, *www.btausa.com*).

REGIONAL TOURIST BOARDS IN ENGLAND

Britain Visitor Centre, 1 Regent St, London SW1Y 4NS (no telephone enquiries; *www.visitbritain.com*).

Cumbria Tourist Board, Ashleigh, Holly Rd, Windermere, Cumbria LA23 2AQ (☎01539/444444, *www.cumbria-the-lake-district.co.uk*).

East of England Tourist Board, Toppesfield Hall, Hadleigh, Suffolk IP7 5DN (☎01473/822922, *www.visitbritain.com*).

Heart of England Tourist Board, Woodside, Larkhill Rd, Worcester WR5 2EZ (☎01905/763436, *www.visitbritain.com*); Premier House, 15 Wheeler Gate, Nottingham NG1 2NA (☎0115/959 8383, *www.visitbritain.com*).

London Tourist Board, Glen House, Stag Place, London SW1E 5LT (no telephone enquiries; *www.LondonTown.com*).

North West England Tourist Board, Swan House, Swan Meadow Road, Wigan Pier, Wigan WN3 5BB (☎01942/821222, *www.visitbritain.com*).

Northumbria Tourist Board, Aykley Heads, Durham DH1 5UX (☎0191/375 3000, *www.ntb.org.uk*).

South East England Tourist Board, The Old Brew House, Warwick Park, Tunbridge Wells, Kent TN2 5TU (☎01892/540766, *www.seetb.org.uk*).

Southern Tourist Board, 40 Chamberlayne Rd, Eastleigh, Hampshire SO50 5JH (☎01703/620006, *www.visitbritain.com*).

West Country Tourist Board, 60 St David's Hill, Exeter, Devon EX4 4SY (☎01392/425426, *www.wctb.co.uk*).

Yorkshire Tourist Board, 312 Tadcaster Rd, York YO24 1GS (☎01904/707961, *www.ytb.org.uk*).

Tourist offices (usually called Tourist Information Centres, or "TICs" for short) exist in virtually every English town – you'll find their phone numbers and opening hours in the relevant sections of the guide. The average opening hours are much the same as standard shop hours, with the difference that in summer they'll often be open on a Sunday and for a couple of hours after the shops have closed on weekdays; opening hours are generally shorter in winter, and in more remote areas the office may well be open fewer days of the week. All centres offer information on accommodation, local public transport, attractions and restaurants as well as town and regional maps. In many cases this is free, but a growing number of offices make a small charge for an accommodation list or a town guide with an accompanying street plan. Areas designated as **National Parks** (such as the Lake District, the North York Moors and Dartmoor) also have a fair sprinkling of information centres, which are generally more expert in giving guidance on local walks and outdoor pursuits. (For information on accommodation-booking services, see p.29).

MAPS

The most comprehensive series of maps is produced by the **Ordnance Survey**, a series

renowned for its accuracy and clarity. The 204 maps in their 1:50,000 (a little over one-inch-to-one-mile) Landranger series cover the whole of Britain and show enough detail to be useful for most walkers. More detailed, and invaluable for serious hiking, are the 1:25,000 Outdoor Leisure maps, which deal with National Parks and areas of outstanding beauty, and the Explorer set of maps which is gradually replacing the Pathfinder series; between them they cover the entire country. Less well known than the Ordnance Survey publications is the Goldeneye series, a range of fairly ordinary road maps for various English counties, but made interesting with the addition of historical and recreational details on the back. The best **road atlases** are the large-format ones produced by the AA, RAC, Collins and Ordnance Survey, which cover all of Britain at around three-miles-to-one-inch and include larger-scale plans of major towns. Virtually every motorway service station in England stocks one or more of the big road atlases.

The full range of Ordnance Survey maps is only available at a few big-city stores (see box on p.22), but in any walking district of England you'll find the relevant maps in local shops or information offices. Check their Web site (see box above) for information on the full range of maps.

MAP OUTLETS

UK

Bath: Whiteman's Bookshop, 7 Orange Grove, BA1 1LP (☎01225/464 029).

Bristol: Stanfords, 29 Corn St, Bristol BS1 1HT (☎0117/929 9966).

Cambridge: Heffers Map Shop, 3rd Floor, in Heffers Stationery Department, 19 Sidney St, CB2 3HL (☎01223/568467).

Liverpool: Blackwell's University Bookshop, Alsop Building, Brownlow Hill, Liverpool, L3 5TX (☎0151/709 8146).

London: Daunt Books, 83 Marylebone High St, London, W1M 3DE (☎0171/224 2295) and 193 Haverstock Hill, London, NW3 4QL (☎0171/794 4006); National Map Centre, 22–24 Caxton St, London, SW1H 0QU (☎0171/222 2466); Stanfords, 12–14 Long Acre, London, WC2E 9LP (☎0171/836 1321); 52 Grosvenor Gardens, SW1W 0AG (☎0171/730 1314); and within the British Airways offices at 156 Regent St, W1R 5TA (☎0171/434 4744); The Travel Bookshop, 13–15 Blenheim Crescent, W11 2EE (☎0171/229 5260).

Manchester: Waterstone's, 91 Deansgate, Manchester, M3 2BW (☎0161/832 1992).

Newcastle Map Centre: 55 Grey St, Newcastle upon Tyne NE1 6EF (☎0191/261 5622).

Oxford: Blackwell's Map and Travel Shop, 53 Broad St, OX1 3BQ (☎01865/792 792).

York: Blackwell's, 32 Stonegate, YO1 8ZS (☎01904/624531).

NORTH AMERICA

Chicago: Rand McNally, 444 North Michigan Ave, IL 60611 (☎312/321-1751).

Los Angeles: Map Link Inc, 30 S LaPatera Lane, Suite 5, Santa Barbara, CA 93117 (☎805/692-6777).

Montreal: Ulysses Travel Bookshop, 4176 St-Denis (☎514/843-9447).

New York: British Travel Bookshop, 551 5th Ave, NY (☎212/490-6688); The Complete Traveler Bookstore, 199 Madison Ave, NY 10016 (☎212/685-9007); Rand McNally, 150 East 52nd St, NY 10022 (☎212/758-7488); Traveler's Choice Bookstore, 22 West 52nd St, NY 10019 (☎212/941-1535).

San Francisco: The Complete Traveler Bookstore, 3207 Filmore St, CA 92123 (☎415/923-1511); Rand McNally, 595 Market St, CA 94105 (☎415/777-3131); Phileas Fogg's Books & Maps, Stanford Shopping Center, Suite 87, Palo Alto, CA 94304 (☎1-800/233-FOGG in California; ☎1-800/533-FOGG elsewhere in US).

Seattle: Elliot Bay Book Company, 101 South Main St, WA 98104 (☎206/624-6600).

Toronto: Open Air Books and Maps, 25 Toronto St, M5C 2R1 (☎416/363-0719).

Vancouver: World Wide Books and Maps, 736 Granville St, BC V6Z 1E4 (☎604/687-3320).

Washington DC: Rand McNally, 7988 Tysons Corner Center, McLean, VA 22102 (☎703/556-8688).

AUSTRALASIA

Adelaide: The Map Shop, 16a Peel St, Adelaide, SA 5000 (☎08/8231 2033).

Auckland: Specialty Maps, 58 Albert St (☎09/307 2217).

Brisbane: Worldwide Maps and Guides 187 George St, Brisbane (☎07/3221 4330).

Melbourne: Mapland, 372 Little Bourke St, Melbourne, VIC 3000 (☎03/9670 4383).

Sydney: Travel Bookshop, Shop 3, 175 Liverpool St, Sydney, NSW 2000 (☎02/9261 8200).

Perth: Perth Map Centre, 891 Hay St, Perth, WA 6000 (☎08/9322 5733).

GETTING AROUND

As you'd expect of such a small and densely populated country, just about every place in England is accessible by train or bus. However, costs are among the highest in Europe – London's commuters spend more on getting to work than any of their European counterparts, while cross-country travel can eat up a large part of your budget. It pays to plan ahead and make sure you're aware of all the passes and special deals on offer – note that some are only available outside England, and must be purchased before you arrive. It's often cheaper to drive yourself around the country though fuel and car rental costs again are among the highest in Europe and will seem prohibitive to North Americans. Congestion around the main cities can be bad, and even the motorways (notoriously the M25, London's orbital road) are liable to sporadic gridlocks, especially on public holidays when what seems like half the population takes to the roads

RAIL TRAVEL

A chronic lack of investment and a foolhardy privatization process caused a severe decline in rail travel over the late Eighties and Nineties. With the track and stations now owned by Railtrack, and the trains and services run by a tangle of private companies, there's also no little confusion when it comes to trying to figure out routes and prices. Still, despite the fears of many, few lines and services have been axed so far, and there aren't many major towns that cannot be reached by rail, although travelling across the country – rather than out from London – can involve making connections with several different services. You can buy tickets at the train station on the day of travel, but it should hardly comes as a surprise to find that booking as far ahead as possible (at

least two weeks) ensures the cheapest fares – or that travelling most places on a Friday, or just turning up at the station to buy a ticket, are the most expensive ways to go. In all instances, an essential first call is National Rail Enquiries on ☎0345/484950, which can advise on routes and services throughout Britain. The booking numbers on p.24 can give you all the information you need.

At the time of going to press, there were five types of reduced-fare ticket – Saver, SuperSaver, SuperAdvanced, Apex and SuperApex – all with byzantine restrictions which are often different from route to route and company to company (for instance, it's often cheaper to travel return from the north to London, rather than from London to the north).

Apex tickets are issued in limited numbers on certain intercity journeys of 150 miles or more, and have to be booked at least 7 days before travelling; a seat reservation is included with the ticket. The rock-bottom **SuperApex** tickets have to be booked fourteen days in advance, and are available in limited numbers on services between London and a few selected towns and cities. To take the London–Newcastle service as an example, an ordinary return fare costs £144; a Saver, £77.40; a SuperSaver, £66; a SuperAdvanced, £54; an Apex, £43; and a SuperApex, £31. For all special-offer tickets you should book as far in advance as you possibly can – many Apex and SuperApex tickets are sold out weeks before the travel date.

Children aged 5–15 inclusive pay half the adult fare on most journeys – but there are no discounts on Apex and SuperApex tickets. Under-5s travel free, although they are not entitled to a seat on crowded trains.

At weekends and on public holidays, many long-distance services have a special deal whereby you can convert your second-class ticket to a first-class one by buying a first class supplement, which costs between £3 and £10 and is well worth paying if you're facing a 5-hour journey on a popular route – every Brit has a horror story about having to stand all the way from London to Newcastle in a smelly second-class carriage.

The ticket offices at many rural and commuter stations are closed at weekends; in these instances there's often a vending machine on the platform. If there isn't a functioning machine, you

RAIL OFFICES AND AGENCIES

NORTH AMERICA

BritRail Travel International, 1500 Broadway, New York, NY 10036 (☎1-800/677-8585, *www.raileurope.com*). All rail passes, rail-drive and multi-country passes and Channel Tunnel tickets. Also sells ferry tickets across the Channel.

Canadian Reservations Centre, 2087 Dundas East, Suite 105, Mississauga, ON L4X 1M2 (☎1-800/361-7245, *www.raileurope.com*). Specializes in Eurail and other rail passes.

CIE Tours International, 108 Ridgedale Ave, PO Box 2355, Morristown, NJ 07962 (☎1-800/243-7687, *www.cietours.ie*). Sells rail passes valid for Britain and Ireland.

CIT Tours, 342 Madison Ave, Suite 207, New York, NY 10173 (☎1-800/223-7987, *www.fs-on-line.com*). Eurail Passes.

Rail Europe, 226–230 Westchester Ave, White Plains, NY 10604 (☎1-800/438-7245, *www.raileurope.com*). Specializes in Eurail Passes.

AUSTRALIA

Rail Plus, Level 8, 114 William St, Melbourne 3000 (☎03/9642 8644 or 1300/555 003); Level 6, 76 Symonds St, Auckland (☎09/303 2484).

RAIL INFORMATION AND BOOKING IN BRITAIN

For all timetable and fare information, contact National Rail Enquiries (☎0345/484950, *www.rail.co.uk*). Calls are charged at local rates,

and are usually answered promptly except at peak times, when you may have to wait up to ten minutes for a reply.

Credit-card **bookings** are made through the privatized rail companies, which means you have to know which network you'll be travelling on – if in doubt, phone the enquiries number above to check. The companies running the principal networks are listed below.

Anglia Railways ☎01603/764776, *www.angliarailways.co.uk*
Central Trains ☎0845/603 9219, *www.centraltrains.co.uk*
GNER ☎08457/225 225, *www.gner.co.uk*
First Great Eastern ☎0645/505000, *www.ger.co.uk*
First Great Western ☎08457/000125, *www.great-western-trains.co.uk*
Midland Main Line ☎08457/125678, *www.mml.co.uk*
Network SouthCentral ☎0181/643 7919.
First North Western Trains ☎0870/606 6007, *www.nwt.co.uk*
Northern Spirit ☎0870/602 3322, *www.northern-spirit.co.uk*
South West Trains ☎01703/213650, *www.swtrains.co.uk*
Thames Trains ☎0345/300700, *www.rail.co.uk*
VirginTrains ☎08457/222333, *www.virgintrains.co.uk*
Wales & West Railways ☎0870/900 0773, *www.walesandwest.co.uk*
West Anglia Great Northern ☎0800/566566.

can buy your ticket on board – but if you've embarked at a station that does have a machine and you've got on the train without buying a ticket, the inspector is entitled to charge you the full fare to your destination and issue you with an on-the-spot fine of £10 or twice the standard single fare.

RAIL PASSES

For foreign visitors who anticipate covering a lot of ground around Britain, a rail pass is a wise investment. The standard **BritRail Pass**, which must be bought before you enter the country, is available from BritRail Travel International (see box above) and many specialist tour operators outside Britain (see pp.6 & 9). It gives unlimited travel in England, Scotland and Wales for 8 days ($265), 15 days ($400), 22 days ($505) or 1 month

($600). The **BritRail Flexipass** is good for travel on 4 days out of 1 month ($235), 8 days out of 1 month ($304), or 15 days out of 2 months ($515). Note that with both these passes there are discounts for those under 25 (BritRail Youth passes) or over 60 (BritRail Senior passes), and the Flexipass has a special 15 days out of 2 months rate for under-26s ($360).

More specialized passes include the **BritRail Family Pass** – buy one of the special passes listed above (such as the Flexipass) and one accompanying child gets a pass of the same type free, other children getting the appropriate pass at half price. There's also a **BritRail SouthEast Pass**, which works like the standard Flexipass, but coverage is limited to the southeast counties. The SouthEast Pass comes in three sizes – valid for 3 days out of 8 ($70), 4 days out of 8 ($100) and 7 days out of 15 ($135). For unlimited bus and tube travel in the capital, there's the **London Visitor Travelcard**, ($32 for 3 days, $41 for 4 days, $63 for a week).

If you are planning to travel widely around Europe by train, then it may be worthwhile buying a **Eurail Pass**, though this is unlikely to pay for itself if you stick to England alone. The pass, which must be purchased before arrival in Europe, allows unlimited free first-class train travel in the UK and sixteen other countries. The **Eurail Youthpass** (for under-26s) costs $388 for 15 days, $499 for 21 days, or $623 for 1 month; if you're 26 or over you'll have to buy a first-class pass, available in 15-day ($554), 21-day ($718), and 1-month ($890) versions. You stand a better chance of getting your money's worth out of a **Eurail Flexipass**, which is valid for a certain number of travel days in a 2-month period. This, too, comes in under-26/first-class versions: 10 days, costing $458/$654 and $599/$862 for 15 days.

Some passes are available only in Britain itself. The **Young Person's Railcard** costs £18 and gives 30 percent reductions on all standard, Saver, SuperSaver and SuperAdvanced fares to full-time students and those aged between 16 and 25. A **Senior Citizens' RailCard**, also £18 and offering 30 percent reductions, is available to those aged 60 or over. The **Family Railcard** costs £20, and gives a variety of discounts from 20 to 30 percent for up to four adults travelling with children. Even more enticingly, it allows up to four children aged 5 to 15 to travel anywhere in the country for a flat fare of £2 each (which includes a seat reservation). Another pass worth mentioning is the **Network Card**, which costs £20 and gives a 33 percent discount on off-peak services throughout London and the south (including Oxford, Cambridge and all the Home Counties). Up to four adults can travel on this card, along with up to four children, who will be charged a flat fare of £1 for each journey.

BUSES AND COACHES

Inter-town **bus** services (known as coaches in England) duplicate many rail routes, very often at half the price of the train or less. The frequency of service is often comparable to rail, and in some instances the difference in journey time isn't great enough to be a deciding factor; buses are comfortable, and the ones on longer routes often have drinks and sandwiches available on board.

There's a plethora of regional companies operating buses and coaches, but by far the biggest national operator is National Express, whose network extends to every corner of the country. With rail prices becoming exorbitant, National Express services are so popular that for busy routes and on any route at weekends and during holidays it's advisable to book ahead, rather than just turn up.

UK residents under 25, in full-time education or over 50 can buy a National Express **Discount Coach Card**, which costs £8, is valid for 1 year and entitles the holder to a 30 percent discount. Foreign travellers of any age can purchase a **Tourist Trail Pass**, which offers unlimited travel on the National Express network for 2 consecutive days (£39 for students and under-23s/£49 for others), 5 days within 10 (£69/£85), 7 days within 21 (£94/£120) or 14 days within 30 (£143/£187). In England you can obtain both passes from major travel agents, at Gatwick and Heathrow airports, at the Britain Visitor Centre in London (see p.55), or at the main National Express office – Victoria Coach Station, Buckingham Palace Rd, London SW1 (☎0990/808080). In North America these passes are available for the dollar equivalent through specialist tour operators (see box on p.6) or direct from British Travel Associates, PO Box 299, Elkton, VA 22827 (☎1-800/327-6097).

Local bus services are run by a bewildering array of companies, most private, a few not. In many cases, timetables and routes are well integrated, but it's increasingly the case that private companies duplicate the busiest routes in an attempt to undercut the commercial opposition, leaving the farther-flung spots neglected. Thus, if you want to get from one end of a big English city to another, you'll probably have a choice of buses all offering cut-price fares, but to get out into the suburbs or to a satellite village, you may have to wait several hours. As a rule, the further away from urban areas you get, the less frequent and more expensive bus services become, but there are very few rural areas which aren't served by at least the occasional privately owned minibus. For all local bus details, call the information and hotline numbers listed in the guide where appropriate.

Many rural areas not covered by other forms of public transport are served by the **Post Bus Network**, which operates minibuses carrying mail and about eight fare-paying passengers. They set off in the morning – usually around 8am

MOTORING ORGANIZATIONS

American Automobile Association (AAA), 4100 E Arkansas Ave, Denver, CO 80222 (☎1-800/222 4357).

Australian Automobile Association, 212 Northbourne Ave, Canberra, ACT 2601 (☎61/6247 7311).

Automobile Association, Fanum House, Basingstoke, Hants RG21 2EA (☎0990/448866).

Canadian Automobile Association, 2 Carlton St, Toronto, ON M4B 1K4 (☎1-800/263-8389 or 905-525-1210).

National Breakdown Green Flag, Green Flag House, Cote Lane, Leeds LS28 5GF (☎0800/000111).

New Zealand Automobile Association, PO Box 1794, Wellington (☎64/473 8738).

Royal Automobile Club, PO Box 100, RAC House, 7 Brighton Rd, South Croydon CR2 6XW (☎0181/686 0088).

CAR RENTAL FIRMS

UK

Avis ☎0990/900500, *www.avis.com*
Budget ☎0800/181181, *www.budget.com*
Europcar BCR ☎0345/222525, *www.europcar.com*
National Car Rental ☎01895/233300, *www.nationalcar.com*
Hertz ☎0990/996699, *www.hertz.com*
Holiday Autos ☎0990/300400, *www.holidayautos.co.uk*
Thrifty ☎0990/168238, *www.thrifty.co.uk*

NORTH AMERICA

Alamo US ☎1-800/522-9696; Canada ☎1-800/GO-ALAMO, *www.goalamo.com*
Avis US ☎1-800/331-1084; Canada ☎1-800/331-1084, *www.avis.com*

Budget US ☎1-800/527-0700; Canada ☎1-800/268-8900, *www.drivebudget.com*
Europe By Car US ☎1-800/223-1516 or 212-245-1713, *www.europebycar.com*
Hertz US ☎1-800/654-3001; Canada ☎1-800/654-3001, *www.hertz.com*
Holiday Autos US ☎1-800/422-7737; Canada ☎1-800/678-0678, *www.kemwel.com*
National Car Rental US ☎1-800/CAR-RENT, *www.nationalcar.com*

AUSTRALIA

Avis ☎1800/225533
Budget ☎1300/362848
Hertz ☎1800/550067

from the main post office and collect mail (or deliver it) from/to the outlying regions. It's a cheap way to travel, and can be a convenient way of getting to hidden-away B&Bs, although it is often excruciatingly slow. You can get a free booklet of routes and timetables from the Royal Mail, Road Transport Consultancy, Room BT 20/3rd Floor, Rowland Hill House, Boythorpe Road, Chesterfield S49 1HQ (☎01246/546329).

A popular service pitched at budget travellers and backpackers is the **"Jump-On-Jump-Off"** **minibus** run by the Stray company. Starting in London, it travels three days each week in a clockwise direction around England, Wales and Scotland via Windsor, Bath, Snowdonia, The Lakes, Liverpool, Edinburgh, York, Stratford, and Oxford before heading back to the capital. Tickets cost £129, and are valid for for up to 4 months. There is also a shorter trip from London to Liverpool. You can use this bus as a "Jump-

On-Jump-Off" option or as a six-day **guided tour**, either arranging accommodation (average price £10 per night) along the way yourself or letting the company do the hard work for you. Contact Stray, 171 Earls Court Road, Earls Court, London SW5 9RF (☎ 0171/373 7737, *www.straytravel.com*).

DRIVING

In order to **drive** in England you need a current full **driving licence**. If you're bringing your own vehicle into the country you should also carry your **vehicle registration** or **ownership document** at all times. Furthermore, you must be **adequately insured**: check your existing insurance policy.

In England you **drive on the left**, a situation which can lead to a few tense days of acclimatization for overseas drivers. Speed limits are 30–40mph (50–65kph) in built-up areas, 70mph

(110kph) on motorways (freeways) and dual carriageways and 60mph (95kph) on most other roads. As a rule, assume that in any area with street lighting the speed limit is 30mph (50kph) unless otherwise stated.

Fuel is expensive compared to North American prices – unleaded petrol (gasoline) costs in the region of 70p per litre, leaded 4-star 78p, and diesel 72p. The lowest prices of all are charged at out-of-town supermarkets; suburban service stations are usually fairly reasonable; and the highest prices are charged by motorway stations.

The Automobile Association (AA), the Royal Automobile Club (RAC) and Green Flag National Breakdown all operate 24-hour emergency **breakdown**. The first two also provide many other motoring services including a reciprocal arrangement for free assistance through many overseas motoring organizations – check the situation with your association before setting out. On motorways, the AA and RAC can be called from roadside booths; elsewhere ring ☎0800/887766 for the AA, ☎0800/828282 for the RAC and ☎0800/400600 for Green Flag. You can ring these emergency numbers even if you are not a member of the respective organization, although a substantial fee will be charged.

Car **parking** in cities and in popular tourist spots can be a nightmare and will also cost you a small fortune. If you're in a tourist city for a day, look out for the **Park-and-Ride schemes** where you can park your car and take a cheap or free bus to the centre. Parking in the long or short stay car parks will be cheaper than using meters which restrict parking time to two hours at the most. As a rule, the smaller the town, the cheaper the parking. A yellow line along the edge of the road indicates parking restrictions; check the nearest sign to see exactly what they are. A double-yellow line means no parking at any time, though you can stop briefly to unload or pick up people or goods (maximum stop two minutes), but if the lines are red, that means absolutely no stopping at all.

CAR AND MOTORBIKE RENTAL

Compared to rates in North America, **car rental** in England is expensive, and you'll probably find it cheaper to arrange things in advance through one

For **bicycle rental**, see "Outdoor Pursuits", p.44.

of the multinational chains, or by opting for a fly/drive deal. If you do rent a car from a company in England, the least you can expect to pay is around £135 a week, which is the rate for a small hatchback from Holiday Autos, the most competitive company; reckon on paying around £40 per day for something direct from one of the multinationals, £10 or so less at a local firm. Rental agencies prefer you to pay by credit card and you may have to leave a deposit of £100 or more on top of the rental charge. There are very few automatics at the lower end of the price scale – if you want one, you should book well ahead. To rent a car you need to show your driving licence; few companies will rent to drivers with less than one year's experience and most will only rent to people between 21 and 70 years of age.

Motorbike rental is ludicrously expensive if you go to a specialized agent such as Scootabout Ltd, 1 Leeke St, London WC1X 9HZ (☎0171/833 4607), which charges around £299 per week for a Deauville, or £365 for a Pan-European ST1100. These prices include insurance cover, 250 miles free (after which it's 10p per mile), and the bikes are kept in top condition. However, you'll save a fortune by taking a chance on an ex-dispatch machine, which can be rented from as little as £50 per week from London-based courier companies such as World's End (☎0181/746 3595), Banjax (☎0171/729 5228) and Mike's Bikes (☎0181/983 4896). The last currently offers the best deals, with a Honda CB350 going for £55 per week (plus a £55 deposit), and NTV650s for £85 per week (£200 deposit). They also have CG125s for pottering around the city at £50 a week, and do very competitive insurance deals, including short-term third-party policies from around £50 per month. You don't have to be a dispatch rider to rent from these companies, although you'll need a full bike licence, and some places only take clients aged 23 or over.

The Auto-Cycle Union, ACU House, Wood St, Rugby, Warwickshire, CV21 2YX (☎01788/566400) can send you a useful free booklet about touring.

CAR AND CAMPER VAN PURCHASE

If you're with a group and visiting for months, rather than weeks, you might consider it worthwhile buying a car or camper van. Both types of vehicle will give you greater independence and flexibility of travel, and the camper van has the added benefit of providing your sleeping needs, too. The best way to get a decent vehicle – a car for under £1000 and a van for £2000 or under – is either to scour the pages of the weekly *Autotrader* or the local ads papers such as *Loot*. If you can find a professional car mechanic to look your bargain over for you, so much the better – a few pounds spent this way could save you a lot in the long run. If the car is more than three years old, make sure it has a Ministry of Transport (MOT) certificate and, if possible, tax, as these are transferred to the new owner. Otherwise you'll end up paying for a minimum six months tax at £85.50, an MOT test and any subsequent repairs necessary for the certificate. Shop around for the compulsory insurance which is probably going to be at least £200. You'll find all information you need about licensing and registering procedures in the form V100, available from any post office.

LIFT SHARING

Due to the decrease in popularity of hitching in the UK, lift-sharing deals have started to appear as a cheap and safer way of getting around the country. There is currently **no organized lift-share agency** in the UK, so the best option is to consult the noticeboards of specialist travellers' bookshops and hostels or put up your own notice; Nomad Books at 781 Fulham Rd, London SW6 5HA (☎0171/736 4000) has a particularly good noticeboard downstairs. The travel magazine *Wanderlust* has a useful "Connections" page worth consulting for possible lift shares/travel companions; you can advertise on this page (£5 for up to 50 words), though you should plan well ahead as the magazine is only published once every two months. Address mail to: Connections, Wanderlust, PO Box 1832, Windsor, SL4 6YP (☎01753/620426). Another option is to look in the small-ads sections of local papers.

TAXIS

Taxis are a useful option for finding that hostel or sight that's off the beaten track or when time is limited. Also, if you're with a group hiring a taxi it can work out as cheap as taking a bus. Reckon on paying around £3 for the first mile and £1 for subsequent miles in cities, and £1.40 a mile in country districts. Black cabs are generally a little more expensive than minicabs, but are usually more reliable. You can hail a black cab on the street, but you must book minicabs by phone – we have given numbers for reliable minicab services throughout the book.

ORGANIZED TOURS

In addition to the "Jump-On-Jump-Off" buses already mentioned (see p.26), Outback, The Cottage, Church Green, Badby, Northants NN11 3AS (☎01327/704115, *www.outbackuk.clara.net*) runs fourteen-day tours, taking in England as well as Scotland and Wales and geared to backpackers. The minibus leaves London on Saturdays and takes in Cornwall and the Lake District, running over the border into Wales (Snowdonia) and up to Scotland (Edinburgh) before returning to London and gives you the option of joining for three, five, seven or ten days only, paying either £35 a day for all travel, accommodation, and two meals a day; £28 for travel and accommodation; or £18 for travel only.

Trafalgar, 22 Craven Terrace, London W2 3QH (☎0171/262 1292) offers round coach trips from London, taking in Stratford-upon-Avon and Hadrian's Wall before nipping up to Scotland and returning via the Lake District. The excursions run all year and include all meals and hotel accommodation; four-day trips cost from £245, six days from £295. Alternatively, between April and September, you could opt for the five-day Devon and Cornwall tour (from £250). Similar escorted tours from London are organized by Insight, Gareloch House, 6 Gareloch Rd, Port Glasgow, PA14 5XH, (☎0990/143433, *www.insighthols.com.au*) who offer a seven-day tour of the south of England (May to October only) which follows a route through Brighton, Devon and Cornwall and Bristol, with detours to Stonehenge, Bath and Glastonbury (£435).

ACCOMMODATION

England has scores of upmarket hotels, ranging from bland business-oriented places to plush country mansions, as well as budget accommodation in the form of hundreds of bed and breakfast places (B&Bs) and youth hostels. Nearly all tourist offices will book rooms for you, although the fee for this service varies considerably. In some areas you will pay a deposit that's deducted from your first night's bill (usually 10 percent), in others the office will take a percentage or flat-rate commission – on average around £3. Another useful service operated by the majority of tourist offices is the "Book-a-bed-ahead" service, which locates accommodation in your next port of call again for a charge of about £3, though the service is sometimes free. For a full explanation of the price-coding system used in this book see the box below.

HOTELS AND B&BS

There is no formalized nationwide system for grading **hotel** accommodation in England, but the tourist authorities and various private organizations classify hotels on a system of stars, crowns, rosettes or similar badges, typically with five stars being the top rank. The grades used by the AA and RAC are the most reliable, as they combine evaluation of facilities with a degree of subjective judgment – thus a hotel offering a whirlpool in each room will not earn its five stars if the management is bloody-minded or the hotel food atrocious. Though there's not a hard and fast correlation between standards and price, you'll probably be paying in the region of £50–60 per night for a double room at a one-star hotel (breakfast included), rising to around £100 in a three-star and from around £200 for a five-star – in London you pay twice that. In some larger towns and cities you'll find that the larger hotels often offer cut-price deals on Saturdays and Sundays to fill the rooms vacated by the week's business trade, but these places tend to be soulless multinational chain operations. If you have money to throw around, stay in a nicely refurbished old building – the historic towns of England are chock-full of top-quality old coaching inns and similar ancient hostelries, while out in the countryside there are numerous converted mansions and manor houses, often with brilliant restaurants attached.

At the lower end of the scale, it's sometimes difficult to differentiate between a hotel and a **bed and breakfast (B&B)** establishment. At their most basic, these typically English places – often known also as **guest houses** in resorts and other tourist towns – are ordinary private houses with a couple of bedrooms set aside for paying guests and a dining room for the consumption of a rudimentary breakfast. At their best, however, B&Bs offer rooms as well furnished as those in hotels costing twice as much, delicious home-prepared breakfasts, and an informal hospitality that a larger place couldn't match. B&Bs are graded by the same organiza-

---

ACCOMMODATION PRICE CODES

Throughout this guide, hotel and B&B accommodation is priced on a scale of ① to ⑨, the number indicating the **lowest price** you could expect to pay per night in that establishment for a **double room** in high season. The prices indicated by the codes are as follows:

① under £40	④ £60–70	⑦ £110–150
② £40–50	⑤ £70–90	⑧ £150–200
③ £50–60	⑥ £90–110	⑨ over £200

tions mentioned above, but using diamonds instead of stars. As a guideline on costs, it's easy to find a one-diamond place for under £40 per night for double B&B, and right at the top end of the scale, there are some four-diamond places for as little as £70 – farmhouse B&Bs are especially good value. As many B&Bs, even the pricier ones, have a very small number of rooms, you should certainly book a place as far in advance as possible. Finally, don't assume that a B&B is no good if it's ungraded. There are so many B&Bs in England that the grading inspectors can't possibly keep track of them all, and in the rural backwaters some of the most enjoyable accommodation is to be found in welcoming and beautifully set houses whose facilities may technically fall short of official standards.

HOSTELS AND CAMPING BARNS

The **Youth Hostels Association** network consists of over 230 properties in England and Wales, offering bunk-bed accommodation in single-sex dormitories or smaller rooms of four to six beds. A few new hostels and many refurbished older ones also now have double and family rooms available, and in cities the facilities are often every bit as good as some hotels. Indeed, although a few places are spartan establishments of the sort traditionally associated with the wholesome, fresh-air ethic of the first hostels, most have moved well away from the old-fashioned, institutional ambience, and boast services like cafés, laundry facilities, Internet access, entertainment and bike rental.

Membership of the YHA costs £5.50 per year for under-18s, £11 for others, and can be obtained either by writing to the YHA (see box below) or in

person at any YHA-affiliated hostel; this gives you membership of the hostelling associations of the sixty countries affiliated to Hostelling International (HI). Foreign visitors who belong to any HI association have automatic membership of the YHA; if you aren't a member of such an organization, you can join the HI at any English or Welsh hostel for a £11 fee or alternatively by collecting six Welcome stamps at £1.80 each from hostels as you go along.

Prices at most English hostels range from £4.20 per night for under-18s and from £6.10 for the over-18s. Students aged 18–25 can get a £1 reduction on production of a valid student card. Length of stay is normally unlimited, and the hostel warden will provide a linen sleeping bag for a small charge. The cost of hostel **meals** is similarly low: breakfast is around £3.20, a packed lunch is about £3.50 and evening meals start at just £4.60. Nearly all hostels have kitchen facilities for those who prefer self-catering.

At any time of year it's best to **book your place** well in advance, and it's essential at Easter and Christmas and from May to August. Most hostels accept payment by Mastercard or Visa; with those that don't, you should confirm your booking in writing, with payment, at least seven days before arrival. Bookings made less than seven days in advance will be held only until 6pm on the day of arrival. If you're tempted to turn up on the spur of the moment, bear in mind that very few are open year-round, many are closed at least one day a week, even in high season, and several have periods during which they take bookings from groups only. We have indicated the months during which individual hostels are closed, but to give the full details of opening times within this guide

YOUTH HOSTEL ASSOCIATIONS

Australia: Australian Youth Hostels Association, 422 Kent St, Sydney (☎02/9261 1111).

Canada: Hostelling International–Canadian Hostelling Association, Room 400, 205 Catherine St, Ottawa, ON K2P 1C3 (☎613/237-7884 or ☎800/663-5777).

England: Youth Hostels Association (YHA), Trevelyan House, 8 St Stephen's Hill, St Albans, Herts AL1 2DY (☎01727/845047, www.yha.org.uk).

Ireland: An Oige, 61 Mountjoy St, Dublin 7 (☎01/830 4555).

New Zealand: Youth Hostels Association of New Zealand, PO Box 436, Christchurch 1 (☎03/799970).

Northern Ireland: Youth Hostels Association of Northern Ireland, 22 Donegal Rd, Belfast BT12 5JN (☎01232/324733).

USA: Hostelling International–American Youth Hostels (HI-AYH), 733 15th St NW, Suite 840, PO Box 37613, Washington, DC 20005 (☎202/783 6161).

would be impossibly unwieldy, so **always phone** to check – we've given the number for every hostel mentioned. Most hostels are closed from 10am to 5pm, with an 11.30pm curfew, although all seven of the London hostels offer 24-hour access.

At best, **independent hostels**, which are more likely to be found in town centres than in the backwoods, offer facilities commensurate with those of YHA places, and at a lower price. However, many of these hostels make their money by over-cramming their rooms with beds, kitchens are often inadequate or nonexistent and washing facilities can be similarly poor. That said, a lot of people find the lack of curfews and lock-outs ample compensation. A useful publication to have is *The Independent Hostel Guide* (£3.95) published by The Backpackers Press, 2 Rockview Cottages, Matlock, Bath, Derbyshire, DE4 3PG, which fills you in on hostels in the UK and Ireland. Some cities have **YMCA** and **YWCA** hostels, though these are only worth considering if you're staying for at least a week, in which case you can get discounts on rates that otherwise are no better than budget B&Bs.

In England's university towns you should be able to find out-of-term accommodation in the **student halls**, usually one-bedded rooms either with their own or shared bathrooms. In some instances, this may be the only budget accommodation on offer in the centre of town – for example, if you were to bowl into Durham in high summer with nothing booked in advance. All the useful university addresses are given in the guide, but if you want a list of everything that's on offer, write to the British Universities Accommodation Consortium, Box 1781, University Park, Nottingham, NG7 2RD (☎0115/950 4571, *www.buac.co.uk*).

In the wilder parts of England, such as the north Pennines, north Yorkshire, Dartmoor and Exmoor, the YHA administers some basic accommodation for walkers in **camping barns**. Holding up to twenty people, these agricultural outbuildings are often unheated and are very sparsely furnished, with wooden sleeping platforms, or bunks if you're lucky, a couple of tables, a toilet and a cold water supply, but they are weatherproof, extremely good value (from £3.35 a night) and perfectly situated for walking tours. You do not have to be a YHA member to stay in any of these. Similar barns, often called **bunkhouses**, are run by private individuals in these areas – the useful ones are mentioned in the guide.

CAMPING AND CARAVANNING

There are hundreds of **campsites** in England, charging from £5 per tent per night to around £12 for the plushest sites, with amenities such as laundries, shops and sports facilities. Some YHA hostels have small campsites on their property, charging half the indoor overnight fee. In addition to these official sites, farmers may offer pitches

---

SELF-CATERING ACCOMMODATION FIRMS

Country Holidays, Spring Mill, Earby, Lancs BB94 0AA (☎01282/445400, *www.country-holidays.co.uk*). More than 5000 properties all over England.

English Country Cottages, Stoney Bank, Earby, Barnoldswick, Lancs BB94 0EF (☎0870/585 1100 or ☎01328/864041). Around 2000 cottages in various parts of rural England.

Landmark Trust, Shottesbrooke, Maidenhead, Berks SL6 3SW (☎01628/825925, *www.landmarktrust.co.uk*). Their brochure (£9.50) lists some 150 converted historic properties, ranging from restored forts and Martello towers to a tiny radio shack used in the last war.

National Trust (Enterprises) Ltd, PO Box 536, Melksham, Wilts SN12 8SX (☎01225/791199). Around 250 NT-owned cottages and farmhouses, most set in their own gardens or grounds.

Northumbria Byways, Crosby House, Crosby on Eden, Carlisle, Cumbria CA6 4QZ (☎01228/573337, *www.northumbria-byways.com*). Take your pick from thatched and slate cottages to castle apartments, situated in Northumberland and Border country.

Rural Retreats, Station Rd, Blockley, Moreton-in-Marsh, Gloucestershire GL56 9DZ (☎01386/701177, *www.ruralretreats.co.uk*). Upmarket apartments in restored old buildings, many of them listed buildings.

Vivat Trust, 61 Pall Mall, London, SW1Y 5HZ (☎0171/930 8030, *www.vivat.org.uk*). Small, select range of historic properties in Shropshire, Dorset, Cumbria and Derbyshire – including North Lees Hall, Charlotte Brontë's inspiration for Mr Rochester's Thornfield Hall in *Jane Eyre*.

for as little as £2 per night, but don't expect tiled bathrooms and hair dryers for that kind of money. Even farmers without a reserved camping area may let you pitch in a field if you ask first, and may even charge you nothing for the privilege; setting up a tent without asking is an act of trespass, which will not be well received. **Free camping is illegal** in National Parks and nature reserves.

The problem with many campsites in the most popular parts of rural England – especially the West Country coast – is that tents have to share the space with **caravans**. Every summer the country's byways are clogged by migrations of these cumbersome trailers, which are still far more numerous than camper vans in England. The great majority of caravans, however, are permanently moored at their sites, where they are rented out to families for self-catering holidays, and the ranks of nose-to-tail trailers in the vicinity of most of England's best beaches might make you think that half the population of Britain shacks up in a caravan for the midsummer break.

Visitors from outside England tend to prefer more robust **self-catering** accommodation, and there are thousands of BTA-approved properties for rent by the week, ranging from city penthouses to secluded cottages. The least you can expect to pay for four-berth self-catering accommodation in summer would be around £200 per week, but for something attractive – such as a small house near the West Country moors – you should budget for twice that amount. The BTA lists include accommodation up to £1200 per week and every regional tourist board has details of cottage rentals in its area; alternatively get hold of a copy of *Self Catering Holiday Homes: Where to Stay in England* (£6.99), published by the English Tourist Board.

Detailed annually revised guidebooks to England's camping and caravan sites include the AA's *Caravan and Camping in Britain and Ireland* (£8.99), which lists their inspected and graded sites, and Cade's *Camping, Touring and Motor Caravan Site Guide* (£4.75), published by Marwain. Alternative sources of information on all types of self-catering accommodation, from canal boats to lighthouses, are *Dalton's Weekly* (available from most newsagents) and the Sunday newspapers, and of course most English travel agents can offer a range of self-catering holiday packages. Some of the firms offering the more interesting accommodation options are listed in the box on p.31.

FOOD AND DRINK

Though the English still tend to regard eating as a functional necessity rather than a focal point of the day, great advances towards a more sophisticated appreciation of the culinary arts have been made in recent years. Every major town has its top-range restaurants, many of them boasting awards for excellence, while it's possible to eat well and inexpensively thanks chiefly to the influence of England's various immigrant communities. However, the pub will long remain the centre of social life in England, a drink in a traditional "local" often making the best introduction to the life of a town.

EATING

In many hotels and B&Bs you'll be offered what's termed an "**English breakfast**", which is basically sausage, bacon and eggs plus tea and toast. This used to be the typical working-class start to the day, but these days the English have adopted the healthier cereal alternative, and most places will give you this option as well. In any town you

RESTAURANT PRICE CODES

Restaurants listed in this guide have been assigned one of four price categories:

Inexpensive under £10   Expensive £20–30
Moderate £10–20   Very Expensive over £30

This is the price you can expect to pay per person for a three-course meal or equivalent, excluding drinks and service. Listed restaurants take credit cards unless otherwise stated.

won't have to walk far to find a so-called "**greasy spoon**" or "**caff**", where the early-day menu will include cholesterol-rich variations on the theme of sausage, beans, fried egg and chips.

For most overseas visitors the quintessential English meal is **fish and chips**, a dish that can vary from the succulently fresh to the indigestibly oily – in many fish-and-chip joints it's little wonder that lashings of salt, vinegar and tomato ketchup or the fruitier brown sauce are common additions. The classier places have tables, but more often they serve **takeaway** (takeout) food only, sometimes supplying a wooden fork so that you can guzzle your roadside meal with a modicum of decorum. Fish-and-chip shops can be found on most high streets and main suburban thoroughfares, although in larger towns they're beginning to be outnumbered by **pizza**, **kebab** and **burger** outlets.

Other sources of straightforward food at lunchtime and early evening are the "greasy spoon" places mentioned above (which tend to close at around 6–7pm), and **pubs** (which often stop serving food at 9pm), where you'll find plain "meat-and-two-veg" dishes: steak-and-kidney pie, chops or steaks, accompanied by boiled potatoes, carrots or some such vegetable. However, a lot of English pubs now take their food very seriously indeed, having separate dining areas and menus that can compete with some of the better mid-range restaurants. Another recent development is the growing number of specialist **vegetarian** restaurants, especially in the larger towns, and the increasing awareness of vegetarian preferences in other eating places. Also on the rise in the major towns are vaguely French **brasseries**, informal bar-restaurants offering simple meals from around £10–12 per head and often with a set lunchtime menu for around half that.

England has its diverse immigrant communities to thank for the range of foods in the mid-range category. Of the innumerable types of ethnic restaurants offering the good-value high-quality

meals you'll find **Chinese**, **Indian** and **Bangladeshi** specialities in every town of any size, with the widest choice in London and the industrial cities of the Midlands and the north. Other Asian restaurants, particularly **Thai** and **Indonesian**, are now becoming more widespread, but are generally a shade more expensive, while further up the economic scale there's no shortage of **French** and **Italian** places – by far the most popular European cuisines, though most cities have their share of more-or-less **Spanish** tapas bars. **Japanese** food has been one of the success stories of recent years, with diners and sushi places joining the expense-account restaurants that have been established for some time in the business centres of England.

The ranks of England's **gastronomic restaurants** grows with each passing year, with cordon-bleu chefs producing high-class French-style dishes, California-influenced menus, internationalist hybrid creations and traditional English meat- and fish-dishes that are as delicious as the more arty creations of their cross-Channel counterparts. London of course has the highest concentration of top-flight places, but wherever you are in England you're never more than half an hour's drive from a really good meal – some of the very best dining rooms are to be found in the countryside hotels. The problem is that fine food costs more in England than it does anywhere else in Europe. If a place has any sort of reputation in foodie circles you're unlikely to be spending less than £30 per head, and for the services of the country's glamour chefs you could be paying a preposterous £120.

Our restaurant listings include a mix of high-quality and good-value establishments, but if you're intent on a culinary pilgrimage, you would do well to arm yourself with a copy of the *Which Good Food Guide* (£14.99), which is updated annually and includes nearly 1300 detailed recommendations. Throughout this book, we've supplied the phone numbers for all restaurants where you may need to book a table. We've also coded restaurants from "Inexpensive" to "Very Expensive"; for details of what this means, see the box on p.33.

DRINKING

The combination of an inclement climate and an English temperamental aversion to casual chat makes the simple **café** a rare phenomenon outside the biggest cities – there are probably more in London's Soho and surrounding area than in the rest of the country combined. A growing number of pubs now serve **tea and coffee** during the day but in most places you'll attract consternation by asking for a cup; in the more genteel tourist towns – such as Stratford, Harrogate and York – you'll find plenty of **tea shops**, unlicensed establishments where the normal procedure is to order a slice of cake or some other pastry with your tea or coffee – the former is far more popular. Increasingly common in the big cities are **brasseries** or equivalent establishments (see p.33), where the majority of customers are there for a bite to eat, but where you're generally welcome to spend half an hour nursing a cappuccino or a glass of wine.

Nothing is likely to dislodge the **pub** from its status as the great English social institution, however. Originating as wayfarers' hostelries and coaching inns, pubs have outlived the church and marketplace as the focal points of English communities, and at their best they can be as welcoming as the full name – "public house" – suggests. Pubs are as varied as the country's townscapes: in larger market towns you'll find huge oak-beamed inns with open fires and polished brass fittings; in the remoter upland villages there are stone-built pubs no larger than a two-bedroomed cottage; and in the more inward-looking parts of industrial England you'll come across nononsense pubs where something of the old division of the sexes and classes still holds sway – the "spit and sawdust" public bar is where working men can bond over a pint or two, the plusher saloon bar, with a separate entrance, is the preferred haunt of mutually preoccupied couples, the middle classes and unaccompanied women. Whatever the species of pub, its **opening hours** are daily 11am–11pm (but in quieter spots, pubs tend to close between about 3 and 5.30pm).

Most pubs are owned by large breweries who favour their own **beers** and **lagers**, as well as some "guest beers", all dispensed by the pint or half-pint. (A pint costs anything from around £1.20 to £2.70, depending on the brew and the locale of the pub.) The most widespread type of English beer is **bitter**, an uncarbonated and dark beverage that should be pumped by hand from the cellar and served at room temperature. (The sweeter, darker "mild" beer is now virtually extinct.) In recent years, boosted by aggressive advertising, **lager** has overtaken beer in popularity, and every pub will have at least two brands on offer, but the major breweries are now capitalizing on a backlash against foreign-sounding, pale, chilly and often tasteless drinks, a reaction in large part due to the work of **CAMRA** (Campaign for Real Ale). Some of the beer touted as good English ale is nothing of the sort (if the stuff comes out of an electric pump, it isn't the real thing), and some of the genuine beers have been adulterated since being taken over by the big companies, but the big breweries do widely distribute some very good beers – for example, Directors, produced by the giant Courage group, is a very classy strong bitter. Guinness, a very dark, creamy Irish stout, is also on sale virtually everywhere, and is an exception to the high-minded objection to electrically pumped beers – though purists will tell you that the stuff the English drink does not compare with the home variety.

Smaller operations whose fine ales are available over a wide area include Young's, Fuller's, Wadworth's, Adnams, Greene King, Flowers and Tetley's. However, if you want to find out how good English beer can be, sample the products of the innumerable small breweries producing real ales to traditional recipes – every region has its distinctive brew, several of which are recommended in this guide. These regional concoctions are frequently available at free houses, independently run establishments that sell what they please and are generally more characterful than so-called "tied pubs". If you see a CAMRA sticker on the window, the beer inside is certainly worth a try, but for serious research the *Good Beer Guide* (£10.99), published annually by CAMRA, is essential. Also useful is the annual *Good Pub Guide* (Ebury Press; £14.99), a thousand-page handbook that rates each pub's ambience and food as well as its beer.

Cider, the fermented produce of apples, is a sweet, alcoholic beverage produced in the West Country, where it's often preferred to beer. The cider sold in pubs all over England is a fizzy drink that only approximates to the far more potent and less refined **scrumpy**, the type of cider consumed by aficionados of the apple. As with beer, the best scrumpy is available within a short radius of the factory, but the drink has nothing like the variety of beer.

Wines sold in pubs are generally appalling, a strange situation in view of the excellent range of wine available in off-licences and supermarkets.

The wine lists in brasseries and wine bars are nearly always better, but the mark-ups are often outrageous, and any members of the party who prefer beer will have to be content with bottled drinks. Nonetheless, many people are prepared to pay the extra in return for a less boozy and male-dominated atmosphere.

POST AND PHONES

Virtually all **post offices** are open Mon–Fri 9am–5.30pm, Sat 9am–12.30 or 1pm; in small communities you'll find sub-post offices operating out of a shop, open the same hours, even if the shop itself is open for longer. Stamps can be bought at post office counters, from vending machines outside, or from an increasing number of newsagents, usually in books of four or ten. A first-class letter to anywhere in the British Isles currently costs 26p and should – in theory, at least – arrive the next day; second-class letters cost 19p, and take from 2 to 4 days. Airmail letters of less than 20g (0.7oz) to European countries cost 30p and elsewhere overseas from 44p for 10g, and 64p for 20g. Pre-stamped aerogrammes conforming to overseas airmail weight limits of under 10g can be bought for 37p from post offices only. For more information about Royal Mail postal services, call ☎0345/740740.

Most public **payphones** are operated by British Telecom (BT) and, at least in the towns, are widespread. Many payphones take all coins from 10p upwards, although an increasing proportion only accept **phonecards**, available from post offices and newsagents which display BT's

green logo. These cards come in denominations of £3, £5, £10; an increasing number of phones also accept **credit cards**.

Inland calls are cheapest at weekends and between 6pm and 8am on weekdays. Reduced rate periods for most **international calls** are 6pm–8am from Monday to Friday and all day Saturday and Sunday. A cheaper way to call is from one of the number of **independent telecom centres**, though you're likely to find these only in the major cities.

Throughout this guide, every telephone number is prefixed by the area code, separated from the subscriber number by an oblique slash, which is omitted if dialling from within the area covered by

---

OPERATOR SERVICES

Domestic operator ☎100
International operator ☎155
Domestic directory assistance ☎192 (free from payphones, otherwise 35p)
International directory assistance ☎153 (free from payphones, otherwise 80p)

INTERNATIONAL CALLS

To call England from overseas dial the international access code (☎011 from the US and Canada, ☎0011 from Australia and ☎00 from New Zealand) followed by 44, the area code minus its initial zero, and then the number. To dial out of England it's ☎00 followed by the country code, area code (with the exception of Italy and Czech Republic, without the zero if there is one) and subscriber number. Country codes are as follows:

Australia ☎61
Ireland ☎353
New Zealand ☎64
US and Canada ☎ 1

TELEPHONE NUMBERS IN THE UK

On April 22, 2000, the UK's telephone-numbering system will change. Six regions will be given **new area codes** – Cardiff, Coventry, London, Northern Ireland, Portsmouth and Southampton – and special-rate numbers will be reconfigured.

Until September 16, 2000, if phoning **from outside an affected area**, you can use either the old number or the new one. However, there is no changeover period for **locally dialled numbers**: the new local numbers won't work until April 22, 2000, and only those numbers will work after that.

The numbers for the affected areas will be reconfigured as follows:

Cardiff:
(01222) xxx xxx becomes **(029) 20**xx xxxx

Portsmouth:
(01705) xxx xxx becomes **(023) 92**xx xxxx

Coventry:
(01203) xxx xxx becomes **(024) 76**xx xxxx

Southampton:
(01703) xxx xxx becomes **(023) 80**xx xxxx

London:
(0171) xxx xxxx becomes **(020) 7**xxx xxxx
(0181) xxx xxxx becomes **(020) 8**xxx xxxx

*Belfast:
(01232) xx xxxx becomes **(028) 90**xx xxxx

The process of reconfiguring **special-rate numbers** (numbers with four-digit prefixes starting 08 or 09) started in autumn 1999, but the latest information is that old and new numbers should work side by side until at least autumn 2000.

*Belfast is used purely as an example. The Northern Ireland code will change to 028, with local 5- and 6-digit numbers all becoming 8 digits long. For changes to other Northern Ireland numbers or queries about special-rate numbers, **call directory enquiries** on ☎192.

that prefix. However, some prefixes relate to the cost of calls rather than the location of the subscriber, and should never be omitted: numbers with ☎0800 and 0808 prefixes are free of charge to the caller; ☎0345 and 08457 numbers are charged at local rates, ☎0870 up to the national rate, irrespective of where in the country you are calling from; and ☎0900 and 0901 are always charged at premium rate.

A **reconfiguration of telephone numbers** is currently taking place in the UK – a process

that began in the summer of 1999, but that is not due to be completed until some time in autumn 2000. Throughout the book we have used the old telephone-numbering system, which will – in most cases – work in tandem with the new numbers throughout the changeover period. Throughout the text, in accounts of areas where numbers will be reconfigured, the relevant changes are outlined in a small box. For full details of the changes, see the box above.

OPENING HOURS AND HOLIDAYS

General **shop hours** are Mon–Sat 9am–5.30pm or 6pm, although there's an increasing amount of Sunday and late-night shopping in the larger towns, with Thursday and Friday the favoured evenings. The big supermarkets also tend to stay open until 8pm or 9pm from Monday to Saturday and open from 10am to 4pm on Sundays, as do many stores in the shopping complexes that are springing up on the outskirts of many major towns. It's also not unusual to find some of the supermarkets in cities and large towns open 24 hours. By contrast, many provincial towns still retain an "early closing day" when shops close at 1pm; Wednesday is the favourite. Note that not all service stations on motorways are open for 24 hours, although you can usually get fuel around the clock in larger towns and cities. Note also

> **PUBLIC HOLIDAYS IN ENGLAND**
>
> January 1
> Good Friday – late March to early April
> Easter Monday – as above
> First Monday in May
> Last Monday in May
> Last Monday in August
> December 25
> December 26
> Note that if January 1, December 25 or December 26 falls on a Saturday or Sunday, the next weekday becomes a public holiday.

that most fee-charging sites are open on **public holidays**, known as **bank holidays** in England, when Sunday hours usually apply.

ADMISSION TO MUSEUMS AND MONUMENTS

Many of England's most treasured sites – from castles, abbeys and great houses to tracts of protected landscape – come under the control of the private **National Trust**, 36 Queen Anne's Gate, London SW1H 9AS (☎0171/222 9251, *www.nationaltrust.org.uk*) or the state-run **English Heritage**, 23 Savile Row, London W1X 1AB (☎0171/973 3000, *www.english–heritage.org.uk*) whose properties are denoted in the guide with "**NT**" or "**EH**" after the opening hours. Both these organizations charge an entry fee for the majority of their sites, and these can be quite high, especially for the more grandiose National Trust estates. If you think you'll be visiting more than half a dozen places owned by the National Trust or more than a dozen owned by English Heritage, it's worth taking **annual membership** (NT £29; EH £26), which allows free entry to their respective properties.

A lot of **stately homes** remain in the hands of the landed gentry, who tend to charge in the region of £5 for admission to edited highlights of their domain – even more if, as at Longleat, they've added some theme-park attractions to the historic pile. Many other old buildings, albeit rarely the most momentous structures, are

owned by the local authorities, which are generally more lenient with their admission charges, sometimes allowing free access. You may find that a history museum or a similar collection has been installed in the local castle or half-rebuilt ruin, and in these cases there's usually a modest entry charge. However, **municipal art galleries and museums** are often free, a situation that holds with many of the great **state museums** – both the British Museum and the National Gallery are free to all visitors, for example. On the other hand, these cash-starved institutions are nowadays obliged to request voluntary donations, as are several of the country's **cathedrals**. Most cathedrals charge a pound or two for admission to the most beautiful parts of the structure – usually the chapter house or cloister.

You will certainly have to pay to visit any of England's burgeoning **heritage museums**, which in some instances are large multi-building sites staffed by people in period costume, but more often consist of interactive displays – some of which take the form of hi-tech animatronic tableaux, while others amount to little more than a few mannequins with video monitors for heads. Tickets for these can cost anywhere between £5 and £10, and expense is not necessarily an indication of quality. However, the most expensive attractions in England are those aimed squarely at tourists with cash to spend – Madame Tussaud's and the London Planetarium, the country's number one earner of foreign cash, now charges £12 for admission.

The majority of fee-charging attractions in England have **reductions** for senior citizens, the unemployed, full-time students and children under 16, with under-5s being admitted free almost everywhere. Proof of eligibility will be required in most cases, though even the flintiest desk clerk will probably take on trust the age of a babe-in-arms. The entry charges given in the guide are the full adult charges – as a rule, adult reductions are in the range of 25–35 percent, while reductions for children are around 50 per-

cent. Most attractions are open daily in summer, with one or two closed days in the winter, though the major state museums are open daily all year. We've given full details of opening hours in the guide.

Finally, foreign visitors planning on seeing more than a dozen stately homes, monuments or gardens might find it worthwhile to buy a **Great British Heritage Pass**, which gives free admission to some six hundred sites, many of which are not run by the National Trust or English Heritage. Costing under £30 for seven days, £42 for fifteen days and £56 for a month. The pass can be purchased through most travel agents at home, on arrival at any large UK airport, from most major tourist offices and the Britain Visitor Centre, 1 Regent St, London W1 (walk-in service only).

THE MEDIA

NEWSPAPERS AND MAGAZINES

English **daily newspapers** are predominantly right wing, with the Murdoch-owned *Times* and the staunchly Conservative *Daily Telegraph* occupying the "quality" end of the market, trailed by the *Independent*, which strives worthily to live up to its self-righteous name, and the *Guardian*, which inhabits a niche marginally to the left of centre. At the opposite end of the scale in terms of intellectual weight and volume of sales is the pernicious *Sun*, the sleaziest occupant of the Murdoch stable; its chief rivals in the sex and scandal stakes are the *Daily Star* and self-consciously ridiculous *Daily Sport*, but the only tabloid that manages anything approximating to a thought-out response to the *Sun's* reactionary politics is the *Daily Mirror*. The middle-brow daily tabloids – the *Daily Mail* and the *Daily Express* – show a depressing preoccupation with the Royal Family and TV celebrities. The scene is a little more varied on a Sunday, when the *Guardian*-owned *Observer*, England's oldest **Sunday newspaper**, supplements the Sunday editions of the dailies, whose ranks are also swelled by the amazingly popular *News of the World*, a smutty rag commonly known as "The News of the Screws".

When it comes to **specialist periodicals**, English newsagents can offer a range covering just about every subject, with motoring, music, sport, computers, gardening and home improvements all well covered. One noticeably poor area is current events – the only high-selling weekly commentary magazine is the *Economist*, which is essential reading in the boardrooms of England. The socialist alternative, the weekly *New Statesman* is subsidized by a few socialist millionaires and is complemented by the glossy monthly *Red Pepper*. The satirical bi-weekly *Private Eye* is a much-loved institution that prides itself on printing the stories the rest of the press won't touch, and on riding the consequent stream of libel suits. If you feel you can stomach a descent into the scatalogical pit of the male English psyche, take a look at *Viz*, a fortnightly comic which has managed to lodge its grotesque caricatures in the collective consciousness.

Australians and New Zealanders in London will be gratified by the weekly free magazine, *TNT*, which provides a résumé of the news from the home countries as well as jobs, accommodation and events in the capital. *USA Today* and the *International Herald Tribune* are widely distributed, as are the magazines *Time* and *Newsweek*.

TELEVISION AND RADIO

In England, terrestrial television stations are divided between the state-owned BBC, with two public service channels, and three independent commercial channels, ITV, Channel 4 and Channel 5. Though assailed by critics in the Conservative party, who think that it maintains a definite left-wing bias, the **BBC** is just about maintaining its worldwide reputation for in-house quality productions, ranging from expensive costume dramas to intelligent documentaries. BBC 2 is the more off-beat and heavyweight BBC channel; BBC 1 is avowedly mainstream. Various regional companies together form the **ITV** network, but they are united by a more tabloid approach to programme-making – necessarily so, because if they don't get the advertising they don't survive. **Channel 4**, a partly subsidized institution, is the most progressive of the bunch, with a reputation for broadcasting an eclectic spread of "arty" and minority-pleasing programmes, and for supporting small-budget motion pictures. The most recent newcomer is **Channel 5**, a self-consciously "young 'n' fun" alternative distinguished by its lurid colour schemes, breathless presenters and mediocre programming. Rupert Murdoch's multi-channel Sky network dominates the **satellite** business, presenting a blend of movies, news, documentaries, sport, re-runs and overseas soaps. It has an increasing number of rivals in the form of **cable** TV companies, which have made inroads throughout the country. These commercial stations are starting to make life uncomfortable for the BBC and ITV networks, but for the time being the old terrestrial stations still attract the majority of viewers. All these services can be accessed by means of the latest technological development, the **digital** system, through which the BBC presents its News 24, Knowledge, Parliament and Choice channels.

Market forces are eating away rather more quickly at the BBC's **radio** network, which has five stations: Radio 1 is almost exclusively pop music, with a chart-biased view of the rock world; Radio 2 is bland music and chat; Radio 3 is predominantly classical music; Radio 4 a blend of current affairs, arts and drama; and Radio 5, a sports and news channel. Radio 1 has rivals on all fronts, with Virgin running a youth-oriented nationwide commercial network, and a plethora of local commercial stations – like London's Capital Radio and Kiss FM – also attracting large sections of Radio 1's target audience. Melody Radio has whittled away at the Radio 2 easy listening market, as has Jazz FM; while Classic FM has lured people away from Radio 3, by offering a less earnest approach to its subject, though it sometimes degenerates into a "Greatest Hits" view of the greats. The BBC also operates several regional stations, but they are usually rather like listening to a broadcast of the local newspapers interspersed with the "Top 20"; the commercial stations, some of them real fly-by-wire operations, tend to be much livelier.

One BBC institution that has stayed in front despite the arrival of downmarket pretenders is the *Radio Times*, a weekly publication that gives full details on all national TV and radio programmes, not just the ones broadcast by the BBC.

ANNUAL EVENTS

In terms of the number of tourists they attract, the biggest occasions in the English calendar are the rituals that have associations with the ruling classes – from the courtly pageant of the Trooping the Colour to the annual rowing race between Oxford and Cambridge universities. Such anachronisms certainly reflect the endemic English taste for nostalgia, but to gauge the spirit of the country you should sample a wider range of events. London's large-scale **festivals** range from the riotous street party of the Notting Hill Carnival to the Promenade concerts, Europe's most egalitarian high-class music season; while every major town has its local arts festival, some of which have attained international status. The best of these festivals, along with various other local fairs and commemorative shows, are mentioned in the main part of the guide, but see also the box below – and for the complete low-down on festivals throughout the country, get a copy of

The Great British Festival Guide (Summersdale Press; £9.99).

To see England at its most idiosyncratic, take a look at one of the numerous regional celebrations that perpetuate **ancient customs**, the origins and meanings of which have often been lost or conveniently forgotten. The sight of the entire population of a village scrambling around a field after a barrel (that they call a bottle), or chasing a cheese downhill is not easily forgotten.

Also included in the list are the main **sports** finals, which may often be difficult to get tickets for, but are invariably televised. In addition to these, there are of course football matches every Saturday (plus some Sundays and mid-week as well) from late August to mid-May, and cricket matches every day throughout the summer – interesting social phenomena even for those unenthralled by team sports.

EVENTS CALENDAR

Mid-February: Chinese New Year. Festivities in London's and Manchester's Chinatown districts.

Mid-March: Cheltenham Gold Cup meeting. The country's premier national-hunt horseracing event.

End of March or early April: University Boat Race. Hugely popular rowing contest on the Thames, between the teams of Oxford and Cambridge.

Shrove Tuesday: Purbeck Marblers and Stonecutters Day, Corfe Castle, Dorset. Ritual football game through the streets of the village.

Maundy Thursday: The Queen dispenses the Royal Maundy Money at a different cathedral annually.

Good Friday: Marbles Championship, Tinsley Green, near Crawley, Sussex.

Easter Monday: Hare Pie Scramble and Bottle-Kicking, Hallaton, Leicestershire.

Saturday in late March or early April: Grand National meeting, Aintree, Liverpool. Cruelly testing steeplechase that entices most of Britain's population into the betting shops.

April 30–May 3: Minehead Hobby Horse, Minehead, Somerset.

May 1: Padstow Hobby Horse, Padstow, Cornwall.

May 8 : Helston Furry Dance, Helston, Cornwall.

Early May: FA Cup Final, Wembley, London. The deciding contest in the premier football tournament.

Spring Bank Holiday Monday: Cheese Rolling, Brockworth, Gloucestershire. Pursuit of a cheese-wheel down a murderous incline – one of the weirdest customs in England.

May–July: Glyndebourne Opera Festival, East Sussex. The classiest and most snobbish arts festival in the country.

Late May and early June: Bath International Festival. International arts jamboree.

Last week of May: Chelsea Flower Show, Royal Hospital, Chelsea, London. Essential event for England's green-fingered legions.

June: Aldeburgh Festival. Jamboree of classical music held on the Suffolk coast; established by Benjamin Britten.

First Friday in June: Cotswold Olimpicks, Chipping Campden, Gloucestershire. Rustic sports festival and torchlight procession.

First week in June: Derby week, Epsom race-course, Surrey. The world's most expensive horseflesh competing in the Derby, the Coronation Cup and the Oaks.

EVENTS CALENDAR (CONTINUED)

First or second Saturday in June: Trooping the Colour, Horse Guards Parade, London. Equestrian pageantry for the Queen's Official Birthday.

Mid-June: Appleby Horse Fair, Appleby-in-Westmorland, Cumbria.

Mid-June: Royal Ascot, Berkshire. High-class horseracing attended by high-class people; the best seats go to royalty and their satellites, while the proles mill around in the outfield.

End of June: World Worm-Charming Championships, Willaston, Cheshire.

Last week of June: Glastonbury Festival, Somerset. Hugely popular festival, with international bands, indie music and loads of hippies.

Last week of June and first week of July: Lawn Tennis Championships, Wimbledon, London. Queues are phenomenal even for the early rounds, and you need to know a freemason or ex-champion to get in to the big games.

First week in July: Henley Royal Regatta, Oxfordshire. Rowing event attended by much the same crew as populates the grandstands at Ascot.

First week of July: Tynwald Ceremony, St Johns, Isle of Man.

Second Saturday in July: Durham Miners' Gala, Durham.

Mid-July: British Open Golf Championship, variable venue. The season's last Grand Slam golf tournament.

Third week in July: Swan Upping, River Thames from Sunbury to Pangbourne. Ceremonial registering of the Thames cygnets.

Last week of July: Royal Tournament, Earl's Court Exhibition Centre, London. Precision military displays.

Last week of July: Cambridge Folk Festival. Biggest event of its kind in England.

Late July: Womad, Reading. Three-day world music festival.

July to early September:The Promenade Concerts, Royal Albert Hall, London. Classical music concerts ending in the fervently patriotic Last Night of the Proms.

August Bank Holiday: Notting Hill Carnival, around Notting Hill, West London. Vivacious celebration by London's Caribbean community – plenty of music, food and floats.

August Bank Holiday: Reading Festival, Berkshire. Three-day hard rock jamboree.

Weekend in mid-August: Bristol Balloon Fiesta. Hundreds of balloons take to the skies early morning and evening.

Last Sunday in August: Plague Memorial, Eyam, Derbyshire.

Early September to early November: Blackpool Illuminations, Lancashire. Five miles of extravagant light displays.

First Monday after September 4: Abbots Bromley Horn Dance, Abbots Bromley, Staffordshire. Vaguely pagan mass dance in mock-medieval costume – one of the most famous ancient customs.

Late October to early November: Huddersfield Contemporary Music Festival. One of Europe's premier showcases for up-to-the-minute highbrow music.

First Sunday in November: London to Brighton Veteran Car Rally. Ancient machines lumbering the 57 miles down the A23 to the seafront.

November 5: Guy Fawkes Night. Nationwide fireworks and bonfires commemorating the foiling of the Gunpowder Plot in 1605 – especially raucous celebrations at York (Fawkes' birthplace), Ottery St Mary in Devon and at Lewes, East Sussex.

Mid-November: Lord Mayor's Procession and Show, the City of London. Cavalcade to mark the inauguration of the new mayor.

December 31: Tar Barrels Parade, Allendale Town, Northumberland.

OUTDOOR PURSUITS

No matter where you are in England, you're never far from a stretch of countryside where you can lose the crowds on a brief walk or cycle-ride. For more hardy types, there are numerous long-distance footpaths, as well as opportunities for the more extreme disciplines of rock climbing and potholing (caving). On the coast and many of the country's inland lakes you can follow the more urbane pursuits of sailing and wind-surfing, and there are plenty of fine beaches for less structured fresh-air activities or just slobbing around.

WALKING

England's finest **walking** areas are the granite moorlands and spectacular coastlines of **Devon and Cornwall** in the southwest, and the highlands of the north – the low limestone and millstone crags of the **Peak District**, between Sheffield and Manchester; the **Yorkshire Dales**, the stretch of the Pennines to the north of the Peak District; the **North York Moors**, a bleak, treeless upland to the east of the Pennines; and the glaciated Cumbrian Mountains, better known as the **Lake District**. On summer weekends the more accessible reaches of these regions can get very crowded with day-trippers, but at any time of the year you'll find yourself in relative isolation if

you undertake one of the **Long Distance Footpaths** (LDPs). Defined as any route over twenty miles long, LDPs exist all over the country and are marked at frequent intervals with an acorn waymarker. Youth hostels are littered along most routes, though you may need a tent for some of the more heroic hikes – like stretches of the Pennine Way, Britain's longest, at over 250 miles. It goes without saying that for any kind of serious walking, and even for day hikes on high ground, you need to be properly equipped and prepared, follow local advice and listen out for the local weather reports. England's climate may be benign on the whole, but people die on the moors and mountains every year.

CYCLING

Despite the recent boom in the sale of mountain bikes, **cyclists** are treated with notorious disrespect by many motorists and by the people who plan the country's traffic systems. Few of England's towns as yet have proper cycle routes and British cyclists are estimated to be twelve times more likely to be killed or injured (per miles cycled) than their counterparts in Denmark, where a network of safe cycle paths and traffic-calming schemes has been created – the organization SUSTRANS (see p.44) is attempting to go some way towards addressing this problem.

WALKING HOLIDAY SPECIALISTS

Adventureline, North Trefula Farm, Redruth, Cornwall TR16 5ET (☎01209/820847, *www. chyycor.co.uk/adventureline*). Small group tours with local guides around the Celtic landscapes of Cornwall.

English Wanderer, 6 George St, Ferryhill, County Durham DL17 0DT (☎01740/653169). Guided or independent walking holidays countrywide.

Footpath Holidays, 16 Norton Bavant, nr Warminster, Wiltshire BA12 7BB (☎01985/840049, *www.dmac.co.uk/footpath.html*). Packages to various hill and coastal districts in England, with experienced group leaders.

Instep Walking Holidays, 35 Cokeham Rd, Lancing, West Sussex BN15 0AE (☎01903/766475, *www.instep.demon.co.uk*). Self-guided holidays with accommodation in small country hotels and guest houses, mainly in the south of England.

HF Walking Holidays, Imperial House, Edgware Rd, London NW9 5AL (☎0181/905 9558 or 905 9388, *www.hfholidays.co.uk*). A wide choice of locations, and lodging in comfortable country houses.

Walker's Britain, 131a Heston Rd, Hounslow, Middlesex TW5 0RD (☎0181/577 2717, *www.sherpa-walking-holidays.co.uk*). At-your-own-pace, self-guided walks between country pubs all over England.

CARRYING YOUR BIKE ON PUBLIC TRANSPORT

The majority of **airlines** will carry bicycles as part of your luggage allowance on plane journeys, although protruding parts, such as pedals and handlebars, have to be removed, and the tyres deflated; some carriers also require you to stash the machine in a bike bag or cardboard cover. Check with your airline well in advance to find out exactly what their terms and conditions are, and bear in mind that you may have to pay excess baggage. Transporting cycles by **ferry** is also free, but a lot more straight-forward; you just wheel them on and off, and reservation is not normally required. **Coach** companies, on the other hand, rarely accept cycles unless they're of the special stowaway variety. One exception is European Bike Express, 31 Baker St, Middlesborough, Cleveland TS1 2LF (☎01642/251440), which tacks trailers on the back of their luxury coaches for journeys to and from a range of destinations on the continent.

Carrying your bike by **train** is a good way of getting to the interesting parts of England without a lot of stressful or boring pedalling. For some reason, however, the newly privatized rail companies seem hell-bent on making life difficult for cyclists by slapping on hefty surcharges. Most suburban trains will carry cycles outside the rush hours of 7.30–9.30am and 4–6pm, but they are not allowed at all on some express trains (or Eurostar), while those that do accept cycles charge between £1 and £3; this usually has to be paid at least 24 hours in advance, and for each separate leg of the trip, which can work out to be ridiculously expensive if your journey involves a couple of changes. If you book 48 hours in advance, Eurotunnel will carry you and your bike for £15 on the 11am or 6pm train from Calais and the 8am or 3.30pm train from Folkestone. Call ☎01303/288933 to book.

CYCLING HOLIDAY SPECIALISTS

For those who want a guaranteed hassle-free cycling holiday, there are various companies offering easy-going packages. These can take all sorts of forms, but generally include transport of your gear to each night's halt, pre-booked accommodation, detailed route instructions, a packed lunch and back-up support. Most companies offer some budget cycling holidays, with hostels or B&Bs instead of hotels. Below is a list of reliable and established operators worth phoning for quotes and brochures:

Activities, PO Box 120, Hereford HR4 8YB (☎01432/830083, *www.acornactivities.co.uk*). Weekend, one-week and fourteen-day tours, with bikes, accommodation, luggage transportation and maps provided.
Bike Rides, Bremhill, Calne SN11 9LA (☎01249/816665, *www.bike-rides.co.uk*). Mountain bike and road tours across the country.
Bike Breaks, 25 Mayville Rd, Liverpool L18 0HG (☎0151/722 8050, *www.byways-breaks.com*). Tours of varying length in the gentle Cheshire countryside.

Compass Holidays, 48 Shurdington Rd, Cheltenham Spa GL53 0JE (☎01242/250642). Guided or independent tours in the Cotswolds and Warwickshire.
Country Lanes, 9 Shaftesbury St, Fordingbridge, Hampshire SP6 1JF (☎01425/655022, *www.countrylanes.co.uk*). Countrywide trips. Also rents out bikes at train stations.
Holiday Lakeland, Dale View, Ireby, Nr Keswick, Cumbria CA5 1EA (☎01697/371871, *www.holiday-lakeland.co.uk*). Tours of three and five nights in the Lake District from May to September.

Surprisingly, cycle **helmets** are not compulsory in Britain – but if you're hellbent on tackling the congestion, pollution and aggression of city traffic, you're well advised to get one. You do have to have a **rear reflector** and front and back **lights** when riding at night, and are not allowed to carry children without a special child seat. It is also illegal to cycle on pavements, or sidewalks, and in most public parks. A secure **lock** (preferably some kind of "D" lock) is also indispensible –

cycle theft in England has become an organized racket in recent years, and it's always a good idea to make a note of your frame number in case you have to report a loss to the police.

The backroads of rural England (those labelled with the prefix "B") are infinitely more enjoyable than trunk routes (or "A" roads), with generally amiable gradients and a sufficient density of pubs and B&Bs to keep the days manageable. Your main problem out in the countryside will be getting hold of any spare parts – only inner tubes and tyres are easy to find.

Off-road cycling is popular in the highland walking areas, but cyclists should remember to keep to rights of way designated on maps as Bridleways, BOATs ("Byways Open To All Traffic") or RUPFs ("Roads Used As Public Footpaths") and to pass walkers at considerate speeds. Footpaths, unless otherwise marked, are for pedestrian use only. Other rules of the road to bear in mind are that cycles are not permitted on motorways (labelled with the prefix "M").

Every region of England offers rich potential for cyclists, with varied scenery and miles of sleepy country lanes to get lost in. Armed with a detailed OS map of any area, you can improvise scenic routes of your own that avoid the main roads – better still, most good bookshops stock a range of cycling guides, featuring suggestions for rides of varying length, with coloured maps and detailed route descriptions.

There are currently around 3000 miles of traffic-free cycle tracks in England. Funded by a £42-million grant by the Millennium Commission, in partnership with local authorities and organizations like the National Trust and Countryside Agency, the charity **SUSTRANS** (which stands for Sustainable Transport) hopes by 2005 to expand this to a 8500-mile National Cycle Network, passing within two miles of some twenty million people. A large proportion of the network is made up of quiet backroads, dubbed "Cycleways", but more than half runs along disused railways and canal towpaths, including the showpiece section connecting the cities of Bath and Bristol. Maps of the network are available from SUSTRANS, 37–41 Prince St, Bristol BS1 4PS (☎0117/929 0888, *www.sustrans.org.uk*).

With more time, you may want to take on one of England's challenging **long-distance routes**. The Cycle Touring Club or CTC (Cotterell House, 69 Meadrow, Godalming, Surrey GU7 3HS; ☎01483/417217, *www.CTC.org.uk*), publishes special maps for some of these, and supplies members with touring and technical advice as well as insurance. The classic cross-Britain route is Land's End, in the far southwest of England, to John O'Groats, on the northeast tip of Scotland – roughly a thousand miles that you can cover in two to three weeks, depending on which of the three CTC-recommended routes you choose. Another favourite coast-to-coast option is the journey from Lowestoft, in the southeast home-

county of Suffolk, to the Ardnamurchan peninsula in northwest Scotland. The CTC suggests a ten-day itinerary, but you could easily spend twice that long scaling the English watershed. The same applies to the wonderful 130-mile Wye Valley route, which winds from the Severn Estuary through the forests and moorlands of the Welsh borders to the rough mountains of mid-Wales. Other tempting long-distance tours could take you around the Yorkshire Dales, Pennines, and Peak District, around Dartmoor and the Cornish coast, or across the austere North York Moors. For a full rundown of tour routes in these and other regions, ask for copies of their leaflets costing £2–4, or hunt out a copy of *Cycling Great Britain* by Tim Hughes and Joanna Cleary (Bicycle Books Inc; £8.95).

Bike rental is available at cycle shops in most large towns, and at villages within National Parks and other scenic areas; the addresses and telephone numbers of these appear in the relevent sections of the guide. Although increasing numbers of rental outfits have quality multi-geared mountain bikes, many of the machines on offer are often old and unwieldy – all right for a brief spin, but not for any serious touring. Expect to pay in the region of £10–15 per day for something sturdy, with discounts for longer periods.

BEACHES

England is ringed by fine beaches and bays, many of the best of which are readily accessible by public transport – though of course that means they tend to get very busy in high summer. For a combination of decent climate and good sand, the southwest is the best area, especially the coast of north Cornwall and Devon. The beaches of England's southern coast become more pebbly as you approach the southeastern corner of the country – resorts round here are more garish than their southwestern counterparts, as exemplified by Brighton. Moving up the east coast, the East Anglian shore is predominantly pebbly and very exposed, making it ideal for those who want to escape the crowds rather than bask in the sun, while right up in the northeast there are some wonderful sandy strands and old-fashioned seaside resorts, though the North Sea breezes often require a degree of stoicism. Over in the northwest, the inland hills of Cumbria are a greater attraction than anything on the coast, though Blackpool has a certain appeal as the apotheosis of the "kiss-me-quick" holiday town.

ENGLAND'S DIRTY BEACHES

This is the list of English beaches where the shore and bathing waters failed to meet EU standards in 1999. An asterisk denotes places that failed for the previous two years as well.

Kent to Dorset
Felpham (West Sussex)
Folkestone* (Kent)
The Warren, Folkestone

The Southwest
Bantham (Devon)
Blue Anchor (Somerset)
Burnham-on-Sea (Somerset)
Cawsand Bay (Cornwall)
Doniford (Somerset)
Harlyn Bay (Cornwall)
Hartland Quay (Devon)
Hope Cove (Devon)
Instow (Devon)
Kingsand Bay (Cornwall)
East Looe (Cornwall)
Minehead – Terminus (Somerset)
Mother Ivey's Bay (Cornwall)
Porthluney Cove (Cornwall)
Plymouth Hoe West* (Devon)
Saunton Sands (Devon)

The East Coast
Alnmouth (Northumberland)
Beadnell (Northumberland)
Blyth – South Beach (Northumberland)
Crimdon Park (Durham)
Saltburn (North Yorkshire)
Sandsend (North Yorkshire)

Seaham Beach (Durham)
Seaham – Remand Home
Seaton Sluice (North Tyneside)
South Shields (North Tyneside)
Spittal (Northumberland)
Staithes* (North Yorkshire)

The Northwest
Aldingham* (Cumbria)
Askham-in-Furness* (Cumbria)
Bardsea* (Cumbria)
Blackpool (North, Central and South*)
(Lancashire)
Haverigg* (Cumbria)
Newbiggin (Cumbria)
Morecambe (South) (Lancashire)
Roan Head (Cumbria)
St Anne's (Lancashire)
St Anne's (North)* (Lancashire)
Walney West Shore* (Cumbria)

Isle of Man
Douglas – Palace
Gansey Bay
Jurby
Kirk Michael
Peel
Port Soderick
Port St Mary
White Strand

It has to be said that English beaches are not the cleanest in Europe, and many of those that the British authorities declare to be acceptable actually fall below EU standards. Although steps are being taken to improve the situation, far too many stretches of the English coastline are contaminated by sea-borne effluent or other rubbish. The box above gives the latest state of play. For annually updated, detailed information on the condition of Britain's beaches, the *Good Beach Guide*, compiled by the Marine Conservation Society (9 Gloucester Rd, Ross-on-Wye, Herefordshire HR9 5BU, ☎01989/566017, *www.goodbeachguide.co.uk*) is the definitive source.

SURFING

For most people, surfing in England means surfing in Newquay. And while it's true that the south-

west is the heartland of the English surf scene, it would be a mistake to think that there aren't decent waves elsewhere. The northeast coast, from Yorkshire to Northumberland, has a growing population of hardy surfers willing to endure temperatures as low as 5°C in winter (and no higher than 14–15°C in summer) to surf clean northerly ground swells breaking over a selection of quality reef and beach breaks. The coastline here is often spectacular, especially in Northumberland, and although the more popular breaks such as Cayton Bay and Saltburn are now crowded, you can find relative isolation off the beaten track.

Nevertheless, the southwest, or more specifically **Newquay** in Cornwall, remains England's undisputed surf centre. Visiting surfers are often amazed to see the hype surrounding this self-styled "surf city". In summer, every other male

TOP TEN ENGLISH BREAKS

1. **Fistral**, Newquay. Hype, crowds, but still a good wave if you can get one to yourself.

2. **Staithes***, Yorkshire. Excellent reef breaks, crowded and jealously guarded by locals.

3. **Croyde Bay**, Devon. Good beach breaks, but again, crowds can be a problem.

4. **Sennen Cove**, Cornwall. Picks up any swell going.

5. **Woolacombe**, Devon. Two miles of fun beach breaks.

6. **Kimmeridge***, Dorset. A popular reef break that doesn't work that often, but is great when it does.

7. **Saltburn**, Cleveland. Another good beach break, with atmosphere to match.

8. **Bamburgh**, Northumberland. A wonderfully scenic quiet beach, with seals in the water and a spectacular castle as a backdrop.

9. **Porthleven***, Cornwall. A heavy reef break, and heavy locals.

10. **Constantine**, Cornwall. Another southwest hot spot that picks up a lot of swell.

* Experienced surfers only.

seems to be a surfer, sporting regulation bleached hair and surf gear, but the majority only turn up to cruise surf babes. It can still be hectic out in the water though, especially at the main break, Fistral, which regularly hosts international contests.

However, head out of town and things quieten down noticeably. Try spots such as **Perranporth** or **Polzeath**, or head up to Devon, which also gets decent waves, despite the overcrowding of its main break, **Croyde**.

The southwest has relatively mild waters (up to 18°C in summer). Even so, you'll still need a wetsuit year round, with a thicker suit from October to May, plus boots and gloves, and maybe a hood (winter water temperatures get down to 9–10°C). There are plenty of places where you can **rent or buy equipment**, which means gear tends to be cheaper in southwest England than elsewhere in the UK. Even if you can escape no further than the Channel coast, you may still be lucky enough to find a wave, especially in winter. It's unlikely to be of good quality, but for the desperate surf traveller places such as **Brighton** and **Bournemouth** may have something worth getting wet for.

GAY AND LESBIAN ENGLAND

Homosexual acts between consenting males were legalized in Britain in 1967, but it wasn't until as recently as 1994 that the **age of consent** was finally reduced from 21 to 18 (still two years older than that for heterosexuals). Lesbianism has never specifically been outlawed, apocryphally owing to the fact that Queen Victoria refused to believe that such a thing existed.

As in so many other aspects of English life, attitudes to homosexuality are riven with contradictions. Despite its draconian laws and the sensationalist trash in the tabloid press, England offers one of the most diverse and accessible lesbian and gay scenes to be found anywhere in Europe. Nearly every town of any size has some kind of organized gay life – pubs, clubs, community groups, campaigning organizations, shops and phone lines – with the major scenes being found in **London**, **Manchester** and **Brighton**.

Many venues are listed in this book, and you'll find a free gay listings sheet in virtually any one of these.

Of the nationwide **publications**, the weekly *Pink Paper* is newsy and contains limited listings; also worth checking are the frothy weekly *Boyz*, and its monthly women's sibling, *Diva*. The best bet for a comprehensive **national directory** of pubs, clubs, groups, gay accommodation and local lesbian and gay switchboards is the glossy monthly *Gay Times*, available from many newsagents and alternative bookstores. Gay Men's Press produces guide books aimed primarily at gay men, although with some lesbian information included too – there's currently *London Scene*, which includes Brighton. Much of the information in such publications applies both to men and women, as the English scene is far more mixed than in most other European nations.

DISABLED TRAVELLERS

England has numerous specialist **tour operators** catering for physically handicapped travellers, and the number of non-specialist operators who welcome clients with disabilities is increasing. For more information on these operators and on facilities for the disabled traveller, you should get in touch with the Royal Association for Disability and Rehabilitation (RADAR), 12 City Forum, 250 City Rd, London EC1V 8AF (☎0171/250 3222, Minicom ☎0171/250 4119, *www.radar.org.uk*), which publishes its own guide to holidays and travel abroad (see below), and is a good source of all kinds of information and advice. There's also the Holiday Care Service, 2nd Floor, Imperial Buildings, Victoria Rd, Horley, Surrey RH6 7PZ (☎01293/774535; Minicom ☎01293/776943), which publishes numerous fact sheets on disabled travel abroad and deals with all sorts of queries. You might also want to contact the charity Tripscope, at the Courtyard, Evelyn Rd, London W4 5JL (☎0181/994 9294), who provide a national telephone information service offering free advice on transport, travel and access in England for those with a mobility problem.

Mobility International also has a **North American office** and is contactable at PO Box 10767, Eugene, OR 97440 (☎541/343-1284). Other useful organizations in North America are the Society for the Advancement of Travel for the Handicapped, 347 5th Ave, New York, NY 10016 (☎212/447-7284), a non-profit-making travel-industry referral service that passes queries on to its members, and the Travel Information Service, Moss Rehabilitation Hospital, 1200 West Tabor Rd, Philadelphia, PA 19141 (☎215/456-9600), a telephone information and referral service.

Disabled travellers in **Australia** and **New Zealand** can get information and advice from ACROD, PO Box 60, Curtin, ACT 2605 (☎02/6282 4333), which has compiled lists of organizations, accommodation, travel agencies and tour operators, Barrier Free Travel, 36 Wheatley St, North Bellingen, NSW 2454 (☎02/6655 1733), a fee-based travel access information service, or the Disabled Persons Assembly, 173 Victoria Terrace, Wellington (☎04/801 9100).

Should you go it alone, you'll find that English attitudes towards travellers with disabilities are often begrudging and guilt-ridden, and are years behind advances towards independence made in North America and Australia. Access to theatres, cinemas and other public places has improved recently, but **public transport** companies rarely make any effort to help disabled people, though some rail services now accommodate wheelchair users in comfort. Wheelchair users and blind or partly sighted people are automatically given 30–50 percent reductions on train fares, and people with other disabilities are eligible for the Disabled Persons Railcard (£14 per year), which gives a third off most tickets, but can take up to two weeks to process. There are no bus discounts for the dis-abled, while of the major **car rental** firms only Hertz offer models with hand controls at the same rate as conventional vehicles, and even these are in the more expensive categories. **Accommodation** is the same story, with modified suites for people with disabilities available only at higher-priced establishments and perhaps at the odd B&B.

Useful **publications** include RADAR's annually updated *Holidays in the British Isles: A Guide For Disabled People* (£7.50), *Getting There: a Guide to Long Distance Travel* (£5) and *Access to the Skies* (£5). The AA publishes the *Disabled Travellers' Guide* (£4.99), free to members. RADAR also produce an *Access Guide to London* (£7.50).

DIRECTORY

Cigarettes The last decade has seen a dramatic change in attitudes towards smoking and a significant reduction in the consumption of cigarettes. Smoking is now outlawed from just about all public buildings and on public transport, and many restaurants and hotels have become non-smoking establishments. Smokers are advised, when booking a table or a room, to check that their vice is tolerated there.

Drugs Likely-looking visitors coming to England from Holland or Spain can expect scrutiny from customs officers on the lookout for hashish (marijuana resin). Being caught in possession of a small amount of hashish or grass will lead to a fine, but possession of larger quantities or of "harder" narcotics could lead to imprisonment or deportation.

Electricity In England the current is 240V AC. North American appliances will need a transformer and adaptor; Australasian appliances will only need an adaptor.

Laundry Coin-operated laundries (launderettes) are to be found in nearly all English towns and are open about twelve hours a day from Monday to Friday, less at weekends. A wash followed by a spin or tumble dry costs about £3, with "service washes" (your laundry done for you in a few hours) about £1 more.

Public toilets These are found at all train and bus stations and are signposted on town high streets. In urban locations a fee of 10p or 20p is usually charged.

Time Greenwich Mean Time (GMT) is used from late October to late March, when the clocks go forward an hour for British Summer Time (BST). GMT is five hours ahead of the US Eastern Standard Time and ten hours behind Australian Eastern Standard Time.

Videos Visitors from North America should note that there is a different format for videotapes in Britain from that in the US and Canada – so even though they look the same, VHS tapes recorded in Britain (in what's called the PAL format) will not work when you get them home and try to play them back on your VCR (which is NTSC format). If you are shooting with your own camera, however, you can use a blank tape purchased in Britain to record your trip's highlights, since your camera will format the tape while it records.

SCOTLAND

CHAPTER 11
**THE
NORTHEAST**

CHAPTER 9
**CUMBRIA
AND THE
LAKES**

CHAPTER 10
YORKSHIRE

CHAPTER 8
**THE
NORTHWEST**

WALES

CHAPTER 7
CENTRAL ENGLAND

CHAPTER 6
EAST ANGLIA

CHAPTER 4
LONDON TO THE SEVERN

CHAPTER 1
LONDON

CHAPTER 3
**HAMPSHIRE,
DORSET &
WILTSHIRE**

CHAPTER 2
**SURREY, KENT
& SUSSEX**

CHAPTER 5
THE WEST COUNTRY

N

CHAPTER ONE

LONDON

What strikes visitors more than anything about LONDON is the sheer size of the place. With a population of around seven million, it is still by far Europe's largest city, spreading across an area of more than 620 square miles from its core on the River Thames. London is also pre-eminent in England: it's where the country's news and money are made and, as far as its inhabitants are concerned, provincial life begins beyond the circuit of the orbital motorway. Londoners' sense of superiority causes enormous resentment in the regions, yet it's undeniable that the capital has an unmatched charisma, a unique aura of excitement and success. In many walks of life, it's still the case that if you want to get on, you've got to get on in London.

Despite its dominant role, London remains the only capital city to have entered the new millennium without its own governing body, a symptom of more than a decade and a half's political indifference from previous Conservative governments. This neglect, compounded by a political culture that penalizes the unfortunate, has resulted in a city of spiralling extremes – ostentatious private affluence and increasing public squalor. At night, the West End is packed with theatregoers, while the doorways and shopfronts continue to serve as dormitories for London's dispossessed. London's problems are perfectly illustrated by the city's chaotic transport system, which is one of the most expensive in the world. Despite the huge expense, the tube network remains at breaking point, and the buses are notoriously unreliable and overcrowded.

London should undoubtedly be better than it is, but it is still a thrilling place. Its museums and galleries are among the finest in the world, while monuments from the capital's more glorious past are everywhere to be seen, from Roman ruins through great Baroque churches to the eclectic Victorian architecture of the triumphalist British Empire. The major sights – from Big Ben to the Tower of London – draw in millions of tourists, but there is enjoyment to be had from the quiet squares, narrow alleyways and surprisingly large expanses of greenery: Hyde Park, Green Park and St James's Park are all within a few minutes' walk of the West End shops.

You could also spend days just shopping in London, hobnobbing with the ruling classes in Harrods, or sampling the offbeat weekend markets, the seedbed of London's famously innovative street fashions, which provides fertile ground for the capital's own home-grown talent. The music, clubbing and gay/lesbian scene is second to none, and mainstream arts are no less exciting, with regular opportunities to catch brilliant theatre companies, dance troupes, exhibitions and opera. Restaurants, these days, are an attraction, too. London has caught up with its European rivals and offers something to suit every taste and budget, from three-star Michelin establishments to low-cost high-quality Indian cafés. Meanwhile, the city's pubs have heaps of atmosphere, especially away from the centre – and an exploration of the farther-flung communities is essential to get the feel of this dynamic metropolis.

A brief history of London

The Romans founded Londinium in 43 AD as a stores depot on the marshy banks of the Thames. Despite frequent attacks – not least by Queen Boudicca, who razed it in 61 AD – the port became secure in its position as capital of Roman Britain by the end of the century. London's expansion really began, however, in the eleventh century, when it

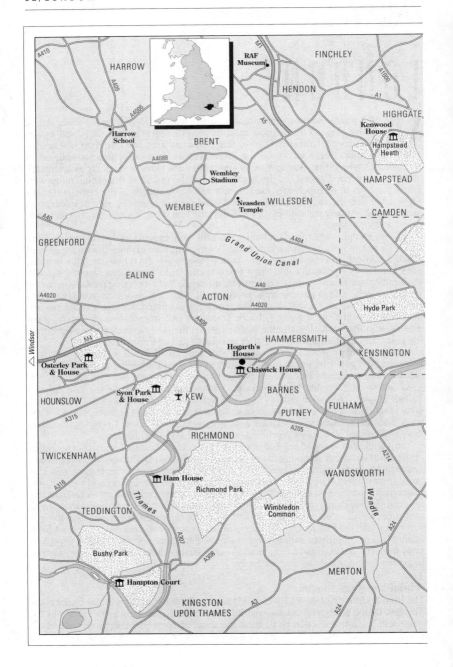

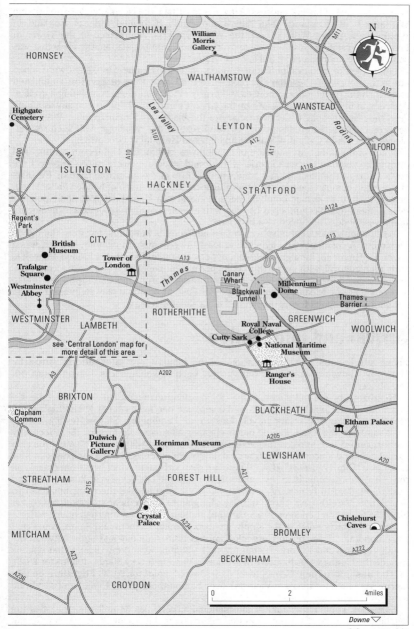

N

TOTTENHAM

William
Morris
Gallery

HORNSEY

WALTHAMSTOW

WANSTEAD

Lea Valley

A12

Highgate
Cemetery

LEYTON

Roding

ILFORD

A400

A1

A10

A107

A12

A11

A118

ISLINGTON

HACKNEY

STRATFORD

A124

Regent's
Park

CITY

A13

British
Museum

Tower of
London

A13

Canary
Wharf

Millennium
Dome

Trafalgar
Square

Thames

Blackwall
Tunnel

Thames
Barrier

Westminster
Abbey

ROTHERHITHE

GREENWICH

WOOLWICH

WESTMINSTER

LAMBETH

Royal Naval
College

see 'Central London' map for
more detail of this area

Cutty Sark

National Maritime
Museum

A3

A202

Ranger's
House

BRIXTON

Clapham
Common

BLACKHEATH

Eltham Palace

Dulwich
Picture
Gallery

Horniman Museum

A205

LEWISHAM

A20

STREATHAM

A215

FOREST HILL

A21

MITCHAM

Crystal
Palace

A234

Chislehurst
Caves

BROMLEY

A23

A222

A236

BECKENHAM

CROYDON

0   2   4miles

Downe ▽

became the seat of the last successful invader of Britain, the Norman duke who became **William I of England** (aka "the Conqueror"). Crowned king of England in Westminster Abbey, William built the White Tower – centrepiece of the Tower of London – to establish his dominance over the merchant population, the class that was soon to make London one of Europe's mightiest cities.

Little is left of medieval or Tudor London. Many of the finest buildings were wiped out in the course of a few days in 1666 when the **Great Fire of London** annihilated more than thirteen thousand houses and nearly ninety churches, completing a cycle of destruction begun the year before by the Great Plague, which killed as many as a hundred thousand people. Chief beneficiary of the blaze was Sir Christopher Wren, who was commissioned to redesign the city and rose to the challenge with such masterpieces as St Paul's Cathedral and the Royal Naval Hospital in Greenwich.

Much of the public architecture of London was built in the eighteenth century and during the reign of Queen Victoria, when grand structures were raised to reflect the city's status as the financial and administrative hub of the invincible **British Empire**. However, in comparison to many other European capitals much of London looks bland, due partly to the German bombing raids in World War II, and partly to some postwar development that has lumbered London with the sort of concrete-and-glass mediocrity that gives modern architecture a bad name.

Yet London's special atmosphere comes not from its buildings, but from the life on its streets. A cosmopolitan city since at least the seventeenth century, when it was a haven for Huguenot immigrants escaping persecution in Louis XIV's France, today it is truly multicultural, with over a third of its permanent population originating from overseas. This century has seen the arrival of thousands from the Caribbean, the Indian subcontinent, the Mediterranean and the Far East, all of whom play an integral part in defining a metropolis that is unmatched in its sheer diversity.

Arrival and information

Flying into London, you'll arrive at one of the capital's four **international airports**: Heathrow, Gatwick, Stansted or City Airport, each of which is less than an hour from the city centre.

Heathrow, twelve miles west of the city, has four terminals, and two train/tube stations: one for terminals 1, 2 and 3, and a separate one for terminal 4. The high-speed **Heathrow Express** trains travel nonstop to Paddington Station (every 15min; 15–20min) for £10 each way. A much cheaper alternative is to take the **Piccadilly Underground line** into central London (every 2–5min; 40–50min) for £3.40. If you plan to make several journeys on your arrival day, buy a multi-zone One-Day Travelcard for £4.50 (see "City Transport", p.56). There are also **Airbuses**, which run from outside all four Heathrow terminals to several destinations in the city (every 20–30min; 1hr) and cost £6 single, £10 return. After midnight, you'll have to take the night bus #N97 to Trafalgar Square (hourly; 1hr 15min) for a bargain £1.50. **Taxis** are plentiful, but cost at least £35 to central London and take around an hour (longer in the rush hour).

Gatwick, thirty miles to the south, has two terminals, North and South, connected by a monorail. The nonstop **Gatwick-Express** train runs day and night between the South Terminal and Victoria Station (every 15–30min; 30min) for £9.50. Other options include the **Connex South Central** service to Victoria (every 30min; 40min) for £8.20, or **Thameslink** to King's Cross (every 15–30min; 50min) for £9.50. **Flightline coaches** run from both terminals to Victoria Coach Station (hourly; 1hr 15min) and cost £7.50 single, £11 return.

Stansted, London's swankiest international airport, lies 34 miles northeast of the capital and is served by the **Stansted Skytrain** to Liverpool Street (every 30min;

TELEPHONE NUMBERS

On April 22, 2000, all **telephone numbers** in London will change. There will be a **new area code, 020,** and all local numbers will become eight digits long: old 0171 numbers being prefixed with a 7, old 0181 numbers with an 8. For further information on the changes to the telephone numbering system in the UK, see the box on p.38.

45min), which costs £10.40. **Flightline coaches** also run to Victoria Coach Station (hourly; 1hr 15min) and cost £9 single, £13 return.

London's smallest airport, **City Airport,** is situated in Docklands, nine miles east of central London. It handles European flights only, and is connected by shuttle bus with Canary Wharf (every 10min; 10min; £2), and Liverpool Street (every 10min; 25–35min; £4). Another option is to take the North London Line to Silvertown, which is ten minutes' walk from the airport.

Arriving by **train** from elsewhere in Britain, you'll come into one of London's numerous main line stations, all of which have adjacent Underground stations linking into the city centre's tube network. **Eurostar** trains arrive at **Waterloo International**, south of the river. Trains from the Channel ports arrive at Liverpool Street, Charing Cross and Victoria train stations; **coaches** terminate at **Victoria Coach Station**, a couple of hundred yards south of the train station, down Buckingham Palace Road.

Information

The **London Tourist Board** (LTB) has a desk in arrivals at Heathrow Terminal 3 (daily 6am–11pm), and another in the Underground station concourse for Heathrow Terminals 1, 2 and 3 (daily 8am–6pm), but the **main central office** is in the forecourt of Victoria Station (Easter–Oct daily 8am–7pm; Nov–Easter Mon–Sat 8am–6pm, Sun 8.30am–4pm). Other centrally located offices can be found near Piccadilly Circus in the British Visitor Centre, 1 Regent St (June–Aug Mon–Fri 9am–6.30pm Sat 9am–5pm, Sun 10am–4pm; rest of year Mon–Fri 9am–6.30pm, Sat & Sun 10am–5pm), in the arrivals hall of Waterloo International (daily 8.30am–10.30pm) and in Liverpool Street Underground station (Mon–Fri 8am–6pm, Sat & Sun 8.45am–5.30pm).

Individual boroughs also run tourist offices at various prime locations. The two most useful are to the south of St Paul's Cathedral (April–Sept daily 9.30am–5pm; Oct–March Mon–Fri 9.30am–5pm, Sat 9.30am–12.30pm; ☎0171/332 1456) and at 46 Greenwich Church St, SE10 (daily: April–Oct 10am–5pm; Oct–March 11am–4pm; ☎0181/858 6376). Both these offices will answer enquiries by phone; the LTB offices can only offer a spread of pre-recorded phone announcements – these are a very poor service indeed, and the calls are charged at an exorbitant rate.

Most information offices hand out a useful reference **map** of central London, plus plans of the public transport systems, but to find your way around every cranny of the city you need to invest in either an *A–Z Atlas* or a *Nicholson Streetfinder*, both of which

LONDON WHITE CARD

Serious museum addicts should consider buying the **London White Card**, which gives you free entry into over fifteen of the big arts and cultural museums, including the V&A, MOMI and the Courtauld Institute. The three-day card costs £16, while the seven-day card costs £26. Even better value is the Family Card, which covers two adults and up to four children and costs £32 for three days or £50 for seven. The cards are available from participating museums and galleries; for more information call ☎0171/923 0807.

have a street index covering every street in the capital; you can get them at most book-shops and newsagents for around £5. The only comprehensive and critical weekly **listings** magazine is *Time Out*, which costs £1.80 and comes out every Tuesday afternoon. In it you'll find details of all the latest exhibitions, shows, films, music, sport, guided walks and events in and around the capital.

City transport

London's transport network is among the most complex and expensive in the world. The **London Transport information office**, at Piccadilly Circus tube station (daily 9am–6pm), will provide free transport maps; there are other desks at Euston, King's Cross, Liverpool Street, Oxford Circus, Piccadilly Circus, St James's Park and Victoria stations. There's also a 24-hour phone line for transport information (☎0171/222 1234). If you can, avoid travelling during the **rush hour** (Mon–Fri 8–9.30am & 5–6.30pm) when tubes become unbearably crowded and some buses get so full, you literally won't be allowed on.

The fastest way of moving around the city is by Underground or **Tube**, as it's known to all Londoners. The eleven different tube lines cross much of the metropolis, although London south of the river is not very well covered. Each line has its own colour and name – all you need to know is which direction you're travelling in: north-bound, eastbound, southbound or westbound. Services operate from around 5.30am until shortly after midnight and you rarely have to wait more than five minutes for a train from central stations. **Tickets** must be bought in advance from the machines or booths in the station entrance hall; if you cannot produce a valid ticket, you will be charged an on-the-spot Penalty Fare of £10. A single journey in the central zone costs an unbelievable £1.40; a **Carnet** of ten tickets costs £10. If you're intending to travel about a lot, a Travelcard is by far your best bet (see box below).

The network of **buses** is very dense, but much slower going than the Tube. Bus tick-ets cost a minimum of 70p, rising to a maximum of £1.20. Normally you pay the driver on entering, but some routes are covered by older Routemaster buses, staffed by a con-ductor and with an open rear platform. Note that at request stops, you must stick your arm out to hail the bus you want. In addition to the Travelcards mentioned in the box below, a **One-Day Bus Pass** is also available and can be used before 9.30am, and costs £2 (Zones 2, 3 & 4) or £2.70 (All Zones). Regular buses run between about 6am and midnight; **Night Buses** (prefixed with the letter "N") operate outside this period. Night bus routes radiate out from Trafalgar Square at hourly intervals, more frequent-ly on some routes and on Friday and Saturday nights. Fares are a flat £1.50 from cen-tral London; one day and weekend Travelcards are not valid.

TRAVELCARDS

To get the best value out of the transport system, buy a **Travelcard**. Available from machines and booths at all tube and train stations and at some newsagents as well (look for the sticker), they are valid for the bus, tube, Docklands Light Railway and suburban rail networks. **One-Day Travelcards**, valid on weekdays from 9.30am and all day at weekends, cost £3.80 (central Zones 1 & 2), rising to £4.50 for All Zones (1–6, including Heathrow); the respective **Weekend Travelcards**, for unlimited travel on Saturdays and Sundays, cost £5.70 and £6.70. If you need to travel before 9.30am on a weekday, but don't need to use suburban trains, you can buy a **One-Day LT Card**, which costs from £4.50 (Zones 1 & 2) to £7.30 (All Zones). **Weekly Travelcards** are even more econom-ical, beginning at £14.30 for Zone 1; for these cards you need a **Photocard**, available free of charge from tube and train stations on presentation of a passport photo.

Large areas of London's suburbs are best reached by the **suburban train** network (Travelcards valid). Wherever a sight can only be reached by overground train, we've indicated the nearest train station and the central terminus from which you must depart. If you're planning to use the railway network a lot, you might want to purchase a **Network Card**, which is valid for a year, costs £20, and gives you up to 33 percent discount on fares to destinations in and around the southeast. To find out about a particular service, phone **National Rail Enquiries** on ☎0345/484950.

If you're in a group of three or more, London's metered **black cabs** can be an economical way of getting around the centre – a ride from Euston to Victoria, for example, should cost around £10. A yellow light over the windscreen tells you if the cab is available – just stick your arm out to hail it. (If you want to book one in advance, call ☎0171/272 0272.)

Minicabs are less reliable than black cabs, but considerably cheaper, so you might want to take one back from a late-night club. Most minicabs are not metered, so always establish the fare beforehand. If you want to be certain of a woman driver, call Ladycabs (☎0171/254 3501), or a gay/lesbian driver, call Freedom Cars (☎0171/734 1313).

Accommodation

There's no getting away from the fact that **accommodation** in London is expensive. Compared with most European cities, you pay over the odds in every category. The city's hostels are among the most expensive in the world, while venerable institutions such as *Claridge's*, *The Dorchester* and *The Connaught* charge the very top international prices – up to £300 or more per luxurious night.

The cheapest places to stay are the dorm beds of the city's numerous independent **hostels**, followed closely by the official YHA hostels. Even the most basic **B&Bs** struggle to bring their tariffs below £40 for a double with shared facilities, and you're more likely to find yourself paying £50 or more.

If you want to avoid the hassle of contacting individual hotels and B&Bs, you could turn to one of the various **accommodation agencies**. All the LTB offices listed on p.55 operate a room-booking service, which costs £5, plus fifteen percent of the room fee in advance; credit card holders can also book through the LTB by phone (☎0171/824 8844). In addition, **Thomas Cook** has accommodation desks at Gatwick airport (☎01293/529372), Victoria (☎0171/828 4646), King's Cross (☎0171/837 5681) and Paddington (☎0171/723 0184) train stations. Most of these are open daily from around 7am till 11pm, and will book anything from youth hostels through to four-star hotels for around £5.

Try also the **British Hotel Reservation Centre** (BHRC) at 13 Grosvenor Gardens (☎0171/828 2425), at either Heathrow Underground station (☎0181/564 8808 or 564 8211), Gatwick airport (☎01293/502433), Victoria train station (☎0171/828 1027) or Victoria coach station (☎0171/824 8232). The Victoria train station office, open daily from 6am to midnight, has the longest opening hours; all offer their services free of charge.

ACCOMMODATION PRICE CODES

Throughout this guide, hotel and B&B accommodation is priced on a scale of ① to ⑨, the number indicating the **lowest price** you could expect to pay per night in that establishment for a **double room** in high season. The prices indicated by the codes are as follows:

① under £40	④ £60–70	⑦ £110–150
② £40–50	⑤ £70–90	⑧ £150–200
③ £50–60	⑥ £90–110	⑨ over £200

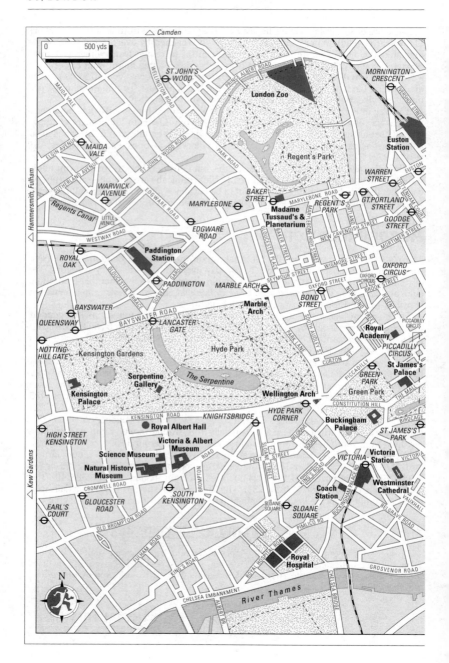

△ Camden

0   500 yds

ST JOHN'S WOOD

MORNINGTON CRESCENT

London Zoo

Regent's Park

△ Hammersmith, Fulham

MAIDA VALE

WARWICK AVENUE

Regents Canal

LITTLE VENICE

WESTWAY ROAD

ROYAL OAK

Paddington Station

PADDINGTON

BAYSWATER

QUEENSWAY

BAYSWATER ROAD

NOTTING HILL GATE

Kensington Gardens

Serpentine Gallery

Kensington Palace

HIGH STREET KENSINGTON

EARL'S COURT

GLOUCESTER ROAD

CROMWELL ROAD

OLD BROMPTON ROAD

Natural History Museum

Science Museum

Victoria & Albert Museum

● **Royal Albert Hall**

KENSINGTON ROAD

SOUTH KENSINGTON

BROMPTON ROAD

SLOANE SQUARE

SLOANE STREET

PONT STREET

Euston Station

WARREN STREET

GT.PORTLAND STREET

GOODGE STREET

BAKER STREET

MARYLEBONE

MARYLEBONE ROAD

REGENT'S PARK

EDGWARE ROAD

Madame Tussaud's & Planetarium

NEW CAVENDISH STREET

MORTIMER STREET

WIGMORE STREET

OXFORD CIRCUS

MARBLE ARCH

OXFORD STREET

BOND STREET

Marble Arch

LANCASTER GATE

Hyde Park

The Serpentine

Wellington Arch

KNIGHTSBRIDGE

HYDE PARK CORNER

PICCADILLY CIRCUS

PICCADILLY CIRCUS

Royal Academy

GREEN PARK

Green Park

St James's Palace

THE MALL

CONSTITUTION HILL

BIRDCAGE

Buckingham Palace

ST JAMES'S PARK

Victoria Station

VICTORIA

Westminster Cathedral

Coach Station

KING'S ROAD

SLOANE SQUARE

PIMLICO RD

BELGRAVE ROAD

VAUXHALL

Royal Hospital

GROSVENOR ROAD

CHELSEA BRIDGE

△ Kew Gardens

EDGWARE ROAD

MARBLE ARCH

SEYMOUR STREET

PARK LANE

SOUTH AUDLEY ST

CURZON ST

N

FULHAM ROAD

KING'S ROAD

CHELSEA EMBANKMENT

ALBERT BR.

River Thames

BUCKINGHAM PALACE RD

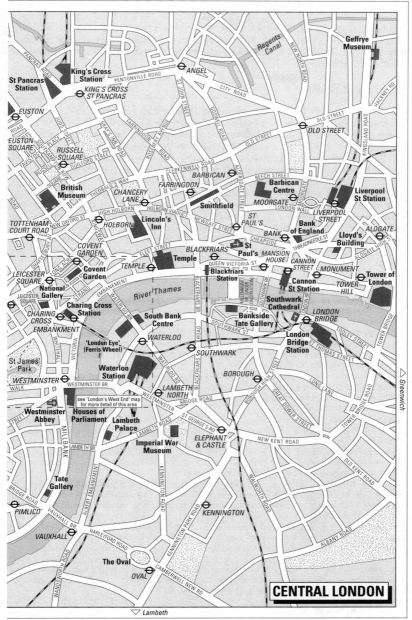

CENTRAL LONDON

A brief word on **London addresses**: the name of each street is followed by a letter giving the geographical location (E for "east", WC for "west central" and so on) and a number that specifies the postal area. However, this is not a reliable indication of the remoteness of the locale – W5, for example, lies beyond the more remote sounding NW10 – so it's always best to check a map before taking a room at what may sound like a fairly central area.

Hotels and B&Bs

With **hotels** you get less for your money in London than elsewhere in the country – generally breakfasts are more meagre and rooms more spartan than in similarly priced places in the provinces. In high season you should phone as far in advance as you can if you want to stay within a couple of tube stops of the West End, and expect to pay no less than £40 for an unexceptional double room without a private bathroom. If travelling with two or more companions, it's always worth asking the price of the family rooms, which generally sleep four and can save you a few pounds.

When choosing your **area**, bear in mind that the West End – Soho, Covent Garden, St James's, Mayfair and Marylebone – and the western districts of Knightsbridge and Kensington, are dominated by expensive, upmarket hotels. For cheaper rooms, the widest choice is close to the main train stations of Victoria and Paddington, and the budget B&Bs of Earl's Court. Those close to King's Cross cater for people on welfare, or charge by the hour, although neighbouring Bloomsbury is both inexpensive and very central.

Victoria

Dover Hotel, 42–44 Belgrave Rd, SW1 (☎0171/821 9085, *dover@rooms.demon.co.uk*). One of the best B&Bs in this area. All rooms are tastefully decorated, and have a shower, toilet, telephone and TV. Victoria tube. ③.

Elizabeth Hotel, 37 Eccleston Square, SW1 (☎0171/828 6812). Comfortable and elegantly furnished hotel, very close to the coach and train stations and providing en-suite and more basic rooms at decent prices. Large TV lounge, and the gardens and tennis courts of Eccleston Square can be used by hotel residents. Victoria tube. ④.

The Goring, 15 Beeston Place, SW1 (☎0171/396 9000). This Edwardian hotel, owned and run by the Goring family for three generations, succeeds in creating an atmosphere of elegance and tranquility. Afternoon tea is served on the delightful private garden-terrace in fine weather; breakfast is not included. Victoria tube. ③.

Limegrove Hotel, 101 Warwick Way, SW1 (☎0171/828 0458). Just about the cheapest decent rooms with washbasins and TVs in this area. Showers and toilets are shared; English breakfast is served in rooms. Victoria tube. ①.

Melbourne House Hotel, 79 Belgrave Rd, SW1 (☎0171/828 3516). One of the best B&Bs along Belgrave Road: family-run, totally refurbished, offering clean and bright rooms, excellent communal areas and friendly service. Victoria or Pimlico tube. ⑤.

Sanctuary House, 33 Tothill St, SW1 (☎0171/799 4044). Situated above a Fuller's pub, run by them and decked out like one, too – smart, pseudo-Victoriana. Breakfast is extra, and is served in the pub, but this is a very central location, right by St James's Park. Ask about the weekend deals. St James's Park tube. ⑥.

Topham's Ebury Court Hotel, 26 Ebury St, SW1 (☎0171/730 8147). Charming family-owned hotel in the English country-house style, just a couple of minutes' walk from the Victoria stations. Sumptuously furnished en-suite twins or doubles, with full English breakfast. Victoria tube. ⑦.

Windermere Hotel, 142–144 Warwick Way, SW1 (☎0171/834 5163). Situated at the western end of Warwick Way, this is a tastefully decorated and quietly stylish place, with a few good-value doubles with shared facilities and en-suite doubles for considerably more. There's a good restaurant downstairs, too. Sloane Square, Pimlico or Victoria tube. ④.

Woodville House & Morgan House, 107 & 120 Ebury St, SW1 (☎0171/730 1048). Two above-average B&Bs, run by the same friendly couple. Great breakfasts, patio garden, with an iron and fridge for guests to use. All rooms at *Woodville* are with shared facilities; some at *Morgan* are en suite. Victoria tube. ③.

Knightsbridge, Kensington and Chelsea

Abbey House Hotel, 11 Vicarage Gate, W8 (☎0171/727 2594). Inexpensive B&B in a quiet street just north of Kensington High Street, maintained to a high standard by its attentive owners. Rooms are large and bright – prices are kept down by sharing facilities. Full English breakfast, with free tea and coffee available all day. High Street Kensington tube. ④.

Aster House, 3 Sumner Place, SW7 (☎0171/581 5888, *asterhouse@btinternet.com*). Pleasant, non-smoking B&B in a luxurious South Ken white-stuccoed street; there's a lovely garden at the back and a large conservatory, where breakfast is served. ⑦.

Blakes, 33 Roland Gardens, SW7 (☎0171/370 6701, *blakes@easynet.co.uk*). Blakes' dramatically designed interior and glamorous suites have long attracted visiting celebs. A faintly *Raffles*esque flavour pervades, with bamboo furniture and old travelling trunks mixing with unusual *objets d'art*, tapestries and prints. Doubles are smart but small; fully equipped suites are spectacular, as they should be for over £300. Gloucester Road tube. ⑧.

The Gore, 189 Queen's Gate, SW7 (☎0171/584 6601, *reservations@gorehotel.co.uk*). Popular, privately owned century-old hotel, awash with oriental rugs, rich mahogany, walnut panelling and other Victoriana. An award-winning restaurant adds to the allure, and it's only a step away from Hyde Park. South Kensington, Gloucester Road or High Street Kensington tube. ⑧.

The Hempel, 31–35 Craven Hill Gardens, W2 (☎0171/298 9000, *the-hempel@easynet.co.uk*). Deeply fashionable minimalist hotel, designed by the actress Anouska Hempel, with a huge and very empty atrium entrance. White-on-white rooms start at around £260 a double, and there's an excellent post-modern Italian/Thai restaurant called *I-Thai*. Lancaster Gate or Queensway tube. ⑨.

Hotel 167, 167 Old Brompton Rd, SW5 (☎0171/373 0672). Nicely furnished Victorian B&B with en-suite facilities, double-glazing and a fridge in all rooms. Breakfast is a continental-style buffet. Gloucester Road tube. ⑤.

The Lanesborough, Hyde Park Corner, SW1 (☎0171/259 5599, *reservations@lanesborough.co.uk*). A former hospital, this early nineteenth-century building has been meticulously restored in Regency style, with all mod cons discreetly hidden amid ornate decor. Service is formal and the overall ambience conservative, in keeping with the tone of the diplomatic neighbourhood. Hyde Park Corner tube. ⑨.

Number Five, 5 Sumner Place, SW7 (☎0171/584 7586, *no.5@dial.pipex.com*). Discreetly luxurious B&B in one of South Ken's prettiest terraces. Breakfast is served in the house's lovely conservatory. South Kensington tube. ⑦.

Vicarage Hotel, 10 Vicarage Gate, W8 (☎0171/229 4030, *jim@vichotel.demon.co.uk*). Ideally located B&B. Clean rooms with shared facilities and a full English breakfast. High Street Kensington tube. ④.

Wilbraham, 1 Wilbraham Place, SW1 (☎0171/730 8296). Superb location, just off Sloane Street, with lots of original Victorian fittings in the rooms. A pleasant, old-fashioned place to stay. Sloane Square tube. ⑥.

Earl's Court

Philbeach Hotel, 30–31 Philbeach Gardens, SW5 (☎0171/373 1244). Friendly gay hotel, with basic and en-suite rooms, a pleasant TV lounge area and popular *Wilde About Oscar* restaurant. Earl's Court tube. ③.

Rushmore Hotel, 11 Trebovir Rd, SW5 (☎0171/370 3839). A cut above the average, with its colourful murals and imaginative room decor in this often dreary area. The attic rooms are especially spacious and comfortable. Full continental breakfast. Earl's Court tube. ⑤.

York House Hotel, 28 Philbeach Gardens, SW5 (☎0171/373 7519). B&B in a quiet crescent right next to the Exhibition Centre; some en-suite rooms and more basic alternatives, all including English breakfast. Friendly service and a lovely garden. Earl's Court tube. ②.

Paddington, Bayswater and Notting Hill

The Columbia, 95–99 Lancaster Gate, W2 (☎0171/402 0021). The spacious public lounge, well-worn decor and useful 24-hour bar make this a rock-band favourite. All rooms are en suite. Lancaster Gate tube. ⑤.

Garden Court Hotel, 30–31 Kensington Garden Square, W2 (☎0171/229 2553). Presentable, family-run B&B close to Portobello market; less expensive rooms with shared facilities also available. English breakfast included. Queensway or Bayswater tube. ②.

The Gresham Hotel, 116 Sussex Gardens, W2 (☎0171/402 2920; *sales@the-gresham-hotel.co.uk*). B&B with a touch more class than many in the area. Rooms are small but tastefully kitted out, and all have TV. Continental breakfast included. Paddington tube. ⑤.

Inverness Court Hotel, 1 Inverness Terrace, W2 (☎0171/229 1444). Late-Victorian facade, reception area, bar and lounges lend a charming ambience, even if most of the bedrooms are in an undistinguished modern style. Bayswater or Queensway tube. ⑥.

Pavilion Hotel, 34–36 Sussex Gardens, W2 (☎0171/262 0905). The successful rock star's home-from-home, with outrageously over-the-top decor and every room individually themed. Paddington tube. ⑥.

Pembridge Court Hotel, 34 Pembridge Gardens, W11 (☎0171/229 9977). Attractively converted town house close to Portobello market, with spacious, fully equipped rooms. Two cats add to the homely feel, as does the lively *Caps Restaurant and Bar*. Notting Hill Gate or Holland Park tube. ④.

St James's, Mayfair and Marylebone

Edward Lear Hotel, 28–30 Seymour St, W1 (☎0171/402 5401, *edwardlear@aol.com*). A great location close to Oxford Street and Hyde Park, lovely flower boxes and a plush foyer. The rooms themselves need a bit of a makeover, but the low prices reflect this and the fact that most only have shared facilities. Kids free at the weekend. Marble Arch tube. ④.

Hotel La Place, 17 Nottingham Place, W1 (☎0171/486 2323). Just off the busy Marylebone Road, this is a small, good-value place; rooms are all en suite, equipped with all the gadgets usually found in grander establishments and comfortably furnished. Baker Street tube. ⑤.

The Metropolitan, Old Park Lane, W1 (☎0171/447 1000, *sales@metropolitan.co.uk*). Very trendy new hotel run by Christina Ong, the *Met* adheres to the current fad for minimalism. The staff are kitted out in DKNY clothes, and the hotel bar was *the* place to be seen when it opened a few years ago. Green Park or Hyde Park Corner tube. ⑨.

Wigmore Court Hotel, 23 Gloucester Place, W1 (☎0171/935 0928). Better than average B&B, boasting a high tally of returning clients. Comfortable rooms with en-suite facilities, plus two doubles with shared facilities for just £45. Unusually, there's also a laundry and basic kitchen for guests' use. Marble Arch or Baker Street tube. ⑤.

Soho, Covent Garden and The Strand

Covent Garden Hotel, 10 Monmouth St, WC2 (☎0171/806 1000, *covent@firmdale.co.uk*). Stylish new conversion from a French Hospital just off Shaftesbury Avenue, with rooms decorated in a fairly traditional English style. All mod cons, including stereo, video, fax and voice mail. Bar and brasserie on the ground floor. Covent Garden or Leicester Square tube. ④.

The Fielding Hotel, 4 Broad Court, Bow St, WC2 (☎0171/836 8305). Quietly situated on a traffic-free and gas-lit court, this excellent hotel is one of Covent Garden's hidden gems. A firm favourite with visiting performers, since it's just a few yards from the Royal Opera House. Breakfast is extra. Covent Garden tube. ⑤.

Hazlitt's, 6 Frith St, W1 (☎0171/434 1771). This early eighteenth-century building is a Soho hotel of real character and charm, offering en-suite rooms decorated and furnished in a style as close to that period as convenience and comfort allow. Continental breakfast is served in the rooms. Tottenham Court Road tube. ⑧.

Manzi's, 1–2 Leicester St, W1 (☎0171/734 0224). Set over the Italian and seafood restaurant of the same name, *Manzi's* is one of very few West End hotels in this price range. Noise might prove to be a nuisance. Continental breakfast is included in the price. Leicester Square tube. ⑤.

One Aldwych, 1 Aldwych, WC2 (☎0171/300 1000, *sales@onealdwych.co.uk*). Following the minimalist trend, this fashionable new luxury hotel is a conversion of one of London's few vaguely Art Nouveau buildings, built in 1907 for the *Morning Post*. Little survives from those days – the draws now are the underwater music in the hotel's vast pool and the TVs in the bathrooms. Covent Garden or Temple tube. ⑨.

Strand Continental Hotel, 143 Strand, WC2 (☎0171/836 4880). This tiny Indian-run hotel near Aldwych offers very basic rooms with shared facilities, plus continental breakfast. Rooms have recently had a lick of paint, but nothing too drastic, making this an unbeatable central London bargain. Covent Garden or Temple tube. ②.

Bloomsbury

Avalon Hotel, 46–47 Cartwright Gardens, WC1 (☎0171/387 2366). Friendly, old-fashioned B&B. All rooms have washbasin and TV, a few are en suite, and English breakfast is included. Euston or Russell Square tube. ③.

Hotel Cavendish, 75 Gower St, WC1 (☎0171/636 9079). A real bargain, with lovely owners, two beautiful overrun gardens and some quite well-preserved original features. All rooms have shared facilities, and there are some good-value family rooms, too. Goodge Street tube. ②.

Crescent Hotel, 49–50 Cartwright Gardens, WC1 (☎0171/387 1515). Very comfortable and tastefully decorated B&B – definitely a cut above the rest. Lovely blacked-up range in the breakfast room. All doubles are en suite, but there are a few bargain singles with shared facilities. Euston or Russell Square tube. ⑤.

Harlingford Hotel, 61–63 Cartwright Gardens, WC1 (☎0171/387 1551). Another good option in this fine Georgian crescent. All rooms are en suite with TV, the lounge has a real fire, and the breakfast room is bright and cheery. Euston or Russell Square tube. ⑤.

Jenkins Hotel, 45 Cartwright Gardens, WC1 (☎0171/837 4654). Smartly kept family-run place with just fourteen fairly small, but well-equipped rooms. The lovely in-house black labrador is a big hit with visitors. Euston or Russell Square tube. ④.

Ridgemount Hotel, 65–67 Gower St, WC1 (☎0171/636 1141). Old-fashioned, family-run place, with small rooms, mostly with shared facilities, a garden, free hot-drinks machine and a laundry. Goodge Street tube. ②.

Hotel Russell, Russell Square, WC1 (☎0171/837 6470, *anon@forte.com*). From its grand 1898 exterior to its opulent interiors of marble, wood and crystal, this late-Victorian landmark fully retains its period atmosphere. No two rooms are identical in size or facilities but all are well appointed and decorated in a homely manner. Half-price weekend deals are available. Russell Square tube. ⑧.

Hampstead

Dillons Hotel, 21 Belsize Park, NW3 (☎0171/794 3360). Bargain B&B in a lovely big Victorian house on a leafy residential street, close to Belsize Park "village". Rooms are very plain, shared facilities only, but quite spacious. TV lounge. Belsize Park tube. ①.

La Gaffe, 107–111 Heath St, NW3 (☎0171/435 4941). Small, warren-like hotel situated over an Italian restaurant and bar in the heart of Hampstead, two minutes' walk from the Heath. All rooms are en suite, and there's a communal roof garden. Hampstead tube. ⑤.

Hampstead Village Guest House, 2 Kemplay Rd, NW3 (☎0171/435 8679, *hvguesthouse@dial.pipex.com*). Lovely non-smoking B&B in an old house set in a quiet backstreet between Hampstead village and the Heath. Rooms have "lived-in" clutter which makes a change from anodyne hotels and spartan B&Bs. Hampstead tube. ⑤.

Sandringham Hotel, 3 Holford Rd, NW3 (☎0171/435 1569). Utterly charming small hotel on a quiet, leafy street right by the Heath. The decor has bags of character, service is relaxed and there's a beautiful garden. Hampstead tube. ⑧.

Hostels, student halls and camping

London's seven **YHA hostels** are generally the cleanest, most efficiently run and most expensive hostels in the capital. They are always busy, so you'll have to arrive as early as possible or book in advance to stand a chance of getting a room. Members of any association affiliated to Hostelling International have automatic membership of the YHA; non-members can join at any of the hostels. In addition to the official hostels, there's a wide range of **private hostels** which charge less and tend to be more laid-back; unlike YHA hostels, however, there's no quality control, so standards can vary wildly. Some accommodation in **student halls of residence** is available outside term time, but the prices aren't all that attractive and the rooms get booked up quickly. London's **campsites** are all out on the perimeters of the city, offering pitches for around £2–4, plus a fee of around £3–4 per person per night (reductions for children and out of season).

YHA hostels

City of London, 36 Carter Lane, EC4 (☎0171/236 4965). Opposite St Paul's Cathedral; 200 beds, mostly in 4 and 5-bed dorms, with triple bunks in larger dorms. St Paul's tube.

Earl's Court, 38 Bolton Gardens, SW5 (☎0171/373 7083). Better than a lot of accommodation in Earl's Court, but only offering dorms of 4–16 beds, and the triple-bunks take some getting used to. Kitchen, restaurant and large garden. No school groups. Earl's Court tube.

Hampstead Heath, 4 Wellgarth Rd, NW11 (☎0181/458 9054). One of the biggest and best-appointed hostels, set in its own grounds near Hampstead Heath. Golders Green tube.

Holland House, Holland Walk, W8 (☎0171/937 0748). Idyllically situated in a converted Jacobean house, and fairly convenient for the centre, this extensive hostel offers a decent kitchen, inexpensive restaurant and Internet access, and tends to be popular with school groups. Holland Park or High Street Kensington tube.

Oxford Street, 14 Noel St, W1 (☎0171/734 1618). Its unbeatable West End location and modest size (90 beds in rooms of 2, 3 and 4 beds) mean that this hostel tends to be full even out of high season. No children. Oxford Circus or Tottenham Court Road tube.

Rotherhithe, Island Yard, Salter Rd, SE16 (☎0171/232 2114). Purpose-built for the YHA, this large hostel is located in a redeveloped area that has little going for it compared to other hostels, but it's only twenty minutes by tube from the West End, and very convenient for the Dome. Rooms have 2, 4, 5 or 10 beds. Rotherhithe tube.

St Pancras, 79–81 Euston Road, NW1 (☎0171/388 9998). London's newest YHA hostel is housed in six floors of a converted police station, directly opposite the new British Library, on the busy Euston Road. Rooms are very clean, bright, triple-glazed and air-conditioned – some even have en-suite facilities. Family rooms available with TVs. King's Cross or Euston tube.

Private hostels

Albert Hotel, 191 Queen's Gate, SW7 (☎0171/584 3019). Battered budget accommodation in a plush area. It's a long walk to the nearest tube, but only a minute or two to Hyde Park and the South Ken museums. No kitchen, but breakfast is included and there's a laundry. South Kensington, Gloucester Road or High Street Kensington tube.

Chelsea Hotel, 33–41 Earl's Court Square, SW5 (☎0171/244 6892). A 260-bed ramshackle hostel offering cheap dorm beds and en-suite twins. Facilities include a TV lounge, restaurant, bar with pool table and a laundry. Breakfast included. Earl's Court tube.

Generator, Compton Place, off Tavistock Place, WC1 (☎0171/388 7666). The neon- and UV-lighting and post-industrial decor may not be to everyone's tastes, but the youthful clientele certainly enjoy the cheap bar that's open daily until 2am. You don't share with strangers, so prices get progressively cheaper the more there are in your posse. Russell Square or Euston tube.

Leinster Hotel, 7–12 Leinster Square, W2 (☎0171/229 9641, *astorhostels@msn.com*). The biggest and liveliest of the Astor Hostels, with a party atmosphere, and two bars open until the wee small hours. Under 30s only. Queensway or Notting Hill Gate tube.

Museum Hostel, 27 Montague St, WC1 (☎0171/580 5360, *astorhostels@msn.com*). In a lovely Georgian house in Bloomsbury, this is the quietest of the Astor hostels. There's no bar, though it's still a sociable, laid-back place, and well situated. Small kitchen, TV lounge and baths as well as showers. Under 30s only. Russell Square tube.

Tonbridge Club, 120 Cromer St, WC1 (☎0171/837 4406). This is a real last resort, but if you're desperate (and a non-British passport holder), you can sleep on a mattress on the floor for £5 per person. Hot showers, TV room. Check-in 9pm–midnight. King's Cross tube.

Student halls

Carr Saunders Hall, 18–24 Fitzroy St, W1 (☎0171/323 9712). Student accommodation belonging to the London School of Economics; prices include breakfast. Open July–Sept. Warren Street tube.

International Student House, 229 Great Portland St, NW1 (☎0171/631 8300, *accom@ish.org.uk*). Hundreds of beds in a vast complex at the southern end of Regent's Park. Open all year round. Great Portland Street or Regent's Park tube.

King's Campus Vacation Bureau, 552 King's Rd, SW10 (☎0171/928 3777). King's College has a range of accommodation mostly in the Kensington, Chelsea and Westminster areas, with some less expensive alternatives in Hampstead, Wandsworth and Denmark Hill. Open July–Sept. All prices including breakfast.

Ramsay Hall, 20 Maple St, W1 (☎0171/387 4537). Fairly central and comfortable, with over 400 beds, mostly singles. Open Easter & June–Sept. Warren Street or King's Cross tube.

Campsites

Abbey Wood, Federation Rd, Abbey Wood, SE2 (☎0181/311 7708). Enormous site east of Greenwich, ten miles from central London. Train from Charing Cross to Abbey Wood.

Crystal Palace, Crystal Palace Parade, SE19 (☎0181/778 7155). Maximum stay of two weeks in summer, three weeks in winter. Train from London Bridge or Victoria to Crystal Palace.

Tent City Acton, Old Oak Common Lane, W3 (☎0181/743 5708). The cheapest beds in London either in your own tent or in dorm accommodation in fourteen large tents. Open June to mid-Sept. East Acton tube.

Tent City Hackney Camping, Millfields Rd, Hackney Marshes E5 (☎0181/985 7656). Dorm tents for £5 a night, plus tent pitches. Big, but very inconvenient, way over in the east of the city with poor transport connections. Open June–Aug. Bus #38 from Victoria or Angel tube, then #236 or #276.

THE CITY

The majority of London's sights are situated to the north of the **River Thames**, which loops through the city from west to east, but there is no single predominant focus of interest, for London has grown not through centralized planning but by a process of agglomeration – villages and urban developments that once surrounded the core are now lost within the amorphous mass of Greater London.

One of the few areas which is manageable on foot is **Westminster and Whitehall**, the city's royal, political and ecclesiastical power base, where you'll find the **National Gallery** and a host of other London landmarks from **Buckingham Palace** to **Westminster Abbey**. The grand streets and squares of **St James's, Mayfair and Marylebone**, to the north of Westminster, have been the playground of the rich since the Restoration, and now contain the city's busiest shopping zones.

East of Piccadilly Circus, **Soho and Covent Garden** form the heart of the **West End** entertainment district, containing the largest concentration of theatres, cinemas, clubs, flashy shops, cafés and restaurants. To the north lies the university quarter of **Bloomsbury**, home to the ever-popular **British Museum** and the secluded quadrangles of **Holborn**'s Inns of Court, London's legal heartland.

The City – the City of London, to give it its full title – is at one and the same time the most ancient and the most modern part of London. Settled since Roman times, it is now one of the world's great financial centres, yet retains its share of historic sights, notably the **Tower of London** and a fine cache of Wren churches that includes **St Paul's Cathedral**. Impoverished and working-class, the **East End**, to the east of the City, is not conventional tourist territory, but to ignore it entirely is to miss out a crucial element of contemporary London. **Docklands** is the converse of the down-at-heel East End, with the Canary Wharf tower, the country's tallest building, epitomizing the pretensions of the Thatcherite dream.

Lambeth and Southwark comprise the small slice of central London that lies south of the Thames. The **South Bank Centre**, London's little-loved concrete culture bunker, is set to be one of the focal points of the millennial celebrations. Neighbouring Southwark is also due to rise into prominence, with a new pedestrian bridge linking the City with **Bankside**, whose former power station is set to become the new **Tate Gallery of Modern Art**.

The largest park in central London is **Hyde Park**, a segment of greenery which separates wealthy **Kensington and Chelsea** from the city centre. The museums of South Kensington – the Victoria and Albert Museum, the Science Museum and the Natural History Museum – are a must; and if you have shopping on your agenda, you'll want to check out the hive of plush stores in the vicinity of **Harrods**.

The capital's trendiest weekend market takes place around **Camden Lock** in North London. Further out, in the literary suburbs of Hampstead and Highgate, there are unbeatable views across the city from half-wild **Hampstead Heath**, the favourite parkland of thousands of Londoners. The glory of **southeast London** is **Greenwich**, with its nautical associations, royal park and observatory. Finally, there are plenty of rewarding day trips along the Thames from **Chiswick to Windsor**, most notably Hampton Court Palace and Windsor Castle.

Westminster and Whitehall

Political, religious and regal power has emanated from **Westminster** and **Whitehall** for almost a millennium. It was Edward the Confessor who first established Westminster as London's royal and ecclesiastical power base, some three miles west of the City of London. The embryonic English parliament met in the abbey in the fourteenth century and eventually took over the old royal palace of Westminster. In the nineteenth century, Whitehall became the "heart of the Empire", its ministries ruling over a quarter of the world's population. Even now, though the UK's world status has diminished, the institutions that run the country inhabit roughly the same geographical area: Westminster for the politicians, Whitehall for the civil servants.

The monuments and buildings in and around Whitehall and Westminster also span the millennium, and include some of London's most famous landmarks – **Nelson's Column**, **Big Ben** and the **Houses of Parliament**, **Westminster Abbey** and **Buckingham Palace**, plus two of the city's finest permanent art collections, the **National Gallery** and the **Tate Gallery**. This is a well-trodden tourist circuit since it's also one of the easiest parts of London to walk round, with all the major sights within a mere half-mile of each other, linked by two of London's most triumphant avenues, **Whitehall** and **The Mall**.

Trafalgar Square

Despite being little more than a glorified, sunken traffic island, infested with scruffy urban pigeons, **Trafalgar Square** is still one of London's grandest architectural setpieces. John Nash designed the basic layout in the 1820s, but died long before the square took its present form. The Neoclassical National Gallery (see opposite) filled up the northern side of the square in 1838, followed five years later by the square's central focal point, **Nelson's Column**; the famous bronze lions didn't arrive until 1868, and the fountains – a rarity in a London square – didn't take their present shape until the eve of World War II.

As one of the few large public squares in London, Trafalgar Square has been both a tourist attraction and a focus for **political demonstrations** since the Chartists assembled here in 1848 before marching to Kennington Common. On a more festive note, the square is graced each December with a giant Christmas tree, donated by Norway in thanks for liberation from the Nazis, and on **New Year's Eve**, thousands of inebriates sing in the New Year.

Stranded on a traffic island to the south of the column, and predating the entire square, is the **equestrian statue of Charles I**, erected shortly after the Restoration on the very spot where eight of those who had signed the king's death warrant were

---

LONDON TOURS

Sightseeing bus tours are run by several rival companies, their open-top double-deckers setting off every thirty minutes from Victoria station, Trafalgar Square, Piccadilly and other tourist spots. Tours take roughly ninety minutes (though you can hop on and off as often as you like) and cost around £12. Alternatively, you can save money and skip the commentary by hopping on a real London bus – the #11 from Victoria will take you past Westminster Abbey, the Houses of Parliament, up Whitehall, round Trafalgar Square, along the Strand and on to St Paul's Cathedral.

Walking tours are infinitely more appealing, mixing solid historical facts with juicy anecdotes in the company of a local specialist. Walks on offer range from a literary pub crawl round Bloomsbury to a tour of places associated with The Beatles. Tours tend to cost £4–5 and usually take two hours. To find out what's on offer for the week, check in the "Around Town" section of *Time Out*. The widest range of walks on offer are run by Original London Walks (☎0171/624 3978).

---

disembowelled. Charles's statue also marks the original site of the thirteenth-century **Charing Cross**, from where all distances from the capital are measured – a Victorian imitation now stands outside Charing Cross train station.

The northeastern corner of the square is occupied by James Gibbs's church of **St Martin-in-the-Fields**, fronted by a magnificent Corinthian portico and topped by an elaborate and distinctly unclassical tower and steeple. Completed in 1726, the interior is purposefully simple, though the Italian plasterwork on the barrel vaulting is exceptionally rich; it's best appreciated while listening to one of the church's free lunchtime concerts. There's a licensed café in the roomy **crypt**, not to mention a shop, gallery and brass rubbing centre (Mon–Sat 10am–6pm, Sun noon–6pm).

The National Gallery

Unlike the Louvre or the Hermitage, the **National Gallery**, on the north side of Trafalgar Square (Mon–Sat 10am–6pm, Wed until 8pm, Sun noon–6pm; free; Leicester Square or Charing Cross tube), is not based on a royal collection, but was begun as late as 1824 when the government bought 38 paintings belonging to a Russian emigré banker, John Julius Angerstein. The gallery's canny acquisition policy has resulted in a collection of more than 2200 paintings, but the collection's virtue is not so much its size, but the range, depth and sheer quality of its contents.

However, with over a thousand paintings on permanent display in the main galleries, you'll need visual endurance to see everything in one day. To view the collection chronologically, begin with the Sainsbury Wing, the softly-softly, postmodern adjunct which playfully imitates elements of the gallery's original Neoclassicism. One welcome innovation is the **Gallery Guide Soundtrack**, a brief audio commentary on each of the more than 1000 paintings on display. The Soundtrack is available free of charge, though you'll be pressured into paying a "voluntary contribution" of £3. Another possibility is to join up with one of the free **guided tours** (Mon–Fri 11.30am & 2.30pm, Wed 6.30pm, Sat 2 & 3.30pm), which set off from the Sainsbury Wing foyer.

THE SAINSBURY WING

Prince Charles was outraged upon seeing the original winning design for the **Sainsbury Wing**, blustering that it would be a "monstrous carbuncle on the face of a much-loved and elegant friend." As a result the structure that was eventually built is only timidly postmodern, blending well with the older building. The first room you enter (room 51) contains the earliest works in the collection, but also boasts the **Leonardo Cartoon**, enshrined behind bullet-proof glass in its own dimly lit side-chapel. The drawing, *The Virgin and Child with St Anne and St John the Baptist*, is a study for a painting commissioned by the king of France; like so many of Leonardo's projects it was never completed. Outside the cartoon's room hangs one he did finish, *The Virgin of the Rocks*, a melancholy scene in a brooding landscape.

Room 53 features the extraordinarily vivid **Wilton Diptych**, a portable altarpiece painted by an unknown fourteenth-century artist for the young King Richard II, who is depicted being presented by saints to Mary, Jesus and assorted angels. During recent restoration, a minuscule map was discovered in the orb atop the banner, showing a green island, a white castle and a boat in full sail, symbolizing Richard's island kingdom.

Paolo Uccello's *Battle of San Romano*, which dominates room 55, is a transitional work, mixing elements of medieval decoration and early Renaissance experiments with linear perspective – note the foreshortened body in the foreground and the broken lances ranged on the ground. Painted for the Medici family, the panel shows a minor skirmish between the Florentines and the Sienese, and is centred on the mercenary captain Niccolò da Tolentino, who races into battle on a delightful white horse.

Room 56 introduces the Dutch contingent, notably **Jan van Eyck's** *Arnolfini Marriage*, one of the few surviving full-length double portraits from the fifteenth century; signed "Van Eyck Was Here" in Latin above the mirror, some have argued that the painting served both as a commemorative portrait and a marriage contract in which the painter is witness.

Botticelli's elongated *Venus and Mars* dominates room 58, with a naked Mars in a deep post-coital sleep, watched over by a beautifully calm Venus, fully clothed and less overcome. Inspired by a Dante sonnet, the painting was a wedding present – some think it was intended as a headboard for the marital bed, others say it was to decorate the lid of a casket. Either way, it is generally agreed to have been painted for the Vespucci family – *vespa* is the Italian for wasp, a swarm of which buzz around Mars' head.

Room 61 holds some fine examples of **Mantegna's** "cameo" paintings, which imitate the effect of classical stone reliefs, reflecting the craze among fashionable Venetian society for collecting antique engraved marbles and gems. The largest of them, *The Introduction of the Cult of Cybele*, the artist's last work, was commissioned by Francesco Cornaro, a Venetian nobleman who claimed descent from one of the greatest Roman families. The Venetian theme is continued with **Bellini's** *Doge Leonardo Loredan*, one of the artist's greatest portraits.

Piero della Francesca's monumental religious paintings are at the opposite end of the wing in room 66. *The Baptism of Christ*, dating from the 1450s, is one of his earliest surviving pictures and displays his immaculate compositional technique, derived from Piero's innovative work as a mathematician.

THE WEST WING

Displayed in the **West Wing** are the National's High Renaissance works. Room 9, linked to the Sainsbury Wing, has a fine array of large-scale Venetian works, including **Titian's** colourful early masterpiece *Bacchus and Ariadne* and his much later, much gloomier *Death of Acteon*, and **Veronese's** lustrous *The Family of Darius Before Alexander*, a remarkable demonstration of his eye for colour.

Next door, in room 8, **Bronzino's** disturbing and erotic *Venus, Cupid, Folly and Time* and **Raphael's** trenchant *Pope Julius II* keep company with the gallery's works by **Michelangelo**, the most startlingly innovative of which is his unfinished *Entombment*. In place of earlier, static lamentations, this painting shows Christ's body being hauled into the tomb, and has no fixed iconography by which to identify the figures – either of the women could be Mary Magdalene, for example, and it is arguable whether the man in red is John the Evangelist or Nicodemus. Michelangelo also provided drawings for the *Raising of Lazarus* by **Sebastiano del Piombo**, the largest painting in the room, which was planned as the altarpiece for Narbonne Cathedral.

Among the north Europeans in room 4, **Holbein** stands out, with his masterfully detailed double portrait, *The Ambassadors*, and his intriguing portrait *A Lady with a Squirrel and a Starling*, painted in 1527 during the artist's first visit to England. The blue background and half-length format are familiar Holbein traits, but the presence of the two animals is more mysterious – they may be oblique references to the name of the unidentified sitter, who was probably a regular at the court of Henry VIII.

THE NORTH WING

The North Wing is particularly strong in seventeenth- and eighteenth-century Dutch painting. The Dutch works in room 16 include **Vermeer**'s serene *A Young Woman Standing at a Virginal*, whose subject is now thought to be Vermeer's eldest daughter Maria, though nobody is quite sure of the relevance of the picture of Cupid above her.

Claude Lorrain's *Enchanted Castle* in room 19 caught the imagination of the Romantics, supposedly inspiring Keats' *Ode to a Nightingale*, while **Turner** left specific instructions in his will for two of his Claude-influenced paintings to be hung alongside a couple of the French painter's landscapes in room 15. Claude's dreamy classical landscapes and seascapes, and the mythological scenes of **Poussin** were favourites of aristocrats on the Grand Tour, and made both artists very famous in their time. Nowadays, though Poussin has a strong academic following, his works strike many people as empty and dull. Hardly surprising then that rooms 19 and 20, which are given over entirely to these two, are among the quietest in the gallery.

Room 27 is completely given over to **Rembrandt**'s works. Two of his self-portraits, painted thirty years apart, regard each other across the room: the melancholic *Self-Portrait Aged 63*, from the last year of his life, making a strong contrast with the sprightly early work. Three adjoining rooms, known collectively as room 28, are dominated by the fleshy expansive canvases of **Rubens**, including his lurid *Samson and Delilah* (which many believe was actually executed by one of his pupils) and the famous portrait of his sister-in-law, known strangely as *Le chapeau de paille* (The Straw Hat) – the hat is actually black felt, decorated with white feathers.

Velázquez dominates the Spanish paintings in room 29, with his astounding portraits and the remarkable *Rokeby Venus*, an ambiguously narcissistic image that was slashed in 1914 by suffragette Mary Richardson, who loved the painting but was revolted by the way it was leered at. Next door, in room 30, **Van Dyck**'s *Portrait of Charles I* is a fine example of the work that made the painter the favourite of the Stuart court, romanticizing the monarch as a dashing horseman. The inscription on the tree declares in Latin that this is Charles, King of England, in case anyone should be confused. Close by in room 32, **Caravaggio**'s melodramatic art is represented by *Christ at Emmaus* and the erotic *Boy Bitten by Lizard*.

THE EAST WING

The East Wing, housing paintings from 1700 to 1900, begins in room 33 with some wistful gallantries from **Watteau** and **Fragonard** and a splendid assembly of portraits, including the dapper self-portrait by **Louise Vigée le Brun**, one of only three women artists in the whole collection.

Next door, room 34 contains a roll-call of the best of English art: **Turner**'s *Fighting Téméraire*, showing the veteran of Trafalgar being towed to the shipyard at sunset; **Gainsborough**'s feathery and translucent *Morning Walk*; and **Constable**'s *Hay Wain*, a painting so familiar that it's difficult to appreciate it properly any more. In room 35 hangs **Hogarth**'s lively satire on loveless marriage, *Marriage à la Mode*. Room 38 contains **Canaletto**'s glittery vistas of Venice and in room 40, there's the airy draughtsmanship of **Tiepolo**, father and son.

Delacroix, who was profoundly impressed by Constable's dappled application of paint, is shown in room 41 alongside **Ingres'** elegant portrait of the banker's wife *Madame Moitessier*, completed when the artist was 76, having taken twelve years to finish. This room also features the only two paintings in the country by **Jacques-Louis David**, as well as the perennially popular, but phoney, *Execution of Lady Jane Grey* by **Paul Delaroche**.

Five magnificent rooms (42–46) of Impressionist and early twentieth-century paintings close the proceedings, starring, in room 43, **Manet**'s unfinished *Execution of Maximilian*. This was one of three versions, and was cut into pieces during the artist's lifetime, then bought and reassembled by Degas after Manet's death. Other major Impressionist works here include seminal works such as **Renoir**'s *Umbrellas* and **Monet**'s *Thames below Westminster* – with, of course, *Waterlilies* close at hand. Also here are **Van Gogh**'s dazzling *Sunflowers*, **Seurat**'s *Bathers at Asnières*, one of Europe's most comprehensive showings of **Cézanne** and a few choice works by **Picasso**, dovetailing the National's collection into that of the Tate (see p.75).

The National Portrait Gallery

Around the back of the National Gallery lurks the **National Portrait Gallery** (Mon–Sat 10am–6pm, Sun noon–6pm; free; Leicester Square or Charing Cross tube), which was founded in 1856 to house uplifting depictions of the good and the great. Though it has some fine works in its collection, many of the studies are of less interest than their subjects and the overall impression is of an overstuffed shrine to famous Brits rather than a museum offering any insight into the history of portraiture. However, it is fascinating to trace who has been deemed worthy of admiration at any moment: aristocrats and artists in previous centuries, warmongers and imperialists in the early decades of this century, writers and poets in the 1930s and 40s and, latterly, footballers and film- and pop-stars.

The NPG's **new extension** opened in the spring of 2000, with new Tudor and contemporary galleries to expand the section that's by far the most popular. To view the gallery chronologically, you need to head for the Tudor gallery, which has the NPG's earliest works. The **Sound Guide**, which gives useful biographical background information to some of the pictures, is provided free of charge, though you're strongly invited to give a "voluntary contribution" of £3.

The Mall and St James's Park

The southwestern exit of Trafalgar Square is marked by the bombastic **Admiralty Arch**, from where you get a fantastic view down the tree-lined sweep of **The Mall**. This dead-straight avenue was laid out early this century as a memorial to Queen Victoria, along with the triumphal arch itself and, half a mile away, the Victoria Memorial in front of Buckingham Palace. There had, however, been a thoroughfare here since 1660, and Regency architect John Nash was responsible for many of its finest buildings. **Carlton House Terrace**, for example, a graceful stretch of town houses just beyond Admiralty Arch, is typical of his best work, and houses the trendy **Institute of Contemporary Arts**, or ICA (Mon–Sat noon–1am, Sun noon–10.30pm; day pass £1.50, Sat & Sun £2.50), the city's main forum for avant-garde exhibitions, films and performances. Many people pay the day membership for access to the bar alone, one of London's hippest bouncer-free meeting places.

Flanking nearly the whole length of the Mall, **St James's Park** was originally created for Henry VIII as recreational land between his palaces at Whitehall and St James's. Developed as a public park by Charles II, it was landscaped by Nash into its present elegant appearance for George IV in 1828, in a style that established the trend for Victorian city parks. Today the pretty tree-lined lake is an inner-city reserve for wildfowl, in particular pelicans (descendants of the pair presented to Charles II by the Russian ambassador), and a favourite picnic spot for the civil servants of Whitehall. The view to Westminster and Whitehall from the bridge is one of the best – and even the ineffably dull facade of Buckingham Palace looks good from here.

Buckingham Palace

The graceless colossus of **Buckingham Palace** (Aug & Sept daily 9.30am–4.15pm; £9.50; Green Park tube) has served as the monarch's permanent London residence since the accession of Victoria. It began its days in 1702 as the Duke of Buckingham's city residence, built on the site of a notorious brothel, and was sold by the duke's son to George III in 1762. The building was overhauled in the late 1820s by Nash and again in 1913, producing a palace that's as bland as it's possible to be. For ten months of the year there's little to do here save watch the **Changing of the Guard**, a thirty-minute ceremony in which a detachment of the Queen's Foot Guards marches to appropriate martial music from St James's Palace (May–Aug daily 11.30am; Sept–April alternate days; no ceremony if it rains).

Since 1993, the hallowed portals have been grudgingly nudged open for two months of the year. Tickets are sold from the tent-like box office in Green Park, at the western end of the Mall; queues vary enormously, but can be long, after which there's a further long wait until your allocated visiting time. Once inside, despite the voyeuristic pleasure of a glimpse behind those forbidding walls, it's a bit of an anticlimax: of the palace's 660 rooms you're permitted to see just eighteen, and there's little sign of life, as the Queen decamps to Scotland every summer.

Beyond the enormous courtyard, from where you can see the Nash portico that looked over St James's Park until it was closed off by Queen Victoria, you hit the **Grand Hall**, the Duke of Buckingham's original hall. Now a frenzy of red and gold decorated

---

THE ROYAL FAMILY

Tourists may still flock to see London's royal palaces, but the British public have become less and less happy about footing the huge tax bill that keeps the **Royal Family** in the style to which they are accustomed. This creeping republicanism can be traced back to 1992, which the Queen herself, in one of her few memorable Christmas Day speeches, accurately described as her *annus horribilis*. This was the year that saw the marriage break-ups of Charles and Di, and Andrew and Fergie, and the second marriage of divorcee Princess Anne.

Matters came to a head, though, over who should pay the estimated £50 million costs of repairs after the fire at Windsor Castle (p.125). Misjudging the public mood, the Conservative government offered taxpayers' money to foot the entire bill. After a furore, it was agreed that some of the cost would be raised from the astronomical admission charges to Windsor Castle and Buckingham Palace. In addition, under pressure from the media, the Queen also reduced the number of royals paid out of the Civil List, and, for the first time in her life, agreed to pay taxes on her enormous personal fortune.

Given the mounting public resentment against the Royal Family, it was hardly surprising that public opinion tended to side with Princess Diana rather than Prince Charles during their various disputes. Diana's subsequent death, and the huge outpouring of grief that accompanied her funeral, further damaged the reputation of the royals, though her demise has also meant the loss of one of the Royal Family's most vociferous critics. Despite the Royal Family's low poll ratings, none of the political parties currently advocates abolishing the monarchy, and public appetite for stories about the adolescent princes (and their potential girlfriends), or trysts between Charles and Camilla, shows no signs of abating.

to the taste of Edward VII, it's dominated by Nash's winding, curlicued **Grand Staircase**. Past a range of dull royal portraits, all beautifully lit by Nash's glass dome, the **Guard Room** is decorated with Gobelin tapestries and nineteenth-century sculpture, leading into the **Green Drawing Room**, a blaze of unusually bright green walls, red carpet and enormous chandeliers. Disappointingly, there's no regal throne in the **Throne Room**, just two pink his'n'hers chairs initialled ER and P.

Nash's vaulted **Picture Gallery**, however, stretching right down the centre of the palace, is breathtaking. On show here is a selection of the Queen's art collection (over three times larger than the National Gallery's) – among them several van Dycks, two Rembrandts and an excellent Vermeer. Of the remaining rooms a few stand out: the stultifyingly scarlet and gilt **State Dining Room**, for example, and Nash's **Blue Drawing Room**, with thirty fake onyx columns, flock wallpaper and an extraordinary Sèvres porcelain table made for Napoleon. The frothy **White Drawing Room**, full of priceless French antiques, is the incongruous setting of an annual royal prank – when hosting the reception for the diplomatic corps, for some mystifying reason the Queen and family emerge from a secret door behind the fireplace to greet the ambassadors.

You can see a further selection of the monarch's art collection at the **Queen's Picture Gallery** (daily 9.30am–4.30pm; £4; Victoria tube), round the side of the palace on Buckingham Palace Road. The exhibitions usually include some works by Reynolds, Gainsborough, Vermeer, Rubens, Rembrandt and Canaletto, which make up the bulk of the collection.

There's more pageantry on show at the Nash-built **Royal Mews** (April–Sept Tues–Thurs noon–4pm; Oct–Dec Wed only; £3.50; Victoria tube), further along Buckingham Palace Road. The royal carriages, lined up under a glass canopy in the courtyard, are the main attraction, in particular the Gold Carriage, made for George III in 1762, smothered in 22-carat gilding and weighing four tons, its axles supporting four life-size figures.

Whitehall

Whitehall, the broad avenue connecting Trafalgar Square to Parliament Square, is synonymous with the faceless, pin-striped bureaucracy charged with the day-to-day running of the country. Since the sixteenth century, nearly all the key governmental ministries and offices have migrated here, rehousing themselves on an ever-increasing scale. The statues dotted about Whitehall recall the days when this street stood at the centre of an empire on which the sun never set. Nowadays, with the Scots, Welsh and Northern Irish all with their own assemblies, Whitehall's remit is greatly reduced.

During the sixteenth and seventeenth centuries Whitehall was also synonymous with royalty, since it was the permanent residence of the kings and queens of England. The original **Whitehall Palace** was the London seat of the Archbishop of York, confiscated and greatly extended by Henry VIII after a fire at Westminster forced him to find alternative accommodation; it was here that Henry celebrated his marriage to Anne Boleyn in 1533, and here that he died fourteen years later.

In 1698, a fire destroyed much of the palace and the royal residence shifted to St James's. The chief section to survive the fire was the **Banqueting House** (Mon–Sat 10am–5pm; £3.50), the first Palladian building to be built in England, begun by Inigo Jones in 1619. The one room now open to the public has no original furnishings, but is well worth seeing for the superlative **Rubens** ceiling paintings glorifying the Stuart dynasty and commissioned by Charles I in the 1630s. Charles himself walked through the room for the last time in 1649 when he stepped onto the executioner's scaffold from one of its windows.

Across the road, two mounted sentries of the Queen's Household Cavalry and two horseless colleagues, all in ceremonial uniform, are posted daily from 10am to 4pm.

Ostensibly they are protecting the **Horse Guards** building, originally built as the old palace guard house, but now guarding nothing in particular. The mounted guards are changed hourly and those standing, every two hours. Try to coincide your visit with the **Changing of the Guard** (Mon–Sat 11am, Sun 10am), when a squad of twelve mounted troops in full livery arrive from Hyde Park Barracks via Hyde Park Corner, Constitution Hill and the Parade Ground to the rear.

Further down this west side of Whitehall is London's most famous road, **Downing Street**. Number 10 has been the residence of the prime minister since the house was presented to Sir Robert Walpole by George II in 1732; along with no. 11 – home of the chancellor of the exchequer – and no. 12, it's the only bit remaining of the original seventeenth-century terrace, the rest of the street dating from 1868. The public have been kept at bay since 1990 when Margaret Thatcher ordered a pair of iron gates to be installed at the junction with Whitehall, a highly symbolic act, and less than effective – a year later the IRA lobbed a mortar into Downing Street, coming within a whisker of killing the Cabinet. Just beyond the Downing Street gates, in the middle of the road, stands Edwin Lutyens' **Cenotaph**, eschewing any kind of Christian imagery, and inscribed simply with the words "The Glorious Dead". The memorial remains the focus of the Remembrance Sunday ceremony in November.

In 1938, in anticipation of Nazi air raids, the basement of the civil service buildings on the south side of King Charles Street were converted into the **Cabinet War Rooms**, now open to the public (daily 10am–6pm; £4.40). It was here that Winston Churchill directed operations and held Cabinet meetings for the duration of World War II. The rooms have been left pretty much as they were when they were finally abandoned on VJ Day 1945, and make for an atmospheric underground trot through wartime London. The museum's free acoustophone commentary helps bring the place to life and includes various eyewitness accounts by folk who worked there.

The Houses of Parliament

Clearly visible at the south end of Whitehall is one of London's best-known monuments, the Palace of Westminster, better known as the **Houses of Parliament**. The city's finest Victorian Gothic Revival building and symbol of a nation once confident of its place at the centre of the world, it is distinguished above all by the ornate, gilded clock tower popularly known as **Big Ben**, after the thirteen-ton main bell that strikes the hour (and is broadcast across the world by the BBC).

The original Westminster Palace was built by **Edward the Confessor** in the first half of the eleventh century, so that he could watch over the building of his abbey. It then served as the seat of all the English monarchs until a fire forced Henry VIII to decamp to Whitehall. The Lords have always convened at the palace, but it was only following Henry's death that the House of Commons moved from the abbey's Chapter House into the palace's St Stephen's Chapel, thus beginning the building's associations with parliament.

In 1834 the old palace burned down. Virtually the only relic of the medieval palace is the bare expanse of **Westminster Hall** (guided tours only, see below), on the north side of the complex. Built by William Rufus in 1099, it's one of the most magnificent secular medieval halls in Europe. The **Jewel Tower** (April–Oct daily 10am–6pm; Nov–March Wed–Sun 10am–4pm; £1.50; EH), across the road from parliament, is another remnant of the medieval palace, now housing an excellent exhibition on the history of parliament.

To watch the proceedings in either the House of Commons or the Lords, simply join the queue for the **public galleries** (known as Strangers' Galleries) outside St Stephen's Gate. The public are let in slowly from about 4.30pm onwards from Monday to Thursday and from 10am on Fridays; the security checks are very tight, and the whole procedure can take an hour or more. If you want to avoid the queues, turn up an hour or more later, when the crowds have usually thinned. Recesses (holiday closures) of both Houses occur at Christmas, Easter, and from August to the middle of October; phone ☎0171/219 4272 for more information.

To see Question Time (Mon–Thurs 2.30–3.30pm) you need to book a **ticket** several weeks in advance from your local MP (if you're a UK citizen) or your embassy in London (if you're not). To contact your MP, simply phone ☎0171/219 3000 and ask to be put through. MPs and embassies can also arrange **guided tours**, which take place in the morning on Mondays, Tuesdays and Thursdays and on Friday afternoons. The full price of a guided tour is around £25, but individuals can usually ask to join up with a pre-booked group, thus cutting the cost to around £2.50 per person. If you want to climb **Big Ben** before or after your tour, say so, as it may be possible to arrange.

Westminster Abbey

The Houses of Parliament dwarf their much older neighbour, **Westminster Abbey** (Mon–Fri 9am–4pm, Sat 9am–2pm & 4–5pm, also Wed 6–7.45pm; £4; Westminster or St James's Park tube), yet this single building embodies much of the history of England. Founded in the eighth century, rebuilt in the eleventh by Edward the Confessor, then again – in honour of Edward – by Henry III in the mid-thirteenth century, it has been the venue for all but two coronations from the time of William the Conqueror onwards and the site of more or less every royal burial during the half-millennium between the reigns of Henry III and George II. Scores of the nation's most famous citizens are honoured here, too – though many of the stones commemorate people buried elsewhere.

Entry is currently via the north transept, cluttered with monuments to politicians and traditionally known as Statesmen's Aisle, shortly after which you come to the abbey's most dazzling architectural set-piece, the **Lady Chapel**, added by Henry VII in 1503 as his future resting place. With its intricately carved vaulting and fan-shaped gilded pendants, the chapel represents the final spectacular gasp of the English Perpendicular style. At the very east end of the chapel, under the Battle of Britain stained glass window, a plaque marks the spot where Oliver Cromwell rested until the Restoration, whereupon his body was disinterred, hanged at Tyburn and beheaded. The aisle north of this chapel is the resting place of Henry VII's granddaughters, Queen Elizabeth I and Queen Mary; in the south aisle you'll find the exquisite tomb of Henry's mother, Margaret Beaufort.

Unfortunately, the public are no longer admitted to the **Shrine of Edward the Confessor**, the sacred heart of the building, though you do get to inspect Edward I's **Coronation Chair**, a decrepit oak throne dating from around 1300, which used to squat above the great slab of the Stone of Scone – the Scottish coronation stone pil-

---

HENRY PURCELL

Henry Purcell (1659–95) is the undisputed father of English classical music and was, until Elgar rose to international prominence in the 1930s, the country's only world-renowned composer. He had a short and fairly remarkable life. His father was a musician in the court of James II, while Henry himself was a chorister at the Chapel Royal. The year after his voice broke in 1673, he became organ tuner at Westminster Abbey and was abbey organist by the tender age of twenty. He wrote the music for the coronations of James II and William and Mary. The music he wrote for Queen Mary's funeral was also performed when Purcell, a notorious alcoholic, died just a few months later at the age of 36 and was laid to rest in the abbey. Legend has it that, following a particularly heavy bout of drinking, his wife locked him out and he caught a cold and died.

fered in 1297 by Edward – until it was given back to the Scots in 1996 as a sop to their nationalism.

Nowadays, the abbey's royal tombs are upstaged by **Poets' Corner**, in the south transept, though the first occupant, **Geoffrey Chaucer**, was in fact buried here not because he was a poet, but because he lived nearby. By the eighteenth century this zone had become an artistic Pantheon, since when the transept has been filled with tributes to all shades of talent. On the south wall stands the memorial to William Shakespeare – who, like T.S. Eliot, Byron, Tennyson and various other luminaries, is not actually buried here.

Doors in the south choir aisle lead to the **Great Cloisters** (daily 8am–6pm), rebuilt after a fire in 1298 and now home to a shop and brass-rubbing centre. At the eastern end of the cloisters lies the octagonal **Chapter House** (daily: April–Oct 10am–5.30pm; Nov–March 10am–4pm; £2.50; EH), where the House of Commons met from 1257 until Henry VIII's reign. The thirteenth-century decorative paving stones and wall-paintings have survived intact. Chapter House tickets include entry to the nearby **Pyx Chamber** (daily 10.30am–4pm), which displays the abbey's plate, and to one of the few surviving Norman sections of the abbey, now the **Undercroft Museum** (daily 10.30am–4pm), filled with generations of royal death masks, including those of Edward III and Henry VII. Wax funeral effigies include representations of Charles II, William III and Mary (the king on a stool to make him as tall as his wife) and Lady Frances Stuart, complete with stuffed parrot.

It's only after exploring the cloisters that you get to see the **nave** itself: narrow, light and, at over a hundred feet in height, by far the tallest in the country. Close by the west door is a doleful fourteenth-century portrait of Richard II, the oldest-known image of an English monarch painted from life. The most famous monument is the **Tomb of the Unknown Soldier**; it stands right in front of the west door, which now serves as the main exit.

Westminster Cathedral

Halfway down Victoria Street, which runs east from Westminster Abbey, you'll find one of London's most surprising churches, the stripey neo-Byzantine concoction of the Roman Catholic **Westminster Cathedral**. Begun in 1895, it is one of the last and wildest monuments to the Victorian era: constructed from more than twelve million terracotta-coloured bricks, decorated with hoops of Portland stone, it culminates in a magnificent tapered campanile which rises to 274 feet, served by a lift (April–Oct daily 9am–5pm; Nov–March Thurs–Sun only; £2). The **interior** is only half finished, so to get an idea of what the place will look like when it's finally completed, explore the series of **side chapels** whose rich, multicoloured decor makes use of over one hundred different marbles from around the world.

The Tate Gallery

From Parliament Square the unprepossessing Millbank runs south along the river to the **Tate Gallery** (daily 10am–5.50pm; free; Pimlico tube). Founded in 1897 with money from Sir Henry Tate, inventor of the sugar cube, the Tate is currently undergoing the biggest period of change in its hundred-year history. Having struggled to perform a difficult dual function as both the nation's chief collection of British art and its primary gallery for international modern art, the Tate is finally going to have two separate buildings to reflect its split personality. The new Tate Gallery of Modern Art opens in spring 2000 in the disused Bankside Power Station (see p.103). The following year, the newly expanded premises on Millbank will officially reopen as the Tate Gallery of British Art.

Until then, the Millbank gallery will continue to house a sampling of modern international art, with first-rate pieces from most of the century's Western art movements.

It's a pretty safe bet that there'll be works by **Surrealists**, Dalí, Magritte and Miró, plus works from the key periods of Picasso's life, one or two by Matisse, and the odd sculpture by Rodin. In addition, the Tate owns works by **Expressionists** such as Munch, Grosz and Kirchner, leading **Abstract** artists Mondrian, Malevich and Kandinsky, and later Abstract Expressionists, Pollock and Rothko. **Pop Art** is represented by Warhol and Lichtenstein, and the **Minimalist** collection includes Carl André's infamous pile of bricks, less well known as *Equivalent VIII*.

The permanent collection of **British art** from Tudor times to the twentieth century includes a fine array of works by Hogarth, Constable, Gainsborough and Reynolds, plus twelve large colour prints of the Creation by Blake, and a range of works by the ever-popular Pre-Raphaelite Brotherhood. From established greats such as Stanley Spencer and Francis Bacon to living artists like David Hockney, R.B. Kitaj and Damien Hirst, twentieth-century British art is currently scattered throughout the modern section described above. It is work by these British artists that will eventually expand to fill the space left by the departure of the international twentieth-century pieces to Bankside.

Lastly, don't miss the Tate's outstanding **Turner collection**, displayed in the Clore Gallery extension. The gallery also offers audioguides, called **TateInform** – one for the British collection 1500–1925 and one for the Turner collection – for £2 each or £3 for both. In its new reincarnation, the Millbank Tate will showcase contemporary British artists and continue to sponsor the **Turner Prize**, the country's most prestigious modern art prize.

St James's, Mayfair and Marylebone

St James's, **Mayfair** and **Marylebone** emerged in the late seventeenth century as London's first real suburbs, characterized by grid-plan streets feeding into grand, formal squares. This expansion set the westward trend for middle-class migration, and as London's wealthier consumers moved west, so too did the city's more upmarket shops and luxury hotels, which are still a feature of the area.

Aristocratic **St James's**, the rectangle of land to the north of St James's Park, was one of the first areas to be developed and remains the preserve of the seriously rich. **Piccadilly**, which forms the border between St James's and Mayfair, is no longer the fashionable promenade it once was, but a whiff of exclusivity still pervades **Bond Street** and its tributaries. **Regent Street** was created as a new "Royal Mile", a tangible borderline to shore up these new fashionable suburbs against the chaotic maze of Soho and the City, where the working population still lived. Now, along with **Oxford Street**, it has become London's busiest shopping district – it's here that Londoners mean when they talk of "going shopping up the West End".

Marylebone, which lies to the north of Oxford Street, is another grid-plan Georgian development, a couple of social and real-estate leagues below Mayfair, but a wealthy area nevertheless. It boasts a very fine art gallery, the **Wallace Collection**, and, in its northern fringes, one of London's biggest tourist attractions, **Madame Tussaud's**, the oldest and largest wax museum in the world.

St James's

St James's, the exclusive little enclave sandwiched between The Mall and Piccadilly, was laid out in the 1670s close to St James's Palace. Royal and aristocratic residences predominate along its southern border, gentlemen's clubs cluster along Pall Mall and St James's Street, while jacket-and-tie restaurants and expense-account gentlemen's outfitters line Jermyn Street. Hardly surprising, then, that most Londoners rarely stray into this area.

St James's does, however, contain some interesting architectural set pieces, such as **Lower Regent Street**, which was the first stage in John Nash's ambitious plan to link George IV's magnificent Carlton House with Regent's Park. Like so many of Nash's grandiose schemes, it never quite came to fruition, as George IV, soon after ascending the throne, decided that Carlton House – the most expensive palace ever to have been built in London – wasn't quite luxurious enough, and had it pulled down. Instead, Lower Regent Street now opens up into **Waterloo Place**, at the centre of which stands the Guards' Crimean Memorial, fashioned from captured Russian cannon and featuring a statue of Florence Nightingale. Clearly visible, beyond, is the "Grand Old" **Duke of York's Column**, erected in 1833, ten years before Nelson's more famous one in Trafalgar Square.

Cutting across Waterloo Place, **Pall Mall** – named after the croquet-like game of *paglio e maglio* (literally "ball and mallet") that was popular at the time – leads west to **St James's Palace**, whose main red-brick gate-tower is pretty much all that remains of the Tudor palace erected here by Henry VIII. When Whitehall Palace burned down in 1698, St James's became the principal royal residence and, in keeping with tradition, an ambassador to the UK is still known as "Ambassador to the Court of St James", even though the court moved down the road to Buckingham Palace when Queen Victoria ascended the throne. The rambling, crenellated complex now provides a bachelor pad for Prince Charles and is off limits to the public, with the exception of the **Chapel Royal** (Oct–Easter Sun 8.30am & 11.15am), situated within the palace, and the **Queen's Chapel** (Easter–July Sun 8.30am & 11.15am), on the other side of Marlborough Road – both are open for services only.

One palatial St James's residence you can visit, however, is Princess Diana's ancestral home, **Spencer House** (Feb–July & Sept–Dec Sun 11.30am–4.45pm; £6), a superb Palladian mansion erected in the 1750s. Inside, tour guides take you through nine of the state rooms, the most outrageous of which is Lord Spencer's Room, with its astonishing gilded palm-tree columns.

Piccadilly Circus and around

Anonymous and congested it may be, but **Piccadilly Circus**, is, for many Londoners, the nearest their city comes to having a centre. A much-altered product of Nash's grand 1812 Regent Street plan and now a major traffic bottleneck, it may not be a picturesque place, but it's prime tourist territory, thanks to its celebrated aluminium statue, popularly known as **Eros**. The fountain's archer is one of the city's top attractions, a status that baffles all who live here. Despite the bow and arrow, it's not the god of love at all but the *Angel of Christian Charity*, erected to commemorate the Earl of Shaftesbury, a bible-thumping social reformer who campaigned against child labour.

If Eros's fame remains a mystery, the regular queue outside the nearby **Rock Circus** (Mon, Wed, Thurs & Sun 10am–8pm, Tues 11am–8pm, Fri & Sat 9am–8pm; £8.25; Piccadilly Circus tube) is a good deal more perplexing. Billed as an all-singing extravaganza, it's little more than an array of Madame Tussaud's waxen rock legends accompanied by snippets of their hits. Next door is the equally tacky **Pepsi Trocadero** (Mon–Fri 11am–midnight, Sat & Sun 10am–1am), Europe's largest indoor virtual-reality theme park. For all the hype, this is really just a glorified amusement arcade with a few virtual-reality rides thrown in.

Regent Street

Regent Street is London's answer to Haussmann's Parisian boulevards. Drawn up by John Nash in 1812 as both a luxury shopping street and a triumphal way between George IV's Carlton House and Regent's Park, it was the city's first attempt at dealing with traffic congestion, and its first stab at slum clearance and planned social segregation, which would later be perfected by the Victorians.

Despite the subsequent destruction of much of Nash's work in the 1920s, it's still possible to admire the stately intentions of his original Regent Street plan. The increase in the purchasing power of the city's middle classes in the last century brought the tone of the street "down" and heavyweight stores catering for the masses now predominate. Among the best known are Hamley's, reputedly the world's largest toy shop, and Liberty, the department store that popularized Arts and Crafts designs at the beginning of this century.

Piccadilly

Piccadilly apparently got its name from the ruffs or "pickadills" worn by the dandies who used to promenade here in the late seventeenth century. Despite its fashionable pedigree, it's no place for promenading in its current state, with traffic careering down it nose to tail most of the day and night. Infinitely more pleasant places to window-shop are the **nineteenth-century arcades**, originally built to protect shoppers from the mud and horse-dung on the streets, but now equally useful for escaping exhaust fumes.

Piccadilly may not be the shopping heaven it once was, but there are still several old firms here that proudly display their royal warrants. One of the oldest institutions is **Fortnum & Mason**, the food emporium at no. 181, established in the 1770s by one of George III's footmen, Charles Fortnum and his partner, Hugh Mason. In a kitsch addition dating from 1964, the figures of Fortnum and Mason bow to each other on the hour every day as the clock over the main entrance clanks out the Eton school anthem.

Further along Piccadilly, with its best rooms overlooking Green Park, stands the **Ritz Hotel**, a byword for decadence since it first wowed Edwardian society in 1906; the hotel's design, with its two-storey French-style mansard roof and long arcade, was based on the buildings of Paris's Rue de Rivoli. For a prolonged look inside, you'll need to be in good appetite (and book in advance) for the famous afternoon tea in the hotel's Palm Court.

Across the road from Fortnum & Mason, the **Royal Academy of Arts** (Mon–Thurs, Sat & Sun 10am–6pm, Fri 10am–8.30pm; £3–6; Green Park or Piccadilly Circus tube) occupies the enormous Burlington House, one of the few survivors from the ranks of aristocratic mansions that once lined the north side of Piccadilly. The Academy itself was the country's first-ever formal art school, founded in 1768 by a group of English painters including Thomas Gainsborough and Joshua Reynolds. Reynolds went on to become the academy's first president, and his statue now stands in the courtyard, palette in hand ready to paint the cars.

The Academy has always had a conservative reputation for its teaching and, until recently, most of its shows. The **Summer Exhibition**, which opens in June each year, remains a stop on the social calendar of upper middle-class England. Anyone can enter paintings in any style, and the lucky winners get hung, in rather close proximity, and sold. Supposed gravitas is added by the RA "Academicians", who are allowed to display six of their own works – no matter how awful. The result is a bewildering display, which gets panned annually by the critics.

Along the west side of the Royal Academy runs the **Burlington Arcade**, built in 1819 for Lord Cavendish, then owner of Burlington House, to prevent commoners throwing rubbish into his garden. It's Piccadilly's longest and most expensive nineteenth-century arcade, lined with mahogany-fronted jewellers, gentlemen's outfitters and the like. Upholding Regency decorum, it is still illegal to whistle, sing, hum, hurry or carry large packages or open umbrellas on this small stretch, and the arcade's beadles (known as Burlington Berties), in their Edwardian frock-coats and gold-braided top hats, take the prevention of such criminality very seriously.

Bond Street

While Oxford Street, Regent Street and Piccadilly have all gone downmarket, **Bond Street,** which runs parallel with Regent Street, has carefully maintained its exclusivity. It is, in fact, two streets rolled into one: the southern half, laid out in the 1680s, is known as Old Bond Street; its northern extension, which followed less than fifty years later, is known as New Bond Street. In contrast to their international rivals, Rue de Rivoli or Fifth Avenue, they are both pretty unassuming streets architecturally: a mixture of modest Victorian and Georgian town houses. The shops that line them, however, are among the flashiest in London, dominated by perfumeries, **jewellers** and designer clothing stores like Prada, Versace, Donna Karan, Gucci, Nicole Farhi, YSL and so on.

In addition to fashion, Bond Street is also renowned for its **auction houses** and for its **fine-art galleries.** Sotheby's, 34–35 New Bond St, is the oldest of the auction houses, and its viewing galleries are open free of charge. Bond Street's art galleries – exclusive mainstays of the street – are actually outnumbered by those on neighbouring **Cork Street.** The main difference between the two locations is that the Bond Street dealers are basically heirloom offloaders, whereas Cork Street galleries sell largely contemporary art. Both have impeccably presented and somewhat intimidating staff, but if you're interested, walk in and look around. They're only shops, after all.

Oxford Street

As wealthy Londoners began to move out of the City in the eighteenth century in favour of the newly developed West End, so **Oxford Street** – the old Roman road to Oxford – gradually became London's main shopping street. Today, despite successive recessions and sky-high rents, this scruffy, two-mile hotchpotch of shops is still one of the world's busiest streets.

East of Oxford Circus, the street forms the border between Soho and Fitzrovia, and features the city's two main record stores, HMV and Virgin Megastore. West of Oxford Circus, the street is dominated by more upmarket stores, including one great landmark, **Selfridge's,** a huge Edwardian pile fronted by giant Ionic columns, with the Queen of Time, riding the ship of commerce and supporting an Art Deco clock, above the main entrance. The store was opened in 1909 by Chicago millionaire Gordon Selfridge, who flaunted its 130 departments under the slogan, "Why not spend a day at Selfridge's?", but was later pensioned off after running into trouble with the Inland Revenue.

Broadcasting House: the BBC Experience

Just north of Oxford Circus, beyond **All Souls,** Nash's simple and ingenious little Bath stone church, lies the totalitarian-looking **Broadcasting House,** BBC radio headquarters since 1931 and now home to the new interactive **BBC Experience** (Mon 1–4.30pm, Tues–Fri 9.30am–4.30pm, Sat & Sun 9.30am–5.30pm; £6.50; Oxford Circus tube). A word of warning is necessary to TV addicts, however, as the museum is almost exclusively concerned with radio (Broadcasting House is the home of BBC radio, but not television). The museum is part guided tour, part hands-on experience, so visits are carefully orchestrated, with tours setting off every thirty minutes (every fifteen at peak times). As well as the usual static displays and audio-visuals extolling the virtues of the "Beeb", you get to record a short radio play with your fellow visitors, and play around in the museum's interactive section, mixing records, fine-tuning your sports commentary and presenting the weather.

The Wallace Collection

One block north of Wigmore Street and just a couple of minutes from Oxford Street, but eons away from its frenetic pace, Hertford House on Manchester Square holds one of London's most important art galleries, the **Wallace Collection** (Mon–Sat 10am–5pm, Sun 2–5pm; free; Bond Street tube). This wonderful array, best known for its eighteenth-century French paintings and decorative art, was bequeathed to the nation by the widow of Sir Richard Wallace, an art collector and, as the illegitimate son of the Fourth Marquess of Hertford, inheritor of the elegant mansion and its treasures. If you visit the collection before the summer of 2000, you'll probably be aware of the museum's new-building works, which are due to be completed around that time.

The ground floor rooms, set around an open-air courtyard, have some interesting medieval and Renaissance pieces, an extensive armoury, and a group of fine nineteenth-century pictures, including **Richard Parkes Bonington**'s translucent watercolours and paintings by his close friend Delacroix. However, the most famous works are on the first floor, the tone of which is set by **Boucher**'s sumptuous mythological scenes over the staircase. Here you'll find furniture from the courts of Louis XV and XVI, decorative gold snuff boxes and fine Sèvres porcelain. Of the paintings, portraits include Sir Joshua Reynolds's doe-eyed moppets and Greuze's winsome adolescents, and two by Louise Vigée le Brun, one of the most successful portraitists of pre-Revolutionary France. Among the Rococo delights are **Fragonard**'s coquettes, the most famous of whom flaunts herself to a smitten beau in *The Swing,* some elegiac scenes by **Watteau** and Boucher's gloriously florid portrait of Madame de Pompadour, Louis XV's mistress and patron of many of the great French artists of the period.

In addition to all this French finery there's a good collection from the Dutch and Venetian schools: **de Hooch**'s *Women Peeling Apples,* the contrasting vistas by **Canaletto** and **Guardi**, **Titian**'s *Perseus and Andromeda,* **Rembrandt**'s affectionate portrait of his teenage son, Titus, who was helping administer his father's estate after bankruptcy charges, and **Hals**'s arrogant *Laughing Cavalier,* the subject of which remains unknown. In the same vast hall as the Hals you'll find **Velázquez**'s typically searching *Lady with a Fan,* and **Gainsborough**'s deceptively innocent portrait of the actress Mary Robinson, in which she insouciantly holds a miniature of the Prince of Wales, her lover (later George IV).

Baker Street, Madame Tussaud's and the Planetarium

A small percentage of tourists emerging from **Baker Street** tube station are on the trail of English literature's languid super-sleuth, Sherlock Holmes, who's celebrated in the **Sherlock Holmes Museum** at no. 239 (the sign on the door actually says 221b). It's a competent exercise in period reconstruction, but the building has no proven connection with Holmes or his creator, Sir Arthur Conan Doyle. Nor is there any attempt to impart any insights, or even basic facts about Holmes or Doyle, yet the narrow staircases are crowded every day with fans from all over the world.

Just round the corner on Marylebone Road, **Madame Tussaud's** (June to mid-Sept daily 9am–5.30pm; mid-Sept to May Mon–Fri 10am–5.30pm, Sat & Sun 9.30am–5.30pm; £9.25; combined ticket with Planetarium £11.50), has been pulling in the crowds ever since the good lady arrived in London from Paris in 1802 bearing the sculpted heads of guillotined aristocrats (she herself only just managed to escape the same fate – her uncle, who started the family business, was less fortunate). The entrance fee might be extortionate, the likenesses occasionally dubious and the automated dummies inept by *Jurassic Park* standards, but you can still rely on finding London's biggest queues here – an hour's wait is the summertime norm.

The best photo opportunities come in the first section, an all-star garden party peppered with contemporary politicians, TV and sports personalities. The next section, called **200 Years**, is more off-beat, with dismembered heads and limbs of outdated personalities – Rudolf Nureyev, Sophia Loren, Nikita Khrushchev – ranged on a shelf as in a butcher's shop, along with a fire-damaged model of George IV with a melted eye. Close by the very first Tussaud figure, Madame du Barry gently respires (thanks to a motorized heart).

The **Grand Hall**, a po-faced gathering of statesmen, clerics, royalty and generals, is lined with oil paintings to add a dash of respectability, but the veracity is a bit suspect – Margaret Thatcher looks like a kindly aunt. The **Chamber of Horrors**, the most popular section of all, is irredeemably tasteless and includes a reconstruction of a foggy East End street, strewn with one of Jack the Ripper's mutilated victims.

The tour of Tussaud's ends with the **Spirit of London**, a manic five-minute romp through the history of London in a miniaturized black taxi. It begins well, dropping witty visual jokes as it careers from Elizabethan times through to Swinging London, ending in a postmodern heritage nightmare, with a cacophony of punks and Beefeaters, before shuddering to a halt by a slobbering Benny Hill.

The adjoining and equally crowded **London Planetarium** (same hours; shows every 40min; £5.65) has a permanent exhibition featuring a giant revolving Earth circled by satellites, live weather satellite transmissions, images from a space telescope and touch-screen computers. All this is just a taster, however, for the thirty-minute virtual-reality presentation, "Planetary Quest", a standard romp through the history of astronomy accompanied by cosmic astro-babble commentary.

Soho

Soho gives you the best and worst of London. It's here you'll find the city's street fashion on display, its theatres, mega-cinemas and the widest variety of restaurants and cafés – where, whatever hour you wander through, there's always something going on. Uniquely, though, Soho retains an unorthodox and slightly raffish air born of an immigrant history as rich as that of the East End. The porn joints that made the district notorious in the 1970s are still in evidence, especially to the west of Wardour Street, as are the yuppies who pushed up the rents in the 1980s.

In the 1990s, Soho transformed itself again, this time into one of Europe's leading gay centres, with bars and cafés bursting out from the Old Compton Street area. Nevertheless, the area continues to boast a lively fruit and vegetable market on **Berwick Street** and a nightlife that has attracted writers and ravers to the place since the eighteenth century. The big movie houses on **Leicester Square** always attract crowds of punters and the tiny enclave of **Chinatown** continues to double as a focus for the Chinese community and a popular place for inexpensive Chinese restaurants.

Leicester Square and Chinatown

By night, when the big cinemas and discos are doing good business, and the buskers are entertaining the crowds, **Leicester Square** is one of the most crowded places in London, particularly on a Friday or Saturday when huge numbers of tourists and half the youth of the suburbs seem to congregate here. By day, queues form for half-price deals at the Society of West End Theatres booth at the south end of the square, while touts haggle with tourists over the price of dodgy tickets for the top shows and clubbers hand out flyers to likely looking punters.

It wasn't until the mid-nineteenth century that the square actually began to emerge as an entertainment zone, with accommodation houses (for prostitutes and their

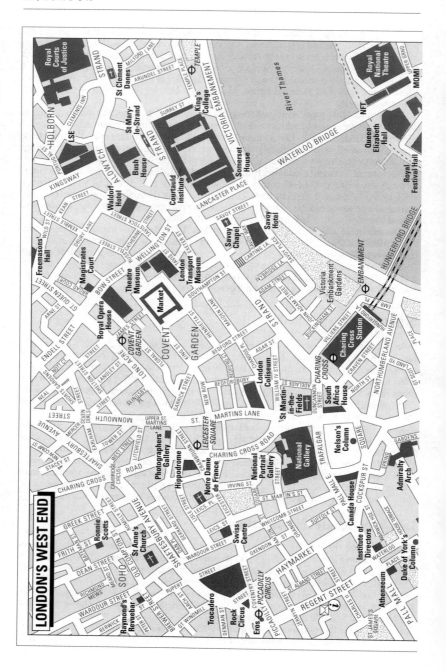

LONDON'S WEST END

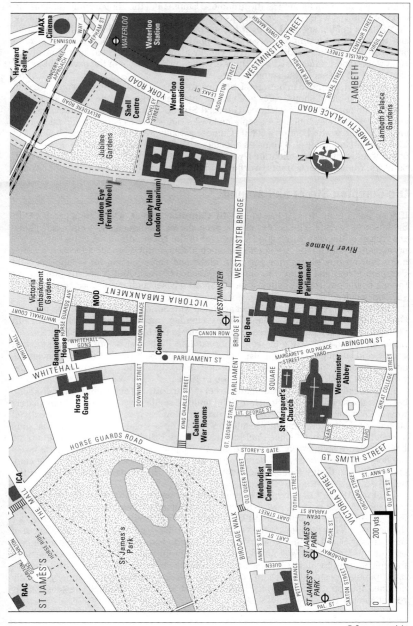

© Crown copyright

clients) and music halls such as the grandiose Empire and the Hippodrome (just off the square), edifices which survive today as cinemas and discos. Cinema moved in during the 1930s, a golden age evoked by the sleek black lines of the Odeon on the east side, and maintains its grip on the area. The Empire, at the top end of the square, is the favourite for the big royal premieres and, in a rather half-hearted imitation of the Hollywood (and Cannes) tradition, there are hand prints visible in the pavement by the southwestern corner of the square.

Chinatown, hemmed in between Leicester Square and Shaftesbury Avenue, is a self-contained jumble of shops, cafés and restaurants that makes up one of London's most distinct and popular ethnic enclaves. **Gerrard Street**, Chinatown's main drag, has been endowed with ersatz touches – telephone kiosks rigged out as pagodas and fake oriental gates – and few of London's 60,000 Chinese actually live in the three small blocks of Chinatown. Nonetheless, it remains a focus for the community, a place to do business or the weekly shopping, celebrate a wedding, or just meet up for meals, particularly on Sundays, when the restaurants overflow with Chinese families tucking into *dim sum*.

Old Compton Street and around

If Soho has a main drag, it has to be **Old Compton Street**, which runs parallel with Shaftesbury Avenue. The corner shops, peep shows, boutiques and trendy cafés here are typical of the area and a good barometer of the latest Soho fads. Soho has been a permanent fixture on the **gay scene** for much of this century, but the approach is much more upfront nowadays, with gay bars, clubs and cafés jostling for position on Old Compton Street and round the corner in Wardour Street. And it doesn't stop there: there's now a gay travel agency, a gay financial adviser and, even more convenient, a gay taxi service.

The streets off Old Compton Street are lined with Soho institutions past and present. One of the best known is London's longest-running jazz club, *Ronnie Scott's*, on Frith Street, founded in 1958 and still capable of pulling in the big names. Opposite is the *Bar Italia*, an Italian café with a big screen for satellite TV transmissions of Italian football games, and late-night hours popular with Soho's clubbers. It was in this building, appropriately enough for such a media-saturated area, that John Logie Baird made the world's first public television transmission in 1926.

At the western end of Old Compton Street is **Wardour Street**, a kind of dividing line between the trendier, eastern half of Soho and the seedier western zone. Immediately west of Wardour Street, the **vice and prostitution** rackets still work the area well staked out. However, straight prostitution makes up a small proportion of what gets sold here, and has been since Paul Raymond – now Britain's richest man – set up his Folies-Bergère style *Revue Bar* in the late 1950s, now complemented by the transvestite floor show next door at *Madame Jo-Jo's*. These last two are paragons of virtue compared with the dodgy videos, short con outfits and rip-off joints that operate in the neighbouring streets.

Until the 1950s, **Carnaby Street** was a backstreet on Soho's western fringe, occupied, for the most part, by sweatshop tailors who used to make up the suits for Savile Row. Then, sometime in the mid-1950s, several trendy boutiques opened catering for the new market in flamboyant men's clothing. In 1964 – the year of the official birth of the Carnaby Street myth – Mods, West Indian Rude Boys and other "switched-on people", as the *Daily Telegraph* noted, began to hang out here. The area quickly became the epicentre of Swinging Sixties' London, and its street sign the image on London's most popular postcard. A victim of its own hype, Carnaby Street equally quickly declined into an avenue of overpriced tack, and so it has remained, despite a fairly recent facelift.

Covent Garden

A little more sanitized and unashamedly commercial than Soho, **Covent Garden** today is a far cry from its heyday when the piazza was the great playground (and red-light district) of eighteenth-century London. The buskers in front of St Paul's Church, the theatres round about and the Royal Opera House on Bow Street are survivors in this tradition, and on a balmy summer evening, Covent Garden Piazza is still an undeniably lively place to be. Another positive side-effect of the market development has been the renovation of the run-down warehouses to the north of the piazza, especially around the Neal Street area, which now boast some of the trendiest shops in the West End, selling everything from shoes to skateboards.

Covent Garden Piazza

London's oldest planned square, laid out in the 1630s by Inigo Jones, **Covent Garden Piazza** was initially a great success, its novelty value alone attracting a rich and aristocratic clientele, but over the next century the tone of the place fell as the fruit and vegetable market expanded, and theatres and coffee houses began to take over the peripheral buildings. When the market closed in 1974, the piazza narrowly survived being turned into an office development. Instead, the elegant Victorian market hall and its environs were restored to house shops, restaurants and arts-and-crafts stalls. Boosted by buskers and street entertainers, the piazza has now become one of London's major tourist attractions, its success prompting a wholesale gentrification of the streets to the north of the market.

Of Jones's original piazza, the only remaining parts are the two rebuilt sections of north-side arcading, and **St Paul's Church**, facing the west side of the market building. The church's proximity to so many theatres has made it known as the "Actors' Church" and it's filled with memorials to international thespians from Boris Karloff to Gracie Fields. The space in front of the Tuscan portico – where Eliza Doolittle was discovered selling violets by Henry Higgins in George Bernard Shaw's *Pygmalion* – is now a legalized venue for buskers and street performers, who must audition for a slot months in advance.

The piazza's history of entertainment goes back to May 1662, when the first recorded performance of Punch and Judy in England was staged by Italian puppeteer Pietro Gimonde, and witnessed by Samuel Pepys. This historic event is commemorated every second Sunday in May by a **Punch and Judy Festival**, held in the gardens behind the church; for the rest of the year the churchyard provides a tranquil respite from the activity outside (access is from King Street, Henrietta Street or Bedford Street).

The piazza's museums

An original flower-market shed on the piazza's east side is occupied by the **London Transport Museum** (daily 10am–6pm, Fri from 11am; £4.95; Covent Garden tube). A herd of old buses, trains and trams make up the bulk of the exhibits, though there's enough interactive fun – touch-screen computers and the odd costumed conductor and vehicles to climb on – to keep most children amused. London Transport's stylish maps and posters are also displayed here in their very own gallery, and you can buy reproductions, plus countless other LT paraphernalia, at the shop on the way out.

The rest of the old flower market now houses the **Theatre Museum** (Tues–Sun 11am–7pm; £3.50), displaying three centuries of memorabilia from every conceivable area of the performing arts in the West (the entrance is on Russell Street). The corridors of glass cases cluttered with props, programmes and costumes are not especially exciting. The long-term temporary shows such as "Slap", a history of stage make-up, tend to be a lot more fun, with a make-up artist on hand to give you a hideous scar or bullet wound. The museum also runs a **booking service** for West End shows and has an unusually good selection of cards and posters.

Not strictly a museum, but more than just a shop, the **Cabaret Mechanical Theatre** (Mon–Sat 10am–6.30pm, Sun 11am–6.30pm; £1.95), on the lower floor of the market building, contains a quirky permanent collection of fifty or so eccentric inventions, hand-made gadgets and witty automata, many of which are for sale. Jokes, from the slapstick to the erudite, are plentiful and the devices within the museum function at the touch of a button.

Bloomsbury

Bloomsbury gets its name from its medieval landowners, the Blemunds, though nothing was built here until the 1660s. Through marriage, the Russell family, the earls and later dukes of Bedford, acquired much of the area and established the many formal, bourgeois squares which are the main distinguishing feature of the area. The Russells named the grid-plan streets after their various titles and estates, and kept the pubs and shops to a minimum to maintain the tone of the neighbourhood.

This century, Bloomsbury acquired a reputation as the city's most learned quarter, dominated by the dual institutions of the **British Museum** and **London University** and home to many of London's chief book publishers, but perhaps best known for its literary inhabitants. Today, the British Museum is clearly the star attraction, but there are other sights, such as the **Dickens House Museum**, that are high on many people's itineraries. In its northern fringes, the character of the area changes dramatically, becoming steadily more seedy as you near the two big main-line train stations of **Euston** and **King's Cross**, where cheap B&Bs and run-down council estates provide fertile territory for prostitutes and drug dealers, and an unlikely location for the new **British Library**.

The British Museum

The **British Museum** (Mon–Sat 10am–5pm, Sun noon–6pm; free; Russell Square, Tottenham Court Road or Holborn tube) is one of the great museums of the world and, after Blackpool, is England's most popular tourist attraction, with in excess of six million visitors a year. With over four million exhibits ranged over two and a half miles of galleries, the BM contains one of the most comprehensive collections of antiquities, prints, drawings and books to be housed under one roof. Its collection of Roman and Greek art is unparalleled, its Egyptian collection is the most significant outside Egypt and, in addition, there are fabulous treasures from Anglo-Saxon and Roman Britain, from China, Japan, India and Mesopotamia – not to mention an enormous collection of prints and drawings, only a fraction of which can be displayed at any one time.

The building itself, begun in 1823, is the grandest of London's Greek Revival buildings, dominated by the giant Ionian colonnade and portico that forms the main entrance. With the British Library now settled into its new premises at St Pancras (see p.90), the museum is currently undergoing a £100 million redevelopment plan, which will allow for the return of its ethnographical department, the opening-up of the British Library's former Round Reading Room – due to reopen at the end of 2000 – where Karl Marx wrote *Das Kapital*, and the surrounding Great Court, which will feature a glass roof designed by Norman Foster. The final completion date for the whole project is 2003.

Greek and Roman antiquities

Greek and Roman antiquities make up the largest section in the museum, spread over three floors. Treasures from Ancient Greece and Rome are ranged to the side of the Assyrian collection on the ground floor, beginning with Cycladic figures, Minoan artefacts, Archaic black-figured vases and later red-figured vases from Greece's Classical age. Beyond here is a glut of wonders: the marble frieze including the **Temple of Apollo at Bassae** (mezzanine room 6) and the reconstructed **Nereid monument**, mighty tomb of a ruler of Xanthos, fronted with Ionic columns and finely carved sea-nymphs.

A huge purpose-built room (no. 8) is devoted to the museum's most famous relics, the **Elgin Marbles**, a series of exquisite friezes, metopes and pedimental sculptures, carved between 447 and 432 BC under the supervision of the great sculptor Pheidias for the **Parthenon**, the sanctuary of the goddess Athena. Removed from Athens in 1801 by Lord Elgin, British ambassador to Constantinople, ostensibly in order to protect them from damage, the sculptures were bought by the British government in 1816 for £35,000 and have caused more controversy than any other of the museum's trophies, with the Greek government repeatedly requesting that they be returned. A CD audioguide (£3) is available to rent, but it's by no means essential as the explanatory panels and video are good enough.

Past the Nereid monument in room 9, you come to two more of Lord Elgin's appropriations: a single column and one of the six caryatids from the **Erechtheum** on the Acropolis. Room 12 contains fragments from one of the Seven Wonders of the Ancient World: two huge figures, an Amazonian frieze and a marble horse the size of an elephant from the tomb of **King Mausolos at Halicarnassus** (source of the word "mausoleum"). A fragment from another Wonder lies in room 14: a giant sculpted marble column drum from the colossal **Temple of Artemis at Ephesus**.

Upstairs, rooms 69 to 73 are dedicated to less spectacular classical artefacts, grouped under specific themes, such as gladiators, music, women and so on. The highlight of these first-floor rooms, though, is the **Portland Vase** (room 70); made from cobalt-blue blown glass and decorated with opaque white cameos, it dates from around the beginning of the first millennium.

The bulk of the British Museum's **Roman statuary** is in the basement, best approached by the west stairs, which are lined with mosaic pavements. The best stuff forms part of the Townley Collection (room 84) and includes two curiously gentle marble greyhounds, a claw-footed sphinx, a chariot-shaped latrine and a Roman copy of the Greek bronze, Discobolus (the discus thrower).

The Western Asiatic antiquities

Just before reaching the Egyptian sculpture on the ground floor, the attendant gods, their robes smothered in inscriptions, fix their gazes on you and serve as a prelude to the **Assyrian sculptures and reliefs** ranged in a corridor (rooms 19–21) parallel to the Egyptian hall. Guarded by two colossal five-legged, human-headed winged bulls, the collection sets off with a full-scale reconstruction of the **Balawat Gates** from Shalmaneser III's palace, leading into room 19 lined with reliefs from the **palace at Nimrud** (883–859 BC); also on display here is a black obelisk carved with hieroglyphs and images of foreign rulers paying tribute to Shalmaneser III.

Another room (no. 17) is lined with splendidly legible friezes, showing **royal lion hunts** of Ashurbanipal, which involved rounding up the beasts before letting them loose in an enclosed arena so the king could kill them, a practice which effectively eradicated the species in Assyria; the succession of graphic death scenes features one in which the king slaughters the cats with his bare hands. From here it's a convenient trot down into the basement (room 89), where smaller **Mesopotamian friezes** and domestic objects include an iron bathtub-cum-coffin from Ur, thought to be the first great city on earth, dating from 2500 BC.

Up the west stairs, in room 56, are some of the BM's oldest artefacts, dating from Mesopotamia in the third millennium BC. The most extraordinary treasures hail from Ur: the enigmatic **Ram in the Thicket**, a midnight blue and white shell statuette of a goat on its hind legs, peering through golden branches; and the equally mysterious **Standard of Ur**, a small hollow box showing scenes of battle on one side, with peace and banqueting on the other, all fashioned in shell, red limestone and lapis lazuli, set in bitumen. A selection of Mesopotamian cuneiform tablets scratched with infinitesimal script includes the **Flood Tablet**, a fragment of the Epic of Gilgamesh, perhaps the world's oldest story.

The Egyptian collection

The BM's collection of Egyptian antiquities is one of the finest in the world. On the ground floor, just past the entrance to the Assyrian section (see p.87), two seated black statues of **Amenophis III** guard the entrance to the main Egyptian Hall (room 25), where the cream of the British Museum's Egyptian antiquities are on display. The name "Belzoni", scratched under the left heel of the larger statue, was carved by the Italian circus strong man responsible for dragging some of the heftiest Egyptian treasures to the banks of the Nile, prior to their export to England.

Beyond, a crowd usually hovers around the **Rosetta Stone**, a black slab found in the Nile delta in 1799, whose trilingual inscription enabled scholars to decode Egyptian hieroglyphs for the first time. Beyond the stone, a sombre trio of life-sized granite statues of **Sesotris III** makes a doleful counterpoint to the colossal pink-speckled granite head of **Amenophis III**, whose enormous arm lies on the floor next to him. Glass cases in the central atrium display a fascinating array of smaller objects, from signet rings to eye-paint containers in the shape of hedgehogs, as well as a bronze of the cat goddess Bastet, with gold nose and earrings. Further on still, another giant head and shoulders, made of two pieces of different-coloured stone, still bears the hole drilled by French soldiers in an unsuccessful attempt to remove it from the mortuary temple of **Rameses II**.

Climbing the west stairs brings you to the **upper floor** and the huge **Egyptian mummy** collection (rooms 60 & 61). The sheer number of exhibits here is overwhelming – one display cabinet to make for is that containing mummies of various animals, including cats, apes, crocodiles and falcons, along with their highly ornate coffins – there's even an eel, whose bronze coffin depicts the deceased as a cobra with a human head.

The Oriental collections

The BM's **Oriental collection** (rooms 33–34 & 91–94) – best approached from the back entrance on Montague Place – is unrivalled in the West, covering Buddhism, Taoism and Confucianism. The Chinese collection is particularly good and the collection of Indian sculpture is easily as good as anything at the V&A (where you now have to pay to get in).

The Chinese collection occupies the eastern half of the Hotung Gallery (room 33), with garish "three-colour" statuary occupying the centre and far end of the room. There's a great cabinet of miniature landscapes popular among bored bureaucrats during the Manchu Empire, and an incredible array of **snuff boxes** in lapis lazuli, jade, crystal, tortoiseshell and quartz. Beyond the superlative collection of **Chinese porcelain**, you enter the **Southeast Asian** half of the room, which kicks off with a beautiful gilt-bronze statue of the Bodhisattva Tara, who, it said, was born from one of the tears wept by Avalokitesvara, a companion of Buddha. At the far end of the room, past the **Tibetan musical instruments** and larger-scale Indian sculptures, is the showpiece of the collection: a dazzling cluster of limestone reliefs, dome sculptures and drum slabs purloined from the **Buddhist stupa of Amaravati**.

The museum's **Islamic antiquities** (room 34), from as far apart as Spain and southern Asia, are in the gallery below, adjacent to the north entrance. The bulk of the collection is made up of thirteenth- to fifteenth-century **Syrian brass** objects, and blue, green and tomato-red **Iznik** ceramics. The best stuff is at the far end of the room, where Moorish lustre pottery resides alongside thirteenth-century astrolobes, scimitars and sabres, and a couple of Mogul hookahs encrusted with lapis lazuli and rubies set in gold. Most unusual, however, is the naturalistic green Kashgar jade terrapin, discovered in Allahabad in 1600.

The other collections

One of the most famous exhibits of the (rather loosely defined) Prehistoric and Romano-British collections, on the first floor, is the **Mildenhall Treasure** (room 49), 28 pieces of silver tableware from the fourth century AD. Further on, in room 50 a glass case holds the remains of the two-thousand-year-old **Lindow Man**, preserved in a Cheshire bog after his sacrificial death at the hands of druids. It's an unsettling introduction to the brilliant displays of **Celtic craftwork**, where two of the most distinctive objects are bronze wine flasks from France, inlaid with coral. Showing Persian and Etruscan influences, they are supreme examples of Celtic art, with happy little ducks on the lip and rangy dogs for handles.

The medieval, Renaissance and modern collections cover more than a millennium, from the Dark Ages to the interwar period. Most visitors, though, come here to see the Saxon **Sutton Hoo** ship burial in room 41. Discovered in Suffolk in 1939, this enormous haul includes silver bowls, gold jewellery decorated with cloisonné enamel and an iron helmet bejewelled with gilded bronze and garnets. Further on, in room 42, among the splendid Viking brooches and coins, are the thickset **Lewis chessmen**, wild-eyed Scandinavian figures carved from walrus ivory and originally painted dark red, which were discovered in the Western Isles.

The BM's ethnography department is gradually returning to Bloomsbury, and will be clustered around the current **Mexican Gallery** (room 33c), a dramatically lit display, covering a huge period of Mexican art from the second millennium BC to the sixteenth century AD. A new gallery for the North American collection has also just opened, and there are further galleries devoted to the Oceanic and Asian collections, due to open over the course of the next few years. In the meantime, an ethnography showcase, in room 35, at the top of the main stairs, will continue to display a few tempting hors d'oeuvres.

The BM also has a new **Money Gallery** (room 68) – sharp right at the top of the main stairs – which traces the history of money from the use of grain in Mesopotamia around 2000BC to the advent of coins in around 625BC in Greek cities in Asia Minor, to printed money in China in the tenth century AD. It's an attractive and informative gallery, and the modern section has coins from all over the world from Siberia to Papua New Guinea.

Minor Bloomsbury museums

A couple of Bloomsbury's lesser museums, although dwarfed by the British Museum, are worth dipping into. The **Dickens House**, 48 Doughty St (Mon–Sat 10am–5pm; £3.50; Russell Square tube) is the area's only house museum – surprisingly, given the plethora of blue plaques marking the residences of local luminaries. Dickens moved here in 1837 shortly before his marriage to Catherine Hogarth, and they lived here for two years, during which time he wrote *Nicholas Nickleby* and *Oliver Twist*. This is the only one of Dickens' fifteen London addresses to survive intact, but only the drawing room has been restored to its original Regency style. Letters, manuscripts, the earliest-known portrait and the annotated books he used during extensive lecture tours in Britain and the States, are the rewards for those with more than a passing interest in the novelist.

Of the various collections linked to university departments, the **Petrie Museum of Egyptian Archeology** (Mon–Fri 10am–noon & 1.15–5pm; free; Goodge Street tube), on the first floor of the Watson building down Malet Place, has a haphazard display of prehistoric to Coptic pottery and jewellery, while tucked away in the southeast corner of Gordon Square at no. 53, the **Percival David Foundation of Chinese Art** (Mon–Fri 10.30am–5pm; free; Russell Square tube) is a fine collection of ceramics ranging from fragile tea cups to opulent bowls glazed with extraordinarily rich colour. The most famous pieces are on the second floor – the vivid blue-and-white "David" vases, made in the fourteenth century, that so influenced Western tastes in crockery.

Gordon Square itself, once the centre of the Bloomsbury Group, is less landscaped and quieter than Russell Square and used mainly by swotting students from the various university departments in the surrounding buildings. Plaques mark the residences of Lytton Strachey (no. 51) and Keynes (no. 46), while another (no. 50) commemorates the **Bloomsbury Group** as a whole (see p.197).

The British Library

After fifteen years of hassle and £500 million of public money, the new **British Library** (Mon & Wed–Fri 9.30am–6pm, Tues 9.30am–8pm, Sat 9.30am–5pm, Sun 11am–5pm; free; King's Cross or Euston tube), located on the busy Euston Road on the northern fringes of Bloomsbury, finally opened to the public in 1998. As the country's most expensive public building, it's hardly surprising that the place has come under fierce criticism from all sides. Architecturally the charge has been led, predictably enough, by Prince Charles, who compared it to an academy for secret policemen. Yet while it's true that the architect, Colin St John Wilson, has a penchant for red-brick brutalism that's horribly out of fashion, and compares unfavourably with its cathedralesque Victorian neighbour, the former *Midland Grand Hotel*, the interior of the library has met with general approval and the new high-tech exhibition galleries are superb.

With the exception of the reading rooms, the library is open to the general public. The three exhibition galleries are to the left as you enter; straight ahead, is the spiritual heart of the BL, a multistorey glass-walled tower housing the vast **King's Library**, collected by George III and donated to the museum by George IV in 1823; to the side of the King's Library is the philatelic collection. If you want to explore the parts of the building not normally open to the public, you must sign up for a **guided tour** (Mon, Wed, Fri & Sun 3pm, Sat 10.30am & 3pm; £3).

The first of the three exhibition galleries to head for is the dimly-lit **John Ritblat Gallery**, where a superlative selection of the BL's ancient manuscripts, maps, documents and precious books, including the richly illustrated Lindisfarne Gospels, are displayed. One of the most appealing innovations is **"Turning the Pages"**, a small room off the main gallery, where you can turn the pages of four selected texts "virtually" on a computer terminal. The **Pearson Gallery of Living Words** houses a more educative exhibition and includes a reading area, where you can peruse a selection of books – for adults and children – on sale in the library's bookshop. The **Workshop of Words, Sounds and Images** is a hands-on exhibition of more universal appeal, where you can design your own literary publication.

Holborn and the Inns of Court

Bounded by Kingsway to the west, the City to the east, the Strand to the south and Theobald's Road to the north, **Holborn** (pronounced "Ho-bun") is a fascinating area to explore. Strategically placed between the royal and political centre of Westminster and the mercantile and financial might of the City, this wedge of land became the hub of the English legal system in the early thirteenth century. Hostels, known as **Inns of Court**, were established where lawyers could eat, sleep and study English Common Law (which was not taught in the universities at the time). Nowadays, the Inns of Court make for an interesting stroll, their archaic, cobbled precincts exuding the rarefied atmosphere of an Oxbridge college, and sheltering one of the city's oldest churches, the twelfth-century **Temple Church**. Close by the Inns, in Lincoln's Inn Fields, is the **Sir John Soane's Museum**, one of the most memorable and enjoyable of London's small museums, packed with architectural illusions and an eclectic array of curios.

Aldwych

The wide crescent of **Aldwych**, forming a neat "D" with the eastern part of the Strand, was driven through the slums of this zone in the last throes of the Victorian era. A confident ensemble occupies the centre, with the enormous **Australia House** and **India House** sandwiching **Bush House**, home of the BBC's World Service since 1940. Despite its thoroughly British associations, Bush House was actually built by the American speculator Irving T. Bush, whose planned trade centre flopped in the 1930s. The giant figures on the north facade and the inscription, "To the Eternal Friendship of English-speaking Nations", thus refer to the friendship between the US and Britain, and are not, as many people assume, the declaratory manifesto of the current occupants.

Somerset House: Courtauld Institute

South of Aldwych and the Strand stands **Somerset House**, sole survivor of the grandiose edifices which once lined this stretch of the riverfront, its four wings enclosing a large courtyard rather like a Parisian *hôtel*. The present building was begun in 1776 by William Chambers as a purpose-built governmental office development. From 2000, the south wing will be open to the public in order to display the **Gilbert Collection** of European silver and gold.

   Part of the north wing has, for some time now, been home to the galleries of the **Courtauld Institute** (Mon–Sat 10am–6pm, Sun 2–6pm; £4, free after 5pm; Temple or Covent Garden tube), chiefly known for its dazzling collection of Impressionist and Post-Impressionist paintings, whose virtue is quality rather than quantity. Among works by Gauguin, Toulouse-Lautrec, Seurat, Van Gogh and Modigliani, are one or two highly prized paintings: a small-scale version of Manet's *Déjeuner sur l'herbe*, Renoir's *La Loge* and Degas' *Two Dancers*, plus a whole heap of Cézanne's canvases, including one of his series of *Card Players*. The Courtauld also boasts earlier works by the likes of Rubens, van Dyck, Tiepolo and Cranach the Elder.

Temple and the Royal Courts of Justice

Temple is the largest and most complex of the Inns of Court, where every barrister in England must study before being called to the Bar. Temple itself is an amalgamation of two Inns – **Middle Temple** and **Inner Temple** – both of which lie to the south of the Strand and, strictly speaking, just within the boundaries of the City of London. A few very old buildings survive here, but the overall scene is dominated by the soulless neo-Georgian reconstructions that followed the devastation of the Blitz. Still, the maze of courtyards and passageways is fun to explore – especially after dark, when Temple is gas-lit.

   There are several points of access, simplest of which is Devereux Court. Medieval students ate, attended lectures and slept in the **Middle Temple Hall** (Mon–Fri 10–11.30am & 3–4pm), across the courtyard, still the Inn's main dining room. The present building was constructed in the 1560s and provided the setting for many great Elizabethan masques and plays – probably including Shakespeare's *Twelfth Night*, which is believed to have been premiered here in 1602. The hall is worth a visit for its fine hammer-beam roof, wooden panelling and decorative Elizabethan screen.

The two Temple Inns share use of the complex's oldest building, **Temple Church** (Wed–Sun 10am–4pm), built in 1185 by the Knights Templar. An oblong chancel was added in the thirteenth century, and the whole building was damaged in the Blitz, but the original round church – modelled on the Church of the Holy Sepulchre in Jerusalem – still stands, with its striking Purbeck marble piers, recumbent marble effigies and tortured grotesques grimacing in the spandrels of the blind arcading.

Across the Strand from Temple, the **Royal Courts of Justice** (Mon–Fri 8.30am–4.30pm), a daunting nineteenth-century Gothic Revival complex, is home to the Court of Appeal and the High Court, where the most important civil cases are tried. Appeals and libel suits are heard here – it was from here that the Guildford Four and Birmingham Six walked to freedom, and it is where countless pop and soap stars have battled it out with the tabloids. The fifty-odd courtrooms are open to the public, though you have to go through stringent security checks first.

Lincoln's Inn Fields

North of the Law Courts lies **Lincoln's Inn Fields**, London's largest square, laid out in the early 1640s, with **Lincoln's Inn** (Mon–Fri 9am–6pm), the first and in many ways the prettiest of the Inns of Court, on its east side. The Inn's fifteenth-century **Old Hall** is open by appointment only (☎0171/405 1393), but you can view the early seventeenth-century **chapel** (Mon–Fri noon–2.30pm), with its unusual fan-vaulted open undercroft and, on the first floor, its late Gothic nave, hit by a Zeppelin in World War I and much restored since.

The south side of Lincoln's Inn Fields is occupied by the gigantic **Royal College of Surgeons**, home to the **Hunterian Museum** (Mon–Fri 9am–5pm; free; Holborn tube), a fascinating collection of pickled bits and bobs. Also on view are the skeletons of the Irish giant, O' Brien (1761–83), who was seven feet, ten inches tall and the Sicilian midget Caroline Crachami (1815–24), who was just one foot ten and a half inches when she died.

A group of buildings on the north side of Lincoln's Inn Fields house **Sir John Soane's Museum** (Tues–Sat 10am–5pm; first Tues of the month also 6–9pm; free; Holborn tube), one of London's best-kept secrets. Soane (1753–1837), architect of the Bank of England, was an avid collector who designed this house not only as a home and office, but also as a place to stash his large collection of art and antiquities – everything from an Egyptian sarcophagus to paintings by the likes of Hogarth and Reynolds. Arranged much as it was in his lifetime, the ingeniously planned house has an informal, treasure-hunt atmosphere, with surprises in every alcove. At 2.30pm every Saturday, a fascinating, hour-long **free guided tour** takes you round the museum and the enormous research library, next door, containing architectural drawings, books and cork and wood models.

Gray's Inn and Staple Inn

North of Lincoln's Inn, **Gray's Inn** (Mon–Fri 10am–4pm), entered from High Holborn, is named for the de Grey family, who owned the original mansion. The entrance is through an anonymous cream-coloured building next door to the venerable *Cittie of Yorke* pub. Established in the fourteenth century, most of what you see today was rebuilt after the Blitz, with the exception of the **Hall** (by appointment only; ☎0171/405 8164), with its fabulous Tudor screen and stained glass, where the premiere of Shakespeare's *Comedy of Errors* is thought to have taken place in 1594.

Heading east along Holborn, it's worth pausing to admire **Staple Inn**, on the right, not one of the Inns of Court, but one of the now-defunct Inns of Chancery, which used to provide a sort of foundation course for those aspiring to the Bar. Its overhanging half-timbered facade and gables date from the sixteenth century and are the most extensive in the whole of London; they survived the Great Fire, which stopped just short of Holborn Circus, but had to be extensively rebuilt after the Blitz.

The City

The City is where London began. Long established as the financial district, it stretches from Temple Bar in the west to the Tower of London in the east – administrative boundaries that are only slightly larger than those marked by the Roman walls and their medieval successors. However, in this Square Mile (as the City is sometimes referred to), you'll find few leftovers of London's early days, since four-fifths of the area burnt down in the Great Fire of 1666. Rebuilt in brick and stone, the City gradually lost its centrality as London swelled westwards, though it has maintained its position as Britain's financial heartland. What you see on the ground is mostly the product of three fairly recent building phases: the Victorian construction boom of the late nineteenth century; the postwar reconstruction following the Blitz and the money-grabbing frenzy of the Thatcherite 1980s, in which nearly fifty percent of the City's office space was rebuilt.

When you consider what has happened here, it's amazing that so much has survived to pay witness to the City's two-thousand-year history. Wren's spires still punctuate the skyline here and there and his masterpiece, **St Paul's Cathedral**, remains one of London's geographical pivots. At the eastern edge of the City, the **Tower of London** still stands protected by some of the best-preserved medieval fortifications in Europe. Other relics, such as the City's few surviving medieval alleyways, Wren's **Monument** to the Great Fire and London's oldest synagogue and church, are less conspicuous, and even locals have problems finding the more modern attractions of the **Museum of London** and the **Barbican** arts complex.

Perhaps the biggest change of all, though, has been in the City's population. Up until the eighteenth century the majority of Londoners lived and worked in or around the City; nowadays 300,000 commuters spend the best part of Monday to Friday here, but only 5000 people remain at night and at weekends. The result of this demographic shift is that the City is fully alive only during office hours. This means that by far the best time to visit is during the week, since many pubs, restaurants and even some tube stations and tourist sights close down at the weekend.

Fleet Street

In 1500 a certain Wynkyn de Worde, a pupil of William Caxton, moved the Caxton presses from Westminster to **Fleet Street**, to be close to the lawyers of the Inns of Court and to the clergy of St Paul's. However, the street really boomed two hundred years later when, in 1702, the now-defunct *Daily Courant*, Britain's first daily newspaper, was published here. By the nineteenth century all the major national and provincial dailies had their offices and printing presses in the Fleet Street district, a situation that prevailed until the 1980s, when the press barons relocated their operations elsewhere.

The best source of information about the old-style Fleet Street is the so-called "journalists' and printers' cathedral", the church of **St Bride's** (Mon–Sat 8am–5pm; Blackfriars tube), which boasts Wren's tallest and most exquisite spire (said to be the inspiration for the tiered wedding cake). The crypt contains a little **museum of Fleet**

Street history, with information on the *Daily Courant* and the *Universal Daily Register*, which later became *The Times*, claiming to be "the faithful recorder of every species of intelligence...circulated for a particular set of readers only".

Numerous narrow alleyways lead off the north side of Fleet Street, two of which – Bolt Court and Hind Court – eventually open out into Gough Square, on which stands **Dr Johnson's House** (May–Sept Mon–Sat 11am–5.30pm; Oct–April Mon–Sat 11am–5pm; £3; Blackfriars tube). Here, the great savant, writer and lexicographer lived from 1747 to 1759, whilst compiling the 41,000 entries for the first dictionary of the English language, two first editions of which can be seen in the grey-panelled rooms of the house. You can also view the open-plan attic, in which Johnson and his six helpers put together the dictionary.

St Paul's Cathedral

St Paul's Cathedral (Mon–Sat 8.30am–4pm; £4, combined ticket with galleries £7.50; St Paul's tube), the City's finest old building, is the fifth church on this site. Its immediate predecessor, a huge Gothic cathedral, was irreparably damaged in the Great Fire and Wren was given the task of building a replacement – just one of over fifty church commissions he received in the wake of the blaze. Topped by an enormous lead-covered dome that's second in size only to St Peter's in Rome, St Paul's remains a dominating presence in the City, despite the encroaching tower blocks – its showpiece west facade is particularly magnificent and is at its most impressive at night when bathed in sea-green arc lights. Westminster Abbey has the edge when it comes to celebrity corpses, pre-Reformation sculpture, royal connections and sheer atmosphere. St Paul's, by contrast, is a soulless but perfectly calculated architectural set-piece, a burial place for captains rather than kings, though it does contain more artists than Westminster Abbey.

The best place from which to appreciate the glory of St Paul's is beneath the **dome**, decorated (against Wren's wishes) by Thornhill's *trompe l'oeil* frescoes. By far the most richly decorated section of the cathedral, however, is the **chancel**, in particular the spectacular, swirling, gilded mosaics of birds, fish, animals and greenery, dating from the 1890s. The intricately carved oak and limewood **choir stalls**, and the imposing organ case, are the work of Wren's master carver, Grinling Gibbons. Meanwhile, in the south-choir aisle, is the only complete effigy to have survived from Old St Paul's, the upstanding shroud of **John Donne**, poet, preacher and one-time Dean of St Paul's.

A series of stairs, beginning in the south aisle, lead to the dome's three **galleries**, the first of which is the internal **Whispering Gallery**, so called because of its acoustic properties – words whispered to the wall on one side are distinctly audible over one hundred feet away on the other, though the place is usually so busy you can't hear very much above the hubbub. The other two galleries are exterior: the **Stone Gallery**, around the balustrade at the base of the dome, and ultimately the **Golden Gallery**, below the golden ball and cross which top the cathedral.

Although the nave is crammed full of overblown monuments to military types, burials in St Paul's are confined to the **crypt**, reputedly the largest in Europe. The white-washed walls and bright lighting, however, make this one of the least atmospheric mausoleums you could imagine. Immediately to your right you'll find **Artists' Corner**, which boasts as many painters and architects as Westminster Abbey has poets, including Christopher Wren himself, who was commissioned to build the cathedral after its Gothic predecessor was destroyed in the Great Fire. The crypt's two other star tombs are those of **Nelson** and **Wellington**, both occupying centre stage and both with more fanciful monuments upstairs.

Paternoster Square to Newgate

The Blitz destroyed the area immediately to the north of St Paul's. In its place the City authorities built the brazenly modernist **Paternoster Square**, a grim pedestrianized piazza whose buildings are currently due for demolition. They will be replaced with Sir William Whitfield's restrained masterplan, seen as a compromise choice in the modernism versus classicism debate.

To the north of Paternoster Square, next to the hollowed-out shell of Wren's **Christ Church** is the **National Postal Museum** (Mon–Fri 9.30am–4.30pm; free), housed in the city's former General Post Office building. The ornate ground floor, where the service counters once were, is now given over to a general history of the postal service, while the museum's world-class collection of stamps is displayed in pull-out drawers on the second floor of the building, along with a short video on the history of post office sorting techniques.

A short distance along Newgate Street, you'll find the Central Criminal Court, more popularly known as the **Old Bailey**. Built on the site of the notoriously harsh Newgate Prison, where folk used to come to watch public hangings, the Old Bailey is now the venue for all the country's most serious criminal court cases; you can watch the proceedings from the visitors gallery (Mon–Fri 10.30am–1pm & 2–4pm), but note that bags and cameras are not allowed in, and there is no cloakroom.

The Museum of London and the Barbican

Despite London's long pedigree, very few of its ancient structures are now standing. However, numerous Roman, Saxon and Elizabethan remains have been discovered during the City's various rebuildings and many of these finds are now displayed at the **Museum of London** (Tues–Sat 10am–5.50pm, Sun noon–5.50pm; £5; free after 4.30pm; St Paul's or Barbican tube), hidden above the western end of London Wall, in the southwestern corner of the Barbican complex. The museum's permanent exhibition is basically an educational trot through London's history from prehistory to the present day. This is interesting enough (and attracts a lot of school groups), but the real strength of the museum lies in the excellent temporary exhibitions, lectures, walks and videos it organizes throughout the year.

The City's only large residential complex is the **Barbican**, a phenomenally ugly and expensive concrete ghetto built on the heavily bombed Cripplegate area. The zone's solitary prewar building is the heavily restored sixteenth-century church of **St Giles Cripplegate** (Mon–Fri 9.30am–5.15pm, Sat 9am–noon), situated across from the famously user-repellent **Barbican Arts Centre**, the "City's gift to the nation", which was formally opened in 1982. The complex does, however, serve as home to the London Symphony Orchestra and the London chapter of the Royal Shakespeare Company, and holds various free gigs in the foyer.

The financial centre

Bank is the finest architectural arena in the City. Heart of the finance sector and the busy meeting point of eight streets, it's overlooked by a handsome collection of Neoclassical buildings – among them, the Bank of England, the Royal Exchange and Mansion House (the Lord Mayor's official residence) – each one faced in Portland Stone.

Sadly, only the **Bank of England**, which stores the nation's vast gold reserves in its vaults, actually encourages visitors. Established in 1694 by William III to raise funds for the war against France, the so-called "Grand Old Lady of Threadneedle Street" wasn't erected on its present site until 1734. All that remains of the building on which Sir John Soane spent the best part of his career from 1788 onwards, is the windowless, outer curtain wall, which wraps itself round the 3.5-acre island site. However, you can view a reconstruction of Soane's Bank Stock Office, with its characteristic domed skylight, in the **museum** (Mon–Fri 10am–5pm; free), which has its entrance on Bartholomew Lane.

East of Bank, beyond Bishopsgate, stands Richard Rogers' glitzy **Lloyd's Building**, completed in 1984. A startling array of glass and blue steel pipes – a vertical version of Rogers' own Pompidou Centre – this is easily the most popular of the new City buildings, at least with the general public. Its claims of ergonomic and environmental efficiency have, however, proved to be false, its open-plan trading floor remains extremely unpopular with the workers themselves and the exterior piping is already in need of extensive repairs.

Just south of the Lloyd's building you'll find the picturesque **Leadenhall Market**, whose richly painted, graceful Victorian cast-ironwork dates from 1881. Inside, the traders cater mostly for the lunchtime City crowd, their barrows laden with exotic seafood and game, fine wines, champagne and caviar.

If you walk down Gracechurch Street from Leadenhall Market, you should be able to make out Wren's **Monument** (April–Sept Mon–Fri 10am–5.40pm, Sat & Sun 2–5.40pm; Oct–March Mon–Sat 10am–5.40pm; £1; Monument tube), which was designed by Wren to commemorate the Great Fire of 1666. Crowned with spiky gilded flames, this plain Doric column stands 202 feet high, making it the tallest isolated stone column in the world; if it were laid out flat it would touch the bakery where the Fire started, east of Monument. The bas-relief on the base, now in very bad shape, depicts Charles II and the Duke of York in Roman garb conducting the emergency relief operation. The 311 steps to the viewing gallery once guaranteed an incredible view; nowadays it is dwarfed by the buildings around it.

The Tower of London and around

The **Tower of London** (March–Oct Mon–Sat 9am–6pm, Sun 10am–6pm; Nov–Feb Mon–Sat 9am–5pm, Sun 10am–5pm; £9.50; Tower Hill tube), one of London's main tourist attractions, overlooks the river at the eastern boundary of the old city walls. Despite all the hype and heritage claptrap, it remains one of London's most remarkable buildings, site of some of the goriest events in the nation's history and somewhere all visitors and Londoners should explore at least once. Chiefly famous as a place of imprisonment and death, it has variously been used as a royal residence, armoury, mint, observatory and – a function it still serves – a safe-deposit box for the Crown Jewels. It was also the home of the royal menagerie: the keeper of the king's leopard during the reign of Edward II was paid sixpence a day for the sustenance of the beast, one penny for himself.

Amidst the crush of tourists and the weight of history surrounding the place, it's easy to forget that the Tower is, above all, the most perfectly preserved (albeit heavily restored) medieval fortress in the country. Begun by William the Conqueror as a simple watchtower, much of what's visible today was already in place by the end of the thirteenth century. Before you set off to explore the Tower complex, it's a good idea to get your bearings by taking one of the free **guided tours**, given every thirty minutes by one of the forty-odd **Beefeaters** (officially known as Yeoman Warders), ex-servicemen in Tudor costume, who can get you into areas otherwise inaccessible.

Visitors today enter the Tower along Water Lane, but in times gone by most prisoners were delivered through **Traitors' Gate**, on the waterfront. The nearby **Bloody Tower**, which forms the main entrance to the Inner Ward, is where the twelve-year-old Edward V and his ten-year-old brother were accommodated "for their own safety" in 1483 by their uncle, the future Richard III, and later murdered.

It's also where **Sir Walter Raleigh** was imprisoned on three separate occasions, including a thirteen-year stretch.

William's **White Tower**, adorned with corner cupolas in Henry VIII's reign, houses a small sample of the **Royal Armouries** collection, the majority of which now reside in Leeds (see p.744). On the second floor, however, you can visit the **Chapel of St John**, London's oldest church, which is said to have been where Henry VI was buried after his murder in 1471. Today the once highly decorated blocks of pale Norman limestone are starkly unadorned, the chapel's beauty coming from its smooth curves and perfect rounded apse.

Surrounding the White Tower, **Tower Green** was where the executions took place of those traitors lucky enough to be spared being put to death in front of jeering crowds on Tower Hill. A brass plate marks the spot where Lady Jane Grey, Anne Boleyn, Catherine Howard and four other privileged individuals met their end (less fortunate folk were hung, drawn and quartered in front of the mob on nearby Tower Hill). They and other noble Tower prisoners, including Thomas More, are buried in the **Chapel of St Peter-ad-Vincula**, a Tudor church close by the scaffold site, only accessible on guided tours. Prisoners at the **Queen's House**, on the far side of Tower Green, included Lady Jane Grey and Rudolf Hess, after his unexplained parachute jump into Scotland in 1941.

The green is also home to two of the Tower's eight famous **ravens**, their wings clipped so they can't fly away – legend says that the Tower and the kingdom will fall if they do. The birds are descendants of early scavengers attracted by the waste from palace kitchens, and are the latest in a long line protected by royal decree since the reign of Charles II. They even have their own graveyard, in the moat near the ticket barrier.

The castellated Waterloo Barracks, just north of the White Tower, holds the **Crown Jewels**, the majority of which postdate the Commonwealth (1649–60), when many of the royal riches were melted down. These days, the displays are efficient and disappointingly swift – visitors are sped along on moving walkways which allow just 28 seconds' viewing. Look out for the **Imperial State Crown**, sparkling with a 317-carat diamond, a sapphire from a ring said to have been buried with Edward the Confessor, and assorted emeralds, rubies and pearls. This mind-blowing display of wealth includes the three largest cut diamonds in the world, the most famous of which, the **Koh-i-Noor**, is set into a crown made for the Queen Mother in 1937 and is displayed separately near the exit. The crowds here are usually phenomenal, so get here as early as possible.

The Lanthorn and Wakefield towers, on the wall of the inmost ward, have been reconstructed to represent Edward I's medieval palace, although the king only lived here intermittently. A few panels in the **Lanthorn Tower** describe the king's domestic and public life, while the **Wakefield Tower**, the second largest in the complex, re-creates two of the king's private chambers, with period-clad actors on hand to answer questions. A tablet on the floor in the state reception room marks the spot where, it is believed, Henry VI was murdered at prayer by Edward IV during the Wars of the Roses. Candlelight and heavy incense enhance the aura of authenticity.

You can also walk along the eastern section of the walls, beginning at the **Salt Tower**, which features prisoners' graffiti. The **Broad Arrow Tower** is decked out as it would have been when Sir Simon de Burley – tutor to Richard II and later to be beheaded on Tower Hill – took refuge here during the 1381 Peasants' Revolt. The **Martin Tower**, at the far end, now houses an exhibition featuring lots of discarded royal crowns, without their precious stones, or with replicas fitted.

Tower Bridge

Tower Bridge (daily: April–Oct 10am–6.30pm; Nov–March 10am–5.15pm; £5.95; Tower Hill tube) is just over one hundred years old, yet it ranks with Big Ben as the most famous of all London landmarks. Completed in 1894, its neo-Gothic towers are clad in Cornish granite and Portland stone, but conceal a steel frame, which, at the time, represented a considerable engineering achievement, allowing a road crossing that could be raised to give tall ships access to the upper reaches of the Thames. The raising of the bascules (from the French for "see-saw") remains an impressive sight (ring ahead to find out when the next opening is). The elevated walkways linking the summits of the towers (intended for public use) were closed from 1909 to 1982 due to their popularity with prostitutes and the suicidal. You can only visit them now on an overpriced **guided tour**, dubbed the "Tower Bridge Experience", that employs videos and an animatronic chirpy Cockney to describe the history of the bridge.

The East End and Docklands

Few places in London have engendered so many myths as the **East End** (a catch-all title which covers just about everywhere east of the City, but has its heart closest to the latter). Its name is synonymous with slums, sweatshops and crime, as epitomized by antiheroes such as Jack the Ripper and the Kray Twins, but also with the rags-to-riches careers of the likes of Harold Pinter and Vidal Sassoon, and whole generations of Jews who were born in the most notorious of London's cholera-ridden quarters and have now moved to wealthier pastures. Old East Enders will tell you that the area's not what it was – and it's true, as it always has been. The East End is constantly changing as newly arrived immigrants assimilate and move out.

The East End's first immigrants were French Protestant Huguenots, fleeing religious persecution in the late seventeenth century. Within three generations the Huguenots were entirely assimilated, and the Irish became the new immigrant population, but it was the influx of Jews escaping pogroms in eastern Europe and Russia that defined the character of the East End in the second half of the nineteenth century. The area's Jewish population has now dispersed throughout London, though the East End remains at the bottom of the pile; even the millions poured into the **Docklands** development have failed to make much impression on local unemployment and housing problems. Unfortunately, racism is still rife, and is directed, for the most part, against the extensive Bengali community, who came here from the poor rural area of Sylhet in Bangladesh in the 1960s and 70s.

Most visitors to the East End come for its famous Sunday **markets** since the area is not an obvious place for sightseeing, and certainly no beauty spot – Victorian slum clearances, Hitler's bombs and postwar tower blocks have all left their mark. However, there's plenty more to get out of a visit, including several **Hawksmoor churches**, and the vast **Docklands** redevelopment, which has to be seen to be believed.

Whitechapel and Spitalfields

The districts of **Whitechapel** and, in particular, **Spitalfields**, within sight of the sleek tower blocks of the financial sector, represent the old heart of the East End, where the French Huguenots settled in the seventeenth century, where the Jewish community was at its strongest in the late nineteenth century, and where today's Bengali community eats, sleeps, works and prays. If you visit just one area in the East End, it should be this zone, which preserves mementoes from each wave of immigration.

The easiest approach is from Liverpool Street Station, a short stroll west of **Spitalfields Market**, the strange-looking red-brick and green-gabled market hall, built in 1893 and extended in the 1920s, which forms the centrepiece of the area. The dominant architectural presence in Spitalfields, however, is **Christ Church** (Mon–Fri noon–2.30pm), built between 1714 and 1729 to a characteristically bold design by Nicholas Hawksmoor and now facing the market hall. Best viewed from Brushfield

EAST END SUNDAY MARKET

Most visitors to the East End come here for the **Sunday markets**. Approaching from Liverpool Street, the first one you come to is **Petticoat Lane**, not one of London's prettiest streets, but one of its longest-running Sunday markets, specializing in cheap (and often pretty tacky) clothing. The authorities renamed the street Middlesex Street in 1830 to avoid the mention of ladies' underwear, though the original name has stuck.

To the north lies **Spitalfields Market**, once the capital's premier wholesale fruit and vegetable market, now specializing in organic food, plus clothes and jewellery. Further east lies **Brick Lane**, heart of the Bengali community, famous for its bric-a-brac Sunday market, wonderful curry houses and non-stop beigel bakery. From Brick Lane's northernmost end, it's a short walk to **Columbia Road**, the city's best market for flowers and plants.

Street, the church's main features are its huge 225-foot-high broach spire and a giant Tuscan portico, raised on steps and shaped like a Venetian window (a central arched opening flanked by two smaller rectangles), a motif repeated in the tower and doors.

Whitechapel Road – as Whitechapel High Street and the Mile End Road are collectively known – is still the East End's main street, shared by all the many races who live in the borough of Tower Hamlets. The East End institution that draws in more outsiders than any other is the **Whitechapel Art Gallery** (Tues & Thurs–Sun 11am–5pm, Wed 11am–8pm; free), a little further up the High Street in a beautiful crenellated 1899 Arts and Crafts building by Charles Harrison Townsend, architect of the similarly audacious Horniman Museum (see p.118). The gallery puts on some of London's most innovative exhibitions of contemporary art, as well as hosting the biennial Whitechapel Open, a chance for local artists to get their work shown to a wider audience.

Just before the point where Whitechapel Road turns into Mile End Road stands the gabled entrance to the former Albion Brewery, where the first bottled brown ale was produced in 1899. Next door lies the **Blind Beggar**, the East End's most famous pub since March 8, 1966, when Ronnie Kray walked into the crowded pub and shot gangland rival George Cornell for calling him a "fat poof". This murder spelled the end of the infamous Kray Twins, Ronnie and Reggie, both of whom were sentenced to life imprisonment, though their well-publicized gifts to local charities created a Robin Hood image that still persists in these parts of town.

East End museums

The East End boasts two fascinating museums, both of them open to the public free of charge. The easiest one to get to is the Bethnal Green **Museum of Childhood** (Mon–Thurs & Sat 10am–5.50pm, Sun 2.30–5.50pm; free), situated opposite Bethnal Green tube station. The open-plan wrought-iron hall, originally part of the V&A (see p.107), was transported here in the 1860s to bring art to the East End. The variety of exhibits means that there's something here for everyone from three to ninety-three, but the museum's most frequent visitors are children. The ground floor is best known for its unique collection of antique dolls' houses dating back to 1673. It's a good idea to take a pile of 20p pieces with you to work the automata – Wallace the Lion gobbling up Albert is always a firm favourite. Elsewhere, there are puppets, a jumble of toys, a vast doll collection and excellent temporary exhibitions.

The **Geffrye Museum** (Tues–Sat 10am–5pm, Sun 2–5pm; free; bus #67, #149 or #242 from Liverpool Street tube), housed in a peaceful little enclave of eighteenth-century ironmongers' almshouses, set back from Kingsland Road, is essentially a furniture museum. A series of period living rooms, ranging from the oak-panelled seventeenth century through refined Georgian and cluttered Victorian, leads to the state-of-the-art

New Gallery Extension, housing the new café and the excellent twentieth-century section, with a room devoted to virtually every decade, and temporary exhibitions in the basement.

Docklands

The architectural embodiment of Thatcherism – a symbol of 1980s smash-and-grab culture according to its critics, a blueprint for inner-city regeneration to its free-market supporters – the **Docklands** redevelopment provokes extreme reactions. Despite its catch-all name, however, Docklands is far from homogeneous. Canary Wharf, with its Manhattan-style skyscraper, is only its most visible landmark; industrial-estate sheds and huge swathes of dereliction are more indicative. Wapping, the westernmost district, has retained much of its old Victorian warehouse architecture, while the Royal Docks, further east, remain a relatively undisturbed industrial wasteland.

The docks were originally built from 1802 onwards to relieve congestion on the Thames quays, eventually becoming the largest enclosed cargo dock system in the world. However, competition from the railways and, later, the development of container ships signalled the closure of the docks in the 1960s. In 1981, at the height of the recession, the **London Docklands Development Corporation** (LDDC) was set up and regeneration began in earnest. No one thought the old docks could ever be rejuvenated; the LDDC, on the other hand, predicted a resident population of over 100,000 and a working population twice that. Seventeen years later, the LDDC was wound up having achieved more than many thought possible, and less than some had hoped.

Travelling through on the overhead railway, Docklands comes over as an intriguing open-air design museum, not a place one would choose to live or work – most people stationed here see it as a bleak business-oriented outpost – but a spectacular sight nevertheless. The best way to view Docklands is from one of the pleasure boats that course up and down the Thames, or from the driverless, overhead **Docklands Light Railway** (DLR), which sets off from Bank, or from Tower Gateway, close to Tower Hill tube. Travelcards are valid on the DLR, or you can get a Docklander ticket for £2.50, giving you unlimited travel on the network after 9.30am. If you're heading for Greenwich, and fancy taking a boat back into town, it might be worth considering a Sail & Rail ticket (£7.20), which allows unlimited travel on the DLR, plus the boat trip between Greenwich and Westminster piers.

From St Katharine's Dock to the Isle of Dogs

An alternative to taking the DLR is to walk from Wapping to Limehouse, along the Riverside Walk, which sticks to, or close to, the riverbank. You begin at **St Katharine's Dock**, immediately east of the Tower of London, and the first of the old docks to be renovated way back in the 1970s. The dock's redeeming qualities are the old swing bridges and the boats themselves, many of them beautiful old sailing ships. Continue along desolate **Wapping High Street**, lined with tall brick-built warehouses, most now tastefully converted into yuppie flats, and you will eventually find yourself in **Limehouse**, beyond which lies the Isle of Dogs. The walk is about two miles in length, and will bring you eventually to Westferry DLR station – for details of riverside pubs along the way, see p.137.

The Thames begins a dramatic horseshoe bend at Limehouse, thus creating the **Isle of Dogs**, currently the geographical and ideological heart of the new Docklands, which reaches its apotheosis in **Canary Wharf**, the strip of land in the middle of the former West India Docks, previously a destination for rum and mahogany, later tomatoes and bananas (from the Canary Islands – hence the name). This is the only really busy bit of the new Docklands, best known as home to Britain's tallest building, Cesar Pelli's landmark tower, officially known as **One Canada Square**, which at 800ft is the highest building in Europe after Frankfurt's Messerturm. The world's first skyscraper to be clad in stainless steel, it's an undeniably impressive sight, both from a distance (its flashing pinnacle is a feature of the horizon at numerous points in London) and close up. Unless you work here, however, there is no public access, except to the marble atrium.

The warehouses to the north of Canary Wharf are to be converted into flats, bars, restaurants and a **Docklands Museum** (scheduled to open in 2000), and will be incorporated into a new complex including a thirty-storey tower block and a multiplex cinema. Until this opens, there's little point in getting off the DLR, which cuts right through the middle of the Canary Wharf office buildings under a parabolic steel and glass canopy.

The rest of the Isle of Dogs remains surreally lifeless, an uneasy mix of drab high-rises, council estates, warehouses converted into expensive apartments and a lot of new architecture – some of it startling, some of it crass, much of it empty. Stay on the DLR and you will eventually come to the southernmost terminus at **Island Gardens**, starting point for the 1902 foot-tunnel to Greenwich (see p.119) and Christopher Wren's favourite spot from which to contemplate his own masterpieces across the river, the Royal Naval College and Old Royal Observatory.

Lambeth and Southwark

Until well into the seventeenth century, the only reason for north-bank residents to cross the Thames, to what is now **Lambeth** and **Southwark**, was to visit the disreputable Bankside entertainment district around the south end of London Bridge, which lay outside the jurisdiction of the City. South London (a catch-all term for everything south of the river) still has a reputation, among north Londoners at least, as a boring, sprawling, residential district devoid of any local culture or life.

As it turns out, this is not too far from the truth: **Lambeth**, for one, is mostly residential, but along its riverbank lie several important cultural institutions, collectively known as the **South Bank Centre**. Although a mess architecturally, these galleries, theatres and concert halls, plus the Museum of the Moving Image, draw large numbers across the river for night-time entertainment.

There are more sights further east in **Bankside**, home to a reconstruction of Shakespeare's Globe Theatre and the new **Tate Gallery of Modern Art** (due to open in the summer of 2000). Neighbouring **Southwark** also has a range of popular museums around Tooley Street. Further east still, **Butler's Wharf** is a thriving little warehouse development, centred on the excellent **Design Museum**.

The South Bank

In 1951, the South Bank Exhibition, held on derelict land south of the Thames, formed the centrepiece of the **Festival of Britain**, an attempt to revive postwar morale by celebrating the centenary of the Great Exhibition (when Britain really did rule over half the world). The most striking features of the site were the Royal Festival Hall (which still stands), the ferris wheel (which returned to the South Bank for the millennium), the saucer-shaped Dome of Discovery (inspiration for the current Millennium Dome), and the cigar-shaped Skylon tower.

The festival's success provided the impetus for the eventual creation of the **South Bank Centre**, home to institutions such as the National Theatre and National Film Theatre. Sadly, the South Bank has become London's much–unloved culture bunker, a mess of "weather-stained concrete, rain-swept walkways, urine-soaked stairs", as one critic aptly put it. On the plus side, the South Bank is currently under inspired artistic direction and stands at the heart of the capital's arts scene. Its unprepossessing appearance is softened, too, by its riverside location, its avenue of trees, and its occasional buskers and skateboarders.

The South Bank is also due to host one of London's highest profile millennium projects, the **BA London Eye** (formerly known as the **Millennium Wheel**), set to dangle over the River Thames from the Jubilee Gardens from 2000 onwards. Standing 495 feet high, it will be the largest ferris wheel ever built, and a ride in one of its 60 capsules, symbolizing seconds and minutes, will cost around £5 for a 20-minute, one-rotation ride.

The Museum of the Moving Image

Slotted adroitly under Waterloo Bridge, the **Museum of the Moving Image (MOMI)** (daily 10am–6pm; £6.25; Waterloo tube) covers an impressive amount in its somewhat cramped space, reeling through a spirited history of film and cinema, with actors on hand to enliven the proceedings. It begins with a vast array of optical toys, but the real fun starts in the following rooms, where, among the memorabilia, cameras, posters and costumes, you can audition for a screen test in a 1920s-style casting session, make your own cartoons in an animation room and watch a shoot on a Hollywood film set, complete with egotistical director.

There's also plenty of opportunity to watch films, often in witty settings: to see the newsreels, for example (including footage of the Hindenberg disaster, Mussolini's pompous posturing and V-Day celebrations) you climb onto the roof of a news van, thus mimicking the logo of the Pathé newsreels. The television section, pandering shamelessly to twenty- and thirty-something Anglo-nostalgia, leads to the bit that's most popular with children, where you get to read the television news and be interviewed by a televisual Barry Norman.

County Hall to the Imperial War Museum

South of the South Bank Centre proper, beyond Jubilee Gardens, stands the colonnaded crescent of **County Hall**, the only truly monumental building in this part of town. Designed to house the London County Council, it was completed in 1933 and enjoyed its greatest moment of fame as the headquarters of the GLC (Greater London Council), abolished by Mrs Thatcher in 1986, leaving London as the only European city without an elected authority. London is due, once more, to get an elected body, and its own mayor, but neither will reside at County Hall, which is now in the hands of a Japanese property company.

Its vast floor space is now home to, among other things, a glorified amusement arcade called Namco Station, a two-hundred-bed Marriott Hotel and, as of 1999, a Football Museum, run by the Premier League. By far the most popular attraction so far, though, is the **London Aquarium** (daily 10am–6pm; £7; Waterloo or Westminster tube), laid out across three floors of the basement. With some super-large tanks, and everything from dog-face puffers to piranhas, this is somewhere that's pretty much guaranteed to please younger kids. The Beach where children can actually stroke the (non-sting) rays is particularly popular. Impressive in scale, the aquarium is fairly conservative in design, however, with no walk-through tanks and only the very briefest of information on any of the fish.

On the south side of Westminster Bridge, in the midst of **St Thomas's Hospital**, on Lambeth Palace Road, is the **Florence Nightingale Museum** (Tues–Sun 10am–5pm; £3.50; Waterloo or Westminster tube), celebrating the woman who revolutionized the nursing profession by establishing the first school of nursing at St Thomas's in 1859. The exhibition hits just the right note, putting the two years she spent in the Crimea in the context of a lifetime of tireless social campaigning.

A short walk south of St Thomas's is the Kentish ragstone church of St Mary-at-Lambeth, which now contains a café and an unpretentious little **Museum of Garden**

History (March–Dec Mon–Fri 10.30am–4pm, Sun 10.30am–5pm; free; Lambeth North tube). The graveyard has been transformed into a small **seventeenth-century garden**, where two interesting sarcophagi lurk among the foliage: one belongs to **Captain Bligh**, the commander of the *Bounty* in 1787; the other is a memorial to **John Tradescant**, gardener to James I and Charles I.

Vauxhall, half a mile south of St Mary-at-Lambeth and once famous for its pleasure gardens, is now a bleak traffic-plagued spot, but it harbours the largest tethered helium balloon in the world, behind the tube station in Spring Gardens. The **London Balloon**, or **Big Bob** as it's affectionately known, rises slowly to a height of 400 feet, to provide the capital's only high viewpoint (until the ferris wheel gets going in 2000). A fifteen-minute ride costs a hefty £12 (daily 10am–dusk, Fri & Sat until midnight; Vauxhall tube).

The domed building at the east end of Lambeth Road, formerly the infamous lunatic asylum of Bethlehem Royal Hospital (better known as Bedlam) is now the **Imperial War Museum** (daily 10am–6pm; £5; free after 4.30pm; Lambeth North, Waterloo or Elephant & Castle tube), by far the best military museum in the capital. The treatment of the subject is impressively wide-ranging and fairly sober, with the main hall's militaristic display of guns, tanks and planes offset by the lower-ground-floor array of documents and images attesting to the human damage of war, including a harrowing section on the liberation of Belsen in 1945. In addition to the static displays, you can walk through re-creations of a World War I trench and a bomb-ravaged street in the Blitz.

Southwark

Southwark, the district ranged around the southern end of London Bridge, was a lively Roman red-light district whose brothels continued to do a thriving illegal trade until 1161 when they were licensed by royal decree. This measure imposed various restrictions on the prostitutes, who could now be fined three shillings for "grimacing to passers-by", and brought in a lot of revenue for the bishops of Winchester, who owned the area for the four centuries after the Norman Conquest. Under the bishops' rule, bull- and bear-baiting, drinking, cockfighting and gambling were also rife, especially on **Bankside** and although, after 1556, Southwark came under the jurisdiction of the City, it was not subject to its regulations on entertainment. So Southwark remained the pleasure quarter of Tudor and Stuart London, where brothels and other disreputable institutions banned in the City – notably theatres – continued to flourish until the Puritan purges of the 1640s.

Bankside

Bankside, east of Blackfriars Bridge, was the most nefarious street in London in Elizabethan times, thanks to its brothels, bearpits and theatres. Nowadays, the biggest crowds currently to be found along Bankside are milling around a spectacular reconstruction of **Shakespeare's Globe Theatre**, the polygonal playhouse where most of the Bard's later works were first performed. The thatched theatre uses only natural light and the minimum of scenery, and currently puts on shows from mid-May to mid-September. Every half an hour, informative **guided tours** (daily: mid-May to mid-Sept 9am–12.15pm & 2–4pm; mid-Sept to mid-Oct 10am–5pm; £5; London Bridge, Southwark or Blackfriars tube) take you round the theatre itself.

Architecturally, Bankside is now dominated by the austere **Bankside power station**. Closed down in 1908, the power station has been redesigned by the Swiss duo Herzog & de Meuron, to become the **Tate Gallery of Modern Art**. The gallery should be open from the summer of 2000 and will house the modern collection from the Tate Gallery at Millbank (see p.75). At the same time, a new pedestrian bridge, designed by Norman Foster, will link the new Tate with the steps of Peter's Hill, below St Paul's Cathedral.

East of Bankside, beyond Southwark Bridge, in the suitably dismal confines of dark and narrow Clink Street, is the **Clink Prison Museum** (daily 10am–4pm; £4; London Bridge tube), built on the site of the former Clink Prison, origin of the expression "in the clink". The prison began as a dungeon for disobedient clerics under the Bishop of Winchester's Palace – the rose window of the palace's Great Hall survives just east of the museum – and later became a dumping ground for heretics, prostitutes and a motley assortment of Bankside lowlife. The exhibition features a handful of prison life tableaux and dwells on the torture and grim conditions within, but, given the rich history of the place, this is a disappointingly lacklustre museum.

In St Mary Overie Dock, round the corner from the Clink, you'll find another timber reconstruction, this time the **Golden Hinde** (daily 10am–7pm; £2.30; London Bridge tube), the galleon in which Sir Francis Drake sailed round the world in 1577–80. The ship is surprisingly small and, with a crew of eighty plus, conditions must have been cramped to say the least. There's a refreshing lack of interpretive panels, so it's worth paying the little bit extra and getting a guided tour from one of the folk in period garb, who will show you the ropes, so to speak, and demonstrate how to fire a cannon, use the ship's toilet and so forth.

Southwark Cathedral

Close by the *Golden Hinde*, bang next door to London Bridge, is **Southwark Cathedral**, originally built in the thirteenth and fourteenth centuries as the Augustinian priory church of St Mary Overie. It miraculously survived the nineteenth century, which saw its East End chapel demolished to make way for London Bridge, railways built within a few feet of its tower and some very heavy-handed Victorian restoration. As if in compensation, the church was granted cathedral status in 1905 and has since had a lot of money spent on it. Of the cathedral's original features, the splendid choir is the most striking. Built in 1207, and thus probably the oldest Gothic structure in London, it has a beautiful sixteenth-century stone altar screen. The building houses hundreds of monuments, including one, in the southwest corner of the nave, to the 47 people who died when the *Marchioness* pleasure boat collided with a barge on the Thames in 1989. Others include a thirteenth-century oak effigy of a knight, the brightly painted tomb of poet John Gower, Chaucer's contemporary, and an early twentieth-century memorial to Shakespeare – for whom a birthday service is held here annually. His younger brother Edmund, an actor at the Globe, was buried here in 1607.

Old Operating Theatre Museum and Herb Garret

The most educative and strangest of Southwark's museums is the **Old Operating Theatre Museum and Herb Garret** on St Thomas Street (daily 10am–4pm; £2.50), built in 1821 at the top of a church tower, where the hospital apothecary's herbs were stored. Despite being entirely gore-free, the museum is as stomach-churning as the London Dungeon (see below), for this theatre dates from the pre-anaesthetics era. The surgeons who used this room concentrated on speed and accuracy (most amputations took less than a minute), but there was still a thirty percent mortality rate, many patients simply dying of shock, many more from bacterial infection, about which very little was known. This is clear from the design of the theatre itself, which has no sink and is made almost entirely of mahogany and pine, which would have harboured bacteria even after vigorous cleaning. Sawdust was sprinkled on the floor to soak up the blood and prevent it dripping onto the heads of the worshippers in the church below.

The London Dungeon, Britain at War and HMS Belfast

A walk past the railway bridges and warehouses of Tooley Street brings you round the back of London Bridge train station to the cold dark vault of the **London Dungeon** (daily: April–Sept 10am–6.30pm; Oct–March closes 5.30pm; £8.95; London Bridge tube), a crowd-pleasing show playing on the foreigners' fascination with English Gothic horror. Among the life-size waxwork tableaux include a hanging at Tyburn gallows, a man being hung, drawn and quartered and one being boiled alive, the general hysteria being boosted by actors dressed as top-hatted Victorian vampires pouncing out of the darkness. Queues form for the "River of Death" boat ride, an historical journey to your execution (not for the faint-hearted); this is immediately followed up by the "Jack the Ripper Experience", an exploitative and voyeuristic trawl through post-mortem photos and wax mock-ups of the victims; lastly you pass through the rather limp "Theatre of the Guillotine".

A little further east on Tooley Street is **Winston Churchill's Britain at War** (daily: April–Sept 10am–5.30pm; Oct–March closes 4.30pm; £5.95; London Bridge tube), which, despite its jingoistic name, is an illuminating exhibition of every aspect of London life during the Blitz. It begins with a rickety lift ride down to a mock-up of a tube air-raid shelter, a prelude to hundreds of sometimes bizarre wartime artefacts. You can sit in an Anderson shelter beneath the chilling whistle of the doodlebugs, tune in to contemporary radio broadcasts and, as a grand finale walk through the chaos of a just-bombed street – pitch dark, noisy, smoky and hot.

There's more World War II history, from a more aggressive angle, at **HMS Belfast** (daily: March–Oct 10am–6pm; Nov–Feb closes 5pm; £4.70; London Bridge tube), a huge cruiser permanently moored between London Bridge and Tower Bridge. Armed with six torpedoes and six-inch guns with a range of over fourteen miles, the *Belfast* spent over two years of the war in the Royal Naval shipyards, after being hit by a mine in the Firth of Forth at the beginning of hostilities. Decommissioned after the Korean War, the ship contains tired-looking historical exhibitions, but the maze of cabins, spread across seven decks, is fun to explore.

Butler's Wharf

In contrast to the brash offices on Tooley Street, **Butler's Wharf**, east of Tower Bridge, has retained its historical character. **Shad Thames**, the narrow street at the back of Butler's Wharf, has kept the wrought-iron overhead gangways by which the porters used to transport goods from the wharves to the warehouses further back from the river, and is one of the most atmospheric alleyways in the whole of Bermondsey. The eight-storey **Butler's Wharf Warehouse** itself, with its shops and restaurants, forms part of Terence Conran's commercial empire and caters for a monied clientele, but the wide promenade on the riverfront is open to the public.

The big attraction of Butler's Wharf is Conran's superb riverside **Design Museum** (daily 10am–6pm; £3.50; Tower Hill or Bermondsey tube), at the eastern end of Shad Thames. The stylish white edifice, a Bauhaus-like conversion of an old 1950s warehouse, is the perfect showcase for an unpretentious display of mass-produced industrial design from classic cars to Tupperware. The constantly evolving Collections Gallery is on the top floor; the first-floor Review Gallery acts as a showcase for new ideas, including prototypes and failures, as well as hosting temporary exhibitions on important designers, movements or single products. The small coffee-bar in the foyer is a great place to relax and there's a pricey Conran restaurant on the top floor.

The **Bramah Tea and Coffee Museum** (daily 10am–6pm; £3.50), housed in an old tea warehouse, Tamarind House, behind the Design Museum on Maguire Street, is not quite in the same league as its neighbour. Still, it's a fun museum and well worth a visit. Founded in 1992 by Edward Bramah, who began his career on an African tea garden in 1950, the museum's emphasis is firmly on tea. There's an impressive array of teapots, from Wedgwood to novelty, and coffee machines, from huge percolator siphons to espresso machines spanning the twentieth century.

Hyde Park, Kensington and Chelsea

Hyde Park, together with its westerly extension, Kensington Gardens, covers a distance of two miles from Speakers' Corner in the northeast to **Kensington Palace** in the southwest. At the end of your journey, you've made it to one of London's most exclusive districts, the Royal Borough of Kensington and Chelsea. Other districts go in and out of fashion, but this area has been in vogue ever since royalty moved into Kensington Palace in the late seventeenth century.

Aside from the shops around Harrods in Knightsbridge, however, the popular tourist attractions lie in **South Kensington**, where three of London's top museums – the **Victoria and Albert**, **Natural History** and **Science museums** – stand on land bought with the proceeds of the Great Exhibition of 1851. **Chelsea**'s character is slightly more bohemian; in the 1960s, the **King's Road**, the district's main thoroughfare, carved out its reputation as London's catwalk, while in the late 1970s it was the epicentre of the punk explosion. Nothing so risqué goes on in Chelsea now, though its residents like to think of themselves as rather more artistic and intellectual than the purely monied types of Kensington.

Hyde Park

Seized from the Church by Henry VIII to satisfy his desire for yet more hunting grounds, **Hyde Park** was first opened to the public by James I and soon became a fashionable gathering place for the beau monde, who rode round the circular drive known as the Ring, pausing to gossip and admire each other's equipage. Hangings, muggings and duels, the Great Exhibition of 1851 and numerous public events have all taken place in Hyde Park – and it is still a popular gathering point or destination for political demonstrations. For most of the time, however, the park is simply a leisure ground – a wonderful open space which allows you to lose all sight of the city beyond a few persistent tower blocks.

Located at the treeless northeastern corner of the park, **Marble Arch** was originally erected in 1828 as a triumphal entry to Buckingham Palace, but now lies stranded on a ferociously busy traffic island at the west end of Oxford Street. This is the most historically charged spot in Hyde Park, as it marks the site of **Tyburn gallows**, the city's main public execution spot until 1783. It's also the location of **Speakers' Corner**, once an entertaining and peculiarly English Sunday tradition, featuring an assembly of characterful speakers and hecklers – now, sadly, a forum for soap-box religious extremists.

A better place to enter the park is at **Hyde Park Corner**, the southeast corner, where **Constitution Arch** stands in the midst of another of London's busiest traffic interchanges. Erected in 1828 to commemorate Wellington's victories in the Napoleonic Wars, the arch originally served as the northern gate into Buckingham Palace grounds. Close by stands **Apsley House** (Tues–Sun 11am–5pm; £3; Hyde Park Corner tube), Wellington's London residence, now a museum to the "Iron Duke". Unless you're a keen fan of the Duke, the highlight of the museum is the art collection, much of which used to belong to the King of Spain. Among the best pieces are works by de Hooch, van Dyck, Velázquez, Goya, Rubens and Murillo, displayed in the Waterloo Gallery on the first floor. The famous, more than twice life-size, nude statue of Napoleon by Antonio Canova stands at the foot of the main staircase.

The park is divided in two by the **Serpentine Lake**, which has a popular **Lido** (May–Sept daily 10am–6pm; £2.50) on its south bank. By far the prettiest section of the lake, though, is the upper section known as the **Long Water**, which narrows until it reaches a group of four fountains, laid out symmetrically in front of an Italianate summerhouse designed by Wren.

The western half of the park is officially known as **Kensington Gardens** and is, strictly speaking, a separate entity, though you hardly notice the change. Its two most popular attractions are the **Serpentine Gallery** (daily 10am–6pm; free), which has a reputation for lively, and often controversial, contemporary art exhibitions, and the richly decorated Gothic **Albert Memorial**, clearly visible to the west. Erected in 1876, the memorial is as much a hymn to the glorious achievements of Britain as to its subject, Queen Victoria's husband (who died of typhoid in 1861). Recently restored to his former gilded glory, Albert occupies the central canopy, clutching a catalogue for the 1851 Great Exhibition that he helped organize.

The Exhibition's most famous feature, the gargantuan glasshouse of the Crystal Palace, no longer exists, but the profits were used to buy a large tract of land south of the park, now home to South Kensington's remarkable cluster of **museums and colleges**, plus the vast **Royal Albert Hall**, a splendid iron-and-glass-domed concert hall, with an exterior of red brick, terracotta and marble that became the hallmark of South Ken architecture. The hall is venue for Europe's most democratic music festival, the Henry Wood Promenade Concerts, better known as the **Proms**, which take place from July to September, with standing-room tickets for as little as £3.

Kensington Palace

On the western edge of Kensington Gardens stands **Kensington Palace** (May–Sept daily 9.45am–5pm; £6; High Street Kensington tube), a modestly proportioned Jacobean brick mansion bought by William and Mary in 1689, and the chief royal residence for the next fifty years. KP, as it's fondly known in royal circles, is, of course, best known today as the place where Princess Diana lived up until her death in 1997. It was, in fact, the official London residence of both Charles and Di until the couple formally separated. In the weeks following Diana's death, literally millions of flowers, mementoes, poems and gifts were deposited at the gates to the south of the palace.

Visitors don't get to see Diana's apartments, which were on the west side of the palace, where various minor royals still live. Instead, they get to view some of the Queen's frocks in the **Royal Ceremonial Dress Collection** and are then given an audio-guide which takes them round the sparsely furnished state apartments. The highlights are the trompe l'oeil ceiling paintings by William Kent, in particular the Cupola Room, and the oil paintings in the King's Gallery. En route, you also get to see the tastelessly decorated rooms in which the future Queen Victoria spent her unhappy childhood. To recover from the above, take tea in the exquisite **Orangery** (daily: Easter–Sept 10am–6pm; Oct–Easter 10am–4pm), to the north of the palace.

The Victoria and Albert Museum

The **Victoria and Albert Museum** (daily 10am–5.45pm; £5, free after 4.30pm; South Kensington tube) began its days as the Museum of Manufactures, a gathering of objects from the Great Exhibition and a motley collection of plastercasts – it being Albert's intention to rekindle Britain's industrial dominance by inspiring factory workers, students and craftspeople with examples of excellence in applied art and design. This notion disappeared swiftly as exotica poured in from around the world, and today, in addition to being the world's finest collection of decorative arts, the museum encompasses sculpture, musical instruments, paintings and photography, all beautifully, if rather haphazardly, displayed across a seven-mile, four-storey maze of halls and corridors. As if all this were not enough, the V&A's temporary shows are among the best in Britain, ranging from surveys of specialized areas of craft and technology to overviews of entire cultures.

Floor plans from the information desks at the **main entrance** on Cromwell Road and the **side entrance** on Exhibition Road can help you decide on which areas to concentrate. There are also free guided orientation tours every day; enquire at the main information desk. Like all London's major museums, the V&A also has big plans for the millennium, with a £75 million multifaceted extension, known as the "**Spiral**" and designed by the controversial Polish-born architect, Daniel Libeskind, in the pipeline.

The ground floor

The ground floor holds the best of the V&A. The **Raphael cartoons** (room 48a), seven full-colour designs for tapestries intended for the Sistine Chapel, are to the left of the main entrance and beyond the museum shop. These drawings, reproduced in countless tapestries and engravings in the seventeenth and eighteenth centuries, were probably more familiar and influential than any of the artist's paintings. Across the hall, the excellent **dress collection** (room 40) starts at 1540 and comes right up to date with clothes by contemporary British designers such as Paul Smith, Helen Storey and Vivienne Westwood.

There follows a string of superb eastern galleries. The Nehru Gallery (room 41), for example – which shows only a fraction of the biggest assembly of **Indian art** outside the subcontinent – features an exquisitely carved white jade wine cup belonging to the Emperor Shah Jahan, a golden chair that belonged to Ranjit Singh, all manner of jewels, sandstone screens and delicate watercolours, not to mention Tippoo's Tiger, a life-size wooden automaton devouring an officer of the East India Company. Next comes the **Islamic gallery** (room 42), a dramatic gathering of vivid blue tiles and carved wooden pulpits, dominated by the stupendous sixteenth-century Ardabil carpet and the exquisite "Chelsea" carpet, bought in Chelsea but of unknown origin.

The **Medieval Treasury** (room 43), full of reliquaries, religious sculpture and other devotional items, including the Norman masterpiece called the Gloucester candlestick, is adjacent to the **Chinese Art** collection (room 44), which ranges from green-tinged Shang bronzes and Tang horses to ceramics produced in the Cultural Revolution. Next door, the most intriguing objects in the understated **Japanese room** (room 45), among all the silk, lacquer and samurai armour, are the tiny carved jade and marble *netsuke* (belt toggles), portraying such quirky subjects as "spider on aubergine" and "starving dog on a bed of leaves".

Turn right at the main information desk and you'll arrive at the **sculpture and architecture** gallery (rooms 50a & 50b), with its array of funerary monuments and portrait busts. The statue of Handel, created in 1738, was highly radical in its day, showing the composer slouching in inspired disarray, one shoe hanging from his foot. Also here is the original plaster model for the tomb of Victoria and Albert, on which they both appear to be 42 years old (the age Albert died) – Albert is raised slightly higher than the Queen, in accordance with her wishes.

Passing from here through the minimalist gallery of **Korean art**, where you are encouraged to touch one of the huge ceramic bowls, you come to the two enormous **Cast Courts** (rooms 46a & 46b), created so that ordinary Londoners, who couldn't afford to travel, would be able to experience the glories of classical and ancient art. Even today, the rooms, still painted in heavy Victorian red and green, are an astonishing sight – a life-size replica of Michelangelo's *David* towers opposite Donatello's smaller bronze of the same subject; the cast of the colossal Trajan's Column, from the forum in Rome, is sliced in half to fit in the room; while the rest of the space is crammed with full-scale replicas of the doors of Hildesheim cathedral, Spanish altars, the pulpit of Pisa's cathedral and scores of other sculptural masterpieces. An interesting little gallery (room 46) between the two cast rooms is lined with **fakes and forgeries**, among them a "fourteenth-century" wooden oratory which the museum bought in good faith in 1912, only to be informed it was a fake by the carpenter's son.

Most of the remainder of the ground floor is given over to the **Italian Renaissance** (rooms 12–20), including a room of Donatello and his followers. Whatever you do, however, don't miss the museum's new **Canon Photography Gallery** (room 38), nor the original refreshment rooms at the back of the main galleries. The eastern **Poynter Room**, a wash of decorative blue tiling, is where the hoi polloi ate; the dark green **Morris Room**, with its Pre-Raphaelite panels, accommodated a better class of diner. In between is the largest and grandest of the rooms, the **Gamble Room**, richly decorated with Minton tiles and now, once more, a cake and coffee halt.

The upper floors

If you go up to the **first floor** you come to a series of rooms covering **Britain 1500 to 1750** (rooms 52–58) and featuring a restored music room, Spitalfields silks and Huguenot silver, an early seventeenth-century oak-panelled interior thought to have been James I's hunting lodge, and the legendary Great Bed of Ware, a king-sized oak monstrosity mentioned by Shakespeare and Ben Jonson and thought to have belonged to Edward IV. Beyond here, the **Twentieth-century Galleries** (rooms 70–74) make a diffident attempt to address contemporary questions of design, ranging from Constructivist fabrics to Olivetti typewriters and Swatch watches.

Beyond the refurbished **Silver Galleries**, which house a dazzling display of silverwork from the medieval to modern, you come to a dimly lit room, hung with medieval tapestries, and the exemplary **Textile Study Rooms** (nos 95–100), displaying all manner of lace, Danish cottons, Chinese damask and robes from Palestine and Afghanistan. The heavily guarded **Jewellery** collection (rooms 91–93) is equally splendid, sparkling with Egyptian amulets, Celtic chokers, Roman snake bracelets, precious gems and 1960s perspex bangles.

There are more works from **Britain 1750–1900** on the **second floor** (rooms 118–126), with a Chippendale bed, a plaster model of the Albert Memorial and furniture shown at the Great Exhibition. A room devoted to William Morris is adorned with his wallpaper, carpets and tiles, as well as furniture designed by his followers, and the collection comes up to date with a small selection of Henry Moore sculptures. Lastly, also on the second floor, there's the high-tech **Glass gallery** (room 131), with touchscreen computers and a spectacular, modern glass staircase and balustrade.

The **top floor** is given almost exclusively to pottery and earthenware, with Far Eastern ceramics, European porcelain and Islamic tiles, but is often closed in the summer.

The Henry Cole Wing

The **Henry Cole Wing**, named after the museum's first director, can easily be overlooked, as its main entrance is on Exhibition Road and it's only linked to the rest of the building on the ground floor. Highlights here include the **Frank Lloyd Wright** gallery on level 2, centred on an office created by the architect for a Pittsburgh department store owner – a typically organic design in luxuriant wood. Also on this floor is the **European ornament** gallery, demonstrating the influences and fashions in decoration of all kinds: antiquities, Rococo figurines and architectural plans share space with 1920s cotton hangings, inspired by Howard Carter's discovery of Tutankhamen's tomb, and kitsch 1950s china.

Portrait miniatures by Holbein, Hilliard and others feature on level 4, the rest of which is, mostly, taken up with nineteenth-century oil paintings, densely hung in the manner of their period. The largest collection of Swiss landscape paintings outside Switzerland and sentimental Victorian genre works are unlikely to pull in the crowds, but persevere and you'll discover Carracciolo's *Panorama of Rome*, paintings by the Barbizon School, an Arts and Crafts piano, a Burne-Jones sideboard and several Pre-Raphaelite works. Level 6 is largely devoted to the paintings of **John Constable**, four hundred of whose works were left to the museum by his daughter. The finished works include *Salisbury Cathedral* and *Dedham Mill*, and there are studies for the *Hay Wain* and *Leaping Horse* plus a whole host of his alfresco cloud studies and sketches. In addition, there's an impressive collection of statues by **Rodin**, most of them donated by the sculptor himself in 1914.

The Science Museum

Established as a technological counterpart to the V&A, the **Science Museum**, on Exhibition Road (daily 10am–6pm; £6.50, free after 4.30pm; South Kensington tube), is undeniably impressive, filling seven floors with items drawn from every conceivable area of science, including space travel, telecommunications, time measurement, chemistry, computing, photography and medicine. Keen to dispel the enduring image of museums devoted to its subject as boring and full of dusty glass cabinets, the Science Museum is gradually updating its galleries with more interactive displays and puts on daily demonstrations to show that not all science teaching has to be deathly dry.

The real problem, though, is that, for a science museum, the whole place remains a long way from the cutting edge of technology. All this is set to change in the summer of 2000, with the opening of the new **Wellcome Wing**, which aims to keep its displays up to date with the latest in computer technology. In the meantime, there's considerable disruption on the ground floor, where the **Power, Space and Transport** exhibition, charting British innovation during the Industrial Revolution, resides.

The **Launch Pad** on the first floor makes a good attempt to present lively, hands-on demonstrations of basic scientific principles and is usually mobbed by kids. Its success has spawned further hands-on galleries in the basement: the "Garden", aimed at 3- to 6-year-olds, and the "Things", for 7- to 11-year-olds. More educative by half, however, is the **Food for Thought** exhibition: interactive displays on nutrition, an exercise bicycle for kids who need to pedal off excess energy and possibly the healthiest branch of *McDonald's* in the world (it doesn't serve food). There's another spectacular new permanent gallery on the first floor, called the **Challenge of Materials**, with some wacky exhibits, including a pair of chocolate shoes, a steel wedding dress and a Bakelite coffin.

One of the most educative and fascinating sections of the whole museum, is the **Science and Art of Medicine** gallery, tucked away right on the top floor. Using an anthropological approach, this is a visual and cerebral feast, galloping through ancient medicine, medieval and Renaissance pharmacy, alchemy, quack doctors, Royal healers, astrology and military surgery. Offbeat artefacts include African fetishes, an Egyptian mummified head, an eighteenth-century Florentine model of a female torso giving birth, and George Washington's dentures.

The Natural History Museum

Alfred Waterhouse's purpose-built mock-Romanesque colossus ensures the **Natural History Museum** (Mon–Sat 10am–5.50pm, Sun 11am–5.50pm; £6, free after 4.30pm; South Kensington tube) its status as London's most handsome museum. Caught up, without huge public funds, in the current enthusiasm for museum redesign and accessibility, the contents are a mishmash of truly imaginative exhibits peppered among others little changed since the museum's opening in 1881.

The main entrance brings you straight into the Central Hall of the **Life Galleries**, dominated by a plaster cast skeleton of a Diplodocus. The "side chapels" are filled with wonders of the natural world – the largest egg, a sabre-tooth tiger – but it's the **Dinosaur gallery** that pulls in the crowds, a show of massive-jawed skeletons and models much enlivened by a stimulating exhibition on Tyrannosaurus Rex and his pea-brained cronies. Best of all is the grisly life-size animatronic tableau of two reptiles tearing apart a tenontosaurus, with much roaring, slurping and oozing blood.

The other firm favourite with kids is the insect room, known as **Creepy-crawlies**, with its giant models of bugs, arachnids and crustaceans, plus real-life displays on the life-cycle of the house fly and other unlovely creatures. Opposite the creepy-crawlies is the entrance to the high-tec **Ecology gallery**, a child-friendly exhibition with a serious message, only slightly marred by the fact that it's sponsored by British Petroleum. The rest of the museum, on the upper floors, is more old-fashioned, and you're best off heading across to the former Geological Museum, now known as the **Earth galleries**, whose main entrance is on Exhibition Road.

From the central hall, an escalator takes you through a revolving, partially-formed globe to "**The Power Within**", a big exhibition on volcanoes and other acts of God. The most popular section is the slightly tasteless Kobe earthquake simulator, where you enter a Japanese supermarket and see the soy sauce bottles wobble while watching an in-store video of the real event. On the other side of the same floor is **Restless Surface**, an interactive display on the earth's elements, soil and rock erosion and, of course, global warming. Other new galleries worth exploring include **Earth's Treasury**, a dimly lit high-tech display of lustrous minerals and crystals, gemstones and jewels.

Kensington

Shopper-thronged **Kensington High Street** is dominated architecturally by the twin presences of Sir George Gilbert Scott's neo-Gothic church of **St Mary Abbots**, whose 250-foot spire makes it London's tallest parish church, and the Art Deco colossus of Barkers department store.

Kensington's sights are mostly hidden away in the backstreets, the one exception being the **Commonwealth Institute** (☎0171/603 4535), housed in a bold 1960s building set back from the High Street. The whole place is currently undergoing a massive restoration and refurbishment programme, aiming to reopen fully in 2000 as a rather more up-to-date, interactive museum.

Two paths along the side of the Commonwealth Institute lead to densely wooded **Holland Park**, the former grounds of a Jacobean mansion, whose east wing alone still stands. Theatrical and musical performances are staged here throughout the summer, and several formal gardens surround the house, most notably the Japanese-style Kyoto Gardens.

A number of wealthy Victorian artists rather self-consciously founded an artists' colony in the streets that lie between the High Street and Holland Park. The most remarkable is **Leighton House** at 12 Holland Park Rd (Mon–Sat 11am–5.30pm; free; Kensington High Street tube). "It will be opulence, it will be sincerity", Lord Leighton opined before starting work on the house in the 1860s – he later became president of the Royal Academy and was ennobled on his deathbed. The big attraction is the domed Arab Hall, decorated with Saracen tiles, gilded mosaics and woodwork drawn from all over the Islamic world. The other rooms are less spectacular but, in compensation, are hung with paintings by Lord Leighton and his Pre-Raphaelite friends.

East of the Commonwealth Institute, two blocks north of the High Street, is **Linley Sambourne House**, 18 Stafford Terrace (March–Oct Wed 10am–4pm, Sun 2–5pm; £3), where the highly successful *Punch* cartoonist lived until his death in 1910. A grand, though fairly ordinary, stuccoed terrace house by Kensington standards, it's less a tribute to the artist and more a showpiece for the Victorian Society, which maintains the house in all its cluttered, late-Victorian excess.

Knightsbridge and Harrods

Knightsbridge is irredeemably snobbish, revelling in its reputation as the swankiest shopping area in London, largely through **Harrods** on Brompton Road (Mon, Tues &

Sat 10am–6pm, Wed–Fri 10am–7pm; Knightsbridge tube). London's most famous department store started out as a family-run grocery store in 1849, with a staff of two. The current 1905 terracotta building is now owned by the Egyptian Mohammed Al Fayed and employs in excess of 3000 staff. Tourists flock to Harrods – it's thought to be the city's third top tourist attraction – though much of what the shop stocks you can buy more cheaply if you can do without the Harrods carrier bag.

The store does, however, have a few sections that are architectural sights in their own right, in particular the Food Hall, with its exquisite Arts and Crafts tiling, and the Egyptian Hall, with its pseudo-hieroglyphs and sphinxes. The Egyptian escalators are an added attraction, now that the Di and Dodi fountain is in place, but don't bother taking them to the first floor "washrooms", unless you want to pay £1 for the privilege of relieving yourself. Note, too, that the store has a draconian dress code: no shorts, no ripped jeans, no vest T-shirts and no backpacks.

Chelsea

It wasn't until the latter part of the nineteenth century that **Chelsea** began to earn its reputation as London's very own Left Bank. Its household fame, however, came through the role of King's Road as the unofficial catwalk of the "Swinging Sixties". The road remained a fashion parade for hippies, too, and in the Jubilee Year of 1977 it witnessed the birth of punk, masterminded from a shop called Sex, run by Vivienne Westwood and Malcolm McLaren. The posey cafés and boutiques still persist, but these days, the area has a more subdued feel, with high rents and house prices keeping things staid, and interior design shops rather than avant-garde fashion the order of the day.

The area's other aspect, oddly enough considering its boho reputation, is a military one. For among the most nattily attired of all those parading down the King's Road are the scarlet or navy-blue clad Chelsea Pensioners, army veterans from the nearby **Royal Hospital** (Mon–Sat 10am–noon & 2–4pm, Sun 2–4pm; free; Sloane Square tube), founded by Charles II in 1681. The hospital's plain, red-brick wings and grassy courtyards became a blueprint for institutional and collegiate architecture all over the English-speaking world.

The concrete bunker next door to the Royal Hospital, on Royal Hospital Road, houses the **National Army Museum** (daily 10am–5.30pm; free; Sloane Square tube). The militarily obsessed are unlikely to be disappointed by the succession of uniforms and medals, but there is very little here for non-enthusiasts. The temporary exhibitions staged on the ground floor are the museum's strong point, but overall it's a disappointing museum – you're better off visiting the infinitely superior Imperial War Museum (see p.103).

Cheyne Walk

The quiet riverside locale of **Cheyne Walk** (pronounced "chainy"), drew artists and writers here in great numbers during the nineteenth century. Since the building of the Embankment and the increase in the volume of traffic, however, the character of this peaceful haven has been lost. Novelist Henry James, who lived at no. 21, used to take "beguiling drives" in his wheelchair along the Embankment; today, he'd be hospitalized in the process.

The chief reason to come here nowadays is to visit the **Chelsea Physic Garden** (April–Oct Wed 2–5pm & Sun 2–6pm; £3.50; Sloane Square tube), which marks the beginning of Cheyne Walk. Founded in 1673, this small walled garden is the oldest botanical garden in the country after Oxford's. At the entrance (on Swan Walk) you can pick up a map of the garden with a list of the month's most interesting flowers and shrubs, whose labels are slightly more forthcoming than the usual terse Latinate tags. The garden also has an excellent tea house, serving tea and delicious home-made cakes.

It's also worth popping into the nearby **Chelsea Old Church** (daily 9.30am–1pm & 2–4.30pm), halfway down Cheyne Walk, where Thomas More built his own private chapel in the south aisle. The church was badly bombed in the last war, but an impressive number of monuments were retrieved from the rubble and continue to adorn the church's interior.

A short distance inland from Cheyne Walk, at 24 Cheyne Row, is **Carlyle's House** (April–Oct Wed–Sun 11am–5pm; £3.20; NT; Sloane Square tube), where the historian Thomas Carlyle set up home, having moved down from his native Scotland in 1834. The house became a museum just fifteen years after Carlyle's death and is a typically dour Victorian abode, kept much as the Carlyles would have had it: the historian's hat still hanging in the hall, his socks in the chest of drawers. The top floor contains the garret study where Carlyle tried in vain to escape the din of the neighbours' noisy roosters in order to complete his final magnum opus on Frederick the Great.

Notting Hill

Forty years ago **Notting Hill** was described as "a massive slum, full of multi-occupied houses, crawling with rats and rubbish", and was populated by offshoots of the Soho vice and crime rackets. These insalubrious dwellings became home to a large contin-

---

NOTTING HILL CARNIVAL

Notting Hill Carnival began unofficially in 1959 as a response to the previous year's race riots. In 1965, Carnival took to the streets and has grown into the world's biggest street festival outside Rio, with an estimated one million revellers turning up each August bank holiday. During the 1960s, it was little more than a few church hall events and a carnival parade, inspired by that of Trinidad – home of many of the area's immigrants. Today the carnival still belongs to West Indians (from all parts of the city), but there are participants, too, from London's Latin American and Asian communities, and, of course, everyone turns out to watch the bands and parades, and hang out.

The main sights of Carnival are the **costume parades**, known as the *mas* (masquarades) which take place on the Sunday (for kids' groups) and Monday (adults) from around 10am until late afternoon. The processions consist of floats, drawn by trucks, with costume themes and steel bands – the "pans" which are one of the chief sounds of the carnival (and have their own contest on the Saturday). The parade makes its way around a three-mile route, starting at the top end of Ladbroke Grove, heading south under the Westway, then turning into Westbourne Grove, before looping north again via Chepstow Road, Great Western Road and Kensal Road. In addition to the parades, there are three or four **stages for live music** – Portobello Green and Powis Square are regular venues – where you can catch reggae, ragga, jungle, a bit of hip-hop and maybe Caribbean soca. And everywhere you go, between Westbourne Grove and the Westway, there are **sound systems** on the street, blasting out reggae and black dance sounds.

Over the last few years, Carnival has been fairly relaxed, considering the huge numbers of people it attracts. However, this is not an event for you if you are at all bothered by crowds – you can be wedged stationary during the parades – and very loud music. It is worth taking more than usual care about crime, too: leave your camera and jewellery at home, and just bring enough money for the day, as pickpockets turn up all over. As far as safety goes, don't worry unduly about the media's horror stories; if there's going to be any trouble, it tends to come after 7pm each day, when the carnival proper winds down and the police look to disperse the sound systems. If you feel at all uneasy, head home early.

Getting to and from Carnival is an event in itself. Ladbroke Grove tube station is closed for the duration, while Notting Hill Gate and Westbourne Park are open only for incoming visitors. The nearest fully operative tube stations are Latimer Road and Royal Oak. Alternatively, there's a whole network of buses running between most points of London and Notting Hill Gate.

gent of Afro-Caribbean immigrants, who had to compete for jobs and living space with the area's similarly down-trodden white residents. Now, the region has been gentrified, with richer folk having taken over large houses in the leafy crescents, and trendy bars and restaurants springing up all over.

Nowadays, Notting Hill is best known for two things – the **Carnival** (see box on p.113) and **Portobello Road market**, a mish-mash of stalls selling anything from valuable antiques to junky bric-a-brac and West Indian vegetables. The initial stretch of London's most popular market contains a mixture of overpriced, touristy stalls and some genuine shops selling classy antiques. In its lower stretches the market gets a lot more funky and the emphasis switches to street clothes and jewellery, odd trinkets, records and books.

Within easy walking distance of Portobello Road, on the other side of the railway tracks, gasworks and canal, is **Kensal Green Cemetery** (daily: April–Sept 8am–6pm; Oct–March 9am–5pm; free), opened in 1833 and still a functioning cemetery. Graves of the more famous incumbents – Thackeray, Trollope and the Brunels – are less interesting architecturally than those arranged on either side of the Centre Avenue, which leads from the easternmost entrance on Harrow Road (Kensal Rise tube).

Regent's Park and Camden

Regent's Park, framed by Nash-designed architecture and home of **London Zoo**, is one of London's finest parks. Within easy walking distance, to the northeast is **Camden Town**, whose vast weekend market has now become one of the city's biggest tourist attractions – a warren of stalls selling street fashion, books, records and ethnic goods.

Regent's Park

As with almost all of London's royal parks, we have Henry VIII to thank for **Regent's Park**, which he confiscated from the Church for yet more hunting grounds. However, it wasn't until the reign of the Prince Regent (later George IV) that the park began to take its current form. According to the masterplan, devised by John Nash in 1811, the park was to be girded by a continuous belt of terraces, and sprinkled with a total of 56 villas, including a magnificent pleasure palace for the Prince himself, which would be linked by Regent Street to Carlton House in St James's. The plan was never fully realized, due to lack of funds, but enough was built to create something of the idealized garden city that Nash and the Prince Regent envisaged.

To appreciate the special quality of Regent's Park, take a closer look at the architecture, starting with the Nash terraces, which form a near-unbroken horseshoe of cream-coloured stucco around the Outer Circle. Within the Inner Circle is the Open Air Theatre, which puts on summer performances of Shakespeare, opera and ballet, and **Queen Mary's Gardens**, by far the prettiest section of the park. A large slice of the gardens is taken up with a glorious rose garden, featuring some 400 varieties, surrounded by a ring of ramblers.

Clearly visible on the western edge of the park is the shiny copper dome and minaret of the **London Central Mosque**, an entirely appropriate addition given the Prince Regent's taste for the Orient. Non-Muslim visitors are welcome to look in at the information centre and glimpse inside the hall of worship, which is packed out with a diversity of communities for the lunchtime Friday prayers.

The northeastern corner of the park is occupied by **London Zoo** (daily: March–Oct 10am–5.30pm; Nov–Feb 10am–4pm; £8.50; Camden Town, Regent's Park or Great Portland Street tube), founded in 1826. It may not be the most uplifting place for ani-

---

REGENT'S CANAL BY BOAT

Three companies run boat services on the Regent's Canal between Camden (Camden Town tube) and Little Venice (Warwick Avenue tube), stopping off at London Zoo on the way and passing through the Maida Hill tunnel en route. The Jenny Wren (Easter–Oct; ☎0171/485 4433) starts off at Camden, while Jason's (Easter–Oct; ☎0171/286 3428) starts off at Little Venice, and the London Waterbus Company (year round; ☎0171/482 2660) sets off from both places. Whichever you choose, you can board at either end; tickets cost around £5–6 return and journey time is 35–45 minutes one-way.

Those interested in the history of the canal should head off to the **London Canal Museum** (Tues–Sun 10am–4.30pm; £2.50), on the other side of York Way, down New Wharf Road, ten minutes' walk from King's Cross Station.

---

mal lovers, but kids will love the place, especially the children's enclosure, where they can actually handle the animals, and the regular "Animals in Action" displays in the Lifewatch House. The zoo boasts some striking architectural features, too, most notably the 1930s modernist, spiral-ramped, concrete penguin pool (where Penguin Books' original colophon was sketched), designed by the Tecton partnership, led by Russian emigré Berthold Lubetkin.

Camden Town

For all the gentrification of the last twenty years, **Camden Town** retains a seedy air, compounded by the various railway lines that plough through the area, the canal, and the market, now the district's best-known attribute.

Having started out as a tiny crafts market in the cobbled courtyard by the lock, **Camden Market** has since mushroomed out of all proportion. More than 100,000 shoppers turn up here each weekend and parts of the market now stay open week-long, alongside a similarly oriented crop of shops, cafés and bistros. The market's overabundance of cheap leather, DM shoes and naff jewellery is compensated for by the sheer variety of what's on offer: from bootleg tapes to furniture, along with a mass of street fashion that may or may not make the transition to mainstream stores. To avoid the crowds, which can be overpowering on a summer Sunday afternoon, you'll need to come either early – before 10am – or late – say, after 4pm, when many of the stalls will be packing up to go.

Despite having no significant Jewish associations, Camden is now home to London's **Jewish Museum** at 129–131 Albert St, just off Parkway (Mon–Thurs & Sun 10am–4pm; £3; Camden Town tube). The purpose-built premises are smartly designed, but the conventional style and contents of the museum are disappointing. Apart from the usual displays of Judaica there's a video and exhibition explaining Jewish religious practices and the history of the Jewish community in Britain. More challenging temporary exhibitions are held in the museum's Finchley branch on East End Road.

Hampstead

Beyond Camden, up Haverstock Hill, the suburb of **Hampstead** developed as a spa resort in the eighteenth century and retains an upper-crust small-town atmosphere. It's long been a bolt-hole of the high-profile intelligentsia, and you can get some idea of its tone from the fact that its MP is the actress Glenda Jackson.

Whichever route you take north of Hampstead tube, you will probably end up at the small triangular green on **Holly Bush Hill**, on the north side of which stands the late-seventeenth-century **Fenton House** (April–Oct Wed–Fri 2–5pm, Sat & Sun 11am–5pm; £4; NT; Hampstead tube). As well as housing a collection of European and Oriental ceramics, the house contains the superb Benton-Fletcher collection of early musical instruments, chiefly displayed on the top floor. Among the many spinets, virginals and clavichords are the earliest extant English grand piano and an Unverdorben lute dating from 1580 (one of only three in the world).

One of the most poignant of London's house museums is the **Freud Museum**, hidden away in the leafy streets of south Hampstead at 20 Maresfield Gardens (Wed–Sun noon–5pm; £3; Finchley Road tube). Having lived in Vienna for his entire adult life, Freud, by now a semi-invalid with only a year to live, was forced to flee the Nazis, arriving in London in the summer of 1938. The ground-floor study and library look exactly as they did when Freud lived here; the collection of erotic antiquities and the famous couch, sumptuously draped in Persian carpets, were all brought here from Vienna. Upstairs, home movies of family life in Vienna are shown continually and a small room is dedicated to his daughter, Anna, herself an influential child analyst, who lived in the house until her death in 1982.

Hampstead's newest attraction is **2 Willow Road** (guided tours April–Oct Thurs–Sat noon–5pm every 45min; £4; NT; Hampstead tube), a modernist red-brick terraced house, built in the 1930s by the Hungarian-born architect Ernö Goldfinger. When Goldfinger moved in, this was a state-of-the-art house, but Goldfinger changed little of it in the following sixty years, so what you see is a 1930s avant-garde dwelling preserved in aspic, a house at once both modern and old-fashioned. An added bonus is that the rooms are packed with works of art by the likes of Max Ernst, Duchamp, Henry Moore and Man Ray. There are a limited number of tickets for the **guided tours**, so it's worth booking ahead. Incidentally, James Bond's adversary is indeed named after Ernö, as Ian Fleming lived close by and had a deep personal dislike of both Goldfinger and his modernist abode.

Hampstead's most lustrous figure is celebrated at **Keats' House** (April–Oct Mon–Fri 10am–1pm & 2–6pm, Sat 10am–1pm & 2–5pm, Sun 2–5pm; Nov–March Mon–Fri 1–5pm, Sat 10am–1pm & 2–5pm, Sun 2–5pm; free; Hampstead tube), an elegant, whitewashed Regency double villa on Keats Grove, a short walk south of Willow Road. Inspired by the peacefulness of Hampstead and by his passion for girl-next-door Fanny Brawne (whose house is also part of the museum), Keats wrote some of his most famous works here, before leaving for Rome, where he died in 1821. The neat, rather staid interior contains books and letters, Fanny's engagement ring and the four-poster bed in which the poet first coughed up blood, confiding to his companion, Charles Brown, "that drop of blood is my death warrant".

Hampstead Heath and Kenwood

Hampstead Heath, north London's "green lung", is the city's most enjoyable public park. It may not have much of its original heathland left, but it packs in a wonderful variety of bucolic scenery in its 800 acres. At its southern end are the rolling green pastures of **Parliament Hill**, north London's premier spot for kite-flying. On either side are numerous ponds, three of which – one for men, one for women and one mixed – you can swim in. The thickest woodland is to be found in the West Heath, beyond Whitestone Pond, as is the most formal section, **Hill Garden**, a secretive and romantic little gem with eccentric balustraded terraces and a ruined pergola. Beyond, lies **Golders Hill Park**, where you can gaze on pygmy goats and fallow deer and inspect the impeccably maintained aviaries, home to flamingos, cranes and other exotic birds.

Finally, don't miss the landscaped grounds of Kenwood, in the north of the Heath, which are focused on the whitewashed, Neoclassical mansion of **Kenwood House** (daily: April–Sept 10am–6pm; Oct 10am–5pm; Nov–March 10am–4pm; free; EH). The house is now home to the *Iveagh Bequest*, a collection of seventeenth- and eighteenth-century art, including a handful of real masterpieces by the likes of Vermeer, Rembrandt, Boucher, Gainsborough and Reynolds. Of the house's period interiors, the most spectacular is Robert Adam's sky-blue and gold **Library**, its book-filled apses separated from the central entertaining area by paired columns. To the south of the house a grassy amphitheatre slopes down to a lake where outdoor **classical concerts** are held on summer evenings.

Highgate

Northeast of Hampstead Heath, and fractionally lower than Hampstead (appearances notwithstanding), **Highgate** lacks the literary cachet of Hampstead, but makes up for it with London's most famous cemetery, resting place of Karl Marx. It also retains more of its village origins, especially around **The Grove**, Highgate's finest row of houses, the oldest dating back as far as 1685.

To get to the cemetery, head south down Highgate High Street and **Highgate Hill**, with its amazing views towards the City. When you get to the copper dome of "Holy Joe", the Roman Catholic Church which stands on Highgate Hill, pop into the pleasantly landscaped **Waterlow Park**, next door, with its fine café and restaurant.

The park provides a through route to **Highgate Cemetery**, which is ranged on both sides of Swain's Lane. Highgate's most famous corpse, that of **Karl Marx**, lies in the **East Cemetery** (daily: April–Sept 10am–5pm; Oct–March 10am–4pm; £1; Archway or Highgate tube). Marx himself asked for a simple grave topped by a headstone, but by 1954 the Communist movement decided to move his grave to a more prominent position and erect the vulgar bronze bust that now surmounts a granite plinth. Close by lies the grave of the author George Eliot.

What the **East Cemetery** lacks in atmosphere is in part compensated for by the fact that you can wander at will through its maze of circuitous paths, whereas to visit the more atmospheric and overgrown **West Cemetery**, with its spooky Egyptian Avenue and terraced catacombs, you must go round with a **guided tour** (Mon–Fri noon, 2pm & 4pm, Sat & Sun hourly 11am–4pm; £3). Among the prominent graves usually visited are those of artist, Dante Gabriel Rossetti and lesbian novelist Radclyffe Hall.

Southeast London: Dulwich to Greenwich

Now largely built-up into a patchwork of Victorian terraces, one area of **southeast London** stands head and shoulders above all the others in terms of sightseeing, and that is **Greenwich**. At its heart is the outstanding architectural set-piece of the **Royal Naval College** and the **Queen's House**, courtesy of Christopher Wren and Inigo Jones respectively. Most visitors, however, come to see the **Cutty Sark**, the **National Maritime Museum** and the **Old Royal Observatory** in Greenwich Park, though Greenwich also pulls in an ever-increasing volume of Londoners in search of bargains at its Sunday market.

Greenwich is, of course, also famous as the "home of time", thanks to its status as the **Prime Meridian of the World** from where time all over the globe is measured. It's partly for this reason that Greenwich was chosen as the centrepiece of the country's millennium celebrations, though the **Millennium Dome** is, in fact, situated in the reclaimed industrial wasteland of North Greenwich, a mile or so northeast of Greenwich town centre.

The only other suburban sights that stand out are the **Dulwich Picture Gallery**, a public art gallery even older than the National Gallery, and the eclectic **Horniman Museum**, in neighbouring Forest Hill.

Dulwich and Forest Hill

Dulwich Village, one of southeast London's prettier patches, is built on land owned in the seventeenth century by the actor *Edward Alleyn, who founded* **Dulwich College** in 1619 as almshouses and a school for poor boys on the profits of his *whorehouses and* bear-baiting pits on Bankside (see p.105). Alleyn is buried in the chapel of the new Dulwich College, a grand Italianate structure with an impressive roll call of old boys, including Raymond Chandler, P.G. Wodehouse and World War II traitor Lord Haw-Haw, though they tend to keep quiet about the last of the trio.

The original college is a short walk away down College Road, right next to the **Dulwich Picture Gallery** (Tues–Fri 10am–5pm, Sat 11am–5pm, Sun 2–5pm; £3, free on Fri; West Dulwich train station, from Victoria), the nation's oldest public art gallery, designed by Sir John Soane and opened in 1817. Soane created a beautifully spacious building, awash in natural light. Crammed with superb paintings from the collection assembled in the 1790s by the French dealer Noel Desenfans, then bequeathed to Francis Bourgeois, who in turn passed it on to the college, highlights include elegiac landscapes by Cuyp; a fine array of Gainsborough portraits (including his famous *Linley Sisters* and a likeness of Samuel Linley, said to have been painted in less than an hour); Rembrandt's *Portrait of a Young Man*; one of the world's finest Poussin series; and splendid works by Tiepolo, Hogarth, Van Dyck, Canaletto and Rubens.

If you walk for a mile or so across Dulwich Park and south down Lordship Lane, you'll reach the wacky **Horniman Museum** (Mon–Sat 10.30am–5.30pm, Sun 2–5.30pm; free; Forest Hill train station, from Victoria or London Bridge), which occupies a striking building designed by Harrison Townsend, architect of the Whitechapel Gallery (see p.99). Horniman, a tea trader with a passion for collecting, financed construction of the purpose-built gallery in 1901, and today the museum revels in its Victorian eclecticism. Ascending the staircase, which is lined with a freshwater aquarium, you reach the old museum with its cases of stuffed birds and skeletons sharing space with half a fruit bat and an orang-utan's foot. The museum has a wide-ranging anthropology section, a musical department, with over 1500 instruments from Chinese gongs to electric guitars, and puts on excellent temporary exhibitions. The newest gallery is its "centre for understanding the environment", known as **"cue"**, a

THE MILLENNIUM DOME

The **Millennium Dome**, clearly visible from the riverside at Greenwich, is located over a mile downstream at North Greenwich, and opened to the public on January 1, 2000. As most grand projects do, it's had a rough ride in the press. Public opinion and the Labour Party – then in opposition – were vehemently against the project, though, of course, once in power, Labour did an abrupt U-turn, and even gave the Dome its own minister. The Church of England, in particular, criticized the project for being "too secular", arguing, with some justification, that, without Jesus, there would be no millennium.

Nevertheless, the Dome, completed at a total cost of something approaching £800 million, is expected to pull in around 12 million punters in 2000 alone. Designed by Richard Rogers (of Lloyd's Building and Pompidou Centre fame), the Dome's geodesic dome is by far the world's largest – 1km in circumference and 50m in height – held up by a dozen, 90-metre tall, yellow, steel masts. The interior is divided into twelve themed zones, each of which is replete with interactive and virtual reality gadgetry. At the centre a high-tech, live, multimedia extravaganza is performed at regular intervals.

Getting to the Dome is an experience in itself. The site has its very own Jubilee line tube station designed by Norman Foster, and part of a tube extension that has cost more to build per mile than the Channel Tunnel. There are also several options of arriving by boat and an aerial cable car link with East India DLR station on the north bank of the Thames.

timber-clad extension with hands-on displays concerned with green issues and aimed primarily at youngsters. In the lovely gardens round the back of the museum there's a graceful Victorian conservatory and a small collection of live animals.

Greenwich

Greenwich is one of London's most beguiling spots and the one place in southeast London that draws large numbers of visitors. It boasts one of the capital's finest architectural set pieces in the former Royal Naval College overlooking the Thames. To the west lies Greenwich town centre, while to the south lies the National Maritime Museum and the Old Royal Observatory, Greenwich's two prime tourist sights. If you're heading straight for either the Maritime Museum or the Observatory, the quickest way to get there is to take the train from Charing Cross (every 30min) to Maze Hill, on the eastern edge of Greenwich Park. Those wanting to start with the town or the *Cutty Sark* should alight at Greenwich station.

A more scenic way of getting to Greenwich is to take a **boat** (every 30–45min) from Charing Cross, Tower Bridge or Westminster piers. At the moment, it's also considerably more expensive, though it is hoped that a new, cheaper "hopper" service from central London will be in place by the millennium. A third possible option is to take the **Docklands Light Railway** (DLR) to Island Gardens, where the Greenwich Foot Tunnel leads under the Thames emerging beside the *Cutty Sark* – the advantage of this approach being the fabulous view of the Wren buildings from across the river.

The town centre

Greenwich town centre, laid out in the 1820s with the Nash-style terraces, is currently plagued with heavy traffic. To escape the busy streets, filled with nautical nick-nack shops and bookshops, head for the old covered market, now at the centre of the weekend **Greenwich Market** (Sat & Sun 9am–5pm), a lively antique, crafts and clothes market which has spread far beyond the perimeters of its predecessor, spilling out up the High Road, Stockwell Road and Royal Hill. The best sections are the indoor secondhand book markets, flanking the Central Market on Stockwell Road; the antiques hall, further down on Greenwich High Road; and the flea market on Thames Street.

A short distance in from the old covered market, on the opposite side of Greenwich Church Street, rises the Doric portico and broken pediment of Nicholas Hawksmoor's **St Alfege's Church** (daily: April–Oct noon–3pm; Nov–March noon–2pm). Built in 1712–18, the church was flattened in the Blitz, but it has been magnificently repaired.

Wedged in a dry dock by the Greenwich Foot Tunnel is the majestic **Cutty Sark** (May–Sept Mon–Sat 10am–6pm, Sun noon–6pm; Oct–March closes 5pm; £3.50), the world's last surviving tea clipper, built in 1869. The *Cutty Sark* lasted just eight years in the China tea trade, and it was as a wool clipper that it actually made its name, making a return journey to Australia in just 72 days. Inside, there's little to see beyond the exhibition in the main hold which tells the ship's story from its inception to its arrival in Greenwich in 1954.

It's entirely appropriate that the one London building that makes the most of its riverbank location should be the former **Royal Naval College** (daily 2.30–4.45pm; free), Wren's beautifully symmetrical Baroque ensemble, initially built as a royal palace, but eventually converted into a hospital for disabled seamen. From 1873 until quite recently, it was home to the Royal Naval College, but is now set to house the University of Greenwich and the Trinity College of Music.

The two grandest rooms, situated underneath Wren's twin domes, are open to the public and well worth visiting; they must be approached from the King William Walk entrance. The magnificent **Painted Hall**, in the west wing, is dominated by James

Thornhill's gargantuan allegorical ceiling painting and his trompe l'oeil fluted pilasters. The **RNC Chapel**, in the east wing, is an altogether colder and more formal affair. The current chapel was designed by James "Athenian" Stuart and features exquisite pastel-shaded plasterwork and spectacular, decorative detailing.

The National Maritime Museum

The west wing of the former Naval Asylum, to the south of the Royal Naval College, now houses the **National Maritime Museum** (daily: 10am–5pm; £7.50), which has undergone a spectacular redevelopment programme for the new millennium. The **Neptune Court** has reopened, so you can now see the museum's four late-seventeenth-century river barges, including the magnificent 63-foot Royal Barge, a gilded Rococo confection designed by William Kent for Prince Frederick, the much-unloved eldest son of George II.

The **Nelson Gallery**, meanwhile, contains the museum's vast collection of Nelson-related memorabilia, including Turner's *Battle of Trafalgar, 21st October, 1805*, his largest work and only royal commission. There's a new hands-on gallery, called **All Hands**, where children can have a go at radio transmission, loading miniature cargo, firing a cannon and so forth. In fact, only a couple of old-fashioned galleries remain now: **Ship of War**, the museum's collection of model sailing ships dating from 1650 to 1815, and **Twentieth-century Seapower**, which employs a tad more theatre to explain modern naval conflicts.

Inigo Jones's **Queen's House**, originally built amidst a rambling Tudor royal palace, is now the focal point of the Greenwich ensemble and an integral part of the Maritime Museum. As royal residences go, it's an unassuming country house, but as the first Neoclassical building in the country, it has enormous architectural significance. An audio commentary on the house is available from the desk in the **Great Hall**, off which is the beautiful **Tulip Staircase**, Britain's earliest cantilevered spiral staircase – its name derives from the floral patterning in the wrought-iron balustrade. The ground floor is given over to temporary exhibitions from the Maritime Museum, while the **Royal Apartments** on the first floor have been decked out with skilful repro furniture, rush matting and damask silk wall hangings.

The Old Royal Observatory

Crowning the hill in Greenwich Park, behind the National Maritime Museum, the **Old Royal Observatory** (daily 10am–5pm; £5; combined ticket with the National Maritime Museum £9.50) was established by Charles II in 1675 to house the first Astronomer Royal, John Flamsteed. Flamsteed's chief task was to study the night sky in order to discover an astronomical method of finding the longitude of a ship at sea, the lack of which was causing enormous problems for the emerging British Empire. Astrologers continued to work here at Greenwich until the postwar smog forced them to decamp to Herstmonceux Castle and the clearer skies of Sussex (they've since moved to the Pacific); the old observatory, meanwhile, is now a very popular museum.

Greenwich's greatest claim to fame is, of course, as the home of Greenwich Mean Time (GMT) and the Prime Meridian – a meridian being any north-south line used as a basis for astronomical observations, and therefore also for the calculation of longitude and time. Since 1884, Greenwich has occupied zero longitude, which means the entire world sets its clocks by GMT. What the Old Royal Observatory don't tell you is that the meridian has, in fact, moved. Nowadays, longitude is calculated by a differential Global Positioning Receiver, served by several US military satellites, which places the meridian 336ft to the east of the brass strip.

The oldest part of the observatory is the Wren-built **Flamsteed House**, whose northeastern turret sports a bright red Time-Ball that climbs the mast at 12.58pm and drops at 1pm GMT precisely; it was added in 1833 to allow ships on the Thames to set their clocks. Passing quickly through Flamsteed's restored apartments and the **Octagon Room**, where the king used to show off to his guests, you reach the **Chronometer Gallery** which focuses on the search for longitude, and displays four different precision clocks designed by **John Harrison**, who eventually won the Longitude Prize in 1763.

Flamsteed's own meridian line is a brass strip in the floor of the Meridian Building. Edmund Halley, Flamsteed's successor, who charted the comings and goings of the famous comet, worked out his own version of the meridian, and the Bradley Meridian Room reveals yet another meridian, standard from 1750 to 1850 and still used for Ordnance Survey maps. Finally, you reach a room that's spliced in two by the present-day Greenwich Meridian, fixed by the cross-hairs in Airy's "Transit Circle", the astrological instrument that dominates the room.

The exhibition ends on a soothing note in the **Telescope Dome** of the octagonal Great Equatorial Building, home to Britain's largest telescope. In addition, there are half-hourly presentations in the **Planetarium** (Mon–Fri 2.30pm; £2), housed in the adjoining South Building.

The Ranger's House and the Fan Museum

Southwest of the observatory and backing onto Greenwich park's rose garden, is the **Ranger's House** (April–Oct daily 10am–6pm; Oct–March Wed–Sun 10am–4pm; £2.50; EH), a red-brick Georgian villa on the southwestern edge of Greenwich Park, that houses a collection of paintings donated by the nineteenth Countess of Suffolk, whose portrait by John Singer Sargent hangs in the foyer. Built in the early eighteenth century, it was lived in after 1749 by the Earl of Chesterfield, who extended the bow window of the large gallery to just within the boundaries of the Royal Park, pushing the rent on the window up to £10 a year, compared to a total rent of six shillings and eight pence on the rest of the house. The high points of the art collection are William Larkin's full-length portraits of a Jacobean wedding party, particularly the twin bridesmaids in slashed silver brocade dresses, and the arrogant Richard Sackville, a dissolute aristocrat resplendent in pompom shoes. The Architectural Study Centre, in the courtyard, is a collection of plaques, mantels, fireplaces and chimneys saved from London's historic buildings – the spiral staircase snaking through the centre of the room was retrieved from the old Covent Garden market hall.

A steepish walk back towards Greenwich proper down Croom's Hill, which runs along the western edge of the park, brings you to the **Fan Museum** at no. 12 (Tues–Sat 11am–4.30pm, Sun noon–4.30pm; £2.50). It's a fascinating little place (and an extremely beautiful house), revealing the importance of the fan as a social and political document. The permanent exhibition on the ground floor traces the history of the materials employed, from peacock feathers to straw. Temporary exhibitions on the first floor explore conditions of production, the fan's link with the Empire and changing fashion.

Out west: Chiswick to Windsor

Most people experience west London en route to or from Heathrow airport, either from the confines of the train or tube, which runs overground at this point, or the motorway. The city and its satellites seem to continue unabated, with only fleeting glimpses of the countryside. However, in the five-mile stretch from Chiswick to Osterley there are several former country retreats, now surrounded by suburbia, which are definitely worth checking out.

The Palladian villa of **Chiswick House** is perhaps the best known of these attractions. However, it draws nothing like as many visitors as **Syon House**, most of whom come for the gardening centre rather than for the **house** itself, a showcase for the talents of Robert Adam, who also worked at **Osterley House**, another Elizabethan conversion, now owned by the National Trust.

Running through much of the area is the **River Thames**, once known as the "Great Highway of London" and still the most pleasant way to travel in these parts during the summer. Boats plough up the Thames all the way from central London via the **botanical gardens of Kew** and the picturesque riverside at **Richmond**, as far as **Hampton Court**, home of the country's largest royal residence and the famous maze. To reach the heavily touristed royal outpost of **Windsor Castle**, however, you really need to take the train.

Chiswick

Chiswick House (April–Sept daily 10am–6pm; first three weeks of Oct daily 10am–5pm; late Oct to March Wed–Sun 10am–4pm; £3; EH; Chiswick train station, from Waterloo), is a perfect little Neoclassical villa, designed in the 1720s by Richard Boyle, Earl of Burlington, and set in one of the most beautifully landscaped gardens in London. Like its prototype, Palladio's Villa Rotonda near Vicenza, the house was purpose-built as a "temple to the arts" – here, amid his fine art collection, Burlington could entertain artistic friends such as Swift, Handel and Pope. Visitors enter via the **lower floor**, where you can pick up an audio guide, before heading up to the **upper floor**, a series of cleverly interconnecting rooms, each enjoying a wonderful view out onto the gardens – all, that is, except the Tribunal, the central octagonal hall, where the earl's finest paintings and sculptures would have been displayed.

To do a quick circuit of the **gardens**, head across the smooth carpet of grass, punctuated by urns and sphinxes that sit under the shadow of two giant cedars of Lebanon. A great place from which to admire the northwest side of the house is from the stone benches of the exedra, the set of yew-hedge niches harbouring lions and copies of Roman statuary, situated beyond the cedars. Elsewhere, there's an Italian garden, a maze of high-hedge alleyways, a lake and a grassy amphitheatre, centred on an obelisk in a pond and overlooked by an Ionic temple.

If you leave Chiswick House gardens by the northernmost exit, beyond the conservatory, it's just a short walk (to the east) along the thunderous A4 road, to **Hogarth's House** (April–Sept Tues–Fri 1–5pm, Sat & Sun 1–6pm; Oct–March closes an hour earlier; closed Jan; free), where the artist spent each summer with his wife, sister and mother-in-law from 1749 until his death in 1764. Nowadays, it's hard to believe that Hogarth came here for peace and quiet, but in the eighteenth century the house was almost entirely surrounded by countryside. In addition to scores of Hogarth's engravings, you can see copies of his satirical series *An Election, Marriage à la Mode* and *A Harlot's Progress*, and compare the modern view from the parlour with the more idyllic scene in *Mr Ranby's House*.

Syon House

Across the water from Kew stands **Syon** (April–Sept Wed–Sun 11am–5pm; Oct Sun only; £5.50, including entry to the gardens; bus #237 or #267, from Gunnersbury tube or Kew Bridge train station), seat of the Duke of Northumberland since Elizabethan times, now more of a working commercial concern than a family home, embracing a garden centre, a wholefood shop, a trout fishery, an aquatic centre stocked with tropical fish, a mini-zoo and a butterfly house, as well as the old aristocratic mansion and its gardens.

From its rather plain castellated exterior, you'd never guess that **Syon House** contains the most opulent eighteenth-century interiors in the whole of London. The splendour of Robert Adam's refurbishment is immediately revealed, however, in the pristine **Great Hall**, an apsed double cube with a screen of Doric columns at one end and classical statuary dotted around the edges. There are several more Adam-designed rooms to admire in the house, plus a smattering of works by van Dyck, Lely, Gainsborough and Reynolds.

While Adam beautified Syon House, Capability Brown laid out its **gardens** (daily 10am–6pm or dusk; £2.50) around an artificial lake, surrounding it with oaks, beeches, limes and cedars. The gardens' chief focus now, however, is the crescent-shaped **Great Conservatory**, an early nineteenth-century addition which is said to have inspired Joseph Paxton, architect of the Crystal Palace. Those with young children will be compelled to make use of the **miniature steam train** which runs through the park at weekends from April to October, and on Wednesdays during the school holidays.

Another plus point for kids is Syon's **Butterfly House** (daily: May–Sept 10am–5pm; Oct–April 10am–3.30pm; £2.90), a small, mesh-covered hothouse, where you can walk amid hundreds of exotic butterflies from all over the world, as they flit about the foliage. However, if your kids show more enthusiasm for life-threatening reptiles than delicate insects, then you could skip the butterflies and go instead for the adjacent **London Aquatic Experience** (daily: April–Sept 10am–6pm; Oct–March 10am–5pm; £3), a purpose-built centre with a mixed range of aquatic creatures from the mysterious basilisk, which can walk on water, to the perennially popular piranhas.

Osterley Park and House

Robert Adam redesigned another colossal Elizabethan mansion three miles northwest of Syon at **Osterley Park** (daily 9am–7.30pm or dusk; free), which maintains the impression of being in the middle of the countryside, despite the presence of the M4 to the north of the house. The park itself is well worth exploring, and there's a great café in the Tudor stables, but anyone with a passing interest in Adam's work should pay a visit to **Osterley House** (April–Oct Wed–Sat 2–5pm, Sun 1–5pm; £4; NT; Osterley tube). If you arrive by public transport, you get a £1 reduction off the price of your ticket.

From the outside, Osterley bears some similarity to Syon, the big difference being Adam's grand entrance portico, with its tall, Ionic colonnade. From here, you enter a characteristically cool **Entrance Hall**, followed by the so-called State Rooms of the south wing. Highlights include the **Drawing Room**, with Reynolds portraits on the damask walls and a coffered ceiling centred on a giant marigold, and the **Etruscan Dressing Room**, in which every surface is covered in delicate painted trelliswork, sphinxes and urns, a style that Adam (and Wedgwood) dubbed "Etruscan", though it is in fact derived from Greek vases found at Pompeii.

Kew and Richmond

Established in 1759, the **Royal Botanical Gardens** (daily 9.30am to 7.30pm or dusk; £5; Kew Gardens tube) have grown from their original eight acres into a 300-acre site in which more than 33,000 species are grown in plantations and glasshouses, a display that attracts over a million visitors every year, most of them with no specialist interest at all. The only drawbacks with Kew are the prohibitive entry fee, and the fact that it lies on the main flight path to Heathrow. There's always something to see whatever the season, but to get the most out of the place, come sometime between spring and autumn, bring a picnic and come for the day.

There are four entry points to the gardens, but the majority of people arrive at Kew Gardens tube and train station, a few minutes' walk east of the **Victoria Gate**. Of all the glasshouses, by far the most celebrated is the **Palm House**, a curvaceous mound of glass and wrought-iron, designed by Decimus Burton in the 1840s. Its drippingly humid atmosphere nurtures most of the known palm species, while in the basement there's a small but excellent tropical aquarium. The largest of the glasshouses, however, is the **Temperate House**, to the south, which contains plants from every continent, including one of the largest indoor palms in the world, the sixty-foot Chilean Wine Palm.

Kew's origins as an eighteenth-century royal pleasure garden are evident in the numerous follies dotted about Kew, the most conspicuous of which is the ten-storey 163-foot-high **Pagoda**. Unfortunately, **Kew Palace**, the three-storey red-brick mansion bought by George II as a nursery for his umpteen children, will be closed for renovation until at least 2000. As a consolation, you could explore **Queen Charlotte's Cottage** (April–Sept Sat & Sun 10.30am–4pm; free), a tiny thatched summerhouse built in the 1770s as a royal picnic spot for George III's wife in the thickly wooded, southwestern section of the park – a sure way to lose the crowds.

On emerging from the station at **Richmond**, you'd be forgiven for wondering why you're here, but the procession of chain stores spread out along the one-way system is only half the story. To see Richmond's more interesting side, take one of the narrow pedestrianized alleyways off busy George Street, which bring you to the wide open space of **Richmond Green**, one of the finest village greens in London, and no doubt one of the most peaceful before it found itself on the main flight path into Heathrow. Handsome seventeenth- and eighteenth-century houses line the south side of the green, where the medieval royal palace of **Richmond** once stood, though only its unspectacular **Tudor Gateway** survives.

The other place to head for in Richmond is the **Riverside**, pedestrianized, terraced and redeveloped by Quinlan Terry, Prince Charles's favourite purveyor of ersatz classicism, in the late 1980s. The real joy of the waterfront, however, is **Richmond Bridge**, London's oldest extant bridge, an elegant span of five arches made from Purbeck stone in 1777. The old town hall, set back from the new development, houses the **tourist office** (Mon–Fri 10am–6pm, Sat 10am–5pm; April–Oct also Sun 10.15am–4.15pm) and, on the second floor, the **Richmond Museum** (April–Oct Tues–Sat 11am–5pm, Sun 2–5pm; Nov–March Tues–Sat 11am–5pm; £2), but most folk prefer to ensconce themselves in the riverside pubs, or head for the numerous boat and bike rental outlets.

Richmond's greatest attraction, though, is the enormous **Richmond Park** (daily: March–Sept 7am–dusk; Oct–Feb 7.30am–dusk; free), at the top of Richmond Hill – 2500 acres of undulating grassland and bracken, dotted with coppiced woodland and as wild as anything in London. Eight miles across at its widest point, this is Europe's largest city park, famed for its red and fallow deer, which roam freely, and for its ancient oaks. For the most part untamed, the park does have a couple of deliberately landscaped plantations which feature splendid springtime azaleas and rhododendrons, in particular the Isabella Plantation.

If you continue along the towpath beyond Richmond Bridge, after a mile or so, you will eventually leave the rest of London far behind and arrive at **Ham House** (April–Oct Mon–Wed, Sat & Sun 1–5pm; £5), home to the Earls of Dysart for nearly three hundred years. Expensively furnished in the seventeenth century, but little altered since then, the house boasts one of the finest Stuart interiors in the country, from the stupendously ornate Great Staircase to the Long Gallery, featuring six "Court Beauties" by Peter Lely. Elsewhere, there are several fine Verrio ceiling paintings, some exquisite parquet flooring and works by van Dyck and Reynolds. Another bonus are the formal seventeenth-century **gardens** (all year Mon–Wed, Sat & Sun 10.30am–6pm; £1.50), especially the Cherry Garden, laid out with a pungent lavender parterre, surrounded by yew hedges and pleached hornbeam arbours. The Orangery, overlooking the original kitchen garden, currently serves as a tea room.

Hampton Court

Thirteen miles southwest of London you'll find the finest of Tudor palaces, **Hampton Court Palace** (mid-March to mid-Oct Mon 10.15am–6pm, Tues–Sun 9.30am–6pm; rest of year closes 4.30pm; £9.25; Hampton Court train station, from Waterloo), a sprawling red-brick ensemble on the banks of the Thames, thirteen miles southwest of London, the finest of England's royal abodes. Built in 1516 by the upwardly mobile **Cardinal Wolsey**, Henry VIII's Lord Chancellor, it was purloined by Henry himself after Wolsey fell from favour. Charles II laid out the gardens, inspired by what he had seen at Versailles, while William and Mary had large sections of the palace remodelled by Wren. Finally abandoned as a royal residence by George III, Hampton Court was opened to the public by Queen Victoria in 1838.

The royal apartments are divided into six thematic walking tours, for which guided tours and audio tours are available at no extra cost. The highlight of **Henry VIII's State Apartments** is the Great Hall, with its astonishing double hammer-beam roof. Further on is the Haunted Gallery, home to the ghost of Henry's fifth wife, nineteen-year-old Catherine Howard. Another high point is the Chapel Royal, which boasts false-timber vaulting wrought in plaster and decorated with gilded, music-making cherubs. The **Queen's Apartments**, approached by the grandiose trompe l'oeil Queen's Staircase, feature several marvellous marble fireplaces, fiery frescoes, Gobelin tapestries and chinoiserie. The tour of the so-called **Georgian Rooms** takes you through the brightly decorated **Wolsey Closet**, one of the few rooms remaining from Wolsey's apartments, and the Cartoon Gallery, hung with Brussels tapestries, some of which are copies of Raphael's cartoons (now in the V&A) for which the room was originally intended.

The **King's Apartments**, approached via the magnificent King's Staircase and the armoury of the King's Guard Chamber, are furnished in the same period as the Queen's, with only the throne-like velvet toilet for light relief. The **Renaissance Picture Gallery** is chock-full of treasures, among them paintings by Tintoretto, Lotto, Titian, Cranach, Bruegel and Holbein. After the opulence of the rest of the palace, the workaday **Tudor Kitchens** come as something of a relief. To make the most of this route, you really do need the audio tour, which sets the vast complex of reconstructed kitchens alight.

Tickets to the Royal Apartments cover entry to the rest of the sites in the grounds. Those who don't wish to visit the apartments are free to wander around the gardens, but will have to pay extra to visit the curious **Royal Tennis Courts** (50p), the palace's famously tricky hedge **Maze** (£2.10), laid out in 1714 north of the palace, and the **South Gardens** (£2.10), where you can view Andrea Mantegna's colourful, heroic canvases, *The Triumphs of Caesar*, housed in the Lower Orangery, and the celebrated **Great Vine**, grown from a cutting in 1768 and now averaging about seven hundred pounds of black grapes per year and sold at the palace each September. Further afield, across Hampton Court Road, Wren's royal road, Chestnut Avenue, cuts through the semi-wild **Bushy Park**, which sustains a few fallow deer.

Windsor and Eton

Every weekend trains from Waterloo and Paddington are packed with people heading for **Windsor**, the royal enclave 21 miles west of London, where they join the human conveyor belt round **Windsor Castle** (daily: March–Oct 10am–5pm; Nov–Feb 10am–4pm; £9.50, £7.50 on Sun). Towering above the town on a steep chalk bluff, the castle is an undeniably awesome sight, its chilly grey walls, punctuated by mighty medieval bastions, continuing as far as the eye can see. Once there, the small selection of state rooms open to the public is unexciting, though the magnificent St George's

Chapel and the chance to see another small selection of the Queen's private art collection make the trip worthwhile. On a fine day, it pays to put aside some time for exploring Windsor Great Park, which stretches for several miles to the south of the castle.

The castle began its days as a wooden fortress built by William the Conqueror, and numerous later monarchs had a hand in its evolution: Henry II rebuilt it in stone, Henry III and Edward III improved it, and George IV restored it. Some of their work was undone by a huge fire in November 1992, which gutted a number of rooms, including St George's Hall. Most have been rebuilt exactly as they were before the fire, but one or two have been redesigned in a safe neo-Gothic style.

Once inside the castle, it's best to head straight for the **St George's Chapel** (Mon–Sat 10am–4pm), a glorious Perpendicular structure ranking with Henry VII's Chapel in Westminster Abbey, and the second most important resting place for royal corpses after the Abbey. Entry is via the south door and a one-way system operates, which brings you out by the **Albert Memorial Chapel**, built by Henry VII as a burial place for Henry VI, completed by Cardinal Wolsey for his own burial, but eventually converted for Queen Victoria into a High Victorian memorial to her husband, Prince Albert.

Before entering the State Apartments, pay a quick visit to **Queen Mary's Dolls' House**, a palatial micro-residence designed for the wife of George V, and the **Gallery**, where special exhibitions culled from the Royal Art Collection are staged. Most visitors just gape in awe at the monotonous, gilded grandeur of the **State Apartments**, while the real highlights – the paintings from the Royal Collection that line the walls – are rarely given a second glance. The **King's Dressing Room**, for example, despite its small size, contains a feast of art treasures, including a dapper Rubens self-portrait, van Dyck's famous triple portrait of Charles I, and *The Artist's Mother*, a perfectly observed portrait of old age by Rembrandt.

You'd hardly know that Windsor suffered the most devastating fire in its history in 1992, so thorough (and uninspired) has the restoration been in rooms such as the **St George's Hall**. By contrast, the octagonal **Lantern Lobby**, beyond, is clearly an entirely new room, a safe neo-Gothic design replacing the old chapel. At this point, those visiting during the winter season are given the privilege of seeing four **Semi-State Rooms**, created in the 1820s by George IV, and still used in the summer months by the Royal Family.

Over the footbridge, at the end of Thames Avenue in Windsor village, is **Eton**, a one-street village lined with bookshops and antique dealers, but famous all over the world for **Eton College** (Easter, July & Aug daily 10.30am–4.30pm; mid-April to June, Sept & Nov daily 2–4.30pm; £2.50; guided tours daily 2.15 & 3.30pm; £3.50), the ultra-exclusive and inexcusably powerful school founded by Henry VI in 1440 and now charged with educating the heirs to the throne, princes William and Harry. Within the rarefied complex you can visit the Gothic chapel, with its medieval wall paintings and a small self-congratulatory museum telling the history of the school – Percy Bysshe Shelley is a rare rebellious figure in the roll call of Establishment greats.

EATING, DRINKING AND NIGHTLIFE

No matter what your taste in food, drink or entertainment, you'll find what you're looking for in London, a city that in many ways becomes a more appealing place after dark. The capital's rich ethnic mix and concentration of creative talent give it a diversity and energy that no other town in England comes close to matching – Birmingham might have a better concert hall, Manchester might have a couple of hot clubs, but nowhere can match the capital's consistent quality and choice. The weekly calendar of gigs, movies, plays and other events is charted most completely in *Time Out*, the main listings magazine, and there are any number of specialist publications for those who want to make sure they are not missing a thing – from solemn books on the foodie shrines of London to esoteric little mags for the rave cognoscenti. However, the listings that follow should be more than enough for any visitor who's planning on spending less than a couple of months in the city.

Eating

London is a great place to eat. You can sample more or less any kind of **cuisine** here, and – wherever you come from – you should find something new and possibly unique. London is home to some of the best **Cantonese** restaurants in Europe, is a noted centre for **Indian and Bangladeshi** food, and has numerous French, Greek, Italian, Japanese, Spanish and Thai restaurants. And within all these cuisines you can choose anything from simple meals to gourmet spreads. Traditional and modern **British** food is available all over town, and some of the best venues are reviewed below. Another bonus is that there are plenty of places to eat around the main tourist drags of the West End – **Soho** has long been renowned for its eclectic and fashionable restaurants and new eateries appear every month, while **Chinatown**, on the other side of Shaftesbury Avenue, offers value-for-money eating right in the centre of town.

There are also plenty of spots to pick up a street **snack** or cheap **lunch** – and some of these quick-stop places are good standbys for an evening filler. The inexpensive places that rely on a rapid turnover are listed under "Snacks, sandwiches, cakes and coffee", and "Breakfasts, lunches and quick meals", but there are plenty more relaxed eateries suitable for a quick bite, such as the pizza and pasta joints, Chinese restaurants, many of which do excellent *dim sum*, and the ever-expanding ranks of London's French-style bistros.

Snacks, sandwiches, cakes and coffee

As well as the places we've listed below, there are several London-wide chains that are well worth checking out. Try **Aroma**, with its bright Aztec colours, designer sandwiches, Portuguese pastries and good coffee in varying strengths; **Caffè Nero**, which serves terrific coffee, a range of Italian cakes, and pasta, calzone and pizza; **Häagen-Dazs**, offering a huge range of interesting ice-cream flavours, plus cakes, sundaes, shakes and coffee; **Pret à Manger**, with its excellent ready-made sandwiches, imaginative salads, hot stuffed croissants and sushi selections; or **Starbucks**, the clean-cut American operation serving some of the best coffee in town.

INTERNET CAFES

Internet cafés are useful if you need to send a quick email to someone and, occasionally, to visit in their own right. Below are a couple worth trying:

Cyberia, 39 Whitfield St, W1 (☎0171/209 0983, *cyberia@easynet.co.uk*). The city's first Internet café, with trip-hop in the background, chilled beers, coffee and cakes for refuelling, and eleven computers lined up for their netizens. Internet access, £3 per half-hour. Goodge Street tube. Daily 9.30am–10pm.

Global Café, 15 Golden Square, W1 (☎0171/287 2242, *webmasters@globalcafe.co.uk*). A pleasant, roomy Soho café, with helpful staff, and a choice of bagels, double-decker sandwiches, coffee, tea and beer. Access to one of the seven terminals costs £2.50 per half-hour; Saturday nights are women-only. Piccadilly Circus tube. Mon–Sat 10am–11pm.

Mayfair and Marylebone

La Madeleine, 5 Vigo St, W1. This is an authentic French patisserie and café with mountains of tempting patisserie from which to indulge yourself while seated at the tables towards the front of the café; those at the back are for punters who want more substantial bistro fare. Green Park or Piccadilly Circus tube. Closed Sun.

Patisserie Valerie at Sagne, 105 Marylebone High St, W1. Founded as *Maison Sagne* in the 1920s, and preserving its wonderful decor from those days, the café is now run by Soho's fab patisserie-makers, and is without doubt Marylebone's finest. Bond Street tube.

Soho

Bar Italia, 22 Frith St, W1. A tiny café that's a Soho institution, serving coffee, croissants and sandwiches more or less around the clock – as it has been since 1949. Popular with late-night clubbers and those here to watch the Italian-league soccer on the giant screen. Leicester Square tube.

Java Java, 26 Rupert St, W1. Wide range of coffee, a staggering array of teas, and free papers and magazines are all on offer in this cross between a French and an American café. Leicester Square or Piccadilly Circus tube.

The Living Room, 3 Bateman St, W1. Hidden away in a Soho backstreet, this is a welcoming, laid-back café with groovy music, sandwiches and cakes, and great armchairs and tatty sofas to chill out in. Tottenham Court Road tube.

Maison Bertaux, 28 Greek St, W1. Long-standing, old-fashioned, downbeat Soho patisserie, with tables on two floors (and one or two outside) and a loyal clientele that keeps them busy. You'll be tempted in by the window full of elaborate cakes, but be warned, when it comes to coffee, they only do café au lait. Leicester Square tube.

Patisserie Valerie, 44 Old Compton St, W1. Popular coffee, croissant and cake emporium dating from the 1920s and attracting a loud-talking, arty, people-watching Soho crowd. The same outfit now run *Maison Sagne* in Marylebone (see above). Leicester Square or Piccadilly Circus tube.

Covent Garden and Bloomsbury

Coffee Gallery, 23 Museum St, WC1. An excellent, if a little small, café close by the British Museum, serving mouth-watering Italian sandwiches and more substantial dishes at lunchtime. Get there early to grab a seat. Tottenham Court Road tube. Closed Sun.

Coffee Matters, 4 Southampton Row, WC1. Campaigning organic café on the edge of Holborn, serving fairly traded espresso, cappuccino or latte to accompany your organic brownies and biscotti. Freshly squeezed organic juices also available. Holborn tube. Closed Sat & Sun.

Mode, 57 Endell St, WC2. The best things about this stylish Covent Garden café are the Italian sandwiches, the cheeses from nearby Neal's Yard Dairy and the laid-back, groovy atmosphere. Covent Garden tube. Closed Sun.

Monmouth Coffee Company, 27 Monmouth St, WC2. The marvellous aroma's the first thing you notice, while the cramped wooden booths and daily newspapers on hand evoke an eighteenth-century coffee-house atmosphere – pick and mix your coffee from a fine selection (or buy the beans to take home). No smoking. Covent Garden or Leicester Square tube.

Notting Hill

Lisboa Patisserie, 57 Golborne Rd, W10. Authentic Portuguese *pastelaria*, with the best custard tarts this side of Lisbon – also coffee, cakes and a friendly atmosphere. The *Oporto* at no. 62a (closed Mon) is a good fallback if this place is full. Ladbroke Grove tube.

Maison Blanc, 102 Holland Park Ave, W11. French patisserie (with other branches in St John's Wood, Hampstead, Chelsea and Richmond) where you can guarantee you'll get the real thing when it comes to croissants and the like. Holland Park tube.

Kensington and Chelsea

Raison d'Etre, 18 Bute St, SW7. Smack in the middle of South Kensington's French quarter, this is a top-notch patisserie/boulangerie, serving excellent coffee. South Kensington tube. Closed Sun.

Camden

Marine Ices, 8 Haverstock Hill, NW3. Splendid old-fashioned Italian ice-cream parlour with a reputation for ices that spreads far and wide; pizza and pasta served in the adjacent restaurant. Chalk Farm tube.

Greenwich

Pistachio's Café, 15 Nelson Rd, SE10. Very good sandwich café in the centre of Greenwich, serving excellent coffee, and with a small garden out back. Greenwich train station.

Breakfasts, lunches and quick meals

There are cafés and small, basic restaurants all over London that can rustle up an **inexpensive meal**. You should be able to fill up at all of the places listed in this section for under £10, including tea or coffee.

Most of these cafés also feature big **English breakfasts**, served most often till 11am, then move over to pies, fish and chips, and the like – a few offer breakfast all day. Some cafés, and many of the Italian places listed, are also open in the evening, but the turnover is fast, so don't expect to linger. They are best seen as fuel stops before – or in a few cases, after – a night out elsewhere.

London-wide chains worth checking out are **Crank's**, the veggie (and vegan) eating house that spawned a thousand imitators with its wholemeal decor, keen staff, lentil bakes, exotic fruit juices and no-smoking policy; **Ed's Easy Diner**, 1950s-theme diners dishing up some of the city's best burgers and fries for middling prices; and **Stockpot**, which serves big portions at rock-bottom prices.

Piccadilly and Soho

Bar du Marché, 19 Berwick St, W1. A weird find in the middle of raucous Berwick Street market: a French café serving quick snacks, meals and fried breakfasts. Licensed bar. Tottenham Court Road tube. Closed Sun.

Bonbonnière, 36 Great Marlborough St, W1. A good find in the Oxford Circus neighbourhood – cheap, plain fry-ups and Italian dishes, served in a no-nonsense dining room. Wine served by the carafe. Oxford Circus tube. Closed Sun.

Centrale, 16 Moor St, W1. Tiny Italian café that serves up huge plates of steaming, garlicky pasta, as well as omelettes, chicken and chops. You'll almost certainly have to wait for – or share – a table. Bring your own booze; there's a 50p corkage charge. Leicester Square tube.

Hotei, 39 Great Windmill St, W1 (plus other branches at 4 Glasshouse St, W1 and 1 Addle St, EC1). Tiny Japanese-run sushi and noodle bar with a simple, inexpensive menu of Rah-men (noodle soup) or Yaki-soba (fried noodles). Piccadilly Circus tube.

Indian YMCA, 41 Fitzroy Square, W1. Don't take any notice of the signs saying the canteen is only for students – this place is open to the public, just press the bell and pile in. The entire menu is portioned up into pretty little bowls; go and collect what you want and pay at the till. The food is great and the prices unbelievably low. Goodge Street tube.

Pollo, 20 Old Compton St, W1. This place has a reputation – some say unjustified – for the best-value Italian food in town, which means that even though there are two floors, you'll either have to wait in line or share a table. Alcohol is served. Leicester Square tube.

Wren at St James's, 35 Jermyn St, SW1 (right by the church). Useful vegetarian café to know about, as the area is short on cheap options. There's outdoor courtyard seating in summer. Piccadilly Circus tube.

Covent Garden and the Strand

Café in the Crypt, St Martin-in-the-Fields, Duncannon St, WC2. Below the church, in the crypt, the good-quality buffet food – including veggie dishes – makes this an ideal spot to fill up before hitting the West End. Charing Cross tube.

Diana's Diner, 39 Endell St, WC2. Cramped wooden benches, a friendly welcome for regulars and improbably large plates of home-made pies, omelettes, grills and chips. A favourite with local office workers. Covent Garden tube.

Food for Thought, 31 Neal St, WC2. A sympatico veggie restaurant and takeaway counter – the food is good, with daily changing specials, and vegan and wheat-free options. Expect to queue and don't expect to linger at peak times. Covent Garden tube. Closed Sun eve.

Frank's Cafe, 52 Neal St, WC2. Italian café/sandwich bar with easy-going service. All-day breakfasts, plates of pasta and omelettes on offer; come either side of lunch to make sure of a table. Covent Garden tube. Closed Sun.

Gaby's, 30 Charing Cross Rd, WC2. Jewish café and takeaway joint serving a wide range of home-cooked veggie and Middle Eastern specialities. Hard to beat for value, choice or long hours. It's licensed, too. Leicester Square tube.

India Club, 143 Strand, WC2. There's a faded period charm to this long-established first-floor Anglo-Indian eatery, whose chilli bhajis are to be taken very seriously. Covent Garden or Temple tube. Lunchtime only; closed Sun.

Juice, 7 Earlham St, WC2. Spartan, antiseptic café serving a wild range of wild juices, quiche, salad and sandwiches that appeals to Covent Garden's clubby crowd, who feel the need to cleanse their bodies. Covent Garden or Leicester Square tube.

Neal's Yard Tearoom, 6 Neal's Yard, WC2. Ramshackle first-floor room above superb organic co-operative bakery. Order your food downstairs before heading for the rickety seats upstairs. Covent Garden tube. Closed Sun.

Clerkenwell

Al's Café Bar, 11–13 Exmouth Market, EC1. This is a trendy little spot – a designer greasy spoon with a media-luvvie clientele, who are served up Italian breads, Mediterranean dishes, nachos, decent coffee and good soups alongside the chips and grills. Angel or Farringdon tube.

Clark & Sons, 46 Exmouth Market, EC1. Exmouth Market is currently undergoing something of a transformation, so it's all the more surprising to find this genuine eel and pie shop still going strong. Angel or Farringdon tube. Closed Sun.

Restaurants

Many of the restaurants we've listed will be busy on most nights of the week, particularly on Thursday, Friday and Saturday, and you're best advised to **reserve a table** wherever you're headed. As for **prices**, you can pay an awful lot for a meal in London, and if you're used to North American portions, you're not going to be particularly impressed by the volume in most places.

St James's, Mayfair and Marylebone

Abu Ali, 136–138 George St, W1 (☎0171/724 6338). Honest Lebanese fare that's terrific value for money from the *tabbouleh* to the kebabs – wash it all down with fresh mint tea. Marble Arch tube. Closed Sun. Moderate.

Browns, 47 Maddox St, W1 (☎0171/495 4565). Bustling, popular chain, whose reputation is founded on its steak, mushroom and Guinness pie, but which also offers pastas, hot sandwiches and salads. Oxford Circus or Bond Street tube. Closed Sun. Moderate.

The Criterion, 224 Piccadilly, W1 (☎0171/930 0488). One of the city's most beautiful restaurants, right by Piccadilly Circus. Refurbishment has made the huge dining room sparkle, and the menu has been devised by scourge of the faint-hearted, Marco Pierre White. Piccadilly Circus tube. Closed Sun lunch. Expensive.

Mandalay, 444 Edgware Rd, W2 (☎0171/258 3696). Pure and unexpurgated Burmese cuisine – a *mélange* of Thai, Malaysian and Indian. The portions are huge, the service friendly and the prices low. Edgware Road tube. Closed Sun. Inexpensive.

Quaglino's, 16 Bury St, SW1 (☎0171/930 6767). Huge 1930s ballroom revived by Terence Conran as one of the capital's busiest and most fashionable eating spots, so you'll need to book well in advance. Dishes don't always work but the splendid surroundings and an unmistakable buzz are the reward. Green Park tube. Expensive.

Sea-Shell, 49–51 Lisson Grove, NW1 (☎0171/723 8703). Top-quality, no-nonsense fish and chips in the heart of Marylebone. Marylebone tube. Closed Sun eve. Moderate.

La Spighetta, 43 Blandford St, W1 (☎0171/486 7340). Not a spaghetti house, in fact, but a pizza and pasta joint – spighetta means wheat – and a very good one at that. Bond Street tube. Moderate.

Soho

China City, White Bear Yard, 25 Lisle St, WC2 (☎0171/734 3388). Large restaurant tucked into a little courtyard off Lisle Street; fresh and bright, with *dim sum* that's up there with the best, service that is "Chinatown brusque", and a menu with eminently reasonable prices. Leicester Square tube. Moderate.

Chuen Cheng Ku, 17 Wardour St, W1 (☎0171/437 1398). Big Cantonese restaurant that's one of the closest in spirit to Hong Kong's cavernous diners. There's a massive range of dishes – the best are on the Chinese-only menu (ask for the day's special). Authentic *dim sum*, too, served from circulating trolleys until 6pm. Leicester Square tube. Moderate.

Kettner's, 29 Romilly St, W1 (☎0171/734 6112). Despite the expensive looking Baroque decor and the pianist, this place serves cheap pizzas and the like. You can't book and might be forced to hang out a while in the noisy Champagne Bar – no great hardship. Leicester Square tube. Closed Sun. Moderate to Expensive.

Kulu Kulu, 76 Brewer St, W1 (☎0171/734 7316). Small, friendly, *kaiten* (or conveyor belt) sushi restaurant, which pulls off the unlikely trick of serving really good sushi without being intimidating. Piccadilly Circus tube. Closed Sun. Moderate.

Mezzo, 100 Wardour St, W1 (☎0171/314 4000). Mezzo is big, busy and very noisy. Considering the numbers served here, the French/Med food is pretty good. The extraction system is so good you can't even smell the Havanas (served by the "cigarette girl") smoked on your own table. Watch out for the £5 "music-cover charge" after 10.30pm. Piccadilly Circus or Tottenham Court Road tube. Moderate to Very Expensive.

Mr Kong, 21 Lisle St, WC2 (☎0171/437 7341). One of Chinatown's finest, with a chef-owner who pioneered many of the modern Cantonese dishes now on menus all over town. You may have to be firm with staff if you want the more unusual dishes – order from the "Today's" and "Chef's Specials" menu and don't miss the mussels in black-bean sauce. Leicester Square tube. Inexpensive to Moderate.

Randall & Aubin, 16 Brewer St, W1 (☎0171/287 4447). Converted butcher's, now a champagne-oyster bar, rotisserie, sandwich shop and charcuterie, to boot – in the summer, this is a wonderfully airy place to eat. Piccadilly Circus tube. Closed Sun. Moderate to Very Expensive.

Zilli Fish, 36–40 Brewer St, W1 (☎0171/734 8649). Bright, brittle and brash, *Zilli Fish* is a hectic place that appeals to Soho's media luvvies. Serves consistently good fish dishes. Oxford Circus or Piccadilly Circus tube. Closed Sat & Sun. Expensive.

Covent Garden

Livebait, 21 Wellington St, WC2 (☎0171/836 7161). Innovative, irrepressible restaurant, with a large, bustling, black-and-white-tiled dining room, and fish so fresh you expect to see it flapping on the slab. Covent Garden tube. Closed Sun. Expensive.

Mon Plaisir, 21 Monmouth St, WC2 (☎0171/836 7243). One of London's best imitations of a Parisian bistro. The set lunch is a bargain at around £15; otherwise pay up for some of the most pleasing French food in town. Covent Garden or Leicester Square tube. Closed Sat lunch & Sun. Moderate to Expensive.

Stephen Bull, 12 Upper St Martin's Lane, WC2 (☎0171/379 7811). The Bauhaus decor and Modern British food are a bold statement and this restaurant has plenty of admirers – the fish dishes and desserts are particularly recommended. Reasonably priced set lunches are a bonus. Leicester Square tube. Closed Sun. Moderate to Expensive.

Fitzrovia and Bloomsbury

Chutney's, 124 Drummond St, NW1 (☎0171/388 0604). Tasty, varied veggie Indian food is guaranteed. The buffet lunch for £5 is a bargain as is the deluxe thali for just £7. Euston Square tube. Inexpensive.

Efes, 80 Great Titchfield St, W1 (☎0171/636 1953). Vast Turkish kebab restaurant with 1970s decor – a reliable and friendly place, with doner and shish kebabs big enough to sink a battleship, and some great starters. There's a takeaway counter at the front. Oxford Circus or Great Portland Street tube. Closed Sun. Moderate.

Great Nepalese, 48 Eversholt St, NW1 (☎0171/388 6737). One of very few places in London serving genuine spicy Nepalese dishes. Euston tube. Inexpensive to Moderate.

Ikkyu, 67a Tottenham Court Rd, W1 (☎0171/636 9280). Busy, basement Japanese restaurant, good enough for a quick lunch or a more elaborate dinner. Either way, prices are infinitely more reasonable than elsewhere in the capital, and the food is tasty and authentic. Goodge Street tube. Closed Sat & Sun lunch. Moderate to Expensive.

Malabar Junction, 107a Great Russell St, WC1 (☎0171/580 5230). Inexpensive Keralan restaurant with two separate kitchens, one serving mouth-watering veggie dishes, the other dishing out meat and fish fare. Tottenham Court Road tube. Inexpensive to Moderate.

Mash London, 19–21 Great Portland St, W1 (☎0171/637 5555). Buzzy modern bar/café/restaurant, with its own micro-brewery, that offers an eclectic rosta of dishes from its wood-fired oven and grill. Oxford Circus tube. Moderate to Expensive.

R. K. Stanley, 6 Little Portland St, W1 (☎0171/462 0099). Sausages from all over the globe, served in modern surroundings, and washed down with ale, lager, stout or porter. Oxford Circus tube. Closed Sun. Moderate.

Wagamama, 4 Streatham St, WC1 (☎0171/323 9223). Austere, minimalist place where the waiters take your orders on hand-held computers. Diners share long benches and slurp huge bowls of noodle soup or stir-fried plates. You may have to queue, however, and the rapid turnover means it's not a place to consider for a long, romantic dinner. Tottenham Court Road tube. Closed Sun. Inexpensive to Moderate.

Clerkenwell and the City

Cicada, 132 St John St, EC1 (☎0171/720 5433). Part bar, part restaurant, *Cicada* offers an unusual Thai-based menu that allows you to mix and match from small, large and side dishes ranging from fishy *tom yum* to ginger noodles or sushi. Farringdon tube. Closed Sat lunch & Sun. Moderate.

St John, 26 St John St, EC1 (☎0171/251 0848). Decidedly English restaurant, only a stone's throw from Smithfield meat market and specializing in offal. All those strange and unfashionable cuts of meat that were once commonplace in rural England – brains, bone marrow, meat from a cow's sternum – are on offer at this white-painted former smokehouse. Farringdon tube. Closed Sat & Sun. Expensive.

Singapura, 1–2 Limeburner Lane, EC4 (☎0171/329 1133). Beautiful, large, modern restaurant off Ludgate Hill specializing in Nonya cuisine – a sort of fusion of Malayan and Chinese traditions – from Singapore. The food is spicy, garlicky and delicious. Blackfriars or St Paul's tube. Closed Sat & Sun. Expensive.

East End

Arkansas Café, 12 Old Spitalfields Market, E1 (☎0171/377 6999). American-barbie fuel stop, using only the very best ingredients. Try Bubb's own smoked beef brisket and ribs, and be sure to taste his home-made barbie sauce (made to a secret formula). Liverpool Street tube. Closed Mon–Sat eve. Inexpensive to Moderate.

Café Spice Namaste, 16 Prescott St, E1 (☎0171/488 9242). Very popular East End Indian, where the menu is a touch more varied than in many of its rivals – Goan and Kashmiri dishes are often included, and you're as likely to find squid or potato cakes as your usual favourites. Tower Hill tube. Closed Sun. Moderate.

Lahore Kebab House, 3 Umberstone St, E1 (☎0171/481 9737). Despite refurbishment, the food is still good and spicy, the prices low, and the service brusque. In addition, the Lahore serves long-stewed sheep's feet – *paya* – (Fridays only) the hallmark of any genuine Pakistani restaurant. Whitechapel tube. Inexpensive.

Viet Hoa Café, 72 Kingsland Rd, E2 (☎0171/729 8293). Large, light and airy Vietnamese café in the wasteland of Shoreditch; serving splendid "meals in a bowl", soups and noodle dishes with everything from spring rolls to tofu. Be sure to try the *Pho* soup, a Vietnamese staple that's eaten at any and every meal. Bus #67, #149 or #242 from Liverpool Street Station. Closed Mon. Inexpensive to Moderate.

Lambeth and Southwark

Blue Print Café, Design Museum, Butler's Wharf, SE1 (☎0171/378 7031). The oldest of Terence Conran's gastrodomes – expect to pay higher than average prices for a higher than average meal, and a fabulous view from the terrace windows (for which you must book ahead). Tower Hill tube. Closed Sat lunch. Very Expensive.

Butlers Wharf Chop House, 36e Shad Thames, SE1 (☎0171/403 3403). Conran-owned restaurant showcasing British meat, fish and cheeses. Prices are high, but the *Chop House* tries to cater for all: you could enjoy a simple dish at the bar, a well-priced set lunch, or an extravagant dinner. You can't reserve the terrace tables but try and book ahead for a window seat. Tower Hill tube. Closed Sat lunch. Moderate to Expensive.

Cantina del Ponte, Butler's Wharf, Shad Thames, SE1 (☎0171/403 5403). Another, cheaper Conran place, offering earthy Italian fare in designer surroundings. Again, to enjoy the window tables, or the alfresco terrace, you should book ahead. Tower Hill tube. Moderate to Expensive.

County Hall Restaurant, Queens Walk, SE1 (☎0171/902 8000). Located within the *Marriot Hotel* that now occupies much of County Hall, this restaurant serves ambitious Med-influenced food in sumptuous surroundings, and offers superb views across the Thames to the Houses of Parliament. Westminster tube. Expensive.

Fina Estampa, 150 Tooley St, SE1 (☎0171/403 1342). This may be London's only Peruvian restaurant, but it also happens to be the very best, bringing a little of downtown Lima to London Bridge. The menu is traditional Peruvian, with a big emphasis on seafood. London Bridge tube. Closed Sun. Moderate to Expensive.

Little Saigon, 139 Westminster Bridge Rd, SE1 (☎0171/207 9747). Great Vietnamese spring rolls, grilled squid-cake and crystal pancakes, all served with a wonderful array of sauces, plus great crispy fried noodles. Waterloo tube. Closed Sat & Sun lunch. Moderate to Expensive.

RSJ, 13a Coin St, SE1 (☎0171/928 4554). Regularly high standards of Anglo-French cooking make this a good spot for a meal after or before an evening at a South Bank theatre or concert hall. The set meals for around £15 are particularly popular. Waterloo tube. Closed Sat lunch & Sun. Moderate to Very Expensive.

Kensington and Chelsea

Hunan, 51 Pimlico Rd, SW1 (☎0171/730 5712). Probably England's only restaurant serving Hunan food, a relative of Szechuan food with the same spicy kick to most dishes, and a fair wallop of pepper in those that aren't actively riddled with chillis. Most people opt for the £21 "leave-it-to-us feast" which lets the chef, Mr Peng, show what he can do. Sloane Square tube. Closed Sun lunch. Expensive.

Jenny Lo's Teahouse, 14 Ecclestone St, SW1 (☎0171/259 0399). Bright, bare, utilitarian Chinese restaurant, whose prices make you think you're in the politest cafeteria in the world. Be sure to check out the therapeutic teas. Victoria tube. Closed Sun. Inexpensive.

New Culture Revolution, 305 King's Rd, SW3 (☎0171/352 9281). Great name, great concept – big bowls of freshly cooked noodles in sauce or soup, dumplings and rice dishes, all offering a one-stop meal at bargain prices in simple, minimalist surroundings. Not a place to linger. Sloane Square tube. Inexpensive.

O Fado, 49–50 Beauchamp Place, SW3 (☎0171/589 3002). Probably the oldest Portuguese restaurant in London, which speaks volumes for its authenticity. It can get rowdy what with the live *fado* ballads, and the family parties, but that's half the enjoyment. You'll need to reserve a table. Knightsbridge tube. Closed Sun eve. Expensive.

Wódka, 12 St Alban's Grove, W8 (☎0171/937 6513). The food is cooked with a little imagination, which makes the smart *Wódka* the place to go if you want to experience the best that Polish cuisine has to offer. It's not an expensive place to eat until you start ladling out the ice-cold, flavoured vodkas. High Street Kensington or Gloucester Road tube. Closed Sat & Sun lunch. Moderate to Expensive.

Bayswater and Notting Hill

Alounak, 44 Westbourne Grove, W2 (☎0171/229 0416). Don't be put off by the dated sign outside – this place turns out really good, really cheap Iranian food. Bayswater tube. Inexpensive.

Hung Toa, 51 Queensway, W2 (☎0171/727 5753). Cantonese and Szechuan barbecued meats, noodle dishes and noodle soups at keen prices on this busy street. Queensway or Bayswater tube. Inexpensive.

The Mandola, 139 Westbourne Grove, W11 (☎0171/229 4734). Strikingly delicious "urban Sudanese" food at sensible prices, served by extremely laid-back staff. Check out the Sudanese spiced coffee at the end. Notting Hill Gate tube. Inexpensive to Moderate.

Rodrizio Rico, 111 Westbourne Grove, W11 (☎0171/792 4035). No menu, no prices, but no problem either as this Brazilian eatery specializes in smoky, grilled meat. Carvers come round and lop off chunks of freshly grilled meats, while you help yourself from the salad bar and hot buffet to prime your plate. Notting Hill Gate or Queensway tube. Closed Sun. Moderate.

Rotisserie Jules, 133a Notting Hill Gate, W11 (☎0171/221 3331). One of three restaurants – the other two being at 6 Bute St, SW7 and 338 King's Rd, SW3 – that excels in freshly roasted chicken at sound prices. Notting Hill Gate tube. Inexpensive to Moderate.

Camden and Hampstead

Cheng Du, 9 Parkway, NW1 (☎0171/485 8058). Probably London's best Szechuan restaurant, full of Camden trendies soaking up the spices in a most un-Chinese-restaurant-like environment, with prices more West End than rustic. Camden Town tube. Moderate to Expensive.

El Parador, 245 Eversholt St, NW1 (☎0171/387 2789). Small, no-frills Spanish restaurant a stone's throw from Camden High Street, serving up tasty *tapas*. Service is friendly and laid-back and there's a lovely garden, with tables for alfresco eating. Mornington Crescent tube. Closed Sat & Sun lunch. Moderate.

Lemonia, 89 Regent's Park Rd, NW1 (☎0171/586 7454). Spirited Greek taverna, doing all the basics well, especially the charcoal-grilled meats and fish – the fish meze is splendid. It's extremely popular, so book ahead. If you can't get in, try the associated *Limani* at no. 154 opposite (☎0171/483 4492), with similarly fine food at roughly the same prices. Chalk Farm tube. Closed Sat lunch & Sun eve. Moderate.

Solly's, 146–150 Golders Green Rd, NW11 (☎0171/455 2121). *Solly's*, downstairs, is a small kosher restaurant and deli specializing in epic falafel; *Solly's Exclusive*, upstairs, is a huge, bustling kosher restaurant. Golders Green tube. Closed Fri eve & Sat lunch. Moderate.

Trojka, 101 Regent's Park Rd, NW1 (☎0171/483 3765). Unpretentious restaurant in the heart of Primrose Hill, offering hearty portions of Russian, Ukrainian and Polish food, to the accompaniment of East European music. Chalk Farm tube. Moderate.

Greenwich

The North Pole, 131 Greenwich High Rd, SE10 (☎0181/853 3020). Pub-like from the outside, bright and bar-like on the ground floor, the *North Pole* offers "East meets West" cuisine upstairs, combining Pacific Rim style cooking with European ingredients. Be sure to check out the goldfish-bowl lamps. Greenwich train station. Closed Mon. Moderate to Expensive.

Tai Won Mein, 49 Greenwich Church St, SE10 (☎0181/858 1668). Good quality fast-food noodle bar that gets very busy at the weekend. Decor is functional and minimalist; choose between rice, fried or soup noodles and *ho fun* (a flatter, softer, ribbon-like noodle). Greenwich train station. Inexpensive.

Chiswick to Richmond

Chez Lindsay, 11 Hill Rise, Richmond, Surrey (☎0181/948 7473). Small, bright authentic Breton crepe and *galetterie*, which also serves more formal French main courses, including lots of fresh fish and shellfish, all washed down with Breton cider in earthenware *bolées*. Richmond tube. Inexpensive to Moderate.

The Gate, 51 Queen Caroline St, W6 (☎0181/748 6932). Gourmet vegetarian dining that's rich, calorific and naughty in a striking little restaurant tucked behind the Hammersmith Apollo. Hammersmith tube. Closed Sat & Sun. Expensive.

Springbok Café, 42 Devonshire Rd, W4 (☎0181/742 3149). Small, informal, authentic South African restaurant, with an open-plan barbie-oriented kitchen. Many of the ingredients are imported, so there's plenty of biltong, smoked ostrich and the like to please ex-pats. Turnham Green tube. Closed Mon–Sat lunch & Sun. Expensive.

Drinking

Virtually every street in central London has its **pub** and, although generally you'll find the best places away from the centre, there are one or two watering holes in the West End that have kept their character. The greatest concentrations of unspoilt pubs within a tube-hop of the centre are to be found on the east side of town, between Aldwych and the City – some can be uncomfortably packed on weekdays before 8pm, but after that, when the City types have gone home, they are far more appealing. The traditional image of London pub food is dire – a pseudo "ploughman's lunch" of bread and cheese, or a murky-looking pie and chips – but the last couple of decades has seen a lot of change for the better. At many of the pubs listed below you can get a palatable **lunchtime meal**, and at a few of them you're looking at cooking worthy of high restaurant praise.

According to English **licensing laws**, pubs are allowed to open Monday to Saturday from 11am to 11pm and Sundays from noon to 10.30pm. Most London pubs stick to these hours, but you may find that some of the less busy establishments still follow the old Sunday hours of noon to 3pm and 7 to 10.30pm. It's also worth noting that many pubs in the City are open from Monday to Friday only, and some close earlier than 11pm. For drinking beyond the standard 11pm last orders at a pub, you're probably best off heading for one of the city's bars, whose numbers have increased enormously over the past few years. These are very different places to your average pub, catering to a somewhat cliquey, often youngish crowd, with designer interiors and drinks; they're also expensive, often levying an entry charge after 11pm. We've listed a fair few – while covering those tied to, or more like, clubs and dance venues on p.139.

Whitehall and Westminster

Albert, 52 Victoria St, SW1. Roomy High-Victorian pub, with big bay windows and glass partitions. Good food, with an excellent upstairs carvery. St James's Park tube.

ICA Bar, 94 The Mall, SW1. You have to be a member to drink at the *ICA Bar* – but anyone can join on the door (Mon–Fri £1.50, Sat & Sun £2.50). It's a cool drinking venue, with a noir dress code observed by the arty crowd and staff. Piccadilly Circus or Charing Cross tube.

Paviour's Arms, Page St, SW1. Original, stylish 1930s Art Deco pub, close to the Tate Gallery and offering Thai food along with the beer. Pimlico tube. Closed Sat & Sun.

St James's, Mayfair and Marylebone

Devonshire Arms, 21a Devonshire St, W1. Beautiful interior with lots of brass, frosted mirrors and original tiling, plus newspapers to read. Baker Street or Regent's Park tube. Closed Sun.

Mulligans, 13–14 Cork St, W1. A fine Irish pub with an odd mix of clientele – Cork Street gallery staff and Irish lads – and the best Guinness in London. Also has a high-class restaurant downstairs, with fine Modern-British cooking. Green Park or Piccadilly tube. Closed Sun.

O'Conor Don, 88 Marylebone Lane, W1. Stripped bare anti-theme Irish pub with table service, excellent Guinness and a pleasantly measured pace. Bond Street tube. Closed Sun.

Red Lion, 2 Duke of York St, SW1. Popular little gin palace, which has preserved its classic Victorian decor. Green Park or Piccadilly Circus tube. Closed Sun.

Soho and Fitzrovia

Coach & Horses, 29 Greek St, W1. Long-standing – and, for once, little-changed – haunt of the ghosts of old Soho, *Private Eye*, nightclubbers, and art students from nearby St Martin's College. Fifties red plastic stools and black formica tables guaranteed. Leicester Square tube.

Dog & Duck, 18 Bateman St, W1. Tiny Soho pub that retains much of its old character, beautiful Victorian tiling and mosaics, and a loyal clientele that often includes jazz musicians from nearby *Ronnie Scott's* club. Leicester Square or Tottenham Court Road tube. Closed Sat & Sun lunch.

French House, 49 Dean St, W1. The tiny French pub has been a Soho institution since before World War I. Free French and literary associations galore, half pints only at the bar (no real ale) and a fine little restaurant upstairs. Leicester Square tube.

The Hope, 15 Tottenham St, W1. Chiefly remarkable for its sausage (veggie ones included), beans and mash lunches, and its real ales. Goodge Street tube.

Newman Arms, 23 Rathbone St, W1. What the *Hope* is to sausages, the *Newman Arms* is to pies, with every sort from gammon to steak-and-kidney. Tottenham Court Road tube. Closed Sat lunch & Sun.

Covent Garden

The Chandos, 29 St Martin's Lane, WC2. If you can get one of the booths downstairs or the leather sofas upstairs in the Opera Room, then you'll find it difficult to leave. Leicester Square tube.

Lamb & Flag, 33 Rose St, WC2. Busy, tiny and highly atmospheric pub, tucked away down an alley between Garrick Street and Floral Street, where John Dryden was attacked in 1679 for writing scurrilous verses about one of Charles II's mistresses. Leicester Square tube.

Punch & Judy, 40 The Market, WC2. Horribly mobbed and expensive, but unbeatable location with a balcony overlooking the Piazza – and a stone-flagged cellar. Covent Garden tube.

Salisbury, 90 St Martin's Lane, WC2. One of the most beautifully preserved Victorian pubs in the capital, with cut, etched and engraved windows, bronze figures and lincrusta ceiling. Leicester Square tube.

Soho Brewing Company, 41 Earlham St, WC2. Busy, brick-vaulted basement brewery with wrought-iron pillars, lots of brushed steel and pricey, strong brews, in particular a very fine wheat beer. Covent Garden tube.

Bloomsbury

Lamb, 94 Lamb's Conduit St, WC1. Pleasant pub with a marvellously well-preserved Victorian interior of mirrors, old wood and "snob" screens. Russell Square tube.

Museum Tavern, 49 Great Russell St, WC1. Large and characterful old pub, right opposite the main entrance to the British Museum, erstwhile drinking hole of Karl Marx. Tottenham Court Road or Russell Square tube.

The Strand, Holborn and Clerkenwell

Café Kick, 43 Exmouth Market, EC1. Stylish take on a local French-style café-bar in the heart of newly fashionable Exmouth Market, with table football to complete the retro theme. Farringdon or Angel tube. Closed Sun.

Eagle, 159 Farringdon Rd, EC1. The first of London's pubs to go foody, this place is heaving at lunch and dinnertimes, as *Guardian* workers tuck into Med dishes, but you should be able to find a seat at other times. Farringdon tube. Closed Sun.

Fox & Anchor, 115 Charterhouse St, EC1. Handsome Smithfield market pub famous for its early opening hours and huge breakfasts (served 7–10am). Farringdon or Barbican tube. Closed Sat & Sun.

Gordon's, 47 Villiers St, WC2. A real, claustrophobic, cave-like wine bar specializing in ports, right next door to Charing Cross station. The excellent and varied wine list, decent buffet food and genial atmosphere make this a favourite with local office workers. Charing Cross or Embankment tube. Closed Sat lunch & Sun.

Jerusalem Tavern, 55 Britton St, EC1. Cosy little converted Georgian parlour, stripped bare and slightly "distressed", serving tasty food along with the beer. Farringdon tube. Closed Sat & Sun.

O'Hanlon, 8 Tysoe St, EC1. Small Irish pub serving its own brews, including the best stout in London, plus great Irish food. Angel tube. Closed Sun.

Princess Louise, 208 High Holborn, WC1. Old-fashioned place, with highly decorated ceilings, lots of glass, brass and mahogany, and a good range of real ales. Holborn tube. Closed Sun.

The City: Fleet Street to St Paul's

Blackfriar, 174 Queen Victoria St, EC4. A gorgeous, utterly original pub, with Art Nouveau marble friezes of boozy monks and a wonderful highly decorated alcove – all original, dating from 1905. Blackfriars tube. Closed Sat eve & Sun.

Old Bank of England, 194 Fleet St, EC4. Not the actual Bank of England, but the former Law Courts' branch, this imposing High Victorian banking hall is now a magnificently opulent ale and pie pub. Temple or Chancery Lane tube. Closed Sat & Sun.

Old Cheshire Cheese, Wine Office Court, 145 Fleet St, EC4. A famous seventeenth-century watering hole, with several snug, dark panelled bars and real fires. Popular with tourists, but by no means exclusively so. Temple or Blackfriars tube. Closed Sun eve.

The City: Bank to Bishopsgate

The Counting House, 50 Cornhill, EC2. Another City bank conversion, with fantastic high ceilings a glass dome, chandeliers and a central oval bar. Naturally enough, given the location, it's wall-to-wall suits. Bank tube. Closed Sat & Sun.

Hamilton Hall, Liverpool Street Station, EC2. Cavernous, gilded, former ballroom of the *Great Eastern* hotel, adorned with nudes and chandeliers. Packed out with City commuters tanking up before the train home, but a great place nonetheless. Liverpool Street tube.

Jamaica Wine House, St Michael's Alley, EC3 (☎0171/626 9496). An old City institution tucked away down a narrow alleyway. Despite the name, this is really just a pub, divided into four large "snugs" by high wooden-panelled partitions. Bank tube. Closed Sat & Sun.

East End and Docklands

Dickens Inn, St Katharine's Way, E1. Eighteenth-century timber-framed warehouse transported on wheels from its original site, and then much altered. Still, it's a remarkable building, with a great view, but very firmly on the tourist trail. Tower Hill tube.

Ferry House, 26 Ferry St, E14. Nice, laid-back, old pub, with no pretensions. Conveniently located near the Greenwich foot tunnel. Island Gardens DLR.

Grapes, 76 Narrow St, E14. The *Grapes'* fame is assured thanks to a mention in Dickens *Our Mutual Friend*; it has a riverside balcony out back, great bar meals and an expensive fish restaurant upstairs. Westferry DLR. Closed Sat lunch.

The Gun, 27 Cold Harbour, E14. An old dockers' pub with lots of maritime memorabilia, and – the main attraction – an unrivalled view of the Millennium Dome. South Quay or Blackwall DLR.

Prospect of Whitby, 57 Wapping Wall, E1. London's most famous riverside pub with a flagstone floor, a cobbled courtyard and great views. Wapping tube.

Town of Ramsgate, 62 Wapping High St, E1. Dark, narrow medieval pub located by Wapping Old Stairs, which once led down to Execution Dock. Captain Blood was discovered here with the crown jewels under his cloak, and Admiral Bligh and Fletcher Christian were regular drinking partners in pre-mutiny days. Wapping tube.

Lambeth and Southwark

Anchor Bankside, 34 Park St, SE1. While the rest of Bankside has changed almost beyond all recognition, this pub still looks much as it did when first built in 1770 (on the inside, at least). Good for alfresco drinking by the river. London Bridge tube.

George Inn, 77 Borough High St, SE1. London's only surviving coaching inn, dating from the seventeenth century and now owned by the National Trust; it also serves a good range of real ales. Borough or London Bridge tube.

NFT Bar, South Bank, SE1. The National Film Theatre's newly refurbished bar is the only riverfront bar on the South Bank between Westminster and Blackfriars bridges – worth checking out not only for the views, but also for the food and the congenial crowd. Waterloo tube.

Knightsbridge, Kensington & Chelsea

Bunch of Grapes, 207 Brompton Rd, SW3. This popular High-Victorian pub, complete with "snob" screens, is the perfect place for a post-V&A pint. South Kensington tube.

Front Page, 35 Old Church St, SW3. Centre of boho Chelsea and infinitely preferable to anything on offer on the King's Road. Sloane Square tube.

Orange Brewery, 37 Pimlico Rd, SW1. The area may be posh, but this is a fairly down-to-earth, gas-lit boozer with its very own micro-brewery. Sloane Square tube.

Paxton's Head, 153 Knightsbridge, SW1. Wonderful Edwardian pub, with lincrusta ceiling tiles, mahogany bar and etched mirrors, and very unpretentious given the locale. Avoid the bar food. Knightsbridge tube.

Notting Hill

The Cow, 89 Westbourne Park Rd, W2. Pub owned by Tom Conran, son of gastro-magnate Terence, which pulls in the beautiful W11 types, thanks to its spectacular food, including a daily supply of fresh oysters. Westbourne Park tube.

Pharmacy, 150 Notting Hill Gate, W11. Don't come here if you despise the work of artist Damien Hurst, as this bar/restaurant is his little conceit. Still, the medicinal joke is worth at least one laugh: stools that look like giant pills, staff in surgical boots. Notting Hill Gate tube. Closed Sun lunch.

Prince Bonaparte, 80 Chepstow Rd, W2. Pared-down, minimalist pub, with acres of space for sitting and supping or enjoying the excellent Mediterranean food. Westbourne Park tube. Closed Tues lunch.

Retro, 183 Portobello Rd, W11. Another trendy Notting Hill bar – lined with old sofas, and serving sushi and cocktails. Ladbroke Grove tube. Closed Sun & Mon.

St John's Wood and Maida Vale

Prince Alfred, 9 Formosa St, W9. A fantastic period-piece Victorian pub with all its original 1862 fittings intact, right down to the glazed "snob" screens. The beer and Thai food are good, too. Warwick Avenue tube.

Warrington, 93 Warrington Crescent, W9. Yet another architectural gem – this time flamboyant Art Nouveau – in an area replete with them. Thai restaurant upstairs. Warwick Avenue or Maida Vale tube.

Camden Town

Crown & Goose, 100 Arlington St, NW1. Cross between a pub, bar and restaurant, situated a block away from the High Street and not too badly mobbed, even during the market. Food's a bit special, too. Camden Town tube.

The Engineer, 65 Gloucester Ave, NW1. Smart, grandiose pub for the smart, grandiose types in Primrose Hill – the food is exceptional though pricey, and it's advisable to book if you're intending to nosh. Chalk Farm tube.

Lansdowne, 90 Gloucester Ave, NW1. Big, bare-boards minimalist pub with comfy sofas, in elegant Primrose Hill. Pricey, tasty food. Chalk Farm tube. Closed Mon lunch.

Hampstead and Highgate

Flask, 14 Flask Walk, NW3. Convivial Hampstead local, which retains its original Victorian "snob" screen. Serves good food and fine ale. Hampstead tube.

Flask, 77 Highgate West Hill, N6. Ideally situated at the heart of Highgate village green, with a rambling low-ceilinged interior and a summer terrace. Highgate tube.

Freemason's Arms, 32 Downshire Hill, NW3. Big, smart pub close to the Heath, of interest primarily for its large beer garden and its basement skittle alley. Hampstead tube.

Holly Bush, 22 Holly Mount, NW3. A lovely old gas-lit pub, tucked away in the steep backstreets of Hampstead village. Mobbed on the weekend. Hampstead tube.

Dulwich and Greenwich

Crown & Greyhound, 73 Dulwich Village, SE21. Grandiose Victorian pub with ornate plasterwork ceiling and a nice summer beer garden. Convenient for the Picture Gallery. North Dulwich train station.

Cutty Sark, Ballast Quay, off Lassell St, SE10. The nicest riverside pub in Greenwich, yet much less touristy than the *Trafalgar Tavern* (it's a couple of minutes walk further east, following the river). Maze Hill train station.

Trafalgar Tavern, 5 Park Row, SE10. Great riverside position and a mention in Dickens *Our Mutual Friend* have made this Regency-style inn a firm tourist favourite. Good whitebait and other snacks. Maze Hill train station.

Chiswick to Richmond

Dove, 19 Upper Mall, W6. Old, old riverside pub with literary associations, the smallest back bar in the UK (4ft by 7ft), and Thai food in the evening. Ravenscourt Park tube.

White Cross Hotel, Water Lane, Richmond. With a longer pedigree and more character than its rivals, the *White Cross* is also closer to the river, has a garden out back and serves filling pub food. Richmond tube.

White Swan, Riverside, Twickenham. Decent food and beer and a quiet riverside location – with a beer pontoon overlooking Eel Pie Island if you want to get even closer to the water. Twickenham train station.

Nightlife

On any night of the week London offers a vast range of things to do after dark, ranging from top-flight opera and theatre to clubs with a life span of a couple of nights. The **listings magazine** *Time Out*, which comes out every Wednesday, is essential if you want to get the most out of this city, giving full details of prices and access, plus previews and reviews.

Don't believe the hype over the last couple of years about the new, Cool Britannia: as far as London is concerned, there's been a bewildering range of places to go after dark for at least the last couple of decades. The live music scene remains amazingly diverse, encompassing all variations of **rock, blues, roots** and **world music**. And although London's **jazz clubs** aren't on a par with those in the big American cities there's a highly individual scene of home-based artists, supplemented by top-name visiting players.

London is seriously into **dance music** – from hardcore to house, from techno to trance. Venues once used exclusively by performing bands now pepper the week with club nights, and you often find dance sessions starting as soon as the band's stopped playing. Bear in mind, then, that there's an overlap between "live music venues" and "clubs" in the listings below; we've indicated which places serve a double function.

London has enjoyed a reputation for quality **theatre** since the time of Shakespeare, and despite the increasing prevalence of fail-safe blockbuster musicals and revenue-spinning star vehicles, the city still provides a platform for innovation. **Cinema** is rather less healthy, for London's repertory film theatres are a dying breed, edged out by the multiscreen complexes, which show mainstream Hollywood fare some months behind America. There are a few excellent independent cinemas, though, including the National Film Theatre, which is the focus of the richly varied **London International Film Festival**, in November.

Live music venues

London is hard to beat for its musical mix: whether you're into **jazz, indie rock, R&B, blues** or **world music** you'll find something worth hearing on almost any night of the week. Entry prices for gigs run from a couple of pounds for an unknown band thrashing it out in a pub to around £30 for the likes of U2, but £10–15 is the average price for a good night out – not counting expenses at the bar.

Rock and blues clubs and pubs

12 Bar Club, 22–23 Denmark Place, WC2. Seven nights a week this club plays a combination of live blues and contemporary country. Tottenham Court Road tube.

Astoria, 157 Charing Cross Rd, WC2. One of London's best and most central venues. A large, balconied one-time theatre that goes for slightly alternative bands, with club nights on Friday and Saturday. *LA2*, next door, is primarily a club, but also attracts less-well-known bands. Tottenham Court Road tube.

Borderline, Orange Yard, off Manette St, W1. Intimate basement joint with diverse musical policy. Good place to catch new bands, although big ones sometimes turn up under a pseudonym. Also has club nights. Tottenham Court Road tube.

Brixton Academy, 211 Stockwell Rd, SW9. This refurbished Victorian hall, complete with Roman decorations, can hold 4000, and usually does, but manages to seem small and friendly, probably because no one is forced to sit down. Hosts mainly mid-league bands, and has renowned club all-nighters too. Brixton tube.

Forum, 9–17 Highgate Rd, NW5. The *Forum* is perhaps the capital's best medium-sized venue – large enough to attract established bands, and with great views and good bars. Kentish Town tube.

The Mean Fiddler, 24–28a Harlesden High St, NW10. An excellent, if unfortunately located, small venue with a main hall and smaller acoustic room. The music veers from rock to world to folk to soul (and even, occasionally, gospel). Willesden Junction tube.

The Orange, 3 North End Crescent, W14. Pub-like venue for serious-minded jazz-funkers. There are also club nights (nights vary). West Kensington tube.

Rock Garden, 35 The Piazza, WC2. Central, loud-music joint where you can get in free if you dine at the attached burger place first. Covent Garden tube.

Roadhouse, 35 The Piazza, WC2. American food, 1950s American decor and a line-up of mainly blues and rock'n'roll bands performing to an older, nostalgic crowd. Covent Garden tube.

Station Tavern, 41 Bramley Rd, W10. Arguably London's best blues venue, with free and occasionally great blues six nights a week. Latimer Road tube.

Subterania, 12 Acklam Rd, W10. One of the original live music/club crossover venues in an arch under a bridge. The crowd is as trendy as the music. Ladbroke Grove tube.

Underworld, 174 Camden High St, NW1. This labyrinthine venue is good for new bands and has sporadic club nights. Camden Town tube.

Jazz, world music and roots

100 Club, 100 Oxford St, W1. After a brief spell as a stage for punk bands, the *100 Club* is once again an unpretentious and inexpensive trad jazz venue. Tottenham Court Road tube.

606 Club, 90 Lots Rd, SW10. A rare for London all-jazz venue, located off the untrendy end of the King's Road. You can book a table, and the licensing laws dictate that you must eat if you want to drink, but there's no cover charge. Fulham Broadway tube.

Africa Centre, 38 King St, WC2. African bands perform here in a packed old hall. The atmosphere is usually great, as most of the audience are London-based Africans. It also has a market. Covent Garden tube.

Jazz Café, 5 Parkway, NW1. Slick modern venue with an adventurous booking policy exploring Latin, rap, funk, hip-hop and other unlikely avenues. Die-hard trad-jazz fans won't be happy. Camden Town tube.

Ronnie Scott's, 47 Frith St, W1. The most famous jazz club in London: small and smoky and still going strong, even though the great man himself has passed away. The place for top-line names, who play two sets – one at around 10pm, the other after midnight. Book a table, or you'll have to stand. Leicester Square tube.

Clubs

More than ten years after the explosion of acid-house, London is still up-for-it. The sheer diversity of dance music has enabled London to maintain its status as Europe's **dance capital** – and is still a port of call for DJs from around the world. Recent relaxations in late-night licensing have allowed many venues to keep serving alcohol until 6am or even later. This resurgence in alcohol in clubland (much to the relief of the breweries) has been echoed by the meteoric rise of the club-bar (see box opposite).

Nearly all **dance clubs** open their doors between 10pm and midnight. Some are open six or seven nights a week, some keep irregular days, others just open at the weekend – and very often a venue will host a different club on each night of the week. Admission **charges** vary enormously, with small midweek nights starting at around £3 and large weekend events charging as much as £25; around £10 is the average for a

CLUB-BARS

The most notable event in the clubbing world of late has been the arrival of the **club-bar**: essentially a bar with modern decor, dance music and a club clientele. Some of the places listed below are more like bars and not all of them have DJs, but all are more about socializing rather than dancing. However, there's no denying it gets tedious when you have to yell.

A.K.A., West Central St, WC1. Minimalist bar, next door to *The End*. Chrome balcony overlooks the main floor, which includes a well-stocked bar where you can eat such delights as Butternut squash and chive soup. Tottenham Court Road tube.

Alphabet, 61–63 Beak St, W1. Upstairs is light and spacious with decadent leather sofas and mouth-watering food; downstairs, the dimmed coloured lights and car seats make for an altogether seedier atmosphere. Oxford Circus tube.

Atlantic, 20 Glasshouse St, W1. Still a popular choice for the glitzy crowd. Three bars designed in the Art Deco style attract a mixed clientele. Oxford Circus tube.

Bar Vinyl, 6 Inverness St, NW1. Funky glass-bricked place complete with record shop downstairs. Has a break-beat and trip-hop vibe. Camden Town tube.

Detroit, 35 Earlham St, WC2. Cavernous underground venue mixing open-plan bar area and secluded Gaudiesque booths. Stocks a huge range of spirits. DJs take over at the weekends, with underground house popular on Saturdays. Covent Garden tube.

Dog House, 187 Wardour St, W1. Dark, smoky basement bar popular for hip-hop, funk and acid-jazz. Leicester Square tube.

Jerusalem, 33–34 Rathbone Place, W1. At the time of writing, this is the place to be seen. Decor is all chandeliers and velvet drapes; astonishing diversity of music. Tottenham Court Road tube.

The Notting Hill Arts Club, 21 Notting Hill Gate, W11. Basement bar, popular for everything from Latin-inspired funk, jazz and disco through to soul, house and garage. Notting Hill Gate tube.

Riki Tik, 23–24 Bateman St, W1. One of the original club-bars. Slightly worn, but still a great place to hang out. House and breakbeats dominate. Tottenham Court Road tube.

Friday and Saturday night, but bear in mind that profit margins at the bar are even more outrageous than at live music venues.

Club venues

333, 333 Old St, EC1. Three floors of drum'n'bass, twisted disco and breakbeat madness. Old Street tube.

Aquarium, 256 Old St, EC1. The place with the pool – when all the beautiful young things get hot and sweaty they can dive in and cool off. Popular for speed garage nights. Old Street tube.

The Arches, 53 Southwark St, SE1. A good place to head if you like your music retro. Soul, funk and disco from the Seventies and Eighties. London Bridge tube.

Astoria, 157 Charing Cross Rd, W1. Massive dance floor packed with up-for-it clubbers on Friday and Saturday nights. Loads of room for everyone and a nice bar area upstairs for those with no energy left. Tottenham Court Road tube.

Bagley's, King's Cross Goods Yard, off York Way, N1. Vast warehouse-style venue. The perfect place for enormous raves, with a different DJ in each of the three rooms, and a chill-out bar complete with sofas. King's Cross tube.

Bar Rumba, 36 Shaftesbury Ave, W1. Small West End venue with a programme of Latin, jazz-based and funk dance. Many of the punters are regulars. An unpretentious place frequented by happy people and well noted in clubbing circles for its amazing diversity. Piccadilly Circus tube.

Blue Note, 1–5 Parkfield St, N1. Everything from Indian music on Mondays to a live acoustic set on Saturdays. Other floors play a funky mix of house, garage, hip-hop and swing, with a great sound system and a lively crowd. The massive Sunday night drum'n'bass session (*Metalheadz*) is always rammed. Angel tube.

Café de Paris, 3 Coventry St, W1. Elegantly restored ballroom that plays house, garage and disco to a smartly dressed, trendy crowd – no jeans or trainers. Leicester Square tube.

Camden Palace, 1 Camden High St, NW1. Most often home to Balearic beats; great lights, great sound, heaving crowds. Camden Town tube.

Chunnel Club, 101 Timworth St, SE1. Chiefly a house venue and justly famous for *Sunny Side Up* which runs all day on Sundays. Dress code is a smile. Vauxhall tube.

Cloud 9, 67–68 Albert Embankment, SE1. Friendly venue, under the arches. One arch for full-on house and techno and the other for the chill out. Vauxhall tube.

The Cross, Goods Way Depot, off York Way, N1. Hidden underneath the arches the favourite flavours of this renowned club are hard-house, house and garage. It's bigger than you imagine, but always rammed with chic clubby types, and there's a fabulous garden – perfect for those chill-out moments. King's Cross tube.

Electric Ballroom, 184 Camden High St, NW1. Attracts a mixed crowd with a wide range of sounds: from rock to hip-hop, jazz to house. Camden Town tube.

The End, 18 West Central St, WC1. A club designed for clubbers, by clubbers – large and spacious with chrome minimalist decor. Well known for all music styles, and especially noted for monthly nights hosted by other clubs or record labels. Holborn tube.

Fridge, Town Hall Parade, Brixton Hill, SW2. South London's big night out, with a musical policy running from funk to garage. Great gay nights and top techno tunes. Occasional home to *Escape from Samsara*, the night with the psychedelic, trancy vibe and hippie market. Brixton tube.

Gardening Club, 4 The Piazza, WC2. Unusually for a central London club, the *Gardening Club* is surprisingly good. A popular choice for house and garage, but be warned, early on you'll be sharing the dance floor with beer-boys and bemused tourists. Covent Garden tube.

Gossips, 69 Dean St, W1. Cave-like basement club that seems to have been around forever. Located deep in the heart of Soho, it's a popular stop for reggae and hip-hop fans. Tottenham Court Road tube.

Hanover Grand, 6 Hanover St, W1. A former Masonic hall, that's now a cool and extravagant club, with a great lights and sound system, a fine dance floor, lots of alcoves – and air conditioning. Popular with the glammed up, glittery and beautiful crew. Oxford Circus tube.

HQs, West Yard, Camden Lock, NW1. Smallish venue by the canal with a range of nights, although the emphasis is on uplifting house through to salsa. Friendly vibe. Camden Town tube.

Iceni, 11 White Horse St, W1. Three-floor club patronized by a slightly older, self-consciously stylish, well-off crowd. Music ranges from funk and rap to house, but is always the last word in drop-dead cool. Green Park tube.

LA2, 157 Charing Cross Rd. Fantastic Nineties-house-meets-disco place with gay and straight nights. The legendary *Carwash* (on Saturdays) is the epitome of all things Seventies – you'll have to dress up to get in. Tottenham Court Road tube.

The Leisure Lounge, 121 Holborn, EC1. This place has had it's share of the big-name nights, and is always a good place to check out the latest grooves. Two dance floors – one a full-on dance zone, the other a more relaxed bar area. Chancery Lane or Farringdon tube.

Ministry of Sound, 103 Gaunt St, SE1. A vast, state-of-the-art club based on New York's legendary *Paradise Garage*, with an exceptional sound system. Corporate clubbing and full of tourists, but it still draws the top talent. Elephant & Castle tube.

Office, 3–5 Rathbone Place W1. Various music styles but noted as home to the original mid week session where you can play silly board games like Ker-Plunk. Booking a table in advance is advised. Tottenham Court Road tube.

Plastic People, 37–39 Oxford St, W1. Surprisingly undiscovered for such a central location. Small, but perfectly formed; funky deep-house, cheerful punters and reasonable prices. Tottenham Court Road tube.

Salsa! 96 Charing Cross Rd, WC2. Funky salsa-based club where you can book a table to eat as you jive. Leicester Square tube.

Subterania, 12 Acklam Rd, W10. In the heart of trendy Notting Hill, worth a visit for its diverse (but dressy) club nights on Fridays and Saturdays. Ladbroke Grove tube.

SW1, 191 Victoria St, SW1. Serious clubbers congregate at this Edwardian oak-panelled dance hall for some hard-house and speed garage. Sunday afternoons attract a less sweaty crowd. Victoria tube.

Turnmills, 63 Clerkenwell Rd, EC1. Swanky coffee bar upstairs, fantastic alien-invasion-style bar and funky split-level dance floor in the main room. *Heavenly Jukebox* on Saturdays is followed at 4am by the awesomely glorious gay extravaganza, *Trade*. Farringdon tube.

The Velvet Room, 143 Charing Cross Rd, WC2. Very cool velvet-dripping interior, with house, techno and drum'n'bass nights. Tottenham Court Road tube.

The Wag Club, 35 Wardour St, W1. In need of an overhaul, but still going strong, with two floors of sounds. The dance music and Eighties-revival nights are popular. Wild, psychedelic interior with funky music to match. Leicester Square or Piccadilly Circus tube.

Gay and lesbian bars and clubs

Lesbian and gay Londoners have a lot to be cheerful about, with a scene that is the envy of most other world capitals and a political climate that seems increasingly to embrace the sexual diversity of its population. **Soho** remains the country's most vibrant "gay village", though it's less male-dominated than it was. Details of most events appear in *Time Out* and the many free gay **listings guides** distributed in bars, clubs and bookshops, or you can tune in to the Thursday night *Lavender Lounge* radio programme on GLR (94.5FM). Another excellent source of information is the London **Lesbian and Gay Switchboard** (☎0171/837 7324), which operates around the clock.

Bars and cafés

There are loads of lesbian and gay watering holes in London, many of them operating as **cafés** by day and transforming into **drinking dens** at night. Lots have **disco nights** and are open until the early hours, making them a fine alternative to the more expensive clubs. This selection will give you a good idea of the range on offer, but almost every corner of London has its own gay local.

79CXR, 79 Charing Cross Rd, WC2. Busy, cruisey men's den on two floors, with industrial decor, late licence and a no-messing atmosphere. Leicester Square tube.

Angel, 65 Graham St, N1. Relaxed, Mediterranean-style lesbian and gay café/bar, attracting a mixed but generally upmarket crowd, and especially popular with women. The food is good, the exhibitions eye-catching, and the sofas comfy. Angel tube.

Balans, 60 Old Compton St, W1. This relaxed (but not especially cheap) café-bar is open all night at weekends, late during the week, and always packed, with a singer or cabaret after 11pm. Be warned though – you may have to promise to eat to get in at busy times, even if you just want a coffee. Leicester Square tube.

Bar Code, 3–4 Archer St, W1. Stylish, busy men's cruise- and dance-bar on two floors in the middle of Soho. Piccadilly tube.

The Black Cap, 171 Camden High St, NW1. North London cabaret institution – a big venue on the drag scene, with live acts almost every night. A friendly mixed (mainly male) crowd joins in the fun. *Mrs Shufflewick's Bar* upstairs is quieter, and opens onto a lush and lovely roof garden. Camden Town tube.

The Box, 32–34 Monmouth St, WC2. Bright, gay-owned café-bar serving good food for a mixed gay/straight crowd during the day, and becoming queerer as the night draws in. *Box Babes* on Sunday nights sees girlpower take it over. Covent Garden or Leicester Square tube.

Brief Encounter, 41–43 St Martin's Lane, WC2. One of the longest-running gay bars in London. One bar is bright and busy, the other dim and busy. A popular pre-*Heaven* or post-opera hang-out (it's next door to the Coliseum). Leicester Square tube.

Candy Bar, 4 Carlisle St, W1. Britain's first seven-day all-girl bar is right in the heart of gay-boys' land and offers three floors of varied lesbo action: a retro-style cocktail bar upstairs, beer and elbows-in-yer-face on ground level, and a range of club nights in the packed basement. Gay men welcome as guests. Be warned, some nights you can queue and queue and queue. Tottenham Court Road tube.

Compton's, 53 Old Compton St, W1. Large, traditional-style pub in the centre of Soho, always busy and with a youngish crowd, but still a relaxed place to cruise or just hang out. Lesbians are a rare, but not unwelcome, sight. Leicester Square or Piccadilly tube.

First Out, 52 St Giles High St, WC2. The first gay café-bar in the West End and still packed, serving good veggie food at reasonable prices. Upstairs is airy and non-smoking, downstairs dark and smoky. *Girl Friday* is a women-only pre-club Friday night session; gay men welcome as guests. Tottenham Court Road tube.

Freedom, 60–66 Wardour St, W1. Hip, busy café-bar, popular and occasionally just a little posey. Fashionably health-conscious beverages complement the more decadent liquids on offer. The theatre space downstairs occasionally transforms itself into a seriously funky basement club. Leicester Square or Piccadilly tube.

The Glass Bar, West Lodge, Euston Square Gardens, 190 Euston Rd, NW1. Difficult to find, but never forgotten, this friendly and intimate women-only bar is housed in a listed building with a wrought-iron spiral staircase. Open to members (you become one once you've found it) Tuesday to Saturday till late, with a mellow soundtrack and live jazz monthly. Euston tube.

Her/She Bar at *Jacomo's*, 88–89 Cowcross St, EC1. This new women's bar boasts stylish but strangely soulless decor, although it does have a good selection of board games. Weekly indie DJs and live music on Sundays jazz it up a bit. Gay men welcome as guests during the week, women-only at weekends. Farringdon tube.

Old Compton Café, 34 Old Compton St, W1. Open all day, every day, this gay coffee-bar is the obvious answer to pre- or post-party peckishness. Tottenham Court Road tube.

Village Soho, 81 Wardour St, W1. Elegant bi-level café-bar attracting more pretty boys than women, but striving to redress the balance. Leicester Square tube.

The Yard, 57 Rupert St, W1. Attractive café-bar, making full use of its courtyard and loft areas. Good food, weekly cabaret – including *Screamers*, the queer comedy club – and fortune tellers. Piccadilly Circus tube.

Clubs

The majority of lesbian and gay **clubs** are still one-nighters at established venues (listed in the mainstream "clubs and discos" above), such as *DTPM* at *The End*, *G.A.Y.* at the *Astoria*, and *Popstartz* at the *Leisure Lounge*. Those listed below are the city's permanent gay and lesbian clubs.

Ace of Clubs, 52 Piccadilly, W1. It calls itself legendary, and it's certainly an institution. This weekly Saturday night women-only club for all ages and styles has been packing them in for years and shows no sign of losing its appeal. Piccadilly Circus tube.

Heaven under The Arches, Villiers St, WC2. This legendary, 2000-capacity club has had major cosmetic surgery of late and emerged with its reputation as the UK's most popular gay club unscathed. Big nights are Mondays (*Popcorn*), Wednesdays (*Fruit Machine*) and Saturdays (*Just Heaven*). More boys than girls. Charing Cross or Embankment tube.

The Hoist, Railway Arch 47c, South Lambeth Rd, SW8. Weekend men's cruise bar with leather/rubber/industrial/uniform dress code. Also hosts *SM Gays* every third Thursday. Vauxhall tube.

Substation Soho, 1a Dean St, W1. Steamy, cruisey, sleazy and mostly boysy late-night haunts offering a diverse seven-day menu of dress codes and musical preferences. Tottenham Court Road tube.

Underground at Central Station, 37 Wharfdale Rd, N1. The basement of this friendly, three-tiered pub yields sleazy late-night cruising seven nights a week and is also host to *Gummi*, Europe's only rubber-only club, every second Sunday of the month. Equally picturesque theme nights include *Blacksmiths*, *Meatpackers*, *Locker Room* and *Glory Hole*. King's Cross tube.

Theatre and cinema

London's two big government-subsidized **theatre** companies are the National Theatre, performing in three theatres on the South Bank (☎0171/452 3000), and the Royal Shakespeare Company, whose productions transfer to the two houses in the Barbican (☎0171/638 8891) after their run in Stratford. For a show that's had good reviews, tickets under £10 are difficult to come by at either, but it's always worth ringing their box offices for details of standby deals, which can get you the best seat in the house for as little as £5 if you're a student, otherwise £10. Similar deals are offered by many of London's scores of theatres. Venues with a reputation for challenging productions include the Almeida, Bush, Donmar Warehouse, Royal Court, Young Vic, Tricycle and the ICA.

The Society of London Theatres ticket booth (Mon–Sat 2.30–6.30pm; noon–2.30pm matinees only) in Leicester Square sells **half-price tickets** for that day's performances at all the West End theatres, but they specialize in the top end of the price range. The Charing Cross Road and Leicester Square areas also have offices that can get tickets for virtually all shows, but the mark-up can be outrageous. Beware that if you buy from touts, there's no guarantee that the tickets aren't fakes.

There are an awful lot of **cinemas** in the West End, but only a very few places committed to non-mainstream movies, and even fewer repertory cinemas programming serious films from the back catalogue. London's main repertory cinemas in the centre are the National Film Theatre (☎0171/928 3232) on the South Bank and the ICA (☎0171/930 3647), both of which charge for day membership on top of the ticket price. It's always worth checking what's on at the Renoir (Brunswick Square; Russell Square tube), the Gate (Notting Hill Gate), the Metro (Rupert Street, near Leicester Square), and the cut-price Prince Charles (Leicester Square). November's **London Film Festival**, which occupies half a dozen West End cinemas, is so popular that most of the films sell out within a couple of days of the publication of the festival's programme.

Classical music, opera and dance

For **classical concerts** the principal venue is the South Bank Centre, where the biggest names appear at the Royal Festival Hall, with more specialized programmes staged in the Queen Elizabeth Hall and Purcell Room (all three halls ☎0171/960 4242). Programmes in the massive concert hall of the Barbican Centre, Silk Street, EC2 (☎0171/638 8891), are too often pitched at the corporate audience, though it has the occasional classy recital. For **chamber music**, the intimate and elegant Wigmore Hall, 36 Wigmore St, W1 (☎0171/935 2141), is many a Londoner's favourite. Tickets for all these venues begin at about £7, with cheap standbys sometimes available to students on the evening of the performance.

From July to September each year, **the Proms** at the Royal Albert Hall (☎0171/589 8212) feature at least one concert daily, with hundreds of standing seats sold for just £3 on the night. The acoustics aren't the world's best, but the calibre of the performers is unbeatable and the programme is a fascinating mix of standards and new or obscure works. The hall is so vast that only megastars like Jessye Norman can pack it out, so if you turn up half an hour before the show starts there should be little risk of being turned away. All year round, from Monday to Friday, there are **free lunchtime concerts** in many of London's churches, with performances of chamber music or solo works by students or professionals.

Covent Garden's **Royal Opera House**, expensively refurbished for the new millennium, is hoping to dispel its elitist, but not its classy, reputation. The **English National Opera** at the Coliseum, St Martin's Lane (☎0171/632 8300), has more radical producers and is a more democratic institution – tickets begin at £8 and any unsold seats are released on the day of the performance at greatly reduced prices; all works are sung in English.

In addition to the big two opera houses, smaller halls often stage more innovative productions by touring companies such as Opera North – the Queen Elizabeth Hall is a regular venue. Nowadays the Royal Opera House has a better reputation for **ballet** than for singing, as its resident **Royal Ballet Company** can call on the talents of Darcy Bussell and Sylvie Guillem, to name just two of its most glamorous stars. Visiting classical companies also appear regularly at the Coliseum, and less frequently at the Royal Albert Hall. London's **contemporary dance** scene is no less exciting – adventurous programmes are staged at the South Bank, the ICA, Sadler's Wells, The Place, as well as at numerous more ad hoc venues.

Listings

Airlines American Airlines (☎0345/789789); British Airways (☎0345/222111); Lufthansa (☎0345/737747); Virgin Atlantic (☎01293/747747).

Airport enquiries Gatwick (☎01293/535353); Heathrow (☎0181/759 4321); London City (☎0171/646 0000); Stansted (☎01279/680500).

American Express 6 Haymarket, SW1 (Mon–Fri 9am–5.30pm, Sat 9am–6pm, Sun 10am–1pm & 2–5pm; ☎0171/930 4411).

Bike rental Bikepark, 14 Stukeley St, WC1 (☎0171/430 0083).

Books Foyles, 119 Charing Cross Rd, WC2, is London's most famous bookshop but is chaotically organized. Neighbouring Waterstones is preferable, as are Books Etc and Blackwells across the road, and the university bookshop Dillons, 82 Gower St, WC1. For more radical publications, call in at Compendium, 234 Camden High St, NW1, a London institution for everything from anarchy to Zen Buddhism. For maps and travel books, go to Stanford's, 12 Long Acre, WC2 or The Travel Bookshop, 13 Blenheim Crescent, W11.

Bus information Long-distance coach services depart from Victoria Coach Station, Buckingham Palace Rd (Victoria tube). National Express have ticket offices here (☎0990/808080) and can tell you about European services operated by Eurolines.

Car rental You'll find cheapish rates at Holiday Autos (☎0990/300400). The multinational firms also have outlets all over London; ring their central switchboards to find the nearest one: Avis (☎0990/900500), Budget (☎0800/181181), Hertz (☎0990/996699).

Dentist Emergency treatment: Guy's Hospital, St Thomas's St, SE1 (Mon–Fri 9am–3pm; ☎0171/955 4317).

Embassies Australia, Australia House, The Strand, WC2 (☎0171/379 4334); Canada, 1 Grosvenor Square, W1 (☎0171/258 6600); Ireland, 17 Grosvenor Place, SW1 (☎0171/235 2171); New Zealand, New Zealand House, 80 Haymarket, SW1 (☎0171/930 8422); South Africa, South Africa House, Trafalgar Square, WC2 (☎0171/930 4488); USA, 24 Grosvenor Square, W1 (☎0171/499 9000).

Exchange Shopping areas such as Oxford Street and Covent Garden are littered with private exchange offices, and there are 24-hour booths at the biggest central tube stations, but their rates are always worse than the banks. Oxford Street, Regent Street and Piccadilly are where you'll find the major branches of all the main banks.

Hospitals The most central hospitals with 24-hour emergency units are: Chelsea & Westminster, 369 Fulham Rd, SW10 (☎0181/746 8000); Royal London Hospital, Whitechapel Rd, E1 (☎0171/377 7000); St Mary's Hospital, Praed St, W2 (☎0171/886 6666); University College Hospital, Grafton Way, WC1 (☎0171/387 9300).

Left luggage AIRPORTS Gatwick: North Terminal (daily 6am–10pm; ☎01293/502013); South Terminal (24hr; ☎01293/502014). Heathrow: Terminal 1 (daily 6am–11pm; ☎0181/745 5301); Terminal 2 (daily 6am–10.30pm; ☎0181/745 4599); Terminal 3 (daily 5.30am–10.30pm; ☎0181/759 3344); Terminal 4 (daily 5.30am–11pm; ☎0181/745 7460). London City Airport (Mon–Fri 6am–9.30pm, Sat 6am–1pm, Sun 10.30am–9.30pm; ☎0171/646 0000). Stansted Airport (24hr; ☎01279/662082). TRAIN STATIONS Charing Cross (daily 7.15am–11pm; ☎0171/839 4282); Euston (daily 6.45am–11.15pm; ☎0171/320 0528); Paddington (Mon–Sat 7am–10pm, Sun 8am–10pm; ☎0171/313 1514); Victoria (daily 7am–10.15pm, plus lockers; ☎0171/928 5151 x29887); Waterloo (daily 7am–11pm; ☎0171/928 2424).

London Transport enquiries 24-hour information on ☎0171/222 1234.

Lost property AIRPORTS Gatwick (daily 7.30am–5.30pm; ☎01293/50316); Heathrow (Mon–Fri 8am–5pm, Sat & Sun 8am–4pm; ☎0181/745 7727); London City (Mon–Fri 6am–9.30pm, Sat 6am–1pm, Sun 10.30am–9.30pm; ☎0171/646 0000); Stansted (daily 5.30am–11pm; ☎01279/680500). TRAIN STATIONS Euston (Mon–Sat 9am–5pm, Sun 11am–7pm; ☎0171/922 6477); King's Cross (daily 8am–7.45pm; ☎0171/922 9081); Liverpool St (Mon–Fri 7am–7pm, Sat & Sun 7am–2pm; ☎0171/928 9158); Paddington (Mon–Sat 7am–10pm, Sun 8am–10pm; ☎0171/313 1514); Victoria (daily 7am–10.15pm; ☎0171/922 9887); Waterloo (Mon–Fri 7.30am–8pm; ☎0171/401 7861). TUBE TRAINS London Regional Transport (☎0171/486 2496).

Markets Camden, Camden High Street to Chalk Farm Road – mainly clothes and cheap jewellery (Wed–Sun 9am–5pm; Camden Town tube); Brick Lane – everything from sofas to antique cameo brooches (Sunday from dawn to around midday; Aldgate East tube); Greenwich, Market Square –

small arty-crafty market (Sat & Sun 9am–5pm; Greenwich train station); Petticoat Lane, Middlesex Street and Goulston Street – cheap and cheerful clothes (Sun 9am–4pm; Aldgate East or Liverpool Street tube); Portobello, Portobello Rd – mostly boho-chic clothes and portable antiques (Sat 9am–5pm; Notting Hill or Ladbroke Grove tube); Spitalfields, Commercial Street – arty-crafty during the week plus organic fruit and veg on Fridays and Sundays (Mon–Fri 11am–3pm, Sun 9am–3pm).

Pharmacies Every police station keeps a list of emergency pharmacies in its area.

Police The most central police station is at 10 Vine St, W1 (☎0171/437 1212), just off Regent Street. In emergencies dial ☎999.

Post offices The Trafalgar Square post office (24–28 William IV St, WC2 4DL) has the longest opening hours (Mon–Fri 8am–8pm, Sat 9am–8pm). It's to this post office that poste restante mail should be sent.

Train stations and information As a broad guide, Euston handles services to northwest England and Glasgow; King's Cross northeast England and Edinburgh; Liverpool Street eastern England; Paddington western England; Victoria and Waterloo southeast England. For information, call national rail enquiries on ☎0345/484950.

Travel agents Campus Travel, 52 Grosvenor Gardens, SW1 (☎0171/730 3402); Council Travel, 28a Poland St, W1 (☎0171/437 7767); STA Travel, 86 Old Brompton Rd, SW7 (☎0171/361 6161); Trailfinders, 42–50 Earl's Court Rd, SW5 (☎0171/938 3366).

travel details

Trains from:

London Charing Cross to: Dover Priory (every 30min; 1hr 45min–2hr).

London Euston to: Birmingham New St (every 30min; 1hr 40min); Carlisle (every 1–2hr; 3hr 50min); Chester (3 daily; 2hr 40min); Crewe (hourly; 2hr); Lancaster (8 daily; 3hr); Liverpool Lime St (hourly; 2hr 45min); Manchester Piccadilly (hourly; 2hr 30min).

London King's Cross to: Brighton (every 10–40min; 1hr 15min); Cambridge (every 30min; 50min); Durham (every 1–2hr; 2hr 50min); Leeds (hourly; 2hr 20min); Newcastle (every 30min; 2hr 40min–3hr); York (every 30min; 1hr 40min–2hr).

London Liverpool St to: Cambridge (hourly; 1hr 20min); Harwich (every 2hr; 1hr 10min); Norwich (hourly; 2hr); Stansted (every 30min; 45min).

London Paddington to: Bath (every 30min–hourly; 1hr 25min); Bristol Parkway (every 30min–1hr; 1hr 20min); Exeter St Davids (hourly; 2hr 10min); Oxford (every 30min–hourly; 50min–1hr); Penzance (7 daily; 5hr); Plymouth (every 1–2hr; 3hr–3hr 40min); Worcester (11 daily; 2hr–2hr 15min).

London St Pancras to: Leicester (every 30min; 1hr 15min); Nottingham (hourly; 1hr 50min); Sheffield (hourly; 2hr 20min).

London Victoria to: Brighton (every 30min; 1hr–1hr 20min); Canterbury East (every 30min; 1hr 30min); Canterbury West (hourly; 1hr 50min); Dover Priory (hourly; 1hr 50min); Gatwick (frequently; 30min) ; Ramsgate (hourly; 1hr 50min);.

London Waterloo to: Portsmouth Harbour (every 30min; 1hr 35min); Southampton Central (every 20min; 1hr 15min); Winchester (every 20min; 55min–1hr 5min).

Buses from Victoria Coach Station to:

Bath (11 daily; 3hr 15min); **Birmingham** (hourly; 2hr); **Brighton** (hourly; 1hr 45min); **Bristol** (hourly; 2hr 20min); **Cambridge** (hourly; 2hr); **Canterbury** (hourly; 1hr 50min); **Carlisle** (3–4 daily; 6hr); **Chester** (5–6 daily; 5hr 30min); **Dover** (hourly; 2hr 45min); **Exeter** (8 daily; 4hr); **Gloucester** (10 daily; 3hr) **Liverpool** (5–6 daily; 4hr 30min); **Manchester** (9 daily; 4hr 15min); **Oxford** (frequently; 1hr 30min); **Plymouth** (7 daily; 4hr 40min); **York** (3 daily; 4hr 20min).

CHAPTER TWO

SURREY, KENT AND SUSSEX

T he southeast corner of England was traditionally where London went on holiday. In the past, trainloads of East Enders were shuttled to the hop fields and orchards of **Kent** for a working break from the city; boats ferried people down the Thames to the beach at Margate; and everyone from royalty to cuckolding couples enjoyed the seaside at Brighton, a blot of decadence in the otherwise sedate county of **Sussex**. **Surrey** is the least pastoral and historically significant of the three counties – the home of wealthy metropolitan professionals prepared to commute from what has become known as the "stockbroker belt".

The late twentieth century has brought big changes to the southeast region. In purely administrative terms the three counties have become four, since local government reorganization split Sussex into East and West. More significantly, many of the coastal towns have faced an uphill struggle to keep their tourist custom in the face of ever more accessible foreign destinations. For the old seaside resorts are still at the mercy of the English weather – in winter, or bad weather, the prom is not a fun place to be. To make matters worse, Brighton, long known as "London beside the sea", now matches the capital with one of the highest proportions of homeless people in the country.

The proximity of Kent and Sussex to the continent has dictated the history of this region, which has served as a gateway for an array of invaders, both rapacious and benign. **Roman** remains dot the coastal area – most spectacularly at **Bignor** in Sussex and **Lullingworth** in Kent – and many roads, including the main London to Dover road, follow the arrow-straight tracks laid by the legionaries. When **Christianity** spread through Europe, it arrived in Britain on the **Isle of Thanet** – the northeast tip of Kent, since rejoined to the mainland by silting and subsiding sea levels. In 597 AD Augustine moved inland and established a monastery at **Canterbury**, still the home of the Church of England and the county's prime historic attraction. (Surprisingly, Sussex was among the last counties to accept the Cross – due more to the region's then impenetrable forest than to its innate ungodliness.)

ACCOMMODATION PRICE CODES

Throughout this guide, hotel and B&B accommodation is priced on a scale of ① to ⑨, the number indicating the **lowest price** you could expect to pay per night in that establishment for a **double room** in high season. The prices indicated by the codes are as follows:

① under £40	④ £60–70	⑦ £110–150
② £40–50	⑤ £70–90	⑧ £150–200
③ £50–60	⑥ £90–110	⑨ over £200

The last successful invasion of England took place in 1066, when the **Normans** over-ran King Harold's army near **Hastings**, on a site now marked by **Battle Abbey**. The Normans left their mark all over this corner of England, and Kent remains unmatched in its profusion of medieval castles, among them **Dover**'s sprawling cliff-top fortress guarding against continental invasion and **Rochester**'s huge, box-like citadel, close to the old dockyards of **Chatham**, power-base of the formerly invincible British navy.

Away from the great historic sites, you can spend unhurried days in elegant old towns such as **Royal Tunbridge Wells**, **Rye** and **Lewes**, or enjoy the less-elevated charms of the traditional resorts, of which **Brighton** is far and away the best, combin-ing the buzz of a university town with a blowsy good-time atmosphere and an excellent range of eating options. Dramatic scenery may be in short supply, but in places the **South Downs Way** offers an expanse of rolling chalk uplands that, as much as any-where in the crowded southeast, gets you away from it all. And of course Kent, Sussex and Surrey harbour some of the country's finest **gardens**, ranging from Kew Botanical Gardens' country home at **Wakehurst Place**, the lush flowerbeds of **Sissinghurst** and the great landscaped estates of **Petworth**, **Sheffield Park** and **Scotney Castle**.

The commuter traffic in this corner of England is the heaviest in Europe, so almost everywhere of interest is close to a **train** station. National Express services from London and other parts of England to the region are pretty good, but local **bus** services are much less impressive.

SURREY

Effectively a rural suburb of southern London, for those who can afford it, **Surrey** is bisected laterally by the chalk escarpment of the **North Downs** which rise west of Guildford, peak around Box Hill near **Dorking**, and continue east into Kent. The por-tion of Surrey within the M25 orbital motorway has little natural and virtually no his-torical appeal, being a collection of satellite towns and light industrial installations serv-ing the capital, although an enjoyable day can be spent at **Sandown Park** or **Epsom** racecourses, or trying the rides at one of Surrey's theme parks, **Thorpe Park** or **Chessington World of Adventures**. Outside the M25's ring, Surrey takes on a more pastoral demeanour, with the county town of **Guildford**, the open heathland of Surrey's western borders and **Farnham**, which has the county's only intact castle.

Guildford and around

Nestling in a gap carved through the North Downs by the River Wey, 35 miles south-west of London, **GUILDFORD** has a reputation as something of a dull town. Yet, while it's true that parts of the town are blighted by the one-way system and a surfeit of shop-ping precincts, the town centre does have a certain charm. Guildford came to promi-nence in the early seventeenth century, when the town became a major staging post halfway along the route from London to the flourishing Portsmouth docks; the canal-ization of the River Wey in 1648 reinforced its position on the trade map, with the High Street's Guildhall being the most significant landmark from this era. Within easy reach of the city are two National Trust properties, **Clandon Park** and **Hatchlands Park**, as well as the Royal Horticultural Society's gardens at **Wisley**.

Arrival, information and accommodation

Guildford's main **train station**, with regular trains from London Waterloo and Portsmouth, lies just over the river to the west of the town centre. Between the town

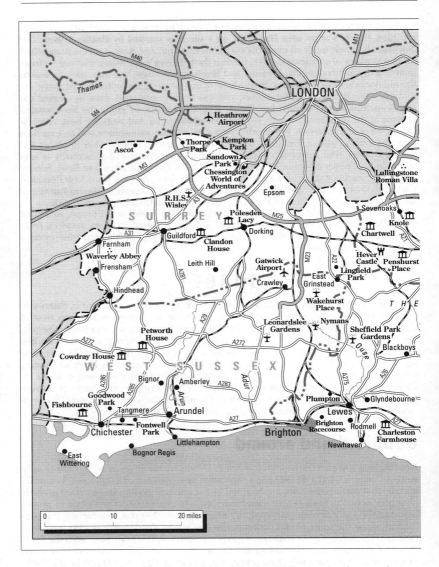

centre and the train station, at the foot of North Street, the **bus station** has regular connections to London, Dorking, Portsmouth and Winchester. The county's main **tourist office** is at 14 Tunsgate (May–Sept Mon–Sat 9am–6pm, Sun 10am–5pm; Oct–April Mon–Sat 9.30am–5.30pm; ☎01483/444333), just off the High Street near the Guildhall.

Inexpensive **accommodation** options in town include *Hillcote*, 11 Castle Hill (☎01483/563324; ①) which offers bargain-rate B&B as does the *Greyfriars* next door

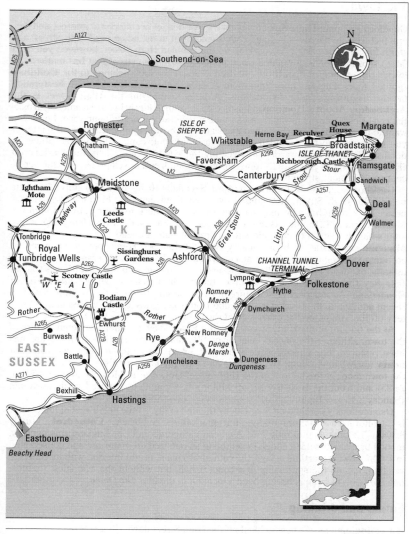

(☎01483/561795; ①). Plusher lodgings can be found at the *Jarvis Guildford Hotel*, Upper High St (☎01483/564511; ⑤) and at the timber-beamed, five-hundred-year-old *Angel Inn* on the High Street (☎01483/564555; ⑦). The nearest **youth hostel** is in the village of Holmbury St Mary, eight miles southeast of Guildford (see p.156). *Loseley Farm* (☎01483/304440), famous for its delicious dairy produce, three miles southwest of the town, also offers basic **camping** facilities.

The Town

Guildford's sloping **High Street** retains a great deal of architectural interest and several picturesque narrow lanes and courts lead off it to the adjoining North Street, and south towards the castle. As you look up the cobbled High Street, however, you can't fail to spot the wonderful gilded clock projecting over the street that has marked the town's time for more than three hundred years. The clock belongs to the **Guildhall** (guided tours Tue & Thurs 2pm, 3pm & 4pm; free) with its elaborate Restoration facade disguising Tudor foundations. A little further up the High Street is the **Archbishop Abbot's Hospital**, a hospice built for the elderly in 1619 fronted by a palatial red-brick Tudor gateway. You can take a peek at the pretty courtyard, but if you want to inspect the Flemish stained glass and oak beams that characterize the interior you must sign up for a guided tour (by appointment; contact the tourist office for details). Back down towards the river on the right, at no. 72, is the **Undercroft** (Easter–Sept Tues & Thurs 2–4pm, Sat noon–4pm; free), a well-preserved thirteenth-century basement of vaulted arches.

Guildford Castle's Norman keep (April–Sept daily 10am–6pm; 85p) sits on its motte behind the High Street, surrounded by flower-filled gardens. Frequently used as a palace by King John, who may have departed from here to Runnymede to sign the Magna Carta in 1215, the castle was enlarged and improved during Henry III's reign, after which it was left to crumble into its present state. Beneath the castle, **Guildford Museum**, in Castle Arch on Quarry Street (Mon–Sat 11am–5pm; free), gives an account of the region's pre-Christian culture and displays cases of ceramic relics as well as some exquisite Saxon jewellery. Upstairs are mementoes to the writer Lewis Carroll (aka Rev Charles Dodgson), author of the children's classic, *Alice's Adventures in Wonderland*. An imaginative sculpture of Alice passing through the looking glass is a recent addition to the Castle Gardens, and Dodgson's grave can be visited in the cemetery off the Mount, on the other side of the river.

At the bottom of the High Street runs the **River Wey**, a rather neglected feature of the town, although the once-crucial River Wey and Godalming Navigation Canal has been restored into a picturesque waterway. From Easter to October, you can **rent boats** (daily 9am–5.30pm; £6 per hour) and take **pleasure cruises** up the river from the town quay, at the bottom of the High Street (July & Aug Mon–Sat 2pm & 3.30pm; £4.25) and from the Boat House, off Millbrook, a couple of hundred yards upstream (Sunday 2.15 & 3.15pm; £2.75).

Ostentatiously perched on Stag Hill by the university, a mile northwest of the centre, is Guildford's monumentally unremarkable red-brick **Cathedral** (daily 8.30am–5.30pm), one of only four Anglican cathedrals built in England this century, topped by a gaudy gilded angel. Resembling an outsized crematorium and consecrated in 1961 following wartime delays, the cathedral's plain, bright interior, with its concrete vaulting, has all the spirituality of a concert hall, but without the acoustics. Its most notable claim to fame is having been a location in the film *The Omen*.

Eating and drinking

For **eating** options, it's best to head off the High Street down Chapel Street, where the stylish Italian-run *Cambio* at no. 10 (☎01483/577702; closed Mon lunch & Sun), offers a set two-course lunch for £10, and the tiny *Café Austria*, at no. 20 (☎01483/537979; closed Sun), serves up everything from free-range Schnitzel to authentic Gugelhupf. Just around the corner, the *Café de Paris* at 35 Castle St (☎01483/564555; closed Sun) is a busy French-style brasserie in a listed building, offering three-course meals from around £14, while *Olivo*, at 53 Quarry St (☎01483/564555; closed Sun), is an innovative *focacceria* serving delicious regional Italian dishes, housed in the town's sixteenth-century dispensary. This place is a foodie's delight: check out their roof-terrace for an alfresco evening meal, but be sure to reserve as they can get very busy, especially at weekends. The same street holds one of Guildford's better **pubs**, the *King's Head*, also with a terrace, serving real ales and inexpensive meals. Guildford's oldest hostelry, *Ye Olde Ship Inn*, is on Portsmouth Road and boasts open fires; alternatively, try the *Jolly Farmer*, a pleasant riverside pub on Millbrook, which offers reasonably priced bar meals and welcomes kids.

Clandon Park and Wisley

Five miles east of Guildford, the Palladian **Clandon Park** (April–Oct Tues–Thurs & Sun 11.30am–4.30pm; £4.30; combined ticket with Hatchlands Park £6.20; NT) was built in the 1730s by Venetian architect Giacomo Leoni, for the second Lord Onslow. The two-storey Marble Hall is particularly impressive as is the Gubbay collection of porcelain, furniture and needlework and the Ivo Forde collection of Meissen Italian comedy figures, also housed here. Within the extensive grounds, landscaped by Capability Brown, there's an outsized souvenir in the form of a Maori meeting house brought back from New Zealand by the fourth Lord Onslow, who had been governor there.

If you're up for another National Trust stately home, buy a combined ticket to get you into **Hatchlands Park** (house: April–Oct Tues–Thurs & Sun 2–5.30pm; grounds April–Oct daily 11.30am–6pm; combined ticket with Clandon £6.20; house £4.30; park & gardens £1.75; NT), a mile or two further along the A246. The grounds are reason enough to come here, with woodland walks and a small Gertrude Jekyll garden, while the **house** itself is a splendid red-brick Palladian pile with richly ornate Robert Adam interiors, a stunning collection of eighteenth- and nineteenth-century keyboard instruments played by the likes of Mozart, Chopin and Mahler, and an exhibition on Admiral Boscawen, who built the house in 1758. Outside, an additional dummy set of windows on the south side of the house adds grandeur, making it look as if there's a third floor, though in fact there are only two.

Five miles northeast of Guildford, signposted off the A3, the Royal Horticultural Society's gardens at **Wisley** (Mon–Fri 10am–6pm or dusk, Sat 9am–6pm or dusk; £5) are a research establishment and a gardeners' garden, with staff on hand to offer advice and solve horticultural queries. The greenhouses contain a vast array of fragile specimens, including orchids and fuchsias; late spring is the best time to visit. The best way to get there by public transport is to catch a train to Woking, from where there is a special bus to Wisley (May–Sept Mon–Fri 11am, returning at 3.30pm; £3).

Farnham and around

Tucked into Surrey's southwestern corner, ten miles west of Guildford along the exposed ridge-top of the Hog's Back, lies **FARNHAM**. Smaller and, in parts, more charming than Guildford, the town moves at a slower pace. Despite its thousand-year history, the majority of Farnham's architecture dates from the eighteenth century, when it enjoyed a boom period based on hop farming.

Yet, Farnham also home to Surrey's only intact **Castle**, built around 1160 by Henry de Blois, Bishop of Winchester, as a convenient residence halfway between his diocese and London. The castle was continuously occupied until 1927, but now houses a conference venue. The **keep** (April–Sept daily 10am–6pm; Oct 10am–5pm or dusk; £2; EH), from where there are good views over the rooftops to the Downs beyond, is the only part of the castle that is open to the public.

Farnham's refined Georgian dwellings are at their best along the broad **Castle Street**, which links the town centre with the castle, but you can actually step inside one of the smart Georgian houses at 38 West St. Once home to one of Farnham's wealthy hop merchants and now containing the **Museum of Farnham** (Tues–Sat 11am–5pm; free) the house on West Street contains a refreshingly succinct rundown on the town's history, its local hero, the eighteenth-century journalist and social reformer William Cobbett, and the highly regarded local art school. On the same street, the town's library is housed in **Vernon House**, where Charles I spent the night in 1648 en route to his trial and eventual execution in London.

Farnham **train station**, with frequent connections to London Waterloo, is five minutes from the centre, over the river on the south edge of town, down South Street and over the bypass. The **tourist office** is housed in the council offices on South St, midway between the station and the centre (Mon–Fri 9.30am–5.15pm, Sat 9am–12.30pm; ☎01252/715109). For **accommodation**, try the excellent *Stafford House Hotel*, 22 Firgrove Hill (☎01252/724336; ②), close to the station, or ask at the tourist office for a list of B&Bs in the area – though most are hard to get to without your own transport. The best of the **B&B** options is *High Wray*, 73 Lodge Hill Rd (☎01252/715589; ②), which lies about a mile south of Farnham Station off the Tilford Road; it's a little off the beaten track, so be sure to ask for clear directions if you're making your own way there, or get a cab there from the station. Once you find it, you'll be rewarded with a peaceful, semi-rural setting, which is conveniently close to the start of the North Downs Way for those that are hiking. Back in town, the French-style brasserie *Café Rouge* on the Borough (☎01252/733688; closed Sun), does decent **food**, while the *Jolly Sailor* **pub** offers reasonable bar meals. Alternatively, if you prefer to eat Italian, there's a choice between the *Pizza Express* (☎01252/733220) or the *Caffé Uno* (☎01252/721193), both on Castle Street.

Waverley Abbey, Frensham and Hindhead

From Farnham station, the B3001 leads two miles southeast to the evocative riverside ruins of **Waverley Abbey**, the first of many Cistercian bases on British soil. Much of the stone was removed from the abbey after the Dissolution to construct Tudor houses in the area, a common fate of such monastic establishments.

Three miles south of Farnham, **FRENSHAM** is set among the heather-covered heathlands that typify the Surrey/Hampshire borders. **Frensham Ponds**, established in medieval times as fish repositories and now popular with anglers, lies just south of town; the land hereabouts is as wild as Surrey gets. Five miles south of here on the A287 lies the village of **HINDHEAD**, whose most famous former resident was Arthur Conan Doyle, creator of the opium-puffing detective Sherlock Holmes. Fans of Conan Doyle can stay in his Edwardian home, now the *Undershaw Hotel* (☎01428/604039; ③), which overlooks Hindhead's main junction. On the northeast edge of town, the curious depression known as the **Devil's Punchbowl** is crisscrossed with walking trails and bridleways. Local legends tell of witches, abductions and satanic rituals in the Punchbowl area, but perpetrators of these stories were most likely cattle thieves and highwaymen preying on the Portsmouth-bound stages. Yak-like Highland cattle graze in the area and the nearby Gibbet Hill, a mile east of the village, a former site of executions, gives the best views of the vicinity.

There is a tiny **youth hostel** (☎01428/604285), on the rim of the Punchbowl, one mile north of Hindhead, signposted off the A3. This secluded hostel, converted from National Trust cottages, makes an idyllic base from which to explore the Punchbowl's trails.

Dorking and around

Set at the mouth of a gap carved by the River Mole through the North Downs, **DORK-ING**, 25 miles from London (frequent trains from Victoria), lies at the intersection of

NORTH SURREY THEME PARKS

Less than an hour's drive southwest of central London lie two popular **theme parks**, both owned by the Tussauds Group and both ranked in the top twenty most visited attractions in the UK – **Chessington** comes in at number five with over one and a half million visitors annually and **Thorpe Park** at number twenty with just under a million visitors. Both parks primarily appeal to the 8–14 age group, and can get extremely crowded during school holidays; an early arrival on summer weekends will avoid long queues for the more popular rides. If it's action you're after, Chessington has the edge, but both easily return their seemingly pricey entrance fees with activities that fill the best part of a day.

Thorpe Park

The purpose-built and water-oriented **Thorpe Park** (times vary, call to check on ☎01932/562633; £17.50) is well signposted off the A320 south of Staines and easily reached by train from London's Waterloo to Staines or Chertsey station, with buses taking you on to the park itself. Set in an old gravel pit next to a concrete works whose machinery is easily mistaken for the latest ride, the park continues to develop new attractions, but is still fairly low-key. Swimwear is a good idea for younger children as the better rides can include a soaking, and it allows them to romp around in the play pool. The watery rides provide grins of amusement rather than screams of delight with the *Loggers Leap* involving an exhilarating fifty-foot drop-off and *Thunder River* being an enjoyable whitish water descent in a huge tyre-like raft. Small children are excluded from these sorts of rides for safety reasons, but are well catered for in the *Octopus's Garden* and the train or boat ride to the small animal farm.

Chessington World of Adventures

Smaller and more animated, but marginally tackier, than Thorpe Park, is **Chessington World of Adventures** (April to mid-July, Sept & Oct daily 10am–5pm; mid-July & Aug daily 10am–9pm; last admission 2hr before closing; £19). The park is signposted off the A243, twelve miles southwest of London, and reached from London's Waterloo train station (to Chessington South) or bus #777 from Victoria. Located in a former zoo, the best way to get the measure of the place is to take the yellow *Safari Skyway* monorail, which introduces you to the few remaining animals, then hop on the *Chessington Railroad* which does a round tour of the rest of the park. Of the better rides the *Dragon River*, *Runaway Minetrain* and *Terrortomb* are all fun rather than frightening, *Seastorm* is a watery favourite, as is *Rameses Revenge*, though it's slightly scarier.

the former Roman Stane Street and the medieval byway known as the **Pilgrim's Way**, which linked Winchester with Canterbury. There's nothing much to see in Dorking itself, but it makes a convenient base for exploring the surrounding countryside. If you want to **stay**, try the *Torridon Guest House* Longfield Rd (☎01306/883724; ②), off Coldharbour Lane, which has just two rooms. For **food**, the *White Horse Inn*, on the High Street, has the best pub meals in town.

Box Hill, on the northern edge of town, is a popular draw for suburban weekenders and a staple of school trips during the week, when the intricacies of the River Mole's contrary flow through the chalk downs are explained. It's a three-hour climb to the top, but the snack-bar (daily 11am–4pm) and the view south over the town and the Weald's sandstone ridges reward the effort. You'll also find the grave of the eccentric local resident Major Peter Labilliere here; the major was famously buried head first, so that, in a topsy-turvy world, he would be the only one to "face his Maker the right way up". The nearest **train station** to Box Hill is Westhumble train station on the Dorking–London line. Box Hill is situated on the 135-mile **North Downs Way**, a tame long-distance footpath stretching from Farnham to Dover and at its best around here with two **youth hostels** nearby.

From the purpose-built **youth hostel** in the village of **Holmbury St Mary** (☎01306/730777; Gomshall train station), six miles southwest of Dorking, it's about an hour's walk to **Leith Hill**, southeastern England's highest point, offering views south to the Channel and north across London. Former local resident Richard Hull built a tower at the hill's summit in 1764, bringing its height up to 1029ft and is now buried beneath it. You can look through a telescope from the top of the **tower** (April–Sept Wed noon–5pm, Sat & Sun 11am–5pm; Oct–March Sat & Sun 11am–3.30pm; 80p; NT). There's a kiosk nearby, selling light refreshments and open the same times as the tower, or you could head for the *Plough* in neighbouring Coldharbour, for real ales and bar meals.

Tanners Hatch **youth hostel**, a basic cottage at the end of a muddy track, two and a half miles northwest of Dorking (☎01372/452528), lies just a mile away from **Polesden Lacey** (house April–Oct Wed–Sun 1.30–5.30pm; grounds daily 11am–6pm or dusk; £3; NT), a Regency-era villa built by Thomas Cubitt in 1824. Renovated in Edwardian times, it houses an assortment of silver, Chinese porcelain, French furniture and paintings, including works by Reynolds.

KENT

Not so long ago Kent's tourist industry was focused chiefly on the resorts of its northern coast and the **Isle of Thanet**. Nowadays these seaside towns have lost much of their gloss, but the county still boasts one of the most popular destinations in the entire country – the county town of **Canterbury**, site of one of the great English cathedrals. Furthermore, Kent can also boast its fair share of alluring castles and gardens, the best known of which are the estate of **Knole**, on the edge of Sevenoaks, **Leeds Castle**, to the west of Maidstone, and **Sissinghurst Gardens** in the heart of the Weald, an inspiration to thousands of amateur horticulturalists. Exploration of the county's other scattered attractions – such as **Scotney Castle**, Winston Churchill's home at **Chartwell**, **Penshurst Place**, **Hever Castle** or the remnants of the Roman villa at Lullingstone – could fill a long and pleasurable weekend.

Transport links from London are good: the A2, M2 and M20 link the Channel ports of Ramsgate, Dover and Folkestone with the capital and rail connections to the county's key towns from London's Charing Cross, Waterloo and Victoria stations are reliable. Sevenoaks, Maidstone, Tunbridge Wells and Canterbury are well served by daily National Express bus services, but local rail and bus links are slow.

The North Kent coast

It's a commonly held view that the northern part of Kent is a scenic and cultural wasteland, a prejudice that stems partly from the fact that most visitors only glimpse the area as they race to or from the Channel ports. However, the region has its fair share of attractions, all of which are easily accessible from the capital. The knot of historic sites at **Chatham** and **Rochester** is followed by the seaside towns of **Whitstable**, **Margate** and **Broadstairs**, once popular resorts that make an interesting mix of the stuffy and the purely frivolous.

Rochester and around

ROCHESTER was first settled by the Romans, who built a fortress on the site of the present **Castle** (daily: April–Sept 10am–6pm; Oct 10am–5pm; Nov–March 10am–4pm; £3.50; EH), at the northwest end of the High Street; some kind of fortification has remained here ever since. In 1077, William I gave Gundulf, architect of the White Tower at the Tower of London, the See of Rochester and the job of improving the defences on the River Medway's northernmost bridge on Watling Street. The castle remains one of the best-preserved examples of a Norman fortress in England. The stark 100-foot-high keep glowers over the town, while its interior is all the better for having lost its floors, allowing clear views up and down the dank interior. It has three square towers and a cylindrical one, the southwest tower, which was rebuilt following its collapse during the siege of the castle in 1215, when the bankrupt King John eventually wrested the castle from its archbishop. The outer walls and two of the towers retain their corridors and spiral stairwells, allowing access to the uppermost battlements.

The foundations of the adjacent **Cathedral** (daily 8.30am–5pm; free) were also Gundulf's work, but the building has been much modified over the past nine hundred years. Plenty of Norman touches have endured, particularly in the cathedral's west front, with its pencil-shaped towers, blind arcading and richly carved portal and tympanum above the doorway. Norman round arches, decorated with zigzags and made from lovely honey-coloured Caen stone, also line the nave. Some fine paintings survived the Dissolution of the Monasteries, most notably the thirteenth-century depiction of the Wheel of Fortune on the walls of the choir (only half of which survives); shown as a treadmill, it is a trenchant image of medieval life's relentless slog. The cathedral once enshrined the remains of St William of Perth, a pious baker from Scotland, who in 1201 embarked on a pilgrimage to the Holy Land, but got only as far as Rochester, where he was robbed and murdered. The monks of Rochester, envying the popular appeal of St Thomas à Becket's shrine at nearby Canterbury, used William's demise as an opportunity to establish a rival shrine – indeed substantial additions to the cathedral were financed by donations from pilgrims paying their respects to the canonized baker's tomb, which has long since disappeared.

Rochester's long, semi-pedestrianized **High Street** is a handsome affair, lined with antique shops, cafés and pubs, many of which are housed within appealingly old half-timbered and weatherboarded buildings. With an *Oliver Twist* bakery and a restaurant called *A Taste of Two Cities*, it's not difficult to guess on a walk along here who Rochester's most famous son is. **Charles Dickens** spent his youth here, but would seem to have been less than impressed by the place – it appears as "Mudfog" in *The Mudfog Papers*, and "Dullborough" in *The Uncommercial Traveller*. Many of the buildings feature in his novels: the *Royal Victoria and Bull Hotel*, at the top of the High Street became the *Bull* in *Pickwick Papers* and the *Blue Boar* in *Great Expectations*, while most of his last book, the unfinished *Mystery of Edwin Drood*, was set in the town.

A gritty picture of Victorian life is conjured up by the tableaux at the **Charles Dickens Centre** in the distinctive red-brick and timber-framed Eastgate House at the southeast end of the High Street (daily 10am–5.30pm; £3.50). Key scenes from his well-known books are enacted at the push of a button and the whole place is entertaining and informative, whether you're a Dickens enthusiast or not. Even if you've no intention of visiting the centre, it's worth taking a look round the back of the building where **Dickens' Chalet** now stands, having been removed from his house at Gad Hill Place. A pretty little two-storey wooden structure with sky-blue gables, balcony and shutters, this Swiss-style chalet was used by Dickens as his summer study and it was here that he was working on *The Mystery of Edwin Drood* just before he died in 1870.

Back up the High Street, past the French Huguenot Hospital, **La Providence**, which moved into this peaceful early Victorian cul-de-sac in 1960, stands **Watts' Charity** (March–Oct Tues–Sat 2–5pm; free), a sixteenth-century almshouse founded by the philanthropist, Richard Watts, for passing travellers and immortalized in Dickens's short story *The Seven Poor Travellers*. The building was used for its original purpose until as late as 1940, and, behind the eighteenth-century stone facade, with its trio of triangular gables, it still boasts a series of galleried Elizabethan bedrooms.

Lastly, it's worth giving Rochester's excellent **Guildhall Museum** at the northwest end of the High Street (daily 10am–5.30pm; free) the once-over. Inside this splendid building, built in 1687, you'll find a vivid model of King John's siege of the castle and a chilling exhibition on the prison ships or hulks. Following American Independence in 1776, England was stuck for a place to transport her growing numbers of convicts – an increase caused as much by desperate poverty and draconian sentencing as any wave of criminality. Until the penal colony of Botany Bay was established a decade or so later, criminals were housed in appalling and overcrowded conditions inside decommissioned naval vessels moored in the Thames. With the clever use of mirrors the exhibit replicates the grim conditions inside these floating prisons.

Practicalities

Rochester **train station**, served by regular trains from London's Charing Cross and Victoria, is at the southeastern end of the High Street. The **tourist office** is halfway along the High Street, opposite the cathedral at no. 95 (Mon–Sat 10am–5pm, Sun 10.30am–5pm; ☎01634/843666). The Charles Dickens centre, near the train station, provides free guided tours of the town (Easter–Sept Wed, Sat & Sun 2.15pm).

As for **accommodation**, you can spend the night with some Dickensian ghosts at the ancient *Royal Victoria and Bull Hotel*, 16–18 High St (☎01634/846266; ⑤) or at the *Blue Boar Guest House* at no. 99 (☎01634/827373; ②). Decent B&Bs include the *Grayling House*, 54 St Margaret's St (☎01634/826593; ①), further up the hill behind the castle. The nearest **youth hostel** (☎01634/400788) is at Capstone Farm, two miles southeast of Chatham; to get there by bus, take the #114 from Chatham Bus Station and get off at the *Waggon at Hale* pub.

Rochester has an unremarkable selection of greasy spoon cafés and indifferent **restaurants**. Your best bet is to go Italian, either at the modest, family-run *Casa Lina,* 146 High St, (☎01634/844993), or at *Giannino's* in the *Royal Victoria and Bull Hotel* (☎01634/828555). For English fare, you could try the *Limehouse*, at 327 High St (☎01634/813 800). As for **pubs** the *Coopers Arms* on St Margaret's Street, which runs uphill between the castle and cathedral, serves good lunches in its small beer garden. A couple of newer **bars** worth checking out are the *City Wall*, 122 High St, with a spicy Tex-Mex-Med menu, and the stylish media hangout *Expressions*, 188 High St. *Amadeus* (☎01634/723370), one of the biggest **nightclubs** in the southeast has recently opened in the Medway Valley Park, a big entertainment complex a couple of miles west of the centre with a multiplex cinema.

Chatham

CHATHAM, less than two miles east of Rochester, has none of the charms of its neighbour. Its chief attraction is its dockyards, originally founded by Henry VIII and once the major base of the Royal Navy, many of whose vessels were built, stationed and victualled here, commanding worldwide supremacy from the Tudor era until the end of the Victorian age. Well sheltered, yet close to London and the sea, and lined with tidal mud flats which helped support ships' keels during construction, the port expanded quickly and by the time of Charles II it had become England's largest naval base. This era of shipbuilding came to an ignominious end when the dockyards were closed in 1984, reopening soon afterwards as a tourist attraction.

The **Historic Dockyard** (April–Oct daily 10am–5pm; Feb, March & Nov Wed, Sat & Sun 10am–4pm; £8.50) occupies a vast eighty-acre site about one mile north of the town centre along the Dock Road; it's a not very pleasant fifteen-minute walk from Chatham town centre, or a short bus ride (ask at the tourist office in Rochester for latest timetable). Behind the stern brick wall you'll find an array of historically and architecturally fascinating buildings dating back to the early eighteenth century. In addition to an impressive display of fifteen historic RNLI lifeboats, there's the "Wooden Walls" gallery, where you can experience life as an apprentice in the eighteenth-century dockyards. Recently introduced to the Historic Dockyards is the Ocelot Submarine, the last warship built at Chatham. The cramped conditions the crew had to endure are hard to believe, and a visit to the sub is a definite no-no for claustrophobes. The main part of the exhibition, however, consists of the Ropery complex including the former rope-making room – at a quarter of a mile long, the longest room in the country.

Signposted to the east of the dockyards, up Wood Street, the **Royal Engineers Museum** (Mon–Thur 10am–5pm, Sat, Sun & public holidays 11.30am–5pm; £3) is devoted to the army's all-purpose construction corps, nicknamed the "sappers", who were responsible for building London's Royal Albert Hall as well as numerous temporary wartime structures. Over the years the museum has acquired several artefacts from the sappers' campaigns, including Wellington's map of Waterloo and General Gordon's silk robes.

Less interesting by far is **Fort Amherst**, back towards the town centre at the bottom of Dock Road (daily: April–Oct 10.30am–5pm; Nov–March 10.30am–4pm; £4). Built to defend the dockyard in the mid-eighteenth century, the fort was extended by prisoners-of-war during the Napoleonic era. The fort's honeycomb of tunnels has been restored, but the one-and-a-half-hour guided tour is overlong and fails to impress – though an amusingly acted World War II Civil Defence "sketch" offers some light relief. The best time to come is on Sundays during the summer, when there's usually some costumed military re-enactment to help bring the place alive.

Boat trips run throughout the summer from Chatham along the River Medway on Britain's last working coal-fired paddle steamer, the *Kingswear Castle* built in 1924. The trips set off from Rochester Pier and the Historic Dockyard, and a cruise to Upnor Castle (April–Sept daily 10am–6pm; Oct daily 10am–5pm; £3.50; EH), an atmospheric sixteenth-century gun fort built on the river to protect Elizabeth I's fleet, costs £5.

Whitstable

Peculiarities of silt and salinity have made **WHITSTABLE** an oyster-friendly environment since classical times, when the Romans feasted on the region's marine delicacies. Indeed, production grew to such levels during the Middle Ages that **oysters** were exported all over Europe, and they were so cheap and plentiful that they became regarded as poor people's food – as Dickens observed, "where there are oysters, there's poverty". However, the whole industry collapsed during the twentieth century, the result of pollution and, in particular, a destructive storm in the 1950s which wrecked all the farms. Though oysters are once more farmed in the area – mostly the faster-growing Pacific Oysters, which have displaced the original Native Oysters – Whitstable is now more dependant on its commercial port, fishing and seaside tourism, while small-scale boat-building and a mildly bohemian ambience make this one of the few pleasant spots along the north Kent coast and a popular day-trip destination for Londoners.

Walking along Whitstable's busy High Street, you'd never guess that you're just a stone's throw from the sea. There's no promenade or bandstand – for that you have to go to Tankerton, Whitstable's easternmost suburb, or Herne Bay, miles further east. Follow the signs at the top of the High Street to reach the seafront, a very pleasant, quiet shingle beach, backed onto by some pretty weatherboard cottages. Most folk come to Whitstable to eat the local oysters (for which, see p.160), but if you want learn more about them, head for the **Oyster and Fishery Exhibition** on the harbour, just off Harbour Street (April–Aug daily 10am–4pm; Sept & Oct Sat & Sun 10am–4pm; £1.50); here kids get to touch some marine life, while the adults can take part in oyster tastings for a further £2.50. One of Whitstable's last surviving wooden oyster yawls

– built in 1890 when there were around 150 working out of the harbour – can be seen along Island Wall, a ten-minute walk west at the end of Harbour Street. If your fascination with Whitstable's maritime history is still not sated, head for the more staid **Whitstable Museum and Gallery** (Mon, Tues & Thurs–Sat 10.30am–1pm & 2–4pm; free), housed in the former Foresters' Hall, heralded by its eye-catching entrance on Oxford Street, with displays on diving and some good photographs and old film footage of the town's heyday. Back in 1830, Whitstable became the northern terminus for one of Britain's first steam-powered passenger railway services – the so-called "Crab & Winkle Line" which linked the town via a half-mile tunnel (the world's longest at that time) with Canterbury, ten miles to the south. Relics of this line still survive today.

Whitstable's **train station** is a five minutes' walk east of the High Street, while the **tourist office** is at 7 Oxford St (Mon–Sat 10am–4pm; ☎01227/275482), the southern continutation of the High Street. For **accommodation** along the seafront, try *Copeland House*, 4 Island Wall (☎01227/266207; ②), west of the High Street, with a garden which backs onto the beach; the *Hotel Continental*, 29 Beach Walk (☎01227/280280; ③); or the simply converted self-contained units, the *Fisherman's Huts*, at Sea Wall (☎01227/280280; ⑤). For **campsites**, you're best off heading to *Seaview Caravan Park* (☎01227/792246; closed Nov–March), which backs onto the beach towards Herne Bay.

Whitstable's fishing background is reflected in its **eating** places, from any number of fish-and-chip outlets along the High Street to the very popular *Royal Native Oyster Stores,* The Horsebridge (☎01227/276856; closed Sun eve & Mon), the town's best restaurant, with main fish dishes starting at £10, and half a dozen oysters costing just £6. A good alternative is *Pearsons Crab and Oyster House*, opposite (☎01227/272005), which offers bar meals downstairs and has a pricier restaurant upstairs. *Tea and Times*, 36 High St, caters for the town's arty fringe, providing free newspapers and serving a decent English breakfast with real coffee. For a **drink** and excellent atmosphere check out the *Old Neptune*, standing alone in its white weatherboards on the shore. Whitstable is at its most lively during its **Oyster Festival**, held annually in the last two weeks of July, featuring lots of crustacean crunching, but also jazz and parades.

Herne Bay and Reculver

Six miles east of Whitstable is the drab seaside resort of **HERNE BAY** which, like its storm-severed pier, is something of a relic from a bygone age when holidaymakers believed that sitting on a patch of shingle and sand was something to look forward to. Certain temperaments may find something stirring in moribund resorts like this, but overall Herne Bay has neither the energetic tackiness nor the discreet refinement of the larger resorts further east. The handsome Neoclassical clock tower on the seafront, and the King's Hall, further east, with its slender wrought-iron colonnade, hint at Herne Bay's halcyon days, but even the prom's new modern Sculpture Trail can't really hide the fact that the resort's glory days are over.

For a brief rundown of the attractions that once drew thousands of tourists here each summer, there's a small exhibition in the back of the **tourist office** at 14 William St (May–Aug daily 10am–5pm; rest of year Mon–Sat 10am–4pm; ☎01227/361911). There are scores of cheap **B&Bs** along the seafront; for better seaviews and en-suite facilities, try the *Carlton Hotel*, a four-storey Victorian house at 40 Central Parade (☎01227/374665; ③). Greasy spoons are plentiful in Herne Bay, but for superior fish and chips, oysters and other seafood, head for *Seawise*, a small **restaurant** (☎01227/361199) with outside seating, by the truncated pier. *The Ship*, near the King's Hall, has more character than most Herne Bay **pubs**, and serves a good range of real ales. One good reason to come to Herne Bay is to go on a **boat trip** to an offshore sandbank, home to a large herd of seals; the trip, in a lovely open yacht, takes four to five hours and costs around £10 per person, depending on the size of the group. Other cruises are also available (☎01227/366712).

For most visitors, though, Herne Bay's main value lies in its proximity to the ruins of England's oldest-known **Roman Fort**, situated inside Reculver Country Park, which occupies an isolated headland two miles east of Herne Bay; to get there, either walk along the coast or catch one of the local buses from the train station. The original fort, built around 280 AD by Carausis, self-styled Emperor of Britain, was used to guard the Wantsum Channel which separated the Isle of Thanet from the mainland and made an easily defended harbour for the Roman fleet. In the seventh century the Saxon **Church of St Mary** was built within the fort's walls, surviving until 1809, when coastal erosion brought about its collapse. Trinity House – the government's maritime navigation authority – bought the ruins the following year, rebuilding the twin twelfth-century **Reculver Towers** in order to render them "sufficiently conspicuous to be useful to navigation". An **interpretation centre** (April–June & Sept Sun 11am–5pm; July & Aug daily 11am–5pm; Oct–March Sun 11am–3pm; free) near the car park tells the full story and provides details on ecological aspects of this part of the coast. The *King Ethelbert* **pub,** close to the towers, provides an important refuelling function for passing tourists.

The Thanet resorts

The **Isle of Thanet**, a featureless plain fringed by low chalk cliffs and the odd sandy bay, became part of the mainland when the navigable Wantsum Channel began silting up around the time of the first Roman invasion. This northeastern corner of Kent has witnessed successive waves of incursions. In 43 AD, nearly a century after Julius Caesar's exploratory visit, the Romans got into their stride when they landed near Pegwell Bay and established Richborough port in preparation for the march inland. The Saxons followed them four hundred years later (the island is named after the "tenets", or fire beacons, which used to warn local residents of the Saxons' raids) and Augustine arrived here in 597 on a divine mission to end Anglo-Saxon paganism. The evangelist is supposed to have met King Ethelbert of Kent and preached his first sermon at a spot three miles west of Ramsgate – a cross marks the location at Ebbsfleet, next to Saint Augustine's Golf Club.

Over the next thousand years or so, civilization advanced to the point at which, in 1751, a resident of Margate, one Mr Benjamin Beale, invented the bathing machine, a wheeled cubicle that enabled people to slip into the sea without undue exhibitionism. It heralded the birth of sea bathing as a recreational and recuperative activity, and led to the growth of **seaside resorts**. By the mid-twentieth century the Isle's intermittent expanses of sand had become fully colonized as the "bucket and spade" resorts of the capital's leisure-seeking proletariat. That heyday has passed, but these earliest of resorts still cling to their traditional attractions to varying degrees.

Getting to the Thanet resorts is straightforward: **trains** and **buses** make the two-hour journey from London Victoria to Margate, Ramsgate and Broadstairs several times a day, and there are local rail and bus services from Canterbury and Dover.

Margate

MARGATE – memorably summarized by Oscar Wilde as "the nom-de-plume of Ramsgate" – is a ragged assortment of cafés, shops and amusement arcades wrapped around a broad bay, a rather less elegant place than the one with which it's been twinned, the Black Sea resort of Yalta. Yet more than two centuries of tourism are embodied in Margate: at its peak thousands of Londoners were ferried down the Thames every summer's day, to be disgorged at the pier – the functional precursor of all such seaside structures. Even today, on a fine summer weekend, the place is heaving with day-trippers enjoying the traditional fish and chips, candyfloss and donkey rides.

Other than the agreeable, if small, sandy beach, Margate's main attraction along its unashamedly tacky seafront is **Dreamland** on Marine Terrace (Easter–June & Sept daily 11am–6pm; July & Aug 10am–10pm), an amusement park heralded by a streamline 1930s' portal, with a rollercoaster dating back to 1863. If this doesn't appeal you could always visit the **Shell Grotto** on Grotto Hill, off Northdown Road (Easter to mid-Oct Mon–Fri 10am–5pm, Sat & Sun 10am–4pm; £1.50), which claims to be the world's only underground shell temple and has been open to the public since it was discovered by some schoolkids in 1835. Its passages are intricately decorated with shell mosaics and its caverns were once linked to the less interesting **Margate Caves** further down Northdown Road (April–June & Oct daily 10am–4pm; July–Sept Mon–Sat 10am–5pm; £1.50) – if nothing else, a good place to cool off on a hot day. The narrow streets of Margate's old town, centred on the Market Place, have potential, but the shopfronts are now mostly boarded up, having been superseded by the town's ugly out-of-town shopping centres. Still, you can take a trip down memory lane in the **Margate Museum** on the Market Place (Easter–Sept daily 10am–5pm; Oct–Easter Mon–Fri 9.30am–4.30pm; £1); the building also served as the town's police station from 1896 to 1959 – you can see several surviving police cells on the ground floor.

The **tourist office** is at 22 High St (Easter–Sept Mon–Fri 9am–5pm, Sat 9am–4pm, Sun 10am–4pm; Oct–Easter Mon–Sat 9am–4pm; ☎01843/220241) and the **train station** is on All Saints' Ave, just a couple of minutes' walk from Dreamland. Margate has plenty of **B&Bs**, the better ones lining the Regency crescents of the Cliftonville area – try the family-run *Ocean View Hotel*, 8–10 Ethelbert Terrace (☎01843/220 641; ①), or *Crescent House*, 24 Fort Crescent (☎01843/223092; ①), which also has sea views. Alternatively, there's the grand 1920s style *Walpole Bay Hotel*, Fifth Ave (☎01843/221703; ⑤). Prosaic **seaside food** is on offer at all of the seafront greasy spoons and fish-and-chip outlets, but you can get very fine **pastries** and snacks from *Batchelor's Patisserie*, at 246 Northdown Rd in Cliftonville. Most of Margate's **pubs** are a bit rough at the edges, so it's worth steering away from the seafront: try the tiny Victorian *Rose in June*, on peaceful Trinity Square, or for real ales (and pizzas), try the *Spread Eagle*, at the top of Victoria Road.

Broadstairs and around

Said to have been established on the profits of smuggling, today **BROADSTAIRS** is the smallest, quietest and most pleasant of Thanet's resort towns, overlooking the pretty little Viking Bay from its cliff-top setting. The town's charm lies in its quiet self-sufficiency: there are no big hotels to dominate and tourism seems to have endured without spoiling the place. Viking Bay is just one of several **sandy coves** which punctuate Thanet's eastern shore; between Broadstairs and Margate you'll find Stone, Joss, Kingsgate and Botany bays with Louisa Bay to the south – all quiet and undeveloped gems that make a good antidote to the busier resort areas.

However, Broadstairs' main claim to fame is as Dickens's holiday retreat – he described it as "one of the freest and freshest little places in the world". Throughout his most productive years he stayed in various hostelries here, and eventually rented an "airy nest" overlooking Viking Bay from Fort Road, since renamed **Bleak House** (daily: March–June & Sept to mid-Dec 10am–6pm; July & Aug 10am–9pm; £3) and opened to the public. It was here that he planned the eponymous novel as well as finishing *David Copperfield*, and three rooms in the house have been preserved as the author would have known them. There's more of the same on the main cliff-top seafront at the **Dickens House Museum**, 2 Victoria Parade, (April to mid-Oct daily 2pm–5pm; £1.20), in the house Dickens used as a model for Betsy Trotwood's House.

If you're in search of further diversions, pay a visit to the **Crampton Tower Museum** (Easter to mid-Oct daily 2–5pm; £1.50), on the other side of the road and railway tracks from the train station. Named after local-born Victorian engineer, Thomas Crampton, who built the town's first water system, it's the museum's buildings rather than its contents that are intriguing: the flint-studded tower, the pumping-engine shed and the nearby "beehive" building are all relics of Crampton's sophisticated water system.

It's a ten-minute walk from the **train station** to Broadstairs' seafront High Street, where you'll find the **tourist office** at no. 6b (April–Sept daily 9am–5pm; Oct–March Mon–Sat 9am–4pm; ☎01843/862242). Many **hotels**, restaurants and other establishments cash in on the Dickens angle; he wrote part of *Nicholas Nickleby* at the family-run *Royal Albion Hotel* on Albion St (☎01843/868071; ⑤), a comfortable treat for Dickens fans – ask about the B&B deal, which includes a meal in the *Marchesi Brothers* restaurant, two doors down. Alternatively, try the *East Horndon Hotel*, 4 Eastern Esplanade (☎01843/868306; ②) or the *Devonhurst Hotel*, also on the Eastern Esplanade (☎01843/863010; ②). There are several ivy-covered Georgian establishments in Belvedere Road, behind the High Street: the *Admiral Dundonald Hotel* at no. 43 (☎01843/862236; ②) and the *Hanson Hotel* next door (☎01843/868936; ②) may lack sea views, but both are good value. There is also a **youth hostel** at 3 Osborne Rd just two minutes' walk from the train station (☎01843/604121); it's housed in a Victorian villa and has a pleasant family atmosphere.

For **food**, there are plenty of fish-and-chip outlets at the bottom of Harbour Street; *Peter's Fish Factory* has outlets throughout the area and claims to be the cheapest and the best. If you're looking for a more congenial setting, try *Harpers Wine Bar*, also on Harbour Street (☎01843/602494; evenings only), which serves moderately priced fish and seafood dishes. Broadstairs' top restaurant is the aforementioned Swiss-run *Marchesi Brothers* restaurant (☎01843/862481), where a main course will set you back at least £10; alternatively, the inexpensive *Osteria Pizzeria Posillipo*, next door (☎01843/601133), does excellent pizzas, pasta and other Italian standards, and has a balcony overlooking the bay. As for **pubs**, the *Bradstowe Bar* at the *Royal Albion Hotel* also has bay views from its garden, while the popular and friendly *Neptune's Hall*, at the top of Harbour Street, serves great beer and has regular live folk-music evenings. The *Tartar Frigate,* also on Harbour Street, with it own seafood restaurant upstairs, and the *Lord Nelson*, round the corner in Albion Street, are solid sociable English pubs.

If you have time to explore the surrounding area, you could spend a rewarding afternoon at **Quex House**, a rambling Regency stately home set in its own gardens in the village of Birchington, four miles from Margate. The building houses the **Powell-Cotton Museum** (April–Oct Tues–Thurs & Sun 2.30–6pm; £3.50), a collection of trophies and artifacts amassed by Major General Powell-Cotton, a nineteenth-century big-game hunter, from his 28 expeditions to the African bush. The major built special galleries to house the dioramas in which over five hundred stuffed animals have been arranged, and there's also a wonderful collection of early photographs documenting the expeditions, along with displays of ethnographic material. In the nearby village of Birchington, the graveyard holds the tomb of Dante Gabriel Rossetti, the Victorian painter and poet, and the village also has a memorial garden to him at Sandles Road, right by the train station.

Ramsgate

If Thanet had a capital, it would be **RAMSGATE**, a handsome resort, rich in robust Victorian red-brick. Most of the town is set high on a cliff linked to the seafront and harbour by broad, sweeping ramps, with the villas on the seaward side displaying wrought-iron verandas and bricked-in windows – a legacy of the tax on glazed windows. Overall the port has avoided Margate's vulgarity while retaining some of Broadstairs' class, and the large-scale regeneration project in the harbour and along the seafront by the Maritime Museum is likely to breath new life into the area.

Currently, the most entertaining sight in Ramsgate is the subterranean **Motor Museum** at West Cliff Hall, on the prom just by the ferry terminal (Easter–Oct daily

10.30am–5.30pm; Nov–Easter Sun 10am–5pm; £2.50), which spices up its eclectic collection of cars and motorbikes by placing each vehicle in historical context. A 1905 Rex pushbike is on show alongside a newspaper proclaiming the increase of third-class steamer fares to the USA to £6, and a 1904 De Dion Bouton is displayed along with details of events from the same year – the founding of Rolls-Royce and the arrest of a New York woman for the heinous crime of smoking in public.

A predictable chronicle of municipal life from Roman times onwards is presented at the **Clock House Maritime Museum**, in the middle of the harbour (April–Sept daily 10am–5pm; Oct–March Mon–Fri 9.30am–4.30pm; £1); the display is brightened by an illuminating section on the Goodwin Sands sandbanks – six miles southeast of Ramsgate – the occasional playing field of the eccentric Goodwin Sands Cricket Club. There's also the newly opened **Thanet Movie Centre**, housed in a converted church near the top of the High Street at Meeting Street (daily 10am–5pm; £3.50) – a film and TV museum covering the early history of the media. You can get hands-on experience of a TV newsroom and editing equipment, and a close-up of all the paraphernalia involved in making a movie.

Ramsgate's **train station** is about a mile northwest of the centre, at the end of Wilfred Road, at the top of the High Street and the **tourist office** is at 19–21 Harbour St (Mon–Sat 9am–5pm, Sun 10am–4pm; ☎01843/591086), For an overnight **stay**, the *York House*, 7 Augusta Rd in Eastcliff (☎01843/596775; ①), offers all the comforts in an 1830s building; while the Victorian *Eastwood Guest House*, 28 Augusta Rd (☎01843/591505; ③) has some rooms with balconies. *Goodwin View*, 19 Wellington Crescent (☎01843/591419; ①), is an attractive seafront option in a terrace originally built to house the duke's officers. The nearest **campsite** is *Nethercourt Touring Park*, just two miles southwest of the town centre (☎01843/595485; closed Nov–March). For **food**, you could go oriental at *Noknoi's Kitchen*, a cosy Thai restaurant overlooking the harbour at 4 Westcliff Arcade (☎01843/852750), with some outside tables and very reasonable prices. Many of Ramsgate's **pubs** also offer good food – try the *Falstaff*, halfway up Addington Street from the seafront, which does a decent ploughman's lunch, or the *Camden Arms* in nearby La Belle Alliance Square, for good-value fish and chips; for cliff-top views, real ales and occasional live music, head for the *Churchill Tavern* on the Paragon.

Canterbury

One of England's most venerable cities, **CANTERBURY** offers a rich slice through two thousand years of history, with Roman and early Christian ruins, a Norman castle and a famous cathedral that dominates a medieval warren of time-skewed Tudor dwellings. The city began as a Belgic settlement that was overrun by the Romans and renamed **Durovernum**, which they established as a garrison and supply base and from where they went on to build a system of roads that was to reach as far as the Scottish borders. With the empire's collapse came the Saxons, who renamed the town **Cantwarabyrig**; it was a Saxon king, Ethelbert, who in 597 welcomed Augustine, despatched by the pope to convert the British Isles to Christianity. By the time of his death, Augustine had founded two Benedictine monasteries, one of which – Christ Church, raised on the site of the Roman basilica – was to become the first cathedral in England.

At the turn of the first millennium Canterbury suffered repeated sackings by the Danes until Canute, a recent Christian convert, restored the ruined Christ Church, only for it to be destroyed by fire a year before the Norman invasion. As the new religion became a tool of control, a struggle for power developed between the archbishops, the abbots from the nearby Benedictine abbey and King Henry II, culminating in the assassination of Archbishop Thomas à Becket in 1170, a martyrdom that effectively established the autonomy of the archbishops and made this one of Christendom's

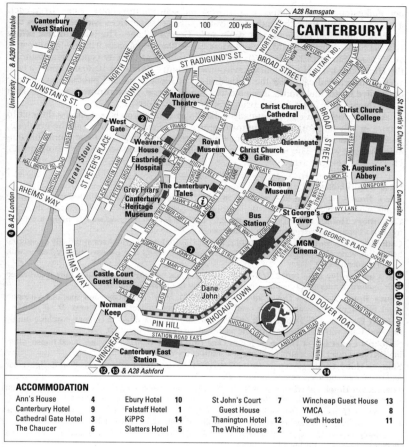

0   100   200 yds

CANTERBURY

ACCOMMODATION

Ann's House	4	Ebury Hotel	10	St John's Court	7	Wincheap Guest House	13
Canterbury Hotel	9	Falstaff Hotel	1	Guest House		YMCA	8
Cathedral Gate Hotel	3	KiPPS	14	Thanington Hotel	12	Youth Hostel	11
The Chaucer	6	Slatters Hotel	5	The White House	2		

© Crown copyright

greatest shrines. Geoffrey Chaucer's *Canterbury Tales*, written towards the end of the fourteenth century, portrays the unexpectedly festive nature of pilgrimages to Becket's tomb, which was later plundered and destroyed on the orders of Henry VIII.

In 1830 a pioneering passenger railway service linked Canterbury to the sea and prosperity grew until the city suffered extensive German bombing on June 1, 1942, in one of the notorious **Baedeker Raids** – the Nazi plan to destroy the most treasured historic sites as described in the German Baedeker travel guides. Today the cathedral and compact town centre, enclosed on three sides by medieval walls, remain the focus for leisure-motivated pilgrims from across the globe.

Arrival, information and accommodation

Canterbury has two **train stations**, Canterbury East for services from London Victoria or Dover Priory, and Canterbury West for slower services from London Charing Cross and Folkestone – the stations are northwest and south of the centre respectively, each a ten-minute walk from the cathedral. National Express services and local **buses** use the bus station just inside the city walls on St George's Lane. The busy **tourist office** is at 34 St Margaret's St (May–Sept Mon–Sat 9.30am–6pm, Sun 9.30am–5pm; rest of year closed Sun; ☎01227/766567), right in the middle of the city centre, just south of the High Street. The Canterbury Environment Centre (Wed–Sat 10.30am–5pm), a converted church and café near the Cathedral on St Alphege's Lane, publishes a number of detailed **historical walks**, available for a small charge. **Bike rental** is available from Canterbury Cycle Mart, Lower Bridge St (☎01227/761488).

Accommodation consists mostly of B&Bs and small hotels and can be difficult to secure in July and August. In the town centre, some old hotels offer all the creaking, authentic antiquity you could ask for, while there's a host of B&Bs to be found just outside the city walls. The tourist office can help you find a place to stay, though they charge £2.50 for the service.

Hotels and B&Bs

Ann's House, 63 London Rd (☎01227/768767). Traditional Victorian villa offering comfortable rooms, most of which are en suite. ①.

Canterbury Hotel, 71 New Dover Rd (☎01227/450551). Fifteen minutes' walk from the town centre with a continental restaurant and friendly service. ④.

Cathedral Gate Hotel, 36 Burgate (☎01227/464381). Built in 1438 and set in the city's medieval heart, this venerable pilgrims' hostelry features crooked floors and exposed timber beams with modern amenities. ②.

The Chaucer, Ivy Lane (☎01227/464427). Big hotel just beyond the city walls, fully refurbished with modern comforts but retaining some of its early Georgian charm. ⑥.

Ebury Hotel, 65–67 New Dover Rd (☎01227/768433). Very comfortable and spacious Victorian hotel, fifteen minutes' walk from the centre; indoor pool and well-appointed rooms. ④.

Falstaff Hotel, 8–10 St Dunstan's St (☎01227/462138). Popular fifteenth-century coaching inn by the West Gate, with four-poster beds and an award-winning restaurant. ⑥.

St John's Court Guest House, St John's Lane (☎01227/456425). Good-value guest house, offering B&B in a quiet but central location, just south of the old town. ①.

Slatters Hotel, St Margaret's St. (☎01227/463271). Luxury hotel with an excellent designer bar and restaurant and great central location. ⑤.

Thanington Hotel, 140 Wincheap (☎01227/453227). Comfortably converted Georgian building, ten minutes' walk from the centre with an indoor pool, games room and friendly, attentive service. ④.

The White House, 6 St Peter's Lane (☎01227/761836). Small and friendly guest house in a fine Regency building, midway between the cathedral and Canterbury West station. ②.

Wincheap Guest House, 94 Wincheap (☎01227/762309) Good-value Victorian B&B, with shared facilities, close to Canterbury East station. ①.

Hostels and campsites

The Caravan and Camping Club Site, Bekesbourne Lane (☎01227/463216). Large year-round caravan park, one and a half miles east of the city off the A257 road to Sandwich.

KiPPS, 40 Nunnery Fields (☎01227/786121). Self-catering hostel-type accommodation in dormitories a few minutes' walk from Canterbury East station; around £10 per person.

Youth Hostel, 54 New Dover Rd (☎01227/462 911, *canterbury@yha.org.uk*). Half a mile out of town, and fifteen minutes' walk from Canterbury East station, this friendly hostel is set in a Victorian villa. Closed Jan.

The City

Despite the presence of a university and art and teacher-training college, England's second most visited city is a surprisingly small place with a population of just 35,000. The town centre, ringed by ancient walls, is virtually car free, but this doesn't stop the High

Street seizing up all too frequently with tourists, two million of whom visit the city each year. Having said that, the very reason for the city's popularity is its rich tapestry of historical sites, combined with a good selection of places to stay, eat and drink, and no visit to southeast England would be complete without, at the very least, a quick stop here.

The cathedral

Mother Church of the Church of England, seat of the Primate of All England, **Canterbury Cathedral** (Mon–Fri 9am–5.30pm, Sat 9am–2.30pm, Sun 12.30–2.30pm & 4.30–5.30pm; closes earlier in winter; £3, free on Sun) is ecclesiastically supreme and fills the northeast quadrant of the city with a befitting sense of authority, even if architecturally it's perhaps not among the country's most impressive. A cathedral has stood here since 602, but in 1070 the first Norman archbishop, Lanfranc, levelled the original Saxon structure to build a new cathedral. Over successive centuries the masterpiece was heavily modified, and with the puritanical lines of the Perpendicular style gaining ascendancy in late medieval times, the cathedral now derives its distinctiveness from the thrust of the 235-foot-high Bell Harry Tower, completed in 1505. The precincts (daily 7am–9pm) are entered through the superbly ornate early-sixteenth-century **Christ Church Gate**, where Burgate and St Margaret's Street meet. This junction, the city's medieval core, is known as the Buttermarket, where religious relics were once sold to pilgrims hoping to prevent an eternity in damnation. Having paid your entrance fee, you pass through the gatehouse and get one of the finest views of the cathedral, foreshortened and crowned with soaring towers and pinnacles.

Once in the magnificent **interior**, look for the tomb of Henry IV and his wife, Joan of Navarre, and for the gilded effigy of Edward III's son, the Black Prince, all of them to be found in the Trinity Chapel, behind the main altar. The **shrine of Thomas à Becket**, in the northwest transept, is marked by the Altar of Sword's Point, where a crude sculpture of the assassins' weapons is suspended above the spot where Becket died and was later enshrined – until Henry VIII's act of ecclesiastical vandalism in 1538. Steps from here descend to the low, Romanesque arches of the **crypt**, one of the few remaining relics of the Norman cathedral and considered the finest such structure in the country, with some amazingly well-preserved carvings on the capitals of the columns.

On the cathedral's north flank are the fan-vaulted colonnades of the **Great Cloister**, from where you enter the **Chapter House**, with its intricate web of fourteenth-century tracery supporting the roof and a wall of stained glass, which illustrates scenes from St Thomas's life and death. In 1935 it was a fitting venue for the inaugural performance of T.S. Eliot's *Murder in the Cathedral*.

St Augustine's Abbey and St Martin's Church

Passing through the cathedral grounds and out through the city walls at the (exit-only) Queningate, you come to the vestigal remains of **St Augustine's Abbey** (daily: April–Sept 10am–6pm; Oct 10am–5pm; Nov–March 10am–4pm; £2.50; EH), occupying the site of the church founded by Augustine in 598. It was built outside the city because of a Christian tradition which forbade burials within the walls, and became the final resting place of Augustine, Ethelbert and successive archbishops and kings of Kent, although no trace remains either of them or of the original Saxon church. Shortly after the Normans arrived, the church was demolished in the same building frenzy which saw the creation of the cathedral. It was replaced by a much larger abbey, most of which was destroyed in the Dissolution so that today only the ruins and foundations remain. To help bring the site to life, pick up an audio tour from the abbey's excellent interpretive centre.

Nearby, on the corner of North Holmes Road and Pretoria Road is **St Martin's Church**, one of England's oldest churches, built on the site of a Roman villa or temple and used by the earliest Christians. Although medieval additions obscure the original Saxon structure, this is perhaps the earliest Christian site in Canterbury – it was here that Queen Bertha welcomed St Augustine in 597, and her husband King Ethelbert was baptized.

Along the High Street

For the most part, the **High Street** is lined with picturesque and ancient buildings – the view up Mercery Lane towards Christ Church Gate is one of the most photographed views in the city: a narrow, medieval street of crooked, overhanging houses behind which loom the turreted gatehouse and the cathedral's towers.

Just before High Street becomes St Peter's St, you come to the **Royal Museum and Art Gallery** (Mon–Sat 10am–5pm; free), housed on the first floor of an awesome mock-Tudor building, with big wooden gables and a mosaic infill between its timbers. There's lots of military memorabilia in the Buffs regimental gallery, which traces the history of the local regiment raised in Tudor times and merged in 1967. The art gallery is worth a quick perusal, with the odd Henry Moore and Gainsborough hidden among the local artists, and interesting temporary exhibitions in the Slater Gallery.

Where the street passes over a branch of the River Stour, stands **Eastbridge Hospital** (Mon–Sat 10am–5pm; £1), founded in the twelfth century to provide poor pilgrims with shelter. Downstairs is an exhibition on Chaucer's life, while storytellers in feudal garb recite parts of his book. Over the road is the wonky, half-timbered **Weavers' House**, built around 1500 and once inhabited by Huguenot textile workers who had been offered religious asylum in post-Reformation England.

St Peter's Street terminates at the two massive crenellated towers of the medieval **West Gate**, between which local buses just manage to squeeze. The only one of the town's seven city gates to have survived intact, its prison cells and guard chambers house a small **museum** (Mon–Sat 11am–12.30pm & 1.30–3.30pm; £1), which displays contemporary armaments and weaponry used by the medieval city guard, as well as giving access to the battlements. In fine weather, you can take a forty-minute trip on a **chauffered punt** (£5 per person) along the gentle River Stour from the nearby bridge.

The Roman Museum, The Canterbury Tales and the Heritage Museum

The redevelopment of the Longmarket area (situated between Burgate and the High Street) in the early 1990s exposed Roman foundations and mosaics that are now part of the **Roman Museum** (June–Oct Mon–Sat 10am–5pm, Sun 1.30–5pm; Nov–May closed Sun; £2.30). The extant remnants of the larger building are pretty dull, and better mosaics can be seen at Lullingstone (see p.184), but the display of recovered artefacts and general design of the museum are tasteful, with Roman domestic scenes re-created, as well as a computer-generated view of Durovernum.

Turning in the other direction down St Margaret's Street leads to the former church that's now **The Canterbury Tales** (March–June, Sept & Oct daily 9.30am–5.30pm; July & Aug daily 9am–5.30pm; Nov–Dec Mon–Fri & Sun 10am–4.30pm; £5.25), a quasi-educational show based on Geoffrey Chaucer's book, which lays claim to being the first original work of English literature ever to be printed. Equipped with a headset, visitors set off on a wander through mildly odour-enhanced galleries in which mannequins occupy idealized fourteenth-century tableaux and recount five of Chaucer's tales.

Genuinely educational and better value is **Canterbury Heritage Museum**, round the corner in Stour Street (June–Oct Mon–Sat 10.30am–5pm, Sun 1.30–5pm; Nov–May Mon–Sat 10.30am–5pm; £2.30), an interactive exhibition spanning local history from the splendour of Durovernum through to the more recent literary figures of Joseph Conrad (buried in the cemetery in London Road) and local-born Mary Tourtel, creator of the check-trousered philanthropist Rupert Bear. An excellent thirty-minute video on the Becket story details the intriguing personalities and events that led up to his assassination, presenting Becket as an overbearing and unpopular figure whose genuine piety was only recognized after his death.

Eating, drinking and nightlife

The combination of a large student population and the tourist trade means Canterbury has a good selection of places to eat and drink, with many **restaurants** and **pubs** in genuinely old settings. However, the Church, which owns much of the city within the walls, keeps a tight rein on any wanton revelry and, bar the odd, agonized yelp of an over-intoxicated student, at night all is as quiet as Becket's tomb.

Snacks

Café St Pierre, 41 St Peter's St. Excellent French patisserie and bakery with tables inside and out on the pavement and garden when the weather's fine.

Caffe Venezia, 60–61 Palace St. Spacious self-service Italian café with decent sandwiches, pasta dishes, pizza slices and good coffee.

Kate's Brasserie 4 Church St. Homely Tudor place near St Augustine's Abbey, serving light lunches, morning coffees and afternoon teas.

Restaurants

Café des Amis, 95 St Dunstan's St (☎01227/464390). Very popular authentic Mexican eatery close to Westgate; try the sizzling chicken *fajitas* or the delicious paella followed by a bubbling chocolate *fondido*. "Phenomenally hot" habanero chillies are only for the brave. Moderate.

Cate's Brasserie, 4 Church St (☎01227/456 655). Cosy, smart French restaurant with set two-course menus from £7.50. Closed Sun. Moderate.

Chaopraya River, 2 Dover St (☎01227/462876). The refined delights of Thai cuisine at a reasonable price – the *Nua pud naman hoy*, beef marinated in oyster sauce and served sizzling with mushrooms, baby corn and spring onions, is delicious. Inexpensive.

Flap Jacques, 71 Castle St. (☎01227/781000). Homely little French bistro offering *moules*, *frites* and Breton pancakes. Live music Sunday lunch and most evenings. Inexpensive to Moderate.

Kudos, 52 Dover St (☎01227/764062). Small, top-notch Chinese restaurant serving excellent food. Inexpensive.

Oranges, 18 St Peter's St (☎01227/464227). Converted pub given a breath of fresh Mediterranean air, polished pine and sunny colours, and offering imaginative Med cooking, too. Inexpensive to Moderate.

Tuo e Mio, 16 The Borough (☎01227/761471). Long-established restaurant offering classy Italian dishes and some delicious, home-made desserts. Moderate.

Tapas en las Trece, 13 Palace St (☎01227/762637). Tasty Spanish tapas at around £4 a dish, with occasional live music. Inexpensive.

Il Vaticano, 35 St Margaret's St (☎01227/765333). A pleasant pasta bar, with a few other basic Italian dishes. Moderate.

Pubs and bars

Alberry's, St Margaret's St. Just up from the tourist office, this lively wine bar has good snacks and occasional live music.

Bell & Crown, 10 Palace St. Authentic and cramped medieval hostelry serving Truman beers.

Canterbury Tales, 12 The Friars. Marble-top bar and lots of polished wood in this tidy little pub opposite the Marlowe Theatre. Nachos and BLTs on the bar menu.

Casey's, 5 Butchery Lane. Cosy, low-ceilinged Irish pub serving oysters and soda bread and other pub grub, with occasional live Irish music.

City Arms, 7 Butchery Lane. Local pub popular with art students and serving very cheap grub.

Miller's Arms, Mill Lane. A pleasant waterside spot for a summertime pint.

New Inn, on the corner of Havelock St, off the Broad St ring road. One of Canterbury's tiniest pubs, popular with students and locals and offering a decent selection of real ale.

Simple Simon's, Radigund's Hall, 3 Church Lane. Old hostelry that's popular with the university and King's School crowd; occasional live music.

Nightlife

Nightlife in Canterbury keeps a low profile – check out what's happening in the free *What Where When* listings magazine available at the tourist office. Opposite Canterbury East station there are two **nightclubs** in the same building: the *Works*, which is a bit of a meat market, and the more civilized *Bizz*, appealing to the over-thirties. *Airlock* at 41 St George's Place, has regular dance nights attracting London DJs. On the other side of town, the university puts on a good range of arty **films** – for details of what's on, call in at Forwood's Music, 35–37 Palace St, where you can also buy a ticket in advance. There are more commercial celluloid offerings at the MGM, a three-screen cinema on the ring road near St George's Place. The university also houses the Gulbenkian Theatre, a venue which shares the city's more edifying cultural events with the Marlowe Theatre in the Friars. In Northgate, the recently revived Penny Theatre presents local and global **live music**. Finally, there's the **Canterbury Festival**, an international potpourri of music, theatre and arts worth catching if you're in the area in the middle two weeks of October.

The Channel Ports: Sandwich to Folkestone

Dover, just 21 miles from mainland Europe (Calais' low cliffs are visible on a clear day), is the southeast's principal cross-Channel port. As a town it is not immensely appealing, even though its key position has left it with a clutch of historic attractions. To the north, lie **Sandwich**, once the most important of the Cinque Ports but now no longer even on the coast, and the pleasant resort towns of **Deal** and **Walmer**, each with its own set of distinctive fortifications as well as a smattering of traditional seaside B&Bs. Sadly, **Folkestone**, Kent's second major port, seven miles southwest of Dover, is even more forlorn than it's neighbour.

There are frequent **train** and **bus** connections to both the main Channel ports during the day – trains leave from London Victoria and Charing Cross, buses from London Victoria. A useful branchline offers train connections from Dover up the coast to Walmer, Deal and Sandwich and on to Ramsgate. However, if you arrive by ferry at either port after 11pm you'll be stuck in town whether you like it or not – the last direct train service leaves for London at 10pm.

THE CINQUE PORTS

In 1278 Dover, Hythe, Sandwich, New Romney and Hastings – already part of a long-established but unofficial confederation of defensive coastal settlements – were formalized under Edward I's charter as the **Cinque Ports** (pronounced "sink", despite its French origin). In return for providing England with maritime support when necessary, chiefly in the transportation of troops and supplies to the Continent during times of war, the five ports were given trading privileges and other liberties, which enabled them to prosper while neighbouring ports struggled to survive. Some took advantage of this during peacetime, boosting their wealth by various nefarious activities such as piracy and the smuggling of tax-free contraband.

Later, Rye and Winchelsea were added to the confederation along with several other "limb" ports on the southeast coast which joined up at various times. The confederation continued until 1685, when the ports' privileges were revoked. Their maritime services were no longer necessary as Henry VIII had founded a professional navy and, due to a shifting coastline, several of the ports' harbours had silted up anyway. Nowadays, only Dover is still a major working port, though the post of Lord Warden of the Cinque Ports still exists. This honorary title, bestowed by the presiding monarch, is currently held by the Queen Mother.

Sandwich and around

SANDWICH, situated on the River Stour four miles north of Deal, is best known nowadays for giving rise to England's favourite culinary contribution when, in 1762, the Fourth Earl of Sandwich, passionately absorbed in a game of cards, ate his meat between two bits of bread for a quick snack. Aside from this incident, the town's main interest lies in its maritime connections – it was chief among the Cinque Ports (see box opposite) until the Stour silted up. Unlike other former harbour inlets, however, the Stour hasn't silted up completely and still flows through town, its grassy willow-lined banks adding to the once great medieval port's present charm.

By the bridge over the Stour stands Sandwich's best-known feature, the sixteenth-century **Barbican**, a stone gateway decorated with chequerwork, where tolls were once collected. Running parallel to the river is **Strand Street**, whose crooked half-timbered facades front antique shops and private homes. The genteel town is separated from the sandy beaches of Sandwich Bay by the **Royal St George Golf Course** – frequent venue of the British Open tournament – and a mile of nature reserves. The reserve that most ornithologists make for is the **Gazen Salts Nature Reserve** – renowned for its diversity of seabirds – three miles north of town, across the Stour.

Overlooking the doleful expanse of Pegwell Bay, two miles northwest of Sandwich, is **Richborough Castle** (April–Sept daily 10am–6pm; Oct daily 10am–5pm; £2.50; EH), one of the earliest coastal strongholds built by the Romans along what later became known as the Saxon Shore on account of the frequent raids by the Germanic tribe. Like Reculver (see p.161), it guarded the southern entrance to the Wantsum Channel, which then isolated the Isle of Thanet from the mainland. Rumour has it that Emperor Claudius, on his way to London, once rode on an elephant through a triumphal arch erected inside the castle, but all that remains now within the well-preserved Roman walls are the relics of an early Saxon church. Richborough's historical significance far outshines its present appearance, especially as Pegwell Bay is now blighted by an ugly chemical works. The nicest way of reaching the castle is to take a boat trip up the Stour from Sandwich Quay (☎01304/820171; £3).

Finding **accommodation** in Sandwich shouldn't be much of a problem – the local **tourist office**, housed in the lovely sixteenth-century Guildhall (April–Oct daily 10am–4pm; ☎01304/613565), will provide you with a list of local hotels and guesthouses. The golfers' choice, the *Bell Hotel* by the Barbican (☎01304/613388; ⑥) is out of most people's range – though its weekend deals are good value; the en-suite rooms at the old coaching inn, the *Fleur de Lis*, near the Guildhall at 6–8 Delf St (☎01304/614944; ③), are much more affordable, though it's recently changed hands and this may well change; or try the modest *Le Trayas* bungalow Poulders Rd (☎01304/611056; ①), a ten-minute walk from the Quay. If you don't mind being a bit further out of town, try the *St Crispin Inn*, an attractive fifteenth-century pub in the village of Worth, a mile or so south of Sandwich (☎01304/612081; ③). Your best choice for top-class **food** is the pricey *Fishermans Wharf* on the quayside (☎01304/613636), which serves excellent seafood; for something less expensive try one of the pubs by the Barbican or the *Haven*, 20A King St, for good coffee, snacks and light meals. For the definitive Sandwich sandwich, head for the twee *Little Cottage Tearooms*, on the quay.

Deal and around

One of the most unusual of Henry VIII's forts is the diminutive castle at **DEAL**, six miles southeast of Sandwich and site of Julius Caesar's first successful landfall in

Britain in 55 BC. The **castle** (April–Sept daily 10am–6pm; Oct daily 10am–5pm; Nov–March Wed–Sun 10am–4pm; £3; EH) is situated off the Strand at the south end of town. Its unusual shape – viewed from the air it looks like a Tudor rose – is as much an affectation as a defensive design, though the premise was that the rounded walls would be better at deflecting missiles; inside, the comprehensive display on the other similar forts built during Henry VIII's reign is well worth a visit. Much more recently, the town was the focal point of Kent's small-scale coal industry, until the pits were closed during the bitterly fought downsizing of the 1980s.

Deal's **tourist office** is situated on the High Street near the sea (mid-May to mid-Sept Mon–Fri 9am–12.30pm & 1.30–5pm, Sat 9am–2pm; rest of year Mon–Fri 9am–12.30pm & 1.30–5pm; ☎01304/369576). There's a whole host of places offering **accommodation** on Beach Street: try the winsome *King's Head* pub at no. 9 (☎01304/368194; ③), or the nearby town house of *Channel View* at no. 17 (☎01304/368194; ③), run by the same proprietor. Another option is *Dunkerley's*, next door at no. 19 (☎01304/375016; ⑤), whose **restaurant** is possibly Deal's finest (and priciest). For more reasonably priced seafood try the *Lobster Pot* (☎01304/374713) on Beach Road, opposite the pier.

Walmer Castle

Walmer Castle, a mile south of Deal (times as above, except restricted access weekdays in Jan & Feb; £4.50; EH), is another rotund Tudor-rose-shaped affair, commissioned when the castle became the official residence of the Lord Warden of the Cinque Ports in 1730. Now it resembles a heavily fortified stately home more than a military stronghold. The best-known resident was the Duke of Wellington, who died here in 1842, and not surprisingly, the house is devoted primarily to his life and times. Busts and portraits of the Iron Duke crowd the rooms and corridors, where you'll also find the armchair in which he expired and the original Wellington boots in which he triumphed at Waterloo. The castle's terraced gardens, overlooking the channel, are a good spot for a picnic, or you can have afternoon tea in The Lord Warden's Tearooms (April–Oct daily; Nov–March Sun).

To get to Walmer Castle from Deal, you can either catch one of the hourly buses or, if the weather's good, make the pleasant walk along the seafront (45min).

Dover

Badly bombed during the war **DOVER**'s town centre and seafront just don't have what it takes to induce many travellers to linger before speeding onwards to Europe, or inland to London or Canterbury. That said, the town authorities have put a lot of effort and money into sprucing the place up, particularly the early Victorian New Bridge

---

CROSS-CHANNEL TRANSPORT SERVICES FROM DOVER AND FOLKESTONE

Dover Eastern Docks to Calais: P&O Stena Line (30 daily; journey time 1hr 15min); Seafrance (15 daily, journey time 1hr 30min).

Dover Western Docks to Calais: Hoverspeed (10 daily; journey time 35min by Hovercraft, 50min by SeaCat).

Folkestone to Boulogne: Hoverspeed SeaCat (4 daily; journey time 55min).

Folkestone to Calais: Eurotunnel (up to 4 hourly; journey time 35min).

Reservations: Eurotunnel (☎0990/353535); Hoverspeed (☎08705/240241 or 01304/865000); P&O Stena Line (☎08706/000600); SeaFrance (☎0990/711711).

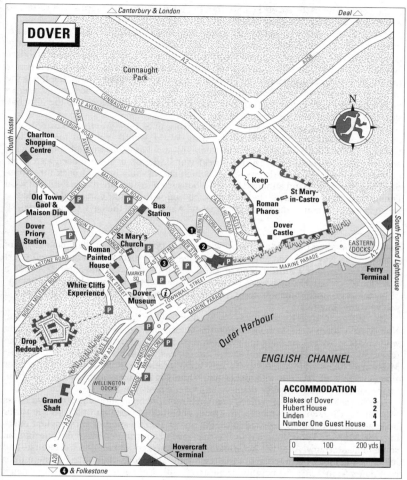

DOVER

Canterbury & London

Deal

Connaught
Park

Youth Hostel

CASTLE AVENUE
CONNAUGHT ROAD
SALISBURY ROAD
PARK AVENUE

Charlton
Shopping
Centre

HIGH STREET

LADWELL PL.
MAISON DIEU ROAD

Old Town
Gaol &
Maison Dieu

Dover
Priory
Station

BIGGIN ST.
LEICESTER ROAD

FOLKSTONE ROAD

CANNON ST.

Roman
Painted
House

St Mary's
Church

YORK STREET

Bus
Station

VICTORIA ST.

WOOLCOMBER STREET

CASTLE HILL ROAD

CASTLE HILL

Keep

Roman
Pharos

St Mary-
in-Castro

Dover
Castle

EASTERN
DOCKS

South Foreland Lighthouse

Ferry
Terminal

CASTLE STREET
RUSSELL STREET

MARKET
SQ

White Cliffs
Experience

NORTH MILITARY ROAD

Dover
Museum

TOWNWALL STREET

MARINE PARADE

MARINE PARADE

Drop
Redoubt

SNARGATE ST.

NEW A20

CAMBRIDGE RD.
WATERLOO CRES.

Outer Harbour

ENGLISH CHANNEL

WELLINGTON
DOCKS

Grand
Shaft

ESPLANADE

A20

ACCOMMODATION

Blakes of Dover 3
Hubert House 2
Linden 4
Number One Guest House 1

0   100   200 yds

Hovercraft
Terminal

& Folkestone

N

A2
A258
A2
A20

development along the Esplanade. Despite such valiant attempts, Dover Castle is still by far the most interesting of the numerous attractions which plug the port's defensive history. Entertainment of a saltier nature is offered by Dover's legendary **White Cliffs**, which dominate the town and have long been a source of inspiration for lovers, travellers and soldiers sailing off to war.

Dover Castle

It was in 1168, a century after the Conquest, that the Normans constructed the keep that now presides over the bulk of **Dover Castle** (daily: April–Sept 10am–6pm; Oct 10am–5pm; Nov–March 10am–4pm; £6.90; EH), a superbly positioned defensive complex that was in continuous use as some sort of military installation from then right up to the 1980s. The castle's a stiff climb from the town centre, and there's a lot to see, so allow up to half a day for a thorough visit.

It was the Romans who put Dover on the map when they chose the harbour as the base for their northern fleet, and erected a **lighthouse** here to guide the ships into the river mouth. Beside the chunky hexagonal remains of the Roman *pharos* stands a Saxon-built church, **St Mary-in-Castro**, dating from the seventh century, with motifs graffitied by irreverent Crusaders still visible near the pulpit. Further up the hill is the impressive, well-preserved **Norman Keep**, built by Henry II as a palace. Inside, there's an interactive exhibition on spying; you can also climb its spiral stairs to the lofty battlements for views over the sea to France.

The castle's other main attraction is its network of **Secret Wartime Tunnels** dug during the Napoleonic war. Extended during World War II, you can tour "Hellfire Corner" – the tunnels' wartime nickname – on a fifty-minute guided tour (leaving approximately every 20min). During World War II, the tunnels were used as a headquarters to plan the Dunkirk evacuation, which successfully brought back three hundred and thirty thousand stranded British troops from the continent in a flotilla of local fishing and pleasure boats. The tour is spiced up with a little gore, and reveals the quaintly low-tech communications systems and war rooms of the navy's command post.

The Town

Postwar rebuilding has made Dover town centre a grim place, but the construction of a car park on New Street in 1970 did at least lead to the discovery of an ancient guest house. The **Roman Painted House** (April–Sept Tues–Sun 10am–5pm; £2), once a hotel for official guests, possesses some reasonable Roman wall paintings, the remains of an underground Roman heating system and some mosaics – it's worth a look if you've some time to kill.

The **White Cliffs Experience**, on Market Square (daily: April–Oct 10am–6pm; Nov–March 10am–4pm, last admission 1hr before closing; £5.75), in fact features no white cliffs at all, but instead employs period-costumed actors to re-create first Roman times, and then wartime days in Dover. Less expensive and less frivolous is the **Dover Museum** below the White Cliffs gift shop (daily: summer 10am–6pm; winter 10am–5.30pm; £1.70, free with ticket for White Cliffs Experience) which has three floors packed with informative displays on Dover's past – and a stuffed polar bear.

As you walk along pedestrianized Cannon Street, the main shopping street, you pass **St Mary's Church**, Victorian for the most part, but of Norman origin as the tower makes clear. Further up the road in Biggin Street, there's another very ancient building, the **Maison Dieu**, founded in the thirteenth century as a place for pilgrims en route to Canterbury. After the Reformation, it was turned into a naval storehouse, and in the last century became part of the town hall. The Stone Hall, with its fine timber roof dates from 1253; the neighbouring neo-Gothic Connaught Hall and the Council Chamber upstairs are the work of the great Victorian architects Poynter and Burges.

There are more historical tableaux at the **Old Town Gaol,** beneath the Town Hall on Biggin Street (May–Sept Tues–Sat 10am–4.30pm, Sun 2–4.30pm; Oct–April Wed–Sat 10am–4.30pm; £3.50); hour-long guided tours describe the misery of penal incarceration during Victorian times. The high ground to the west of town, originally the site of a Napoleonic-era fortress, retains one interesting oddity, the **Grand Shaft** (July & Aug Tues–Sun 2–5pm; £1.25), a 140-foot triple staircase by which troops could go down at speed to defend the port in case of attack.

Dover's cliffs

As the first and last sight of England for travellers throughout the centuries, the **white cliffs of Dover** hold a complex role in the English psyche. Matthew Arnold invoked their massive grandeur in his famous elegy for a lost time, *Dover Beach*, written in the 1860s. Today, the beach has little of the romance invested in the spot by Arnold, but the cliffs flanking the town retain their majesty, even if pollution has taken some of the edge off their whiteness. The best views, of course, are to be had from several miles out to sea, but if you haven't the time or resources to catch a boat, a good vantage point on land is the Prince of Wales pier in the harbour.

There are some great **walks** to be had along the cliffs themselves. To reach **Shakespeare Cliff**, catch bus #D2A from Worthington Street towards Aycliff. Alternatively, there's a steep two-and-a-half-mile climb to Shakespeare Cliff from North Military Road, off York Street, taking you by the **Western Heights**, a series of defensive battlements built into the cliff in the nineteenth century. From here there is a sweeping panorama of the Straits of Dover – the world's busiest shipping lanes – and a bird's-eye view of the harbour and the surrounding cliffs. It's even possible to catch a glimpse of France on a clear day.

Another exhilarating two-mile walk from Langdon Cliffs takes you above the Eastern Docks towards St Margarets Bay and the **South Foreland Lighthouse** (April–Oct Sat, Sun & school holidays 12.30–5.30pm; £1.50; NT). This Victorian construction, that looks somewhat like a minaret, was built to warn shipping off the dangerous Goodwin Sands; it was also where Marconi conducted his first ship-to-shore radio experiments in 1898. Having recently celebrated Marconi's centenary, the lighthouse is set to be the first place in Britain to see the dawn of the new millennium, at 7.56am on January 1, 2000.

Practicalities

There are frequent train services from both Charing Cross and Victoria stations in London to Dover Priory **train station**, a ten-minute walk northwest of the centre; there are regular shuttle buses to the Eastern Docks, but none to the Western Docks. Buses from London (hourly; 2hr 30min) run to the Eastern Docks and the town-centre **bus station** on Pencester Road.

The **tourist office**, in the town centre underneath the high-rise *County Hotel* on Townwall Street (daily: July & Aug 8am–7.30pm; rest of year 9am–6pm;

THE CHANNEL TUNNEL

In the autumn of 1994 passenger services through the Channel Tunnel finally began, 160 years after the idea was first suggested by French engineer Aime Thome de Gamond, whose geological survey of the seabed concluded that such a link was feasible. As a result of his work, a tunnel over a mile long was driven out from the English coast in 1882, while French engineers began to dig from Sangatte – the present location of the French terminal. All was going remarkably well until Queen Victoria became paranoid about the possibility of invasion, and work was halted.

In 1973 a pang of Euro-optimism led to another attempt, until cash problems forced the British to pull out of the "Chunnel", as it was dubbed, and things didn't go any smoother when the French and British finally agreed on proposals at the end of the Eighties for a pair of rail tunnels and a third service tunnel. Britain's biggest-ever civil engineering project was dogged by delays, overspending and disagreements between Trans Manche Link (the tunnellers) and Eurotunnel (who put up the money), while the British government dithered over the routeing of a new high-speed rail link to London, which is not expected to be completed until well into the next century. In the meantime the Eurostar travels at close to 200mph from Paris or Brussels to the tunnel, zips through at 100mph to surface at Folkestone and then crawls with the commuter traffic to its terminal at Waterloo.

☎01304/205108), can advise about accommodation, which is plentiful. It also has a free *White Cliffs Trails* pamphlet that outlines many good walks near Dover, both coastal and inland. **Bikes** can be rented from Andy's Shop, 156 London Rd (☎01304/204401).

The biggest concentrations of small **hotels and B&Bs** are on the Folkestone Road, close to Priory station, but the ones around the base of Castle Hill Road on the other side of town are generally nicer. *Hubert House*, 9 Castle Hill Rd (☎01304/202253; ②), is a friendly B&B, convenient for the Eastern Dock, as is the good-value *Number One Guesthouse*, opposite, at 1 Castle St (☎01304/202007; ②). *Blakes of Dover* further up Castle Street, at no. 52 (☎01304/202194; ③), is a lovely wood-panelled wine bar, restaurant and hotel with a genial owner; *Linden*, at no. 231 (☎01304/205449; ①), is one of the better B&Bs along the Folkestone Road. There's a very busy **youth hostel** in a listed Georgian house at 306 London Rd (☎01304/201314), a mile up the High Street from Dover Priory station. Cheaper and more central is the **YMCA** at 4 Leyburne Rd – though they may soon move to premises on Princes Road, so phone ahead to check (☎01304/206138), where bunkhouse beds go for £6 a night. The most convenient **campsite** is *Hawthorn Farm* (☎01304/852658; closed Dec–Feb) close to Martin Mill train station, one stop up the line towards Ramsgate.

Given the town's uninspiring appearance, Dover's **pubs** are surprisingly characterful, although the town gets a rather rough reputation from its shift-workers servicing the docks and ferries. There are two decent pubs near the town hall: *Park Inn* a big old place on Park Street with plenty of real ales, and the *Prince Albert*, on the corner of Biggin Street and Priory Road. *The White Horse* is a nice old eighteenth-century pub at the foot of the castle. Dover's culinary offerings are poor, and you could do worse than eat pub **food** at *The Eight Bells*, a big Weatherspoon's pub on Cannon Street. Despite its garish exterior, *Topo Gigio*, 1–2 King St (☎01304/201048), offers acceptable and inexpensive Italian food, as does *Dino's*, 58 Castle St (☎01304/204678). The French restaurant, *Fleur-de-Lis* at 10 Effingham St (☎01304/240224; eve only, closed Sun), is the best place in town, though it is quite pricey. If you want to learn more about the local **nightlife**, pick up the free monthly *What's On* leaflet from the tourist office.

Folkestone

Seven miles down the coast from Dover, **FOLKESTONE** started life as a fishing village and rose to prominence as a resort in the nineteenth century, when the grandiose terraces which still dominate the town were built. In theory, Folkestone, with its narrow cobbled streets and cliff-top marine promenade, should be a more appealing place than, say, Dover, but the truth is that, rather like the Channel Tunnel itself, the good times seem to have passed Folkestone by.

Aside from the **Folkestone Museum and Art Gallery** (Mon–Sat 9.30am–5pm; free), whose main virtue is that it's free, Folkestone's only major tourist attraction is the **Russian Submarine**, U-475 Foxtrot (daily 10am–dusk; £3.95), docked at the South Quay, beside the Hoverspeed terminal. This sinister Soviet sub carried nuclear weapons and could operate at a depth of 250 yards, making it almost impossible to detect. Very little has been altered inside which means that visitors must be prepared to squeeze through numerous awkward hatches and claustrophobics should stay away.

The Victorian **Leas Lift**, to the west along the run-down Marine Parade (Easter–Sept daily 9am–6pm; Oct–Easter Sun 9am–5pm; 50p), will transport you to the **The Leas**, the town's justly famous marine promenade. It's worth persevering to the far end of the Leas to admire the fantastically ornate red-brick and terracotta Metropole Hotel, and its architectural cousin and neighbour, the Grand – sadly neither function as hotels any more, though the Metropole now houses an **arts centre and gallery** (April–Oct Mon–Sat 10am–5pm, Sun 2.30–5pm; Nov–March Tues–Sat 10am–4pm, Sun 2.30–5pm).

Up on Folkestone's East Cliff is **Martello Tower No. 3** (Easter–Sept daily 10.30am–5pm; £1), one of 74 similar towers along this stretch of coast, about which you can learn more from the tower's small exhibition (see also p.178). Further east along the cliffs, at Capel-le-Ferne on the B2011, you should be able to spot the new **Battle of Britain Memorial**, a giant seated figure of an RAF pilot gazing out to sea, with the various squadron badges carved onto the sandstone base. Those with a further interest in the subject should head three miles inland on the A260 to the **Kent Battle of Britain Museum** (Easter–Sept daily 10am–5pm; Oct daily 11am–4pm; £3), at Hawkinge airfield, where several hangars house World War II memorabilia, including a crashed Messerschmitt and replica Spitfires and Hurricanes.

Practicalities

The only passenger vessels that arrive in Folkestone these days are the Hoverspeed SeaCats from Boulogne, which dock near to **Folkestone Harbour train station** and connect with trains to London Charing Cross via **Folkestone Central**, a twenty-minute walk northwest of the harbour, off Cheriton Road. Eurostar passengers for Paris and Brussels can climb aboard at the new, pompously named, Ashford International train station, just up the line from Folkestone. National Express **coaches** to London leave from the **bus station** on Bouverie Square, between the Central and Harbour stations.

The **tourist office** is in Harbour Street, near the quayside (daily: July–Aug 9am–7pm; Sept–June Mon–Sat 9am–5.30pm, Sun 9am–1pm & 2–4pm; ☎01303/258594). For **overnight** stays, the nicest part of town is to the west along the Leas, which were once patrolled by the local Lord Radnor's own police force. The red-brick and terracotta *Burlington* Earls Ave (☎01303/255301; ⑤), the *Chilton House Hotel*, 14–15 Marine Parade (☎01303/249786; ①) and *Westward Ho!*, at 13 Clifton Crescent (☎01303/221515; ②) are the best among the scores of hotels and B&Bs. The *Guildhall*, on the Bayle, is a nice **pub** to relax in; for **food**, head for the excellent and reasonably priced Italian joint *Osteria Posillipo*, 18 Rendezvous Street at the top of the Old High St (☎01303/246666; closed Tues), or the expensive, but exquisite *Paul's*, 2a Bouverie Rd West (☎01303/259697) for Modern-British cuisine.

Hythe to Dungeness: the Romney and Denge marshes

In Roman times, the **Romney and Denge marshes** – now the southernmost part of Kent – were submerged beneath the English Channel. Then the lowering of the sea levels in the Middle Ages and later reclamation created a forty-square-mile area of shingle and marshland which, until the last century, was afflicted by malaria and various other malaises. Contrasting strongly with the wooded pastures of Kent's interior, the sheepspeckled marshes have an eerie, forlorn appearance, as if still unassimilated with the mainland and haunted by their maritime origins. The ancient town of **Hythe** is on the eastern edge of the reclaimed marshes and is linked with Rye in East Sussex (see p.189) on the marsh's western edge, by the arc of the twenty-three-mile Napoleonic-era **Royal Military Canal**.

Hythe and Lympne

Separated from Folkestone by the massive earthworks of the Channel Tunnel, **HYTHE** is a sedate seaside resort bisected by the disused waterway of the Royal Military Canal, which was built as a defensive obstacle during the perceived threat of Napoleonic invasion. Hythe's receding shoreline reduced its usefulness as a port and the nearby coast is now just a sweep of beach punctuated by **Martello Towers**, part of the chain of 74 such towers built along the south and east coasts in the early nineteenth century as a defence against potential French invasion.

The nicest part of Hythe is not the seafront, but the old town, and in particular the quiet backalleys to the north of the High Street. To give purpose to your wandering, follow the signs to the macabre collection of various ancient bones and skulls in the **crypt** (May–Sept Mon–Sat 10.30am–noon & 2.30–4pm; 50p) of the eleventh-century St Leonard's Church. A ride on the world's largest toy train – or smallest public railway – the **Romney, Hythe and Dymchurch Railway** (R, H & DR), a fifteen-inch-gauge line which runs the fourteen miles from Hythe to Dungeness (Easter–Sept daily; March & Oct Sat & Sun; ☎01797/362353), is also a must. Built in the 1920s as a tourist attraction linking the resorts along the shore, its fleet of steam locomotives – mainly one-third scale models from the Twenties and Thirties – are now maintained by volunteers. The station is to the west of the town centre, on the south bank of the canal by Station Bridge.

LYMPNE (pronounced "lim"), set on top of a rise that was once lapped by the sea, three and a half miles inland from Hythe, was the site of the Roman **Portus Lemanis**, which continued to be an important harbour until the Channel receded and stranded the settlement at its present location. Little remains of the Roman port, bar some stonework scattered at the foot of the hill, but on top of the hill, offering fine views over the marshes, is a small Norman church and the much modified **Lympne Castle** (June to mid-Sept Mon–Thurs 10.30am–5.30pm; £2.50), both built by Archbishop Lanfranc, the Norman architect of Canterbury's cathedral. The castle served as a residence for later archbishops, and retains its fourteenth-century Grand Hall. Two miles west of the castle, the overpriced **Port Lympne Wild Animal Park** (daily: summer 10am–dusk; winter 10am–4pm, last admission 2hr before closing; £8.90) houses more than five hundred beasts, including gorillas, elephants, wolves, lions, tigers and rhinos.

Practicalities

Hythe's **tourist office** is, bizarrely, situated in the old public toilets in Red Lion Square (April–June & Sept daily 9am–5.30pm; July & Aug daily 9am–7pm; Oct–March Mon–Sat 9am–5.30pm, Sun 10am–4pm; ☎01303/267799). For **accommodation** check out the secluded *White House*, 27 Napier Gardens (☎01303/266252; ④), overlooking the cricket green just a couple of minutes from the sea, the *Swan Hotel*, a friendly pub on the High Street (☎01303/266311; ②), or the Edwardian *Fern Lodge*, a mile east of the town centre at 87 Seabrook Rd (☎01303/267 315; ②), or if you've got more money to spend, the very superior *Hythe Imperial* (☎01303/267441; ⑦). For high-class **fish and chips**, eat-in or takeaway, drop into *Torbay of Hythe*, 81 High St (closed Sun & Mon); alternatively, the *Capri*, 32–34 High St (☎01303/269898) serves good pizzas and other **Italian dishes**.

Along the coast to Dungeness

The Romney, Hythe and Dymchurch Railway stops at nine stations along the bleak stretch of coastline en route to Dungeness, the first of which is Dymchurch, a tacky seaside resort worth passing over in favour of the sandy strand of **St Mary's Bay**, an easy walk from the next station, **St Mary-in-the-Marsh**; if you need to stop for lunch, head for the excellent *Star* pub opposite the village church, not far from the station.

Next stop on the railway is one of the original Cinque Ports, **NEW ROMNEY**, nine miles southwest of Hythe. It's now really only of interest to connoisseurs of miniature railways, who will be enthralled by the R, H & DR's **Toy and Model Train Museum** (same days as the railway; 10am–5pm; £1) at New Romney station, halfway between the town and the seafront. There's a **tourist office** on the High Street (April–June & Sept daily 9am–5.30pm; July & Aug daily 9am–7pm; Oct–March Mon–Sat 9am–5.30pm, Sun 10am–4pm; ☎01797/364044), where you'll also find the sixteenth-century *Cinque Ports Arms* (☎01797/361894; ①), a nice-looking pub with inexpensive rooms; for something a bit more special, head for *Romney Bay House* (☎01797/364747; ⑤), a wonderfully secluded place to stay by the beach in neighbouring Littlestone-on-Sea.

Dungeness

DUNGENESS, six miles south of Romney and the southern terminus for the R, H & DR, is set in the sort of wasteland normally used as an army firing range, but in this case British Nuclear Fuels grabbed the tip of the Denge Marsh site and built a nuclear power station here in the 1960s. Ten minutes' walk from the station a **BNF Visitor Centre** (Easter–Oct daily 10am–4pm; Nov–Easter Sun–Fri 10am–4pm; guided tours only; last admission 2.45pm; free) with an upbeat "harnessing nature's forces" message, even offers free reactor tours, which will probably only appeal to children (no under-5s), who'll enjoy wearing the yellow hard hats with retractable ear defenders. Another landmark you can visit, right by the station, is the **Old Lighthouse** (June–Sept daily 10.30am–5pm; March–May & Oct Sat & Sun; £2.20), built in 1904 and the fourth one on the site since 1615 – the fifth and present one is visible half a mile away.

The spooky, shingle-swathed expanse of Dungeness has become the abode of eccentric and reclusive characters living in basic fishermen's cabins or disused railway carriages, apparently relishing the area's bleak austerity and carcinogenic threat. The barren environment of the Denge Marsh also supports a unique floral ecology and all around you'll see tiny communities of wildflowers struggling against the unrelenting breeze. If you follow the road back towards Lydd, past the two lighthouses, you will eventually come to **Prospect Cottage**, where the avant-garde film director, writer and artist, Derek Jarman, spent much of his time until his death in 1995 from AIDS. The cottage is still privately owned and not a tourist attraction as such, but a steady stream of pilgrims come here to pay their respects. The flotsam sculptures and unusual flora in the shingle garden make an eye-catching sight – as does the poem "The Sunne Rising" by John Donne, which adorns the southern wall – and were the subject of one of Jarman's last books, *The Garden* (1995).

A few houses up the road from Prospect Cottage, there's a traditional oak-fired smokery where you can buy delicious picnic fodder; alternatively, you can refuel at the unprepossessing, but welcoming *Britannia* pub, which lies between the two lighthouses. The Dungeness shingle bank also attracts huge colonies of gulls and terns, as well as smews and gadwalls – if you're interested in finding out more, pop into the **RSPB visitor centre** (daily: March–Oct 10am–5pm, Nov–Feb 10am–4pm; £2.50), off the road from Dungeness to Lydd.

The Kent Weald

The Weald is usually taken to refer to the region around the spa town of **Royal Tunbridge Wells**, but in fact it stretches across a much larger area between the North and South Downs and includes parts of both Kent and Sussex, though the majority of its attractions are just inside Kent. We've taken the wider definition to include the medieval manor at **Penshurst** and nearby **Hever Castle**, just northeast of Tunbridge Wells, as well as the towns of **Sevenoaks** and **Maidstone**, on the edge of the North Downs.

During Saxon times, much of the Weald was covered in thick forest – the word itself derives from the Germanic word *Wald*, meaning forest, and the suffixes -hurst (meaning wood) and -den (meaning clearing) are commonly found in Wealden village names. Now, however, the region is epitomized by gentle hills, sunken country lanes and somnolent villages as well as some of England's most beautiful gardens – **Sissinghurst**, fifteen miles east of Tunbridge Wells, being the best known.

Public transport to the area is good, but in order to explore the Wealden countryside in any depth, you'll need your own vehicle. If you are driving or on a bicycle, you may want to follow the signs indicating the **High Weald Country Tour**, a seventy-mile back-country loop stretching through the best of the Kentish Weald, from Penshurst in the west to Tenterden in the east. Ask for the leaflet and map at tourist offices in the area.

Regular **trains** from London's Victoria, Waterloo and Charing Cross stations run to Sevenoaks, Maidstone and Tunbridge Wells, and take under an hour. National Express operates several **bus** services daily to the above towns from Victoria Coach Station. Regional bus companies also run regular services from Victoria to the major Wealden towns as well as providing an adequate service between the major towns in Kent.

Royal Tunbridge Wells and around

ROYAL TUNBRIDGE WELLS – not to be confused with the more mundane Tonbridge, a few miles to the north – is the home of the mythical whingeing right-wing letter-writer known as "Disgusted of Tunbridge Wells". Most British people, therefore, view it with derision, but don't be misled – this prosperous spa town, surrounded by gorgeous countryside, is an elegant and diverting place.

In 1606 Lord North discovered a bubbling spring while riding through the Waterdown Forest, which covered the area at that time. From the claim that this spring had curative properties a spa resort evolved: Charles I's wife camped out here for several weeks after giving birth to the future Charles II, whose own wife later came here in an attempt to cure her infertility. The spa reached its height of popularity during the Regency period when such restorative cures were in vogue. The distinctively well-mannered architecture of that period, generously surrounded by parklands in which the rejuvenated gentry exercised, gives the southern and western part of town its special character. The architecture also has an effect on the locals. If you turn up around the beginning of August, you'll find that many of the townsfolk have taken to the streets in eighteenth-century garb for the five-day **Georgian Festivities**.

The spa and the town

The icon of those genteel times, and the best place to start your wanderings, is the **Pantiles**, an elegant colonnaded parade of shops, ten minutes' walk south of the train station, where the fashionable once gathered to promenade and take the waters. The name stems from the chunky Kent tiles made of baked clay, which were put down as paving during Queen Anne's reign. Hub of the Pantiles is the original **Chalybeate Spring**, in the Bath House (March–Sept daily 10am–5pm), where a "Dipper" has been employed since the late eighteenth century to serve the ferrous waters. A period-dressed incumbent will fetch you a glass from the cool spring for 25p – or, if you bring your own cup, you can help yourself for free from the adjacent source. The Bath House itself was built in 1804, but failed as an enterprise as the water turns a nasty colour when heated; it closed in 1847 and now houses a pharmacy.

You can view one of the original "pantiles" in the exhibition, **A Day at the Wells** (daily: April–Oct 10am–5pm; Nov–March 10am–4pm; £4.95), situated in the basement of the nearby Corn Exchange. An audio tour, narrated as if by Richard "Beau" Nash – self-appointed arbiter of good taste (see box on p.350) – attempts to re-create, with the help of various historical tableaux, spa life in the eighteenth century. In bad weather, a stroll along the museum's reconstruction of the Pantiles might seem preferable to the real thing.

Apart from tiles, Tunbridge also produced domestic ceramics, on view with other local relics and historical artefacts in the **Museum and Art Gallery** built in the 1950s at the top of Mount Pleasant Road (Mon–Sat 9.30am–5pm; free), a fifteen-minute walk up the old-fashioned High Street, from the Pantiles. The museum's main attraction is a superb collection of locally made wooden boxes, known as "Tunbridge Ware", introduced in the 1830s, whose "mosaic-style" inlaid lids are decorated with rural scenes and ornamental borders. The gallery also puts on excellent temporary exhibitions in its one-room art gallery.

On the east side of the High Street, the Grove and, to the north, Calverley Grounds are havens of urban tranquillity, while **The Common**, spreading out on the west side of town, is laced with pathways carved by the original visitors to the spa. You can trace the course of the old horse-racing track, or simply sit among the strange sandstone formations of Wellington Rocks. If you fancy a more energetic scramble, head three miles west of Tunbridge Wells to **High Rocks** (daily 9am–6pm or dusk; £1), another fissured outcrop of towering rocks linked by stairways and bridges and bursting with rhododendrons; traces of a Neolithic settlement are also visible here.

Practicalities

The Tunbridge Wells **tourist office** is housed in the Old Fish Market, in the Pantiles (Oct–April Mon–Sat 9am–5pm, Sun 10am–4pm; May & Sept Mon–Sat 9am–5pm, Sun 10am–5pm; June–Aug Mon–Sat 9am–6pm, Sun 10am–5pm; ☎01892/515675) and will hand out a map of the town. The **train station**, on the London Charing Cross to Hastings line, is south of the town centre, where High Street becomes Mount Pleasant Road.

Tunbridge Wells has a fair number of very plush **hotels**, relics of the good old days, like the exemplary *Royal Wells Inn*, overlooking the Common from Mount Ephraim (☎01892/511188; ⑤), or the *Swan Hotel*, a worthwhile splurge in the Pantiles itself (☎01892/541450; ⑤). For **B&B** the elegant *Ephraim Lodge* on the Common (☎01892/523053; ③), and the nearby *Clarken Guest House*, a large Victorian house with gardens at 61 Frant Rd (☎01892/533397; ②) are both good value.

For a small town, Tunbridge Wells has a fair selection of **restaurants**, one of the best (and most expensive) being *Thackeray's House*, one-time home of the writer, at 85 London Rd (☎01892/511921; closed Sun eve & Mon). At the other end of the cultural spectrum, there's *Gracelands*, a Chinese restaurant on Cumberland Walk (☎01892/540754; closed Sun & Mon), with a live Chinese Elvis show. The cheaper end of the market is dominated by the chains: the reliable *Pizza Express* have a branch at 81 High St, and *Pierre Victoire*, on Mount Pleasant Rd, offers a bargain three-course lunch. *Flippers*, 9 High St (closed Sun), fry superior fish and chips, while there are great veggie options at the *Trinity Arts Centre Café* in a converted church on Church Road (lunch & pre-theatre deals only; closed Sun).

One **pub** you're unlikely to miss is the popular *Opera House*, a new Weatherspoon's conversion in the town's former 1902 theatre on Mount Pleasant Road – you can sit in the foyer, the stalls or even on stage and gaze up at the balconies. The *Duke of York*, in the Pantiles, is much smaller and snugger, as is the pleasant *Grape Vine* wine bar on the High Street. For a cocktail or beer, check out the stylish *Bar Zia* at the bottom of the High Street.

Penshurst and Hever Castle

Tudor timber-framed houses and shops line the high street of the attractive village of **PENSHURST**, five miles northwest of Tunbridge Wells (bus #231 or #233; not Sun). Its village church, **St John the Baptist**, is capped by an unusual four-spired tower and is entered under a beamed archway which conceals a rustic post office. However, the main reason for coming here is to visit **Penshurst Place** (house: March Sat & Sun noon–5.30pm; April–Sept daily noon–5.30pm; grounds same days 11am–6pm; house &

grounds £5.70; grounds only £4.20), home to the Sidney family since 1552 and birth-place of the Elizabethan soldier and poet, Sir Philip Sidney. The fourteenth-century Barons Hall, built for Sir John de Pulteney, four times Mayor of London, is the chief glory of the interior, with its sixty-foot-high chestnut roof still in place. The ten acres of grounds include a formal Italian garden with clipped box hedges, and double herba-ceous borders mixed with an abundance of yew hedges.

The moated and much-altered **Hever Castle**, three miles further west (daily: April–Nov noon–5pm; £7.30), is where Anne Boleyn, second wife of Henry VIII, grew up, and where Anne of Cleves, Henry's fourth wife, lived after their divorce. In 1903, having fallen into disrepair, the castle was bought by William Waldorf-Astor, American millionaire owner of *The Times*, who had the house assiduously restored, panelling the rooms with fine reproductions of Tudor woodcarvings. In the Inner Hall hangs a fine portrait of Henry VIII by Holbein; a further Holbein painting of Elizabeth I has recent-ly been restored and is hanging on the middle floor. Upstairs, in Anne Boleyn's room, you can see her book of prayers which she carried with her to the executioner's block, but more impressive is the Anne of Cleves room, which houses an unusually well-pre-served tapestry, illustrating the marriage of Henry's sister to King Louis XII of France, with Anne Boleyn as one of the ladies-in-waiting.

Outside in the grounds, next to the gift shop, is the absorbing **Guthrie Miniature Model Houses Collection**, showing the development of aristocratic seats from feudal times on. However, the best feature of the grounds is Waldorf-Astor's beautiful **Italian Garden**, built on reclaimed marshland and decorated with Roman statuary. For kids (and adults) there's a traditional **yew hedge maze** to figure out, an adventure play-ground and a **water maze**. Also in the grounds is a twenty-bedroom mock-Tudor annexe, built by Waldorf-Astor, who decided that the castle didn't have enough rooms to accommodate the guests of a thrusting newspaper magnate in style; it's now used solely as a conference venue.

Scotney Castle and Sissinghurst

Picturesque **Scotney Castle**, eight miles southeast of Tunbridge Wells (April–Oct Wed–Fri 11am–6pm, Sat & Sun 2–6pm; £4; NT), sits half-ruined within romantically landscaped gardens on the edge of a small lake (bus #256 then a mile's walk southeast; not Sun). The only part of the small castle still intact is the Jacobean wing (open May to mid-Sept), which houses artefacts from the sixteenth century, but the real reason to visit is to admire the castle's delightful setting and its superb grounds.

Sissinghurst, twelve miles east of Tunbridge Wells (April to mid-Oct Tues–Fri 1–6.30pm, Sat & Sun 10am–5.30pm; £6; NT), was described by Vita Sackville-West as "a garden crying out for rescue" when she and her husband took it over in the 1920s. Over the following years they transformed the five-acre plot into one of England's greatest and most popular modern gardens.

Spread over the site of a medieval moated manor (which was rebuilt into an Elizabethan mansion of which only one wing remains today), the gardens were designed around the linear pattern of the former buildings' walls. A major part of Sissinghurst's appeal derives from the way that the flowers are allowed to spill over onto the narrow walkways, defying the classical formality of the great gardens that pre-ceded it. The brick tower that Vita had restored and used as her study acts as a focal point and offers the best views of the walled gardens. Most impressive are the **White Garden**, composed solely of white flowers and silvery-grey foliage, and the **Cottage Garden**, featuring flora in shades of orange, yellow and red.

The reputation of the gardens, as well as its limited capacity for visitors, is such that Sissinghurst gets extremely busy in summer when timed tickets for half-hourly visits are issued. Food options in the gardens are limited and overpriced – your best bet is to bring a picnic. **Bus** #297 from Royal Tunbridge Wells (not Sun) takes you within two miles of the gardens, and buses #4 and #5 run between Maidstone and Hastings (not Sun), stopping in Sissinghurst en route.

Sevenoaks and around

Set among the green sand ridges of west Kent, 25 miles from London, **SEVENOAKS** was once a small Kent village – it is now a very popular commuter town, with trains reaching London in under an hour. Sadly, the place lost all but one of the ageing oaks from which it derives its name in the storm that struck southern England in October 1987 (see box below). With mere saplings having taken their place, the only real reason to come to the town is to visit the immense baronial estate of Knole.

Knole (April–Oct Wed–Sat noon–4pm, Sun 11am–5pm; £5; NT) is entered from the south end of the Sevenoaks High Street, making it very nearly half an hour's walk from the train station. The house was created in 1456 by Archbishop Thomas Bourchier, who transformed the existing dwelling into a palace for himself and succeeding archbishops of Canterbury. The palace, numerically designed to match the calendar with 7 courtyards, 52 staircases and 365 rooms, was appropriated by Henry VIII, who lavished further expense on it and hunted in the thousand acres of parkland, still home to several hundred deer. Henry's daughter, Elizabeth I, passed the estate on to her cousin, Thomas Sackville, who remodelled the house in 1605. Part of Knole's allure is that it has preserved its Jacobean exterior and remained in the family's hands ever since. Vita Sackville-West, who in 1923 penned a definitive history of her family entitled *Knole and the Sackvilles*, was brought up here, and her one-time lover Virginia Woolf derived inspiration for her novel *Orlando* from her frequent visits to the house. Only thirteen rooms are open to the public, featuring an array of fine, if well-worn, furnishings and tapestries. Paintings by Gainsborough and Van Dyck are on display, as are Reynolds's depictions of George III and of Queen Charlotte – between them hangs a painting of their strutting, dandified progeny, George IV, one of the fifteen children she bore the king. Note that the deer park is open for free daily throughout the year, whereas the garden is open from May to September on the first Wednesday of the month from 11am to 4pm; entry costs £1.

Sevenoaks' **tourist office** is in the library building (April–Sept Mon–Sat 9.30am–5pm; Oct–March Mon–Fri 9.30am–5pm, Sat 9.30am–4.30pm; ☎01732/450305), just beyond the **bus station** in Buckhurst Lane; the **train station** is fifteen minutes' walk north of the town centre on the London Road. The town's priciest and smartest **accommodation** is at the excellent *Royal Oak Hotel*, a seventeenth-century coaching inn at the south end of the High Street (☎01732/451109; ⑤), beyond the entrance to

---

THE GREAT STORM

On the evening of October 15, 1987, a BBC weatherman gave a forecast that he has never been able to live down, predicting the possibility of "some strong winds in the southeast", but rejecting the rumour that a gale was on its way. An unusually low depression had developed over the Bay of Biscay earlier that evening and was expected to weaken as it moved up into the North Sea, avoiding the mainland. Instead, it headed directly towards England's southern coast. The storm reached its peak, with hurricane-force gusts of up to 110mph, at around 6am, which kept the death toll to just eighteen, in contrast to the last such recorded storm in 1703, described by Daniel Defoe as "the most violent Tempest the World ever saw", which killed eight thousand people. However, property damage from Cornwall to East Anglia ran into millions of pounds and many of the southeast's landscaped gardens were utterly ravaged. An estimated three million trees were felled by the winds, leaving scars that still testify to that night's carnage.

Knole. In most people's range is the self-catering "family room" at the elegant *Red House* 23 Bayhem Rd (☎01732/460506; ②), ten minutes northeast of the High Street, or the spacious room at *Burley Lodge*, close to the entrance to Knole (☎01732/455761; ①). The nearest **youth hostel** (☎01732/761341) is an imposing Victorian vicarage set in its own grounds in Kemsing, four miles northeast of Sevenoaks; it's a two-mile hike from Kemsing station or you can take bus #425/6 or #433 from Sevenoaks to Kemsing post office, which is close by – note that no public transport runs to Kemsing on Sundays.

For inexpensive filling **food**, you can't fault *Pizza Express*, 146 High St, but for something more snackish (and a really good coffee), pop inside *Coffee Call*, on Dorset Street. The menu at the nearby *Dorset Arms* is better than your average pub, but for some truly delicious food, you need to go to *No. 5* (☎01732/455555), the restaurant at the *Royal Oak Hotel*, which offers a two-course lunch for just over £10, though in the evening one main dish will cost you more than that; for an inexpensive evening meal, head for the hotel's bistro (in other words the bar), which is also good – and half the price.

Lullingstone Roman Villa

Lullingstone Roman Villa, seven miles north of Sevenoaks and half a mile south of the village of Eynsford train station (daily: April–Sept 10am–6pm; Oct 10am–5pm; Nov–March 10am–4pm; £2.50; EH), has some of the best-preserved Roman mosaics in southeast England on show, in a pleasant location alongside the trickle of the River Darent. Believed to have been the first-century residence of a farmer, the site has yielded some fine marble busts – these are now on display in the British Museum in London, but a superb floor remains depicting the killing of the Chimera, a mythical fire-breathing beast with a lion's head, goat's body and a serpent's tail. Excavation in a nearby chamber has revealed early Christian iconography, which suggests that the villa may have become a Romano-Christian chapel in the third century, pre-empting the official arrival of that religion by three hundred years and making Lullingstone one of the earliest sites of clandestine Christian worship in England.

Chartwell

The residence of Winston Churchill from 1924 until his death in 1965, **Chartwell**, six miles west of Sevenoaks (April–June, Sept & Oct Wed–Sun 11am–5pm; July & Aug Tues–Sun 11am–5pm; £5.50; NT), is one of the most visited of the National Trust's properties. It's an unremarkable, heavily restored Tudor building whose main appeal is the wartime premier's memorabilia, including his paintings, which show an unexpectedly contemplative side to the famously gruff statesman. Entry to the house is by timed ticket at peak times – expect long queues. Metrobus #246, which passes Bromley South station, stops near the gates.

Ightham Mote

The secluded, moated manor house of **Ightham Mote** (pronounced "I-tam"), six miles southeast of Sevenoaks just off the A227 (April–Oct Mon, Wed–Fri, Sun & public holidays 11am–5.30pm; £5; NT), originates from the fourteenth century and is one of the southeast's most picturesque National Trust properties, though the original defensive appearance of this half-timbered ragstone building has been muted by Tudor alterations. A tour of the interior reveals a mixture of architectural styles ranging from the fourteenth-century Old Chapel and crypt, through a barrel-vaulted Tudor chapel with a painted ceiling to an eighteenth-century Palladian window. This idyllically situated medieval dwelling is being restored by the National Trust, whose efforts are described in a small exhibition on the ground floor. Igtham is tricky to get to by bus, with only the infrequent #404 from Sevenoaks (not Sat or Sun) making the trip.

Maidstone and around

If you missed out **MAIDSTONE**, you wouldn't be missing much. A minor Roman and later a Saxon settlement, Maidstone is Kent's principal commercial, industrial and agricultural centre, but the only bit of town that holds any interest at all is the cluster of ancient buildings south of the High Street down Mill Street, by the banks of the River Medway, a spot whose charm is somewhat tempered by the fact that it lies right by a six-lane highway.

Of most interest is the **Archbishop's Palace** (daily 10.30am–4pm; free), built around 1348 and formerly used as a stopping-off point for the Archbishop of Canterbury on journeys to London. Although the building is now used as a registry office, with a café upstairs, it's worth checking out the impressive oak-panelled function rooms. Close by is **All Saints' Church**, a good example of late-fourteenth-century Perpendicular architecture. Standing on its very own traffic island, opposite the Archbishop's Palace, is a wonderful old red-brick, ragstone and timber building, originally the archbishop's stables, and now appropriately enough the **Tyrwhitt-Drake Museum of Carriages** (April–Oct daily 10.30am–5pm; £1.50), housing every type of carriage from infant perambulators to royal wagons. If you've time to spare, it's worth paying a visit to **Maidstone Museum and Art Gallery** (Mon–Sat 10am–5.15pm, Sun 11am–4pm; free), which occupies a grandiose red-brick Elizabethan mansion built by the local MP on St Faith's Street, two blocks north of the High Street. The highlights of the museum's vast collection are a half-unravelled Egyptian mummy, a statue of Lady Godiva and a whole cabinet of curiosities brought back from around the globe by the local-born Victorian explorer, Julius Brenchley.

The **tourist office** is situated in the gatehouse of the Archbishop's Palace (April–Oct Mon–Sat 9am–5pm; Nov–March Mon–Fri 9.30am–5pm, Sat 9.30am–2pm; ☎01622/602169). Maidstone has no fewer than three **train stations**: Maidstone East, served by trains from London Victoria, is ten minutes' walk north of the High Street up pedestrianized Week Street; while Maidstone Barracks and Maidstone West, both on the west bank of the Medway and less than ten minutes' walk from the High Street, are served by local trains from Tonbridge and Strood.

Maidstone's **accommodation** is fairly limited: the *Rock House Hotel*, 102 Tonbridge Rd (☎01622/751616; ②), west of the centre, is one of the better options; otherwise you're best off heading out of town, to somewhere with more character, such as the converted oast houses on Barn Hill in Hunton (☎01622/829852; ③), seven miles southwest of Maidstone. **Food** options in town include *Bar Coast*, Middle Row (☎01622/606941), which has a tasty and moderately priced menu. Otherwise, there's reliable pub grub and real ales at the *Muggleton Inn*, a big Weatherspoon's pub on the High Street, and a branch of *Pizza Express* in the old Conservative Club on Earl Street. If you're in the mood for a pricey gastronomic treat, *Le Soufflé*, on the Green in Bearsted (☎01622/737065; closed Sun eve & Mon), two miles east of Maidstone on the A20, specializes in classic French dishes.

Cobtree Museum of Kent Life

Though too close to the M20 to re-create any rural idyll, the **Cobtree Museum of Kent Life** two miles north (March Sat & Sun 10am–4pm; April–Oct daily 10am–5.30pm; £4.20) offers a fascinating account of rural life in the county over the last hundred years or so. The farm was bought in 1904 by local bigwigs, the Tyrwhitt-Drakes, and was at one time a zoo – today, the animals are purely livestock. The section on hop-picking in the traditional oast house, is particularly fascinating. Nearby, you can view a series of hopper huts, in which East Enders from London used to spend their hop-picking "holidays". To get to the museum, you need to take **bus** #155 (Mon–Sat only) from Maidstone; or on a Sunday, you can catch a **boat** instead (hourly noon–4pm; £3 return).

Leeds Castle

Leeds Castle, five miles east of Maidstone, off the A20 (daily: March–Oct 10am–5pm; Nov–Feb 10am–3pm; castle, park & gardens £9.30; park & gardens £7.30), more closely resembles a fairytale palace than a defensively efficient fortress. Named after the local village, work on the castle began around 1120. The present stone castle dates from Norman times and is set half on an island in the middle of a lake and half on the mainland surrounded by landscaped parkland. Following centuries of regal and noble ownership (and, less glamorously, service as a prison) the castle is now run as a commercial concern, hosting conferences as well as sporting and cultural events. Its interior fails to match the castle's stunning, much-photographed external appearance and, in places, twentieth-century renovations have quashed any of its historical charm; possibly the most unusual feature inside is the dog collar museum in the gatehouse. In the grounds, there's a fine aviary with some superb and colourful exotic specimens, as well as manicured gardens and a mildly challenging maze. The easiest way to get to Leeds Castle by public transport is to buy an all-inclusive rail ticket to Bearsted station, which pays for a shuttle service and entry to the castle; services run from London Victoria via Maidstone East.

SUSSEX

Although now separated into two counties, East and West, **Sussex** (deriving from "land of the south Saxons") retains a unified identity. Most of the region was covered in dense forest until the Tudor era, when the huge demand for timber and charcoal began its deforestation. However, large areas of woodland still exist in inland parts of the counties and contribute to Sussex's bucolic character. Nowhere is this rural atmosphere more evident than on the southeast's main long-distance footpath, the **South Downs Way**, which runs along the grassy ridge of the South Downs, giving dramatic views over some fine countryside as well as over the coast, where the Downs meet the sea at the chalk cliffs of **Beachy Head** and **Seven Sisters**.

However, Sussex also has its fair share of urban centres, many of which are populated by London commuters. The best known is the traditional seaside resort of **Brighton**, the counties' biggest and brashest town, while a few miles inland more sedate **Lewes**, the county town of East Sussex, is famed for its bonfire night celebrations. **Hastings**, farther east, is renowned for its historical connections, although the eponymous fight actually took place six miles away at **Battle**. Farther east still, on the edge of the Romney marshes, the former Cinque Port of **Rye** exemplifies rustic English tweeness. In West Sussex, the main centres of interest are the attractive hilltop town of **Arundel**, surrounded by unspoilt countryside, and the county town of **Chichester**.

Hastings and around

During the twelfth and thirteenth centuries, **Hastings** flourished as an influential Cinque Port (see p.170). In 1287 its harbour creek was silted up by the same storm which washed away nearby **Winchelsea**, forcing the settlement to be temporarily abandoned. These days, Hastings is a curious mixture of unpretentious fishing port, traditional seaside resort and arty retreat popular with painters (there's even a street and quarter named Bohemia). In 1066, William, Duke of Normandy, landed at Pevensey Bay, a few miles west of town, and made Hastings his base, but his forces met Harold's army – exhausted after quelling a Nordic invasion near York – at **Battle**, six miles northwest of Hastings. Battle today boasts a magnificent abbey built by William in thanks for his victory, which makes a good afternoon's excursion from Hastings. Farther north, **Batemans**, home of Rudyard Kipling and the classic **Bodiam Castle** are both easily reached from Hastings in a day-trip.

Hastings

Hastings' **old town**, east of the pier, holds most of the appeal of this part tacky, part pretty seaside resort. With the exception of the oddly neglected Regency architecture of **Pelham Crescent**, directly beneath the castle ruins, **All Saints Street** is by far the most evocative thoroughfare, punctuated with the odd, rickety, timber-framed dwelling from the fifteenth century. The thirteenth-century **St Clement's Church** stands in the High Street, which runs parallel to All Saints Street, on the other side of the Bourne. By a louvred window at the top of the church's tower rests a cannonball that was lodged there by a Dutch galleon in the 1600s – its poignancy rather dispelled by a companion fitted in the eighteenth century for the sake of symmetry. On the right as you walk up the High Street, you'll see **Starr's Cottages**, one of which is wedge-shaped and painted to resemble a piece of cheese, while the **Old Town Hall Museum** on the High Street (Mon–Fri 10am–5pm, Sat 10am–1pm & 2–5pm, Sun 3–5pm; free) offers the customary spread on local history.

Down by the seafront, the area known as **The Stade** is characterized by its tall, black weatherboard **net shops**, most dating from the mid-nineteenth century (and still in use), but which first appeared here in Tudor times. To raise Hastings' tone, the town council attempted to shift the fishermen and their malodorously drying nets from the beach by increasing rents per square foot, and these sinister-looking towers were their response. Somewhat remarkably, Hastings still boasts a working fishing fleet, the boats being dragged up onto the shingle, and you can still buy fresh fish from several of the net shops.

There's a trio of nautical attractions on nearby Rock-a-Nore Road. The **Fisherman's Museum** (daily: April–Oct 10am–5pm; Nov–March 11am–4pm; free), a converted seaman's chapel, offers an account of the port's commercial activities and displays one of Hastings' last clinker-built luggers – exceptionally stout trawlers able to withstand being winched up and down the shingle beach. The neighbouring **Shipwreck Heritage Centre** (daily 10.30am–5pm; £2.20), details the dramas of unfortunate mariners, focusing on the wreck of the *Amsterdam*, beached in 1749 and now embedded in the sand three miles west of town awaiting a proposed excavation. Opposite is the **Hastings Sea-Life Centre** (daily 10am–5pm; £5.25), one of a popular chain of aquariums with walk-through tunnels, magnified tanks housing marine creatures and an excellent and sympathetic film on sharks.

Castle Hill, separating the old town from the visually less-interesting modern quarter, can be ascended by the **West Hill Cliff Railway**, from George Street, off Marine Parade, one of two Victorian funicular railways in Hastings (daily: April–Sept 10.30am–5.30pm; Oct–March 11am–4pm; 80p); The East Cliff Railway, on Rock-a-Nore Rd is open in summer only. This hilltop is where William the Conqueror erected his first **Castle** in 1066, one of several prefabricated wooden structures brought over from Normandy in sections. Built on the site of an existing fort, probably of Saxon origins, it was soon replaced by a more permanent stone structure, but in the thirteenth century storms caused the cliffs to subside, tipping most of the castle into the sea; the surviving ruins, however, offer an excellent prospect of the town. The castle is home to **The 1066 Story** (daily: April–Sept 10am–5pm; Oct–March 11am–3.30pm; £3), in which the events of the last successful invasion of the British mainland are described inside a mock-up of a siege tent. The twenty-minute audiovisual details the history of the castle and corrects a few myths about the famous battle.

More fun is the **Smugglers' Adventure**, over the hill (daily: Easter–July & Sept 10am–5pm; Aug 10am–5.30pm; Oct–Easter 11am–3.30pm; £4.50; combined ticket with

The 1066 Story £6.45). Here the labyrinthine St Clement's caves, named after a carving resembling St Clement but probably predating Christianity, have been converted to house a number of amusing and educational dioramas depicting the town's long history of duty dodging. During the eighteenth century, smuggling – especially of alcohol and tobacco – was the region's biggest source of income after agriculture and a farm worker could earn more than a week's wages with one night's contraband. Large-scale smuggling waned in the 1830s when a more efficient coastguard and diminishing taxes reduced its viability.

Hastings also has its fair share of traditional English seaside activities – mini-golf, boating, go-karts and **Hastings Pier**, west of the old town, where bingo and palm-reading are on offer, along with the usual video games and slot machines.

Practicalities

The **train station**, served by regular trains from both London's Charing Cross (via Ashford International) and Victoria (via Lewes) stations, is a ten-minute walk from the seafront along Havelock Road; National Express **bus** services operate from the station at the junction of Havelock Road and Queen's Road. The **tourist office** is located within the Town Hall on Queen's Road (daily: June–Aug 9.30am–6pm; Sept–May 10am–5pm; ☎01424/781111); there's also a smaller seafront office (April–Sept daily 9.30am–6pm; Oct–March Sat & Sun 11am–4pm; ☎01424/781120) near the Boating Lake on East Parade by the old town.

There are lots of inexpensive **accommodation** choices away from the seafront, particularly along Cambridge Gardens, near the station, but for sea views you have to pay a little extra. *Argyle Guest House*, 32 Cambridge Gardens (☎01424/421294; ①), has good value rooms with sea views; the cosy timber-framed *Lavender and Lace*, 106 All Saints St (☎01424/716290; ①), is right in the middle of the old town and books up fast; as is the *Jenny Lind Hotel*, 69 High St (☎01424/421392; ②), which has pleasantly uncluttered, clean rooms above its own pub-restaurant; *West Hill Cottage*, an attractive listed cottage with friendly hosts and generous breakfasts, is also well located in Exmouth Place near the bottom of West Hill (☎01424/716021; ①). Hastings' **youth hostel** (☎01424/812373) is in the large manor house of Guestling Hall set in its own grounds (with camping available), three miles out of Hastings on the road to Rye; bus #711 from the main tourist office will take you there.

By far the best prospects for **eating and drinking** are on the High Street and its pedestrianized offshoot, George Street. The *Jenny Lind Hotel*, offers imaginative, moderately priced fish and seafood dishes; *Harris* 58 High St (closed Sun), with its wood-panelled walls and potted plants, does decent tapas; while the waft of garlic from *Bella Napoli* 9 George St (☎01424/429211) is positively enticing. The best fish and chips in town are at the eat-in *Mermaid*, 2 Rock-a-Nore, right by the beach, or from the neighbouring takeaway *Blue Dolphin*; jellied eels can be sampled from the adjacent net shop. *Rösers*, 64 Eversfield Place, on the seafront in St Leonards-on-Sea, a short walk west of central Hastings (☎01424/712 218), is a classy, and expensive, option specializing in fish.

There are more than thirty **pubs** to choose from in Hastings: the local fishermen's favourite is the *Lord Nelson* right by the front on the Bourne; others to check out are the ever-popular *First In Last Out*, 15 High St in the old town, the creaky-beamed hostelry, *Ye Olde Pump House*, George St, or the trendy clubby bar, *The Street*, Robertson St, accessible via a tiny entrance on Cambridge Road in the new town centre. Hastings' one and only decent club is *The Crypt*, on Havelock Road (closed Mon, Tues & Sun), popular with students from the town's thirty-odd language schools.

Battle

The town of **BATTLE** – a ten-minute train ride inland from Hastings – occupies the site of the most famous land battle in British history. Here, on October 14, 1066, the invading Normans swarmed up the hillside from Senlac Moor and overcame the Anglo-Saxon army of King Harold, who was killed not by an arrow through the eye – a myth resulting from the misinterpretation of the Bayeux Tapestry – but by a workaday clubbing about the head. Before the battle took place, William vowed that, should he win the engagement, he would build a religious foundation on the very spot of Harold's slaying to atone for the bloodshed, and, true to his word, **Battle Abbey** (daily: April–Sept 10am–6pm; Oct 10am–5pm; Nov–March 10am–4pm; £4; EH) was built four years later and subsequently occupied by a fraternity of Benedictines. The magnificent structure, though partially destroyed in the Dissolution and much rebuilt and revised over the centuries, still dominates the town, with the huge gatehouse, added in 1338, now containing a good audiovisual exhibition on the battle. You can also wander through the ruins of the abbey to the spot where Harold was clubbed – the site of the high altar of William's abbey, now marked by a memorial stone.

Though nothing can match the resonance of the abbey, the rest of the town is worth a stroll. **St Mary's Church**, on the High Street, has a fine Norman font and nave and the churchyard contains the grave of one Isaac Ingall who, according to the inscription on his tomb, was 120 years old when he died in 1798. At the far end of the High Street, packed with antique shops and other tourist outlets, is the fourteenth-century **Almonry** (Mon–Sat 10am–4.30pm; £1) – the present town hall – which contains a miniature model of Battle and the oldest Guy Fawkes in the country. Every year, on the Saturday nearest to November 5, this three-hundred-year-old effigy is paraded along the High Street at the head of a torchlit procession culminating at a huge bonfire in front of the abbey gates – similar celebrations occur in Lewes (see p.195).

The **tourist office** is at 88 High St (April–Oct daily 10am–6pm; Nov–March Mon–Sat 10am–4pm, Sun 10am–2pm; ☎01424/773721). Battle's **accommodation** tends to be agreeable but expensive, for example the *George Hotel*, an old coaching inn with fully en-suite rooms at 23 High St (☎01424/774466; ⑤), or the luxurious country house, *Powdermills Hotel*, Powdermill Lane (☎01424/775511; ⑧). For less pricey B&B deals try the elegant *Abbey View*, Caldbec Hill (☎01424/775513; ③) only two minutes' walk from town; or the 270-year-old Georgian *Kitchenham Farm* (☎01424/892221; ②), a working farm near the village of Ninfield, about seven miles southwest of Battle. For town-centre **pubs** in Battle, all serving decent food, try the fifteenth-century *Old King's Head* on Mount Street, the *1066* at 12 High St, or the *Chequers Inn* at Lower Lake, on the High Street.

Rye and Winchelsea

Perched on a hill overlooking the Romney Marshes, ten miles east of Hastings, sits the ancient town of **RYE**. Added as a "limb" to the original Cinque Ports (see p.170), the town then became marooned two miles inland with the retreat of the sea and the silting-up of the River Rother. It is now one of the most popular places in East Sussex – half-timbered, skew-roofed and quintessentially English, but also very commercialized.

From Strand Quay, head up The Deals to Rye's most picturesque street, the sloping cobbled lane of **Mermaid Street**, which will bring you eventually to the peaceful oasis of Church Square. Henry James, who strangely suggested that "Rye would . . . remind you of Granada", spent the last years of his life at **Lamb House** at the east end of Mermaid Street (April–Oct Wed & Sat 2pm–6pm; £2.50; NT). The house's three rooms and garden are of interest chiefly to fans of James's novels, or to admirers of E.F. Benson, who lived here after James. A blue plaque in the High Street also testifies that Radclyffe Hall, author of the seminal lesbian novel, *The Well of Loneliness*, was also once a resident of the town. At the centre of Church Square stands **St Mary's Church**, boasting the oldest functioning pendulum clock in the country; the ascent of the church tower – whose bells were looted by French raiders in 1377 and then retrieved with similar audacity – offers fine views over the clay-tiled roofs and grid of narrow lanes. In the far corner of the square, stands the **Ypres Tower**, formerly used to keep watch for cross-Channel invaders, and now a part of the **Rye Castle Museum** on nearby East Street (April–Oct daily 10.30am–5.30pm; Nov–March Sat & Sun 10.30am–4pm; £3). Both sites house a number of relics from Rye's past, including an eighteenth-century fire-engine. Also worth seeking out is **Rye Art Gallery** (daily 10.30am–5pm; free), located in two lovely houses off the High Street, beyond East Street; the Easton Rooms stage exhibitions by local contemporary artists, while the Stormont Studio has a small permanent collection, including works by artists associated with Rye, such as Burra and Nash.

WINCHELSEA, perched on a hill two miles southwest of Rye and easily reached by train, bus, foot or bike, shares Rye's indignity of having become detached from the sea, but has a very different character. Rye gets all the visitors, whereas Winchelsea feels positively deserted, an impression augmented as you pass through the medieval Strand Gate and see the ghostly ruined **Church of St Thomas à Becket**. The original settlement was washed away in the great storm in 1287, after which Edward I planned a new port with a chequerboard pattern of streets. Even at the height of Winchelsea's economic activity, however, not all the plots on the grid were used. The town also suffered from incursions by the French in the fourteenth and fifteenth centuries, at which time the church was pillaged; the remains of the church constitute Sussex's finest example of the Decorated style. Head south for a mile and a half and you get to **Winchelsea beach**, a long expanse of pebbly sand.

Practicalities

Hourly **trains** run to Rye and Winchelsea from Hastings; the bus station is just outside Winchelsea. **Bus** #711 runs into the centre of both towns from Hastings. Rye's **tourist office**, on Strand Quay (daily: April–Oct 9am–5.30pm; Nov–March 10am–4pm; ☎01797/226696), has masses of information on local attractions. The same building houses Rye's **museum** (same hours; £2) with an interesting twenty-minute audiovisual about the town and a scaled-down model of Rye on show – they also rent out audio tours to take you round the town itself (£2). The town's popularity with weekending Londoners gives it an excellent choice of **accommodation**. The most luxurious option is the *Mermaid Inn* (☎01797/223065; ⑦), a fifteenth-century pub on Mermaid Street; and there's also the handsomely furnished rooms in *Jeake's House*, also on Mermaid Street (☎01797/222828; ②). Both are deservedly popular. Alternatively, there's *Old Vicarage*, 66 Church Square (☎01797/222119; ②), a lovely pink Georgian house next to the church; the *Playden Cottage Guest House* Military Rd (☎01797/222234; ③), off the A268, is another charming guest house; and finally, *Owlet* B&B, 37 New Rd (☎01797/222544; ①), east of the centre on the A259 and one of Rye's least expensive options. The fourteenth-century *Strand House* (☎01797/226276; ②), at the foot of the cliff below Strand Gate, is the best accommodation option in Winchelsea. The *Mermaid* is by far the most atmospheric **pub**, with heavy exposed timbers throughout; a younger crowd frequents the more laid-back *Strand Quay*, at the bottom of Mermaid Street. The best **restaurant** in town is the pricey *Landgate Bistro* at 5 Landgate (☎01797/222829; closed Sun & Mon), which serves good steaks, but if you want something a touch less expensive try the seafood at the *Old Forge* in Wish Street (☎01797/223227; closed Mon & Sun, also Tues & Wed lunch) or the small and intimate *Gatehouse Restaurant*, 1 Tower St (☎01797/222 327; closed Mon lunch). For more excellent seafood dishes, head for the *Flushing Inn* on Market Street (☎01797/223292). *The Peacock*, 8 Lion St (☎01797/226702), serves up everything from beans on toast to moderately priced fresh Rye Bay plaice in a suitably ancient setting – it's also a Good place for delicious cream teas.

Bodiam Castle

Ask a child to draw a castle and the outline of **Bodiam Castle**, nine miles north of Hastings (Feb–Oct daily 10am–6pm or dusk; Nov–Dec Tues–Sun 10am–4pm or dusk; £3.50; NT), would be the result: a classically stout square block with rounded corner turrets, battlements and a moat. When it was built in 1385 to guard what were the lower reaches of the River Rother, Bodiam was state-of-the-art military architecture, but during the Civil War a company of Roundheads breached the fortress and removed its roof to reduce its effectiveness as a possible stronghold for the king. Over the next 250 years Bodiam fell into neglect until restoration earlier this century by Lord Curzon. Nowadays, the castle particularly appeals to children who enjoy clambering up the narrow spiral staircases which lead to crenellated battlements, and watching the absorbing fifteen-minute video portraying medieval life in a castle.

If you've got money to burn and/or children to entertain, it's worth knowing about the **Kent and East Sussex Railway** (July & Aug daily; April–June, Sept & Oct Sat & Sun; plus school holidays throughout the year; ☎01580/765155; £6.80), which runs full-scale steam trains from Northiam station, a mile to the south of Bodiam Castle, for seven miles northeast to Tenterden.

The best **accommodation** and **food** options are a couple of miles southeast, in the lovely village of Ewhurst, which houses a quaint country pub, the *White Dog Inn* (☎01580/830264; ②).

Burwash and Bateman's

Fifteen miles north of Hastings on the A265, halfway to Tunbridge Wells, **BURWASH**, with its red brick and weatherboarded cottages and Norman church tower exemplifies the pastoral idyll of inland Sussex. Half a mile south of the village lies the main attraction, **Bateman's** (April–Oct Mon–Wed, Sat, Sun & public holidays 11am–5pm; £5; NT), home of the Nobel Prize-winning writer and journalist Rudyard Kipling from 1902 until his death in 1936. Built by a local ironmaster in the seventeenth century and set amid attractive gardens, the house features a working watermill converted by Kipling to generate electricity, and which now grinds corn every Saturday at 2pm. Inside, the house is laid out as Kipling left it, with letters, early editions of his work and mementos from his travels on display. Next to the house, a garage houses the last of Kipling's Rolls-Royces, one of the many that he owned during his lifetime, although he never actually drove them, preferring the services of a chauffeur.

Eastbourne and around

Like so many of the southeast's seaside resorts, **EASTBOURNE** was kick-started into life in the 1840s, when the Brighton, Lewes and Hastings Rail Company built a branch line from Lewes to the sea. The Seventh Duke of Devonshire, William Cavendish, promptly developed the resort, an achievement zealously commemorated in the town's Devonshire Park, Devonshire swimming baths and Devonshire Place, where a self-satisfied statue of the duke stands. Past holidaymakers include George Orwell, the composer Claude Debussy, who finished writing *La Mer* here, as well as Marx and Engels. Nowadays Eastbourne has a solid reputation as a retirement town – albeit one that's a touch livelier than the nearby custom-built Peacehaven. Eastbourne's elegant three-mile seafront consists of houses and hotels and is tainted by barely a shop, but the greatest draw around is the South Downs, which the sea has ground into a series of dramatic chalk cliffs around **Beachy Head**, just west of town.

THE SOUTH DOWNS WAY

Following the undulating crest of the South Downs, from the village of Buriton on the Sussex–Hampshire border, two miles southwest of Petersfield train station, to their spectacular end at Beachy Head, the **South Downs Way** rises and dips over eighty miles along the chalk uplands, offering the southeast's finest walks. If undertaken in its entirety, the bridleway is best traversed from west to east, taking advantage of the prevailing wind, Eastbourne's better transport services and accommodation, and the psychological appeal of ending at the sea. **Steyning**, the halfway-point, marks a transition between predominantly wooded sections and more exposed chalk uplands – to the east of here you'll pass the modern **youth hostel** at Truleigh Hill (☎01903/813419). Other hostels along the way are at Telscombe and at Alfriston, where a southern loop can be taken which brings you to Eastbourne along the cliffs of the Seven Sisters, and an old bothy at Gumber Farm (☎01243/814484; closed Nov–Easter), near Bignor Hill.

The OS Landranger **maps** 198 and 199 cover the eastern end of the route; you'll need 185 and 197 as well to cover the lot. Half a dozen guides are available, the best being *South Downs Way* by Miles Jebb (Cicerone Press), or the more detailed *South Downs Way* by Paul Millmore (Aurum Press).

Conforming to tradition, the **Pier** is the focal point of the seafront: opened in 1872, it was intended to match the best on the south coast, which it certainly does. To the west, along the Grand Parade, is the ever-popular sunken **Bandstand**, with its regular (frequently military) band concerts (June–Aug daily 3–4.30pm; May & Sept Sun only). Further along the promenade, the **Wish Tower**, the first of the prom's two prominent redbrick Martello Towers – whose name derives from an old Sussex word meaning "marsh" – has been transformed into a **puppet museum** (Easter–Nov daily 10am–5pm; £1.80), while the **Redoubt Fortress**, east of the pier, now houses a military museum (Easter–Nov daily 9.30am–5.30pm; £2.10) and is the venue for regular fireworks displays throughout the summer.

One bright spark in sedate Eastbourne is the **Towner Art Gallery and Museum** (Tues–Sat noon–5pm, Sun 2–5pm; free) a ten-minute walk northwest of the train station; it shows a refreshingly contemporary and ever-changing range of work. Close by is a good wet weather retreat for those with kids, the **Scale Rail Model Centre** (Mon–Sat 9.30am–5pm, Sun 10am–2.30pm; £2), featuring no fewer than ten separate layouts. Another possible place of distraction is the **Museum of Shops** at 20 Cornfield Terrace (daily 10am–5pm; £2.50), just down from the tourist office. The amount of artefacts – old packages, coronation cups, toys – from the last hundred years of consumerism is just staggering, all crammed into mock-up shops spread over several floors. Finally, a more serious attempt to tackle the history of the town is made at the **Eastbourne Heritage Centre** (May–Sept daily 2–5pm; £1), in a distinctive corner house opposite the Winter Gardens.

Practicalities

Eastbourne is served by hourly trains from London Victoria (via Lewes and continuing to Hastings), with the **train station**, a splendid Italianate terminus, ten minutes' walk from the seafront up Terminus Road; there are also frequent services between here and Brighton (see p.198). The **bus station**, on Cavendish Place right by the pier, receives daily services from London, and has hourly services to Brighton via Newhaven. The **tourist office** is at 3 Cornfield Rd, just off Terminus Road (Mon–Sat 9.30am–5.30pm, Sun 10am–1pm; ☎01323/411400), with a smaller seasonal office on the pier itself (May–Sept daily 11am–5pm).

There are hundreds of places to **stay** here: a couple of good choices are *Sea Breeze Guest House*, 6 Marine Rd (☎01323/725440; ①), a cheap and cheerful place just a hundred yards from the sea, and *Sea Beach House Hotel*, 39–40 Marine Parade (☎01323/410458; ③), on the seafront. A mile and a half west along the A259 to East Dean there's a **youth hostel** (☎01323/721081) with spectacular views across Eastbourne; take bus #712 from the train station. You can camp right by a sandy beach at the secluded *Bay View* **campsite** (☎01323/768688; closed Nov–March), off the A259 east to Pevensey.

The Terminus Road area, between the train station and the sea, has the highest concentration of **restaurants**, with an excellent Thai place, *Seeracha*, at 94 Seaside Rd (☎01323/642867), and the town's best Italian, *Luigi's*, nearby at no. 72 (☎01323/736994; closed Sun); both are moderately priced. If you're in need of a large ice-cream sundae, go to *Fusciardi's* opposite the Winter Gardens on Carlyle Road.

The best **pubs** are some distance from the seafront: the *Hurst Arms* at 76 Willingdon Rd, a ten-minute walk inland from the station up Upperton Road, has Harvey's locally brewed beers on tap, with the same brew also available at the *Lamb*, a slightly over-enthusiastic but very pleasant version of a traditional English inn situated in the near-by High Street. Slightly out of the centre at 220 Seaside, is the ornate Victorian *Black Horse* pub (along the A259 to Bexhill), one of Eastbourne's least touristy places, offering wholesome food.

Beachy Head, Seven Sisters and the Cuckmere

A short walk west from Eastbourne takes you out along the most dramatic stretch of coastline in Sussex, where the chalk uplands of the Sussex Downs are cut by the sea into a sequence of splendid cliffs. The most spectacular of all, **Beachy Head**, is 575ft high, with a diminutive-looking lighthouse below, but no beach – the headland's name derives from the French *beau chef* meaning "beautiful head". The beauty certainly went to Friedrich Engels' head; he insisted his ashes be scattered here, and depressed individuals regularly try to join him by leaping to their doom from this well-known suicide spot.

West of the headland the scenery softens into a diminishing series of cliffs, a landmark known as the **Seven Sisters**. The country park after which they are named provides some of the most impressive walks in the county, taking in the cliff-top walk and the lower valley of the meandering River Cuckmere, into which the Seven Sisters subside. At **LITLINGTON**, five miles up the Cuckmere, the idyllic *Litlington Tea Gardens* provide a beautiful refreshment halt. On the opposite bank of the river in **ALFRISTON**, is the wonderfully ancient timber-framed and thatched **Clergy House** (April–Oct Mon, Wed–Thurs, Sat & Sun 10am–5pm; £2.50; NT), built in the fourteenth century and the first property to be acquired by the National Trust in 1896. Less edifying, but potentially more fun for kids, a mile or so up the valley, is **Drusillas Park** (daily: summer 10am–5pm; winter 10am–4pm; £6.95), where visitors can get to look at penguins and meerkats, milk a cow, touch snakes, and lark about on the adventure playground and miniature railway.

If you'd rather stay round this neck of the woods than in Eastbourne, check in at the *Birling Gap Hotel* (☎01323/423197; ③), overlooking the dramatic cliffs between Seven Sisters and Beachy Head, or bed down at the **youth hostel** (☎01323/870423) in a traditional Sussex flint building in Alfriston.

Herstmonceux

Twelve miles northeast of Eastbourne is the huge partially moated, castellated castle of **Herstmonceux** (tours only, call ahead to confirm times ☎01323/834444; £2.50; gardens April–Oct daily 10am–6pm; £3;), whose Elizabethan grounds, featuring a formal walled garden and extensive woodland, make an ideal picnic spot. Tours are of a restricted area of the house only, as most of it forms part of Queen's University of

Canada. Highlights include the Ballroom, Medieval Room and a stunning staircase – claimed to be one of the finest in the country – from the Elizabethan era, though most of the building has been extensively renovated and is very plain. Also in the grounds is the **Science Centre** (April–Oct daily 10am–6pm; £3.50; combined ticket with grounds £5.70), former home of the Royal Observatory, which moved here from Greenwich in the 1950s to escape the postwar smog, only to be forced to leave for the clearer skies over the Pacific Ocean in the 1980s. The observatory's domes and telescopes are now open to the public and make an enjoyable day's outing for budding astronomers.

Lewes and around

East Sussex's county town, **LEWES** straddles the River Ouse as it carves a gap through the South Downs on its final stretch to the sea. Though there's been some rebuilding in the riverside Cliffe area (the place where Lewes started), and new housing estates are spreading from the town's fringes, the core of Lewes remains remarkably good-looking: Georgian and crooked older dwellings still line the High Street and the narrow lanes – or "Twittens" – lead off this main street and its continuations, with views onto the downs. With some of England's most appealing chalkland right on its doorstep, and numerous traces of a history that stretches back to the Saxons, Lewes is a worthwhile stopover on any tour of the southeast – and an easy one, with good rail connections with London and along the coast.

Following the Norman Conquest, William's son-in-law, William de Warenne, built a priory and castle here, the latter still dominating the High Street. In 1264 Henry III's incompetence caused a baronial revolt led by Simon de Montfort which culminated in the king's surrender at the Battle of Lewes, although de Montfort and his reduced force were annihilated within a year at the Battle of Evesham. De Montfort's name crops up all over the town, as do references to the Lewes Martyrs, the seventeen Protestants burned here in 1556, at the height of Mary Tudor's militant revival of Catholicism – an event commemorated in spectacular fashion every November 5 (see box opposite). Intellectual non-conformity is something of a Lewes trademark, its roll call of free-thinkers featuring pioneer paleontologist Gideon Mantell and the radical humanist Tom Paine, whose *Common Sense* and *The Rights of Man* inspired or supported the revolutions in France and America. The conservative spirit triumphed in 1914, however, after a pair of local enthusiasts commissioned a version of Rodin's majestic sculpture *The Kiss*, depicting Paolo and Francesca – lovers from Dante's *Inferno* – clinched in a full-on embrace. Local sentiment was outraged when the piece was unveiled in Lewes town hall, leading to its rapid removal amid a flurry of controversy (the sculpture was re-exhibited in the town hall in June 1999, 85 years after the scandal).

The town

The best way to begin a tour of the town from the train station, is to walk up Station Road, then left down the High Street. Lewes' **Castle** (Mon–Sat 10am–5.30pm or dusk, Sun 11am–5.30pm or dusk; £3.50) is hidden from view behind the houses on your right. Inside the castle complex – unusual for being built on two mottes, or mounds – the shell of the eleventh-century keep remains, and both the towers can be climbed for excellent views over the town to the surrounding downs. Tickets for the castle include admission to the **museum** (same hours as castle), by the castle entrance, which is much better than the usual stuffy town museum.

A few minutes' walk further west along the High Street past St Michael's Church, with its unusual twin towers – one wooden and the other flint – brings you to the steep cobbled and much photographed **Keere Street**, down which the reckless Prince Regent is alleged to have driven his carriage. Keere Street leads to **Southover Grange** (Mon–Sat

THE BONFIRE SOCIETIES

Each November 5, while the rest of Britain lights small domestic bonfires or attends municipal firework displays to commemorate the foiling of a Catholic plot to blow up the Houses of Parliament, Lewes puts on a more dramatic show, whose origins lie in the deaths of the town's Protestant martyrs. By the end of the eighteenth century, Lewes' **Bonfire Boys** had become notorious for the boisterousness of their anti-Catholic demonstrations, in which they set off fireworks indiscriminately and dragged rolling tar barrels through the streets – a tradition still practised today, although with a little more caution. In 1845 events came to a head when the incorrigible pyromaniacs of Lewes had to be read the Riot Act, instigating a night of violence between the police and Bonfire Boys. Lewes' first **bonfire societies** were established soon afterwards, to try to get a bit more discipline into the proceedings, and earlier this century they were persuaded to move their street fires to the town's perimeters.

Today's tightly knit bonfire societies, each with its quasi-militaristic motto ("Death or Glory", "True to Each Other", etc), spend much of the year organizing the Bonfire Night shenanigans, when their members dress up in traditional costumes and parade through the town carrying flaming torches, before marching off onto the downs for their society's big fire. At each of the fires effigies of Guy Fawkes and the pope are burned alongside contemporary, but equally reviled, figures – Chancellors of the Exchequer and Prime Ministers are popular choices.

8am–dusk, Sun 9am–dusk; free), with its lovely gardens. Built in 1572 from the priory's remains, the Grange was also the childhood home of the diarist John Evelyn. Past the gardens, a right turn down Southover High Street leads to the Tudor-built **Anne of Cleves House** (mid-Feb to Oct Mon–Sat 10am–5pm, Sun noon–5pm; Nov–Dec Tues–Sat 10am–5pm, Sun noon–5pm; Jan to mid-Feb Tues, Thurs & Sat 10am–5pm, Sun noon–5pm; £2.50; combined ticket with the castle £5), given to her in settlement after her divorce from Henry VIII – though she never actually lived there. The magnificent oak-beamed Tudor bedroom is impressive, with its cumbersome "bed wagon", a bed-warming brazier which would fail the slackest of fire regulations and which the four-hundred-year-old Flemish four-poster has managed to survive. The house's decor dates from the sixteenth century when the Wealden iron industry was flourishing and Sussex produced most of England's iron, with Lewes being a centre of cannon manufacture.

On the opposite side of the road and closer to the train station is the church of **St John the Baptist**, with its squat, brick tower capped by a six-foot shark for a weather vane; inside there's some superb stained glass and a tiny chapel with the lead coffins of William de Warenne and his wife Gundrada, William I's daughter. De Warenne was one of the six barons presiding over the new administrative provinces – known as the **Rapes of Sussex** – created by the Normans soon after the Conquest. Behind the church are the ruins of de Warenne's **St Pancras Priory**, once one of Europe's principal Cluniac institutions, with a church the size of Westminster Abbey. Sadly it was dismantled to build town houses following the Dissolution and is now an evocative ruin surrounded by playing fields.

Back in the town centre, the **Star Brewery Studio** off Fisher Street, north of the High Street, displays the creative talents of a collective of artists, bookbinders, carpenters and other artisans; the attached **Star Gallery** (Mon–Sat 10.30am–5.30pm; free) presents a changing series of exhibitions. At the east end of the High Street, School Hill descends towards Cliffe Bridge, built in 1727 and entrance to the commercial centre of the medieval settlement. For the energetic, a path leads up onto the Downs from the end of Cliffe High Street – site of England's worst avalanche disaster in 1836, when a bank of snow slid onto Cliffe village, killing eight people. The path passes close to an obelisk, commemorating the town's seventeen Protestant martyrs.

Practicalities

The **train station**, south of the High Street down Station Road, has regular services from London Victoria and along the coast to Brighton, Eastbourne, Hastings and the **ferry port** at Newhaven, from where Hoverspeed run catamarans to Dieppe (☎08705/240241). Buses leave from the **bus station** on Eastgate Street near the foot of School Hill. The **tourist office** is at the junction of the High Street and Station Road (Easter–Sept Mon–Fri 9am–5pm, Sat 10am–5pm, Sun 10am–2pm; Oct–Easter Mon–Fri 9am–5pm, Sat 10am–2pm; ☎01273/483448).

For **accommodation** try *Millers*, a timber-framed house at 134 High St (☎01273/475631; ②), or *Castle Bank Cottages*, 4 Castle Banks (☎01273/476291; ③); a beamed period house with great views. The *Crown Hotel*, High St, close to the tourist office (☎01273/480670; ③), is a reasonable fallback. The nearest **youth hostel** is in the village of Telscombe, six miles south of Lewes (see p.197); there's another – a rustic wooden cabin with basic facilities – eleven miles northeast of town at Blackboys, near Uckfield (☎01825/890607).

Lewes is home of the excellent Harvey's brewery and most of the **pubs** serve its wares – try the *Brewers' Arms*, opposite St John the Baptist, the *Lewes Arms* tucked behind the Star Brewery Studios, or the *King's Head*, down on Southover High Street; the last also specializes in game and fish dishes. Other **Food** alternatives include the inexpensive Indian *Dilraj,* 12 Fisher St (☎01273/479279), *La Cucina*, a moderately priced Italian joint at 13 Station St (☎01273/476707), or the inexpensive *Pailin Thai* restaurant, opposite at no. 20 (☎01273/473906). Pricier options include the brasserie *Twenty Fisher Street*, to be found, unsurprisingly, at 20 Fisher St (☎01273/487568), and *Thackery's* at 3 Malling St (☎01273/474634; closed lunch & all Mon & Sun), over the river on the east side of town, which serves traditional English and French-style food at moderate prices.

Glyndebourne

Glyndebourne, Britain's only unsubsidized opera house, is situated near the village of Glynde, three miles east of Lewes. Founded sixty years ago, the Glyndebourne season is an indispensable part of the high-society calendar, with ticket prices and a distribution system that excludes all but the most devoted opera-lovers. On one level, Glyndebourne is a repellent spectacle, its lawns thronged with gentry and corporate bigwigs ingesting champagne and smoked salmon – the productions have massive intervals to allow an unhurried repast. On the other hand, the musical values are the highest in the country, using young talent rather than expensive star names, and taking the sort of risks Covent Garden wouldn't dream of taking – for example, *Porgy and Bess* is now taken seriously as an opera largely as a result of a great Glyndebourne production. The recent arrival of a new, award-winning theatre (seating 1200) has broadened the appeal of this exclusive venue to a wider audience. There are tickets available at reduced prices for dress rehearsals or for standing-room-only tickets (call ☎01273/813813, for details).

Rodmell

Three miles south of Lewes lies the village of **RODMELL**, whose main source of interest is the **Monk's House** (April–Oct Wed & Sat 2–5.30pm; £2.50; NT), former home of Virginia Woolf, a leading figure of the Bloomsbury Group (see box opposite). She and her husband, Leonard, moved to the weatherboarded cottage in 1919 and Leonard stayed there until his death in 1969; both Virginia's and Leonard's remains are interred in the gardens. Nearby, you can see the River Ouse where Virginia killed herself in 1941 by walking into the water with her pockets full of stones. The house's interior is nothing special and will only really be of interest to ardent Bloomsbury fans; admirers can look round the study where Virginia wrote several of her novels, and her

THE BLOOMSBURY GROUP

The **Bloomsbury Group** were essentially a bevy of upper-middle-class friends, who took their name from the Bloomsbury area of London, where most of them lived before acquiring houses in the Sussex countryside. The Group revolved around Virginia, Vanessa, Thoby and Adrian Stephen, who lived at 46 Gordon Square, the London base of the Bloomsbury Group. Thoby's Thursday evening gatherings and Vanessa's Friday Club for painters attracted a whole host of Cambridge-educated snobs who subscribed to Oscar Wilde's theory that "aesthetics are higher than ethics". Their diet of "human inter- course and the enjoyment of beautiful things" was hardly revolutionary, but their behav- iour, particularly that of the two sisters (unmarried, unchaperoned, intellectual and artis- tic), succeeded in shocking London society, especially through their louche sexual prac- tices (most of the group swung both ways).

All this, though interesting, would be forgotten were it not for their individual work. In 1922 Virginia declared, without too much exaggeration, "Everyone in Gordon Square has become famous": Lytton Strachey had been the first to make his name with *Eminent Victorians*, a series of unprecedentedly frank biographies; Vanessa, now married to the art critic Clive Bell, had become involved in Roger Fry's prolific design firm, Omega Workshop; and the economist John Maynard Keynes had become an adviser to the Treasury (he later went on to become the leading economic theorist of his day). The Group's most celebrated figure, Virginia, married Leonard Woolf and became an estab- lished novelist; she and Leonard also founded the Hogarth Press, which published T.S. Eliot's *Waste Land* in 1922.

Eliot was just one of a number of writers, such as Aldous Huxley, Bertrand Russell and E.M. Forster, who were drawn to the interwar Bloomsbury set, but others, notably D.H. Lawrence, were repelled by the clan's narcissism and snobbish narrow-mindedness. Whatever their limitations, the Bloomsbury Group were Britain's most influential intel- lectual coterie of the interwar years, and their appeal shows little sign of waning – even now, scarcely a year goes by without the publication of the biography or memoirs of some Bloomsbury peripheral.

bedroom which is laid out with period editions of her work. To get there, catch a train to **Southease**, from where it's a mile northwest to Rodmell village, across the river.

Three miles south of Rodmell, in the village of Telscombe, is a quiet **youth hostel** (☎01273/301357), whose simple accommodation is in two-hundred-year-old cottages; take bus #123 from Lewes.

Charleston Farmhouse

Six miles east of Lewes, off the A27, is another Bloomsbury Group shrine, **Charleston Farmhouse** (April–June, Sept & Oct Wed–Sun 2–5pm; July & Aug Wed–Sat 11.30am–5pm, Sun 2–5pm; £5.50), home to Virginia Woolf's sister Vanessa Bell, Vanessa's husband, Clive Bell, and her lover, Duncan Grant. As conscientious objec- tors, the trio moved here during World War I so that the men could work on local farms (farm labourers were exempted from military service). The farmhouse became a gath- ering point for other members of the Bloomsbury Group, including the biographer Lytton Strachey, the economist Maynard Keynes and the novelist E.M. Forster. Duncan Grant continued to live in the house until his death in 1978. Unless it's a Sunday, you have to join a fifty-minute guided tour in order to view the interior of the farmhouse, where almost every surface is painted and the walls are hung with paint- ings by Picasso, Renoir and Augustus John, alongside the work of the markedly less tal- ented residents. Many of the fabrics, lampshades and other artefacts bear the unmis- takable mark of the Omega Workshop, the Bloomsbury equivalent of William Morris's artistic movement.

Brighton

Recorded as the tiny fishing village of Brithelmeston in the Domesday Book, **BRIGHTON** seems to have slipped unnoticed through history until the mid-eighteenth-century sea-bathing trend established a resort that has never looked back. The fad received royal approval in the 1770s when the decadent Prince Regent, later George IV, began patronizing the town in the company of his mistress, thus setting a precedent for the "dirty weekend", Brighton's major contribution to the English collective consciousness. Trying to shake off this blowsy reputation, Brighton now highlights its Georgian charm, its upmarket shops and classy restaurants, and its thriving conference industry. Yet, however much it tries to present itself as a comfortable middle-class town, the essence of Brighton's appeal is its faintly bohemian vitality, a buzz that comes from a mix of English holidaymakers, thousands of young foreign students from the town's innumerable language schools, a thriving gay community and an energetic local student population from the art college and two universities.

Arrival, information and accommodation

Brighton is served by numerous trains from London's Victoria, London Bridge and King's Cross stations. There are also regular services along the coast from Hastings, Eastbourne via Lewes, and from Portsmouth via Chichester. The **train station** is at the head of Queen's Road, which descends to the Clock Tower and then becomes West Street which eventually leads to the seafront – a distance of about half a mile. National Express and Southdown **bus services** arrive at Pool Valley **bus station**, tucked just in from the seafront on the south side of the Old Steine.

The **tourist office** is at 10 Bartholomew Square (June–Sept Mon–Fri 9am–6pm, Sat 10am–5pm, Sun 10am–4pm; Oct–May Mon–Sat 9am–5pm, Sun 10am–4pm; ☎01273/292599), behind the town hall on the southern side of the Lanes – the maze of narrow alleyways marking Brighton's old town. You'll find most budget **accommodation** clustered around the **Kemp Town** district, to the east of the Palace Pier, with the more elegant and expensive hotels west of the town centre around Regency Square, opposite the West Pier; many places offer reductions for stays of two nights or more so it's always worth enquiring. Brighton's official **campsite** is the *Sheepcote Valley* site (☎01273/626546), just north of Brighton Marina; take bus #1 or #1A to Wilson Avenue, or take the Volks railway and walk up Arundel Road to Wilson Avenue.

Hotels, B&Bs and guest houses

Adelaide Hotel, 51 Regency Square (☎01273/205286). Top-notch guest house in the fancier part of town. One room has a four-poster bed. ④.

Ainsley House, 28 New Steine (☎01273/605310). Friendly, upmarket guest house in an attractive Regency terrace. ②.

Andorra Hotel, 15–16 Oriental Place (☎01273/321787). At the west end of town, this hotel has comfortable rooms with good facilities. ②.

Arlanda Hotel, 20 New Steine (☎01273/699300). Plusher than average choice in the New Steine square, with wide price range depending on the room; the cheapest are on the top floor and quite poky. ③.

Ascott House Hotel, 21 New Steine (☎01273/688085). Very comfortable, but pricey, guest house just a few yards from the sea, that's recently undergone new ownership. ③.

Cavalaire House, 34 Upper Rock Gardens (☎01273/696899). Average B&B, just off Marine Parade, which has triples and offers the seventh night free. ②.

Cornerways Hotel, 18–20 Caburn Rd (☎01273/731882). Inexpensive and friendly B&B, a couple of minutes west of the train station. ①.

Four Seasons, 3 Upper Rock Gardens (☎01273/681496). Cosy B&B in the Kemp Town area, with good vegetarian breakfast options. ①.

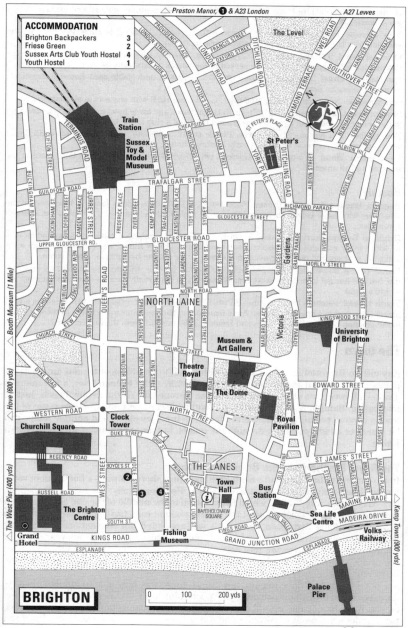

ACCOMMODATION

Brighton Backpackers	**3**
Friese Green	**2**
Sussex Arts Club Youth Hostel	**4**
Youth Hostel	**1**

△ Preston Manor, ❶ & A23 London   △ A27 Lewes

The Level

Train Station

Sussex Toy & Model Museum

St Peter's

NORTH LAINE

Museum & Art Gallery

Theatre Royal

Victoria Gardens

University of Brighton

The Dome

Royal Pavilion

Clock Tower

Churchill Square

THE LANES

Town Hall

Bus Station

Sea Life Centre

Volks Railway

The Brighton Centre

Fishing Museum

Grand Hotel

Palace Pier

BRIGHTON

△ Booth Museum (1 Mile)
△ Hove (600 yds)
△ The West Pier (400 yds)
△ Kemp Town (900 yds)

0	100	200 yds

© Crown copyright

Hudsons, 22 Devonshire Place (☎01273/683642). Relaxed, centrally situated and exclusively gay guest house. ②.

New Europe Hotel, 31–32 Marine Parade (☎01273/624462). Large, buzzing, gay hotel on the seafront, with late bar and regular cabaret nights. ③.

Oriental Hotel, 9 Oriental Place (☎01273/205050). Friendly, laid-back staff and very funky decor throughout; full veggie breakfasts are served in the hotel's mellow café. ③.

Queensbury Hotel, 58 Regency Square (☎01273/325558). Comfortable guest house in Brighton's definitive Georgian district. ③.

Sea Spray, 25 New Steine (☎01273/680332). Good-value B&B with showers in all rooms. ②.

Sussex Arts Club, 7 Ship St (☎01273/727371). Laid-back and lively hotel in a Regency house right in the centre of town, with a pub on the ground floor and a club in the basement. ④.

Twenty One, 21 Charlotte St, off Marine Parade (☎01273/686450). Classy Kemp Town B&B with very comfortable rooms in an ornate, early Victorian house. ③.

Westbourne Hotel, 46 Upper Rock Gardens (☎01273/686920). Well-appointed B&B close to the seafront and all amenities. ②.

Hostels

Baggies Backpackers, 33 Oriental Place (☎01273/733740). Spacious house a little west of the West Pier with large bright dorms, starting at £9 a night, decent showers and plenty of room to spread out.

Brighton Backpackers, 75 Middle St (☎01273/777717). Brighton's established independent hostel with a lively, easy-going atmosphere and vivid murals. A new annexe just round the corner overlooks the seafront and offers a quieter alternative; £9 for a dorm bed, £25 for a twin room.

Friese Green, 20 Middle St (☎01273/747551). The folk here are friendly enough, and it's very central, but this has got to be a last resort really, unless you don't really care how lumpy your mattress is. £10 a night.

Youth Hostel, Patcham Place, London Rd (☎01273/556196, *brighton@yha.org.uk*). Brighton's YHA hostel is housed in a splendid Queen Anne mansion, in parkland four miles north of the sea, close to the junction of the roads to Lewes and London. Take bus #5A from the town centre.

The town

Any visit to Brighton inevitably begins with a visit to its two most famous landmarks – the exuberant **Royal Pavilion** and the wonderfully tacky **Palace Pier**, a few minutes away – followed by a stroll along the seafront promenade or the pebbly beach. Just as interesting, though, is an exploration of Brighton's car-free **Lanes**, where some of the town's diverse restaurants, bars and tiny bric-a-brac, jewellery and antique shops can be found, or an idle meander through the quaint, but more bohemian streets of **North Laine**.

The Royal Pavilion and the Brighton Museum

In any survey to find England's most loved building, there's always a bucketful of votes for Brighton's exotic extravaganza, the **Royal Pavilion** (daily: June–Sept 10am–6pm; Oct–May 10am–5pm; £4.50), which flaunts itself in the middle of the Old Steine, a main thoroughfare along which most of the seafront-bound road traffic gets funnelled. Until 1787, the building that stood here was a well-appointed but conventional farmhouse, which was first rented by the fun-loving Prince of Wales in the previous year. He then commissioned its conversion into something more regal, and for a couple of decades the prince's south-coast pied-à-terre was a Palladian villa, with mildly oriental embellishments.

Upon becoming Prince Regent, however, George was fully able to indulge his taste for excess, and in 1815 his patronage fell upon John Nash, architect of London's Regent Street. What Nash came up with was an extraordinary confection of slender minarets, twirling domes, pagodas, balconies and miscellaneous motifs imported from India and

China and supported on an innovative cast-iron frame, creating an exterior profile that defines a genre of its own – Oriental-Gothic. George had the time of his life here, frolicking with his mistress, Mrs Fitzherbert, whom he installed in a house on the west side of the Old Steine.

On ascending the throne in 1837 the dour Queen Victoria was not amused by George's taste in architecture, and she shifted the royal seaside residence to the Isle of Wight. All the Pavilion's valuable fittings were carted off to Buckingham and Kensington palaces and Victoria sold the gutted building to the town. The Pavilion was then pressed into a series of humdrum roles – tea room, hospital, concert hall, radar station, ration office – but has now been brilliantly restored, completely eradicating damage caused by an arson attack in 1975, and by the storm in October 1987 (see p.183), which hurled a dislodged minaret through the roof and floor of the nearly completed Music Room.

Inside the Pavilion the exuberant compendium of Regency exotica has been enhanced by the return of many of the objects which Victoria had taken away. One of the highlights – approached via the restrained Long Gallery – is the **Banqueting Room**, which erupts with ornate splendour and is dominated by a one-tonne chandelier hung from the jaws of a massive dragon cowering in a plantain tree. Next door, the huge, high-ceilinged kitchen, fitted with the most modern appliances of its time, has iron columns disguised as palm trees.

Nearby, the stunning **Music Room**, the first sight of which reduced George to tears of joy, has a huge dome lined with more than twenty-six thousand individually gilded scales and hung with exquisite umbrella-like glass lamps. After climbing the famous cast-iron staircase with its bamboo-look banisters, you can go into Victoria's sober and seldom-used bedroom and the North Gallery where the king's portrait hangs, along with a selection of satirical cartoons. More notable, though, is the **South Gallery**, decorated in sky blue with trompe l'oeil bamboo trellises and a carpet which appears to be strewn with flowers.

Across the gardens from the Pavilion stands the **Dome**, once the royal stables and now the town's main concert hall, it adjoins the **Brighton Museum and Art Gallery** (Mon, Tues & Thurs–Sat 10am–5pm, Sun 2–5pm; free), which is entered just around the corner on Church Street. It houses an eclectic mix including modern fashion and design, archeology, painting and local history, including a large collection of pottery, from basic Neolithic earthenware to delicate porcelain figurines popular in the eighteenth century. The collection of classic Art Deco and Art Nouveau furniture stands out, the highlight being Dalí's famous sofa based on Mae West's lips. The Balcony Café is the perfect setting for a coffee or tea, perched above a sea of exhibits from which you can enjoy the lines of this lovingly restored Victorian building.

The Lanes and North Laine

Tucked between the Pavilion and the seafront is a warren of narrow, pedestrianized thoroughfares known as **the Lanes** – the core of the old fishing village from which Brighton evolved. Long-established antiques shops, designer outlets and several bars, pubs and restaurants generate a lively and intimate atmosphere in this part of town. **North Laine** – "laine" was the local term for a strip of land – which spreads north of North Street along Kensington, Sydney, Gardner and Bond streets, is more bohemian with its hub along pedestrianized Kensington Gardens. Here the shops are more eclectic, selling secondhand records, clothes, bric-a-brac and New Age objects, and mingle with earthy coffee shops and downbeat cafés. Slightly to the north of here is the **Sussex Toy and Model Museum** (Mon–Fri 10am–1pm & 2–5pm, Sat 11am–1pm & 2–5pm; £3), housed in an old stables underneath the train station. The collection is impressive, ranging from an entire cabinet full of Smurfs to a set of Pelham puppets, but it's the working model railways that are likely to be the focus of most children's attention.

The seafront

Most of the seafront is an ugly mix of shops, entertainment complexes and hotels, ranging from the impressively pompous plasterwork of the *Grand Hotel* – scene of the IRA's attempted assassination of the Conservative Cabinet in October 1984 – to the green-glass monstrosity on the seaward side of the Lanes. To appreciate fully the tackier side of Brighton, you must take a stroll along the **Palace Pier**. The pier has yet to gain a replacement for the splendid theatre that once occupied its seaward end, but every inch of the structure is devoted to fun and money-making, from the cacophonous Palace of Fun to the Pleasure Dome, from the state-of-the-art video games to the fairground rides and karaoke sessions at the end of the pier. Brighton's architecturally superior West Pier, built in 1866 half a mile west along the seafront, was damaged in World War II and then fell into disrepair, but looks set to be restored to its former glory by 2002.

Underneath the arches between the Palace and West piers, there are two small museums: the **National Museum of Penny Slot Machines** (Easter–Sept daily noon–6pm; rest of year Sat & Sun, plus school holidays noon–6pm; free), which houses decrepit antique slot machines which struggle to function; and the **Brighton Fishing Museum** (May–Oct daily 10am–5pm; free), which has old photos and video footage of the golden days of the local fishing industry and shelters a large Sussex clinker, once a common boat on Brighton beach.

Across the road from the Palace Pier, on Marine Parade, is the **Sea Life Centre** (daily 10am–5pm; £5.50), one of the best marine life displays of its kind, with a transparent tunnel passing through a huge aquarium – a walk along the bottom of the sea with sharks and rays gliding overhead. Nearby, the antiquated locomotives of **Volk's Electric Railway** (April to mid-Sept; £1) – the first electric train in the country – run eastward towards the Marina and the nudist beach, usually the preserve of just a few thick-skinned souls. En route, you pass the **Madeira Lift** (Easter to mid-Sept 9.45am–7.15pm; free), a pagoda-like Victorian tower built in 1890 from which you can enjoy a great view over Brighton and out to sea.

Booth Museum and Preston Manor

In the north of Brighton's suburbs there are two museums worth a look. The big municipal museum, the **Booth Museum of Natural History** (Mon–Wed, Fri & Sat 10am–5pm, Sun 2–5pm; free), is a mile up Dukes Road from the centre of town (bus #10 or #10A). Purpose-built to house Mr E.T. Booth's prodigious collection of stuffed birds, this is a wonderfully fusty old Victorian museum with beetles, butterflies and animal skeletons galore, but which also displays very imaginative temporary shows.

The delightful **Preston Manor** (Mon 1–5pm, Tues–Sat 10am–5pm, Sun 2–5pm; £3), was originally built in 1250, though the present building dates from 1738 and 1905. Inside a series of period interiors evokes the life of the Edwardian gentry, from the servants' quarters downstairs to the luxury nursery upstairs. The house is two miles north of Brighton on the A23, but only a short walk from Preston Park train station.

Eating, drinking and nightlife

Brighton has the greatest concentration of **restaurants** anywhere in the southeast, outside London. Around North Laine are some great, inexpensive cafés, while for classier establishments head to the Lanes and out towards neighbouring Hove. Many of the cheaper places fight hard to attract the large student market with discounted deals of around ten percent, so if you have a student ID, use it.

Nightlife is hectic and compulsively pursued throughout the year, making Brighton unique in the sedate southeast. There are a couple of outstanding **clubs**, lots of **live music** and more cinema screens per head than anywhere else in Britain. Midweek entry into the clubs can cost just a couple of pounds and cinema seats are similarily priced before 6pm.

For up-to-date details of **what's on,** pick up a copy of the glossy monthly magazine *Impact* (50p) from the tourist office or newsagents. If you've got access to the Internet, you can log on to the highly praised **Web site,** *www.brighton.co.uk* – you can get on line at the Brighton Media Centre on Middle Street. Other listings for the town are available monthly in the trendy magazine *The Latest* (30p) or the flimsier *New Insight* (45p).

Every May the three-week-long **Brighton Festival** (☎01273/706771) takes place in various venues around town. This arty celebration includes funfairs, exhibitions, street theatre and concerts from classical to jazz. Running at the same time is the **Brighton and Hove Fringe Festival** (☎01273/295590), which also stages live music and drama, literature readings and tons of club nights.

Brighton has one of the longest established and most thriving gay communities in Britain, with a variety of lively clubs and bars drawing people from all over the southeast. It also hosts a number of gay events including the annual Gay Pride Festival, held over two weeks at the beginning of July. It's a great excuse for a party with loads going on from the performing arts to exhibitions, not to mention the **Brighton Parade,** a day-and-night-long jamboree. For details on all events, call ☎0906/683642.

Arts centres and comedy clubs

Akademia, 14–17 Manchester St (☎01273/622633). Stand-up comedy and late bar.

Brighton Media Centre/Cinematheque, 9–12 Middle St (☎01273/384300). Art-house cinema and exhibition space, with Internet facilities available.

Gardner Arts Centre, University of Sussex, Falmer (☎01273/685861, *gardner-arts@pavilion.co.uk*). Performing and visual arts; theatre, cinema, workshops, exhibition space and café.

Komedia, Gardner St, North Laine (☎01273/647100). Lively alternative theatre-café notable for its regular roll call of stand-up comedy and live music. Late bar.

Sussex Arts Club, Ship St (☎01273/727371). Live bands, theatre and performance, plus exhibition space. The building includes a late bar and hotel.

Ray Tindle Centre, 40–42 Upper Gardner St (☎01273/607171). Experimental music and drama, also live bands.

Cafés and bars

Bar Centro, Ships St. Brighton's biggest, most spacious pre-club bar with occasional in-house DJs spinning tunes.

Disco Biscuit Café, 14 Queen's Rd. Clubbers' choice with big bright sofas, furry Dalmatian chairs and all-day breakfasts.

Dorset Street Bar, corner of Gardner St and North Rd. Bar, café and restaurant rolled into one, with delicious French and international dishes to tempt you. They also do real cream teas.

Gemini, 127–132 King's Rd Arches. Great beach bar to lounge around at, with big sarnies and table service.

Good Bean, 16 Prince Albert St. Great tasting coffee in uncluttered surroundings.

Grinder, 10 Kensington Gardens. Upstairs trip-happy café serving tasty cheap snacks and great soups, with a balcony for watching life in North Laine go by, and lots of club fliers to hand.

Innocent Bystander, 54 Preston St, off King's Road, near the West Pier. Hungry clubbers' favourite greasy spoon with all the usuals plus vegan breakfasts and the infamous "Gut Buster" breakfast, with a background of MTV; open till 3am.

Mock Turtle, 4 Pool Valley. Old-fashioned tea shop crammed with bric-a-brac and cheap, home-made cakes. Closed Sun & Mon.

The Sanctuary, 51 Brunswick St East, Hove. Cool and arty vegetarian café with soft furnishings and a cosy, relaxed ambience. Deservedly popular, despite its not-very-central location.

The Squid, 78 Middle St. A self-styled pre-club bar in those ever popular primary colours, with drinks at £2.50 a shot to fire you up for the night.

Zanzibar, 129 St James's St. Premier pre-club gay bar out towards Kemp Town.

Restaurants

Al Duomo, 7 Pavilion Buildings (☎01273/326741). Brilliant pizzeria, with a genuine wood-burning oven. Has a more intimate sister restaurant, *Al Forno* at 36 East St. Inexpensive.

Black Chapati, 12 Circus Parade (☎01273/699011). Innovative Asian cooking with Japanese and Thai influences as well as more conventional Indian dishes, which are brilliantly executed. Something of a Brighton landmark despite its out-of-the-way location, more than a mile inland, at the point where the London road enters town. Moderate.

Bombay Aloo, 39 Ship St (☎01273/776038). No flock wallpaper and an all-you-can-eat veggie buffet for a fiver – what more could you ask for? Inexpensive

Browns, 3–4 Duke St (☎01273/323501). A mixture of steak, seafood and pasta dishes as well as traditional favourites like Guinness-marinated steak-and-mushroom pie, served in a sophisticated continental setting with wooden floors, palms and background jazz. Moderate.

Casa Don Carlos, 5 Union St (☎01273/327177). Small, long-established tapas bar in the Lanes with outdoor seating and daily specials. Also serves more substantial Spanish dishes and drinks. Inexpensive.

English's Oyster Bar, 29–31 East St (☎01273/327980). Three fishermen's cottages knocked together to house a marble and brass oyster bar and a red velvet dining room. Seafood's the speciality with a mouthwatering menu and better value than you might expect, especially the set menus. Brighton institution famed for its atmosphere as much as its food. Expensive.

Food for Friends, 17 Prince Albert St (☎01273/202310). Brighton's ever-popular wholefood veggie eatery is imaginative enough to please die-hard meat-eaters. It's usually busy, but well worth the squeeze and offers discounts for students. Inexpensive.

Le Gastronome, 3 Hampton Place (☎01273/777399). Well known for its good-value classic French cuisine, friendly service and outstanding selection of wines; choose the dish of the day for £8 or a five-course blow-out for £22.50. Closed Sun & Mon. Moderate.

Havana, 33 Duke St (☎01273/773388). Very stylish continental brasserie with just a hint of colonial ambience – palms and rattan chairs – to evoke tropical luxury and a feeling of being pampered. The menu is eclectic, ranging from Med to Thai – the lunchtime menu is particularly good value. Moderate.

Melrose Restaurant, 132 King's Rd (☎01273/326520). Traditional and decent seafront establishment which has been serving seafood, roasts and custard-covered puddings for over forty years. The *Regency Restaurant* next door is a similar and smaller option. Inexpensive.

Piccolo, 56 Ship St (☎01273/380380). Informal Italian restaurant with pizza and pasta dishes from around £4 and special deals for students. Inexpensive.

Sumo 8–12 Middle St (☎01273/823344). Recently opened, designer-cool Pacific-rim restaurant with late-night bar. The imaginative menu features a delicious choice of starters to whet the appetite, and such exotic main courses as Piri-Piri Chicken with peanut sauce. Moderate.

Tamarind Tree, 48 Queen's Rd (☎01273/298816). Mellow Carribean café decked in turquoise and wickerwork, with a surprisingly large range of veggie dishes. Main dishes around £8, or you could just have a filling starter. Moderate.

Terre-à-Terre, 7 Pool Valley (☎01273/729051). Imaginative, global, veggie cuisine in a small and modern arty setting, just off Old Steine. Closed Mon lunch & Sun. Moderate.

Thai Spice Market, 13 Boyces St (☎01273/325195). Classical Thai interior and cuisine, serving meat, seafood and vegetarian varieties. Inexpensive to Moderate.

Tin Drum 95–97 Dyke Rd (☎01273/777575). Buzzing new continental-style café-bar and restaurant with a taste for Baltic-rim cooking and a blend of Eastern European influences; fresh seasonal ingredients and speciality vodkas are distilled on the premises. Moderate.

Wai Kika Moo Kau, 11 Kensington Gardens (☎01273/671117). Slightly distressed decor at this funky global veggie café/restaurant with everything from Thai curry to aubergine bake – all for under a fiver. Inexpensive.

Yum Yum Noodle Bar, 22–23 Sydney St (☎01273/606777). Serves anything Southeast Asian – Chinese, Thai, Indonesian and Malaysian noodle dishes at good-value prices – situated above a Chinese supermarket. Lunchtimes only. Inexpensive.

Pubs

The Albert, 48 Trafalgar St. A listed building, right by the train station, popular with students. Live rock upstairs, real ale downstairs; free pool in the afternoon.

Aquarium, 1 Steine St. Who said the gay scene is like living in a fish bowl? Another Steine Street staple.

Cricketers, 15 Black Lion St. Just west of the Lanes, this is Brighton's oldest pub and it looks it too; very popular with good pub grub.

Dr Brighton's, 16 King's Rd. Popular gay venue.

Druids Head, 9 Brighton Place. Great, old pub in the heart of the Lanes with a flagstone floor and a raucous jukebox.

Font & Firkin, Union St. Spacious converted chapel with a bar in place of the altar.

Free Butt Inn, 8 Phoenix Place. Busy pub with a full calendar of live music.

Great Eastern, 103 Trafalgar St. Relaxing pub with bare boards and bookshelves, lots of real ales, and no fruit machines or TV.

The Greys, 105 Southover St. Old-fashioned pub with an open fire, stone floors and wooden benches – with some great food available courtesy of the Belgian chef. Frequent live bands.

Hand in Hand, 33 Upper St James St. An agreeable pub with its own brewery out the back.

Hector's House, Grand Parade. Big bare-boards-and-sofa student pub that has the odd pre-club night with in-house DJs; vibrators instead of condoms in the loos. Lush.

Marlborough, Prince's St. Friendly pub just off Old Steine, popular with a gay and mixed crowd.

O'Donovan's of Cork, 80 East St. Slightly more genuine than *O'Neill's*, with Irish music and open stage nights.

O'Neill's, 27 Ship St. Big Irish-themed pub, but popular and with occasional live music.

Queens Head, 10 Steine St. Popular gay pub in the heart of the town centre.

Smugglers, 10 Ship St. A young crowd packs out this place, with a good jazz club upstairs, dance club downstairs, and free pool during the day.

Nightlife

BN1, 1 Preston Rd (☎01273/323161). Newly refurbished club with a serious surround-sound system, currently attracting the best DJs around, playing mainly drum'n'bass, house and garage.

The Beach, King's Road Arches (☎01273/722222). R'n'b, classic grooves and occasional stand-up comedy nights.

Casablanca, *Churchill Palace Hotel*, 2–5 Middle St (☎01273/321817). Basement venue featuring live bands and all types of funk, including latin and jazz.

Cuba, 160 King's Rd Arches (☎01273/770505). Disco, salsa, techno and hip-hop nights at this lofty bar/club by the beach opposite West Street.

Escape, 10 Marine Parade (☎01273/606906). Brighton's trendiest nightclub packs them in night after night, specializing in funk and techno.

Honey Club, 214 King's Rd Arches (☎01273/202807). Garage, house and hip-hop – and a lively crowd.

The Jazz Place, *Smugglers Inn*, 10 Ship St (☎01273/328439). Popular jazz venue in the basement, with the livelier *Enigma* upstairs catering for active ravers and fronting the occasional abstract dance troupe.

The Joint, 37 West St (☎01273/321692). Indie and disco sounds.

Lift, above the *Pig in Paradise*, 11–12 Queens Rd (☎01273/779411). Regular and varied jazz, jungle and funk events.

Paradox, 78 West St (☎01273/321628). The best option after the *Zap Club*. Its *Wild Fruits* gay nights on first Mondays of the month are particularly popular.

Revenge, 32 Old Steine (☎01273/606064). The south's largest gay club with Monday night cabarets plus upfront dance and retro boogie on two floors.

Swifts Club, West St (☎01273/327701). Popular venue for retro sounds from the 1960s onwards with the *Cavern*, below, playing hip-hop, ragga jungle and the like.

The Tavern, Castle Square (☎01273/827641). Classic soul, funk and disco go down a treat at this central club, off Old Steine.

Volks Tavern, 3 Madeira Drive (☎01273/682828). Under the colonnades on Marine Parade, you'll find a groovy crowd with live bands, reggae revival nights and some break beats. There's even a fetish night if you're up for it.

Zap Club, 188–193 Kings Road Arches (☎01273/821588). Brighton's most durable club, right on the seafront opposite Ship Street.

Listings

Bike Rental Freedom Bikes, 96 St James's St (☎01273/681698); Rayment's Cycles, 13–14 Circus Parade, New England Rd (☎01273/697217); Sunrise Cycle Hire, West Pier, King's Rd Arches (☎01273/748881). Rental costs around £12 a day and £30 a week, with £20 deposit.

Books Border's, Churchill Sq (☎01273/731122); Waterstone's, 55 North St (☎01273/327867).

Buses 1 Stop Travel, 16 Old Steine (Mon–Fri 8.30am–5.45pm, Sat 9am–5pm; ☎01273/700406); Brighton and Hove Buses ☎01273/886200; Stagecoach South Coast Buses ☎01424/433711; National Express ☎0990/808080.

Car rental Affordable Car Hire, 1–2 Victoria Terrace, Kingsway, Hove (☎01273/724464); Sixt Rent a Car, *Metropole Hotel*, King's Rd, Brighton (☎01273/418512).

Dentist ☎01273/777790.

Exchanges American Express, 82 North St (Mon–Sat 9am–5.30pm; ☎01273/203766); Thomas Cook, 58 North St (Mon–Sat 9am–5.30pm; ☎01273/367700).

Hospitals Brighton General, Elm Grove; for emergencies, Royal Sussex County, Eastern Rd (call ☎01273/696955 for both).

Internet Sumo restaurant, 8–12 Middle St (☎01273/823344); Brighton Reference Library, Church St (☎01273/296968); The Arena, 36 Preston St (☎01273/245105).

Laundry Wash-a-Rama, 12 Elm Grove; Bubbles 1, 75 Preston St; KG Launderette, 116 St George's Rd.

Left Luggage At the train station (24-hour service).

Lesbian and Gay Switchboard ☎01273/204 050 (daily 6–11pm).

Pharmacies Ashton's, 98 Dyke Rd (daily till 10pm; ☎01273/325020).

Police John St, off Edward St, near the Pavilion (☎01273/606744).

Post offices 51 Ship St (Mon–Sat 9am–5.30pm).

Taxis ☎01273/204060, 205205 or 202020.

Trains National Rail Enquiries ☎0345/484950.

Travel agents Going Places, 125 Queens Rd (☎01273/202676); STA Travel, 38 North St (☎01273/728282); Thomas Cook, 58 North St (☎01273/367700).

Mid-Sussex

The principal attraction of **Mid-Sussex** is its wealth of fine gardens, ranging from the majestic **Sheffield Park** to the tree plantations of **Wakehurst**, the luscious flowerbeds of **Nymans** to the landscaped lakes of **Leonardslee**. Exploring this region by public transport isn't really feasible unless you take your bike on the train; tourist information is thin on the ground too – it's best to get clued up at Brighton's tourist office beforehand, if you're interested in doing a thorough tour.

Sheffield Park and the Bluebell Railway

Around twenty miles northeast of Brighton lies the country estate of **Sheffield Park**, its centrepiece a Gothic mansion built for Lord Sheffield by James Wyatt. The house is closed to the public, but you can roam around the hundred-acre **gardens** (Jan & Feb Sat & Sun 10.30am–4pm or dusk; April–Oct Tues–Sun & public holidays 10.30am–6pm or sunset; March, Nov & Dec Tues–Sun 10.30am–4pm; £4.20; NT), which were laid out by Capability Brown, the Christopher Wren of the grassy knoll. The gardens and pathways are based around a series of five landscaped ponds – vestiges of Sussex's industrial iron-smelting days. At their best in spring and autumn, the gardens feature a wide range of exotic plants and trees, with the taller conifers mimicking the house's spires.

A mile southwest of the gardens lies the southern terminus of the **Bluebell Railway** (May–Sept daily; Oct–April Sat, Sun & school holidays; day ticket £7.40; ☎01825/723777), whose vintage steam locomotives chuff nine miles north via Horsted Keynes to Kingscote. Although the service gets extremely crowded at weekends – especially in May, when the bluebells blossom in the woods through which the line passes – it's an entertaining and nostalgic way of travelling through the Sussex countryside and your day ticket lets you go to and fro as often as you like. A vintage bus service connects the northern terminus of Kingscote (no car access) with East Grinstead train station (hourly trains from London Victoria), though plans are afoot to re-lay the remaining two miles of track and link the Bluebell directly with East Grinstead.

Wakehurst Place and Nymans

Wakehurst Place, eighteen miles north of Brighton (daily: Feb & Oct 10am–5pm; March 10am–6pm; April–Sept 10am–7pm; Nov–Jan 10am–4pm; £5; NT), is the country home of Kew Royal Botanic Gardens. The 25-acre site is given over mainly to trees and shrubs but, like many gardens in the area, was badly hit by the storm of 1987 (see box on p.183) when it lost more than fifteen thousand trees. However, the collection has been gradually replenished and now features a variety of horticultural environments, including a Himalayan Glade and an Asian Heath Garden. The gardens spread down from the Jacobean mansion to beyond Westwood lake, from where paths then lead back to the house, making a pleasant hour-and-a-half's round walk. The nearest station is Haywards Heath, on the London–Brighton line, from where you can catch bus #772 – a limited daily service, which actually starts its journey from Old Steine in Brighton.

For one of the southeast's greatest gardens, head five miles southwest of Wakehurst Place to **Nymans** (March–Oct Wed–Sun 11am–6pm or sunset; £5; NT), near the village of Handcross; bus #773 from Brighton to Crawley can drop you off on the A23 beside the village. Created by Ludwig Messel, an inspired gardener and plant collector, the gardens contain a valuable collection of exotic trees and shrubs as well as more everyday plants, of which the colourful rhododendrons are particularly prolific. Nymans consists of a series of different enclosures and gardens, the highlight of which is the large, romantic walled garden, almost hidden from sight by an abundance of climbing plants and housing a collection of rare Himalayan magnolia trees. The gardens are centred around the picturesque ruins of a mock-Tudor manor house, now covered in wisteria, roses and honeysuckle, and are laced with gently sloping paths linking the huge beds of rhododendrons, azaleas and roses.

Leonardslee Gardens

The most picturesque of all the mid-Sussex gardens are those at **Leonardslee** (daily: April–Oct 9.30am–6pm; £4, £5 during May), four miles southwest of Nymans, near the village of Crabtree; bus #107 from Brighton to Horsham passes by the garden gates. Set in a wooded valley, the seventy-acre gardens are crisscrossed by steep paths, which link six lakes created – like those at Sheffield Park – in the sixteenth century to power waterwheels for iron foundries. The range of flora is especially impressive here, featuring many hybrid species of rhododendron that were created specifically for this garden and are at their best in May. Wallabies, sika and fallow deer roam freely, adding to the Edenic atmosphere.

Arundel and around

The hilltop town of **ARUNDEL**, eighteen miles west of Brighton, has for seven centuries been the seat of the dukes of Norfolk, whose fine castle looks over the valley of the River Arun. The medieval town's well-preserved appearance and picturesque setting draws in the crowds on summer weekends, but at any other time a visit reveals one of West Sussex's least-spoilt old towns. Arundel also has a unique place in English cricket: traditionally, the first match of every touring side is played against the Duke of Norfolk's XI on the ground beneath the castle.

The town

Arundel Castle, towering over the High Street (April–Oct Mon–Fri & Sun noon–5pm; castle, grounds & chapel £6.70; grounds & chapel £2), is what first catches the eye and, despite its medieval appearance, most of what you see is only a century old. The structure dated from Norman times, but was ruined during the Civil War, then lavishly reconstructed during the nineteenth century by the eighth, eleventh and fifteenth dukes. From the top of the keep, you can see the current duke's spacious residence and the pristine castle grounds. Inside the castle, the renovated quarters include the impressive **Barons Hall** and the **library**, which boasts paintings by Gainsborough, Holbein and Van Dyck. On the edge of the castle grounds, the fourteenth-century **Fitzalan Chapel** houses tombs of past dukes of Norfolk including twin effigies of the seventh duke – one as he looked when he died and, underneath, one of his emaciated corpse. The Catholic chapel belongs to the Norfolk estate, but is actually physically joined to the **Church of St Nicholas**, the parish church, whose entrance is in London Road. It is separated from the altar of the main Anglican church by an iron grille and a glass screen. Although traditionally Catholics, the dukes of Norfolk have shrewdly played down their papal allegiance in sensitive times – such as during the Tudor era when two of the third duke's nieces, Anne Boleyn and Catherine Howard, became Henry VIII's wives.

West of the parish church, further along London Road, is Arundel's other major landmark, the towering Gothic bulk of **Arundel Cathedral**. Constructed in the 1870s by the fifteenth duke of Norfolk over the town's former Catholic church, the cathedral's spire was designed by John Hansom, inventor of the hansom cab, the earliest taxi. Inside are the enshrined remains of St Philip Howard, the fourth duke's son, exhumed from the Fitzalan Chapel after his canonization in 1970. Following a wayward youth, Howard returned to the Catholic fold at a time when the Armada's defeat saw anti-Catholic feelings soar. Caught fleeing overseas and sentenced to death for praying for Spanish victory, he spent the next decade in the Tower of London, where he died. The cathedral's impressive outline is more appealing than the interior, but it fits in well with the townscape of the medieval seaport.

The rest of Arundel is pleasant to wander round, with the antique shop-lined Maltravers and Arun streets being the most attractive throughfares. Halfway up the High Street, in the same building as the tourist office is the **Arundel Heritage Museum** (April–Sept Mon–Sat 10.30am–5pm, Sun 2–5pm; £1), a surprisingly interesting local museum with a history of medicine on the ground floor and lots of information on Arundel's days as a busy port, once connected by canal to Weybridge on the Thames.

Practicalities

Arundel is served by regular trains from London Victoria, Portsmouth, Brighton and Chichester. The **train station** is half a mile south of the town centre over the river on the A27, with **buses** arriving either in the High Street or River Road. The **tourist office** is at 61 High St (June–Aug Mon–Fri 9am–5pm, Sat & Sun 10am–5pm; Sept–May Mon–Fri 9am–5pm, Sat & Sun 10am–3pm; ☎01903/882268). **Boat rental** and riverboat **cruises** upstream to the village of Amberley are available from the riverside *Tea Rooms* by the bridge.

For **accommodation**, try *Bridge House*, just south of the Queen Street bridge (☎01903/882142; ②), a friendly place offering good-value en-suite rooms, or the venerable *Swan Hotel* at the bottom of High Street (☎01903/882314; ④), a fine old house with a cosy adjoining restaurant. *Castle View* (☎01903/883029; ②), next door to the tourist office above the tea rooms of the same name, is reasonable, and neighbouring *Dukes Restaurant*, with its spectacular gilded ceiling, also has a few rooms available (☎01903/883847; ④). Three miles west of town in Walburton, is the three-hundred-year-old thatched cottage, *Beam Ends*, Hedgers Hill (☎01243/551254; no credit cards; ②), offering friendly B&B accommodation. For a real splurge, head for Amberley, four miles north, where you can get a luxury double room at the six-hundred-year-old *Amberley Castle* (☎01798/831992; ⑦). Arundel's **youth hostel** (☎01903/882204) is in a large Georgian house by the river at Warningcamp, a mile and a half northeast of town. You can **camp** at the hostel, or try the *Maynards* site (☎01903/882075) at the top of the hill on the A27 two miles southeast of town.

First choice for reasonably priced, good-quality food is the **restaurant** attached to the *White Hart* pub over the river at 3 Queen St (☎01903/882374); alternatively try the *Red Lion*, on the High Street, for solid pub grub and real ales. Out of keeping with the rest of Arundel is the modernist *Mac's Wine and Champagne Bar* and restaurant, 18 Tarrant St (☎01903/885100; closed Sun eve & all Mon), which offers an eclectic Med-influenced menu; à la carte is very reasonably priced with no main course over £10. The best real-ale **pub** in town is the *Eagle*, 41 Tarrant St, which dispenses King and Barnes beer from nearby Horsham and Fuller's London Pride.

Bignor and Petworth

Six miles north of Arundel, the excavated second-century ruins of the **Bignor Roman Villa** (March–May & Oct Tues–Sun 10am–5pm; June–Sept daily 10am–6pm; £3.35) include some well-preserved mosaics, of which the Ganymede is the most outstanding. The site, first excavated between 1811 and 1819, is superbly situated at the base of the South Downs and features the longest extant section of mosaic in England, as well as the remains of a hypocaust, the underfloor heating system developed by the Romans.

Adjoining the pretty little village of **PETWORTH**, eleven miles north of Arundel, is **Petworth House** (April–Oct Mon–Wed, Sat & Sun 1–5.30pm; park daily 8am–dusk; house £5.50; park free; NT), one of the southeast's most impressive stately homes. Built in the late seventeenth century, the house contains an outstanding art collection, including paintings by Van Dyck, Titian, Gainsborough, Bosch, Reynolds, Blake and Turner – the last a frequent guest here. Highlights of the interior decor are Louis Laguerre's murals around the **Grand Staircase** and the **Carved Room**, where carvings by Grinling Gibbons and Holbein's full-length portrait of Henry VIII can be seen. The seven-hundred-acre grounds were landscaped by Capability Brown and are considered one of his finest achievements.

Petworth's **tourist office** is on the Market Square (April–Sept Mon–Sat 10am–5pm Sun 11am–4pm; March & Oct Mon–Sat 10am–4pm; Nov–Feb Fri–Sat 11am–3pm; ☎01798/343523). For a memorable night's **stay**, book in at Petworth's converted *Old Railway Station* (☎01798/342346; ④).

Chichester and around

The county town of West Sussex and its only city, **CHICHESTER** is an attractive, if stuffy, market town, which began life as a Roman settlement – the Roman cruciform street plan is still evident in the four-quadrant symmetry of the town centre, spread around the Market Cross. The city has built itself up as one of southern England's cultural centres, hosting the **Chichester Festival** in early July, its focus a fairly safe programme of middlebrow plays, though the studio theatre is a bit more adventurous. The racecourse at **Goodwood Park**, north of the city, hosts one of England's most fash-

HORSE RACING IN SOUTHEAST ENGLAND

A popular way to spend a day out in southeast England is to go to the races at one of the many tracks in the region. **Glorious Goodwood** and the **Derby week** are the fashionable meetings to attend, as is **Royal Ascot**, in Berkshire, but the less well-known courses, such as Brighton, Fontwell Park and Kempton Park, offer equally entertaining meetings throughout the year. For course locations, see chapter map on pp.148–149. Generally it'll cost you around £8–10 to get into a "basic" enclosure, but you can pay much higher prices for admission into the grandstand and more exclusive enclosures, where the social event often takes precedence over the racing.

Ascot (☎01344/622211; 10min walk from Ascot train station). No account of racing in southeast England would be complete without Ascot, the jewel in the crown of English racecourses. Admission is rather expensive, but the facilities and atmosphere make it worth the price. The week-long Royal Meeting in mid-June is the one to attend, and to dress up for, with a selection of outrageous hats, outfits and royals on display, especially on Ladies' Day. The racecourse hosts less glamorous meetings throughout the rest of the year.

Brighton (☎01273/603580; Brighton train station with connecting buses on race days). Overlooking Brighton Marina at the east end of town, Brighton's racecourse has a U-shaped track and is one of the few courses in England that doesn't form a complete circuit; binoculars are useful and can be rented. The racecourse's situation, on top of the South Downs overlooking the English Channel, makes it particularly appealing for a day out. Up to twenty meetings take place from April to November every year with the three-day meeting in early August providing the best action.

Epsom Downs (☎01372/726311; Epsom Downs or Tattenham Corner train station with connecting buses on race days). Home of two of England's most famous races, the Derby and the Oaks, both of which take place during Derby week, the first week in June. The Derby has been run for nearly two hundred years and is the time when Epsom really comes alive – a fun day out for all classes of persons. There are very few meetings at other times: evening meetings at the end of June and July and a two-day event at the end of August.

Fontwell Park (☎01243/543335; Barnham train station with connecting buses on race days). Midway between Arundel and Chichester, Fontwell Park, which held its first meet-

ionable racing events at the same time (see box above). The Gothic cathedral is the chief permanent attraction in the city, but two miles west of the town are the restored Roman ruins of **Fishbourne**, one of the most visited ancient sites in the county. To the south is the flat headland of Selsey Bill, a dull section of coast, fringed with retirement estates for the well-to-do; if you want some fresh sea air, your best bet is to make for the inlets of **Chichester Harbour** or the Witterings, east of the harbour mouth, though there's little here of interest other than the sandy expanses of beach.

The City

The main streets lead off to the compass's cardinal points from the Gothic **Market Cross**, a bulky octagonal rotunda topped by ornate finials and a crown lantern spire, and built in 1501 to provide shelter for the market traders, although it appears far too small for its function.

A short stroll down West Street brings you to the neat form of the **Cathedral** (daily: Easter to mid-Sept 7.30am–7pm; mid-Sept to Easter 7.30am–5pm), whose slender spire – a nineteenth-century addition – is visible out at sea. Building began in the 1070s, but the church was extensively rebuilt following a fire a century later and has been only minimally modified since about 1300, except for the spire and the unique, freestanding fifteenth-century bell tower, which now houses the cathedral shop. The **interior** is ing in the 1920s, is a lesser-known racecourse which makes it a friendly and welcoming venue for first-time race-goers. It's one of only two figure-of-eight racecourses in Britain. One-day meetings take place once or twice a month from August to May, with up to seventeen fixtures a year.

Goodwood Park (☎01243/774107; four miles from Chichester train station with connecting buses on race days). Goodwood boasts a wonderful location, on a lush green hill overlooking Chichester with the South Downs as a backdrop. Even if you have only the mildest interest in the sport, and no interest in betting, it's worth a visit for the main meeting, Goodwood Week – or "Glorious Goodwood" to its fans; held in late July, it's second only to Ascot in its social cachet. There are plenty of other meetings from May to late September.

Kempton Park (☎01932/782292; a five-minute walk from Kempton Park train station). Just fifteen miles from London, this popular course has excellent facilities, including covered enclosures for inclement meetings; the majority of the fixtures are run on the flat. Racing takes place all year with evening meetings in April and from June to August. A highlight is the very popular two-day Christmas Festival which starts on Boxing Day.

Lingfield Park (☎01342/834800; a ten-minute walk from Lingfield train station). Has an all-weather synthetic track so races can be run here when they would have to be abandoned elsewhere, but unfortunately this hasn't really caught on with the public, and crowds are poor. If you want a lively atmosphere, stick to the turf (grass) events – especially the Turf National Hunt at the beginning of December and the Turf Flat in early May.

Plumpton (☎01273/890383; a short walk from Plumpton train station). Eight miles out of Brighton, this course has one of the sharpest tracks in the country (leading to its being nicknamed the "Wall of Death"), with extremely tight bends and a downhill back straight. Facilities here are good and races take place all year except in June and July.

Sandown Park (☎01372/470047; a ten-minute walk from Esher train station). Only fourteen miles from Central London, this hugely popular venue near Esher has been frequently voted "Racecourse of the Year" over the past decade. Atmosphere, an excellent location and superb facilities all add up to a great day's racing, with the Whitbread Gold Cup towards the end of April and the Coral-Eclipse Stakes in early June bringing out the crowds and being well worth attending.

renowned for its contemporary devotional art, which includes a stained glass window by Marc Chagall and an enormous altar-screen tapestry by John Piper. Other points of interest are the sixteenth-century painting in the north transept of the past bishops of Chichester, and the fourteenth-century Fitzalan tomb which inspired a poem by Philip Larkin. However, the highlight is a pair of reliefs in the south aisle, close to the tapestry – created around 1140, they show the raising of Lazarus and Christ at the gate of Bethany. Originally highly coloured, the reliefs once featured semi-precious stones set in the figures' eyes and are among the finest Romanesque stone carvings in England.

There are several fine buildings up **North Street**, including a dinky little Market House, built by Nash in 1807 and fronted by a Doric colonnade and a tiny flint Saxon church – now an ecclesiastical bookshop – with a diminutive wooden shingled spire. Finally, you come to the appealingly dumpy red-brick **Council House**, built in 1731, with Ionic columns and delightful intersecting tracery on its street facade, and crowned by a wonderful stone lion. East off South Street, in the well-preserved Georgian quadrant of the city known as the Pallants, you'll find **Pallant House**, 9 North Pallant (Tues–Sat 10am–5pm; Sun & public holidays 12.30am–5pm; £2.80). Stone dodos stand guard over the gates of this fine mansion, which houses artefacts and furniture from the early eighteenth century. Modern works of art are also included, among them pieces by Henry Moore and Barbara Hepworth and George Sutherland's portrait of

Walter Hussey, the former Dean of Chichester, who commissioned much of the cathedral's contemporary art.

Continuing in an anticlockwise direction around the town and crossing East Street to head north up Little London, brings you to the **Chichester District Museum** (Tues–Sat 10am–5.30pm; free), housed in an old white weatherboarded corn store. Inside, the modest but entertaining display on local life includes a portable oven carried by Joe Faro, the city pieman, as well as the portable stocks used for the ritual humiliation of petty criminals. The **Guildhall** (June–Aug Sat noon–4pm; free), a branch museum within a thirteenth-century Franciscan church in the middle of Priory Park, at the north end of Little London, has some well-preserved medieval frescoes. It was formerly a town hall and court of law, and the poet, painter and visionary William Blake was tried here for sedition.

Practicalities

A regular service runs from London Victoria to Chichester's **train station** at the foot of South Street, with the **bus station** next door. From either station it's a ten-minute walk north to the Market Cross, passing the **tourist office** at 29a South St (April–Sept Mon–Sat 9.15am–5.15pm, Sun 10am–4pm; Oct–March closed Sun; ☎01243/775888).

Every other house on the main roads out of Chichester seems to offer B&B **accommodation**, so there's no problem finding a place to stay other than during the festival. If you want to splash out, try the *Ship* North St (☎01243/778000; ⑥), a comfortable and characterful inn in the centre of town. Less expensive central B&B options include the brick and flint *Riverside Lodge*, 7 Market Ave, in the Pallants quarter (☎01243/783164; ②) or *Friary Close*, Friary Lane (☎01243/527294; ③), east of the town centre. You can **camp** at the *Red House Farm*, Brookers Lane, Earnley (☎01243/512959; closed Nov–Easter), six miles southwest of town, a mile or so from the beach.

As well as offering excellent accommodation, the *Ship* is a good place for a **drink**, or you could try the *Rainbow*, 56 St Paul's Rd, northwest of the town centre, which also has an excellent range of Sussex beers. For something to **eat**, the *Medieval Crypt Brasserie* at 12 South St (☎01243/537033) has wonderful stone vaulting and main courses for around £8; and further down the street there's a branch of *Pizza Express*. For authentic French/Med food, go for the stylish *Little London* brasserie (☎01243/771771), housed in an eighteenth-century vaulted cellar just off East Street in Little London, which offers set-price two- and three-course dinners. Staying with Mediterranean cuisine, *The Sicilian*, 14 St Pancras (☎01243/538282; closed lunch, plus all Mon & Sun), specializes in pasta and seafood dishes.

Fishbourne Roman Palace

Fishbourne, two miles west of Chichester (March–July, Sept & Oct daily 10am–5pm; Aug daily 10am–6pm; Nov to mid-Dec daily 10am–4pm; mid-Dec to Feb Sat & Sun 10am–4pm; £4.20), is the largest and best-preserved Roman palace in the country. Roman relics have long been turning up in Fishbourne and in 1960 a workman unearthed their source – the site of a depot used by the invading Romans in 43 AD which is thought later to have become the vast, hundred-room palace of the Romanized Celtic aristocrat, Cogidubnus. A pavilion has been built over the north wing of the excavated remains, where floor mosaics depict Fishbourne's famous dolphin-riding cupid as well as the more usual geometric patterns.

Like the more evocative remains at Bignor (see p.209), only the residential wing of the former quadrangle has been excavated – other parts of the dwelling fulfilled mundane service roles and probably lacked the mosaics which give both sites their singular appeal. The underfloor heating system has also been well restored and an audiovisual programme gives a fuller picture of the palace as it was in Roman times. The extensive gardens attempt to re-create the appearance of the palace grounds as they would have been then.

To get to Fishbourne take the train to Fishbourne station, turn right as you leave the station and the palace is a few minutes' walk away.

Tangmere Military Aviation Museum

Three miles east of Chichester, signposted off the A27, is **Tangmere Military Aviation Museum** (daily: Feb & Nov 10am–4.30pm; March–Oct 10am–5.30pm; £3; bus #58 from Chichester), sited at one of England's earliest airfields, which was established in 1917 and closed in 1970. On display are a number of aircraft including replicas of the legendary Hurricane and Spitfire fighters which took off from Tangmere airfield during the Battle of Britain. Early supersonic jets are also housed, with a display about Neville Duke whose Hawker Hunter reached 727mph along the nearby coast in the early 1950s. Up the road the *Bader Arms* is a reasonable **pub**, which commemorates the famous Battle of Britain pilot Douglas Bader who survived the war and continued flying after having been shot down and losing both his legs.

Sculpture at Goodwood

Three miles north of Chichester, just to the east of Goodwood House, **Sculpture at Goodwood** (March–Oct Thurs–Sat 10.30am–4.30pm; £10) is an absolute must for anyone interested in contemporary art – the entry fee appears deliberately designed to put off casual punters. Since 1994 Wilfred and Jeanette Cass, long-time collectors of sculpture, have created a unique woodland environment for more than forty large-scale works, some of which have been specially commissioned and each of which is sited to allow you to appreciate it in isolation. The selection of pieces on display changes from year to year, but has been known to include Turner Prize winners.

Weald and Downland Open-Air Museum

Five miles north of Chichester, the **Weald and Downland Open-Air Museum** (March–Oct daily 10.30am–5pm; Nov–Feb Wed, Sat & Sun 10.30am–4pm; £5.20), just outside the village of Singleton, is one the best rural museums in the southeast. More than forty old buildings – from a Tudor market hall to a medieval farmstead have been saved from destruction and reconstructed at the forty-acre museum site. A substantial lottery award in the late 1990s has gone towards the construction of a new visitor's centre, due to open in 2001. Besides a whole range of livestock as permanent residents there are also numerous special events and activities to visit, particularly in July and August, so it's worthwhile ringing for details of the current season's programme (☎01243/811348). There's a half-hourly bus from Chichester (#60), which will drop you off in Singleton.

travel details

Trains

Battle to: Hastings (Mon–Sat 2 hourly, Sun hourly; 15min); London Charing Cross (2 hourly; 1hr 15min); Sevenoaks (Mon–Sat 2 hourly, Sun hourly; 45min); Tunbridge Wells (Mon–Sat 2 hourly, Sun hourly; 30min).

Brighton to: Chichester (2 hourly; 1hr); Gatwick Airport (every 10–20min; 25–40min); Hastings (2 hourly; 1hr 10min); Lewes (Mon–Sat every 10–20min, Sun hourly; 15min); London Victoria (2 hourly; 1hr–1hr 20min); London King's Cross (Mon–Sat 4 hourly, Sun 2 hourly; 1hr 15min); Oxford (3 hourly; 2hr 50min); Portsmouth Harbour (hourly; 1hr 25min).

Broadstairs to: London Victoria (hourly; 2hr 45min); Ramsgate (2 hourly; 5min).

Canterbury East to: Dover Priory (Mon–Sat 2 hourly, Sun hourly; 30min); London Victoria (1 hourly; 1hr 30min).

Canterbury West to: London Charing Cross (hourly; 1hr 40min); London Victoria (hourly; 1hr 40min); Ramsgate (hourly; 20min).

Chatham to: Dover Priory (hourly; 50min); London Charing Cross (2 hourly; 1hr 10min); London Victoria (every 10–30min; 40min–1hr).

Chichester to: London Victoria (2 hourly; 1hr 45min); Portsmouth Harbour (Mon–Sat 4 hourly, Sun 2 hourly; 40min).

Dorking to: Farnham (hourly; 1hr); London Waterloo (2 hourly; 40min).

Dover Priory to: Folkestone Central (2 hourly; 15min); London Charing Cross (Mon–Sat 2 hourly, Sun hourly; 1hr 40min); London Victoria (2 hourly; 1hr 50min).

Eastbourne to: Gatwick Airport (2 hourly; 1hr); Hastings (Mon–Sat 3 hourly, Sun hourly; 30min); Lewes (Mon–Sat every 10–25min, Sun hourly; 20–25min); London Victoria (Mon–Sat 2 hourly, Sun hourly; 1hr 30min).

Folkestone Central to: London Charing Cross (2 hourly, Sun hourly; 1hr 30min).

Folkestone West to: London Charing Cross (2 hourly; 1hr 30min).

Gatwick Airport to: London Victoria (very frequent; 30min).

Guildford to: London Waterloo (3 hourly; 35–55min).

Hastings to: Gatwick Airport (hourly; 1hr 30min); London Charing Cross (Mon–Sat 2 hourly, Sun hourly; 1hr 40min); London Victoria (hourly; 2hr); Rye (railbus every 20min); Tunbridge Wells (2 hourly; 35–45min).

Herne Bay to: London Victoria (2 hourly; 1hr 30min); Ramsgate (Mon–Sat 2 hourly, Sun hourly; 30min).

Lewes to: London Victoria (Mon–Sat 2 hourly, Sun hourly; 1hr 15min).

Maidstone East to: London Victoria (Mon–Sat 2 hourly, Sun hourly; 1hr); London Charing Cross (hourly; 1 hr).

Margate to: Canterbury West (hourly; 35–45min); London Victoria (hourly; 1hr 10min).

Ramsgate to: London Charing Cross (2 hourly; 2hr–2hr 20min); London Victoria (hourly; 2hr 30min).

Rochester to: Dover Priory (Mon–Sat 2 hourly, Sun hourly; 1hr 10min); Herne Bay (Mon–Sat 2 hourly; Sun hourly; 1hr); London Victoria (hourly; 40min) London Charing Cross (Mon–Sat 2 hourly; Sun hourly; 1hr 10min).

Rye to: Hastings (railbus every 20min).

Sandwich to: Dover Priory (hourly; 30min); Ramsgate (hourly; 15min).

Sevenoaks to: London Blackfriars (Mon–Sat 2 hourly; 1hr); London Charing Cross (Mon–Sat 4 hourly, Sun 2 hourly; 30min).

Tunbridge Wells to: London Victoria (Mon–Fri 2 hourly; 50min).

Whitstable to: London Victoria (hourly; 1hr 20min); Ramsgate (every 30min; 40min).

Woking to: London Waterloo (every 10–40min; 35min).

Buses

All buses go to Victoria Coach Station
Brighton to: London (hourly; 2hr).
Canterbury to: London (hourly; 1hr 50min).
Chichester to London (2 daily; 3hr)
Dover Eastern Docks to: London (hourly; 2hr 45min).
Eastbourne to: London (3 daily; 2hr 40min).
Folkestone to: London (4 daily; 2hr 30min).
Hastings to: London (2 daily; 2hr 40min).
Ramsgate to: London (4 daily; 2hr 50min).
Rochester to: London (hourly; 1hr 30min).
Tunbridge Wells to: London (1 daily; 1hr 40min).

CHAPTER THREE

HAMPSHIRE, DORSET AND WILTSHIRE

The distant past is perhaps more tangible in **Hampshire**, **Dorset** and **Wiltshire** than in any other part of England. Predominantly rural, these three counties overlap substantially with the ancient kingdom of **Wessex**, whose most famous ruler, Alfred, repulsed the Danes in the ninth century and came close to establishing the first unified state in England. Before Wessex came into being, however, many earlier civilizations had left their stamp on the region. The chalky uplands of Wiltshire boast several of Europe's greatest Neolithic sites, including **Stonehenge** and **Avebury**, while in Dorset you'll find **Maiden Castle**, the most striking Iron Age hill fort in the country, and the **Cerne Abbas Giant**, source of many a legend. The Romans tramped all over these southern counties, leaving the most conspicuous signs of their occupation at the amphitheatre of **Dorchester** – though that town is more closely associated with the novels of Thomas Hardy and his distinctively gloomy vision of Wessex.

None of the landscapes of this region could be described as grand or wild, but the countryside is consistently seductive, its appeal exemplified by the crumbling fossil-bearing cliffs around **Lyme Regis**, the managed woodlands of the **New Forest** and the gentle, open curves of **Salisbury Plain**. Its towns are also generally modest and slow-paced, with the notable exceptions of the two great maritime bases of **Portsmouth** and, to a lesser extent, **Southampton**, a fair proportion of whose visitors are simply passing through on their way to the more genteel pleasures of the **Isle of Wight**. This is something of an injustice, though neither place can compete with the two most interesting cities in this part of England – **Salisbury** and **Winchester**, each of which possesses a stupendous cathedral amid an array of other historic sights. Of the region's great houses, **Wilton**, **Stourhead**, **Longleat** and **Kingston Lacy** are the ones that attract the crowds, but every cranny has its medieval church, manor house or unspoilt country inn – there are few parts of England in which an aimless meander can be so rewarding. If it's straightforward seaside fun you're after, **Bournemouth** leads the

ACCOMMODATION PRICE CODES

Throughout this guide, hotel and B&B accommodation is priced on a scale of ① to ⑨, the number indicating the **lowest price** you could expect to pay per night in that establishment for a **double room** in high season. The prices indicated by the codes are as follows:

① under £40	④ £60–70	⑦ £110–150
② £40–50	⑤ £70–90	⑧ £150–200
③ £50–60	⑥ £90–110	⑨ over £200

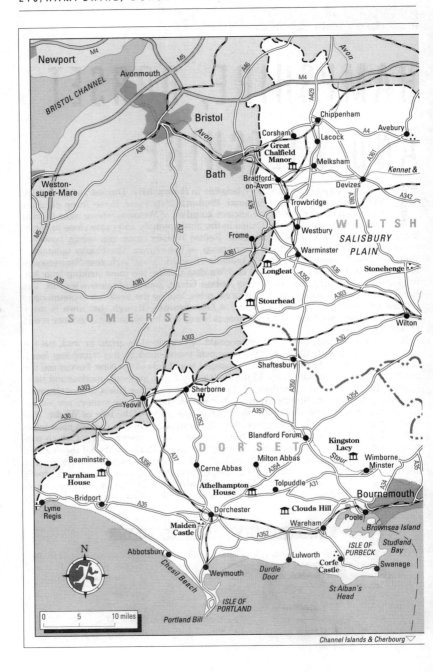

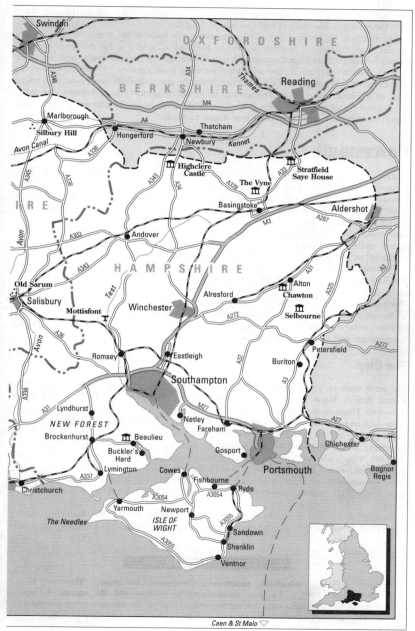

Caen & St Malo ▽

way, with Weymouth and Lyme Regis heading the ranks of the minor resorts, along with the yachties' havens over on the Isle of Wight.

The roads in this area get choked in summer, the bulk of the traffic heading either for the more celebrated holiday centres of the West Country or for the ferry ports of Poole, Portsmouth and Southampton. If you're heading for one particular spot, it's often easier to reach it by rail, on the fast direct services from London's Waterloo station. To tour the area extensively and conveniently, though, you definitely need your own transport, as the hinterland is not well served by public transport. Keen walkers can avoid the hordes by taking to the New Forest's quieter spots or to the **Dorset Coast Path**, which stretches all the way from Lyme Regis to Poole.

Portsmouth

Britain's foremost naval station, **PORTSMOUTH** occupies the bulbous peninsula of Portsea Island, on the eastern flank of a huge, easily defended harbour. The ancient Romans raised a fortress on the northernmost edge of this inlet, and a small port developed during the Norman era, but this strategic location wasn't fully exploited until Tudor times, when Henry VII established the world's first dry dock here and made Portsmouth a royal dockyard. It has flourished ever since and nowadays Portsmouth is a large industrialized city, its harbour clogged with naval frigates, ferries bound for the continent or the Isle of Wight, and swarms of dredgers and tugs.

Portsmouth was heavily bombed during the last war due to its military importance and, although the Victorian slums got what they deserved, bland tower blocks from the nadir of British architectural endeavour now give the city an ugly profile. Only **Old Portsmouth**, based around the original harbour, preserves some Georgian and a little Tudor character. East of here is **Southsea**, a residential suburb of terraces with a half-hearted resort strewn along its shingle beach, where a mass of B&Bs face stoic naval monuments and tawdry seaside amusements.

The City

For most visitors, a trip to Portsmouth begins and ends at the **Historic Ships**, in the **Royal Naval Base** at the end of Queen Street (daily: March–Oct 10am–5.30pm; Nov–Feb 10am–5pm; last entry 1hr before closing). The complex comprises three ships and as many museums, with each ship visitable separately (£5.95 each) – though most people do the lot on an all-ships ticket (£11.90), including the Royal Naval Museum; or all-inclusive ticket, taking in various exhibitions and a harbour-tour (£14.90), which will easily take half a day. Note that visits to the *Victory* are guided, with limited numbers at set times, and you may have to wait up to two hours for your turn. Also, visitors with disabilities will have a hard time moving between decks on the two complete ships; a virtual tour by video (call ☎01705/722562 for details) is a good alternative.

Nearest the entrance to the complex is the youngest ship, **HMS Warrior**, dating from 1860. It was Britain's first armoured, or "iron-clad" battleship, complete with sails

---

TELEPHONE NUMBERS

On April 22, 2000, all **telephone numbers** in Portsmouth will change. There will be a **new area code, 023**, and all local numbers will be prefixed with **92**, making the new local numbers eight digits long. For further information on the changes to the telephone numbering system in the UK, see the box on p.36.

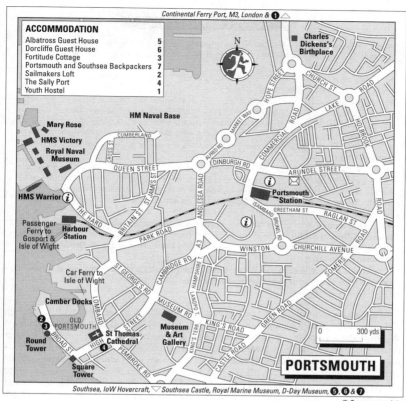

ACCOMMODATION

Albatross Guest House	5
Dorcliffe Guest House	6
Fortitude Cottage	3
Portsmouth and Southsea Backpackers	7
Sailmakers Loft	2
The Sally Port	4
Youth Hostel	1

Continental Ferry Port, M3, London & ❶

Charles Dickens's Birthplace

HM Naval Base

Mary Rose

HMS Victory

Royal Naval Museum

HMS Warrior ⓘ

Passenger Ferry to Gosport & Isle of Wight

Harbour Station

Car Ferry to Isle of Wight

Camber Docks

OLD PORTSMOUTH

Round Tower

St Thomas Cathedral

Square Tower

Museum & Art Gallery

Portsmouth Station ⓘ

PORTSMOUTH

0   300 yds

Southsea, IoW Hovercraft, ▽ Southsea Castle, Royal Marine Museum, D-Day Museum, ❺, ❻ & ❼

and steam engines, and was the pride of the fleet in its day. Longer and faster than any previous naval vessel, and the first to be fitted with washing machines, the *Warrior* was described by Napoleon III as a "black snake amongst the rabbits". You can wander around its main deck and see where eighteen seamen ate, slept and relaxed in the tiny spaces between each of the ship's thirty-six cannons. Not surprisingly, the captain's cabin, at the stern of the ship, resembles a sumptuous four-star suite, while the navigator also had a cabin to himself, although he shared it with a massive cannon. Other weaponry, including rifles, pistols and sabres, is all neatly stowed, but the *Warrior* was never challenged nor even fired a cannon in her twenty-two years at sea.

HMS Victory was already forty years old when she set sail from Portsmouth for Trafalgar on September 14, 1805, returning victorious three months later, but bearing the corpse of Admiral Nelson. Shot by a sniper from a French ship at the height of the battle, Nelson expired below decks three hours later, having been assured that victory was in sight. The usual fate of casualties at sea was to be sewn into their hammocks with a cannon ball and thrown overboard, but Nelson didn't wish to be buried at sea, so his body was preserved in a huge vat of brandy pending his eventual burial in St Paul's Cathedral. Although badly damaged during the battle, the *Victory* continued in service for a further twenty years, before being retired to the dry dock where she rests today.

NAVAL VERNACULAR

Many phrases in today's English language owe their origins to the country's seafaring heritage. Below are some of the more familiar expressions whose daily use has blurred their naval ancestry:

• "Three square meals a day". Sailors aboard the *Victory* were served a meagre trio of daily meals on square wooden plates.

• "Let the cat out of the bag" and "Not enough room to swing a cat". Both refer to the cat-o'-nine-tails, a nine-thonged whip with knots at the end of each thong. Taking the "cat" out of its baize bag made subsequent intentions obvious, and floggings were carried out on the upper deck where the bosun could get a good swing at the wrongdoer.

• "Limeys". This nickname for Brits derives from the casks of lime juice ships carried to prevent scurvy.

• "Grog". Slang for alcohol still current in Australia. In Nelson's time sailors were allocated a gallon of beer or a pint of rum per day; in the early 1700s, Admiral Vernon, noted for his coat made of grogram and so nicknamed "Old Grog", became notorious for diluting the daily servings with water, producing an insipid brew akin to some Australian beers.

• "Turn a blind eye". Part of Nelson's early reputation was made on his irreverent attitude to authority. At the Battle of Copenhagen, the arrogant second-in-command thought he knew best and "ignored" unnecessary signals from other ships by holding the telescope to his blind eye.

• "Son of a gun". A scoundrel. Women unfortunate enough to give birth on ship, did so between the cannons to keep the gangways clear.

In a shed behind the *Victory* are the remains of the **Mary Rose**, Henry VIII's flagship, which capsized before his eyes off Spithead in 1545 while engaging French intruders. Whether she was top-heavy (she was certainly overloaded at the time) or took in water through her lower gunports, having reeled from a broadside, is uncertain, but the *Mary Rose*, named after Henry's daughter and the Tudor rose, sank swiftly with almost all her seven-hundred-strong crew. In 1982 a massive conservation project successfully raised the remains of the hull, which silt had preserved beneath the seabed, and it was moved to its present position. This may be a sterling bit of history and the successful culmination of a painstaking archeological recovery, but you can't help feeling it's the techniques of retrieval and preservation that are being celebrated here, rather than the ship itself. Many of the thousands of objects which were found near the wreck are now displayed in a rather more absorbing exhibition close to the *Warrior*. Videos of the recovery operation are shown, as well as depictions of life aboard a sixteenth-century warship.

Opposite the *Victory*, various buildings house the exhaustive **Royal Naval Museum** (£3.50). Tracing the story from Alfred the Great's fleet to the present day, this is the most resistible attraction in the complex. One building contains a collection of jolly figureheads, Nelson memorabilia and numerous nautical models, but coverage of a more recent conflict, the Falklands War of 1982, is treated very lightly.

The naval theme is continued at **Submarine World** on Haslar Jetty in Gosport (daily: April–Oct 10am–5.30pm; Nov–March 10am–4.30pm; last tour 1hr before closing; £3.75), reached by taking the passenger ferry from Harbour train station jetty (daily 5.30am–midnight; £1.50 return), just south of the entrance to the Royal Naval Base, or, from the same place, the water-bus, which gives you a half-hour tour of the harbour before dropping you in Gosport (Easter–Oct 10.30am–5pm; £3). Allow yourself a couple of hours to explore these slightly creepy vessels – a guided tour inside *HMS Alliance* gives you an insight into life on board and the museum elaborates evocatively on the long history of submersible craft.

From the pontoon beside HMS *Warrior*, regular ferries depart (Wed & Sat 1.30pm, Sun 2pm; £6.50, including entry to the fort) for the mile-long ride to **Spitbank Fort**, an offshore bastion of granite, iron and brick little altered since its construction in the 1860s. With over fifty rooms linked by passages and steps on two floors, the complex includes a 430-foot deep well, which still draws fresh water from below the seafloor, and an inner courtyard complete with a café and sheltered terrace. The artificial island hosts theme nights – ask at the tourist office for details – and you can also stay here (see p.222).

Back at the Harbour train station in Portsmouth, it's a well-signposted twenty-minute walk south to what remains of **Old Portsmouth**. Along the way, you pass the simple **Cathedral of St Thomas** on the High Street, whose original twelfth-century features have been obscured by rebuilding after the Civil War and in this century. The High Street ends at a maze of cobbled Georgian streets huddling behind a fifteenth-century wall protecting the **Camber**, or old port, where Walter Raleigh landed the first potatoes and tobacco from the New World. Nearby, the Round and Square Towers, which punctuate the Tudor fortifications, are popular vantage points for observing nautical activities. There's also a couple of lively shoreside pubs, the *Still & West Country House* and *Spice Island* (see p.223), with seats outside for viewing the comings and goings in the Solent.

Southsea's main attraction is the **D-Day Museum** on Clarence Esplanade (April–Oct daily 10am–5.30pm; Nov–March Mon 1–5pm, Tues–Sun 10am–5pm; £4.75), relating how Portsmouth had a chance to avenge its wartime bombing by being the main assembly point for the D-Day invasion, code-named "Operation Overlord". The museum's most striking exhibit is the 270-feet long *Overlord Embroidery*, which tells the tale of the Normandy landings. Next door to the museum, the squat profile of **Southsea Castle** (April–Oct daily 10am–5.30pm; Nov–March Sat & Sun 10am–4.30pm; £2), built from the remains of Beaulieu Abbey (see p.245), may have been the spot from where Henry VIII watched the *Mary Rose* sink in 1545. A mile further along the shoreside South Parade, just past South Parade pier, the **Royal Marines Museum** (daily 10am–4.30pm; £3.75) describes the origins and greatest campaigns of the navy's elite fighting force. Outside, a junior assault course gives aspirant young commandos a chance to get in shape.

The remainder of Portsmouth has little else of interest apart from **Dickens's Birthplace** at 393 Commercial Rd (daily: April–Oct 10.30am–5.30pm; Dec 1–20 10am–4.30pm; £2) half a mile north of the town centre, where the writer was born in 1812. A couple of rooms have been fitted out as they were during his lifetime but for true fans, there's far more of interest in Rochester (see p.157) and, to a lesser extent, Broadstairs (see p.162), where Dickens wrote many of his greatest books.

The city's outstanding monument is six miles out of the centre – just past the burgeoning marina development at Port Solent. **Portchester Castle** (daily: April–Sept 10am–6pm, Oct 10am–5pm; Nov–March 10am–4pm; £2.70; EH) was built by the Romans in the third century and is the finest surviving example in northern Europe. It's walls are over twenty feet high and incorporate some twenty bastions, making it so robust that the Normans felt no need to alter it when they moved in. Later, a castle was built within Portchester's precincts by Henry II, which Richard II extended and Henry V used as his garrison when assembling the army that was to fight the Battle of Agincourt. Today its grassy enclosure makes a sheltered spot for a congenial game of cricket or a kickabout with a football.

Practicalities

Portsmouth's main **train station** is in the city centre, but the line continues to **Harbour Station**, the most convenient stop for the main sights and old town. There are regular fast services from London Waterloo, and a frequent bus and train service between Portsmouth and Winchester, 25 miles northwest. Passenger ferries leave from the jetty at the Harbour station for Ryde, on the Isle of Wight (see p.227) and Gosport, on the other side of Portsmouth Harbour. Wightlink car ferries depart from the ferry port off Gunwharf Road for Fishbourne on the Isle of Wight (see p.227). There are three **tourist offices** in Portsmouth, one on the Hard, by the entrance to the dockyards (daily: Easter–Sept 9.30am–5.45pm; Oct–Easter 9.30am–5.15pm; ☎02392/826722); another opposite the main train station, at 103 Commercial Rd (Mon–Sat 10am–5pm; ☎02392/838382); and a third on Southsea's seafront, next to the Sea Life Centre (Easter–Sept daily 9.30am–1.30pm & 2.30–5.45pm; ☎02392/832464).

Hotels and guest houses

Albatross Guest House, 51 Waverley Rd, Southsea (☎02392/828325). One of many good-value B&Bs in this part of Southsea. ①.

Dorcliffe Guest House, 42 Waverley Rd, Southsea (☎02392/828283). Family-run guest house overlooking a small park, close to restaurants and seafront. En-suite rooms are available. ①.

Fortitude Cottage, 51 Broad St, Old Portsmouth (☎02392/823748). Harbourside cottage offering three comfortable rooms, all en suite, and a beamed breakfast room overlooking the boats. ②.

Sailmakers Loft, 5 Bath Square, Old Portsmouth (☎02392/823045). Spithead views from this small B&B in a quiet location next to the *Spice Island Inn*. Most rooms are en suite. ②.

The Sally Port, 57–58 High St, Old Portsmouth (☎02392/821860). Opposite the cathedral, this old pub with sloping floors serves good bar food and has fully equipped, extremely comfortable bedrooms, most of which are en suite. ③.

Spitbank Fort (☎01329/664286). One mile from Portsmouth Harbour and accessible by ferry, this man-made island in the middle of the Solent has one four-bed apartment for nightly or weekly rent between May and September. £120 per night.

Hostels and campsites

Portsmouth and Southsea Backpackers, 4 Florence Rd, Southsea (☎02392/832495 or 822963). Fifty-bed hostel with full facilities, including a large kitchen, at the east end of Clarence Esplanade. Dorm beds go for £9, doubles and twins for £22, and en suite for £25. A twenty-minute walk from the city centre, or catch bus #4, #6, #7, or any bus to South Parade Pier.

Southsea Caravan Park, Melville Rd, Southsea (☎02392/735070). Well-appointed campsite right at the east end of Southsea Esplanade (bus #16 or #25).

Youth Hostel, Wymering Manor, Old Wymering Lane, Cosham (☎02392/375661, *portsmouth@yha.org.uk*). Housed in an attractive Tudor manor, ten minutes west of Cosham train station or bus #1, #5, #5a or #12 from city centre.

Eating and drinking

Bistro Montparnasse, 103 Palmerston Rd, Southsea (☎02392/816754). Stands out from the many restaurants in this part of Southsea for its good-quality French and seafood dishes. Closed lunchtimes, plus all Sun & Mon. Moderate.

Country Kitchen, 59a Marmion Rd, Southsea (☎02392/811425). Wholefood restaurant with vegetarian specialities. Closed Sun. Inexpensive.

Frisco Bay Café, 40 South Parade, Southsea (☎02392/872587). American-themed diner with an adjacent bar and nightclub. Inexpensive.

Quayhaven, Broad St (☎02392/820607). Good-looking old-town restaurant offering traditional English and seafood dishes; the same management runs the humbler *Slipway Café*, next door. Closed Mon. Moderate.

Sherrees Diner, the Hard. Inexpensive hole-in-the-wall snack bar just down from the Harbour train station.

Sorrento Pizzeria, Port Solent (☎02392/201473). Swish Italian restaurant in Portsmouth's prestige marina development, six miles north of the city centre, near Porchester Castle. Moderate.

Spice Island Inn, Bath Square, Old Portsmouth (☎02392/870543). Old hostelry in a quiet location in the oldest part of town, boasting a handsome front and cosy interior; serves a great range of hot and cold dishes.

Still & West Country House, Bath Square, Old Portsmouth (☎02392/821567). Adjacent pub to the *Spice Island*, and of similar age, with an innovative seafood menu and a range of Gale's beers, as well as tables outside overlooking the Solent.

Sur La Mer, 69 Palmerston Rd, Southsea (☎02392/876678). A good-value French and seafood restaurant with set-price three-course meals for around £12. Closed Sun.

Trafalgar, the Hard. Brightly painted and lively old tavern close to the naval heritage area offering daily lunchtime specials.

Southampton and around

A glance at the map gives some idea of the strategic maritime importance of **SOUTHAMPTON**, which stands on a triangular peninsula formed at the place where the rivers Itchen and Test flow into Southampton Water, an eight-mile inlet from the Solent. Sure enough, Southampton has figured in numerous stirring events: it witnessed the exodus of Henry V's Agincourt-bound army, the Pilgrim Fathers' departure in the *Mayflower* in 1620 and the maiden voyages of such ships as the *Queen Mary* and the *Titanic*. Unfortunately, since its pummelling by the Luftwaffe and some disastrous postwar planning, the thousand-year-old city has changed beyond recognition. Now a sprawling conurbation easily bypassed by motorways, it'll be pretty low on your list of places to visit in southern England, but you may pass through on your way to the Isle of Wight, and it has enough of interest to occupy a couple of hours while you wait for the ferry.

King Canute is alleged to have commanded the waves to retreat at Southampton – not, as legend has it, from a misguided sense of his kingly powers, but to rebuke his obsequious courtiers. Whatever his motive, the task would have been especially difficult here, for Southampton, like other Solent ports, enjoys the phenomenon of "double tides" – a prolonged period of high water as the Channel swirls first up the westerly side of the Solent, then, two hours later, backs up round Spithead. This means that exceptionally large vessels can berth here and, even though ocean-going liners are pretty much a rarity nowadays, there'll certainly be some sort of large-scale vessels floating by, either to the Eastern Docks at the tip of the promontory, or in the **Western Docks**, which has the largest commercial dry dock in England.

Core of the modern town is the **Civic Centre**, a short walk east of the train station. Its clock tower is the most distinctive feature of the skyline, and it houses an excellent **art gallery** that's particularly strong on twentieth-century British artists such as Sutherland, Piper and Spencer (Tues–Sat 10am–5pm, Sun 1–4pm; free). The **Western Esplanade**, curving southward from the station, runs alongside the best remaining bits of the old city **walls**. Rebuilt after a French attack in 1338, they feature towers with evocatively chilly names like Windwhistle, Catchcold and **God's House Tower** – the last of these, at the southern end of the old town in Winkle Street, houses a good **Museum of Archeology** (Tues–Fri 10am–noon & 1–5pm, Sat 10am–noon & 1–4pm, Sun 2–5pm; free). Best preserved of the city's seven gates is **Bargate**, at the opposite end of the old town, at the head of the High Street; an elaborate structure, cluttered with lions, classical figures and machicolations (defensive apertures through which missiles could be dropped), it was formerly the guildhall and court house.

Other ancient buildings survive amid the piecemeal redevelopment of the High Street area. The oldest church is **St Michael's**, to the west of the High Street, with a twelfth-century font of black Tournai marble. The nearby **Tudor House Museum**, in Bugle Street (same times as God's House Tower), is an impressive fifteenth-century, timber-framed building, its grand banqueting hall and reconstructed Tudor garden outshining the sundry exhibits of Georgian, Victorian and early twentieth-century social history, which include a 680-cc Ackland motor-bike from 1923. On the opposite side of the High Street, the ruined **Holy Rood** church, bomb-damaged in World War II, stands as a monument to the merchant navy men killed in that war; it also has a memorial fountain to the crew of the *Titanic*, many of whom came from Southampton. Down at the southwest corner of the old town, by the seafront, the **Wool House** is a fine fourteenth-century stone warehouse; formerly used as a jail for Napoleonic prisoners, it now houses a **Maritime Museum** (Tues–Fri 10am–1pm & 2–5pm, Sat 10am–1pm & 2–4pm, Sun 2–5pm; free) with accounts of the heyday of ocean liners, and includes a huge model of the *Queen Mary* and various mementos from the *Titanic*. The museum also offers the opportunity to listen to the recorded voices of various survivors of the *Titanic* tragedy relating their experiences, while *Titanic* obsessives can follow a "*Titanic* Trail" walking tour around Southampton – ask for the free pamphlet at the tourist office.

If you're an aviation enthusiast you should visit the **Hall of Aviation** in Albert Road South, by the car ferry terminal (June–Sept Mon–Sat 10am–5pm, Sun noon–5pm; Oct–May closed Mon; £3). Dedicated to local aviation designer R.J. Mitchell, it has sixteen of his aircraft on display, including the Spitfire, the Sandringham Flying Boat and the Supermarine seaplane, which in 1931 won the Schneider Trophy by whizzing round the Isle of Wight at an average speed of 340mph.

Practicalities

Services from London Waterloo arrive twice-hourly at the central **train station** in Blechynden Terrace, west of the Civic Centre; the **bus** and **coach stations** are immediately south and north of the Civic Centre. The **tourist office** is at 9 Civic Centre Rd (Mon–Wed, Fri & Sat 9am–5pm, Thurs 10am–5pm; ☎02380/221106).

Southampton isn't a wildly attractive **place to stay**, but there are plenty of business hotels and commercial guesthouses in the centre – there's *Elizabeth House* at 43–44 the Avenue (☎02380/224327; ⑤) or *Linden*, just north of the train station on the Polygon (☎02380/225653; no credit cards; ①). For grander lodging, try the four-hundred-year-old *Star* (☎02380/339939; ⑤) or the slightly younger *Dolphin* (☎02380/339995; ⑧); both hotels are halfway down the High Street and provide accommodation with atmosphere.

There's not a great choice of original **eating** places in town either. You could try *Buon Gusto*, 1 Commercial Rd, an attractive and inexpensive Italian restaurant (☎02380/331543; closed Sun); the *Town House*, 59 Oxford St, for vegetarian specialities; *Kuti's Brasserie*, 39 Oxford St, a moderately priced top-class Bengali restaurant with occasional live music (☎02380/221585); Oxford St (☎02380/635043; closed Sun). As for pubs, the tiny old *Platform Tavern* in Winkle Street, at the south end of the High Street, and the ancient *Red Lion*, complete with minstrels' gallery at 55 High St, are more charismatic alternatives to the bars at the *Star* or *Dolphin* hotels.

Around Southampton

There are a few places in the immediate vicinity of Southampton which are well worth a visit, and all are easily accessible by bus. **NETLEY**, three miles southeast on Southampton Water, has a picturesquely ruined Cistercian abbey (open during daylight; free; EH), a Solent fortress and the Royal Victoria Country Park, which makes a good picnic spot overlooking the water. **ROMSEY**, ten miles northwest (bus #15 from Southampton), offers a largely original Norman **abbey church** (daily 8.30am–5.30pm), completed in 1150 and bought by the townsfolk a few years after the Dissolution. Just south of the town is the stately home of **Broadlands**, a Palladian mansion on the River Test which was the birthplace and country residence of Lord Palmerston (his statue adorns Romsey's main square) and former home of Lord Mountbatten (mid-June to early-Sept daily noon–5.30pm, last admission 4pm; £5.50), who lies buried in the abbey and whose family still live in the house. Five miles north of Romsey, **Mottisfont Abbey House and Garden** (April to mid-June & July–Oct Mon–Wed, Sat & Sun noon–6pm or dusk; last two weeks of June Mon–Wed, Sat & Sun noon–6pm 11am–8.30pm; £4.50; NT) enjoy a lovely location right by the Test. The house of this former twelfth-century Augustinian priory (open 1–5pm) is noted for the drawing room decorated by Whistler and the medieval cellarium, but it's the gardens which are the real draw, particularly for their old-fashioned rose collection, at its best in June. Mottisfont is accessible by train from Southampton – get off at Dunbridge, from where it's a fifteen-minute walk – or by bus from Romsey.

Another horticultural attraction **Houghton Lodge Gardens** lies another five miles north of Mottisfont (March–Sept Mon, Tues, Thurs & Fri 2–5pm, Sat & Sun 10am–5pm; £5), one and a half miles south of Stockbridge. Surrounded by gardens which sweep down to the River Test – and a choice trout-fishing spot – the Lodge is a rare example of an eighteenth-century cottage *orné*, or rural retreat for rich townsfolk. Should you wish to join it, your admission charge also includes a tour of the hydro-ponicum, a talk on the art of hydroponics (a system of growing plants in water).

The Isle of Wight

Having achieved county status after years of being lumped in with Hampshire, the **ISLE OF WIGHT** still has difficulty in shaking off its image as a mere adjunct of rural southern England – comfortably off, scrupulously tidy and desperately unadventurous. However, in recent years expensive ferry prices and unimaginative marketing have

---

SEA ROUTES TO THE ISLE OF WIGHT

Wightlink Ferries, PO Box 59, Portsmouth PO1 2XB (☎0990/827744) has three year-round ferry routes to the Isle of Wight, including a faster but more expensive catamaran service to Ryde.
Portsmouth–Ryde: 4.30am–12.20am every 30–60min; 15min; £10.50 for foot passengers only.
Portsmouth–Fishbourne: 3am–1.30am every 30–60min; 35min; £8.20 for foot passengers; £58.10–£72.30 for car and driver plus £8.20 per passenger.
Lymington–Yarmouth: every 30–60min 6.15am–9.30pm; 30min; £8.20 for foot passengers; £58.10–£72.30 for car and driver plus £8.20 per passenger.

Hovertravel, Quay Road, Ryde, Isle of Wight PO33 2HB (☎02392/811000 or 01983/811000) runs a year-round hovercraft service from Southsea to Ryde.
Southsea–Ryde: Mon–Fri 7.10am–8.10pm, Sat & Sun 8.15am–8.10pm every 15–30min; 9min; £10.20 for foot passengers only.

Red Funnel, 12 Bugle Street, Southampton, SO14 2JY (☎02380/334010) operates year-round ferries on two routes, one of them a high-speed service.
Southampton–East Cowes: daily 4am–1am every 1–2hr; 55min; £7.80 for foot passengers; £60 for car and driver plus £7.80 per passenger.
Southampton–West Cowes: daily 5.55am–10.30pm every 30min–1hr; 22min; £11.80 for foot passengers only.

All the prices quoted are for a 90-day (Red Funnel and Hovertravel) or 1-year (Wightlink) return ticket. Wightlink and Red Funnel both offer overnight or 5-day deals for cars, with discounts of around 35 percent.

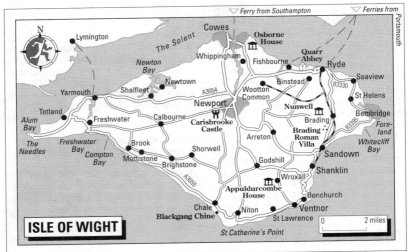

© Crown copyright

seen the Isle of Wight's holidaymaking hordes diminish and related services sell up. Surviving hotels are converting into retirement homes, a dependable, year-round enterprise for which the island's mild climate is well suited.

Measuring less than 23 miles at its widest point and divided fairly neatly by a chalk spine that runs east to west across its centre, the Isle of Wight packs a surprising variety of landscapes and coastal scenery within its bounds. North of the ridge is a terrain of low-lying woodland and pasture, deeply cut by meandering rivers; southwards is open chalky downland fringed by high cliffs. Two **Heritage Coast** paths follow the best of the shoreline, one running from Totland to St Lawrence on the south coast, the other from east of Yarmouth to west of Cowes along the north coast. What's more, the island harbours several historic buildings and a splendid array of well-preserved Victoriana clad in fretted bargeboards and pseudo-Gothic gables. The Victorian character of the Isle of Wight is scarcely surprising, for the founding Victorian herself felt most at home here – **Osborne House**, near Cowes, originally designed as a summer retreat for the royal family, became Queen Victoria's permanent home after Albert died. Several other great Victorians also had close associations with the island: Tennyson lived at Freshwater in a frowsty old mausoleum that is now a hotel, Dickens stayed and wrote in Winterbourne House (now also a hotel) in Bonchurch, the town where Swinburne grew up and is now buried.

Arrival and information

If you're dependent upon **public transport**, pick up the Southern Vectis bus route map and timetable (50p) from the tourist office or bus station at your point of arrival. The company's hourly Island Explorer buses (routes #7 and #7A) run all round the island in about four hours. A Rover Ticket allows you unlimited travel on the bus network, costing £6.25 for a Day Rover and £25.50 for a Weekly Rover; tickets are available from any train station or tourist office. The **rail line** is a short east-coast stretch linking Ryde, Sandown and Shanklin.

St Paul's Cathedral, from Fleet Street

Highgate Cemetery, London

Notting Hill Carnival, London

Chinatown, London

Ightham Mote, Kent

The Royal Pavilion, Brighton

Net lofts in Hastings, East Sussex

Durdle Door, Dorset

Westbury White Horse, Wiltshire

B&B in Broadway, the Cotswolds

Forest of Dean sculpture trail

The market and Guild Hall, Norwich

The Bridge of Sighs, Cambridge

Brasenose College, Oxford

Harvesting lavender, Norfolk

The Roman Baths, Bath

Cycling is a very popular way of getting around the Isle of Wight, especially as bikes are carried free on all ferry services, but beware that in summer the narrow lanes can get very busy. For **bike rental**, you can expect to pay around £10 a day; ask at any tourist office for the yellow leaflet on cycling (20p) which lists a dozen outlets as well as clubs, cycle ways and recommended routes. If you're planning to do a lot of cycling, it may be worth getting hold of Ron Crick's detailed *Cyclist's Guide to the Isle of Wight* (£3.15). Off-road cyclists should check out the four pamphlets (£3.95 the set) or Ian Williams's book, *Cycling Wight* (£3.40) sold by Offshore Sports, Orchardleigh Rd, Shanklin (☎01983/866269) and 2–4 Birmingham Rd, Cowes (☎01983/290514); both outlets rent out **mountain bikes**.

Ryde and around

As a major ferry terminal, **RYDE** is the first landfall many visitors make on the island, but one where few choose to linger. A working town which came to prominence as a resort in the Victorian era, Ryde offers some grand nineteenth-century architecture and decent beach amusements, but is unexceptional by island standards.

Reaching out over the shallows of Ryde Sands, the functional half-mile-long **pier** is where the ferries dock and former London Underground rolling stock carries the seasonal throngs inland. Union Street rises steeply from the pier's base to the town centre and at its crest sits All Saints' church whose spire acts as a landmark from vantage points all across the east of the island and even from parts of the mainland. The **Esplanade** extends eastwards from the pier, and along it are found traditional diversions: Ryde Arena and Ice Rink, the Eastern Pavilion (mimicking Brighton's original) and boating lake, all backed by sandy beaches. At the Esplanade's far end is the small Gothic Revival folly of Appley Tower, celebrating the sailing of the First Fleet to Botany Bay from Mother Bank, off Ryde, in 1787. It was once part of Appley House (now an expensive country hotel) built in the 1720s on the vast ill-gotten gains of arch-smuggler, Daniel Boyce. Successful in bribing witnesses, sheriffs and juries at his many trials, he was finally convicted in 1733 when the law introduced the random appointment of jurors.

Practicalities

The **tourist office** (Aug Mon–Thurs & Sun 9am–7pm, Fri & Sat 9am–9pm; rest of year daily 9am–5pm; ☎01983/562905), **bus station**, **Hovercraft terminal** and **Esplanade train station** (the northern terminus of the Island Line train line, which runs south to Shanklin) are all located near the base of the pier; there's also a **taxi** rank nearby. **Boat trips** to the Solent forts leave from Ryde jetty; for details contact Solent Cruises (☎01983/564602).

Accommodation is available just over the road from the jetty in St Thomas Street, where the *Biskra House Hotel and Restaurant* at no. 17 (☎01983/567913; ④) offers balconied rooms and a terrace looking out to sea as well as fine Italian cooking. *Yelf's Hotel* on Union St (☎01983/564062; ④) is one of Ryde's oldest hotels, right in the town centre, but is mainly geared up for business travellers. Inexpensive **B&Bs** don't exactly jump out at you in Ryde: try the great-value *Trentham Guest House*, 38 The Strand (☎01983/563418; no credit cards; ③) or the similar *Vine Guest House*, 16 Castle St (☎01983/566633; ③; closed Jan) – both are just south of the Esplanade. The nearest **campsites** are the *Pondwell Caravan Park* two miles east of town on the way to Seaview (☎01983/612330), and *Beaper Farm*, three miles south on the Sandown road (☎01983/615210).

Union Street offers the best **eating** opportunities. *Joe Daflo's Café Bar* at no. 24 has an appealing continental air, the *Redan* at no. 76–7 is an unusual and inexpensive pub/coffee shop combination that has live bands on Saturday nights. Try the moderately priced *Ryde Tandoori*, 45 Union St, for something more substantial.

Around Ryde

As elsewhere on the island, just a couple of miles can remove you from an undistinguished urban setting into one of idyllic rusticity. Just outside the village of **Binstead**, two miles west of Ryde's centre, lies one of the island's earliest Christian relics. In 1132 **Quarr Abbey** was founded by Richard de Redvers for Savigny monks; its name was derived from the quarries nearby, where stone was mined for use in the construction of Winchester and Chichester cathedrals. Subsequently the abbey was occupied by Benedictine and, later, Cistercian monks. Only stunted ruins survived the Dissolution and ensuing plunder of ready-cut stone, although an ivy-clad archway still hangs picturesquely over a farm track. In 1907 a new abbey was founded just west of the ruins – it's a striking rose-brick building with Byzantine overtones, and is open to the public (daily 9am–9pm; Vespers 5pm).

Two miles south of Binstead, the village of **Havenstreet** houses the **Brickfields Horse Country** (daily 10am–5pm; £4.50), a centre for all things equine. Its attractions include a horse museum with a carriage collection, saddlery and blacksmith and wagon rides pulled by huge, docile Shires.

Three miles west of Havenstreet, **Wootton Bridge** is the end-stop of the **Isle of Wight Steam Railway** (late March to Oct 10.30am–4.15pm; £6.50; ☎01983/882204), which starts its delightful ten-mile round trip at Smallbrook on the main Ryde–Shanklin line to the east. Though it doesn't stop anywhere of interest along the way, the impeccably restored carriages in traditional green livery pass through lovely unspoilt countryside, and the ride makes a nostalgic way of spending an afternoon.

Two miles east of Ryde's centre, the quiet village of **SEAVIEW** used to be dominated by maritime industries, before the popularity of sea bathing elevated it to a select resort in the middle of the nineteenth century. And so it remains today, a discreet hideaway of holiday homes and quiet pubs, looking across to the rotund naval forts sitting in the Solent. For an **overnight stay** in Seaview try the *Spring Vale Hotel* (☎01983/612533; ⑥), along the seafront west of town, a grand late-Georgian building with a lovely terrace overlooking the garden. Slightly cheaper, the *Seaview Hotel* on High St (☎01983/612711, *seaview.hotel@virgin.net*; ⑤) is a charming, privately owned hotel with a superb and moderately priced restaurant, serving traditional English dishes.

Bembridge and around

BEMBRIDGE, a residential area set around its own harbour in the east of the island, has little to attract visitors, save for its **Shipwreck Centre and Maritime Museum**, Sherbourne St (late March to Oct daily 10am–5pm; £2.50), stuffed with nautical odds and ends salvaged from the seabed by the museum's deep-sea-diving owner. A couple of old **pubs** make for a good refreshment break: the *Pilots' Boat Inn* by the mouth of Bembridge harbour and the *Crab & Lobster,* tucked away at the very eastern tip of the Foreland and renowned for its locally caught seafood.

In summer a ferry runs from Bembridge across the mouth of the harbour to the spit of land and adjacent beach known as the **Duver**, where you'll find the seasonal *Baywatch Café*. At the Duver's northern edge are the buttressed remains of St Helen's Church, built by the Normans on the site where Hildila, an early Saxon missionary, set about converting the islanders to Christianity. From the church, follow the path southwest, which curls round the harbour past an old mill and returns to Bembridge along the boat-lined Embankment, built to reclaim from the sea the former inlet which once extended all the way to Brading (see p.229).

The island's easternmost tip, the **Foreland**, is a rather dreary corner, although the tidal beach at **Whitecliff Bay**, to the south, lightens the pallid air. From Whitecliff Bay a path gradually ascends towards the chalk cliffs of Culver and then onto **Bembridge Down**. A monument to Lord Yarborough, first commodore of the Royal Yacht

Squadron at Cowes, caps the down, with refreshments available at the adjacent *Culver Haven Inn*. If you're not up to walking up the steep two-mile path, you can drive to the top of the down (there's no bus service) and then stroll around up there; leave Bembridge on the Sandown road, the B3395, and soon after the airport a sharp left turn leads steeply upwards past a mid-nineteenth-century fort (now occupied by an electronics company). The road ends in a warren of World War II emplacements – now colonized by rabbits – with island-wide views.

Brading

On the busy Ryde to Sandown road (A3055), the ancient village of **BRADING** boasts a surprisingly disparate collection of ancient and modern sites. Just south of the village are the remains of **Brading Roman Villa** (April–Oct daily 9.30am–5pm; £2.50), one of two such villas on the island (the other is in Newport; see p.236), both of which were probably sites of bacchanalian worship. The Brading site is renowned for its superbly preserved mosaics, including intact images of Medusa and depictions of Orpheus – associated with the cult of Bacchus – as well as the mysterious and unique man with a cockerel's head.

In the centre of Brading, what is believed to be the island's oldest intact dwelling – dating from 1228 – now houses the **Isle of Wight Wax Museum** (daily: mid-May to mid-Sept 10am–10pm; mid-Sept to mid-May 10am–5pm; £4.50). Inside, various dioramas portray island celebrities from Vespasian, the conqueror of Vectis (the Roman name of the island), to Tennyson. The Chamber of Horrors is as gruesome as you'd expect, with Animal World offering a little relief until you get to the "freaks of nature" section. Next door is the **Old Town Hall** which still has the original stocks and whipping post once used to immobilize miscreants. Across the road, *Penny Plain* is a good place for snacks and teas in its walled garden (closed Nov–Easter), or try the *Bugle Inn*, formerly a smugglers' rendezvous. From behind the pub, a path leads to Brading Haven, once an inlet connected to the sea, where the smugglers used to land their contraband.

Nunwell House (July to mid-Sept Mon–Wed 1–5pm; £4), signposted off the A3055 less than a mile northwest of Brading, was where, in 1647, Charles I spent his last night of freedom before being taken to Carisbrooke Castle and thence to his eventual execution in Whitehall. The house has been in the Oglander family for nearly nine hundred years, with the present building being a mix of Jacobean and Georgian styles with Victorian additions. It sits in five acres of lovely gardens and remains very much the family home of the present owners, whose military legacy is reflected inside in a small exhibition commemorating the Home Guard, the voluntary defence force recruited during the early years of World War II when the island prepared to resist Nazi occupation.

Sandown and Shanklin

The two eastern resorts of Sandown and Shanklin merge into each other across the sandy reach of Sandown Bay, representing the island's holidaymaking epicentre. Frequently recorded as among Britain's sunniest spots, Sandown is a relic of a traditional Sixties bucket-and-spade resort, while Shanklin, with its auburn cliffs, Old Village and scenic Chine, has a marginally more sophisticated aura.

Appropriately, **SANDOWN** possesses the island's only surviving pleasure **Pier**, bedecked with amusement arcades, cafeterias, dodgems and a large theatre with nightly entertainment in season – but out of season the town becomes rather desolate. The illuminating **Geological Museum** at the east end of the High Street (Mon–Fri 9.30am–5pm, Sat 9.30am–4.30pm; free), displaying some massive ammonites recovered locally, and the **Tiger Sanctuary and Isle of Wight Zoological Gardens** at

Yaverland, just east of town (daily: Easter–Nov 10am–5pm; call for winter opening times; ☎01983/403883; £4.95), are both worth a visit. The zoo contains several species of tigers, panthers and other big cats, some of which are heading for extinction in the wild, as well as some frisky lemurs and monkeys. The zoo's reptile house has an exhaustive selection of spiders and snakes, and in summer TV snakeman Jack Corney or a member of his family puts on snake-handling displays.

Possibly being separated from the shore by hundred-foot cliffs has preserved **SHANKLIN** from the tawdry excesses of its northern neighbour – though it hasn't stopped the promotion of the **Old Village**'s rose-clad, thatched charm with the same zeal as Sandown's pier. The real thing can be found in any number of inland villages, but with the adjacent **Shanklin Chine** (daily: Easter–May & Oct 10am–5pm; June–Sept 10am–10pm; £2), a twisting pathway descending a mossy ravine and decorated at night with fairy lights, it all adds up to a picturesque spot, popular since early Victorian times when local resident John Keats drew his Romantic imagery from the environs.

Sandown's **tourist office** is located at 8 High St (Easter to late July, Sept & Oct daily 9am–6pm; late July & Aug daily 9am–8.45pm; Nov–Easter Mon–Sat 10am–4pm; ☎01983/403886); Shanklin's is at 67 High St (same hours; ☎01983/862942). Both towns have Island Line train stations about half a mile inland from their beachfront centres.

Hotels and B&Bs

Grange Hall Hotel, Grange Rd, Sandown (☎01983/403531). Good-value cliff-top hotel in its own grounds, with all rooms en suite. Closed Jan. ③.

Holliers Hotel, 3 Church Rd, Shanklin Old Village (☎01983/862764). Well-appointed old hotel in the Old Village with indoor and outdoor swimming pools and a good restaurant. ④.

Luccombe Hall, Luccombe Rd, Shanklin (☎01983/862719, *reservations@luccombehall.co.uk*). Originally built as the summer palace for the Bishop of Portsmouth, the Hall is now a secluded and finely situated hotel with two pools, a mile from the Old Village. ⑤.

Mount Brocas, 15 Beachfield Rd, Sandown (☎01983/406276). Good-value B&B at the west end of High Street, very close to the beach. ①.

Ocean Hotel, Esplanade, Sandown (☎01983/402351, *oceanhotel@aol.com*). Grand seafront hotel right in town with good deals and facilities for children. Closed Jan & Feb. ④.

Osborne House Hotel, 20 Esplanade, Shanklin (☎01983/862501). Attractive Victorian hotel, a stone's throw from the beach. All rooms are en suite with TV and tea/coffee-making facilities. Closed Nov & Dec. ③.

St Catherine's Hotel, 1 Winchester Park Rd, Sandown (☎01983/402392). Comfortable B&B with en-suite rooms, just five minutes walk from the beach. ②.

Hostels and campsites

Cheverton Copse Holiday Park, Sandown (☎01983/403161). Spacious park set among woodland, two miles from the town. Signposted off the A3056 road. Closed Oct–April.

Fairway Holiday Park, Sandown (☎01983/403462). Inexpensive and well-equipped campsite, ten-minutes' walk northeast of the train station. Closed Nov–Feb.

Landguard Camping Park, Landguard Manor Rd, Shanklin (☎01983/867028). Similar to the above and just ten minutes' walk north of the train station. Closed Oct–April.

Sandown Youth Hostel, Fitzroy St, Sandown (☎01983/402651). Converted house right in the town centre, but only a few minutes walk from the beach. Dorm beds £9.15 per night.

Restaurants and cafés

Barnaby's Restaurant, 4 Pier St, Sandown. Good-looking eatery, close to the pier with meals and snacks under £5. Closed Nov–Feb. Inexpensive.

Cottage Restaurant, 8 Eastcliff Rd, Shanklin Old Village (☎01983/862504). Olde-worlde restaurant serving English and French dishes. Closed Sun & Mon. Moderate.

Fisherman's Cottage Free House, Esplanade, Shanklin. Atmospheric seafaring pub at the southern end of the Esplanade, on Appley Beach, serving wholesome food. Closed Nov–Feb. No credit cards. Moderate.

Francine's Restaurant, 16 High St, Sandown (☎01983/403289). Licensed restaurant with a good variety of English and seafood dishes. Closed Dec–Easter. Inexpensive to Moderate.

King's Bar Café, High St, Sandown. Continental-style licensed café with great views over the sea; snacks plus a dish of the day available from noon to 2pm. No credit cards. Moderate.

Salad Bowl, Esplanade, Sandown. Seaside bangers-and-mash joint with an outdoor patio. No credit cards. Inexpensive.

Ventnor and around

The attractive seaside resort of **VENTNOR** and its two village suburbs of **Bonchurch** and **St Lawrence** sit at the foot of St Boniface Down, the island's highest point at 787ft. The Down periodically disintegrates into landslides, creating the jumbled terraces known locally as the **Undercliff**, whose sheltered, south-facing aspect, mild winter temperatures and thick carpet of undergrowth have contributed to the former fishing village becoming a fashionable health spa. Thanks to these unique factors, the town possesses rather more character than the island's other resorts, its Gothic Revival buildings clinging dizzily to zigzagging bends.

The floral terraces of the **Cascade** curve down to the slender Esplanade and narrow beach, where former boat builders' cottages now provide more recreational services. Among them the **Longshoreman's Museum** (Easter–Christmas daily 9.30am–5pm; 50p) offers a peep into Ventnor's bygone days with a collection of nautical objects, models and old photographs. From the shoreside *Spyglass Inn* (see below) on the Esplanade, it's a pleasant mile-long stroll to Ventnor's famous **Botanical Gardens**, where 22 landscaped acres of subtropical vegetation flourish. Displays are divided thematically, including the South African and Australian banks, the Culinary Herb and the Medicinal gardens. There's also a **Smuggling Museum** inside the gardens (April–Sept daily 10am–5pm; £2.20), which capitalizes on Ventnor's long history of "owling", as the nefarious nocturnal activity was once known.

To the east of Ventnor, the ancient village of **Bonchurch** exudes an alluring rustic charm with its duck pond and rows of quaint cottages set on the Undercliff's wooded slopes. Behind high stone walls loom grand Victorian country houses where writers such as Dickens, Thackeray and Swinburne once stayed. At Bonchurch's east end is the spartan, towerless edifice of the eleventh-century **Old Church of St Boniface** with its wreath of skewed gravestones and mature trees further enhancing the village. Above the village the **Landslip Footpath** descends the Undercliff. It's recently been restored and reopened to the public, but remains prone to subsidence, so it's still worth checking with the tourist office that it's open before you set off on an exploration.

Heading west from Ventnor the road, still prone to subsidence, winds its way along the wooded hillside where the village of **St Lawrence** appears lost in the tumbling Undercliff. The studios of **Isle of Wight Glass** in the Old Park (summer Mon–Fri 9am–5pm, Sat & Sun 10am–4.30pm; winter Mon–Fri 9am–5pm; 50p) give a rare chance to observe the process of glassblowing.

Practicalities

Ventnor's **tourist office** is at 34 High St (Easter–Oct daily 9.30am–5.30pm; ☎01983/853625). For **accommodation** options, try the *Spyglass Inn* on Ventnor's Esplanade (☎01983/855338; ②), which has a few self-contained rooms and balconies, and offers a small discount for week-long stays. A few doors down is *St Martin's* (☎01983/852345; no credit cards; ②), with comfortable rooms and sea views, right next to the little wooden cottage where, in 1860, Turgenev started his novel *Fathers and Sons*. Alternatively, the *Bonchurch Inn* (☎01983/852611; ②), a quieter pub than the

Spyglass, with a few rooms upstairs, lies off the Shute in Bonchurch. Also in Bonchurch, on Shore Rd, is the *Under Rock Hotel* (☎01983/855274; no credit cards; ②), a small Georgian country house in a sub tropical rock garden. On the main A3055, at Undercliff Drive, *Lisle Combe* (☎01983/852582; no credit cards; ①), former home of poet Alfred Noyes, offers B&B accommodation in a beautifully preserved early-Victorian villa. Apart from *St Martin's* – which does do cream teas and snacks – and *Lisle Combe*, all the above have dining facilities. Alternatively, you may like to sample the moderately priced seafood at the seasonal *Horseshoe Bay* **restaurant** in Horseshoe Bay, Bonchurch. The best of the many restaurants in Ventnor town centre is the *Thistle Café*, 30 Pier St (☎01983/852681), offering inexpensive seafood and vegetarian meals as well as an all-day breakfast.

Appuldurcombe House and Godshill

Follow the B3327 for a couple of miles inland, over St Boniface Down, through arable farmland and past market gardens, to **Wroxall**, where a track leads left for half a mile to the ruins of **Appuldurcombe House** (April–Oct daily 10am–6pm or dusk; Nov to mid-Dec & March Sat & Sun 10am–4pm; £2; EH), the island's grandest pre-Victorian house. The present mansion was built in the late eighteenth century in the Palladian style on the site of an eleventh-century priory and an Elizabethan manor. Its gardens landscaped by Capability Brown (which included the erection of a "scenic" castle ruin – since dismantled – across the valley), the house was the home of Lord Yarborough before impecuniousness and neglect led to its semi-abandonment earlier this century. What makes Appuldurcombe unusual is that it has been preserved in this state of decay, a partially roofed but intact shell where the evidence of a former owner's extravagant raising of all floor levels and doorways can clearly be seen. The house's stately eastern facade, spring-fed fountain and impressive situation, overlooking a fold in the downs, make for an illuminating visit. Back down the track, *Appuldurcombe Holiday Park* (☎01983/852597; closed Nov–Feb) offers facilities for campers.

Pass through Freemantle Gate, an Ionic triumphal arch reputedly designed by James Wyatt and formerly the entrance to Appuldurcombe House, then follow the old carriage drive across the fields for a couple of miles and you'll come out opposite the village car park in **GODSHILL**. By road it's twice the distance to this "tourist village", jammed with summertime day-trippers come to appreciate the fairytale cuteness of its old core where the square-towered **Church of the Lily Cross** overlooks a cluster of thatched cottages and high-walled lanes. The church contains a very rare fifteenth-century painting, rediscovered in 1857, depicting Christ crucified on a triple-branched lily, as well as effigies of past owners of Appuldurcombe House, the Leighs and the Worsleys.

Other attractions have sprung up to capitalize on Godshill's enduring popularity. **Godshill Model Village** (April to late July & Sept daily 10am–5pm; late July to Aug 10am–6pm; March & Oct daily 10.30am–4pm; £2.50) is just what it says; and there's an Old Smithy, antique shops and a brace of quaint tea- and scone-shops on site, too.

St Catherine's Point to the Needles

The western Undercliff begins to recede at the village of **Niton**, where a footpath continues to the most southerly tip of the island, **St Catherine's Point**, marked by a modern lighthouse. A prominent landmark on the downs behind is **St Catherine's Oratory**, known locally as the "Pepper Pot". In fact it's a medieval lighthouse, reputedly built in 1325 as an act of expiation by Walter de Goditon who had attempted to pilfer a cargo of wine owned by a monastic community whose ship was wrecked off Atherfield Point in 1313. An adjacent oratory was also constructed but demolished during the Dissolution, although the crude lighthouse remained in use for over three hundred years.

A short distance west, there's accommodation at the very popular *Clarendon Hotel and Wight Mouse Inn*, **Chale** (☎01983/730431; ④), a cluttered, family-run combination of pub, restaurant and hotel which welcomes children. The inn is only half a mile from **Blackgang Chine** (daily: end March to late-May & mid-Sept to end Oct 10am–5.30pm; late May to mid-Sept 10am–10pm; £5.50), which, having opened as a landscaped garden in 1843, gradually evolved into a theme park – possibly the world's first – and now offers a half-dozen exhibits from Smugglerland to Dinosaurland, a giant maze, a rendition of a Victorian Quay and a high-speed water ride.

From Chale, Military Road continues west along the coast, a flat windswept drive with occasional turn-offs to small bays and chines of which **Hanover Point** is the most impressive. Along this coastline, the narrow beaches backed by low cliffs are too exposed for safe swimming. Several old buildings in the area – including the *Wight Mouse Inn* – were once extended using timber salvaged from wrecks which foundered here.

Inland to Shorwell, Brighstone and Calbourne

A leisurely and rewarding inland detour westwards can fill a half-day or more and passes through many of the island's prettiest villages, containing nothing more than picturesque, typically English village greens, ancient churches and country pubs. **SHORWELL**, for example, has its terrace of thatched cottages, the *Crown Inn*'s delectable ales and a fine walk through the woodlands up onto Chillerton Downs, signposted near the wooden footbridge on the village's northern exit. For an overnight stay in the village, *North Court* (☎01983/740415; no credit cards; ②) is an impressive mansion with six bedrooms, mostly en suite, a music room, lovely gardens, a tennis court and croquet lawn, and offers bicycle rental.

Between Shorwell and the pretty village of **BRIGHSTONE**, a couple of miles west with its fine pub the *Three Bishops,* is **Yafford Mill and Farm Park** (daily 10am–6pm or dusk if earlier; £3.50) with lots for kids to see and do, including the internal workings of a still-operational watermill. Three miles north of Brighstone, **CALBOURNE**'s quaint Winkle Street makes a much photographed rural, thatched scene with *Swainston Manor Hotel* a mile and a half east of the village (☎01983/521121, *hotel@swainstonmanor.freeserve.co.uk*; ⑥), being the best place for a memorably grand overnight stay. For those on a smaller budget, there are **campsites** at *Chine Farm*, Atherfield (☎01983/740228; closed Oct–April), *Grange Farm*, Brighstone Bay (☎01983/740296; closed Nov–Feb) and at *Compton Farm*, Brook (☎01983/740215; closed Oct–April). At the village of Brook, the inland route rejoins Military Road – look back up the valley at the impressive Brook House – which then ascends the flank of Compton Down before descending into Freshwater Bay.

Dimbola Lodge, Alum Bay and the Needles

The western tip of the Isle of Wight holds sundry traces of some of the venerable Victorians who were drawn to the area. On the coastal road at Freshwater Bay, on the corner with Terrace Lane, **Dimbola Lodge** (Tues–Sun 10am–5pm; £2.50) was the home of pioneer photographer Julia Margaret Cameron. After visiting local resident Tennyson in 1860, Cameron immediately bought adjacent land on the nearby coast, joining two cottages to make a substantial home for herself and her family, where she practised her art until moving to Ceylon in 1875. The building now houses a gallery of her work, including an impressive range of her portraits of some of the foremost society figures of her day and also features changing exhibitions. There's also a bookshop, a vegetarian restaurant and a tea room on the premises. If you want **accommodation** around here and are prepared to fork out, book into *Farringford Hotel*, on Bedbury Lane (☎01983/752500, *farringford@netgates.co.uk*; ⑥), Tennyson's former home, where the facilities now include an outdoor pool, putting green and tennis courts as well as several cottage suites. On the way, you'll pass Freshwater's unusual ninety-year-old thatched Church of St Agnes; Tennyson's wife is buried in the churchyard. Inside, there are memorials to Tennyson as well as Thackeray's daughter, Lady Ritchie.

Between Freshwater Bay and the Needles, the breezy four-mile ridge of **Tennyson Down** is one of the island's most satisfying walks, with yet another monument to the poet at its 485-feet summit and vistas onto rolling downs and vales. There's a **youth hostel** a short walk northeast from the Needles, at Totland Bay (☎01983/752165; closed Sun in winter), where beds are available for £10.15 a night. By public transport, take buses #7A, #11, #12 or #42, alighting at Totland War Memorial, and walk a quarter-mile up Weston Road and Hurst Hill.

The focal points of the isle's western tip are **Alum Bay**'s multichrome cliffs and the chalk stacks of the Needles where Tennyson Down slips into the Channel. The road ends at **The Needles Pleasure Park** (April–Oct daily 10am–5pm), a collection of fairground amusements, a glass studio and companies running boat trips out around the Needles. There's a plinth commemorating Marconi's first telegraph messages to a tug moored in the bay, a little less than a century ago. A chair lift (£2.60 return) runs down to the foot of the cliffs of Alum Bay whose ochre-hued sands, used as pigments for painting local landscapes in the Victorian era, contrast brightly with the chalk face of the Needles headland.

It's a twenty-minute walk to the lookout on top of the three tall chalk stacks known as **the Needles**, best seen from a boat trip leaving from Alum Bay (Needles Pleasure Cruises; ☎01983/754477; 25min; £2.50), or from the tunnel by the **Old Battery**, a fort dating from 1862 (end March to June, Sept & Oct Mon–Thurs & Sun 10.30am–5pm; July & Aug daily 10.30am–5pm; £2.50; NT). During the Fifties the fort was a military establishment where rockets were strapped down and their engines tested. The fort is sometimes closed in bad weather; call to check (☎01983/754772).

Yarmouth and around

Situated at the mouth of the River Yar, the pleasant town of **YARMOUTH** was the island's first purpose-built port. Although razed by the French in 1377 on their way to Newtown and Carisbrooke, the port began to prosper again after **Yarmouth Castle** (April–Sept daily 10am–6pm, Oct 10am–5pm; £2.10; EH), tucked between the quay and the pier, was built on the command of Henry VIII. Although there is little more to see in town, Yarmouth, linked to Lymington in the New Forest by car ferry, makes an appealing arrival or departure point; for details of ferry departures see p.225.

The **tourist office** is on Yarmouth Quay (Easter–Oct daily 9.30am–5.45pm; Nov–Easter Mon & Fri–Sun 10am–4pm; ☎01983/760015). There's a decent range of affordable **accommodation** in town. *Jireh House* in St James's Square (☎01983/760513; ②) is a pretty seventeenth-century stone guesthouse and tea room, which serves evening meals in summer, or try *Wavell's*, also St James's Square (☎01983/760738; no credit cards; ②) which has bright, contemporary-style rooms. Alternatively, there's the cosy *Bugle Hotel* (☎01983/760272; ⑤) opposite, which holds one of the town's many good **pubs**. There's good food too at the moderately priced *Bugle*'s *Poacher's Restaurant,* and the less expensive *Fender's Bistro* in Bridge Road.

Two miles west of town **Fort Victoria Country Park** (Easter–Sept daily 10am–5pm) is a Palmerston-era fort looking out to Hurst Castle on the mainland, less than a mile away. Besides footpaths through the woodlands and along the coast, there's an **aquarium** (Easter–Oct daily 10am–6pm; £1.90), a **planetarium** (Easter to mid-Sept daily 10am–5pm; mid-Sept to Easter Sat & Sun 10am–5pm; shows on the hour, last tickets 1hr before closing; £3), a **Seabed Heritage Exhibition** (Easter–Oct daily 10am–5pm; £1) and a **model railway**, claimed to be the largest in England (April–Sept daily 10am–5pm; Oct Sat & Sun 10am–5pm; £3.30).

Newtown and Shalfleet

At the time of the fourteenth-century raids on the island, **NEWTOWN**, sitting on an inlet of the eponymous estuary on the northwest coast, had been the Isle of Wight's capital for 150 years. This purpose-built medieval settlement never fully recovered from the French sacking in 1377 and nothing remains of the ancient town, bar a trace of its gridded street pattern and an incongruously stranded Jacobean **town hall** (April–June, Sept & Oct Mon, Wed & Sun 2–5pm; July & Aug Mon–Thurs & Sun 2–5pm; £1.30; NT). North of the town, a jetty leads out around a nature reserve, past the disintegrating quays of Newtown's former harbour, where curlews, geese and other waterfowl nest.

Just a mile's walk away, at the head of one of the estuary's inlets, **SHALFLEET**'s position on the Newport road makes it more lively than Newtown. The *New Inn*, just opposite the largely unrestored Norman church, serves delicious seafood dishes and over the road, the *Old Malthouse* (☎01983/531329; no credit cards; ①) is a quiet and comfortable **B&B**. Heading north up Mill Road, you'll pass the old watermill and the stunted remains of the quays which once lined the inlet. At the end of Mill Road a boatyard looks out onto the tidal creeks, another popular spot for birdwatchers.

Cowes and around

COWES, at the island's northern tip, is inextricably associated with sailing craft and boat building: Henry VIII built a castle here to defend the Solent's expanding naval dockyards from the French and Spanish, and in the 1950s the world's first hovercraft made its test runs here. In 1820 the Prince Regent's patronage of the yacht club gave the port its cachet with the *Royal Yacht Squadron*, now one of the world's most exclusive sailing clubs, permitted to fly the St George's Ensign guaranteeing free entry to all foreign ports. Only its three hundred members and their guests are permitted within the hallowed precincts of the club house in the remains of Henry VIII's castle, and the club's landing stage is sacrosanct. The first week of August sees the international yachting festival known as **Cowes Week**, which visiting royalty turns into a high-society gala, although most summer weekends see some form of yachting or powerboat racing off Cowes.

The town is bisected by the River Medina, with West Cowes being the older and more interesting half, its High Street meandering up from the waterfront Parade. Along the High Street you'll find shops reflecting the town's gentrified heritage, with boatyards, chandlers and Bekens's famous yachting gallery – a photo by Bekens of your yacht is considered as prestigious as a family portrait by Lord Snowdon.

Practicalities

The Cowes **tourist office** is at the Arcade, Fountain Quay (April–Oct Mon–Sat 9am–5pm, Sun 10am–4pm, with extended hours during Cowes Week; Nov–March Mon–Sat 10am–4pm; ☎01983/291914). **Boat trips** upriver and around the harbour leave from the Parade; for details contact Solent Cruises (☎01983/564602).

Central **accommodation** options include the *Union Inn* in Watch House Lane (☎01983/293163; ①), the *Wishing Well Guest House*, 10b High St (☎01983/297322; ②), and in East Cowes, there's the *Doghouse*, (☎01983/293677; ②) Crossways Rd, opposite Osborne House, and, nearby, the *Crossways Hotel* (☎01983/298282; ③). Prices rise steeply during Cowes Week, and most places are booked up well in advance. The town has a decent selection of places to **eat**: *Baan Thai*, 10 Bath Rd, and the *Ocean Tandoori*, 38 Birmingham Rd (the east end of the High Street), both offer good-quality oriental food at moderate prices. There are numerous wholesome snack and sandwich shops along the High Street, as well as traditional **pub** meals served at the *Fountain, Anchor* and *Harbour Lights*, all in the High Street. The *Fountain* also has rooms (☎01983/292397; ④), while the *Anchor* has a garden and live music at weekends.

Osborne House and Whippingham

A floating bridge (pedestrians free; cars £1.30) connects West Cowes to the more industrial East Cowes, where the only place of interest is Queen Victoria's family home, **Osborne House** (April–Sept daily 10am–6pm; Oct daily 10am–5pm; last admission 1hr before closing; grounds 10am–6pm or dusk; £6.90, including carriage ride to the Swiss Cottage; EH), signposted one mile southeast of town (bus #4 from Ryde or #5 from Newport). The house was built in the late 1840s by Prince Albert and Thomas Cubitt, with extensions such as the Household Wing, the Swiss Cottage – where Victoria's children played and studied – and the exotic Durbar Room with its elaborate Indian plasterwork, were all added over the next half-century. Albert designed the private family home as an Italianate villa, with balconies and large terraces overlooking the landscaped gardens towards the Solent. The state rooms, used for entertaining visiting dignitaries, exude an expected formality, while the private apartments feel more homely, like the affluent family holiday residence that Osborne was – far removed from the pomp and ceremony of state affairs in London. Following Albert's death, the desolate Victoria spent much of her time here, where she eventually died in 1901. Since then, according to her wishes, the house has remained virtually unaltered, allowing an unexpectedly intimate glimpse into Victoria's family life.

At Whippingham, a mile south of Osborne, there's another of Albert's architectural extravaganzas, the Gothic Revival **Royal Church of St Mildred** (May–Sept Mon–Fri 10am–5pm; April & Oct closes 4pm). Its exterior evokes the many-pinnacled Rhine castles of Albert's homeland, while the interior boasts huge rose windows, a finely carved altarpiece of the Last Supper and a large octagonal lantern. The German Battenberg family, who later adopted the anglicized name Mountbatten, have a chapel here and the parents of the present Queen's late uncle, Earl Mountbatten, the island's last governor, are buried in the churchyard.

Newport and Carisbrooke Castle

NEWPORT, the capital of the Isle of Wight, sits at the centre of the island at a point where the River Medina's commercial navigability ends. Apart from a few pleasant old quays dating from its days as an inland port, the town serves as the island's municipal and commercial centre, where familiar chain stores draw in the shoppers. Newport offers little of cultural interest apart from a cinema, the Medina and Apollo theatres and the remains of the **Roman villa** in Cypress Road (March–Oct Mon–Sat 10am–4.15pm; £2). A well-signposted ten minutes' walk southeast of the town centre, a few rudimentary foundations of the third-century villa are on show, as well as some excavated artefacts in the museum, but frankly you'd be better off visiting its sister villa in Brading (see p.229).

The town's main attraction, however, lies in the hilltop fortress of **Carisbrooke Castle** (daily: April–Sept 10am–6pm; Oct 10am–5pm; Nov–March 10am–4pm; £4.50; EH), on the southwest outskirts (bus #9 from Newport). The austere Norman keep was greatly extended over the years, first in the thirteenth century by the imperious Countess Isabella who inherited much of the island and ruled it as a petty kingdom. Having tolerated her excesses, the Crown bought her estates as she lay dying in 1293 and appointed governors to defend the island, rather than risking its security to the vagaries of birthright. This precaution proved timely as the following century saw repeated French raids right across the island.

Carisbrooke's most famous visitor was Charles I, detained here (and caught one night ignominiously jammed between his room's bars while attempting escape) prior to his execution in London. The **museum** in the centre of the castle features many relics from his incarceration, as well as those of the last royal resident, Princess Beatrice, Queen Victoria's youngest daughter. The castle's other notable curiosity is the sixteenth-century well-house, where donkeys still trudge inside a huge, hamster-like, treadmill to raise a barrel 160ft up the well shaft. A stroll around the battlements provides several lofty perspectives on the castle's interior as well as sweeping views across the centre of the island.

Newport's **tourist office** is on South St (April–June, Sept & Oct Mon–Sat 9.15am–5pm, Sun 10am–4pm; July & Aug Mon–Sat 9.15am–6pm, Sun 10am–4pm; Nov–March Mon–Sat 9.15am–5pm; ☎01983/813818). Your best option for a **meal** or a **drink** is to stick around Carisbrooke: try the *New Eight Bells* pub, near the castle, or the ever-popular, moderately priced *Valentino's* Italian restaurant (closed Sun), both on Carisbrooke High Street, at the bottom of the hill.

Winchester

Nowadays a tranquil, handsome market town, set amid docile hay-meadows and watercress beds, **WINCHESTER** was once one of the mightiest settlements in England. Under the Romans it was Venta Belgarum, the fifth largest town in Britain, but it was **Alfred the Great** who really put Winchester on the map, when he made it the capital of his Wessex kingdom in the ninth century. For the next couple of centuries Winchester ranked alongside London, its status affirmed by William the Conqueror's coronation in both cities and by his commissioning of the local monks to prepare the **Domesday Book**. As the shrine of St Swithun, King Alfred's tutor, Winchester attracted innumerable pilgrims, and throughout the medieval era the city continued to command enormous ecclesiastical and political influence – Bishop **William of Wykeham**, founder of Winchester College and Oxford's New College, was twice chancellor of England. It wasn't until after the Battle of Naseby in 1645, when Cromwell took the city, that Winchester began its decline into provinciality.

Hampshire's county town now has a scholarly and slightly anachronistic air, embodied by the ancient almshouses that still provide shelter for senior citizens of "noble poverty" – the pensioners can be seen wandering round the town in medieval black or mulberry-coloured gowns with silver badges. A trip to this secluded old city is a must – not only for the magnificent **cathedral**, chief relic of Winchester's medieval glory, but for the all-round well-preserved ambience of England's one-time capital.

The City

The first minster to be built in Winchester was raised by Cenwalh, the Saxon king of Wessex in the mid-seventh century, and traces of this building have been unearthed near the present **Cathedral** (daily 7.15am–6.30pm; £2.50 donation requested), which was begun in 1079 and completed some three hundred years later, producing a church whose elements range from early Norman to Perpendicular styles. The exterior is not its best feature – squat and massive, the cathedral crouches stumpily over the tidy lawns of the Cathedral Close. The interior is rich and complex, however, and its 556-foot nave makes this Europe's longest medieval church. Outstanding features include its carved Norman font of black Tournai marble, the fourteenth-century misericords (the choir stalls are the oldest complete set in the country) and some amazing monuments – **William of Wykeham's Chantry**, halfway down the nave on the right, is one of the best. Jane Austen, who died in Winchester, is commemorated by a stone close to the font, though she's recorded simply as the daughter of a local clergyman. Above the high altar lie the mortuary chests of pre-Conquest kings, including Canute; William

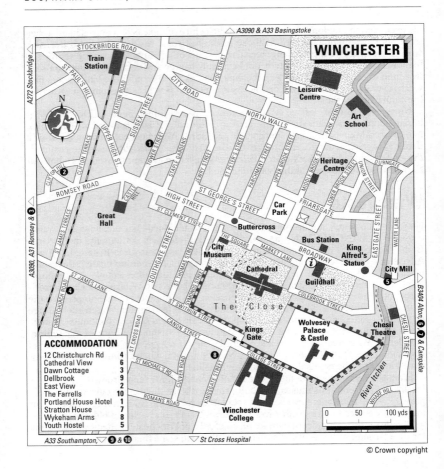

△ A3090 & A33 Basingstoke

WINCHESTER

STOCKBRIDGE ROAD

Train Station

ST PAUL'S HILL

CITY ROAD

HYDE STREET

GORDON ROAD

Leisure Centre

PARK AVENUE

Art School

STATION ROAD

UPPER HIGH ST

SUSSEX STREET

TOWER STREET

STAPLE GARDENS

LEWIS STREET

ST PETER'S STREET

PARCHMENT STREET

NORTH WALLS

UPPER BROOK STREET

MIDDLE BROOK STREET

LOWER BROOK STREET

UNION STREET

DURNGATE

❶

CLIFTON HILL

CLIFTON TERRACE

ROMSEY ROAD

❷

HIGH STREET

ST GEORGE'S STREET

Heritage Centre

FRIARSGATE

Car Park

A272 Stockbridge

N

ST JAMES TERRACE

CASTLE HILL

Great Hall

ST CLEMENT STREET

SOUTHGATE STREET

ST THOMAS STREET

STAPLE STREET

City Museum

THE SQUARE

MARKET LANE

Buttercross

Bus Station

BROADWAY

King Alfred's Statue

EASTGATE STREET

WATER LANE

A3090, A31 Romsey & ❸

ST JAMES LANE

Cathedral

Guildhall

City Mill

❺

B3404 Alton, ❻ ❼ & Campsite

CHRISTCHURCH ROAD

❹

The Close

COLEBROOK STREET

CHESIL STREET

ST SWITHUN STREET

CANON STREET

Kings Gate

Wolvesey Palace & Castle

Chesil Theatre

ST CROSS ROAD

CULVER ROAD

KINGSGATE STREET

ST MICHAEL'S RD

COLLEGE STREET

❽

River Itchen

WHARF HILL

ACCOMMODATION

12 Christchurch Rd	4
Cathedral View	6
Dawn Cottage	3
Dellbrook	9
East View	2
The Farrells	10
Portland House Hotel	1
Stratton House	7
Wykeham Arms	8
Youth Hostel	5

ROMANS ROAD

Winchester College

0   50   100 yds

A33 Southampton, ▽ ❾ & ❿

▽ St Cross Hospital

Rufus, killed while hunting in the New Forest in 1100 (see p.244), lies in the presbytery. To appreciate the Cathedral at its most atmospheric, try to be here for Evensong, currently 5.30pm most days, 3.30pm on Sundays.

The Norman **crypt** is open only in the summer, since it's flooded for much of the winter – the cathedral's original foundations were dug in marshy ground, and at the beginning of this century a steadfast diver, William Walker, spent five years replacing the rotten timber foundations with concrete (Deep Sea Adventure in Weymouth gives you the full story; see p.258). If you catch it open, though, have a look inside at the fourteenth-century statues of William of Wykeham and St Swithun as well as Anthony Gormley's standing figure, one of the country's most adventurous recent ecclesiastical commissions. The tomb of St Swithun is also here, originally buried outside in the churchyard. When his remains were interred inside the cathedral where the "rain of heaven" could no longer fall on him, he took revenge and the heavens opened for forty days, hence the legend that if it rains on St Swithun's Day (July 15) it will continue for another forty.

Outside the cathedral, the **City Museum**, a basic local history display, sits on the Square (Mon–Fri 10am–5pm, Sat 10am–1pm & 2–5pm, Sun 2–5pm; Oct–March closed Mon; free). The nearby High Street is a standard municipal mishmash of ancient and modern facades. Walk west along here and you'll eventually arrive at **Great Hall** on Castle Street (April–Oct daily 10am–5pm; Nov–March Mon–Fri 10am–5pm, Sat & Sun 10am–4pm), the vestigial remains of a thirteenth-century castle destroyed by Cromwell. Sir Walter Raleigh heard his death sentence here in 1603, though he wasn't finally dispatched until 1618, and Judge Jeffreys held one of his Bloody Assizes in the castle after Monmouth's rebellion in 1685. The main interest now, however, is a large, brightly painted disc slung on one wall like some curious antique dartboard. This is alleged to be King Arthur's Round Table, but the wood-work is probably fourteenth-century, later repainted as a PR exercise for the Tudor dynasty – the portrait of Arthur at the top of the table bears an uncanny resemblance to Henry VIII. Below the table, the floor of the Great Hall is dominated by a huge and gaudy sculpture of Queen Victoria, carved by Sir Alfred Gilbert (responsible for *Eros* in London's Piccadilly Circus) to mark her Golden Jubilee in 1887, and deposited here for lack of anywhere else in town large enough to hold it. Adjoining the Great Hall, an illuminating exhibition relates the history of the Norman castle and Great Hall, and you can also take a brief wander in Queen Eleanor's Medieval Garden – a re-creation of a noblewoman's shady retreat.

Head east along the High Street, past the Guildhall and the august bronze statue of King Alfred on the Broadway, to reach the River Itchen and the **City Mill** (March Sat & Sun 11am–4.45pm; April–Oct Wed–Sun 11am–4.45pm; £1; NT), now part-occupied by a youth hostel. Turning right before the bridge you pass what remains of the Saxon walls, which bracket the ruins of the twelfth-century **Wolvesey Castle** (April–Sept daily 10am–6pm, Oct daily 10am–dusk; £1.80) and the Bishop's Palace, built by Christopher Wren. Immediately to the west up College Street stand the buildings of **Winchester College**, the oldest public school in England – established in 1382 by William of Wykeham for "poor scholars", it now educates few but the wealthy and privileged. The cloisters and chantry are open during term time and the chapel is open all year. Jane Austen moved to the house at 8 College St from Chawton (see p.241) in 1817, when she was already ill with Addison's Disease, dying there later the same year. The thirteenth-century **Kings Gate**, at the top of College Street, is one of the city's original medieval gateways, housing the tiny St Swithun's Church.

About a mile south of College Walk, reached by a pleasant stroll across the water-meadows of the Itchen, lies **St Cross Hospital** (Easter–Sept Mon–Sat 9.30am–12.30pm & 2–5pm; Oct–Easter 10.30am–12.30pm & 2–3.30pm; £2). Founded in 1136 as a hostel for poor brethren, it boasts a fine church, begun in that year and com-pleted a century or so later. Needy wayfarers may still apply for the "dole" at the Porter's Lodge – a tiny portion of bread and beer.

Practicalities

Winchester **train station** is about a mile northwest of the cathedral on Stockbridge Road. If you arrive by **bus**, you'll find yourself on the Broadway, conveniently opposite the **tourist office** in the imposing Guildhall (late May to Sept Mon–Sat 10am–6pm, Sun 11am–2pm; Oct–May Mon–Sat 10am–5pm; ☎01962/840500). The tourist office has plenty of information about the city and its environs, including an excellent visitor's guide (£1). Ask here about the daily, **guided walks** of the city (1hr 30min; £2.50).

Hotels and guest houses

12 Christchurch Rd (☎01962/854272). There are just two rooms at this neat and homely B&B. No credit cards. ①.

Cathedral View, 9a Magdalen Hill (☎01962/863802). Good central choice, with views of the cathe-dral from three of its six rooms. The fractionally cheaper rooms have private facilities, though they're not en suite. No credit cards. ②.

Dawn Cottage, Romsey Rd (☎01962/869956). Classy non-smoking B&B about a mile west of the centre and connected by frequent bus services. The comfortable rooms – one with a spa bath at a slightly higher rate – have great views over the Itchen Valley. ②.

Dellbrook, Hubert Rd (☎01962/865093). Pleasant Edwardian-era, family-run B&B by the water-meadows near St Cross Hospital, a mile south of the city centre. ④.

East View, 16 Clifton Hill (☎01962/862986). Small Victorian town house overlooking the city and surrounding countryside. ③.

The Farrells, 5 Ranelagh Rd (☎01962/869555). Small, inexpensive B&B in a Victorian house off St Cross Road. ②.

Portland House Hotel, 63 Tower St (☎01962/865195). Georgian house in a quiet mews between the cathedral and train station. All rooms are en suite with TV and tea/coffee-making facilities. No credit cards. ②.

Stratton House, Stratton Rd, St Giles Hill (☎01962/863919, *Strattongroup@btinternet.com*). Hundred-year-old house in its own grounds with good views of the city. Large grounds and car park. ③.

Wykeham Arms, 75 Kingsgate St (☎01962/853834). Fine old hostelry where the art of classy inn-keeping has not yet vanished. Quirkily shaped rooms with beams and assorted antiques enhance the flavour. ⑥.

Hostels and campsites

Morn Hill Caravan and Camping Site, Morn Hill (☎01962/869877). Take Bus #X64 or #67 to reach this campsite three miles east of town towards Alton and Chawton. Closed Nov–March.

Youth Hostel, City Mill, 1 Water Lane (☎01962/853723). Lovely eighteenth-century mill, which is one of the original YHA hostels and very popular, so book ahead. Beds cost £9.15. Closed Jan & Feb.

Eating and drinking

Bhu-Thai, 3 Eastgate St. Thai dishes. Inexpensive.

Cathedral Refectory, The Close. Good-value lunch-spot run by the Friends of Winchester Cathedral. Inexpensive.

Courtyard Café, The Guildhall, Broadway. Casual café with outdoor eating; more substantial food and ales are served at the indoor bistro. Inexpensive.

Eclipse Inn, The Square. Picturesque old inn specializing in pies and casseroles. Inexpensive.

The Mash Tun, 60 Eastgate St. Riverside ale-house with a terrace. Food and music daily, and discounts for students.

Nine The Square, 9 Great Minster St. Light meals at the downstairs wine bar, opposite Cathedral. Closed Sun. Inexpensive

Noah's, Jewry St. Good-value café/restaurant, serving home-cooked dishes with Thai, Caribbean and Mediterranean influences. Closed Mon–Thurs eve, & all Sun. Inexpensive.

Old Chesil Rectory, 1 Chesil St (☎01962/851555). Fifteenth-century oak-beamed restaurant serving traditional English cooking. Moderate.

Pappagallo Restaurant, 1 City Rd (☎01962/841117). The better of the city's two Italian restaurants. Closed Sun. Moderate.

Suhel's Balti House, 8 St George's St. Excellent-value, well-presented Indian and Tibetan dishes. Inexpensive.

Wykeham Arms 75 Kingsgate St. Winchester's best pub, unprepossessing from the outside but inside it's a maze of characterful, intimate spaces with gourmet-standard food. Moderate.

Central and northern Hampshire

Aside from a few centres of population of little interest to the visitor, such as Petersfield and Basingstoke, central and northern Hampshire is a relatively rural region. It holds a few points of interest, such as the village of **Chawton**, where Jane Austen wrote most of her books, and **Alton**, the jumping-off point for the Mid-Hants Watercress Railway

Line. Hampshire's northern reaches are most notable for their stately homes: **Stratfield Saye**, Wellington's reward for winning at Waterloo; the superbly preserved Tudor manor house, **the Vyne**; and the outstanding excess of **Highclere Castle** in the county's northwest corner. Although Alton, Petersfield and Basingstoke are all easily accessible by train from Waterloo, getting to the sites described below is far more easily accomplished with your own transport.

Queen Elizabeth Country Park

Petersfield, situated on the Portsmouth to London road, originally grew up as a staging post on the old coach road and today is an unassuming provincial town with little appeal for tourists. Its main attraction lies three miles south of town where the A3 cuts through the South Downs. The **Queen Elizabeth Country Park** (free access; information centre April–Oct daily 10am–5.30pm; Nov–March Sat & Sun 10am–dusk) marks the official western end of the eighty-mile South Downs Way (see p.192), although the path actually continues another quarter of a mile to Buriton. A mixture of chalk downland and managed forest, the park is crisscrossed with marked trails which you can explore on foot, horse or mountain bike; the more adventurous can try hang- and paragliding from Butser Hill on the other side of the A3.

Local information is available from Petersfield's **tourist office** housed in the library on Petersfield Square (Mon–Fri 10am–5pm, Sat 10am–4pm; ☎01730/268829) and **mountain bikes** can be rented from Owen Cycles, Lavant St, Petersfield (£10 per day; ☎01730/260446). Bed and breakfast **accommodation** is available at the nearby village of Buriton, on the north side of the park; try the secluded fifteenth-century cottages comprising *Toad's Alley* in South Lane (☎01730/263880; no credit cards; ①), or the eighteenth-century farmhouse *Nursted Farm* (☎01730/264278; no credit cards; ①) a few minutes' drive northeast of the village off the B2146. Alternatively, in the pretty village of East Meon, three miles west of Buriton, *South Farm* (☎01730/823261; no credit cards; ②) offers B&B rooms in a lovely, five-hundred-year-old building.

Alton, Chawton and Selborne

Thirteen miles north of Petersfield and accessible hourly by train from London Waterloo or bus from Winchester, **ALTON** is an attractive town, whose major point of interest is the fifteenth-century Church of St Lawrence (daily 9am–6pm). The church is notable for its austere Perpendicular style; its south door still bears the marks of the shot which killed Royalist commander Colonel Boles, who had been chased by Roundheads through the streets of Alton and into the church during the Civil War. In the church's cemetery lies the grave of Fanny Adams, a little girl brutally hacked to death in 1867, whose name gave rise to the expression "sweet Fanny Adams" – meaning something negligible or without value; sailors at that time used the murder victim's name to describe the recent issue of tinned mutton, whose nutritional value they doubted.

Alton is the terminus for the **Mid–Hants Watercress Line** (☎01962/733810; £8), a jolly, steam-powered train, so named because it passes through the former watercress beds which once flourished here. The train chuffs ten miles to Alresford, east of Winchester, with gourmet dinners served on board on Saturday evenings and traditional Sunday lunches too.

A mile southwest of Alton, lies the village of **CHAWTON**, where Jane Austen lived from 1809 to 1817 during the last and most prolific years of her life and where she wrote or revised almost all her six books, including *Sense and Sensibility* and *Pride and Prejudice*. **Jane Austen's House** (Jan & Feb Sat & Sun 11am–4.30pm; March–Dec daily 11am–4.30pm; £2.50), in the centre of the village, is a plain red brick building, containing first editions of some of her greatest works.

Four miles south of Chawton is the little village of **SELBORNE** where the eighteenth-century naturalist Gilbert White wrote his ecological treatise, *The Natural History and Antiquities of Selborne*. In the High Street his house, **The Wakes** (daily 11am–5pm; £4), is preserved as a memorial to his work and contains the original manuscript. White constructed the Zig Zag Path with his brother and made many of his observations on Selborne Hill, just southwest of the village. The house also contains a museum commemorating Captain Oates, a member of Scott's ill-fated Antarctic expedition in 1912. It's a pleasant hour's walk up to the top of the hill from here.

The Vyne

A couple of miles north of Basingstoke, just outside the village of Sherborne St John, **the Vyne** is a distinguished country house dating from several different periods (April–Oct Wed–Sun 1.30–5.30pm; £5; NT). The original Tudor building was started in 1520, and the classical portico, supposedly the oldest in England, was added in 1645. Inside the superbly preserved rooms, some featuring their original oak panelling, are many unusual antiques, among them two late-seventeenth-century maps of London and England, a camera obscura and a portrait of a dashing young Isaac Newton. The Chute family owned the house for two hundred years (ancestral portraits decorate many walls) until an heirless Charles Chute bequeathed the house to the National Trust in the 1950s.

Outside the sombre Tudor chapel, which features its original Flemish glass and tiles, a row of truncheons inscribed with the letter "P" line one wall. These are a relic from the civil unrest which took place in protest at the Corn Laws. The weapons were securely stored here at the Vyne in order to arm local officers in the event of trouble. The "P" refers to Robert Peel, founder of the Metropolitan Police, whose officers were commissioned to suppress any popular discontent. Ironically, as prime minister, Peel repealed the Corn Laws in 1846.

Stratfield Saye

Stratfield Saye House, five miles northeast of the Vyne (June–Aug Mon–Thurs, Sat & Sun 11.30am–4pm; May & Sept Sat & Sun 11.30am–4pm; £5), was given to the Duke of Wellington as a reward for victory at Waterloo in 1815. The house, still home of the current duke, contains a plethora of "Wellingtonia" as well as copious Regency ornaments, many originating from dispossessed French aristocrats. The mosaics in the entrance hall were taken from the Roman ruins at nearby Silchester. In the former stables is an absorbing exhibition of Wellington's life and times, ending in the Gothic monstrosity of his funeral carriage which bore him to his final resting place at St Paul's, where his nautical counterpart Admiral Nelson already lay.

Highclere Castle

The "Gothic" profile of **Highclere Castle**, four miles south of Newbury off the A34 Winchester road (July to early Sept daily 11am–5pm; last admission 4pm; £6), results from its lavish remodelling by Sir Charles Barry, co-architect of the Houses of Parliament. Formerly a Georgian mansion set in parkland designed by Capability Brown, this ancestral home of the earls of Carnarvon was completely refurbished inside and out by Barry and others in the 1840s. Inside the house, the ostentatious style continues unbridled, from the Gothic "Saloon" or entrance hall to the adjacent state rooms, one of them in the Rococo style – all examples of the excessive opulence so beloved of the Victorian aristocracy. The house also contains a collection of personal mementos of the Fifth Earl of Carnarvon who, along with Howard Carter, unearthed Tutankhamun's tomb near Luxor in 1922. There are artefacts from that excavation as well as his earlier Egyptian treasures, which were discovered after the Earl's death in Egypt in 1923. His tomb is situated atop Beacon Hill, a mile southeast of the house. Also on view here is Napoleon's desk and chair and a collection of old master paintings, including by Reynolds and Van Dyck.

Sandham Memorial Chapel

Four miles east of Highclere on the A34, the **Sandham Memorial Chapel** at Burghclere (April–Oct Wed–Sun 11.30am–5pm; March & Nov Sat & Sun 11.30am–4pm; £2) houses murals by the artist Stanley Spencer, inspired by his experiences as a medical orderly in Macedonia during World War I. Working for over four years here *in situ*, on what he described as "a mixture of real and spiritual fact", Spencer abandoned his initial decision to paint in fresco in imitation of Giotto – whose Scrovegni chapel in Padua was the model for this one – in favour of his usual medium of oils on canvas. Above the altar, the dominating central *Resurrection of the Soldiers*, with its jumble of white crosses, is flanked by scenes of a soldier's daily routine – scrubbing floors, making sandwiches, shaving under mosquito nets and scraping the dead skin off frost bitten feet. It's best to come here on a sunny day if you can, as only natural light illuminates Spencer's subdued tones.

The New Forest

The name of the **NEW FOREST** is misleading, for much of this region's woodland was cleared for agriculture and settlement long before the Normans arrived, and its poor sandy soils support only a meagre covering of heather and gorse in many areas. The forest was requisitioned by William the Conqueror in 1079 as a game reserve, and the rights of its inhabitants soon became subservient to those of his precious deer. Fences to impede their progress were forbidden, and terrible punishments were meted out to those who disturbed the animals – hands were lopped off, eyes put out. Later monarchs less passionate about hunting than the Normans gradually restored the forest-dwellers' rights, and today the New Forest enjoys a unique patchwork of ancient laws and privileges, enveloped in an arcane vocabulary dating from feudal times. The forest boundary is the "perambulation", and owner-occupiers of forest land have common rights to obscure practices such as "turbary" (peat-cutting), "estover" (firewood collecting), and "mast" (letting pigs forage for acorns and beech mast), as well as the more readily comprehensible right of pasture, permitting domestic animals to graze freely.

The **trees** of the New Forest are now much more varied than they were in pre-Norman times, with birch, holly, yew, Scots pine and other conifers interspersed with the ancient oaks and beeches. The main wooded areas are around **Lyndhurst**, the "capital" of the New Forest, and one of the most venerable trees is the much-visited **Knightwood Oak**, just a few hundred yards north of the A35 three miles southwest of Lyndhurst, which measures about 22ft in circumference at shoulder height. The most obvious species of New Forest **fauna** are the New Forest **ponies** (reputedly descendants of the Armada's small Spanish horses which survived the battle), now thoroughly domesticated – you'll see them grazing nonchalantly by the roadsides and ambling through some villages. The local deer are less likely to be seen now that some of the faster roads are fenced, although several species still roam the woods, including the tiny **sika deer**, descendants of a pair which escaped from nearby Beaulieu in 1904.

Covering about 144 square miles – a third now in private ownership, the rest administered by the Forestry Commission – the New Forest is one of southern England's main rural playgrounds, and about eight million visitors annually flock here to enjoy a breath of fresh air, often after spending hours in traffic jams. To get the best from the region, you need to walk or ride through it, avoiding the places cars can reach. There are 150 miles of car-free gravel roads in the forest, making cycling an appealing prospect. The Ordnance Survey Leisure Map 22 of the New Forest is worth getting if you want to explore in any detail, and in Lyndhurst you can pick up numerous specialist walking books and natural history guides. **Trains** from London Waterloo serve Brockenhurst twice-hourly; for Lyndhurst you have to alight at Lyndhurst Road station, a couple of miles east of the town proper. Lyndhurst and nearby Brockenhurst are centres of County Bus routes to most parts of the forest, and both have plenty of reasonably priced accommodation, though there are also several expensive country house hotels and restaurants scattered in isolated settings. The forest has ten **campsites** run by the Forestry Commission, most closed between October and Easter – to get the full list, write to 231 Corstorphine Rd, Edinburgh EH12 7AT (☎0131/334 0066) – and there's a **youth hostel** in Cottesmore House, Cott Lane, Burley, in the west of the Forest (☎01425/403233; limited opening Nov–Feb), which offers beds for £9.15 a night.

Lyndhurst and Brockenhurst

LYNDHURST, its town centre skewered by an agonizing one-way system, isn't a particularly interesting place, though the brick **parish church** is worth a glance for its William Morris glass, a fresco by Lord Leighton and the grave of one Mrs Reginald Hargreaves, better known as Alice Liddell, Lewis Carroll's model for Alice. The town is of most interest to visitors for the **New Forest Museum & Visitor Centre** in the central car park off the High Street (daily: summer 10am–6pm; winter 10am–5pm; ☎02380/282269), where you can buy Explorer bus passes and maps for cycling and riding; AA Bike Hire, nearby in Gosport Lane (☎02380/283349), rents **bikes** for £8 a day. For **accommodation** try the clean and airy *Clarendon Villa*, also in Gosport Lane (☎02380/282803; ②); *Forest Cottage*, a B&B at the west end of the High Street (☎02380/283461; no credit cards; ①); or *Ormonde House* in Southampton Road (☎02380/282806; ⑤), offering discounts on longer stays. *Le Café Parisien* on High Street, sells **snacks** which you can eat in its small garden in summer; for larger meals, head for the nearby *Crown Hotel*.

The forest's most visited site, the **Rufus Stone**, stands a few hundred yards from the M27 motorway, three miles northwest of Lyndhurst. Erected in 1745, the monument marks the putative spot where the Conqueror's ghastly son and heir, **William II** – aka William Rufus after his ruddy complexion – was killed in 1100. The official version is that a crossbow bolt fired by a member of the royal hunting party glanced off a stag and struck the king in the heart. Sir William Tyrrell took the rap for the "accident" and fled incriminatingly to France, though he later swore on his deathbed that he had not fired the fatal arrow. As William II was a tyrant with many enemies, his death probably was a political assassination – a strong suspect was William's brother Henry, also in the shooting party, who promptly raced to Winchester to claim the crown, leaving Rufus to be carted ignominiously to the cathedral by a passing charcoal burner. The stone is remarkably unimpressive for such a landmark: the Victorians encased it in a protective layer of metal to deter vandals, and now it can't be seen at all clearly.

Three miles southwest of Lyndhurst you'll find the popular **Ornamental Drives** of Bolderwood and Rhinefield. These Victorian plantations of exotic trees were badly damaged by the hurricane of October 1987 (see p.183), but passing along them gives you an impression of overgrown ancient woodland. If you fancy a guided woodland hike, ask at the visitor centre in Lyndhurst about the ranger-led walks organized by the Forestry Commission, or call ☎02380/283141.

BROCKENHURST, four miles to the south of Lyndhurst, is a useful centre for visitors without their own transport. There's a train station right in town and by the level-crossing New Forest Cycle Experience (☎01590/624204) offers **bikes for rent** for £9.50 a day. The town also has some decent places to **stay**; try the *Cottage Hotel* on Sway Road (☎01590/622296; ⑤; closed Dec & Jan) or *Cater's Cottage*, Latchmoor (☎01590/623225; no credit cards; ②), an above-average B&B on the southern outskirts of Brockenhurst. A short distance farther south in Sway, there's a quiet B&B at *Little Purley Farm* in Chapel Lane (☎01590/682707; no credit cards; ①), with views over to the Isle of Wight. The *Snakecatcher* on Lyndhurst Road is a good **pub** that also serves terrific bar food.

Beaulieu and Buckler's Hard

The village of **BEAULIEU** (whose name originates from the French meaning "Beautiful Place", but is pronounced "Bewley"), in the southeast corner of the New Forest, was the site of one of England's most influential monasteries, a Cistercian house founded in 1204 by King John – in remorse, it is said, for ordering a group of supplicating Cistercian monks to be trampled to death. Built using stone ferried from Caen and Quarr on the Isle of Wight, the **abbey** managed a self-sufficient estate of ten thousand acres and became a famous sanctuary, offering shelter to Queen Margaret of Anjou among many others. The abbey was dismantled soon after the Dissolution, and its refectory now forms the parish church, which, like everything else in Beaulieu has been subsumed by the Montagu family who have owned a large chunk of the New Forest since one of Charles II's illegitimate progeny was created duke of the estate.

The estate has been transformed with a prodigious commercial vigour into **Beaulieu** (daily: Easter–Sept 10am–6pm; Oct–Easter 10am–5pm; £9), a tourist complex comprising **Palace House**, the attractive if unexceptional family home, the abbey and the main attraction, Lord Montagu's **National Motor Museum**. An undersized monorail and an old London bus ease the ten-minute walk between the entry point and Palace House. The house, formerly the abbey's gatehouse, contains masses of Montagu-related memorabilia while the undercroft of the adjacent abbey houses an exhibition depicting medieval monastic life. Inside the celebrated Motor Museum, a collection of 250 cars and motorcycles includes a £650,000 McLaren F1, spindly antiques and recent classics, as well as a couple of svelte land-speed racers, including the record-breaking *Bluebird*. The entertaining "Wheels", a dizzying ride-through display, takes you on a trip through the history of motoring.

If Beaulieu amply deserves its name, **Buckler's Hard**, a couple of miles downstream on the River Beaulieu (daily: summer 10am–6pm; winter 10am–4.30pm; £3.20), has an even more wonderful setting. It doesn't look much like a shipyard now, but from Elizabethan times onwards dozens of men o' war were assembled here from giant New Forest oaks. Several of Nelson's ships, including *HMS Agamemnon*, were launched here, to be towed carefully by rowing boats past the sandbanks and across the Solent to Portsmouth. The largest house in this hamlet of shipwrights' cottages, which forms part of the Montagu estate, belonged to Henry Adams, the master builder responsible for most of the Trafalgar fleet; it's now an upmarket hotel and restaurant, the *Master Builder's House Hotel* (☎01590/616253; ⑦). At the top of the village, the **Maritime Museum** traces the history of the great ships and incorporates a labourer's cottage as it was in the 1790s, as well as the *New Inn*, shipwright's cottage and chapel – all preserved in their eighteenth-century form.

Lymington

The most pleasant point of access for the Isle of Wight (for ferry details, see p.225) is **LYMINGTON**, a sheltered haven that's linked by ferry to Yarmouth and has become one of the busiest leisure harbours on the south coast. Rising from the quay area, the old town is full of cobbled streets and Georgian houses and has one unusual building – the partly thirteenth-century church of **St Thomas the Apostle**, with a cupola-topped tower built in 1670.

Information is available in summer from the local **visitor centre** in New Street, off the High Street (Easter–Sept & school holidays Mon–Sat 9am–4pm; ☎01590/672422).

Places to **stay** in town include *Jack in the Basket*, 7 St Thomas St (☎01590/673447; ①), an old building off the High Street with a café/restaurant attached; *Albany House*, Highfield (☎01590/671900; no credit cards; ③), a Regency house near the public gardens, and *Wheatsheaf House*, Gosport Lane (☎01590/679208; no credit cards; ③), a quaint listed building offering decent B&B. For **snacks**, try the *Jack in the Basket* (see above), or the cheap and cheerful *Coffee Mill*, opposite the visitor centre on New Street. Lymington's best **pubs** are the *Chequers* on Ridgeway Lane, on the west side of town, the *Bosun's Chair*, on Station Road and the harbourfront *Ship Inn*, on the quayside, with seats outside looking over the water.

Signposted two miles east of Lymington, the **Sammy Miller Museum**, in New Milton (daily 10am–4.30pm; £3.50) gives classic motorcycles the "Beaulieu" treatment. Many of the once-eminent British marques from Ariel to Vincent are displayed, as well as exotica from MV, NSU and several acclaimed trials bikes ridden by Sammy Miller himself, one of Britain's most successful trials riders.

Bournemouth and around

Renowned for its clean sandy beaches, the resort of **Bournemouth** is the nucleus of Europe's largest non-industrial conurbation stretching between Lymington and Poole harbour. The resort has a single-minded holidaymaking atmosphere, though neighbouring **Poole** and **Christchurch** are more interesting historically. North of this coastal sprawl, the pleasant old market town of **Wimborne** has one of the area's most striking churches, while the stately home of **Kingston Lacy** contains an outstanding collection of old masters and other paintings.

Arrival, information and accommodation

Trains from London Waterloo stop just under a mile east of the centre, but frequent **buses** run into town from the bus station opposite. The **tourist office**, right in the centre of town on Westover Road (mid-July to mid-Sept Mon–Sat 9.30am–7pm, Sun 10.30am–5pm; rest of year Mon–Sat 9.30am–5.30pm; ☎0906/8020234), exchanges money and books National Express tickets.

There's no shortage of **accommodation** in the Bournemouth area – the town has more than four hundred hotels and guest houses covering all budget ranges. There are no **campsites** in central Bournemouth; the nearest is just north of Christchurch (see p.249).

Boo's, 31 Dalmeny Rd, Southbourne (☎01202/428189). This small independent hostel, which takes its name from the resident cat, is very close to the beach, is open all year round and has 24-hour access. Beds cost £10 per night. From Bournemouth take bus #25 or #68 to Church Road, Southbourne, and then continue down Church Road into Dalmeny Road.

Connaught Hotel, West Hill Rd, West Cliff (☎01202/298020, *sales@connaught.co.uk*). Well-equipped three-star hotel, five minutes' walk from the town centre and beach, with excellent leisure facilities and restaurant. ⑥.

Grove Hotel, 2 Grove Rd, East Cliff (☎01202/552233, *hotelgrove@aol.com*). Well-positioned family-run hotel attractively set in its own grounds. Minimum two-night stay in high season. ④.

Kensington Hotel, 18 Durley Chine Rd, West Cliff (☎01202/557434, *raykazemzadeh@virgin.net*). Inexpensive hotel in a characterful Victorian villa situated in this pleasant part of town, a few minutes walk from the beach. Minimum one-week stay in high season. ④.

Langtry Manor, 26 Derby Rd, East Cliff (☎01202/553887, *lillie@langtrymanor.com*). Former hide-away of Edward VII and his mistress, Lillie Langtry, this comfortably equipped hotel has Edwardian furnishings, and period-style banquets on Saturday evenings. ⑦.

Mon Bijou, 47 Manor Rd, East Cliff (☎01202/551389). Cosy hotel a mile east of the centre providing good value and friendly service. ③.

Royal Bath Hotel, Bath Rd (☎01202/555555, *devere.royalbath@airtime.co.uk*). This grand, late-

Victorian hotel is among the town's finest, and also one of the most expensive – but it's right in the centre with excellent sea views. Guests can use the fully equipped leisure complex, which includes a pool and gym. ⑧.

Sandbanks, 15 Banks Rd (☎01202/707377, *reservations@sandbankshotel.co.uk*). Large and modern, right on the Sandbanks beach, between Bournemouth and Poole. ⑦.

Sea Dene Hotel, 10 Burnaby Rd, Alum Chine (☎01202/761372). Inexpensive and friendly guest house near the beach. Vegetarians and vegans are catered for. ②.

Tudor Grange, 31 Gervis Rd, East Cliff (☎01202/291472). Tudor-style house with attractive interior and gardens, situated on the east side of town. ③.

The City

BOURNEMOUTH dates only from 1811, when a local squire, Louis Tregonwell, built a summer house on the wild, unpopulated heathland that once occupied this stretch of coast, and planted the first of the pine trees that now characterize the area. By the end of the century Bournemouth's mild climate, sheltered site and glorious sandy beach had attracted nearly sixty thousand inhabitants. Today the resort has twice that number of residents, and an unshakably genteel, elderly image, though its geriatric nursing homes are counterbalanced by burgeoning numbers of language schools and a nightclub scene fuelled by a transient youthful population.

The blandly modern town that you see today has little to remind you of Bournemouth's Victorian heyday, though the River Bourne still runs down through a park to the town's centre, which consists of a network of one-way streets running around the Square and down to **Bournemouth Pier**. Other than sunbathing along the pristine sandy beach – one of southern England's cleanest – the town's greatest attraction is its unusually high proportion of green space, set aside during the boom years at the end of the last century. As well as having more than three million pine trees, a sixth of the town – around two thousand acres – is given over to horticultural displays, and exploring Bournemouth's **public gardens** can easily fill a day. The best known of Bournemouth's gardens is **Compton Acres** (March–Oct daily 10am–6pm or dusk; £4.95), at the west end of town, signposted off the Poole road. Here you'll find seven gardens, each with a different international theme, the best of which, the elegantly understated Japanese Garden, contrasts with the more familiar classical symmetry of the Italian Garden.

The excellent **Russell-Cotes Art Gallery and Museum** on East Cliff Promenade (Tues–Sun 10am–5pm; free) is central Bournemouth's sole non-horticultural attraction. It houses a collection of oriental souvenirs gathered from around the world by the Russell-Cotes family, hoteliers who grew wealthy during Bournemouth's late-Victorian tourist boom. The benefactors' lavishly decorated former home, featuring unusual stained glass and ornate painted ceilings, is jam-packed with their eclectic collections, of which the Japanese artefacts are especially interesting.

About a mile and a half east of the museum in the suburb of Boscombe, the **Shelley Rooms** in Shelley Park off Beechwood Avenue (Tues–Sun 2–5pm; free) house memorabilia from the life of the Romantic poet Percy Bysshe Shelley, former resident of Boscombe and the husband of Mary Shelley, who wrote the Gothic horror tale *Frankenstein* in 1818 when aged only 21. She is buried with the poet's heart in the graveyard of St Peter's church, just east of the Square; the tombs of Mary's parents – radical thinker William Godwin and early feminist Mary Wollstonecraft – are also here.

Eating and drinking

Bistro on the Beach, Esplanade, Southbourne end. Situated right on the beach and specializing in freshly prepared steak and seafood. Closed Mon, Tues & Sun. Moderate.

Brass House, Westover Rd. One of Bournemouth's most popular pubs, also serving meals. Can be rowdy.

CH2, 37 Exeter Rd. Modern, elegant restaurant specializing in steaks and mussels with a variety of sauces, and with a good fish selection. Closed Sun & Mon. Moderate.

Chablis, 6a Christchurch Rd. Young and trendy wine bar with dance music and DJs, and food in the daytime. Moderate.

Chez Fred, 10 Seamoor Rd, Westbourne. Well-known fish-and-chips outlet offering deals such as a bread roll, mushy peas and a glass of wine to accompany your meal. Inexpensive.

Goat and Tricycle, 27–29 West Hill Rd. Worth a trek up the hill for the real ales and home-made food in this quiet and unpretentious pub. Inexpensive to Moderate.

Mr Pang's, 234 Holdenhurst Rd. Better than average Chinese situated just east of the train station. Closed Tues. Moderate.

Salathai, 1066 Christchurch Rd, Boscombe. Authentically spicy Thai dishes, including chilli-laced chicken and fried noodles. Closed Sun. Moderate.

Nightlife and entertainment

The university, foreign-language students and young holidaymakers have helped liven up Bournemouth's **nightlife** – though the traditional entertainment scene continues to throw up a steady stream of dire pier-end comedians well past their prime. Chief among the established venues all lie just north of the pier – the Pavilion Theatre, with its own ballroom; the Winter Gardens, home of Bournemouth's symphony orchestra; a multiplex cinema; and an ice-skating rink. Pick up a copy of the listings magazine *Live Wire* for news of live gigs in the town.

Of the **nightclubs**, the best known are the *Zoo* and *The Cage*, both housed in the same building in Firvale Road, right in the centre of town (Mon, Wed, Fri & Sat). Mainstream club and house sounds predominate, along with soul and revival evenings and an over-25s night on Fridays at the *Zoo*. Hard house and techno get an airing at the *Rendezvous*, 1a Avenue Rd, while, the *K-Bar*, Terrace Rd (Thurs–Sat) caters for the over-23s and offers a regular diet of r'n'b, garage, funk and soul. Sample Art Deco style at the *Slam Bar*, on Firvale Rd, which plays everything from garage to Eurotrash, has a brasserie menu and shows sport on a big screen TV. In Boscombe, the opulence of the converted *Opera House*, 570 Christchurch Rd is reflected in the dressed-up clientele; the place now reverberates to diverse club sounds, with drum'n'bass upstairs. *Bumbles* on Poole Hill (Wed, Fri & Sat) plays both dance and Seventies and Eighties music; Wednesday is dedicated to tribute bands.

On a more sedate note, the fortnight at the end of June and the beginning of July sees the **Bournemouth International Festival** draw performers of every musical genre. There's also a buskers' festival that takes place around the second weekend of May – check at the tourist office for further details.

Christchurch

CHRISTCHURCH, five miles east of Bournemouth is best known for its colossal parish church, **Christchurch Priory** (Mon–Sat 9.30am–5pm, Sun 2.15–5.30pm; £1 donation requested), bigger than most cathedrals. Built on the site of a Saxon minster dating from 650 AD, but exhibiting chiefly Norman and Perpendicular features, the church is the longest in England, at 311ft, and its fan-vaulted North Porch is the country's biggest. Legend tells of how the building materials were moved overnight to the present location and of the hand of a mysterious carpenter who assisted in the work, hence the priory's name. The choir, beautifully lit by huge, clear-glass windows and separated from the nave by a finely carved Jesse Screen, contains what is probably the oldest misericord in England, dating from 1210, and complemented by a 1960s mural by Hans Feibush above the stone reredos. Fine views can be gained from the top of the 120-foot tower (ask at desk; 50p).

The area round the old town quay has a carefully preserved charm. The **Red House Museum and Gardens** on Quay Road (Tues–Sat 10am–5pm, Sun 2–5pm; £1) contain an affectionate collection of local memorabilia, and **boat trips** (Easter to mid-Oct daily; ☎01202/429119) can be taken from the grassy banks of the riverside quay east to Mudeford (25min; £4 return) or up the river to the *Tuckton Tea Rooms* outside Bournemouth (15 mins; £2 return).

The **Visitor Information Centre**, 23 High St (June–Sept Mon–Fri 9.30am–5.30pm, Sat 9.30am–5pm; July & Aug Mon–Fri 9.30am–5.30pm, Sat 9.30am–5pm, Sun 10am–2pm; Oct to May Mon–Fri 9.30am–5pm, Sat 9.30am–4.30pm; ☎01202/471780) can supply you with a town map and a Visitor's Guide. Good **accommodation** options in or around town can be fairly pricey, though a few minutes northwest of the centre, Barrack and Stour roads are lined with a selection of unexciting but reliable guest hous-es, for example *Grosvenor Lodge*, 53 Stour Rd (☎01202/499008; ①). In the centre, try the *King's Arms Toby Hotel*, 18 Castle St (☎01202/484117; ③); eastwards lie more exclu-sive choices, such as the *Avonmouth Hotel*, 95 Mudeford (☎01202/483434; ⑥), and *Waterford Lodge* Bure Lane, Friars Cliff, Highcliffe (☎01425/278801; ⑥), two miles east of the town centre. **Campers** should head out to *Mount Pleasant Caravan and Camping Park*, Matchams Lane, Hurn, Christchurch (☎01202/475474; closed Nov–Feb), five miles northeast of town on the road to Ringwood. For something **to eat**, try *La Mamma Pizzeria*, 51 Bridge St (☎01202/471608; closed Sun lunch & Mon in winter), where you can enjoy candle-lit Italian classics at moderate prices, with alfresco eating in summer, or the slightly pricier French restaurant, *Le Petit St Tropez*, 3 Bridge St (☎01202/482522). Recommended **pubs** include the *King's Arms Hotel*, right by the pri-ory, with a nice garden area; or check out Christchurch's oldest pub, *Ye Olde George Inn*, 2a Castle St, which has a beer garden and serves meals at lunchtime.

Poole

POOLE, west of Bournemouth, is an ancient seaport on a huge, almost landlocked har-bour. The town developed in the thirteenth century and was successively colonized by pirates, fishermen and timber traders, more recently replaced by companies prospect-ing for oil in the shallow waters – the harbour's environmental significance ensures that the extraction process is carefully disguised. The old quarter by the quayside is worth exploring: the old Custom House, Scaplen's Court and Guildhall are the most striking of over a hundred historic buildings within a fifteen-acre site.

At the bottom of Old High Street, near the Poole Pottery showroom and crafts centre, is **Scaplen's Court** (Aug Mon–Sat 10am–5pm, Sun noon–5pm; combined ticket with Waterfront Museum £4), a late medieval building where Cromwell's troops were once billeted (you can see their graffiti around the fireplace). It has now been restored as an educational centre, with reconstructions of a Victorian kitchen, pharmacy and school room and displays of old-time toys and games. Over the road, local history is further elaborated at the **Waterfront Museum** (Mon–Sat April–Oct 10am–5pm, Sun noon–5pm; Nov–March Mon–Sat 10am–3pm, Sun noon–3pm; £2; combined ticket with Scaplen's Court £4), tracing Poole's development over the cen-turies and featuring well-displayed local ceramics and tiles and a rare Iron Age log boat, as well as changing exhibitions.

In the middle of the harbour between Poole and the Isle of Purbeck, **Brownsea Island** (April–Sept daily 10am–6pm or dusk; £2.50) is linked by regular boats ferrying visitors over from Poole's quayside (25min; £3.80 return). Now a National Trust prop-erty, this five-hundred-acre island is famed for its red squirrels, wading birds and other wildlife, which you can spot along themed trails that reveal a surprisingly diverse land-scape – including heath, woodland and fine beaches – and good views. One shore holds a grand pile of a castle, rebuilt after the original was gutted by fire in 1896; it's now leased to a large retail group for staff holidays. But the most regular visitors to Brownsea are scouts and guides: the Boy Scout movement was formed in the wake of a camping expedition to the island led by Lord Baden-Powell in 1907, and scouts are now the only people allowed to camp here.

From Poole Quay, you can also join a **cruise** to the Isle of Wight (Mon, Tues & Thurs–Sat 9am; £14 return), allowing excellent views over Poole Bay to Bournemouth and Christchurch, and a four-hour stop in Yarmouth (see p.234). From Poole Harbour, reached across the bridge at the end of Poole Quay, **ferries** leave for France and the Channel Islands. Brittany Ferries (☎0990/360360) leave for Cherbourg once or twice daily all year, while Condor Ferries (☎01305/761551) operate a Fast Ferry and cata-maran service to Jersey and Guernsey between April and October, with connections to St Malo in Brittany between May and September.

Poole's **tourist office** is in the Waterfront Museum (summer daily 10am–5pm; winter Mon–Sat 10am–3pm, Sun noon–3pm; ☎01202/253253). Best choice for **accommodation** is the *Antelope Hotel* at the quay end of the High Street (☎01202/672029; ③), a handsome old hostelry in the old town centre; if you fancy a stay in a former mayoral residence, try the eighteenth-century *Mansion House* Thames St (☎01202/685666, *enquiries@theman-sionhouse.co.uk*; ⑦). Cheaper rooms can be had at the *Crown Hotel* (☎01202/672137; no credit cards; ①), an inn on the parallel Market Street. Further out, at Canford Cliffs, smaller hotels worth trying include the *Sea Witch* at 47 Haven Rd (☎01202/707697; ④), and *Norfolk Lodge*, 1 Flaghead Rd, (☎01202/708614; ③), both of which are convenient for the Sandbanks beaches. Less central, but great value, is the *Harbour Lights Hotel*, 121 North Rd, Parkstone (☎01202/748417; ①), a mile or so north of the centre. There's a col-lection of good **restaurants** at the southern end of the High Street; look out for *Mez Creis* seafood restaurant at no. 16 (evenings only, closed Sun & Mon) – it's flanked by *Hardy's* (closed Mon) and *Toppers*, which are both good for light lunches and sandwiches. At the top end of the High Street, *Alcatraz* is a trendy Italian brasserie with outdoor tables, while, at the other end, on the Quayside, *Corkers* has a café and bar downstairs and a restaurant above, serving traditional English dishes and seafood; it also has five en-suite rooms avail-able (☎01202/681393; ②). For **pubs** try the medieval hall in the *King Charles* on Thames Street, with its leather armchairs and big screen, or the green tile-fronted *Poole Arms* which serves fresh cockles and other inexpensive pub grub.

Wimborne Minster and Kingston Lacy

An ancient town on the banks of the Stour, just a few minutes' drive north from the sub-urbs of Bournemouth, **WIMBORNE MINSTER**, as the name suggests, is mainly of interest for its great church, the **Minster of St Cuthberga**. Built on the site of an eighth-century monastery, its massive twin towers of mottled grey and tawny stone dwarf the rest of the town, and at one time the church was even more imposing – its spire crashed down during morning service in 1602, though amazingly no one was injured, and since then Wimborne has not risked heavenly ire by replacing it. What remains today is basically Norman with later features added – such as the Perpendicular west tower, which bears a figure dressed as a grenadier of the Napoleonic era, who strikes every quarter-hour with a hammer. Inside, the church is crowded with memorials and eye-catching details – look out for the orrery clock inside the west tower, with the sun marking the hours and the moon marking the days of the month, and for the organ with trumpets pointing out towards the congregation instead of pipes. The **Chained Library** above the choir vestry (Mon–Fri 10am–noon & 2–4pm; 50p), dating from 1686, is Wimborne's most prized possession and one of the oldest public libraries in the country.

Wimborne's older buildings stand around the main square near the minster, and are mostly from the late eighteenth or early nineteenth century. The **Priest's House** on the High Street started life as lodgings for the clergy, then became a stationer's shop. Now it is an award-winning **museum** (April, May & Oct Mon–Sat 10.30am–5pm; June–Sept Mon–Sat 10.30am–5pm, Sun 2–5pm; £2.20), each room furnished in the style of a different period. A working Victorian kitchen, a Georgian parlour and an ironmonger's shop are among its exhibits, and a walled garden at the rear provides an excellent place for summer teas.

Kingston Lacy (house April–Oct Mon–Wed, Sat & Sun noon–5.30pm; grounds April–Oct daily 11am–6pm or dusk if earlier; Nov–Dec Fri–Sun 11am–4pm; house & grounds £6, grounds only £2.50; NT), one of the country's finest seventeenth-century country houses, lies two miles northwest of Wimborne Minster, in 250 acres of parkland grazed by a herd of Red Devon cattle. Designed for the Bankes family, who were exiled from Corfe Castle (see p.252) after the Roundheads reduced it to rubble, the Queen Anne brick building was clad in grey stone during the nineteenth century by Sir Charles Barry, co-architect of the Houses of Parliament. William Bankes, then owner of the house, was a great traveller and collector, and the **Spanish Room** is a superb scrapbook of his Grand Tour souvenirs, lined with gilded leather and surmounted by a Venetian ceiling. Kingston Lacy's **picture collection** is also outstanding, featuring Titian, Rubens, Velázquez and many other old masters. Be warned, though, that this place gets so swamped with visitors that the National Trust has to issue timed tickets on busy weekends.

You'll find Wimborne's **tourist office** at 29 High St (summer: Mon–Sat 9.30am–5.30pm; winter 9.30am–4.30pm; ☎01202/886116). This is a place that is unlikely to hold your attention for longer than half a day, but if you want to **stay**, try *Homestay* at 22 West Borough (☎01202/849015; no credit cards; ②), above a pie shop whose sausages and savouries find their way into the customized breakfasts. Otherwise, there's the *King's Head* on The Square, which offers comfortable if pricey rooms (☎01202/880101; ⑤), or the three-hundred-year-old *Henbury Farmhouse* (☎01258/857306; no credit cards; ①), four miles west of Wimborne in Sturminster Marshall. For bistro **lunches** or suppers try *Primizia* (closed Sun & Mon eve) on West Borough, and for **snacks** or teas *Cloisters* on East Street.

The Isle of Purbeck

Though not actually an island, the **ISLE OF PURBECK** – a promontory of low hills and heathland jutting out beyond Poole Harbour – does have an insular and distinctive feel. Reached from the east by the **ferry from Sandbanks**, at the narrow mouth of Poole harbour, or by a long and congested landward journey via the bottleneck of **Wareham**, Purbeck can be a difficult destination to reach, but its villages are immensely pretty, none more so than **Corfe Castle**, with its majestic ruins. **Swanage**, a low-key seaside resort, is flanked by more exciting coastlines, all accessible on the Dorset Coast Path: to one side the chalk stacks and soft dunes of Studland Bay, to the other the cliffs of Durlston Head and Dancing Ledge, leading to the oily shales of Kimmeridge Bay and the spectacular cove at Lulworth. Like Portland, further west, the area is pockmarked with stone quarries – Purbeck marble is the finest grade of the local oolitic limestone.

Wareham and around

The grid pattern of its streets indicates the Saxon origins of **WAREHAM**, and the town is surrounded by even older earth ramparts known as the **Walls**. A riverside setting adds greatly to its charms, though the major road junction at its heart causes horrible traffic queues in summer, and the scenic stretch along the Quay also gets fairly overrun. Nearby lies an oasis of quaint houses around **Lady St Mary's Church**, which contains the marble coffin of Edward the Martyr, murdered at Corfe Castle in 978 by his stepmother, to make way for her unready son Ethelred. **St Martin's Church**, at the north end of town, dates from Saxon times and the chancel contains a faded twelfth-century mural of St Martin offering his cloak to a beggar, but the church's most striking feature is a romantic effigy of T.E. Lawrence in Arab dress, which was originally destined for Salisbury Cathedral, but was rejected by the dean there who disapproved of Lawrence's sexual proclivities. Lawrence was killed in 1935 in a motorbike accident on the road from Bovington, after returning to Dorset from his Middle Eastern adventures. His simply furnished cottage is at **Clouds Hill**, seven miles northwest of Wareham (April–Oct Wed–Fri & Sun noon–5pm or dusk; £2.30; NT). In Wareham the small **museum** next to the town hall in East Street (Easter–Oct Mon–Sat 11am–1pm & 2–4pm; free) displays some of Lawrence's memorabilia, as does the absorbing but over-priced **Tank Museum** in Bovington Camp, five miles west of Wareham (daily 10am–5pm; £6.50). You can walk through a replica trench of the Somme, and catch the first tanks that went into battle in action (July & Sept Thurs at noon; Aug Thurs & Fri at noon).

A much-advertised local tourist honeypot is the **Blue Pool**, an intensely coloured clay-pit lake near Furzebrook, some three miles south of Wareham. A small museum (Easter to early Oct daily 10am–5pm; £3) gives the background to the local clay industry, and there are cream teas, nature trails and other amenities for less studious customers.

Holy Trinity Church, on South Street, contains Wareham's **tourist office** (June–Sept Mon–Sat 9.30am–5pm, Sun 10am–1pm; Oct–May Mon–Sat 9.30am–1pm & 1.45pm–5pm; ☎01929/552740). From the nearby Quay, row- and motor-boats are available to rent (£8–12 an hour). The best **accommodation** options are the *Anglebury Hotel*, 15 North St (☎01929/552988; ③) and the *Maltings*, 2 Abbots Quay, offering riverside views right by the tourist office (☎01929/552092; no credit cards; ②). The *Old Granary* **restaurant** on the Quay (☎01929/552010; ②) also has rooms, with views over the river and the meadows beyond. *Kemps*, one and a half miles west of town in East Stoke (☎01929/462563), serves imaginative but unpretentious food and is particularly good value at lunchtime – rooms are also available here (②).

Corfe Castle

The romantic ruins crowning the hill behind the village of **CORFE CASTLE** (daily: March & late Oct 10am–4.30pm; April to late Oct 10am–5.30pm or dusk; Nov–Feb 11am–3.30pm; £4; NT) are perhaps the most evocative in England. The family seat of Sir John Bankes, Attorney General to Charles I, this Royalist stronghold withstood a Cromwellian siege for six weeks, gallantly defended by Lady Bankes. One of her own men, Colonel Pitman, eventually betrayed the castle to the Roundheads, after which it was reduced to its present gap-toothed state by gunpowder. Apparently the victorious Roundheads were so impressed by Lady Bankes's courage that they allowed her to take the keys to the castle with her – they can still be seen in the library at the Bankes's subsequent home, Kingston Lacy (see p.251).

The village is well stocked with tearooms and gift shops and has a couple of good **pubs** too: the *Fox* on West Street, where you can drink or have lunch in a large garden with views to the castle, and, below the castle ramparts, the *Greyhound*. If you can't afford the high **room** rates and expensive dinners at the Elizabethan *Mortons House Hotel* on East Street (☎01929/480988, *mortonshouse@aol.com*; ⑥), you can still enjoy a reasonably priced bar meal or tea. For more moderately priced accommodation, head for *Brook Cottage*, 5 East St (☎01929/480347; no credit cards; ①), or the *Bankes Arms Hotel* (☎01929/480206; ②), an old inn outside the castle entrance. Three miles west, outside Church Knowle, the Tudor-beamed *Cartshed Cottage* at Whiteway Farm (☎01929/480801; ②) has a couple of rooms in a panoramic setting.

Shell Bay to St Alban's Head

Purbeck's most northerly coastal stretch, **Shell Bay**, is a magnificent beach of icing-sugar sand backed by a remarkable heathland ecosystem that's home to all six British species of reptile – adders are quite common, so be careful. At the top end of the beach a **ferry** (daily 7am–11pm every 20min; pedestrians 90p, bikes 80p, cars £2.20) crosses the mouth of Poole harbour connecting the Isle of Purbeck with Sandbanks in Poole.

To the south, beyond the broad sweep of Studland Bay, is **SWANAGE**, a traditional seaside resort with a pleasant sandy beach and an ornate town hall, the facade of which once adorned the Mercer's Hall in the City of London and was brought back here as ballast on a cargo ship. The town's station is the southern terminus of the **Swanage Steam Railway** (April–Oct daily; Nov–March Sat & Sun; £6 return), which is slowly being restored to run as far as Wareham, but has currently only reached Norden (on the A351).

Swanage's **tourist office** is by the beach on Shore Road (Easter–Oct daily 10am–5pm; Nov–Easter Mon–Thurs 10am–5pm, Fri 10am–4pm; ☎01929/422885), and there's a **youth hostel**, with good views across the bay, on Cluny Crescent (☎01929/422113, *swanage@yha.org.uk*; closed Nov to mid-Feb). There are scores of **B&Bs** in Swanage; you'll find a handy trio on King's Road near the train station or try the *Purbeck Hotel,* 19 High St (☎01929/425160; ①), which also has a decent pub. Swanage has a wide variety of places **to eat**, ranging from fish-and-chip shops to upmarket restaurants, the best of which is the excellent *Galley,* 9 High St (☎01929/427299), which specializes in well-prepared local fish dishes served at moderate prices. If you're interested in exploring on the Purbeck Cycleway (map available from the tourist office), **rent bikes** from Bikeabout, 71 High St (☎01929/425050), opposite the town hall (£10 a day, £35 a week).

Highlights of the coast beyond Swanage are the cliffs of **Durlstone Head**, topped by a lighthouse. Nearby stands a vast stone globe weighing forty tonnes, installed by George Burt, an eccentric Victorian building contractor from Swanage, who also erected the local folly castle. The cliffs continue to **St Alban's Head**, their ledges crowded with seabirds and rare wildflowers in spring. Paths lead inland to the attractive villages of **Langton Matravers**, where the **Coach House Museum** interprets the local stone-quarrying industry (April–Sept Mon–Sat 10am–noon & 2–4pm; 85p), and **Worth Matravers**, where there's a fine Norman church and a great **pub**, the *Square & Compass*, which produces filling, unfancy bar food at reasonable prices.

Kimmeridge Bay to Durdle Door

Beyond St Alban's Head the coastal geology suddenly changes as the grey-white chalk and limestone give way to darker beds of shale. **Kimmeridge Bay** may not have a sandy beach but it does have a remarkable marine wildlife reserve much appreciated by divers – there's a Dorset Wildlife Trust **information centre** by the slipway (April–Oct daily 10am–5pm; ☎01929/481044). The amazing range of species is all the more surprising because the bay has been the site of small-scale industry for centuries. The Saxons crafted amulets from the shale and the extraction of alum (for glassmaking) and coal followed. Today a low-tech "nodding donkey" oil well fits unobtrusively into the landscape. In the village, the sixteenth-century *Kimmeridge Farmhouse* (☎01929/480990; no credit cards; ②) is a quiet spot for an overnight **stay**.

The Lulworth artillery ranges west of Kimmeridge are inaccessible during weekdays but generally open at weekends and in school holidays – watch out for the red warning flags and notices and always stick to the path. Roads in this area have similar restrictions, but generally open before 9am and after 5pm to allow commuters through. The coastal path passes close to the deserted village of **Tyneham**, whose residents were summarily evicted by the army in 1943; the abandoned stone cottages have an eerie fascination, and an exhibition in the church explains the history of the village. Ironically, the army's presence has actually helped to preserve the local habitat which plays host to many species of flora and fauna long since vanished from farmed or otherwise developed areas.

The quaint thatch-and-stone villages of East and West Lulworth form a prelude to **Lulworth Cove**, a perfect shell-shaped bite formed when the sea broke through a weakness in the cliffs and then gnawed away at them from behind, forming a circular cave which eventually collapsed to leave a bay enclosed by sandstone cliffs. Lulworth's scenic charms are well known, and as you descend the hill through West Lulworth in summer the sun glints off the metal of a thousand car roofs in the parking lot behind the cove. At the **Lulworth Heritage Centre** the mysteries of the local geology are explained (March–Oct daily; 10am–6pm, Nov–Feb 10am–4pm; free; parking £3).

Immediately west of the cove you come to **Stair Hole**, a roofless sea cave riddled with arches that will eventually collapse to form another Lulworth, and a couple of miles west is **Durdle Door**, a famous limestone arch that appeals to serious geologist and casual sightseer alike. Most people take the uphill route to the arch which starts from the car park but, if you want to avoid the steep climb, you can drive a mile from the village towards East Chaldon and park at the *Durdle Door Holiday Park* for a small fee. An alternative, if tide-dependent, route goes up the private drive from the Heritage Centre and down into the secluded St Oswald's Bay which separates Lulworth from Durdle Door. If you've timed it right you can slip round the headland and climb up to the arch although you may prefer to stay on the more agreeable St Oswald's beach.

West Lulworth is the obvious place to stay or eat on this section of coast. The *Castle Inn* (☎01929/400311; ②), *Cromwell House Hotel* (☎0929/400253; ③), right on the coast path, and *Ivy Cottage* (☎01929/400509; no credit cards; ①), a seventeenth-century cottage with inglenook fireplace, all make for good stop-offs. You'll find a **youth hostel** at the end of School Lane West (☎01929/400564); a plain chalet with small rooms, it's a stone's throw away from the Dorset Coast Path. **Campers** can find a pitch at the above-mentioned *Durdle Door Holiday Park* (☎01929/400200; closed Nov–Feb). In **East Lulworth**, the *Weld Arms* also has rooms (☎01929/400211; ①) and the easily overlooked *Sailor's Return* in East Chaldon, four miles northwest of Lulworth Cove, is unsurpassed locally for its mouthwatering pub food.

Dorchester and around

The county town of Dorset, **DORCHESTER** still functions as the main agricultural centre for the region, and if you catch it on a Wednesday when the market is in full swing you'll find it livelier than usual. For the local tourist authorities, however, this is essentially **Thomas Hardy**'s town; he was born at Higher Bockhampton, three miles east of here, his heart is buried in Stinsford, a couple of miles northeast (the rest of him is in Westminster Abbey), and he spent much of his life in Dorchester itself, where his statue now stands on High West Street. Even without the Hardy connection, Dorchester makes an attractive stop, with its pleasant central core of mostly seventeenth-century and Georgian buildings, and the prehistoric Maumbury Rings on the outskirts. To the southwest of town looms the massive hill fort of **Maiden Castle**, the most impressive of Dorset's many pre-Roman antiquities and the Tudor **Athelhampton House**, near the village of Puddletown, six miles east of Dorchester, stands out because of its decorative gardens.

The Town

Dorchester was Durnovaria to the Romans, who founded the town in about 70 AD. The original Roman walls were replaced in the eighteenth century by tree-lined avenues

HARDYS' WESSEX

Thomas Hardy (1840–1928) resurrected the old name of **Wessex** to describe the region in which he set most of his fiction. In his books, the area stretched from Devon and Somerset ("Lower" and "Outer Wessex") to Berkshire and Oxfordshire ("North Wessex"), though its central core was Dorset ("South Wessex"), the county where Hardy spent most of his life. His books richly depict the life and appearance of the towns and countryside of the area, often thinly disguised under fictional names. Thus Salisbury makes an appearance as "Melchester", Weymouth (where he briefly lived) as "Budmouth Regis", and Bournemouth as "Sandbourne" – described as "a fairy palace suddenly created by the stroke of a wand, and allowed to get a little dusty" in *Tess of the d'Urbervilles*. But it is **Dorchester**, the "Casterbridge" of his novels, which is portrayed in most detail, to the extent that many of the town's buildings and landmarks that still remain can be identified in the books (especially *The Mayor of Casterbridge* and *Far From the Madding Crowd*). Hardy knew the town well; he attended school here (walking daily from the family home at Higher Bockhampton) and set up as an architect (his father and grandfather were both stonemasons), a profession which he later practised in Cornwall and London. He returned to Dorchester in 1885, spending the rest of his life in a house built to his own designs at Max Gate, on the Wareham Road.

Today, the Hardy industry takes two forms; the bookish and low-profile activities of the Thomas Hardy Society, whose diehard zealots help to preserve the relics and places with which the author is associated, and the high-profile overkill of the tourist mandarins who have made sure that some reminder of Hardy and his works greets the visitor to Dorchester at every turn. The Thomas Hardy Society (Box 1438, Dorchester, Dorset DT1 1YH, ☎01305/251501) can provide plenty of material for enthusiasts to pore over, and organizes walks and tours, including a fifteen-mile hike which follows in the steps of Tess on her Sunday mission to her father-in-law, Parson Clare of Beauminster, in an attempt to rescue her failed marriage.

Alternatively, you could read the **books**. Recommended reading includes *Under the Greenwood Tree* (1872) for an evocation of Hardy's childhood in and around Higher Bockhampton; *Tess of the d'Urbervilles* (1891), for elegiac descriptions of the Frome Valley; *The Return of the Native* (1878), for wild Egdon Heath and the eerie yew forest of Cranborne Chase, and *The Mayor of Casterbridge* (1886) for Dorchester and Maumbury Rings.

called "Walks" (Bowling Alley Walk, West Walk and Colliton Walk), but some traces of the Roman period have survived. At the back of County Hall excavations have uncovered a fine Roman villa with a well-preserved mosaic floor, and on the southeast edge of town you'll find **Maumbury Rings**, where the Romans held vast gladiatorial combats in an amphitheatre adapted from a Stone Age site. The gruesome traditions continued into the Middle Ages, when gladiators were replaced by bear-baiting and public executions or "hanging fairs".

Continuing the sanguinary theme, after the ill-fated rebellion of the Duke of Monmouth (another of Charles II's illegitimate offspring) against James II, Judge Jeffreys was appointed to punish the rebels. His "Bloody Assizes" of 1685, held in the Oak Room of the **Antelope Hotel** on Cornhill, sentenced 292 men to death. In the event, 74 were hanged, drawn and quartered, and their heads then stuck on pikes throughout Dorset and Somerset; the luckier suspects were merely flogged and transported to the West Indies. Judge Jeffreys lodged just round the corner from the *Antelope* in High West Street, where a half-timbered restaurant now capitalizes on the lurid association.

In 1834 the **Shire Hall**, further down High West Street, witnessed another *cause célèbre*, when six men from the nearby village of **Tolpuddle** were sentenced to transportation for banding together to form the Friendly Society of Agricultural Labourers, in order to present a request for a small wage increase on the grounds that their families were starving. After a public outcry the men were pardoned, and the Tolpuddle Martyrs passed into history as founders of the trade union movement. The room in which they were tried is preserved as a memorial to the martyrs, and you can find out more about them in Tolpuddle itself, eight miles east on the A35, where there's a fine little **museum** (April–Oct Tues–Sat 10am–5.30pm, Sun 11am–5.30pm; Nov–March closes at 4pm; free).

The best place to find out about Dorchester's history is in the engrossing **Dorset County Museum** on High West Street (July & Aug daily 10am–5pm; rest of year closed Sun; £3), where archeological and geological displays trace Celtic and Roman history, including a section on Maiden Castle. Pride of place goes to the re-creation of Thomas Hardy's study, where his pens are inscribed with the names of the books he wrote with them. Other museums in town include the formidably turreted **Keep Military Museum** (Easter–Oct Mon–Sat 9.30am–5pm; £2), just west of Hardy's Monument, which traces the fortunes of the Dorset and Devonshire regiments over three hundred years and offers sweeping views over the town; and a small **Dinosaur Museum** off High East Street on Icen Way (daily: April–Sept 9.30am–5.30pm; Oct–March 10am–4.30pm; £3.50), that appeals chiefly to children. Best of all is **Tutankhamun: The Exhibition** High St (daily 9.30am–5.30pm; £3.50), a fascinating and thorough exploration of the young pharaoh's life and afterlife through to the eventual discovery of his tomb in 1922. Everything from the mummified remains, complete burial chamber and the celebrated golden mask has been carefully and atmospherically re-created with painstaking detail.

If you're on the Hardy trail, you'll want to visit **Thomas Hardy's Cottage** (April–Oct Mon–Thurs & Sun 11am–5pm or dusk; £2.60; NT), where the writer lived from 1840 to 1862 and from 1867 to 1870, and his last and longest abode, **Max Gate** (April–Sept Sun, Mon & Wed 2–5pm; £2.10; NT), though you may be disappointed by the paucity of what there is to see. The nearer of the two, Max Gate, where the writer completed *Tess of the D'Urbervilles*, *Jude the Obscure* and much of his poetry, is a twenty-minute walk east from the centre on the Wareham road (A352), but only the garden and dining and drawing rooms are open to the public. Hardy's birthplace in Higher Bockhampton, about three miles northeast of Dorchester, has even less on offer: bits of period furniture and some original manuscripts. Infrequent buses (#184–189) all pass within half a mile – otherwise you can walk (on the A35 and Bockhampton Road) or take a taxi.

Practicalities

Dorchester has two **train stations**, both of them to the south of the centre: trains from Weymouth and London arrive at Dorchester South, while Bristol trains use the Dorchester West station. Most **buses** stop around the car park on Acland Road, to the east of South Street; there are about four services daily from Poole, Salisbury and Weymouth, as well as National Express services from London. Dorchester Coachways (☎01305/262992) offers a cheaper daily service to London as well as connections throughout the county. The **tourist office** is in Antelope Walk (April–Sept Mon–Sat 9am–5pm, Sun 10am–5pm; Oct Mon–Sat 9am–5pm; Nov–March Mon–Sat 9am–4pm; ☎01305/267992). **Bikes for rent** are available at Dorchester Cycles, 31 Great Western Rd (☎01305/268787), for £10 per day or £50 per week.

Dorchester has a good selection of **accommodation**, including top of the range *Casterbridge Hotel*, 49 High East St (☎01305/264043; ⑤), a superior Georgian guesthouse, and the best budget option, *Maumbury Cottage,* 9 Maumbury Rd (☎01305/266726; no credit cards; ①), a small, friendly and central B&B. The *King's Arms*, High East St, (☎01305/265353; ②), a historic local landmark, also serves good food, including vegetarian dishes. Out of town, try the *Old Rectory* in Winterbourne Steepleton three miles to the west (☎01305/889468; no credit cards; ②), or, two miles north of town in Charminster, *Slades Farm*, North Street (☎01305/265614; no credit cards; ①), a converted barn with en-suite rooms. The nearest **youth hostel** is at Litton Cheney (☎01308/482340), halfway between Dorchester and Bridport, and the closest **campsite** is the *Giant's Head Caravan and Camping Park*, Old Sherborne Rd (☎01300/341242; closed Nov–Easter), about five miles north of town, above the Cerne Abbas giant (see p.264).

When it comes to **food**, your best bet is a pub meal; try the *Royal Oak* or the *Old Ship Inn*, both on High West Street and both highly recommended. The famous *Judge Jeffreys Restaurant* is inevitably touristy, but offers fair value, while *Panini's* on Trinity St (daytime only), and the *Mock Turtle*, on High West Street, both offer quality cuisine at reasonable prices. Across the road, the *Old Tea House* serves teas and snacks. Dorchester's **nightlife** is limited, but there is *Paul's Nightclub* at 33 Trinity St, which lays on comedy and live music nights as well as club sounds.

Maiden Castle and Athelhampton House

One of southern England's finest prehistoric sites, **Maiden Castle** (free access) stands on a hill two miles or so south of Dorchester. Covering about 115 acres, it was first developed around 3000 BC by a Stone Age farming community and then used during the Bronze Age as a funeral mound. Iron Age dwellers expanded it into a populous settlement and fortified it with a daunting series of ramparts and ditches, just in time for the arrival of Vespasian's Second Legion. The ancient Britons' slingstones were no match for the more sophisticated weapons of the Roman invaders, and Maiden Castle was stormed in a bloody massacre in 43 AD.

What you see today is a massive series of grassy concentric ridges about sixty feet high, creasing the surface of the hill. The site is best visited early or late in the day, when the low-angled sun casts the earthworks in shadow, showing them up more clearly. The main finds from the site are displayed in the Dorset County Museum (see opposite).

Five miles east of Dorchester on the A35, just past the village of Puddletown, lies **Athelhampton House** (March–Oct Mon–Fri & Sun 10.30am–5pm; Nov–Feb Sun 10.30am–5pm; £4.95), a fine fifteenth-century house surrounded by walled gardens resplendent with fountains and unusual topiary pyramids of yew. Inside, the oak-panelled Great Hall is Athelhampton's most outstanding feature, with its hammer-beam ceiling, original fireplace and oriel window. Other rooms don't quite live up to the Hall's Tudor grandeur, but feature an interesting collection of antiques which the house was bought to display.

Weymouth to Bridport

Whether George III's passion for sea bathing was a symptom of his eventual madness is uncertain, but it was at the bay of **Weymouth** that in 1789 he became the first reigning monarch to follow the craze. Sycophantic gentry rushed into the waves behind him, and soon the town, formerly a workaday harbour, took on the elegant Georgian stamp which it bears today. A likeness of the monarch on horseback is even carved into the chalk downs northwest of the town, like some guardian spirit. Weymouth nowadays plays second fiddle to the vast resort of Bournemouth to the east, but it's still a lively family holiday destination, with several costly new attractions to augment its more sedate charms.

Just south of the town stretch the giant arms of Portland Harbour, and a long causeway links Weymouth to the strange five-mile-long excrescence of the **Isle of Portland**. West of the causeway, the eighteen-mile bank of pebbles known as **Chesil Beach** runs northwest in the direction of **Bridport**.

Weymouth

WEYMOUTH had long been a port before the Georgians popularized it as a resort – it's possible that a ship unloading a cargo here in 1348 first brought the Black Death to English shores, and on a happier note it was from Weymouth that John Endicott sailed in 1628 to found Salem in Massachusetts. A few buildings survive from these pre-Georgian times: the restored **Tudor House** on Trinity Street (June–Sept Tues–Fri 11am–3.45pm; Oct–May first Sun of month 2–4pm; £1.50) and the ruins of **Sandsfoot Castle** (free access), built by Henry VIII, overlooking Portland Harbour. But Weymouth's most imposing architectural heritage stands along the Esplanade, a dignified range of bow-fronted and porticoed buildings gazing out across the graceful bay, an ensemble rather disrupted by the garish **Clock Tower** commemorating Victoria's jubilee. The more intimate quayside of the Old Harbour, linked to the Esplanade by the main pedestrianized throroughfare St Mary's Street, is lined with waterfront pubs from where you can view the passing yachts, trawlers and ferries.

Like most British seaside resorts, Weymouth has had to supply more than sand and saucy postcards to its clientele in recent years. Its slightly faded gentility is now counterbalanced by a number of "all-weather" attractions, the most high-profile of which is the **Sea Life Park** in Lodmoor Country Park east of the Esplanade (daily 10am–4pm, last admission 1hr before closing; £5.50, £4.95 from tourist office), where you can get close to sharks and rays and wander among multichrome birds in the tropical house. Other attractions include the **Deep Sea Adventure** at the Old Harbour (summer 9.30am–8pm; winter 9.30am–7pm; £3.50), which describes the origins of modern diving and the sobering story of the *Titanic* disaster. Over the river on Hope Square, **The Timewalk** housed in Brewer's Quay (daily 10am–5.30pm; public & school holidays open until 9.30pm; £3.95), contains an entertaining and educational walk-through exhibition of Weymouth's maritime and brewing past. A fifteen-minute walk southwards leads to the Palmerston-era **Nothe Fort** (mid-May to mid-Sept daily 10.30am–5.30pm; hours are variable in winter, call to check; ☎01305/787243; £3) which has a number of displays on military themes, as well as a museum detailing the centuries-old practice of coastal defence, made obsolete in 1956 by advancing technology. If you're interested in exploring the bay, check out the glass-bottomed *Fleet Observer*, which sails from the Ferrybridge pub near Abbotsbury Oysters on the A354 Portland Rd (June–Sept 6 daily; 1hr 30min; £4; ☎01305/773396).

Practicalities

Weymouth is easily reached by public transport: there is a regular **train** service from London, Bournemouth and Poole, and less frequent services from Bristol and Cardiff via Yeovil. There are also good **bus** services between Weymouth and Dorchester, eight miles north, a hub for many other routes. The town's **tourist office** is at King's Statue, the Esplanade (daily: April–Sept 9am–5pm; Oct–March 10am–3pm; ☎01305/785747).

A cluster of the town's **accommodation** options lies at the south end of the Esplanade, between the bay and harbour, for instance *Chatsworth*, 14 Esplanade (☎01305/785012; ④), which also serves decent food, and the good-value *Cavendish House*, 5 Esplanade (☎01305/782039; ②; closed Nov–March), in a detached Georgian terrace overlooking the bay with harbour views at the back. Just a few steps from the seafront, the *Globe Hotel* is an unpretentious place with good-value rooms on the corner of East and Mitchell streets (☎01305/785849; no credit cards; ①). At the quieter northern end of the Esplanade, *Bay Lodge*, at 27 Greenhill (☎01305/782419; ④; closed Nov), is a better-than-average B&B with good sea views. There are some excellent choices a little further from the centre, such as the *Beehive*, Church Lane, Osmington (☎01305/834095; no credit cards; ①; closed Jan), a lovely and quiet thatched cottage in a small village three miles northeast of Weymouth, with discounts for longer stays; two miles northeast of the centre at 29 Preston Rd, the pleasant *Streamside Hotel* serves well-prepared traditional British fare, with added French flair – higher-priced en-suite rooms are also available (☎01305/833121; ③).

Weymouth is also well served by its refreshment outlets and **restaurants**. If it's seafood you're after, you can't do better than *Perry's*, a moderately priced place overlooking the quayside at 4 Trinity Rd (☎01305/785799; closed Sun eve in winter), or try the nearby *Rendezvous*, The Quay, an inexpensive first-floor bar/restaurant by Town Bridge, above the popular Irish bar *O'Malley's*. Other cheaper places include *Criterion* at 63 Esplanade, a useful self-service restaurant near the beach with all-day breakfasts, and the *Seagull Café*, 10 Trinity Rd, a family-run chippie with fresh fish and lashings of chips (closed Mon). On St Mary's St, *Bon Appetit* and *Crusty's* both make good lunchspots with a range of hot baguettes and sandwiches and some outdoor seating, while *Cafe 21* at 21 East St is Weymouth's only vegetarian restaurant – open every lunchtime, but only Saturday and Sunday evenings (no credit cards). On the corner of St Nicholas St and Commercial Rd, *Sailor's Return* is one of a number of amenable **pubs** in town, a harbourside tavern with in-your-face angling paraphernalia and fresh fish on the menu; others include the *Old Rooms Inn* on Trinity Rd, an inexpensive lunch venue, again with a strong maritime theme, and the *Nothe Tavern*, buried among Nothe Gardens (south of the harbour on Barrack Rd), which offers bar meals and Eldridge Pope beer and has views from the garden.

Portland

Stark, wind-battered and treeless, the **ISLE OF PORTLAND** is famed above all for its hard white limestone, which has been quarried here for centuries – Wren used it for St Paul's Cathedral, and it clads the UN headquarters in New York. It was also used for the six-thousand-foot breakwater that protects Portland Harbour – the largest artificial harbour in Britain, which was built by convicts in the mid-nineteenth century. Poorer grades of Portland stone are pulverized for cement – the industrial stone-crushing plant is a prominent and unlovely feature of the island.

The causeway road by which Portland is approached stands on the easternmost section of the Chesil shingle. To the east you get a good view of the harbour, a naval base since 1872, but now jeopardized by the post-Cold War rundown of Britain's defences. The first settlement you come to, **Fortuneswell**, overlooks the huge harbour and is itself surveyed by a 450-year-old Tudor fortress, **Portland Castle** (April–Sept 10am–6pm; Oct 10am–5pm; £2.50; EH), commissioned by Henry VIII. South of **Easton**, the main village on the island, Wakeham Road holds Pennsylvania Castle (now a private house), built in 1800 for John Penn, governor of the island and a grandson of the founder of Pennsylvania. A couple of hundred yards beyond the house, the seventeenth-century *Avice's Cottage*, a gift of Marie Stopes, the pioneer of birth control, is home to a small **museum** (April–July, Sept & Oct Mon, Tues & Fri–Sun 10.30am–1pm & 1.30–5pm; Aug daily 10.30am–1pm & 1.30–5pm; £1.70), with exhibitions on local shipwrecks, smuggling and quarrying. The cottage owes its name to Thomas Hardy, who described it in his novel, *The Well-Beloved*. Nearby, in Church Ope Cove, you can see the ruins of St Andrew's Church and eleventh-century Rufus Castle.

The craggy limestone of the island rises to 496 feet at **Portland Bill**, where a lighthouse has guarded the promontory since the eighteenth century. The present one, dating from 1906, now houses Portland's **tourist office** (Easter–Sept Mon, Tues & Thurs–Sun 10am–4pm, Wed 11am–4pm; ☎01305/861233), which can update you on **accommodation** options in the area, for instance *Sturt Corner* (☎01305/822846; no credit cards; ①) or the *Pulpit Inn* (☎01305/821237; ①), both nearby on Portland Bill. If you want to stay in a lighthouse, the *Old Higher Lighthouse* (☎01305/822300) offers self-catering facilities, as do the *Old Coastguard Cottages* (☎01903/785052) and *Hobbiton*

Cottage in Church Ope Cove (☎01305/820388). Expect to pay £175–450 per week, depending on season, and book well in advance.

Chesil Beach and Bridport

Chesil Beach is the strangest feature of the Dorset coast, a two-hundred-yard-wide, fifty-foot-high bank of pebbles that extends for eighteen miles, its component stones gradually decreasing in size from fist-like pebbles at Portland to "pea gravel" at Burton Bradstock in the west. This sorting is an effect of the powerful coastal currents, which make this one of the most dangerous beaches in Europe – churchyards in the local villages display plenty of evidence of wrecks and drownings. Though not a swimming beach, Chesil is popular with sea anglers, and its wild, uncommercialized atmosphere makes an appealing antidote to the south coast resorts. To explore it, you need your own transport or plenty of time – infrequent bus services connect the main villages, and the Dorset Coast Path runs close to the shore for most of the way.

Chesil Beach encloses a brackish lagoon called The Fleet for much of its length – it was the setting for J. Meade Faulkner's classic smuggling tale, *Moonfleet*. Overlooking the lagoon, *Moonfleet Manor* (☎01305/786948; ⑤), a hotel and large sports resort three miles west of Weymouth, capitalizes on the Faulkner connection. At the point where the shingle beach attaches itself to the shore is the pretty village of **ABBOTSBURY**, all tawny ironstone and thatch. Its Tithe Barn is a fifteenth-century building, the last remnant of the village's Benedictine abbey, and today the centre of a **Children's Farm** (daily: Easter–Oct 10am–6pm; last admissions 1hr before closing; Nov–Easter Sat & Sun 11am–dusk; £3.75), and the venue for occasional exhibitions. The village **Swannery** (April–Oct daily 10am–6pm; last admissions 1hr before closing; £4.80), a wetland reserve for mute swans, dates back to medieval times, when presumably it formed part of the abbot's larder. The eel-grass reeds through which the swans paddle were once harvested to thatch roofs throughout the region. Other attractions are the hilltop **Chapel of St Catherine**, also dating from the fifteenth century, and the **Sub-Tropical Gardens** (daily: April–Oct 10am–6pm, last admission 1hr before closing; Nov–March 10am–dusk; £4.40), where delicate species thrive in the micro-climate created by Chesil's stones, which act as a giant radiator to keep out all but the worst frosts. Up on the downs a couple of miles inland from Abbotsbury is a monument to Thomas Hardy, not the usual one associated with Dorset, but the flag captain in whose arms Admiral Nelson expired.

If you want to **stay** in Abbotsbury try *Swan Lodge*, 1 Rodden Row, for good B&B accommodation (☎01305/871249; no credit cards; ②) or the *Ilchester Arms* in the village centre, a handsome stone inn with comfortable rooms and fine food (☎01305/871243; ②). West of the village three miles along the coast at **West Bexington**, the *Manor Hotel* is an excellent unpretentious hostelry offering accommodation and a sumptuous range of food (☎01308/897616, *manorhotel@btconnect.com*; ⑥). Inland and further west, in the lovely village of **Shipton Gorge**, the *Innsacre Restaurant with Rooms* (☎01308/456137; ③) provides similar services.

BRIDPORT, just beyond the far end of Chesil Beach, is a nice old town of brick rather than stone, with unusually wide streets, a hangover from its rope-making days when cords made of locally grown hemp and flax were stretched between the houses. Bridport has several fine buildings: a medieval church, a Georgian town hall, a fourteenth-century chantry and a Tudor building housing the local **museum** (April–Oct Mon–Sat 10am–6pm; £1.50). If you want to know about the rope and net industry head for the fishing resort of **West Bay**, Bridport's access to the sea, where majestic red cliffs rear up above the sea. The **Harbour Life Exhibition** (April–Oct daily 10am–6pm; £1), will fill you in about "Bridport daggers" (hangmen's nooses) and more besides. West Bay also has the area's best place to **eat**, the *Riverside Restaurant*, a renowned but informal fish place with good views out to sea (closed Sun eve & Mon). Across the harbour, the *Bridport Arms Hotel* (☎01308/422994; ②) offers good **accommodation** near the beach; also worth trying is the *Britmead House*, 154 West Bay Rd (☎01308/422941; ③), on the road back to Bridport. In the centre of town, try *Cranston Cottage*, 27 Church St (☎01308/456240; no credit cards; ①). The Bridport **tourist office** is at 32 South St (April–Oct Mon–Sat 9am–5pm; Nov–March Mon–Sat 10am–3pm; ☎01308/424901).

Lyme Regis and around

From the end of Chesil Beach an ever more dramatic sequence of cliffs runs westward, followed as closely as possible by the **Dorset Coast Path**, which has to deviate inland in a few places to avoid areas of landslip. The most prominent feature along this coast is **Golden Cap**, an outcrop of sandstone close to west Dorset's main resort, **Lyme Regis**. On summer days it can seem that tourism is threatening to choke the life out of Lyme – but you can quickly find refuge inland, where **Beaminster** makes a good base for exploring scenic little Dorset villages of golden stone and thatched cottages.

Lyme Regis

LYME REGIS, Dorset's most westerly town, shelters snugly between steep hills, just before the grey, fossil-filled cliffs lurch into Devon. Its intimate size and undeniable photogenic qualities make Lyme so popular that in high summer car-borne crowds jostle with pedestrians for the limited space along its narrow streets. For all that, the town lives up to the classy impression created by its regal name, which it owes to a royal charter granted by Edward I in 1284. It has some upmarket literary associations to further bolster its self-esteem – Jane Austen penned *Persuasion* in a seafront cottage here, while novelist John Fowles is the town's most famous current resident; but it was the film adaptation of his book, *The French Lieutenant's Woman*, shot on location here, that did more than any tourist board production ever could to place the resort firmly on the map.

Though Lyme Regis now relies mostly on holidaymakers for its keep, it was for centuries a port for the wool traders of Somerset, and shipbuilding thrived here until Victorian times. Colourwashed cottages and elegant Regency and Victorian villas line its seafront and flanking streets, but Lyme's best-known feature is a briskly practical reminder of its commercial origins. **The Cobb**, the curving harbour wall, was first constructed in the thirteenth century but has suffered many alterations since, most notably in the nineteenth century, when its massive boulders were clad in neater blocks of Portland stone.

As you walk along the seafront and out towards The Cobb, look for the outlines of ammonites in the walls and paving stones. The cliffs around Lyme are made up of a complex layer of limestone, greensand and unstable clay, a perfect medium for preserving fossils, which are exposed by landslips of the waterlogged clays. One of the most famous landslides occurred in 1839, when a large block of land, complete with a crop of turnips, was severed from its neighbouring fields by a chasm so dramatic that Queen Victoria came to inspect the scene from her yacht. In 1811, after a fierce storm caused parts of the cliffs to collapse, twelve-year-old Mary Anning, a keen fossil-hunter, discovered an almost complete dinosaur skeleton, a thirty-foot ichthyosaurus now displayed in London's Natural History Museum (see p.110).

Hammering fossils out of the cliffs is frowned on by today's conservationists, and in any case is rather hazardous. Hands-off inspection of the area's complex geology can be enjoyed on both sides of town: to the west lies the **Undercliff**, a fascinating jumble of overgrown landslips, now a nature reserve. East of Lyme, the Dorset Coast Path is closed as far as jaded **Charmouth** (Jane Austen's favourite resort), but at low tide you can walk for two miles along the beach, then, just past Charmouth, rejoin the coastal path to the headland of **Golden Cap**, whose brilliant outcrop of auburn sandstone is crowned with gorse.

Lyme's excellent **Philpot Museum** on Bridge Street (April–Oct Mon–Sat 10am–5pm, Sun 10am–noon & 2.30–5pm; Nov–March Sat 10am–5pm, Sun 10am–noon & 2.30–5pm, also open school half-terms at same times; £1.20) provides a crash course in local history and geology, while **Dinosaurland** on Coombe Street (daily: Aug 10am–6pm; rest of year 10am–5pm; £3.20) fills out the story on ammonites and other local fossils. Also worth seeing is the small **marine aquarium** on The Cobb (Easter–Oct 10am–5pm, later closing in July & Aug; £1.50), where local fishermen bring unusual catches, and the fifteenth-century **parish church** of St Michael the Archangel, up Church Street, which contains a seventeenth-century pulpit and a massive chained Bible.

Practicalities

Lyme's nearest **train station** is in Axminster, five miles north; the #31 **bus** runs from here to Lyme Regis (Mon–Sat hourly; on Sun take the #378, which runs three times) or a **taxi** will cost around £8. National Express runs a daily service from Exeter. The **tourist office** is at Church St (May–Sept Mon–Fri 10am–6am, Sat & Sun 10am–5pm; April & Oct daily 10am–5pm; Nov–March Mon–Fri 10am–4pm, Sat 10am–2pm; ☎01297/442138).

Lyme's sole seafront hotel is the pricey *Bay Hotel* on Marine Parade (☎01297/442059; ⑤), but you don't have to walk far for more moderately priced accommodation. The *Old Monmouth Hotel* is centrally located at 12 Church St (☎01297/442456; ②), and *Cliff Cottage* Cobb Rd (☎01297/443334; no credit cards; ①) also has a tea garden and fish restaurant; the *Red House*, a ten-minute walk out of town on Sidmouth Road, (☎01297/442055; ③; closed mid-Nov to mid-March), offers an especially warm welcome as well as fabulous views. Other choices include the *White House,* 47 Silver St (☎01297/443420; no credit cards; ②; closed Oct–Easter), the *New Haven B&B*, 1 Pound St (☎01297/442499; ②) and the *Cobb Arms* Marine Parade (☎01297/443242; ②). For inexpensive daytime meals, try the *Bell Cliff Restaurant* at 5–6 Broad St. Reasonably priced choices in the evening include the *Kersbrook Hotel* Pound Rd (☎01297/442596; ④), which is also a pleasant place to stay, or the moderately priced *Millside Restaurant and Wine Bar*, 1 Mill Lane (☎01297/442049) serving good pasta and fish dishes. The best **pubs** are the *Royal Standard* on Ozone Parade, and the *Pilot Boat* on Bridge Street, which also does smashing seafood and vegetarian meals.

Beaminster

There isn't a great deal to detain you in **BEAMINSTER**, a handsome little stone town in the Brit Valley, ten miles northeast of Lyme. A quick look at its sculpted church-tower and picturesque seventeenth-century and Georgian houses, and you may feel ready to pass on. With some fine places to stay and eat, however, Beaminster makes a convenient base for exploring West Dorset's hinterland.

The outstanding local sight is **Parnham House** (April–Oct Tues–Thurs & Sun 10am–5pm; £5), just south of town. It's a glorious Tudor manor house surrounded by velvety lawns and immaculate topiary yew cones, and provides a palatial setting for one of Britain's most successful revivals of a dying craft – furniture-making. John Makepeace's workshops and Parnham College are renowned, though most of the inspired products are too costly for any but wealthy connoisseurs. Those of more limited means can watch the holly, yew, mulberry and burr oak being worked on, wander round the well-furnished house, sample a decent lunch in the Buttery or take a picnic in the grounds.

The best place to **stay** in Beaminster is *Bridge House,* (☎01308/862200, *enquiries@bridge-house.co.uk*; ⑥), just outside the gates over the bridge on the Bridport side of town; it also has an excellent, if pricey **restaurant**. *Pickwicks Inn,* overlooking Market Square is a friendly pub which provides good food and less expensive rooms (☎01308/862094; ②) and the *Greyhound* on the Square offers a wide choice of decent pub food, including vegetarian dishes. For more rural accommodation, try *Higher Langdon Farm* up on the downs, two miles northeast of town (☎01308/862537; ②).

Inland Dorset and southern Wiltshire

The main pleasures of inland Dorset come from unscheduled meandering through its ancient landscapes and tiny rural settlements, many of which boast preposterously winsome names such as Ryme Intrinseca, Piddletrenthide, Up Sydling and Plush. Two of the most interesting of these villages are **Milton Abbas** and **Cerne Abbas**, the former attractive on account of its curious artificiality, the latter for its rumbustious chalk-carved giant. The major tourist honeypots, though, are the towns of **Blandford Forum**, **Shaftesbury** and **Sherborne**, the landscaped garden at **Stourhead** across the county boundary in Wiltshire, and the brasher stately home at **Longleat**, an unlikely hybrid of safari park and historic monument.

Blandford Forum

BLANDFORD FORUM, the gateway into mid-Dorset from Bournemouth, owes its latinate name not to the Romans but to medieval pedantry – the original Saxon name Cheping, meaning "market", was translated as Forum by Latin-speaking tax officials in the thirteenth century. The Romans weren't far away, however – their main route from Old Sarum to Dorchester ran through the Iron Age fortification of Badbury Rings, just east of the town, where it made an uncharacteristic bend.

In 1731 Blandford was all but destroyed by fire, the fourth such conflagration since the end of the sixteenth century. The phoenix that rose from these ashes – as the Fire Monument near the church puts it – was designed by the unfortunately named Bastard brothers, John and William, whose "Blandford School" produced buildings characterized by mellow dapplings of brick and stone. Sleepy Blandford still boasts one of the most harmonious and complete Georgian townscapes in England, with its centrepieces being the **Town Hall** and the **Church of St Peter and St Paul**, built in 1739. Outside, the church's distinguishing feature is the cupola perched on its handsome square tower; inside, it has fine box pews and huge Ionic columns. It doesn't quite look as John Bastard intended, though: the church was daringly altered at the end of the nineteenth century, when the chancel was sawn off the nave, stuck on wheels, rolled out of the way so that a new section could be built in the gap, and then stuck back onto the extension. The town **museum** in Bere's Yard, opposite the church (closed until mid-2000; call ☎01297/450710, or ask at the tourist office for information) offers a pithy account of local history, while **Mrs Penny's Cavalcade of Costume** at Lime Tree House, The Plocks (Easter–Sept Mon & Thurs–Sun 11am–5pm; Oct–Easter Mon & Thurs–Sun 11am–4pm; £3) presents over five hundred items of costume and accoutrements from 1730 to the 1950s, collected throughout the lifetime of a local woman, Mrs Penny.

Blandford's **tourist office** is in the car park on West Street (Mon–Sat April–Oct 10am–5pm; Nov–March 10am–1pm; ☎01258/454770). There are numerous **B&B**s along Whitecliff Mill Street to choose from, or try *Gone Walkabout*, at 3 Alexandra St (☎01258/455699, *101454.1674@compuserve.com*; no credit cards; ①), a Georgian house close to the town centre and welcoming walkers and cyclists. The local Hall & Woodhouse brewery supplies many local **hostelries** – the *Greyhound*, in quiet

Greyhound Place, is a good-looking pub with outdoor seating and great food. Other eating options include the moderately priced *Ottoman* Turkish restaurant, at 65 East St.

Milton Abbas and Cerne Abbas

The village of **MILTON ABBAS**, six miles southwest of Blandford, is an unusual English rural idyll. It owes its model-like neatness to the First Earl of Dorchester who, in the eighteenth century, found the medieval squalor of former "Middleton" a blot on the landscape of his estate. Although some see the earl as an enlightened advocate of modern town planning, the more likely truth is that he simply wanted to beautify his land, so he had the village razed and rebuilt in its present location as thirty semi-detached, whitewashed and thatched cottages on wide grassy verges. No trace remains of the old village which once surrounded the fourteenth-century **abbey church** (dawn–dusk; small charge during school holidays), a mile's walk away near the lake at the bottom of the village. Delayed by the Black Death and cut short by the Dissolution, the unfinished abbey church lacks much internal decoration, and instead retains a spacious, uncluttered feel.

Not far from the village, the brick and flint cottage *Dunbury Heights* (☎01285/880445; no credit cards; ①), about a mile towards Blandford, and the eighteenth-century thatched farmhouse *Park Farm* (☎01258/880828; no credit cards; ②), near Milton Abbey, both offer B&B **accommodation**. The *Dorset Tea Rooms* provides light lunches and the *Hambro Arms* **pub** at the top of the hill is the best bet for more substantial evening meals.

The most visited site in Dorset lies a further ten miles west, just off the A352, on the regular bus route between Dorchester and Sherborne (#216). **CERNE ABBAS** has bags of charm in its own right, with gorgeous Tudor cottages and abbey ruins, not to mention a clutch of decent pubs. Its main attraction, however, is the enormously priapic **giant** carved in the chalk hillside, standing 180-feet high and flourishing a club over his disproportionately small head. The age of the monument is disputed, some authorities believing it to be pre-Roman, others thinking it might be a Romano-British figure of Hercules, but in view of his prominent feature it's probable that the giant originated as some primeval fertility symbol. Folklore has it that lying on the outsize member will induce conception, but the National Trust, who now own the site, do their best to stop people wandering over it and eroding the two-foot trenches that form the outlines.

Shaftesbury

Ten miles north of Blandford, **SHAFTESBURY** perches on a spur of lumpy green-gold hills, with severe gradients on three sides of the town. On a clear /day, views from the town are terrific – one of the best vantage points is **Gold Hill**, quaint, cobbled and very steep. The local history **museum** at the top of Gold Hill (Easter–Sept daily 10.30am–4.30pm; also some weekends in winter, call ☎01747/854146 to check; £1) is worth a glance – its contents include a collection of locally made buttons, for which the area was once renowned.

Pilgrims used to flock to Shaftesbury to pay homage to the bones of Edward the Martyr, which were brought to the **Abbey** in 978, though now only the footings of the abbey church survive, just off the main street (Easter–Sept daily 10.30am–4.30pm; £1). **St Peter's Church** on the market place is one of the few reminders of Shaftesbury's medieval grandeur, when it boasted a castle, twelve churches and four market crosses.

The **tourist office** is on Bell Street (mid-March to Oct daily 10am–5pm; Nov to mid-March Mon–Wed 10am–1pm, Thurs–Sat 10am–5pm; ☎01747/853514). The *Mitre Inn* on the High Street serves good pies and has **rooms** (☎01747/852488; ②) as has the *Knoll* in Bleke Street (☎01747/855243; no credit cards; ②). Three miles south of town in the village of **Compton Abbas**, on the scenic A350 to Blandford, the *Old Forge*, on

Chapel Hill (☎01747/811881; no credit cards; ②), offers B&B in an eighteenth-century cottage with log fires. For a **snack** or main **meal** in Shaftesbury, the *Salt Cellar* at the top of Gold Hill makes a great place to sit, without suffering from over-quaintness.

Stourhead

Landscape gardening – the creation of an artificially improved version of nature – was a favoured mode of display among the grandest eighteenth-century landowners, and **Stourhead**, ten miles northwest of Shaftesbury, is one of the most accomplished survivors of the genre (house April–Oct Mon–Wed, Sat & Sun noon–5.30pm or dusk; garden daily 9am–7pm or dusk; tower April–Oct Tues–Fri 2–5.30pm or dusk, Sat & Sun 11.30am–5.30pm or dusk; house £4.50; garden £4.50; tower £1.50; combined ticket £8; NT). The Stourton estate was bought in 1717 by Henry Hoare, who commissioned Colen Campbell to build a new villa in the Palladian style. Hoare's heir, another Henry, returned from his Grand Tour in 1741 with his head full of the paintings of Claude and Poussin, and determined to translate their images of well-ordered, wistful classicism into real life. He dammed the Stour to create a lake, then planted the terrain with blocks of trees, domed temples, stone bridges, grottoes and statues, all mirrored vividly in the water. In 1772 the folly of King Alfred's Tower was added and today affords fine views across the estate and into neighbouring counties. The rhododendrons and azaleas that now make such a splash in early summer are a later addition to this dream landscape. The house, in contrast, is fairly run-of-the-mill, though it has some good Chippendale furniture.

A mile to the southeast, in the showpiece village of **Stourton**, also now owned by the National Trust, the *Spread Eagle Inn* has five en-suite **rooms** available (☎01747/840587; ⑤) – it's also a good place to have **lunch**. However, Stourton is difficult to reach without your own transport – the nearest train station is at Gillingham, over six miles away.

Longleat

If Stourhead is an unexpected outcrop of Italy in Wiltshire, the African savannah intrudes even more bizarrely at **Longleat** (house Easter–Oct 10am–6pm; Nov–Easter 10am–4pm; safari park Easter–Oct 10am–5pm; house £5; safari park £6; combined ticket £13), two and a half miles south of the road from Warminster to Frome. In 1946 the sixth marquess of Bath raised eyebrows among his peers as the first stately-home owner to open his house to the paying public on a regular basis to help make ends meet. In 1966 he caused even more amazement when Longleat's Capability Brown landscapes were turned into a drive-through **safari park** – the first in the country. (The carless visitor can survey the lions, tigers, giraffes, elephants, zebras and hippos from a safari bus for an extra £1.) Once committed to such commercial enterprise, the bosses of Longleat knew no limits: other attractions now include the world's largest hedge maze, a Doctor Who exhibition, a hi-tech simulation of the world's most dangerous modes of travel and the seventh marquess's steamy murals encapsulating his interpretation of life and the universe (children may not be admitted). Beyond the brazen razzmatazz, though, there's an exquisitely furnished Elizabethan house, built for Sir John Thynne, Elizabeth's High Treasurer, with the largest private library in Britain and a fine collection of pictures, including Titian's *Holy Family*.

Longleat is about four miles from the train stations of Frome and Warminster and is currently served by a Lion-Link bus that leaves Warminster train station at 11.10am and returns from the Information Centre at Longleat at 5.15pm – the service is provided free to coach- and rail-ticket holders, and otherwise costs £1.50. Alternatively, there's the #53 bus (Mon–Sat) which shuttles roughly every hour between Warminster and Frome train stations – though be prepared to walk the two and a half miles from the entrance of the house to its grounds.

Sherborne

Tucked away in the northwest corner of Dorset, the pretty town of **SHERBORNE** was once the capital of Wessex, its church having cathedral status until Old Sarum (see p.270) usurped the bishopric in 1075. This former glory is embodied by the magnificent **Abbey Church** (daily: summer 10am–6pm; winter 10am–4pm), which was founded in 705, later becoming a Benedictine abbey. Most of its extant parts date from a rebuilding in the fifteenth century, and it is one of the best examples of Perpendicular architecture in Britain, particularly noted for its outstanding **fan vaulting**. The church also has a famously weighty peal of bells, led by "Great Tom", a tenor bell presented to the abbey by Cardinal Wolsey. Among the abbey church's many tombs are those of Alfred the Great's two brothers, Ethelred and Ethelbert, and the Elizabethan poet Thomas Wyatt, all located in the northeast corner. The **almshouse** on the opposite side of the Abbey Close was built in 1437 and is a rare example of a medieval hospital; another wing provides accommodation for Sherborne's well-known public school.

Sherborne also has two "castles", both associated with Sir Walter Raleigh. Queen Elizabeth I first leased, then gave, Raleigh the twelfth-century **Old Castle** (April–Sept daily 10am–6pm; Oct daily 10am–1pm & 2–5pm; Nov–March Wed–Sun 10am–1pm & 2–4pm; £1.50; EH), but it seems that he despaired of feudal accommodation and built himself a more comfortably domesticated house, **Sherborne Castle**, in adjacent parkland (April–Oct Tues, Thurs, Sat & Sun 12.30–5pm; £4.80). When Sir Walter fell from the queen's favour by seducing her maid of honour, the Digby family acquired the house and have lived there ever since; portraits, furniture and books are displayed in a whimsically Gothic interior, remodelled in the nineteenth century. The Old Castle fared less happily, and was pulverized by Cromwellian cannonfire for the obstinately Royalist leanings of its occupants. The **museum** on Half Moon Street (Tue–Sat 10.30am–4.30pm, Sun 2.30–4.30pm; £1) includes a model of the Old Castle and photographs of parts of the fifteenth-century Sherborne Missal, a richly illuminated tome weighing nearly fifty pounds, now housed in the British Library.

The **tourist office** is at 3 Tilton Court, Digby Rd (Mon–Sat: Easter–Nov 9.30am–5.30pm; Nov–Easter 10am–3pm; ☎01935/815341). For an **overnight stay** try the *Half Moon Hotel*, Half Moon St (☎01935/812017; ②), the *Britannia Inn*, on Westbury, just down from the abbey (☎01935/813300; ③), or the *Cross Keys Hotel*, 88 Cheap St (☎01935/812492; ④), which has a few tables out front for drinks and meals. *Oliver's* on Cheap Street and the *Church House Gallery* close to the abbey on Half Moon Street are both good for teas and light lunches.

Salisbury

SALISBURY, huddled below Wiltshire's chalky plain in the converging valleys of the Avon and Nadder, looks from a distance very much as it did when Constable painted his celebrated view of it from across the water meadows, even though traffic may clog its centre and military jets scream overhead from local air bases. Prosperous and well-kept, Wiltshire's only city is designed on a pleasantly human scale, with no sprawling suburbs or high-rise buildings to challenge the supremacy of the cathedral's immense spire – unusually, the local planners have imposed a height limit on new construction. Unfortunately, the condition of the cathedral itself remains problematic, and scaffolding is likely to remain a feature of its elegant silhouette for the foreseeable future.

The town sprang into existence in the early thirteenth century, when the bishopric was moved from **Old Sarum**, an ancient Iron Age hillfort settled by the Romans and their successors. The deserted remnant of Salisbury's precursor now stands on the northern fringe of the town, just a bit closer in than **Wilton House** to the west, one of Wiltshire's great houses.

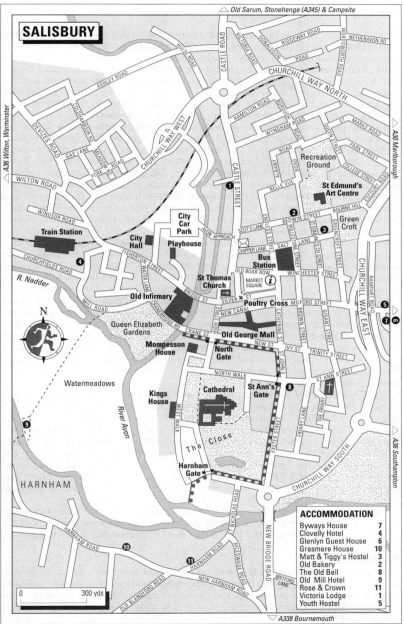

SALISBURY

Old Sarum, Stonehenge (A345) & Campsite

A36 Wilton, Warminster

A38 Marlborough

CHURCHILL WAY NORTH

Recreation Ground

St Edmund's Art Centre

Green Croft

Train Station

City Hall

City Car Park

Playhouse

Bus Station

St Thomas Church

Market Square

Poultry Cross

Old Infirmary

Queen Elizabeth Gardens

Mompesson House

Old George Mall

North Gate

Watermeadows

Kings House

Cathedral

St Ann's Gate

Harnham Gate

The Close

HARNHAM

R. Nadder

River Avon

CHURCHILL WAY EAST

A38 Southampton

CHURCHILL WAY SOUTH

A338 Bournemouth

0   300 yds

ACCOMMODATION

Byways House	7
Clovelly Hotel	4
Glenlyn Guest House	6
Grasmere House	10
Matt & Tiggy's Hostel	3
Old Bakery	2
The Old Bell	8
Old Mill Hotel	9
Rose & Crown	11
Victoria Lodge	1
Youth Hostel	5

© Crown copyright

The City

Begun in 1220, **Salisbury Cathedral** (daily: May–Sept 7am–8.15pm; Oct–April 7am–6.15pm; £3 suggested donation) was mostly completed within forty years and is thus uniquely consistent in its style, with one extremely prominent exception – the **spire**, which was added a century later and at 404ft is the highest in England. Its survival is something of a miracle, for the foundations penetrate only about six feet into marshy ground, and when Christopher Wren surveyed it he found the spire to be leaning almost two and a half feet out of true. The tie-rods inserted by Wren arrested the problem, but didn't cure it, and engineers are once more at work on it.

The interior is over-austere after James Wyatt's brisk eighteenth-century tidying, but there's an amazing sense of space and light in its high nave, despite the sombre pillars of grey Purbeck marble, which are visibly bowing beneath the weight they bear. Monuments and carved tombs line the walls, where they were neatly placed by Wyatt, and in the north aisle there's a fascinating clock dating from 1386, one of the oldest functioning clock mechanisms in Europe. Other features not to miss are the vaulted colonnades of the **cloisters**, and the octagonal **chapter house** (late April to early Sept Mon–Sat 9.30am–7.45pm, Sun 9.30am–5.30pm; rest of year daily 9.30am–5.30pm; 30p), which displays a rare original copy of the Magna Carta, and whose walls are decorated with a frieze of scenes from the Old Testament.

Surrounding the cathedral is the **Close**, the largest and most impressive in the country, a peaceful precinct of lawns and mellow old buildings. Most of the houses have seemly Georgian facades, though some, like the Bishop's Palace and the deanery, date from the thirteenth century. **Mompesson House** (April–Oct Mon–Wed, Sat & Sun noon–5.30pm; £3.40; NT), built by a wealthy merchant in 1701, is a fine example of a Queen Anne house and contains some beautifully furnished eighteenth-century rooms and a superbly carved staircase – the entry price includes a thirty-minute guided tour. The other building to head for in the Close is the **King's House**, in which you'll find the **Salisbury and South Wiltshire Museum** (July & Aug Mon–Sat 10am–5pm, Sun 2–5pm; rest of year closed Sun; £3) – an absorbing account of local history. It includes a good section on Stonehenge and also focuses on the life and times of General Pitt-Rivers, the father of modern archeology, who excavated many of Wiltshire's prehistoric sites, including Avebury (see p.273).

The Close's **North Gate** opens onto the centre's older streets, where narrow pedestrianized alleyways bear names like Fish Row and Salt Lane, indicative of their trading origin. Many half-timbered houses and inns have survived all over the centre, and the last of four market crosses, **Poultry Cross**, stands on stilts in Silver Street, near the Market Square. The market, held on Tuesdays and Saturdays, still serves a large agricultural area, as it did in earlier times when the city grew wealthy on wool. Nearby, the church of **St Thomas** – named after Thomas à Becket – is worth a look inside for its carved timber roof and "Doom painting" over the chancel arch, depicting Christ presiding over the Last Judgment. Dating from 1475, it's the largest of its kind in England. Opposite the church, *Snell's* sells memorable chocolates and cakes.

Lastly, to best appreciate the city's inspiring silhouette – the view made famous by Constable – take a twenty-minute walk through the water meadows southwest of the centre to **Harnham**; the *Old Mill* here serves drinks and modestly priced meals.

Practicalities

Salisbury is a major transport hub, with regular **trains** from London, Exeter, Bristol, Southampton and Portsmouth; National Express **bus** services from London; and local buses to such sights as Stonehenge and Avebury. Trains arrive half a mile west of the centre, on South Western Road; the bus station is a short way north of the Market Place, on Endless Street, with an adjacent office (Mon–Sat 8.15am–5.15pm;

☎01722/336855) providing details of services throughout the region, including tours to Stonehenge and around. For details on all Wiltshire bus routes, ring ☎08457/090899. For a **taxi**, call ☎01722/744744.

The **tourist office** is on Fish Row, just off the Market Place (May, June & Sept Mon–Sat 9.30am–6pm, Sun 10.30am–4.30pm; July & Aug Mon–Sat 9.30am–7pm, Sun 10.30am–5pm; Oct–April Mon–Sat 9.30am–5pm; ☎01722/334956) and is the starting point for informative and inexpensive **guided walks** of the city (daily April–Oct 11am & 6pm; 1hr 30min; £2.50); the tourist office also has details of the Cathedral Walk and Ghost Walk, costing about the same. A.S. Tours (☎01980/862931) runs frequent minibus tours to Stonehenge and Old Sarum (£12); to Stonehenge and Avebury (£20); and to Glastonbury and "King Arthur Country" (£22). If you want to **rent a bike**, go to Hayball's Cycle Shop, 30 Winchester St (☎01722/411378), which charges £9 per day, £55 for a week. There's a dedicated Cycling and Walking Hotline which provides information on itineraries around Salisbury (Mon–Fri 9am–5pm; ☎01980/623255).

Hotels and B&Bs

Byways House, 31 Fowlers Road (☎01722/328364). Victorian house in a quiet location, offering rooms with or without bath. Two rooms have a view of the cathedral. ②.

Clovelly Hotel, 17 Mill Rd (☎01722/322055, *clovelly.hotel@virgin.net*). Good-value hotel close to the train station. ③.

Glen Lyn Guest House, 6 Bellamy Lane, Milford Hill (☎01722/327880, *glen.lyn@btinternet.com*). Elegant Victorian house in quiet lane a ten-minute walk east of the centre. ②.

Grasmere House, 70 Harnham Rd, (☎01722/338388). One of Salisbury's best hotels, this late-Victorian red-brick hotel has a large garden and views over the river to the cathedral. ⑦.

Old Bakery, 35 Bedwin St (☎01722/320100). Oak-beamed city-centre B&B in a five-hundred-year-old building. You can save a few pounds by skipping breakfast. ②.

The Old Bell, 2 St Ann St (☎01722/327958). Attractive inn right opposite St Ann's Gate, near the cathedral. ②.

Old Mill Hotel, Town Path, Harnham (☎01722/327517). Great views across the meadows to the cathedral from this riverside pub with real ales and an adjoining eight-hundred-year-old restaurant; about a mile from the centre. ⑤.

Rose & Crown, Harnham Rd (☎01722/399955). Upmarket riverside hostelry dating from the thirteenth century. ⑥.

Victoria Lodge, 61 Castle Rd (☎01722/320586, *viclodge@interalpha.co.uk*). One of several good-value B&Bs along this main road to Stonehenge. All rooms with bath, and there's a good restaurant, too.③.

Hostels and campsites

Salisbury Camping and Caravanning Club Site, Hudson's Field (☎01722/320713). Well-appointed campsite a mile and a half north of Salisbury close to Old Sarum. Closed Oct to mid-March.

Matt and Tiggy's Hostel, 51 Salt Lane (☎01722/327443). Eighteen beds available in two properties (one a four-hundred-year-old cottage) run by a young couple; expect to pay around £10 for a dorm bed, breakfast available at £1.50 extra, and sheets cost 80p. Close to the bus station.

Youth Hostel, Milford Hill (☎01722/327572, *salisbury@yha.org.uk*). A 220-year-old building in its own spacious grounds, a ten-minute walk east of the cathedral, on Milford Hill. Beds cost £10.15.

Eating and drinking

Bishop's Mill, Bridge St. Popular pub with outdoor seating, right in the city centre. Morland's, Ruddles and Old Speckled Hen beer on tap, and food, tea and coffee available until 7pm.

Café Prague, 2 Salt Lane. Comfortable café-pub behind the bus station, with good atmosphere, mellow sounds and a range of breakfasts and pies served until 7pm.

Harper's, Market Square (☎01722/333118). Serves good-value, traditional English lunches and evening meals. Closed Sun eve in winter. Inexpensive.

Haunch of Venison, Minster St. One of the city's most atmospheric pubs which also serves good food. Look out for the mummified hand of a nineteenth-century card player still clutching his cards.

Michael Snell Tea Rooms St Thomas's Square. Established and popular tearooms in the city centre, with outdoor tables. Closed Sun.

Milford Hall Restaurant, 206 Castle St (☎01722/417411). Good-value restaurant that is part of the eponymous hotel, with set menus for £9.95. Also serves morning coffees and afternoon teas. No smoking. Moderate.

Moloko Café, 5 Bridge St. Cool café and cocktails bar with croissants, panini and salads also available.

Pheasant Inn, Salt Lane. This down at heel but atmospheric fifteenth-century inn serves traditional pub food and good vegetarian dishes. Inexpensive.

Old Sarum and Wilton

The ruins of **Old Sarum** (daily: April–Sept 10am–6pm; Oct 10am–5pm; Nov–March 10am–4pm; £2; EH) occupy a bleak hilltop site two miles north of the city centre – an easy walk, but there are plenty of buses: #3, #5, #7, #8, #9 and #X19 (Sat only). Possibly occupied up to five thousand years ago, then developed as an Iron Age fort whose double protective ditches remain, it was settled by Romans and Saxons before the Norman bishopric of Sherborne was moved here in the 1070s. Within a couple of decades a new cathedral had been consecrated at Old Sarum, and a large religious community was living alongside the soldiers in the central castle. Old Sarum was an uncomfortable place, parched and windswept, and in 1220 the dissatisfied clergy – additionally at loggerheads with the castle's occupants – appealed to the pope for permission to decamp to Salisbury (still known officially as New Sarum). When permission was granted, the stone from the cathedral was commandeered for Salisbury's gateways, and once the church had gone the population waned. By the nineteenth century Old Sarum was deserted, but it continued to exist as a political constituency (William Pitt was one of its representatives). The most notorious of the "rotten boroughs", it returned two MPs at a time to Westminster up until the 1832 Reform Act put a stop to it.

WILTON, five miles west of Salisbury, is renowned for its carpet industry and the splendid **Wilton House** (Easter–Oct daily 10.30am–5.30pm; last entry 1hr before closing; £6.75), of which Daniel Defoe wrote: "One cannot be said to have seen any thing that a man of curiosity would think worth seeing in this county, and not have been at Wilton House." The Tudor house, built for the First Earl of Pembroke on the site of a dissolved Benedictine abbey, was ruined by fire in 1647 and rebuilt by Inigo Jones, whose classic hallmarks can be seen in the sumptuous Single Cube and Double Cube rooms, so called because of their precise dimensions. Sir Philip Sidney, illustrious Elizabethan courtier and poet, wrote part of his magnum opus *Arcadia* here – the dado round the Single Cube Room illustrates scenes from the book – and the Double Cube room was the setting for the ballroom scene in Emma Thompson's film, *Sense and Sensibility*. The easel **paintings** are what makes Wilton really special, however – the collection includes Van Dyck, Rembrandt, two of the Brueghel family, Poussin, Andrea del Sarto and Tintoretto. In the grounds, the famous **Palladian Bridge** has been joined by ancillary attractions including an adventure playground, garden centre and an audiovisual show on the colourful earls of Pembroke, all designed to subsidize a massive programme of structural renovation.

Salisbury Plain and northwards

The Ministry of Defence is the landlord of much of **Salisbury Plain**, the hundred thousand acres of chalky upland to the north of Salisbury. Flags warn casual trespassers away from MoD firing ranges and tank training grounds, while rather stricter security cordons off such secretive establishments as the research centre at Porton Down, Britain's centre for chemical and biological warfare. As elsewhere, the army's presence has ironically saved much of the plain from modern agricultural chemicals, thereby inadvertently nurturing species that are all but extinct in more trampled landscapes.

Though now largely deserted except by forces families living in ugly, temporary-looking barracks quarters, Salisbury Plain once positively throbbed with communities. Stone Age, Bronze Age and Iron Age settlements left hundreds of burial mounds scattered over the chalklands, as well as major complexes at Danebury, Badbury, Figsbury, Old Sarum (see opposite), and, of course, the great circle of **Stonehenge**. North of Salisbury Plain, beyond the A342 Andover–Devizes road, lies the softer Vale of Pewsey, traversed by the Kennet canal. **Marlborough**, to the north of the Vale, is the centre for another cluster of ancient sites, including the huge stone circle of **Avebury**, the mysterious grassy mound of **Silbury Hill** and the chamber graves of **West Kennet**. Malmesbury, though in Wiltshire, is covered in the following chapter (see p.320), as it feels more closely allied to the Cotswolds area than to the rest of its county, from which it's cut off by the M4 and the rail line.

Stonehenge

No ancient structure in England arouses more controversy than **STONEHENGE** (daily mid-March to May & Sept to mid-Oct 9.30am–6pm; June–Aug 9am–7pm; mid-Oct to end Oct 9.30am–5pm; end Oct to mid-March 9.30am–4pm; £4; NT & EH), a mysterious ring of monoliths nine miles north of Salisbury. While archeologists argue over whether it was a place of ritual sacrifice and sun-worship, an astronomical calculator or a royal palace, the guardians of the site struggle to accommodate its year-round crowds who are resentful at no longer being able to walk among the stones. Annual battles between the police and gatherings of druids and New Age travellers trying to celebrate the summer solstice are a thing of the past since the passage of the draconian Criminal Justice Act in 1994 – but the site is nonetheless securely patrolled at that time of year.

Conservation of Stonehenge, one of UNESCO's 380 designated World Heritage Sites, is obviously an urgent priority, and the current custodians are trying to address the dissatisfaction that many feel on visiting this landmark. A new visitors' centre is planned a mile and a half from the stones at Larkhill, and a re-routeing of the nearby roads is projected. In the meantime, visitors are issued with handsets programmed to dispense a range of information on the site – some of the soundtrack is interesting, but much is misleading and patronizing.

What exists today is only a small part of the original prehistoric complex, as many of the outlying stones were plundered by medieval and later farmers for building materials. The construction of Stonehenge is thought to have taken place in several stages. In about 3000 BC the outer circular bank and ditch were constructed, and the massive Heel Stone placed outside the entrance to the central enclosure; just inside the ditch was dug a ring of 56 pits, which at a later date were filled with a mixture of earth and human ash. Around 2100 BC the first stone circle was raised within the earthworks, comprising approximately eighty great blocks of dolerite (bluestone), whose ultimate source was Preseli in Wales. Some archeologists have suggested that these monoliths were found lying on Salisbury Plain, having been borne down from the Welsh mountains by a glacier in the last Ice Age, but the lack of any other glacial debris on the plain would seem to disprove this theory. It really does seem to be the case that the stones were cut from quarries in Preseli and dragged or floated here on rafts, a prodigious task in view of the fact that some are 25ft high and weigh as much as forty tons. Scientists recently claimed to have dated a bluestone's removal from its source, which may finally solve some part of the enigma.

The crucial phase in the creation of the site came in 1500 BC, when the incomplete bluestone circle was transformed by the construction of a circle of twenty-five trilithons (two uprights crossed by a lintel) and an inner horseshoe formation of five trilithons. Hewn from Marlborough Downs sandstone, these colossal stones (called sarsens) were carefully dressed and worked – for example, to compensate for perspectival distortion the uprights have a slight swelling in the middle, the same trick as the builders of the Parthenon were to employ several hundred years later. More bluestones were used to form a small circle and horseshoe within the trilithons, but the purpose of all this work remains baffling. The symmetry and location of the site (a slight rise in a flat valley with even views of the horizon in all directions) as well as its alignment towards the points of sunrise and sunset on the summer and winter solstices tend to support the supposition that it was some sort of observatory or time-measuring device.

There's a lot less charisma about the reputedly significant Bronze Age site of **Woodhenge** (dawn–dusk; free), two miles northwest of Stonehenge. The site consists of a circular bank about 220ft in diameter enclosing a ditch and six concentric rings of post holes, which would originally have held timber uprights, possibly supporting a roofed building of some kind. The holes are now marked more durably if less romantically by concrete pillars. A child's grave was found at the centre of the rings, suggesting that it may have been a place of ritual sacrifice.

Marlborough

An obvious base from which to explore Salisbury Plain is **MARLBOROUGH**, a peaceful spot now that the M4 deflects traffic from the old stagecoach route passing through the town. It's a handsome town too: the wide High Street, a dignified assembly of Georgian buildings, has a fine Perpendicular church standing at each end and half-timbered cottages rambling up the alleyways behind. The famous public school is not especially old – it was established in 1843 – but incorporates an ancient coaching inn among its red-brick buildings.

Marlborough **tourist office** is in the car park on George Lane, accessible from the High Street via Hilliers Yard (Easter–Oct Mon–Sat 10am–5pm, Sun 10.30am–4.30pm; Nov–Easter Mon–Sat 10am–4.30pm; ☎01672/513989) and there are several inns and guesthouses offering **accommodation** along the High Street. Top of the range are *Ivy House* (☎01672/515333; ⑤), the antique *Castle and Ball* (☎01672/515201; minimum two-night stay; ④) and the *Merlin* pub (☎01672/512151; ④). Less expensive options include the B&B at 5 Reeds Ground, London Rd (☎01672/513926; no credit cards; ①), while with your own transport you could try one of a couple of excellent B&Bs outside town: *Clench Farmhouse* (☎01672/810264; no credit cards; ②), an eighteenth-century farmhouse four miles south near Wootton Rivers, or *Rosegarth* in West Grafton (☎01672/810288; no credit cards; ①), seven miles to the southeast. **Eating** is no problem in central Marlborough: the bistro food at *Ivy House* is reasonable, while *Polly Tea Rooms* serves good snacks and ice cream.

If you fancy a woodland walk or picnic, head out southeast of town into **Savernake Forest**, an ancient royal forest of oak and beech, crossed by eight long avenues that converge at its centre. You can walk there in less than thirty minutes, or else take a bus to Great Bledwyn from Marlborough (about every two hours), asking the driver to let you off en route.

Silbury Hill, West Kennet and Avebury

The neat green mound of **Silbury Hill**, five miles west of Marlborough, is probably overlooked by the majority of drivers whizzing by on the A4. At 130ft it's no great height, but when you realize it's the largest prehistoric artificial mound in Europe, and was made by a people using nothing more than primitive spades, it commands more respect. It was probably constructed around 2600 BC, but like so many of the sites of

Salisbury Plain, no one knows quite what it was for, though the likelihood is that it was a burial mound. You can't actually walk on the hill – so having admired it briefly from the car park, cross the road to the footpath that leads half a mile to the **West Kennet Long Barrow**. Dating from about 3250 BC, this was definitely a chamber tomb – nearly fifty burials have been discovered at West Kennet.

Immediately to the west, the village of **AVEBURY** stands in the midst of a **stone circle** (free access; NT & EH) that rivals Stonehenge – the individual stones are generally smaller, but the circle itself is much wider and more complex. A massive earthwork 20 feet high and 1400 feet across encloses the main circle, which is approached by four causeways across the inner ditch, two of them leading into wide avenues stretching over a mile beyond the circle. The best guess is that it was built soon after 2500 BC, and presumably had a similar ritual or religious function to Stonehenge's. The structure of Avebury's diffuse circle is quite difficult to grasp, but there are plans on the site, and you can get an excellent overview at the **Alexander Keiller Museum**, at the western entrance to the site (April–Oct daily 10am–6pm; Nov–March Mon–Sat 10am–4pm; £1.70; NT & EH), which displays excavated material and explanatory information. Nearby, the Great Barn is soon to hold a permanent exhibition of Avebury and the surrounding country. Thus clued up, you can wander round the peaceful circle, accompanied by sheep and cattle grazing unconcernedly among the stones. To the southeast, an avenue of standing stones leads half a mile beyond West Kennet towards a spot known as the Sanctuary, though there is little left to see here.

Back in the placid **village** of Avebury, you might drop into **Avebury Manor** (April–Oct Tues, Wed & Sun 2–5.30pm; £3; NT), behind the Alexander Keiller Museum. This sixteenth-century house – incorporating later alterations – has four or five panelled and plastered rooms, for which you are issued with over-shoes to protect the wooden floors from the chalk dust, and a garden with topiary and medieval walls. House and garden are distinctly low-key attractions, however, and little to do with the spirit of Avebury; you might find it more satisfying poking around the small village, half inside the circle, and having a **snack** or cream tea at *Stone's Restaurant*, or a drink in the *Red Lion* pub which also serves reasonable meals as well as providing a few rooms should you wish to **stay** over (☎01672/539266; ②). There's a **tourist office** (☎01672/539425) currently housed in a Portakabin near the Great Barn, but soon to move to a permanent office. Good bus routes connect Avebury with Salisbury, Marlborough and Devizes, and A.S. Tours runs guided trips here from Salisbury four times weekly (see p.269).

Devizes

DEVIZES, seven miles down the A361 from Avebury at the mouth of the Vale of Pewsey, is a pleasant place, with some attractive eighteenth-century houses, a stately semicircular market place and a couple of fine churches, St Mary's and St John's. It's chiefly worth a stop, however, for the excellent **Museum** at 41 Long St (Mon–Sat 10am–5pm; £2, free Mon), housing an exceptional collection of prehistoric finds from barrows and henges throughout the county. Star exhibit is the so-called Marlborough Bucket, decorated with bronze reliefs from the first century BC.

The town offers some appealing nooks to explore: seek out the timbered and jettied row of Elizabethan-era houses on the cobbled St John's Alley, tucked away behind St John's Street. Out of town, you can enjoy a pleasant canalside stroll along the **Kennet and Avon Canal** which boasts 29 locks at Caen Hill, about a ninety-minute walk heading westwards, but easily cyclable too.

Devizes has a very helpful **tourist office** at Cromwell House, Market Place (Mon–Sat 9.30am–5pm; ☎01380/729408). The best place **to stay** is the *Castle Hotel*, on New Park Street, a former coaching inn with a bar and restaurant (☎01380/729300; ④);

less expensive are the *Craven* B&B Station Rd (☎01380/723514; no credit cards; ①), where all the rooms are en suite; and the *White Bear Inn*, Monday Market St (☎01380/722583; no credit cards; ①). For **eating**, try the *Wiltshire Kitchen*, St John's St, which serves good lunches and snacks, as does the *The Cheesecake* in Market Place. Also in Market Place, you'll find *Seafoods Restaurant,* a fish-and-chip takeaway which also provides more substantial sit-down meals at cheap prices.

Lacock and around

LACOCK, ten miles northwest of Devizes, is the perfect English feudal village, albeit one gentrified by the National Trust to within a hair's breadth of natural life, and besieged by tourists all summer. Appropriately for so photogenic a spot, it has a fascinating museum dedicated to the founding father of photography, Henry Fox Talbot, a member of the dynasty which has lived in the local **Abbey** since it passed to Sir William Sharington on the Dissolution of the Monasteries in 1539. Ten years later Sharington was arrested for colluding with Thomas Seymour, Treasurer of the Mint, in a plot to subvert the coinage: he narrowly escaped with his life by shopping his partner in crime – who was beheaded – and after a period of disgrace managed to buy back his estates. His descendant, William Henry Fox Talbot, was the first to produce a photographic negative, and the **Fox Talbot Museum**, in a sixteenth-century barn by the abbey gates, (March–Oct daily 11am–5.30pm; Nov–Feb Sat & Sun 11am–4pm; £3.60; NT), captures something of the excitement he must have experienced as the dim outline of an oriel window in the abbey steadily imprinted itself on a piece of silver nitrate paper. The postage-stamp-sized result is on display in the museum. The **abbey** itself (April–Oct Wed–Mon 1–5.30pm; £3.60; £5.70 including museum; NT), preserves a few monastic fragments amid the eighteenth-century Gothic, while the church of **St Cyriac** (free access) contains the opulent tomb of the nefarious Sir William Sharington, buried beneath a splendid barrel-vaulted roof.

The village's delightfully Chaucerian-sounding hostelry, *At the Sign of the Angel*, is a good, if expensive, **hotel** and **restaurant** (☎01249/730230; ⑥).

Corsham Court and Bowood House

The main sight within a short drive of Lacock is **Corsham Court** (April–Oct Tues–Sun 11am–5.30pm; Nov & Jan–March Sat & Sun 2–4.30pm; £4.50), three miles west. It dates from Elizabethan times, though what you see now bears the Georgian stamp of Nash and Capability Brown, and the house contains a fine collection of art, including pieces by Caravaggio, Rubens, Reynolds and Michelangelo. The village of **Corsham** is another dignified little cloth-making town of Bath stone, riddled with underground limestone quarries and a long railway tunnel engineered by Brunel.

Ten miles east of Corsham, off the A342 Chippenham–Devizes road and just outside the village of Calne, **Bowood House** (April–Oct daily 11am–5.30pm; £5.50) was designed in the eighteenth century by, among others, Henry Keene, Charles Barry and Robert Adam. Adam was primarily responsible for the great south front and the Orangery, and, inside the house, the library – though the present appearance of this owes more to Charles Robert Cockerell, architect of Oxford's Ashmolean Museum, who also built the Neoclassical chapel. But it is the magnificent grounds of Bowood that are the real draw, with rhododendron gardens, a Doric temple on the banks of its placid lake and a waterfall in the woods; there's also an adventure playground for kids, and a restaurant.

Bradford on Avon and around

With its buildings of mellow auburn stone, reminiscent of the townscapes just over the county border in Bath and the Cotswolds, **BRADFORD ON AVON** is the most appealing town in the northwest corner of Wiltshire, offering far more than the dull county town of Trowbridge, or the slightly more distant Chippenham and Warminster. Sheltering against a steep wooded slope, it takes its name from its "broad ford" across the Avon, though the original fording place was replaced in the thirteenth century by a **bridge** that was in turn largely rebuilt in the seventeenth century. The domed structure at one end is a quaint old jail converted from a chapel.

The local industry, based on textiles like that of its Yorkshire namesake, was revolutionized with the arrival of Flemish weavers in 1659, and many of the town's handsome buildings reflect the prosperity of this period. Yet Bradford's most significant building is the tiny **St Laurence Church** on Church Street, an outstanding example of Saxon architecture dating from about 700 AD. Wrecked by Viking invaders, and later used as a school and a simple dwelling, it was rehabilitated by a local vicar in 1856. Its distinctive features are the carved angels over the chancel arch.

Trains call regularly at Bradford from Weymouth, Dorchester, Bath and Bristol; the **train station** is on St Margaret's Street close to the town centre, while regular **bus** services from Bath, Trowbridge and Frome arrive at town bridge. **Bike rental** is available at *Lock Inn Cottage*, 48 Frome Rd (☎01225/868068), for £10 a day. The well-equipped **tourist office** lies near the bridge at 34 Silver St (daily: April–Oct 10am–5pm; Nov–March 10am–4pm; ☎01225/865797). Bradford has a good range of **accommodation**, none more characterful than *Bradford Old Windmill*, a B&B up the hill at 4 Mason's Lane (☎01225/866842; ⑤), where an imaginative vegetarian menu is served house-party style; winter opening is irregular. *Priory Steps*, closer to the centre on Newtown (☎01225/862230; ⑤), is a family home with bags of personality, well-prepared dinners and excellent views over a roofscape of weavers' cottages. The *Riverside Inn*, 49 St Margaret's St (☎01225/863526; ②), lives up to its name, with private facilities in all rooms. For light lunches or cakes, try the *Bridge Tea Rooms* on Bridge Street, or *Scribbling Horse* at 34 Silver St. For alcohol or more substantial food, head for the *Bunch of Grapes* **pub** on Silver Street, also a venue for jazz, folk and blues every other Tuesday.

Great Chalfield

Great Chalfield Manor (guided tours April–Oct Tues–Thurs 12.15pm, 2.15pm, 3pm, 3.45pm & 4.30pm; £3.60; NT), two and a half miles northeast of Bradford, is a splendid moated complex of house, church and outbuildings dating from about 1470, sensitively restored at the beginning of the century as a family home. The exterior looks like a typical Cotswold manor, all gables and mullions; inside, the Great Hall is overlooked by a minstrels' gallery from which three gargoyle-like masks gaze down into the hall, the eyes cut away so that the womenfolk could inspect the proceedings below without jeopardizing their modesty. The interior of the church features some fifteenth-century wall paintings.

travel details

Trains

Bournemouth to: Brockenhurst (3 hourly; 25min); Dorchester (hourly; 40min); London (2 hourly; 1hr 45min–2hr); Poole (2–4 hourly; 10–15min); Southampton (3 hourly; 30min); Weymouth (hourly; 1hr); Winchester (3 hourly; 1hr).

Dorchester to: Bournemouth (hourly; 40min); Brockenhurst (hourly; 1hr); London (hourly; 2hr 30min); Weymouth (hourly; 10min).

Portsmouth to: Guildford (2 hourly; 1hr); London (3 hourly; 1hr 30min–2hr); Southampton (2 hourly; 40–50min); Winchester (hourly; 1hr).

Ryde (Isle of Wight) to: Shanklin (2 hourly; 30min).

Salisbury to: Exeter (10 daily; 1hr 45min); London (hourly; 1hr 30min); Portsmouth (hourly; 1hr 15min); Southampton (2 hourly; 30min).

Southampton to: Bournemouth (3 hourly; 30min); Bristol (hourly; 1hr 50min); Brockenhurst (2 hourly; 15min); London (2 hourly; 1hr 15min); Portsmouth (2 hourly; 40–50min); Salisbury (2 hourly; 30min); Weymouth (hourly; 1hr 30min); Winchester (4 hourly; 20min).

Winchester to: Bournemouth (3 hourly; 1hr); London (2 hourly; 1hr–1hr 30min); Portsmouth (hourly; 1hr); Southampton (2 hourly; 20min).

Buses

Bournemouth to: London (hourly; 2hr 30min); Lyndhurst (8 daily; 1hr 30min); Poole (6 hourly; 20min).

Dorchester to: Bournemouth (3 daily; 1hr 15min); London (3 daily; 3hr–4hr 40min); Poole (4 daily; 1hr 15min); Salisbury (2 daily; 1hr 45min); Weymouth (every 15min; 30min).

Lymington to: Beaulieu (6 daily; 40min).

Lyndhurst to: Bournemouth (7 daily; 1hr 20min); Southampton (hourly; 30min–1hr).

Poole to: Bournemouth (6 hourly; 20min); Corfe (hourly; 1hr).

Portsmouth to: Brighton (2 daily; 1hr 40min–2hr); London (10 daily; 2hr 30min); Southampton (hourly; 30min); Winchester (hourly; 1hr 40min).

Salisbury to: Bath (Mon–Sat hourly; 2hr); Bristol (1 daily; 2hr); London (2–3 daily; 2hr 30min–3hr); Poole (5 daily; 1hr 40min); Stonehenge (hourly; 40min).

Southampton to: Bristol (1 daily; 2hr 45min); Exeter (2 daily; 4hr 15min–5hr 15min); London (hourly; 2hr 30min); Winchester (3 hourly; 50min).

Weymouth to: Dorchester (4 hourly; 30min).

Winchester to: London (7 daily; 2hr); Portsmouth (hourly; 1hr 40min); Southampton (3 hourly; 50min).

Ferries and Hovercraft

Lymington to: Yarmouth, Isle of Wight (1–2 hourly; 30min).

Poole to: Cherbourg (Jan–Nov 1–2 daily; 4hr 15min); Jersey (1 daily May to mid-Oct; 3hr 45min) Guernsey (1 daily May to mid-Oct; 2hr 30min).

Portsmouth to: Bilbao (2 weekly; 11hr); Caen (Jan to mid-Nov 2–3 daily; 6hr); Cherbourg (up to 7 daily; 5hr); Fishbourne, Isle of Wight (2 hourly; 40min); Le Havre (2–3 daily; 6hr); Ryde, Isle of Wight (1–2 hourly; 15min); St Malo (1 daily Jan to mid-Nov; 8hr 45min).

Southampton to: East Cowes, Isle of Wight (March to early Jan hourly; 1hr); West Cowes, Isle of Wight (March–Dec 2 hourly; 20min).

Southsea To: Ryde, Isle Of Wight (2–4 hourly;10min).

Weymouth to: St Malo (May to mid-Oct 1 daily; 5hr); Jersey (May to mid-Oct 1 daily; 3hr 15min) Guernsey (May to mid-Oct 1 daily; 2hr).

CHAPTER FOUR

FROM LONDON
TO THE SEVERN

S outhern central England, the slab of land running west **from London to the River Severn**, is a disparate region of Roman towns and new towns, tree-clad hills and rolling downs, encompassing no fewer than six counties. The chief physical link within this swathe of England is the **River Thames**, whose 215-mile course from its source in the western Cotswolds makes it the second longest river in the country. Transport routes create a further continuity, the oldest of them being the **Ridgeway**, a prehistoric track – and now a national trail – running northeast from Wiltshire and continuing along the length of the Chiltern Hills. Of more practical use to the majority of visitors, the M40/A40 slices right through the heart of the region, linking London to Gloucester via Oxford and the Cotswolds, while the M4 motorway and the rail line between London and Bristol marks the region's approximate southern edge. Densely populated, this is one (especially well-heeled) part of England where remote and "undiscovered" spots are thin on the ground.

Of the places covered in this chapter, a prime target is Hertfordshire's **St Albans**, an ancient and dignified town with Roman remains and a superb cathedral – but marooned amidst a knot of motorways and new towns on the fringes of London. These new towns – places like **Welwyn Garden City** and **Hemel Hempstead** – have little obvious appeal, but there are a few surprises hereabouts, not least **Hatfield House**, one of the country's finest ancestral homes. Neighbouring Bedfordshire, mostly flat agricultural land with a hint of industrial Midlands, is not a county you'd cross England to visit, but **Bedford** is a good stopping-off place, amidst quiet and pleasant villages.

Though **Milton Keynes** is worth seeing as a curiosity of modern urban design, the best of adjacent **Buckinghamshire** lies in the **Chiltern Hills**. These picturesque chalk uplands, with their heavy covering of beech trees, rise near Luton, beside the M1, and stretch south-west across Buckinghamshire before petering out at the Thames in Oxfordshire. The range

---

ACCOMMODATION PRICE CODES

Throughout this guide, hotel and B&B accommodation is priced on a scale of ① to ⑨, the number indicating the **lowest price** you could expect to pay per night in that establishment for a **double room** in high season. The prices indicated by the codes are as follows:

① under £40	④ £60–70	⑦ £110–150
② £40–50	⑤ £70–90	⑧ £150–200
③ £50–60	⑥ £90–110	⑨ over £200

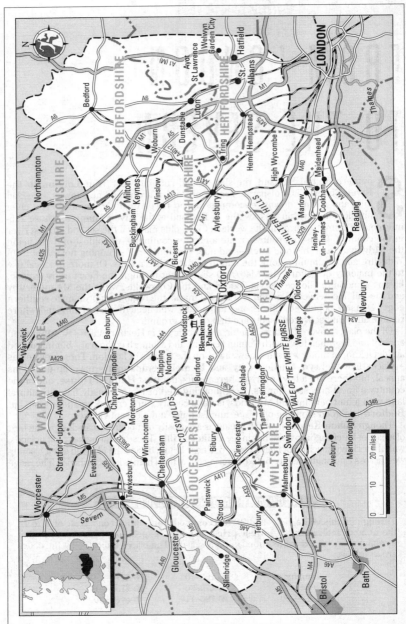

© Crown copyright

provides some of the best walking in the region, chiefly around **Marlow** and **Henley-on-Thames**, either of which makes a convenient base, with the tiny villages that dot the Chilterns possessing a scattering of accommodation too. **Berkshire**, which extends west from the M25 to just beyond Newbury, is blighted in its eastern part by workaday towns such as **Reading** and Slough, though the former does host two of the most prestigious rock festivals in Europe. By contrast, the Berkshire Downs, divided from the Chilterns by the Thames but linked to them by the Ridgeway, stretch west beyond the county boundary to include the **Vale of White Horse**, one of the highlights of this whole region.

Bordering Berkshire to the north, **Oxfordshire** is firmly centred on its county town. With its ancient university, superb museums and lively student population, **Oxford** can keep you busy for days, and it's an excellent base for the **Cotswolds**, which lie mostly in **Gloucestershire**. Throughout the Cotswolds, beautifully preserved mansions and churches attest to the fortunes made through the medieval wool trade, and the remarkable continuity of Cotswold architecture has created villages as attractive as any in England, though the tourist deluge makes some spots nightmarish in summer. Tourism is less of a nuisance in the southern areas of the Cotswolds, around the busy working towns of **Cirencester** and **Stroud**, and of course there's plenty of good walking country in which to escape the crowds.

In the west, the land drops sharply from the Cotswold escarpment down to **Cheltenham**, an elegant Regency spa town most famous these days for its horse racing. It's a rather staid place, however, with much less to offer than **Gloucester**, with its superb cathedral and rejuvenated docklands. From here, the Vale of Gloucester follows the route of the **River Severn** northeast towards Worcestershire, the stone cottages of the Cotswolds giving way to the thatched, half-timbered and redbrick houses which are characteristic of **Tewkesbury**, a solidly provincial town with a superb abbey.

The line between London's Paddington station and Bristol provides the backbone of the **rail network** through this region, with branch lines running north from Reading, Maidenhead, Didcot and Swindon. Trains from King's Cross, St Pancras, Euston and Marylebone stations serve the northeasterly area, including St Albans, Bedford and the northern Chilterns. The area covered in this chapter is threaded by four motorways, the M1, M40, M4 and M25, giving swift access from all sides, whether by private car or **bus**.

St Albans

ST ALBANS is one of the most appealing towns on the peripheries of London, its well-blended medley of medieval and modern features grafted onto the site of Verulamium, the town founded by the Romans soon after the invasion of 43 AD. Boudicca and her followers burned this settlement to the ground eighteen years later, but reconstruction was swift and the town grew into a major administrative base. It was here, in 209 AD, that a Roman soldier became the country's first Christian martyr when he was beheaded for giving shelter to a priest. Pilgrims later flocked to the town that had come to bear his name, where the place of execution was marked by a hilltop cathedral, once one of the largest churches in the Christian world.

Not just a religious centre, St Albans also flourished as a trading town and a staging post on the route to London from the north, its economy further buttressed by two local industries, brewing and straw-hat-making. In the nineteenth century, the coaching trade faded away with the coming of the railways, but when St Albans was connected to London by train in 1868, it rapidly reinvented itself as a prosperous and pleasant commuter town, a description that fits it well today.

St Albans' best-known attraction is its **cathedral**, but the town also possesses the outstanding **Verulamium Museum**, home to several breathtaking Roman mosaics, as well as a likeable riverside park and a number of charming old streets. All the town's main sights are within easy walking distance of each other, making St Albans an ideal day out, but if you do decide to stay the night be sure to try out some of the excellent pubs.

The City

You can begin a tour of the city by climbing the 93 steps to the top of the fifteenth-century **Clock Tower** on the High Street (Easter to Sept Sat & Sun 10.30am–4.30pm; 30p), a tight squeeze but worth it for the view. The colossal brick and flint **Cathedral** (daily 9am–5.30pm; £2.50 donation requested), looming to the south, is accessible down a narrow passageway across from the foot of the tower. An abbey was constructed here in 1077, on the site of a Saxon abbey founded by King Offa of Mercia, and despite subsequent alterations – including the ugly nineteenth-century west front – the legacy of the Normans remains the most impressive aspect. The sheer scale of their design is breathtaking: the nave, almost 300-foot long, is the longest medieval nave in Britain, even if it isn't the most harmonious – the massive Norman pillars on the north side stand out from those in the later Early English style opposite. Some of the Norman pillars retain thirteenth- and fourteenth-century paintings, the detail clear though the ochre colours are much faded. Two- and three-tone geometric designs decorate the Norman arches in the nave and at the central crossing, where the impact of the original design reaches its peak with the mighty Norman tower. Behind the high altar an elaborate stone reredos (a clumsy construction compared with the splendid Gothic rood screen) hides Saint Alban's fourteenth-century shrine. The tomb was smashed up during the Dissolution, but the Victorians discovered the pieces and gamely put them all together again. Some of the carving on the Purbeck marble is now remarkably clear – look out for the scene on the west end depicting the saint's martyrdom.

A few yards to the west of the cathedral's main entrance, the **abbey gateway** is the only other part of the original complex to have survived the Dissolution. From here, Abbey Mill Lane leads down past the *Fighting Cocks* (one of the oldest pubs in the country) and across the trickle of the River Ver to **Verulamium Park**, whose sloping lawns and duck-happy ponds occupy the site of the Roman city. The park holds a scattering of Roman remains – primarily fragments of the old Roman wall and the remains of a town house with its underfloor heating system (hypocaust) – but these are hardly riveting. Instead, follow the signs to the **Verulamium Museum** (Mon–Sat 10am–5pm, Sun 2–5pm; £3), which occupies an attractive circular building on the northern edge of the park. Inside, a series of well-conceived displays illustrate and explain life in Roman Britain, but these are eclipsed by the **mosaic** room, containing five wonderful floor mosaics unearthed here on the site of Verulamium in the 1930s and 1950s. Dated to about 200AD, the *Sea God Mosaic* has created its share of academic debate, with some arguing it depicts a god of nature with stag antler horns rather than a sea god with lobster claws, but there's no disputing the subject of the *Lion Mosaic*, in which a lion carries the bloodied head of a stag in its jaws. The most beautiful of the five is the *Shell Mosaic*, a simply gorgeous work of art whose semicircular design depicts a beautifully crafted scallop shell within a border made up of rolling waves.

Close by, the **Verulamium Theatre** (April–Sept daily 10am–5pm; Oct–March 10am–4pm; £1.50), across the busy road from the museum, was built around 140 AD but reduced to the status of municipal rubbish dump by the fifth century. It's nothing but a small hollow in comparison with the Colosseum, but the site is impressive if only for the fact that nothing else quite like it exists in Britain. From here, you can walk back to the centre along St **Michael's Street**, over one of the prettier stretches of the Ver, past a sixteenth-century watermill (now a museum and café; Easter–Oct Tues–Sat 11am–6pm, Sun noon–6pm; Nov–Easter closes 4.45pm; free), and up the gently curving **Fishpool Street**, a quiet road lined with medieval inns and handsome Georgian houses.

On the other side of the city centre, off the northern end of St Peter's Street, Hatfield Road is home to the **City Museum** (Mon–Sat 10am–5pm, Sun 2–5pm; free), which provides a thorough history of St Albans from Boudicca to the building of the M25. You can also learn about Matthew Paris, the most famous occupant of St Albans abbey – his chronicles, covering events before and during his own lifetime in the thirteenth century, are some of the wittiest and most detailed written in medieval Europe. The museum uses reproductions of some of his manuscripts to tell the city's early history, including an illustration of the martyrdom of Alban which leaves absolutely nothing to the imagination.

Practicalities

Trains bound for Bedford from London King's Cross arrive at St Albans' City Station, from where it's a ten-minute walk up the hill to the main drag, St Peter's Street. Trains from Euston serve the small Abbey Station a similar distance from the centre at the bottom of Holywell Hill, a southerly continuation of St Peter's Street. Most **buses** terminate at City Station, but virtually all services stop along St Peter's Street too. The **tourist office** is in the Town Hall, on the Market Place at the bottom of St Peter's Street (Easter–Oct Mon–Sat 9.30am–5.30pm; Nov–Easter Mon–Sat 10am–4pm; ☎01727/864511).

As for accommodation, there are several inexpensive **B&Bs** near City Station, including the *Care Inns*, 29 Alma Rd (☎01727/867310; no credit cards; ②), a Victorian house with three comfortable and attractively furnished en-suite bedrooms. Fishpool Street is, however, a much prettier spot to head for and it's here you'll find the pleasant *Black Lion Inn*, at no. 198 (☎01727/851786; ②), an ancient pub with sixteen agreeable rooms. Indeed, you can't move for **pubs** in St Albans – the Campaign for Real Ale has its headquarters here, and seems to have a benign influence. Benskins is, by most accounts, the brew to look for. *The Goat*, on Sopwell Lane off Holywell Hill, serves some of the best food (not Fri–Sun eve) and beer in town, and has jazz on Sunday lunchtimes, while the *Blue Anchor*, on Fishpool Street, is a more solidly local pub with an open fire in winter and garden seating in summer. The antique *Fighting Cocks*, on Abbey Mill Lane, has been chopped around a bit and does get mightily crowded on sunny summer days, but still has lots of enjoyable nooks and crannies to nurse a pint. As for **restaurants**, the low prices at *La Cosa Nostra*, a no-nonsense Italian place at 62 Lattimore Rd (☎01727/832658; closed Sun), off Victoria Street out near City Station, is a popular spot, and the best Indian restaurant in town is the moderately priced *New Gulshan Tandoori*, 141 Victoria St (☎01727/830201).

Around St Albans

St Albans lies just five minutes' drive outside the M25 and is flanked by the M1 and A1. The best day-trips take you away from the traffic, where you can find pockets of Hertfordshire which are thoroughly unsuburban – to the east **Hatfield House** and to the north, **Ayot St Lawrence**, site of George Bernard Shaw's old home, **Shaw's Corner**.

Hatfield House and Hatfield town

Hatfield House, six miles east of St Albans (late March to late Sept Tues–Thurs & Sat noon–4pm, Sun 1–4.30pm; £6), is one of the most impressive houses in England. Henry VIII and his heirs used the original building as a country retreat, though for Elizabeth, kept here by her half-sister Mary, it was more a prison than a home. James I, on inheriting the throne, decided he disliked Hatfield and did a house-swap with his chief minister, Sir Robert Cecil. The new owner, fancying himself as an architect, proceeded to destroy most of the Tudor house, but he died in 1612 shortly before the completion of his work. Cecil's descendants still live here.

From the awesome brick exterior to the dark wood panelling inside, Hatfield House has a grand and heavy atmosphere, but some magnificent Tudor and Jacobean portraits bring the **interior** alive, supplying a roll call of the important people of the day. Elizabeth I provides a central theme, her memorabilia including a pair of the queen's silk stockings and an extraordinary pedigree tracing her descent from Adam and Eve via Noah and King Lear. The banqueting hall survives from the Tudor building but is rarely open, being used mainly for "Elizabethan banquets". The extensive grounds include part of the **formal gardens** laid out by John Tradescant, the greatest gardener ever engaged by the Stuarts.

Hatfield House can be reached easily on public transport. Its entrance is opposite the train station of **HATFIELD** town, on the King's Cross–Cambridge line, and frequent local buses run from here to St Albans, the surrounding towns and also to London. At first sight Hatfield smacks of suburbia, but the old centre – a short walk south of the station – is well worth exploring. Climb the steep Fore Street to the **church**, which has a window by the Pre-Raphaelite artist Edward Burne-Jones, and the tomb of Sir Robert Cecil, a macabre affair with Cecil's effigy resting over a skeleton. The *Eight Bells* pub at the bottom of Fore Street serves a good pint and a reasonable lunch.

Ayot St Lawrence and Shaw's Corner

The tiny village of **AYOT ST LAWRENCE**, hiding among gentle hills in one of the prettiest corners of Hertfordshire, boasts the romantic ruins of a Gothic church and a fine pub, but its fame stems from its association with **George Bernard Shaw**, who lived in the house known as **Shaw's Corner** from 1906 until his death in 1950. The house (April–Oct Wed–Sun 1–5pm; £3.30; NT) has been left much as it was – Shaw's fans may be particularly delighted at the chance to have a pee in the playwright's loo. The shed at the bottom of the garden, where Shaw used to write, is little more than a cell, the only luxuries being a telephone and the hut's ability to revolve in order to maximize the available sunlight.

Ayot St Lawrence lies nine miles northeast of St Albans, accessible along some of the county's narrowest lanes. The closest public transport gets is Wheathampstead (B653), two miles to the west and served by weekday buses from Hatfield, St Albans and other nearby towns.

Bedford and around

The untidy landscapes of Bedfordshire herald a transition between the satellite towns of London and the Midlands. The county's most distinctive feature is the wriggling River Ouse, whose banks were once lined with dozens of watermills, though these were not nearly as important as the brickworks that long underpinned the local economy. For the casual visitor, the county might not warrant a major detour, but **Bedford** itself deserves more than just a sideward glance, if for no other reason than for its links with John Bunyan. It is also within easy striking distance by car of **Woburn Abbey and Safari Park** as well as **Milton Keynes**, a sprawling new town just across the county boundary in Buckinghamshire.

Thirty miles north of St Albans, **BEDFORD** epitomizes the county, struggling to retain a modicum of character in the face of redevelopment. The town need not detain you long, but it has an excellent art gallery, and makes the most of its connections with **John Bunyan**, a seventeenth-century blaspheming tinker turned Nonconformist preacher, who lived most of his life in and around Bedford. Bunyan fought for Parliament in the Civil War and became a well-known public speaker during Cromwell's Protectorate, but the Restoration proved disastrous for him. In 1660, he was arrested for breaking Charles II's new religious legislation, which restricted the activities of Nonconformist preachers. Bunyan spent most of the next seventeen years in Bedford prison, where he wrote *The Pilgrim's Progress*, a seminal text whose simple language and powerful allegories were to have a profound influence on generations of

Nonconformists. The **Bunyan Meeting Free Church** on Mill Street (Tues–Sat 10am–4pm) was built in the 1840s on the spot where Bunyan organized his Independent Congregation after his release from prison. The building still functions as a Nonconformist church and its splendid bronze doors have ten finely worked panels depicting scenes from *Pilgrim's Progress*. The adjacent **Bunyan Museum** (March–Nov Tues–Sat 11am–4pm; free) has more on the book and its author's life and times.

Near by, the **Cecil Higgins Art Gallery**, in Castle Close (Tues–Sat 11am–5pm & Sun 2–5pm; free), is perhaps of more general interest, its wide-ranging collection featuring porcelain, glass and local lace. There's also a first-rate watercolour and print collection as well as a display on Victorian life. The latter includes the extraordinary Burges Room, a colourful fantasy of fake-medieval decoration created by William Burges, one of the leading figures in the Gothic Revival movement.

Practicalities

Bedford lies on the London St Pancras–Sheffield rail line, and most **trains** arrive at Midland station, from where it's a ten-minute walk east to the centre. **Buses** arrive at the station on All Hallows, a brief stroll west across the pedestrianized shopping area from the High Street. The **tourist office** is located at 10 St Paul's Square, in the same pedestrianized area (Mon–Sat 9.30am–5pm, Sun 11am–3pm; ☎01234/215226).

For **accommodation** you needn't look beyond De Pary's Avenue, a short walk north of the centre along the High Street. There are a string of **B&Bs** here, including the straightforward *De Pary's Guest House* at no. 48 (☎01234/261982; ①). The *Swan*, down on the Embankment beside the River Ouse (☎01234/346565; ⑨), is the town's most famous **hotel** and merits at least a peek – its main staircase was designed by Christopher Wren. Bedford's large Italian community adds a bit of zip to the local **restaurant** scene. There are two good places on Newnham Street, a short walk east of the High Street along Mill Street, the *Pizzeria Santaniello*, at no. 9, which serves some of the tastiest pizzas and pasta in town, and the *Bar Cappuccino*, at no. 36, where they sell good coffees and Italian ice creams as well as pizzas and other snacks.

Woburn Abbey and Safari Park

Fourteen miles southwest of Bedford, the grandiloquent Georgian facade of **Woburn Abbey** (guided tours: late March to Sept Mon–Sat 11am–4pm & Sun 11am–5pm; Jan to late March & Oct Sat & Sun 11am–4pm; house & grounds £7; half price if you've already paid to get into the safari park) overlooks a huge area of parkland just to the east of the eponymous village. Called an "abbey" since it was built on the site of a Cistercian foundation, the house is the ancestral pile of the dukes of Bedford, whom Queen Victoria once dismissed as a dull lot. Judging from the family's penchant for canine portraits, she may have had a point, but the lavish state rooms also contain some wonderful paintings, including an exquisite set of **Tudor portraits** hanging in the Long Gallery, most notably the famous *Armada Portrait* of Elizabeth I by George Gower. Elsewhere are works by Van Dyck, Velazquez, Gainsborough and Rembrandt, whilst Reynolds and Canaletto each have a room to themselves.

You can explore the grounds immediately around the house on foot, but only motorists can enter the part given over to **Woburn Safari Park** (March–Oct daily 10am–dusk; Nov–Feb Sat & Sun 11am–3pm; £11.50 in summer; £6.50 rest of year; half price if you've already paid to get into the abbey), the largest drive-through wildlife reserve in Britain. The animals include endangered species such as the African white rhino and bongo antelope, and appear to be in excellent health. A posse of guards tours around on the lookout for drivers in distress, but the main danger is an overheated engine rather than an attack by an enraged animal. The Safari Park is extraordinarily popular and in high season the traffic can achieve rush-hour congestion, so turn up as early as possible for a quieter experience.

Milton Keynes

MILTON KEYNES, fourteen miles southwest of Bedford and six miles northwest of Woburn, is Britain's largest new town, but it wasn't built from scratch – in fact it swallowed up thirteen existing villages. These old communities have been left virtually intact, but they are now very much an appendage to the modern industrial and commercial nucleus, encircled by a web of bypasses. The town represents the epitome of 1960s planning, and nowhere else in the country has been conceived so obviously with the convenience of the motorist in mind. The network of footpaths and subways, which totally separates pedestrians from traffic, makes getting about relatively easy for those without cars, but you can't really walk around the town simply because it is so dispersed, covering an area of almost fifty square miles. From its inception, Milton Keynes has attracted wildly differing reviews. For some, the town was an unfolding horror story of hi-tech madness which discarded all the traditions of the English town, for others it was a prosperous way forward that left the terraced slums of the inner city far behind. Both have elements of truth, but the end result has little to entice the casual visitor and – as it has turned out – has even failed to lure enough business: more than a quarter of a century after its foundation, a chunk of the city is still awaiting development, and only the area around the huge shopping centre, bounded by Midsummer and Avebury boulevards, lives up to its popular image of grid-plan streets and an almost clinical tidiness. If you do visit, the town is seen to best advantage by walking or cycling along the **Grand Union Canal**, which runs through here on its way from London to the industrial Midlands.

Trains arrive at Central Station to the west, with direct links from London Euston and Birmingham. **Buses** terminate at Coach Way, but virtually all services stop on Midsummer Boulevard and at the train station. Milton Keynes **tourist office**, a few minutes' walk east of the train station (Mon–Fri 9.30am–5pm, Sat 9.30am–4pm; ☎01908/232525), has town maps and a comprehensive list of local accommodation.

Buckingham and around

The unassuming market town of **BUCKINGHAM** overlooks a sharp bend in the River Ouse about twenty-five miles southwest of Bedford. The town centre is at its prettiest amongst the higgledy-piggledy streets edging Market Hill, where the **Old Gaol Museum** (Mon–Sat 10am–4pm; £1) focuses on local history and has an imaginative programme of temporary exhibitions. Otherwise, Buckingham is short of sights, though there is a pleasant footpath running along sections of the Ouse and the town is only a short drive from three National Trust properties – **Stowe Landscape Gardens**, **Claydon House** and **Waddesdon Manor**.

There is no train service to Buckingham, but there are frequent bus links from all the surrounding towns, including Milton Keynes and Northampton. **Buses** drop passengers close to Market Hill, the site of the **tourist office** (July & Aug Mon–Sat 10am–4pm, Sun 10am–4pm; rest of year Mon–Sat 10am–4pm; ☎01280/823020), which shares its premises with the Old Gaol Museum. The best **hotel** in town is the *Villiers*, 3 Castle St (☎01280/822113; ⑤), a spick-and-span, medium-sized place at the foot of Market Hill.

Stowe Landscape Gardens

Just three miles northwest of Buckingham off the A422 Banbury road, **Stowe Landscape Gardens** (late March to mid-April, July & Aug daily 10am–5pm or dusk;

mid-April to June, Sept & Oct Mon, Wed, Fri & Sun 10am–5pm or dusk; £4.50; NT) contain an extraordinary collection of outdoor sculptures and decorative buildings by some of the greatest designers and architects of the eighteenth century, working for the Temple and Grenville families and later the dukes of Buckingham and Chandos. This ornamental miscellany has a partly naturalistic setting, representing one of the first breaks with the strictly formal garden tradition that had dominated Europe for decades. On display is work by Sir John Vanbrugh, James Gibbs and William Kent, and the grounds incorporate one of only three Palladian bridges in the country, as well as the "Grecian valley" that was Capability Brown's first large-scale design. The curious obelisk surmounted by a monkey that stands on an island in the middle of the Octagonal Lake is a monument to the dramatist William Congreve, erected in 1736 by William Kent.

The irregular opening hours reflect the fact that the main house has been occupied by Stowe school since 1923.

Claydon House and Waddesdon Manor

One of the region's least spoilt buildings, **Claydon House** lies five miles south of Buckingham in Middle Claydon (April–Oct Sat–Wed 1–5pm; £4.10; NT). A deceptively plain Neoclassical facade conceals an exuberant Rococo interior, commissioned in the eighteenth century by the second earl Verney and said to be the only work of a craftsman called Lightfoot. The intricacy of his woodcarving peaks in the Chinese Room – one of the finest examples of chinoiserie in Britain – where the ornamentation drips like icing. An adjacent room contains mementoes of the Verney family and of Florence Nightingale, who spent her summers at Claydon.

Located a few miles south of Claydon House, off the A41, **Waddesdon Manor** (April–June, Sept & Oct Thurs–Sun 11am–4pm; July & Aug Wed 1–4pm, Thurs–Sun 11am–4pm; house & grounds £10 timed ticket; grounds only £3; NT) looks like an exiled chateau from the Loire Valley. From 1874 to 1889, minions of Baron Ferdinand de Rothschild laboured to transform a barren hill into a palatial country home suitable for one of Europe's richest families. The end result is perhaps too pompous and conceited for most tastes, even after a recent five-million-pound restoration financed by the baron's descendants, but there's no denying the magnificence of the contents. The interior holds a vast collection of French eighteenth-century decorative arts including Savonnerie carpets, some of the finest examples of Sèvres porcelain in England, Beauvais tapestries and furniture once owned by the French royal family. There are also paintings by early Dutch and Flemish masters and portraits by major English artists including Gainsborough and Reynolds. The extravagance is overwhelming – even the cast-iron aviary in the **grounds** (March–Dec Wed–Sun 10am–5pm; £3) is a work of art.

The Chilterns

The chalk downs of the **Chiltern Hills** extend southwest from the humdrum town of Luton, beside the M1, rolling across Buckinghamshire and Oxfordshire as far as the River Thames. Dotted with pretty villages and homely pubs, the Chilterns are particularly delightful just to the south of High Wycombe (and the M40) in the vicinity of **Marlow** and **Henley**, two smart Thameside towns that make good bases for exploring the range, though there are hotels and B&Bs in the hills too. This is magnificent walking country and some of the best hikes incorporate stretches of the **Ridgeway National Trail**. Beside the Thames at the southern tip of the Chilterns is **Reading**, skirted by the M4 and of interest for its two big festivals, Reading Rock Festival and the World Music extravaganza, WOMAD.

THE RIDGEWAY

The **Ridgeway** has existed for several thousand years and was probably once part of a route extending from the Dorset coast to the Wash in Norfolk. Today, it comprises one of England's fourteen national trails, running from **Overton Hill**, near Avebury in Wiltshire (see p.273), to **Ivinghoe Beacon**, 85 miles to the northeast near Tring, which is itself just a few miles southwest of Luton. Crossing five counties, the trail avoids densely populated areas, following the top of the chalk downland ridge for most of its course, except where the Thames slices through the ridge at **Goring Gap**, which marks the transition from the wooded valleys of the Chilterns to the more open Berkshire Downs. By and large, the Ridgeway is fairly easy hiking and over half of it is accessible to cyclists and RVs. The prevailing winds mean that it is best walked in a northeasterly direction. The Ridgeway is strewn with prehistoric monuments of one description or another, though the finest archeological remains are in the **Vale of White Horse** and around **Avebury** (see p.304 and p.273). There are several youth hostels within reach of the Ridgeway – most notably the *Ridgeway Centre Youth Hostel* (see Wantage, p.304) – and numerous B&Bs. A *Ridgeway Information and Accommodation Guide* is available from the National Trails Office, Cultural Services, Holton, Oxford OX33 1QQ (☎01865/810224). There's also a useful Web site: *www.nationaltrails.gov.uk*

Whipsnade Zoo

Whipsnade Zoo (Mon–Sat 10am–6pm or dusk, Sun 10am–7pm or dusk; £9.50), the free-range menagerie of the Zoological Society of London, perches high up on the downs about six miles southwest of Luton, at the northern end of the Chilterns. Whipsnade takes its educational role seriously and runs a number of major breeding programmes – there's a flourishing cheetah population, and the rare Burmese elephant has also been bred successfully. Most animals, from tigers to wallabies, are kept in large enclosures, separated from the public by a fence or a ditch. You can drive around the zoo (March–Nov £7.50 per car; rest of year free), but it's possible to see everything perfectly well on foot. Alternatively, you could hop on the free Safari bus that stops at the main enclosures, or take a ride in the little steam train which offers an "Asian Railway Safari" as it puffs past herds of elephants and one-horned rhinos.

To reach Whipsnade by **car**, leave the M1 at Junction #9 (approaching from the south) or #12 (from the north) and follow the elephant signs. The nearest **train station** is at Luton, from where there are regular **buses** to the zoo (for details, call ☎0345/788788).

Marlow and around

MARLOW, just a couple of miles south of the M40 (Jtn #4), pushes up against the north bank of the Thames, its riverside streets flanked by Georgian buildings and dominated by the Victorian spire of All Saints' church. Swarms of tourists congregate here in summer and Marlow has its own regatta, but it is smaller and more relaxed than Henley (see p.288), and you can while away an hour watching boats go through the lock or tracing Marlow's literary connections. In 1817 Percy Bysshe Shelley and his wife Mary moved to a house on West Street (between Hayes Place and the school) and stayed for a year – just long enough for him to compose the *Revolt of Islam* and for her to write *Frankenstein*. T.S. Eliot lived down the road at no. 31 for a time in 1918, and Jerome K. Jerome wrote parts of *Three Men in a Boat* in the *Two Brewers* on St Peter's Street, Marlow's best **pub**. Even so, the nearby Chilterns are the main attraction along with Cookham (see opposite), a few minutes' away by train from Marlow station.

There are regular **trains** from London Paddington to Maidenhead, where you change for Marlow, which is also connected by **bus** to Henley-on-Thames every thirty minutes. Buses drop passengers in the centre. From Marlow train station, it's a short walk west along Station Road to the **tourist office**, at 31 High St (Mon–Fri 9.30am–5pm, Sat 9.30am–4.30pm & Sun 10am–5pm; ☎01628/483597). They have a full range of local leaflets including a B&B list and public transport timetables. Marlow has lots of accommodation with the cream of the crop being the *Compleat Angler*, a swish **hotel** down by the bridge (☎01628/484444; ⑧). A more economical alternative is the pleasant and convenient *Fisherman's Reach* **B&B**, in a modern house in between the train station and the river on Gossmore Lane (☎01628/482290; ②).

Cookham

On sunny weekends people flock to **COOKHAM**, three miles southeast of Marlow, for its riverside setting, for its pubs, and because this quaint village was once the home of **Stanley Spencer**, one of Britain's greatest – and most eccentric – artists. The Bible dominated Spencer's education, and in many of his later works he transposes the biblical tales to his own surroundings, transforming Cookham into an earthly paradise in which even the most ordinary objects and people are holy. Spencer's Christianity was extremely unorthodox, however, following a private religious system he called the "Church of Me", and making no distinction between sacred and profane love. In his paintings, the result is a world in which mundane scenes become overwhelmingly sensual, but Spencer's fixation with sexuality had less happy consequences: he divorced his first wife, Hilda, in order to marry his bisexual mistress, Patricia Preece, who exploited him financially and constantly humiliated him. Throughout this miserable second marriage Spencer continued writing to Hilda, a passionate correspondence that continued even after her death in 1950.

Spencer's greatest achievement is generally considered to be his murals in the Sandham Memorial Chapel at Burghclere in Hampshire, but several of his visionary Cookham-based pictures, including the wonderful but unfinished *Christ Preaching at Cookham Regatta*, are on display in the old **Wesleyan Chapel** on the High Street (Easter–Oct daily 10.30am–5.30pm; Oct–Easter Sat & Sun 11am–5pm; 50p). Spencer and Patricia lie together in the churchyard, just to the left of the path leading up to the south porch.

From Cookham Rise, two stops on the **train** from Marlow, it's a ten-minute walk east across the common to the main village. The *Bel & Dragon* pub, with ancient beams and ample leather chairs, pulls a good pint and serves home-made food.

Cliveden

High up on a ridge and across the Thames just to the east of Cookham, **Cliveden** was designed in the middle of the nineteenth century by Sir Charles Barry, architect of the Houses of Parliament – a connection reinforced by the fact that Nancy Astor, the first woman to sit in the House of Commons, once lived here. Dubbed by the left-wing press as the "Cliveden set", Lord and Lady Astor hosted weekend gatherings of influential politicians in the run up to World War II. Their ability to appreciate the difficulties faced by Hitler was not readily understood by many of their compatriots, but this didn't stop Churchill appointing Lord Astor a minister in his wartime cabinet. Impressive if only for its size, Cliveden's redeeming feature is its position, which provides the country's finest views of the Thames. The National Trust has been reduced to leasing Cliveden as a £300-a-night hotel (☎01628/605069), but you can visit the west wing of the **house** (April–Oct Thurs & Sun 3–6pm; £6, including grounds; NT) and glimpse guests sipping tea in the oak-panelled hall or waiters laying tables in the gilt-laden dining rooms – an echo of the period when Nancy Astor hosted lavish social gatherings here. The **grounds** (March–Oct daily 11am–6pm; Nov & Dec closes 4pm; £5) teem with tourists at weekends, but you can find peace and quiet in the woods along the river.

Henley-on-Thames and around

Three counties – Oxfordshire, Berkshire and Buckinghamshire – meet at **HENLEY-ON-THAMES**, a long-established stopping place for travellers between Oxford and London. Henley is a good-looking, affluent commuter town that is at its prettiest among the brick and half-timbered buildings which flank the main drag, Hart Street, with the Market Place at one end and the easy Georgian curves of Henley Bridge at the other. The bridge is also overlooked by the parish church of St Mary, whose sturdy square tower sports a set of little turrets worked in chequerboard flint and stone. A pleasant spot for most of the year, Henley becomes positively arrogant during the **Royal Regatta**, the world's most important amateur rowing tournament. Established in 1839, it's the boating equivalent of the Ascot races (see p.210), a quintessentially English parade ground for the rich, aristocratic and aspiring, whose champagne-swilling antics are inexplicably found thrilling by larger numbers of the hoi polloi. The competitions, featuring past and potential Olympic rowers, run from the last Wednesday in June through to the first week in July. Information is available from the Regatta Headquarters on the Berkshire side of the Thames (☎01491/572153).

Practicalities

The Paddington–Reading rail line runs through Twyford, where you change trains for the five-mile journey north along the branch line to Henley; there are no services on Sundays between September and May. From the **train station**, it's a five-minute walk north to Hart Street, Henley's short main street and most useful reference point. Henley is easy to reach by bus with regular services from Oxford, London and Marlow. **Buses** stop in New Street, just to the north of Hart Street. The **tourist office** is in the basement of the town hall (daily April–Sept 10am–7pm; Oct–March 10am–4pm; ☎01491/578034), on the Market Place, at the top of Hart Street. Henley has several first-rate **B&Bs**, including the smart and tastefully furnished *Alftrudis*, 8 Norman Ave (☎01491/573099; no credit cards; ②), which occupies a Victorian town house a couple of minutes' walk south of Hart Street – take Duke Street and watch for the turning on the right. Another good option is *Lenwade*, 3 Western Rd (☎01491/573468, *lenwadeuk@compuserve.com*; no credit cards; ②), which has three comfortable guest rooms in an attractive, semidetached, Victorian house about five minutes' walk from Hart Street. The best **hotel** is the *Red Lion*, an old wisteria-clad coaching inn near the bridge on Hart Street (☎01491/572161; ⑤).

For **food**, stick to the pubs on Hart Street. The *Angel* by the bridge, the *Three Tuns* and the *Argyll* further up all offer good quality, reasonably priced bar food and the tasty brews of Brakspears, the local brewery.

Stonor House

The tranquillity of **Stonor House** (May & June Sun 2–5.30pm; July & Aug Wed 2–5.30pm, Sun 2–5.30pm; £4.50), a Tudor mansion nestling in a fold of the Chiltern Hills five miles north of Henley, on the edge of the village of Stonor, belies its turbulent history. After the Reformation, the Stonor family remained steadfastly Catholic, refusing to take the oath acknowledging the monarch as head of the Church of England. Stonor became a haven for refugee Catholics, among them, the Jesuit scholar and evangelist Edmund Campion, who was eventually hunted down and executed for high treason in 1581. Though punished for their Catholicism and deprived of their land, the Stonors were later reinstated, and their descendants still live here today.

The **house**, with its Tudor facade superimposed onto the original medieval building, presents an harmonious exterior, the rich ochre brickwork punctuated by towers and backdropped by a lightly forested hill. However, the interior lacks cohesion and contains little old family furniture, its mediocrity only redeemed by Campion memorabilia and the occasional surprise, such as the chapel frieze carved from tea chests by a Polish artist during World War II. The frieze was given by Graham Greene, a family friend who was staying here when he wrote *Our Man in Havana*, a book of far greater renown than poor old Campion's *Ten Reasons for Being a Catholic*.

There is a **bus** from Henley to Stonor, but it only runs four times a week and returns before the house has even opened.

Reading

READING is a modern, prosperous town on the south bank of the River Thames, ten miles south of Henley. Guarding the western approaches to the capital, it has always been important, a stopping-off point for kings and queens from earliest times and once home to one of the country's richest abbeys. Henry VIII took care of the abbey, seizing its lands and hanging the abbot from the main gate, and today almost nothing remains of the old town except the shattered remains of the aforementioned abbey, a short walk to the east of the pedestrianized shopping centre.

There is a flourishing **arts scene** in the town, with both the Reading Film Theatre (☎0118/9868497) and the Hexagon Theatre (☎0118/9606060) offering a good programme of shows, but you wouldn't make a beeline for the place were it not for its two big summertime **music festivals**. The first, the three-day **WOMAD** festival, held each July, is a celebration of World Music Arts and Dance originally inspired by Peter Gabriel. Since the first WOMAD in 1982, there have been about a hundred spin-off events in twenty countries, but the Reading festival remains the focus, held at the Rivermead Leisure Complex, Richfield Ave, just to the north of the town centre. For details on WOMAD, write to Millside, Mill Lane, Wiltshire SN13 8PN (☎01225/744494, ticket line ☎0118/9390930, *www.realworld.on.net/womad*). Also held at the Rivermead Leisure Complex, but a little later in the summer, is the **Reading Festival**, also held over three days and featuring many of the big names of contemporary music. Details of who is performing are published in the music press at least a couple of months in advance and tickets are available from record shops across the country. The vast majority of festival-goers **camp** on site and special buses run there in their hundreds, or you can walk from Reading train station – it only takes fifteen minutes.

Reading can be reached by train from London Paddington and Waterloo. The **tourist office**, in the town hall, in the town centre on Blagrave Street (Mon–Fri 10am–5pm; ☎0118/9566226), runs an accommodation-booking service – be sure to reserve a room months in advance if you're planning on being here for either festival.

Oxford

The image of **OXFORD** that crystallizes in the minds of most British people is one of upper-class students talking in nasal accents, living in oak-panelled rooms and drinking port into the early hours. While such a vision cannot be dismissed as entirely obsolete, it would be a mistake to reduce the city simply to a bastion of privileged scholarship. The average Oxford student looks much the same as a student from any other university, and what fills the local press is not the latest college gossip but reports of joy-riding on local housing estates. The university might dominate central Oxford both physically and mentally, yet the wider city has developed out of the prosperity generated not by the colleges but by the nearby Cowley factory, which launched Britain's first mass-produced car in the 1920s. Thousands of workers have been laid off over the last decade, but the motor industry remains vital to the city's economy.

Oxford started life late, in Saxon times, and blossomed even later, under the Normans, when the cathedral was built and Oxford was chosen as the royal residence.

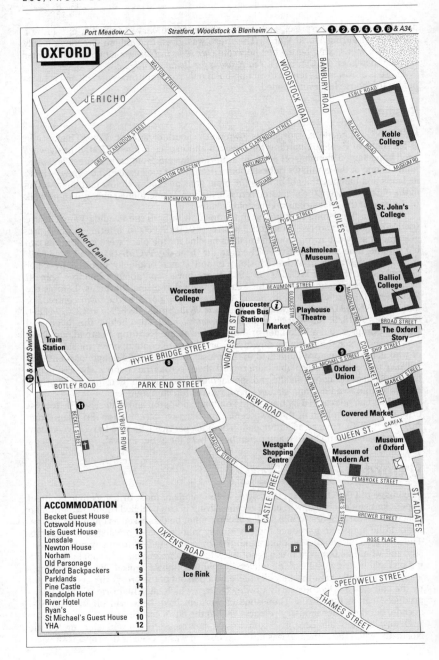

OXFORD

Port Meadow△   Stratford, Woodstock & Blenheim △   △ ❶ ❷ ❸ ❹ ❺ ❻ & A34,

JERICHO

WALTON STREET

GREAT CLARENDON STREET

LITTLE CLARENDON STREET

WALTON CRESCENT

RICHMOND ROAD

WELLINGTON SQUARE

WOODSTOCK ROAD

BANBURY ROAD

KEBLE ROAD

BLACKHALL ROAD

MUSEUM RD

Keble College

WALTON STREET

ST. JOHN'S STREET

PUSEY STREET

PUSEY LANE

ST. GILES

MAGDALEN STREET

St. John's College

Ashmolean Museum

Balliol College

Oxford Canal

Worcester College

BEAUMONT STREET

GLOUCESTER STREET

❼

Gloucester Green Bus Station (i) **Playhouse Theatre**

Market

BROAD STREET

The Oxford Story

SHIP STREET

WORCESTER ST

Train Station

HYTHE BRIDGE STREET

GEORGE STREET

CORNMARKET STREET

MARKET STREET

❽

ST. MICHAEL'S STREET

❾

Oxford Union

◁ ⓫ & A420 Swindon

BOTLEY ROAD

PARK END STREET

NEW INN HALL STREET

NEW ROAD

Covered Market

⓫

HOLLYBUSH ROW

BECKET STREET

QUEEN ST.

CARFAX

PARADISE STREET

Westgate Shopping Centre

Museum of Modern Art

Museum of Oxford

ST. ALDATES

CASTLE STREET

PEMBROKE STREET

ST. EBBE'S STREET

BREWER STREET

ACCOMMODATION

Becket Guest House	11
Cotswold House	1
Isis Guest House	13
Lonsdale	2
Newton House	15
Norham	3
Old Parsonage	4
Oxford Backpackers	9
Parklands	5
Pine Castle	14
Randolph Hotel	7
River Hotel	8
Ryan's	6
St Michael's Guest House	10
YHA	12

OXPENS ROAD

ROSE PLACE

Ice Rink

SPEEDWELL STREET

THAMES STREET

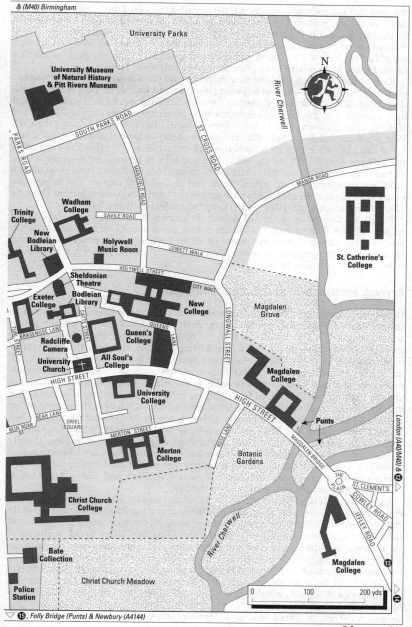

& (M40) Birmingham

University Parks

University Museum
of Natural History
& Pitt Rivers Museum

N

River Cherwell

SOUTH PARKS ROAD

ST CROSS ROAD

MANSFIELD ROAD

PARKS ROAD

MANOR ROAD

Wadham
College

SAVILE ROAD

Trinity
College

St. Catherine's
College

New
Bodleian
Library

Holywell
Music Room

JOWETT WALK

HOLYWELL STREET

Sheldonian
Theatre

CITY WALL

Magdalen
Grove

Exeter
College

Bodleian
Library

New
College

BRASENOSE LANE

CATTE STREET

QUEENS

LONGWALL STREET

TURL STREET

Radcliffe
Camera

Queen's
College

QUEENS LANE

Magdalen
College

University
Church

All Soul's
College

HIGH STREET

BEAR LANE

BLUE BOAR ST

University
College

ORIEL
SQUARE

HIGH STREET

ROSE LANE

Punts

MAGDALEN BRIDGE

London (A40/M40) & 12

MERTON STREET

Merton
College

Botanic
Gardens

THE
PLAIN

ST CLEMENT'S

COWLEY ROAD

Christ Church
College

River Cherwell

Magdalen
College

13

IFFLEY ROAD

Bate
Collection

Police
Station

Christ Church Meadow

0   100   200 yds

12

15 , Folly Bridge (Punts) & Newbury (A4144)

© Crown copyright

It seems that the presence of **Henry I**, the so-called "Scholar King", helped attract students in the early twelfth century, their numbers increasing with the expulsion of English students from the Sorbonne in 1167. The first colleges, founded mostly by rich bishops, were essentially ecclesiastical institutions – reflected in both their design (most had cloisters and a chapel) and discipline (until 1877 lecturers were not allowed to marry, and women have been granted degrees only since 1920).

Each of the 39 colleges has its own character and often a particular label, whether it's the richest (St John's), most left-wing (Wadham and Balliol) or most public-school-dominated (Christ Church). Collegiate rivalries are long established, usually based upon success in sports, and tension between the university and the city – or "Town" and "Gown" – has existed as long as the university itself, a fact epitomized during the **Civil War**, when the colleges sided with Charles I (who turned Oxford into the Royalist capital of England) while the city backed the Parliamentarians. The privileges enjoyed by the colleges – until 1950 the university had two MPs of its own, for example – have stoked resentment that still flares into the occasional confrontation, but a non-communicative coexistence is more typical. Given that thousands of tourists and foreign language students also invade the city throughout the year, it is no surprise that Oxford's 120,000 permanent inhabitants tend to keep themselves to themselves.

For all its idiosyncrasies, Oxford should not be missed, and can keep you occupied for several days. The university buildings include some of England's greatest architecture, and the city can also boast some excellent museums and numerous bars and restaurants. Getting there is easy too: from London the journey takes just an hour by train and ninety minutes by bus.

Arrival, information and accommodation

Oxford **train station** is fifteen minutes' walk west of the centre, linked by a shuttle bus. Long-distance National Express **buses** terminate at the Gloucester Green bus station at the bottom of George Street, less than five minutes from the centre; many services, including private buses from London (see "Listings", p.302), make other city stops prior to arriving at Gloucester Green, while some buses from the surrounding area, including the Cotswolds, terminate on St Giles instead. Intense competition between companies means that **city buses** run reasonably frequently, most leaving from Cornmarket and the High Street. The Oxford Bus Company produces a useful map of routes within the city, which you can pick up at the Gloucester Green station or at the **tourist office** in the Old School, also in Gloucester Green (summer Mon–Sat 9.30am–5pm, Sun 10am–3.30pm; rest of year Mon–Sat 9.30am–5pm; ☎01865/726871), where you can find copies of the free annual *Oxford Guide*, containing a wealth of information about the city sights, as well as services, pubs and restaurants in the area (copies are less easy to find in winter). Oxford's frustrating one-way system and lack of convenient parking space means **driving** around town can be a hassle, so use the **Park and Ride** scheme which operates from the main access routes into the city.

Expensive **hotels** predominate in the heart of Oxford, although there are a few cheaper options close to the train station. While you won't find a great number of **B&Bs** right in the centre, there are plenty scattered along all the main roads heading out of the city, mostly within a half-hour walk or a short bus ride. **Iffley Road**, southeast of the centre, offers the biggest choice of inexpensive places and gives easy access to the Cowley Road, a gritty student ghetto and the liveliest part of Oxford away from the centre; there is little to choose between the B&Bs along this street, though standards rise the farther up Iffley Road you go. South of St Aldate's, **Abingdon Road** is a quieter residential area with a good range of guest houses. Wherever you stay, book ahead in high season; you can do this yourself by telephone, or through the tourist office, which levies a £2.50 charge (plus a returnable ten-percent deposit).

Hotels & B&Bs

Becket House, 5 Becket St (☎01865/724675). Close to the train station, but less convivial than most. ①.

Cotswold House, 363 Banbury Rd (☎01865/310558). A top-notch B&B, three miles north of the centre (bus #2 or #7). ④.

Isis Guest House, 45–53 Iffley Rd (☎01865/741024). Large college house, just across Magdalen Bridge, open from late June to September; good value. ①.

Lonsdale, 312 Banbury Rd (☎01865/554872) Away from the centre, but good transport links into town. No credit cards. ②.

Newton House, 82–84 Abingdon Rd (☎01865/240561). The most central of the south Oxford B&Bs, and well placed for evening strolls along the Thames. ②.

Norham Guest House, 16 Norham Rd (☎01865/515352). A quiet and genteel place in north Oxford, an area dominated by large Victorian houses belonging mostly to academics. Fifteen minutes' walk from town, just off the Banbury Rd. ③.

Old Parsonage Hotel, 1 Banbury Rd (☎01865/310210). A small classy hotel in a handsome house at the top of St Giles. ⑦.

Parklands, 100 Banbury Rd (☎01865/554374). Homely place with a garden, licensed restaurant and bar; a good deal at this price. Standard or en-suite rooms. ⑤.

Pine Castle, 290–292 Iffley Rd (☎01865/241497). A spacious Victorian house in a similar mould to *Parklands*, although marginally closer to the centre. ③.

Randolph Hotel, 1 Beaumont St (☎01865/247481). The most famous, most overrated and most overpriced hotel in the city, suffering from all the disadvantages of being part of a chain. Scenes from the *Inspector Morse* TV series and *Shadowlands* were shot here. ⑧.

River Hotel, 17 Botley Rd (☎01865/243475). Friendly, comfortable, convenient for the train station and the only hotel in Oxford with river frontage. ④.

Ryan's, 164 Banbury Rd (☎01865/558876). Well appointed, with mostly en-suite rooms. A long walk from the centre, but on the bus route and close to the shops. No credit cards. ②.

St Michael's Guest House, 26 St Michael's St (☎01865/242101). Almost permanently full, but the most central of the B&Bs. ②.

Hostels and camping

Oxford Backpackers, 9A Hythe Bridge Rd (☎01865/721761, *oxford@hostels.demon.co.uk*). An eighty-bed independent hostel that's far more central and less institutional than the YHA. There's a late-night bar. Advance booking recommended.

Oxford Camping International, 426 Abingdon Rd (☎01865/244088). The closest campsite to the city, just over a mile south of Carfax. Take bus #35 or #36 from St Aldate's.

Youth Hostel, 32 Jack Straw's Lane (☎01865/762997, *oxford@yha.org.uk*). Off the Marston Road a couple of miles east of the centre, accessible on minibuses #13, #14 or #14A from the High Street, or bus #10 from the bus station. Beds are in great demand, but camping is available in the attractive wooded garden. Inexpensive meals available in addition to good self-catering facilities.

The City

Oxford straddles the confluence of the **Thames** and the **Cherwell** rivers. In theory, and on most maps, the former is known within the city as the "Isis", but few locals actually use the term. Central Oxford's main point of reference is **Carfax**, overlooked by the Saxon remnant of St Martin's tower, from which the city's main axes radiate: the **High** runs east to Magdalen Bridge and the Cherwell, **Cornmarket** north to the broad avenue of St Giles, and **St Aldate's** south to the Thames. Many of the oldest colleges face onto the High, a lovely, though busy, road running through the centre, or onto streets on either side of it: most can be spotted from the tangle of bikes around the entrance. Owing to the ever-growing number of visitors, colleges have restricted opening hours to the afternoon only and a few charge admission too, though in some cases only at weekends and during holiday periods.

ON THE RIVER

Punting is a favourite summer pastime both among students and visitors, but handling a punt – a traditional flat-bottomed boat ideal for the shallow waters of the Thames and Cherwell – requires some practice. The punt is propelled and steered with a long pole, which beginners inevitably get stuck in riverbed mud: if this happens, let go and paddle back, otherwise you're likely to be pulled overboard. The Cherwell, though much narrower than the Thames and therefore trickier to navigate, provides more opportunities for pulling to the side for a picnic – an essential part of the punting experience. For **boat rental**, Magdalen Bridge, at the east end of the High, is the most central place (☎01865/202643), but in summer it's so busy that you're better off going a mile or so north to the Cherwell Boat House by Wolfson College off Banbury Road (☎01865/515978). From the Thames boat station at Folly Bridge (☎01993/868190), south of St Aldate's, you'll have to punt a fair way along a broad stretch of river before being able to turn off into the Cherwell. Expect to pay about £10 per hour for a boat plus a £25 deposit, and sometimes ID is required. Five people make an ideal group – four sitting and one punting – though there is room for six. If you're determined not to do any actual punting, chauffeured punts are available for around £20 per half-hour, with free booze. Other types of craft are also available for rent. Call the boathouses for more information or if there are any doubts about the weather.

The other boats most commonly seen on the Thames belong to the university **rowing clubs**, which started up in the early nineteenth century, when top hats were *de rigueur*: the first Oxford vs Cambridge boat race (now staged in Putney, London) took place in 1829. Rowers practise mainly along the stretch between Folly Bridge and Iffley, also used for college races. The so-called **Torpids** are held at the end of February and the **Eights** at the end of May – the latter are the most important and therefore attract the largest crowds.

South of Carfax

The **Town Hall**, an ostentatious Victorian creation, spreads down the hill from Carfax, with a staircase on the south side giving access to the **Museum of Oxford** (Tues–Fri 10am–4pm, Sat 10am–5pm; £1.50), which makes good use of photographs to tell the history of the city. In the face of tough competition this museum often gets ignored, but you'll learn far more here than at the "Oxford Story" in Broad Street (see p.298).

Just down from the museum, the huge Tom Tower, designed by Christopher Wren, marks the entrance to **Christ Church** (Mon–Sat 9am–5pm, Sun 9am–1pm; £3), Oxford's largest, most prestigious and some would say most pretentious college. The former college of Albert Einstein, William Gladstone and no fewer than twelve other British prime ministers, it claims the distinction of having been founded twice, first by Cardinal Wolsey in 1525, and then again in 1546 following the cardinal's fall from grace and decease. Men in bowler hats are assiduous at guarding the main entrance: visitors must enter via the **Memorial Garden**, which takes you directly to the **Cathedral**, which is also the college chapel. This largely Norman building once formed part of a priory said to have been founded by the Saxon princess later canonized as St Frideswide, whose shrine was the impetus to Oxford's growth. The cathedral has been hacked about – Wolsey destroyed part of the west end to make space for a quad and Sir Gilbert Scott made alterations last century – but it still possesses a lovely freshness and sense of space. The Norman legacy remains in the glorious choir, where massive Norman columns rise to delicate fifteenth-century stone vaulting. Much fine medieval carving and several impressive tombs have also survived. The shrine of St Frideswide, by the Lady Chapel, had to be rebuilt following its destruction during the Dissolution, but it retains the first known example of natural foliage in English sculpture, a splendid confection of leaves dating from around 1290. A window in the adjacent Latin Chapel depicts the life of the saint, one of the earliest works by Pre-Raphaelite luminary Edward Burne-Jones, who also created some windows in the south aisle.

From the cathedral you enter the striking but unfinished **Tom Quad**; the raised terrace was originally designed to be a cloister. A staircase in the southeast corner serves the dining hall, the grandest refectory in Oxford with an array of stern portraits of scholars. Through the smaller Peckwater quad you reach Canterbury quad, where the **Christ Church Picture Gallery** (Easter–Sept Mon–Sat 10.30am–1pm & 2–4.30pm, Sun 2–5.30pm; Oct–Easter Mon–Sat 10.30am–1pm & 2–4.30pm, Sun 2–4.30pm; £1) provides a pokey home for works by many of Italy's finest artists from the fifteenth to eighteenth centuries, including some by Leonardo da Vinci and Michelangelo.

Christ Church Meadow stretches south from the college, where you can follow a shady path first south along the Thames and then north by the Cherwell. Back on St Aldate's and just south of Christ Church, the **Bate Collection** (Mon–Fri 2–5pm, Sat during term 10am–noon; free) contains England's most comprehensive collection of European woodwind instruments. Though only music buffs will make sense of some of the explanatory notes, you don't have to be an expert to enjoy this place. In addition to rows of flutes and clarinets, there are all sorts of other instruments on show, from medieval crumhorns, looking like rejected walking sticks, to the country's finest gamelan, which is played regularly.

Back towards Carfax and off to the left along Pembroke Street, the **Museum of Modern Art** or Moma (Tues–Sun 11am–6pm, Thurs 11am–9pm; £2.50, free Wed till 1pm & Thurs from 6pm) is always worth checking out. The gallery usually has two exhibitions on the go, featuring international contemporary art in a wide variety of media; the basement café serves good coffee and vegetarian food. The gallery may be closed in between exhibitions.

East of Carfax – the High Street and around

As you walk east along the High from Carfax, the first building to demand attention is **St Mary's** or the University Church. Its handsome Baroque porch, flanked by chunky corkscrewed pillars, and the elaborately pinnacled tower take precedence over an unexceptional interior. (You can climb the tower from Radcliffe Square; see p.297.) Across the High from St Mary's, an alley called Magpie Lane leads to Merton Street, cobbled and uncharacteristically tranquil, and to **Merton College** (Mon–Fri 2–4pm, Sat & Sun 10am–4pm; free), historically the city's most important college. Balliol and University colleges may have been founded earlier, but it was Merton – opened in 1264 – which set the model for colleges in both Oxford and Cambridge, being the first to gather its students and tutors together in one place. Furthermore, unlike the other two, Merton retains some of its original medieval buildings, which are therefore the oldest part of the university. Famous Merton alumni include T.S. Eliot, J.R.R. Tolkien and Kris Kristofferson.

The best of the thirteenth-century architecture can be seen in **Mob Quad**, a delightful courtyard complete with mullioned windows and Gothic doorways, and in the Chapel, where the painted windows in the choir, dating from around 1300, were donated by Henry de Mamesfeld, an egocentric who appears as a kneeling figure 24 times. A curious monument in the antechapel shows Thomas Bodley (founder of Oxford's most important library) surrounded by masculine-looking women in classical garb. Merton's other gem is its fourteenth-century **Library**, one of the finest medieval libraries in Britain. Much of the woodwork, including the panelling, screens and bookcases, dates from the Tudor period, but some fittings are original.

Back on the High, **University College** (known as "Univ"), founded in 1249, has a rightful claim to be the city's first college, but nothing of that period survives – what you see dates mostly from the seventeenth century. A year Univ may prefer to forget is 1811, when it expelled **Percy Bysshe Shelley** for distributing a paper called *The*

Necessity of Atheism. Guilt later induced Univ to accept a memorial to the poet after he drowned in Italy in 1822: the white marble monument, showing the limp body of the poet borne by winged lions and mourned by the Muse of Poetry, occupies a shrine-like room by Staircase 3. The college's most famous recent alumnus was Bill Clinton, the non-inhaling Rhodes Scholar; former Australian premier Bob Hawke also studied here.

Queen's College, across the High from Univ (and closed to the public), cuts an altogether more impressive figure. The only Oxford college to have been built in one period (1672–1760), Queen's benefited from the skills of some of the country's finest architects: Nicholas Hawksmoor did much of the work and his teacher, Christopher Wren, designed the chapel, a grand room with a ceiling of cherubs and foliage and a massive oak screen. Unfortunately, the chapel can be visited only on a tour arranged at the tourist office.

Oscar Wilde's college, **Magdalen** (daily 2–6pm; £2.50), pronounced "Maudlin", dominates the eastern end of the High, its majestic medieval tower worthy of a cathedral. A handsome reredos saves the **Chapel** from complete gloom, but you must admire it from a distance since a stone screen confines you to the rather spiritless antechapel. The adjacent **cloisters**, with bizarre and grotesque stone figures perched atop delicate buttresses, are the best in Oxford, and Magdalen boasts better **grounds** than most too: a bridge across the Cherwell joins **Addison's Walk**, which you can follow around a water meadow where rare wild fritillaries flower in spring. Deer graze in a fenced-off park on the river's west bank, some of them destined for the college dining tables. Magdalen also has a fine choir, whose annual duties include singing madrigals from the top of the church tower at 6am on May 1. Pubs open especially for this May Day event and the din made by drunken students often drowns out the singing.

The small **Botanic Gardens** (daily: summer 9am–5pm; rest of year 9am–4.30pm; greenhouses daily 2–4pm; £2, free in winter) opposite Magdalen predate all others in the country, being first planted in 1621 on the site of a medieval Jewish cemetery. Bounded by a curve of the Cherwell, they provide a peaceful escape from the High.

Retracing your steps back to Queen's, you can cut north up Queen's Lane, past some of the best gargoyles in Oxford, to **New College** (April–Oct 11am–5pm; Nov–March 2–4pm; £2, free in winter). Founded in 1379, the college has splendid Perpendicular architecture in the Front Quad, though the addition of an extra storey in 1675 spoiled the overall effect. The **Chapel** has been mucked about too, yet it remains perhaps the finest in Oxford after the cathedral, not so much for its design as its contents. The antechapel contains some original fourteenth-century glass, but the Nativity in its west window was designed by Sir Joshua Reynolds in 1777, a not entirely successful departure for perhaps England's most famous portrait painter. Beneath it, shoved up against the wall, stands the wonderful *Lazarus* by Jacob Epstein – Khrushchev, after a visit to the college, claimed that the memory of this haunting sculpture kept him awake at night. On the south wall a war memorial crafted in 1921 by Eric Gill lists 228 students killed in World War I. A magnificent nineteenth-century stone reredos takes up the entire east wall of the main chapel, consisting of about fifty canopied figures, mostly saints and apostles, with Christ for a centrepiece. The misericords, the other highlight, sadly are cordoned off.

An archway on the east side of Front Quad leads through to the grounds, a pleasant lawn skirted by the best-preserved part of the thirteenth-century **city walls**. You can leave the college either through the north entrance into Holywell Street or back the way you came and into New College Lane: heading west along either street brings you to the top of Broad Street.

The Broad Street area

Oxford's most monumental architecture prevails over the eastern end of Broad Street. The semicircular **Sheldonian Theatre** (Mon–Sat 10am–12.30pm & 2–4.30pm; £1.50), placed with its facade directed away from the street, was Christopher Wren's first major work: a reworking of the Theatre of Marcellus in Rome, it was conceived in 1663, when the 31-year-old Wren's main job was as professor of astronomy. Designed as a stage for university ceremonies, nowadays it functions mainly as a concert hall. The interior, painted in gold and a dull brown, lacks any sense of drama, and even the views from the cupola (50p) are disappointing.

Wren's colleague Hawksmoor designed the **Clarendon Building**, set at right angles to the Sheldonian and now part of the university library. Across the courtyard, a doorway leads to the **Old Schools Quad**, a beautifully proportioned, symmetrical space created in the seventeenth century by an unknown architect. On the east side, the so-called Tower of the Five Orders of Architecture gives a lesson in design, with tiers of columns built according to the five classical styles: from top to bottom, Tuscan, Doric, Ionic, Corinthian and Composite. The heart of one of the country's great centres of learning occupies the building opposite. Set up by Thomas Bodley in the seventeenth century, the **Bodleian Library** has expanded greatly since then, becoming the second largest library in the UK. An estimated eighty miles of shelves are distributed among various buildings, including the ugly modern annexe on the other side of Broad Street. Though only members can enter the main part, you can go on a guided tour of Duke Humfrey's library (summer Mon–Fri 10.30am, 11.30am, 2pm & 3pm, Sat 10.30am & 11.30am; winter Mon–Fri 2pm & 3pm, Sat 10.30am & 11.30am; £3.50), founded in 1439 and restored by Bodley – sign up for a tour in the Exhibition Room, on the south side of the quad. The painted beams are glorious, and you'll be shown a selection of precious manuscripts and books, but an aura of ancient scholarship is far more tangible in the less visited Merton library (see p.293). Entered through the shop on the west side of the quad, the **Divinity School** (Mon–Fri 9am–4.30pm, Sat 9am–12.30pm; free), has a fifteenth-century vaulted ceiling, a riot of pendants and decorative bosses that should be seen on a bright sunny day, when light streams onto the still fresh stone.

The **Radcliffe Camera** (closed to the public) seems rather isolated behind the Old Schools Quad, but this only adds to the majesty of this mighty Italianate rotunda, built from 1737 to 1749 by James Gibbs, architect of London's St Martin-in-the-Fields. For a less intimidating perspective, climb the 125-step tower of the **University Church** (July & Aug daily 9am–7pm; rest of year Mon–Sat 9am–5pm, Sun 11.30pm–5pm; £1.60), which backs onto Radcliffe Square. The views can't be bettered, particularly over **All Souls College** (Mon–Fri 2–4pm; closed Aug; free), with its twin mock-Gothic towers (the work of Hawksmoor) and a coloured sundial designed by Wren.

Back on Broad Street, a series of classical heads, their eyes blackened by pollution, stare menacingly across the street at Blackwells, Oxford's largest and most famous bookshop. The heads continue along the front of the **Museum of the History of Science** (Tues–Sat noon–4pm; free), where microscopes and early calculators are immaculately displayed alongside Islamic and European astrolabes that seem more like works of art than tools of science. The museum is due to reopen in April 2000, a Lottery grant having funded the addition of new galleries and visitor facilities.

Exeter College (daily 2–5pm; closed Christmas week; free), next to the museum but entered from Turl Street, has Oxford's most elaborate **chapel**: modelled by Sir Gilbert Scott on Sainte Chapelle in Paris, it's a cramped conglomeration of fussy neo-Gothic features. A tapestry of the *Adoration of the Magi*, a fine collaboration between William Morris and Edward Burne-Jones, who met at Exeter, is ill-served by its setting. The chapel in **Trinity College** (daily 10.30am–noon & 2–5pm; £2), on the north side of Broad Street, couldn't be more different. Grinling Gibbons did some of his finest carving here, a distinctly secular performance with cherubs' heads peering out from delicate foliage. **Balliol** (daily 2–5pm; £1), next door, is as left-wing as Trinity is conservative, and the two are bitter rivals, ritualizing their traditional antipathy in the tradition of Gordouli, when Balliol students chant abuse at their adversaries across the wall, usually at unsociable hours of the night. Architecturally, Balliol is an unexceptional assembly of buildings, haphazardly gathered around two quads.

The **Oxford Story** (daily: April–June, Sept & Oct 9.30am–5pm; July & Aug 9am–6pm; Nov–March Mon–Fri 10am–4.30pm, Sat & Sun 10am–5pm; £5.50), towards the Cornmarket end of Broad Street, involves sitting at a desk and being pulled sluggishly past scenes illustrating the history of the university, while listening to a commentary through headphones. You can spend a more pleasurable half-hour around the corner at the **Oxford Union** in St Michael's Street, home of the university debating society, where many budding politicians – Edward Heath and Tony Benn among them – have tried out their oratorical skills. The Union has also hosted a mixed bag of internationally famous celebrity speakers in recent years, among them Yasser Arafat, Archbishop Desmond Tutu, Ronald Reagan, Mother Theresa, O.J. Simpson and Diego Maradona. The original debating hall, shaped rather like an upturned boat and now the union library (closed to the public), is decorated with Pre-Raphaelite murals illustrating the Arthurian legend, created (but never completed) in the 1850s by William Morris, Rossetti, Burne-Jones and a few like-minded friends. The position of the windows between the badly faded panels makes a full appreciation of the murals difficult, but they remain a fascinating oddity. The union bar makes a pleasant change from the city cafés, with tables outside in summer.

The Ashmolean, University and Pitt-Rivers museums

The university's best museums grew up around the collections of **John Tradescant**, gardener to the kings James I and Charles I. During extensive travels around the world he built up a huge collection of artefacts and natural specimens which became known as Tradescant's Ark. The collection eventually passed to the university, was split up – mainly between the Ashmolean and the Pitt-Rivers museums – and has been added to ever since.

The **Ashmolean** (Tues–Sat 10am–5pm, Sun 2–5pm; free), the oldest public museum in the country, was established as a home for Tradescant's Ark in 1683. Originally, the university's vast collection of art and archeology, which includes some of Britain's greatest treasures, was housed in the History of Science Museum in Broad Street but was later moved to a mammoth Neoclassical building on Beaumont Street. If you don't have time to make more than one visit, you'll have to just pick out the highlights. Until late 1998, however, the museum will be in a state of flux pending the completion of work on three new ground-floor galleries (to accommodate Islamic, ancient Greek and Oriental artefacts hitherto locked in the vaults), and many of its prize pieces are difficult to locate. Nor is the glossy "Museum Guide" (50p) much help; the best way to find something is to ask one of the attendants.

Downstairs, the **Egyptian** displays should not be missed: in addition to the well-preserved mummies and coffins, there are unusual frescoes, rare textiles from the Roman and Byzantine periods and several fine examples of relief carving, such as on the shrine of Taharqa. The **Eastern Art** section includes superb Islamic ceramics and early Chinese pottery: the simple monochrome pots of the Sung dynasty (960–1279) look surprisingly modern. On the first floor, the archeological displays have been rather crammed together, though the Beazley Room contains an excellent display of ceramics from the Geometric Period (ninth and eighth centuries BC), while the Arthur Evans or "Minoan" room (no. 28) houses the largest collection of ancient Cretan objects outside Greece. A small part of the Ashmolean's original exhibits can be seen in the **Tradescant Room**, an offbeat group of exhibits including Guy Fawkes's lantern and Oliver Cromwell's death mask. The oldest-known North American Indian garment, known as Powhatan's mantle, and other ethnographical objects give a taste of what you'll find in the Pitt-Rivers.

The Department of Western Art straddles the first and second floors. The Fortnum Gallery has the best of the **Italian art**, notably Piero di Cosimo's *Forest Fire* and Paolo Uccello's *Hunt in the Forest*, and it's followed by a strong showing of **French paintings**, with Pissarro, Monet, Manet and Renoir well represented alongside Cézanne and Bonnard, plus a dash of Picasso and Van Gogh. Look out for what's on in the Eldon Gallery, which stages exhibitions from the Ashmolean's vast hoard of **prints**, and for the Michelangelo and Raphael drawings by the staircase: these include some of Raphael's finest sketches. Up on the second floor, the Combe Gallery is devoted to mostly nineteenth-century **British paintings**: Samuel Palmer's visionary paintings run rings around the rest, though there's lashings of Pre-Raphaelite stuff from Rossetti, Holman Hunt and cohorts.

By the *Lamb & Flag* pub on the far side of St Giles from the Ashmolean, an alley cuts through to Parks Road and the **University Museum of Natural History** (daily noon–5pm; free), opposite the mottled brick facade of Keble College. The building, constructed under the guidance of John Ruskin, looks more like a cross between a railway station and a church than a museum – particularly inside, a high Victorian-Gothic fusion of cast iron and glass, featuring soaring columns and capitals decorated with animal and plant motifs.

Exhibits include a working beehive and some impressive fossil dinosaurs, though the museum's natural history displays are outdone by the **Pitt-Rivers Museum** (Mon–Sat 1–4.30pm; free), reached through a door at the far end. Founded in 1884 from the bequest of grenadier guard turned archeologist Augustus Henry Lane Fox Pitt-Rivers, this is one of the world's finest ethnographic museums and an extraordinary relic of the Victorian age, arranged like an exotic junk shop with each bulging cabinet labelled meticulously by hand. The exhibits, brought to England by several explorers, Captain Cook among them, range from totem poles and mummified crocodiles to African fetishes and gruesome shrunken heads from Ecuador. For a breather afterwards, go and sit in the nearby University Parks on the banks of the Cherwell.

Eating, drinking and nightlife

With so many students to cater for, Oxford has developed a huge choice of places to eat and drink. For a midday bite, the numerous **sandwich bars** are ideal – the best are listed below, and you'll find several others in the Covered Market between the High and Cornmarket, an Oxford institution as essential to local shoppers as the Bodleian is to academics. If you prefer to make your own picnic, *Parmenters*, 58 High, and *Taylors* at the top of St Giles, are recommended delicatessens. Reasonable food is served at most **pubs** – those listed below have been singled out for their ambience or selection of beers rather than for their menus, which are pretty uniform. For **restaurant** meals, Oxford is not exactly a gourmet haven, but it does have a few high-class choices amid the welter of unpretentious and good-value places.

This is not a town for wild nights: lovers of **classical music** are well catered for, but the city has a fairly paltry offering of other forms of entertainment – which is why at weekends so many young people hang around on Cornmarket after the pubs have shut, or head off to queue at one of the kebab vans for a late-night snack. In addition to the city's main concert halls, certain college chapels – primarily Christ Church, Merton and New College – are good venues for classical recitals. The proximity to London and Stratford-upon-Avon means that most Oxonians head out of town to go to the **theatre**. Student productions dominate the city repertoire, but the quality of acting varies, particularly when they tackle Shakespeare, the favourite for the open-air college productions put on for tourists during the summer.

Having spawned both Supergrass and Radiohead in recent years, you'd think Oxford would be hot on popular music these days. Sadly, the star quality of its local heroes is not reflected in either the live-music or club scene which, aside from a couple of noteworthy venues, is lame for a university city. Part of the reason for this is that the students tend to fall back on college discos, an option closed to the rest. **Listings** are given in the *Oxford Times*, out on Friday; in *Daily Information* (weekly out of term time), a broadsheet posted up in pubs and cafés, and in *This Month in Oxford*, a monthly booklet which you can pick up free at the tourist office. In addition, there is the free monthly *Oxford Magazine* which lists forthcoming gigs and club nights in and around Oxford; you can usually get copies at the train station, the tourist office and other places around town. **Tickets** to most musical events are on sale at Blackwells Music Shop, 38 Holywell St (☎01865/792792).

Snacks and cafés

Café Coco, Cowley Rd. Chic American-style brasserie just off the Plain, offering a great selection of aperitifs, classy shorts and delicious coffee. The food is mainly Mediterranean (mezes, pizzas and *merguez*), and a touch pricey, but the service is slick and the atmosphere lively.

Café Rico, Gloucester Green, near the bus station. Modern, chrome-decorated place for baguettes and soups, where you can sit outside and watch the market goings-on.

Carfax Fish and Chips, Carfax Passage, off the High. Oxford's best-loved chippy. Open Mon–Fri until midnight.

Convocation Coffee House, Radcliffe Square, attached to the University Church. Ideal for coffee and cake or quiche-and-salad lunches, served in an atmospheric stone-vaulted room. No smoking.

Felson's, 32 Little Clarendon St. Another hot contender for Oxford's best sandwich bar, this tiny, friendly place has a huge range of fillings in massive baguettes and rolls.

George and Davies, Little Clarendon St. An old-established ice-cream parlour that stays open well after the pubs and cinemas.

Heroes, 8 Ship St. Sandwich bar with some of the best (and most adventurous) fillings in town.

Kebab Kid, Gloucester Green. The city's best kebab stand is close to the bus station, has tables (a rarity), and serves its grilled lamb and chicken in freshly baked *naan* breads rather than the usual limp pittas. Plenty of vegetarian options, too.

News Café, 1 Ship St. Breakfasts, bagels and daily specials offered here, as well as beers and wines. As the name suggests, food for thought is provided by the newspapers and two TVs tuned to news broadcasts. Open till 9pm daily.

Nosebag, 6 St Michael's St. A civilized but unassuming place, with Laura Ashley decor and classical background music. The hot and cold food attracts queues at lunchtime; not so in the evening, when it is a good place for a quick but wholesome meal. Good selection of veggie food.

St Giles' Café, 52 St Giles. Oxford's favourite greasy spoon. The huge fry-ups and quality coffee pulls an interesting mix of people, including the poet Elizabeth Jennings, who is said to be a regular here.

Restaurants

Aziz, 228–230 Cowley Rd (☎01865/798033). Lively, spacious and bright Bangladeshi restaurant, with bamboo furniture and rugs. The food's delicious, too, and they do an exceptional range of vegetarian dishes. Reservations recommended at weekends. Inexpensive.

Bangkok House, 42a Hythe Bridge St (☎01865/200705). Best Oriental restaurant in town, with superb Thai food and excellent service. The mixed starter and the coconut-milk curries are particularly good. Closed Sun & Mon lunch. Moderate.

Browns, 5–9 Woodstock Rd (☎01865/511995). Buzzing and stylish restaurant with abundant foliage. Main courses from hamburgers to fresh salmon, in addition to legendary Guinness pies. No booking allowed, although queueing is part of the experience. Also open for breakfast. Moderate.

La Capannina, 247 Cowley Rd (☎01865/248200). Oxford's most authentic Italian is cosy and unpretentious (in spite of being the favourite haunt of local pop stars Supergrass). It's a mile or so up the Cowley Road, but easy to find thanks to the extravagant mock-log-cabin facade. Inexpensive.

Cherwell Boathouse, Bardwell Rd, off Banbury Rd (☎01865/552746). A deservedly popular spot for an unhurried meal at a riverside setting, about a mile north of town. Closed all Mon & Tues, plus Sun eve. Reservations essential. Moderate.

Gee's Brasserie, 61A Banbury Rd (☎01865/558346). Chic conservatory setting, but not as expensive as it looks. The unusual menu includes chargrilled vegetables with polenta, a variety of steaks and a wide choice of breads. Open daily for lunch and dinner plus brunch at weekends. Moderate.

Hi-Lo Jamaican Eating House, 70 Cowley Rd (☎01865/725984). Legendary West Indian restaurant with oodles of atmosphere and imported Jamaican beer; the menu's meat-oriented (curried goat often features), the lighting low and the background music heavy reggae. Moderate.

Oriental Condor, 20 Park End St (☎01865/250988). Modernistic place opposite the train station with cool murals and the kitchen on view, offering very tasty authentic Chinese food. Inexpensive.

Le Petit Blanc, 71–72 Walton St (☎01865/510999). Renowned French chef Raymond Blanc's affordable, and much hyped, alternative to his famous *Manoir aux Quat' Saisons* in Great Milton, east of Oxford. It's been criticized for lack of space but the food is a refreshing mix of French gourmet (corn-fed quail with lime leaf and ginger) and traditional English (pan-fried Gloucester old spot pork). If you want to splash out, this is the place to do it. Expensive.

Pizza Express, Golden Cross, Cornmarket (☎01865/790442). Lovely Tudor building and the best-value pizzas in central Oxford, with superb garlic bread starter, but a pricey wine list. Expect a long wait at weekends. Inexpensive.

Shimla Pinks, 16 Turl St (☎01865/245564). One of the best Indian restaurants in the centre and part of a fashionable chain. This one has excellent-value set lunches, friendly service and good tandoori dishes, with vegetarian versions of most curries. Inexpensive.

Pubs and bars

Eagle & Child, 49 St Giles. Known variously as the "Bird & Baby", "Bird & Brat" or "Bird & Bastard", this pub was once the haunt of J.R.R. Tolkien, C.S. Lewis and other Anglican literary types, and attracts a fairly genteel mix of professionals and academics.

Isis, by Iffley Lock. Lovely spot amid the flood meadows, just under two miles' walk southeast along the Thames from Folly Bridge: definitely a summer pub. Iffley village nearby has one of the finest Romanesque churches in the country. Bus #4 from Queen Street or any service running along the Abingdon Road to Donnington Bridge, from which it's a ten-minute walk along the river.

Jolly Farmers, 20 Paradise St, behind the Westgate Centre. Oxford's most popular gay pub; mainly male and packed at weekends.

King's Arms, 40 Holywell St. Prone to student overkill over term-time weekends, but otherwise very pleasant, with snug rooms at the back. Good choice of beers.

The Perch, Binsey. Big garden, good – though not particularly cheap – food, busy at Sunday lunchtime. It's a pleasant thirty-minute walk northwest of the centre across Port Meadow, a large area of common land between the Thames and the rail line.

The Turf, Bath Place, off Holywell St. Small seventeenth-century pub with a fine range of beers, and mulled wine in winter, but slowish service because of the tiny bar. Abundant seating outside.

Victoria Arms, 90 Walton St. Northwest of the centre in Jericho, formerly where college servants resided and now Oxford's most atmospheric suburb. At one stage very run down, the area is now popular among students, academics, yuppies and hippies.

White Horse, 52 Broad St. A tiny pub that was used as a set for the *Inspector Morse* series.

Clubs, music venues and discos

The Coven (☎01865/242770), Oxpens Rd. Formerly a gay disco, but now gone more or less straight. Tacky grottoes for tête-a-têtes, but generally a good atmosphere and decent music. Thursday is best night for techno/acid/hard house. Open 9pm–2am.

Northgate Hall, 16 St Michael's St. A lesbian and gay centre with discos on certain nights (eg women only on Friday, mixed on Saturday). Vastly improved since it got a late licence, but still unpredictable.

Old Fire Station (aka OFS), 40 George St (☎01865/794490). Has found a niche for itself as a testing-ground for West End musicals; tickets for these workshop productions are cheap by London standards. DJs play dance sounds on Friday and Saturday, and there's a popular 1970s cheese night on Thursday. Admission £4–6.

Park End Club (☎01865/250181), 37 Park End St. A slick outfit, currently the most popular mainstream club in Oxford, with a couple of prosecutions for overcrowding, neckless heavies on the door and a cattle-market atmosphere at weekends. Open until 2am.

Philanderer and Firkin, 56 Walton St (☎01865/727265). Good indie bands play here, both local and moderately well-known ones on nationwide tours. The small room above the pub cannot cope with the crowds attracted by the latter. Go prepared to sweat.

Zodiac, 190 Cowley Rd (☎01865/420042). Far and away Oxford's most respected indie and dance venue, with live bands throughout the week, and the excellent *Transformation club* (guitar-driven indie pop) on Saturday.

Theatre, classical music, opera and dance

Apollo, George St (☎01865/244544). Known locally as the "Appalling", but the UK's top opera and ballet companies occasionally break up the monotonous programme of ageing pop acts and pantomimes.

Holywell Music Room, 32 Holywell St (☎01865/798600). This small, plain, Georgian building opened in 1748 as the first public music hall in England. Haydn once conducted here. It has a varied programme, from straight classical to experimental music, with occasional jazz.

Pegasus Theatre, Magdalen Rd (☎01865/722851). Low-budget, avant-garde productions dominate the programme of this east Oxford theatre.

Playhouse, Beaumont St (☎01865/798600). The city's best theatre. Professional touring companies (including the excellent Oxford Stage Company) perform a mixture of plays, opera and concerts, with the odd production by Oxford University Dramatic Society (OUDS), the top student group.

Sheldonian Theatre, Broad St. Hard seats and less-than-perfect acoustics, but still Oxford's top concert hall. Tickets and programme available from Blackwells Music Shop (see p.300).

Listings

Banks and exchanges All the major banks are on or near Cornmarket; American Express is at 4 Queen St (☎01865/792066).

Bike rental Bikezone, 6 Lincoln House, Market St, off Cornmarket (☎01865/728877); and Cycle King, 55 Walton St (☎01865/516122).

Books and maps Blackwells Travel Shop and Dillons, both on Broad Street, are the best source of literature on Oxford and the surrounding area.

Bus information Buses to London are operated by Oxford Tube (☎01865/772250) and Citylink (☎01865/785400), both running every 20 minutes or so during the day and hourly in the evening; the Oxford Tube continues through the night. These companies also serve Birmingham, Gatwick, Heathrow, Henley and Stratford-upon-Avon, but most other long-distance services are in the hands of National Express (☎0990/808080). Buses within Oxfordshire are run by the Oxford Bus Company (☎01865/785400) and a number of private companies including Swanbrook (☎01452/712386).

Car rental Avis, 1 Abbey Rd (☎01865/249000); Budget, Park End St, next to the train station (☎01865/724884); Hertz, City Motors, Wolvercote Roundabout, Woodstock Rd (☎01865/319972); National Car Rental, 2 Dawson St, bottom of Cowley Rd (☎01865/240471).

Cinema The ABC cinemas on Magdalen Street and George Street (both ☎01865/251998) show the latest blockbusters, while the best arts cinema is the Ultimate Picture Palace (UPP) on Jeune St, off Cowley Rd (☎01865/245288). The Phoenix on Walton Street (☎01865/512526) shows mainstream and arts films, and screens foreign-language films on Monday evenings.

Hospital John Radcliffe Hospital, Headington (☎01865/741166).

Internet Daily Information, 31 Warnborough Rd (Mon–Wed 9am–9pm, Thurs–Sat 9am–6pm, Sun 2–6pm; ☎01865/310011); Internet Exchange Café, Costa Coffee, 8–12 George St (daily 9am–5.30pm; ☎01865/241601); Pickwick Papers, 90 Gloucester Green (daily 9am–6pm; ☎01865/793149).

Laundry Coin Wash Launderette, 127 Cowley Rd; Safari Launderette, 113 Walton St, Jericho.

Pharmacies Boot's, 6 Cornmarket St (Mon–Wed, Fri & Sat 8.45am–6pm, Thurs 8.45am–7pm, Sun 11am–5pm; ☎01865/247461).

Police St Aldate's (☎01865/266000).

Post Office 102 St Aldate's (Mon–Fri 9am–5.30pm, Sat 9am–6pm; ☎01865/202863). All services, including fast cash currency transactions.

Taxis ABC (☎01865/775577); City Taxis (☎01865/201201); Euro Taxis (☎01865/430430).

Train enquiries For all enquiries, call ☎0345/484950.

Around Oxford

If you have a car, it is possible to go on day trips into the Chilterns and Cotswolds from Oxford. Those reliant on the buses will be more restricted, though **Blenheim Palace** is a straightforward ride from the city. Renting a bicycle is strongly recommended as, in addition to Blenheim and the **Vale of White Horse**, there are several interesting churches within easy reach of Oxford: such as the Norman abbey at Dorchester-on-Thames, eight miles southeast, and the church at South Leigh, nine miles west, with remarkable wall paintings dating from the fourteenth and fifteenth centuries.

Woodstock and Blenheim

WOODSTOCK, seven miles north of Oxford, has royal associations going back to the Saxon kings, who were first attracted by the area's potential for hunting. Henry I built the first royal lodge here, which was enlarged by Henry II into the palace in which the Black Prince was born in 1330. During the Civil War the Woodstock estate became a Royalist garrison, and in the following century Blenheim Palace was built on the site. The town has clearly benefited from the traffic of successive monarchs and grandees, though its handsome stone buildings and spruce streets are maintained nowadays mainly as a provider of food, drink and beds for visitors to Blenheim. Nonetheless, it's worth having a stroll around and spending half an hour at the **Oxfordshire Museum** on Park Street (Tues–Sat 10am–5pm, Sun 2–5pm; £1), a neat review of the archeology, social history and industry of the county. A refurbishment programme lasting until summer 2000 means that the permanent exhibition will be closed until then, though temporary exhibitions will still be taking place.

There are plenty of good **pubs** in the town, the best being the *Black Prince*, a five-minute walk north along Oxford Street away from the crowds; it has a varied menu and serves real ale. **Buses** from Oxford run every thirty minutes (reduced service on Sun), with some continuing to Stratford.

Blenheim Palace

Military achievement nowadays is rewarded with a medal or promotion, but in 1704, as a thank-you for his victory over the French in the Battle of Blenheim, John Churchill, First Duke of Marlborough, got money to build himself the only non-royal residence in the country grand enough to bear the name "palace". The chosen site was the royal estate at Woodstock, where the old residence was demolished to make way for the gargantuan **Blenheim Palace** (mid-March to Oct daily 10.30am–5.30pm; £8.50), designed by Sir John Vanbrugh, architect of Castle Howard in Yorkshire.

Acrimony on all sides characterized the building of Blenheim. Vanbrugh found himself at loggerheads with the duke's formidable wife, Sarah Jennings, who had wanted Christopher Wren as architect, while Queen Anne's Parliament, which had reluctantly approved the sum of £300,000 to finance the project, never paid the full amount. The house was finished only after the death of the man for whom it was built, owing its completion to the widowed duchess, who made up the financial shortfall and was responsible for much of the interior design. The Italianate palace, the country's greatest example of Baroque civic architecture, as well as its largest private residence, is too awesome to be beautiful and is more a monument than a house – as was always Vanbrugh's intention.

The present heir to the £100,000,000 estate is the Marquess of Blandford, whose antics – ranging from possession of drugs to burglary and assault – fill the tabloids from time to time, and may even result in his disinheritance. He's sadly not untypical of the clan. Other than the first duke of Marlborough, one of the few members of the family to have made anything but a poor impression was **Sir Winston Churchill**, born here in 1874. Several rooms are dedicated to the wartime prime minister, who is buried with his parents and wife in the graveyard of **Bladon church**, visible from the palace.

Highlights of the **interior** of the palace include the dining salon with murals by Louis Laguerre, furniture from Versailles, stone and marble carvings by Grinling Gibbons and several fine goldleaf ceilings by Nicholas Hawksmoor. Unfortunately, you don't get much of a chance to relish it all: guides whisk visitors through Blenheim in around 45 minutes, reeling off stultifying statistics that make the Chippendale chairs, family portraits and tapestries all merge into a spiritless inventory.

Formal **gardens** stretch southwards from the palace, but the open parkland remains the chief attraction, especially just north of the house, where the ground falls away dramatically to an exquisite artificial lake. It's said that Capability Brown, who landscaped the grounds, laid out the trees and avenues to represent the Battle of Blenheim. Whatever the truth of the tale, fine vistas fan out in every direction, including one from Vanbrugh's own bridge up to the Column of Victory, erected by Sarah Jennings and topped by a statue of her husband posing heroically in a toga.

There are two **entrances** to Blenheim Palace, one just south of Woodstock on the Oxford road and another through the Triumphal Arch at the west end of Park Street. If you wish to visit the **grounds** only (daily 9am–5pm; £6 with car, £2 for pedestrians) and are driving, use the free car park in Woodstock.

The Vale of White Horse

Extending southwest from Oxford, the **Vale of White Horse** takes its name from the prehistoric figure carved into the chalk of the Berkshire Downs above Uffington, eighteen miles from the city. Burial mounds and Iron Age forts pepper the downs, linked by the **Ridgeway National Trail** which runs along the top – paralleled below by the London–Swindon rail line and the A420 Oxford–Swindon road. In addition to the attraction of the White Horse and adjacent prehistoric sites, the downs provide fine and breezy walking country. Most paths follow the old drove roads, along which sheep were once taken to and from market, but nowadays horses are a more common site. The well-drained downland turf provides an ideal training ground for racehorses, and special areas known as "gallops" are used by numerous local stables, particularly around **Lambourn** on the southern slopes. You can see the horses in action at Newbury racecourse, just off the M4 to the south.

Wantage

Twelve miles southwest of Oxford, **WANTAGE** is a sleepy, slightly run-down market town, useful above all as a base from which to begin exploring the downs and Ridgeway. Its main claim to fame is as the birthplace of King Alfred the Great, whose statue dominates the Market Place. **Buses** from Oxford and Didcot pull in here every hour or so; for timetable information, call Thames Transit on ☎01865/772250. The *Alfred Lodge* at 23 Ormond St (☎01235/762409; ①) is an unassuming, friendly B&B, about five minutes' walk east of the centre, or, a mile south of Wantage in the hamlet of Letcombe Regis (ask directions for the footpath or catch bus #38), try *The Old Vicarage* (☎01235/765827; no credit cards; ②), a spacious Victorian house with a pretty garden opposite the village pub. A mile further south there's the Ridgeway Centre **youth hostel** (☎01235/760253) converted from five former barns, with spectacular views over the vale and just a stone's throw from the Ridgeway; take bus #38 from Wantage to Letcombe Regis, and walk a mile and a half uphill to the hostel from there.

Wantage has a fair selection of **places to eat**, including a passable Chinese and an Indian, but the pick of the restaurants is *Fox's* (☎01235/760568), just off the square on Newbury Street, which serves a constantly changing menu of gourmet food in cosy, congenial surroundings. For a less expensive pub meal, try *The Lamb* (☎01235/766768), a recently revamped thatched seventeenth-century building at the bottom of Mill Street (head northwest from the square).

The quickest way to reach the **Ridgeway** direct from Wantage is to take bus #38 beyond Letcombe Regis to **Letcombe Bassett**, less than a mile from the path – and the model for Cresscombe village in Hardy's *Jude the Obscure*. The best walks along the Ridgeway take you westwards from Letcombe, the stretch between Wantage and Wayland's Smithy via White Horse Hill being one of the finest along the whole route. Before setting off, it's worth visiting the **Vale and Downland Museum** on Church Street (Tues–Sun 10.30am–4.30pm; £1.50), which gives an excellent history of the local landscape and has a shop with useful books and maps.

White Horse Hill and Uffington

White Horse Hill, six miles along the Ridgeway west of Wantage, follows close behind Stonehenge and Avebury in the hierarchy of Britain's ancient sites, though it attracts nothing like the same number of visitors. Carved into the north-facing slope of the downs, the 374ft-long **horse** looks like something created with a few swift strokes of an immense brush, and there's been no lack of weird and wonderful theories as to the origins of this stylized creature. Some people have suggested it was a glorified signpost, created to show travellers where to join the Ridgeway. The idea that it was supposed to represent the horse (or even the dragon) of St George is scarcely less fanciful, though the saint's story is associated with other parts of this region. In Victorian and Edwardian times the best-loved legend, popularized in a ballad by G.K. Chesterton, claimed that it was cut by King Alfred as an emblem of his victory over the Danes at the Battle of Ashdown, fought nearby in 871 AD. The first record of the horse's existence dates from the time of Henry II, but recent research has suggested that its origin goes back some two thousand years earlier, as far back as the second millennium BC, making it by far the oldest chalk figure in Britain. A 1994 study showed that the carving could have been the work of people of the late Bronze Age, who dug out the soil to a depth of a metre, filling the hollow with clear white chalk taken from a nearby hilltop. Burial sites excavated in the surrounding area point to the horse representing some kind of sacred function, owing its survival to its use by successive incoming cultures.

Legend has it that the small flat-topped and possibly artificial hillock below the horse, known as **Dragon Hill**, was where St George killed and buried the dragon, a theory supposedly proved by the bare patch at the top and the channel down the side, where blood trickled from the creature's wounds.

Uffington Castle, the prehistoric fort above the Horse, now shown to date back to the same era, provides a grazing ground for sheep and the best vantage point in the area for visitors. The Ridgeway runs along its south side and continues west two miles to **Wayland's Smithy**, a five-thousand-year-old burial mound encircled by trees. It is one of the best Neolithic remains along the Ridgeway, though heavy restoration has rather detracted from the mystery of the place. Among a number of conflicting myths, the most romantic suggests that Wayland's Smithy was named after an invisible smith who made invincible armour and reshod travellers' horses. It's more probable that it was named by invading Saxons who stumbled upon it and, ignorant of its real function, appropriated it for their God, Wayland the Smith.

PRACTICALITIES

White Horse Hill can be reached up two narrow roads leading off the B4507, a Roman road otherwise known as the Portway, which follows a lovely undulating route along the foot of the downs. Getting to White Horse Hill on public transport is difficult, the only **bus service** to speak of being the #68 bus between Wantage and Faringdon on Wednesday and Friday. Uffington, six miles west of Wantage, is the closest village to the horse, thirty minutes' walk due south. A metropolis compared with the other villages along the Portway, Uffington has a couple of **B&Bs**, the better being the *Craven* on Fernham Road (☎01367/820449, *carol.wadsworth@cwcom.net*; ②); a less pricey option is the pleasant *Norton House*, next to the post office on the main street (☎01367/820230, *106436.145@compuserve.com*; no credit cards; ①). The *White Horse* **pub** (☎01367/820726; ④) in Woolstone, a hamlet hidden among the trees about a mile southwest, has overpriced rooms but serves tastier food than its counterparts in Uffington. There is limited **camping** space at Britchcombe Farm, in a fabulous spot by the Portway just east of the Uffington turn-off.

The Cotswolds

The limestone hills of the **Cotswolds** are preposterously photogenic, strewn with countless picture-book villages built by merchants enriched by the wool trade. Wool was important here as far back as the Roman era, but the greatest fortunes were made between the fourteenth and sixteenth centuries, during which period many of the region's fine manors and churches were built. Largely bypassed by the Industrial Revolution, which heralded the area's commercial decline, much of the Cotswolds is a relic, its architecture preserved in often immaculate condition. Numerous churches are

---

WILLIAM MORRIS AND THE PRE-RAPHAELITES

William Morris, the nineteenth-century socialist, writer and craftsman, had a profound influence on his contemporaries and on subsequent generations. In some respects he was an ally of Karl Marx, railing against the iniquities of private property and the squalor of industrialized society. Where he differed from Marx, however, was in his belief that machines necessarily enslave the individual, and in his vision of a world in which each person would be liberated through a sort of communistic, crafts-based economy. His prose/poem story *News from Nowhere* vaguely described his Utopian society, but his main legacy was the **Arts and Crafts Movement**, a direct offshoot of his work and a lasting influence on British crafts.

His career as an artist began at Oxford, where he met Edward Burne-Jones, who shared his admiration for the arts of the Middle Ages. After graduating they both ended up in London, painting under the direction of Dante Gabriel Rossetti, the leading light of the **Pre-Raphaelites** – a loose grouping of artists intent on regaining the spiritual purity characteristic of art before Raphael and the Renaissance tainted the world with humanism. In 1861 Morris founded **Morris & Co** ("The Firm"), whose designs came to embody the ideas of the Arts and Crafts Movement, one of whose basic tenets was formulated by its founder: "Have nothing in your houses that you do not know to be useful or believe to be beautiful." Rossetti and Burne-Jones were among the designers, though the former remains better known for his paintings of Jane Morris, his friend's wife and his own mistress, whom he turned into the archetypal Pre-Raphaelite woman. Morris's own designs for fabrics, wallpapers and numerous other products were to prove a massive – some would say negative – influence in Britain, as evidenced by the success of the Laura Ashley aesthetic, a lineal descendant of Morris's rustic nostalgia.

Morris's energy was not exhausted by his work for The Firm. In 1890 he set up the **Kelmscott Press**, named after but not located at his summer home, whose masterpiece was the so-called *Kelmscott Chaucer*, the collected poems of one of the Pre-Raphaelites' great heroes, with woodcuts by Burne-Jones. Morris also pioneered interest in the architecture of the Cotswolds – it was in response to hideous restoration work in this region that Morris instigated the **Society for the Protection of Ancient Buildings**, still an active force in preserving the country's architectural heritage.

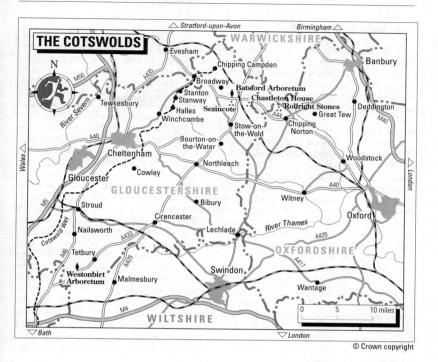

THE COTSWOLDS

N

△ Stratford-upon-Avon · Birmingham △

WARWICKSHIRE

· Evesham · Chipping Campden · Banbury

· Broadway · Batsford Arboretum · Chastleton House · Rollright Stones · Deddington

· Stanton · Stanway · Sezincote · Great Tew

· Halles · Winchcombe · Stow-on-the-Wold · Chipping Norton

Tewkesbury · River Severn

Wales △

· Bourton-on-the-Water

Cheltenham · Northleach · Woodstock

Gloucester · Cowley

GLOUCESTERSHIRE

Stroud · Bibury · Witney

Cirencester · Lechlade · River Thames · Oxford

London △

Nailsworth · Tetbury

Westonbirt Arboretum · Malmesbury · Swindon

OXFORDSHIRE

· Wantage

WILTSHIRE

0   5   10 miles

▽ Bath · ▽ London

© Crown copyright

decorated with beautiful Norman carving, for which the local limestone was ideal: soft and easy to carve when first quarried, but hardening after long exposure to the sunlight. The use of this local stone is a strong unifying characteristic, though its colour modulates as subtly as the shape of the hills, ranging from a deep golden tone in **Chipping Campden** to a silvery grey in **Painswick**.

The consequence of all this is that the Cotswolds have become one of the country's main tourist attractions, with many towns afflicted by plagues of tea and souvenir shops – this is Morris Dancing country. To see the Cotswolds at their best, you should visit in winter or avoid the most popular towns and instead escape into the hills themselves. This might be a tamed landscape, but there is good scope for walks, either in the gentler valleys that are most typical of the Cotswolds or along the dramatic escarpment which marks the boundary with the Severn Valley. A long-distance path called the **Cotswold Way** runs along the top of the ridge, stretching about one hundred miles from Chipping Campden past Cheltenham, Gloucester and Stroud as far as Bath. A number of prehistoric sites provide added interest along the route, with some – such as **Belas Knap** near Winchcombe – being well worth a diversion.

There are few large settlements in this region, the biggest true Cotswold town being **Cirencester**, a buzzing community dating back to the Romans. Nearby **Cheltenham** actually sits on the wrong side of the western escarpment and has little in common with Cotswold wool towns, but it likes to present itself as a gateway to the hills and is included here for that practical reason.

Lechlade and around

LECHLADE marks the westernmost navigable point of the Thames and thus in summer is teeming with pleasure boats, but for most people it's handy as a springboard for exploring the southern fringe of the Cotswolds. For **overnight stops** try the *Cambrai Lodge* (☎01367/253173; no credit cards; ②), the *New Inn* (☎01367/252296, *newinnlech@aol.com*; ②) or the *Flour Bag* B&B (☎01367/252322; no credit cards; ①), which doubles as a bakery. You can pitch a tent either at the St John's Priory **campsite** (☎01367/252360), a mile southeast along the A417 (follow the signs for Faringdon) or in the field by the *Trout* pub (☎01367/252313) next door. The boating fraternity congregates at the *Trout*, a real anglers' pub with stuffed fish on the wall (and live jazz on Tuesday and Sunday) a footpath leads there across the meadow from by the church.

There's lots to see around Lechlade, with the tiny church at **Inglesham**, by a farm about a mile south, one of the best sights in the entire region. Its oldest parts are Saxon and the whole building breathes history, its wooden screens twisted with age, its stone floor worn and uneven. You can walk to the church along the east bank of the Thames, though you must rejoin the A361 for a short distance at the end. Two other churches well worth visiting nearby are the one at **Fairford**, four miles west, which retains its beautiful medieval stained-glass windows, and at **Quenington**, two miles north of Fairford, with lovely Romanesque carvings. Isolated among fields just three miles east of Lechlade, **Kelmscott** has become a place of pilgrimage for devotees of **William Morris**, who used the Tudor manor as a summer home from 1871 to his death in 1896. The simple beauty of the house (April–Sept Wed 11am–1pm & 2–5pm; £6; ☎01367/252486) is enhanced by the furniture, fabrics, wallpapers and tapestries – some rescued from dog baskets – that were created by Morris or his Pre-Raphaelite friends, including Burne-Jones and Rossetti. Morris and his wife Jane are buried in the southeast corner of the churchyard, in the shadow of the minuscule church. If you intend to visit, it's wise to call first to confirm the very erratic opening hours. You can't reach Kelmscott on public transport, but it's a pleasant stroll along the north bank of the Thames from Lechlade.

Burford and the Windrush Valley

The A40 runs west from Oxford, whisking traffic through the heart of the Cotswolds. The **River Windrush**, flanked by gentle hills, meanders between willows alongside it, a contrastingly peaceful valley – at least until you reach **BURFORD**, twenty miles from Oxford. The time to appreciate the town's magnificent sloping High Street is not in summer, when cars battle for space while tourists fight it out on the pavements and in the antique shops. But the huge **parish church**, originally Norman but remodelled in the fifteenth century, is a delight at any time. An unusual monument to Henry VIII's barber, Edmund Harman, shows four Amazonian Indians, said to be the first representation of native Americans in Britain.

Spare a morning to follow the footpath along the Windrush through **WIDBROOK**, a hamlet with an idyllic medieval chapel built in the middle of a field on the site of a Roman villa, and on to **SWINBROOK**, just under three miles east of Burford. The church in this immaculate village contains a monument showing six members of the Fettiplace family reclining comically on their elbows: the Tudor effigies rigid and stony-faced, their Stuart counterparts stylish and rather camp. The best place for lunch or a drink in Swinbrook is the *Swan Inn*.

Burford straddles several main Cotswold routes. **Buses** along the A40 between Oxford and Cheltenham stop several times a day, and there are buses daily except Sunday from Lechlade; buses along other routes are mostly once-a-week market-day services. Many of Burford's old inns have metamorphosed into expensive **hotels**, but the *Highway Hotel* at 117 High St (☎01993/822136, *rbx20@dial.pipex.com*; ②) is good value. There are several **B&Bs**, including the *Chevrons* on Swan Lane (☎01993/823416; no credit cards; ①), parts of which date back to the sixteenth century; it's on a side street off the High St. A good fallback is *Langley Farm* (☎01367/878686; ①; closed Oct–April), a former hunting lodge three and a half miles northeast near the village of Leafield: head north along the A361, turn right at the crossroads onto the B4437, then first right and first left – the farm is one mile on the left.

Motorists heading to Cirencester, ten miles southwest (see p.317), should take the B4425 via **BIBURY**: this village is completely overrun with visitors, but anyone interested in the early industrial age should make a point of going to the seventeenth-century **Arlington Mill**, for a close-up demonstration of the workings of water power (daily: Easter–Oct 10am–6pm; Nov–Easter 10am–5pm; £2.50).

Stow-on-the-Wold

Straddling eight roads, including the Roman Fosse Way (now the A429), windswept **STOW-ON-THE-WOLD** sucks in a disproportionate number of visitors for its size and attractions, which essentially comprise an old marketplace surrounded by brassy pubs, antiques shops and souvenir boutiques. The narrow walled alleyways, or "tunes", running into the square were designed for funnelling sheep into the market, dominated by an imposing Victorian hall and, just to the south, a medieval cross allegedly raised to instil honesty among the traders.

Stow is the logical springboard for trips deeper into the region with its good bus connections from Moreton-in-Marsh and Cheltenham, and its abundant selection of accommodation options. The **tourist office** on the market square (April–Oct Mon–Sat 9.30am–5.30pm, Sun 10.30am–4pm; Nov–March Mon–Sat 9.30am–4.30pm; ☎01451/831082), sells National Express bus tickets and keeps a list of local **B&Bs**, among them the conveniently central and good value *Pear Tree Cottage*, on High St (☎01451/831210; no credit cards; ①). Tucked away on Union Street (take the short cut passage through the *King's Arms* pub from the square) is secluded *Clover Cottage* (☎01451/832210; no credit cards; ①), a good option for non-smoking vegetarians, or you could try *Tall Trees* (☎01451/831296; no credit cards; ③), on the edge of town off the Oddington road (A436), which has sweeping views, central heating and a cosy wood burner in its modern sitting room annexe. Close to the tourist office stands the popular **youth hostel** (☎01451/830497), but if you're **camping** you'll have to press on a mile or so east along the Oddington road (A436) to the Stow Rugby Club (☎01451/830887), the nearest campsite. For **food**, you've a choice of several old coaching inns on the square, including the *White Hart*, which specializes in down-to-earth meat-and-two-veg meals for under £6. Nearby, the *Royalist*, on the corner of Park and Digbeth streets, is yet another pub billing itself the oldest in Britain, a claim in part substantiated by wooden beams carbon-dated at around one thousand years old.

Moreton-in-Marsh and around

MORETON-IN-MARSH, five miles north of Stow and fifteen miles northwest of Burford, has more of a buzz than most Cotswold towns, particularly on Tuesdays, when the High Street disappears beneath a huge market. But the thing not to miss in Moreton is the **Batsford Arboretum** (March to mid-Nov daily 10am–5pm; £3.50), a fifteen-minute walk from the High Street. The largest private collection of rare trees in the country, it was planted in the 1880s by Lord Redesdale following his return from a posting in Tokyo. The hilly gardens have a distinctly Japanese flavour, and you can sit here amid magnolias and Chinese pocket-handkerchief trees enjoying wonderful views. Beside the entrance to the arboretum is the **Cotswold Falconry Centre** (March–Nov daily 10am–5pm; £3) which, in addition to a collection of beautiful birds of prey, gives flying displays (at 11.30am, 1.30pm, 3pm & 4.30pm; no 4.30pm flight in Nov) against a backdrop of the sweeping Evenlode Valley.

Moreton has better **public transport** services than most other towns in the region, with daily **buses** (except Sun) to Stow-on-the-Wold, Chipping Campden, Evesham, Malvern, Stratford and Cheltenham. In addition, Moreton is on the London–Oxford–Worcester **train** line. There's little in the way of **hotels**, however, *Moreton House* (☎01608/650747, *moretonhouse@msm.com*; ②) being the best value of those on the High Street. For **B&B**, try *Acacia*, an attractive period cottage on New Road, on the way to the station (☎01608/650130; no credit cards; ①). **Places to eat** line the main street, where blackboards advertise any number of inexpensive pub lunches. For a splash-out gourmet meal, head for the *Marsh Goose* **restaurant** (☎01608/652111), on the east side of the thoroughfare, which serves superb fresh seafood and game dishes, with an à la carte menu or set dinners for around £25 per head. **Bike rental** is available from Brian Jeffrey's toyshop on the High Street (☎01608/650756).

Two miles southwest along the A44, just before you reach Bourton-on-the-Hill, are the blue onion domes and miniature minarets of **Sezincote** (May–July & Sept Thurs & Fri 2.30–5.30pm; garden Jan–Nov Thurs & Fri 2–6pm; house & garden £4.50; garden only £3), tucked gracefully if incongruously among the Cotswold hills. This extraordinary house, built in the early nineteenth century, was the result of a collaboration between architect Samuel Pepys Cockerell (a distant relative of the diarist), and artist Thomas Daniell, both of whom had spent some time in India and been inspired by Moghul architecture. The end result so impressed the Prince Regent on a visit in 1806 that he ordered the designs for Brighton Pavilion to be changed along these exotic lines. Inside, a curious classical-cum-Chinese style takes precedence; outside, temples, statues and unusual trees and shrubs are scattered about the small but exquisite garden – and in the early months of the year the snowdrops and aconites make a glorious display.

The other stately home in this area worth a visit is **Chastleton House**, three miles southeast of Moreton off the A44 (April–Oct Wed–Sat noon–4pm; £5; all tickets must be pre-booked, call ☎01608/674284 Mon–Fri 10am–1pm; NT). Built between 1605 and 1612 by Walter Jones, the wealthy Welsh wool merchant and member of parliament for Worcester, this ranks among the most splendid Jacobean properties in the country, set amid ornamental gardens that include England's first-ever croquet lawn (the rules of this eccentric and most English of games were codified here in 1865). Inside, the house looks as if it's been in a time warp for four hundred years, with unwashed upholstery, unpolished wood panelling and even cobwebs clogging some corners. The air of general shabbiness derives in part from the fact that the Jones family lost their fortune after the Civil War (they supported the losing side), and could not subsequently afford to clutter their home with fancy Renaissance fittings; and in part because the National Trust, who took on the property in 1991, wisely decided the beguiling "lived-in look" should be retained. Three million pounds later, the house and its treasures – which include elaborate plaster friezes, priceless Florentine tapestries, family portraits, furniture and some exquisite glassware – are safely preserved, although without the rope barriers and surface sheen that can sometimes mar NT properties. If you're intending to visit, note that entry is by timed ticket only.

Northleach

Secluded in a shallow depression just off the Fosse Way, **NORTHLEACH**, seven miles southwest of Stow-on-the-Wold, is one of the most attractive, and least spoilt, villages in the Cotswolds. This fact, together with its location at the heart of the plateau, within easy reach of Oxford, Stratford and the picturesque Windrush Valley, makes it a perfect base from which to explore the region. Rows of immaculate late-medieval cottages cluster around a spacious central square, many of them with traditional stone-tiled roofs, but the village's most outstanding feature is its handsome Perpendicular **church**, erected in the fifteenth-century at the height of the wool boom, when the surrounding fields of rich limestone grasses supported a vast population of sheep. The local breed, known as the Cotswold Lion, was a descendant of flocks introduced by the Romans, and by the thirteenth century had become the largest in the country, producing heavy fleeces that were exported to the Flemish weaving towns. The income from this lucrative trade, initially controlled by the clergy but later by a handful of wealthy merchants, financed the construction of three major churches in the region, of which the one at Northleach is arguably the most impressive (the others are in Cirencester and Chipping Campden). Inside, the floor of the nave is inlaid with an exceptional collection of **memorial brasses** marking the tombs of the merchants whose endowments paid for the church. On several, you can make out the woolsacks laid out beneath the corpse's feet – a symbol of wealth and power that features to this day in the House of Lords, where a woolsack is placed on the Lord Chancellor's seat.

Two minutes' walk up the main street from the village square, **Keith Harding's World of Mechanical Music** (daily 10am–6pm; £5) is Northleach's other main attraction, comprising a bewildering collection of antique musical boxes, automata, barrel organs and mechanical instruments. The admission charge includes an hour-long demonstration tour of the collection, of which the highlight is hearing Rachmaninov and Gershwin playing versions of their own masterpieces on reproduction pianos.

A list of **places to stay** in Northleach is posted outside the **tourist office** (April–Oct Mon–Sat 10am–5pm & Sun 2–5pm; ☎01451/860715) in the otherwise missable Cotswold Heritage Centre at the turning off the main road (£2.50). Pick of the places in the village centre itself has to be *Cotteswold House* on the Market Place (☎01451/860493; ②), a wonderfully well-preserved Tudor cottage with exposed stone arches and thirteenth-century oak panelling on the walls; all the rooms have en-suite bathrooms. Less luxurious options on the square include *Market House* (☎01451/860557; no credit cards; ②), and *Banks Villas* on West End (☎01451/860464; ①). For **food**, your best bets are a bar meal either at the *Wheatsheaf Hotel* (☎01451/860244) just down from the square on West End, which also does a more sophisticated à la carte menu, or at the *Sherborne Arms* on the Market Place (☎01451/860241). In addition, *The Country Wine Merchant* on the square offers its clients the use of a barbecue in their back garden, where you can grill your own food provided you buy a bottle of wine from them first. Those for whom money is no object, however, may prefer to splurge on a meal at the famous *Old Woolhouse* restaurant on the Market Place (☎01451/860366; reservations essential), where you can expect to spend around £40 per head on top-notch French cuisine; the food is superb, but be warned that wine starts at £40 per half-bottle.

Chipping Norton and around

The bustling market town of Chipping Norton, 22 miles northwest of Oxford, presides over one of the least explored, but most scenic, corners of the Cotswolds – a region of rambling limestone uplands latticed by long dry-stone walls and dotted with picturesque villages. The western approach to the town, via the A44 from Moreton-in-Marsh, is dominated by the extraordinary chimney stack of the **Bliss Tweed Mill**, mounted on a domed tower and the quirkiest of a crop of monuments dating from the boom of the textile trade. Granted a charter in the twelfth century by King John to hold a wool fair, Chipping Norton reached its peak three hundred years later, when it acquired most of the stalwart stone houses and half-timber-framed coaching inns lining the market square. Also paid for by wealthy wool merchants, **St Mary's Parish**

Church, just below the square, harbours one of the country's finest fifteenth-century Perpendicular naves, in addition to some well-preserved brasses and tombs. More remnants of the town's former prominence are housed in the small **museum** at the top of the square (Easter–Oct Tues–Sun 2–4pm; Nov–Easter Tues–Sat 2–4pm; £1), among them a carved head of a Roman river god unearthed by a local farmer, and equipment salvaged from the Victorian wool mill and brewery.

Buses to Chipping Norton from Oxford drop passengers in front of the town hall, at the opposite end of the square to the **tourist office** (March–Oct Mon–Sat 9.30am–5.30pm; Nov–Feb Mon–Sat 10am–3pm; ☎01608/644379), where you can book **accommodation** in the area's plentiful hotels and B&Bs. Among the best options is *Kingsmoor Cottage*, two miles west along the A44 in the sleepy village of Salford (☎01608/643276; no credit cards; ①). Closer to town, but a little pricier, is *Southcombe Lodge*, a modern bungalow one mile east in the hamlet of Southcombe (☎01608/643068; ②). The best of the numerous **pubs** surrounding the square is the stone-tiled *Blue Boar*, which serves imaginative bar food and real ales. For a more sophisticated meal, try *Foggies/La Cantina* (☎01608/643363; closed Sun & Mon), a classy pasta **restaurant** and wine bar just along from the tourist office on Middle Row, where a three-course meal will cost around £15.

A labyrinth of lanes spreads east of Chipping Norton through a string of well-manicured villages and valleys to tiny **GREAT TEW**, the perfect target for a pub walk. Hidden deep amid woodland, this hamlet of honey-coloured houses contains one of England's most idyllic pubs, the *Faulkland Arms*, which serves a dozen or so real ales (including the legendary local bitter, Hook Norton), a fine selection of single malts, home-made herbal wines, plus snuff and clay pipes you can fill with tobacco for a smoke in the flower-filled garden. Little has changed in the flagstone-floored bar since the sixteenth century, although the adjacent snug was recently converted into a small restaurant serving snacks and evening meals.

Another local expedition takes in the **Rollright Stones**, high up on the wolds about five miles northwest of Chipping Norton, and the third most important stone circle in Britain after Stonehenge and Avebury. Legend recounts that these gnarled Bronze Age rocks are a king and his army (of unknown identity), petrified by a witch while on a campaign to conquer England.

Chipping Campden

CHIPPING CAMPDEN, six miles northwest of Moreton-in-Marsh, gives a better idea than anywhere else in the Cotswolds as to what a prosperous wool town might have looked like in the Middle Ages. The houses have undulating, weather-beaten roofs and many retain their original mullioned windows, while the fine Perpendicular **church** dates from the fifteenth century, the zenith of the town's wool-trading days. Inside, an ostentatious monument commemorates the family of Sir Baptist Hicks, a local benefactor who built the nearby almshouses and the market hall in the High Street. His own home was burnt down during the Civil War, but you can glimpse the ruins over the wall beside the church.

A fine panoramic view rewards those who make the short but severe hike up the Cotswold Way northwest to **Dover's Hill** (follow Hoo Lane north off the High Street). Since 1610 this natural amphitheatre has been the stage for an Olympics of rural sports, though the event was suspended last century when games such as shin-kicking became little more than licensed thuggery. A more civilized version, the **Cotswold Games**, has been staged each June since 1951: no shin-kicking, but still the odd bit of hammer-throwing.

Such a museum-piece as Chipping Campden must inevitably cope with a bevy of visitors in summer. Try to stay overnight and explore in the evening or at dawn, when the streets are empty and the golden hues of the stone at their richest. **Public transport** to the area is good, with frequent bus services to Moreton, Evesham and Stratford. You can't move for **guest houses** along the High Street, most of which can be booked through the **tourist office** (daily 10am–5.30pm; ☎01368/841206). Distinguished by its blue door, *Mrs Benfield's* on Lower High Street (☎01386/840163; no credit cards; ②) has fewer lacy trimmings than most (with correspondingly low prices), as does the *Volunteer Inn* on Park Road (☎01386/840688; no credit cards; ③). Most other **pubs** have rooms but are in a different price bracket, such as the *Noel Arms* (☎01386/840317; ⑥). The standard of **pubs** is good, but the *Eight Bells Inn*, around the corner from the church, is particularly cosy, and it serves top food. There's a window in the floor showing the passage once used by Catholic priests escaping from the church.

Winchcombe and around

The journey to **WINCHCOMBE**, twelve miles southwest of Chipping Campden, is stunning, whether you take the dramatic descent over the escarpment or the exhilarating ride down the B4632, which weaves along the lower folds of the cliff. Under the Saxons, Winchcombe became the provincial capital of the kingdom of **Mercia**, and it was the most important town in the Cotswolds until the early Middle Ages. The Saxon abbey didn't survive the Dissolution, and the town's main place of worship is the rather plain fifteenth-century church, most notable for its gargoyles. Apart from that, Winchcombe has an attractive blend of stone and half-timbered buildings and a couple of museums, but the real attractions are Sudeley Castle, Belas Knap and Hailes Abbey, all located just outside the town (see p.314). These, together with some of the finest scenery in the region and Tewkesbury only a short hop away, make Winchcombe a much more appealing place to base yourself than Cheltenham, or indeed, any number of more touristy towns and villages in the Cotswolds.

Bus #606 runs about once an hour through the day from Cheltenham to Winchcombe bound for Broadway; services from Chipping Campden run three times

---

SHORT WALKS FROM WINCHCOMBE

Drained by the sinuous River Isbourne, the scenic valley around Winchcombe is riddled with rewarding and well-marked trails, among them the **Cotswold Way** (see p.307), which cuts through the town before climbing to Belas Knap and the plateau of Cleve Common and West Down. From the edge of the escarpment, reached after a stiff sixty-to ninety-minute hike, the views over Cheltenham and the Severn Valley to the distant Malverns are superb.

A less strenuous, but equally inspiring, option is the three-and-a-half-hour round route to **Spoonley Farm**, just over two miles southeast of town, which takes in a ruined Roman villa where you can see a beautifully preserved **Roman mosaic** *in situ*. The existence of this antiquity was one of the area's best kept secrets until the American travel writer Bill Bryson featured it in his chart topping *Notes From A Small Island*, since when the tourist office has been inundated with requests for its *Country Walks Around Winchcombe* booklet (£1.25), which describes the route in detail. If you can't get hold of one of these, check OS Outdoor Leisure Map 45. The footpath to Spoonley Farm starts in the same place as the Cotswold Way, opposite the church at the south end of the main street, but shortly after peels left towards Sudeley Castle. After crossing the castle grounds, it follows the contour of the hill to Waterhatch Woods, site of the old villa; the mosaic is covered in sheets of plastic held down with stones, which you have to remove yourself (be sure to replace them afterwards). From the ruin, strike uphill as far as a farm track, which you can follow southwest, turning right at Cole's Hill towards Waterhatch Farm. The path then drops gently down to river level and eventually back to Winchcombe.

a day. Winchcombe's efficient **tourist office** (April–Oct Mon–Sat 10am–1pm & 2–5pm, Sun 10am–1pm & 1.30–4pm; ☎01242/602925), has a list of virtually all the **B&Bs** in Winchcombe. Among the best is the Jacobean *Great House* on Castle Street (☎01242/602490; no credit cards; ②), whose rooms all have four-poster beds; the *Gower House* at 16 North St (☎01242/602616; no credit cards; ①) offers a good, though noisier, alternative (it's on the main road), while *Clevely*, three miles out of the village on Corndean Lane (☎01242/602059; no credit cards; ②), is the least expensive option in the area. The nearest campsite is *Winchcombe Caravan Club Site* at Alderton (☎01242/620259), three miles north along the Stow road (B4077).

There's little to choose between the town's two main **pubs**, the *White Hart* and the *Plaisterers Arms*, which are both on the main street and serve food, but *Harvest Home* in the hamlet of Greet, one and a half miles along the Evesham road, sometimes includes delicious German specialities on its eclectic menu.

Sudeley Castle

A short walk west of Winchcombe, **Sudeley Castle** (March–Oct daily 10.30am–5.30pm; castle & garden £6; castle only £4.95) was once a favourite country retreat of Tudor and Stuart monarchs, though it never belonged to the royal family. It has a particularly strong connection with Catherine Parr, the sixth wife of Henry VIII, who came to live here after her marriage to Thomas Seymour, Lord of Sudeley, following the king's death. During the Civil War the house became a base for the Royalists (Charles I sought refuge here several times), then was later all but destroyed by the Parliamentarians. What remained stood empty until 1830, when the ruins were bought by the Dent family, whose work re-created an extremely handsome exterior but not the atmosphere of a fifteenth-century home. The motley collection inside includes paintings by Turner and Constable, a bed Charles I once slept in and one of Catherine Parr's teeth – her tomb is in the chapel. The real joy of Sudeley lies outside: in the **Queen's Garden** (closed March), with its huge yew hedges cut like masonry; in the creeper-covered ruins of the banqueting hall; and, above all, in the setting, with the green slopes of the escarpment behind.

Belas Knap

Up on the ridge overlooking Winchcombe, the Neolithic long barrow of **Belas Knap** occupies one of the most breathtaking spots in the Cotswolds. Dating from around 3000 BC, this is the best-preserved burial chamber in England, stretching out like a strange sleeping beast cloaked in green velvet. The two-mile climb up the Cotswold Way from Winchcombe contributes to the fun, giving good views back over Sudeley Castle. The path strikes off to the right near the entrance to Sudeley; when you reach the road at the top, turn right and then left up into the woods, from where it's a ten-minute hike to Belas Knap.

Hailes Abbey

Hailes Abbey (April–Sept daily 10am–6pm; Oct daily 10am–5pm; Nov–March Sat & Sun 10am–4pm; £2.60), a two-mile stroll northeast of Winchcombe, was once one of England's great Cistercian monasteries. Pilgrims came here from all over the country to pray before the abbey's phial of Christ's blood, a relic shown to be a fake at the time of the Dissolution, when the thirteenth-century monastery was demolished. Not much of the original complex remains beyond the foundations, but some cloister arches survive, worn by wind and rain. The ruin is undramatic, but Hailes is still worth visiting for the attached museum, for the tranquillity of the spot and for the nearby **church**, which is older than the abbey and contains beautiful wall paintings dating from around 1300. The cartoon-like hunting scene was probably a warning to Sabbath-breakers.

Cheltenham

Until the eighteenth century **CHELTENHAM** was like any other Cotswold town, but then the discovery of a spring in 1716 transformed it into Britain's most popular **spa**. During Cheltenham's prime, a century or so later, the royal, the rich and the famous descended in hordes to take the waters, which were said to cure anything from constipation to worms. These days a fair proportion of Cheltenham's hundred thousand inhabitants are above retirement age, and the town projects a rather smug, White, upper-class image – encapsulated by the row that arose over the selection of a Black barrister as Conservative candidate for the 1992 general election. A Black face wasn't acceptable to a large number of Tory voters, whose desertion cost the party a previously safe seat.

Though not a place you're likely to want to linger in, Cheltenham is a natural stopping-off place en route to the Severn Valley, and the haughty elegance of the Regency architecture, characterized by fancy ironwork and Greek columns, can be a pleasant change after the homely Cotswolds. The town is also a thriving arts centre, famous for its festivals of **jazz** (April), **classical music** (July) and **literature** (October) – and then, of course, there are the races (see box below). In addition, Coopers' Hill, six miles southwest on the A46, is the venue for the region's most bizarre, and established, competitions. On the second bank holiday in May, a steep section of the Cotswold escarpment hosts the village's annual **Cheese Rolling Festival**, when a large Double Gloucester cheese is rolled down the one-in-two incline and chased by dozens of drunken folk; the first to grab the cheese is the winner. The damage to life and limb has resulted in the race being banned in recent years, but it has been reinstated by popular demand, and now there are four races run, three for men and one for women.

Arrival, information and accommodation

All long-distance **buses** arrive at the station in Royal Well Road, just west off the Promenade. The **train station** is on Queen's Road, southwest of the centre; buses G and F run into town every fifteen minutes, otherwise it's a twenty-minute walk. Among the many leaflets and brochures handed out at the **tourist office**, at 77 Promenade (July & Aug Mon–Sat 9.30am–5.15pm, Sun 9.30am–1.30pm; rest of year Mon–Sat 9.30am–5.15pm; ☎01242/522878), is one giving a rundown of bus services to and from most destinations in the area. They also sell tickets for walking **tours** of the town

---

CHELTENHAM RACES

Cheltenham racecourse, a ten-minute walk north of Pittville Park at the foot of Cleeve Hill, is Britain's main steeplechasing venue. The principal event of the season, the three-day **National Hunt Festival** in March, attracts forty thousand people each day. A fair proportion of them come from Ireland, the birthplace of some of the greatest horses to have raced here, including the supreme steeplechaser, **Arkle**. Other meetings take place in December, January, March, April and November: a list of fixtures is posted up at the tourist office. For the cheapest but arguably the best view, pay £5 (rising to £15 during the Festival) for entry to the Courage Enclosure, as the pen in the middle is known. For schedules and other information, call ☎01242/226226.

A popular pre-meet watering hole is the *King's Arms*, a short walk east of the racecourse in **Prestbury**, an old Cotswold village with a reputation for being the most haunted village in England, and which has now been subsumed into the town. **Fred Archer**, considered by many to have been the finest Flat jockey of all time, was brought up here, and he features prominently among the pub's racing memorabilia. The pub has sadly lost much of its character since becoming part of a chain, and you might find the nearby *Royal Oak* more congenial.

(Mon–Fri at 2.15pm, £2.50), and for guided bus tours stopping at several destinations in the Cotswolds that are otherwise difficult to reach on public transport (mid-June to mid-Oct Tues, Wed, Thurs & Fri; £12); they're popular so book in advance.

Cheltenham makes an excellent base for exploring the Cotswolds by **bike**: rental shops include Crabtree's, 50 Winchcombe St (☎01242/515291) and Cotswold Cycling Company, 48 Shurdington Rd (☎01242/250642), which also arranges cycling holidays. Hotels and guest houses abound, many of them in fine Regency houses, and rooms are easy to come by – except during the races, when you should book weeks in advance. There are several B&Bs on or near Bath Road, east of the promenade.

HOTELS & B&BS

Brennan, 21 St Luke's Rd (☎01242/525904). Small Regency building, one of the best choices on this road. Non-smoking dining room. ②.

Crossways, 57 Bath Rd (☎01242/527683, *crossways@lynch.co.uk*). Non-smoking Regency house, two minutes walk from the centre. ②.

Lawn Hotel, 5 Pittville Lawn (☎01242/526638). Near the park, this choice is quiet and excellent value, with TVs in all rooms. No credit cards. ①.

Lypiatt House, Lypiatt Rd (☎01242/224994). This place in its own grounds wins the prize for comfort and personal attention. Open fires and a conservatory with a small bar sets the tone. ⑤.

Regency House, 50 Clarence Square (☎01242/582718, *penny@regency1.demon.co.uk*). Upmarket choice with period furnishings and leafy views from its well-equipped rooms. ④.

Willoughby Hotel, 1 Suffolk Square (☎01242/522798). South of the centre, this smart place has high-class home comforts, at fairly steep prices. Self-catering available. ⑥.

HOSTELS AND CAMPING

YMCA, 6 Victoria Walk (☎01242/524024). Cheltenham's cheapest central option is a short walk from the town hall. There are also extremely good-value lunches on offer.

Longwillows, Woodmancote (☎01242/674372). The nearest campsite, three miles north and accessible on Stagecoach bus #51 from Pittville Street. If you're driving, follow the signs for Prestbury/Winchcombe/B4362 and continue until you see a sign pointing left to Woodmancote village.

The Town

The focus of Cheltenham, the broad **Promenade**, sweeps majestically south from the High Street, lined with the town's grandest houses, smartest shops and most genteel public gardens. A short walk north of the High Street, through the ugliest part of the centre, brings you to **Pittville**. Planned as a spa town to rival Cheltenham, it was never completed and is now mostly parkland, where you can stroll along a few solitary Regency avenues and visit the grandest spa building, the domed **Pump Room** (Sat & Sun: May–Sept 10am–4.30pm, Oct–April 11am–4pm), whose chief function is as a concert hall – though you can sample England's only naturally alkaline water for free here. Once you've had your fill of old spa architecture, the **Art Gallery and Museum** on Clarence Street (Mon–Sat 10am–5.20pm; free) marks the high point of Cheltenham. It is good on social history, demonstrating particular enjoyment in showing the privileged lives of the Victorian upper classes, and has a fine room dedicated to the Arts and Crafts Movement, containing several pieces by Charles Voysey and Ernest Gimson, two of the period's most graceful designers. Also on display is an array of rare Chinese ceramics and a section devoted to the story of Edward Wilson, a local man who died on Scott's ill-fated expedition to the Antarctic. This is also one of the few museums in the world to have special exhibits for the blind and partially sighted.

For a matchless view over the town, catch a bus #606 out to Southam, one mile north of Prestbury village on the B4632, and follow the public footpath east up the sheer face of the Cotswold escarpment to the top of **Cleeve Common**. The summit, known as

Cleeve Cloud and topped by a cluster of radio masts, is the highest point along the Cotswold escarpment (1083ft). To round off the walk, head north along the ridge to Cleeve Hill, from where you can pick up buses back into town via the main road.

Eating, drinking and nightlife

Restaurants in central Cheltenham cater mainly for the upper end of the market, the best value is *Below Stairs* at 103 Promenade (☎01242/234599; closed Sun), which serves scrumptious fish and seafood at moderate prices. Two other places worth trying are *Le Champignon Sauvage* at 24 Suffolk Rd (☎01242/573449; closed Sun & Mon), which is very expensive, but has a quite reasonable fixed-price menu at lunch; and *Le Petit Blanc* by the side of the Queen's Hotel on the Promenade (☎01242/266800; closed Sun), an outpost of Raymond Blanc's famed *Manoir Aux Quat' Saisons* where you can eat contemporary French cooking at prices which become distinctly affordable at lunchtime (their three-course fixed-price menu costs £15 per head). At the stylish *Café Rouge*, 33 Promenade (☎01242/529989), three courses weigh in at £7.50 and breakfast is served all day; you can sit outside to relax over a coffee. *Boogaloo* at 16 Regent St, also has all-day breakfasts, musical accompaniment and a separate floor for smokers. Vegetarians and vegans are well catered for at the *Axiom Art Centre's* bright little café on Winchcombe Street where you can enjoy wholesome salads, snacks and main meals at bargain prices.

On the whole, Cheltenham's **pubs** are dreary; the *Restoration Inn* on the High Street, is worth a visit if only as one of the few survivals from the town's pre-spa days; less formal is the *Old Swan*, a few doors along, which serves fairly standard bar food as well as tea and coffee. For **live music**, your best bet is the *Axiom*, on Winchcombe Street near the Odeon cinema. This is the hub of the town's alternative scene, hosting bands most weekday evenings and DJs at weekends; their bar is also a cool place to hang out, with stripped-wood floors and a good choice of real ales.

Cirencester and around

Fifteen miles south of Cheltenham, on the very fringes of the Cotswolds, **CIRENCES-TER** makes a refreshing change from its neighbours – you'll see groups of young people around here, and for once green wellies and Barbours are not the predominant fashion. Nor does the town peddle the "olde-worlde" image that many Cotswold towns indulge in, though it has an endearingly old-fashioned atmosphere, generated partly by shops that haven't changed for decades.

Under the Romans, the town was called Corinium and ranked second only to Londinium in size and importance. A provincial capital and a centre of trade, it flourished for three centuries and had one of the largest forums north of the Alps. Few Roman remains are visible in Cirencester itself thanks to the destruction meted out by the Saxons in the sixth century. The new occupiers built an abbey (the longest in England at the time), but the town's prosperity was restored only with the wool boom of the Middle Ages, when the wealth of local merchants financed the construction of one of the finest Perpendicular churches in England. Cirencester has survived as one of the most affluent towns in the area, hence the much-vaunted title "Capital of the Cotswolds".

Nine roads radiate from Cirencester, five of them Roman. **Bus** services to the town could be better given its position, but there are daily connections from Swindon, fourteen miles southeast, and Cheltenham, fifteen miles north. All services stop in the Market Place.

The Town

Cirencester's heart is the delightful swirling **Market Place**, on Mondays and Fridays packed by traders' stalls. An irregular line of eighteenth-century facades along the north side contrasts with the heavier Victorian structures opposite, but the parish church of **St John the Baptist**, built in stages during the fifteenth century, dominates. The extraordinary flying buttresses which support the tower had to be added when it transpired that the church had been constructed upon a filled-in ditch. Its three-tiered south porch – large enough to function as the town hall at one stage – leads to the nave, where slender piers and soaring arches create a superb sense of space, enhanced by clerestory windows that bathe the nave in a warm light. The church contains much of interest, including a wineglass **pulpit**, carved in stone in around 1450 and one of the few pre-Reformation pulpits to have survived in Britain. North of the chancel, superb fan vaulting hangs overhead in the **chapel of St Catherine**, who appears in a still vivid fragment of a fifteenth-century wall painting. In the adjacent **Lady Chapel** are two good seventeenth-century monuments, to Humphrey Bridges and his family and to the dandified Sir William Master. Outside, one of the best views of the church is from the **Abbey Grounds**; site of the Saxon abbey, it's now a small park skirted by the modest river Churn and a fragment of the Roman city wall.

Few medieval buildings other than the church have survived in Cirencester. The houses along the town's most handsome streets – Park, Thomas and Coxwell – date mostly from the seventeenth and eighteenth centuries. One of those on Park Street houses the **Corinium Museum** (April–Oct Mon–Sat 10am–5pm, Sun 2–5pm; Nov–March Tues–Sat 10am–5pm, Sun 2–5pm; £2.50), which devotes itself mainly to the Roman era. Given that the museum has one of the largest Roman collections in Britain, the number of exhibits on display is disappointing, but a lot of space is taken up by **mosaic pavements**, which are among the finest in the country.

A yew hedge the height of telegraph poles runs along Park Street, concealing **Cirencester House**, the home of the Earl of Bathurst. At no point can you see the building (it is plain anyway), but the attached three-thousand-acre park is open to the public: you enter it from Cecily Hill, a lovely street except for the eccentric Victorian barracks. Although the avenues in the park restrict the scope for walks, you can still enjoy a pleasant stroll. The polo pitches attract some of the country's top players, with games held almost daily from May to September.

The **Brewery Arts Centre**, off Cricklade Street, is occupied by more than a dozen resident artists, whose studios you can visit and whose work you can buy in the shop. The centre's theatre hosts high-calibre plays and concerts (from jazz to classical), and there is a buzzing café on the first floor, open Monday to Saturday.

Practicalities

The **tourist office** (April–Dec Mon–Sat 9.30am–5.30pm; Jan–March Mon–Sat 9.30am–5pm; ☎01285/654180), in the Corn Hall on the Market Place, is excellent and has an **accommodation** list outside. A string of **B&Bs** lines Victoria Road, a short walk east: choose the house you fancy, since facilities and prices barely differ, though the non-smoking *Abbeymead*, at no. 39a (☎01285/653740; no credit cards; ①), *Warwick Cottage* at no. 75 (☎01285/656279; no credit cards; ①) and *The Leauses*, at no. 101 (☎01285/653643; no credit cards; ①) are cheaper than most. For a little more luxury, stay at the *Crown of Crucis Hotel* in Ampney Crucis (☎01285/851806; ④), a sixteenth-century former coaching inn with riverside gardens, a good restaurant and a no-smoking rule; to reach it, head two-and-a-half miles east on the A417. There's a **youth hostel** in Duntisbourne Abbots (☎01285/821682), a lovely rural spot five miles west reachable by infrequent buses. The most accessible **campsite** is at the *Mayfield Touring Park* at Perrotts Brook (☎01285/831301), two miles north on the A435; any Cheltenham-bound bus will drop you there.

For **snacks** you can't do much better than *Keith's Coffee Shop* on Blackjack Street, which also serves the best coffee in town. The *Café Bar* **restaurant**, next to the Brewery Centre, is inexpensive and goes out of its way to make its vegetarian dishes interesting (no credit cards; closed Sun). The best choice for a relaxing evening meal, however, is *Harry Hare's* at 3 Gosditch St (☎01285/652375), just behind the church, which specializes in classy renditions of down-to-earth English dishes; most three-course meals cost under £20, and they offer a good selection of wines. If you're splashing out and have transport, the *Crown of Crucis* in Ampney Crucis (see accommodation, above) is another option also worth considering.

Cirencester has plenty of **pubs**, their clientele swollen by tweedy students from the nearby Royal Agricultural College. Try the *Kings Head* on the Market Place or, for bar meals, the *Waggon & Horses* on Blackjack Street, and the *Butcher's Arms* in Ampney Crucis.

The Dunt Valley and Elkstone

The area northwest of Cirencester has a number of delightful churches well worth seeing, particularly in the **Dunt Valley**, one of the quietest corners of the Cotswolds yet just a stone's throw from the A417. Barn conversions and new houses attest to the number of cityfolk who've come here to escape the rat race, but few villages are large enough even to have a pub. Those without a car or a bike should not be discouraged from exploring: to visit the two best churches in the valley, at Daglingworth and Duntisbourne Rouse, will involve just a seven-mile walk. An excellent Ramblers' Association pamphlet, available from the tourist office, describes the route, or else use OS Landranger Map 163.

The hilltop church at **Daglingworth**, just two miles from Cirencester, has an unremarkable exterior, but inside there are three small **stone panels** – of Christ in Majesty, the Crucifixion and St Peter – that are among the best preserved Anglo-Saxon carving in the country. The simplicity and eccentric proportions of the figures, carved in deep relief, appear disconcertingly modern. Less than a mile beyond (you can walk along the Dunt for most of the way), the Saxon church of **Duntisbourne Rouse** perches on a steep bank beneath the road: a minute church for a minute valley, the Dunt being more a stream than a river. The interior of the church can't quite live up to the setting, but it has a finely carved Norman chancel arch and a delightful thirteenth-century wall painting of daisies. The road follows the valley north past Duntisbourne Leer, gathered around a ford, and **Duntisbourne Abbots** (two miles beyond Duntisbourne Rouse), where the houses tumble prettily down the hillside but the church is a disappointment by local standards.

On the other side of the A417, eight miles north of Cirencester and out of the Dunt Valley, **Elkstone** boasts the most beautiful **Norman church** in the Cotswolds. The nasty fifteenth-century tower aside, the church retains its original Norman structure and carving, the latter at its best in the south porch. Inside, the simple harmony of the vaulted chancel outshines even the exquisite carving around the arches and east window. A tiny spiral staircase on the left of the altar leads to a dovecote above the chancel.

Westonbirt Arboretum

About twelve miles southwest of Cirencester, **Westonbirt Arboretum** (daily 10am–8pm or sunset; £3.50) claims one of the largest collections of temperate trees and shrubs in the world: the maple trees, which set the place ablaze in autumn, and the blankets of bluebells and anemones in spring draw the biggest crowds. Azaleas, rhododendrons and camellias provide other great splashes of colour. Numerous paths criss-cross the six-hundred-acre garden: an average circular walk takes about an hour and a half, but you can easily stroll about for much longer than that. The arboretum flanks the A433, just west of Westonbirt village and three miles southwest of Tetbury, a handsome but untouristy Cotswold town. (Keen royalists should keep an eye open for the Prince of Wales and Princess Anne, who live nearby, at Highgrove and Gatcombe Park respectively.) The most useful public transport is the twice-daily #X55 Cirencester–Bath **bus**, which runs past the arboretum.

Malmesbury

The striking half-ruin of a Norman abbey presides over the small hilltown of **MALMESBURY**, one of the oldest boroughs in England. Lying eleven miles south of Cirencester (and only five miles north off the M4 motorway), it's not part of the Cotswolds geologically, though the town's early wealth was based on wool. Malmesbury certainly lacks the tweeness of the Cotswold towns to the north, with new housing estates encircling the centre, and modern developments marring views over the Avon. But none of this can detract from the splendour of the abbey, a majestic structure with some of the finest Romanesque sculpture in the country. **Buses** connect Cirencester and Malmesbury every one or two hours Monday to Saturday. Coming from Bath, it's best to catch a train to Chippenham and pick up a bus from there.

The High Street, which begins at the bottom of the hill by the old silk mills (converted into flats) and heads north across the river and up past a jagged row of ancient cottages, ends up at the octagonal **Market Cross**. Built in around 1490 to provide shelter from the rain, nowadays it is a favourite haunt of the local youth, whatever the weather. Nearby, the eighteenth-century **Tolsey Gate** leads through to the **Abbey** (daily: April–Oct 10am–6pm; Nov–March 10am–4pm). Founded in the seventh century and once a powerful Benedictine foundation, the abbey burnt down in about 1050; the twelfth-century building which replaced it was damaged during the Dissolution, and other parts collapsed at a later date. The **nave** is the only substantial Norman part to have survived, which it has done beautifully. A multitude of figures, in three tiers depicting scenes from the Creation, the Old Testament and the life of Christ, surround the doorway of the south porch, the pride of the abbey, while inside the porch, the apostles and Christ are carved in deep relief. Within the main body of the church, the pale stone brings a dramatic freshness, particularly to the carving of the nave arches and of the clerestory. To the left of the high altar, the pulpit virtually hides the **tomb of King Athelstan**, grandson of Alfred the Great and the first Saxon to be recognized as king of England; the tomb is empty, the location of the king's remains is unknown. The abbey's greatest surviving treasures are housed in the parvise, reached via a narrow spiral staircase right of the main doorway, where pride of place is given to four **medieval Bibles**, written on parchment and sumptuously illuminated with gilt ink and exquisite miniature paintings.

As well as harbouring the tomb of a former king of England, Malmesbury was the birthplace of **Thomas Hobbes**, the moral and political philosopher who suggested in his book *Leviathan* that the only way to avoid social chaos was for people to surrender their rights to an all-powerful authority, an ideology that has led to his being claimed as a precursor by the Left and Right alike. Another local celebrity is **Elmer the Monk**, who in 1005 attempted to fly from the abbey tower with the aid of wings: he limped for the rest of his life, but won immortal fame as the "flying monk".

There are several **B&Bs** in town. The **tourist office** in the town hall off Cross Hayes car park (Easter–Sept Mon–Thurs 8.30am–4.50pm, Fri 8.30am–4.20pm & Sat 10am–4pm; ☎01666/823748) has an accommodation list outside. The *Whole Hog*, a stone-walled tearoom-cum-pub overlooking the Market Place, serves good, inexpensive **food**, including Wiltshire ham and Malmesbury sausages, and a selecton of real ale. *Summer Café* on the High Street, is better for teas and coffees and also does food. The *Guild Hall Bar* on Oxford Street, opposite the tourist office, is a free house with good ale and pool.

Stroud and around

Five heavily populated valleys converge at **STROUD**, twelve miles west of Cirencester, creating an exhausting jumble of hills and a sense of high activity untypical of the Cotswolds. The bustle is not a new phenomenon. During the heyday of the wool trade the Frome River powered 150 mills, turning Stroud into the centre of the local cloth industry. Even now, Stroud is very much a working town, and one which doesn't need to peddle its heritage to the tourists in order to survive. While some of the old mills have been converted into flats, others contain factories – a few even continue to make cloth, including the so-called Stroudwater Scarlet used for military uniforms. That said, a string of boarded-up shop fronts in the High Street bears witness to a sharp economic decline over past decades, as employment possibilities have dwindled and shoppers travel to malls and out-of-town commercial complexes around Gloucester. The local council are poised to initiate a high-profile regeneration scheme – including a controversial housing development that threatens to engulf the picturesque Painswick Valley to the north in new estates – but for the time being the down trend seems firmly entrenched, and Stroud, in spite of its scenic setting, remains the dowdiest of the region's towns.

For visitors, interest centres around Stroud's industrial past: as a primer, you could spend half an hour at the **Lansdown Hall Museum**, which is due to move to new premises at the Mansion House, in Stratford Park Leisure Centre – check the current situation with the tourist office. Industrial archeology is strewn the length of the Frome Valley – the so-called Golden Valley. Council offices occupy one of the valley's finest mills, **Ebley Mill**, a twenty-minute walk west of the centre along the old Stroudwater Canal – for the best view you should then walk south across the field to the village of **Selsley**.

The unused **Severn and Thames Canal** east of Stroud cuts a more picturesque route, particularly beyond Chalford, three miles east, where houses perch precariously on the hillside. Walk thirty minutes along the towpath from here and you'll end up at the mouth of the **Sapperton tunnel**, more than two miles long and a great feat of eighteenth-century engineering. It is unsafe to go inside, so seek sustenance at the nearby *Daneway Inn* instead, or head for the hilltop village of **Sapperton**, a world away from the hurly-burly of the Frome Valley.

Trains on the London–Gloucester rail line stop at Stroud, which is also well served by **buses** from Cirencester. These and other bus services arrive at the station on Merrywalks. The **tourist office** is in the Subscription Rooms on Kendrick Street (April–Sept Mon–Sat 10am–5.30pm; Oct–March Mon–Sat 10am–4.30pm; ☎01453/765768). Most **guest houses** are at the top of steep hills, but the B&B at *Wilmington* (☎01453/752366, greg@gholder.free-online.co.uk; no credit cards; ①) is on a level street five minutes' east of the centre on the Cirencester road. The (non-smoking) *Lay-Bye* at 7 Castlemead Rd (☎01453/751514; no credit cards; ①), fifteen minutes' walk south of the centre, offers the best value among the places further out of town, while the *Downfield Hotel* at 134 Cainscross Rd (☎01453/764496; ②), in a Georgian building five minutes from the High Street, is a dependable choice further up the scale. You'll find the nearest **youth hostel** and **campsite** at Slimbridge (see p.322).

Many artists and New Agers live in the local valleys, and they make their mark on Stroud's restaurants. For **food** in the daytime go straight to *Mills Café* in Withey's Yard off High Street, which sells scrumptious cakes, home-made soups and other wholesome concoctions. Vegetarian and organic meals are also served in the town on Union Street at the *Pelican*, which calls itself an "ethnic pub" and has live jazz and folk. For more conventional surroundings, eat at the *Retreat* wine bar in Church Street, which is smartish but not overpriced.

Uley

The B4066 cuts a glorious route along the valley ridge southwest of Stroud, passing through **ULEY**, six miles from town. Boasting one of the best settings in the region, the village **church** lords it over the small green and the *Old Crown* pub, where the local brews include one called Pigor Mortis. **Uley Bury**, among the largest hill forts in

Britain, extends along the ridge above the village. The path from the church takes you up the shortest and steepest route, though motorists can opt to drive up to the car park right by the fort. Fences prevent you from clambering on top of the bury, but you can walk around the edge – a distance of about two miles altogether – and take in some staggering views. The atmosphere peaks on a winter's day, when bracing winds blow across the ridge while mist gathers in the valley below.

Slimbridge

Eight miles southwest of Stroud, out of the Cotswolds, **SLIMBRIDGE** sits in a narrow corridor between the M5 and the Severn – a surprising location for the **Slimbridge Wildfowl and Wetlands Centre** (daily: summer 9.30am–5pm; winter 9.30am–4pm; £5.25), covering 880 acres between Sharpness Canal and the river. Since ornithologist Sir Peter Scott created it in 1946, the centre has become Britain's largest **wildfowl sanctuary**, and a breeding ground with an important conservation role. Geese, swans, ducks and a huge gathering of flamingos make up the bulk of the birdlife. While some birds are resident all year round, many are migratory: the greatest numbers congregate in the winter months, when Bewick swans, for example, migrate from Russia. There is an extensive network of trails around the sanctuary, with hides for observation.

There is a comfortable, purpose-built **youth hostel** (☎01453/890275), with beds for £10.15, and a **campsite**, the *Tudor Caravan Park* (☎01453/890483), midway between the village and the wildfowl centre, about half a mile from each. The only **buses** to go anywhere near Slimbridge are those between Gloucester and Bristol or Dursley, which stop by the turn-off on the A38, just over a mile east of the village.

Painswick

The A46 and the B4070 are equally attractive routes linking Stroud and Cheltenham, but the former has the edge because after four miles you reach the old wool town of **PAINSWICK**, where ancient buildings jostle for space on narrow streets running downhill off the busy main street. The fame of Painswick's **church** stems not so much from the building itself as from the surrounding **graveyard**, where 99 yew trees, cut into bizarre bulbous shapes resembling lollipops, surround a collection of eighteenth-century table-tombs unrivalled in the Cotswolds. However, it's the **Rococo Garden** (mid-Jan to June & Sept–Nov Wed–Sun 11am–5pm; July & Aug daily 11am–5pm; £3), about half a mile north up the Gloucester road and attached to Painswick House (not open to the public), that ranks as the town's main attraction. Created in the early eighteenth century and later abandoned, the garden is being restored to its original form with the aid of a painting dated 1748. Although unfinished, it is already beautiful and the country's only example of Rococo garden design – a short-lived fashion typified by a mix of formal geometrical shapes and more naturalistic, curving lines. With a vegetable patch as an unusual centrepiece, the Painswick garden spreads across a sheltered gully – for the best vistas, walk around anticlockwise. In February and March people flock to see the snowdrops which smother the slopes beneath the pond.

The best **bus** service to Painswick is the #46 between Stroud and Cheltenham, which runs hourly during the week and four times on Sundays. The number of **guest houses** and **hotels** attests to the amount of people who find Painswick a more congenial place than Stroud, and the **tourist office**, housed in an old school at the bottom of the main street (Tues–Fri 10am–4pm, Sat & Sun 10am–1pm; ☎01452/813552), can help you find somewhere at the right price if the following places are booked: for quiet and reasonable rooms try the *Thorne Guest House* on Friday St (☎01452/812476; no credit cards; ②) or *Cardynham House* on St Mary's St (☎01452/814006; ③), where all rooms have four-posters, one of which has a private pool, open fires and lounge, and is available for £100 a night. Nearby, the *Royal Oak* **pub** is reckoned to be the best in town.

Alternatively, you might consider heading out of Painswick, to the village of Edge, half a mile west, where *Upper Dorey's Mill* (☎01452/812459, *sylvia@painswick.co.uk/doreys*; ②) offers plenty of rural atmosphere in a converted eighteenth-century cloth mill by the riverside (non-smokers only).

Gloucester

For centuries life was good for **GLOUCESTER**. The Romans chose the spot for a garrison to guard the Severn and spy on Wales, and later for a *colonia* or home for retired soldiers – the highest status a provincial Roman town could dream of. Commercial prestige came with trade up the River Severn, which developed into one of the busiest trade routes in Europe. The city's political importance hit its peak under the Normans, when William the Conqueror met here frequently with his council of nobles. The Middle Ages saw Gloucester's rise as a religious centre, and the construction of what is now the cathedral, but also saw its political and economic decline: navigating the Severn as far up as Gloucester was so difficult that most trade gradually shifted south to Bristol. In a brave attempt to reverse the city's decline, a canal was opened in 1827 to link Gloucester to Sharpness, on a broader stretch of the Severn further south. Trade picked up for a time, but it was only a temporary stay of execution.

Today, the canal is busy once again, though this time with pleasure boats. The Victorian dockyards too have undergone a facelift and are touted as the city's great new tourist attraction – and indeed they house some of the region's best museums. Gloucester's most magnificent possession, however, is the **cathedral**, its tower visible for miles around. Few other buildings in the city have survived the ravages of history and the twentieth century, with the centre a mish-mash of medieval ruins swallowed up by ugly new buildings. Gloucester is solidly downmarket, discount stores taking the place of the boutiques that characterize nearby Cheltenham. Yet this comes almost as a relief: Gloucester is without airs, and as variegated culturally as it is architecturally; you can mingle with farmers at the livestock market on Priory Road (Mon & Thurs) and then head along to the Guildhall on Eastgate Street, a buzzing arts centre with a cinema, regular exhibitions and a full and varied programme of concerts.

A web of roads engulfs Gloucester, surrounding the city like the tentacles of an octopus. If you're **driving**, head for the docks (well signposted) and park there. National Express runs **buses** from all neighbouring cities and beyond, and there are additional local services from Cheltenham (bus #94). **Trains** arrive every one or two hours from London, Cheltenham, Cardiff, Worcester and Bristol (for a full rundown see "Travel Details" on p.329).

The City

Gloucester lies on the east bank of the Severn, its centre spread around a curve in the river. **The Cross**, once the entrance to the Roman forum, marks the heart of the city and the meeting-point of Northgate, Southgate, Eastgate and Westgate streets, all Roman roads. **St Michael's Tower**, the remains of an old church, overlooks it. The main shopping area lies east of the Northgate–Southgate axis, with the **cathedral** and the **docks**, the focus of interest, to the west of it. The bus and train stations are opposite one another across Bruton Way, five minutes' walk east of the Cross.

Southgate and Westgate streets

The most interesting parish church in Gloucester is **St Mary de Crypt** on Southgate Street, mostly late medieval but with some of its original Norman features. A soft, soothing light filters through the stained-glass windows, and a sixteenth-century wall

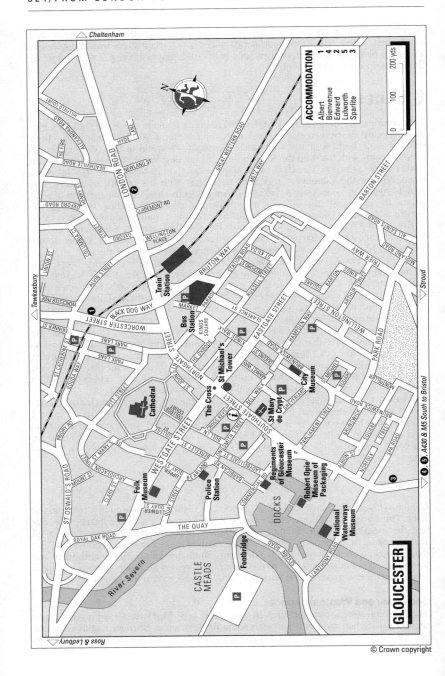

© Crown copyright

painting of the Adoration of the Magi in the chancel shows unusual detail for work of that period. Greyfriars runs alongside St Mary's, past the ruins of a Franciscan church and the Eastgate Market to the **City Museum** on Brunswick Road (July–Sept Mon–Sat 10am–5pm, Sun 10am–4pm; rest of year Mon–Sat 10am–5pm; £2; combined ticket with Folk Museum £3), with a good archeological collection including a fragment of the Roman city wall, preserved *in situ* below ground level. Westgate Street, quieter and many times more pleasant than its three Roman counterparts, retains several medieval buildings. One of them, a creaking timber-framed house at the bottom of the street, contains the **Folk Museum** (July–Sept Mon–Sat 10am–5pm Sun 10am–4pm; rest of year Mon–Sat 10am–5pm; £2; combined ticket with City Museum £3), which illustrates the social history of the Gloucester area using an impressive collection of objects, from huge wrought-iron cheese presses to salt-filled rolling pins used to scare off witches. College Court alley leads from Westgate Street to the haven of the cathedral, passing the Beatrix Potter shop and museum – the house sketched by the children's artist and author while she was on holiday here in 1897 and subsequently appearing in every copy of *The Tailor of Gloucester* – but it's really only for the seriously obsessed.

The Cathedral

The superb condition of Gloucester **Cathedral** (daily 8am–6pm) is striking in a city that has lost so much of its past. An abbey was founded on this spot by the Saxons, but four centuries later Benedictine monks came and built their own church, begun in 1069. As a place of worship it shot to importance after the murder at Berkeley Castle of Edward II in 1327: Bristol and Malmesbury wouldn't take his body, but Gloucester did, and the king's shrine became a major place of pilgrimage. The money generated helped to finance the conversion of the church into the country's first and greatest example of the **Perpendicular style**: the magnificent 225ft tower crowns the achievement. Henry VIII recognized the church's prestige by conferring on it the status of cathedral.

Beneath the reconstructions of the fourteenth and fifteenth centuries, some Norman aspects remain, best seen in the **nave**, flanked by sturdy pillars and arches adorned with immaculate zigzag mouldings. Only when you reach the choir and transepts can you see how skilfully the new church was built inside the old, the Norman masonry hidden beneath the finer lines of the Perpendicular panelling and tracery. The **choir** has extraordinary fourteenth-century misericords, and also provides the best vantage point for admiring the east window, completed in around 1350 and – at almost eighty feet tall – the **largest medieval window** in Britain. Beneath it, to the left (as you're facing the east window) is the **tomb of Edward II**, immortalized in alabaster and marble and in good fettle apart from some graffiti. In the nearby **Lady Chapel**, delicate carved tracery holds a staggering patchwork of windows, virtually creating walls of stained glass. There are well-preserved monuments here too, but the tomb of Robert II, back in the **presbytery**, is far more unusual. Robert, eldest son of William the Conqueror, died in 1134, but the painted wooden effigy dates from around 1290. Dressed as a crusader, he lies in a curious pose, with his arms and legs crossed, his right hand gripping his sword ready to do battle with the infidel.

The innovative nature of the cathedral's design can perhaps be best appreciated in the beautiful **cloisters**, completed in 1367 and featuring the first fan vaulting in the country. The fine quality of the work is outdone perhaps only by Henry VII's Chapel in Westminster Abbey, which it inspired. Back inside, an **exhibition** in the upstairs galleries, reached from the north transept (April–Oct Mon–Fri 10.30am–4pm, Sat 10.30am–3pm; £1) traces the history of the cathedral, putting it into context with that of the city as a whole. Try out the **Whispering Gallery** here, where you can pick up the tiniest sounds from across the vaulting.

The Docks

The **Docks** complex was developed during the fifty years following the opening of the Sharpness canal in 1827. The import of corn represented the bulk of the port's business at that time, and huge **warehouses** were built for storing the grain. Fourteen of them have survived, mostly now converted into municipal offices, shops and museums, a redevelopment at its most crudely commercial in the **Merchants' Quay** shopping centre, an oversized greenhouse full of forlorn shoppers.

The museums, however, are excellent. The **Robert Opie Museum of Packaging and Advertising** (March–Sept daily 10am–6pm; Oct–Feb Tues–Sun 10am–5pm; £3.50) gathers together a collection of packets and tins spanning almost a century, from late Victorian times to the 1990s. The first part takes you through the last hundred years decade by decade – something of a nostalgia trip, going back to the good old days of British manufacturing industry. Look out for the "Nasti" toilet roll, with a picture of Hitler and the catchphrase "a unique sanitary bum paper". The museum café is mundane by comparison, but it's worth sitting a while to enjoy the old commercials shown on the television.

The much bigger **National Waterways Museum** (daily 10am–5pm; £4.75), in the southernmost Llanthony Warehouse, completely immerses you in the canal mania which swept Britain in the eighteenth and nineteenth centuries, touching on everything from the engineering of the locks to the lives of the horses that trod the towpaths. You walk round to a lively background of recordings, including imaginary dialogues spoken in good West Country accents and readings of contemporary accounts; there's also a series of excellent hands-on displays, particularly on the top floor where you can steer your own narrow boat (harder than it looks) or build a canal on a computer.

The **Regiments of Gloucestershire Museum** in the old customs house (June–Sept daily 10am–5pm; Oct–May Tues–Sun 10am–5pm; £4), does an award-winning job of making a potentially dull or alienating subject fascinating. It doesn't rely on the displays of uniforms and miscellaneous memorabilia used in most military museums, but concentrates on all aspects of life as a soldier, both in war and during peacetime.

Practicalities

The **tourist office** is at 28 Southgate St (Mon–Sat 10am–5pm; ☎01452/421188). Judging from the amount of **accommodation** in the city centre, Gloucester doesn't expect many visitors to stay overnight. Of the few **hotels** within easy walking distance of the train station and centre, the *Albert* at 56–58 Worcester St (☎01452/502081; ②) and the *Edward* at 88 London Rd (☎01452/525865; ②), offer the best value. A central, inexpensive B&B is *Spalite* (☎01452/380828; ②), at the bottom of Southgate Street near the docks, although it's right on the main road and a bit prone to traffic noise. For organic breakfasts and evening meals, try *Bienvenue* at 54 Central Rd (☎01452/523284; no credit cards; ②; closed Nov & Jan), half a mile south of the centre off the Stroud road. There are more B&Bs on or near London Road, north of the centre, but this area has little to recommend it beyond slightly cheaper room rates and proximity to the train station; elsewhere, a good-value choice is *Lulworth* at 12 Midland Rd (☎01452/521881; ①), in a quiet location behind the Park.

The selection of **restaurants** is only slightly more remarkable than its hotels, and many places are open only during the day. You'll find some of the best food in the city at the *Undercroft Restaurant* in the cathedral, open until 4pm and at the café-bar in the Guildhall on Eastgate Street – open until 11pm and always lively. *Ye Olde Fish Shoppe* on Hare Lane, even more of a Gloucester institution, occupies a sixteenth-century building and is the fanciest take-away for miles; it serves excellent crispy fish until 6.30pm, though the attached restaurant stays open later (☎01452/255502; no credit cards; closed all Sun & Mon eve). You'll hunt in vain for a more conventional restaurant serving classier food, though the *College Green Eating House* at 9 College St is reasonably good (☎01452/520739; closed Sun in winter). For pizzas go to *Pizza Piazza* at Merchants' Quay – the only reason to venture to the docks in the evening.

There isn't a huge choice of **pubs**, the best are all within spitting distance of the Cross. The rambling fifteenth-century *New Inn* in Northgate Street has a good atmosphere, a splendid galleried courtyard and cheap meals, but for really tasty hot food at rock bottom prices go to the *Fountain Inn*, down a narrow alley off Westgate Street, this pub pulls a sublime pint of Abbot ale and has tables in an olde-worlde adjacent courtyard – ideal for a sunny day.

Tewkesbury and around

The small market town of **TEWKESBURY**, ten miles north of Gloucester, stands hemmed in by the Avon and Severn rivers, which converge nearby, and the threat of floods has curbed expansion more efficiently than any conservation-conscious planning office could. In addition to the pressure of space, the comparatively unchanging face of Tewkesbury is also due to the fact that it almost completely missed out on the Industrial Revolution. Elegant Georgian houses and medieval timber-framed buildings still line several of the town's main streets – especially Church Street – and the Norman **abbey** has survived as one of the greatest in England. Some old buildings inevitably fell to postwar bulldozers, however, particularly along the High Street, and recent years haven't been kind to the town's economy. Tewkesbury is still recovering from the recession which hit local aerospace and electronics industries particularly badly – its title "The Silicon Chip Valley of the West Country" rings rather hollow these days.

The constant rumble of traffic through Tewkesbury can be troublesome, but the fact that four main roads meet here (Gloucester, Worcester, Evesham and Ledbury are all within fifteen miles) means that getting to the town is fairly easy. Stagecoach, Swanbrook and Midland Red operate most **buses** to Tewkesbury, running from Gloucester, Cheltenham, Worcester and Evesham; for current timetable information, call the tourist office (see p.328).

Tewkesbury Abbey

The site of **Tewkesbury Abbey** was first selected for a Benedictine monastery in the eighth century, but virtually nothing of the Saxon complex survived a sacking by the Danes, and a new abbey was founded by a Norman nobleman in 1092. The work took about sixty years to complete, with some additions made in the fourteenth century. Two hundred years later the Dissolution brought about the destruction of most of the monastic buildings, but the abbey itself survived thanks to a buy-out in which the local people paid Henry VIII £453 for the property.

The sheer scale of the abbey's exterior makes a lasting impact: its colossal **tower** is the largest Norman tower in the world, while the west front's soaring recessed arch – 65 feet high – is the only exterior arch in the country to boast such impressive proportions. In the nave, fourteen stout Norman pillars steal the show, graceful despite their size and despite the vaulted ceiling, which bears down too heavily overhead. The roof of the fourteenth-century **choir** on the other hand is staggering. The brightly painted bosses include a ring of Yorkist suns, said to have been put there by Edward IV after the defeat of the Lancastrians at Tewkesbury in 1471, the last important battle of the Wars of the Roses. (The battlefield, known as Bloody Meadow, is off Lincoln Green Lane, southwest of the abbey.) South of the choir is the **Milton Organ**, played by the poet when he was secretary to Oliver Cromwell at Hampton Court and bought by the townspeople in 1727. The abbey's medieval **tombs** celebrate Tewkesbury's greatest patrons, the Fitzhamons, De Clares, Beauchamps and Despensers, who turned the building into something of a mausoleum for themselves. The Despensers have the best monuments, particularly Sir Edward, standard-bearer to the Black Prince, who died in 1375 and is shown as a kneeling figure on the roof of the **Trinity Chapel** to the right of the high altar: you can see it best from beside the Warwick Chantry Chapel in the north aisle. Nearby, in the ambulatory, the macabre so-called **Wakeman Cenotaph**, carved in the fifteenth century but of otherwise uncertain origin, represents a decaying corpse being consumed by snakes and other creatures.

Practicalities

The **tourist office** at 64 Barton St (April–Oct Mon–Sat 9am–5pm, Sun 10am–4pm; rest of year closed Sun; ☎01684/295027) has inexpensive town and walking maps, plus a small museum upstairs. You won't have to look far to find a **room**, though noise can be a problem. There are several guest houses and B&Bs on Barton Road, including the cheap and cheerful *Bali-Hai* at no. 5 (☎01684/292049; no credit cards; ①). More genteel are the *Two Back of Avon*, a beautiful period building on Riverside Walk (☎01684/298935; no credit cards; ②), or the quiet *Carrant Brook House* on Rope Walk (☎01684/290355; no credit cards; ③). The *Malvern View Guest House* at 1 St Mary's Lane (☎01684/292776; no credit cards; ①) has nice views but little character. Most of Tewkesbury's smart old **hotels** are run by chains: the *Abbey Hotel* at 67 Church St (☎01684/294247; ③) is the friendliest, but for style you can't beat Tewkesbury's two top hotels, the *Tudor House*, High St (☎01684/297755; ④), and the *Bell* at 52 Church St (☎01684/293293; ⑤); both are housed in splendid old buildings, but the latter, overlooking the abbey, has the edge. There are no fewer than five **camping sites** within striking distance of the city, the most easily accessible being the *Abbey Caravan Club* in the park at the bottom of Gander Lane (☎01684/294035).

The town has a curious line in **teashops**, several of which make you feel as if you're in someone's sitting room; try the one in the *Bible Bookshop* on Nelson St (closed Sun & Mon), or the *Hen and Chicken* on Barton St (closed Sun am & all Mon). Its **pub** equivalent is the ancient *Berkeley Arms* on Church Street, which is popular with pensioners and serves astoundingly cheap but distinctly basic food. If quality takes priority over local colour, you'll do better at *Ye Olde Black Bear* at the top of the High Street, which also pulls some of the best pints in town. *Le Bistro André* at 78 Church St (☎01684/290357; closed Sun & Mon) is a lively, moderately priced French restaurant serving anything from snails to venison; credit cards entail a five-percent surcharge.

Deerhurst

Before the construction of Tewkesbury's Norman abbey, **Deerhurst**, just south of the town, was the most prestigious religious centre in the area. As the chief monastery in the Saxon kingdom of Hwicce, it was considered a suitable venue for the meeting in 1016 between the English king Edmund Ironside and Cnut (Canute) the Dane, at which the partition of England was agreed. Deerhurst's importance declined after 1100, but two outstanding buildings date back to the village's heyday.

The monastery church of **St Mary's** is a chronological jumble: some masonry dates back to the eighth century, but the Saxon work was done mainly in the tenth. The Normans then chopped the insides about a bit (they had the nerve to knock arches into the nave walls, which somehow didn't collapse), and other additions came later. The interior remains remarkably simple considering, and contains several very rare features, none more so than the series of curious **windows and holes** which puncture the nave walls: these small triangular piercings, cut by the Saxons, are said to represent the eyes of God. In the north aisle, a ninth-century **font** of golden Cotswold stone has intricate spiral decoration unique for that period. Outside, a sign directs you to a stylized carved angel high up on the wall of the ruined apse; though also Saxon, the relief looks more Celtic in inspiration. The adjoining house once formed part of the monastery's cloister.

The nearby **Odda's Chapel**, which also clings to another building (in this case a half-timbered cottage), lay neglected until last century, its Saxon masonry smothered underneath plaster. It is only slightly younger than St Mary's, having been built in 1056 by Odda in honour of his brother Aelfric, both relatives of the king. The small chapel, just forty feet long, has survived in good condition apart from a few damp patches. The original dedicatory inscription is in the Ashmolean Museum in Oxford, but a copy has been put in its original place.

Deerhurst is four miles south of Tewkesbury by road, but only two miles on foot across the fields or along the Severn. Alternatively, you can catch the #372 **bus** (not Sun) from Tewkesbury to Gloucester, which stops within a mile of Deerhurst.

Bredon Hill

The most important Iron Age fort in the area once crowned **Bredon Hill**, six miles northeast of Tewkesbury and visible for miles around in the flat Severn Vale. Excavation of the site revealed more than fifty bodies, all hacked to pieces, seemingly the victims of a final assault by unknown attackers in the first century AD. Inside the rampart, a huge expanse covering eleven acres, an eighteenth-century tower called Parson's Folly is an incongruous centrepiece, but the views are supreme, with deer often grazing on the slopes.

Bredon Hill can be approached from various places around the southern foot of the hill. From **Overbury**, one of the prettier villages, the climb takes less than an hour. If you're relying on public transport, buses bound for Evesham from Tewkesbury pass through the village of **Bredon** (except Sun), from where you should allow about three hours to walk to the hill and back.

travel details

Trains
Bedford to: London (1–2 hourly; 30min–1hr); St Albans (1–2 hourly; 40min).
Cheltenham to: Birmingham (1–2 hourly; 40min–1hr); Bristol (hourly; 1hr); Gloucester (1–2 hourly; 10min); London (1–2 hourly; 2hr); Worcester (every 2hr; 30min).
Gloucester to: Birmingham (1–2 hourly; 1hr); Bristol (hourly; 40min); Cheltenham (1–2 hourly; 15min); London (1–2 hourly; 2hr); Stroud (7 daily; 20min).
Henley to: London, via Reading (hourly; 30min–1hr).
Milton Keynes to: Birmingham (hourly; 1hr 20min); London (2 hourly; 40min); Twyford (7 daily; 30min–1hr).
Oxford to: Birmingham (hourly; 1hr 30min); London (1–2 hourly; 1hr); London (1–2 hourly; 1hr); Moreton-in-Marsh (hourly; 40min); Worcester (hourly; 1hr 10min).

St Albans to: Bedford (1–2 hourly; 40min); London (14 daily; 20–40min).

Buses
Bedford to: Cambridge (4–10 daily; 45min); London (4 daily; 2hr); Milton Keynes (every 2hr; 45min); Northampton (hourly; 50min).
Cheltenham to: Bath (daily; 2hr); Birmingham (4 daily; 1hr 10min); Bristol (5 daily; 1hr 15min); Broadway (4 daily; 1hr); Burford (3 daily; 45min); Chipping Campden (Thurs & Sat, also Wed July–Sept; 1hr); Cirencester (Mon–Sat 5 daily; 40min); Evesham (Mon–Sat 4 daily; 1hr 10min); Gloucester (2–4 hourly; 30–45min); London (11 daily; 2hr 40min); Malvern (Sat 3 daily; 1hr 30min); Moreton-in-Marsh (5 daily, 1 on Sun; 1hr); Oxford (5 daily, 3 on Sun; 1hr 30min); Painswick (10 daily, 3 on Sun; 40min); Stow-on-the-Wold (7–9 daily, 1 on Sun; 50min); Stratford-upon-Avon (2 daily; 1hr 30min); Stroud (10 daily; 45min);

Swindon (5 daily; 1hr 40min); Tewkesbury (9 daily; 30min); Warwick (1 daily; 2hr); Winchcombe (hourly; 30min).

Cirencester to: Cheltenham (Mon–Sat 5 daily; 40min); Gloucester (7 daily; 50min); Lechlade (8 daily; 20min); London (8 daily; 2hr 30min); Malmesbury (4 daily; 45min); Stroud (7 daily, 1 on Sun; 45min); Swindon (5–12 daily; 50min); Tetbury (6–9 daily, 2 on Sun; 45min).

Gloucester to: Bath (Wed & Sat; 1hr 30min); Birmingham (4 daily; 1hr 15min); Bristol (5 daily; 50min); Cheltenham (2–4 hourly; 30–45min); Cirencester (7 daily; 50min); Exeter (4 daily; 3hr 10min); Hereford (2 daily; 50min); Ledbury (Mon–Sat 3 daily; 1hr); Oxford (5 daily, 3 on Sun; 2hr); Stroud (hourly; 30min); Tewkesbury (10 daily, 5 on Sun; 40min–1hr); Worcester (5 daily; 1hr 30min).

Henley to: Aylesbury (Mon–Sat 2 daily; 1hr 20min); Marlow (2 hourly; 20min); Milton Keynes (2 daily; 2hr 30min); Oxford (9 daily; 1hr 15min); London (8 daily; 1hr 40min).

Milton Keynes to: Aylesbury (Mon–Sat hourly; 1hr–1hr 20min), Bedford (Mon–Sat every 2hr; 45min); Buckingham (Mon–Sat hourly, 3 on Sun; 20min); Dunstable (Mon–Sat 4 daily; 45min); Henley (2 daily; 2hr 30min), London (hourly; 1hr 30min); Oxford (4 daily; 1hr 15min).

Oxford to: Aylesbury (hourly; 1hr 10min); Bath (3 daily; 2hr); Birmingham (9–12 daily; 1hr 30min); Bristol (5 daily; 2hr 30min); Burford (11 daily; 30–50min); Cambridge (9 daily; 3hr); Cheltenham (Mon–Sat 5 daily, 3 on Sun; 1hr 10min–1hr 30min); Gloucester (Mon–Sat 5 daily, 3 on Sun; 1hr 30min–2hr); Henley (15 daily; 1hr); London (hourly; 1hr 45min); Stratford (3 daily; 1hr 30min); Swindon (Mon–Sat 5 daily; 1hr); Tewkesbury (1 daily; 2hr 30min); Woodstock (2 hourly; 30min); Worcester (1 daily; 2hr).

Stroud to: Cheltenham (Mon–Sat 7 daily; 45min); Cirencester (7 daily, 1 on Sun; 45min); Gloucester (hourly; 30min); Painswick (8 daily, 4 on Sun; 10min); Tetbury (6–8 daily; 40min).

Tewkesbury to: Cheltenham (9 daily; 30min); Gloucester (10 daily, 5 on Sun; 40min–1hr); Oxford (1 daily; 2hr 30min–3hr); Worcester (Mon–Sat 10 daily; 40min–1hr 10min).

CHAPTER FIVE

THE WEST COUNTRY

E ngland's **West Country** – comprising the counties of Somerset, Devon and Cornwall and the city of Bristol – is a region encompassing everything from genteel, cosy villages to vast Atlantic-facing strands of golden sand and wild expanses of granite moorland. It would be impossible to do justice to this great peninsula by basing yourself in any one place – the country beckons ever westwards into rural backwaters where increasingly exotic place-names and idiosyncratic pronunciations recall that this was England's last bastion of Celtic culture.

The biggest city in the West Country is also its easternmost – **Bristol**, a cosmopolitan and sophisticated place which, although overrun by traffic and defaced by office blocks, preserves traces of every phase in its long maritime history. Bristol is within reach of some superb countryside, and only a few miles from Georgian **Bath**, whose symmetrical honey-toned terraces perfectly complement its scenic location. The exquisite cathedral city of **Wells** lies close at hand, over the Somerset border and just up the road from **Glastonbury**, one of many sites steeped in Arthurian legend in this part of the country. Straddling the border with Devon, **Exmoor** offers a foretaste of the wilderness to be found on **Dartmoor**, which takes up much of the southern half of inland Devon. The greatest of the region's massifs, Dartmoor lies between **Exeter** and **Plymouth**, the West Country's only major cities except for Bristol. Exeter is by far the more interesting, dominated by the twin towers of its medieval cathedral; Plymouth, though holding some reminders of its role as an Elizabethan naval port, is for the most part spoiled by postwar development.

Warmed by the Gulf Stream, and enjoying more hours of sunshine than virtually anywhere else in England, this part of the country can sometimes come fairly close to the atmosphere of the Mediterranean, and indeed Devon's principal resort, **Torquay**, styles itself the capital of the "English Riviera". Cornwall too has its concentrations of tourist development – chiefly at **Newquay**, **Falmouth** and **St Ives** – but this county is essentially less domesticated than its agricultural neighbour. In part this is due to the overbearing presence of the turbulent Atlantic, which is never more than half an hour's drive away, and gives Cornwall's old fishing ports an almost embattled character, especially on the north coast. The fortified headland of **Tintagel** and the clenched little harbour of **Boscastle** are typical of Cornwall's craggy appeal, but the full elemental power of the ocean can best be appreciated on the twin pincers of **Lizard Point** and **Land's End**, where the splintered

---

ACCOMMODATION PRICE CODES

Throughout this guide, hotel and B&B accommodation is priced on a scale of ① to ⑨, the number indicating the **lowest price** you could expect to pay per night in that establishment for a **double room** in high season. The prices indicated by the codes are as follows:

① under £40	④ £60–70	⑦ £110–150
② £40–50	⑤ £70–90	⑧ £150–200
③ £50–60	⑥ £90–110	⑨ over £200

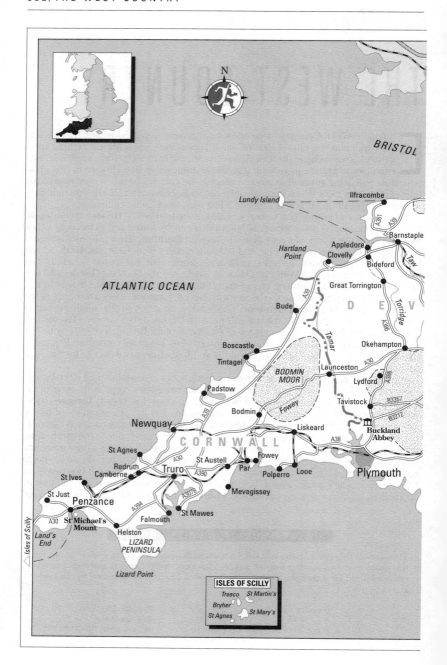

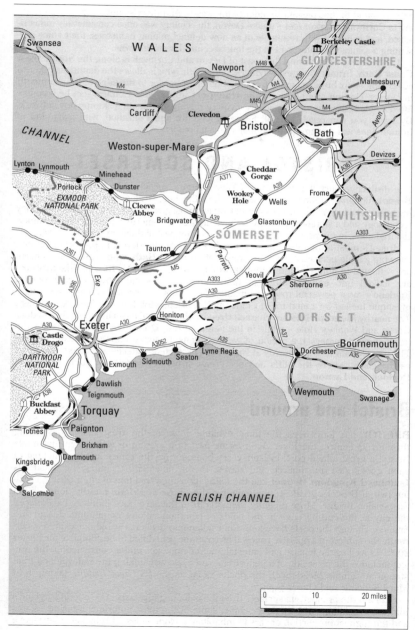

© Crown copyright

cliffs resound to the constant thunder of the waves. And there's another factor contributing to Cornwall's starker feel – unlike Devon, this county was once considerably industrialized, and is dotted with remnants of its now defunct mining industries, their ruins presenting a salutary counterpoint to the tourist-centred seaside towns.

The best way of exploring the coast of Devon and Cornwall is along the **South West Coast Path**, Britain's longest waymarked footpath, which allows the dauntless hiker to cover almost six hundred miles from the Somerset border to the edge of Bournemouth in Dorset. Getting around by **public transport** in the West Country can be a convoluted and lengthy process, especially if you're relying on the often skimpy bus network. By train, you can reach Bristol, Exeter, Plymouth and Penzance, with a handful of branch lines wandering off to the major coastal resorts.

BRISTOL AND SOMERSET

The distinctive burr that is typical of West Country speech is immediately audible in **Bristol**. Alongside it, however, you will also hear the more strident tones of fast money and big business which made this city one of Britain's most go-ahead centres in the 1990s. New technology and a vibrant youth culture have helped to re-energize the city's old commercial traditions, in the process generating some of the best nightlife in the southwest.

Bristol's most attractive neighbourhoods are those developed in the Georgian era, showing a style perfected over the Somerset border in **Bath**, whose grace and charm are reflected in a much higher tourist profile. To the south, **Wells** and **Glastonbury** are locked into entirely different time-frames, Wells's cathedral offering one of England's most powerful medieval images, Glastonbury's ruined abbey possessing a mystique fuelled by a mixture of Celtic myth, Christian folklore and New Age fantasy. The nearby **Mendip Hills** are characterized by chasms and caverns – notably Cheddar Gorge and Wookey Hole – while in the neighbouring **Quantock Hills** you enter the heartlands of Somerset, a region of verdant glens, thatched pubs and village greens. The mood changes very quickly at **Exmoor**, a protected wilderness that extends as far as the coast, where the cliffs and sea create a perfect setting for such villages as **Porlock** and **Lynton**.

Bristol and around

BRISTOL has long been the most dynamic town in the West Country. Weaving through its centre, the River Avon forms part of a system of waterways that made Bristol a great inland port, in later years booming on the transatlantic trafficking of such goods as rum, tobacco and slaves. In the nineteenth century the illustrious **Isambard Kingdom Brunel** laid the foundations of a tradition of engineering, creating two of Bristol's greatest monuments – the *SS Great Britain* and the lofty Clifton Suspension Bridge. More recently, spin-offs from the aerospace industry have placed the city at the cutting edge in the fields of communications, computing, design and finance. Though the ports have long since fallen into decline, the old docks area is currently the subject of a massive renewal programme scheduled to be complete for Easter 2000. As well as the leisure and entertainment complexes under construction, the project includes the provision of a pedestrian- and cycle-way linking the redeveloped train station at Temple Meads with the docks as far as the *SS Great Britain*, taking in St Mary Redcliffe and Queen Square.

Beneath the prosperous surface, Bristol has its negative aspects – one of England's highest populations of homeless people, some of the most notorious housing estates and the highest proportion of cars to inhabitants. Nonetheless it remains an attractive city, predominantly hilly, and surrounded by rolling countryside which you can get a taste of on day-trips to a couple of nearby aristocratic homes – **Berkeley Castle** and **Dyrham Park**. For a total change of mood you might spend a day by the sea, at the Victorian resorts of **Clevedon** and the much grander **Weston-super-Mare**, though be warned that the Bristol Channel is not the most inspiring place to swim, the sea sometimes reduced to a distant ribbon on the horizon.

Arrival, information and accommodation

Bristol is an easy place to get to. Twice-hourly **trains** from London Paddington arrive at either Bristol Parkway or Bristol Temple Meads. The latter, a twenty-minute walk from the centre, is used by services to and from the west, and served by frequent buses #8, #9, #508 and #509, which pass through the centre on their way to Clifton. Parkway is too far out of town to walk in: take bus #73 (on Sundays, #573 or #583). The **bus station**, where National Express coaches from London arrive hourly, is in Marlborough Street, right next to Broadmead, the modern shopping centre. Cheaper Bakers Dolphin Coaches (☎01934/413000) also connect Bristol with London's Marble Arch, stopping around the corner from the bus station on the Haymarket. For bus timetables and routes in the Bristol and Bath area, call ☎0117/955 5111.

The **tourist office** is in the Georgian-Gothic St Nicholas church on St Nicholas Street (June–Sept daily 9.30am–5.30pm; Oct–May Mon–Sat 9.30am–5.30pm, Sun 11am–4pm; ☎0117/926 0767); they offer a free booking service for rooms in hotels and B&Bs – though you'll have to leave a ten percent deposit. Most of Bristol's **accommodation** is in the leafy Georgian areas of Cotham and Clifton, which are also the districts where the majority of the city's students live.

Hotels and B&Bs

Arches Hotel, 132 Cotham Brow (☎0117/924 7398, *ml@archeshotel.demon.co.uk*). In an attractive area of town, though a good bus ride from the centre. Small but comfortable rooms with or without bath. Non-smoking. ②.

Clifton Hotel, St Paul's Rd (☎0117/973 6882). In Lower Clifton, near the centre, this is one of a row of smart, Georgian-style hotels, all with similar prices. This one, sporting comfortable rooms with period furnishings, is enlivened by *Rack's*, a popular pavement café and nightspot. ⑤, ③ at weekends.

Downs View, 38 Upper Belgrave Rd (☎0117/973 7046). As the name implies, this B&B enjoys a good view over Clifton Downs, though the view from the back is even better. Rooms are plain, but adequate. ②.

Glenroy Hotel, Victoria Square (☎0117/973 9058, *admin@glenroyhotel.demon.co.uk*). The choice location near Clifton Village and the attractive exterior promise more than the diminutive rooms deliver, though it's adequate for an overnight stay. ⑤, ③ at weekends.

K Linton Homes, 3 Lansdown Rd (☎0117/973 7326). There's nothing very special about this unmarked B&B, but the location is excellent, in one of Clifton's leafiest nooks near the university. No credit cards. ③.

Naseby House Hotel, 105 Pembroke Rd (☎0117/973 7859). This plush Victorian building is comfortable and beautifully furnished, located in Clifton but within walking distance of the centre. ⑤.

Oakfield Hotel, 52 Oakfield Rd (☎0117/973 5556). In Clifton, about a mile from the city centre; the public rooms are gloomy, though the bedrooms are fine. ③.

St Michael's Guest House, 145 St Michael's Hill (☎0117/907 7820). Simple accommodation situated over one of Cotham's most popular cafés, near the university. Tea- and coffee-making facilities, plus cable-linked TVs in all rooms. ③.

Hostel, university accommodation and campsites

Baltic Wharf, Cumberland Rd (☎0117/926 8030). The prime riverside location of this campsite in the centre of town compensates for the cramped space, which is dominated by caravans. Unless you

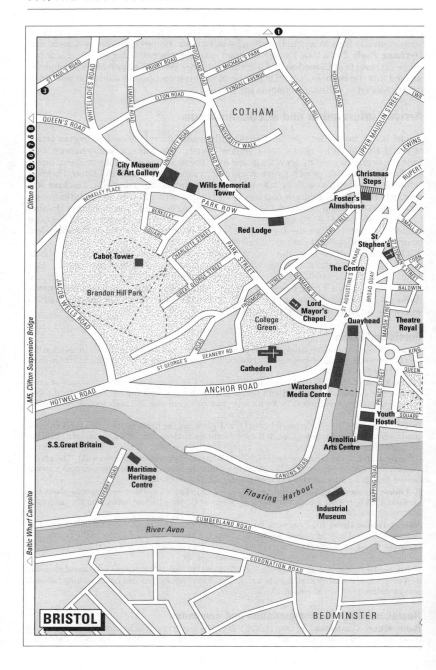

BRISTOL

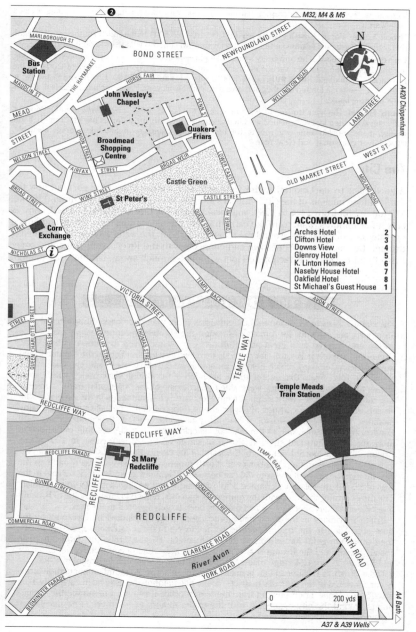

ACCOMMODATION

Arches Hotel	2
Clifton Hotel	3
Downs View	4
Glenroy Hotel	5
K. Linton Homes	6
Naseby House Hotel	7
Oakfield Hotel	8
St Michael's Guest House	1

© Crown copyright

bag one of the nine grass pitches, you'll have to cope with unforgiving stone chippings. Closed Oct–March.

Brook Lodge Farm, Cowslip Green, Redhill (☎01934/862311). Nine miles southwest of Bristol, this is the nearest rural campsite to town, a mile southwest of the village of Redhill off the A38.

University of Bristol. The university's main hall of residence opens its doors to non-students during the Easter and summer vacations (usually April & July–Sept). In the heart of Cotham, the Hawthorns (Woodland Road, ☎0117/954 5900) rents out singles (£23.50, £26 en suite) and twins (£33, £45 en suite); a limited number of rooms are available all year. Prices include breakfast. Rooms must be prior booked.

Youth Hostel, Hayman House, 14 Narrow Quay (☎0117/922 1659, *bristol@yha.org.uk*). Modern and central, located in a refurbished warehouse on the quayside; most dorms have four or six beds, though there are also some twin rooms. Kitchen, laundry, games room and bike storage available. Closed over Christmas and New Year.

The City

A good place to start exploring **the Centre**, once an extension of the port but now the traffic-ridden nucleus of the city, with cars swirling round the statues of Edmund Burke, MP for Bristol from 1774 to 1780, and local benefactor Edward Colston. The Centre is only a few minutes' walk from the cathedral and the oldest quarter of town, and linked by water-taxi to the sights around the Floating Harbour, the waterway network that runs through the southern part of town and connects with the River Avon. You could cover Bristol's other central attractions on foot without too much sweat, but there are enough

---

THE SLAVE TRADE IN BRISTOL

The statue of Edward Colston in the Centre has more than once been the subject of graffiti attacks and calls for its removal. Although the eighteenth-century sugar magnate is known and revered as a great philanthropist – his name given to numerous buildings, streets and schools in Bristol – for many he is reviled as a leading light in the London-based Royal African Company, which held the monopoly on the **slave trade** until the market was opened in 1698. From that date until the abolition of the British slave trade in 1807, merchants throughout the country were able to participate in the "triangular trade" whereby vast numbers of slaves were shipped from West Africa to plantations in the Americas, the vessels returning with cargoes of sugar, cotton, tobacco and other slave-produced commodities. By the 1730s, Bristol, a leading transatlantic port, had become, along with London and Liverpool, one of the main beneficiaries of the trade, sending out a total of more than two thousand ships in search of slaves on the African coast; in 1750 alone, Bristol ships transported some eight thousand of the twenty thousand slaves sent that year to British colonies in the Caribbean and North America. Few slaves actually came to the city, though the grave of one who did can be seen in Henbury churchyard: a servant to the Earl of Suffolk, the slave was named Scipio Africanus and was aged just 18 when he died. The direct profits, together with the numerous spin-offs, helped to finance some of Bristol's finest Georgian architecture – a fact that has been largely ignored in the past.

Bristol's primacy in the trade had already been long supplanted by Liverpool by the time opposition to the trade began to gather force: first the Quakers and Methodists, then more powerful forces voiced their discontent. By the 1780s the Anglican Dean Josiah Tucker and the Evangelical writer Hannah More had become active abolitionists, and Samuel Taylor Coleridge made a famous anti-slavery speech in Bristol in 1795.

Today Bristol's Caribbean link is maintained by an active West Indian population largely concentrated in the St Paul's district – scene of a flamboyant carnival in early July. Pick up a "Slave Trade Trail" booklet from the tourist office if you want to pursue the various points around the city connected with the trade, though as yet there is no permanent memorial or exhibition devoted to it.

steep hills to make it worthwhile using the bus network for more distant sights, especially in the Clifton district, at the highest part of town, on the edge of the Avon Gorge.

From the cathedral to the city museum

A short walk west of the Centre lies College Green, dominated by the crescent-shaped Council House and by the **cathedral**. Founded around 1140 as an abbey on the supposed spot of St Augustine's convocation with Celtic Christians in 603, it became a cathedral church with the Dissolution of the Monasteries. Among the many additions in subsequent centuries are the two towers on the west front, erected in the last century in a faithful act of homage to Edmund Knowle, architect and abbot at the start of the fourteenth century. Inside the cathedral, Abbot Knowle's **choir** offers one of the country's most exquisite examples of the early Decorated style of Gothic, while the adjoining **Elder Lady Chapel**, dating from the early thirteenth century, contains some fine tombs and some eccentric carvings of animals, including a monkey playing the bagpipes accompanied by a ram on the violin. The ornate **Eastern Lady Chapel** has some of England's finest examples of heraldic glass. From the south transept, a door leads through to the **Chapter House**, a strongly carved piece of late Norman architecture.

Opposite the cathedral's west front, take a look at the Norman **Abbey Gateway**, which blends harmoniously with the cathedral on one side and the city library – constructed at the beginning of this century – on the other, though nothing on this side of College Green can completely efface the brutal effect of the Council House opposite. There is one more vestige from the Middle Ages, however, on the northeast side of the green, where the **Lord Mayor's Chapel** (Tues–Sat 10am–noon & 1–4pm) has some lovely French and Flemish stained glass, and striking effigies of the thirteenth-century founders of the hospital of which this church once formed a part.

Climbing steeply up from the green, the shop-lined **Park Street** has some elegant Georgian streets leading off it – for instance Great George Street and Berkeley Square, from either of which you can enter **Brandon Hill Park**, site of the landmark **Cabot Tower**, built at the end of the last century to commemorate the four-hundredth anniversary of John Cabot's voyage to America. You can clamber up the 105-foot tower for the city's best panorama.

At the top of Park Street stands central Bristol's other chief landmark, the **Wills Memorial Tower**, erected in the 1920s to lend some stature to the newly opened university. One of the last great neo-Gothic buildings in England, the tower was the gift of the local Wills tobacco dynasty, the university's main benefactors.

Next to the tower, on Queen's Road, the **City Museum and Art Gallery** (daily 10am–5pm; free) occupies another building donated by the Wills clan. The sections on local archeology, geology and natural history are pretty well what you'd expect, but the scope of the museum is occasionally surprising – it has the largest collection of Chinese glass on show outside China itself, and some magnificent Assyrian reliefs, carved in the eighth century BC. The second-floor gallery of paintings and sculptures includes work by English Pre-Raphaelites and French Impressionists, as well as a few choice older pieces, among them a portrait of Martin Luther by Cranach and Giovanni Bellini's *Descent into Limbo*.

Opposite the tower, on Park Row, you can visit the **Red Lodge** (April–Oct Sat–Wed 10am–5pm; free), a sixteenth-century building that was originally a merchant's home and later a finishing school for young ladies, then England's first girls' reform school. Highlight is the Great Oak Room, featuring a splendid carved stone fireplace and sumptuous oak panelling.

From the Centre to Broadmead

There are some niches of older architecture off the northern end of the Centre. Hidden behind offices, leading steeply up from Rupert Street on the west side of the Centre,

Christmas Steps is a stepped shop-lined alley with a cramped, timeworn flavour, though none of the present buildings dates further back than the eighteenth century. At the top stands **Foster's Almshouse**, a red brick gabled and turreted affair built in 1481 but remodelled in the last century on a Burgundian Gothic pattern. Founder of the almshouse was Bristol merchant and mayor John Foster, also responsible for the adjacent **Chapel of the Three Kings of Cologne**, a tiny church named after a chapel in Cologne Cathedral, which was no doubt admired on Foster's Rhineland journeys. The three kings carved on the facade were added in the 1960s.

One of Bristol's oldest churches, **St Stephen's**, stands on the opposite side of the Centre. Established in the thirteenth century, rebuilt in the fifteenth and thoroughly restored with plenty of neo-Gothic trimmings in 1875, the parish church has some flamboyant tombs inside, mainly of various members of the merchant class who were the church's main patrons. Especially good are those of Justice Snygge and Edmund Blanket, a fourteenth-century cloth merchant.

On nearby **Corn Street**, the city's financial centre, you'll find the Georgian Corn Exchange, designed by John Wood of Bath (see p.351), which holds the covered St Nicholas markets. Outside the entrance stand four engraved bronze pillars, dating from the sixteenth and seventeenth centuries and transferred from a nearby arcade where they served as trading tables – thought to be the "nails" from which the expression "pay on the nail" is derived.

Beyond the market, Wine Street runs along the site of the old **Bristol Castle**, an eleventh-century structure that was completely dismantled at the end of the Civil War. The site is now a park, with the hollow shell of the fourteenth-century **St Peter's Church** – gutted during World War II – the only thing still standing, though the castle's moat is still visible. The park, which runs alongside a stretch of Bristol waterways, attracts lunchers from the surrounding shops and offices, and is the occasional venue for summer concerts and fairs.

North of Castle Green extends Bristol's **Broadmead** shopping centre, an uninspiring development laid out on the ruins left by wartime bombing. A couple of relics from before that period survive. Accessible from both the central strip of Broadmead and the Horsefair, **John Wesley's Chapel** was the country's first Methodist chapel, established in 1739 by Wesley himself (Jan & Feb Mon–Sat 11am–2.30pm; rest of year Mon–Sat 10am–4pm). Lying very much as Wesley left it, the chapel has a double-deck pulpit beneath a hidden upstairs window, from which the evangelist could observe the progress of his trainee preachers. Tours of the chapel and some of the rooms used by Wesley and his acolytes are available for £2. Outside the chapel is an equestrian statue of Wesley, and, in the main courtyard, another one representing John's brother Charles, also a leading Methodist and hymn-writer. Nearby, another testimony to Bristol's close links with nonconformist sects has also survived: **Quakers' Friars**, a thirteenth-century construction whose name derives from the Dominican friars who first used the building, and the Quakers who took it over from the sixteenth century. William Penn, founder of Pennsylvania, was married here, as was the Quaker founder George Fox.

King Street to St Mary Redcliffe

King Street, a short walk east from the Centre, was laid out in 1633 and still holds some fine seventeenth-century buildings, among them the **Merchant Venturers' Almshouses** for retired seamen, founded in the fifteenth century but restored in 1699 by Edward Colston. Further down is the **Theatre Royal**, the oldest working theatre in the country, opened in 1766 and preserving many of its original Georgian features. The theatre hosted most of the famous names of its time, including Sarah Siddons, whose ghost is said to stalk the building.

In a different architectural style, one of King Street's most prominent buildings is the timber-framed **Llandoger Trow** pub, its name taken from the flat-bottomed boats that traded between Bristol and the Welsh coast. Traditionally the haunt of seafarers, it is reputed to have been the meeting place of Daniel Defoe and Alexander Selkirk, the model for Robinson Crusoe. The area around here and the *Old Duke* jazz pub opposite has Bristol's thickest profusion of pubs, restaurants and nightclubs, and brims with life at weekends and summer evenings.

Behind King Street spreads **Queen Square**, an elegant grassy area focused on a statue of William III by Rysbrack, reckoned to be the best equestrian statue in the country. The square was the site of some of the worst civil disturbances ever seen in England when the Bristolians rioted in support of the Reform Bill of 1832, burning houses on two sides of the square; among the survivors was no. 37, where the first American consulate was established in 1792. The square has a decent pub at its southeastern corner, the *Hole in the Wall*, so-called after the narrow window at the back of the building used to keep watch for press gangs – it was reputedly the model for the *Spyglass Inn* in Robert Louis Stevenson's *Treasure Island*.

The southeast corner of the square leads to Redcliffe Bridge and on to the area of Redcliffe, where the spire of **St Mary Redcliffe** provides one of the distinctive features of the city's skyline. Described by Elizabeth I as "the goodliest, fairest, and most famous parish church in England", the church was largely paid for and used by merchants and mariners who prayed here for a safe voyage. The present building was begun at the end of the thirteenth century, though it was added to in subsequent centuries and the spire was constructed in 1872. Inside, memorials and tombs recall some of the figures associated with the building, including the arms and armour of Sir William Penn, admiral and father of the founder of Pennsylvania, on the north wall of the nave; and the Handel Window in the North Choir aisle, installed in 1859 on the centenary of the death of Handel, who composed on the organ here. The whale bone above the entrance to the Chapel of St John the Baptist is thought to have been brought back from Newfoundland by John Cabot. The poets Samuel Taylor Coleridge and Robert Southey were both married in St Mary, within six weeks of each other in 1795.

Above the church's north porch is the muniment room, where **Thomas Chatterton** claimed to have found a trove of medieval manuscripts; the poems, distributed as the work of a fifteenth-century monk named Thomas Rowley, were in fact dazzling fakes. The young poet committed suicide when his forgery was exposed, thereby supplying English literature with one of its most glamorous stories of self-destructive genius. The "Brilliant Boy" is remembered by a memorial stone in the south transept, and there is another one to his family, who were long associated with the church, in the churchyard. Chatterton's birthplace is just across the busy Redcliffe Way, administered by the city museum and viewable only on application there – though there is precious little to see inside.

A few minutes' walk away, Bristol's **Old Station** stands outside Temple Meads station, the original terminus of the Great Western Railway linking London and Bristol. The terminus, like the line itself, was designed by Brunel in 1840, and was the first great piece of railway architecture. The train shed is due to open as a museum of the British Empire and Commonwealth.

Bristol's waterways

Bristol's **Harbourside** is the focus of a grand development project which is due to be completed in early 2000. The twin pivots of the scheme are Explore@Bristol, an interactive science centre, and Wildscreen@Bristol, a multimedia wildlife complex, though plans encompass a range of other consumer-friendly installations: contact the tourist office for the latest information.

At the southern end of the Centre, the River Frome disappears underground at the **Quayhead**, a spot marked by a statue of Neptune and a memorial plaque to Samuel Plimsoll, inventor of the eponymous line that's painted on the hulls of merchant ships.

St Augustine's Reach, the central part of the Floating Harbour, is flanked by the **Arnolfini** and **Watershed** arts centres, bastions of Bristol's cultural scene and both housed in refurbished Victorian warehouses. Outside the Arnolfini is a statue of **John Cabot**, the Genoan-born explorer licensed by Henry VII to sail from Bristol in 1497; his landing at Newfoundland formed the basis of England's later claims on the New World. He disappeared on his second expedition the following year.

Moored onto the quays adjacent to St Augustine's Reach are several boats converted into pubs, restaurants and music venues. To explore further afield take advantage of the ferry service, leaving from near Neptune's statue at the Quayhead (April–Sept daily 11am–4pm every 40min; Oct–March Sat & Sun 11am–4pm every 40min; £1 single flat fare, £2.80 40-minute round trip, or £3.30 for one hour). The first stop is the **Industrial Museum**, featuring a diverse collection of vehicles, mostly with Bristol connections, and a display of maritime models and reconstructions (April–Oct Mon–Wed, Sat & Sun 10am–5pm; Nov–March Sat & Sun 10am–5pm; free). On some summer days you can take a thirty-minute cruise of the harbour from here, on a steam tug built in 1861, which is rumoured to be the oldest in the world (£3).

From the museum, you can either catch the ferry or use the infrequent steam train of the **Bristol Harbour Railway** (March–Oct occasional weekends noon–5pm; every 15min; £1 return; ☎0117/925147) to the **SS Great Britain**. Built in 1843 by Brunel, the *Great Britain* was the first propeller-driven, ocean-going iron ship, used initially between Liverpool and New York, then between Liverpool and Melbourne, circumnavigating the globe 32 times over a period of 26 years. Her ocean-going days ended in 1886 when she was caught in a storm off Cape Horn, and abandoned in the Falkland Islands; she was recovered from there and returned to Bristol in 1968. Now berthed in the same dry dock where she was constructed, the *Great Britain* is still undergoing restoration work, but is open to visitors (daily: April–Sept 10am–5.30pm; Oct–March 10am–4.30pm; £6). Some cabins have been restored, the bunks occupied by eerily breathing mannequins, and you can peer into the immense engine room. Alongside is docked a much smaller affair: a replica of the **Matthew** (same times as *SS Great Britain*; entry covered by that ticket), the vessel in which John Cabot sailed to America in 1497. The boat was rebuilt in time for the voyage to be re-enacted on the 500th anniversary, and may be moved again, this time to a new anchorage. The adjoining **Maritime Heritage Centre** (same times as *SS Great Britain*; entry covered by that ticket) gives the full history of both the *Great Britain* and the *Matthew*, and the few facts which are known about Cabot and his exploits. The museum also illustrates the port's long shipbuilding history from the eighteenth century, when it was second only to London, to its decline in the last century, when Bristol's inability to berth the increasingly large vessels led to its decline.

Clifton

North and west of the Wills Tower (see p.339) extends **Clifton**, once an aloof spa resort, now Bristol's most elegant quarter. Clifton Village, its select enclave, is centred on the Mall, close to **Royal York Crescent**, the longest Georgian crescent in the country, offering splendid views over the steep drop to the River Avon below.

A few minutes' walk behind the Crescent is Bristol's most famous symbol, **Clifton Suspension Bridge**, 702ft long and poised 245ft above high water. Money was first put forward for a bridge to span the Avon Gorge by a Bristol wine merchant in 1753, though it was not until 1829 that a competition was held for a design, won by Isambard Brunel on a second round, and not until 1864 that the bridge was completed, five years after Brunel's death. Hampered by financial difficulties, the bridge never quite matched the engineer's original ambitious design, which included Egyptian-style towers topped by sphinxes on each end. You can see copies of his plans in the **Visitor Centre** on Sion Place (daily: Easter–Sept 10am–5.30pm; Oct–Easter 11am–4pm; £1.20) – the original drawings are in the university's Brunel Collection and can be viewed on application. The three rooms here give the full background on the competitions and the vicissitudes which accompanied the bridge's construction.

Just above the bridge in Clifton, a small **Observatory** sits on an arm of Clifton Downs overlooking the gorge, and contains a working camera obscura (daily: summer 11am–5.30pm; winter 11am–4pm; £1). Adjoining the Downs is **Bristol Zoo** (daily: summer 9am–6pm; winter 9am–5pm; £6), renowned for its animal conservation work, and also featuring a collection of rare trees and shrubs.

Cross the bridge for the view, and continue over to reach the thick Leigh Woods, and Bristol's widest expanse of parkland, **Ashton Court**, scene of a free music festival held each July.

Eating, drinking and nightlife

Bristol's numerous **pubs** and **restaurants** are nearly always buzzing – especially those around King Street. Nightlife is equally lively; if you want to check out the **clubs**, look for the music that suits your tastes rather than simply turning up at a venue – and be prepared to queue. You can usually find something happening every night until late – pick up a copy of *Venue*, the Bristol and Bath fortnightly listings magazine (£1.90) for details of what's on where.

Restaurants

Bell's Diner, 1 York Rd (☎0117/924 0357). In the heart of the fashionable Montpelier district (ten minutes from the Centre), this corner bistro offers an inventive menu with good-value, award-winning food. No smoking in dining area. Closed Sat & Mon lunch, plus Sun eve. Moderate.

Blue Goose, 344 Gloucester Rd (☎0117/942 0940). It's worth the ten-minute bus ride north of the Centre to this popular place serving English and Mediterranean cuisine with Pacific elements. Closed lunchtimes, plus all Sun & Mon. Moderate.

Browns, 38 Queen's Rd (☎0117/930 4777). Spacious and relaxed place for a cocktail or a hamburger; it's housed in the former university refectory, a Venetian-style structure next to the City Museum. Moderate.

Byzantium, 2 Portwall Lane (☎0117/922 1883). A riverside warehouse that's been transformed into a highly theatrical dining area, allegedly based on a Beirut hotel circa 1930. The food is superb, with a good-value set-price menu, and there's an equally extravagant downstairs bar that stays open late. Closed Sun.

Harvey's, 12 Denmark St (☎0117/927 5034). Owned by a famous name in the world of wines and sherries, this is a showcase restaurant in a medieval cellar complex adjoining a museum of wine that's an attraction in itself, and can be visited while waiting for food. The atmosphere is formal, the food French and the wine list both encyclopedic and outstanding. Closed Sat lunch & all Sun. Very Expensive.

Las Iguanas, 10 St Nicholas St (☎0117/927 6233). Boisterous Mexican joint where the fajitas are highly recommended; there's also a swinging basement bar with DJs Thurs, Fri & Sat. Closed Sun lunch. Moderate.

Michael's Fusion Restaurant, 129 Hotwell Rd (☎0117/927 6190). A range of innovative dishes that blend ingredients and techniques from the farthest corners of the globe served in beautifully furnished Victorian surroundings. Closed all Mon, Tues–Sat lunch & Sun eve. Moderate.

River Station, The Grove (☎0117/914 4434). A former river-police station that has been artfully transformed by the founders of *Bell's* (see above) into two great restaurants: downstairs you can chew on deli-type snacks or just have a drink, while the upstairs restaurant offers a bigger range of international dishes. Inexpensive to Moderate.

Pubs, bars and cafés

Arnolfini, Narrow Quay. This art centre serves excellent vegetarian and meat dishes, plus drinks at the bar.

Avon Gorge Hotel, Sion Hill. On the edge of the Gorge in Clifton Village, this mediocre bar has a broad terrace with tables from which to contemplate the magnificent views. Snacks available.

Bristol Comedy Pub, 117 Stokes Croft Rd. Modern lines and green tones for this stand-up venue, run by the management of *Jester's*, Bristol's main stage for comics further up the road.

Café Tasca, 12 York Rd. A Montpelier institution for breakfasts, lunches and evening meals Closed Mon–Wed & Sun.

Cadbury House, 68 Richmond Rd, Montpelier. Loud and crowded with a good jukebox.

The Farm, Hopetoun Rd, St Werburgh's. A country pub in the city, off Ashley Hill to the northeast of the centre; vegetarian cooking, baguettes and DJs at weekends make this a popular spot, especially in summer when the beer garden is usually buzzing.

Fleece and Firkin, 12 St Thomas St. Stone-flagged ex-wool warehouse, this loud and sweaty pub offers good beer and regular live music and comedy.

Mud Dock Café, 40 The Grove. A winning if unlikely combination of bike shop and café-bar/restaurant by the river. There's a barbecue on the balcony in summer, and DJs most nights.

Nova Scotia, Cumberland Basin. Traditional dockside pub with seats by the nineteenth-century lock. Inexpensive food available.

Old England, Bath Buildings (bottom of Picton Street). Pool tables inside, benches outside, good beer and often packed, in an area of Montpelier rich with drinking-holes.

Star and Garter, 33 Brook Rd, Montpelier. Smoky, loud and cramped – an excellent reggae pub.

Taverna dell'Artista, King St. A haunt of theatrical folk as well as a rowdy bunch of regulars, this is a successful Anglo-Italian dive with a late licence. The pizzas, pastas and salads are only mediocre though.

Watershed, 1 Canons Rd, St Augustine's Reach. A good bar and café in the arts complex, occasionally hosting live music.

Clubs and venues

Bierkeller, All Saints St, off Broadmead. Steamy venue for live music from thrash metal to world sounds.

Colston Hall, Colston Ave (☎0117/922 3686). Major names appear in this stalwart of mainstream venues. Most of the events in the classical Proms Festival, at the end of May, take place here.

Fiddlers, Willway St, Bedminster. Mainly live folk and world music at this relaxed and well-run club on the south side of the river, off Bedminster Parade.

Lakota, 6 Upper York St. Bristol's most celebrated club, attracting the biggest DJs and often generating queues to get in. Dress up on Saturdays.

New Trinity Community Centre, Trinity Rd, off Old Market. Happening club sounds in this converted church, including good drum'n'bass nights.

Po Na Na, Queen St. Underground club with Moroccan decor; it's near the university and popular with students. Mainly house sounds and techno. Closes at 2am.

Powerhouse, 4 Stokes Croft. Garage, indie and drum'n'bass nights.

Thekla, Phoenix Wharf, off Queen Square. A steamy, youthful riverboat venue staging regular club nights Thurs–Sat, open until 2am or 4am.

Listings

Banks and Exchanges Barclays, 40 Corn St; Lloyds, 55 Corn St; HSBC, 24 College Green; National Westminster, 32 Corn St; American Express 74 Queen's Rd (☎0117/975 0750) and 31 Union St, Broadmead (☎0117/927 7788).

Bike rental Mud Dock Cycleworks, 40 The Grove (☎0117/929 2151). Mountain bikes £15 a day; £100 deposit.

Books Waterstone's, The Galleries, Union St (Mon, Tues, Fri & Sat 9am–6pm, Wed 10am–6pm, Thurs 9am–7pm, Sun 11am–5pm; ☎0117/925 2274).

Buses Local services ☎0117/955 5111; National Express ☎0990/808080.

Car rental Avis, Rupert St (☎0117/929 2123); Speedway, 654 Fishponds Rd (☎0117/965 5555); Victoria Car Hire, 155 Victoria St (☎0117/927 6909).

Hospital Bristol Royal Infirmary, 2 Marlborough St (☎0117/920 0000).
Internet Netgates Café, 51 Broad St (☎0117/907 4040).
Laundry 78 Alma Rd, Clifton; 34 Princess Victoria St, Clifton.
Left luggage Temple Meads station (Mon–Sat 6.30am–9.30pm, Sun 9.30am–9.30pm).
Pharmacy Boots, 19 St Augustine's Parade, the Centre (Mon–Fri 8am–8pm, Sat 8.30am–5.30pm, Sun 6pm–8pm).
Police Broad St (☎0117/927 7777).
Post office The Galleries, Wine Street (Mon–Sat 9am–5.30pm).
Taxis AA Taxis (☎0117/955 5000); Ace Taxis (☎0117/977 7477).
Trains ☎0345/484950.
Travel agents STA Travel, 25 Queen's Rd, Clifton (☎0117/929 4399); Usit CAMPUS, 39 Queen's Rd, Clifton (☎0117/929 2494).

Around Bristol

There are two obvious half-day jaunts from Bristol – to **Berkeley Castle** and to **Dyrham Park**, though to get to the latter from Bristol you'll need your own transport. To the south of town, the Bristol Channel gives the first taste of the West Country's coastal resorts: the nearest, **Clevedon**, also offers the opportunity of seeing a fine Tudor manor house, while **Weston-super-Mare** is a full-blown beach town, a frenetic whirl in summer.

Berkeley Castle

Though quite secluded within a swathe of meadows and neat gardens, **Berkeley Castle** (April & May Tues–Sun 2–5pm; June & Sept Tues–Sat 11am–5pm, Sun 2–5pm; July & Aug Mon–Sat 11am–5pm, Sun 2–5pm; Oct Sun only 2–5pm; castle & grounds £4.80, grounds only £1.70) dominates the little village of Berkeley, twenty miles north of the city on the A38. The fortress has an agreeably turreted medieval look, the robust twelfth-century walls softened by later accretions acquired in its gradual transformation into a family home. The interior is packed with mementos of its long history, including its grisliest moment in 1327, when Edward II was murdered here – apparently by a red-hot iron thrust into his bowels. You can view the cell where the event took place, along with dungeons, dining room, kitchen, picture gallery and the Great Hall. Outside, the grounds include an Elizabethan terraced garden and a Butterfly Farm (£1.75), and within easy walking distance, in Berkeley village, is the **Jenner Museum** (April–Sept Tues–Sat 12.30–5.30pm, Sun 1–5.30pm; Oct Sun 1–5.30pm; £2), dedicated to Edward Jenner, discoverer of the principle of vaccination.

From Bristol the #308 **bus** runs every two hours (not Sun) to Berkeley Castle en route to the Slimbridge bird sanctuary (see p.322) and Gloucester (see p.323).For a lunchtime stop, follow the narrow High Street out of the centre of the village for about a mile to reach the *Salutation*, an unpretentious country **pub** with a garden, serving up bacon sandwiches and the like.

Dyrham

A visit to **Dyrham Park**, twelve miles east of Bristol (daily noon–5.30pm or dusk; house April–Oct Mon, Tues & Fri–Sun noon–5.30pm; grounds & house £5.50, grounds £2.50, park only £1.80; NT), is almost worth it for the journey alone, which takes in a far-reaching panorama at the top of Tog Hill, where the A420 intersects with the A46. Standing on the site of a calamitous defeat of the Britons by the Saxons in 677, the house is a late seventeenth-century Baroque mansion, finely decorated and panelled in oak, cedar and walnut. Alongside furniture used by the diarists Pepys and Evelyn, many of the contents reflect the career of the first owner William Blathwayt, a diplomat who collected pieces from Holland and North America. The name Dyrham means "deer enclosure", and the surrounding 268 acres of parkland are still grazed by fallow deer – the deer park gives views as far as the Welsh hills.

Bus connections are limited to two daily from Bath, currently leaving the bus station at 10am and 2.30pm, returning at 1.14pm and 5.44pm (25-minute journey): the route passes through Dyrham village, half a mile from the park.

Clevedon

Fifteen miles south of Bristol, **CLEVEDON** is centred on hills inland from the sea, but its handsome beach promenade invites a stroll, with wind-bent trees and views across to Wales. Focal point is the **pier** (April–Oct daily 9am–5pm; Nov–March closed Wed; 75p), from where you can take cruises to Bristol, Gloucester, along the coast to Devon, and over to Wales; tickets can be obtained from the pier's Tollhouse, which also houses the **tourist office** (same hours as pier; ☎01275/878846). Pick up a leaflet at the tourist office on the **Poet's Walk**, an easy stroll you can make round the headland. The path, which was supposed to have provided inspiration for Tennyson and Coleridge, winds round Church Hill, passing St Andrew's churchyard and climbing Wain's Hill, taking in some bracing views en route – about a mile in all.

Clevedon is also the site of **Clevedon Court** (April–Sept Wed, Thurs & Sun 2–5pm; £4; NT), a fourteenth- and fifteenth-century manor house a couple of miles inland. Since 1709 it has been the property of the Elton family, among whose offspring were Sir Arthur Hallam Elton – inspiration for Tennyson's elegy *In Memoriam* – and his son Edmund, whose internationally known pottery is displayed here. You'll also find a fascinating collection of glassware, some fine specimens of furniture spanning three hundred years and portraits of and drawings by William Makepeace Thackeray, who wrote much of *Vanity Fair* here, as well as making it the setting of *Henry Esmond*. The chapel is worth a look for its fine tracery, and the terraced gardens give good views seaward.

There are a few **pubs and restaurants** on or around Clevedon's seafront, including *Il Giardino* (☎01275/878832; closed Sun & Mon). If you wanted to stay, *Clarence House* is a comfortable **B&B** overlooking the sea at 10 The Beach (☎01275/873623; no credit cards; ②). One room is en suite, and smoking is not allowed. **Buses** from Bristol depart at least hourly – as well as services exclusively for Clevedon, you can take many of the buses bound for Weston-super-Mare.

Weston-super-Mare

Buses and trains from Bristol – and a regular bus service from Clevedon – run frequently to the major resort on this coast, **WESTON-SUPER-MARE**, eight miles south of Clevedon. A tiny fishing village at the beginning of the nineteenth century, Weston boomed to become one of the chief West Country seaside towns of the Edwardian era. It is rather moth-eaten today, though its sandy beaches and seafront amusements still attract busloads of trippers. If the crowds get you down, you can always climb up into Weston Woods, rising to the north of the main beach and reachable just around the point on Kewstoke Road. Beyond the point lies **Sand Bay**, a less-developed beach zone bounded to the north by Sand Point, a headland maintained by the National Trust. More adventurously, you can cross to the southern end of Weston – walk or bus to Uphill (#5a to Links Rd) – to join the **West Mendip Way** footpath, following the Mendip hills for thirty miles to Wells and beyond (see p.357).

Trains arrive at Neva Road, a ten-minute walk from the seafront; the **bus station** is nearer, on Beach Road, though some buses stop in the streets around. The **tourist office** is on Beach Lawns, a traffic island between Beach Road and Marine Parade (April–Sept daily 9.30am–5.30pm; Oct–March Mon–Fri 9.30am–5pm, Sat 9.30am–1pm & 1.45–4pm; ☎01934/888800). If you want to stay in Weston, you can take your pick from a good selection of **B&Bs**: try *Conifers*, some way back from the seafront at 63 Milton Rd (☎01934/624404; no credit cards; ①), with rooms with or without bathroom; closer is the non-smoking *Edelweiss* at 24 Clevedon Rd (☎01934/624705; no credit cards; ①), where all rooms are en suite. There are a couple of **campsites** in the area: *Country View* in Sand Bay (☎01934/627595; closed Nov–Feb) north of town and, some way inland and south of town, *Slimbridge* on Links Rd (☎01934/641641; closed Nov–Feb) – very close to the Mendip Way.

Bath

Though only twelve miles from Bristol, **BATH** has a very different feel from its neighbour – more harmonious, compact, leisurely and complacent. Jane Austen wrote *Persuasion* and *Northanger Abbey* here, it is where Gainsborough established himself as a portraitist and landscape painter, and the city's elegant crescents and Georgian buildings are studded with plaques naming Bath's eminent inhabitants from its heyday as a spa resort. Nowadays Bath ranks as one of Britain's top ten tourist cities (the Baths are the busiest fee-charging historic site outside London), yet the place has never lost the exclusive air those names evoke.

Bath owes its name and fame to its **hot springs** – the only ones in the country – which made it a place of reverence for the local Celtic population, though it had to wait for Roman technology to create a fully-fledged bathing establishment. The baths fell into decline with the departure of the Romans, but the town later regained its importance under the Saxons, its abbey seeing the coronation of the **first king of all England**, Edgar, in 973. A new bathing complex was built in the sixteenth century, popularized by the visit of Elizabeth I in 1574, and the city reached its fashionable zenith in the eighteenth century, when **Beau Nash** ruled the town's social scene. It was at this time that Bath acquired its ranks of Palladian mansions and town houses, all of them built in the local **Bath stone** which is now enshrined in building regulations as an obligatory element in any new constructions in the city.

The swathes of parkland between the Regency developments lend the city a spacious feel, but the sheer weight of traffic pouring through the central streets can often counteract the pleasures of these open spaces. Drivers are advised to use one of the **Park-and-Ride** car parks around the periphery – and if you're coming from Bristol, note that you can **cycle** all the way along a cycle-path that follows the route of a disused railway line and the course of the Avon.

Arrival, information and accommodation

Bath Spa **train station** and the city's **bus station** are both on Manvers Street, a short walk from the centre. The **tourist office** is right next to the abbey on Abbey Churchyard (June–Sept Mon–Sat 9.30am–6pm, Sun 10am–4pm; Oct–May Mon–Sat 9.30am–5pm, Sun 10am–4pm; ☎01225/477101). Here you can find a detailed list of **accommodation**; most establishments are small, so always phone first.

Hotels and B&Bs

Alderney Guest House, 3 Pulteney Rd (☎01225/312365). One of the cheapest of a row of guest houses close to the train station, between the river and canal. Adequate and convenient. No credit cards. ①.

Bath Tasburgh Hotel, Warminster Rd (☎01225/425096, *reservations@bathtasburgh.co.uk*). This Victorian mansion about one mile east of the centre is decidedly posh, but the views and location are excellent, with access to the Kennet and Avon Canal at the bottom of six acres of gardens and meadows. Gourmet meals and picnics are provided. ⑥.

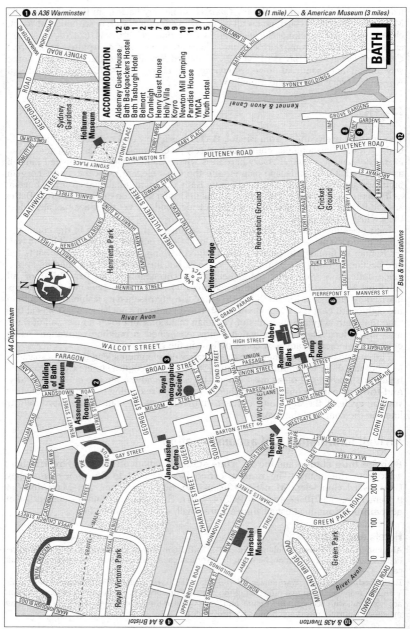

BATH

ACCOMMODATION

Alderney Guest House	12
Bath Backpackers Hostel	6
Bath Tasburgh Hotel	1
Belmont	2
Cranleigh	4
Henry Guest House	7
Holly Villa	8
Koyro	9
Newton Mill Camping	10
Paradise House	11
YMCA	3
Youth Hostel	5

© Crown copyright

Belmont, 7 Belmont, Lansdown Rd (☎01225/423082). Huge rooms – though the single's a bit poky – with or without shower in a house designed by John Wood, very near to the Assembly Rooms, Circus and Royal Crescent. No credit cards. ①.

Cranleigh, 159 Newbridge Hill (☎01225/310197, *cranleigh@btinternet.com*). Above the city, with fine views from some of the back rooms. *Objets d'art* abound, and period fittings include original fireplaces. No smoking. ⑤.

Henry Guest House, 6 Henry St (☎01225/424052). Just round the corner from the abbey, with more rooms than most (none en suite), but its location means that availability is limited. No credit cards. ②.

Holly Villa, 14 Pulteney Gardens (☎01225/310331). High-class B&B, close to the Kennet and Avon Canal, with a nice garden and six rooms (all en suite). No smoking and no credit cards. Closed Jan & Feb. ②.

Koyro, 7 Pulteney Gardens (☎01225/336712). The name means "Sunshine" in Japanese – the mother-tongue of the landlady, who has made cleanliness and simplicity the keynotes. No smoking. No credit cards. ③.

Paradise House, 88 Holloway (☎01225/317723, *paradise@apsleyhouse.easynet.co.uk*). The wonderful view justifies the ten-minute uphill trudge from the centre. Croquet or boules in the lush garden and open fires in the winter are other attractions, and all rooms are en suite. ⑤.

Hostels and campsite

Bath Backpackers Hostel, 13 Pierrepoint St (☎01225/446787). Cheap right in the centre of things. There's no curfew, no lockout, a kitchen, bar and pool room, but no breakfast.

Newton Mill Touring Centre (☎01225/333909). The nearest campsite, three miles west of the centre at Newton St Loe (bus #5 to Newton Mill). The site holds a laundry, restaurant and shop (open summer only), and the price includes use of showers.

YMCA, International House, Broad St (☎01225/460471, *info@ymcabath.u-net.com*). Clean, central, with lots of room and convenient prices, this place offers good central accommodation, charging £11 for dorm beds, £15 for singles, £28 for doubles, and with reductions for two nights or more; all prices include breakfast.

Youth Hostel, Bathwick Hill (☎01225/465674, *bath@yha.org.uk*). An Italianate mansion a mile from the centre, with gardens and panoramic views. Dorm beds and double rooms with evening meals also available. Take buses #18 or #418 from the station.

The City

Although Bath could easily be seen on a day-trip from Bristol, it really deserves a couple of days on the spot, particularly to explore some of the out-of-town attractions. The city itself is chock-full of museums, but some of the greatest enjoyment comes simply from the streets, with their pale gold architecture and sweeping vistas. With limited time you might consider viewing these on an open-top bus tour leaving from Grand Parade, or one of the free walking tours from outside the Pump Room in the Abbey Church Yard. Otherwise you could see much under your own steam by renting a bike from Avon Valley Cyclery at the back of the train station.

The Baths and the Abbey

Bath's centrepiece is, naturally enough, the **Roman Baths** located in front of the abbey in the pedestrianized Abbey Church Yard (April–July & Sept daily 9am–6pm; Aug daily 9am–6pm & 8–10pm; Oct–March daily 9.30am–5pm; £6.70, £8.70 combined ticket with Museum of Costume). Although the tickets are pricey, there's two or three hours-worth of well-balanced, informative entertainment here, with a taped commentary provided on handsets allowing you to wander at your own pace around the temple and bathing complex, where a spring still issues water at a constant 46.5°C. Highlights of the remains are the open-air (but originally covered) Great Bath, its vaporous waters surrounded by nineteenth-century pillars, terraces and statues of famous Romans; the

BEAU NASH AND REGENCY BATH

Richard "Beau" Nash was an ex-army officer, ex-lawyer, dandy and gambler, who became Bath's Master of Ceremonies in 1704, conducting public balls of an unprecedented splendour. Wielding dictatorial powers over dress and behaviour, Nash orchestrated the social manners of the city and even extended his influence to cover road improvements and the design of buildings. In an early example of health awareness, he banned smoking in Bath's public rooms at a time when pipe-smoking was a general pastime among men, women and children. Less philanthropically, he also encouraged gambling and even took a percentage of the bank's takings. Nonetheless, he was generally held in high esteem and succeeded in establishing rules such as the setting of specific hours and procedure for all social functions. Balls were to begin at six and end at eleven and every ball had to open with a minuet "danced by two persons of the highest distinction present". White aprons were banned, gossipers and scandalmongers were shunned, and, most radical of all, the wearing of swords in public places was forbidden, a ruling referred to in Sheridan's play *The Rivals*, in which Captain Absolute declares, "A sword seen in the streets of Bath would raise as great an alarm as a mad dog." By such measures, Nash presided over the city's greatest period, during the first four decades of the eighteenth century. He lived in Bath until his death at the age of 87, by which time he had been reduced to comparative poverty.

Next to the innovations of Nash and the architectural creations of the two John Woods, the name of **William Oliver** should not be forgotten in the story of Regency Bath. A physician and philanthropist, Oliver did more than anyone to boost the city's profile as a therapeutic centre, thanks to publications such as his *Practical Essay on the Use and Abuse of Warm Bathing in Gouty Cases* (1751), and by founding the Bath General Hospital to enable the poor to make use of the waters. He is remembered today by the Bath Oliver biscuit, which he invented, and by the use of Olivers as the exchange currency in a local community bartering scheme.

Circular Bath, where bathers cooled off; the Norman King's Bath; and part of the temple of Minerva. Among a quantity of coins, jewellery and sculpture exhibited are the gilt bronze head of Sulis Minerva, the local deity, and a grand, Celtic-inspired gorgon's head from the temple's pediment. Models of the complex at its greatest extent give some idea of the awe which it must have inspired, while the graffiti salvaged from the Roman era – mainly curses and boasts – give a nice personal slant on this antique leisure centre. You can get a free glimpse into the baths from the next-door **Pump Room**, the social hub of the Georgian spa community and still redolent of that era, housing a tearoom and restaurant.

Although there has been a church on the site since the seventh century, **Bath Abbey** did not take its present form until the end of the fifteenth century, when Bishop Oliver King began work on the ruins of the previous Norman building, some of which were incorporated into the new church. The bishop was said to have been inspired by a vision of angels ascending and descending a ladder to heaven, which the present facade recalls on the turrets flanking the central window. The west front also features the founder's signature in the form of carvings of olive trees surmounted by crowns, a play on his name.

Much of the building underwent restoration following the destruction that took place under Henry VIII; his daughter, Queen Elizabeth, played a large part in the repairs. The interior is in a restrained Perpendicular style, and boasts splendid fan vaulting on the ceiling, which was not properly completed until the nineteenth century. The floor and walls are crammed with elaborate monuments and memorials, and traces of the grander Norman building are visible in the Norman Chapel.

To the Circus and the Royal Crescent

From Abbey Church Yard, the elegantly colonnaded Bath Street leads onto Westgate Street and Sawclose, where you can take a glance at the **Theatre Royal**, opened in 1805 and one of the country's finest surviving Georgian theatres. Next door is the house where Beau Nash spent his last years, now a restaurant. Up from the Theatre Royal, off Barton Street, the gracious **Queen Square** was the first Bath venture of the architect **John Wood**, who with his son (also John) was chiefly responsible for the Roman-inspired developments of the areas outside the confines of the medieval city. Wood himself lived at no. 24, giving him a vista of the northern terrace's palatial facade.

Just north of the square, at 40 Gay St, the **Jane Austen Centre** (daily: April–Sept 9.30am–5.30pm; Oct–March 9.30am–5pm; £3) collects various objects associated with the writer in a Georgian town house just down from one of the many places Austen inhabited in Bath (at no. 25). The Centre gives a good overview of Jane Austen's various connections with the town, though the gift shop takes up a good proportion of it. West of Queen Square, at 19 New King St, another typical Bath townhouse was where the musician and astronomer Sir William Herschel, in collaboration with his sister Caroline, discovered the planet Uranus in 1781. You can take a brisk whirl around the small **Herschel Museum** here (March–Oct daily 2–5pm; Nov–Feb Sat & Sun 2–5pm; £2.50), showing contemporary furnishings, musical instruments, a replica of the telescope with which Uranus was identified and various knick-knacks from the Herschels' life.

Up from Queen Square, at the end of Gay Street, is the elder John Wood's masterpiece, **The Circus**, consisting of three crescents arranged in a tight circle of three-storey houses, with a carved frieze running round the entire circle. Wood died soon after laying the foundation stone for this enterprise, and the job was finished by his son. The painter Thomas Gainsborough lived at no. 17 from 1760 to 1774.

The Circus is connected by Brock Street to the **Royal Crescent**, grandest of Bath's crescents, begun by the younger John Wood in 1767. The stately arc of thirty houses is set off by a spacious sloping lawn from which a magnificent vista extends to green hills and distant ribbons of honey-coloured stone. The interior of **No. 1 Royal Crescent**, on the corner with Brock Street, has been restored to reflect as nearly as possible its original Georgian appearance (mid-Feb to Oct Tues–Sun 10.30am–5pm; Nov to mid-Dec Tues–Sun 10.30am–4pm; £4).

At the bottom of the Crescent, Royal Avenue leads onto **Royal Victoria Park**, the city's largest open space, containing an aviary and botanical gardens.

The Assembly Rooms, the Paragon and Milsom Street

The younger John Wood's **Assembly Rooms**, east of the Circus on Bennett Street, were, with the Pump Room, the centre of Bath's social scene. A fire virtually destroyed the building in 1942, but it has now been perfectly restored and houses a **Museum of Costume** (daily 10am–5pm; £3.90), an entertaining collection of clothing from the Stuart era to the latest Japanese designs.

From the Assembly Rooms, Alfred Street leads to the area known as the **Paragon**, at the top of Milsom Street. Here, an old Methodist chapel houses the **Building of Bath Museum** (mid-Feb to Nov Tues–Sun 10.30am–5pm; £3), an educational explanation of the construction and architecture of Bath. At the bottom of the Paragon, off George Street, lies **Milsom Street**, a wide shopping strand designed by the elder Wood as the main thoroughfare of Georgian Bath. A former private chapel from the period now contains the **Royal Photographic Society** (daily 9.30am–5.30pm, last entry 4.45pm; £2.50), with regular exhibitions tracing the history of the art and its technology.

The river and Great Pulteney Street

The flow of the River Avon – a crucial ingredient in the city's charm – is interrupted by a graceful V-shaped weir just below the shop-lined **Pulteney Bridge**, an Italianate structure designed by the eighteenth-century Scottish architect Robert Adam. The bridge was intended to link the city centre with **Great Pulteney Street**, a handsome avenue originally planned as the nucleus of a large residential quarter on the eastern bank. The work ran into financial difficulties, however, so the roads running off it now stop short after a few yards, though there is a lengthy vista to the imposing classical facade at the end of the street (mid-Feb to mid-Dec Mon–Sat 11am–5pm, Sun 2.30–5.30pm; mid-Feb to Easter closed Mon; £3.50). The three-storey building contains an impressive range of decorative and fine art, mostly furniture, silverware, porcelain and paintings (one by Gainsborough) from the eighteenth century, plus a good collection of twentieth-century craftwork. Behind Holburne House, **Sydney Gardens** make a delightful place to take a breather. When Holburne House was a bustling hotel, the pleasure gardens were the venue for concerts and fireworks, as witnessed by Jane Austen, a frequent visitor here – the family had lodgings across the street at 4 Sydney Place in the autumn of 1801. Today, the bosky slopes are cut through by the railway and the Kennet and Avon Canal. From here, it's a pleasant one-and-a-half mile saunter along the canal to the *George* pub (see opposite).

If you want to explore the river itself, rent a skiff, punt or canoe in summer from the **Victorian Bath Boating Station** at the end of Forester Road, behind the Holburne Museum. Organized river trips can be made from Pulteney Bridge and weir, and there are cruises on the Kennet and Avon Canal from Sydney Wharf, near Bathwick Bridge. A two-mile **nature trail** winds along the banks of the restored canal, which itself extends east as far as Reading.

Eating, drinking and nightlife

Bath has a reputation for gourmet cuisine, even if too many of the town's **restaurants** do over-exploit the period trappings. In the less exalted regions of the price scale, there are several decent, inexpensive places to eat, and coffee shops and snack bars are ubiquitous in the centre, as are pubs offering lunchtime fare. Try and be in Bath for the **Bath International Festival** (two weeks in May or June), which features big names in classical music, jazz, folk and blues, with a plethora of fringe events accompanying the official programme, plus fireworks, literary and art events and lots of busking. For concerts, gigs and other events during the rest of the year, refer to *Venue*, the fortnightly listings magazine (£1.90).

Restaurants

Circus Restaurant, 34 Brock St (☎01225/318918). Homely but elegant, just around the corner from the Circus, serving mainly French cuisine. Non-smoking. Moderate.

Demuth's, 2 North Parade Passage (☎01225/446059). Bath's favourite eating place for veggies and vegans, offering original and delicious dishes, as well as organic beers and wines. Decor is bright and modern, and there is no smoking. Booking advisable on Fri, Sat & Sun. Moderate.

The Hole in the Wall, 16 George St (☎01225/425242). Smart, select and classy Modern-British cuisine guaranteed in this basement retreat. Closed Sun. Moderate to Expensive.

Maxson's Diner, 7 Argyle St (☎01225/444440). Lively American-style burger bar off Pulteney Bridge, also offering nachos, BLT and pecan pie, but can get very crowded. Inexpensive to Moderate.

No. 5 Bistro, 5 Argyle St (☎01225/444499). Decent wine bar and restaurant with jazz soundtrack, two doors down from *Maxson's Diner*. BYOB Mon & Tues; Wed is fish night, and the desserts are always good. Closed Sun, plus Mon lunch. Moderate.

Pierre Victoire, 16 Argyle St (☎01225/334334). Great location, next to the river under Pulteney Bridge, plus competitive prices make this a good bet for a cosy soirée, and there's a set-price lunch for under £6. Closed Sun eve in winter. Moderate.

Pimpernel's, *Royal Crescent Hotel*, 16 Royal Crescent (☎01225/319090). English-based classics with Asian influences make this the best restaurant in Bath, or you can sample similarly excellent fare in the less formal *Brasserie*. All non-smoking. Very Expensive.

Popjoy's Restaurant, Sawclose (☎01225/460494). Touristy and twee, this restaurant is still worth sampling for its prime location next to the Theatre Royal, and for the curiosity value of being Beau Nash's house (it's named after his mistress). The food is Modern-British and there's a good-value pre-theatre menu. Closed Sun. Expensive.

Pump Room, Abbey Church Yard (☎01225/444477). If you don't want to splash out on a champagne breakfast or a full meal here, make sure you have at least a sandwich or tea to absorb the atmosphere, though be prepared to queue. Open daytime only, plus evenings during the Bath Festival. Moderate.

Rascals, 8 Pierrepont Place (☎01225/330280). Music and high-quality bistro food, in this network of snug cellars off Manvers Street, near Parade Gardens. Moderate.

Tilley's Bistro, 3 North Parade Passage (☎01225/484200). Informal, rather cramped French restaurant with starter-sized and -priced portions to allow more samplings, good set-price lunchtime menus and a separate vegetarian menu. Closed Sun lunch. Moderate.

Walrus and Carpenter, 25 Barton St. Popular spot near the Theatre Royal, serving steaks, burgers, poultry dishes and a full vegetarian menu. Inexpensive to Moderate.

Pubs and cafés

The Bath Tap, 19–20 St James's Parade. Home of Bath's gay and lesbian scene, though without so much of the "scene". It's lively but relaxed, with a mixed crowd enjoying the regular cabaret (strippers currently on Friday) as well as Club Eros in the cellar (see below). For news and events, see their Web site *www.welcome.to/thebathtap*

The Bell, Walcot St. Grungy atmosphere, with live music three times a week (Mon & Wed eve, plus Sun afternoon) and table football.

Café Retro, 18 York St. A trendy spot to sip a cappuccino near the Abbey. Fish pie and crepes are also on hand, and there's a full evening menu with an upstairs dining area.

Coeur de Lion, Northumberland Place (off High Street). Centrally located tavern on a flagstoned shopping alley; this is Bath's smallest boozer and is invariably packed, but it makes for a good lunchtime stop, with some bench seating outside.

The George, Mill Lane, Bathampton. Popular canal-side pub twenty minutes' walk from the centre. Better than average bar food.

Grapes, Westgate St. Again, popular, sometimes touristy, but usefully located old pub. Fruit machines and jukebox are present.

Hat and Feather, London St. Further up from Walcot Street, this drinking hole continues the quarter's alternative theme, with plenty of atmosphere and live music on some nights.

Pig and Fiddle, corner of Saracen and Walcot streets. Real ales and outside terraces, north of Pulteney Bridge. Table football and food helps to pull in the crowds.

Porters, Miles Buildings, George St. Part of *Moles* club (see below), this is the only vegetarian pub in Bath – serving only veggie food and some organic ales – though it feels more like a café.

St James' Wine Vaults, St James' St. A varied clientele is attracted to this dive north of the Circus, which has music in the basement.

Nightlife and entertainment

Town-centre **clubs** include *T's* (under Pulteney Bridge), popular with students and younger clubbers; *Moles* on George Street, which has live music for half the week and DJs playing dance sounds the other half; the *Walcot Palais*, literally a garage venue behind the *Porter Butt* pub on London Road, embracing roots and punk; the *Hush*, The Paragon, a pre- and post-club hangout with three bars, lots of tables and chairs and a small dance area; *Po Na Na*, 8 North Parade, basement dive playing club sounds to a largely student crowd; and the *Venue*, at Bath University, with techno and drum'n'bass on Friday and Saturday. The best gay and lesbian venue is *Club Eros*, situated under the *Bath Tap* pub (see above) at 19 St James's Parade, open on Fridays and Saturdays until 2am. There are three floors in all, including a chill-out zone.

Theatre and ballet fans should check out what's showing at the Theatre Royal on Sawclose (☎01225/448844), which stages more experimental productions in the Ustinov Studio.

Around Bath: Claverton and Frome

For a quick sample of the lovely countryside around Bath you could make an easy excursion to **CLAVERTON**, on the eastern edge of Bath, where the **American Museum** (late March to July & Sept–Nov Tues–Sun 2–5pm; Aug daily 2–5pm; grounds Tues–Fri 1–6pm, Sat & Sun noon–6pm; musuem & grounds £5, grounds only £2.50) merits at least half a day. Occupying the early nineteenth-century Claverton Manor, where Winston Churchill made his maiden political speech in 1897, this was the first museum of Americana to be established outside the US, and consists of a series of reconstructed rooms illustrating life in the New World from the seventeenth to the nineteenth centuries, as well as special sections devoted to textiles, whaling, the open-ing of the West, Native Americans and Hispano-American culture. The glorious **grounds** contain a replica of George Washington's garden, an arboretum and assorted relics resembling items from a movie set. University buses #18 and #418 run through-out the year to the Avenue (the stop before the campus), from where it's a ten-minute walk to the museum.

Fifteen miles south of Bath, at the eastern end of the Mendip Hills, the town of **FROME** (pronounced "Froom") is a picturesque ensemble of steep cobbled streets, yellow-stone weavers' cottages, Georgian rows and some dusty old shops. You could spend a pleasant hour or two roaming Frome's nooks and crannies, such as Gentle Street, or perusing the old gravestones in the churchyard of St John's. Buses #184 and #267 connect Bath with Frome every hour (not Sun). From here, it's only five miles across the Wiltshire border to Longleat (see p.263).

Wells, Glastonbury and the Mendips

Wells, twenty miles south of Bristol across the Somerset border and the same distance southwest from Bath, is a miniature cathedral city that has not significantly altered in eight hundred years. You could spend a good half-day kicking around here, and you might decide to make it an accommodation stop for visiting nearby attractions in the **Mendip Hills**, such as the **Wookey Hole** caves or **Cheddar Gorge**. On the southern edge of the range, the town of **Glastonbury** has for centuries been one of the main Arthurian sites of the West Country, and is now the country's most enthusiastic centre of New Age cults.

Wells

Technically the smallest city in the country, **WELLS** owes its celebrity entirely to its **Cathedral**. Hidden from sight until you pass into its spacious close from the central Market Place, the building presents a majestic spectacle, the broad lawn of the former graveyard providing a perfect foreground. The **west front** teems with some three hun-dred thirteenth-century figures of saints and kings, once brightly painted and gilded, though their present honey tint has a subtle splendour of its own. Close up, the impact is slightly lessened, as most of the statuary is badly eroded and many figures were dam-aged by Puritans in the seventeenth century.

The facade was constructed about fifty years after work on the main building was begun in 1180. The **interior** is a supreme example of early English Gothic, the long nave punctuated by a dramatic "scissor arch", one of three that were constructed in 1338 to take the extra weight of the newly built tower. Though some wax enthusiastic about the ingenuity of these so-called "strainer" arches, others argue that they're "grotesque intrusions" from an artistic point of view.

Other features worth scrutinizing are the narrative carvings on the **capitals and corbels** in the transepts – including men with toothache and an old man caught pilfering an orchard. In the north transept, don't miss the 24-hour astronomical clock, dating from 1390, whose jousting knights charge each other every quarter-hour, as announced by a figure known as Jack Blandiver, who kicks a couple of bells from his seat high up on the right – on the hour he strikes the bell in front of him. Opposite the clock, a doorway leads to a graceful, much-worn flight of steps rising to the **Chapter House**, an octagonal room elaborately ribbed in the Decorated style. There are some gnarled old tombs to be seen in the aisles of the **choir**, at the end of which is the richly coloured stained glass of the fourteenth-century **Lady Chapel**.

The row of clerical houses on the north side of the cathedral green are mainly seventeenth- and eighteenth-century, though one, the **Old Deanery**, shows traces of its fifteenth-century origins. The chancellor's house is now a **museum** (April–June, Sept & Oct daily 10am–5.30pm; July & Aug daily 10am–8pm; Nov–Easter Wed–Sun 11am–4pm; £2), displaying, among other items, some of the cathedral's original statuary, placed here for conservation reasons (and replaced by replicas), as well as a good geological section with fossils from the surrounding area, including Wookey Hole.

A little further along the street, the cobbled medieval **Vicars' Close** holds more clerical dwellings, linked to the cathedral by the Chain Gate and fronted by small gardens. The cottages were built in the mid-fourteenth century – though only no. 22 has not undergone outward alterations – and have been continuously occupied by members of the cathedral clergy ever since.

On the other side of the cathedral – and accessible through the cathedral shop – are the cloisters, from which you can enter the tranquil grounds of the **Bishop's Palace** (April–Oct Tues–Fri 10.30am–6pm, Sun 2–6pm; Aug daily 10.30am–6pm; £3), also reachable from Market Place through the Bishop's Eye archway. The residence of the Bishop of Bath and Wells, the palace was walled and moated as a result of a rift with the borough in the fourteenth century, and the imposing gatehouse still displays the grooves of the portcullis and a chute for pouring oil and molten lead on would-be assailants. Its tranquil gardens contain the springs from which the city takes its name – and which still feed the moat as well as the streams flowing along the gutters of Wells's High Street – and the ruined **Great Hall**, built at the end of the thirteenth century and despoiled during the Reformation.

Practicalities

Wells is not connected to the rail network, but its **bus station**, off Market Street, receives hourly buses from Bristol and Bath (less frequent on Sunday). The **tourist office** is on Market Place (daily: April–Oct 9.30am–5.30pm; Nov–March 10am–4pm; ☎01749/672552).

There are several central choices of **accommodation**: of the B&Bs, try *Tor Guest House*, 20 Tor St, a restored seventeenth-century building overlooking the cathedral (☎01749/672322; ②), or *Bekynton House*, a little farther out at 7 St Thomas St (☎01749/672222, *desmond@bekynton.freeserve.co.uk*; ②), with six rooms available. The High Street has some nice old coaching inns, including the *Market Place Hotel*, near the tourist office (☎01749/672616; ⑤), and the *Star Hotel*, 18 High St (☎01749/670500; ④).

For a coffee or **snack**, *Crofter's* tea rooms on Market Place is the best bet close to the cathedral. If you need something more substantial, head for *Chapel's* in Union

Street (off High St), a modern café-bar offering dishes like prawn vol-au-vents and fisherman's pie. Good Italian dishes as well as traditional English ones are available from the Italian-run *Ancient Gate House*, Sadler St (☎01749/672029); at no. 5 on the same street, *Ritcher's* (☎01749/679085) combines a downstairs bistro with a restaurant in a plant-filled loft serving top-notch dishes. Excellent wholefood is served at the *Good Earth* on Priory Road, near the bus station (☎01749/678600; closed Sun), with inexpensive three-course meals on offer at lunchtime. You can eat decent, inexpensive meals in the upstairs restaurant as well as **pub** fare at the *City Arms* on Cuthbert Street, formerly the city jail.

The area around Wells makes good cycling country: you can **rent a mountain bike** at *The Bicycle Company*, 80 High St (☎01749/675096; £9 for first day, £5 for each subsequent day) or *Bike City*, 31 Broad St (☎01749/671711; same prices).

The Mendips

The **Mendip Hills**, rising to the north of Wells, are chiefly famous for Wookey Hole – the most impressive of many caves in this narrow limestone chain – and for the **Cheddar Gorge**, where a walk through the narrow cleft might make a starting point for more adventurous trips across the Mendips. From Monday to Saturday there's an hourly bus to Wookey Hole from Wells (#172), from where there's also an hourly bus to the gorge (#126 or #826) – every two hours on Sunday.

Wookey Hole

Hollowed out by the River Axe a couple of miles outside Wells, **Wookey Hole** is an impressive cave complex of deep pools and intricate rock formations, but it's folklore rather than geology that takes precedence on the guided tours (daily: April–Oct 10am–5pm; Nov–Feb 10.30am–4.30pm; closed Dec 17–25; £7). Highlight of the tour is the alleged petrified remains of the Witch of Wookey, a "blear-eyed hag" who was said to turn her evil eye on crops, young lovers and local farmers until the Abbot of Glastonbury intervened; he despatched a monk who drove the witch into the inner cave, sprinkled her with holy water and turned her into stone. Some substance was lent to the legend when an ancient skeleton – in fact Romano-British – was unearthed here in 1912, together with a dagger, sacrificial knife and a big rounded ball of pure stalagmite, the so-called witch's ball. Beside her were found two skeletons, the remains of goats tied to a stake. The guides point out several other fancied resemblances to people and things during the hour-long tour, at the end of which you can use your ticket to visit a functioning Victorian paper mill by the river, and rooms containing speleological exhibits. On a less earnest note is the range of amusements laid on by Madame Tussauds, owners of the complex – notably a collection of gaudy, sometimes ghoulish, Edwardian fairground pieces.

A walkable couple of miles uphill west of Wookey Hole, **Ebbor Gorge** offers a wilder alternative to the more famous Cheddar Gorge, with tranquillity guaranteed on the wooded trails that follow the ravine up to the Mendip plateau.

Cheddar Gorge

Six miles west of Wookey on the A371, **CHEDDAR** has given its name to Britain's best-known cheese – most of it now mass-produced far from here – and is also renowned as a centre for strawberry growing. However, the biggest selling point of this rather plain village is the **Cheddar Gorge**, lying beyond the neighbourhood of Tweentown about a mile to the north.

Cutting a jagged gash across the Mendip Hills, the limestone gorge is an impressive geological phenomenon, though its natural beauty is undermined by the minor road running through it and by the Lower Gorge's mile of shops, coach park and **tourist**

office (daily: summer 10am–5pm; winter Sat & Sun 10am–5pm; ☎01934/744071). Few trippers venture further than the first few curves of the gorge, beyond the shops, which admittedly holds its most dramatic scenery, though each turn of the two-mile length presents new, sometimes startling vistas. At its narrowest the path squeezes between cliffs towering almost five hundred feet above, and if you don't want to follow the road as far as **Priddy**, the highest village in the Mendips, you can reach more dramatic destinations by branching off onto marked paths to such secluded spots as **Black Rock**, just two miles from Cheddar, or **Black Down**, at 1067ft the Mendips' highest peak. Cliff-top paths winding along the rim of the gorge provide an alternative to walking next to the road. The tourist office can give you details of a two-and-a-half-hour circular walk and of the **West Mendip Way**, a forty-mile route extending from Uphill, near Weston-super-Mare, to Wells and Shepton Mallet.

Beneath the gorge, the **Cheddar Caves** (daily: May to mid-Sept 10am–5pm; mid-Sept to May 10am–4.30pm; £7.50) were scooped out by underground rivers in the wake of the Ice Age, and subsequently occupied by primitive communities. The bigger of the two main groups, **Gough's Caves**, is a sequence of chambers with names like Solomon's Temple, Aladdin's Cave and the Swiss Village, all arrayed with tortuous rock formations that resemble organ pipes, waterfalls and giant birds. **Cox's Caves** (same ticket), entered lower down the main drag, have floodlighting that picks out subtle pinks, greys, greens and whites in the rock, and a set of lime blocks known as "the Bells", which produce a range of tones when struck. The Fantasy Grotto, attached to Cox's Caves, is the kids' favourite, with high-tech light and laser effects playing on its gushing waterfall.

Outside again, close to Cox's Caves, the 274 steps of **Jacob's Ladder** (same ticket as caves) lead to a cliff-top viewpoint towards Glastonbury Tor, Exmoor and the sea. It's a muscle-wrenching climb – anyone not in a state of honed fitness can reach the same spot with a great deal more ease via the narrow lane winding up behind the cliffs. You can also survey the panorama from **Pavey's Lookout Tower** nearby.

PRACTICALITIES

Among Cheddar's handful of **B&Bs**, there's *Chedwell Cottage* Redcliffe St (☎01934/743268; no credit cards; ①) which has two en-suite rooms; and the *Innishbeg*, West Lynne, off Tweentown (☎01934/743494; no credit cards; ①; closed Sept–Easter), which also has just two en-suite rooms, so booking ahead is recommended. Other options include the **youth hostel**, opposite the fire station, off the Hayes (☎01934/742494; closed Jan); and three **campsites**, two near the centre of Cheddar – *Froglands* (☎01934/742058; closed mid-Oct to Easter), a hundred yards past the church, and *Church Farm* opposite (☎01934/743048; closed Sept–Easter) – and the fully equipped *Broadway House* on the northwestern outskirts of the village off the A371 to Axbridge (☎01934/742610; closed Dec–Feb).

Glastonbury

Six miles south of Wells, and reachable from there in twenty minutes on frequent buses, **GLASTONBURY** lies at the centre of the so-called **Isle of Avalon**, a region rich with mystical associations. At the heart of it all is the early Christian legend that the young Christ once visited this site, a story that is not as far-fetched as it sounds. The Romans had a heavy presence in the area, mining lead in the Mendips, and one of these mines was owned by **Joseph of Arimathea**, a well-to-do merchant said to have been related to Mary. It's not completely impossible that the merchant took his kinsman on one of his many visits to his property, in a period of Christ's life of which nothing is recorded. It was this possibility to which William Blake referred in his *Glastonbury Hymn*, better known as *Jerusalem*: – "And did those feet in ancient times/Walk upon England's mountains green?"

Another legend relates how Joseph was imprisoned for twelve years after the Crucifixion, miraculously kept alive by the **Holy Grail**, the chalice of the Last Supper, in which the blood was gathered from the wound in Christ's side. The Grail, along with the spear which had caused the wound, were later taken by Joseph to Glastonbury, where he founded the abbey and commenced the conversion of Britain.

According to the official version, however, **Glastonbury Abbey** (June–Aug 9am–6pm; Sept–May 10am–dusk; £3) was a Celtic monastery founded in the fourth or fifth century – making this the oldest Christian foundation in England and enlarged by St Dunstan, under whom it became the richest Benedictine abbey in the country. Three Anglo-Saxon kings (Edmund, Edgar and Edmund Ironside) were buried here, the library had a far-reaching fame, and the church had the longest known nave of any monastic church at the time of the Dissolution (580ft – Wells Cathedral's nave reaches 415ft). The original building was destroyed by fire in 1184 and the ruins are the rather scanty remains of what took its place, reduced to their present state at the Dissolution. Hidden behind walls at the centre of town, surrounded by grassy parkland and shaded by trees, the ruins only hint at the extent of the building, which was financed largely by a constant procession of medieval pilgrims. Most prominent and photogenic remains are the transept piers and the shell of the Lady Chapel, with its carved figures of the Annunciation, the Magi and Herod.

The abbey's **choir** introduces another strand to the Glastonbury story, for it holds what is alleged to be the tomb of **Arthur and Guinevere**. As told by William of Malmesbury and Thomas Malory, the story relates how, after being mortally wounded in battle, King Arthur sailed to Avalon where he was buried alongside his queen. The discovery of two bodies in an ancient cemetery outside the abbey in 1191 – from which they were transferred here in 1278 – was taken to confirm the popular identification of Glastonbury with Avalon. In the grounds, the fourteenth-century abbot's kitchen is the only monastic building to survive intact, with four huge corner fireplaces and a great central lantern above. Behind the main entrance to the grounds, look out for the thorn-tree that is supposedly from the original **Glastonbury Thorn** said to have sprouted from the staff of Joseph of Arimathea when he landed here to convert the country. The plant grew for centuries on a nearby hill known as Wyrral, or Weary-All, and despite being hacked down by Puritans, lived long enough to provide numerous cuttings whose descendants still bloom twice a year (Easter & Dec). Only at Glastonbury do they flourish, it is claimed – anywhere else they die after a couple of years.

On the edge of the abbey grounds, the medieval abbey barn forms the centrepiece of the engaging **Somerset Rural Life Museum** (April–Oct Tues–Fri 10am–5pm, Sat & Sun 2–6pm; Nov–March Tues–Sat 10am–3pm; £2.50, valid for multiple entry for one year), illustrating a range of local rural occupations, from cheese- and cider-making to peat-digging, thatching and farming.

From the ruins it's a mile-long hike to **Glastonbury Tor**, at 521ft a landmark for miles around. The conical hill is topped by the dilapidated **St Michael's Tower**, sole remnant of a fourteenth-century church; it commands stupendous views encompassing Wells, the Quantocks, the Mendips, the once-marshy peat moors rolling out to the sea, and sometimes the Welsh mountains. Pilgrims once embarked on the stiff climb here with hard peas in their shoes as penance – nowadays people come to feel the vibrations of crossing ley-lines. If you don't fancy the steep ascent, there's an easier path farther up Wellhouse Lane, the road that leads to the Tor Park from the centre of town.

At the bottom of Wellhouse Lane, in the middle of a lush garden intended for quiet contemplation, the **Chalice Well** (daily April–Oct 10am–6pm; Nov–March noon–4pm; £1.50) is alleged to be the hiding-place of the Holy Grail. The iron-red waters were considered to have curative properties, making the town a spa for a brief period in the eighteenth century, and they are still prized – there's a tap in Wellhouse Lane.

Back in town, you might take a glance at the fifteenth-century church of **St John the Baptist**, halfway along the High Street. The tower is reckoned to be one of Somerset's finest, and the **interior** has a fine oak roof and stained glass illustrating the legend of St Joseph of Arimathea, both from the period of the church's construction. The Glastonbury thorn in the churchyard is the biggest in town.

Further down the street, the fourteenth-century **Tribunal** was where the abbots presided over legal cases; it later became a hotel for pilgrims, and now holds a small museum of finds from the Iron Age lake villages that once fringed the marshland below the Tor (April–Sept Mon–Thurs & Sun 10am–5pm, Fri & Sat 10am–5.30pm; Oct–March Mon–Thurs & Sun 10am–4pm, Fri & Sat 10am–4.30pm; £1.50).

Glastonbury is of course best known for its **music festival** which takes place most years over three days at the end of June outside the nearby village of Pilton. Having started in the 1970s, the festival has become one of the biggest and best organized in the country, without shedding too much of its alternative feel. Bands range from huge acts like REM and Tricky, to up-and-coming indie groups. Ticket prices are steep (around £85) and are snapped up early: for general information, contact the promoters on ☎01749/890470, or Glastonbury's tourist office (see below), which is also licensed to sell tickets.

Practicalities

Bus #376 runs once or twice an hour from Wells. Glastonbury's **tourist office** is housed in the Tribunal on the High Street (April–Sept Mon–Thurs & Sun 10am–5pm, Fri & Sat 10am–5.30pm; Oct–March Mon–Thurs & Sun 10am–4pm, Fri & Sat 10am–4.30pm; ☎01458/832954, or, for information on tickets for the festival, call ☎01458/832020). There is a rich assortment of good-value **accommodation** in town; among the budget B&Bs, the seventeenth-century *Waterfall Cottage*, 20 Old Wells Rd (☎01458/831707; no credit cards; ①), boasts a garden and views, while close to the Chalice Well and Rural Life Museum at 32 Chilkwell St, the *Bolthole* (☎01458/832800; no credit cards; ①), caters for vegetarians. Far grander is the *Ramala Centre* on nearby Dod Lane (☎01458/832459; ②). This old manor house is the headquarters of a meditation group and offers accommodation without strings, including use of a library of esoteric philosophy – smokers and carnivores are not welcome. Another retreat, the *Shambhala Healing Centre* on Coursing Batch, abutting the Tor (☎01458/831797, *isisandargon@shambhala.co.uk*; ②), has Tibetan, Egyptian and Chinese guestrooms, offers four types of massage and a water garden, and specializes in short breaks to replenish your spiritual batteries. If you prefer a more medieval mood, head straight for the *George & Pilgrims*, an old oak-panelled inn on the High Street (☎01458/831146; ⑤). Beautifully furnished bedrooms make for a stylish stay at 3 Magdalene St (☎01458/832129; ⑤), a listed Georgian house right next to the abbey. Just as centrally located, *Glastonbury Backpackers*, 4 Market Place (☎01458/833353, *glastonbury@backpackers-online.com*) offers a livelier atmosphere, with clean pastel-coloured doubles costing £26 with shared bath, or £30 with private facilities, while dorm beds go for £9. There's a café, restaurant, pool room and no curfew, plus occasional bands playing in the bar. The nearest YHA **hostel**, at the Chalet, Ivythorn Hill (☎01458/442961; closed Sept–March), lies a couple of miles outside the nearby village of **Street**, an easy bus ride on the #376 between Wells and Glastonbury. There's also a decent **campsite** within sight of the Tor, the *Isle of Avalon* (☎01458/833618), ten minutes' walk up Northload Street on Godney Road.

Wedged between the esoteric shops of Glastonbury's High Street are several decent **cafés** serving inexpensive homemade meals, including the *Excalibur* at no. 52; the *Global Café*, at no. 24, whose felafel and bean salads are accompanied by live music Thursday to Saturday evenings; and the *Blue Note Café* at no. 4, another good place to hang out over coffees and cakes with live or recorded music. Halfway up the High Street, the Assembly Rooms has a wholefood café, but is better known as the venue for talks and musical and theatrical **performances**. You can also buy tickets for concerts and miracle plays staged within the abbey grounds between mid-June and mid-September – call ☎01458/832267 for details.

If you're spending a few days in the area, think about renting a **bike**; cycling is an ideal way of getting around the Somerset Levels – the area of reclaimed marshes between Glastonbury and the sea. Bikes can be rented at Pedalers, 8 Magdalene St (☎01458/831117), for about £7 a day.

Bridgwater, Taunton and the Quantocks

Travelling west through the Somerset Levels, your route could take you through both **Bridgwater** and **Taunton**, each of which would make a handy starting point for excursions into the gently undulating **Quantock Hills**, a mellow landscape of snug villages set in scenic wooded valleys or "combes". Public transport is fairly minimal round here, but you can see quite a lot on the **West Somerset Railway** between Bishops Lydeard and the coastal resort of Minehead, with stops at some of the thatched, typically English villages along the west flank of the Quantocks; and there are **horse-riding** facilities at many local farms.

Bridgwater

Sedate **BRIDGWATER** has seen little excitement since it was embroiled in the Civil War and its aftermath, in particular the events surrounding the **Monmouth Rebellion** of 1685. Having landed from his base in Holland, the Protestant Duke of Monmouth, an illegitimate son of Charles II, was enthusiastically proclaimed king at Taunton, and was only prevented from taking Bristol by the encampment of the Catholic James II's army there. Monmouth turned round and attempted to surprise the king's forces on **Sedgemoor**, three miles outside Bridgwater. The disorganized rebel army was mown down by the royal artillery, Monmouth himself was captured and later beheaded, and a period of repression was unleashed under the infamous Judge Jeffreys, whose Bloody Assizes created a folk-memory in Somerset of gibbets and gutted carcasses displayed around the county.

The town was once one of Somerset's major ports and, despite some ugly outskirts, still has some handsome redbrick buildings around its centre. Northgate leads to the River Parrett and King's Square, which occupies the site of the keep of Bridgwater Castle, built in the thirteenth century but fallen into decay after the Civil War. A few traces remain above ground: part of the main wall is visible on West Quay, and a lesser wall on Queen Street – much of the original material was recycled for the construction of other houses in town. The thirteenth- to fourteenth-century St Mary's church (Mon–Wed & Sat 10.30am–noon, Thurs 10.30am–noon & 2–3.30pm), immediately identifiable by its polygonal, acutely angled steeple that soars over the town centre, has an oak pulpit and a seventeenth-century Italian altarpiece. The church is starkly contrasted by the Neoclassical Baptist church opposite, dating from 1600 but rebuilt in 1837. Bridgwater's **Blake Museum**, by the River Parrett on Blake Street (Tues–Sat 10am–4pm; free) shows relics, models and a video-documentary relating to the Battle of Sedgemoor. The sixteenth-century building is reputedly the birthplace of local hero Robert Blake, admiral under Oliver Cromwell, whose swashbuckling career against Royalists, Dutch and Spanish is chronicled and illustrated here.

You can spend a rewarding hour or two here and the surrounding area: equip yourself with the Bridgwater Castle Trail pamphlet from the **tourist office**, at the Town Hall on the High Street (March–Oct Mon–Sat 10am–5pm, reduced hours in winter; ☎01278/427652), which can also tell you about available **accommodation** hereabouts. An atmospheric and central choice would be the *Old Vicarage* right opposite St Mary's

Church (☎01278/458891; ③), which calls itself one of Bridgwater's oldest buildings – and you can still see some of the wattle and daub of the original walls on the left of the gateway into the courtyard. One of the best local **B&Bs** is *Chinar*, 17 Oakfield Rd (☎01278/458639; no credit cards; ②), a modern house in a quiet neighbourhood offering one single and two double rooms; or try the *Acorns*, 61 Taunton Rd (☎01278/445577; no credit cards; ①), on the banks of the Bridgwater–Taunton Canal, which has thirteen rooms, half of them en suite. For **snacks** head for the *Nutmeg House* in Angel Crescent, off the High Street, which does full evening meals Thursday to Saturday (closed Sun); alternatively, pick up a bag of fish and chips at the *West Quay Fish Bar*, by the river at the bottom of Castle Street. You can also eat well, or just have a **drink**, at the *Old Vicarage*, while St Mary's Street has a few more places to while away an evening, including *Toff's*, a mainstream club; the *Rock Garden*, a café-bar/brasserie; and the *Three Crowns* pub, which often has live bands.

A good time to be in Bridgwater would be for the **carnival** celebrations, which usually take place on the nearest Thursday to Guy Fawkes Day (one of the Catholic conspirators of the Gunpowder Plot hailed from nearby Nether Stowey; see p.360). Grandly festooned floats of the local Carnival Clubs roll through town, before heading off to do the same in various other Somerset towns and villages, including North Petherton, Glastonbury, Wells and Shepton Mallet.

Taunton

Twelve miles from Bridgwater, Somerset's county town of **TAUNTON** lies in the fertile Vale of Taunton, wedged between the Quantock, Brendon and Blackdown hills. The region is famed for its production of cider and scrumpy (cider's less refined cousin), while Taunton itself is host to one of the country's biggest cattle markets.

Taunton's **Castle**, started in the twelfth century, staged the trial of royal claimant Perkin Warbeck, who in 1490 declared himself to be the Duke of York, the younger of the "Princes in the Tower" – the sons of Edward IV, who had been murdered seven years earlier. Most of the castle was pulled down in 1662, but a part of it now houses the **County Museum** (Tues–Sat: April–Oct 10am–5pm, Nov–March 10am–3pm; £2.50), which includes a portrait of Judge Jeffreys among other memorabilia of local interest. Overlooking the county cricket ground are the pinnacled and battlemented towers of the town's two most important churches: **St James** and **St Mary Magdalene**, both fifteenth-century though remodelled by the Victorians. St Mary's is worth a look inside for its roof-bosses carved with medieval masks.

Otherwise Taunton should only detain you as a base to visit the Quantock villages or Exmoor. Information is on hand at the **tourist office** on Paul Street (April–Sept Mon–Thur 9.30am–5.30pm, Fri 9.30am–7pm, Sat 9.30am–5pm; Oct–March Mon–Fri 9.30am–5.30pm, Sat 9.30am–5pm; ☎01823/336344), in the library building. If you want to stay here, head for Wellington Road at the centre of town, where there are three **B&Bs** within a few steps of each other: *Brookfield* at no. 16 (☎01823/272786; no credit cards; ②), *Beaufort Lodge* at no. 18 (☎01823/326420; no credit cards; ②) – both with all rooms en suite – and *Acorn Lodge* at no. 22 (☎01823/337613; no credit cards; ①) with shared bathrooms for its two single and three twin rooms, all of which have TVs. The most atmospheric place in town is next to the museum: the *Castle*, Castle Green (☎01823/272671, *reception@the-castle-hotel.com*; ⑦), a wisteria-clad, three-hundred-year-old hotel exuding old-fashioned good taste – the place to stop for a cup of tea if nothing else. On a more down-to-earth note, *Prockters Farm*, a couple of miles outside town, near the village of West Monkton (☎01823/412269; no credit cards; ①), is a comfortable old country retreat with brass beds and antiques plus a large garden, offering rooms with or without private bathroom. For a snack or **meal**, head down East Street from Fore Street to *Porter's*, a congenial and inexpensive wine bar at 49 East Reach (closed Sun). Vegetarian dishes are served at the *Brewhouse Theatre and Arts Centre* on Coal Orchard, by the cricket ground, a good place to come in the evening, when there's usually something going on.

The Quantock Hills

Geologically closer to Devon than Somerset, the **Quantock Hills** are a cultivated outpost of Exmoor, similarly crossed by clear streams and grazed by red deer. Just twelve miles in length and mostly between 800 and 900 feet high, the range is enclosed by a triangle of roads leading up from Bridgwater and Taunton, within which snake a tangle of narrow lanes connecting secluded hamlets, reached by local buses from Taunton and Bridgwater. Along the western edge of the range, a restored steam railway is also a useful transport link, originally built to serve the harbour of Watchet, now used by tourists, birdwatchers and trekkers.

Bishops Lydeard and Combe Florey

North of Taunton, the first villages you pass through on the A358 give you an immediate introduction to the flavour of the Quantocks. **BISHOPS LYDEARD**, four miles up, has a splendid church tower in the Perpendicular style; the church's interior is also worth a look for its carved bench-ends, one of them illustrating the allegory of a pelican feeding its young with blood from its own breast – a symbol of the redemptive power of Christ's blood. The village is the terminus of the **West Somerset Railway**, linked by buses #28 and #28A from Taunton's train station. From mid-March to the first week of November (plus some dates in December) steam and diesel trains depart up to eight times daily, stopping at renovated stations on the way to Minehead, some twenty miles away (see p.364). For a talking timetable call ☎01643/707650, for other enquiries call ☎01643/704996.

A couple of miles north, **COMBE FLOREY** is almost exclusively built of the pink-red sandstone characteristic of Quantock villages. For over fifteen years (1829–45), the local rector was the unconventional cleric Sydney Smith, called "the greatest master of ridicule since Swift" by Macaulay; more recently it's been home to Evelyn Waugh.

Nether Stowey and around

Eight miles west of Bridgwater on the A39, on the edge of the hills, the pretty village of **NETHER STOWEY** is best known for its association with **Samuel Taylor Coleridge**, who walked here from Bristol at the end of 1796, to join his wife and child at their new home. This "miserable cottage", as Sara Coleridge called it, was visited six months later by William Wordsworth and his sister Dorothy, who soon afterwards moved into Alfoxton House, near Holford, a couple of miles down the road. The year that Coleridge and Wordsworth spent as neighbours was extraordinarily productive – Coleridge composed some of his best poetry at this time, including *The Rime of the Ancient Mariner* and *Kubla Khan*, and the two poets in collaboration produced the *Lyrical Ballads*, the poetic manifesto of early English Romanticism. Many of the greatest figures of the age made the trek down to visit the pair, among them Charles Lamb, Thomas De Quincey, Robert Southey, Humphry Davy and William Hazlitt, and it was the coming and going of these intellectuals that stirred the suspicions of the local authorities in a period when England was at war with France. Spies were sent to track them and Wordsworth was finally given notice to leave in June 1798, shortly before *Lyrical Ballads* rolled off the press. In **Coleridge Cottage** (April–Sept Tues–Thurs & Sun 2–5pm; £2.50; NT), not such an "old hovel" now, you can see the man's parlour and reading room, and, upstairs, his bedroom and an exhibition room containing various letters and first editions.

The village library in nearby Castle Street has a **Quantock Information Centre** (Mon 2.30–5pm, Wed 10am–12.30pm & 2–5pm, Fri 10am–12.30pm, 2–5pm & 5.30–7pm;

☎01278/732845), which can provide walking itineraries and local information. As for **accommodation**, a good choice in the village is *Castle Cottage*, 12 Castle St (☎01278/733453; no credit cards; ①), a seventeenth-century house which also serves light meals and teas to non-guests. **Campers** should head for *Mill Farm* (☎01278/732286), a couple of miles east of Nether Stowey on the A39, outside the village of Fiddington. There's also a stables here, and a heated pool is laid on for campers and riders.

The nearby village of **HOLFORD** makes for a good place to stop. There's *Quantock House* (☎01278/741439; no credit cards; ②), a beautiful Elizabethan thatched cottage, and a signposted two-mile walk from the village centre is a **youth hostel** (☎01278/741224; closed Sept–March), where you can also **camp** in the grounds. Holford's *Plough Inn*, where Virginia and Leonard Woolf spent their honeymoon, serves simple **snacks**, and is also a stop on the #15 Bridgwater–Minehead bus route.

From Nether Stowey, a minor road winds south off the A39 to the highest point on the Quantocks at **Wills Neck** (1260ft); park at Triscombe Stone, on the edge of Quantock Forest, from where a footpath leads to the summit about a mile distant. Stretching between the Wills Neck and the village of Aisholt, the bracken- and heather-grown moorland plateau of **Aisholt Common** is the heart of the Quantocks – the best place to begin exploring this central tract is near **West Bagborough**, where a five-mile path starts at Birches Corner. Lower down the slopes, outside the village of Aisholt, the banks of **Hawkridge Reservoir** make a lovely picnic stop.

The Quantocks make wonderful riding country, and the hills are notorious for confrontations between hunting parties and anti-hunt activists. If you want to do some horse back trekking, contact Mill Farm at Fiddington, near Nether Stowey (see above). **Mountain bikes** can be rented for £9 per day from the *Quantock Orchard Caravan Park* (☎01984/618618), between Crowcombe – a stop on the West Somerset Railway – and Triscombe.

Kilve, Watchet and Cleeve Abbey

The Quantock seaboard can be seen at its best at **Kilve Beach**, signposted off the A39 below Holford. Not so much a beach as a grand shale-studded foreshore, it's perfect for messing about in the rock pools and roaming the seaweedy shore.

Six miles to the west, **WATCHET** is Somerset's only port of any consequence, and the place from which Coleridge's Ancient Mariner set sail. Having made a halt at the harbour, the quiet heart of the village, you can get a good all-round view from **St Decuman's** church above it, built on the site of the saint's martyrdom. Decuman, who floated over the sea from Wales, was decapitated by a Danish invader who was instantly converted when the saint picked up his bleeding head, washed it in a stream, and gently placed it next to him as he lay down to die. Watchet is only a stop away on the West Somerset Railway from **Washford**, from where it's a ten-minute walk to **Cleeve Abbey** (daily: April–Sept 10am–6pm; Oct 10am–5pm; Nov–March 10am–1pm & 2–4pm; £2.60; EH), a Cistercian house founded in 1198. Although the church itself has been mostly destroyed, the convent buildings are in excellent condition, providing the country's most complete collection of domestic buildings belonging to this austere order. An exhibition on the premises illustrates how the monks lived and how the local population unsuccessfully pleaded with Henry VIII for the abbey's survival.

Exmoor

A high bare plateau sliced by wooded combes and splashing rivers, **EXMOOR** can be one of the most forbidding landscapes in England, especially when its sea-mists fall. When it's clear, though, the moorland of this National Park reveals rich swathes of colour and an amazing diversity of wildlife, from buzzards to the unique **Exmoor ponies**, a species closely related to prehistoric horses. In the treeless heartland of the moor around **Simonsbath**, in particular, it is not difficult to spot these short and stocky animals, though fewer than twelve hundred are registered, and of these only about two hundred are free-living on the moor. Much more elusive are the **red deer**, England's largest native wild animal, of which Exmoor supports England's only wild population. The effect of hunting through the centuries has accounted for a drastic depletion in numbers, though they have a strong recovery rate, and about 2500 are thought to inhabit the moor today, their annual culling by stalking as well as hunting is a regular point of issue among conservationists and nature-lovers.

Endless permutations of **walking routes** are possible along a network of some six hundred miles of footpaths and bridleways. In addition, the National Park Authority and other local organizations have put together a programme of guided walks, graded according to distance, speed and duration and costing from £1–£3.50 per person. Contact any of the Visitor Centres or else phone the National Park base at Dulverton (☎01398/323665) for details. **Horseback** is another option for getting the most out of Exmoor's desolate beauty, and stables are dotted throughout the area – the most convenient are mentioned below; expect to pay around £10 an hour. Whether walking or riding, bear in mind that over seventy percent of the National Park is privately owned and that access is theoretically restricted to public rights of way; special permission should certainly be sought before doing anything like camping, canoeing or fishing.

There are four obvious bases for inland walks: **Dulverton** in the southeast, site of the main information facilities and useful also for excursions into the neighbouring Brendon Hills; **Simonsbath** in the centre; **Exford**, near Exmoor's highest point of Dunkery Beacon; and the attractive village of **Winsford**, close to the A396 on the east of the moor. Exmoor's coastline offers an alluring alternative to the open moorland, all of it accessible via the **South West Coast Path**, which embarks on its long coastal journey at **Minehead**, though there is more charm to be found farther west at the sister-villages of **Lynmouth** and **Lynton**, just over the Devon border.

Minehead stands at the end of the **West Somerset Railway**, but otherwise you have to rely on often infrequent local **buses** for public transport. The main lines are run in the summer only; for the winter you'll have to rely on once- or twice-weekly community buses connecting Dulverton, Minehead and Lynton. From late May until the end of September, the most useful lines are the #285, looping between Minehead, Dunster, Wheddon Cross, Exford and Porlock (not Sat); and the #295 connecting Dulverton with Lynton via Tarr Steps, Exford and Simonsbath (not Sat or Sun); while the #398 runs throughout the year (not Sun) between Minehead, Dulverton and Tiverton. On the coast, the most useful route is the summer-only #300, connecting Minehead with Lynton and Ilfracombe three times daily, extending as far as Taunton on one of its journeys. If you're planning to make good use of the buses, enquire about the money-saving "Explorer" (£5) and "3-Day" (£9.50) tickets from Visitor Centres or bus operators.

The Brendon Hills

Sandwiched between the Quantocks and Exmoor, the **Brendon Hills** are effectively an extension of the moor, separated from it by the rivers Avill and Exe. The A396, which runs alongside the rivers, offers opportunities to take woodland paths rising to such scenic spots as **Wimbleball Lake**, accessible from the village of **Brompton Regis**. Exmoor's major reservoir, the lake is the habitat of herons and kingfishers, and footpaths lead from its southern shores up **Haddon Hill**, enjoying sweeping panoramas from its 1164ft summit.

Overlooking Wimbleball Lake, *Lower Holworthy Farm* offers plain but comfortable **accommodation** and traditional farmhouse food to its guests (☎01398/371244; no credit cards; ②). Further north, **Wheddon Cross** has the excellent *Rest and Be*

Thankful inn, with a beer garden, good food and several rooms (☎01643/841222, *rbtinn@btconnect.com*; ③). There's also a **riding stables** nearby at Huntscott House Stables (☎01643/841272) which arranges two-hour rides in small groups for £20.

Dulverton

The village of **DULVERTON**, on the southern edge of the National Park near Brompton Regis, is the Park Authority's headquarters and so makes a good introduction to Exmoor. Information on the whole moor is available at the **visitor centre**, 7 Fore St (daily: Easter–Oct 10am–1.15pm & 1.45–5pm; Nov–Easter 10.30am–2.30pm; ☎01398/323841). **Accommodation** in Dulverton includes *Town Mills* (☎01398/323124; no credit cards; ①), an old millhouse in the centre of the village. If the handful of other options are full, or you hanker after beams and four-posters, try the central but slightly costlier *Lion Hotel* in Bank Square (☎01398/323444; ③). *Crispin's*, in a nook off 26 High St, does moderately priced carnivorous and vegetarian **food**, while further down the High Street, *Lewis's Tea Rooms* serves teas and snacks. Moorland **horse-riding** and tuition is offered at West Anstey Farm, (☎01398/341354), a couple of miles west of Dulverton; a day's trekking costs £60 and a two-day riding break £130.

Winsford

Just west of the A396 five miles north of Dulverton, **WINSFORD** – birthplace of the renowned Labour politician Ernest Bevin – lays good claim to being the moor's prettiest village. A scattering of thatched cottages ranged around a sleepy green, it is watered by a confluence of streams and rivers – one of them the Exe – giving it no fewer than seven bridges. *Larcombe Foot* (☎01643/851306; no credit cards; ②; closed Jan & Feb), one mile to the north, offers excellent **B&B** overlooking the Exe, and there's a well-equipped **campsite** nearby at *Halse Farm* (☎01643/851259; closed Nov–Feb). The *Royal Oak*, a thatched and rambling old inn on the village green, can offer you drinks, snacks and full restaurant **meals**, though the rooms are pricey (☎01643/851455, *royaloak.winsfordsom@virgin.net*; ⑤).

WALKS FROM DULVERTON

The most popular short walk from Dulverton goes along the east bank of the Barle to the seventeen-span medieval bridge at **Tarr Steps**, five miles to the northwest.

You could combine this walk with a hike up **Winsford Hill**, a circular walk of less than four hours from Tarr Steps. Follow the riverside path upstream from Tarr Steps, turning right after about half a mile along Watery Lane, a rocky track that deteriorates into a muddy lane near Knaplock Farm. Stay on the track until you reach a cattle-grid, on open moorland. Turn left here, cross a small stream and climb up Winsford Hill, a heather moor whose 1400-foot summit is invisible until you are almost there. At the top, from where there are views as far as Dartmoor, you can see the **Wambarrows**, three Bronze Age burial mounds. If you want a refreshment stop, descend the hill on the other side to the village of Winsford (see above).

A quarter-mile due east of the barrows, the ground drops sharply by over 200ft to the Punchbowl, a bracken-grown depression resembling an amphitheatre. Keep on the east side of the B3223 which runs up Winsford Hill, following it south for a mile, until you come across the **Caratacus Stone**, an inscribed stone just by Spire Cross. The stone is thought to date from between 450 and 650, the damaged inscription reading "Carataci Nepos" – that is, "kinsman of Caratacus", the first-century British king.

Continue south on the east side of the road, cross it after about a mile, and pass over the cattle grid on the Tarr Steps road, from which a footpath takes you west another one and a half miles back to Tarr Steps. The *Tarr Farm* café here provides food and refreshment.

Exford and Dunkery Beacon

The hamlet of **EXFORD**, an ancient crossing-point on the River Exe, is popular with walkers for the four-mile hike from here to **Dunkery Beacon**, Exmoor's highest point at 1700ft. The village also holds Exmoor's main **youth hostel**, a large Victorian house in the centre (☎01643/831288; closed Nov to mid-Feb). Three miles east at Luckwell Bridge, and convenient for Dunkery Beacon, *Cutthorne* (☎01643/831255; ③) is a secluded eighteenth-century farmhouse offering comfortable **B&B**, while *Westermill Farm* (☎01643/831238) provides a tranquil **campsite** on the banks of the Exe, two and a half miles outside Exford. **Horse-riding** can be arranged at Stockleigh Stables (☎01643/831166), half a mile north of the village.

Exmoor Forest and Simonsbath

At the centre of the National Park stands **Exmoor Forest**, the barest part of the moor, scarcely populated except by roaming sheep and a few red deer – the word "forest" denotes simply that it was a hunting reserve. In the middle of it stands the village of **SIMONSBATH** (pronounced "Simmonsbath"), at a crossroads between Lynton, Barnstaple and Minehead on the River Barle. The village was home to the Knight family, who bought the forest in 1818 and, by introducing tenant farmers, building roads and importing sheep, brought systematic agriculture to an area that had never before produced any income. The Knights also built a wall round their land – parts of which can still be seen – as well as the intriguing Pinkworthy (pronounced "Pinkery") Pond, four miles to the northwest, whose exact function has never been explained.

Simonsbath would make a useful base for the heart of the moor. The *Exmoor Forest Hotel* (☎01643/831341, *helen@exforest.freeserve.co.uk*; ①) offers clean and comfortable accommodation, and also space for free **camping**. For snacks, coffee and lunches, there's a decent and inexpensive **restaurant** here too, *Boevey's*, in a converted barn near the *Simonsbath House Hotel* (☎01643/831259; ⑤), a cosy bolt-hole offering seven agreeably gnarled rooms, all en suite, and a good restaurant. A couple of miles outside the village on the Brayford road, the *Poltimore Arms* at **Yarde Down** is a classic country **pub**, serving excellent food including vegetarian dishes.

Minehead and around

A chief port on the Somerset coast, **MINEHEAD** quickly became a favourite Victorian watering-hole with the arrival of the railway, and it has retained a cheerful holiday-town atmosphere ever since. Steep lanes containing some of the oldest houses link the two quarters of **Higher Town**, on North Hill, and the livelier **Quay Town**, the harbour area. It is in Quay Town that the **Hobby Horse** performs its dance in the town's three-day May Day celebrations, snaring maidens under its prancing skirt and tail in a fertility ritual resembling the more famous festivities at the Cornish port of Padstow (see p.430).

The **tourist office** is midway between Higher Town and Quay Town at 17 Friday St, off the Parade (April–June, Sept & Oct Mon–Sat 9.30am–5pm; July & Aug Mon–Sat 9.30am–5.30pm, Sun 10am–1pm; Nov–March Mon–Sat 10am–4pm; ☎01643/702624). If you want to **stay** in Minehead, try *Avill House* on Townsend Road (☎01643/704370; no credit cards; ①), a short walk from the seafront past the tourist office; or the *Mayfair Hotel*, 25 The Avenue (☎01643/702719; closed Dec–March; ③), which enjoys a central location. There's a **youth hostel** a couple of miles southeast, outside the village of Alcombe (☎01643/702595; closed Nov–March), in a secluded combe on the edge of Exmoor.

As well as being the start of the **South West Coast Path** (see box opposite), Minehead is a terminus for the **West Somerset Railway**, which curves eastwards into the Quantocks as far as Bishops Lydeard (see p.360). The Minehead area's major attraction, the old village of **DUNSTER**, is about a mile from the line's first stop, three miles inland of Minehead. The main street is dominated by the towers and turrets of

---

THE SOUTH WEST COAST PATH

The South West Coast Path, the longest footpath in Britain, starts at Minehead and tracks the coastline as closely as possible along Devon's northern seaboard, round Cornwall, back into Devon, and on to Dorset, where it finishes close to the entrance to Poole Harbour. The path was conceived in the 1940s, but it is only in the last twenty years that – barring a few significant gaps – the full **six-hundred-mile route** has been open, much of it on land owned by the National Trust, and all of it well signposted with the acorn symbol of the Countryside Agency.

Some degree of planning is essential for any long walk along the South West Coast Path, in particular on the south Devon stretch, where there are six ferries to negotiate and one ford to cross between Plymouth and Exmouth. Accommodation needs to be considered too: don't expect to arrive late in the day at a holiday town in season and immediately find a bed. Even campsites can fill to capacity, though campers have the flexibility of asking farmers for permission to pitch in a corner of a field.

The relevant Ordnance Survey maps can be found at most village shops on the route, while many newsagents, bookshops and tourist offices will stock books or pamphlets containing route plans and details of local flora and fauna. The Countryside Agency (John Dower House, Crescent Place, Cheltenham, GL50 3RA; ☎01242/521381, *www.countryside.gov.uk*) in conjunction with Ordnance Survey produces a series of books (published by Aurum Press) describing different parts of the path, while the **South West Coast Path Association** publishes an annual guide (£5.99) to the whole path, including accommodation lists, ferry timetables and transport details; contact them at Windlestraw, Penquit, Ermington, Devon PL21 0LU (☎01752/896237).

Dunster Castle (April–Sept Mon–Wed, Sat & Sun 11am–5pm; Oct Mon–Wed, Sat & Sun 11am–4pm; grounds daily April–Sept 10am–5pm; Oct–March 11am–4pm; house & grounds £5.40, grounds only £2.90; NT), most of whose fortifications were demolished after the Civil War. After that the castle became something of an architectural showpiece, and Victorian restoration has made it into something more like a Rhineland Schloss than a Norman stronghold.

On a tour of the castle you can see various pompous portraits of the Luttrells, owners of the house for six hundred years before the National Trust took over in the 1970s, as well as a bedroom once occupied by Charles I, a fine seventeenth-century carved staircase and a richly decorated banqueting hall. The grounds include terraced gardens and riverside walks – and drama productions are periodically staged here in the summer (call ☎01985/843601 for details). The nearby hilltop tower is a folly, **Conygar Tower**, dating from 1776.

Despite the influx of seasonal visitors, Dunster village preserves relics of its woolmaking heyday; the octagonal **Yarn Market**, in the High Street below the castle, dates from 1609, while the three-hundred-year-old **water mill** at the end of Mill Lane is still used commercially for milling the various grains which go to make the flour and muesli sold in the shop (July & Aug daily 10.30am–5pm; April–June, Sept & Oct Mon–Fri & Sun 10.30am–5pm; £2.10; NT) – the café, overlooking its riverside garden is a good spot for lunch. For somewhere to **stay**, try the elegant old *Dollons House*, 10 Church St (☎01643/821880, *hannah.bradshaw@virgin.net*; non-smoking; ③). There's a **visitor centre** at the top of Dunster Steep by the main car park (Easter–Oct daily 10am–5pm; Nov–Easter Sat & Sun 11am–3pm; ☎01643/821835).

Porlock

The real enticement of **PORLOCK**, six miles west of Minehead, is its extraordinary position in a deep hollow, cupped on three sides by the hogbacked hills of Exmoor. The thatch-and-cob houses and dripping charm of the village's long main street have led to invasions of tourists, some of whom are also drawn by the place's literary links. According to Coleridge's own less than reliable testimony, it was a "man from Porlock" who broke the opium trance in which he was composing *Kubla Khan*, while the High Street's beamed *Ship Inn* prides itself on featuring prominently in the Exmoor romance *Lorna Doone* and, in real life, having sheltered the poet Robert Southey, who staggered in rain-soaked after an Exmoor ramble.

Porlock's **tourist office** is at West End, High Street (March–Oct Mon–Sat 10am–6pm, Sun 10am–1pm; Nov–Feb Tues–Sat 10am–1pm; ☎01643/863150). The best **accommodation** in town is on the High Street, where the *Ship* (☎01643/862507, *the-ship@btconnect.com*; ③) has plenty of atmosphere and the Victorian *Lorna Doone Hotel* (☎01643/862404, *lorna@doone99.freeserve.co.uk*; ②) offers king-sized rooms, all with private bath and TV. Further down, *The Cottage* is smaller and quainter, but a little pricier (☎01643/862687; ③). Both *The Cottage* and the *Lorna Doone* serve snacks, meals and teas – as does *Lowerbourne House*, a tearoom and bookshop with useful local information, also on the High Street. Porlock has a central **campsite** *Sparkhayes Farm* (☎01643/862470; closed Nov–March), signposted off the main road near the *Lorna Doone*.

If you walk two miles west over the reclaimed marshland, you'll come to the tiny harbour of **PORLOCK WEIR**, which gives little inkling of its former role as a hard-working port trafficking with Wales. It's a peaceful spot, giving onto a bay that enjoys the mildest climate on Exmoor. An easy two-mile stroll west from here along the South West Coast Path brings you to **St Culbone**, a tiny church – claimed to be the country's smallest – sheltered within woods once inhabited by a leper colony.

Lynton and Lynmouth

West from Porlock, the road climbs 1350ft in less than three miles, though cyclists and drivers might prefer the gentler and more scenic toll road alternative to the direct uphill trawl (cars £2, bikes 50p). Nine miles along the coast, on the Devon side of the county line, the Victorian resort of **LYNTON** perches above a lofty gorge with splendid views over the sea. Almost completely cut off from the rest of the country for most of its history, the village struck lucky during the Napoleonic wars, when frustrated Grand Tourists – unable to visit their usual continental haunts – discovered in Lynton

---

WALKS FROM LYNTON AND LYNMOUTH

The major year-round attraction in these parts is walking, not only along the coast path but inland. The one-and-a-half-mile tramp to **Watersmeet**, for example, follows the East Lyn River to where it is joined by Hoar Oak Water, a tranquil spot transformed into a roaring torrent after a bout of rain. From the fishing lodge here – now owned by the National Trust and open as a café and shop in summer – you can branch off on a range of less-trodden paths, such as the three-quarters-of-a-mile route south to **Hillsford Bridge**, the confluence of Hoar Oak and Farley Water.

North of Watersmeet, a path climbs up **Countisbury Hill** and the higher **Butter Hill** (nearly 1000ft) giving riveting views of Lynton, Lynmouth and the north Devon coast, and there is also a track leading to the lighthouse at **Foreland Point**, close to the coastal path. East from Lynmouth you can reach the point via a fine sheltered shingle beach at the foot of Countisbury Hill – one of a number of tiny coves that are easily accessible on either side of the estuary.

From Lynton, an undemanding expedition takes you west along the **North Walk**, a mile-long path leading to the **Valley of the Rocks**, a steeply curved heathland dominated by rugged rock formations. At the far end of the valley, herds of wild goats range free, as they have done here for centuries.

a domestic piece of Swiss landscape. Coleridge and Hazlitt trudged over to Lynton from the Quantocks, but the greatest spur to the village's popularity came with the publication in 1869 of R.D. Blackmore's Exmoor melodrama *Lorna Doone*, a book based on the outlaw clans who inhabited these parts in the seventeenth century. Since then the area has become indelibly associated with the swashbuckling romance.

Lynton's imposing **town hall** on Lee Road epitomizes the Victorian–Edwardian accent of the village. It was the gift of publisher George Newnes, who also donated the nearby **cliff railway** connecting Lynton with Lynmouth (March to mid-July & mid-Sept to Nov Mon–Sat 9am–7pm, Sun 9am–7pm; mid-July to mid-Sept Mon–Sat 9am–10pm, Sun 9am–10pm; 80p, £1 after 7pm). The device is an ingenious hydraulic system, its two carriages counter balanced by water tanks which fill up at the top, descend, and empty their load at the bottom.

Five hundred feet below, **LYNMOUTH** lies at the junction and estuary of the East and West Lyn rivers, in a spot described by Gainsborough as "the most delightful place for a landscape painter this country can boast". The picturesque scene was shattered in August 1952 when Lynmouth was almost washed away by floodwaters coming off Exmoor, a disaster of which there are many reminders around the village. Having recovered its calm, Lynmouth is only ruffled now by the summer crowds, though nothing could compromise the village's unique location. Shelley spent his honeymoon here with his sixteen-year-old bride Harriet Westbrook, making time in his nine-week sojourn to write his polemical *Queen Mab* – two different houses claim to have been the Shelleys' love-nest. R.D. Blackmore, author of *Lorna Doone*, stayed in **Mars Hill**, the oldest part of the town, its creeper-covered cottages framing the cliffs behind the Esplanade. In summer, the harbour offers boat trips and fishing expeditions, and you can explore the **Glen Lyn Gorge** up the wooded valley with its walks and waterfalls and displays of the uses and dangers of water-power (daily 9am–dusk; exhibition Easter–Oct 9am–dusk; £2) – this was the course taken by the destructive floods of 1952.

PRACTICALITIES

Lynton's **tourist office** is in the town hall (daily: summer 9.30am–5.30pm; winter 9.30am–4pm; ☎01598/752225), while Lynmouth has a **National Park Visitor Centre** on the harbour (April–Oct daily 10am–5pm; ☎01598/752509).

Lynton has the better choice of less expensive **B&Bs**, among them the Victorian *The Turret*, 33 Lee Rd (☎01598/753284; no credit cards; ①), one of the cheapest options of the row of accommodation lining this street, built by the same engineer who built the cliff railway. It's run by a friendly Scot and has six spacious rooms, four of them en suite including the turreted room at the top. Also cheap, but more central, is *St Vincent* (☎01598/752244, *keenstvincent@lineone.net*; ①), a whitewashed, Georgian house on Castle Hill with spacious bedrooms and a garden. The *Lynhurst*, Lyn Way (☎01598/752241, *lynhurst@demon.co.uk*; ②), is farther out from the centre, but has striking views over the valley. There is a **youth hostel** (☎01598/753237; closed Jan to mid-Feb) in a homely Victorian house about one mile inland from Lynton's centre, and signposted off Lynbridge Road. **Snacks** and coffees are served at the *Lily May's*, 1 Castle Hill.

In **Lynmouth**, the most inspiring place to stay is *Harbour Point*, a **B&B** right on the harbour at 1 The Esplanade, (☎01598/752321; no credit cards; ②) – the slightly pricier Turret Room and the Balcony Room are the best choices here. Other good options include the posh *Bath Hotel*, Harbourside (☎01598/752238; ③) and the *Orchard House Hotel*, 12 Watersmeet Rd (mid-Feb to mid-Nov; ☎01598/753247; ①). The *Rock House Hotel*, Harbourside (☎01598/753508, *dave@rockh.freeserve.co.uk*; ③), serves scones in the garden, snacks at the bar and meals in its **restaurant**. The *Village Inn*, Lynmouth St, does inexpensive lunches and dinners, including vegetarian options, though you'll find better food at the *Rising Sun* and at the *Bath Hotel* (see above), which charges £19 for a five-course dinner in its no-smoking restaurant.

From April to October you can take a **boat trip** with Exmoor Coast Boat Cruises (☎01598/753207) from Lynmouth harbour, an excellent way to view the bird-life on the cliffs; excursions last from 45 minutes (£4) to 4 hours (£8).

DEVON

With its rolling meadows, narrow lanes and remote thatched cottages, **Devon** has long been the urbanite's ideal vision of a pre-industrial, "authentic" England, and a quick tour of the county might suggest that this is largely a region of cosy, gentrified villages inhabited mainly by retired folk and urban refugees. Certainly Devon suffers from an excess of cloying nostalgia and an abundance of commercialism, but its popularity has a positive side to it as well – chiefly that zealous care is taken to preserve the undeveloped stretches of countryside and coast in the condition that has made them so popular. Pockets of genuine tranquillity are still to be found all over the county, from Dartmoor villages with an appeal that goes deeper than mere picturesqueness, to quiet coves on the spectacular coastline.

Devon has played a leading part in England's **maritime history**, and you can't go far without meeting some reminder of the great names of Tudor and Stuart seafaring, particularly at the two cities of **Exeter** and **Plymouth**. These days the nautical tradition is perpetuated on a domesticated scale by yachtspeople taking advantage of Devon's numerous creeks and bays, especially on its southern coast. Land-bound tourists flock to the sandy beaches and seaside resorts, of which **Torquay** on the south coast and **Ilfracombe** on the north are the busiest, though the most attractive are those which have retained something of their nineteenth-century elegance, such as Sidmouth, Dartmouth and Salcombe. Other seaside villages retain a low level of fishing activity but otherwise live on a stilted Old World image, of which **Clovelly** is the supreme example. **Inland**, Devon is characterized by swards of lush pasture and a scattering of sheltered villages, the county's low population density dropping to almost zero on **Dartmoor**, the wildest and bleakest of the West's moors.

Exeter and Plymouth are on the main **rail** lines from London and the Midlands, with a branch line from Exeter linking the north coast at Barnstaple. **Buses** from the chief stations fan out along the coasts and into the interior, though the service can be extremely rudimentary for the smaller villages.

Exeter

EXETER's sights are richer than those of any other town in Devon or Cornwall, the legacy of an eventful history since its Celtic foundation and the establishment here of the most westerly Roman outpost. After the Roman withdrawal, Exeter was refounded by Alfred the Great and by the time of the Norman Conquest had become one of the largest towns in England, profiting from its position on the banks of the River Exe. The expansion of the wool trade in the Tudor period sustained the city until the eighteenth century, and Exeter has maintained its status as commercial centre and county town, despite having much of its ancient centre gutted by World War II bombing.

You are likely to pass through this transport hub for Devon at least once on your West Country travels, and Exeter's sturdy cathedral and the remnants of its compact old quarter would repay an overnight stay.

Arrival, information and accommodation

Exeter has two **train stations**, Exeter Central and St David's, the latter a little further out from the centre of town, though closer to some of the cheaper B&Bs. South West

Coast Path trains on the London Waterloo–Salisbury line stop at both, as do trains on the Tarka Line to Barnstaple (see p.396) and those to Exmouth, though Exeter Central is not served by Great Western trains from London Paddington. **Buses** stop at the station on Paris Street, where there are **left luggage** lockers, and it's right across from the **tourist office** (April–June & Sept Mon–Sat 9am–5pm; July & Aug Mon–Sat 9am–5pm, Sun 10am–4pm; Oct–March Mon–Fri 9am–5pm, Sat 9am–1pm & 2–5pm; ☎01392/265700). There's a second visitor centre in The Quay House on Exeter's Quayside (Easter–Oct daily 10am–5pm; ☎01392/265213). The city is best negotiated on foot, but if you envisage using the buses on an intensive one-day visit, pick up a bus map from the tourist office and buy a £2.80 all-day bus ticket from the bus station. Most of Exeter's B&B **accommodation** lies north of the centre, near the two stations.

Hotels and B&Bs

Bendene Hotel, 15 Richmond Rd (☎01392/213526). Full daytime access and the heated outdoor swimming pool are the main lures in this terrace house near Central Station. ②.

Cyrnea, 73 Howell Rd (☎01392/438386). Cheerful management and clean, spacious rooms for good prices. No credit cards. ①.

The Edwardian, 30 Heavitree Rd (☎01392/276102). Restored Edwardian hotel handy for the bus station but not so good for the trains. Rooms are mostly en suite; three have four-poster beds. ②.

Maurice, 5 Bystock Terrace (☎01392/213079). Close to Exeter Central Station, offering good value. Non-smoking. ①.

Park View Hotel, 8 Howell Rd (☎01392/271772). Conveniently located for St David's Station, this listed Georgian building has some chintzy furnishings but the rooms are spacious and quiet. ①.

Raffles, 11 Blackall Rd (☎01392/270200). An elegant Victorian house with rooms individually furnished with Pre-Raphaelite etchings and other items from the owner's antique business. Does a good fixed-price evening meal using garden produce. ②.

Rougemont Thistle Hotel, Queen St (☎01392/254982). Chandeliers, moulded ceilings and deep-pile carpets. ⑥.

The Royal Clarence Hotel, Cathedral Yard (☎01392/319955). Built in 1769, reputedly the first inn in England to be described as a "hotel". Superb location, with rates to match. ⑦.

St Olave's Court, Mary Arches St (☎01392/217736). Among Exeter's top-notch hotels, this is central and friendly, all rooms en suite with a Georgian flavour; there's also an excellent restaurant. Good weekend deals are offered. ⑥.

Telstar Hotel, 77 St David's Hill (☎01392/272466). Ordinary but adequate, and a useful location, midway between the train stations. ①.

Trees, 2 Queen's Crescent (☎01392/259531). Close to the bus station off York Rd, an old-fashioned and reliable choice. ①.

The White Hart, 65 South St (☎01392/279897). Old coaching inn with period trappings, centrally located. ④, ③ at weekends.

Youth hostel and university accommodation

University Halls of Residence (☎01392/211500, *Conferences@exeter.ac.uk*). Accommodation on the campus or on Heavitree Rd for £13 per person or £16 with your own bath in mostly single rooms. Available Easter & July–Sept. Book in advance.

Youth Hostel 47 Countess Wear Rd (☎01392/873329, *exeter@yha.org.uk*) A country house two miles outside the city centre; take minibus #J, #K or #T from High Street or South Street, or #57 from the bus station, to the Countess Wear post office on Topsham Road, a fifteen-minute ride, plus a ten-minute walk. Alternatively, you could do the whole journey on foot on a path following the River Exe from the Quayside.

The City

The most distinctive feature of Exeter's skyline, **St Peter's Cathedral** is a stately monument made conspicuous by the two great Norman towers flanking the nave. Close up,

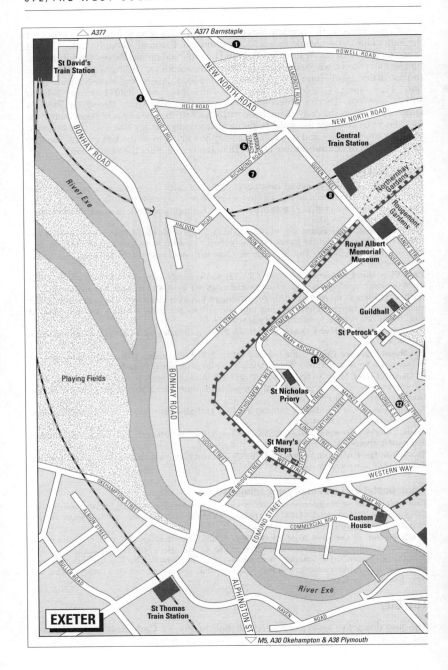

△ A377   △ A377 Barnstaple

St David's Train Station

HOWELL ROAD

NEW NORTH ROAD

ELMGROVE ROAD

HELE ROAD

BONHAY ROAD

ST DAVID'S HILL

River Exe

NEW NORTH ROAD

Central Train Station

BYSTOCK TERRACE

RICHMOND ROAD

QUEEN STREET

Northernhay Gardens

HALDON ROAD

IRON BRIDGE

NORTHERNHAY STREET

Rougemont Gardens

Royal Albert Memorial Museum

GANDY STREET

QUEEN STREET

EXE STREET

PAUL STREET

NORTH STREET

HIGH STREET

Guildhall

St Petrock's

BARTHOLOMEW ST EAST

MARY ARCHES STREET

Playing Fields

BONHAY ROAD

BARTHOLOMEW ST WEST

St Nicholas Priory

FORE STREET

MARKET STREET

ST GEORGE'S S.

SOUTH STREET

St Mary's Steps

KING STREET

STEPCOTE HILL

SMYTHEN STREET

PRESTON STREET

TUDOR STREET

WEST STREET

WESTERN WAY

OKEHAMPTON STREET

NEW BRIDGE STREET

QUAY HILL

ALBION STREET

EDMUND STREET

COMMERCIAL ROAD

Custom House

BULLER ROAD

St Thomas Train Station

ALPHINGTON ST

River Exe

HAVEN ROAD

EXETER

▽ M5, A30 Okehampton & A38 Plymouth

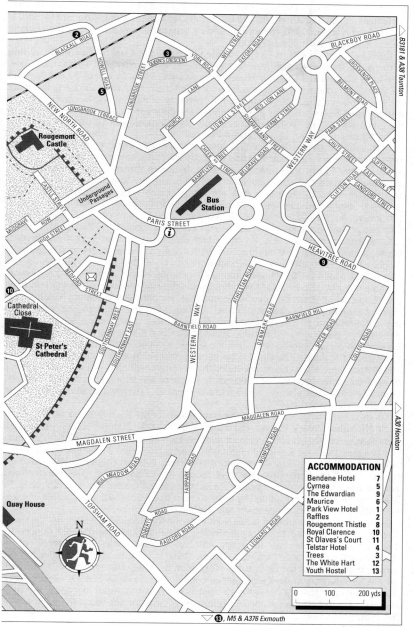

ACCOMMODATION

Bendene Hotel	7
Cyrnea	5
The Edwardian	9
Maurice	6
Park View Hotel	1
Raffles	2
Rougemont Thistle	8
Royal Clarence	10
St Olaves's Court	11
Telstar Hotel	4
Trees	3
The White Hart	12
Youth Hostel	13

© Crown copyright

it is the facade's ornate Gothic screen that commands attention: its three tiers of sculpted figures – including Alfred, Athelstan, Canute, William the Conqueror and Richard II – were begun around 1360, part of a rebuilding programme which left only the Norman towers from the original construction.

Entering the cathedral, you're confronted by the longest unbroken **Gothic ceiling** in the world, its **bosses** vividly sculpted – one shows the murder of Thomas à Becket. The **Lady Chapel** and **Chapter House** – respectively at the far end of the building and off the right transept – are thirteenth-century, but the main part of the nave, including the lavish rib-vaulting, dates from the full flowering of the English Decorated style, a century later. There are many fine examples of sculpture from this period, including, in the minstrels' gallery on the left side, angels playing musical instruments, and, below them, figures of Edward III and Queen Philippa.

Dominating the cathedral's central space are the huge organ pipes installed in the seventeenth century and harmonizing perfectly with the linear patterns of the roof and arches. In the **Choir** don't miss the sixty-foot **bishop's throne** or the **misericords** – decorated with mythological figures around 1260, they are thought to be the oldest in the country. Near the entrance stands a comparatively recent addition to the many medieval tombs and memorials lining the cathedral's walls: a monument to R.D. Blackmore, author of *Lorna Doone*. If you want to make sure you don't miss a thing, take one of the twice-daily tours (April–Sept 11am & 2.30pm; £2.50 donation).

Outside, a graceful statue of the theologian Richard Hooker surveys the **Cathedral Close**, a motley mixture of architectural styles from Tudor to Regency, though most display Exeter's trademark red brickwork. One of the finest buildings is the Elizabethan **Mol's Coffee House**, impressively timbered and gabled, now a bookshop.

Some older buildings are still standing amid the banal concrete of the modern town centre, including Exeter's finest civic building, the fourteenth-century **Guildhall** – claimed to be England's oldest municipal building in regular use. Standing not far from the cathedral on the pedestrianized **High Street**, it's fronted by an elegant Renaissance portico, and the main chamber merits a glance for its arched roof timbers, which rest on carved bears holding staves, symbols of the Yorkist cause during the Wars of the Roses. The Guildhall is usually visitable Monday–Saturday 11am–1pm and 2–4pm, and when things are quiet the doorman will give you a brief tour. Just down from here, opposite **St Petrock's** – one of Exeter's six surviving medieval churches in the central area – you'll find the impossibly narrow Parliament Street, just 25 inches wide at this end.

On the west side of Fore Street, the continuation of the High Street, a turning leads to **St Nicholas Priory** (Easter–Oct Mon, Wed & Sat 3–4.30pm; free), part of a small Benedictine foundation that became a merchant's home after the Dissolution; the interior has been restored to what it might have looked like in the Tudor era. On the other side of Fore Street, trailing down towards the river, cobbled **Stepcote Hill** was once the main road into Exeter from the west, though it is difficult to imagine this steep and narrow lane as a main thoroughfare. Another of central Exeter's ancient churches, **St Mary Steps**, stands surrounded by mainly Tudor houses at the bottom, with a fine seventeenth-century clock on its tower and a late Gothic nave inside.

Exeter's centre is bounded to the southwest by the River Exe, where the port area is now mostly devoted to leisure activities, particularly around the old **Quayside**. Pubs, shops and cafés share the space with handsomely restored nineteenth-century warehouses and the smart **Custom House**, built in 1681, its opulence reflecting the former importance of the cloth trade. Next door, the Quay House from the same period has an information desk and, upstairs, a video on Exeter's history (Easter–Oct). The area comes into its own at night, but is worth a wander at any time, the river crossed by a pedestrian suspension bridge or regular ferries (summer daily; winter Sat & Sun only; 20p).

Back at the north end of the High Street, Romansgate Passage (next to Boots) holds the entrance to a network of **underground passages** first excavated in the thirteenth century to bring water to the cathedral precincts. The passages, which resemble a public toilet from the outside, can be visited as part of a 35-minute guided tour (July–Sept & school holidays Mon–Sat 10am–5.30pm; Oct–June Mon–Sat 2–5.30pm, Sat 10am–5.30pm; £2.50, £3.50 in July & Aug) – not recommended to claustrophobes. Nearby, Castle Street leads to what remains of **Rougemont Castle**, now little more than a perimeter of red-stone walls that are best appreciated from the surrounding Rougemont and Northernhay Gardens. Following the path through this park, exit at Queen Street to drop in at the excellent **Royal Albert Memorial Museum** (Mon–Sat 10am–5pm; free), the closest thing in Devon to a county museum. Exuding the Victorian spirit of wide-ranging curiosity, this motley assortment includes everything from a menagerie of stuffed animals to fascinating examples of the building styles used at different periods in the city. The collections of silverware, watches and clocks contrast nicely with the colourful ethnography section, and the picture gallery has some good specimens of West Country art alongside work by other artists associated with Devon.

Eating and drinking

The café inside the Royal Albert Memorial Museum would be reason enough to come here, with its wholesome **snacks** served in a convivial atmosphere. Round the corner from the museum, in medieval Gandy Street, *Coolings Wine Bar* (closed daytime Sun) is a popular lunch stop that's also open until late evening, while *Mad Meg's* (closed Mon & Tues lunch) is more basic but has plenty of olde worlde atmosphere; once a nunnery, it's now buried beneath the Pickwick shopping arcade on Fore Street. *Herbie's*, 15 North St (☎01392/258473; closed all day Sun & Mon eve), is the only wholefood **restaurant** in town, and has organic ice cream on the menu; alluring garlic smells waft out of *Maryam*, 28 South St (☎01392/496776; closed Sun), an unpretentious trattoria; and good-value Mexican and Italian staples are on the menu at *Harry's*, in a converted church at 86 Longbrook St (☎01392/202 234).

The *Well House*, in front of the cathedral, is an old **pub** offering reasonably priced lunches. Nearby, the *Ship Inn*, in St Martin's Lane, also serves food, and prides itself on the claim that it was once Francis Drake's local. The pubs and clubs on Exeter's Quay make this a lively spot to while away an evening. You can eat and drink sitting outside at the seventeenth-century *Prospect Inn* and the more contemporary *On the Waterside*.

Nightlife and entertainment

You'll find three of Exeter's most popular **clubs** on the Quay; the *Warehouse* and the adjacent *Boxes* are two studenty places, playing a mix of dance music, while *Volts* plays more mainstream disco sounds. Some of the best dance and live music venues are in the centre, including the *Cavern Club*, with entrances in Queen Street and Gandy Street (also open 10.30am–4pm for snacks) and the *Timepiece*, Little Castle St, formerly a prison that now also has a good daytime bar with a garden. For live music, you could also try the university's *Lemon Grove* (term-time only) and the *Fizgig & Firkin*, a pub on Lower North Street which has live music on Fridays and Saturdays.

The **Phoenix Exeter Arts Centre** (☎01392/667080), behind the Royal Albert Memorial Museum, is the focus of a medley of cultural pursuits, including regular non-mainstream films, exhibitions, gigs and various workshops, and there's a good café here. Of the town's theatres, the **Northcott**, near the university on Stocker Road (☎01392/493493), and the Barnfield, on Barnfield Road (☎01392/271808), have the best productions, with the former also staging ballet and opera performances. The **Exeter Festival** takes place during the first three weeks of July, and features jazz and blues concerts as well as classical performances and cabaret, at various venues around town.

Around Exeter

The coast south and east of Exeter holds an architectural oddity, **A La Ronde**, and a string of old-fashioned seaside resorts, none of them over-commercialized, though still best seen outside the summer peak. **Sidmouth** would be a good choice for an overnight stop, as would the neighbouring villages of **Beer** and **Seaton**.

A La Ronde, Exmouth and Budleigh Salterton are all served by **bus** #57 running every twenty minutes from Exeter, while #52, #52A and #52B are best for Sidmouth (the #57 also connects Exmouth with Sidmouth). A minibus service, the hourly #899, connects Sidmouth with Beer and Seaton. You can also get to Exmouth by **train**, and from the train station at **Honiton**, eight miles inland, #340 runs every couple of hours to Sidmouth.

A La Ronde

The Gothic folly of **A La Ronde**, (April–Oct Mon–Thurs & Sun 11am–5.30pm; £3.20), a couple of miles outside Exmouth off the A376, was the creation of two cousins, Jane and Mary Parminter, who in the 1790s were inspired by their European Grand Tour to construct a sixteen-sided house possibly based on the Byzantine basilica of San Vitale in Ravenna. The end product, sketchily related to its alleged source, is filled with mementos of the Parminters' tour as well as a number of their more offbeat creations, such as a frieze made of feathers culled from game birds and chickens. In the upper rooms are a gallery and staircase completely covered in shells, too fragile to be visited, though part can be glimpsed from the completely enclosed octagonal room on the first floor – a closed-circuit TV system enables visitors to home in on details.

The women intended that the house should be inherited only by female descendants, though the conditions of Mary Parminter's will (she died in 1849) were broken at the end of the nineteenth century when the building was inherited by the Reverend Oswald Reichel, the only male owner of the house in its history. Reichel gave it a refurbishment that in some ways actually improved the building, for instance by the addition of dormer windows on the second floor, which had previously not enjoyed any natural light, let alone the superb views over the Exe Estuary to Haldon Hill and Dawlish Warren.

Exmouth and Budleigh Salterton

EXMOUTH started as a Roman port and went on to become the first of the county's resorts to be popularized by holidaymakers in the late eighteenth century. Overlooking lawns, rock pools and a respectable two miles of beach, Exmouth's Georgian terraces once accommodated such folk as the wives of Nelson and Byron – installed at no. 6 and 19 The Beacon respectively. The town's still unhurried air contrasts sharply with the cranes and warehouses of the docks beyond the Esplanade. **Staying** here is a good option, with plenty of choice: best for location is the *Manor Hotel*, The Beacon (☎01395/274477; ③). In July and August, Exmouth is linked by ferry to Star Cross, on the other side of the Exe estuary (hourly service; £2 single fare), where you can pick up a bus route to Dawlish and Teignmouth (see p.376).

Four miles east of Exmouth, bounded on each side by red sandstone cliffs, **BUDLEIGH SALTERTON** continues the genteel theme – its thatched and white-washed cottages attracted such figures as Noël Coward and P.G. Wodehouse, and John

Millais painted his famous *Boyhood of Raleigh* on the shingle beach here. (Sir Walter Raleigh was born in the pretty East Budleigh, a couple of miles inland.) Three miles east, **Ladram Bay** is a popular pebbly beach sheltered by woods and beautiful eroded cliffs. If you want to stay in the area, contact the **tourist office** on Fore Street (Easter–June, Sept & Oct Mon–Sat 10am–5pm; July & Aug Mon–Sat 10am–5pm, Sun 11am–5pm; Nov–Easter Mon–Thurs & Sat 10am–1pm, Fri 10am–3pm; ☎01395/445275).

Sidmouth

Set amidst a shelf of crumbling red sandstone, cream-and-white **SIDMOUTH** is the chief resort on this stretch of coast and boasts nearly five hundred buildings listed as having special historic or architectural interest, among them the stately Georgian homes of **York Terrace** behind the Esplanade. Moreover, the **beaches** are better tended than many along this coast, not only the mile-long main town beach but also Jacob's Ladder, a cliff-backed shingle and sand strip beyond Connaught Gardens to the west of town. To the east, the South Devon Coast Path (part of the South West Coast Path) climbs steep Salcombe Hill to follow cliffs that give sanctuary to a range of birdlife including yellowhammers and green woodpeckers, as well as the rarer grasshopper warbler. Farther on, the path descends to meet one of the most isolated and attractive beaches in the area, **Weston Mouth**.

The **tourist office** is on Ham Lane, off the eastern end of the Esplanade (March & April Mon–Thurs 10am–4pm, Fri & Sat 10am–5pm, Sun 10am–1pm; May–July & Sept Mon–Sat 10am–5pm, Sun 10am–1pm; Aug & Oct Mon–Sat 10am–6pm, Sun 10am–4pm; Nov–Feb Mon–Sat 10am–1.30pm; ☎01395/516441). Of the **B&Bs**, *Ferndale*, 92 Winslade Rd (☎01395/515495; no credit cards; ②; closed Nov–Feb), a modernized Victorian house about a mile from the sea, is one of the cheapest; closer to the seafront, the *Old Farmhouse*, on Hillside Road (☎01395/512284; no credit cards; ②; closed Dec & Jan) offers attractive rooms with plenty of atmosphere, and delicious meals if required. There's more choice in the string of decent guesthouses along Salcombe Road, including *Berwick House* (☎01395/513621; no credit cards; ②), which offers evening meals. For **snacks** in town, *Osborne's* on Fore Street has teas, milkshakes and light meals, while two hundred yards from the seafront, on Old Fore Street, the *Old Ship* and *Anchor* pubs provide excellent bar meals and suppers as well as a good range of ales. Sidmouth hosts what many consider to be the country's best **folk festival** during about eight days at the beginning of August. Folk and roots artists from around the world as well as dance and theatre companies take over various venues including the *Arena Theatre* and various pubs and parks. A campsite is laid on outside Sidmouth with shuttle buses to the centre, and tickets can be bought for specific days, for the weekend or the entire week. For detailed information, call the tourist office, or call ☎01296/433669. Book early for the main acts.

Beer and Seaton

Eight miles east along the coast, the fishing village of **BEER** lies huddled within a small sheltered cove between gleaming white headlands. A stream rushes along a deep channel dug into Beer's main street, and if you can ignore the crowds in high summer much of the village looks unchanged since the time when it was a smugglers' eyrie, its inlets used by such characters as Jack Rattenbury, who published his *Memoirs of a Smuggler* in 1837. The village is best known for its quarries, which were worked from Roman times until the last century: **Beer Stone** was used in many of Devon's churches and houses, and also went into the construction of some London buildings. You can visit the complex of **underground quarries** (Easter–Sept 10am–6pm; Oct 11am–5pm; last entry 1hr before closing; £3.50) a mile or so west of the village on a guided tour, along with a small exhibition of pieces carved by medieval masons, among others. Take a jumper. *Bay View* (☎01297/20489; no credit cards; ①; closed Nov–Easter), overlooking the sea on Fore Street, is easily the best of the **B&B**s and Beer's **youth hostel** is on a hillside half a mile northwest, at Bovey Combe, Townsend (☎01297/20296; closed Nov–March).

SEATON, a smooth stroll less than a mile eastwards, has a steep, pebbly beach like Beer's, but this is a much more developed resort, mutating from a placid, slow-moving haven at its western end to a much gaudier affair to the east. One of the main attractions is the open-top **tramway** which follows the path of the old railway line to the inland village of Colyton. Seaton's **tourist office** is on the Underfleet, in the main car park on Harbour Road (April–June, Sept & Oct Mon–Sat 10am–5pm, Sun 1.30–5.30pm; Nov–March Mon–Fri 10am–2pm; ☎01297/21660). On Trevelyan Road, at the far end of the Esplanade on the eastern edge of town, you'll find *Beach End* (☎01297/23388; ②; closed Nov–March), a bright and roomy Edwardian **B&B** or, just across from the tourist office, *Beaumont* on Castle Hill (☎01297/20832, *tony@lymebay.demon.co.uk*; no credit cards; ②), on the west side – both have sea views.

Across Seaton Bridge and the Axe estuary, the coast stretches a cliffy six miles beyond Axmouth to Lyme Regis in Dorset (see p.261).

The "English Riviera" region

The wedge of land between Dartmoor and the sea contains some of Devon's most fertile pastures, backing onto some of the West's most popular coastal resorts. Chief of these is **Torbay**, an amalgam of **Torquay**, **Paignton** and **Brixham**, together forming the nucleus of an area optimistically known as "The English Riviera". To the north of the Torbay conurbation lie small-scale **Teignmouth** and **Dawlish**, while to the south the port of **Dartmouth** offers another calmer alternative, linked by riverboat to historic and almost unspoilt **Totnes**. West of the River Dart, the rich agricultural district of **South Hams** extends as far as Plymouth, cleft by a web of rivers flowing off Dartmoor. The main town here is **Kingsbridge**, at the head of an estuary down which you can ferry to the sailing resort of **Salcombe**.

Trains from Exeter to Plymouth run down the coast as far as Teignmouth before striking inland for Totnes – to get to Torbay, change at Newton Abbot. The hourly #X46 **bus** connects Exeter and Torquay in 55 minutes, while the #85 and #85A serve Teignmouth and Dawlish. For the hinterland and points south and west along the coast, you can rely on a network of buses from Torquay, and travellers to Totnes and Dartmouth could make use of the **South Devon Railway** and **boats** along the River Dart.

Teignmouth and Dawlish

The estuary town of **TEIGNMOUTH** (pronounced "Tinmouth"), once a terminus for shipments of Dartmoor granite, still has a thriving harbour along the banks of the Teign, and fishing boats are still hauled up onto the pebble beach from which juts a pier that formerly segregated male and female bathers. The town began to attract holidaymakers at the end of the eighteenth century – Fanny Burney and John Keats both stayed – and some dainty Georgian and Victorian villas adorn Powderham Terrace and the Den. Behind the town centre, the lanes hold some interesting old pubs, while the estuary crossing to **Shaldon**, either by road bridge or by passenger ferry (last one at around 8.45pm), deposits you in a smaller version of Teignmouth, relatively unscathed by the seasonal crowds.

Teignmouth's **tourist office** is near the pier (May–Sept daily 9.30am–5.30pm; Oct–April Mon–Fri 9am–1pm & 2–5pm; ☎01626/779769). The *Hill Rise Hotel*

(☎01626/773108; no credit cards; ①) provides great-value **accommodation** on Winterbourne Road, a quiet cul-de-sac away from the sea but handy for the station. Nearer the thick of things is the memorable *Riverbeach House*, 3 Ivy Lane (☎01626/772198; no credit cards; ①), a few steps away from the estuary. For **food and drink**, Teignmouth's backstreets and alleys unearth some choice pubs, notably the *Ship Inn* on Queen Street, overlooking the water and opposite the reasonable *Harbour Lights* snack bar, which offers seafood salads.

North of Teignmouth, **DAWLISH** is a smaller, more sedate resort, known to Jane Austen and Charles Dickens, whose character Nicholas Nickleby was born here. The seafront, a mile from the older inland centre, is spanned by a granite railway viaduct built by Brunel, under which you pass to reach a beach of sand and shingle. A better beach lies a little further south, at Coryton Cove. If you want to **stay**, make for the *Walton Guest House*, a Georgian building five minutes from the seafront on Plantation Terrace (☎01626/862760; no credit cards; ②).

Torquay

Five miles south of Teignmouth, the coast is heavily urbanized around **Torbay**, a tourist conglomeration entirely dedicated to the exploitation of the bay's sheltered climate and exuberant vegetation. **TORQUAY**, the largest component of the super-resort, comes closest to living up to the self-penned "English Riviera" sobriquet, sporting a mini-corniche and promenades landscaped with flowerbeds. The much-vaunted palm trees (actually New Zealand cabbage trees) and the coloured lights that festoon the harbour by night contribute to the town's unique flavour, a slightly frayed combination of the exotic and the classically English. Torquay's transformation from a fishing village began with its establishment as a fashionable haven for invalids, among them the consumptive Elizabeth Barrett Browning, who spent three years here. In recent years the most famous figures previously associated with Torquay – crimewriter Agatha Christie and traveller Freya Stark – have given way to the fictional TV hotelier Basil Fawlty, whose jingoism and injured pride perfectly encapsulate the town's adaptation to the demands of mass tourism.

Arrival, information and accommodation

The **train station** is off Rathmore Road, next to the Torre Abbey gardens; most **buses** leave from outside the Pavilion, including the #X80 to Totnes and Plymouth, and the frequent #12 and #12A service linking Torquay with Paignton and Brixham. Torquay's **tourist office** is on Vaughan Parade, near the Pavilion (late May to Sept Mon–Sat 9am–6pm, Sun 10am–6pm; Oct to late May Mon–Sat 9am–5.15pm; ☎01803/297428). Torquay has plenty of **accommodation**, but you'll need to book in advance during peak season. If you want to stay centrally and aren't too fussed about views, try the *Devon Arms*, 29 Park Hill Rd (☎01803/292360; no credit cards; ①), whose two twin rooms share a bathroom. Otherwise there's more choice along Belgrave Road and, slightly further out, Avenue Road; two good choices are the *Chesterfield Hotel*, 62 Belgrave Rd (☎01803/292318; ②), and *Kingston House*, 75 Avenue Rd (☎01803/212760; ②), close to the train station and the marina. Farther back behind the station, on Old Mill Road, the Victorian *Torbay Rise* (☎01803/605541; ③; Nov–March), on a hill overlooking the sea, has a terrace and outdoor pool. On the other side of the harbour, the spacious Victorian *Sea Point Hotel* on Old Torwood Road offers excellent value (☎01803/211808; no credit cards; ①; closed Oct–Easter), with all rooms sharing bathroom and shower. Midway between Torquay's train station and the village of Cockington, the *Fairmount House Hotel*, on Herbert Road, Chelston (☎01803/605446; ④; closed Nov–Feb), makes an attractive alternative to staying in central Torquay: chief advantages are its restaurant and garden. If you're looking for cheap and friendly **hostel** accommodation, make a bee-line for *Torquay Backpackers*, 119 Abbey Rd (☎01803/299924; no credit cards). It's very central for the town, and just a ten-minute walk from the station – there's a free pick-up service offered if you ring ahead.

The Town

Torquay is focused on the small **harbour** and marina, where the mingling crowds can seem almost Mediterranean, especially at night. To one side stands the copper-domed **Pavilion**, an Edwardian building that originally housed a ballroom and assembly hall, now refurbished with shops. Behind the Pavilion, limestone cliffs sprouting white high-rise hotels and apartment blocks separate the harbour area from Torquay's main beach, **Abbey Sands**. Good for chucking a frisbee about but too busy for serious relaxation, it takes its name from **Torre Abbey**, sited in ornamental gardens behind the beachside road. The Norman church that once stood here was razed by Henry VIII, though a gatehouse, tithe barn, chapter house and tower escaped demolition. The present **Abbey Mansion** (Easter–Oct daily 9.30am–6pm; £3) is a seventeenth- and eighteenth-century construction, now containing the mayor's office, a suite of period rooms with collections of paintings, silver and glass, and one devoted to Agatha Christie. There's more material relating to the Mistress of Murder at the main **Torquay Museum**, 529 Babbacombe Rd (Easter–Oct Mon–Sat 10am–4.45pm, Sun 1.30–4.45pm; Nov–Easter Mon–Fri 10am–4.45pm; £2), but most of the space is given over to the local history and natural history collections. Bus #32 stops outside.

You'll probably find the walk round the promontory at Torbay's north end more stimulating, as it leads to some good sand beaches. To reach the nearest, follow the pretty half-mile coastal walk that takes you through Daddyhole Plain, a large chasm in the cliff caused by a landslide locally attributed to the devil ("Daddy"). The path descends to meet the seawall at **Meadfoot Beach**, where boats and pedalos can be hired. If you're searching for something a little more low-key, continue round the point to where a string of beaches extends along the coast as far as the cliff-backed coves of **Watcombe** and **Maidencombe**.

Eating, drinking and nightlife

There is a surprisingly high standard of cuisine in Torquay's **restaurants**, one of the best being the *Mulberry Room*, 1 Scarborough Rd, where the moderately priced English and Continental menu is colour-coded according to its cholesterol content; there are also three en-suite **rooms** available here (☎01803/213639; ③), with discounts for longer stays. Unless you're staying, the restaurant closes Monday, Tuesday and Sunday evenings. The earthier *Jingles*, 34 Torwood St, offers low-priced Tex-Mex meals, or you can go Continental at *Flynn's Bistro*, 14 Parkhill Road, where French provincial cuisine is served at moderate prices, and there's a small garden for dining out in summer (evenings only; closed Sun). Nearby on Park Lane, the cobbled *Hole in the Wall* **pub** serves some vegetarian dishes and has sing-songs round the piano – it was the Irish playwright Sean O'Casey's boozer when he lived in Torquay.

Torquay's main **clubs** are the *Bar Rio* by the harbour on Victoria Parade and *Claire's* on Torwood Street, while *Valbonne's* on Higher Union St and *Club Rainbow* at the *Rainbow International Hotel* in Belgrave Road both cater to over-25s. The *Monastery*, in Torwood Gardens, caters for a younger crowd, with all-night sessions on Saturdays. *Rocky's*, near the Pavilion on Rock Road (off Abbey Road), is a long-established gay club.

Paignton

Not so much a rival to Torquay as its complement, **PAIGNTON** lacks the gloss of its neighbour, but also its pretensions. Activity is concentrated at the southern end of the wide town beach, around the small harbour that nestles in the lee of the appropriately named Redcliffe headland. Otherwise, diversion-seekers could wander over to **Paignton Zoo** (daily: summer 10am–6pm; winter closes at dusk; £7), a mile out on Totnes Road, or board the **Paignton & Dartmouth Steam Railway** at Paignton's Queen's Park train station near the harbour. Running daily from June to September, with a patchy service in April, May, October and December, the line connects with Paignton's other main beach – **Goodrington Sands** – before trundling alongside the Dart estuary to Kingswear, seven miles away. The accent is on Victorian nostalgia, with railway personnel in period uniforms, but it's a pleasant way to view the scenic countryside, and you could make a day of it by taking the ferry connection from Kingswear to Dartmouth (see p.383), then taking a river boat up the Dart to Totnes, from where you can take any bus back to Paignton – a "Round Robin" ticket (£9.90) lets you do this.

Paignton's bus and train stations are next to each other off Sands Road. Five minutes away, the seafront has a **tourist office** (late May to Sept Mon–Sat 9am–6pm, Sun 10am–6pm; Oct to late May Mon–Sat 9am–5.15pm; ☎01803/558383). If you're stuck for a place **to stay**, you could do worse than *St Weonard's Hotel*, 12 Kernou Rd (☎01803/558842; ③), a couple of minutes walk from the seafront. The harbour area has a few pubs and restaurants, including the inexpensive *Harbour Light*, and the nearby *Pier Inn*.

Brixham

From Paignton, it's a fifteen-minute bus ride down to **BRIXHAM**, the prettiest of the Torbay towns. Fishing was for centuries Brixham's life-blood, its harbour extending some way farther inland than it does now to afford a safe anchorage – a function performed today by an extensive breakwater. Indeed, at the beginning of the nineteenth century, this was the major fish-market in the West Country, and it still supplies fish to restaurants as far away as London. Among the trawlers on Brixham's quayside is moored a full-size reconstruction of the **Golden Hind**, the surprisingly small vessel in which Francis Drake circumnavigated the world – it has no real connection with the port, however. The harbour is overlooked by an unflattering statue of William III, a reminder of his landing in Brixham to claim the crown of England in 1688. From here, steep lanes and stairways thread up to the older centre around Fore Street, where the bus from Torquay pulls in.

From the harbour, you can reach the promontory of **Berry Head** along a path winding up from the *Berry Head House Hotel*. Fortifications built during the Napoleonic wars are still standing on this southern limit of Torbay, which is now a conservation area, attracting colonies of nesting seabirds and affording fabulous views.

The town's **tourist office** (June to mid-Oct Mon–Sat 9.30am–6pm, Sun 10am–6pm; mid-Oct to May Tues–Sat 9.30am–5.15pm; ☎01803/852861) is on the quayside, next to William's statue. **Accommodation** is listed on the door when the office is closed. Of the B&Bs, try those on King Street, overlooking the harbour: *Sampford House*, at no. 59 (☎01803/857761; no credit cards; ②), and the *Harbour View Hotel*, at no. 65 (☎01803/853052; ②), where all rooms are en suite. Behind the quayside, the *Brioc Hotel*, 11 Prospect Rd (☎01803/853540; no credit cards; ①) also offers good value, and has a cottage attached for those looking for a bit more space (⑤). The nearest **youth hostel** is four miles away outside the village of **Galmpton**, on the banks of the Dart (☎01803/842444; closed Nov–March), a one-and-a-half-mile walk from Churston Bridge, accessible on bus #12 or #12A (every 15min) – you can also get there on the Paignton & Dartmouth Steam Railway (see above). There is a landscaped **campsite** at **Hillhead** (☎01803/853204; closed Nov–Easter), two and a half miles south of Brixham on the Kingswear road.

Brixham offers fish and more fish, from the stalls selling cockles, whelks and mussels on the harbourside to the moderate-to-expensive *Poopdeck* **restaurant** at 14 The

Quay (☎01803/852254; open Fri & Sat eve, & alternate Sun for lunch), above the Harbourside Bookshop. A few doors up, the *Sprat & Mackerel* offers staple **pub** snacks. For a more relaxed pint, try out the *Blue Anchor* on Fore Street, with coal fires and low beams.

Totnes

Most of the Plymouth buses from Paignton and Torquay make a stop at **TOTNES**, on the west bank of the River Dart. The town has an ancient pedigree, its period of greatest prosperity occurring in the sixteenth century when this inland port exported cloth to France and brought back wine. Some handsome structures from that era remain, and there is still a working port down on the river, but these days Totnes has mellowed into a residential market town, enjoying an esoteric fame as a centre of the New Age arts-and-crafts crowd. With its arcaded High Street and secretive flowery lanes, Totnes has its syrupy side, partly the result of its proximity to the Torbay tourist machine, but so far its allure has survived more or less intact.

Totnes centres on the long main street that starts off as Fore Street, site of the town's **museum** (April–Oct Mon–Fri 10.30am–5pm; £1.50), which occupies a four-storey Elizabethan house at no. 70. Showing how wealthy clothiers lived at the peak of Totnes's success, it is packed with domestic objects and furniture, and also has a room devoted to local mathematician Charles Babbage, whose "analytical engine" was the forerunner of the computer. There are a number of other houses along Fore and High streets in an equally good state of preservation: the late eighteenth-century, mustard-yellow "Gothic House", a hundred yards up Fore Street on the left; 28 High St, overhung by some curious grotesque masks; and 16 High St, a house built by pilchard merchant Nicholas Ball, whose initials are carved outside. His wealth, inherited by his widow, was eventually bequeathed by her second husband, Thomas Bodley, to found Oxford's Bodleian Library.

Fore Street becomes the **High Street** at the East Gate, a much retouched medieval arch. Beneath it, Rampart Walk trails off along the old city walls, curling round the fifteenth-century church of **St Mary**. Inside, an exquisitely carved roodscreen stretches across the full width of the red sandstone building. Behind the church, the eleventh-century **Guildhall** (April–Sept Mon–Fri 10.30am–1pm & 2–4.30pm; 90p) was originally the refectory and kitchen of a Benedictine priory. Granted to the city corporation in 1553, the building still houses the town's Council Chamber, which you can see together with the former jail cells, used until the end of the last century, and the courtroom, which ceased its function only in 1974.

Totnes **Castle** (April–Sept daily 10am–6pm; Oct daily 10am–5pm; Nov–March Wed–Sun 10am–1pm & 2–4pm; £1.60; EH) on Castle Street – leading off the High Street – is a classic Norman structure of the motte and bailey design, its simple crenellated keep atop a grassy mound offering wide views of the town and Dart valley. Totnes assumes a much livelier air at the bottom of Fore Street, at river level. This is the highest navigable point on the **River Dart** for seagoing vessels, and there is constant activity around the craft arriving from and leaving for European destinations. More locally, there are also cruises to Dartmouth between Easter and October, leaving from Steamer Quay, on the other side of the Dart. Riverside walks in either direction pass some congenial pubs, and near the railway bridge you can board a steam train of the **South Devon Railway** on its run along the course of the Dart to Buckfastleigh, adjacent to Buckfast Abbey (see p.392).

A walkable couple of miles out of Totnes, both rail and river pass near the estate of **Dartington Hall**, the arts and education centre set up in 1925 by US millionairess Dorothy Elmhirst and her husband. A constant programme of films, plays, concerts, dance and workshops is run here, but you can walk through the sculpture-strewn gardens and – when it's not in use – visit the fourteenth-century Great Hall, rescued from dereliction by the Elmhirsts.

Practicalities

Totnes's **tourist office** is in the Town Mill, off the Plains near the Safeway car park (summer Mon–Sat 9.30am–5pm, Sun 10am–1pm; winter Mon–Fri 10am–12.30pm & 1.30–4pm; ☎01803/863168). You'll find a good **B&B** below the castle at 2 Antrim Terrace (☎01803/862638; no credit cards; ①), which offers organic breakfasts and does not permit smoking. For a bit extra, pamper yourself at the *Royal Seven Stars Hotel* on The Plains (☎01803/862125; ③), or, just over the river in Seymour Place, at the *Old Forge* (☎01803/862174; non-smoking; ③) – a working medieval forge with comfortably modernized rooms and a large garden. Opposite the castle car park on North Street, the *Elbow Room* (☎01803/863480; no credit cards; ③) occupies a two-hundred-year-old converted cottage and cider press. If you want to stay nearer to Dartington, try the *Cott*, Shinner's Bridge, (☎01803/863777; ④) – two miles west of Totnes on the A385 – outwardly almost unchanged since its construction in 1320. The local **youth hostel** (☎01803/862303; closed Nov–March), in a sixteenth-century cottage, lies next to the River Bidwell two miles from Totnes and half a mile from Shinner's Bridge, one stop on the #X80 Torquay–Plymouth bus route.

You don't need to stray off the Fore Street/High Street axis to find a good place to **eat** in Totnes. *Willow*, 87 High St (☎01803/862605), and *Tolivers*, 67 Fore St (☎01803/862604), are two inexpensive vegetarian wholefood restaurants with a relaxed atmosphere and occasional live music (both closed Sun in winter and some weekday evenings). Indonesian food is on offer at *Rickshaws*, 98 High St (closed evenings and all Sun & Mon), while *Café Sobranie*, 82 High St, serves good-value snacks and meals (closed evenings and all Sun & Mon). There are also several decent **pubs**: the lively *Castle Inn* on Fore Street, the *Bull Inn*, at the top of the High Street and the *Kingsbridge Inn* on Leechwell Street (off Kingsbridge Hill) all have a warm atmosphere, bar snacks and good ale. Another good pub is the riverside *Steampacket*, on St Peter's Quay.

Dartmouth

South of Torbay, and eight miles downstream from Totnes, **DARTMOUTH** has thrived since the Normans recognized the potential of this deepwater port for trading with their home country, and today its activities embrace fishing, freight and a booming leisure industry – as well as the education of the senior service's officer class at the Royal Naval College, built at the start of this century on a hill overlooking the port. Coming from Torbay, visitors to Dartmouth can save time and a long detour through Totnes by using the frequent ferries crossing over the Dart's estuary from Kingswear (50p, £2 for cars with passengers), the last one at around 10.45pm.

Behind the enclosed boat basin at the heart of town stands Dartmouth's most photographed building, the four-storey **Butterwalk**, built in the seventeenth century for a local merchant. Richly decorated with wood carvings, the timber-framed construction was restored after bombing in World War II, though still looks precarious as it overhangs the street on eleven granite columns. This arcade now holds shops and Dartmouth's small **museum** (Mon–Sat: April–Sept 11am–5pm; Oct–March noon–3pm; £1), mainly devoted to maritime curios, including old maps, prints and models of ships. Nearby **St Saviour's**, rebuilt in the 1630s from a fourteenth-century church, has long been a landmark for boats sailing upriver. The building stands at the head of Higher Street, the old town's central thoroughfare and the site of another tottering medieval structure, the *Cherub* inn. More impressive is **Agincourt House** on the parallel Lower Street, built by a merchant after the battle for which it is named, then restored in the seventeenth century and again in the twentieth.

Lower Street leads down to **Bayard's Cove**, a short cobbled quay lined with well-restored eighteenth-century houses, where the Pilgrim Fathers touched en route to the New World. A twenty-minute walk from here along the river takes you to **Dartmouth Castle** (April–Sept daily 10am–6pm; Oct daily 10am–5pm; Nov–March Wed–Sun 10am–1pm & 2–4pm; £2.60; EH), one of two fortifications on opposite sides of the estuary. The site includes coastal defence works from the last century and from World War II, though the main interest is in the fifteenth-century castle, the first in England to be constructed specifically to withstand artillery. The castle was never actually tested in action, and consequently is excellently preserved. If you don't relish the return walk, you can take advantage of a ferry back to town, leaving roughly every fifteen minutes from Easter to October (£1).

Continuing south along the coastal path brings you through the pretty hilltop village of **Stoke Fleming** to **Blackpool Sands** (45min from the castle), the best and most popular beach in the area. The unspoilt cove, flanked by steep, wooded cliffs, was the site of a battle in 1404 in which Devon archers repulsed a Breton invasion force sent to punish the privateers of Dartmouth for their raiding across the Channel.

From Dartmouth there are regular ferries across the river to **Kingswear**, terminus of the **Paignton & Dartmouth Steam Railway** (see p.379). There are also various summer cruises from Dartmouth's quay up the River Dart to Totnes (75min; £6.20 return); this is the best way to see the river's deep creeks and the various houses overlooking the river, among them the **Royal Naval College** and **Greenway House**, birthplace of Walter Raleigh's three seafaring half-brothers, the Gilberts, and later rebuilt for Agatha Christie.

Practicalities

Dartmouth's **tourist office** is opposite the car park at Mayor's Avenue (Easter–Oct Mon–Sat 9.30am–5.30pm, Sun 10am–4pm; Nov–Easter Mon–Sat 10am–4pm; ☎01803/834224). Cheaper **accommodation** is either at the top of steep hills or strung along the uninspiring Victoria Road, a continuation of Duke Street. The hill-top choices are far preferable for their views: try the spacious and elegant *Avondale* at 5 Vicarage Hill (☎01803/835831; no credit cards; ②), or the comfortable *Campbells*, slightly further out at 5 Mount Boone, where home-baked bread and fruit from the garden are offered (☎01803/833438; no credit cards; ③). *Capritia* is a convenient and friendly B&B at 69 Victoria Road (☎01803/833419; no credit cards; ①), as is nearby *Sunny Banks* at 1 Vicarage Hill (☎01803/832766; no credit cards; ②). Alternatively, splurge on the *Royal Castle Hotel* (☎01803/833033; ⑤), right on the central quay, converted from two seventeenth-century merchants' houses.

For a **snack**, the *Frying Pan* is a decent fish-and-chip shop at 11 Broadstone, behind the quay, while the casual *Café Alf Resco* on Lower Street is good for breakfasts and coffees and has outdoor tables (closed Mon & Tues). Dartmouth has a good range of **restaurants**; *Bayard's*, 28 Lower St (☎01803/833523), serves moderately priced fish and vegetarian dishes, or you could try *Cutter's Bunch*, a French bistro a few doors down at no. 33 (☎01803/832882; evenings only, closed Mon). The expensive *Carved Angel*, at 2 South Embankment (☎01803/832465; closed Sun eve, all Mon & Jan to mid-Feb), is a high-class fish restaurant with views over the riverfront; it also excels in game in winter. If you're put off by the prices and ambience, drop into its inexpensive offshoot at 7 Foss St, the *Carved Angel Café* (closed Sun & Jan). The menu may lack the sparkle of its parent, but it offers some great soups and puddings.

The South Hams

The area between the Dart and Plym estuaries, the **South Hams**, holds some of Devon's comeliest villages and most striking coastline. The "capital" of the region,

KINGSBRIDGE, is easily accessible by hourly buses from Dartmouth or Totnes, and is the hub of local services to the South Hams villages. Fine Tudor and Georgian buildings distinguish this busy market town, especially along the steep Fore Street, where the colonnaded Shambles is largely Elizabethan on the ground floor, its granite pillars supporting an upper floor added at the end of the eighteenth century. The town hall hosts a craft **market** on Tuesdays and Fridays, and **information** on the region is available at the tourist office on the Quay (summer Mon–Sat 9am–5pm, Sun 10am–4pm; winter closed Sun; ☎01548/853195).

A summer ferry runs from Kingsbridge to Devon's southernmost resort of **SAL-COMBE**, almost at the mouth of the Kingsbridge estuary. Once a nondescript fishing village, Salcombe is now a full-blown sailing and holiday resort, its calm waters strewn with small craft and the steep streets awash with leisurewear. There is still some fishing activity here, and a few working boatyards, but a certain serenity prevails, with the ruined Fort Charles at the entrance to the harbour injecting a touch of romance amid the villas and hotels. Most of the **hotels** are above the central Fore Street, enjoying excellent estuary views, for example *Rocarno* on Grenville Road (☎01548/842732; no credit cards; ①). Lower down, there's a good B&B round the corner from Fore Street at 7 Courtenay St (☎01548/842276; no credit cards; ①): ask for the balcony room. A brief walk outside town, *Woody's Place* on Devon Road (left past the post office on Fore Street) offers relaxed accommodation in dorms or twin rooms, with access to a private beach – out-of-season rates are nearly fifty percent cheaper (☎0468/847352; ④). **Campers** have a good choice in the area, the nearest site being *Ilton Farm*, off the Malborough road (☎01548/842858), while *Sun Park* at Soar Mill Cove (☎01548/561378) and *Higher Rew* at Rew Cross, south of Salcombe (☎01548/842681), are both within good walks of two of the area's finest beaches. Back in town, fish is top of the menu at *Spinnaker's Restaurant* (closed Sun), a moderately priced place that shares a building with the *Salcombe Hotel* on Fore Street, looking out over the river.

From a quay off Fore Street, a regular ferry crosses the narrow channel from here to **East Portlemouth**, from where you can follow the coastal path past the craggily photogenic Gammon Point to Devon's most southerly tip at **Prawle Point**, where a broken-backed freighter is a reminder of the hazards of this stretch of coast. A couple of miles inland from Lannacombe Bay, which links Prawle Point with Start Point, the headland at the top of Start Bay, you can find a quiet nook to stay at *South Allington House* (☎01548/511272; non-smoking; ③).

At **SHARPITOR**, a couple of miles south of Salcombe, the National Trust runs **Overbecks Museum** (April–July & Sept Mon–Fri & Sun 11am–5.30pm; Aug daily 11am–5.30pm; Oct Mon–Thurs & Sun 11am–5pm; £3.90; NT), which is mainly given over to natural history and houses a capacious **youth hostel** (☎01548/842856; closed Nov–March) in its grounds. South of here, the six-mile hike from Bolt Head to Bolt Tail takes you along a ragged coast where shags, cormorants and other marine birds swoop over the rocks, and wild thyme and sea thrift grow underfoot.

Seven miles east of Kingsbridge, the lagoon of the **Slapton Ley nature reserve** supports heron, terns, widgeon and – rarest of all – great crested grebes. A bus links Torcross with Kingsbridge, though of course you could walk from Prawle Point round the dramatic headland at Start Point, or from Dartmouth, five miles along the coast from the lagoon's northern tip.

West of Kingsbridge, **THURLESTONE** is a chocolate-box village of pink-washed thatched cottages, with a splendid undeveloped sandy beach backed by rolling farmland. Surfers prefer the extensive sands to the opposite side of the Avon estuary at **BIGBURY-ON-SEA**, reachable in summer by a ferry between the hamlets of Bantham and Cockleridge – or by wading the river at low tide. A special tractor-like vehicle ferries visitors the short distance from Bigbury's beach to Burgh Island, where a grand Art Deco hotel and the atmospheric *Pilchard Inn* are the main attractions. For an **overnight stay** in the area, Bantham's *Sloop Inn* (☎01548/560489; no credit cards; ④) has several low-slung rooms overlooking the sea and estuary, and a restaurant serving good seafood.

Plymouth

PLYMOUTH's predominantly bland and modern face belies its great historic role as a naval base, a role assured in the sixteenth century by the patronage of such national heroes as John Hawkins and Francis Drake. It was from here that the latter sailed to defeat the Spanish Armada in 1588, and 32 years later the port was the last embarkation point for the Pilgrim Fathers, whose New Plymouth colony became the nucleus for the English settlement of North America. The sustained prominence of the city's Devonport dockyards as a shipbuilding and military base made it a target in World War II, when the Luftwaffe reduced the old centre to rubble, apart from the compact area around the Barbican. Subsequent reconstruction, spurred on by growth that has made Plymouth by far Devon's biggest town, has done nothing to enhance the place. That said, it would be difficult to spoil the glorious vista over **Plymouth Sound**, the basin of calm water at the mouth of the combined Plym, Tavy and Tamar estuaries, which has remained largely unchanged since Drake played his famous game of bowls on the Hoe before joining battle with the Armada. This alone makes a visit to Plymouth a memorable one, and you could also spend a couple of hours wandering around the Elizabethan warehouses and inns of the **Barbican**. The latter is the focus of occasionally raucous nightlife, and a gamut of excellent restaurants specializing in freshly caught seafood. Although this area is easy to stroll around, you could also make use of the regular and frequent circular **bus** service (#25) for getting around the town, which stops at the train station, Sutton Harbour, the Hoe, and the Citadel. Plymouth makes a good starting point for forays onto Dartmoor, and a base for visiting a trio of elegant country houses with both aesthetic appeal and historical resonance, though transport connections are not always easy.

Arrival, information and accommodation

Plymouth's **train station** is off Saltash Road, from where bus #25 leaves every fifteen minutes for the central Royal Parade. The **bus station** (☎01752/222666) is just over St Andrew's Cross from Royal Parade, at Bretonside, and holds **left-luggage lockers** (maximum stay 24 hours). The **tourist office** is off Sutton Harbour at 9 The Barbican (summer Mon–Sat 9am–5pm, Sun 10am–4pm; winter Mon–Fri 9am–5pm, Sat 10am–4pm; ☎01752/304849). Ask here about guided tours, a useful way to get an informed view of the city and surrounding areas: *Blue Badge* (☎01752/775841), for example, operates walking tours of the Royal Citadel and the old town on Sunday afternoons for about £3 a head (May–Sept).

Plymouth has plenty of choice when it comes to **accommodation**: try first the row of B&Bs edging the Hoe on Citadel Road if you want to be near the sights, though you won't be more than a twenty-minute walk from the Hoe and Barbican areas if you prefer to stay close to the train station. Ferry passengers might want to be nearer the docks in the Millbay district, on the western side of town.

Hotels and B&Bs

Acorns and Lawns, 171 Citadel Rd (☎01752/229474). One of the terrace of competitively priced B&Bs off the eastern side of Plymouth Hoe, this one offering good-value accommodation and constant access. All doubles are en suite, most rooms with shower. No credit cards. ③.

Avalon, 167 Citadel Rd (☎01752/668127). All rooms have TV and tea/coffee facilities, one is en suite. No credit cards. ①.

The Beeches, 175 Citadel Rd (☎01752/266475). A good choice on this row close to the Barbican, with access at all times. No credit cards. ③.

Bowling Green Hotel, 9–10 Osborne Place, Lockyer St (☎01752/209090). Smart establishment overlooking Francis Drake's fabled haunt on the west side of the Hoe. ②.

Dudley Hotel, 42 Sutherland Rd (☎01752/668322). Simple accommodation near the train station. Services offered include secure parking, early breakfasts for ferry passengers and evening meals. ①.

Georgian House, 51 Citadel Rd (☎01752/663237). Small hotel with all rooms en suite, and a good restaurant attached. ①.

Grosvenor Park Hotel, 114 North Road East (☎01752/229312). Most convenient stop for the train station, off the North Cross roundabout. Excellent value. ②.

Oliver's Hotel, 33 Sutherland Rd (☎01752/663923). A few minutes from the train station, with a good restaurant. ②.

Osmond Guest House, 42 Pier St (☎01752/229705). Comfortable choice close to the Great Western Docks, offering a pick-up service from the bus and train stations. ①.

Phantele, 176 Devonport Rd (☎01752/561506). Unpretentious budget choice towards the Torpoint ferry on the west side of town, near the youth hostel; useful if everywhere central is booked up (which is not unknown). No credit cards. ①.

Hostels

Backpackers Hotel, 172 Citadel Rd (☎01752/225158). Relaxed place in a convenient location on the hotel strip near the Hoe and Royal Parade. Call ahead, as beds fill up quickly.

Plymouth YHA, Belmont House, Devonport Rd (☎01752/562189, *plymouth@yha.org.uk*). Walk a quarter-mile from Devonport train station, or catch a bus from the centre (Citybus #33 or #34, or First Western National #15A or #81).

The City

A good place to start a tour of the city is **Plymouth Hoe**, an immense esplanade studded with reminders of the great events in the city's history. Resplendent in fair

FRANCIS DRAKE

Born around 1540 near Tavistock, **Francis Drake** worked in the domestic coastal trade from the age of thirteen, but was soon taking part in the first English slaving expeditions between Africa and the West Indies, led by his Plymouth kinsman John Hawkins. Later Drake was active in the secret war against Spain, raiding and looting merchant ships in actions unofficially sanctioned by Elizabeth I. In 1572 he became the first Englishman to sight the Pacific, and soon afterwards, on board the *Golden Hind*, became the first one to **circumnavigate the world**, for which he received a knighthood on his return in 1580. The following year Drake was made mayor of Plymouth, settling in Buckland Abbey (see p.390), but was back in action before long – in 1587 he "singed the king of Spain's beard" by entering Cadiz harbour and destroying 33 vessels that were to have formed part of Philip II's **armada**. When the replacement invasion fleet appeared in the English Channel in 1588, Drake – along with Raleigh, Hawkins and Frobisher – played a leading role in wrecking it. The following year he set off on an unsuccessful expedition to help the Portuguese against Spain, but otherwise most of the next decade was spent in relative inactivity in Plymouth, Exeter and London. Finally, in 1596 Drake left with Hawkins for a raid on Panama, a venture that cost the lives of both captains.

Drake has come to personify the Elizabethan Age's swashbuckling expansionism and patriotism, but England's naval triumphs were as much the result of John Hawkins' humbler work in building and maintaining a new generation of warships as they were of the skill and bravery of their captains. Drake was simply the most flamboyant of a generation of reckless and brilliant mariners who broke the Spanish hegemony on the high seas, laying the foundations for England's later imperialist pursuits.

weather, with glorious views over the sea, the Hoe can also attract some pretty fero-cious winds, making it well-nigh impossible to explore in wintry conditions. Approaching from the Civic Centre – the hub of the town centre – the most distinc-tive landmark is a tall white naval war memorial, standing alongside smaller monu-ments to the defeat of the Spanish Armada and to the airmen who defended the city during the wartime blitz, and a rather portly statue of Sir Francis Drake, gazing grandly out to the sea. Appropriately, there's a bowling green back from the brow.

In front of the memorials the red-and-white striped **Smeaton's Tower** (Easter–Sept 10.30am–4.30pm; 75p, free for Plymouth Dome visitors) was erected in 1759 by John Smeaton on the treacherous Eddystone Rocks, fourteen miles out to sea. When replaced by a larger lighthouse in 1882, it was reassembled here, where it gives the loftiest view over Plymouth Sound. Below Smeaton's Tower is the **Plymouth Dome** leisure complex (daily April–Sept 9am–5pm; Oct–March 11am–5pm; £3.95), which includes tricksy audiovisual exhibitions of Plymouth's history and the lives of local heroes such as Drake, the Mayflower Pilgrims and Captain Cook. On the seafront, Plymouth's **Royal Citadel** is an uncompromising fortress constructed in 1666 to intim-idate the populace of the only town in the southwest to be held by the Parliamentarians in the Civil War. The stronghold is still used by the military, though there are guided tours through some of its older parts, including the seventeenth-century Governor's House and the Royal Chapel of St Katherine (tours May–Sept 2.30pm; £3); tickets are available from the Plymouth Dome or the tourist office.

Round the corner, the old town's quay at **Sutton Harbour** is still used by the trawler fleet and is the scene of a boisterous early-morning fish market. The **Mayflower Steps** here commemorate the sailing of the Pilgrim Fathers and a nearby plaque lists the names and professions of the 102 Puritans on board. All three of Captain Cook's voy-ages to the South Seas, Australia and the Antarctic also started from here, as did the nineteenth-century transport ships to Australia, carrying thousands of convicts and colonists. Nowadays the harbour is the starting point for cruises, ranging from one-hour tours around the Sound and the Devonport naval dockyard, to longer sea trips and the four-hour cruise up the Tamar to the Cornish village of Calstock.

The **Barbican** district, which edges the harbour, is the heart of old Plymouth. Most of the buildings are now shops and restaurants, but off the quayside, New Street holds most of the oldest buildings, among them the **Elizabethan House** (April–Sept Wed–Sun 10am–5.30pm; £1; NT), a captain's dwelling retaining most of the original architectural features, including a lovely old pole staircase. The Pilgrim Fathers are thought to have spent their last night in England in Island House, at the end of the par-allel Southside Street, now home to the tourist office.

Cross the bridge over Sutton Harbour to reach Plymouth's newest exhibit, the grand **National Marine Aquarium** (daily: April–Oct 10am–5pm; Nov–March 11am–5pm; £6.50). On three levels, the complex represents a range of marine environments from moorland stream to coral reef and deep-sea ocean, including sharks and Europe's largest collection of seahorse species. Talks and presentations take place throughout the day, and the feeding-times – carried out by divers – are among the highlights. Back in the centre of town, the handsome timber-framed, mainly seventeenth-century **Merchant's House Museum**, 33 St Andrew St (April–Sept Tues–Fri 10am–1pm & 2–5.30pm, Sat 10am–1pm & 2–5pm; 90p) goes into various aspects of Plymouth's his-tory. Behind it, off Royal Parade, stands the city's chief place of worship, **St Andrew's**, a reconstruction of a fifteenth-century building that was almost completely gutted by a bomb in 1941. The entrails of the navigator Martin Frobisher are buried here, as are those of Admiral Blake, the Parliamentarian who died as his ship entered Plymouth after destroying a Spanish treasure fleet off Tenerife (see p.360). Local boy William Bligh, of *Mutiny on the Bounty* fame, was baptized here.

Eating and drinking

You'll find a wildly eclectic range of **restaurants** in and around Plymouth's Barbican area. One of the best fish restaurants is *Piermaster's*, at 3 Southside St (☎01752/229345; closed Sun), whose kitchen is supplied straight from the nearby harbour; it's plain but elegant, if a little expensive. Across the road, the *Barbican Pasta Bar* attracts the crowds, while Notte St, at the top of Southside, has the inexpensive *Revival*, a Mexican/Italian/American diner with lots of jazzy ambience. The next-door *Eastern Eye* is a good-value Indian, and a few doors down at 54 Notte St, the area's cosmopolitan tone is taken to new lengths at *Pavarotti's*, which has French, English, Greek and Italian items on the menu, and features a good-value fixed-price selection of *meze* (☎01752/250240). If you hanker for simple English cuisine, the cramped *Queen Anne Eating House* in the Barbican's White Lane serves budget meals (closed Sun eve & Mon), while the similarly priced unlicensed *Tudor Rose*, 36 New St, is good for cottage pies and teas and opens its garden in summer. *Plymouth Arts Centre*, 38 Looe St, has a self-service vegetarian restaurant open until around 8pm, though the major reason for coming here is to see its films and live performances.

The *Dolphin* **pub** on Southside Street is a landmark in the Barbican, and is crowded with fishermen in the morning and locals and boisterous boozers at night, and serves simple lunchtime snacks. On the other side of town, the *Brown Bear* on Chapel Street is a local haunt in the Devonport dock district, a traditional beamed pub patronized by naval folk, beer aficionados and foodies attracted by the lively evening menu.

Around Plymouth

One of the best local day excursions from Plymouth is to **Mount Edgcumbe**, where woods and meadows provide a welcome antidote to the urban bustle, and are within easy reach of some fabulous sand. East of Plymouth, the aristocratic opulence of **Saltram House** includes some fine art and furniture, while to the north of town you can visit Drake's old residence at **Buckland Abbey**.

Mount Edgcumbe

Lying on the Cornish side of Plymouth Sound and visible from the Hoe, **Mount Edgcumbe** features a Tudor house, landscaped gardens and acres of rolling parkland and coastal paths. The **house** (April to mid-Oct Wed–Sun 11am–5pm; £4) is a reconstruction of the bomb-damaged Tudor original, though inside the predominant note is eighteenth-century, the rooms elegantly restored with authentic Regency furniture. The house alone, however, would not merit the expedition here: far more enticing are the **grounds**, which include impeccable gardens divided into French, Italian and English sections – the first two a blaze of flowerbeds adorned with classical statuary, the last an acre of sweeping lawn shaded by exotic trees. The **park**, which is free and open all year, covers the whole of the peninsula facing the estuary and the sea, including a part of the Cornish Coastal Path. From the peninsula's two headlands, Rame Head and Penlee Point, extensive views show Plymouth in its best light.

You can reach the house by the passenger **ferry** to Cremyll, leaving at least hourly from Admiral's Hard, a small mooring in the Stonehouse district of town, reachable on bus #33 or #34 from outside the Guildhall; in summer there's also a direct motor launch (four daily) between the Mayflower Steps and the village of **Cawsand**, an old smugglers' haunt two hours' walk from the house. Cawsand itself is just a mile from the southern tip of the huge **Whitsand Bay**, the best bathing beach for miles around.

Saltram House

The remodelled Tudor mansion **Saltram House** (April–Oct Mon–Thurs & Sun noon–5pm; garden also open March weekends 11am–4pm; £5.70; garden only £2.70; NT), two miles east of Plymouth off the A38, is Devon's largest country house, featuring work by the great architect Robert Adam and fourteen portraits by **Joshua Reynolds**, who was born nearby in Plympton. Showpiece is the Saloon, a fussy but exquisitely furnished room dripping with gilt and plaster, and set off by a huge Axminster carpet especially woven for it in 1770. Saltram's landscaped park provides a breather from this riot of interior design, though it is marred by the proximity of the road. You can get here on the hourly #22 bus (not Sun) from Royal Parade to Cott Hill, from where it's a ten-minute signposted walk.

Buckland Abbey

Six miles north of Plymouth, close to the River Tavy and on the edge of Dartmoor, stands **Buckland Abbey** (April–Oct Mon–Wed & Fri–Sun 10.30am–5.30pm; Nov–March Sat & Sun 2–5pm; house & grounds £4.40; grounds only £2.30; NT), once the most westerly of England's Cistercian abbeys. After its dissolution Buckland was converted to a private home by the privateer Richard Grenville (cousin of Walter Raleigh), from whom the estate was acquired by Sir Francis Drake in 1582, the year he became mayor of Plymouth. It remained his home until his death, but the house reveals few traces of Drake's residence, as he spent most of his retirement years plundering on the Spanish main. There are, however, numerous maps, portraits and mementos of his buccaneering exploits on show, most famous of which is Drake's Drum, which was said to beat a supernatural warning of impending danger to the country. Apart from Drake's knick-knacks, the collection includes some stirring relics of the Elizabethan era of seafaring, as well as a gallery filled with model ships. The house stands in majestic grounds which contain a fine fourteenth-century **Great Barn**, buttressed and gabled and larger than the abbey itself. The abbey is reachable from Plymouth on the #83, #84 or #86 bus to Tavistock, changing at Yelverton to the hourly #55 minibus (not Sun).

Dartmoor

The longer one stays here the more does the spirit of the moor sink into one's soul, its vastness, and also its grim charm. When you are once out upon its bosom you have left all traces of modern England behind you, but on the other hand you are conscious everywhere of the homes and the work of the prehistoric people. . . . If you were to see a skin-clad, hairy man crawl out from the low door, fitting a flint-tipped arrow on to the string of his bow, you would feel that his presence there was more natural than your own.

Arthur Conan Doyle, *The Hound of the Baskervilles*

Occupying the main part of the county between Exeter and Plymouth, **DARTMOOR** is southern England's greatest expanse of wilderness, some 365 square miles of raw granite, barren bogland, sparse grass and heather-grown moor. It was not always so desolate, as testified by the remnants of scattered Stone Age settlements and the ruined relics of the area's nineteenth-century tin-mining industry. Today desultory flocks of sheep and groups of ponies are virtually the only living creatures to be seen wandering over the central fastnesses of the National Park, with solitary birds – buzzards, kestrels, pipits, stonechats and wagtails – wheeling and hovering high above.

The core of Dartmoor, characterized by tumbling streams and high tors chiselled by the elements, is **Dartmoor Forest**, which has belonged to the Duchy of Cornwall since 1307, though there is almost unlimited public access as long as certain guidelines are

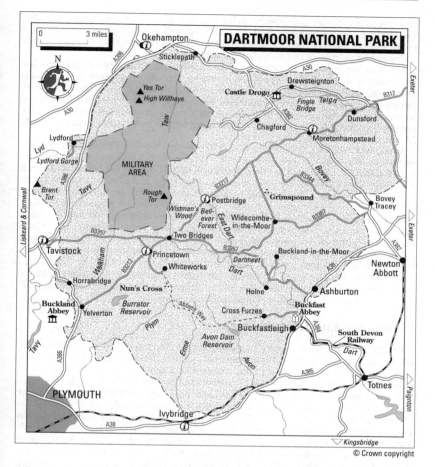

followed – for instance, you are not allowed to park overnight in unauthorized places, and no vehicles are allowed farther than fifteen yards from the road. Camping is permitted out of sight of houses and roads, but fires are strictly forbidden. Though networks of signposts or painted stones do exist to guide **walkers**, map-reading abilities are a prerequisite for any but the shortest walks, and a good deal of experience is essential for longer distances – it is not uncommon for search parties to have to be rounded up to look for hikers gone astray. Information on walks and on pony-trekking centres can be found at the National Park Visitor Centres in Dartmoor's major towns and villages, and from information points in smaller villages.

    Princetown, at the heart of the moor, has the Dartmoor National Park's main information centre and a selection of stores, pubs and places to stay. A few other villages, such as **Postbridge** and **Widecombe**, have B&Bs and shops, though for the widest choice of accommodation you have to go to the towns and villages circling the moor – chief of them **Tavistock**, **Lydford** and **Okehampton**. It would not be impossible to base yourself in Exeter or Plymouth, neither more than an hour's ride from the central **Two Bridges**, at the intersection of the B3312 and B3357, which gives access to some of the wildest tracts of Dartmoor. Always plan ahead and book places to stay – availability can be extremely restricted in high season.

Much to the irritation of locals and visitors alike, the **Ministry of Defence** has appropriated a significant portion of northern Dartmoor, an area that contains Dartmoor's highest tors and some of its most famous beauty spots. The MoD firing ranges are marked by red and white posts; when firing is in progress, red flags or red lights signify that entry is prohibited. As a general rule, you can assume that if no warning flags are flying by 9am between April and September, or by 10am from October to March, there is to be no firing on that day.

In summer, a Transmoor **bus** service (#82) operates between Exeter and Plymouth, with stops at Two Bridges and Princetown – for most of the year it runs on Saturdays only, but there are at least three daily services from late May to the end of September. Also from Exeter, the regular #359 runs to Castle Drogo and Chagford, on the northeast side of the moor, while National Express coaches and private Cornish lines serve Okehampton. There are three daily buses from Okehampton to Tavistock via Lydford. Bus #98 connects Princetown with Tavistock three times daily from Monday to Friday, and buses run from Tavistock to Plymouth roughly every twenty minutes. Apart from these, there's little except once-weekly runs to remote villages. Ask about the *Ride-and-Ramble* scheme which combines two- to six-hour guided walks with bus routes and timetables: the booklet, available from Princetown's tourist office or Exeter and Plymouth bus stations, gives full details. Any tourist office in the area also stocks the free *Dartmoor Visitor* newspaper with info on camping, accommodation, events, facilities for the disabled, and military firing-range schedules.

Princetown and the central moor

PRINCETOWN owes its growth to the proximity of Dartmoor Prison, a high-security jail originally constructed for POWs captured in the Napoleonic wars. The grim presence seeps into the village, which has a somewhat oppressed air and functional grey stone houses, some of them – like the parish church of St Michael – built by French and American prisoners. What Princetown lacks in beauty is amply compensated for by the surrounding country, the best of which lies immediately to the north.

Information on all of Dartmoor is given by the main **National Park information centre**, on the village's central green (daily April–Oct 10am–5pm; Nov–March closes 4pm; ☎01822/890414). The best place to stay is right in the centre of the village at *Lamorna*, a friendly **B&B** on Two Bridges Road (☎01822/890360; no credit cards; ③). Alternatively, you might head for *Duchy House*, 200 yards from the centre, on Tavistock Road (☎01822/890552; no credit cards; ③), which has rooms with or without private bath, and also runs a **café**. Two pubs in Princetown's central square also offer accommodation, the *Railway Inn* (☎01822/890232; ③) and the *Plume of Feathers* (☎01822/890240; ③); the latter claims to be the oldest building in town, and also has dormitory accommodation in two bunkhouses as well as a convenient **campsite** – staple bar-food is always available.

Northeast of Princetown, two miles north of the crossroads at Two Bridges, the dwarfed and misshapen oaks of **Wistman's Wood** are an evocative relic of the original Dartmoor Forest, cluttered with lichen-covered boulders and a dense undergrowth of ferns. The gnarled old trees are alleged to have been the site of druidic gatherings, a story unsupported by any evidence but quite plausible in this solitary spot.

Three miles northeast of Two Bridges, the largest and best preserved of Dartmoor's **clapper bridges** crosses the East Dart river at **POSTBRIDGE**, to which it gives its name. Used by tin-miners and farmers since medieval times, these simple structures consist of huge slabs of granite supported by piers of the same material; another more basic example is at Two Bridges. Walkers from Postbridge can explore up and down the river, or press further south through **Bellever Forest** to the open moor beyond. On the edge of the forest, a couple of miles south of Postbridge on the banks of the East Dart river, lies one of Dartmoor's two **youth hostels** (☎01822/880227; closed Nov–March) – it's on a minor road from Postbridge, but there's no public transport. There's also a **camping barn** close to Bellever Forest at Runnage Farm with a bunkhouse and outdoor camping facilities alongside – for this and any of Dartmoor's other camping barns, it's wise to book ahead, particularly at weekends: ☎01271/324420. You'll find more luxury in the *Lydgate House Hotel*, signposted off the main road half a mile southwest of Postbridge and offering easy access to Bellever Forest (☎01822/880209; ④; closed Dec–Feb).

Two miles northeast of Postbridge, the solitary *Warren House Inn* offers warm, fire-lit comfort in an unutterably bleak tract of moorland. To the east of the B3212, reach-able on a right turn towards Widecombe-in-the-Moor, the Bronze Age village of Grimspound lies below Hameldown Tor, about a mile off the road. Inhabited some three thousand years ago, when Dartmoor was fully forested and enjoyed a consider-ably warmer climate than it does today, this is the completest example of Dartmoor's prehistoric settlements, consisting of twenty-four circular huts scattered within a four-acre enclosure. A stone wall nine feet thick surrounds the huts, several of which have raised bed-places, and you can see how the villagers ensured a constant water supply by enclosing part of a stream with a wall. Grimspound itself is thought to have been the model for the Stone Age settlement in which Sherlock Holmes camped in *The Hound of the Baskervilles*, while **Hound Tor**, an outcrop three miles to the southwest, was the inspiration for Conan Doyle's tale – according to local legend, phantom hounds were sighted racing across the moor to hurl themselves on the tomb of a hated squire at his death in 1677.

Buckland-in-the-Moor and the southeastern moor

Four miles east of the crossroads at Two Bridges, **Dartmeet** marks the place where the East and West Dart rivers merge after tortuous journeys from their remote sources. Crowds home in on this beauty spot, but the valley is memorably lush and you don't need to walk far to leave the car park and ice-cream vans behind. From here the Dart pursues a more leisurely course, joined by the River Webburn near the pretty moorland village of **BUCKLAND-IN-THE-MOOR**, one of a cluster of moorstone-and-thatched hamlets on this southeastern side of the moor.

Four miles north is another candidate for most popular Dartmoor village, **WIDE-COMBE-IN-THE-MOOR**, set in a hollow amid high granite-strewn ridges. Its church of **St Pancras** provides a famous local landmark, its pinnacled tower dwarfing the four-teenth-century main building, whose interior boasts a beautiful painted roodscreen. Look out here too for the carved one-eared rabbits above the communion rail. The nearby **Church House** was built in the fifteenth century for weary churchgoers from outlying districts, and was later converted into almshouses. Widecombe's other claim to fame is the traditional song, *Widdicombe Fair*: the **fair** is still held annually on the second Tuesday of September, but is now primarily a tourist attraction. You could **stay** in Widecombe in the plain and pleasant *Sheena Tower* on the outskirts of the village (☎01364/621308; non-smoking; no credit cards; ①; closed Dec & Jan); half a mile out, *Higher Venton Farm* (☎01364/621235; no credit cards; ②) is a peaceful thatched long-house close to a couple of good pubs. You can **camp** at *Cockingford Farm*, one and a half miles south of Widecombe (☎01364/621258; closed mid-Nov to mid-March). There is also a **pony-trekking** centre near the village at Shilstone Rocks Riding and Trekking Centre (☎01364/621281).

South of Buckland, the village of **HOLNE** is another rustic idyll surrounded on three sides by wooded valleys. The vicarage here was the birthplace of Charles Kingsley, author of such Devon-based tales as *Westward Ho!* and *The Water Babies*. A window commemorates him in the village church, which also has a whimsical epitaph on the grave of Edward Collins, landlord of the next-door *Church House* inn until 1780. The pub itself was built three hundred years before that, and offers excellent meals and some **accommodation** (☎01364/631208; ②). Oliver Cromwell is said to have stayed here. On the edge of Holne, on the route of the Two Moors Way, there is a **camping** barn with good facilities (☎01364/631544), backing onto a small camping field.

A couple of miles east, the Dart weaves through a wooded green valley to enter the grounds of **Buckfast Abbey** (daily: May–Oct 9am–5.30pm; Nov–April 10am–4pm; free), a modern monastic complex occupying the site of an abbey founded in the eleventh century by Canute, abandoned two hundred years later, refounded, and finally dissolved by Henry VIII. The present buildings were the work of a handful of French Benedictine monks who consecrated their new abbey in 1932, though work on the other monastic buildings has continued until recently. The church itself is in a traditional Anglo-Norman style, following the design of the Cistercian building razed in 1535, and shows examples of the monks' dexterity in making stained glass windows – which, along with honey, handicrafts and tonic wine, help to keep the community funded. An exhibition covers the abbey's history and displays its treasures.

The northeastern moor

The essentially unspoilt market town of **MORETONHAMPSTEAD**, lying on the northeastern edge of the moor, makes an attractive entry point from Exeter – and, incidentally, shares with Woolfardisworthy (near Bideford) the honour of having the longest single-word place-name in England. Local **information** is handled by a Community Information Point on The Square (March–Oct daily 10am–1pm & 2–5pm; Nov–Easter Fri–Sun 10am–1pm & 2–4pm; ☎01647/440043). There is classy **accommodation** in the central *White Hart* (☎01647/440406; ③), a Georgian posting inn that also provides coffees and meals, and at *Cookshayes*, on the edge of the village at 33 Court St (☎01647/440374; ②; closed Nov–Feb), offering good home cooking. A mile or two outside Moreton in the hamlet of Doccombe, *Great Doccombe Farm* (☎01647/440694; no credit cards; ①) is a comfortable three-hundred-year-old farmhouse.

The Steps Bridge **youth hostel** (☎01647/252435; closed Oct–March) sits on the outskirts of **Dunsford**, three miles northeast of Moretonhampstead and right on the boundary of the National Park – buses #359 (not Sun) and #82 stop nearby. Its woodland setting overlooking the Teign Gorge makes it a popular overnight stop for hikers.

Moretonhampstead has a historic rivalry with neighbouring **CHAGFORD**, a Stannary town (a chartered centre of the tin trade) that also enjoyed prosperity as a centre of the wool trade. It stands on a hillside overlooking the River Teign, with a fine fifteenth-century church on its edge and enough attractions within and around to keep its pubs and hotels in business. The ancient *Three Crowns*, next door to the former guildhall on the main square, is one of a number of decent pubs in the village, and offers some pricey accommodation in raftered rooms (☎01647/433444; ⑤). An alternative is the thatched, seventeenth-century *Lawn House* (☎01647/433329; closed Nov–Feb; no credit cards; ①), close to the centre on Mill Street – non-smokers only.

There are numerous walks to be made in the immediate vicinity, for instance to Fernworthy Reservoir, four miles to the southwest along signposted narrow lanes, or downstream along the Teign to the twentieth-century extravaganza of **Castle Drogo** (April–Oct Mon–Thurs, Sat & Sun 11am–5.30pm; grounds daily 10.30am–dusk; £5.30; grounds only £2.50; NT), which occupies a stupendous site overlooking the Teign

DARTMOOR'S NORTHERN TORS

A seven-mile, three-hour walk from Okehampton skirts the east of the MoD's Okehampton Range, brings you within view of the highest points on the moor, then plunges you into the recesses of the East Okement River, before rounding Belstone Common and returning north to Okehampton via the village of Belstone. From Okehampton, get onto the north bank of the Okement River, passing Simmond's Park and Okehampton School on the right, and walking under Ball Hill on a woody path as far as **Fatherford Viaduct**. Follow a well-defined path for about a mile through Halstock Wood, sloping down diagonally until meeting the East Okement River, which you can cross at **Chapel Ford**.

Walk up the eastern bank of the East Okement for five hundred yards before passing through an opening in the hedge, leaving the valley to head towards **Winter Tor**, a little more than a mile due south of the ford. At the tor, carry on up to the top of the ridge, from which a splendid panorama unfolds, with Dartmoor's highest peaks of **Yes Tor** and **Willhays Tor** about three miles southwest. To the east the great bowl of Taw Marsh can be seen.

After a couple of hundred yards, take a left turn northwards, climbing along the ridge to the rocky pinnacles of **Belstone Common**. Between **Higher Tor** and **Belstone Tor** you'll pass **Irishman's Wall**, the vestige of an attempt to enclose part of the moor against the wishes of the locals, who waited until the wall was nearly complete before gathering to push the structure down. Carry on heading north, descending sharply towards the **Nine Stones** cairn circle, seven hundred yards below Belstone Tor. This Bronze Age burial ground was popularly held to be the petrified remains of nine maidens turned to stone for dancing on Sunday (there are in fact twelve stones). North, a nearby track brings you northeast to the village of Belstone, half a mile away.

From Belstone, follow the road signed "Okehampton Indirect" for about half a mile northwest; you can then either turn left to Cleave House, descend to the river and return northwards up the East Okement to Okehampton, or continue along the road.

---

gorge. Having retired at the age of thirty-three, grocery magnate Julius Drewe unearthed a link that suggested his descent from a Norman baron, and set about creating a castle befitting his pedigree. Begun in 1910, to a design by **Sir Edwin Lutyens**, it was not completed until 1930, but the result was an unsurpassed synthesis of medieval and modern elements. The croquet lawn is available for use, with mallets for hire.

Paths lead from Drogo east to **Fingle Bridge**, one of Dartmoor's most noted beauty spots, where shaded green pools hold trout and the occasional salmon. The *Angler's Rest* pub has an adjoining **restaurant**.

The north and northwestern moor

The main centre on the northern fringes of Dartmoor, **OKEHAMPTON** grew prosperous as a market town for the medieval wool trade, and some fine old buildings survive between the two branches of the River Okement that meet here, among them the prominent fifteenth-century tower of the **Chapel of St James**. Across the road from the seventeenth-century town hall, a granite archway leads into the **Museum of Dartmoor Life** (Easter–May & Oct Mon–Sat 10am–5pm; July–Sept daily 10am–5pm; Nov–Easter Mon–Fri 10am–4pm; £2), an excellent overview of habitation on the moor since earliest times. Four miles east of Okehampton at Sticklepath (bus #X9 or #X10), **Finch Foundry** (April–Oct Mon & Wed–Sun 11am–5.30pm; £2.70; NT) is a Victorian forge with working machinery and demonstrations. Loftily perched above the West Okement on the other side of town, **Okehampton Castle** (April–Sept daily 10am–6pm;

Oct daily 10am–5pm; £2.30; EH) is the shattered hulk of a stronghold laid waste by Henry VIII; its ruins include a gatehouse, Norman keep and the remains of the Great Hall, buttery and kitchens.

Between May and September, an old goods line provides Okehampton with a useful Sunday **rail** connection, linking the town with Exeter via Crediton in about forty minutes: ask about the Sunday Rover ticket (£5) which also covers the Plymouth–Gunnislake rail link and bus travel on Dartmoor (☎01837/55330). The station is a fifteen-minute walk up Station Road from Fore Street in Okehampton's centre, where the **tourist office** (Easter–June & Oct Mon–Sat 10am–5pm; July–Sept daily 10am–5.30pm; Nov–Easter Mon, Fri & Sat 10am–5pm; ☎01837/53020) sits next to the museum. Alongside them lies the expensive *White Hart* (☎01837/52730; ③), though cheaper **accommodation** can be found further up Fore Street at the *Fountain Hotel*, offering basic rooms (☎01837/53900; no credit cards; ①). Views towards Exmoor and an outdoor heated pool push up the rates at *Heathfield House* on Klondyke Road above the station (☎01837/54211; ②), or opt for the more economical *Meadowlea* lower down at 65 Station Rd (☎01837/53200; ①). If all else fails, you'll have to stay a little out of Okehampton, for example at the comfortable and spacious *Upcott House* on Upcott Hill, half a mile north of the centre (☎01837/53743; no credit cards; ①). Okehampton's new **youth hostel** (☎01837/53916) provides four- and six-bed bunkrooms in a converted goods shed at the station. There's a small **campsite** three-quarters of a mile east of Okehampton on the B3260, *Yertiz* (☎01837/52281). In the centre of town, the *Coffee Pot* in Fairplace Terrace is a cheap retreat for breakfasts, coffees and meals, tucked away behind the museum (Oct–May closed evenings). For **riding** on the moor, contact Skaigh Riding Stables (☎01837/840917) or Eastlake (☎01837/52513), both east of town in the Belstone/Sticklepath area.

Lydford

Five miles southwest of Okehampton, the village of **LYDFORD** boasts the sturdy but small-scale Lydford Castle, a Saxon outpost, then a Norman keep and later used as a prison. The chief attraction here, though, is **Lydford Gorge** (April–Sept 10am–5.30pm; Oct 10am–4pm; Nov–March 10.30am–3pm as far as the White Lady Waterfall only; £3.40; NT), whose main entrance is a five-minute walk downhill. Two routes – one above, one along the banks – follow the ravine burrowed through by the River Lyd as far as the hundred-foot White Lady Waterfall, coming back on the opposite bank. Overgrown with thick woods, the one-and-a-half-mile gorge is alive with butterflies, spotted woodpeckers, dippers, herons and clouds of insects. The full course would take you roughly two hours at a leisurely pace, though there is a separate entrance at the south end of the gorge if you only want to visit the waterfall. In winter months, when the river can flood, the waterfall is the only part of the gorge open.

Back in the village, the picturesque *Castle Inn* sits right next to the castle, and provides a fire-lit sixteenth-century bar where you can drink and snack. The inn also offers en-suite accommodation in low-ceilinged oak-beamed rooms (☎01822/820242; ④), and there is a rather pricey but first-rate restaurant too, in a back room cluttered with curios and memorabilia. **Horse-riding** in the area is on offer at the *Lydgate House Hotel* (☎01822/820321).

The western moor

Southwest from Princetown, walkers can trace the grassy path of the defunct rail line to **Burrator Reservoir**, four miles away; flooded in the 1890s to provide water for Plymouth, this is the biggest stretch of water on Dartmoor. The wooded lakeside teems with wildlife, and the boulder-strewn slopes are overlooked by the craggy peaks of **Sharpitor** (1312ft) and **Sheep's Tor** (1150ft). From here, the best walk is to strike northwest to meet the valley of the **River Walkham**, which rises in a peat bog at Walkham Head, five miles north of Princetown, then scurries through moorland and woods to join the River Tavy at Double Waters, two miles south of Tavistock. The fast-flowing water attracts herons, kingfishers and other colourful birdlife, to be seen darting in and out of dense woods of alder, ash and sycamore.

The river crosses the B3357 Tavistock road at **MERRIVALE**, a tiny village with a decent pub (the *Dartmoor Arms*), four miles west of Princetown. Merrivale makes another good starting point for moorland walks – there's a decent **campsite** at *Higher Longford Farm*, Moorshop, a mile out of Merrivale on the Tavistock Road (☎01822/613360) – and it is only half a mile west of one of Dartmoor's most spectacular stone rows, at **Long Ash**. Just a few yards from the B3357, the upright stones form a stately procession, stretching 850ft across the bare landscape. Dating from between 2500 BC and 750 BC, and probably connected with burial rites, the rows are known locally as "Potato Market" or "Plague Market" in memory of the time when provisions for plague-stricken Tavistock were deposited here. A mile to the southwest, on the western slopes of the Walkham valley, the sphinx-like pinnacle of **Vixen Tor** looms over the barren moor.

Tavistock

The main town of the western moor, **TAVISTOCK** owes its distinctive Victorian appearance to the building boom that followed the discovery of copper deposits here in 1844. Originally, however, this market and Stannary town on the River Tavy grew around what was once the West Country's most important Benedictine abbey, established in the eleventh century and, at the time of its dissolution, owning land as distant as the Isles of Scilly. Some scanty remnants survive in the churchyard of **St Eustace**, a mainly fifteenth-century building with some fine monuments inside and a William Morris window in the south aisle.

Half a mile south of Tavistock, on the Plymouth Road, stands a statue of Francis Drake, who was born and raised on Crowndale Farm, a mile south of town; the statue on Plymouth Hoe is a replica of this one. On the same road, at no. 48, is a reliable **B&B**, *Mallards Guesthouse* (☎01822/615171; no credit cards; ①); another good choice is the Georgian *Eko Brae* at 4 Bedford Villas, in the Springhill quarter of town (☎01822/614028; no credit cards; ①). Tavistock's **tourist office** is in the town hall on Bedford Square (Easter–June, Sept & Oct Mon–Sat 10am–5pm; July & Aug daily 10am–5.30pm; Nov–Easter Mon, Tues, Fri & Sat 10am–4pm; ☎01822/612938) and **bikes** can be rented from Tavistock Cycles, Paddons Row, Brook St (☎01822/617630).

North of Tavistock, a four-mile lane wanders up to **Brent Tor**, 1130-foot high and dominating Dartmoor's western fringes. Access to its conical summit is easiest along a path gently ascending through gorse on its southwestern side, leading to the small church of St Michael at the top. Bleak, treeless moorland extends in every direction, wrapped in silence that's occasionally pierced by the shrill cries of stonechats and wheatears. A couple of miles eastwards, **Gibbet Hill** looms over Black Down and the ruined stack of the abandoned Wheal Betsy silver and lead mine.

North Devon

From Exeter the A377 runs alongside the scenic Tarka Line railway to **North Devon**'s major town, **Barnstaple**. Within easy reach of here, the resorts of **Ilfracombe** and **Woolacombe** draw the crowds, though the fine sandy beaches surrounding the latter give ample opportunity to find your own space. The river port of **Bideford** gives its name to a long bay that holds another beach resort, **Westward Ho!**, as well as the precipitous village of **Clovelly**, perhaps Devon's most famous beauty spot. Inspiring coastal walks follow the bay, particularly to the stormy **Hartland Point** and beyond. Away from the coast, there is plenty of scope for walking and cycling along the Tarka Trail long-distance path, passing through some of the region's loveliest countryside, while for a complete break, the tiny island of **Lundy** provides further opportunities for stretching the legs and clearing the lungs.

Barnstaple

BARNSTAPLE, at the head of the Taw estuary, makes an excellent springboard, being well connected to the resorts of Bideford Bay, Ilfracombe and Woolacombe, as well as to the western fringes of Exmoor. The town's centuries-old role as a marketplace is perpetuated in the daily bustle around the huge timber-framed **Pannier Market** off the High Street, alongside which runs **Butchers Row**, its 33 archways now converted to a variety of uses. Also off the High Street, in the pedestrianized area between that and Boutport Street, lies Barnstaple's **parish church**, itself worth a look, and the fourteenth-century **St Anne's Chapel**, converted into a grammar school in 1549 and later numbering among its pupils John Gay, author of *The Beggar's Opera*; it's now closed to the public. At the end of Boutport Street, make time to visit the **Museum of North Devon** (Tues–Sat 10am–4.30pm; £1, free on Sat 10am–noon), a lively miscellany including wildlife displays and a collection of eighteenth-century pottery for which the region was famous. The museum lies alongside the Taw, where footpaths make for a pleasant riverside stroll, with the colonnaded eighteenth-century **Queen Anne's Walk** – built as a merchants' exchange – providing some architectural interest.

Barnstaple's well-equipped **tourist office** lies opposite Butchers Row on Boutport Street (May–Sept Mon–Sat 9.30am–5.30pm; Oct–April Mon–Sat 9.30am–5pm; ☎01271/375000). There are plenty of **places to stay** in town, two of them five hundred yards south of Long Bridge, at the bottom of the High Street: the Georgian *Nelson*

THE TARKA LINE AND THE TARKA TRAIL

Henry Williamson's *Tarka the Otter* (1927), rated by some as one of the finest pieces of nature writing in the English language, has been appropriated as a promotional device by the Devon tourist industry. As parts of the book are set in the Taw valley, it was inevitable that the Exeter to Barnstaple rail route – which follows the Taw for half of its length – should be dubbed the **Tarka Line**. Leaving almost hourly from Exeter St David's station, trains on this branch line cut through the sparsely populated heart of Devon, the biggest town en route being **Crediton**, ancient birthplace of Saint Boniface (patron saint of Germany and the Netherlands) and site of the bishopric before its transfer to Exeter in the eleventh century.

Barnstaple forms the centre of the figure-of-eight traced by the **Tarka Trail**, which tracks the otter's wanderings for a distance of over 180 miles. To the north, the trail penetrates Exmoor then follows the coast back, passing through Williamson's home village of **Georgeham** on its return to Barnstaple. South, the path takes in Bideford (see p.400), following a disused rail line to Meeth, and continuing as far as Okehampton (see p.395), before swooping up via Eggesford, the point at which the Tarka Line joins the Taw valley.

Twenty-three miles of the trail follow a former rail line that's ideally suited to **bicycles**, and there are rental shops at Barnstaple (near the train station), and Bideford (see p.401). A good ride from Barnstaple is to **Torrington** (fifteen miles south), where you can eat at the *Puffing Billy* pub, formerly the train station.

Tourist offices give out leaflets on individual sections of the trail, but the best overall book is *The Tarka Trail Guide* (Devon Books, £4.95), available from tourist offices or bookshops.

House, 99 Newport Rd (☎01271/345929; no credit cards; ③), backing onto Rock Park and the river, and, around the corner on Victoria Road, *Ivy House* (☎01271/371198; no credit cards; ③) is similarly well equipped but has more capacity. A little further out, on Landkey Road – a continuation of Newport Road – is the first-rate *Mount Sandford* (☎01271/342354; no credit cards; ③), which has a beautiful garden. Convenient for the station, *Herton* (☎01271/323302; no credit cards; ③) is a semi-rural B&B out on Lake Road (left onto Sticklepath Terrace, then left again) that boasts its own tennis court, but is difficult to find in the dark and a twenty-minute walk from the centre. On a plusher note, the Victorian *Royal and Fortescue Hotel* off the square on Boutport Street (☎01271/342289, *info@royalfortescue.co.uk*; ④) is a rather formal place with a decent restaurant.

Among the best inexpensive **restaurants** in town are the Italian *La Viennetta* on Boutport Street and *Chamber's Brasserie* at the bottom of Boutport Street, good for baguettes and salads until about 9pm. After that time, when it becomes a normal pub and wine bar, try the *Golden Lion Tap* next door, for basic meals upstairs or in the bar. For gourmet dining, head a mile south of the centre, to *Lynwood House*, on Bishops Tawton Road, which serves a moderate set lunch, though in the evenings you'll have to splash out on the expensive, but choice, seafood dishes; there is also accommodation here (☎01271/343695, *thelynwood@email.com*; ④). Cyclists on the Tarka Trail can **rent bikes** from Tarka Trail Cycle Hire at the train station (£8.50 per day) or Rolle Quay Cycle Hire on Rolle Street (£9 per day), at the top end of the High Street, conveniently placed for the northern section of the Trail towards Braunton. The *Rolle Quay Inn* can provide lunches to eat there or take as a picnic.

Ilfracombe and around

The most popular resort on Devon's northern coast, **ILFRACOMBE** is essentially little changed since its evolution into a Victorian and Edwardian tourist centre, large-scale development having been restricted by the surrounding cliffs. Nonetheless, the relentless pressure to have fun and the ubiquitous smell of chips can become oppressive, though in summer you can always pop down to the small harbour and escape on a coastal tour, a cruise to Lundy Island (see p.401) or a fishing trip. An attractive stretch of coast runs east out of Ilfracombe, beyond the grassy cliffs of Hillsborough, where a succession of undeveloped coves and inlets is surrounded by jagged slanting rocks and heather-covered hills. Three miles to the east, above the almost enclosed Watermouth Bay, lies **Watermouth Castle** (April–Oct Mon–Fri & Sun 10am–4pm; £5.50), an imposing nineteenth-century mansion, best admired from the outside unless you have kids, who will appreciate the water shows, dungeons and carousel.

The pick of the **beaches** in the area – indeed the best on Devon's northern coast – are round **Morte Point**, five miles west of Ilfracombe, from which the view takes in the island of Lundy, fifteen miles out to sea. Below the promontory stretches a rocky shore whose menacing sunken reef inspired the Normans to give it the name Morte Stone. A break in the rocks makes space for the pocket-sized **Barricane Beach**, famous for the tropical shells washed here from the Caribbean by the Atlantic currents, and a popular swimming spot. Luckily there's room for everyone on the two miles of **Woolacombe Sand**, a broad, west-facing expanse much favoured by surfers and families alike. The beach can get crowded towards its northern end, where a cluster of hotels, villas and retirement homes makes up the summer resort of **WOOLACOMBE**. The quieter southern end is bracketed by **Baggy Point**, where from September to November the air is a swirl of gannets, shags, cormorants and shearwaters. Round the point, **Croyde Bay** is another surfers' delight, more compact than Woolacombe, with stalls on the sand renting surfboards and wet-suits.

Practicalities

From Barnstaple, First Red Bus #3 runs daily several times an hour to Ilfracombe, and the frequent #303 runs to Woolacombe. From Minehead and Lynton, take the three-times-daily DevonBus #300. For Woolacombe, take the First Red Bus #31 and #31a from Ilfracombe, while DevonBus #308 travels from Barnstaple to Croyde. The Ilfracombe **tourist office** is at the Landmark on the Seafront (May, June, Sept & Oct daily 10am–6pm; July & Aug 10am–8pm; Nov–April Mon–Fri 10am–5pm, Sat 10am–4pm, Sun 10am–2pm; ☎01271/863001).

One of Ilfracombe's less expensive **hotels** is *Kinvara*, very central at 6 Avenue Rd (☎01271/863013; no credit cards; ①; closed Nov–Easter), but if you want views, try the *Cavendish* at 9 Larkstone Terrace (☎01271/863994; ②; closed Nov–Feb), or, on the same road, *Harbourside Hotel* (☎01271/862231; ④). Ilfracombe's **youth hostel**, *Ashmour House* (☎01271/865337; closed Nov–March) is a Georgian building above the harbour on Hillsborough Terrace. The area's best **campsites** are around Morte Point – good choices are *North Morte Farm* (☎01271/870381; closed Oct–Easter), five hundred yards from the beach, also offering caravans for rent; and *Napps*, three and a half miles east towards Combe Martin (☎01271/882557), complete with tennis courts and swimming pool – bus #30 goes there. Near Ilfracombe's bus station on Broad Street, the *Landpiper Inn* has a good selection of **food**.

In **Woolacombe**, the *Combe Ridge Hotel* on the Esplanade, on the outskirts of town (☎01271/870321; no credit cards; ②) offers standard rooms, while in **Croyde**, you might try *West Winds*, on Moor Lane (☎01271/890489, *chris@croydewestwinds.freeserve.com*; ③), which has access to the beach. The **tourist office** is on the Esplanade (Easter–Oct Mon–Sat 10am–5pm, Sun 10am–4pm; reduced hours Nov–Easter; ☎01271/870553).

Bideford Bay

Bideford Bay (sometimes called Barnstaple Bay) encapsulates the variety of Devon, encompassing the downmarket beach resort of **Westward Ho!**, the savage windlashed rocks of **Hartland Point** and the photogenic village of **Clovelly**. **Instow** and **Appledore**, sheltered towns in the mouth of the Torridge estuary, have a lower-key attraction, while **Bideford** itself is mainly a transit centre, with some decent accommodation and bus connections to all the towns on the bay, and regular boats for Lundy.

Bideford

Like Barnstaple, nine miles to the east, the estuary town of **BIDEFORD** formed an important link in the north Devon trade network, mainly due to its **bridge**, which still straddles the River Torridge. First built in 1300, the bridge was reconstructed in stone in the following century, and subsequently reinforced and widened, hence the irregularity of its twenty-four arches, no two of which have the same span. Bideford's greatest prosperity arose in the seventeenth and eighteenth centuries, when it enjoyed a flourishing trade with the New World, and today the tree-lined quay along the west riverbank is still the focal point for the knot of narrow shop-lined streets.

From the Norman era until the eighteenth century, the port was the property of the Grenville family, whose most celebrated scion was **Richard Grenville**, commander of the ships that carried the first settlers to Virginia, and later a major player in the defeat of the Spanish Armada. Grenville also featured in *Westward Ho!*, the historical romance by **Charles Kingsley** who wrote part of the book in Bideford and is thus commemorated by a statue at the quay's northern end. Behind, **Victoria Park** extends up the riverbank, containing guns captured from the Spanish in 1588.

Alongside the park is the **tourist office** (Easter–June & Sept Mon–Sat 10am–5pm, Sun 10am–1pm; July & Aug Mon–Sat 10am–5pm, Sun 10am–4pm; Oct–Easter Mon–Fri

10am–4.30pm, Sat 10am–4pm; ☎01237/477676), from which you can pick up an accommodation list as well as information on coastal cruises and the boat to Lundy (see p.403) – tickets from here or the booths along the quayside. A useful **B&B** nearby is the *Cornerhouse*, 14 The Strand, two minutes from Victoria Park (☎01237/473722; no credit cards; ①). Further out, on Northam Road, the attractive *Mount* (☎01237/473748, *alex@laugharne1.freeserve.com*; ②) is set in its own walled gardens, while the classy *Royal Hotel* (☎01237/472005, *info@royalbideford.co.uk*; ⑤), just over the old bridge on Barnstaple Street, offers comfortable rooms but no views. Cooper Street, running up from the quay, has a good-value **restaurant**, the *Vagabond Cavalier*, and further up that street, *Cooper's* serves up coffees and daytime snacks. Round the corner on Mill Street, the *Heavitree Arms* has bar snacks.

For exploring the Tarka Trail by **bike**, there's Bideford Bicycle Hire, Torrington St (☎01237/424123), two hundred yards south of the bridge on the far riverbank (£9 per day).

Appledore and Instow

The old shipbuilding port of **APPLEDORE**, near the confluence of the Taw and Torridge rivers, still has several operating boatyards and a small sailing fleet moored in the river, but the peaceful pastel-coloured Georgian houses give little hint of the extent of the industry in earlier times. There are a few **B&Bs** overlooking the estuary on Marine Parade, including *Regency House* at no. 2 (☎01237/473689; ①); otherwise try the pleasant *Seagate Hotel* right on the Quay (☎01237/472589; ①), where rooms with a view slip up a couple of price codes.

In summer, foot passengers can take the five-minute ferry journey (April–Oct; every 15min during high tide; £1.50) across to **INSTOW**, whose sandy beach stretches in a long line, broadening to a muddy flat at low tide. There's another good accommodation option here – *Pilton Cottage*, Victoria Terrace, Marine Parade (☎01271/860202; no credit cards; ②), across the road from the beach. *Worlington House* **youth hostel** (☎01271/860394; closed Nov–March) occupies a large Victorian country house overlooking the estuary three-quarters of a mile inland from here.

Westward Ho!

WESTWARD HO!, three miles northwest of Bideford, is the only English town to be named after a book. After the publication of Kingsley's historical romance in 1855, speculators recognized the tourist potential of what was then an empty expanse of sand and mud pounded by Atlantic rollers, and the town's first villa was built within a decade. Rudyard Kipling spent four years of his youth here, as described by him in *Stalky and Co*, and his presence is recalled in Kipling Terrace – the site of his school – and **Kipling Tors**, the heights at the west end of the three-mile sand and pebble beach.

Kingsley didn't think much of the new resort when he paid a visit, and he certainly wouldn't care for it now, with its spawning amusement arcades, caravan sites and holiday chalets, and its substandard seawater. You might content yourself with the walk along the beach towards the west, or the excellent views from the Tors.

Clovelly

The impossibly picturesque village of **CLOVELLY**, which must have featured on more calendars, biscuit boxes and tourist posters than anywhere else in the West Country, was put on the map in the second half of the nineteenth century by two books: Charles Dickens's *A Message From the Sea* and, inevitably, *Westward Ho!* Charles Kingsley's father was rector here for six years. To an extent, the tone of the village has been preserved since then by limiting hotel accommodation and precluding holiday homes, but on summer days it's impossible to see past the artifice. Although the strict commercial control has meant that the presence of coach parties has been contained, there's still a fairly regular stream of visitors.

The first hurdle to surmount is the horrific **visitors centre** (daily 9am–5pm), where you are charged £2.50 for access to shops, snack bars and an audiovisual show, and also for use of the car park (it's well-nigh impossible to leave your motor anywhere else). Walkers, cyclists and users of public transport have right of way to the village, even if it means a tiresome detour round the oversized complex. Below the centre, the cobbled, traffic-free main street plunges past neat, flower-smothered cottages where sledges are tethered for transporting goods – the only way to carry supplies since the use of donkeys ceased.

At the bottom lies Clovelly's stony beach and tiny harbour, snuggled under a cleft in the cliff wall. A lifeboat operates from here, and a handful of fishing boats are the only remnants of a fleet which provided the village's main business before the herring stocks became depleted. The jetty was built in the fourteenth century to shelter the coast's only safe harbour between Appledore and Boscastle in Cornwall. If you can't face the return climb, take the Land Rover which leaves about every fifteen minutes from behind the *Red Lion* (Easter–Oct 9am–5.30pm; 80p) back to the top of the village. It is here, immediately below the visitors centre, that Hobby Drive begins, a three-mile walk you can make along the cliffs through woods of sycamore, oak, beech, rowan and the occasional holly, with grand views over the village.

You can reach Clovelly by Western National #319, which traces a route from Barnstaple to Bude, also passing through Hartland and Bideford. There are just two **hotels** in the village, both pricey: the *New Inn* halfway down the High Street (☎01237/431303; ⑤), and, enjoying the best position of all, the *Red Lion* at the harbour (☎01237/431237; ⑥). Below the *New Inn* is a small **B&B**, *Donkey Hill Cottage* (☎01237/431601; no credit cards; ①) which you should book a long way in advance. There's a greater selection of guesthouses a twenty-minute walk up from the visitors centre in Higher Clovelly; go for the *Old Smithy*, on the main road (☎01237/431202; no credit cards; ①) or, farther out, *Fuchsia Cottage* on Burscott Lane (☎01237/431398; no credit cards; ①), a modern house enjoying views from its first-floor rooms. Clovelly's best **eating** option is the *Red Lion*, which offers a three-course dinner for £17.50.

Hartland Point and around

You could drive along minor roads to **Hartland Point**, ten miles west of Clovelly, but the best approach is on foot along the coastal path. Shortly before arriving, the path touches at the only sandy beach between Westward Ho! and the Cornish border, **Shipload Bay**. The headland presents one of Devon's most dramatic sights, its jagged black rocks battered by the sea and overlooked by a solitary lighthouse 350ft up. South of Hartland Point, the saw-toothed rocks and near-vertical escarpments defiantly confront the waves, with spectacular waterfalls tumbling over the cliffs. This sheer stretch of coast has seen dozens of shipwrecks over the centuries, though many must have been prevented by the sight of the fourteenth-century tower of **St Nectan's** – a couple of miles south of the point in the village of Stoke – which acted as a landmark to sailors before the construction of the lighthouse. At 128ft, it is the tallest church tower in north Devon, and overlooks a weathered old graveyard containing memorials to various members of the Lane family – of the Bodley Head and Penguin publishing empire – who were associated with the area; inside, the church boasts a finely carved roodscreen and a Norman font, all covered by a repainted wagon-type roof. Tea and home-made scones are served on Wednesdays, Thursdays and weekends in summer at *Stoke Barton Farm*, just opposite, which also provides **B&B** (☎01237/441238; no credit cards; ①) and basic camping facilities.

Half a mile east of the church, gardens and lush woodland surround **Hartland Abbey** (May–Sept Wed, Thurs & Sun 2–5.30pm; also Tues 2–5.30pm in July & Aug;

£4.25), an eighteenth-century country house incorporating the ruins of an abbey dissolved in 1539, and displaying fine furniture, old photographs and recently uncovered frescoes. There are three pubs and a café in **HARTLAND** itself, further inland, while **HARTLAND QUAY** is a scatter of houses around the remains of a once-busy port, financed in part by the beneficence of the mariners Raleigh, Drake and Hawkins, but mostly destroyed by storms in the last century. About one mile south of here, **Speke's Mill Mouth** is a select surfers' beach. The *Hartland Quay* hotel is a great place to stay in the area (☎01237/441218; ②), and there is a **youth hostel** in a converted Victorian schoolhouse at Elmscott, two miles south and about half a mile inland (☎01237/441367; closed Sept–March). The only public transport is the Western National bus #319; alight at Hartland.

Lundy Island

There are fewer than twenty full-time residents on **Lundy**, a tiny windswept island twelve miles north of Hartland Point. Now a refuge for thousands of marine birds, Lundy has no cars, just one pub and one shop – indeed little has changed since the Marisco family established itself here in the twelfth century, making use of the shingle beaches and coves to terrorize shipping along the Bristol Channel. The family's fortunes only fell in 1242 when one of their number, William de Marisco, was found to be plotting against the king, whereupon he was hanged, drawn and quartered at Tower Hill in London.

After the Mariscos, Lundy's most famous inhabitants were Thomas Benson, MP for Barnstaple in the eighteenth century – who was discovered using slave labour to work the granite quarries, and later found guilty of a massive insurance fraud – and **William Hudson Heaven**, who bought the island in 1834 and established what became known as the "Kingdom of Heaven". His home, **Millcombe House**, an incongruous piece of Georgian architecture in the desolate surroundings, is one of many relics of former habitation scattered around the island, though a recent addition compared with the castle standing on Lundy's southern end, erected by Henry III following the downfall of the Mariscos.

Tracks and footpaths interweave all over the island, and walking is really the only thing to do here. Inland, the grass, heather and bog is crossed by drystone walls and grazed by ponies, goats, deer and the rare soay sheep. The shores – mainly cliffy on the west, softer and undulating on the east – shelter a rich variety of **birdlife**, including kittiwakes, fulmars, shags and Manx shearwaters, which often nest in rabbit burrows. The most famous birds, though, are the **puffins** after which Lundy is named – from the Norse *Lunde* (puffin) and *ey* (island). They can only be sighted in April and May, when they come ashore to mate. Offshore, grey seals can be seen all the year round.

Practicalities

The Oldenburg crosses to Lundy from Bideford throughout the year apart from a few weeks in January and February, with additional sailings from Ilfracombe and from Clovelly from April to September (1–4 weekly). From Bideford, sailings increase in frequency from twice a week in winter to four times in midsummer, taking two and a quarter hours; day return tickets cost around £24, period returns £35 (reservations ☎01237/470422). A quicker but extravagant alternative is to go by **helicopter**, which makes the journey in just ten minutes from Lake Heliport, near Abbotsham, between Bideford and Westward Ho!, and will cost you around £330 return (☎01237/421054).

Accommodation on the island can be booked up months in advance, and B&B is only available in houses which have not already been taken for weekly rentals. Since B&B bookings can only be made within two weeks of the proposed visit, this limits the options, though outside the holiday season it is still eminently possible to find a double room for under £45 per night. **Bookings** must be made through the Landmark Trust's Shore Office in Bideford (☎01237/470422). Options range from the remote *Admiralty Lookout* (lacking electricity and with only hand-pumped water) to the two-storey granite *Barn*, a hostel sleeping fourteen. More comfort can be found at the *Old House*, where Charles Kingsley stayed in 1849, or the *Old Light*, a lighthouse built in 1820 by the architect of Dartmoor Prison. A single person might find the *Radio Room* cosy; it once housed the radio transmitter that was the island's only link with the outside world. There's also a **campsite** on the island open throughout the year, though it can get pretty rain- and windswept in winter.

CORNWALL

When D.H. Lawrence wrote that being in **Cornwall** was "like being at a window and looking out of England", he wasn't just thinking of its geographical extremity. Virtually unaffected by the Roman conquest, Cornwall was for centuries the last haven for a **Celtic culture** elsewhere eradicated by the Saxons – a land where princes communed with Breton troubadours, where chroniclers and scribes composed the epic tales of Arthurian heroism, and where itinerant monks from Welsh and Irish monasteries disseminated an elemental and visionary Christianity. Primitive granite crosses and a crop of Celtic saints remain as traces of this formative period, and though the Cornish language had ebbed away by the eighteenth century, it is recalled in Celtic place names that in many cases have grown more exotic as they have become corrupted over time.

Another strand of Cornwall's folkloric character comes from the **smugglers** who thrived here right up until the last century, exploiting the sheltered creeks and hidden anchorages of the southern coasts. For many fishing villages, such as Polperro and Mousehole, contraband provided an important secondary income, as did the looting of the ships that regularly came to grief on the reefs and rocks. Further distinguishing it from its neighbour, Cornwall has also had a strong **industrial economy**, based mainly on the mining of **copper** and **tin** in the north, centred on the towns of Redruth and St Agnes, and in the south on the deposits of **china clay**, which are still being mined in the area around St Austell.

Nowadays, of course, Cornwall's most flourishing industry is tourism. The repercussions of the holiday business on Cornwall have been uneven, for instance shamefully defacing **Land's End** with a clutter of pseudo-historical twaddle but leaving Cornwall's other great promontory, **Lizard Point**, untainted. Examples of what happens when all the stops are pulled out can be seen in the thronged resort of **Falmouth** and its north-coast equivalent, **Newquay**, the West's chief surfing centre, though in some ways the full-blown resorts have a greater air of authenticity than the quainter villages that have succumbed to the sell-out, such as **Mevagissey**, **Polperro** and **Padstow**. Others, such as **Boscastle** or **Charlestown**, are hardly touched, however, and you couldn't wish for anything more remote than **Bodmin Moor**, a tract of wilderness in the heart of Cornwall – and even **Tintagel**, site of what is fondly known as King Arthur's castle, has preserved its sense of desolation. Other places have reached a happy compromise with the seasonal influx, like **St Ives**, **Fowey** and **Bude**, or else are saved from over-exploitation by sheer distance, as is the case with the **Isles of Scilly**. Throughout the county, though, it only requires a shift of a few miles to escape the crowds, and there are enough good beaches around for everyone to find a space.

The best way to reach the quietest spots is along the **South West Coast Path**, but a car is almost indispensable for anyone wanting to see a lot in a short time, as the system of public transport is limited to a couple of **rail** branch lines off the main line to Penzance and a thin network of local bus services.

From Looe to Veryan Bay

The southeast strip of the Cornish coast from Looe to Veryan Bay holds a string of medieval harbour towns tarnished by various degrees of commercialization, but there are also a few spots where you can experience the best of Cornwall, including some wonderful coastline. The main rail stop is **St Austell**, the capital of Cornwall's china clay industry, though there is a branch line connecting nearby **Par** with the north coast at Newquay. To the east of St Austell Bay, the touristy **Polperro** and **Looe** are easily accessible by bus from Plymouth, and there's a rail link to Looe from Liskeard. The estuary town of **Fowey**, in a niche of Cornwall closely associated with the author Daphne Du Maurier, is most easily reached by bus from St Austell and Par, as is **Mevagissey**, to the west.

Looe and Polperro

LOOE was drawing crowds as early as 1800, when the first "bathing-machines" were wheeled out, but the arrival of the railway in 1879 was what really packed its beaches. Though Looe now touts itself as something of a shark-fishing centre, most people come here for the sand, the handiest stretch being the beach in front of East Looe – the busier half of the river-divided town. If you walk a mile eastwards you'll find a cleaner spot to swim at **Millendreath**. Most of Looe's attractions are in boating and bathing, though if the weather's bad you could always shelter in the **Old Guildhall Museum** (May–Sept Mon–Fri & Sun 11.30am–4.30pm; £1), a diverse collection of maritime models and exhibits, though none so interesting as the building itself, a fifteenth-century construction preserving its prisoners' cells and raised magistrates' benches.

East Looe's **tourist office** is at the Guildhall on the main Fore Street (Easter & May to mid-Sept daily 10am–5pm; April & mid-Sept to Oct daily 10am–2pm; ☎01503/262072). There's plenty of **accommodation** here: for estuary views, try the *Dolphin Hotel* (☎01503/262578; no credit cards; ①), but for more character, head for *Osborne House*, a converted cottage in Lower Chapel Street, close to the harbour (☎01503/262970; ②; closed Nov & Jan), or *Sea Breeze*, a three-storey B&B further up the same street (☎01503/263131; ③) – both of which have moderately priced **restaurants**. Other places to eat include the *Cellar Wine Bar* for inexpensive lunches on the harbourside, and, opposite on Buller Quay, the posher *Trawlers* (☎01503/263593; closed Sun), whose French-inspired menu concentrates mainly on lobster and other seafood, at moderate-to-expensive prices. For plainer food, try the inexpensive *Golden Guinea* on Fore Street, a seventeenth-century building that does a brisk trade in staple seaside meals as well as cream teas.

Looe is linked by hourly buses with neighbouring **POLPERRO**, a smaller and quainter place, but with a similar feel. From the bus stop and car park at the top of the village, it's a five- or ten-minute walk alongside the River Pol to the minuscule harbour. The tightly packed houses rising on each side of the stream present an undeniably pretty sight, little changed since the village's heyday of smuggling and pilchard fishing, but the "discovery" of Polperro has almost ruined it, and its straggling main street – the Coombes – is now an unbroken row of tourist shops and fast-food outlets.

Polperro's best places to **stay** are *New House* on Talland Hill (☎01503/272206; no credit cards; ②), right on the harbour with a garden, or *Lanhael House*, a period building with gardens and pool in a quiet spot above the car park (☎01503/272428; ④; closed Nov–May). Closer to the harbour but still relatively secluded, the *Old Mill House* is an agreeable old pub on Mill Hill offering eight comfortable rooms (☎01503/272362; ③), and good **food**. The non-smoking *Kitchen* on the Coombes is good for evening dining, especially if you're a vegetarian or seafood fan. Also on the main road, the *Plantation Café* provides cream teas and snacks (closed Sat).

Fowey and around

The ten miles west from Polperro to **Polruan** are among the best stretches of the coastal path in south Cornwall, giving access to some beautiful secluded sand beaches. There are frequent ferries across the River Fowey from Polruan, giving a fine view of the quintessential Cornish port of **FOWEY** (pronounced "Foy"), a cascade of neat, pale terraces at the mouth of one of the peninsula's greatest rivers. The major port on the county's south coast in the fourteenth century, Fowey finally became so ambitious that it provoked Edward IV to strip the town of its military capability, though it continued to thrive commercially, coming into its own as the leading port for china clay shipments in the last century. In addition to the bulkier freighters sailing from wharves north of the town, the harbour today is crowded with trawlers and yachts, giving the town a brisk, purposeful character lacking in many of Cornwall's south-coast ports.

Fowey's steep layout centres on the church of **St Fimbarrus**, a distinctive fifteenth-century construction replacing a church that was sacked by the French. The church marks the traditional end of the ancient **Saints' Way footpath** from Padstow, linking the north and south Cornish coasts (see p.431). Beside St Fimbarrus, the **Literary Centre** on South Street is a small exhibition including a twelve-minute video of Daphne Du Maurier's life and work (mid-May to mid-Sept daily 10am–5pm; free), while behind the church stands **Place House**, an extravagance belonging to the local Treffry family, with a Victorian Gothic tower grafted onto the fifteenth- and sixteenth-century fortified building. Below the church, the **Ship Inn**, sporting some fine Elizabethan panelling and plaster ceilings, was originally home to the Rashleighs – a recurring name in the annals of this region – and held the local Roundhead HQ during the Civil War. From here, Fore Street, Lostwithiel Street and the Esplanade fan out, the **Esplanade** leading to a footpath that gives access to some splendid walks around the coast. Past the remains of a blockhouse that once supported a defensive chain hung across the river's mouth, the small beach of **Readymoney Cove** is soon reached – so-called either because it was where smugglers buried their ill-gotten gains, or because it was where the flotsam of shipwrecks came ashore. Close by stand the ruins of **St Catherine's Castle**, built by Thomas Treffry on the orders of Henry VIII, and offering fine views across the estuary.

You don't have to take on the entire thirty miles of the Saints' Way to get the flavour of this trail, though if you prefer a circular route you can try the **Hall Walk**, a scenic four-mile hike north of Fowey. More details are available from the tourist office, though it's simple enough: cross the river on the car ferry (at the car park north of town) to **Bodinnick**, walk downstream on the other side, crossing the footbridge over the narrow creek of Pont Pill, then take the passenger ferry back from Polruan. The route passes a memorial to "Q", alias Sir Arthur Quiller-Couch, who lived on Fowey's Esplanade between 1892 and 1944, and whose writings helped popularize the place he called "Troy Town". Fans of Daphne Du Maurier can join a guided walk (summer only) around scenes described in the author's books – contact the tourist office for details.

Beyond the west bank ferry stage you come to **Golant**, a riverside hamlet a little more than a mile from the Iron Age fort of **Castle Dore**, which features in Arthurian romance as the residence of King Mark of Cornwall, husband of Iseult. You can also get to the fort from Fowey on bus #24, though there is still a ten-minute walk from the stop on the crossroads.

LOSTWITHIEL, three miles further upriver (train from Par, or bus or train from St Austell), is an old market town on the lowest bridging point of the Fowey. It's an appealing mixture of Georgian houses and dark cobbled passageways, with a peculiar, Breton-inspired octagonal spire on St Bartholomew's church. The town lies below the watchful eye of **Restormel Castle** (April–Sept daily 10am–6pm; Oct daily 10am–5pm; £1.60; EH), a shale-built shell of a circular keep that crowns a hill a mile or so north. It's a peaceful, panoramic spot, last seeing service when Royalist forces prised it out of the hands of the Earl of Essex's Parliamentarian army in 1644.

Practicalities

Separated from eastern routes by its river, Fowey is most accessible by twice-hourly #24 **buses** from St Austell. There is a small **tourist office** in the town's post office on Custom House Hill (May–Sept Mon–Fri 9am–5.30pm, Sat 9am–5pm, Sun 10am–5pm; Oct–April Mon–Fri 9am–1pm & 2pm–5pm, Sat 9am–1pm; ☎01726/833616). All of the central pubs offer **B&B**; on Lostwithiel Street, try the *Ship* (☎01726/833751; ④) or the *Safe Harbour* (☎01726/833379; no credit cards; ②), both offering en-suite rooms and parking. At 6 Fore Street is the *Dwelling House* (☎01726/833662; ②), with three en-suite rooms, the best of them in the attic. The *Marina Hotel*, on the Esplanade (☎01726/833315; ⑤), is a plusher place, also with a garden and river views; rooms with views cost more. Outside Fowey, *Coombe Farm* (☎01726/833123; no credit cards; ①) provides perfect rural isolation while being only about twenty minutes' walk from town, at the end of a lane off the B3269 – and there's a bathing area just three hundred metres away. There is a **youth hostel** outside Golant at *Penquite House*, a Georgian mansion with views over the valley (☎01726/833507, golant@yha.org.uk; closed Dec & Jan). The nearest **campsite** is at *Yeate Farm* (☎01726/870256; closed Nov–Feb), on the eastern bank of the river, three-quarters of a mile up from the Bodinnick ferry crossing.

Fowey has some good seafood **restaurants**; among the best is *Ellis's* at 3 the Esplanade (☎01726/832359), specializing in lobster, and *Food For Thought* on the quay, which offers a weekday fixed-price menu of fish dishes (☎01726/832221) – both are quite formal, expensive places. The area is also well provided with worthy **pubs**, some of which can be sampled on walkabouts, such as Golant's *Fisherman's Arms*, the *Old Ferry Inn* at Bodinnick and Polruan's excellent *Lugger Inn*. The *Old Ferry* also has comfortable rooms (☎01726/870237; ②, ⑤ for a room with a view).

St Austell and its bay

It was the discovery of china clay, or kaolin, in the downs to the north of **ST AUSTELL** that spurred the town's growth in the eighteenth century. An essential ingredient in the production of porcelain, kaolin had until then only been produced in northern China, where a high ridge, or *kao-lin*, was the sole known source of the raw material. Still a vital part of Cornwall's economy, the clay is now mostly exported for use in the manufacture of paper, as well as paint and medicines. The conical spoil heaps left by the mines are a feature of the local landscape, especially on Hensbarrow Downs to the north, the great green and white mounds making an eerie sight.

St Austell's nearest link to the sea is at **CHARLESTOWN**, an easy downhill walk from the centre. This unassuming and unspoilt port is named after the entrepreneur Charles Rashleigh, who in 1791 began work on the harbour in what was then a small fishing community two miles south of St Austell, widening its streets to accommodate the clay wagons daily passing through. The wharves are still used, loading clay onto vessels that appear oversized beside the tiny jetties. Behind the harbour, the **Shipwreck Museum** (March–Oct daily 10am–6pm; £4.45) is entered through tunnels once used to convey the clay to the docks, and shows a good collection of photos and relics as well as tableaux of historical scenes.

On each side of the dock the coarse sand and stone **beaches** have small rock pools, above which cliff walks lead around St Austell Bay. Eastwards, you soon arrive at overdeveloped **Carlyon Bay**, whose main resort is **Par**. The beaches here get clogged with clay – the best swimming is to be found by pressing on to the sheltered crescent of **Polkerris**. The easternmost limit of St Austell Bay is marked by **Gribbin Head**, near which stands Menabilly House, where Daphne Du Maurier lived for 24 years – it was the model for the "Manderley" of *Rebecca*. The house is not open to the public, but you can walk down to Polridmouth Cove, where Rebecca met her watery end.

Practicalities

Trains on the main London–Penzance line serve St Austell, with most services also stopping at Par, which is also connected to Newquay on the north coast. Western National run an hourly **bus** service linking St Austell, Charlestown, Par and Polkerris.

Charlestown has two really attractive places **to stay**: *T'Gallants* (☎01726/70203; ②), a smart Georgian B&B at the back of the harbour where cream teas are served in the garden; and the *Pier House Hotel* (☎01726/67955; ④), with a premium harbourside location and a restaurant offering a good-value Carvery lunch on Sunday. Behind *T'Gallants*, the *Rashleigh Arms* offers real ale and a range of food, though the most highly commended **pub** in the area is the *Rashleigh Inn* at Polkerris. The best **campsite** in St Austell Bay is *Par Sands* (☎01726/812868; closed Nov–March), next to Par beach.

Mevagissey to Veryan Bay

MEVAGISSEY was once known for the construction of fast vessels, used for carrying contraband as well as pilchards. Today the tiny port might display a few stacks of lobster pots, but the real business is tourism, and in summer the maze of backstreets is saturated with day-trippers, converging on the inner harbour and overflowing onto the large sand beach at **Pentewan** a mile to the north, despite the poor water quality.

Past the headland to the south of Mevagissey, the small sandy cove of **Portmellon** retains little of its boatbuilding activities but is freer of tourists. Further still, **GORRAN HAVEN** was formerly a crab-fishing village but now looks merely suburban, though it has a neat rock-and-sand beach, and a footpath that winds round to the even more attractive **Vault Beach**, half a mile south. South of here juts the most striking headland on Cornwall's southern coast, **Dodman Point**, cause of many a wreck and topped by a stark granite cross built by a local parson as a seamark in 1896. The promontory holds the substantial remains of an Iron Age fort, with an earthwork bulwark cutting right across the point.

Curving away to the west, the elegant parabola of **Veryan Bay** is barely touched by commercialism. Just west of Dodman Point lies one of Cornwall's most beautiful coves, **Hemmick Beach**, an excellent swimming spot with rocky outcrops affording a measure of privacy. Visually even more impressive is **Porthluney Cove**, a crescent of sand whose centrepiece is the battlemented **Caerhays Castle**, (mid-March to mid-April Mon–Fri 2–4pm; gardens mid-March to mid-May Mon–Fri 10am–4pm; house £3.50; garden £3.50; combined ticket £6) built in 1808 by John Nash and surrounded by beautiful gardens which are open in spring and on occasional charity days only.

A little farther on, the minuscule and whitewashed **Portloe** is fronted by jagged black rocks that throw up fountains of seaspray, giving it a good, end-of-the-road kind of atmosphere. Sequestered inland, **VERYAN** has a pretty village green and pond, but is best known for its curious circular white houses built in the last century by one Reverend Jeremiah Trist. A lane from Veryan leads down to one of the cleanest swimming spots on Cornwall's southern coast, **Pendower Beach**. Two-thirds of a mile long and backed by dunes, Pendower joins with the neighbouring **Carne Beach** at low tide to create a long sandy continuum.

Practicalities

From St Austell's train station, **bus** #26 or #26A leave hourly for Mevagissey, sometimes continuing to Gorran Haven. Veryan and Portloe are reachable on #51 from Truro. Right in the heart of Mevagissey, the old *Ship Inn* (☎01726/843324; ③) offers reasonable **accommodation**; alternatively try *Mevagissey House* (☎01726/842427;

no credit cards; ③; closed Nov–Feb), a nineteenth-century vicarage on Vicarage Hill. You might appreciate the coast better by staying in Portmellon, where the weathered old *Rising Sun Inn* (☎01726/843235; ③; closed Nov to mid-March) confronts the sea. In Gorran Haven, the well-situated *Llawnroc Inn* (☎01726/843461; ③) is the only budget option; all rooms here are en suite. The nearest **youth hostel** (☎01726/843234; closed Nov–March) is in a former farmhouse at **Boswinger**, a remote spot half a mile from Hemmick Beach. Difficult to reach without your own transport, it's about a mile from the bus stop at Gorran Church Town, served infrequently by some #26 buses. Boswinger also has a **campsite**, *Sea View* (☎01726/843425; closed Oct–Easter), with, as the name implies, a panoramic position overlooking Veryan Bay; book ahead here in July and August. If you want to stay in **Veryan**, head for the *New Inn*, a friendly pub which serves wholesome meals and provides B&B (☎01872/501362; ②).

There's no shortage of **restaurants** in Mevagissey, most specializing in fish – for location you might try the large harbourfront *Shark's Fin Hotel*. The *Cellar Bar* on Church Street and the *Fountain Inn* on Fore Street are pubs with grub.

St Mawes to Falmouth

Lush tranquillity collides with frantic tourist activity around **Carrick Roads**, the complex estuary basin to the south of **Truro**, the region's main centre for transport and accommodation. On the eastern shore, the luxuriant **Roseland** peninsula is a backwater of woods and sheltered creeks between the River Fal and the sea. **St Mawes** is the main draw here, chiefly on account of its castle, a twin of Pendennis across the neck of the estuary in **Falmouth**, a major resort at the end of a branch line from Truro, itself a stop on the main line to Penzance.

St Mawes and the Roseland peninsula

Stuck at the very end of a prong of land down at the bottom of Carrick Roads, the secluded, unhurried town of **ST MAWES** has an attractive walled seafront lying below a hillside of villas and abundant gardens. Just out of sight at the end of the seafront stands the small and pristine **St Mawes Castle** (April–Sept daily 10am–6pm; Oct daily 10am–5pm; Nov–March Mon–Wed & Fri–Sun 10am–1pm & 2–4pm; £2.50; EH). Built during the reign of Henry VIII, the castle owes its excellent condition to its early surrender during the Civil War when it was placed under siege by Parliamentary forces in 1646, a move which hastened the bloody occupation of Pendennis Castle over in Falmouth. Both castles adhere to the same clover leaf design, with a central round keep surrounded by robust gun-emplacements, but this is the more attractive of the pair. The dungeons and gun installations contain various artillery exhibits as well as some background on local social history.

Moving away from St Mawes, you could spend a pleasant afternoon poking around the Roseland peninsula between the Percuil River and the eastern shore of Carrick Roads. It's only two and a half miles to the scattered hamlet of **ST JUST-IN-ROSE-LAND**, where the strikingly picturesque church of St Just stands right next to the creek, surrounded by palms and subtropical shrubbery, its gravestones tumbling down to the water's edge.

A couple of miles farther north, the chain-driven King Harry **ferry** (summer daily 8am–9pm; winter Mon–Sat 8am–7pm, Sun 10am–5pm; £2.50 per car; foot-passengers 20p) crosses the River Fal about every twenty minutes, docking close to **Trelissick Garden** (April–Sept Mon–Sat 10.30am–5.30pm, Sun 12.30–5.30pm; March & Oct closes at 5pm; £4.20; NT), which is celebrated for its hydrangeas and other Mediterranean species, and has a splendid woodland walk along the Fal (free access). Take buses #51B or #T7 to get here.

In summer, there's a **ferry** from St Mawes to the southern arm of the Roseland Peninsula, which holds the twelfth- to thirteenth-century church of St **Anthony's** and the **lighthouse** on St Anthony's Head, marking the entry into Carrick Roads. There's also a ferry crossing from St Mawes to Falmouth (every 30min in summer, less frequent in winter).

Practicalities

St Mawes makes an attractive – though fairly pricey – place to **stay**. Located right on the seafront, *St Mawes Hotel* (☎01326/270266; ⑨; closed Nov to mid-Feb) enjoys a glorious view over the estuary, but you'll find a more relaxed reception down the road at the *Rising Sun* (☎01326/270233; ③), which also has a good restaurant. Less expensive rooms can be found away from the sea; one good budget choice is the *Malt House* (☎01326/270129; ④), which offers a spacious en-suite room with sea views. There's a decent **campsite** at Trethem Mill, three miles inland from St Mawes (☎01872/580504; closed Nov–March). Back in St Mawes, the *Victory Inn* is a fine old oak-beamed **pub** just off the seafront.

Truro

TRURO, seat of Cornwall's law courts and other county bureaucracies, has a distinctly small-scale provincial feel, even if its Georgian houses do reflect the prosperity that came with the tin-mining boom of the 1800s. Blurring the town's overall identity, its modern shopping centre stands alongside the powerful but chronologically confused **Cathedral**. Completed in 1910, this was the first Anglican cathedral to be built in England since St Paul's, but it incorporates part of the fabric of the old parish church that previously occupied the site. The airy interior's best feature is the neo-Gothic baptistry, with its emphatically pointed arches and elaborate roof vaulting. To the right of the choir, St Mary's aisle is a relic of the original Perpendicular building, other fragments of which adorn the walls, including – in the north transept – a colourful Jacobean memorial to local Parliamentarian John Robartes and his wife.

The only other item to keep you in Truro is the **Royal Cornwall Museum** (Mon–Sat 10am–5pm; £2.50) housed in an elegant Georgian building on River Street. The exhibits include minerals, toys and paintings by Cornish artists. In summer, passenger **ferries** depart four times daily from the quayside on a scenic river cruise to Falmouth (about £5 return).

Practicalities

Truro's **tourist office** is on Boscawen Street (Easter–May, Sept & Oct Mon–Fri 9am–5.15pm, Sat 10am–1pm; June–Aug Mon–Fri 9am–6pm, Sat 10am–5pm; Nov & Feb–Easter Mon–Thurs 9am–5.15pm, Fri 9am–5.45pm; Dec & Jan Mon–Fri 9am–4.45pm; ☎01872/274555). Buses stop nearby at Lemon Quay, or near the train station on Richmond Hill. Best **accommodation** near the train station is the *Gables*, at the bottom of Station Road at 49 Treyew Rd (☎01872/242318; ①), where all rooms have showers; near the centre of town, the *Bay Tree* is a restored Georgian house halfway between the station and the centre at 28 Ferris Town (☎01872/240274; ①). Much of Truro's inexpensive accommodation is on or around the pleasant Lemon Street: *Patmos*, 8 Burley Close, off Barrack Lane, where Lemon Street meets Falmouth Road, is a good non-smoking choice, with views over the river (☎01872/278018; ①). On the other side of the river, to the northwest of town, there are several more B&Bs on Tregolls Road, including the elegant *Conifers* at no. 36 (☎01872/279925; ①) and

Karenza at no. 72 (☎01872/274497; ①). The nearest **campsite** is *Carnon Downs*, three miles outside Truro on the A39 Falmouth road (☎01872/862283; closed Nov–March).

A good selection of Truro's **restaurants** lie on or around Kenwyn St, including *Number Ten* at no. 10, where you can choose wholesome dishes from around the world at inexpensive prices (☎01872/272363); teas, coffees and healthy fruit drinks are on the menu, or bring your own booze. There's an outdoor eating area round the back, as there is at the *Feast*, 15 Kenwyn St, which cooks up excellent wholefoods to eat in or take away, and offers a choice of Belgian beers (daytime only; closed Sun). Elsewhere in town, *Saffron* at 5 Quay St offers inexpensive brunches and an especially good-value pre-theatre menu (☎01872/263771; closed Sun), or you can stick with strictly Cornish fare at the *Oggy Oggy Pasty Company* on River Street, whose alluring range of freshly baked pasties draws queues at lunchtime (closed Sun). On the corner of Frances Street and Castle Street, *Oliver's* is an award-winning restaurant with moderate-to-expensive fixed-price menus (☎01872/273025; closed Sun). The adjoining *Wig and Pen* is a decent **pub** with bar food, real ale and jazz on Wednesdays and Fridays, and next door to that, the *Globe Inn* also serves hot snacks.

Falmouth

The construction of Pendennis Castle on the southern point of Carrick Roads in the six-teenth century prepared the ground for the growth of **FALMOUTH**, then no more than a fishing village. The building of its deepwater harbour was proposed a century later by Sir John Killigrew, and Falmouth's prosperity was assured when in 1689 it became chief base of the fast Falmouth Packets, which sped mail to the Americas. This century, though, Falmouth has shed most of its Cornishness, and, barring its castle, has little to offer anyone who wants to get away from the hard sell.

The long **High Street** and its continuations Market and Church streets are crammed with humdrum bars and cafés, though at the southern end, Arwenack Street does have the Tudor remains of the Killigrews' **Arwenack House**. The peculiar granite pyramid standing opposite the house, built in 1737, is probably intended to commemorate the local family, though its exact significance has never been clear. The dynasty's most eminent member was Thomas Killigrew, an indifferent Restoration dramatist who was also manager of the king's company of actors. The founder of London's Theatre Royal in Drury Lane, Charles II's former companion-in-exile obtained permission to use female actors for the first time on stage – thereby introducing Nell Gwyn to the king's notice. Apart from this, the centre of town only offers a clamber up the precipitous 111 steps of **Jacob's Ladder** from the Moor, the old town's main square, to give a bird's-eye view of the harbour. From the Prince of Wales Pier, below the Moor, frequent ferries leave for St Mawes, accompanied in summer by boats touring the local estuaries.

Standing sentinel at the tip of the promontory that separates Carrick Roads from Falmouth Bay, **Pendennis Castle** (daily: April–June & Sept 10am–6pm; July & Aug 9am–6pm; Oct 10am–5pm; Nov–March 10am–4pm; £2.70; EH) shows little evidence of its five-month siege by the Parliamentarians during the Civil War, which ended only when half its defenders had died and the rest had been starved into submission. Though this is a less-refined contemporary of the castle at St Mawes, its site wins hands down, facing right out to sea on its own pointed peninsula, the stout ramparts offering the best all-round views of Carrick Roads and Falmouth Bay. In August, the castle grounds stay open until 8pm.

Beyond Pendennis Point stretches a long sandy bay with various **beaches** backed by expensive hotels. If you wanted to swim, the best spot is from **Swanpool Beach**, accessible by cliff path from the more popular **Gyllyngvase Beach** – or walk a couple of miles farther on to **Maenporth**, from where there are some fine cliff-top walks.

Practicalities

Falmouth's **tourist office** is off the Moor, on Killigrew Street (Easter–June & Sept Mon–Thurs & Sat 9am–5pm, Fri 9am–4.45pm; July & Aug Mon–Thurs & Sat 9am–5pm, Fri 9am–4.45pm, Sun 10am–4pm; Oct–Easter Mon–Thurs 9am–1pm & 2–5pm, Fri 9am–1pm & 2–4.45pm; ☎01326/312300). Most of the town's **accommodation** is south, near the train station and beach area: on Melvill Rd, the *Ivanhoe* at no. 7 (☎01326/319083; ②) and the *Melvill House Hotel* run by a Franco-Scottish couple at no. 52 (☎01326/316645; ②) are good value, the latter also providing dinners by prior arrangement. If you prefer to be near the centre, you can't do better than the *Arwenack Hotel* at 27 Arwenack St (☎01326/311185; no credit cards; ①). Expect to pay more for places nearer the beaches: *Gyllyngvase House Hotel* is a staid but comfortable choice on Gyllyngvase Road (☎01326/312956; ③), two minutes from the sea, with a restaurant and views from two of its rooms, and *Chellowdene* (☎01326/314950; no credit cards; ③; closed Oct–April) on the parallel Gyllyngvase Hill has very similar rates, its well-equipped rooms just 50m from the sea. There's a perfectly sited **youth hostel** inside Pendennis Castle (☎01326/311435, *pendennis@yha.org.uk*; closed Dec to mid-Feb). Among the overdeveloped caravan parks on the coast south of Falmouth, the nearest **campsite** is *Tremorvah Tent Park* (☎01326/318311), about a mile outside town behind Swanpool Beach and on the coast path.

Pasties, pizzas and chips are available everywhere in Falmouth, but if you prefer to **eat** in congenial surroundings try *Bon Ton Roulet* on the High Street (closed Sun lunch) which has a good selection of fish and pasta dishes, as well as light snacks. Cheaper and simpler food is on offer down the steps opposite at the unlicensed *Simply Sugar* (closed Sun & Mon eve). The best fish in town is to be found off the main drag at the *Seafood Bar*, Lower Quay Hill (☎01326/315129; closed lunch, and all Sun & Mon), where thick crab soup is a speciality. The *Quayside Inn*, further up on Arwenack Street, is the pick of the **pubs**. Drivers might like to head out of town to the *Pandora Inn* at Mylor Bridge, four miles north of Falmouth, where you can drink by the water-side; superior bar food is available at lunchtime, or you can eat in the formal restaurant – good for fresh seafood (☎01326/372678).

The Lizard peninsula

The **Lizard peninsula** – from the Celtic *lys ardh*, or "high point" – preserves a thankfully undeveloped appearance in contrast to many other areas of Cornwall. If this flat and treeless expanse can be said to have a centre, it is **Helston**, a junction for buses running from Falmouth and Truro to the spartan villages of the peninsula's interior and the tiny fishing ports on its coast. From Falmouth, Truronian's #T4 takes about an hour to reach Helston, with a stop at Gweek. From Helston, which is linked to Penzance by the frequent Western National #2, bus routes into the Lizard peninsula are run by Truronian: #T1 – whose route takes in St Agnes, Redruth and Truro – goes to the village of **The Lizard** via Porthleven and **Mullion** and #T2 connects the east-coast villages of St Keverne and **Coverack** (neither service runs on Sun in winter).

The east coast to Lizard Point

To the north of the peninsula, the snug hamlets sprinkled in the valley of the **River Helford** are a complete contrast to the rugged character of most of the Lizard. At the river's mouth stands **MAWNAN**, whose granite church of St Mawnan-in-Meneage is dedicated to the sixth-century Welsh missionary Saint Maunanus – Meneage, rhyming with vague, means "land of monks". Upstream on the south side, **Frenchman's Creek** is one of a splay of creeks and arcane inlets running off the river, and was the inspira-

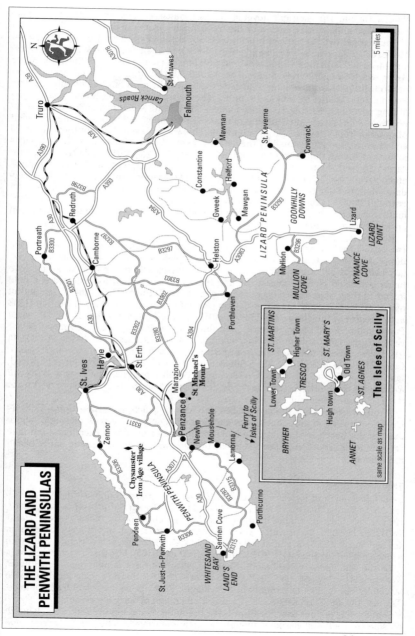

THE LIZARD AND
PENWITH PENINSULAS

The Isles of Scilly

same scale as map

© Crown copyright

tion for Daphne Du Maurier's novel of the same name – her evocation of it holds true: "still and soundless, surrounded by the trees, hidden from the eyes of men".

You can get over to the south bank by the seasonal ferry from Helford Passage to **Helford**, an agreeable old smugglers' haunt worth a snack-stop – *Rose Cottage* provides teas and light meals, or you can eat **pub** lunches in the garden of the *Shipwright's Arms,* overlooking the river. South of here, on the B3293, the broad windswept plateau of **Goonhilly Downs** is interrupted by the futuristic saucers of Goonhilly Satellite Station, and the nearby ranks of wind turbines. East, the road meets the coast at the fishing port of **COVERACK**, whose name – "Hideaway" – gives some indication of its one-time role as a centre of contraband. Three miles offshore lurk the dreaded **Manacles** rocks, the cause of numerous shipwrecks over the centuries, many of which were gleefully claimed by the local wreckers. Coverack has a few decent places to stay, including the pleasant and friendly *Bakery Cottage* (☎01326/280474; no credit cards; ①), with home cooking; at the seafront, ask in the *Harbour Lights* restaurant about vacancies in a neighbouring cottage that sleeps four, usually available for three-day minimum stays though occasionally available for one or two nights only (☎01326/280507; ①). There's a **youth hostel** just west of Coverack's centre overlooking the bay (☎01326/280687; closed Nov–March); the hostel also has information on windsurfing courses.

Beyond the safe and clean swimming spot of **Kennack Sands** – where *Sea Acres* (☎01326/290064; closed Nov–Feb) is one of a cluster of **campsites** – the south tip of the promontory, **Lizard Point**, is marked by a plain lighthouse and a couple of low-key cafés and gift shops. Sheltered from the ceaselessly churning sea, a tiny cove holds a disused lifeboat station. Behind the point, a road and footpath leads a mile inland to the nondescript village called simply **THE LIZARD**, holding a handful of places to sleep and eat: the non-smoking *Caerthillian* is a comfortable Victorian **B&B** in the centre of the village (☎01326/290019, *caerthillian@connexions.co.uk*; ②), while Penmenner Road has several possibilities, including *Parc Brawse House* (☎01326/290466; ①) and the non-smoking *Penmenner House Hotel* (☎01326/290370; ②), both a twenty-minute walk from Lizard Point and forty minutes from Kynance Cove. The *Caerthillian* also has a fine **restaurant** with a range of moderately priced, tasty dishes, though it's usually closed from October to June. The nearby *Witchball Restaurant* is slightly cheaper, and a better choice than the tired meals served up at the *Top House* pub in the village centre.

A mile westward lies the peninsula's best-known beach, **Kynance Cove**. With its sheer hundred-foot cliffs, its stacks and arches of serpentine rock and its offshore islands, the beach has a wild grandeur, and the water quality is excellent – but take care not to be stranded on the islands by the tide, which submerges the entire beach at its flood.

The west coast

Four miles north of Kynance Cove, **MULLION**, the Lizard's biggest village, has a fifteenth- to sixteenth-century church dedicated to the Breton **Saint Mellane** (or Malo), with a dog-door for canine churchgoers. In the centre of the village, *Alma House* (☎01326/240509; ②) provides good **accommodation** and has a good restaurant (closed Sun & Mon), or, a brief distance outside, *Campden House* is a friendly B&B with a fuschia-filled garden (☎01326/240365; no credit cards; ①), less than ten minutes' walk from the sea, and serves dinners. Near the village of Cury, a mile north of Mullion, *Riverside* is a pleasant rural B&B (☎01326/241027; ①), where evening meals are also available. For snacks and **meals** in the village, *Stock's* provides some decent choice. Try also the shop across the road for a glorious range of dairy ice cream.

A mile away on the coast, **Mullion Cove** has more rock sculptures and a small beach outside its sheltered harbour, though the neighbouring beaches of **Polurrian** and

Poldhu are more popular with surfers. At the cliff-edge, the Marconi Monument marks the spot from which the first transatlantic radio transmission was made in 1901. To the north stretch more sandy beaches at **Church** and **Dollar coves**, though these can be unsafe at low tide. The freshwater **Loe Pool**, three miles north, is separated by a shingle bar from the sea, and is one of the two places claiming to be where the sword Excalibur was restored to its watery source (the other is on Bodmin Moor). The beaches hereabouts are rated highly by surfers.

Nearby **Porthleven** is a sizeable port that once served to export tin ore from the Stannary town of **HELSTON**, three miles inland. This transport junction is best known for its **Furry Dance** (or Floral Dance), which dates from the seventeenth century. Held on May 8 (unless this falls on a Sunday or Monday, when the procession takes place on the nearest Saturday), it's a stately procession of top-hatted men and summer-frocked women performing a strange, rather solemn dance through the town's streets and gardens. Other than this, the town's most famous attraction is the garish **Flambards Theme Park** (April to mid-July, Sept & Oct daily 10.30am–5pm; mid-July to Aug daily 10am–6pm; may close Mon and Fri in April, May, Sept & Oct, call to check ☎01326/564093; £7.50), which is a riot of pseudo-Victoriana. Helston has the peninsula's only **tourist office** at 79 Meneage St (Easter–Sept Mon–Sat 10am–1pm & 2–5pm; Oct–Easter Mon & Sat 10am–1pm, Tues, Thurs & Fri 10am–1pm & 2–5pm; ☎01326/565431). Just along from the tourist office at 95 Meneage Rd is *Hutchinson's*, an award-winning fish-and-chip shop. For a drink or a **pub** snack, check out the *Blue Anchor*, 50 Coinagehall St, a fifteenth-century monastery rest house, now a cramped pub with flagstone floors and mellow beer brewed on the premises: try the Spingo Special. For those wanting to explore the Lizard peninsula **by bike** – a great way to get the best out of the network of tiny lanes connecting the villages and coastal tracts – apply to Helston's Bike Services on Meneage Road (☎01326/564564), which rents out mountain bikes (£8 a day), provides a repair service and supplies accessories.

The Penwith peninsula

Though more densely populated than the Lizard, the **Penwith peninsula** is a more rugged landscape, with a raw appeal that is still encapsulated by **Land's End**, despite the commercial paraphernalia superimposed on that headland. The seascapes, the quality of the light and the slow tempo of the local fishing communities made this area a hotbed of artistic activity towards the end of the nineteenth century, when the painters of **Newlyn**, near **Penzance**, established a distinctive school of painting. More innovative figures – among them Ben Nicholson, Barbara Hepworth and Constructivist Naum Gabo – were soon afterwards to make **St Ives** one of England's liveliest cultural communities, and their enduring influence is illustrated in the St Ives branch of the Tate Gallery, showcasing the modern artists associated with the locality.

Penwith is far more easily toured than the Lizard, with a road circling its coastline and a better network of public transport from the two main towns, St Ives and Penzance, which have most of the accommodation. From Penzance – the terminus for **rail** services from London and Birmingham – **buses** #1 and (Sun only) #10A go straight to Land's End in about an hour, whereas the #5A, #5B and #6B take in Newlyn, Mousehole and Lamorna (#6C also goes to Lamorna). North of Land's End, the comparatively neglected headland of Cape Cornwall is served by the #10 bus from Penzance to St Just, while Zennor, St Just, Sennen Cove and Land's End are served by #15 from St Ives (not Sun). St Ives can be reached by branch rail line or numerous buses from Penzance and Truro. Hikers might consider walking the eight miles separating Penzance from St Ives along the old St Michael's Way, a waymarked pilgrim's route for which the tourist office in both these towns can provide a free route-map.

Penzance and around

Occupying a sheltered position at the northwest corner of Mount's Bay, **PENZANCE** has always been a major port, but most traces of the medieval town were obliterated at the end of the sixteenth century by a Spanish raiding party. Today the dominant style of Penzance is Georgian, particularly at the top of **Market Jew Street** (from *Marghas Jew*, meaning "Thursday Market"), which climbs from the harbour and the train and bus stations. At the top of the street stands the green-domed Victorian **Market House** before which stands a statue of **Humphry Davy** (1778–1829), the local woodcarver's son who pioneered the science of electrochemistry and invented the life-saving miners' safety-lamp, which his statue holds.

Turn left here into **Chapel Street**, which has some of the town's finest buildings, including the flamboyant **Egyptian House**, built in 1835 to contain a geological museum but subsequently abandoned until its restoration twenty-odd years ago. Across the street, the **Union Hotel** dates from the seventeenth century, and originally housed the town's assembly rooms: the news of Admiral Nelson's victory at Trafalgar and the death of Nelson himself were first announced from the minstrels' gallery here in 1805. At no. 19, the **Maritime Museum** (Easter–Oct Mon–Sat 10.30am–4.30pm; £2) holds a good collection of seafaring articles, including an array of items salvaged from local wrecks and a full-size section of an eighteenth-century man o' war.

If your interest is roused by the art scene that flourished hereabouts at the turn of the century, head for Morrab Road, between the Promenade and Alverton Street (a continuation of Market Jew Street), where the **Penlee House Gallery and Museum** (July & Aug Mon–Sat 10.30am–4.30pm, Sun 12.30–4.30pm; rest of year closed Sun; £2, free on Sat) holds the biggest collection of the works of the Newlyn School – impressionistic maritime scenes, frequently sentimentalized but often bathed in an evocatively luminous light.

Newlyn itself, Cornwall's biggest fishing port, lies immediately south of Penzance, protected behind two long piers. The colony of artists who gathered here around the Irish painter Stanhope Forbes is represented in the collection in Penzance, but Newlyn's **art gallery**, near the harbour at 24 New Rd (Mon–Sat 10am–5pm; free), which concentrates on contemporary art, gives an often stimulating insight into how that tradition has evolved.

Information and accommodation

Penzance's **tourist office** (May–Sept Mon–Fri 9am–5pm, Sat 10am–4pm, Sun 10am–1pm; Oct–April Mon–Fri 9am–5pm, Sat 10am–1pm; ☎01736/362207) is right next to the train and bus stations on the seafront. Drivers can deposit their vehicles during excursions to the Isles of Scilly at Avalon **car park** near the harbour at South Place (☎01736/364622), for about £2.50 per day. For **bike rental** head for Blewett & Pender at the bottom of Market Jew Street on Albert Street (☎01736/333243).

Guest houses nearest the bus and train stations include *Honeydew* at 3 Leskinnick St (☎01736/364206; no credit cards; ①), at the bottom of Market Jew Street. On Chapel Street, there's the seventeenth-century *Trevelyan Hotel* (☎01736/362494; no credit cards; ①) – ask for a top-floor room for the view – or you could soak up the atmosphere in the *Union Hotel* (01736/362319; ④) or at the *Penzance Arts Club*, at the bottom of Chapel Street (☎01736/363761; ④), where four tasteful rooms are available in what was once the Portuguese embassy; there's a good café in the basement too. For a top-of-the-league treat, the seventeenth-century *Abbey Hotel*, owned by former model Jean Shrimpton and her husband, has lashings of old-fashioned comfort, superb views and an excellent restaurant, off Chapel Street on Abbey Street (☎01736/366906; ⑥). Most cheaper B&Bs are along Morrab and Alexandra Roads to the west of the centre: on Morrab Road, try *Kimberley House* at no. 10 (☎01736/362727; no credit cards; ①); on Alexandra Road, the *Minalto* offers good value for its spacious rooms (☎01736/362923; ②). On the seafront, the non-smoking *Camilla House Hotel* is useful for the harbour at Regent Terrace, on a parallel road to the Promenade (☎01736/363771; ③); most rooms have sea views, and the top room is cosiest. Alexandra Road is also the location of the *Blue Dolphin hostel* (☎01736/363836). The official YHA hostel is out of town, housed in a Georgian mansion at Castle Horneck, Alverton (☎01736/326666, *penzance@yha.org.uk*; closed Jan), a two-mile hike from the station up Market Jew Street into Alverton Road, then turn right at the *Pirate Inn*, or take bus #5B, #6B or #10B from Penzance station as far as the *Pirate Inn*.

Eating and drinking

Penzance's most congenial **restaurant** is *Co-Co's Tapas Bar* on Chapel Street, good for coffees and cakes as well as beers and tapas. Apart from the quality cuisine served up in the more formal *Harris's* nearby at 46 New St (☎01736/364408; closed Mon, plus Sun in winter), the town has few other places that rise above the average, though there are some other reasonably priced eateries in the centre: *Michelangelo's* in Market Jew Street Place and *Carwardine's Brasserie* (closed Sun & Mon–Wed eve) in the pedestrianized Causeway Head are both inexpensive brasseries that stay open late. Vegetarians can head further up the Causeway to the tiny *Dandelions* or make for *Brown's* in the basement of a gallery in Bread Street, both daytime only and closed all day Sunday.

Penzance has a couple of characterful **pubs**, including one of the most famous in the country, the *Admiral Benbow* on Chapel Street, crammed with gaudy ships' figureheads and other nautical items, though the authenticity is spoiled by fruit machines and video games. The *Turk's Head*, on the same street, is the town's oldest inn, reputed to date back to the thirteenth century, and has a garden with the remains of a contrabanders' tunnel to the harbour.

St Michael's Mount

Buses from Penzance bus station leave every thirty minutes for Marazion, five miles east, from where the medieval chimneys and towers of **St Michael's Mount** (April–Sept Mon–Fri 10.30am–5.30pm, plus most weekends; Oct–March phone for opening times ☎01736/710507; £4.40; NT) can be seen a couple of hundred yards offshore. A vision of the archangel Michael led to the building of a church on this granite pile around the fifth century, and within three centuries a Celtic monastery had been founded here. The present building derives from a chapel raised in the eleventh century by Edward the Confessor, who handed over the abbey to the Benedictine monks of Brittany's Mont St Michel, whose island abbey – also founded after a vision of Saint Michael – was the model for this one. The complex was appropriated by Henry V during the Hundred Years' War, and it became a fortress after its dissolution a century later. After the Civil War, when it was used to store arms for the Royalist forces, it became the residence of the St Aubyn family, who still inhabit the castle.

The fortress-isle has a milder, more pedestrian feel than its prototype off the Breton coast, but there's no doubting its eye-catching site, which demands a first-hand inspection from anyone travelling along this part of the Cornish littoral. A good number of its buildings date from the twelfth century, but the later additions are more interesting, such as the battlemented **chapel** and the seventeenth-century decorations of the Chevy Chase Room, the former refectory. Other rooms are crowded with paintings of the castle, portraits of various St Aubyns and general memorabilia.

At low tide the promontory can be approached via a cobbled causeway; at high tide there are boats from Marazion (£1).

Mousehole to Land's End

Accounts vary as to the derivation of the name of **MOUSEHOLE** (pronounced "Mowzle"), though it may be from a smugglers' cave just south of town. In any case, the name evokes perfectly this minuscule harbour, cradled in the arms of a granite breakwater three miles south of Penzance. The village attracts more visitors than it can handle, so hang around until the crowds have departed before you walk through its tight tangle of lanes to take in Mousehole's oldest house, the fourteenth-century Keigwin House (a survival of the 1595 attack when the village was burned by the Spaniards), and/or a drink at the *Ship Inn*, which also has **rooms** (☎01736/731234; no credit cards; ②) – those with a view cost slightly more. Half a mile inland, the churchyard wall at **Paul** holds a monument to Dolly Pentreath, a resident of Mousehole who died in 1777 and was reputed to have been the last person to speak the Cornish language. The inscription includes a Cornish translation of a verse from the Bible.

Three miles south round the coast, **Lamorna Cove** is squeezed between granite headlands, linked by a flower-bordered lane to the tiny village of **LAMORNA**, where you can see an old flour mill and drink at the comfortable old *Lamorna Wink* pub – as the sign shows, it was the wink that signified that contraband spirits were available. There's also a sequestered, high-quality hotel in the area, the *Lamorna Cove Hotel* (☎01736/731411; closed Nov to mid-March except Christmas period; ⑤), about half a mile above the cove; it has a pool, gardens and marvellous views.

PORTHCURNO's name means "Port Cornwall", but its beach of tiny white shells suggests privacy and isolation rather than the movement of ships. Steep steps lead up from here to the cliff-hewn **Minack Theatre**, created in the 1930s and since enlarged to hold 750 seats, though the basic Greek-inspired design has remained intact. The spectacular backdrop of Porthcurno Bay makes this one of the country's most inspiring theatres – providing the weather holds. The summer season lasts seventeen weeks from May to September, presenting a gamut of plays, opera and musicals, with tickets costing just £5.50 and £6.50 for afternoon or evening performances (box office Mon–Fri from 9.30am; ☎01736/810181). Bring a cushion and a rug. You can also visit the **Exhibition Centre** (daily: April–Sept 9.30am–5.30pm; Oct–March 10am–4pm; closed during matinée performances; £2), which allows you to see the theatre and follow the story of its creation through photographs and audiovisual displays.

The peculiar white pyramid on the shore to the east of Porthcurno marks the spot where the first transatlantic cables were laid in 1880. On the headland beyond lies an Iron Age fort, **Treryn Dinas**, close to the famous rocking stone called **Logan's Rock**, a seventy-ton monster that was knocked off its perch by a nephew of playwright Oliver Goldsmith and a gang of sailors in 1824. Somehow they replaced the stone, but it never rocked again.

The best way to approach **Land's End** is unarguably on foot along the coastal path. Although nothing can completely destroy the potency of this extreme western tip of England, the colossal theme park built behind this majestic headland in 1987 comes close to violating irreparably the spirit of the place. The trivializing **Land's End Experience** (daily: summer 10am–6pm; winter 10am–5pm; £8.95) substitutes a tawdry panoply of lasers and unconvincing sound effects for the real open-air experience, but the location is still a public right of way (though you'll have to pay to use the car park: £2), and once past the paraphernalia, nature takes over. Turf-covered cliffs sixty feet high provide a platform to view the Irish Lady, the Armed Knight, Dr Syntax Head and the rest of the Land's End outcrops, beyond which you can spot the Longships lighthouse, a mile and a half out to sea, and sometimes the Wolf Rock lighthouse, nine miles southwest, or even the Isles of Scilly, 25 miles away.

Whitesand Bay to Zennor

To the north of Land's End the rounded granite cliffs fall away at **Whitesand Bay** to reveal a glistening mile-long shelf of beach that offers the best swimming on the Penwith peninsula. The rollers make for good surfing and boards can be rented at **Sennen Cove**, the more popular southern end of the beach. There are a few places to **stay** around the southern end of the strand, including *Myrtle Cottage* (☎01736/871698; no credit cards; ①), which also has a cosy café open to non-residents, and the nearby *Polwyn Cottage*, tucked away on Old Coastguard Row (☎01736/871349; no credit cards; ①). If you don't mind being a few minutes' walk inland, *Whitesands Lodge* would make a good base for the whole area, offering dormitory accommodation and single, twin or family rooms (☎01736/871776; ①). As well as the self-catering facilities, there's a relaxed café-restaurant (also open to non-residents), a library, studio workspace, and access to bike rental and land and sea tours. When all else fails, try the *Sennen Cove Hotel*, visible from the strand, which has low rates and great views, but is otherwise fairly second-rate (☎01736/871275; ③).

Cape Cornwall, three miles northward, shelters another superb beach, overlooked by the chimney of the Cape Cornwall Mine, which closed in 1870. Half a mile inland the grimly grey village of **ST JUST-IN-PENWITH** was a centre of the tin and copper industry, and the rows of trim cottages radiating out from Bank Square are redolent of the close-knit community that once existed here. The tone is somewhat lightened by the grassy open-air theatre where the old Cornish miracle plays were staged; it was later used by Methodist preachers as well as Cornish wrestlers. The village has a **youth hostel** on its outskirts (☎01736/788437; closed Nov–Feb) – take the left fork past the post office. Three out of the four pubs in and off Bank Square have **accommodation**, best of them the traditional *Star Inn* (☎01736/788767; no credit cards; ①). For snacks, lunches and inexpensive dinners, stop off at the *St Just Tea Rooms*.

A couple of miles north of St Just, outside **PENDEEN**, you can get a close-up view of the Cornish mining industry at **Geevor Tin Mine** (March–June, Sept & Oct daily 10.30am–5pm; £5), where you can tour the surface machinery and explore the innards of an underground mine and visit the museum, which is the only part of the site open for visits in winter (reduced hours; £2). East of here, the landscape is all rolling moorland and an abundance of granite, the chief building material of **ZENNOR**. D.H. Lawrence and Frieda came to live here in 1916: "It is a most beautiful place," Lawrence wrote, "lovelier even than the Mediterranean." The Lawrences were soon joined by John Middleton Murry and Katherine Mansfield, with the hope of forming a writers' community, but the new arrivals soon left for a more sheltered haven near Falmouth. Lawrence stayed on to write *Women in Love*, spending in all a year and a half in Zennor before being given notice to quit by the local constabulary, who suspected Lawrence and his German wife of unpatriotic sympathies. His Cornish experiences were later described in *Kangaroo*.

At the bottom of the village, the **Wayside Museum** is dedicated to Cornish life from prehistoric times (mid-April to Sept daily 10am–6pm; Oct Mon–Fri & Sun 11am–5pm; £2.20). Note the "plague stone" on the road outside the building, where a hole containing vinegar was used to disinfect visiting merchants' money during cholera outbreaks in the nineteenth century. At the top of the lane, the church of **St Sennen** displays a sixteenth-century bench-carving of a mermaid who, according to local legend, was so entranced by the singing of a chorister that she lured him down to the sea, from which he never returned – though his singing can still occasionally be heard. Nearby, the *Tinners Arms*, where Lawrence stayed before moving into Higher Tregerthen, is a homely place to drink and eat. If you don't mind sleeping up to six to a room, the *Old Chapel Backpackers Hostel* makes a fun place **to stay**, right next to the Wayside Museum (☎01736/798307).

The Iron Age village of **Chysauster** (April–Sept daily 10am–6pm; Oct daily 10am–5pm; £1.60; EH), located on a windy hillside a couple of miles inland from Zennor, off the minor road to Penzance, is the best-preserved ancient settlement in the southwest. Dating from about the first century BC, it contains two rows of four buildings, each consisting of a courtyard with small chambers leading off it, and a garden that was presumably used for growing vegetables.

St Ives

East of Zennor, the road runs four hilly miles on to the steeply built town of **ST IVES**, a place that has smoothly undergone the transition to holiday haunt from its previous role as a centre of the fishing industry. So productive were the offshore waters that a record sixteen and a half million fish were caught in one net on a single day in 1868, and the diarist Francis Kilvert was told by the local vicar that the smell was sometimes so great as to stop the church clock. Virginia Woolf, who spent every summer here to the age of twelve, described St Ives as "a windy, noisy, fishy, vociferous, narrow-streeted town; the colour of a mussel or a limpet; like a bunch of rough shell fish clustered on a grey wall together." By the time the pilchard reserves dried up around the early years of this century, the town was beginning to attract a vibrant **artists' colony**, precursors of the wave later headed by Ben Nicholson, Barbara Hepworth (second of Nicholson's three wives), Naum Gabo and the potter Bernard Leach, who in the 1960s were followed by a third wave including Terry Frost, Peter Lanyon, Patrick Heron, Bryan Winter and Roger Hilton.

Sunday painters dominate the dozens of galleries sandwiched between the town's restaurants and bars; the place to view the better work created in St Ives is the **St Ives Tate Gallery**, opened in 1993, overlooking Porthmeor Beach on the north side of town (Tues–Sun 10.30am–5:30pm; £3.90; combined ticket with Barbara Hepworth Museum £6). The beachfront, viewed through a grand concave window, is a constant presence inside the airy and gleaming white building, creating a dialogue with the gallery's paintings, sculptures and ceramics, most of which date from the period 1925 to 1975. Apart from these, the Tate has some specially commissioned contemporary works on view. The museum's rooftop **café** is one the best places in town for tea and cake.

A short distance away on Barnoon Hill, the **Barbara Hepworth Museum** (July, Aug & public holidays daily 10.30am–5.30pm; rest of year closed Mon; £3.50) gives another insight into the local arts scene. One of the foremost non-figurative sculptors of her time, Hepworth lived in the building from 1949 until her death in a studio fire in 1975. Apart from the sculptures, which are arranged in positions chosen by Hepworth in the house and garden, the museum has masses of background on her art, from photos and letters to catalogues and reviews. A few Hepworths are scattered around the town, including a tender *Madonna* in the harbourside church of **St Ia** – a fifteenth-century building dedicated to the female missionary who was said to have floated over from Ireland on an ivy leaf.

After doing the Tate, devotees of Bernard Leach's Japanese-inspired ceramics can visit his studio, the **Leach Pottery**, in the village of Higher Stennack, three-quarters of a mile outside St Ives on the Zennor road (bus #16, #17 or #17A). Products of the pottery can also be found in the New Craftsman shop in Fore Street with some examples of Leach's work alongside that of his wife Janet, who died in 1997.

The wide expanse of **Porthmeor Beach** dominates the northern side of St Ives, the stone houses tumbling almost onto the yellow sands. Unusually for a town beach, the water quality is excellent, and the rollers make it popular with surfers (boards available for rent below the gallery); there's also a good open-air café here. South of the station, **Porthminster Beach** is another favourite spot for sunbathing and swimming, but if you hanker for a quieter stretch you need to head east out of town to the string of magnificent golden beaches lining **St Ives Bay** – the strand is especially fine on the far side of the port of Hayle, at the mouth of the eponymous river.

Practicalities

To reach St Ives by **train**, change at St Erth on the main line to Penzance or there are direct services from Penzance. **Buses** #16, #17 and #17A, B or C connect Penzance with St Ives, but the only service from here to Truro is run by National Express. The train station is off Porthminster Beach, just north of the bus station on Station Hill. The **tourist office** is in the Guildhall, in the narrow Street An Pol, two minutes' walk away (July & Aug Mon–Sat 9.30am–6pm, Sun 10am–1pm; Sept Mon–Sat 9.30am–5.30pm; Oct to mid-May Mon–Thurs 9.30am–5.30pm, Fri 9.30am–5pm; mid-May to June Mon–Sat 9.30am–5.30pm, Sun 10am–1pm; ☎01736/796297). Among the places where you can rent **surfing equipment** are Porthmeor Beach and the surf specialist Wind an Sea on Fore Street, with an outlet on the harbour. The St Ives **Festival** of folk, jazz and blues, also taking in classical music and theatre, takes place over twelve days in mid-September.

HOTELS AND B&BS

Chy-Roma, 2 Seaview Terrace (☎01736/797539, *jenny@omshanti.demon.co.uk*). Convenient for the bus and train stations, among a cluster of similar lodgings, this one boasts home cooking and great panoramic views. A week's notice needs to be given for cheque payments. No credit cards. ②.

The Cobbles, 33 Back Rd West (☎01736/798206). Slightly cramped accommodation, but near Porthmeor Beach and with a relaxed and friendly atmosphere. No credit cards. ②.

Garrack Hotel, Burthallan Lane (☎01736/796199). One of the best hotels in the area, outside the town's bustle, but within walking distance of Porthmeor Beach. Family-run, the hotel has an indoor pool and sauna, and an excellent restaurant (see below; the atmosphere is polite but friendly. ⑦.

The Grey Mullet, 2 Bunkers Hill (☎01736/796635). Oak-beamed and bedecked with flowers and prints, this eighteenth-century house – said to be the oldest in town – is twenty yards from the harbour on a cobbled lane. No credit cards. ②.

Kandahar, 11 The Warren (☎01736/796183). Best choice among the B&Bs edging the seafront below the bus station; four rooms have a view. Closed Nov to mid-Feb. ②.

Kynance, 24 The Warren (☎01736/796636). Another good choice in this area of town near Porthminster Beach, with some parking space. The top-floor rooms have good views but get booked up early. Closed mid-Nov to early March. ②.

Penclawdd, 1 Sea View Place (☎01736/796869). In the picturesque Downalong area of town, north of the harbour, with excellent views. ②.

CAMPSITES AND HOSTEL

Ayr, Higher Ayr (☎01736/795855, *andy@ayrholidaypark.demon.co.uk*). St Ives has no campsites right on the seafront, but this one has a good sea-prospect, half a mile west of the centre, above Porthmeor Beach. Closed Nov–March.

Higher Chellew, Nancledra (☎01736/364532). Good out-of-town alternative to the above, and much cheaper. Facilities are basic but clean, and include washing machines. Located on the B3311 road, equidistant between St Ives and Penzance.

St Ives Backpackers, The Stennack (☎01736/799444, *st-ivesbackpackers@dial.pipex.com*). Restored Wesleyan chapel school from 1845, usefully located in the centre opposite the cinema. Comfortable and clean, with barbecues and free tours around the area. Dorms have four, six or eight beds, and there's currently one double room – more are planned.

RESTAURANTS AND CAFÉS

The Café, Island Square (☎01736/793621). Vegetarian snacks and full evening meals, reasonably priced and served with a smile. Inexpensive.

Garrack Hotel, Burthallan Lane (☎01736/796199). A bit out of the way, but worth the detour. The kitchen excels at fish but meat dishes are also excellent, and there are some astounding desserts. Expensive.

The Grapevine, 7 High St (☎01736/794030). Bistro serving breakfasts and lunches and fresh local fish at night, all in a pleasant woody decor. Moderate.

Peppers, 22 Fore St (☎01736/794014). Up-to-date pizza and pasta parlour, also serving fish and steaks. Inexpensive.

Pig 'n' Fish, Norway Lane (☎01736/794204). A great spot for seafood. The oysters are good value and the desserts are wonderful. Closed Sun & Mon, plus Nov to mid-March. Moderate.

Seafarer, 45 Fore St (☎01736/797686). Seafood at low prices, with cosy decor. Moderate.

The Spinning Wheel, Street An Pol. Teas, coffees and full meals served right opposite the Guildhall. Inexpensive.

Wilbur's Café, St Andrew's St (☎01736/796661). Movie stars on the walls and a lively atmosphere with pastas and fish prominent on the menu, and a vegetarian option. Moderate.

The Isles of Scilly

The **Isles of Scilly** are a compact archipelago of about a hundred islands 28 miles southwest of Land's End, none of them bigger than three miles across, and only five of them inhabited – **St Mary's**, **Tresco**, **Bryher**, **St Martin's** and **St Agnes**. In the annals of folklore, the Scillies are the peaks of the submerged land of Lyonesse, a fertile plain that extended west from Penwith before the ocean broke in, drowning the land and leaving only one survivor to tell the tale. In fact they form part of the same granite mass as Land's End, Bodmin Moor and Dartmoor, and despite rarely rising above a hundred feet, they possess a remarkable variety of landscape. All are swept by an energizing briny air filled with the cries of seabirds, and though the water is cold the beaches are well-nigh irresistible, ranging from small coves to vast untrammelled strands. Other points of interest include Cornwall's greatest concentration of prehistoric remains, some fabulous rock formations, and masses of **flowers**. Along with tourism, the main source of income here is flower-growing, for which the equable climate and the long hours of sunshine – their name means "Sun Isles" – make the islands ideal. The profusion of wild flowers is even more noticeable than the fields of narcissi and daffodils, and the heaths and pathways are often dense with marigolds, gorse, sea thrift, trefoil and poppies, not to mention a host of more exotic varieties introduced by visiting foreign vessels.

Free of traffic, theme parks and amusement arcades, the Scillies are a welcome respite from the tourist trail, the main drawbacks being the high cost of reaching the islands and the shortage of accommodation – making advance booking essential at any time. Note that most B&Bs offer – and often insist on – a dinner, bed and breakfast package, and this option should not be automatically rejected, considering the tiny choice of places to eat (St Mary's Hugh Town is better supplied), though basic groceries are always available. If you're coming between May and September, try to time your visit to be here on a Wednesday or Friday evening to witness the **gig races**, the most popular sport on the Scillies, performed by six-oared vessels some thirty feet in length. Some of the boats used are over a hundred years old, built originally to carry pilots to passing ships.

Getting to the islands

The islands are accessible by sea or air. **Boats from Penzance to St Mary's** are operated by the Isles of Scilly Steamship Company on the South Pier (☎0345/105555). Sailings, which can be nauseatingly rough, take place daily and last about two-and-three-quarter hours; single tickets cost £37, day returns £30–34, short-break returns (one to three nights) £42–52, and period returns £62–72, with discounts for students, families and children. There are ferries between each of the inhabited islands (about £5 return fare), though these are sporadic in winter.

The main departure points for **flights** (also operated by the Isles of Scilly Steamship Company; ☎0345/105555) are **Land's End**, near St Just (Mon–Sat; 15min; £54–92 return), **Newquay** (Mon–Sat; 30min; £65–99 return), **Plymouth** (Mon, Wed & Fri; 45min; £102–139 return), **Exeter** (Mon–Sat; 50min; £133–180 return) and **Bristol** (Mon, Tues, Thurs & Fri; 1hr 10min; £148–199 return). In winter, there is no service from Newquay or Plymouth, and a much reduced service from Bristol and Exeter, with only Land's End operating a full timetable. British International also runs **helicopter** flights (☎01736/363871) from the heliport a mile east of Penzance to St Mary's (not Sun) and Tresco (not Sun) taking about twenty minutes, with return fares costing about £95 – though you can get discounted "Late Saver Returns" if you buy them the day before departure for a one- to three-night stay.

St Mary's

The island of **ST MARY'S** holds the overwhelming majority of the archipelago's population and most of its tourist accommodation. From the airport there are buses to shuttle passengers the mile to **HUGH TOWN**, straddling a neck of land at the southwestern end of the island. Ferries from Penzance dock on the north side of town, under a knob of land still known as the Garrison, where the eight-pointed **Star Castle**, built in Elizabeth I's reign after the scare of the Spanish Armada, has been converted into a hotel. The rampart walk hereabout is a good place to gain your bearings, affording views over all the islands and the myriad rocky fragments around them.

Hugh Town itself is nothing to shout about, and once you've exhausted the pubs and shops there's little to occupy your time apart from the engaging **Isles of Scilly Museum** on Church Street, well worth an hour or two's wander (summer Mon–Sat 10am–noon & 1.30–4.30pm & 7.30–9pm; rest of year Mon–Sat 10am–noon & 1.30–4.30pm; £1). Most of the exhibits are relics salvaged from the many ships foundered on or around the islands, including the happy miscellany of finds recovered from the most recent wreck, the *Cita*, which sank off St Mary's Porth Hellick in March 1997 en route from Southampton to Belfast, much of its cargo, ranging from trainers to tobacco, finding its way into the islanders' homes. Hugh Town's best bathing **beach** is in the sheltered bay of Porthcressa, where you can also find Buccabu Bike Hire (☎01720/422289), which offers a good way to get around the island if you don't want to take advantage of the circular **bus** service leaving from nearby at the end of the main street (4–7 daily) – though neither bike nor bus is ideal for exploring the remoter coastal sections.

From Porthcressa a path wanders south to skirt the **Peninnis Headland**, passing some impressive sea-sculpted granite rocks. Other weathered boulders stand behind the Peninnis Lighthouse, notably the formation known as the **Kettle and Pans**, where a rock said to resemble a kettle stands close to some massive rounded basins. The path follows the coast to **Old Town Bay**, around which the modern houses of **OLD TOWN** give little hint of its former role as the island's chief port. The town has cafés and a sheltered south-facing beach, where there's a **diving** school, with equipment for hire (☎01720/422732).

Three-quarters of a mile east, **Porth Hellick** is the next major inlet on the island's southern coast, marked by a rugged quartz monument to the fantastically named Sir Cloudesley Shovell, who in 1707 was washed up here from a shipwreck which claimed four ships and nearly 1700 lives. On one side of the bay is another rock shape, the **Loaded Camel**; near it a gate leads to a four-thousand-year-old **barrow**, probably used by Bronze Age people from the Iberian peninsula who were the Scillies' first colonists.

Pelistry Bay, on the northeastern side of St Mary's, less than two miles from Hugh Town, is one of the most secluded spots on the island, its sandy beach and crystal-clear waters sheltered by the outlying **Toll's Island**. The latter, joined to St Mary's at low tide by a slender strand, holds the remains of an old battery known as Pellow's Redoubt as well as several pits in which kelp was burned to produce a substance used for the manufacture of soap and glass. Grey seals are a common sight here.

The best remnants of early human settlement on the Scillies are to be found at **Halangy Down**, a mile or so north of Hugh Town, overlooking the sea. Dating from around 200 BC, it's an extensive complex of stone huts, chief of them a structure built around a courtyard with interconnecting buildings. Most complete is **Bant's Carn**, part of a much earlier site, probably contemporaneous with the one at Porth Hellick, comprising a long rectangular roofed chamber where cremations were carried out.

Practicalities

Hugh Town's **tourist office**, on Porthcressa Beach (Easter to June, Sept & Oct Mon–Sat 8.30am–5.30pm; July & Aug Mon–Sat 8.30am–6pm, Sun 10am–noon; Nov–Easter Mon–Thurs 8.30am–5pm, Fri 8.30am–4.30pm; ☎01720/422536), has information on available accommodation for all the Scillies. The town is relatively well supplied with **B&Bs**: Porthcressa Road has the small, non-smoking *Pieces of Eight* (☎01720/422163; no credit cards; ②), while *The Boathouse*, on the Thoroughfare, enjoys a good view over the harbour and has a restaurant (☎01720/422688; ③; closed Nov–Feb). Right on the quay where the ferries dock, the *Harbourside Hotel* is one of St Mary's priciest options (☎01720/422352; ⑦; closed Dec–Feb), though if you can afford that you can probably stretch to the island's most atmospheric hotel, the *Star Castle* (☎01720/422317; ⑧; closed Nov–Feb), high up on the Garrison. In the same area is the more modest *Veronica Lodge*, The Garrison (☎01720/422585; no credit cards; ②; closed Dec & Jan), a comfortably solid house with a spacious garden and excellent views. There is much to be said for staying outside Hugh Town, for example at *Atlantic View* (☎01720/422684; no credit cards; ②), in the centre of the island on High Lanes (right off Telegraph Road heading north), which also offers **riding** excursions and **bike rental**. The island's **campsite** is at *Garrison Farm* near the playing field at the top of the eponymous promontory in Hugh Town (☎01720/422670; closed Dec–Feb). Camping elsewhere is not allowed.

There are plenty of places to eat in Hugh Town. The *Pilot's Gig* is a basement **restaurant** below the Garrison Gate at the end of Hugh Street, specializing in fish but offering more modest snacks at lunchtime. In the middle of the main street, the *Kavorna Bakery* has simple snacks as well as coffees and buns. In the Garrison, the *Star Castle Hotel* has a good-value fixed-price menu, and you can also snack cheaply in the hotel's *Dungeon Bar*. Out of town, *Juliet's Restaurant* serves light meals and moderately priced early dinners in its garden between Porthmellon and Porthloo beaches.

Tresco

After St Mary's, **TRESCO** is the most visited island of the Scillies, yet the boatloads of visitors somehow manage to lose themselves on the two-miles-by-one island, the second largest in the group. Once the private estate of Devon's Tavistock Abbey, Tresco still retains a cloistered, slightly privileged air, and it has none of St Mary's short-term budget accommodation.

According to the tide, boats pull in at **New Grimsby**, halfway up the west coast, or the smaller quay at Old Grimsby, on the east coast, or the southernmost point of Carn Near. Whichever the case, it is only a few minutes' walk to the entrance to **Abbey Gardens** (daily 10am–4pm; £5.50), featuring a few ruins from the priory amid subtropical gardens first laid out in 1834. Many of the plants were grown from seeds taken from London's Kew Gardens, others were brought here from Africa, South America and the Antipodes. The entry ticket also admits you to a collection of figureheads and name plates taken from the numerous vessels that have come to grief around here.

You don't need to walk far to find alluring sandy beaches: one of the best – **Appletree Bay** – is only a few steps from the southern ferry landing at Carn Near. **Old Grimsby**, on the island's eastern side, has another couple of sand beaches, looking out to a submarine-shaped rock offshore, though the wide strands south of here are the island's best, and good for shell-hunting.

There is another gorgeous sandy bay around the cluster of cottages that make up **New Grimsby**, on the island's eastern shore. North of here, Tresco's tidy fields give way to an untended heathland of heather and gorse, while a narrow path traces the coast to **Charles' Castle**, built in the 1550s. Strategically positioned on a height to cover the lagoon-like channel separating Tresco from Bryher, the castle was in fact badly designed, its guns unable to depress far enough to be effective, and it was superseded in 1651 by the much better-preserved **Cromwell's Castle**, actually no more than a gun-tower, built at sea level next to a pretty sandy cove.

The shore path winds northwest from here, round to **Piper's Hole**, a deep underground cave accessible from the cliff-edge on the northern coast. The entrance can be a little difficult to negotiate but it's worth pressing ahead to its freshwater pool. A torch would be useful.

Practicalities

Apart from the exclusive *Island Hotel* at the centre of the island (☎01720/422883; ⑨; closed Nov–Feb), and the *New Inn* at New Grimsby (☎01720/422844; ⑦), the only **accommodation** on the island comprises self-catering homes, usually available for weekly rent only, though it's worth asking if you want a place for less time. Prices run from £250 to £400 a week: contact *Boro Farm* (☎01720/422843; closed Jan & Feb); *Borough Farm* (☎01720/422840; closed Nov–Feb), or Tresco's Estate Office (☎01720/422849) for bookings and further details. The *New Inn* has a **restaurant** with a three-course set menu, and you can eat pub snacks in its garden. For gourmet cuisine, head for the restaurant at the *Island Hotel*, where fresh fish is the speciality.

Bryher and Samson

Covered with a thick carpet of bracken, heather and bramble, **BRYHER** is the wildest of the inhabited islands, but the seventy-odd inhabitants have introduced some pockets of order in the form of flower plantations, mostly confined to the small settlement around the quay and climbing up the slopes of **Watch Hill** on Bryher's eastern side, from which you can enjoy a grand panorama of the whole group of islands.

It is the exposed western seaboard that takes the full brunt of the Atlantic, and nowhere more spectacularly than at the aptly named **Hell Bay**, cupped by a limb of land on the northwestern shore, and worth catching when the wind's up. In contrast to this sound and fury, peace reigns in the southern cove of **Rushy Bay**, one of the best beaches on the island.

From the quay, there is a daily boat service to the other islands, and frequent tours to seal and bird colonies as well as fishing expeditions. You could make a quick hop to the small isle of **SAMSON**, deserted since 1855 when the last impoverished inhabitants were ordered off by the island's proprietor. Most of the abandoned cottages are on the **South Hill**, site of several primitive burial chambers dating from the second millennium BC. The North Hill has a stone coffin from the same period, thought to be the sepulchre of a tribal chief. Most of the famous **gig races** start off from Nut Rock, to the east of Samson, finishing at St Mary's quay.

Practicalities

Soleil D'Or, on the eastern side of the island with views over to Tresco, is one of the cheapest of Bryher's **B&Bs** (☎01720/422003; ②; closed Nov–Feb); another reliable choice is

Chafford, also on the eastern side of the island, near Watch Hill (☎01720/422241; ②; closed Nov–March) – both places offer meals. There is a **campsite** at Jenford Farm on Watch Hill (☎01720/422886; closed Nov–March). For refreshment, the island's one hotel, the *Hell Bay* (☎01720/422947; ⑨; closed Nov–Feb) – actually a safe distance away from Hell Bay, near the pool below Gweal Hill – has a bar and restaurant. You can also eat inexpensively at the *Vine Café*, below Watch Hill, and the *Fraggle Rock Café*, near the post office, which has an upstairs restaurant – Friday is fish-and-chips night.

St Martin's

The main landing stage at **ST MARTIN'S** is on the southern promontory, at the head of the majestic sweep of **Par Beach** – a fitting entry to the island that boasts the best of the Scillies' beaches. From the quay, a road leads up past a public tennis court (rackets and balls for rent) to **HIGHER TOWN**, the main concentration of houses and location of the only shop. Here you can also find St Martin's Diving Centre (☎01720/422848), giving tuition at all levels. The water here is among the clearest in Britain, and is much favoured by scuba enthusiasts.

Beyond the church, follow the road westwards along the island's long, narrow ridge to **LOWER TOWN**, little more than a cluster of cottages on the western extremity, where there's a second quay for coming and going. The town overlooks the uninhabited isles of **Teän** and **St Helen's**, the latter holding the remains of a tenth-century oratory, monks' dwellings and a chapel, as well as a pest house, erected in 1756 to house plague-carriers entering British waters.

Along the southern shore, the gentler side of the island, you'll find the long strand of **Lawrence's Bay** and large areas of flowerbeds. On the northern side, the coast is rougher, with the exception of **Great Bay**, a beautiful half-mile recess of sand, utterly secluded and ideal for swimming. From its western end, you can climb across boulders at low tide to the hilly and wild **White Island**, on the northeastern side of which is a vast cave, **Underland Girt**, accessible at low tide.

At **St Martin's Head** on the northeastern tip of the main island lies the red and white Daymark erected in 1683 (not 1637 as inscribed) as a warning to shipping. On a clear day you can see the foam breaking against the Seven Stones Reef seven miles distant, where the tanker *Torrey Canyon* was wrecked in 1967, causing one of the world's worst oil spills. Below St Martin's Head, on the southeastern shore, lies another fine beach, **Perpitch**, looking out to the scattered Eastern Isles, slivers of rock to which boats take trippers to view puffins and grey seals.

Practicalities

St Martin's has two good **B&Bs**; *Glenmoor Cottage* (☎01720/422816; no credit cards; ②) and *Polreath* (☎01720/422046; ③), both in Higher Town. In Middletown, between Higher Town and Lower Town, you'll find a **campsite** (☎01720/422888; closed Nov–Feb), just off the road near Lawrence's Bay – the only Scillies' campsite enjoying some degree of shelter. *Polreath* also has a simple **café** serving light meals, or you could venture down the valley south of Higher Town to the wholefood café and restaurant at *Little Arthur Farm* for a range of delicious home-baked cakes, organic salads and hot meals (April–Sept). The only **pub** on the island is the *Sevenstones Inn* in Lower Town, where snacks are available.

St Agnes

Visitors to the southernmost inhabited island of **ST AGNES** disembark at **Porth Conger**, from where a road leads to the western side of the island, on the way passing the disused **Old Lighthouse**, one of the oldest in the country – dating from 1680 – and the most significant landmark on St Agnes. From here the right-hand fork leads to **Periglis Cove**, a mooring for boats on the western side of the island, while the left-hand fork goes to **St Warna's Cove**, where the patron saint of shipwrecks is reputed to have landed from Ireland, the exact spot being marked by a holy well. Between the two coves is a fine coastal path which passes the miniature **Troy Town Maze**, thought to have been created a couple of centuries ago, but possibly much older. Beyond St Warna's Cove, the path continues down over Wingletang Down to the southern headland of **Horse Point**, where there are some tortuous wind-eroded rocks. **Beady Pool**, an inlet on the eastern side of the headland, gained its name from the trove of beads washed ashore from the wreck of a seventeenth-century Dutch trader; some of the reddish-brown stones still occasionally turn up. The eastern side of St Agnes has one of the best beaches, the small, sheltered **Covean** (accessible from the path opposite *Covean Cottage*). Between here and Porth Conger a sand bar appears at low tide to connect the smaller isle of **Gugh**, the strand creating another lovely sheltered beach. You can walk across the bar to see a scattering of untended Bronze Age remains, and there is a good panorama of the islands from the hill at Gugh's northern end; take care not to be marooned by the incoming tide, which is extremely fierce.

St Agnes's western side looks out onto the **Western Rocks**, a horseshoe of islets that can be explored on boat tours. Biggest of them is Annet, a nesting-place for a variety of birds such as the stormy petrel and Manx shearwater, as well as colonies of puffins and shags, though many have been chased out or slaughtered in recent years by the predatory great black-beaked gull – largest of the gull family. The islands forming the western arm of the group are the best place to see grey seals. The island of **Rosevean** has the remains of houses used by the builders of the Bishop Rock Lighthouse, five miles out – at 175ft the tallest in Britain and the westernmost one on this side of the Atlantic.

Practicalities

Best of the **B&Bs** on St Agnes is the *Coastguards*, one of a smart row of cottages past the Old Lighthouse and post office on the island's western side (☎01720/422373; ③). Others include *Covean Cottage*, above Porth Conger (☎01720/422620; ③; closed Dec–Feb), *Downs Cottage* (☎01720/422704; ④; closed Dec–Feb), near the post office, and the *Parsonage* (☎01720/422370; no credit cards; ②), nestled below the lighthouse behind a copse of Cornish elms. There's a good **campsite** at *Troy Town Farm* above Periglis Cove (☎01720/422360; closed Nov–Feb), enjoying first-rate views over to the Western Rocks. Just above the jetty at Porth Conger, the *Turk's Head* serves superb St Agnes pasties to go with its beer.

Redruth to Bude

Though generally harsher than the county's southern seaboard, the north Cornish coast is punctuated by some of the finest beaches in England, the most popular of which are to be found around **Newquay**, the surfers' capital. Other major holiday centres are to be found down the coast at the ex-mining town of **St Agnes** and north around the Camel estuary, where the port of **Padstow** makes a good base for some remarkable beaches as well as a fine inland walk. North of the Camel, the coast is an almost unbroken line of cliffs as far as the Devon border, the gaunt, exposed terrain making a melodramatic setting for **Tintagel**, though the wide strand at **Bude** attracts legions of surfers and family holidaymakers.

Offsetting the beaches and caravan parks, parts of the more westerly stretches are littered with the derelict stacks and castle-like ruins of the engine-houses that once powered the region's **copper** and **tin mines**, industries that at one time led the world.

Also prominent are the grey nonconformist chapels that reflect the impact of John Wesley on Cornwall's mining communities. His open-air meetings attracted thousands of listeners in such places as Gwennap Pit outside **Redruth**, the centre of the industry.

North Cornwall's network of public transport leaves a lot to be desired. Newquay is the terminus for the cross-peninsula **train** route from Par, while the main line to Penzance stops at Redruth and Camborne, which are connected to St Agnes on the #43 and #57 **bus** routes, while Redruth is linked to Falmouth on #41. Truronian runs a regular #T1 service (no Sun) from St Agnes to Truro, Helston and The Lizard, while Western National's #57, which starts in Penzance, also takes in St Ives and continues on to Perranporth and Newquay. Bus #56 runs between Newquay and Padstow, the latter also served by the regular #55 from Bodmin (not Sun in winter). Services #122, #125 and #X4 link Bude, Boscastle and Tintagel, and #124 runs between Port Isaac, Polzeath and Wadebridge (not Sun in winter). Finally, Okehampton and Exeter are linked to Bude by #X9, and to Boscastle by #X10 (no Sun).

Redruth and around

In the 1850s **REDRUTH** and neighbouring **CAMBORNE**, with which it is now amalgamated, accounted for two-thirds of the world's copper production, the 350 pits employing some fifty thousand workers, many of whom were forced to emigrate when cheaper deposits of tin and copper were discovered overseas at the turn of the century. The simple granite mine buildings bear a family resemblance to the numerous Methodist chapels in the area – testimony to the success enjoyed by the nonconformist sects in Cornwall. Between 1762 and 1786 the grassy hollow of Gwennap Pit, outside **St Day**, a mile southeast of Redruth, was the scene of huge gatherings of miners and their families to hear John Wesley preach. The first visits to Cornwall by the founder of Methodism were met with derision and violence, but he later won over the tough mining communities who could find little comfort in the gentrified established church. At one time Wesley estimated that the congregation at Gwennap Pit exceeded thirty thousand, noting in his diary, "I shall scarce see a larger congregation till we meet in the air." The present tiered amphitheatre was created in 1805, and is today the venue of Methodist meetings for the annual Whit Monday service.

The town's former harbour lies two and a half miles away at **PORTREATH**, a surfing beach that enjoys the cleanest water on this stretch. The village is within walking distance of the awe-inspiring **Hell's Mouth**, a cauldron of waves and black rocks at the base of two-hundred-foot cliffs five miles down the coast at the top of St Ives Bay; it's also just three miles south of **Porthtowan**, another popular surfing beach.

You can find a good selection of **B&Bs** in Redruth, among them the attractive *Lansdowne House*, five minutes from the bus and train stations at 42 Clinton Rd (☎01209/216002; no credit cards; ①). Portreath has the basic *Cliff House*, just off the harbourside (☎01209/842008; no credit cards; ①), and *Sycamore Lodge* on Primrose Terrace (☎01209/842784; closed Dec; no credit cards; ①).

St Agnes and around

Though the village is surrounded by ruined engine houses, **ST AGNES** today gives little hint of the conditions in which its population once lived, the straggling streets of uniform grey cottages now housing retired people, whose immaculate flower-filled gardens are admired by the troops of holidaymakers striding up and down the steep terrace called Stippy-Stappy.

Well connected by bus to Truro, St Ives, Redruth and Newquay, St Agnes makes a useful stopover for exploring the coast in the area. At the end of a steep valley below St

Agnes, **Trevaunance Cove** is the site of several failed attempts to create a harbour for the town. Its fine sandy beach is a favourite with surfers and other bathing enthusiasts, despite the poor water quality. West of St Agnes lies one of Cornwall's most famous vantage points, **St Agnes Beacon**, 630ft high, from which views extend inland to Bodmin Moor and even across the peninsula to St Michael's Mount. A short distance away, the headland of **St Agnes Head** has the area's largest colony of breeding kittiwakes, and the nearby cliffs also shelter fulmars and guillemots, while grey seals are a common sight offshore. Past the old World War II airfield three miles north of St Agnes, the resort of **Perranporth** lies at the southern end of Perran Beach, a three-mile expanse of sand enhanced by caves and natural rock arches, very popular with surfers (boards and equipment to rent at Surf Shack on Beach Rd).

A good **place to stay** in St Agnes is *Penkerris*, a spacious Edwardian house near the centre on Penwinnick Road (☎01872/552262; ①); there are log fires in winter and you can also eat here. The most interesting **pub** is the *Railway Inn* on Vicarage Road; decorated with an idiosyncratic collection of shoes, horsebrasses and naval memorabilia, it also has a good selection of ales and snacks. One of the area's choicest **hotel-restaurants** occupies a spectacular position at Trevaunance Point overlooking Trevaunance Cove: the ivy-clad *Trevaunance Point Hotel* (☎01872/553235; ⑤), ex-home of actor Claude Rains, serves wonderful moderately priced fish dishes as well as some vegetarian choices. In Perranporth, the *Cellar Cove Hotel* represents great value, with bird's-eye views over the beach (☎01872/572110; ②), while, right next to the beach, the *Seiners' Arms* is a huge pub and restaurant where you can sit outside and also sleep (☎01872/573118; ④). On the cliff-top outside Perranporth, the **youth hostel** (☎01872/573812; closed Oct–March), in a former coastguard station, enjoys great views towards Ligger Point at the north end of the beach.

Newquay

It is difficult to imagine a lineage for **NEWQUAY** that extends more than a few years back, but the "new quay" was built in the fifteenth century in what was already a long-established fishing port. Up to then it had been more colourfully known as Towan Blistra, and was concentrated in the sheltered west end of the bay. The town was given a boost in the nineteenth century when its harbour was expanded for coal import and a railway was constructed across the peninsula for china clay shipments. With the trains came a swelling stream of seasonal visitors, drawn to the town's superb position on a knuckle of cliffs overlooking fine golden sands and Atlantic rollers, natural advantages which have made Newquay the premier resort of north Cornwall.

The centre of town is a somewhat tacky parade of shops and restaurants, partly pedestrianized, from which lanes lead to ornamental gardens and sloping lawns on the cliff-tops. Below, adjacent to the small harbour in the crook of the massive Towan Head, **Towan Beach** is the most central of the seven miles of firm sandy beaches that follow in an almost unbroken succession. You can reach all of them on foot, though for some of the farther ones, such as **Porth Beach**, with its grassy headland, or the extensive **Watergate Bay**, you might prefer to make use of local buses #53 and #56. The beaches can all be unbearably crowded in full season, and all are popular with surfers, particularly Watergate and – west of Towan Head – **Fistral Bay**, the largest of the town beaches. On the other side of East Pentire Head from Fistral, **Crantock Beach** – reachable over the Gannel River by ferry or upstream footbridge – is usually less crowded, and has a lovely backdrop of dunes and undulating grassland. This is one of the beaches in the Newquay area that pass EU guidelines, the others being Towan and Watergate. Try to coincide your visit to Newquay with one of the surfing competitions and events that run right through the summer – contact the tourist office for details.

Practicalities

Newquay's train station is off Cliff Road, a couple of hundred yards from the bus station on East Street. All buses for the beaches stop on Cliff Road and its extension Narrowcliff. The **tourist office** lies opposite the bus station at Marcus Hill (May–Sept Mon–Sat 9am–6pm, Sun 10am–4pm; Oct–April Mon–Sat 9am–5pm; ☎01637/871345). There's loads of **accommodation** in Newquay, though rooms can still be at a premium in July and August. In the centre of town, the *Bay View House Hotel* offers good value and superb views (☎01637/871214; ③), while fans of Fistral Beach will appreciate the proximity of *Links Hotel* on Headland Rd (☎01637/873211; no credit cards; ②). Newquay has a handful of independent **hostels** offering beds in dorms and some double rooms, the most impressive of which is *Newquay International Backpackers*, 69 Tower Rd (☎01637/879366, *newquaybackpackers@dial.pipex.com*); it's run by the same people who run *St Ives Backpackers*, who also arrange free tours and entertainment. Other hostels operate to varying standards, including *Towan Backpackers Hostel*, 16 Beachfield Ave (☎01637/874668), *Rick's Hostel*, 8 Springfield Rd (☎01637/851143), where rooms can only be rented by the week in summer, and *Matt's Surf Lodge*, 110 Mount Wise Rd (☎01637/874651). All hostels have TVs, kitchens, and places to store your surfboard. The **campsites** in the area are all mega-complexes, but many of them are unwilling to take same-sex groups or even couples. The most convenient site, *Porth Beach* (☎01637/876531; closed Nov to mid-March), behind the beach of the same name to the east of town, falls into this category, and a little further back, on Trevelgue Rd, *Trevelgue* (☎01637/851851) is also family-oriented. The next-door *Smugglers Haven* (☎01637/852000), however, run by the same management, has a more relaxed attitude, while the *Sunnyside* on Quintrell Downs (☎01637/873338) goes out of its way to attract the 18 to 30 singles crowd – it's a couple of miles inland, close to a stop on the train line.

Newquay is filled with places to eat, but most are mediocre. There are a few casual cafés just up from the beach on Tower Road, including the *Lifebuoy Café*, which serves all-day **breakfasts** for £3 (vegetarians pay a little more). Just above Towan Beach, *Chy-an-Mor* is a large café-bar on Beach Road, serving various **snacks**, including burgers and ploughman's lunches on its terrace. For something more substational, try the *Bay View House Hotel* (see above), which offers good-value set-price **meals** with views.

The hippest place to rent or buy **surfing equipment** is Tunnel Vision, 6 Alma Place, off Fore Street, which offers a huge range of gear. Other shops include Fistral Surf Shop, 1 Beacon Rd, on the harbour side of the headland, or Newquay Surfing Centre nearby at 72 Fore St, which gives lessons (☎01637/850737; closed Nov–April) as does Offshore Surfing School (☎01637/851487; closed Nov–April). If you're more interested in **biking**, head for the rental place on Towan Beach (☎01637/874668) or try Newquay Bike Hire at Unit 1, Wesley Yard (☎01637/874040), which will deliver a bike free. Newquay has become Cornwall's biggest centre for **nightclubbing**: the town's current hot spots are *Berties* on East St and the *Sailors Arms* and *The Beach* on Fore St, though these places tend to be fairly glittery and overwhelmed in summer. The *Red Room*, at Foster's pub in Narrowcliff and the *Kaola* on Beach Rd have more underground sounds; otherwise ask around and watch for the posters for the current venues.

Padstow and around

The small fishing port of **PADSTOW** is nearly as popular as Newquay, but has a very different feel. Enclosed within the estuary of the Camel – the only river of any size that empties on Cornwall's north coast – the town long retained its position as the principal fishing port on this coast, and still has something of the atmosphere of a medieval town. Its chief annual festival is also a hangover from times past, the **Obby Oss**, a May Day romp when one of the locals garbs himself as a horse and prances through the town

THE SAINTS' WAY

Padstow's St Petroc church is the traditional starting point for one of Cornwall's oldest walking routes, the **Saints' Way**. Extending for some thirty miles between Cornwall's north and south coasts, and connecting the principal ports of Padstow and Fowey, the path originates from the Bronze Age when traders preferred the cross-country hike to making the perilous sea journey round Land's End. The route was later travelled by Irish and Welsh missionaries crossing the peninsula between the fifth and eighth centuries, on pilgrimage to the principal shrines of Cornwall's Celtic culture.

Skirting Bodmin Moor, the reconstructed Saints' Way is rarely dramatic, though it passes a variety of scenery and several points of interest along the way, from Neolithic burial chambers to medieval churches and the more austere lines of Wesleyan chapels. The route is well marked and can be walked in stages, the country paths that constitute it stretching for two to six miles each; although it crosses several trunk roads, these do not impinge too much. Pick up guides and leaflets giving detailed directions in Padstow, Bodmin and Fowey tourist offices.

From St Petroc's, follow Hill Street, crossing New Street, and continue along Dennis Lane to the lake at Dennis Cove, from where the path climbs through fields to the monument to Queen Victoria, the point at which most people stop. If you choose to continue, you'll find that seven or eight miles out of Padstow, the route crosses the **St Breock Downs** with views stretching from the Camel estuary to the white clay mountains around St Austell. From here the path veers southeast to pass through **Lanlivet**, the halfway point of the Way lying a couple of miles outside Bodmin. There is an inexpensive **B&B** here at *Lower Woon Farm* (☎01208/831756; no credit cards; ①), which also serves three-course evening meals for £12.

South of here, **Helman Tor** (674ft) holds the trail's most impressive scenery, studded with bare boulders and wind-eroded rocks and flanked by acres of gorse. At Helman Tor Gate, the path divides, giving you the choice of reaching Fowey via **Lanlivery** – home of St Brevita's church with one of Cornwall's landmark towers – or **Luxulyan**, which boasts a lush gorge crossed by a viaduct and aqueduct built in 1842 and a holy well below the fifteenth-century church. The eastern route through Lanlivery takes you through the wooded estuary of the River Fowey – legendary meeting place of Tristan and Iseult – to the port. The longer western route follows an old cobbled causeway for part of the way, and passes through **Tywardreath**, which once marked the inland extent of the sea before the port of Par was built by industrialist Joseph Treffry (builder of the viaduct at Luxulyan). Tywardreath means "house on the strand", and was described by Daphne Du Maurier in her novel of that name. Fowey is four miles southeast of here. The end of the route is the church of St Fimbarrus in Fowey; see p.407 for accommodation hereabouts.

preceded by a masked and club-wielding "teaser" – a spirited if rather institutionalized re-enactment of old fertility rites.

On the hill overlooking Padstow, the church of **St Petroc** is dedicated to Cornwall's most important saint, a Welsh or Irish monk who landed here in the sixth century, died in the area and gave his name to the town – "Petrock's Stow". The building has a fine fifteenth-century font, an Elizabethan pulpit and some amusing carved bench-ends. The walls are lined with monuments to the local Prideaux family, who still occupy nearby **Prideaux Place**, an Elizabethan manor house with grand staircases, richly furnished rooms full of portraits, fantastically ornate ceilings and formal gardens (Easter–Sept Mon–Thurs & Sun 1.30–5pm; house & grounds £4.50, grounds only £2.50), all of which have been used as settings for a plethora of recent films, such as *Twelfth Night* and *Oscar and Lucinda*. The grounds contain an ancient deer park, and give good views over the Camel estuary.

The harbour is jammed with launches and boats offering cruises in Padstow Bay, while a regular **ferry** (daily 10am–6pm; not Sun in winter; £1.60 return) carries people across the river to **ROCK** – close to the sand-engulfed church of **St Enodoc** (John Betjeman's burial place) and to the good beaches around Polzeath. The ferry leaves from the harbour's North Pier except at low water when it goes from near the war memorial downstream.

The coast on the **south side** of the estuary also offers some good **beach** country, which you can reach in summer on bus #56 (not Sat), though walking would enable you to view some terrific coastline. Out of Padstow, the rivermouth is clogged by **Doom Bar**, a sand bar that was allegedly the curse of a mermaid who had been mortally wounded by a fisherman who mistook her for a seal. Apart from thwarting the growth of Padstow as a busy commercial port, the bar has scuppered some three hundred vessels, with great loss of life. Round **Stepper Point** you can reach the sandy and secluded Harlyn Bay and, turning the corner southwards, **Constantine Bay**, the area's best surfing beach. The dunes backing the beach and the rock pools skirting it make this one of the most appealing bays on this coast; moreover it boasts the best water quality, though the tides can be treacherous and bathing hazardous near the rocks. Surfers are attracted to other beaches in the neighbourhood too, but the surrounding caravan-sites can make these claustrophobic in summer - the sands around **Porthcothan** are worth exploring.

Three or four miles further south lies one of Cornwall's most dramatic beaches, **Bedruthan Steps**. Traditionally held to be the stepping-stones of a giant called Bedruthan (a legendary figure conjured into existence in the nineteenth century), these slate outcrops can be readily viewed from the cliff-top path, at a point which drivers can reach on the B3276. You'll be hard put to resist walking down the path, but take extreme care as the rock is unstable: access is closed in bad weather.

Padstow is also the start of an excellent **cycle-track** converted from the old railway line between Wadebridge and Padstow, forming part of the **Camel Trail**, a fifteen-mile traffic-free path that follows the river up as far as Wenfordbridge, on the edge of Bodmin Moor, with a turn-off for Bodmin. The five-mile Padstow–Wadebridge stretch offers glimpses a variety of birdlife, especially around the small **Pinkson Creek**, habitat of terns, herons, curlews and egrets. You can **rent bikes** from Brinham's on Padstow's South Quay. Further down the estuary, on the Camel Trail outside Wadebridge, Bridge Bike Hire has a greater stock, though it's still advisable to book (☎01208/813050). **Walkers** can set out from Padstow on the thirty-mile **Saints' Way** across the peninsula to Fowey (see box on p.431).

Practicalities

Padstow's **tourist office** is on the harbour (April–Sept Mon–Fri 10am–5pm, Sat 10am–4pm, Sun 11am–4pm; Oct–March Mon–Fri 10am–4pm; ☎01841/533449). Central **accommodation** includes the *London Inn* on Landewell Street (☎01841/532554; no credit cards; ①), converted from a row of fishermen's cottages in 1802, and the posher *Old Ship Hotel*, Mill Square (☎01841/532357; ⑥). The *Alexandra*, above the town at 30 Dennis Rd (☎01841/532503; no credit cards; ②; closed Nov–Easter), is a solid Victorian house with a good prospect of the Camel estuary. The nearest **youth hostel** has stunning views and is excellently sited almost on the beach at Treyarnon Bay (☎01841/520322; closed Nov–March); to get there, take a bus to Constantine (#55 or #56, also from Newquay) then walk for half a mile. Behind the hostel there is a **campsite** at Trethias Farm (☎01841/520323; closed Oct–March). Nearer Padstow, there is another alongside the estuary about a ten-minute walk south of town, *Dennis Cove* (☎01841/532349; closed Oct–Easter).

Padstow's quayside is lined with snack bars and pasty shops as well as pubs where you can sit outside, such as the *Shipwright's* on the harbour's north side. But foodies know the town best for its high-class **restaurants**, particularly those associated with star chef Rick Stein, whose *Seafood Restaurant*, at Riverside (☎01841/532485; closed

Sun), is one of England's top fish restaurants – and very expensive. The waiting list for a table here can be months long, though a reservation on a weekday out of season can mean booking only a day or two ahead, and there's always the chance of a cancellation if you turn up on spec. The TV chef has responded to the demand by opening up another couple of places in town, *St Petroc's Bistro* at 4 New St (☎01841/532700; closed Mon), which has a slightly cheaper, more French-inspired version of the *Seafood Restaurant's* menu, and the casual *Middle Street Café* nearby, whose round marble tables lend it the style of a Milanese bar (except that you can't smoke), and which serves snacks at lunch and moderate set-price meals at night (closed Sun). All three establishments also offer accommodation (⑤).

Rick Stein doesn't have a monopoly of classy restaurants in Padstow; the harbourside also has the expensive *Old Custom House*, serving meat and game alongside the usual fish choices (☎01841/532359); book ahead in summer. For cheaper eats, head for *Rojano's* on Mill Square, which serves up pizza and pasta (closed Mon). Otherwise, the nautical-flavoured *London Inn* (see p.432) does sandwiches, pasties and more substantial meals, as does the *Old Ship*, where you can eat outside. And if you really can't leave Padstow without sampling some of Rick Stein's creations, you could always feast on a gourmet picnic, supplied by the master's **delicatessen** next to the *Middle Street Café*.

Polzeath to Port Isaac

Facing west into Padstow Bay, the beaches of and around **POLZEATH** are the finest in the vicinity, pelted by rollers which make this one of the best surfing sites in the West Country – though be warned that Daymer Bay still falls short of EU standards of water cleanliness. *Pheasants Rise*, Trebetherick (☎01208/863190; no credit cards; ①; closed Nov–Easter), is a useful **B&B** a few minutes' walk from both Polzeath and Daymer bays, and the *Tristram* **campsite** (☎01208/862215; closed Nov–Easter) sits on a cliff overlooking the beach. In recent years, Polzeath campsites, like those in Newquay, have barred groups of young people owing to past fracas, though *Trenant Steading* (☎01208/862407; closed Nov–Easter) between Polzeath and New Polzeath is currently still admitting them, but check first. Polzeath has a small **tourist office** behind the beach (Easter to mid-Oct Mon–Sat 10am–5pm; ☎01208/862488). On the beach, the *Galleon* does various snacks and takeaways, and *Finn's* does full meals as well as cream teas. *Mother's Kitchen*, just off the beach next to the *Spar* supermarket, offers a range of ice cream, pasta and takeaway pizzas (not chips), and the *Oyster-Catcher* bar is a lively evening hangout just up the hill. *Surf's Up* on the beach offers **surfing** tuition; the gear can be rented from shops.

Heading east, the coastal path brings you through cliff-top growths of feathery tamarisk, which flower spectacularly in July and August. From the headland of **Pentire Point**, views unfold for miles over the offshore islets of **The Mouls** and **Newland**, with their populations of grey seals and puffins. Half a mile east, the scanty remains of an Iron Age fort stand on the humpy back of **Rump's Point**, from where the path descends a mile or so to **Lundy Bay**, a pleasant sandy cove surrounded by green fields. Climbing again, you pass the shafts of an old antimony mine on the way to **Doyden Point**, which is picturesquely ornamented with a nineteenth-century castle folly once used for gambling parties.

The inlet of **Port Quin** has a few cottages but no shops – the next settlement of any size is **PORT ISAAC**, wedged in a gap in the precipitous cliff-wall and dedicated to the crab and lobster trade. Only seasonal trippers ruffle the surface of life in this cramped harbour town, whose narrow lanes focus on a couple of pubs at the seafront, where a pebble beach and rock pools are exposed by the low tide. The village offers a range of **accommodation**, best of all the *Slipway Hotel* (☎01208/880264; ②), a sixteenth-century building right opposite the harbour; the management is youthful and friendly, and there's a bar and excellent restaurant too. Cheaper choices are outside the centre and away from the sea, among them the basic *Fairholme*, 30 Trewetha Lane (☎01208/880397; no credit cards; ①), or, overlooking the neighbouring Port Gaverne Bay, *Rockmount*, 12 The Terrace (☎01208/880629; non-smoking; ①). Further along, *St Andrew's Hotel* at 18 The Terrace has plain but adequate rooms, those with a sea view going for higher prices (☎01208/880240; ③). The *Old School* also has wonderful views and a mediocre seafood restaurant (☎01208/880721; ③). The *Golden Lion* is Port Isaac's most cheerful **pub** and has an adjoining bistro and balcony seating overlooking the harbour. Crab is what Port Isaac does best; try it here or to take away on the harbourfront; other places to sample crab or lobster include the *Slipway Hotel*. The *Old School* is a good place for snacks and teas, or you might be tempted by basic but fresh fish and chips across the road at the *Old Drugstore*.

At the main car park at the top of the village, a kiosk which alternates between Port Isaac and Tintagel provides **information** on walking along the heritage coast on either side of the town. **Port Gaverne**, the next cove to the east, is a serene cluster of houses, with a snug bar at the *Port Gaverne Hotel* (☎01208/880244; ⑥), which also has a great restaurant and quaint rooms – both expensive.

Tintagel

East of Port Isaac, the coast is wild and unspoiled, making for some steep and strenuous walking, and interspersed with some stupendous strands of sandy beaches such as that at **Trebarwith**. A few miles further north, the rocky littoral provides an appropriate backdrop for the black, forsaken ruins of **Tintagel Castle** (daily: April–Sept 10am–6pm; Oct 10am–5pm; Nov–March 10am–4pm; £2.80; EH). It was the twelfth-century chronicler Geoffrey of Monmouth who first popularized the notion that this was the **birthplace of King Arthur**, son of Uther Pendragon and Ygrayne, but by that time local folklore was already saturated with tales of King Mark of Cornwall, Tristan and Iseult, Arthur and the knights of Camelot. Twin influences were at work in Geoffrey's story, which merges the historic figure of Arthur with a separate body of legend centring on the missionary activity of the Celtic monastery that occupied this site in the sixth century. Tintagel is certainly a plausibly resonant candidate for the abode of the Once and Future King, but the **castle** ruins in fact belong to a Norman stronghold occupied by the earls of Cornwall, who after sporadic spurts of rebuilding allowed it to decay, most of it having been washed into the sea by the sixteenth century. The remains of the **Celtic monastery** are still visible on the headland and are an important source of knowledge of how the country's earliest monastic houses were organized. Digs begun in 1998 on the eastern side of the island have also revealed glass fragments dating from the sixth or seventh centuries believed to originate in Malaga, as well as a 1500-year-old section of slate bearing two Latin inscriptions, one of them attributing authorship to one "Artognou, father of Coll's descendant".

The best approach to the site is from **Glebe Cliff** to the west, where the parish church of **St Materiana** sits in isolation; the South West Coast Path passes the church, and for drivers it's a good place to park before descending to the castle. From the village of **TINTAGEL** the shortest access is from the signposted path, a well-trodden route. The only item of note in this dreary collection of cafés and B&Bs is the **Old Post Office** (April–Sept daily 11am–5.30pm, Oct daily 11am–5pm; £2.20; NT), a rickety-roofed slate-built construction dating from the fourteenth century, now restored to its appearance in the Victorian era when it was used as a post office. The village has plenty of **accommodation**, including the fairly basic *Bosayne*, Atlantic Rd (☎01840/770514; no credit cards; ①), one of a tier of B&Bs looking out over the cliff. The *Old Malt House* (☎01840/770461; ②; closed Jan) and the *Tintagel Arms Hotel* (☎01840/770780; ②),

KING ARTHUR IN CORNWALL

Did **King Arthur** really exist? If he did, it is likely that he was an amalgam of two people; a sixth-century Celtic warlord who united the local tribes in a series of successful battles against the invading Anglo-Saxons, and a local Cornish saint. Whatever his origins, his role was recounted and inflated by poets and troubadours in later centuries (particularly in Welsh poems, the earliest of which is *Gododdin*). Though there is no mention of him in the ninth- to twelfth-century *Anglo-Saxon Chronicle*, his exploits were elaborated later by the unreliable medieval chronicler Geoffrey of Monmouth, who made Arthur the conqueror of western Europe, and was the first to record the belief that **Tintagel** was his birthplace. Twelfth-century chronicler William of Malmesbury narrated the story of Glastonbury, including the popular legend that, after being mortally wounded in battle, Arthur sailed to Avalon (Glastonbury), where he was buried alongside Guinevere. The Arthurian legends were crystallized in Thomas Malory's epic, *Morte d'Arthur* (1485), further romanticized in Tennyson's *Idylls of the King* (1859–85) and resurrected in T.H. White's saga, *The Once and Future King* (1937–58).

Although there are places throughout Britain and Europe which claim some association with Arthur, it is England's West Country, and **Cornwall** in particular, that has the greatest concentration of places boasting a link. Relatively untouched by the Saxon invasions, Cornwall has practically appropriated the hero as its own, a far more authentic bond than the efforts of the county's tourist industry might suggest. Here, the legends – fertilized by fellow Celts from Brittany and Wales – have established deep roots, so that, for example, the spirit of Arthur is said to be embodied in the Cornish chough – a bird now almost extinct. Cornwall's most famous Arthurian site is **Tintagel**, which is said to be the birthplace of Arthur. Meanwhile, Merlin is thought to have lived in a cave under the castle – and also on a rock near Mousehole, south of Penzance. Nearby Bodmin Moor is full of places with names like "King Arthur's Bed" and "King Arthur's Downs", while Camlan, the battlefield where Arthur was mortally wounded fighting against his nephew Mordred, is thought to lie on the northern reaches of the moor at Slaughterbridge, near Camelford (which is also sometimes identified as Camelot itself). Nearby, at Dozmary Pool, the knight Bedivere was dispatched by the dying Arthur to return the sword Excalibur to the mysterious hand emerging from the water – though Loe Pool in Mount's Bay also claims this honour. According to some, Arthur's body was transported after the battle to Boscastle, on Cornwall's northern coast, from where a funeral barge transported the body to Avalon. Cornwall is also the presumed home of King Mark, at the centre of a separate cycle of myths which later became interwoven with the Arthurian one. It was Mark who sent the knight Tristan to Ireland to fetch his betrothed, Iseult; his headquarters is supposed to have been at Castle Dore, north of Fowey. Out beyond Land's End, the fabled, vanished country of Lyonesse is also said to be the original home of Arthur, as well as being (according to Spenser's Faerie Queene) the birthplace of Tristan.

Much of the Cornish tourist office's celebration of the Arthurian sagas has the same cynical basis as the more ancient desire to claim Arthur by the various villages and sites throughout England and Wales: the cachet and hence profit to be had from the veneration of a secular saint. Witness the "discovery" of the tomb of Arthur and Guinevere by the Benedictine monks of Glastonbury in the twelfth century, which helped to boost the profile of this powerful abbey. Today in Tintagel you will find Arthurian tack galore, including every kind of Merlin-esque hogwash (crystal balls, sugar-coated wands, etc), and even Excaliburgers.

both on Fore Street, are conveniently located for the castle. Three-quarters of a mile outside the village at Dunderhole Point, past St Materiana, the offices of a former slate quarry now house a **youth hostel** with great views of the coastline (☎01840/770334; closed Oct–March). At the end of Atlantic Road, the *Headland* site offers scenic **camping** (☎01840/770239; closed Oct–March).

Boscastle

Three miles east of Tintagel, the port of **BOSCASTLE** lies compressed within a narrow ravine drilled by the rivers Jordan and Valency, its tidy riverfront bordered by thatched and lime-washed houses giving on to the twisty harbour. Above and behind, a collection of seventeenth- and eighteenth-century cottages can be seen on a circular walk, starting either from Fore Street or the main car park, where there is a local map. The walk traces the valley of the Valency for about a mile to reach Boscastle's graceful **parish church**, tucked away in a peaceful glen. A mile and a half further up the valley lies another church, **St Juliot's**, restored by Thomas Hardy when he was plying his trade as a young architect. It was while he was working here that he met Emma Gifford, whom he married in 1874, a year after the publication of *A Pair of Blue Eyes*, the book that kicked off Hardy's literary career. It opens with an architect arriving in a Cornish village to restore its church, and is full of descriptions of the country around Boscastle.

Among Boscastle's most attractive **accommodation** is *St Christopher's Hotel* (☎01840/250412; ②; closed Jan), a restored Georgian manor house at the top of the High Street. The *Old Coach House*, on Tintagel Road (☎01840/250398; ①) is another well-equipped old building, and has very friendly staff. The harbour has a lovely old **youth hostel** (☎01840/250287; closed Nov to mid-March) which is right by the sea. Nearby, you can eat at the *Harbour Restaurant*, which serves hot meals all day, as well as sandwiches and teas, or you could pick up an ice cream from the *Harbour Light*, whose splendidly saggy roof marks it out as one of Boscastle's oldest buildings. The village has three good **pubs**, though the *Napoleon* has the advantage of a good vegetarian menu among its bar meals and a spacious garden with distant views of the sea. The *Cobweb* is busier but rates highly on atmosphere and has live music on Saturdays.

Bude and around

There is little distinctively Cornish in Cornwall's northernmost town of **BUDE**, four miles west of the Devon border. Built around an estuary surrounded by a fine expanse of sands, the town has sprouted a crop of holiday homes and hotels, though these have not unduly spoiled the place nor the magnificent cliffy coast surrounding it.

Of the excellent beaches hereabouts, the central **Summerleaze** is clean and wide, growing to such immense proportions when the tide is out that a sea water swimming pool has been provided near the cliffs. The mile-long **Widemouth Bay**, two and a half miles **south** of Bude, is the main focus of the holiday hordes – it has the cleanest water monitored between Bude and Polzeath, though bathing can be dangerous near the rocks at low tide. Surfers also congregate five miles down the coast at **Crackington Haven**, wonderfully situated between 430-foot crags at the mouth of a lush valley, though the water quality is poor. The cliffs on this stretch are characterized by remarkable zigzagging strata of shale, limestone and sandstone, a mixture which erodes into vividly contorted detached formations.

To the **north** of Bude, acres-wide **Crooklets** is the scene of **surfing** and lifesaving demonstrations and competitions. A couple of miles farther on, **Sandy Mouth** holds a pristine expanse of sand with rock pools beneath the encircling cliffs. The water quality is up to EU standards despite the seaborne litter, and myriad wildflowers dot the country around. It is a short walk from here to another surfers' delight, **Duckpool**, a tiny sandy cove flanked by jagged reefs at low tide. The beach is dominated by the three-hundred-foot **Steeple Point**, at the mouth of a stream that flows through the **Coombe Valley**. Once the estate of the master Elizabethan mariner Sir Richard Grenville, the valley is now managed by the National Trust, who have laid out a one-and-a-half-mile nature trail alongside the wooded stream, half a mile inland.

Between Duckpool and the Devon border stretch five miles of strenuous but exhilarating coast. The only village along here is **Morwenstow**, just south of **Henna Cliff**, at 450ft the highest sheer drop of any sea-cliff in England after Beachy Head, affording magnificent views along the coast and beyond Lundy to the Welsh coast.

Practicalities

Bude's **tourist office** is in the centre of town at the Crescent (April–Sept Mon–Sat 10am–5pm, Sun 10am–4pm; Oct–March Mon–Fri 10am–4pm, Sat 10am–2pm; ☎01288/354240). For **accommodation**, *Clovelly House*, 4 Burn View (☎01288/352761; no credit cards; ②), and *Links View*, 13 Morwenna Terrace (☎01288/352561; no credit cards; ①), are close to each other near the golf course; the former also has a coffee shop open all day for "Celtic" organic food, fresh fish dishes and cream teas. There's a very homely B&B at 16 The Rowans, off Hawthorne Ave, (☎01288/355151; no credit cards; ①), while the best of the lot is the *Falcon Hotel* on Breakwater Rd (☎01288/352005; ⑧), supposed to be the oldest coaching house in north Cornwall. If proximity to bathing is your priority, try the hotels around Crooklets Beach, such as the comfortable and capacious *Inn on the Green* (☎01288/356013; ③). Bude's nearest **campsite** is *Wooda Park* (☎01288/352069; closed Nov–March), away from the sea at Poughill (pronounced "Poffil"), two miles north of Bude. Slightly farther, at Widemouth Bay, the *Widemouth Bay* site sits amidst a host of others (☎01288/361208; closed Nov–Feb).

The *Falcon Hotel* offers good food at its bar and has a more formal and expensive **restaurant**, which specializes in seafood. For snacks and salads, try the central *Carriers Inn* on the Strand, which has seating outside. A mile inland from Bude, in the village of **Stratton**, the *Tree Inn* was used as the Royalist headquarters during the battle of Stamford Hill, an engagement re-enacted annually on the nearest weekend to 16 May. The pub was the home of the "Cornish Giant" Anthony Paine, manservant of Lord Grenville, who commanded the king's forces at their victory. There's a choice of **surfing equipment rental** outlets, including Zuma Jay on Belle Vue Lane and, visible at the end of the street, XTC on Princes Street. On a different note, the **Bude Jazz Festival** attracts a range of stomping sounds from around the world for a week at the end of August.

Bodmin and Bodmin Moor

Bodmin Moor, the smallest, mildest and most accessible of the West Country's great moors, has some beautiful tors, torrents and rock formations, but much of its fascination lies in the strong human imprint, particularly the wealth of relics left behind by its **Bronze Age** population, including such important sites as Trethevy Quoit and the stone circles of the Hurlers. Separated from these by some three millennia, the churches in the villages of St Neot's, Blisland and Altarnun are among the region's finest examples of fifteenth-century art and architecture.

The biggest centre in the area, **Bodmin**, stands outside the moor but can provide information on walking routes on the moor and on the Camel Trail, which touches here. With the north moor village of **Camelford**, Bodmin has the area's widest choice of accommodation, and is the most accessible town, sitting on the main A30 and within reach of the main rail line. Thanks to its central position, Bodmin is also well connected on bus routes, but the only services onto the moor are the sporadic #X3 from Bodmin to Launceston via Bolventor (Tues & Thurs, plus Sat in summer), Tilley's Coaches #225, running three times daily on weekdays between Launceston and Altarnun, and the more frequent #77 and #X77 from Liskeard (also a train stop) to St Neot (not Sun). Still on the moor's southeastern corner, the #73 runs hourly between Liskeard and Pensilva via St Cleer and Darite (not Sun).

Bodmin

The town of **BODMIN** lies on the western edge of Bodmin Moor, equidistant from the north and south Cornish coasts and the Fowey and Camel rivers, a position that encouraged its growth as a trading town. It was also an important ecclesiastical centre after the establishment of a priory by Saint Petroc, who moved here from Padstow in the sixth century. The priory disappeared but Bodmin retained its prestige through its church of St Petroc, built in the fifteenth century and still the largest in Cornwall. Though officially the county town, Bodmin sacrificed much of its administrative role by refusing access to the Great Western Railway in the 1870s, as a result of which much local business transferred down the road to Truro. **Bodmin Parkway** station lies three miles outside town, with a regular bus connection to the centre. By **bus** you can reach the town between Monday and Saturday from Padstow or Wadebridge on Western National #55 and from St Austell on any of the #29s; on Sunday the #55 connects St Austell, Bodmin and Wadebridge four times a day. From Penzance, Plymouth or Newquay it is easiest to take the National Express coaches, which go to Bodmin three times a day.

Bodmin's most prominent landmark is the **Gilbert Memorial**, a 144ft obelisk honouring a descendant of Walter Raleigh and occupying a commanding location on Bodmin Beacon, a high area of moorland near the centre of town. Below, at the end of Fore Steet, stands **St Petroc's** church; inside, it has an extravagantly carved twelfth-century font and an ivory casket that once held the bones of Petroc, while the south-west corner of the churchyard holds a sacred well. Close by, the notorious **Bodmin Jail** (Easter to mid-Oct Mon–Fri & Sun 10am–5pm, Sat 11am–5pm; mid-Oct to Easter daily 11am–4pm; £3) glowers darkly on Berrycombe Road, redolent of the public executions that were guaranteed crowd-pullers until 1862, when the hangings continued behind closed doors until the jail's closure in the early years of this century. You can visit part of the original eighteenth-century structure, including the condemned cell and some grisly exhibits chronicling the lives of the inmates.

Further up Berrycombe Road begins a section of the **Camel Trail** (see p.432), linking the town by cycle- and footpath to the main route along the Camel river at Boscarne Junction a mile up, which is itself connected by steam locomotives of the **Bodmin & Wenford Railway** to the restored station on St Nicholas Street and beyond to Bodmin Parkway (April–Sept 2–4 daily). The trains make a stop at Colesloggett, a good place to get off to explore **Cardinham Woods**, an excellent place for a day's rambling (see below for bike rental).

From Parkway it's less than two miles' walk to one of Cornwall's most celebrated country houses, **Lanhydrock** (April–Sept Tues–Sun 11am–5.30pm; Oct Tues–Sun 11am–5pm; house & grounds £6.40; grounds only £3.20; NT), originally seventeenth-century but totally rebuilt after a fire in 1881. The granite exterior remains true to its original form, but the 42 rooms show a very different style, including a long picture gallery with a plaster ceiling depicting scenes from the Old Testament, and – most illuminating of all – servants' quarters that reveal the daily workings of a Victorian manor house. The grounds have magnificent beds of magnolias, azaleas and rhododendrons, and a huge area of wooded parkland bordering onto the River Fowey.

Practicalities

Bodmin's **tourist office** (May–Sept Mon–Sat 10am–5pm; Oct–April Mon–Fri 10am–1pm; ☎01208/76616) is near the main car park at the bottom of St Nicholas Street. Basic **B&B** is available at *Higher Windsor* Cottage, 18 Castle St (☎01208/76474; no credit cards; ①); you'll also find rooms at the *George and Dragon* pub, 3 St Nicholas St (☎01208/72514; no credit cards; ①). Outside town, close to the Lanhydrock estate, the handsome *Bokiddick Farm* at Lanivet (☎01208/831481; no credit cards; ②) has rooms and fantastic views. There's a decent **campsite** on Old Callywith Road, a fifteen-minute walk from the centre (☎01208/73834; closed Dec–Feb).

Off Fore Street, the *Hole in the Wall* **pub** in Crockwell Street has a pleasant backroom bar in what used to be the debtors' prison, with exposed fourteenth-century walls enclosing a collection of antiquities and bric-a-brac. In summer you can drink in the courtyard, where there's a stuffed lion, and bar lunches are available or fuller meals in the upstairs **restaurant**. Good snacks are also served at the *Maple Leaf*, just across from St Petroc's at 14 Honey St. If you want to **rent a bike**, Glyn Valley Cycle Hire in Cardinham Woods has off-roaders available for the cycle route here or beyond to the moor (☎01208/74244).

Bodmin Moor

Just ten miles in diameter, **BODMIN MOOR** is a wilderness on a small scale, its highest tor rising to just 1375ft from a platform of 1000ft. Yet the moor conveys a sense of loneliness quite out of proportion to its size, with scattered ancient remains providing in places the only distraction from an empty horizon. Aside from its tors, the main attractions of the landscape are the small Dozmary Pool, a site steeped in myth, and a quartet of rivers – the Fowey, Lynher, Camel and De Lank – that rise from remote moorland springs and effectively bound the moor to the north, east and south.

Blisland and the western moor

BLISLAND stands in the Camel valley on the western slopes of Bodmin Moor, three miles northeast of Bodmin. Georgian and Victorian houses cluster around a village green and a church whose well-restored interior has an Italianate altar and a startlingly painted screen. On **Pendrift Common** above the village, the gigantic **Jubilee Rock** is inscribed with various patriotic insignia commemorating the jubilee of George III's coronation in 1809. From this seven-hundred-foot vantage point you look eastward over the De Lank gorge and the boulder-crowned knoll of **Hawk's Tor**, three miles away. On the shoulder of the tor stand the Neolithic **Stripple Stones**, a circular platform once holding 28 standing stones, of which just four are still upright.

Blisland lies just a couple of miles east of the **Merry Meeting** crossroads, a point near the end of the Camel Trail. The most convenient **place to stay** is *Lavethan* (☎01208/850487; no credit cards; ③), a plain but comfortable B&B, ten minutes' walk from the village towards St Mabyn. If you want to spend longer in the area, you could try *Lower Helland Farm*, a couple of miles outside the village off the A30 and near the Camel river and the Camel Trail (☎01208/72813) – two peaceful cottages have been converted from a barn and stable, rented at £100–250 a week according to season. The nearest **campsite** is *Glenmorris Park*, on Longstone Road, St Mabyn (☎01208/841677; closed Nov–Easter).

Bolventor and Dozmary Pool

The village of **Bolventor**, lying at the centre of the moor midway between Bodmin and Launceston, is an uninspiring place close to one of the moor's chief focuses for walkers and sightseers alike – **Jamaica Inn** (☎01566/86250; ③). A staging-post even before the precursor of the A30 road was laid here in 1769, the inn was described by Daphne Du Maurier as being "alone in glory, four square to the winds", and the combination of its convenient position and its association with her has led to its growth into a hotel and restaurant complex. One corner exhibits the room where the author stayed in 1930, soaking up inspiration for her smugglers' yarn. At the other end of the building is the silly but highly entertaining **Museum of Curiosities** (daily: Easter–Oct 10am–5pm, until 8pm during school holidays; winter 11am–4pm; closed Jan; £2.50; combined ticket with Smuggler's Museum

£4) a fairground miscellany of Victorian toys, mummified and stuffed animals, a collection of pipes and a guinea pigs' cricket match. The **Smuggler's Museum** across the road (same hours; £2.50), shows sundry relics associated with the contrabanders.

The inn's car park is a useful place to leave your vehicle and venture forth on foot. Just a mile away, along what must be the most travelled path on the moor, **Dozmary Pool** is another link in the West Country's Arthurian mythologies – after Arthur's death Sir Bedevere hurled Excalibur, the king's sword, into the pool, where it was seized by an arm raised from the depths. Loe Pool, near Porthleven on the Lizard, also claims the honour (see p.415). Despite its proximity to the A30, the diamond-shaped lake usually preserves an ethereal air, though it's been known to run dry in summer, dealing a bit of a blow to the legend that the pool is bottomless.

The lake is also the source of another, more obviously Cornish legend, that of John Tregeagle, a steward at Lanhydrock, whose unjust dealings with the local tenant farmers in the seventeenth century brought upon his spirit the curse of endlessly baling out the pool with a perforated limpet shell. As if this were not enough, his ghost is further tormented by a swarm of devils pursuing him as he flies across the moor in search of sanctuary; their infernal howling is sometimes audible on windy nights.

Liskeard and St Neot

LISKEARD, a bus and rail junction just off the southern limits of the moor, makes a decent overnight stop, with **accommodation** at two decent B&Bs *Elnor*, 1 Russell St (✆01579/342472; no credit cards; ①), and the *Nebula*, 27 Higher Lux St (✆01579/343989; ③), which also serves evening meals. From here, buses go on to **ST NEOT**, one of Bodmin Moor's prettiest villages, approached through a lush wooded valley. Its seventeenth-century **church** contains some of the most impressive stained glass windows of any parish church in the country, the oldest glass being the fifteenth-century **Creation Window**, at the east end of the south aisle. Next along, **Noah's Window** continues the sequence, but the narration soon dissolves into windows portraying patrons and local bigwigs, while others present cameos of the ordinary men and women of the village.

This southern edge of the moor is far greener and more thickly wooded than the northern reaches, due to the confluence of a web of rivers into the Fowey. One of the moor's best-known beauty spots is a couple of miles east, below Draynes Bridge, where the Fowey tumbles through the **Golitha Falls**, less a waterfall than a series of rapids. Dippers and wagtails flit through the trees, and there's a pleasant woodland walk you can take to the dam at the Siblyback Lake reservoir just over a mile away: follow the river up to Draynes Bridge, then walk north up a minor road until a path branches off on the right after a half-mile, leading down to the water's edge.

Camelford and the northern tors

The northern half of Bodmin Moor is dominated by its two highest tors, both of them easily accessible from **CAMELFORD**, a town once associated with King Arthur's Camelot, while Slaughterbridge, which crosses the River Camel north of town, is one of the contenders for his last battleground. The town has resisted trading on the Arthurian myths, but does have a couple of museums providing some diversion: the **British Cycling Museum** (daily Mon–Thurs & Sun 10am–5pm; £2.40), housed in the old station one mile north of town on the Boscastle road, is a cyclophile's dream, containing some four hundred examples of bikes through the ages and a library of books and manuals. Meanwhile the more conventional **North Cornwall Museum** (April–Sept Mon–Sat 10am–5pm; £1.50) in Camelford's centre contains domestic items and exhibits showing the development of the local slate industry, and also has a **tourist office** (same hours; ✆01840/212954).

Although it lacks excitement, Camelford makes a useful touring base. Among its **accommodation** is the central *Countryman Hotel*, at 7 Victoria Rd (✆01840/212250;

②), and the *Trenarth* (☎01840/213295; no credit cards; ①), much further up this long road, roughly fifteen minutes' walk from the centre. Back in town, *Silvermoon* is a well-equipped B&B on Lane End, just off the main road (☎01840/213736; no credit cards; ①), the The *Mason's Arms* on Market Place has rooms and a beer garden (☎01840/213309; no credit cards; ①) and the *Orangery*, opposite Camelford House, makes a convenient coffee stop. There are two **campsites** in the area, at *King's Acre* (☎01840/213561; closed Nov–Easter) and *Lakefield Caravan Park*, Lower Pendavey Farm (☎01840/213279; closed Nov–March), the latter also providing **horse-riding**.

Rough Tor, the second highest peak on Bodmin Moor at 1311ft, is four miles' walk southeast from Camelford. The hill presents a different aspect from every angle: from the south an ungainly mass, from the west a nobly proportioned mountain. A short distance to the east stand the Little Rough Tor, where there are the remains of an Iron Age camp, and Showery Tor, capped by a prominent formation of piled rocks.

Easily visible to the southeast, **Brown Willy** is, at 1375ft, the highest Bodmin peak in Cornwall, as its original name signified – Bronewhella, or "highest hill". Like Rough Tor, Brown Willy shows various faces, its sugarloaf appearance from the north sharpening into a long multi-peaked crest as you approach. The tor is accessible by continuing from the summit of Rough Tor across the valley of the De Lank, or, from the south, by footpath from Bolventor. The easiest ascent is by the worn path which climbs steeply up from the northern end of the hill.

Altarnun and the eastern moor

ALTARNUN is a pleasant, granite-grey village snugly sheltered beneath the eastern heights of the moor. Its prominent **church**, dedicated to St Nonna, mother of David, patron saint of Wales, contains a fine Norman font and 79 bench-ends carved at the beginning of the sixteenth century, depicting saints, musicians and clowns. The village also has a Methodist chapel, over the door of which there is an effigy of John Wesley – a regular visitor to the neighbourhood – by Nevill Northey Burnard (1818–78), a local sculptor who, despite the praise of his contemporaries, ended his days in a Redruth poorhouse. Outside the village, *Trecollas Farm* (☎01566/86386; no credit cards; ①; closed Nov–Feb) offers good accommodation and a four-course breakfast.

South of Altarnun, **Withey Brook** tumbles four hundred feet in less than a mile of gushing cascades before meeting up with the River Lynher, which bounds Bodmin Moor to the east. Beyond the brook, on **Twelve Men's Moor**, lie some of Bodmin Moor's grandest landscapes. The quite modest elevations of Hawk's Tor (1079ft) and the lower Trewartha Tor appear enormous from the north, though they are overtopped by **Kilmar**, highest of the hills on the moor's eastern flank at 1280ft.

Withey Brook starts life about six miles from Altarnun on **Stowe's Hill**, site of the moor's most famous stone pile, **The Cheesewring**, a precarious pillar of balancing granite slabs, marvellously eroded by the wind. Gouged out of the hillside nearby, the disused Cheesewring Quarry is a centre of rockclimbing. A mile or so down Stowe's Hill stands an artificial rock phenomenon, **The Hurlers**, a wide complex of three circles dating from about 1500 BC. The purpose of these stark upright stones is not known, though they owe their name to the legend that they were men turned to stone for playing the Celtic game of hurling on the Sabbath.

The Hurlers are easily accessible just outside **MINIONS**, Cornwall's highest village, three miles south of which stands another Stone Age survival, **Trethevy Quoit**, a chamber tomb nearly nine feet high, surmounted by a massive capstone. Originally enclosed in earth, the stones have been stripped by centuries of weathering to create Cornwall's most impressive megalithic monument. Bus #73 from Liskeard calls at St Cleer and Darite, both of which are close to Trethevy Quoit; alternatively, it's a three-mile walk from Liskeard.

travel details

Trains

Barnstaple to: Exeter (5–9 daily; 1hr).

Bath to: Bristol (every 20min; 20min); London (hourly; 1hr 30min); Salisbury (hourly; 1hr); Southampton (1–2 hourly; 1hr 30min).

Bodmin to: Exeter (1–2 hourly; 1hr 40min); London (hourly; 4hr); Penzance (hourly; 1hr 20min); Plymouth (hourly; 40min).

Bristol to: Bath (every 20min; 20min); Birmingham (hourly; 1hr 30min); Exeter (1–2 hourly; 1hr 20min); London (2 hourly; 1hr 40min); Penzance (9 daily; 4hr); Plymouth (8 daily; 2hr); Truro (9 daily; 3hr 20min).

Exeter to: Barnstaple (5–9 daily; 1hr); Birmingham (6 daily; 2hr 20min–2hr 40min); Bodmin (1–2 hourly; 1hr 40min); Bristol (1–2 hourly; 1hr 20min); Exmouth (2 hourly; 25min); Honiton (hourly; 30min); Liskeard (hourly; 1hr 30min); London (hourly; 2hr 30min); Par (hourly; 1hr 50min); Penzance (hourly; 3hr); Plymouth (2 hourly; 1hr); Salisbury (9–13 daily; 1hr 45min–2hr 20min); Torquay (hourly; 45min); Truro (7 daily; 2hr 15min).

Falmouth to: Truro (10–12 daily; 23min).

Honiton to: Exeter (hourly; 30min); Salisbury (every 1–2 hours; 1hr 20min).

Liskeard to: Exeter (hourly; 1hr 30min); London (8 daily; 4hr); Looe (8 daily, no Sun service in winter; 30min); Penzance (hourly; 1hr 30min); Plymouth (hourly; 30min); Truro (hourly; 50min).

Newquay to: Par (5 daily, no Sun service in winter; 45min).

Par to: Exeter (hourly; 1hr 50min); Newquay (5 daily, no Sun service in winter; 50min); Penzance (hourly; 1hr 10min); Plymouth (hourly; 1hr).

Penzance to: Bodmin (hourly; 1hr 20min); Bristol (9 daily; 4hr); Exeter (hourly; 3hr); Liskeard (hourly; 1hr 30min); London (9 daily; 5hr 15min–6hr 30min); Par (hourly; 1hr 10min); Plymouth (hourly; 2hr); St Ives (3–5 daily; 20min); Truro (1–2 hourly; 40min).

Plymouth to: Birmingham (6 daily; 3hr 30min); Bodmin (hourly; 40min); Bristol (8–9 daily; 2hr); Exeter (2 hourly; 1hr); Liskeard (hourly; 30min); London (9 daily; 3hr–3hr 45min); Par (hourly; 1hr); Penzance (hourly; 2hr); St Erth (hourly; 1hr 50min); Truro (hourly; 1hr 15min).

St Ives to: Penzance (3–5 daily; 20min); St Erth (2 hourly; 15min).

Torquay to: Exeter (hourly; 45min).

Truro to: Bristol (9 daily; 3hr 20min); Exeter (7 daily; 2hr 15min); Falmouth (10–12 daily; 25min); Liskeard (hourly; 50min); London (9 daily; 4hr 40min); Penzance (1–2 hourly; 40min); Plymouth (hourly; 1hr 15min).

Buses

Bath to: Bristol (2–4 hourly; 50min); Frome (hourly; 50min); London (8 daily; 3hr 20min); Salisbury (Mon–Sat hourly; 1hr 20min–2hr 20min); Wells (hourly; 1hr 20min).

Bodmin to: Bristol (1 daily; 4hr); Newquay (2–3 daily; 45min–1hr); Plymouth (2–4 daily; 1hr 10min); St Austell (Mon–Sat hourly, no Sun service in winter; 45min).

Bridgwater to: Taunton (4 daily; 30min); Wells (Mon–Sat hourly; 1hr 30min).

Bristol to: Bath (2–4 hourly; 50min); Birmingham (6 daily; 1hr 50min); Bodmin (1 daily; 3hr 50min); Exeter (5 daily; 1hr 40min–2hr); Glastonbury (hourly; 1hr 20min); London (hourly; 2hr 25min); Newquay (2–3 daily; 4hr–4hr 40min); Plymouth (5 daily; 2hr 30min–3hr); St Austell (1 daily; 4hr 30min); Salisbury (1 daily; 1hr 50min); Southampton (1 daily; 2hr 45min); Torquay (2–3 daily; 3hr); Truro (1 daily; 5hr); Wells (hourly; 1hr).

Exeter to: Birmingham (4 daily; 3hr 45min–4hr 20min); Bristol (5 daily; 1hr 45min–2hr); Falmouth (1 daily; 3hr 40min); London (8 daily; 4hr–4hr 30min); Plymouth (2 hourly; 1hr); St Austell (3 daily; 2hr 30min–3hr 40min); Southampton (2 daily; 4hr 15min–5hr 10min); Torquay (1–2 hourly; 1hr); Truro (3 daily; 3hr 10min).

Falmouth to: Exeter (1 daily; 4hr); Helston (8 daily; 1hr); Penzance (7 daily; 1hr 45min); Plymouth (2 daily; 2hr 30min); St Austell (2 daily; 1hr 30min); Truro (2–3 hourly; 30–40min).

Frome to: Bath (hourly; 1hr); Wells (hourly; 1hr).

Glastonbury to: Bristol (hourly; 1hr 20min); Taunton (Mon–Sat 5 daily; 1hr 40min); Wells (2 hourly; 20min).

Newquay to: Bodmin (2–3 daily; 45min–1hr); Bristol (2–3 daily; 4hr–4hr 40min); Plymouth (5 daily; 1hr 30min–2hr); St Austell (hourly; 1hr).

Penzance to: Plymouth (7 daily; 2hr 50min–3hr 30min); St Austell (6–7 daily; 1hr 30min–2hr 10min); St Ives (2–3 hourly; 40min); Truro (hourly; 1hr 45min).

Plymouth to: Bodmin (2–4 daily; 1hr 10min); Bristol (5 daily; 2hr 30min–3hr); Exeter (2 hourly; 1hr 10min); Falmouth (2 daily; 2hr 30min); London

(8 daily; 4hr 40min–5hr 30min); Newquay (5 daily; 1hr 30min–2hr); Penzance (7 daily; 2hr 50min–3hr 30min); St Austell (7–9 daily; 1hr 15min–2hr); St Ives (4 daily; 2hr 30min–3hr); Torquay (hourly; 2hr); Truro (7 daily; 1hr 30min–1hr 50min).

St Austell to: Bodmin (hourly, no Sun service in winter; 45min); Bristol (1 daily; 4hr 30min); Exeter (3 daily; 2hr 30min–3hr 40min); Falmouth (2 daily; 1hr 30min); Newquay (hourly; 1hr); Penzance (6–7 daily; 1hr 30min–2hr 10min); Plymouth (7–9 daily; 1hr 15min–2hr); St Ives (3 daily; 1hr 40min); Truro (1–2 hourly; 40–50min).

St Ives to: Penzance (2–3 hourly; 30min); Plymouth (4 daily; 2hr 30min–3hr); St Austell (3 daily; 1hr 40min); Truro (12 daily; 1hr 15min–1hr 45min).

Taunton to: Bridgwater (Mon–Sat 4 daily; 30min); Glastonbury (Mon–Sat 5 daily; 1hr 40min); Wells (Mon–Sat 5 daily; 1hr 45min).

Torquay to: Bristol (2–3 daily; 2hr 45min–3hr); Exeter (1–2 hourly; 1hr); London (8 daily; 5hr 15min); Plymouth (hourly; 2hr).

Truro to: Bristol (1 daily; 5hr); Exeter (2 daily; 3hr 10min); Falmouth (2–3 hourly; 30–40min); Penzance (hourly; 1hr 45min); Plymouth (7 daily; 1hr 30min–2hr); St Austell (1–2 hourly; 40–50min); St Ives (12 daily; 1hr 15min–1hr 45min).

Wells to: Bath (hourly; 1hr 20min); Bridgwater (Mon–Sat 5–9 daily; 1hr 20min); Bristol (4–12 daily; 1hr); Frome (Mon–Sat 5–8 daily; 1hr); Glastonbury (hourly; 15min); Taunton (Mon–Sat 5 daily; 1hr 50min).

CHAPTER SIX

EAST ANGLIA

S trictly speaking, **East Anglia** is made up of just three counties – Suffolk, Norfolk and the old county of Cambridgeshire – which were settled by Angles from Holstein in the fifth century, though in more recent times, it's come to be loosely applied to parts of Essex and Huntingdonshire too. As a region it's renowned for its wide skies and flat landscapes, and of course such generalizations always contain more than a grain of truth – if you're looking for mountains, you've come to the wrong place. That said, East Anglia often fails to conform to its stereotype: parts of Suffolk are positively hilly, and its coastline can induce vertigo; the north Norfolk coast holds steep cliffs as well as wide sandy beaches; and even the pancake-flat fenlands are broken by wide, muddy rivers and hilly mounds, on one of which perches Ely's magnificent cathedral. Indeed, the whole region is sprinkled with fine medieval churches, the legacy of the days when this was England's most progressive and prosperous region.

Of all the East Anglian counties, **Suffolk** is the most varied. Its undulating southern reaches, straddling the River Stour, are home to a string of picturesque, well-preserved little towns – **Lavenham** and **Kersey** are two excellent examples – which enjoyed immense prosperity during the thirteenth to sixteenth centuries, the heyday of the wool trade. Elsewhere, **Bury St Edmunds** can boast not just the ruins of its once-prestigious abbey, but also some fine Georgian architecture on its grid-plan streets. Even the much maligned county town of **Ipswich** has more to offer than it's generally given credit for. Nevertheless, for many visitors it's the north Suffolk coast that steals the local show. In **Southwold**, with its comely Georgian high street, Suffolk possesses a delightful seaside resort, elegant and relaxing in equal measure, while neighbouring **Aldeburgh** hosts one of the best music festivals in the country.

Norfolk, as everyone knows thanks to Noël Coward, is very flat. It's also one of the most sparsely populated and tranquil counties in England, a remarkable turnaround from the days when it was an economic and political powerhouse – until, that is, the Industrial Revolution simply passed it by. Its capital, **Norwich**, is still East Anglia's largest city, renowned for its Norman cathedral and castle, and for its high-tech Sainsbury Centre, a provocative collection of twentieth-century art. The one part of Norfolk which has been well and truly discovered is the **Broads**, a unique landscape of reed-ridden waterways that has been over-exploited by farmers and boat-rental companies for the last twenty years. Too far from London to attract day-trippers, the Norfolk coast – with the exception of touristy **Great Yarmouth** and, to a lesser extent, the

---

ACCOMMODATION PRICE CODES

Throughout this guide, hotel and B&B accommodation is priced on a scale of ① to ⑨, the number indicating the **lowest price** you could expect to pay per night in that establishment for a **double room** in high season. The prices indicated by the codes are as follows:

① under £40	④ £60–70	⑦ £110–150
② £40–50	⑤ £70–90	⑧ £150–200
③ £50–60	⑥ £90–110	⑨ over £200

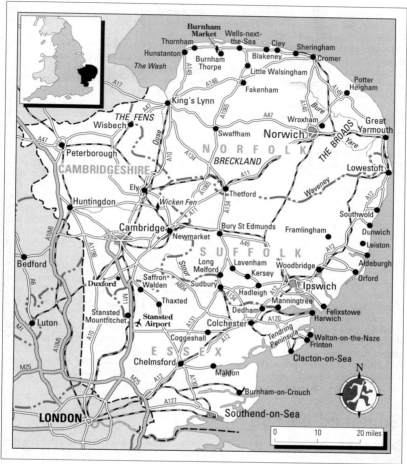

© Crown copyright

Victorian resort of **Cromer** – remains one of the most unspoilt in England, with **Blakeney Point** and the surrounding marshes among the country's top nature reserves. Meanwhile, sheltering inland, are two outstanding stately homes – **Blickling Hall** and **Holkham** – with several more within easy striking distance of **King's Lynn**, a strange, almost disconcerting mixture of fenland town and ancient seaport.

Cambridge is, however, the one place in East Anglia everyone visits, largely on account of its world-renowned university, whose ancient colleges boast some of the finest medieval and early modern architecture in the country. The rest of Cambridgeshire is dominated by the landscape of the **Fens**, for centuries an inhospitable marshland, which was eventually drained to provide rich alluvial farming land. The one great highlight here is the cathedral town of **Ely**, settled on one of the few areas of raised ground in this region and an easy and popular day-trip from Cambridge.

The old county of Huntingdonshire, now the western part of Cambridgeshire, has its moments too, most notably in **Peterborough**'s splendid cathedral and at the Oliver Cromwell Museum in **Huntingdon**.

Heading into the region from the south, almost inevitably takes you through Essex, though there's little here to divert you. Not properly part of East Anglia but generally lumped together with the region, Essex's proximity to London has turned many places into soulless commuter towns, while its inhabitants – "Essex man and woman" – are dubbed archetypally brash, conservative and uncultured by the rest of the English. The county capital, Chelmsford, is no great shakes and instead it's in historic towns like **Colchester** and the coastal resort of **Southend-on-Sea** where Essex is at its most appealing.

Getting around

The **train** network is at its best to and from London, with quick and frequent services from the capital to all the major towns. As places like Colchester, Ipswich and Norwich, or Cambridge, Ely and Peterborough, are linked on the same train lines, it's also relatively easy to move from one major town to another. Once you get away from the major towns, however, you're going to have to rely on local **buses**, whose services are often restricted in winter and on Sundays. In parts of north Norfolk and inland Suffolk, you may find the only way to get about is to take your own transport. Major bus routes are dominated by a handful of major operators like Eastern National in Essex, First Eastern Counties in Norfolk and Stagecoach Cambus in Cambridgeshire. Each of these companies sells rover tickets of some description, providing unlimited travel for one day or more on their buses and sometimes on services operated by other companies too. For instance, First Eastern Counties' BusRanger ticket is valid on Eastern National and some Thamesway routes. For more information, contact the operators' offices, as listed in the text.

Hiking, naturally enough, is less strenuous here than in most English regions, and there are several **long-distance footpaths** worth considering. The main routes run through Norfolk, starting with the **Peddars Way**, from Knettishall near Thetford and heading north to the coast at Hunstanton. The route then continues east as the **Norfolk Coast Path** as far as Cromer, from where the **Weaver's Way** then wends through the Broads to Great Yarmouth. Any local tourist office can provide trail guides.

Southend-on-Sea

SOUTHEND-ON-SEA owes its existence to the Prince Regent, who in 1809 decided that the village of Prittlewell – now a suburb of Southend – would provide a healthier atmosphere for his wife, Princess Caroline, than London, forty miles to the west. Caroline lodged at Prittlewell's "south end", which henceforth became the town's official name. As the nearest sandy beach to London, Southend has doggedly maintained the popularity that followed from its royal patronage, though nowadays it has come to epitomize the downmarket English seaside resort of fish and chips, candyfloss and slot machines.

With a population of over a hundred and fifty thousand, Southend today incorporates many of the neighbouring towns along a seven-mile stretch of sand, which faces south onto the muddy Thames estuary. It's a rather dull geographical backdrop, with little in the town itself to raise the spirits and nothing on the promenade that isn't repeated up and down the English coast in dozens of comparable resorts. Nothing, that is, save for Southend's **pier** (summer daily 8am–10pm; winter Mon–Fri 8am–5pm, Sat & Sun 7pm), which, at one and a third miles in length, is reputedly the longest in the world. Paul Theroux finished his grumpy circuit of Britain here, recounted in *The Kingdom By*

The Sea, and to emulate him you can either walk or take the special pier shuttle train. Gazing out over the Thames estuary is not perhaps the most enduring of scenic experiences, but it's pleasant enough and afterwards you can wander the seafront, with its amusement arcades, brash pubs and fast-food joints. Just west of the pier, the resort's early days are recalled by the Georgian **Royal Terrace**, with its distinctive wrought-iron verandas, on the embankment above the seafront; Princess Caroline stayed here, at nos. 7 and 9.

The beach to the east of the pier is best for **bathing** and it's here that you'll find the **Sea Life Centre** (☎01702/601834), about half a mile along, and, a short walk beyond, the Marine Activity Centre (☎01702/612770), which offers sailing, windsurfing and canoeing. Needless to say, the resort has its share of **amusement parks**, the two major ones being Peter Pan's Adventure Island (☎01702/468023) and the tiny tots' Never Never Land (☎01702/460618), both of which are near the pier on the Western Esplanade.

Practicalities

Trains from London's Fenchurch Street station take just under an hour to reach Southend Central Station, which lies at the top of the pedestrianized High Street, a good ten minutes' walk from the pier: head down the High Street onto Pier Hill and you can't miss it. Services from Liverpool Street arrive a little further out of the centre at Southend Victoria. The **bus station** is at the junction of High Street and Heygate Avenue, opposite the Royals Shopping Centre – the best place for drivers to aim for, since it has a large multistorey **car park**. The **tourist office** is located about five minutes' walk from the pier at 19 High St (July & Aug Mon–Sat 9.30am–5pm, Sun 10am–4pm; rest of year closed Sun; ☎01702/215120).

The bulk of Southend's visitors are day-trippers and it's difficult to conceive of a reason to buck the trend. Nevertheless, if you're determined to find **accommodation**, Southend abounds in inexpensive B&Bs, many along the Eastern Esplanade, though by far the nicest places to stay are the few Georgian properties on the Royal Terrace. Here, the flower-decked *Mayflower Hotel*, at no. 6 (☎01702/340489; ①), or the *Terrace Hotel*, at no. 8 (☎01702/348143; ①), are probably the best budget options. The nearest **campsite** is the *East Beach Caravan and Camping Park* (☎01702/292466; closed Nov–Feb) in Shoeburyness, the easternmost suburb of Southend.

Southend's proximity to London has had a beneficial effect on the quality of its **restaurants**. One of the best places to eat is the *Fleur de Provence*, just west of the High Street at 52 Alexandra St (☎01702/352987), where the Provençal food is delicious, if expensive. Alternatively, for a cheap fill-up, *Bailey's Fry-Inn* on the Eastern Esplanade is a traditional Southend chippy. Various **festivals** throughout the year add more focus to a visit. One of the best is the annual summer jazz festival (dates vary, check with the tourist office), followed by carnival week in August, complete with processions and a fireworks display. The biggest event each year, though, is the **Air Show** held over the May bank holiday weekend, with aerial displays and fly-overs along the Thames estuary.

Colchester and around

If you visit anywhere in Essex, it should be **COLCHESTER**, an agreeable town with a castle, a university and a large army base, fifty miles or so northeast of London. More than anything else, Colchester prides itself on being England's oldest town and there is documentary evidence of a settlement here as early as the fifth century BC. By the first century AD, the town was the region's capital under King Cunobelin – better known as Shakespeare's Cymbeline – and when the Romans invaded Britain in 43 AD they chose Colchester (Camulodunum) as their new capital, though it was

BOUDICCA

Boudicca – aka Boadicea – was the wife of Prasutagus, chief of the Iceni tribe of Norfolk, who allied himself to the Romans during the conquest of Britain in 43 AD. Five years later, when the Iceni were no longer useful, the Romans attempted to disarm them and, although the Iceni rebelled, they were soon brought to heel. On Prasutagus's death, the Romans ignored his will and confiscated his property – and when Boudicca protested, the Romans flogged her and raped her daughters. Boudicca quickly rallied the Iceni and their allies and set off on a rampage through southern Britain in 60 AD.

As the ultimate symbol of Roman oppression, the Temple of the Deified Claudius in Colchester was the initial focus of hatred, but once Colchester had been demolished Boudicca turned her sights elsewhere. She laid waste to London and St Albans, massacring over seventy thousand citizens and inflicting crushing defeats on the Roman units stationed there. She was far from squeamish, ripping traitors' arms out of their sockets and torturing every Roman and collaborator in sight. She was eventually defeated by the Roman governor Suetonius Paulinus in a pitched battle which cost the Romans just four hundred lives, and the Britons countless thousands. Boudicca committed suicide, while the Romans took their revenge on the surviving rebel tribes.

soon eclipsed by London, becoming a retirement colony for legionaries instead. The first Roman temple in the country was erected here, and in 60 AD the colony was the target of Boudicca's abortive revolt (see box above). A millennium later, the conquering Normans built one of their mightiest strongholds in Colchester, but the conflict that most marked the town was the Civil War. In 1648, Colchester was subjected to a gruelling siege by the Parliamentarian army led by Lord Fairfax; after three months, during which the population ate every living creature within the walls, the town finally surrendered and the Royalist leaders were promptly executed for their pains.

Today, Colchester makes a good base for further explorations of the surrounding countryside – particularly the Stour valley towns of Constable country (see pp.453–458), within easy reach to the north, and the handsome little village of **Coggeshall** a short way inland.

Arrival, information and accommodation

Colchester has two **train stations**. Services from London and Harwich arrive at the mainline Colchester North Station, from where it's a fifteen-minute walk south into town – follow North Station Road and its continuation North Hill until you reach the west end of the High Street. Trains from Frinton, Walton and Clacton-on-Sea arrive at Colchester Town Station, to the south of the centre at the bottom of St Botolph's Street. The **bus station** is off Queen Street, the northerly continuation of St Botolph's Street, and is a couple of minutes' walk from the High Street. You can get bus timetables here from the First Eastern National office (Mon–Fri 9am–5pm, Sat 9am–1pm; ☎01206/572478), which also sells Bus Ranger tickets (£5.50) valid for a day's travel throughout much of East Anglia.

The **tourist office** is at 1 Queen St (April–Sept Mon–Sat 9.30am–6pm, Sun 10am–5pm; Oct–March Mon–Sat 10am–5pm; ☎01206/282920), just behind the castle. As well as helping with accommodation, they sell leaflets detailing local walks and co-ordinate daily **guided walks** around town (June–Sept; £2). You can rent a **bike** from Bicycle Breaks (☎01206/868 254; £6 per day) – who deliver the bikes to you if you're staying in or close to the town centre – a good way of getting out to see the nearby "Constable Country" (see p.454).

Accommodation

For **accommodation**, Colchester has more than its fair share of old hotels as well as a cluster of pleasant, well-located B&Bs. *Colchester Mill Hotel*, East St (☎01206/865022; ③) is located in a refurbished flourmill down by the River Colne, a few minutes' walk east from the High Street; the *George Hotel*, 116 High St (☎01206/578494; ⑤), is an attractive old coaching inn, whose recently refurbished rooms come with all mod cons; *The Old Manse*, 15 Roman Rd (☎01206/545154; no credit cards; ①) is the best of the many B&B options along Roman Road, with three pleasant guestrooms; and the *Red Lion*, 43 High St (☎01206/577986; ③) is another old-timer, a fifteenth century timber building containing 24 modernized en-suite rooms.

The Town

Most visitors start off at the town's rugged, honey-coloured **Castle**, the perfect introduction to Colchester's long history, set in attractive parkland, which stretches down to the River Colne. Begun less than ten years after the Battle of Hastings, it boasts a phenomenally large keep – the largest in Europe at the time – built on the site of the defunct Roman temple. The castle's **museum** (March–Nov Mon–Sat 10am–5pm, Sun 2–5pm; Dec–Feb Mon–Sat 10am–5pm; £3.60) contains the best of the region's Romano-British archeological finds, although, apart from a fine bronze of Mercury, the messenger of the gods, this amounts to little more than a smattering of coins, tombstones, statues and mosaics. Perhaps the most impressive mosaic – depicting sea beasts pursuing dolphins – is on display at the castle entrance, next to the castle well. The museum also covers the Boudicca revolt and the 1648 siege, and you can sign up for a **guided tour** of the underground tunnels (45min; £1), which give access to the foundations of the Roman temple and the Norman chapel and walls – parts not otherwise accessible to regular visitors.

The castle stands at the eastern end of the wide, and largely pedestrianized, **High Street**, which lies pretty much along the same route as it did in Roman times. The most arresting building here is the flamboyant **Town Hall**, built in 1902 and topped by a statue of Saint Helena, mother of Constantine the Great and daughter of "Old King Cole" of nursery-rhyme fame – after whom, some say, the town was named. Immediately north of the High Street is the so-called **Dutch Quarter**, where Flemish refugees settled in the sixteenth century giving a boost to the town's ailing cloth trade. The area's lofty buildings still make this a pleasant place to stroll, particularly along West and East Stockwell streets. South of the High Street, much of the medieval street plan has been subsumed within a vast open-air shopping precinct, complete with three separate indoor shopping centres and an open-air **market** held every Friday and Saturday in Vineyard Street. Nearby, narrow Trinity Street is home to the **Tymperleys Clock Museum** (April–Oct Tues–Sat 10am–1pm & 2–5pm; free), featuring locally made clocks and housed in a wonderful fifteenth-century timber-framed building with its own little garden.

Looming above the western end of the High Street is the town landmark, "**Jumbo**", a disused nineteenth-century water tower, considerably more imposing than the nearby **Balkerne Gate**, which once marked the western entrance of Roman Colchester. Built in AD 50, this is the largest surviving Roman gateway in the country, though with the remains at only a touch over six feet in height, it's far short of spectacular. The town's **Roman Walls**, to which the gate is joined, are somewhat more impressive – erected only after Boudicca had sacked the city in AD 60 and, as such, a case of too little too late. The overall effect of this particular section is spoiled by the adjacent ring road, but there are other more tranquil fragments in the park below the castle.

With a little time to spare, it's worth strolling down **East Hill**, a continuation of the High Street east of the castle. Splendid Georgian houses line the top end of the hill, one of which – opposite the tourist office – is now the **Hollytrees Museum** (Tues–Sat 10am–noon & 1–5pm; free), containing a modest collection of costumes, toys, domestic items, trade implements and decorative arts from the eighteenth to the twentieth century. Over the road at the **Minories** (Mon–Sat 10am–4pm; free) another Georgian exterior conceals a contemporary arts centre, with a changing exhibition programme and a decent café.

A few yards away, Queen Street heads south, becoming St Botolph's Street before it reaches Colchester Town Station. Just before the station are the ruins of **St Botolph's Priory**, beside the squat, quasi-fortified church of the same name. As the first Augustinian priory built in England, St Botolph's became head of the black-clad order until the Dissolution. It was reduced to rubble, like so much of the town, in 1648, though the twelfth-century western doorway and the thick piers of the nave give some idea of its Romanesque glory.

Eating, drinking and nightlife

Colchester's oysters have been highly prized since Roman times and the local vineyards have an equally long heritage, so it's no surprise to find the town has a good choice of first-rate **restaurants**. Pickings are slim on Sundays, however, when most places are closed. The best food in town is to be had at the *Warehouse Brasserie*, on Chapel Street North (☎01206/765656; closed Sun eve), which offers tasty dishes at moderate prices from a wide-ranging, contemporary menu. Alternatively, try *Ruan Thai*, 82a East Hill (☎01206/870770), an excellent and moderately priced Thai restaurant near the top of East Hill; or *Tilly's*, 22 Trinity St (closed Sun), a Victorian tearoom that serves snacks and full English meals. *The Lemon Tree*, 48 St John's St (☎01206/767337; closed Sun), is a moderately priced option, popular for its lunch specials and sunny courtyard seating. For pizza, try *Pizza Express*, 1 St Runwald's St, off West Stockwell (☎01206/760680), or *Toto's*, 5–7 Museum St (☎01206/573235).

Colchester's town centre is crowded with **pubs**, with three of the best being the *Red Lion*, 43 High St, the *Foresters Arms*, a nice backstreet local on Castle Road, and the *Goat and Boot*, just one of several lively spots down East Hill. And, as you'd expect in a university town, the town rates reasonably well when it comes to the **arts and nightlife**. The Colchester Arts Centre, on Church Street next to the Balkerne Gate (☎01206/500900), puts on a good programme of rock, folk, jazz, theatre and dance, plus some club nights – all in a converted Victorian church. Nearby is the Mercury Theatre (☎01206/573948), the town's main drama venue. In term time it's also worth checking what's on at the university's Lakeside Theatre (☎01206/873261), a mile or so east of the centre, where they provide a varied programme of theatre and music.

Coggeshall

COGGESHALL, eight miles west of Colchester, boasts a wealth of sixteenth- and seventeenth-century timber-framed housing, the legacy of its days as a prosperous lace town. The most interesting buildings sport fine decorative pargeting, a once-fashionable style in which the faults of any building could be concealed by plasterwork with incised patterns – the more ornate the pattern, the wealthier the householder. This makes for some enjoyable viewing, as does the Victorian clocktower, faced with deep-blue weatherboarding and surmounted by a dinky white belfry, which lords it over the main square.

The village also contains two National Trust properties. The first, **Paycocke's House** on West Street (April to early Oct Tues, Thurs & Sun 2–5pm; £2, £3 with combined ticket for Grange Barn), is a rambling, cloth merchant's house dating from around 1500. The half-timbered facade, with its oriel windows and woodcarvings, is charming, but the interior is even more appealing, containing a wide variety of decorative carving – look for the detail in the linenfold panelling of the dining room and over the main fireplace. A small sample of locally made lace is on display here too. The second property, **Grange Barn** (same times and prices as Paycocke's House), a twelfth-century timber-framed barn, the oldest in Europe, lies half a mile south of the village centre across the River Blackwater.

For **lunch**, head for any one of Coggeshall's antique pubs, the oldest of which is the medieval *Woolpack Inn* at the far end of Church Street.

The Tendring Peninsula

East of Colchester a nub of land juts out into the North Sea to form the **Tendring Peninsula**. The clean sandy beaches strung along the peninsula's southeast shore, the so-called "Essex Sunshine Coast," have been thoroughly developed over the last hundred years, resulting in a series of brash resorts, the most famous of which is **Clacton-on-Sea**. All are accessible by train from Colchester (or London's Liverpool Street), but in truth, none stands out, with the flat hinterland providing little visual relief from the dull seascape. By contrast, the attractive old quarter of **Harwich**, the international ferry terminal at the northeastern tip of the peninsula, is worth at least an hour or two of anyone's time.

It's disappointing that, for the moment at least, Tendring's most alluring historical sight, the privately owned medieval remains and gardens of **St Osyth Priory**, just west of Clacton, are closed to the public. The priory is associated with the gruesome legend of Osyth, daughter of Frithwald, the first king of East Anglia, who, as the story goes, refused to renounce her Christianity when asked to do so by Viking raiders. In response they lopped off her head, which she then carried to the church (that then stood here) before collapsing.

Clacton-on-Sea

CLACTON-ON-SEA, the Tendring's chief town, is a tad more polished than Southend and immediately more attractive, with its floral promenade gardens and broad sands. Attempts to lure you onto its pier with precisely phrased promises – the "largest" (as opposed to Southend's "longest") pleasure pier in the UK – and to "the new shopping experience at Clacton Common", are a tad desperate, but actually it has little need of such boosterism. Clacton is a pleasant, unassuming family resort – it's as straightforward as that.

The **train station** is a couple of blocks east of the resorts main drag, Pier Avenue. **Buses** mostly stop near the seafront promenade. The **tourist office** at 23 Pier Ave (June to mid-Sept Mon–Fri 9am–5pm, Sat 9am–4.30pm, Sun 9am–4.30pm; mid-Sept to May closed Sun; ☎01255/423400), can dish out details on accommodation, campsites and local attractions. The *Royal Hotel*, 1 Marine Parade East, on the promenade in front of the pier (☎01255/421215; ④), is the best **accommodation** option, its cast-iron balconies providing the perfect spot to sip a drink once the sun has sunk over the yardarm.

Frinton and Walton

FRINTON-ON-SEA, five miles further up the coast from Clacton, is a smaller, slightly snootier resort, sporting manicured lawns, sea views and a clutch of sedate-looking hotels and B&Bs. There's nothing so downmarket as an amusement arcade here. Indeed the main street, Connaught Avenue, was once pronounced the "Bond Street of East Anglia" – though this claim seems more than a little far-fetched today.

Nearby **WALTON-ON-THE-NAZE** is a quiet place with a garish pier and a rather forlorn air. Its most appealing aspect is **The Naze** itself, a spatulate promontory which pokes north of the resort to form the eastern perimeter of **Hamford Water**, a large area of muddy creeks and salt marshes that produces the tastiest of oysters. It is also a major wintering area for wildfowl, and thousands of migrating birds pause here during spring and autumn. A few footpaths nudge into the area from the nearest minor roads – the B1034 to the south, the B1414 in the west – enabling visitors to get a closer look at the birdlife.

To reach Frinton and Walton-On-The-Naze by **train**, change at Thorpe-le-Soken on the Colchester–Clacton line – both resorts are on a tiny branch line. Neither resort has a tourist office, but finding your way around is hardly problematic and there are lots of reasonably priced **B&Bs** to choose from. In Frinton, an especially good choice is the *Uplands Guest House*, 41 Hadleigh Rd (☎01255/674889; ②), a pleasant 1920s dwelling with eight attractively furnished bedrooms; it's located in a quiet residential area, just a couple of hundred yards from the beach. Walton's best hotel – not perhaps a zealously fought-for title – is the seafront *Regency Hotel*, 45 The Parade (☎01255/676300; ③), an amiable seaside guest house with its own bar – ask for a room with sea views.

Harwich

HARWICH, on the northeastern tip of the Tendring Peninsula, has a long history as a sea and river port. It equipped Elizabethan mariners like Drake and Hawkins and provided the dockyards that built the *Mayflower*, the ship that took the Pilgrim Fathers to America. Sitting at the estuary of the rivers Stour and Orwell, it also prospered from the proceeds of the Essex wool trade, slipping into prolonged decline when the focus of English trade moved from Europe to the Americas in the eighteenth century. Today, it's Britain's main North Sea ferry terminal, though since ferry traffic goes no further than Parkeston Quay, this has left the old town, a mile or so to the east, relatively undisturbed.

The most interesting sites of old Harwich are conveniently clustered on the east side of a stumpy little headland. Start on King's Quay Street, a short walk from the train station – take Main Road up along the headland and turn right down Wellington Road – where you'll find the brightly painted **Electric Palace**, a purpose-built cinema fashioned in Edwardian Baroque in 1911 that's still going strong. A short distance away to the south, on the green abutting the esplanade, is the only surviving **Treadwheel Crane** in the world, a seventeenth-century wooden structure from the local shipyards, with two giant wheels operated by men walking inside them. South again, it's only a few yards across the green to the **Low Lighthouse**, now home to the local maritime museum (May–Aug daily 10am–5pm; 50p), and, on the other side of the green, inland at West Street, the more imposing **High Lighthouse**. This now serves as a television and wireless museum (late May to Sept daily 12.30–4.30pm; £1). From here head south down Main Road past the train station to the **Harwich Redoubt** (May–Aug daily 10am–5pm; Sept–April Sun 10am–noon & 2–4pm; £1), a well-preserved circular fort constructed in 1808 as part of the coastal defences against Napoleon's expected invasion.

Harwich has two **train stations**: one at Parkeston Quay, the other just off Main Road, not far from the High Lighthouse. The **bus** service from Colchester to Parkeston Quay and Harwich old town is fast and frequent. For help with finding accommodation, Harwich **tourist office** is at the Safeway supermarket store, off the A120 between Parkeston Quay and Harwich old town (April–Sept daily 8.30am–7.30pm; Oct–March Mon–Fri 8.30am–5.30pm & Sat 9am–4pm; ☎01255/506139). There are only a handful of **hotels** and **B&Bs** to choose from and the nicer places are well away from the ferry terminal. Easily the best option is *The Pier*, down on the old town quayside (☎01255/241212; ⑤), a hotel with just six en-suite rooms, each decorated in a broadly nautical style. Downstairs, the eponymous **restaurant** is an outstanding but moderately priced place specializing in the freshest of seafood.

The ferry agents at Parkeston Quay can provide up-to-date details of **continental ferry services** to the Hook of Holland (Stena Line), and Hamburg and Esbjerg in Denmark (Scandinavian Seaways).

The Stour Valley and the old wool towns of south Suffolk

A few miles north of Colchester, the **Stour Valley** forms the border between Essex and Suffolk for much of its length, and signals the beginning of East Anglia proper. Compared with much of the region it is positively hilly, a handsome landscape of farms and woodland latticed by dense, well-kept hedges and thick grassy banks that once kept the Stour in check. The valley is dotted with lovely little villages, where rickety, half-timbered Tudor houses and elegant Georgian dwellings cluster around medieval churches, proud buildings with square, self-confident towers. The Stour's prettiest villages are concentrated along its lower reaches – to the east of the A134 – in **Dedham Vale**, with **Stoke-by-Nayland** and **Dedham** arguably the most appealing of them all. This is also known as "**Constable Country**", as it was the home of John Constable, one of England's greatest artists, and the subject of his most famous works. Inevitably, there's a Constable shrine – the much-visited complex of old buildings down by the river at **Flatford Mill**.

The villages along the River Stour and its tributaries were once busy little places at the heart of East Anglia's weaving trade, which boomed from the thirteenth to the fifteenth century. By the 1490s, the region produced more cloth than any other part of the country, but in Tudor times production shifted to Colchester, Ipswich and Norwich and, although most of the smaller settlements continued spinning cloth for the next three hundred years, their importance slowly dwindled. Bypassed by the Industrial Revolution, south Suffolk had, by the late nineteenth century, become a remote rural backwater, an impoverished area whose decline had one unforeseen consequence. With few exceptions, the towns and villages were never well enough off to modernize, and the architectural legacy of medieval and Tudor times survived. The two best-preserved villages are **Lavenham** and **Kersey**, both of which heave with sightseers on summer weekends, but there are other attractive spots too, notably **Long Melford** and **Sudbury**. The latter boasts an excellent museum devoted to the work of Thomas Gainsborough, another great English artist and a native of the town who spent much of his time painting the local landscape.

Seeing the region by **public transport** is problematic – distances are small (Dedham Vale is only about ten miles long), but buses between the villages are infrequent and you'll find it difficult to get away from the towns. Several rail lines cross south Suffolk, the most useful being the London–Colchester–Sudbury route. The area is crisscrossed by **footpaths**, some of the most enjoyable of which are in the vicinity of Dedham village.

Manningtree and Mistley

At the turn of the eighteenth century work was undertaken to make the **River Stour** navigable between Manningtree, where the river suddenly narrows, and Sudbury about fifteen miles inland. All manner of goods were to be transported into the Essex and Suffolk hinterland by this route over the next two centuries, including regular supplies of grindstones supplied to the mills which lined the river. One of the beneficiaries of the scheme was **MANNINGTREE**, around seven miles northeast of Colchester (and connected by a regular train service), whose largely Georgian High Street is evidence of its heyday as a river port. Only a small quay has survived, but a much larger working dockyard exists a mile or so to the east at **MISTLEY**, where the air is pungent with malt from the local maltings. The B1352 between the two forms a pleasant riverside promenade, passing by the incongruous Neoclassical **Mistley Towers**, Robert Adam's only foray into church architecture. Built as embellishments to the local church, which was later demolished, the towers remaining as a reminder of the man who footed the bill, a local bigwig by the name of Richard Rigby. Rigby's pet idea was to turn Mistley into a fashionable spa resort, but his grandiose plans never got off the ground – all that's left is an unusual swan fountain with an oval basin just beyond the towers on the main road. More peculiar still, and signposted off the B1352, is Mistley's **Secret Bunker** (Feb–Easter, Oct & Nov Sat & Sun 10.30am–4.30pm; Easter to Sept daily 10.30am–4pm; £4.95), formerly Essex's nuclear battle-planning centre, only decommissioned in 1993. Archive film and tours of the underground system let you into all the awful secrets of a place designed to withstand megaton bomb damage and be self-supporting for months following an attack.

With much prettier places close at hand, there's really no need to stay hereabouts, but *The Crown* pub, at 51 High St, is a pleasant place for a drink. It also offers B&B accommodation.

East Bergholt, Flatford Mill and John Constable

"I associate my careless boyhood to all that lies on the banks of the Stour" wrote **John Constable**, who was born to a miller in **EAST BERGHOLT**, nine miles northeast of Colchester in 1776. The house in which he was born has long since disappeared, so it has been left to **Flatford Mill**, a mile or so to the south, to take up the painter's cause. The mill was owned by his father and was where Constable painted his most famous canvas, *The Hay Wain* (now in the National Gallery, London), which created a sensation when it was exhibited in 1824. To the chagrin of many of his contemporaries, Constable turned away from the landscape-painting conventions of the day, rendering his scenery with a realistic directness that harked back to the Dutch landscape painters of the seventeenth century. Typically, he justified this approach in unpretentious terms, observing that, after all "no two days are alike, nor even two hours; neither were there ever two leaves of a tree alike since the creation of the world." The mill itself – not the one he painted, but a Victorian replacement – is not open to the public, but the sixteenth-century thatched **Bridge Cottage** (March, April & Oct Wed–Sun 11am–5.30pm; May–Sept daily 10am–5.30pm; Nov to early Dec Wed–Sun 11am–3pm; Jan & Feb Sat & Sun 11am–3pm; free, but parking £1.80), which overlooks the scene, has been painstakingly restored and stuffed full of Constabilia. Unfortunately, none of Constable's paintings are displayed here, though the adjacent granary contains mezzotints of the artist's works and there's a pleasant riverside tearoom to take in the view. Beyond stands **Willy Lott's Cottage** (also closed to the public), which does actually feature in *The Hay Wain*.

In summer, the National Trust organizes **guided walks** (£1.80) around the sites of Constable's paintings (call ☎01206/298260 for details), but there are many other pleasant walks to be had along this deeply rural bend in the Stour – not least the footpaths connecting the mill to the train station at Manningtree, two miles to the east, and the village of Dedham a mile and a half to the west.

Dedham

Constable went to school in **DEDHAM**, just upriver from Flatford Mill. It's one of the region's most attractive villages, with a scattering of ancient timber-framed houses strung along the wide main street. The only sights as such are the **St Mary's Church**, an early sixteenth-century structure which Constable painted on several occasions, and the **Sir Alfred Munnings Art Museum**, in Castle House (May–July & Sept Wed & Sun 2–5pm; Aug Wed, Thurs, Sat & Sun 2–5pm; £3), just south of the village on the road to Ardleigh, which displays works of the locally born academician, best known for his portraits of horses. Barely remembered today, Munnings was a controversial figure in the 1940s when, as President of the Royal Academy, he savaged almost every form of modern art there was. Few would say his paintings were inspiring, but seeing them is a pleasant way to fill a rainy afternoon. It is, however, the general flavour of Dedham which appeals most.

The only way to reach Dedham by **bus** is on the twice-weekly service from Colchester, but Stratford St Mary, just over a mile to the west, is easily reached on the regular Colchester–Ipswich bus route. Dedham has one of the smartest **hotels** in the area, *Maison Talbooth* (☎01206/322367; ⑦), which occupies a good-looking Victorian country house about fifteen minutes' walk southwest of the village on the road to Stratford St Mary. Each of the hotel's ten large bedrooms are individually decorated in sumptuous style and dinner can be had close by at *Le Talbooth* (☎01206/323150), an expensive, but top-notch **restaurant** in an ancient timber-framed house down by the River Stour. Alternatively, there's *Dedham Hall* (☎01206/323027; ⑤), an old manor house set in its own grounds on the east side of the village off Brook Street – be sure to ask for a room in the house itself. The restaurant here is very good too (closed Mon). You can also stay in the heart of Dedham itself at the *Marlborough Head* pub (☎01206/323250; ③), where a handful of very pleasant rooms are available above the bar, and excellent, moderately priced **food** can be had from its inventive and wide-ranging menu.

Stoke-by-Nayland and Nayland

Heading northwest from Dedham, the B1029 dips beneath the A12 to reach the byroad to Higham, an unremarkable hamlet where you pick up the road to **STOKE-BY-NAY-LAND**, four miles to the west. This is the most picturesque of villages, where a knot of half-timbered, pastel-painted cottages snuggle up to **St Mary's Church**. With its pretty brick and stone-trimmed tower, the church was one of Constable's favourite subjects. The doors of the south porch are sumptuously covered by the carved figures of a medieval Jesse Tree. The village also boasts a great old pub, the *Angel Inn* (☎01206/263245; ④), known for its adventurous food (eat in the bar or book for the restaurant) and cosy rooms. There are several other good places to stay in and near the village, including *Thorington Hall* (☎01206/337329; ②), which offers four bedrooms in a seventeenth-century house.

Southwest from here, it's two miles back to the River Stour at **NAYLAND**, a workaday little place that is chiefly remarkable for its church's altar painting, *Christ Blessing the Bread and Wine*. It's one of only two attempts by Constable at a religious theme – and, dated to 1809, it was completed long before he found his artistic rhythm. There's also a fine, largely Norman church a mile or so to the west at tiny **Wissington**, where the nave is decorated with a rare series of thirteenth-century frescoes. Back in Nayland, you can wet your whistle and sample quality bar food at the venerable *White Hart*, 11 High St. Local **accommodation** is available at *Hill House*, Gravel Hill (☎01206/262782; ②) on the edge of the village and at *Gladwins Farm*, Harper's Hill (☎01206/262261; ③), a secluded timber-framed farmhouse with its own indoor pool.

Sudbury

SUDBURY – the fictional "Eatanswill" of Dickens's *Pickwick Papers* – has doubled in size in the last thirty years, to become easily the most important town in this part of the Stour Valley. A handful of timber-framed houses hark back to its days of wool-trade prosperity, but its three Perpendicular churches were underwritten by another local industry, silk weaving, which survives on a small scale to this day. Sudbury's most famous export, however, is **Thomas Gainsborough**, the leading English portraitist of the eighteenth century, whose statue, with brush and palette, stands on Market Hill, the town's predominantly Victorian market place. A superb collection of the artist's work is on display in the house where he was born – **Gainsborough's House** at 46 Gainsborough St (April–Oct Tues–Sat 10am–5pm, Sun 2–5pm; Nov–March Tues–Sat 10am–4pm, Sun 2–4pm; £3). Gainsborough left Sudbury when he was just thirteen, moving to London where he was apprenticed to an engraver. But it seems he was soon moonlighting and the earliest of his surviving portrait paintings – his *Boy and Girl*, a remarkably self-assured work dated to 1744 – is displayed here. In 1752, Gainsborough moved on to Ipswich, where he soon established himself as a portrait painter to the Suffolk gentry – though, sadly, none of the portraits of high-society ladies with which he made his name are to be found in the museum's collection.

Sudbury is just seven miles northwest of Nayland – and twice that from Colchester – along the A134. It's accessible by **train** from Colchester (change at Marks Tey) and is the hub of **bus** services to and from neighbouring towns and villages including Colchester and Ipswich. Once you've seen Gainsborough's house, though, there's little reason to hang around. If you do decide to stay, the **tourist office** in the town hall on Market Hill (Easter–Sept Mon–Sat 10am–4.45pm; Oct–Easter Mon–Sat 10am–2.45pm; ☎01787/881320) can provide **accommodation** details.

Long Melford

True to its name, **LONG MELFORD**, three miles north of Sudbury on the A134, has possibly the longest main street in the country. That in itself is not much of a recommendation, but more to the point, for much of its two miles the street is lined with handsome timber-framed houses. At its northern end, it opens up into a wide sloping green, beyond which stands a collection of sixteenth-century almshouses presided over by the mighty stone and flint **Holy Trinity Church**. Built in the fifteenth century, around the same time as Lavenham's, it's one of the most majestic of the so-called wool churches, with huge windows which flood the nave with light. For centuries, rich benefactors have left their legacy here in the form of brightly coloured stained glass, including one window decorated with three rabbits representing the Holy Trinity. A guide is usually on hand during the day.

To the east of the green, behind a high brick wall, is **Melford Hall** (April & Oct Sat & Sun 2–5.30pm; May–Sept Wed–Sun 2–5.30pm; £4.20; NT), a turreted redbrick Tudor mansion, once a country retreat for the abbots of nearby Bury St Edmunds (see p.458). The interior is mostly eighteenth century and Regency, and there's a display of watercolours by Beatrix Potter, a distant relative of the owners. Half a mile north of the green, a mile-long lime-tree drive leads to **Kentwell Hall** (April to mid-June, Sept & Oct Sun noon–5pm; mid-June to Aug daily noon–5pm; £4.90), a moated Tudor mansion that's still in private hands. From mid-June to mid-July, and on most summer weekends and bank holidays, the grounds are given over to touristy "historical re-creations", with admission prices rising to match the event. Aside from the house itself, there's a brick rose maze, a fifteenth-century moathouse and a working "Tudor" farm.

If you want to **stay** in Long Melford, the *George & Dragon* on Hall Street (☎01787/371285; ④) – a continuation of the High Street – is the best option. *The Bull* on the same stretch of road (☎01787/378494) is a real heavyweight among old inns, shouting its Elizabethan credentials throughout and serving decent, reasonably priced **food** in its public bar.

Lavenham

Four miles northeast of Long Melford, off the A134, lies **LAVENHAM**, formerly a centre of the region's wool trade and today one of the most visited villages in Suffolk, thanks to its unrivalled ensemble of perfectly preserved half-timbered houses. The whole place has changed little since the demise of the wool industry in the seventeenth century, owing in part to the zealous local preservation society, which has carefully maintained the village's museum-like quality by banning from view such excrescences of twentieth-century life as TV aerials.

The village is at its most beguiling in the triangular **Market Place**, an airy spot flanked by pastel-painted, medieval dwellings whose beams have been bent into all sorts of wonky angles by the passing of the years. It's here you'll find Lavenham's most celebrated building, the pale-white, timber-framed **Corpus Christi Guildhall** (April–Oct daily 11am–5pm; £2.80; NT), erected in the sixteenth century as the head-quarters of one of Lavenham's four guilds. In the much-altered interior (used successively as a prison and workhouse), there's an exhibition on the woollen industry, but most visitors quickly reach the walled garden and the teashop. Just to the east across the plaza is the mostly fifteenth-century **Little Hall** (April–Oct Wed, Thurs, Sat & Sun 2–5.30pm; £1.50), which contains a modest collection of furniture and *objets d'art*; close by – from beside the *Angel Hotel* – there's a stunning view down Prentice Street with a line of antique, timber-framed dwellings dipping into the deep green countryside beyond. The other building worthy of special notice is the Perpendicular church of **St Peter and St Paul** (daily: summer 8.30am–5.30pm; winter 8.30am–3.30pm), though it's sited a short walk southwest of the centre, at the top of Church Street. Local merchants endowed the church with a nave of majestic proportions and a mighty flint tower, at 141ft the highest for miles around, partly to celebrate the Tudor victory at the Battle of Bosworth in 1485 (see p.594), but mainly to show off their wealth.

There are fairly frequent **buses** to Lavenham from Colchester via Sudbury and Long Melford, with the service continuing on to Bury St Edmunds. The **tourist office** is located on Lady Street (Easter to Oct daily 10am–4.45pm; ☎01787/248207), just south off Market Place. They can help with accommodation and sell a detailed, street-by-street walking guide. Rooms at the *Swan* **hotel** (☎01787/247477; ⑦), a splendid old inn on the High Street, are some of the most comfortable in town; the building incorporates part of the Elizabethan Wool Hall and has a whole host of cosy lounges and courtyard gardens. There's more luxury accommodation at *Lavenham Priory*, on Water Street (☎01787/247404; ⑤), where four immaculate rooms are contained within the old Benedictine priory. Less expensive options on the Market Place include the ancient *Angel Hotel* (☎01787/247388; ④), which has eight pleasant rooms above its bar, and the dinky *Angel Gallery* (☎01787/248417; ②), where the three guest rooms are situated above a pocket-sized art shop. For cheaper B&B options, you'll probably end up staying outside Lavenham itself; the tourist office will provide you with details. For **food**, the *Angel Hotel* serves up excellent, moderately priced bar meals, as does the *Swan*. The other choice in Market Place is the *Great House* (☎01787/247431; closed Sun eve), whose outstanding restaurant serves moderately priced food on both its à la carte and set menus.

Kersey and Hadleigh

Eight miles southeast off the A1141, **KERSEY** vies with Lavenham as the most photographed village in Suffolk. Little more than one exquisite street of timber-framed houses, which dips in the middle to cross a ford that's inhabited by a family of fearless ducks, Kersey is another old wool town, with an austere parish church visible for miles around, on high ground above the village. Today, the village is little more than prime real estate, though there are two good pubs, the *White Horse* and the *Bell*, both of which serve good, reasonably priced bar food.

Another two miles southeast, the market town of **HADLEIGH** is a positive metropolis compared to Kersey, but the focus of interest here – around the **Parish Church of St Mary's** – is equally compact. The church, one block west of the elongated High

Street, is mainly fifteenth century, a replacement for several earlier versions – legend asserts that Guthrum, the Danish chieftain and arch-rival of Alfred the Great, was buried underneath the south aisle in 889. Opposite the church, across the graveyard, is the half-timbered **Guildhall**, every bit as immaculate as Lavenham's, with the earliest sections dating from 1438, while at the back of the church is the highly ornate **Deanery Tower**, a fifteenth-century gatehouse whose palace was never completed. In the garret room at the top of the tower, the Oxford Movement, which opposed liberal tendencies within the Anglican Church and sought to promote Anglo-Catholicism, was founded in 1833 by local rector Hugh Rose.

Hadleigh is easy to reach by **bus** with regular services from Sudbury, Lavenham, Ipswich and Colchester, though Sundays can be a bit tricky. Several Hadleigh-bound buses pass through Kersey too. Tourist information on Hadleigh is available at the library on the High Street and the town is also home to the **East of England Tourist Board**, just off the High Street at Toppesfield Hall (Mon–Fri 9am–5pm; ☎01473/822922). Both can help with local **accommodation**, though there's no real reason to tarry once you've seen the sights. For a bite to eat, *Ferguson's Delicatessen*, 48 High St (closed Sun), sells delicious sandwiches.

Bury St Edmunds

BURY ST EDMUNDS started out as a Benedictine monastery, founded to house the remains of Edmund, the last Saxon king of East Anglia, who was tortured and beheaded by the marauding Danes in 869. Almost two centuries later, England was briefly ruled by the kings of Denmark and the shrewdest of them, King Canute, made a gesture of reconciliation to his Saxon subjects by conferring on the monastery the status of abbey. It was a popular move and the abbey prospered, so much so that before its dissolution in 1539, it had become the richest religious house in the country. Most of the abbey disappeared long ago, and nowadays Bury is better known for its graceful Georgian streets, its flower gardens and its sugar beet plant than for its ancient monuments. Nonetheless, it's an amiable, eminently likeable place, one of the prettiest towns in Suffolk, and with good transport connections on to Cambridge, Colchester, Ipswich or Norwich it demands at least half a day of anyone's time.

The Town

The town centre has preserved its Norman street plan, a grid plan in which Churchgate was aligned with – and sloped up from – the abbey's high altar. It was the first planned town of Norman Britain and, for that matter, the first example of urban planning in England since the departure of the Romans. Beside the abbey grounds is **Angel Hill**, a broad, spacious square partly framed by Georgian buildings, the most distinguished being the ivy-covered **Angel Hotel**, which features in Dickens' *Pickwick Papers*. Dickens also gave readings of his work in the **Athenaeum**, the Georgian assembly rooms at the far end of the square (occasionally open for exhibitions and sales). A twelfth-century wall runs along the east side of Angel Hill, with the bulky fourteenth-century **Abbey Gate** forming the entrance to the abbey gardens and ruins.

The **abbey ruins** themselves are like nothing so much as petrified porridge, with little to remind you of the grandiose Norman complex that dominated the town. Thousands of medieval pilgrims once sought solace at St Edmund's altar and the cult was of such significance that the barons of England gathered here to swear that they would make King John sign their petition – the Magna Carta of 1215. The only significant remnants of the abbey are behind the more modern cathedral (see below) on the far side of the public **gardens** – the suntrap rose garden, hemmed in by giant yew hedges, is a particular delight. Here, the rubbled remains of a small part of the old **abbey church** have been integrated into a set of unusual Georgian houses, one of which holds the **Abbey Visitor Centre** (Easter–Oct daily 10am–5pm; free). The centre traces the history of the abbey and rents headsets (£1.50) for an audiotape tour of the grounds and ruins. In front, across the green, is the imposing **Norman Tower**, once the main gateway into the abbey and now a solitary monument with dragon gargoyles and fancily decorated capitals.

Incongruously, the tower is next to the front part of Bury's **Cathedral of St James** (daily: June–Aug 8.30am–8pm; rest of year 8.30am–5.30pm; £2 donation requested), with chancel and transepts added as recently as the 1960s. That its thousand-odd kneelers are often cited as one of its major highlights gives an idea of the paucity of the interior, notwithstanding the hammer-beam roof and a couple of quality stained glass windows. In fact, it was a toss-up between this place and **St Mary's Church**, further down Crown Street, as to which would be given cathedral status in 1914. The presence of the tomb of Mary Tudor in the latter was probably the clinching factor.

Round the corner from St Mary's, just off Crown Street on Honey Hill, the **Manor House Museum** (Tues–Sun 10am–5pm; £2.70), occupies a grand Georgian mansion built by the wife of the First Earl of Bristol as a pied-à-terre party house. A superb collection of clocks and watches forms the core of the museum's collection and although the accompanying paintings are less compelling, the whole place is well served by a computerized public information system. The museum also mounts extremely popular temporary exhibitions on art and textiles, often based on TV and film costume dramas. At the far end of Crown Street stands Bury's most important industrial concern, the pungent **Greene King Brewery**, whose powerful Abbot Ale is an intense bittersweet beer to be quaffed with caution. The brewery and the National Trust are joint owners of the Regency **Theatre Royal**, at the junction of Crown and Westgate streets, built in 1819 by William Wilkins and still staging plays.

The town's main commercial area is on the west side of the centre, a five-minute walk up from Angel Hill at the top of Abbeygate Street. There's been some intrusive modern planning here, but dignified Victorian buildings flank both Cornhill and Buttermarket, the two short main streets, as well as the narrower streets in between. Older still is the Cornhill's flint-walled **Moyse's Hall**, one of the few surviving Norman houses in England, while the streets to the south are lined by an attractive medley of architectural styles, from elegant Georgian town houses to Victorian brick terraces. You'll see the best by strolling along Guildhall and turning left down Churchgate, which brings you back to Angel Hill.

Practicalities

Bury St Edmunds' **train station** is ten minutes' walk from Angel Hill, south along Northgate Street, and the **bus station** is on St Andrew Street North, near Cornhill. The town's **tourist office**, at 6 Angel Hill (Easter–May Mon–Fri 9.30am–5.30pm, Sat 10am–3pm; June–Sept 9.30am–5.30pm, Sat & Sun 10am–3pm; Oct–Easter Mon–Fri 10am–4pm, Sat 10am–1pm; ☎01284/764667), provides free town maps.

The pick of the town's **hotels** is the *Angel*, on Angel Hill (☎01284/753926; ⑤), an immaculately maintained, county-set hotel with thick carpets, oodles of wood panelling and suitably luxurious rooms. A good alternative is the *Chantry Hotel*, 8 Sparhawk St (☎01284/767427; ④), which has fifteen comfortable rooms in a converted Georgian building near the Manor House Museum. The town has a good supply of **B&Bs**, including the excellent *South Hill House*, 43 Southgate St (☎01284/755650; no credit cards; ②), a handsome old town house with many Georgian features and three large en-suite bedrooms.

For **restaurants**, *Maison Bleue at Mortimer's*, 31 Churchgate St (☎01284/760 623; closed Sat lunch & Sun), serves wonderfully fresh seafood at moderate prices. *The*

Vaults, inside the medieval undercroft at the *Angel Hotel*, is also first-rate, with tasty main dishes from £6.50. Otherwise, aim for coffee, cakes and snacks in the Cathedral Refectory (closed Sun), or at the café in the Manor House Museum, which has court-yard garden seating.

Of the **pubs**, one you shouldn't miss is the *Nutshell* (closed Sun), on The Traverse at the top of Abbeygate, which, at sixteen feet by seven and a half, claims to be Britain's smallest. Greene King's brewery tap is the ancient-looking *Dog & Partridge*, 29 Crown St. For entertainment, there's a year-round programme of cultural events held at the **Theatre Royal**, on Westgate St (☎01284/769505).

Ipswich and around

Situated at the head of the Orwell estuary, **IPSWICH** was a rich trading port in the Middle Ages, but its appearance today is mainly the result of a revival of fortunes in the Victorian era. The town centre itself has been mauled by the developers in the last few decades, but two surviving reminders of old Ipswich – **Christchurch Mansion** and the splendid **Ancient House** – plus the recently renovated quayside are all reason enough to spend at least an afternoon here. Ipswich also boasts a wealth of medieval flint churches, some now locked and slowly rusting away, but others sympathetically restored. One now houses the tourist office, from where **guided walks** depart a couple of times a week during the season (May–Sept, Tues & Thurs 2.15pm; £1.50) – perhaps the best way to see the town on a quick visit.

The Town

The ancient Saxon market place, **Cornhill**, is still the town's focal point, a likeable urban space flanked by a bevy of imposing Victorian edifices – the Italianate town hall, the old Neoclassical Post Office and the pseudo-Jacobean Lloyds building. To get to Ipswich's most famous building, walk halfway along Tavern Street and duck down the mock-Tudor arcade on the right, known as the Walk, to pedestrianized Buttermarket, a little way along which stands the **Ancient House**. The exterior of this Tudor building was decorated around 1670 in extravagant style, a riot of pargeting and stucco work that is one of the finest examples of Restoration artistry in the country. There are plasterwork reliefs of pelicans and nymphs as well as representations of the four continents known at the time. Europe is symbolized by a Gothic church, America a tobacco pipe, Asia an Oriental dome and Africa, eccentrically enough, by an African astride a crocodile. Since the house is now a shop, you're free to take a peek inside to view yet more of the decor, including the hammer-beam roof on the first floor.

From the Ancient House, head up Dial Lane past the fifteenth-century church of **St Lawrence** and back onto Tavern Street, where two wonderful mock-Tudor shops, built in the 1930s, face the **Great White Horse Hotel**, the "overgrown tavern" which appears in Dickens's *Pickwick Papers*. Heading north from here up Northgate Street takes you past the much-restored sixteenth-century, half-timbered **Oak House**, once an inn and now housing office space, to busy St Margaret's Plain and the gates of **Christchurch Mansion** (Tues–Sat 10am–5pm, Sun 2.30–4.30pm; free). This handsome, if much-restored, Tudor building, sporting seventeenth-century Dutch gables, is set in 65 acres of parkland, an area larger than the town centre itself. The mansion's labyrinthine interior is well worth exploring, with period furnishings and a good collection of paintings by Constable and Gainsborough, as well as more contemporary arts exhibitions.

Back in the town centre, the western half of old Ipswich has been transformed by some fairly hideous, postwar development along **Civic Drive**, but there is one modern building which puts the rest to shame. It's the **Willis Corroon Building**, designed by

Norman Foster in the 1970s, whose smoked glass exterior snakes its way along Princes Street at Franciscan Way, reflecting the older buildings around it by day but allowing a startling X-ray vision of the illuminated interior after dusk. From here, it's a short stroll to College Street, named after the college that Cardinal Wolsey, a native of Ipswich, established here in 1528, but failed to complete before his fall from grace. All that remains of Cardinal College now is the solitary **Wolsey's Gateway**, next to the four-teenth-century St Peter's Church.

Pressing on, head east along College Street and, after rounding St-Mary-at-Quay, another medieval church, follow Key Street one block north to reach the **Wet Dock**, the largest in Europe when it opened in 1845 and looking much as it did then, apart from the rash of yachts in the marina. The smell of malt and barley still wafts across the dockside, and several of the granaries continue to function, though other warehouses have been turned into pubs, restaurants and offices. Halfway along the quayside stands the proud Neoclassical **Customs House**, built for the opening of the dock.

Fifteen minutes' walk southeast of the Wet Dock, along Cliff Road, the **Tolly Cobbold Brewery** (tours: May–Sept daily at noon; ☎01473/231723; £3.90) rewards visitors with a sample of its brew after the tour of its Victorian premises. If this whets your thirst, pop into the *Brewery Tap* pub next door.

Practicalities

Ipswich **train station** is on the south bank of the Orwell, ten minutes' walk from Cornhill along Princes Street. The **bus station** is more central, occupying part of the Old Cattle Market, one block south of the Ancient House. The **tourist office** (Mon–Sat 9am–5pm; ☎01473/258070) is in the converted St Stephen's Church in St Stephen's Lane, between the bus station and the Ancient House. The town is compact enough to walk around, though a special summer **bus** (June to late July Sun only; late July to Aug daily) runs a circular route, connecting the train station to all the main sights, including the Wet Dock and the brewery on Cliff Road.

There's no real need **to stay**, especially with the Suffolk coast so close, but a full list of B&Bs is available from the tourist office. One of the best is *Burlington Lodge*, 30 Burlington Rd (☎01473/251868, *nortonburlodge@msn.com*; ①), an attractive Victorian detached house with five comfortable bedrooms about ten minutes' walk west of the Cornhill. Alternatively, try the ultra-modern, spick and span *Novotel Hotel*, in the centre near Wolsey's Gateway, Grey Friars Rd (☎01473/232400; ⑤).

There are several good **restaurants** down by the Wet Dock. *Il Punto* (☎01473/289748), which offers good quality French cuisine at moderate prices, has the most distinctive premises – on board a Dutch pleasure boat – while the more expensive *Mortimer's Seafood Restaurant* (☎01473/230225), in one of the old redbrick warehouses down on Wherry Quay, specializes in seafood. Meals here range from £20–30 a head, though it's cheaper at lunch. **Cafés** in town include *Bensons* at 1 St Stephen's Lane and *Pickwick's*, 1 Dial Lane, with courtyard seating next to St Lawrence's Church.

For a **drink**, try either the *Black Horse* on Black Horse Lane, or the busy *Brewery Tap*, next to the Tolly Cobbold brewery, at the far end of Cliff Road. For **entertainment**, try the Ipswich Film Theatre, in the Corn Exchange complex (☎01473/215544), behind the town hall, which shows mainstream and art movies.

Woodbridge to Framlingham

Beyond Ipswich, the obvious destination is the Suffolk coast, but on the way it's worth considering two short stops – the breezy little town of **Woodbridge** and the archeological finds at nearby **Sutton Hoo**, and the tranquil village of **Framlingham**, a delightful place with a gaunt, ruined castle.

Woodbridge and around

Stringing along the banks of the River Deben eight miles northeast of Ipswich, **WOODBRIDGE** is a pleasant if somewhat unremarkable town whose easy access to the sea – along the river's long and sheltered estuary – once nourished a thriving seaport and shipbuilding industry. These heady nautical days are recalled by the yachts in the marina and the adjacent **Tide Mill** (April & Oct Sat & Sun 11am–5pm, May–Sept daily 11am–5pm; £1), which comes complete with its antique milling machinery. From the waterfront, it's an easy five-minute walk up Quay and Church streets to **Market Hill**, the heart of the town since the Middle Ages. Here you'll find two moderately diverting museums, the **Woodbridge Museum** (Easter–Oct Thurs–Sat 10am–4pm, Sun 2.30–4.30pm; £1), tracing the town's history and the discovery of the Sutton Hoo treasure; and the **Suffolk Horse Museum** (Easter–Sept daily 2–5pm; £1.50) housed in the eye-catching, sixteenth-century Shire Hall and featuring paintings, photographs and exhibits celebrating the Suffolk Punch breed, heavy working horses bred in the town since the fifteenth century.

Woodbridge **train station** is handily located at the foot of Quay Street, beside the waterfront. **Buses** pull in here too. The **tourist office** is at the train station (Easter–Sept Mon–Fri 9am–5.30pm, Sat & Sun 9.30am–5pm; Oct–Easter Mon–Fri 9am–5.30pm, Sat 10am–4pm, Sun 10am–1pm; ☎01394/382240) and can help with accommodation as well as providing sketch maps of the town. Among several **hotels** and **B&Bs**, two of the more appealing are the *Old Station House Hotel*, at the station (☎01394/384831; ③), which has pleasant en-suite rooms and river views, and the *Bull Hotel* on Market Hill (☎01394/382089; ④), a well-run seventeenth-century coaching inn opposite Shire Hall. There are several first-rate **restaurants**, but the best is *Spice*, 17 The Thoroughfare (☎01394/382557; closed Sun), which serves delicious Malaysian and eastern-influenced dishes at moderate prices; it also has a **bar** with a buzz. Alternatively, there's the *Bull Hotel*, on Market Hill, which offers tasty bar meals and prides itself on its puddings, while the *King's Head*, 17 Market Hill, has good beer and bar meals which make full use of the products of nearby Orford's fine smokehouses (see p.464).

Sutton Hoo

In the summer of 1939, at **Sutton Hoo**, a couple of miles east of Woodbridge on the opposite side of the River Deben, a local landowner stumbled across the richest single archeological find in Britain, an Anglo-Saxon royal burial site belonging to Raedwald, king of East Anglia, who died around 625 AD. A forty-oar open ship was discovered, containing a wooden tomb stuffed with gold and jewelled ornaments. Further archeological research was conducted on the site in the 1980s, and in November 1991 a second undisturbed grave was uncovered. The artefacts are now on display in the British Museum in London. The National Trust, who now own Sutton Hoo, are currently revamping visitor facilities and constructing an exhibition area explaining the history and significance of the finds, but the work won't be completed until 2001. In the meantime, the only access is provided on hour-long **guided tours** organized by the Sutton Hoo Society (Easter–Oct Sat & Sun 2pm & 3pm; £2). To join the tour, take the A1152 out of Woodbridge, cross the railway line and then turn down the B1083, the Bawdsey road, at the roundabout. After nearly one mile, opposite the junction to Hollesley, you'll find the footpath to Sutton Hoo signposted on the right; the walk takes twenty minutes.

Framlingham and around

FRAMLINGHAM, ten miles north of Woodbridge, boasts a magnificent **Castle** (daily: April–Oct 10am–6pm; Nov–March 10am–4pm; £2.95; EH), whose severe, turreted walls date from the twelfth century. The original seat of the Dukes of Norfolk, the fortress is little more than a shell inside, but the curtain-wall, with its thirteen towers, has survived almost intact, a splendid example of medieval military architecture topped by ornamental Tudor chimney stacks. Footpaths crisscross the earthen banks encircling the castle and from the internal wall walkways, there are sweeping views across town to the imposing redbrick mass of Framlingham College, but nothing remains of the Great Hall where Mary Tudor was proclaimed Queen of England in 1553.

The sleepy little village next to the castle is a real pleasure to visit, its elongated main street, **Market Hill**, flanked by a harmonious ensemble of sedate old buildings, including the *Crown Hotel* (☎01728/723521; ④), a traditional seventeenth-century inn with roaring fires, wood panelling and snug bedrooms. The parish **Church of St Michael** is also intriguing, its finely crafted hammer-beam roof sheltering several wonderful, sixteenth-century tombs belonging to the Howard family, who owned the castle at the time. They were a turbulent clan. During the reign of Henry VIII, both Thomas Howard, the Duke of Norfolk and his son Henry Howard, the Earl of Surrey, schemed away, determined to be the leading nobles of their day. They brought down the powerful Chancellor of the Exchequer, Thomas Cromwell, in 1540 and their position seemed secure when the king married one of their kin, Catherine, later the same year. But the Howards had overreached themselves. In 1542, the king had Catherine beheaded for adultery and, from his deathbed in 1547, he ordered that Henry Howard should be executed. The same fate would have befallen Howard's father had the king lived a few days longer.

In the hamlet of **Dennington**, a couple of miles to the north of Framlingham along the B1116, stands another interesting church. St Mary's Church holds a fantastical series of fifteenth-century bench-end carvings – one shows a one-legged man using his foot as a sunshade – and an elaborate canopy for the pyx (the vessel in which the Holy Sacrament was kept); one of only two such canopies in Europe.

The district is also a centre of East Anglia's flourishing wine industry and several local vineyards offer tours and tastings. The well-established **Shawsgate Vineyard** (tours: Easter–Oct daily 10am–5.30pm; ☎01728/724060) is situated one mile north of Framlingham along the B1120.

The Suffolk coast

The **Suffolk coast** feels detached from the rest of the county: the road and rail lines from Ipswich to Lowestoft funnel traffic five miles inland for most of the way, and patches of marsh and woodland make the separation still more complete. Dotting the empty coastline are remnants of the circular brick **Martello towers** built to repel Napoleonic invasion at the turn of the nineteenth century, part of a chain of defences deemed necessary along the sparsely inhabited Suffolk and Essex littoral. Coastal erosion continues to plague the region, and has contributed to the virtual extinction of the local fishing industry, and, in the case of **Dunwich**, has destroyed virtually the entire town. What is left, however, is undoubtedly one of the most unspoilt shorelines in the country, if you leave aside the **Sizewell** nuclear power station. The sleepy isolation of **Orford** is rarely broken even in the height of summer, and even more well-established resorts like **Southwold** have managed to escape the lurid fate of other English seaside towns. There are scores of delightful **walks** hereabouts, easy routes along the coast that are best followed with either OS map 156 or 169, or the simplified *Footpath Maps*

(£1) available at most tourist offices. The Suffolk coast is also host to East Anglia's most compelling cultural gathering, the three-week-long **Aldeburgh Festival**, which takes place every June.

Orford

Twelve miles east of Woodbridge, on the far side of the storm-racked Forest of Rendlesham, the tiny village **ORFORD** is dominated by two buildings, both of them medieval. The more impressive is the twelfth-century **Castle** (April–Oct daily 10am–6pm; Nov–March Wed–Sun 10am–4pm; £2.30; EH), built on high ground to the southwest of the village by Henry II, and under siege within months of its completion from Henry's rebellious sons. Most of the castle disappeared centuries ago, but the lofty keep remains, its impressive stature hinting at the scale of the original fortifications. Orford's other medieval edifice, on the far side of the main square, is **St Bartholomew's Church**, where Benjamin Britten premiered his most successful children's work, *Noye's Fludde*, as part of the 1958 Aldeburgh Festival (see box opposite).

From the top of the castle keep, there's a great view across **Orford Ness**, a six-mile-long spit of shingle deposits that has all but blocked off Orford from the sea since Tudor times. Its mud flats and marshes harbour sea lavender beds, which act as feeding and roosting areas for wildfowl and waders. The National Trust offers **boat trips** (April–Oct Thurs–Sat 10am–2pm; last ferry back 5pm; £5.20; NT members £3.20; call ☎01394/450057) across to the Ness from Orford Quay, four hundred yards down the road from the church, and a five-mile hiking trail threads its way along the spit, passing the occasional military building. Some of the pioneer research on radar was carried out here, but the station was closed at the beginning of World War II because of the threat of German bombing. There are also plenty of walks to be had around Orford itself. One of the best is the five-mile hike north along the river wall that guards the west bank of the River Alde, returning via Ferry Road, a narrow country lane.

Orford's gentle, unhurried air is best experienced on a night's stay. **Rooms** are available at the *Crown & Castle* (☎01394/450205; ④), an attractive inn across from the castle with comfortable bedrooms kitted out with all mod cons, and at the marginally less enticing *King's Head* (☎01394/450271; ②), on Market Hill, the main square. For **meals**, don't miss the Butley Orford Oysterage, also on Market Hill. This has a very reasonably priced café-restaurant, whose menu focuses on fresh oysters and oak-wood smoked fish. Finally, down near the quay, the *Jolly Sailor Inn* serves bar meals, teas and coffee.

Aldeburgh and around

ALDEBURGH is best known for its annual arts festival, the brainchild of composer **Benjamin Britten**, who is buried in the village churchyard alongside the tenor Peter Pears, his lover and musical collaborator. They lived by the seafront in Crag House on Crabbe Street – the street named for the poet who provided Britten with his greatest inspiration (see box opposite). Outside of June, when the festival takes place, and November, when the international poetry festival fills the town, Aldeburgh is the quietest of places, with just a small fishing fleet selling its daily catch from wooden shacks along the pebbled shore. The wide main street, parallel to the sea, and its backstreets are, in fact, all that's left of a once extensive medieval town, scoured away by centuries of erosion. Consequently, the seafront is something of a hotchpotch as it was not designed to face the sea.

Aldeburgh's oldest building, the sixteenth-century **Moot Hall** (Easter–May & Sept Sat & Sun 2.30–5pm; June & Sept daily 2.30–5pm; July & Aug daily 10.30am–12.30pm & 2.30–5pm; 50p), which began its days in the centre of town, now finds itself on the

BENJAMIN BRITTEN AND THE ALDEBURGH FESTIVAL

Benjamin Britten was born in Lowestoft in 1913, and was closely associated with this part of Suffolk for most of his life. However, it was during his self-imposed exile in the USA during World War II – he was a conscientious objector – that Britten first read the work of the nineteenth-century Suffolk poet, George Crabbe. Crabbe's *The Borough*, a grisly portrait of the life of the fishermen of Aldeburgh, was the basis of the libretto of Britten's best-known opera, *Peter Grimes*, which was premiered in London in 1945 to great acclaim.

In 1947 Britten founded the English Opera Group and the following year launched the **Aldeburgh Festival** as a showpiece for his own works and those of his contemporaries. He lived in the town for the next ten years, achieving much of his best work as a conductor and pianist there. For the rest of his life he composed many works specifically for the festival, including his masterpiece for children, *Noye's Fludde*, and the last of his fifteen operas, *Death in Venice*.

By the mid-1960s, the festival had outgrown the parish churches in which it began, and moved into a collection of disused malthouses, five miles west of Aldeburgh on the River Alde, just south of the small village of **Snape** along the B1069. **Snape Maltings** were subsequently converted into one of the finest concert venues in the country. In addition to the concert hall, there is now a recording studio, a music school, various craft shops and galleries, a tearoom, and a nice pub, the *Plough & Sail*. Even if there's nothing specific on, it's worth calling into the complex to browse in the shops or perhaps take one of the daily summer **river trips** (Easter–Oct; 1hr; £3.50) along the Alde estuary to see the birdlife.

For more information on the Aldeburgh Festival, contact the **festival box office** on Aldeburgh High Street (Mon–Fri 10am–4pm, Sat 10am–2pm; ☎01728/453543; *www.aldeburgh.co.uk*). Tickets for the concerts, talks, exhibitions and other special events go on sale to the public around the middle of April, and often sell out fast for the big-name recitals; prices range from £8 to £25. There are concerts at other times of the year too – again details are available from the booking office – with showcase events including the Easter Music Festival, the Proms season in August, the week-long Britten Festival at the end of October and December's Winter Concerts.

seashore. It's a handsome building made out of a mixture of redbrick, flint and timber and the interior accommodates a modest museum of local finds and history. Aldeburgh's newest building, the **RNLI Lifeboat Station**, is situated bang in the middle of the seafront opposite the Jubilee Hall. From the public viewing deck you can look at the town's lifeboat and the tractor used to drag it out to sea.

Several **footpaths** radiate out from Aldeburgh, with the most obvious trail leading along the seashore north to Thorpeness (see p.466), with others leading southwest to the winding estuary of the River Alde, an area rich in wildfowl.

Practicalities

Aldeburgh's **tourist office** is located in the half-timbered cinema at 51 High St (April–Oct Mon–Fri 9am–5.15pm, Sat & Sun 10am–5.15pm; ☎01728/453637). The Festival Box Office (see box above) is further down the street at no. 150 (Mon–Fri 10am–4pm, Sat 10am–2pm) and can answer general enquiries when the tourist office is closed. Getting hold of **accommodation** should be no problem, except of course during the festivals when you should book months in advance. The town boasts several splendidly sited **hotels**, including the *Wentworth*, (☎01728/452312; ⑥), a family-owned hotel along the seafront from the Moot Hall. Of the **B&Bs**, the *Ocean House*, 25 Crag Path (☎01728/452094; no credit cards; ③) is probably the best. An immaculately maintained Victorian dwelling right on the seafront in the centre of town, it's decorated in period style, with two of its three guest rooms overlooking the beach; dinner is available by prior arrangement. Also in the town centre is *East Cottage*, 55 King St (☎01728/453010; ①), a brightly painted Victorian cottage a block back from the sea. Another option is the *Wateringfield*, on Golf Lane (☎01728/453163; ①), a spacious 1930s house overlooking the golf course on the edge of town. There's also a **youth hostel** on Heath Walk in the hamlet of Blaxhall (☎01728/688206; closed Nov–March), a couple of miles west of the concert facilities at Snape Maltings (see box on p.465). The hostel has forty beds and is housed in a former village school.

There are tearooms and takeaway fish-and-chip shops on the High Street, but Aldeburgh is the place for miles around to splash out on a decent meal – the town's highbrow leanings sustaining a glut of terrific **restaurants**. *Café 152*, 152 High St (☎01728/454152), is the most moderately priced, a simple painted wooden café where stylishly cooked fresh fish is served at lunch and dinner. There are more Mediterranean flavours and adventurous use of local ingredients at both the *Lighthouse*, 77 High St (☎01728/453377), and the *Regatta*, 171–173 High St (☎01728/452011; closed Mon & Tues through winter), each moderately priced and the latter open to the pavement in summer. For **drinks**, head for the *White Lion Hotel*, just along the seafront from the Moot Hall.

Thorpeness

THORPENESS, two miles up the coast from Aldeburgh, is a strange little resort, planned as a "fantasy" holiday village in 1910 by local landowner Stuart Ogilvie "for people who want to experience life as it was in Merrie England". This eccentricity explains the mock-Tudor style of much of the architecture, eye-catching follies like the watertower-shaped *House in the Clouds* and, less tangibly, the sense of keep-out privacy that pervades the place. The large pleasure lake at the centre of the village, the "Meare", has its islets named after characters from *Peter Pan*, whose author, J.M. Barrie, was an Ogilvie family friend. For further details on the history of Thorpeness, head for the **windmill** (May, June & early Sept Sat & Sun 11am–1pm; July & Aug Mon–Fri 2–5pm; free), a few hundred yards back from the sea and signposted down a lane from the main street, The Whinlands.

Sizewell and Leiston

It's impossible to wander along the shore around Aldeburgh without noticing the ominous presence of the **Sizewell nuclear power station**, whose superstructure, topped by what looks like a giant golf ball, is located two miles beyond Thorpeness. The gas-cooled reactor, Sizewell A, has been producing electricity since 1966, and will continue to do so into the next century. It was the plan to build a second pressurized-water reactor (PWR), **Sizewell B** – the first of its kind in the UK – that provoked one of the longest public enquiries in the country's history, lasting 340 days. Work began shortly after the disaster at Chernobyl, and the reactor was completed in the early part of 1995. In an attempt to assuage public unease, there's a plush **information centre** (Easter–Oct Mon–Fri 10am–4pm; free; tours need to be booked in advance, call ☎01728/653890), which cheerfully explains how unbelievably safe nuclear power is, and how the disaster which struck at the PWR on Three-Mile Island in the US couldn't possibly happen to Sizewell's American-designed PWR.

A couple of miles inland from Sizewell, the small town of **LEISTON** was synonymous with the agricultural engineering firm Garretts for over two centuries, until the company closed in 1980. Much of the original plant has been removed, but the main iron- and timber-framed factory building, built in 1852 and nicknamed "the cathedral", now forms part of the **Long Shop Museum** on Main Street (April–Oct Mon–Sat 10am–5pm, Sun 11am–5pm; £2.50), a few yards from the B1069. Here, you can view a selection of Garretts finest products from steamrollers and trolleybuses to bakers' ovens and dry-cleaning machines.

Dunwich

Seat of the king of East Anglia, a bishopric and once the largest port on the Suffolk coast, the ancient city of **DUNWICH**, about twelve miles up the coast from Aldeburgh, reached its peak of prosperity in the twelfth century. Over the last millennium, however, something like a mile of land has been lost to the sea, a process that continues at the rate of about a yard a year. As a result, the whole of the medieval city now lies under the ocean, including all twelve churches, the last of which toppled over the cliffs in 1919. All that survives are fragments of the Greyfriars monastery, which originally lay to the west of the city and now dangles at the sea's edge. For a potted history of the lost city, head for the **museum** (Easter–Sept daily 11.30am–4.30pm; Oct daily noon–4pm; free) in Dunwich village – little more than one small street of terraced houses built by the local landowner in the nineteenth century.

A sprawling, coastline car park gives ready access to this part of the seashore and is also where fishing boats still sell their daily catch off the shingle beach. From the car park, it's a short stroll west to the village and south to Greyfriars. Or you can hike further south, out along the beach to **Dunwich Heath**, where the coastguard cottages have been turned into a National Trust information centre (May–Oct daily; rest of year weekends only) with displays on medieval Dunwich and local wildlife. The heath is itself next to the **Minsmere RSPB reserve**, whose star attraction is a colony of avocets. You can rent binoculars from the RSPB **visitor centre** (mid-March to Sept Mon & Wed–Sun 9am–5pm) and strike out on the trails to the birdwatching hides; there's a café on site, too.

The coastline and its heaths have an eerie quality – P.D. James distils this perfectly in her *Unnatural Causes*, portraying the coast as the "battlefield where for nearly nine centuries the land had waged its losing fight against the sea". This atmosphere is best appreciated by **staying** at Dunwich's one and only pub, the *Ship Inn* (☎01728/648219; ③). With its low wooden beams and open fire, the bar here is a great place for a drink and the **food** is both moderately priced and very tasty with seafood the main event. There are also **rooms** available

Southwold and around

Perched on more robust cliffs just to the north of the River Blyth, **SOUTHWOLD** gained what Dunwich lost, and by the sixteenth century it had overtaken all its local rivals. Its days as a busy fishing port are now long gone, though a small fleet still brings in herring, sprats and cod, and nowadays it's a genteel seaside resort, an eminently appealing little town with none of the crassness of many of its competitors. There are fine old buildings, a long sandy beach, open heathland, a dinky harbour and even a little industry – in the shape of the Adnams brewery – but no burger bars and certainly no amusement arcades. This gentility was not to the liking of George Orwell, who lived for a time at his parents' house at 36 High St (a plaque marks the house). Orwell heartily disliked the town's airs and graces, and has left no trace of his time here – apart from disguised slights in a couple of early novels.

Southwold's breezy High Street is framed by attractive, mainly Georgian buildings, which culminate in the pocket-sized Market Place. From here, it's a brief stroll along East Street to the curious **Sailors' Reading Room** (daily 9am–5pm; free), decked out with model ships and nautical texts, and the bluff above the **beach**, where row upon row of candy-coloured huts march across the sands. Queen Street begins at the Market Place too, quickly leading to **South Green**, the prettiest of several greens dotted across town. In 1659, a calamitous fire razed much of Southwold and when the town was rebuilt the greens were left to act as firebreaks. Beyond, both Ferry Road and the Ferry Footpath lead down to the **harbour**, at the mouth of the River Blyth, an idyllic spot, where fishing smacks rest against old wooden jetties and nets are spread out along the banks to dry. There's a footpath along the harbourside that leads to a tiny **ferry** (Easter–May Sat & Sun 10am–12.30pm & 2–4.30pm; June–Aug daily 10am–12.30pm & 2–4.30pm; 30p), which pops across the river to Walberswick (see below).Turn right after the Harbour Inn and right again to walk back into town across **Southwold Common**. The whole circular walk takes about thirty minutes.

Back on the Market Place, it's a couple of hundred yards north along Church Street to East Green, with Adnam's Brewery on one side and the stumpy lighthouse on another. Close by is Southwold's architectural pride and joy, the **Church of St Edmund** (daily June–Aug 9am–6pm; Sept–May 9am–4pm; free), a handsome fifteenth-century structure whose solid symmetries are balanced by its long and elegantly carved windows. Inside, the slender, beautifully proportioned nave is distinguished by its panelled roof, embellished with praying angels, and its intricate rood screen. The latter carries paintings of the apostles and the prophets, though the Protestants defaced them during the Reformation. Beyond the screen, the choir stalls carry finely carved human and animal heads as well as grotesques – look out for the man in the throes of toothache. Look out also for "Southwold Jack", a brightly painted, medieval effigy of a man in armour nailed to the wall beside the font. No one knows when or why this very military carving was moved into the church – it certainly doesn't fit in – but the betting is that he was once part of a clock, nodding belligerently as he struck the hours.

Practicalities

With frequent services from other towns along the coast, Southwold is easy to reach by **bus**. These stop on the Market Place, opposite the **tourist office** (Easter–Sept Mon–Sat 10am–1pm & 1.45–5pm, Sun 11am–1.15pm & 1.45–4pm; ☎01502/724729), which has details of local attractions and sells walking maps. The town has two well-known **hotels** beside the Market Place, both owned and operated by Adnams. The smarter of the two is the *Swan* (☎01502/722186; ⑥), which occupies a splendid Georgian building with lovely period rooms, though the bedrooms – in the main house and in a garden annexe behind – are a little on the small side. The *Crown,* just along the High Street (☎01502/722275; ⑤), has just twelve simple bedrooms, nine of which are en suite. The best **B&B** in town is the delightful *Acton Lodge,* 18 South Green (☎01502/723217; no credit cards; ②), which occupies a grand Victorian house complete with its own neo-Gothic tower. The interior is decorated in period style and the three comfortable bedrooms are all en suite. Breakfasts are delicious, too. Alternatively, there's a string of **guesthouses** down along the seafront on North Parade: try the *North Parade,* at no. 21 (☎01502/722573; ②), a well-tended Victorian house with sprucely decorated bedrooms; or the attractive *Dunburgh,* at no. 28 (☎01502/723253; ③), housed in a rambling building with its own mini-tower.

Southwold has two outstanding **places to eat**. The *Crown*'s front bar provides superb informal meals, encompassing daily fish and meat specials combined with an enlightened wine list where all the choices are available by the glass. Turn up, wait for a table and expect to pay just £12 or so for two courses; you'll have to make a booking if you want to eat in the adjacent restaurant, which is pricier, slightly more adventurous and just as terrific. The *Swan*'s more formal dining room is the place for a gourmet blow-out, offering a choice of set dinners at £20–30 a head. For a **drink**, sample Adnams' brews in the *Crown*'s wood-panelled back-bar or stroll along to the *Red Lion* on South Green.

Walberswick and Blythburgh

Just across the River Blyth from Southwold lies the leafy little village of **WALBER-SWICK**, another once-prosperous port, now fallen into peaceful decline. For many years, it was the home of the English Impressionist painter, Philip Wilson Steer, and is now a seaside escape popular with well-heeled holidaymakers, who consider its larger neighbour too boisterous. As such, there's not much to see and most visitors make a bee-line for the *Bell*, an old village pub close to the riverfront which offers tasty bar food and Adnams beer. There are two ways for walkers to get here from Southwold – either via ferry (see opposite) or over the Bailey bridge about a mile further inland. The foot-path to the bridge begins on Station Road, a continuation of Southwold's High Street.

In the sixteenth century, the silting up of the River Blyth effectively marooned **BLYTHBURGH**, now an inconsequential hamlet but once a thriving port at the head of a wide estuary, five miles west of Southwold. The **Church of the Holy Trinity**, a handsome flint and stone structure dating from the 1440s, recalls the village's previ-ous prosperity – it's sheer bulk earning it the moniker, "Cathedral of the Marshes". Inside, the light and airy nave is decorated with carved angels and brightly painted flower patterns similar to St Edmund's in Southwold. The bench-ends depict the Seven Deadly Sins with gusto and, in another echo of Southwold, there's a "Jack-o'-the-Clock" here, too.

Lowestoft

LOWESTOFT, the easternmost point in the British Isles, is a world apart from the likes of Southwold and Aldeburgh. It's a fishing port and has been so since the railway arrived here in 1847, when Lowestoft began seriously to challenge its Norfolk neighbour, Great Yarmouth. The town is bisected by its Inner Harbour with the older part to the north. Here, the narrow alleyways, known locally as "scores", once lined with fishermen's huts and smokehouses, run east off the High Street towards the giant Bird's Eye factory, des-tination of much of the trawlers' haul. If you've an interest in Lowestoft's history, visit the **Maritime Museum** on Whapload Road (May–Oct daily 10am–5pm; 50p), near the light-house on the north side of town. Alternatively, you could take a **guided harbour tour** in a trawler, details of which can be found at the **tourist office**, East Point Pavilion (April–Sept daily 9.30am–5.30pm; Oct–March Mon–Fri 10.30am–5pm, Sat & Sun 10am–5pm; ☎01502/523000), on the south side of the harbour.

Norwich

One of the five largest cities in Norman England, **NORWICH** once served a vast hin-terland of cloth producers in the eastern counties, whose work was brought here by river and exported to the continent. Its isolated position beyond the Fens meant that it enjoyed closer links with the Low Countries than with the rest of England – it was, after all, quicker to cross the North Sea than to go cross-country to London. The local tex-tile industry, based on worsted cloth (named after the nearby village of Worstead), was further enhanced by an influx of Flemish and Huguenot weavers, who made up more than a third of the population in Tudor times. By 1700, Norwich was the second rich-est city in the country after London.

With the onset of the Industrial Revolution, Norwich lost ground to the northern manufacturing towns – the city's famous mustard company, Colman's, is one of its few industrial success stories. This, and its continuing geographical isolation, has helped preserve many of the city's older buildings and much of its ancient street plan. It has also meant that the population has never swelled to any great extent and today, with just 130,000 inhabitants, Norwich remains an easy and enjoyable city to negotiate. Yet the city is no provincial backwater. In the 1960s, the foundation of the University of East Anglia (UEA) made Norwich more cosmopolitan and bolstered its arts scene, while in the 1980s it's attracted new high-tech companies, who created something of a mini-boom, making the city one of England's wealthiest. As East Anglia's unofficial capital,

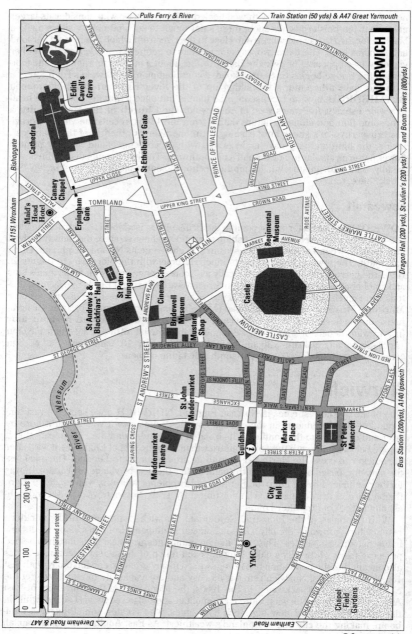

NORWICH

© Crown copyright

Norwich also lies at the hub of the region's transport network and serves as a useful base for visiting the Broads, and even as a springboard for the north Norfolk coast.

Arrival and information

Norwich's grandiose **train station** is on the east bank of the River Wensum, ten minutes' walk from the city centre along Prince of Wales Road. Long distance **buses** pull in at the Surrey Street station, also little more than ten minutes' walk from the town centre, but this time north via Surrey and St Stephen's streets. Information on local and regional bus services is provided by the Norfolk Bus Information Centre, 4 Goal Hill (Mon–Sat 8.30am–5pm; ☎0500/626116). The First Eastern Counties' Bus Ranger ticket (£5.50), valid for a day's unlimited travel on most East Anglian bus routes, is available here, as is the three-day ticket for unlimited travel on three days in seven (£13.50). The **tourist office** is in the Guildhall on the Market Place (June–Sept Mon–Sat 9.30am–5pm; Oct–May Mon–Fri 9.30am–4.30pm, Sat 9.30am–1pm & 1.30–4.30pm; ☎01603/666071). The **Broads Authority Office**, 18 Colegate (☎01603/610734), is a useful source of information for those heading for the Broads.

The best way to see the city is on foot – the tourist office's **city walking tours** (1hr 30min; £2.25) is a good way of getting the lie of the land – though it's also worth bearing in mind the **riverbus** (May–Sept, 3–4 daily; £1.50), which runs from Elm Hill to the Thorpe Road Quay, opposite the train station, providing an inexpensive means of cruising Norwich's central waterway. For longer **cruises**, contact Southern River Steamers (Easter & May–Sept daily; from £2.50; ☎01603/624051), which runs city cruises and trips to the Broads from Elm Hill and the Thorpe Road quay.

Accommodation

As you might expect, Norwich has **accommodation** to suit all budgets, but there's precious little in the town centre. Most **B&Bs** and **guest houses** are strung along the Earlham Road, a tedious, mostly Victorian street running west towards UEA, which itself offers **rooms**, primarily during the summer and Easter vacations.

The Beeches Hotel, 4–6 Earlham Rd (☎01603/621167, *reception@beeches.co.uk*). Just across the ring road from the centre, this medium-sized hotel occupies a fully modernized Victorian townhouse. All 25 rooms are en suite and the place is popular with visiting business folk. ⑤.

Earlham Guest House, 147 Earlham Rd (☎01603/454169). Spick-and-span lodgings at this family-run guest house, located in a two-storey Victorian house a good ten minutes' walk from the centre. Seven bedrooms, each with a TV. ②.

Maid's Head Hotel, Tombland (☎01603/209955). Bang in the centre, opposite the cathedral, this smart hotel incorporates all sorts of architectural bits and pieces from Art Deco flourishes through to heavy Victorian-style wood panelling. The end result is quite pleasing and the bedrooms come complete with modern furnishings and fittings. The most expensive rooms have ancient beamed ceilings, open fires and four-poster beds. ⑥.

Hotel Nelson, Prince of Wales Rd (☎01603/760260). This modern, riverside hotel, directly opposite the train station, caters to a mainly business clientele. It offers spick-and-span rooms, some of which overlook the water, an indoor pool and a health club. ⑥.

Norwich youth hostel, 112 Turner Rd (☎01603/627647). This seventy-bed hostel is located two miles west of the centre. There are self-catering and laundry facilities. ①.

Rosedale Guest House, 145 Earlham Rd (☎01603/453743, *drcbac@aol.com*). Typical Victorian guest house containing eight frugal but perfectly adequate bedrooms, each with a TV. A good ten-minute walk from the town centre. ②.

University of East Anglia (☎01603/592092). There are sixty en-suite rooms available year-round in Nelson Court (②), the rest are student rooms with shared bathrooms (①), available during Easter and summer vacations. The campus is four miles west of the centre along the Earlham Road; of the many buses running here from the centre, the #104 from Castle Meadow is the most frequent.

The City

Norwich is surprisingly hilly, tucked into a sweeping bend of the River Wensum, and with its irregular street plan, a Saxon legacy, orientation in the city can be confusing. There are, however, some obvious landmarks to help you find your way: the cathedral with its giant spire, the Norman castle on its commanding mound and the distinctive clocktower of City Hall. The **cathedral** and the **castle** are the town's premier attractions and the latter also holds one of the region's most satisfying collections of fine art. Finally, note that **Sunday** can be a disastrous day to visit if you want to see anything other than the cathedral: most museums and attractions are closed, not to mention most restaurants.

The Cathedral

Norwich **Cathedral** (daily 7.30am–6pm; free tours June–Oct Mon–Sat; £2 donation requested) is distinguished by its prickly octagonal spire which rises to a height of 315ft, second only to Salisbury. It's best viewed from Bishopgate to the east, where the thick curves of the flying buttresses, the rounded excrescences of the ambulatory chapels – unusual in an English cathedral – and the straight symmetries of the main body can all be seen to perfection.

The **interior** is pleasantly light thanks to the pale pink stone and clear glass of much of the nave, where the thick pillars are a powerful legacy of the Norman builders who began the cathedral in 1096 for Bishop Herbert de Losinga. Look up to spy the nave's fan vaulting, delicate and geometrically precise carving adorned by several hundred roof **bosses** recounting – from east to west – the story of the Old and New Testaments. In **St Luke's Chapel**, on the ambulatory's east side, is the cathedral's finest work of art, the *Despenser Reredos*, a superb painted panel commissioned to celebrate the crushing of the Peasants' Revolt of 1381. Norman bishops were barons as much as religious leaders, and to emphasize their direct relationship with Almighty God they positioned their thrones directly behind the high altar. Though most were later relocated, the one here occupies its original position and, just in case the bishop ran short of inspiration, a flue runs down from the back to the reliquary recess in the ambulatory behind to transport divine essences up to him. Accessible from the south aisle of the nave are the cathedral's unique **cloisters**. Built between 1297 and 1310, and the only two-storey cloisters left standing in England, they contain a remarkable set of sculpted **bosses** depicting scenes from the Bible, similar to the ones in the main nave, but close enough to be scrutinized without binoculars.

Outside, beside the main entrance, stands the medieval **Canary Chapel**. This is the original building of Norwich School, whose blue-blazered pupils are often visible during term time – the rambling school buildings are next door. A statue of the school's most famous boy, Horatio Nelson, faces the chapel, standing on the green of the Upper Close, which is guarded by two ornate and imposing medieval gates, **Erpingham** and, a few yards to the south, **St Ethelbert**. These lead onto the old Saxon market place, **Tombland**, a wide and busy thoroughfare whose name derives from the Saxon word for an open space. Beside the Erpingham gate is a memorial to Edith Cavell, a local woman who was a nurse in occupied Brussels during World War I. She was shot by the Germans in 1915 for helping allied prisoners to escape, a fate that made her an instant folk hero; her grave is beside the cathedral ambulatory. The Upper Close itself is but a small part of the much larger **Cathedral Close**, which extends east to the river, covering around one-fifth of the old walled city. Crisscrossed by footpaths, the Close is a pleasant place for a stroll, beginning with the Upper Close and then the adjoining Lower Close, where a scattering of silver birches and cherry trees is flanked by an attractive terrace of Georgian buildings. Keeping straight, the footpath continues east to **Pull's Ferry**, a landing stage at the city's medieval watergate, named after the last ferryman to work this stretch of the river. It's the most picturesque spot in town and from here you can wander along the riverbank either south to the railway station or north to Bishopgate.

From Elm Hill to the Market Place

At the north end of Tombland, fork left at the Maid's Head Hotel and **Elm Hill,** more a gentle slope than a hill, will eventually appear on the left. Priestley, in his *English Journey* of 1933, thought this part of Norwich to be overbearingly Dickensian, that it was "difficult to believe that behind those bowed and twisted fronts there did not live an assortment of misers, mad spinsters, saintly clergymen, eccentric comic clerks, and lunatic sextons". It's a powerful image and as you pass along Elm Hill's cobbles, admiring the half-timbered houses which make it Norwich's most photographed spot – be sure to take a look at **Wright's Court**, down a passageway at no. 43, one of the few remaining enclosed courtyards which were once a feature of the street. At the far end Elm Hill opens out into a triangular space centred on a plane tree, planted on the spot where the eponymous elm tree from Henry VIII's time once stood.

Beyond, veering left up Elm Hill, you soon reach **St Peter Hungate** (April–Sept Mon–Sat 10am–5pm; free), a good-looking flint church dating from the fifteenth century and now a brass-rubbing centre and museum of church art. Turn right at the church and it's just a few yards to **St Andrew's Hall** and **Blackfriars Hall**, two adjoining buildings that were originally the nave and chancel, respectively, of a Dominican monastery church. Imaginatively recycled, the two halls are now used for a variety of public events, including concerts, weddings and antique fairs; the crypt of the former now serves as a café (closed Sun).

South of here, off St Andrew's Street and along Bridewell Alley, stands the **Bridewell Museum** (April–Sept Tues–Sat 10am–5pm; £1.30), one of the city's more enjoyable museums. Formerly the city jail, the Bridewell holds a pot-pourri of old machines, adverts, signs, and reconstructed shops celebrating Norwich's old trades and industry. Inevitably, there's much on the all-important mustard industry and there's even more just up the alley at no. 3, where the Colman's-run **Mustard Shop** (closed Sun), sells all sorts of unlikely permutations on the basic mustard theme.

From the top of Bridewell Alley, Bedford Street and then Pottergate lead west to **St John Maddermarket** (June–Sept Wed–Fri 10am–4pm), one of thirty medieval churches standing within the boundaries of the old city walls. Most are redundant and are rarely open to the public, but this is one of the more accessible, courtesy of a dedicated volunteer. St John is a good example of the Perpendicular style. Apart from the stone trimmings, the church is almost entirely composed of flint rubble, the traditional building material of east Norfolk, an area chronically short of decent stone. By comparison, the interior is something of a disappointment, its furnishings and fittings thoroughly remodelled at the start of the twentieth century. It's from this period that the heavy-duty oak altar canopy and the extensive wood panelling date. Back outside, the arch under the church tower leads through to the **Maddermarket Theatre**, built in 1921 in the style of an Elizabethan playhouse. Incidentally, Maddermarket is named after the yellow flower that the weavers used to make red vegetable dye, or madder.

From Pottergate, several narrow alleys lead to the city's **Market Place**, site of one of the country's largest open-air markets (closed Sun), with stalls selling everything from bargain-basement clothes to local mussels and whelks. Three very different but equally distinctive buildings oversee the market's stripy awnings, the oldest of them being the fifteenth-century **Guildhall**, an attractive flint and stone structure that now houses the tourist office. Opposite, commanding the heights of the market place, is the austere **City Hall**, a lumbering brick pile with a landmark clocktower built in the 1930s in a Scandinavian style – it bears a striking resemblance to the city hall in Oslo. On the south side is the finest of the three buildings, **St Peter Mancroft** (Mon–Fri

9.30am–4.30pm, Sat 10am–12.30pm), whose long and graceful nave leads to a mighty stone tower, an intricately carved affair surmounted by a spiky little spire. The church once delighted John Wesley, who declared "I scarcely ever remember to have seen a more beautiful parish church", a fair description of what remains an exquisite example of the Perpendicular style with the slender columns of the nave reaching up towards the delicate groining of the roof. Completed in 1455, the open design of the nave was meant to express the mystery of the Christian faith with light filtering in through the stained-glass windows in a kaleidoscope of colours. Much of the original glass has survived, most notably in the east window which boasts a cartoon strip of Biblical scenes from the Virgin nursing the baby Jesus, through to the Crucifixion and Resurrection.

Back outside and just below the church is the bubble-gum-pink **Sir Garnet Wolseley** pub, sole survivor of the 44 ale houses that once crowded the Market Place – and stirred the local bourgeoisie into endless discussions about the drunken fecklessness of the working class. Opposite the pub, across **Gentlemen's Walk**, the town's main promenade, which runs along the bottom of the market place, is the brightly painted **Royal Arcade**, an Art Nouveau extravagance from 1899. The arcade has been beautifully restored to reveal the swirl and blob of the tiling, ironwork and stained glass, though it's actually the eastern entrance, further from the Walk, which is the most appealing section.

The Castle

High on a mound in the centre of town above an incongruous modern shopping mall, stands the twelfth-century **Castle Keep** (Mon–Sat 10am–5pm, Sun 2–5pm; July–Sept £3.40; Oct–June £2.50, includes entry to Regimental Museum) replete with blind arcading, an unusually decorative touch on a military structure. You can join a guided tour (an extra £2) of the battlements and dungeons (the castle served as the county jail for over six hundred years), or simply wander at will around the museum and art gallery inside. The latter contains a selection of work by the early nineteenth-century **Norwich School** of landscape painters, whose leading lights were John Sell Cotman and John Crome.

A long and dark (and one-way) tunnel leads down from the Castle Museum to the **Royal Norfolk Regimental Museum** (same times as castle), which tracks through the history of the regiment with remarkable candour – including an even-handed account of the Norfolks' police-keeping role in Northern Ireland. The exit leaves you below the castle on Market Avenue.

King Street and the river

Behind the castle, **King Street** possesses one or two surprises, beginning with the **Dragon Hall**, at no. 115–123 (April–Oct Mon–Sat 10am–4pm; Nov–March Mon–Fri 10am–4pm; £1.50), an extraordinarily long, half-timbered showroom built for the cloth merchant Robert Toppes in the fifteenth century. Bowed and bent by age, you get a good impression of the building from the outside, but enthusiasts can pop in to have a closer look at the roof – there's nothing else to see. A right turn opposite the hall up St Julian's Alley leads to **St Julian's Church** (daily 7am–6pm; free) and an adjoining monastic cell, thatched and standing in open countryside as late as the mid-nineteenth century. One of the smallest of the city's religious foundations, this was the retreat of St Julian, a Norwich woman who took to living here after experiencing visions of Christ in 1373. Her mystical *Revelations of Divine Love* – written after twenty years' meditation on her visions – was the first widely distributed book written by a woman in the English language, and has been in print ever since.

Still further down King Street, at Carrow Bridge near the football ground, are the ruins of two medieval **boom towers**, which formed part of the city's defences. From here, a **riverside walk** – initially on the east bank – follows the Wensum around the city centre to Bishopgate, switching to the inner (west) bank at Foundry Bridge, beside the train station. The walk is at its most appealing between Pull's Ferry (see p.472) and **Cow Tower**, a 50-foot-high watchtower where the bishop's retainers collected river tolls. This is one of the few survivors of Norwich's **fortified walls**, which once stretched for over two miles, surrounding the city and incorporating thirty such circular towers and ten defensive gates. Up until the 1790s, the gates were closed at dusk and all day on Sundays.

The University

The **University of East Anglia** (UEA) occupies a sprawling campus on the western outskirts of the city. Its buildings are resolutely modern concrete-and-glass blocks of varying designs – some quite ordinary, others like the prize-winning "ziggurat" halls of residence, designed by Denys Lasdun, eminently memorable. The high-tech **Sainsbury Centre for Visual Arts** (Tues–Sun 11am–5pm; £2) is an amazing piece of architectural art built by Norman Foster in 1978. The hangar-like interior houses one of the most unusual collections of sculpture and painting in the country, donated by the family which owns the Sainsbury supermarket chain, in which the likes of Giacometti, Bacon and Henry Moore rub shoulders with Mayan and Egyptian antiquities. The centre also runs a first-rate programme of temporary exhibitions (call ☎01603/593199 for further details). **Buses** #26, #27 and #35 run to the UEA from the train station and Castle Meadow.

Eating, drinking and entertainment

There are plenty of **cafés and restaurants** in the city centre – most of them very good value. Decent **pubs**, though, are harder to find – maybe because previously serviceable places have been turned into ersatz "traditional" drinking dens for students. The **arts scene** in Norwich is a tad self-conscious, but the city does possess several first-rate **theatres**.

Cafés and restaurants

Adlard's, 79 Upper Giles St (☎01603/633522). Engaging Modern-British restaurant with accomplished seasonal cooking. Closed all Sun & Mon lunch. Expensive.

Briton Arms, 9 Elm Hill. Home-made quiches, tarts, cakes and scones in a quaint Elm Hill house. Closed Sun. Inexpensive.

The Last Wine Bar, 72 St George's St (☎01603/626626). Converted factory building holding a smart wine bar, which serves up tasty bistro-style dishes. A couple of minutes' walk north of the river. Closed Sun. Moderate.

Marco's, 17 Pottergate (☎01603/624044). The city's oldest and finest Italian restaurant, serving all the classics with panache. Smart and formal. Closed Sun & Mon. Expensive.

Pinocchio's, 11 St Benedict St (☎01603/613318). Relaxed Italian restaurant with inventive food combinations and featuring live music a couple of times a week. Occupies a pleasantly converted old general store. Closed Sun. Moderate.

Pizza Express, 15 St Benedict's St. No surprises, of course, on the menu, but you get the city centre's best pizzas. Inexpensive.

St Andrew's Hall Crypt Coffee Bar, St Andrew's Plain at St George's St. Very cheap spot for budget meals or just a coffee and cake. Closes 4.30pm & all Sun. Inexpensive.

Take 5, at Cinema City, St Andrew's Plain. Imaginative, budget bistro food served in amenable surroundings. There's courtyard seating and a friendly bar, too. Closed Sun. Inexpensive.

Tree House, 14 Dove St, above the Rainbow wholefood shop. Vegetarian wholefood café-restaurant offering a daily changing menu of soups, salads and main courses, plus organic wines and beers. Closed Sun. Inexpensive.

Pubs, bars and clubs

Adam & Eve, Bishopgate. There's been a pub on this site for seven hundred years and it's still the top spot in town for the discerning drinker – with a changing range of real ales and an eclectic wine list supplied by Adnams.

Coach & Horses, Bethel St. Pleasant city-centre pub – across the street from City Hall – with lived-in furnishings and fittings. Good for a quiet drink.

Fat Cat, 49 West End St. Award-winning real-ale pub, twenty-minutes' walk west of the centre, down the Dereham Road. Lots of great beer in traditional surroundings.

Pottergate Tavern, Pottergate. Traditional, neighbourhood pub in a rather odd-looking Art Deco building just west along the street from St John Maddermarket Church.

Ribs of Beef, Wensum St. Boisterous riverside drinking haunt popular with students and townies alike. Well-kept ales and inexpensive bar food.

Waterfront, 139–41 King's St (☎01603/632717). Norwich's principal club and alternative music venue, with gigs and DJs most nights. Sponsored by UEA.

Entertainment

Predictably, Norwich has its fair share of multi-screen **cinemas** showing Hollywood blockbusters, but it also has the art-house Cinema City, in Suckling House on St Andrew's Plain (☎01603/622047). For **theatre**, there's the mainstream Theatre Royal, on Theatre Street (☎01603/630000), while the Maddermarket, St John's Alley, off Pottergate (☎01603/620917), offers an interesting programme of modern plays. There's also the Norwich Arts Centre, Reeves Yard off St Benedict's Street (☎01603/660352), which hosts a **jazz festival** in the last two weeks of November and features an eclectic year-round programme of cultural events, with everything from acid jazz to small-scale theatre. Predictably enough, **UEA** is a major source of entertainment for students and locals alike, with gigs at the Union and classical concerts at the Music Centre. The annual **Norfolk and Norwich Festival** each October (call the Ticket Shop ☎01603/764764 for details) features music, film, theatre, comedy, dance, walks and talks at venues all over the city.

The Norfolk Broads

Three rivers – the Yare, Waveney and Bure – meander across the flatlands to the east of Norwich, converging on Breydon Water before flowing into the sea at Great Yarmouth. In places these rivers swell into wide expanses of water known as "broads", which for years were thought to be natural lakes. In fact they're the result of extensive peat cutting, several centuries of accumulated diggings made in a region where wood was scarce and peat a valuable source of energy. The pits flooded when sea levels rose in the thirteenth and fourteenth centuries to create the **Norfolk Broads**, now one of the most important wetlands in Europe – a haven for such species as swallowtail butterflies, kingfishers, great crested grebes and Cetti's warblers – and the county's major tourist attraction.

The Broads' delicate ecological balance suffered badly during the 1970s and 1980s. The careless use of fertilizers poisoned the water with phosphates and nitrates, encouraging the spread of algae; the decline in reed cutting – previously in great demand for thatching – made the broads partly unnavigable; while the enormous increase in pleasure-boat traffic began to erode the banks. National Park status was, however, accorded to the area in 1988, and efforts are now under way to clear the waters and protect the ecosystem. Co-ordinating the clean up is the **Broads Authority**, which maintains a series of information centres throughout the region. At any of these locations, you can pick up a free copy of the *Broadcaster*, a useful newspaper guide to the Broads as a whole.

The region is crossed by several **train** lines, with connections from Norwich to Wroxham, Acle and Reedham, as well as Berney Arms, near Breydon Water, one of the few places in England that can be reached by rail but not road. The best – really the only – way to see the Broads themselves is **by boat**, and you could happily spend a week or so exploring the 125 miles of lock-free navigable waterways, visiting the various churches, pubs and windmills en route. Among many **boat rental** companies, two of the more established are Blakes Holidays (☎01603/784458) and Broads Tours Ltd (☎01603/782207), both of whom operate out of Wroxham (see below). Prices start at £600 a week for four people in peak season, but less expensive, short-term rentals are widely available, too.

Trying to explore the Broads by car is – as you might imagine – pretty much a waste of time, but cyclists and walkers have a much better time, taking advantage of the region's network of footpaths and cycling trails.. There are eight Broads Authority **bike rental** points dotted round the Broads (£8 per day; ☎01603/782281). **Walkers** should head for the 56-mile Weavers' Way, a long-distance footpath that winds through the best parts of the Broads on its way from Cromer to Great Yarmouth. The easiest boating centre to reach from Norwich is **WROXHAM**, accessible by train, bus and car. Seven miles northeast of the city, the village itself is short on charm, but it has a useful **information centre**, on Station Road (Easter–Oct daily 9am–1pm & 2–5pm; ☎01603/782281), and plenty of places where you can stock up with food before heading out on a cruise.

Five miles east of Wroxham, the village of **LUDHAM** straggles along the roadside at the tip of Womack Water, an offshoot of the River Thurne. Just north of the village is How Hill, where the Broads Authority maintain **Toad Hole Cottage** (Easter–May & Oct daily 11am–5pm, June–Sept 10am–5pm; free), an old eel catcher's cottage housing a small exhibit on the history of the trade, which was common hereabouts until the 1940s. Behind the cottage is the narrow River Ant where there are hour-long boat trips in the *Electric Eel* (Easter–May & Oct Sat & Sun 11am–3pm, June–Sept daily 10am–5pm; £2.50; reservations advised, call ☎01692/678763) to view the wildlife. **Bus** #54 runs to Ludham from Norwich.

A couple of miles east of Ludham, **POTTER HEIGHAM** is the nominal capital of the Broads, taking its name from the pottery which once stood here on the River Thurne and from the Saxon lord of Heacham who founded the first settlement. Again, there's not much to keep your attention, though you can watch boaters struggling with the village's fourteenth-century bridge, regarded as one of the most difficult passages in the Broads. All the major boat rental companies have outlets here and there's also an **information centre** (Easter–Oct daily 9am–1pm & 2–5pm; ☎01692/670779). The only public transport to Potter Heigham is by bus from Great Yarmouth.

Tiny **RANWORTH**, on Ranworth Broad around twelve miles east of Norwich, is a quieter spot altogether. There's no point in coming here if you're after a boat. The village does, however, have its own **information office** (Easter–Oct daily 9am–1pm & 2–5pm; ☎01603/270453), with stacks of stuff on local walking and wildlife, and a **church**, graced by a much-admired fifteenth-century rood screen. If travelling by boat, you will also be able visit the isolated ruins of St Benet's Abbey, a couple of miles downstream beside the River Bure.

Great Yarmouth

First and foremost, **GREAT YARMOUTH** is a seaside resort, its promenade a parade of amusement arcades and rainy-day attractions, deserted in winter, heaving in summer. But it's also a port with a long history and, despite extensive wartime bomb damage, it retains a handful of sights that give some idea of the place Daniel Defoe thought "far superior to Norwich".

Yarmouth was a major trading port by the fourteenth century, its economy underpinned by its control of the waterways leading inland to Norwich. It also benefited from fishing, especially during the nineteenth century when there was a spectacular boom in the herring industry. The fishing finally fizzled out in the 1960s, but the town was saved by the timely discovery of gas and oil deposits off the Norfolk coast, and these have since made it a major base for the offshore gas industry, second only to Aberdeen for North Sea oil.

The Town

Arriving by train or car from Norwich, initial impressions are favourable thanks to the appealing silhouette of the church of **St Nicholas**, which boasts one of the widest naves in the country and, consequently, an impressive west front. The church stands at the northern end of the broad marketplace, centre of what was medieval Yarmouth, but now mostly undistinguished. The one exception is the **Hospital for Decayed Fishermen**, founded in 1702, which opens out into a lovely little courtyard flanked by Dutch gables, its central cupola topped by a chilly looking statue of the fishermen's friend himself, St Peter. Next to the hospital is Sewell House, the childhood home of Anna Sewell, author of *Black Beauty*.

Despite considerable wartime damage, sections of the **medieval walls** remain, with one of the best-preserved portions located along Ferrier Road, just north of St Nicholas. Other interesting features of the old town are the narrow parallel alleys, known locally as "rows", which used to link the River Yare with the seashore. Sixty-nine have survived, and at the **Old Merchant's House** in Row 117 (Easter–Oct daily 10am–5pm; £1.75; EH), three blocks west of the town hall along South Quay, you can join up with one of English Heritage's guided tours of several of them. For more on Yarmouth's past, head for the **Elizabethan House Museum**, at 4 South Quay (June–Sept Mon–Fri 10am–5pm, Sun 2–5pm; £1.90; NT), whose period rooms concentrate on domestic life and include a Tudor bedroom and dining room. Here also is the Conspiracy Room where legend has it that Cromwell and his Puritan colleagues plotted the trial and execution of Charles I.

The vast majority of tourists simply head for the Victorian-built seafront, **Marine Parade**, whose wide sandy beach was the unlikely setting for many of the most dramatic events in Dickens's *David Copperfield*. There are the usual promenade gardens and seafront attractions here, bolstered by the presence of the town's **Maritime Museum** (June–Sept Mon–Fri & Sun 10am–5pm), which traces the history of the herring industry and the inland waterways. Great Yarmouth also shares the last steam herring-drifter, the 1930s *Lydia Eva*, with Lowestoft, and when it's here you'll find it berthed on South Quay.

Practicalities

It's a good ten-minute walk east from Great Yarmouth's **train station** to the central Market Place – cross the river by the footbridge and you'll find yourself on North Quay from where The Conge leads straight there. **Buses** terminate one block from the sea on Wellesley Road. There are two **tourist offices**: one in the town hall, on South Quay (Mon–Fri 9am–5pm; ☎01493/846345), and a seasonal office on Marine Parade (June–Sept Mon–Sat 9.30am–5.30pm, Sun 10am–5pm; April & May daily 10am–1pm & 2–5pm; ☎01493/842195). There's also a useful **Broads Information Centre** in the North West Tower, North Quay (July–Sept daily 10am–4pm; ☎01493/332095).

B&Bs line every street, with price a fair indication of quality, but if you don't have much luck, call in at the tourist office for assistance. Among many, the Willow Guest House, 26 Trafalgar Rd (☎01493/332355; ①), offers sea views from several of its ten bedrooms, while Senglea Lodge, 7 Euston Rd (☎01493/859632; ①), is a cosy, well-maintained terraced house with seven pleasant bedrooms a short walk from Marine Parade. For a **hotel**, try the Royal, 4 Marine Parade (☎01493/844215; ③), arguably Yarmouth's grandest – and where Dickens stayed. Yarmouth's **youth hostel** is in a large Victorian house near the bus station at 2 Sandown Rd (☎01493/843991; closed Sept–March).

Far and away the best **restaurant** in town is the reasonably priced *Seafood Restaurant*, 85 North Quay (☎01493/856009; closed Sun), which does a superb fish soup and Mediterranean-influenced seafood dishes.

The north Norfolk coast

For thirty miles beyond Yarmouth, there are no estuaries, harbours and very little in the way of habitation along the **north Norfolk coast**. The first place of any note is **Cromer**, a down-at-heel seaside town whose bleak and blustery cliffs have drawn tourists for over a century. A few miles to the west is another well-established resort, **Sheringham**, but thereafter the shoreline becomes a ragged patchwork of salt marshes, dunes and shingle spits which form an almost unbroken series of nature reserves, supporting a fascinating range of flora and fauna. It's a lovely stretch of coast and the villages bordering it, principally **Cley-next-the-Sea**, **Blakeney** and **Wells** are prime targets for an overnight stay. The other major attraction along this northern stretch of the coast is the large number of stately homes a short distance inland – some, like **Felbrigg** and **Holkham Hall**, among the finest in the region.

Cromer and Sheringham are the only places connected by **train**, with an hourly service from Norwich on the Bittern Line. Local **bus** services fill in the gaps, connecting most of the towns and villages. There's also the **Coastliner bus** (June–Sept Tues–Fri & Sun; ☎0500/626116), which provides regular services along the whole length of the coast from Cromer to Hunstanton, with some buses continuing to Great Yarmouth, King's Lynn and Sandringham. The Norfolk Coast Rover ticket (£3.50) gives a day's unlimited travel on the route. For **walkers**, there's also the **Norfolk Coast Path**, which runs from Hunstanton to Cromer (where it joins the Weavers' Way), an exhilarating route through the dunes and salt marshes; a National Trail Guide covers the route in detail, otherwise you'll need OS Landranger maps 132 and 133.

Cromer and around

Dramatically poised on a high bluff, **CROMER** should be the most memorable of the Norfolk coastal resorts, but its fine aspect is undermined by a dispiriting shabbiness in the streets and shopfronts – an "atrophied charm" as Paul Theroux called it. The tower of **St Peter and St Paul**, at 160ft the tallest in Norfolk, attests to the port's medieval wealth, but it was the advent of the railway in the 1880s that heralded the most frenetic flurry of building activity. A bevy of grand Edwardian hotels was constructed along the seafront and for a moment Cromer became the most fashionable of resorts, but the gloss soon wore off and only the seen-better-days **Hotel de Paris** has survived. A small fleet of crab boats resting on the beach with their attendant tractors is all that remains of the town's traditional industry. Cromer's **pier** was badly damaged in a storm in November 1993, but has since been repaired and struggles gamely on.

Somewhat miraculously Cromer has managed to retain its rail link with Norwich; the **train station** is a five-minute walk west of the centre. **Buses** terminate on Cadogan Road, next to the **tourist office** (daily: Easter–Oct 10am–5pm; Nov–March 10am–1pm & 1.30–4pm; ☎01263/512497), which is just 200 yards from the cliff-top promenade. An hour or two in Cromer is probably enough, though the beach is first-rate and the cliff-top walk exhilarating. There's no shortage of inexpensive **accommodation** – the tourist office has all the details.

Felbrigg Hall

Just a couple of miles southwest of Cromer off the A148, **Felbrigg Hall** (April–Oct Mon–Wed, Sat & Sun 1–5pm; £5.50; NT) is a charming Jacobean mansion. The main facade is particularly appealing, the soft hues of the ageing limestone and brick intercepted by three bay windows which together sport a large, cleverly carved inscription – Gloria Deo in Excelsis – in celebration of the reviving fortunes of the family who then owned the place, the Windhams. The interior is splendid too, with the studied informality of both the dining room and the drawing room enlivened by some magnificent seventeenth-century plasterwork ceilings and sundry *objets d'art*. Many of the paintings in the hall were purchased by William Windham II, who did his Grand Tour in the 1740s. In the drawing room are several marine scenes, notably two paintings of the "Battle of the Texel" by Willem van de Velde the Elder, hung just as William had them, with pride of place going to the six oils and twenty-odd gouaches of Rome and southern Italy by Giovanni Battista Busiri.

The surrounding **parkland** (daily dawn to dusk) divides into two, with woods to the north and open pasture to the south. Footpaths crisscross the park – a popular spot to head for is the medieval church of **St Margaret's** in the southeastern corner, which contains a fine set of brasses and a fancy memorial to William Windham I and his wife by Grinling Gibbons. Nearer the house, there's the extensive **walled garden**, which features flowering borders and an octagonal dove house, and the stables, which have been converted into very pleasant **tearooms**.

Blickling Hall

Blickling Hall (April–Oct Tues & Wed–Sun 1–4.30pm; house & gardens £6.20; gardens only £3.50; NT), set in a sheltered, wooded valley ten miles south of Cromer is another grand Jacobean pile. Built for Sir Henry Hobart, a Lord Chief Justice, the hall dates from the 1620s and although it was extensively remodelled over a century later, the modifications respected the integrity of the earlier design. Consequently, the long facade, with its slender chimneys, high gables and towers, is the apotheosis of Jacobean design. Inside, highlights include a superb plasterwork ceiling in the Long Gallery and an extraordinarily grand main staircase. There's also a gargantuan tapestry depicting Peter the Great defeating the Swedes, given to one of the family by Catherine the Great.

The surrounding **parkland** (daily dawn to dusk) incorporates a mile-long lake and a weird pyramidal mausoleum holding the earthly remains of the last of the male Hobarts.

Sheringham

SHERINGHAM, a popular seaside town four miles west of Cromer, has an amiable, easy-going air and makes a reasonable overnight stop, though frankly you're still only marking time until you hit the more appealing places further west. One of the distinctive features of the town is the smooth local beach pebbles that face and decorate the houses, a flinting technique used frequently in this part of Norfolk – the best examples here are off the High Street. The down-side is that the power of the waves which makes the pebbles smooth has also forced the local council to spend thousands rebuilding the sea defences. The resultant mass of reinforced concrete makes for a less than pleasing seafront – all the more reason to head, instead, for **Sheringham Park**, the 770-acre woodland park a couple of miles southwest of the town, laid out by Humphrey Repton in the early 1800s. The park boasts a wonderful array of rhododendrons and azaleas, at their best in late May to early June, and a series of look-out posts from which you can admire the view down to the coast. The other out-of-town jaunt is on the **North Norfolk Railway**, whose steam trains operate along the five miles of track from

Sheringham to the modest market town of Holt (June–Sept daily; all-day ticket £6.50; ☎01263/822045).

Sheringham's two **train stations** are opposite each other on either side of Station Road. The main station, the terminus of the Bittern Line from Norwich, is just to the east, the North Norfolk Railway station to the west. The **tourist office** (Easter–Oct Mon–Sat 10am–5pm, Sun 10am–4pm; ☎01263/824329) is in between them on Railway Approach. From the tourist office, it's a five-minute walk north to the seafront, straight down Station Road and its continuation, the High Street. You can rent **bikes** from Bike Riders, 7 St Peter's Rd (☎01263/821906), adjacent to the North Norfolk Railway station.

There are plenty of **B&B** options, with one of the best being *Oak Lodge* at 2 Morris St (☎01263/823158; ②), a smart Edwardian house with four attractive bedrooms right in the centre of town. A good alternative is the *Two Lifeboats*, 2 High St (☎01263/822401; ②), a small hotel on the promenade offering sea views from most of its bedrooms. The **youth hostel** is a short walk south of the main train station at 1 Cremer's Drift (☎01263/823215), set in its own grounds just off the Cromer road. The *Two Lifeboats* serves inexpensive **bar meals** and more formal dinners in its **restaurant**, and prides itself on its fresh fish.

Cley-next-the-Sea and Blakeney Point

Travelling west from Sheringham, the A149 meanders through a pretty rural landscape offering occasional glimpses of the sea and a shoreline protected by a giant shingle barrier erected after the catastrophic flood of 1953, a disaster which claimed over a thousand lives. After seven miles you reach **CLEY-NEXT-THE-SEA**, once a busy wool port but now little more than a row of flint cottages and Georgian mansions set beside a narrow, marshy inlet that (just) gives access to the sea. The original village was destroyed in a fire in 1612, which explains why Cley's fine medieval **Church of St Margaret** is located half a mile inland at the very southern edge of the current village, overlooking the green. The Black Death brought church construction to a sudden halt, hence the contrast between the stunted, unfinished chancel and the splendid nave, which boasts several fine medieval brasses and some folksy fifteenth-century bench ends depicting animals and grotesques. Cley's other great draw – housed in an old forge on the main street – is the excellent Cley Smoke House, selling local smoked fish and other delicacies, while nearby Picnic Fayre has long been one of the finest delis in East Anglia.

It's about 400 yards east from the village to the mile-long byroad that leads to the shingle mounds of **Cley beach**. This is the starting point for the four-mile hike west out along the spit to **Blakeney Point**, a nature reserve famed for its colonies of terns and seals. The seal colony is made up of around four hundred common and grey seals and the old lifeboat house, at the end of the spit, is now a National Trust information centre. The shifting shingle can, however, make the going difficult, so keep to the low-water mark – which also means that you won't accidentally trample any nests. The easier alternative is to take one of the boat trips to the point from Blakeney or Morston. The Norfolk Coast Path passes close to the beach too, continuing south along the edge of the **Cley Marshes**, which attract a bewildering variety of waders – and, of course, "twitchers".

Cley has several great places **to stay**, beginning with the *Cley Mill B&B* (☎01263/740209; ③) housed in a converted windmill complete with sails and a balcony offering wonderful views over the surrounding salt marshes and seashore. Other options in the village include the attractive *Whalebone House*, on the main street (☎01263/740336; ②), and the *Three Swallows* pub (☎01263/740526; ②) on the green by the church, which has several pleasant en-suite rooms and serves good **food**.

Blakeney

BLAKENEY is delightful. Once a bustling port exporting fish, corn and salt, it's now a dreamy little place of pebble-covered cottages sloping up from a narrow harbour just a mile west of Cley. Crab sandwiches are sold from stalls at the quayside, the meandering high street is flanked by family-run shops, and footpaths stretch out along the sea wall to east and west, allowing long, lingering looks over the salt marshes. The only sight as such is the **Church of St Nicholas**, beside the A149 at the south end of the village, whose sturdy tower and nave are made of flint rubble with stone trimmings, the traditional building materials of north Norfolk. Curiously, the church has a second, much smaller tower at the back. In the nineteenth century this was used as a lighthouse to guide ships into harbour, but its original function is unknown. Inside, the oak and chestnut hammer-beam roof and the delicate rood screen are the most enjoyable features of the nave, which is attached to a late thirteenth-century chancel, the only survivor from the original Carmelite friary church. With its seven stepped lancet windows, the east window is a rare example of Early English design, though the stained glass is much later.

Blakeney **harbour** is linked to the sea by a narrow channel, which pierces its way through the salt marshes. The channel is, however, only navigable for a few hours at high tide – at low tide the harbour is no more than a muddy creek. Depending on the tides, there are **boat trips** from Blakeney or Morston quay, a mile or two to the west, to Blakeney Point; as well as the two-hour round trips which land passengers at the National Trust information centre on Blakeney Point there are also hour-long seal-watching trips. The main operators advertise departure times on blackboards by the quayside.

For **accommodation**, the quayside *Blakeney Hotel* (☎01263/740797; ⑦) is one of the most charming hotels in Norfolk, a rambling building with high-pitched gables and pebble-covered walls. The hotel has a heated indoor swimming pool, a secluded garden, cosy lounges decorated in soft pastel colours, sea views and serves excellent food. The cheaper rooms can be poky and somewhat airless, but you can pay a little more to get a room with splendid views across the harbour and the marshes. There are discounts for longer stays with full board. A very good alternative is the *Manor Hotel* (☎01263/740376; ④), which occupies a low-lying courtyard complex a few yards to the east of the harbour; or the *King's Arms*, just back from the quay on Westgate (☎01263/740341; ③), a traditional pub, with low, beamed ceilings and seven pleasant en-suite bedrooms, that also serves up excellent, reasonably priced **bar food**. For longer stays, contact *Blakeney Cottage Holidays* (☎01692/405188), who rent some super local cottages – there's an office halfway up the High Street.

Wells-next-the-Sea and around

Despite its name, **WELLS-NEXT-THE-SEA** is situated a good mile or so from open water. In Tudor times, when it enjoyed much easier access to the sea, it was one of the great ports of eastern England, a major player in the trade with the Netherlands. It's still one of the more attractive towns on the north Norfolk coast, and the only one to remain a commercially viable port. There's nothing specific to see among its narrow lanes, but it makes a very good base for exploring the surrounding coastline.

The town divides into three distinct areas, starting with the broad rectangular green to the south, lined with oak and beech trees and some very fine Georgian houses, and known as **The Buttlands** since the days when it was used for archery practice. North from here, across Station Road, are the narrow lanes of the town centre with **Staithe Street**, the tiny main drag, flanked by quaint old-fashioned shops. At the bottom end of Staithe Street stands the **quay**, a slightly forlorn affair inhabited by a couple of amusement arcades and fish-and-chip shops. A few yards away is the mile-long road to the **beach**, a handsome sandy tract backed by pine-clad dunes. The road is shadowed by a high flood defence and a tiny narrow-gauge railway, which scoots down to the beach every forty minutes or so during the season.

Buses to Wells stop on the Buttlands, a short stroll from the **tourist office** at the foot of Staithe Street (March to mid-July, Sept & Oct Mon–Sat 10am–5pm, Sun 10am–4pm; mid-July to Aug Mon–Sat 9.30am–7pm, Sun 9.30am–6pm; ☎01328/710885). Several of the best **guest houses** are along Standard Road, which runs up from the eastern end of the quayside. First choice should be the elegant *Normans* (☎01328/710657; ②), whose seven spacious and tastefully decorated rooms are all en suite; the TV lounge has a log fire and racks of games and the first-floor look-out window provides a wide view over the marshes – binoculars are provided. Other options include *Mill House*, a dignified old millowner's home on Northfield Lane (☎01328/710739; ①), and *Ilex House* on Bases Lane (☎01328/710556; ②); the latter is a good-looking Georgian villa sitting in its own grounds, just to the west of the centre. There's also a **campsite**, the sprawling Pinewoods Caravan and Camping Park, by the beach (☎01328/710439; closed Nov to mid-March).

Wells' best **restaurant** is the *Moorings*, by the quay on Freeman Street (☎01328/710949), which offers unusual and beautifully prepared dishes (local fish a speciality) at moderate prices. *Nelson's*, 21 Staithe St, is a tea- and coffee shop which serves inexpensive meals. For **pub** food, head straight for the *Crown* on the Buttlands, the best pub in town.

Holkham Hall

One of the most popular outings from Wells is to **Holkham Hall** (June–Sept Mon–Thurs & Sun 1–5pm; £4), three miles to the west and a stop on the Coastliner bus (see p.479). This grand and self-assured stately home was designed by the eighteenth-century architect William Kent for the first earl of Leicester and is still owned by the family. The severe sandy-coloured Palladian exterior belies the warmth and richness of the interior, which retains much of its original decoration, notably the much-admired marble hall, with its fluted columns and intricate reliefs. The rich colours of the state rooms are an appropriate backdrop for a fabulous selection of **paintings**, including canvases by Van Dyck, Rubens, Gainsborough and Gaspar Poussin. One real treat is the Landscape Room where around twenty landscape paintings are displayed in the cabinet style of the eighteenth century. Most depict classical stories or landscapes, a poetic view of the past that enthralled the English aristocracy for decades.

The **grounds** are laid out on sandy, saline land, much of it originally salt marsh. The focal point is an 80-foot-high obelisk, atop a grassy knoll, from where you can view both the hall to the north and the triumphal arch to the south. In common with the rest of the north Norfolk coast, there's plenty of **birdlife** to observe in and around the park – Holkham's lake attracts Canada geese, heron and grebes and several hundred deer graze the open pastures.

A footpath leads north from the estate across the marshes to **Holkham Bay**, where one of the finest sandy beaches on this stretch of coast is fringed by pine-studded sand dunes. Waders inhabit the mud and salt flats, while farther inland you can see warblers, flycatchers and redstarts.

Little Walsingham

For centuries **LITTLE WALSINGHAM**, five miles south of Wells, rivalled Canterbury as the foremost pilgrimage site in England. In 1061 the Lady of the Manor, Richeldis de Faverches, was prompted to build a replica of the **Santa Casa** (Mary's home in Nazareth) here – inspired, it is said, by visions of the Virgin Mary. Whatever the reason for her actions, it brought instant fame and fortune to this little Norfolk village. By the fourteenth century, the Augustinians and Franciscans had established themselves here and every English king since Henry III had visited the place, walking barefoot for the last mile. Henry VIII followed in his predecessors' footsteps in 1511, though he subsequently destroyed the shrine during the Dissolution and brought the village's principal trade to an abrupt halt. Pilgrimages resumed in earnest after 1922, when the local vicar, Alfred Hope Patten, organized an Anglo-Catholic pilgrimage, the prelude to the building of an Anglican shrine in the 1930s. Today the village does good business out of its holy connections and the narrow-gauge **steam railway** from Wells (Easter–Sept daily; ☎01328/710631).

Little Walsingham now has a number of shrines catering to a variety of denominations – there are even two Russian Orthodox shrines – though the main one is the **Anglican shrine** inside the heavily restored parish church, a few yards from the main square beside the road to Holt. It's a strange-looking building – a cross between an English village hall and a Greek Orthodox church – and inside the candle-lit Santa Casa contains the statue of Our Lady of Walsingham.

Shrines apart, Little Walsingham has an attractive **High Street**, overlooked by handsome Georgian and half-timbered houses, several of which are given over to shrine shops and religious bookstores. At its southern end is Friday Market, a pretty little square which backs onto the grounds and ruins of the old Franciscan Friary. Along the High Street itself are yet more ecclesiastical ruins, those of **The Abbey** – more accurately the Augustinian Priory – whose landscaped grounds stretch east to the River Stiffkey. The abbey ruins are not much to look at, but the fifteenth-century **gatehouse**, on the High Street, is an impressive affair – look up and you'll spy Christ peering out from a window. At the north end of the High Street is the main square, the **Common Place**, whose half-timbered buildings surround a quaint octagonal structure built around the village **pump** in the sixteenth century.

The Coastliner **bus** stops outside the Anglican shrine and the **train station** (for the steam train from Wells) is a five-minute walk from the north end of the village: from the station, turn left along Egmere Road and take the second major right down Bridewell Street. The **tourist office** is on Common Place (Easter–Sept daily 10am–4.30pm; ☎01328/820510). It's difficult to find accommodation during major **pilgrimages**: the main ones are the national pilgrimage on May 31 and the pilgrimage for the sick and handicapped on August 30. That said, the *Black Lion* pub on Friday Market (☎01328/820235; ④) has comfortable en-suite rooms and a restaurant, as does the *Bull Inn* on Common Place (☎01328/820333; ③).

Burnham Market and Burnham Thorpe

A quick diversion off the A149 five miles west of Wells puts you in the picturesque village of **BURNHAM MARKET**, whose Georgian houses are ranged around an appealing green. The target here is the *Hoste Arms* (☎01328/738777; ⑤), an old coaching inn which offers some of the best restaurant and bar food on the coast – and attracts a well-heeled crew to match.

A mile or so to the east, **BURNHAM THORPE** was the birthplace of **Horatio Nelson**, who was born in the parsonage on September 29, 1758. Nelson joined the navy at the tender age of twelve, and was sent to the West Indies, where he met and married Frances Nisbet, retiring to Burnham Thorpe in 1787. Back in action by 1793, his bravery cost him first the sight of his right eye, and shortly afterwards his right arm. His personal life was equally eventful – famously, his infatuation with Emma Hamilton, wife of the ambassador to Naples, caused the eventual break-up of his marriage. His finest hour was during the Battle of Trafalgar in 1805, when he led the British navy to victory against the combined French and Spanish fleet, a crucial engagement that set the scene for Britain's century-long domination of the high seas. The victory, as everyone knows, didn't do Nelson much good – he was shot in the chest during the battle and even the kisses of Hardy failed to revive him.

The parsonage was demolished years ago, but Nelson is celebrated in the **All Saints Parish Church**, where the lectern is made out of timbers taken from the *Victory*, the chancel sports a Nelson bust, and the south aisle has a small exhibition on his life. It was actually Nelson's express wish that he should be buried here, but instead he was laid in state at Greenwich and then buried at St Paul's. The other place to head for here is the **village pub** (no prizes for guessing the name) where Nelson held a farewell party for the locals in 1793.

Titchwell Marsh and Thornham

Beyond Burnham Market there's more rich marshland filled with wildfowl, especially at **Titchwell Marsh** where the RSPB maintains a reserve based around reed beds and fresh and saltwater lagoons. **TITCHWELL** itself has the excellent *Titchwell Manor Hotel* (☎01485/210221; ⑤), beside the A149, where the bar offers great seafood – from grilled oysters and mussels to monkfish and plaice. Lunch can easily be had for under a tenner and though the rooms are a little pricey, dinner, bed and breakfast deals are better value. **THORNHAM**, a mile further west, has three more likely looking pubs, including the splendid *Lifeboat Inn* on Ship Lane (☎01485/512236; ⑤), again with great food and good all-in deals.

Hunstanton

The Norfolk coast pretty much ends at **HUNSTANTON**, a Victorian seaside resort that grew up to the southwest of the original fishing village. Like Yarmouth, it has its fair share of amusement arcades, crazy golf, and entertainment complexes, but it has also hung on to its genteel origins – and its sandy beaches, backed by stripy gateau-like cliffs, are among the cleanest in Norfolk. Incidentally, in "The World of Fun" on Greevegate, Hunstanton possesses the self-proclaimed largest joke shop in Britain with more whoopee cushions and Dracula fangs than even the most unpleasant ten-year-old could want.

The **tourist office** is in the town hall (daily: April–Sept 9.30am–5pm; Oct–March 10.30am–4pm; ☎01485/532610) on the wide sloping green, the focal point of the town, and can help out with **accommodation**, though it's easy enough to find. The nicest and priciest places, like *Le Strange Arms* (☎01485/534411; ⑤), whose gardens run down to the beach, are to be found among the cottages of Old Hunstanton, a mile northeast of the town centre. At the other end of the market, the **youth hostel** occupies a Victorian town house at 15 Avenue Rd (☎01485/532061; closed Nov–March), south of the green.

King's Lynn and around

An ancient port built on an improbably marshy location, **KING'S LYNN** straddles the mouth of the Great Ouse, a mile or so before it flows into the Wash. Strategically placed for easy access to seven English counties, the merchants of Lynn grew rich importing fish from Scandinavia, timber from the Baltic and wine from France, while exporting wool, salt and corn to the Hanseatic ports. The town stagnated when the focus of maritime trade moved to the Atlantic seaboard, but its port facilities have been reinvigorated since the UK joined the EU. Much of the old centre was demolished during the 1950s and 1960s to make way for commercial development. As a result, Lynn lacks the concentrated historic charm of towns such as Bury St Edmunds, though it does have a number of well-preserved buildings, the oldest guildhall in the country and a handful of excellent stately homes and medieval castle ruins within easy reach.

Arrival, information and accommodation

From the **train station**, it's a short walk west along Waterloo Street to Railway Road, the principal thoroughfare, which borders the eastern edge of the town centre. The **bus station** is nearer the centre, a few yards to the west of Railway Road from where signs point you to the **tourist office** in the Custom House (April–Oct Mon–Sat 9.15am–5pm, Sun 10am–5pm; Nov–March daily 10.30am–4pm; ☎01553/763044).

Accommodation presents few problems except during the arts festival at the end of July. Most of the budget **B&Bs** lie southeast of the train station, easily reached by walking through the park behind the station. Aim for Tennyson Avenue and Goodwins Road, its continuation to the south. Here you'll find the *Old Rectory*, 33 Goodwins Rd (☎01553/768544; ②), and *Fairlight Lodge*, 79 Goodwins Rd (☎01533/762234; ②), and the more upmarket *Russet House Hotel*, 53 Goodwin Rd (☎01553/773098; ④). Lynn's finest **hotel** is the *Duke's Head* on the Tuesday Market Place (☎01533/774996; ⑧) – make sure you get a room overlooking the square – which offers good-value year-round deals where evening meals are included. The town's **youth hostel** enjoys a central location in the converted Thorseby College on College Lane (☎01533/772461; closed Sept–March).

The Town

Lynn's historic core lies in the two blocks between the High Street and the quayside. A good place to begin is the **Saturday Market Place**, the older and smaller of the town's two marketplaces, presided over by the hybrid **Church of St Margaret**, which contains two of the most fanciful medieval brasses in East Anglia. These are the Walsoken brass, adorned with country scenes, and the Braunche brass, named after a certain Robert Braunche and depicting the lavish feast he laid on for Edward III. Across the square is Lynn's prettiest building, the **Trinity Guildhall**, its wonderful chequered flint and stone facade dating to 1421 and repeated in the Elizabethan addition to the left and in the adjoining Victorian Town Hall. Next door to the Guildhall is the entrance to the **Old Gaol House** (April–Oct daily 10am–5pm; Nov–March Mon, Tues & Fri–Sun 10am–4pm; £2.20), which incorporates a series of eighteenth-century cells within a small museum on local baddies. There's also access to the Guildhall undercroft, which displays an exhibition of the town's rich collection of civic regalia. This is actually more stimulating than you might think, since the treasures include King John's Cup and Sword, the latter a gift to the town prior to the king's ill-fated and ill-timed dash across the Wash, during which he caught the incoming waters and saved himself, but lost the crown jewels.

Of the medieval warehouses which survive along the quayside, the most evocative is the **Hanseatic Warehouse**, built around 1475, whose half-timbered upper floor juts unevenly over the cobbles of St Margaret's Lane. The other architectural highlight is a short stroll north, at the end of the gentle Georgian curve of Queen Street. It's here you'll find the splendid **Custom House**, erected in 1683 in a style clearly influenced by the Dutch. There are classical pilasters, petite dormer windows and a roof-top balustrade, but it's the dinky little cupola that catches the eye. The Custom House holds the tourist office (see below) and overlooks **Purfleet Quay**, a short and stumpy harbour once packed with merchant ships.

Beyond the Custom House, King Street, with its much wider berth, continues where Queen Street left off. On the left, just after Ferry Lane, stands Lynn's most precious building, **St George's Guildhall** (Mon–Sat 10am–5pm; free), dating from 1410 and the oldest surviving guildhall in England. It was a theatre in Elizabethan times and is now part of the King's Lynn Arts Centre. Beyond the Guildhall is the later and much larger **Tuesday Market Place**, with the pastel-pink Duke's Head Hotel, dating from 1689, and the Neoclassical **Corn Exchange** – imaginatively converted into a second arts centre for the town – standing out against an otherwise unspectacular assemblage.

Eating, drinking and entertainment

Weekly **markets** still attract large fenland crowds to the Saturday Market Place (Sat only) and the larger Tuesday Market Place (Tues & Fri). Tasty **pub meals** are available at the *Tudor Rose* on St Nicholas St, off Tuesday Market Place, and this is also the best place for a **drink**. There's a good café, *Crofter's*, in the undercroft of the Guildhall arts centre, and the town has two highly recommendable, if expensive, **restaurants**. The first is the *Riverside Rooms*, 27 King St (☎01553/773134; closed Sun), in an old fifteenth-century warehouse round the back of the arts centre, where the food – light lunches and dinner – is excellent; you get river views and tables outside in decent weather too. The second is *Rococo*, a modish little outfit on the Saturday Market Place (☎01533/771483; closed all Sun, & Mon lunch), which offers everything from game to veggie dishes.

Entertainment in Lynn revolves around the King's Lynn Arts Centre, housed in St George's Guildhall on King Street (☎01553/764864). Its galleries, cinema and theatre stage much of the annual festival held in July. The Corn Exchange, on the Tuesday Market Place (same number as Guildhall), offers a wide-ranging programme from theatre and music to comedy and dance.

Around King's Lynn

Within a ten-mile radius of King's Lynn are several notable attractions. The architectural highlight is **Houghton Hall**, an extravagant Palladian mansion with baroque flourishes, but it's **Sandringham**, one of the Queen's country residences, that pulls in the crowds. The area also holds some fine Norman ruins at **Castle Rising** and **Castle Acre**.

Castle Rising

Situated at the centre of extensive earthworks five miles northeast of Lynn, the shell of the twelfth-century keep of **Castle Rising** (April–Oct daily 10am–6pm; Nov–Easter Wed–Sun 10am–4pm; £2.30; EH) is in remarkably good condition. Towering over the surrounding flatlands, it's a powerful, imposing structure and some of its finer architectural details have survived as well – from the blind arcading and ox-eye windows on the outside to the vaulted ceilings and ornamented fireplaces within. The nearby village is laid out on a grid plan and contains a quadrangle of beautiful seventeenth-century **almshouses**, whose elderly inhabitants still go to church in red cloaks and pointed black hats, the colours of the original benefactor, the Earl of Northampton. **Buses** #410 and #411 (hourly) from King's Lynn to Hunstanton stop off at the *Black Horse* pub in the village.

Sandringham House

Another four miles on from Castle Rising looms the seven-thousand-acre estate of **Sandringham House** (Easter–Sept daily 11am–4.45pm; closed for two weeks late-July or early Aug; £5), bought in 1861 by Queen Victoria for her son, the future Edward VII. The house is billed as a private home, but few families have a drawing room crammed with Russian silver and Chinese jade. The **museum**, housed in the old coach and stable block, contains an exhibition of royal memorabilia from dolls to cars, but much more arresting are the beautifully maintained **grounds**, a mass of rhododendrons and azaleas in spring and early summer. The estate's sandy soil is also ideal for game birds, which was the attraction of the place for the terminally bored Edward, whose tradition of New Year shooting parties is still followed by the royals. Local **buses** #410 and #411 make the journey from King's Lynn, as does the summer Coastliner service (see p.479).

Houghton Hall

Five miles due east of Sandringham is the early Palladian masterpiece of **Houghton Hall** (Easter–Sept Thurs & Sun 2–5.30pm; £6), rejected by the future Edward VII in favour of Sandringham. It was built in the 1720s for Sir Robert Walpole, a leading Whig politician whose roller-coaster career included a couple of terms as prime minister and a period of imprisonment for corruption. As at Holkham, the exterior, with its classical portico, is formal and severe, though the four corner domes do add a touch of frivolity. Inside, the lavishness of the state rooms is at its most overpowering in the stone hall and saloon, the ceilings dripping with fancy plasterwork. Look out also for the overmantels in the parlour, the work of Grinling Gibbons. The original Walpole art collection was flogged to Catherine the Great of Russia in 1779 to pay off family debts, but there are still plenty of *objets d'art* on display, notably Sèvres porcelain and Mortlake tapestries.

There's no bus service to the hall – the nearest you'll get is the village of **Harpley**, a mile or so to the south.

Castle Acre

The remote hamlet of **CASTLE ACRE** stands in the shadow of one of the few hilltops in Norfolk, nineteen miles east of King's Lynn. Taking advantage of the terrain, one of William I's most trusted lieutenants, William Warenne, built a fortified manor house here shortly after the Conquest. The site was refortified as a stone **castle** (free access; EH) in the 1140s, but little remains from either period – except, that is, for the Norman earthworks. These are some of the most complete in the whole of England, with the mound of the keep and the circular bailey easy to discern. To the west, on the banks of the River Nar, there are more medieval ruins, those of the Cluniac **priory** (April–Oct daily 10am–6pm; Nov–March Wed–Sun 10am–4pm; £2.95; EH) founded by Warenne's son in 1090. The most significant remains are at the west front of the priory church, an excellent illustration of the way different medieval styles were blended together, with the Norman doorway and delicate blind arcading set beneath an arching Early English window.

The *Ostrich* **pub** on the village green makes a great target for lunch, not so much for the food as for its ancient atmosphere and good location. There is a bus service linking Castle Acre with King's Lynn, but it runs infrequently and can't be relied upon.

Breckland

Until the late eighteenth century **Breckland** was a sparsely populated district characterized by open heaths and pastureland grazed by thousands of sheep. The animals had to contend with frequent sandstorms as the wind whipped the dry, sandy soils and travellers had the added problem of the highwaymen who plagued the area. The next century saw some hard-won agricultural gains, but it was the work of the Forestry Commission that changed the character of the area in the 1920s when they launched a vast tree-planting programme, covering the heathland with the assorted conifers of **Thetford Forest**. Further dramatic change came during World War II when the establishment of a mock "battle area" destroyed five villages and thousands of acres of farmland. The end result was the largest concentration of military bases in the country. All of this hardly makes the area seem alluring, but in **Thetford** the district has a pleasant market town with one or two historical curiosities and there are lots of woodland walks to be enjoyed. The district also holds one first-rate medieval manor house, **Oxburgh Hall**, one notable country house, **Euston Hall**, and the tomb of the last Sikh Maharajah in **Elveden**.

Thetford

Breckland's chief town is **THETFORD**, birthplace of the radical eighteenth-century ideologue **Thomas Paine**, and, way back in the eleventh century, seat of the kings and bishops of East Anglia. It's a pleasant place, with riverside walks and gardens, though the remains of the Cluniac priory and the giant earthworks of Castle Hill – at opposite ends of the pedestrianized town centre – are the only reminders of the town's former importance. On King Street, there's also a striking gilt statue of Paine, paid for by the Thomas Paine Foundation of America. For years disowned by his native town, Paine was the chief British apologist for the French Revolution, and a prominent theorist for the American one, publishing his most famous tract, *The Rights of Man*, in 1791. In this, he advocated, among other things, the abolition of the monarchy and the establishment of a social welfare system to succour the poor. His books were subsequently banned and his effigy burned in many towns, and then, accused of sedition, he was forced to flee the country, going first to France and then to America. Paine's birthplace, on White Hart Street, was pulled down long ago – the Thomas Paine Hotel now stands on the site – but the timber-framed **Ancient House Museum**, close by at 21 White Hart St (June–Aug Mon–Sat 10am–12.30pm & 1–5pm, Sun 2–5pm; Sept–May Mon–Sat 10am–12.30pm & 1–5pm; July & Aug 80p; rest of year free), has an interesting display on Paine. It also possesses replicas of the Thetford treasure of Roman gold and silverwork (the originals are in the British Museum) and a herb garden.

    Trains arrive at the station off the Norwich road, at the top of White Hart Street. The **bus station** is south of the river, from where it's a short walk over the bridge and up Bridge Street to King Street. The Ancient House Museum doubles as the **tourist office** (same hours as museum; ☎01842/752599). For **accommodation** there's *The Bell*, a fifteenth-century inn on King St (☎01842/754455; ⑤), which is also a good place to eat; the *Thomas Paine Hotel*, White Hart St (☎01842/755631; ④); and the *Wereham House Hotel*, opposite at no.24 (☎01842/761956; ④).

Elveden

The tiny village of **ELVEDEN**, strung out along the A11 three miles southwest of Thetford, is – strange though it may seem – a place of pilgrimage for Britain's 250,000-strong Sikh community. The pilgrims come to pay homage to the last Sikh Maharajah, **Prince Duleep Singh**, who is buried, beside his wife and son in the local churchyard. Having been forced to sign away his Punjab kingdom and the famous Koh-i-Noor diamond to the British, he was sent to England and handed the seventeen-thousand-acre estate at Elveden in 1863. He became a favourite of Queen Victoria, who thought him "extremely handsome", and with his state pension he transformed Elveden Hall (no public access) into an oriental extravaganza.

Euston Hall

About three miles southeast of Thetford on the A1088, **Euston Hall** (June–Sept Thurs 2.30–5.00pm; £3) is the ancestral pile of the Dukes of Grafton, the first of whom was the illegitimate son of Charles II. Built in the seventeenth century, the hall has a long, somewhat sombre facade, whose straight lines are broken up by towers and a protruding pediment. The interior holds a large collection of family portraits by the likes of Van Dyck, Lely and Stubbs, but many visitors make straight for the **grounds**, laid out by John Evelyn and Capability Brown.

Thetford Forest and Oxburgh Hall

The biggest change affecting the Breckland has been the creation of **Thetford Forest**, eighty thousand acres planted with unerring regularity in the 1920s immediately to the west of Thetford town. Realizing the error of their ways, the Forestry Commission (FC) is currently engaged in more imaginative replanting, and has laid out several **forest walks**, wildlife hides and other recreational facilities to try and entice people to come here. Call in at **High Lodge Forest Centre**, five miles west of Thetford (Easter–Oct daily 10am–5pm; Nov–Easter Sat & Sun 11am–4pm; ☎01842/810271), for trail maps or to rent a bike to get you around the forest.

A mile or so to the west of High Lodge, the main road leaves the forest as it approaches the outskirts of Brandon. From here, it's about eleven miles northwest to **Oxburgh Hall** (April–Oct Mon–Wed, Sat & Sun 1–5pm; gardens open 11am; £5; gardens only £2.50; NT), a medieval manor house of postcard prettiness, whose dappled brickwork overlooks a reed-choked moat. The hall was built in 1482 for the Bedingfeld family, staunch Catholics whose religious sympathies gave them all sorts of trouble from the Reformation onwards. The approach to the hall is via an 80-foot-high ceremonial gateway, matched by the main gate tower of the house itself, but the interior is something of a disappointment. Aside from the tapestries executed by the imprisoned Mary Queen of Scots, the rooms are routinely Victorian, the product of extensive renovations in the middle of the nineteenth century. The most exquisite Bedingfeld legacy – a set of terracotta tombs – is just outside the grounds of the hall in the partly ruined parish church.

Ely and around

ELY began its life as a seventh-century Benedictine abbey built on the Isle of Ely, a rare patch of upland in the soggy fens. Until the draining of the fens in the seventeenth century, this was to all intents and purposes a true island – the name Ely means "eel island" – surrounded by treacherous marshland, accessible only with the aid of "fen-slodgers" who knew the terrain. Under Hereward the Wake, the island became a centre of Anglo-Saxon rebellion, holding out against the Norman invaders until 1071. To mark their victory, the Normans constructed a new "cathedral of the fens", a towering structure visible for miles across the flat landscape. With a population of less than ten thousand, Ely has changed very little since medieval times, and the cathedral remains its main attraction. You could easily see the town on a day-trip from Cambridge, but it makes a pleasant night's stop in its own right, and is close to a couple of Cambridgeshire's other historic sights – namely the cathedral at **Peterborough** and the small town of **Wisbech**.

The Town

Ely **Cathedral** (June–Sept daily 7am–7pm; Oct–May Mon–Sat 7.30am–6pm, Sun 7.30am–5pm; £3.50) is seen to best advantage from the south, the crenellated towers of the west side perfectly balanced by the prickly finials to the east with the distinctive timber lantern rising above them both. To approach from this direction, follow the footpath leading up the hill into the cathedral precincts from **Broad Street**, the second turning on the right as you walk up Station Road from the train station. At the top of the footpath, pass through the medieval **Porta**, once the principal entrance to the monastery

THE FENS

One of the strangest of all English landscapes, the **Fens** cover a vast area from just north of Cambridge right up to Boston in Lincolnshire. For centuries, they were an inhospitable wilderness of quaking bogs and marshland, punctuated by clay islands on which small communities eked out a livelihood cutting peat for fuel, using reeds for thatching and living on a diet of fish and wildfowl. Piecemeal land reclamation took place throughout the Middle Ages, but it wasn't until the seventeenth century that the systematic draining of the fens was undertaken – amid fierce local opposition – by the Dutch engineer **Cornelius Vermuyden**. The transformation of the fens had unforeseen consequences: as it dried out, the peaty soil shrank to below the level of the rivers, causing further flooding, a situation only exacerbated by the numerous windmills, erected to help drain the fens, but which actually resulted in further shrinkage. The problem of shrinkage was only resolved in the 1820s with the introduction of steam-driven pumps, as these leviathans could control water levels with much greater precision, enabling the fens to be turned into the valuable agricultural land that you see today.

At **Wicken Fen** (visitor centre daily 9am–5pm; ☎01353/720274; £3.50; NT), nine miles south of Ely, you can visit one of the few remaining areas of undrained fenland. Its survival is thanks to a group of Victorian entomologists who donated the land to the National Trust in 1899, making it the oldest nature reserve in the UK. The seven hundred acres are undrained but not uncultivated – sedge and reed cutting are still carried out to preserve the landscape as it is – and the reserve also features one of the last surviving fenland wind pumps. Traditional "droves" (wide footpaths) enable visitors to explore the fen and a boardwalk nature trail gives access to several hides. The NT also organizes a variety of events and guided walks – call ahead for details.

complex, and turn right to reach the main entrance on the lopsided **west front** – one of the transepts collapsed in a storm in 1701.

The first things to strike you as you enter the **nave** are the sheer length of the building and the lively nineteenth-century painted ceiling, largely the work of amateurs. The procession of plain late-Norman arches, built around the same time as Peterborough, leads to the architectural feature that makes Ely so special, the **octagon** – the only one of its kind in England – built in 1322 to replace the collapsed central tower. Its construction, employing the largest oaks available in England to support some four hundred tons, is one of the wonders of the medieval world, and the effect, as you look up into this Gothic dome, is simply breathtaking. **Octagon tours** (£2.50) depart several times a day from the desk at the entrance up into the octagon itself.

When the central tower collapsed, it fell eastwards, and the choir was rebuilt in a fussier decorative style. The thirteenth-century presbytery, beyond, houses the relics of **St Ethelreda**, founder of the abbey in 673, who, despite being twice married, is honoured liturgically as a virgin. At the east end are three chantry chapels, the most charming of which (on the left) is an elaborate Renaissance affair dated to 1533. The other marvel at Ely is the **Lady Chapel**, in actual fact a separate building accessible via the north transept. It lost its wealth of sculpture and all its stained glass during the Reformation, but its fan vaulting remains an exquisite example of the English Gothic style. Retracing your steps, the south triforium near the main entrance holds the **Stained Glass Museum** (April–Sept Mon–Sat 10.30am–5pm, Sun noon–6pm; Oct–March Mon–Sat 10.30am–4.30pm, Sun noon–4.15pm; £2.50), another Anglican money-spinner exhibiting examples of this applied art from 1240 to the present day.

The **precincts** of the cathedral boast a fine ensemble of medieval domestic architecture, a higgledy-piggledy assortment of old stone, brick and half-timbered buildings that runs south from the Infirmary complex, abutting the presbytery, to the Prior's buildings near the Porta gate. Many of the buildings are used by the King's boarding school – where the cathedral's choristers are trained – others by the clergy, but although you can't go in any of them, it's still a pleasant area to stroll; a free map and brochure is available from the cathedral.

The rest of Ely is pretty enough, but hardly compelling after the wonders of the cathedral. To the north, the **High Street**, with its Georgian buildings and old-fashioned shops, makes for an enjoyable browse and, if you push on past the Market Place down Forehill, you'll soon reach the riverside **Maltings arts centre**, where you can grab a bite to eat. Alternatively, head west from the cathedral entrance across the triangular Palace Green, to **Oliver Cromwell's House** at 29 St Mary's St (April–Sept daily 10am–5.30pm, Oct–March Mon–Sat 10am–5pm; £2.70), a timber-framed former vicarage, which holds a small exhibition on the Protector's ten-year sojourn in Ely, when he was employed as a tithe collector.

Practicalities

Ely lies on a major rail intersection, with direct **trains** from as far afield as Liverpool, Norwich and London, as well as from Cambridge, just twenty minutes to the south. The **train station** is a ten-minute walk from the cathedral straight up Station Road and its continuation Back Hill. **Buses** (from King's Lynn and Cambridge) stop on Market Street immediately to the north of the cathedral. The **tourist office** is in Oliver Cromwell's House (April–Sept daily 10am–5.30pm, Oct–March Mon–Sat 10am–5pm; ☎01353/662062).

Ely has several appealing **B&Bs**, the best being the handy *Cathedral House*, 17 St Mary's St (☎01353/662124; ②), an attractive Georgian town house with three comfortable, en-suite bedrooms. Other good options are concentrated along Egremont Street, about five minutes' walk north from the cathedral via the Lynn Road. Possibilities here include the spacious *Old Egremont House*, at no. 31 (☎01353/663118; ②), with cathedral views and a walled garden, and the more modern *Post House*, at no. 12a (☎01353/667184; ①).

Of the numerous **tearooms** in town, the *Almonry*, in the grounds to the north of the cathedral, is by far the best sited, with garden seats granting great views of the cathedral. Another good choice is the *Steeplegate Tea Rooms* on Steeple Row (closed Sun), backing onto the cathedral grounds from the High Street. For **restaurants**, there's a choice of *Dominique's*, 8 St Mary's St (☎01353/665011; closed Sun eve, Mon & Tues), a café by day and a reasonably priced bistro by night; and the *Old Fire Engine House*, 25 St Mary's St (☎01353/662582; closed Sun eve), a long-standing and more expensive gourmet English restaurant. Ely's friendliest **pub** is the Prince Albert, on Silver Street. For **entertainment**, the Maltings arts centre has a cinema (☎01353/666388), as well as a waterfront brasserie and bar.

Wisbech

The small town of **WISBECH** sits in the middle of an agricultural area some twenty miles north of Ely. The town first developed as Peterborough's seaport, but the silting up of the Wash has slowly pushed it back from the coast, which is now twelve miles away along the navigable River Nene. The Nene slices through the heart of old Wisbech with the town's most interesting buildings to either side or "brink". The North Brink has the edge architecturally, thanks partly to **Peckover House** (April–Oct Wed, Sat & Sun 12–5.30pm; £3.50; gardens only £2; NT), a substantial early Georgian property which was bought by a wealthy local banker named Jonathan Peckover towards the end of the eighteenth century. The exterior of the house is typically plain, and the interior is only sparsely furnished – it's the Rococo woodwork and plaster decorations that make the trip worthwhile, as well as the Victorian garden with its orangery, summer-houses, reed barn and herbaceous borders. It's an easy drive to Wisbech from Ely, though rather more complicated by **public transport**: take the train to March (20min) and catch a local bus on to Wisbech, but note that services are infrequent so check out times before you depart. Wisbech is only twelve miles west of King's Lynn (see p.485) and daily buses make the onward journey from there.

Peterborough

There are direct train services from Ely to **PETERBOROUGH**, thirteen miles from Wisbech in the far northwestern corner of Cambridgeshire, whose distinct and unmissable attraction is its superb Norman **Cathedral** (daily 8.30am–5.15pm; £3 suggested donation). A site of Christian worship since the seventh century, the first two churches were destroyed – the original Saxon monastery by the Danes in 870, its replacement by fire in 1116. Work on the present structure began a year after the fire and was pretty much completed within the century. The one significant later addition is the thirteenth-century **west facade**, one of the most magnificent in England, made up of three grandiloquent, deeply recessed arches, though the purity of the design is marred slightly by an incongruous central porch added in 1370.

The **interior** is a wonderful example of Norman architecture – round-arched rib vaults and shallow blind arcades line the nave, while up above the painted wooden ceiling, dating from 1220, is an exquisite example of medieval art, one of the most important in Europe. There are several notable tombs here too, beginning with that of **Catharine of Aragon**, who is buried in the north aisle of the presbytery under a slab of black Irish marble. Catharine was Henry VIII's first wife and the king's determination to divorce her in favour of Anne Boleyn precipitated the English Reformation. The marriage was finally declared void in 1533, but much to the king's chagrin, Catharine insisted till her death (in 1536) that she remained Henry's lawful wife. Mary Queen of Scots was also interred here, in the south aisle, after her execution in 1587, but twenty-five years later she was transferred to Westminster Abbey.

The cathedral lies immediately to the east of Peterborough's pedestrianized town centre. To reach it from the **train station**, follow the signs, which bring you to the top of Cowgate in a couple of minutes from where the cathedral is visible straight ahead. The **tourist office** is at 45 Bridge St, to the left as you emerge from the cathedral gate (Mon–Fri 9am–5pm, Sat 10am–4pm; ☎01733/452336).

Cambridge

An agricultural market town at heart, **CAMBRIDGE** is, on the whole, a much quieter and more secluded place than Oxford, though for the visitor, what really sets it apart from its scholarly rival "the Backs" – the green swathe of land straddling the languid River Cam – which overlook the backs of the old colleges, and provide the town's most enduring image. Cambridge is an extremely compact place, and you can walk round the historic centre in an afternoon – though once you begin to explore the individual colleges, pay a visit to the Fitzwilliam Museum and spend a leisurely afternoon on a punt, you could easily find yourself staying here for several days.

If possible you should avoid coming in high summer when the students are replaced by hordes of sightseers and posses of foreign language students. Faced with such crowds the more popular colleges have had to restrict their opening times, and are now introducing summer admission charges. Bear in mind, too, that during the exam period (May to early June), most colleges close their doors to the public.

Tradition has it that Cambridge was founded in the late 1220s by scholastic refugees from Oxford who fled the town after one of their number was lynched by hostile townsfolk – the first proper college wasn't founded until 1271, however. Rivalry has existed

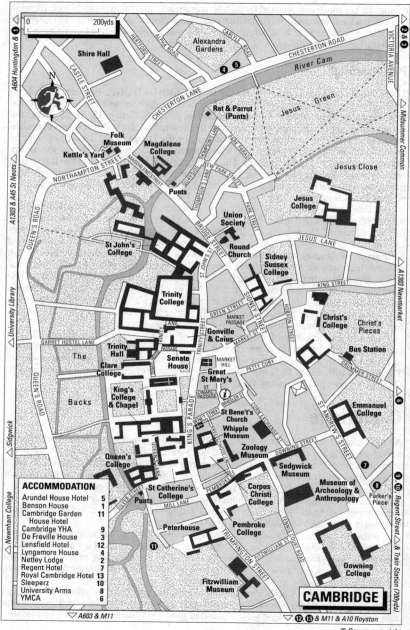

ACCOMMODATION

Arundel House Hotel	5
Benson House	1
Cambridge Garden House Hotel	11
Cambridge YHA	9
De Freville House	3
Lensfield Hotel	12
Lyngamore House	4
Netley Lodge	2
Regent Hotel	7
Royal Cambridge Hotel	13
Sleeperz	10
University Arms	8
YMCA	6

CAMBRIDGE

© Crown copyright

between the two institutions ever since – epitomized by the annual Boat Race on the River Thames – while internal tensions between "town and gown" have inevitably plagued a place where, from the late fourteenth century onwards, the university has tended to dominate local life. The first (but by no means the last) rebellion against the scholars occurred during the Peasants' Revolt of 1381, and had to be put down with armed troops by the Bishop of Norwich; five townsfolk were hanged as a result.

In the sixteenth century, Cambridge became a centre of church reformism, educating some of the most famous Protestant preachers in the country, including Cranmer, Latimer and Ridley, all of whom were martyred in Oxford by Mary Tudor. Later, during the Civil War, Cambridge once again found itself at the centre of events: Cromwell himself was both a graduate of Sidney Sussex and the local MP, while the university was largely Royalist. After the Restoration, the university regained most of its privileges, though by the eighteenth century it was in the doldrums, better known, as Byron put it, for its "din and drunkenness" than for its academic record.

The nineteenth century witnessed the biggest changes in the balance between town and gown, as the number of students increased dramatically with the broadening of the curriculum to include new subjects such as natural science and history. The university finally lost its ancient privileges over the town, which was expanding rapidly thanks to the arrival of the railway; the population quadrupled in the years between 1800 and 1900. This century, change has been much slower in coming to Cambridge, particularly when it comes to equality of the sexes. The first two women's colleges were founded in the 1870s, yet it was only after 1947 that women were actually awarded degrees. Another women's college, New Hall, was established in 1954, but these three remained the only colleges to accept women until the mid-1970s, with some colleges holding out until the late 1980s. In the meantime, the city and university have been rapidly acquiring a reputation as a **high-tech centre** of excellence, what locals refer to half-seriously as "Silicon Fen". Cambridge has always been in the vanguard of scientific research – its alumni have garnered no fewer than 90 Nobel prizes over the years – and it's currently poised to corner the lucrative electronic communications industry, with the recent announcement that Bill Gates is to establish a Microsoft development centre in the city.

Arrival and transport

The **train station** is a mile or so southeast of the city centre, off Hills Road. It's an easy but tedious twenty-minute walk into the centre, or take shuttle bus #1, which runs into town every eight minutes or so (not Sun). The **bus station** is centrally located on Drummer Street, right by Christ's Pieces. **Stansted**, London's third airport, with its striking terminal building designed by Norman Foster, is just thirty miles south of Cambridge on the M11; there are hourly trains from here to the city, and regular bus services too. Arriving by **car**, you'll find much of the city centre closed to traffic and on-street parking well-nigh impossible – for a day trip, at least, the best option is a **Park-and-Ride** car park; they are signposted on all major approaches.

The city centre is small enough to walk round comfortably, so apart from getting to and from the train station, you shouldn't have to use the city buses. Instead, you'll immediately be confronted by the fact that Cambridge is a cycling city, with almost every student and local owning one. **Bike rental** outlets are dotted all over town (see p.506), including a handy summer desk right outside the train station. Whenever you leave your bike, padlock it to something immovable – bike theft is rampant.

Information and tours

Cambridge **tourist office** is conveniently situated in the ornate, domed former public library on Wheeler Street, off King's Parade (April–Oct Mon–Fri 10am–6pm,

Sat 10am–5pm, Sun 11am–4pm; Nov–March Mon–Fri 10am–5.30pm, Sat 10am–5pm; ☎01223/322640). They issue city maps, have lots of leaflets on local attractions and sell an in-depth guide to the city (£4). They can also help with accommodation (see below), which is a useful service especially in the summer when vacant rooms can be hard to find. The best source of information on eating out and entertainment is Adhoc's pocket *What's On?*, a free, monthly brochure available at the tourist office and larger bookshops.

The tourist office runs very popular **walking tours** of the centre (2hr; April–Sept daily; Oct Mon–Sat; Nov–March Sat; £6.25), which are expensive but include entrance to at least one college that normally charges for the privilege. Book well in advance in summer. The other high-profile tour is Guide Friday's open-top **bus tour** (daily; £8; ☎01223/362444), which runs in a continuous loop around the city centre – tickets allow you to get on and off at will and are on sale from the driver, at the tourist office and from the Guide Friday Tourism Centre in the train station.

Accommodation

Cambridge is short of central accommodation and those few **hotels** that do occupy prime locations are expensive. That said, Chesterton Road, the busy street running east from the top of Magdalene Street, has several reasonably priced hotels and guest houses. There are lots of **B&Bs** on the outskirts of town, especially along Huntingdon Road, a ten-minute walk north of the centre, and near the train station on Tenison Road, a right turn a couple of hundred yards down Station Road, where you'll also find the **youth hostel**. In high season, when rooms are often difficult to find, the tourist office's **accommodation booking service** can be very useful (Mon–Fri 9.30am–4pm; ☎01223/457581).

Hotels, guest houses and B&Bs

Arundel House Hotel, 53 Chesterton Rd (☎01223/367701). A converted row of late-Victorian houses overlooking Jesus Green makes for one of the better mid-range B&B choices. Neat and tidy rooms with mundanely modern furnishings. Breakfasts are good. ④.

Benson House, 24 Huntingdon Rd (☎01223/311594). The best of the B&Bs in the neighbourhood, opposite New Hall and just five minutes from Magdalene Bridge. Some rooms are en suite. ②.

Cambridge Garden House Hotel, Granta Place, Mill Lane (☎01223/259988). Cambridge's best central hotel, set in its own gardens with a fine riverside location, rooms with balconies, indoor pool and health club. ⑧.

De Freville House, 166 Chesterton Rd (☎01223/354993). Six large and tastefully furnished en-suite rooms in an attractive, high-gabled Victorian house. A little bit too far out from the centre for comfort, but otherwise a very good choice. No credit cards. ③.

Lensfield Hotel, 53 Lensfield Rd (☎01223/355017). Small, family-owned hotel on the ring road just round the corner from the Fitzwilliam Museum. ⑤.

Lyngamore House, 35–37 Chesterton Rd (☎01223/312369, *karen.dowling@lineone.net*). Inexpensive, comfortable B&B whose front rooms overlook Jesus Green. No credit cards. ①.

Netley Lodge, 112 Chesterton Rd (☎01223/363845). Cosy B&B, in an Edwardian town house not far from the river and Midsummer Common. Three attractively furnished bedrooms, one en suite. No credit cards. ②.

Regent Hotel, 41 Regent St (☎01223/351470, *reservations@regenthotel.co.uk*). Small-scale, family-owned hotel in a historic town house and with a nice café-bar on the south side of the centre over-looking Parker's Piece. ⑤.

Royal Cambridge Hotel, Trumpington St (☎01223/351631, *royalcambridge@msihotels.co.uk*). One of the city's more gracious old hotels, with a slightly heavy hand in the traditionally decorated rooms, but no quibbles about the location, just down from the Fitzwilliam. ⑦.

Sleeperz Hotel, Station Rd (☎01223/304050, *info@sleeperz.com*). A popular hotel occupying an imaginatively converted granary warehouse, right outside the train station. Most of the rooms are bunk-style affairs done out in the manner of a ship's cabin, though there are a few doubles too. All are en suite, with shower and TV. ③, doubles ②.

University Arms Hotel, Regent St (☎01223/351241, *devere.uniarms@airtime.co.uk*). The traditionalist's choice, this comfortable Victorian pile lords it over Parker's Piece, on the south side of the city centre. Most rooms enjoy the view, as does the *Parker's Bar*. ⑤.

Hostels and campsites

Cambridge YHA, 97 Tenison Rd (☎01223/354601). Close to the train station, with a small courtyard garden and games room.

Cherry Hinton Caravan Club Site, Lime Kiln Road, Cherry Hinton (☎01223/244088). Three miles east of the city centre in the village of Cherry Hinton, this pleasantly landscaped camping and caravan site spreads over five acres. Closed Nov–March.

YMCA, Gonville Place, at Parker's Piece (☎01223/356998). Central singles and doubles, with breakfast included in the price, but very busy during summer – book well in advance.

The City

Cambridge's main shopping street is Bridge Street, which becomes Sidney Street, St Andrew's Street and finally Regent Street; the other main thoroughfare is the procession of St John's Street, Trinity Street, King's Parade and Trumpington Street. The university developed on the land west of this latter route along the banks of the Cam, and now forms a continuous half-mile parade of **colleges** from Magdalene to Peterhouse, with sundry others scattered about the periphery. The **Fitzwilliam Museum**, easily the city's best, is just along Trumpington Street south of Peterhouse. The account below starts with **King's College**, whose chapel is the university's most celebrated attraction, and covers the rest of the town in a clockwise direction.

King's College

The first buildings of **King's College** (☎01223/331212), founded in 1441 by Henry VI, are no longer part of the college, but lie tucked away behind the glum-looking facade of the Old Schools building, now administrative offices immediately to the north on Trinity Lane. Not content with his initial effort, Henry cleared away half of medieval Cambridge to make room for a much grander foundation, one of the few successes of a spectacularly unsuccessful reign. Henry spared no expense, but although the overall layout of his Great Court survives, the existing college – facing King's Parade – is largely neo-Gothic, built in the 1820s to a design by William Wilkins. The main exception is the much celebrated **King's College Chapel** (term time Mon–Fri 9.30am–3.30pm, Sat 9.30am–3.15pm, Sun 1.15–2.15pm; rest of year Mon–Sat 9.30am–4.30pm, Sun 10am–5pm; £3), on the north side of Great Court, though visitors usually enter via Trinity Lane. Committed to canvas by Turner and Canaletto, and eulogized in three

COLLEGE ADMISSION CHARGES AND OPENING TIMES

All of the more visited colleges now impose an **admission charge**, partly to control the number of tourists and partly to raise cash. It is, however, a creeping trend, so don't be surprised if other, lesser-known colleges follow suit. **Opening times** are fairly consistent throughout the year, though term-time hours tend to be a little more restrictive than out of term especially at the weekend. It's also worth noting that during the exam season, which stretches from late April to early June, all the colleges have periods when they are closed to the public. Where no opening hours are given, you're usually free to tour the grounds at any time during the day. For more specific information, call the relevant college; **phone numbers** are given in the text.

sonnets by Wordsworth, it's now best known for its **boys' choir**, whose members process across the college grounds during term time in their antiquated garb to sing evensong (Tues–Sat 5.30pm) and carols on every Christmas Eve. Begun in 1446 and over sixty years in the making, the chapel is an extraordinary building. From the outside, it seems impossibly slender, its streamlined buttresses channelling up to a dainty balustrade and four spiky turrets, but the exterior was, in a sense at least, a happy accident – its design predicated by the carefully composed interior. Here, in the final flowering of the Gothic style, the mystery of the Christian faith was expressed by a long, uninterrupted **nave** flooded with kaleidoscopic patterns of light filtering in through copious stained-glass windows. Paid for by Henry VIII, the **stained glass** was largely the work of Flemish glaziers, with the lower windows portraying scenes from the New Testament and the Apocrypha, and the upper windows displaying the Old Testament. Henry VIII also paid for the intricately carved wooden choir screen, one of the earliest examples of Italian Renaissance woodcarving in England, but the choir stalls beyond date from the 1670s. Above the altar hangs Rubens' *Adoration of the Magi*. Finally, an exhibition in the chantries puts more historical flesh on Henry's grand plans.

Like Oxford's New College, King's enjoyed an exclusive supply of students from one of the country's public schools – in this case, Eton – and until 1851 claimed the right to award its students degrees without taking any examinations. The first non-Etonians were only accepted in 1873. Times have changed since those days, and if anything, King's is now one of the more progressive colleges, having been one of the first to admit women in 1972. Among its most famous alumni are E.M. Forster, who described his experiences in *Maurice*; film director Derek Jarman; poet Rupert Brooke; and John Maynard Keynes, whose economic theories did much to improve the college's finances when he became the college bursar.

From King's Parade to Clare College

King's Parade, originally the medieval High Street, is inevitably dominated by King's College and Chapel, but the higgledy-piggledy shops opposite are an attractive foil to William Wilkins's architectural screen. At the northern end of King's Parade is **Great St Mary's**, the university's pet church, a sturdy Gothic structure dating from the fifteenth century. Its tower (Easter–Sept Mon–Sat 9am–6pm, Sun 10am–4pm; Oct–Easter Mon–Sat 9am–4.15pm, Sun 10am–2pm; £1.50) offers a good overall view of the colleges and a bird's-eye view of **Market Hill**, east of the church, where food and bric-a-brac stalls are set out from Monday to Saturday. Opposite the church stands **Senate House**, an exercise in Palladian classicism by James Gibbs, and the scene of graduation ceremonies on the last Saturday in June, when champagne corks fly around the rabbit-fur collars and black gowns. It's not usually open to the public, though you can wander around the quad if the gate's open.

The northern continuation of King's Parade is Trinity Street, a short way along which is the main entrance to **Gonville and Caius College** (☎01223/332400), known simply as Caius (pronounced "keys"), after the co-founder John Keys, who latinized his name, as was the custom with men of learning. The design of the college owes much to Keys, who placed a gate on three sides of two adjoining courts, each representing a different stage on the path to academic enlightenment: the Gate of Humility, through which the student entered the college, now stands in the Fellows' Garden; the Gate of Virtue, sporting the female figures of Fame and Wealth, marks the entrance to Caius Court; while the Gate of Honour, capped with sundials and decorated with classical motifs, leads to Senate House Passage and on to Senate House.

Senate House Passage continues west beyond the Gate of Honour to Trinity Lane, which gives access to the North Gate of King's (for the chapel) and to two other well-concealed colleges. The first, **Trinity Hall** (☎01223/332500) – not to be confused with Trinity College – offers little to detain you, though its Elizabethan library

Tintagel, Cornwall

Appledore, Devon

Polperro, Cornwall

Ironbridge, Shropshire

Lanyon Quoit, Cornwall

Centenary Square, Birmingham

Lincoln Cathedral

Swan Theatre, Stratford-upon-Avon

Derwent Water

Football badges

Tarn Hows, Lake District

BOWNESS PIER
(FOR WINDERMERE)

Bowness Pier, Windermere

retains several of its original chains designed to prevent students from purloining the texts. **Clare College** (daily 10am–5pm; £1.75; ☎01223/333200), just to the south, is much more interesting. One of seven colleges founded, rather surprisingly, by women, its plain period-piece courtyards, completed in the early eighteenth century, lead to one of the most picturesque of all the bridges over the Cam, **Clare Bridge**. Beyond lies the Fellows' Garden, one of the loveliest college gardens open to the public (times as college).

Trinity and St John's

Trinity College, on Trinity Street (daily 10am–6pm; £1.75; ☎01223/338400), is the largest of the Cambridge colleges and to ram home the point it also has the largest courtyard. It comes as little surprise then that its list of famous alumni is longer than any other college: literary greats, including Dryden, Byron, Tennyson and Vladimir Nabokov; the Cambridge spies Blunt, Burgess and Philby; two prime ministers, Balfour and Baldwin; William Thackeray, Isaac Newton, Lord Rutherford, Vaughan Williams, Pandit Nehru, Bertrand Russell, Ludwig Wittgenstein, Edward VII, George VI and Prince Charles.

A statue of Henry VIII, who founded the college in 1546, sits in majesty over Trinity's Great Gate, his sceptre replaced with a chair leg by a student wit. Beyond lies the vast asymmetrical expanse of **Great Court**, which displays a fine range of Tudor buildings, the oldest of which is the fifteenth-century clock tower – the annual race against its midnight chimes is now common currency thanks to the film *Chariots of Fire*. The centrepiece of the court is the delicate fountain, in which, legend has it, Lord Byron used to bathe naked with his pet bear – the college forbade students from keeping dogs.

To get through to **Nevile's Court** – where Newton first calculated the speed of sound – you must pass through "the screens", a passage separating the hall from the kitchens, a common feature of Oxbridge colleges. The west end of the court is enclosed by the university's most famous building after King's College Chapel, the **Wren Library** (term time Mon–Fri noon–2pm, Sat 10.30am–12.30pm; rest of year Mon–Fri noon–2pm; free). Viewed from the outside, it's impossible to appreciate the scale of the interior thanks to Wren's clever device of concealing the internal floor level. In contrast to many modern libraries, natural light pours into the white stuccoed interior, which contrasts wonderfully with the dark lime-wood bookcases, also Wren-designed and housing numerous valuable manuscripts including Milton's *Lycidas*, Wittgenstein's journals and A.A. Milne's *Winnie the Pooh*.

Next door, **St John's College**, on St John's St (daily 10am–5.30pm; £1.75; ☎01223/338600), sports a grandiloquent Tudor gatehouse, distinguished by the coat of arms of the founder, Lady Margaret Beaufort, the mother of Henry VII, held aloft by two spotted, mythical beasts. Beyond, three successive courts lead to the river, but there's an excess of dull reddish brickwork here – enough for Wordsworth, who lived above the kitchens on F staircase, to describe the place as "gloomy". The arcade on the far side of Third Court leads through to the celebrated **Bridge of Sighs**, a covered bridge built in 1831 but in most other respects very unlike its Venetian namesake. The wooden bridge is closed to the public, and in any case is best viewed either from a punt or from the much older, more stylish Wren-designed bridge a few metres to the south. The Bridge of Sighs links the old college with the fanciful nineteenth-century **New Court**, a crenellated neo-Gothic extravaganza topped by a feast of pinnacles and a central cupola – and known as "the wedding cake".

From the Round Church to Magdalene

Back on St John's Street, it's a few seconds' walk to Bridge Street and the **Round Church** (daily: summer 10am–5pm; winter 1–4pm), built in the twelfth century on the model of the Holy Sepulchre in Jerusalem. It's a curious-looking structure, squat with

---

ON THE RIVER

Punting is the quintessential Cambridge activity, though it's a good deal harder than it looks. First-timers find themselves zigzagging across the water and "punt jams" are very common on the stretch of the Cam beside the Backs in summer. Punt rental is available at several points, including the boatyard at Mill Lane (beside the Silver Street bridge), at Magdalene Bridge, and at the *Rat & Parrot* pub on Jesus Green. It costs around £8 an hour (and most places charge a deposit of £40), with up to six people in each punt. If you find it all too daunting you can always hire a **chauffeur punt** from most of the rental places, which usually works out at around a fiver a head.

Cambridge is also famous for its **rowing clubs**, which are clustered along the north bank of the river on Midsummer Common, the only stretch of water that is punt-free. The most important inter-college races are the **May Bumps**, which, confusingly, take place in June; fight your way to the bar of the *Fort St George* on Midsummer Common and watch the spectacle.

---

an ill-considered nineteenth-century spire, but the Norman pillars remain inside. The church now accommodates the town's brass-rubbing centre, whose staff will instruct you in the art, and it's also the starting point for Christian heritage walks around the city (Feb–Nov Wed 11am, Sun 2.30pm; free).

Set back from the road, down a footpath beside the church, is the **Union Society**, a bastion of male-dominated debating culture, founded in 1815, which only admitted women in the 1960s. The society likes to think of itself as a miniature House of Commons – its debating chamber is designed as such – and its debates continue to attract many of the leading politicians and speakers of the day. These are presided over by the Union's officers, who tend to be made up of the university's more ambitious, conservative elements. In the normal scheme of things, election to the Union presidency leads about twenty years later to a place in Cabinet – the last Tory administration barely contained a Minister who hadn't been Union president.

Saving nearby Jesus College till later (see below), it only takes a minute or two to stroll up from the Round Church to Magdalene Bridge, site of the old Roman ford, and then **Magdalene College** (☎01223/332100) – pronounced "maudlin" – founded as a hostel by the Benedictines and a university college since 1542. Magdalene was the last of the colleges to admit women, finally succumbing in 1988. Here, the main focus of attention is the **Pepys Building** (Oct to early-Dec & mid-Jan to mid-March Mon–Sat 2.30–3.30pm; late April to Aug Mon–Sat 11.30am–12.30pm & 2.30–3.30pm; free), in the second of the college's ancient courtyards. Samuel Pepys, a Magdalene student, bequeathed his entire library to the college, where it has been displayed ever since in its original red-oak bookshelves – though his famous diary, which also now resides here, was only discovered in the nineteenth century.

A short walk away at the top of Magdalene Street are two less-touristed sites: the **Folk Museum**, 2–3 Castle St (April–Sept Mon–Sat 10.30am–5pm, Sun 2–5pm; Oct–March closed Mon; £1) and, further up Castle Street, the grassy mound which is all that remains of **Cambridge Castle**. Between the two, adjacent to the Folk Museum is **Kettle's Yard** a deceptively spacious open-plan conversion of some old slum dwellings, originally owned by the art critic and curator Jim Ede. The house is packed full of works of art, including many by the St Ives primitivist Alfred Wallis, but it is much more than a simple gallery – it's the sense of art within a living space, amid house plants, lounge chairs and an extensive library of art books, which make the place so special. In 1970 a formal exhibition gallery (Tues–Sat 12.30–5.30pm, Sun 2–5.30pm; free) was added as a forum for contemporary artists.

Jesus and Sidney Sussex

Back down Magdalene Street then Bridge Street, take the first left after the Round Church to reach **Jesus College** (☎01223/339339), whose wide open spaces and intimate cloisters are reminiscent of a monastic institution. This is not too surprising as the Bishop of Ely founded the college on the grounds of a suppressed Benedictine nunnery in 1496. The main redbrick gateway is approached via a distinctive walled walkway strewn with bicycles and known as "the Chimney". Beyond, much of the ground plan of the nunnery has been preserved, especially around **Cloister Court**, the prettiest of the college's courtyards, dripping with ivy and overflowing hanging baskets. The college chapel, entered from the court, occupies the former priory chancel and looks more like a medieval parish church; it was imaginatively restored in the nineteenth century, using ceiling designs by William Morris and Pre-Raphaelite stained glass. The poet Samuel Taylor Coleridge was the college's most famously bad student, absconding in his first year to join the Light Dragoons, and returning only to be kicked out for a combination of bad debts and unconventional opinions.

From Jesus Lane, Bridge Street becomes Sidney Street and soon after **Sidney Sussex College** (☎01223/338800) appears on the left, its sombre facade engulfed by mock-Gothic cement rendering that was plastered over the college walls in the 1830s. The college's main claim to fame is that Oliver Cromwell studied here, and in 1960 it was the lucky recipient of the Protector's head, now buried in a secret location in the college chapel.

St Andrew's Street

Just beyond Sidney Sussex, on St Andrew's Street, you hit the hustle and bustle of the town's central shopping area, dominated by the **Lion Yard** shopping centre – one of the few town-planning mistakes in the centre of Cambridge. The greatest outrage was foisted upon **Petty Cury**, formerly a cobbled curve of leaning half-timbered houses and now a dreary string of modern shops. To escape from all this, head through the turreted gateway of **Christ's College** (☎01223/334900), which features the coat of arms of the founder, Lady Margaret Beaufort, who also founded St John's. Passing through First Court you come to the Fellows' Building, attributed to Inigo Jones, whose central arch gives access to the **Fellows' Garden** (Mon–Fri 10.30am–12.30pm & 2–4pm; free). The poet John Milton is said either to have painted or composed beneath the garden's elderly mulberry tree, though there's no definite proof that he he did either; Christ's other famous undergraduate was Charles Darwin, who showed little academic promise and spent most of his time hunting and shooting. If you continue walking through the college, you come to its modern adjunct, Denys Lasdun's concrete pyramidal accommodation block, dubbed "the typewriter". A little further along St Andrew's Street is **Emmanuel College** (☎01223/334200), whose stolid Neoclassical facade hides a pair of Wren buildings – the cloister gallery and chapel on the Front Court. The college was founded in 1584 to train a new generation of Protestant clergy following the Reformation. Emmanuel men were numbered among the Pilgrims who settled New England, which not only explains the derivation of the place name Cambridge in Massachusetts but also accounts for Harvard University – John Harvard, another alumnus, is remembered by a memorial window in Wren's chapel.

Still further along the street, but on the opposite side, is the uncompromisingly Neoclassical ensemble of **Downing College** (☎01223/334800), established in 1800 after more than eighty years of costly litigation between the university and the heirs of the original benefactor, Sir George Downing. It is unique among Cambridge colleges in being laid out like a campus around a central lawn, rather than enclosed in separate courtyards.

Downing Street and the museums

A group of scientific and specialist museums occupy the land either side of **Downing Street** and its continuation Pembroke Street, which run between St Andrew's and Trumpington. Each is connected to one of the university faculties and forms an important resource for students, but is also open to the public. There's the **Sedgwick Geology Museum** (Mon–Fri 9am–1pm & 2–5pm, Sat 10am–1pm; free), which displays fossils and skeletons of dinosaurs, reptiles and mammals, plus the oldest geological collection in the world; the **Museum of Zoology** (Mon–Fri 2.15–4.45pm; free); the **Whipple Museum of Science** (Mon–Fri 1.30–4.30pm; free), crammed with hundreds of scientific instruments; and the **Museum of Archeology and Anthropology** (Mon–Fri 2–4pm, Sat 10am–12.30pm; free). The last is probably the pick of the bunch for the non-specialist, covering the development of the city from prehistoric times to the nineteenth century and, better still, holding a superb ethnographical gallery. This is centred on a soaring 50-foot native totem pole and many of the exhibits derive from the "cabinets of curiosities" collected by eighteenth-century explorers. Several pieces on show were gathered on Captain Cook's first voyage to the South Pacific between 1768 and 1771.

From St Catherine's to Peterhouse

There are four more town-centre colleges clustered around the foot of King's Parade and the top of Trumpington Street. One of them is **St Catherine's College** (☎01223/338300) – popularly known as "Catz" – founded in 1473 by the provost of King's on land just to the south of that college. In contrast to its glamorous neighbour, the Principal Court here is a cheerless affair, whose dour, heavy-duty buildings mirror the college's relative impecuniousness – in 1880 St Catherine's was so broke that it was nearly forced to merge with King's. Much more enticing is **Corpus Christi College** (☎01223/338000), just across King's Parade, founded by two of the town's guilds in 1352. Ignore the first court and head north into Old Court, which dates from the foundation of the college and is where Christopher Marlowe wrote *Tamburlane* before graduating in 1587. The college library, on the south side, contains a priceless collection of Anglo-Saxon manuscripts, while the north side is linked by a gallery to **St Bene't's Church**, which served as the college chapel, but is of much earlier Saxon origin. Inside, Thomas Hobson's Bible is exhibited in the case in the right-hand corner; Hobson was the owner of a Cambridge livery stable, where he would only allow customers to take the horse nearest the door – thus giving rise to the phrase "Hobson's choice".

Queens' College (daily 10am–4.30pm; £1; ☎01223/335511), accessed through the gate on Queen's Lane, just off Silver Street, is the most popular college with university applicants, and it's not difficult to see why. In the Old Court and the Cloister Court, Queens possesses two fairy-tale Tudor courtyards, with the first of the two the perfect illustration of the original collegiate ideal with kitchens, library, chapel, hall and rooms all set around a tiny green. Cloister Court is flanked by the Long Gallery of the President's Lodge, the last remaining half-timbered building in the university, and, in its southeast corner, by the tower where Erasmus is thought to have beavered away during his four years here, probably from 1510 to 1514. Be sure to pay a visit to the college hall, off the screens passage, which holds mantel tiles by William Morris, and portraits of Erasmus and one of the co-founders, Elizabeth Woodville, wife of Edward IV. Equally eye-catching is the wooden **Mathematical Bridge** over the Cam (visible for free from the Silver Street Bridge), a copy of the mid-eighteenth-century original which, it was claimed, would stay in place even if the nuts and bolts were removed.

Back on Trumpington Street, **Pembroke College** (☎01223/338100) contains Wren's first ever commission, the college **chapel**, paid for by his Royalist uncle, erstwhile Bishop of Ely and a college fellow, in thanks for his deliverance from the Tower of London after seventeen years' imprisonment. It boasts a particularly fine, though modern, stained-glass East Window and a delicate fifteenth-century marble relief of St Michael and the Virgin, the product of an unusually skilled early English workshop. Outside the library there's a statue of William Pitt the Younger, clad here in a toga, who entered the college at fifteen and was prime minister at twenty-five, and is just one of a long list of college alumni, which includes poets Edmund Spenser, Thomas Gray and Ted Hughes.

Across the road from Pembroke is the oldest and smallest of the colleges, **Peterhouse** (✿01223/338200), founded in 1284. Few of the original buildings have survived, the principal exception being the thirteenth-century hall, entered from the main court, whose interior was remodelled by William Morris. As at Corpus Christi, Peterhouse used the church next door – in this case Little St Mary's – as the college chapel, until the present one, with its light-hearted Baroque gables, was erected in the main court in 1632.

The Fitzwilliam Museum

Of all the museums in Cambridge, the **Fitzwilliam Museum**, on Trumpington Street (Tues–Sat 10am–5pm, Sun 2.15–5pm; £3 donation suggested), stands head and shoulders above the rest. The building itself is a splendidly grandiloquent interpretation of Neoclassicism, built in the mid-nineteenth century to house the vast collection bequeathed by Viscount Fitzwilliam in 1816. Since then, the museum has been gifted a string of private collections, most of which are focused on a particular specialism. Consequently, the Fitzwilliam says much about the changing tastes of the British upper class. The **Lower Galleries** contain a wealth of antiquities including Egyptian sarcophagi and mummies, fifth-century BC black- and red-figure Greek vases, plus a bewildering display of European porcelain. Further on, there are rooms dedicated to armour, glass and pewterware, fans, portrait miniatures and illuminated manuscripts, and – right at the far end – galleries devoted to Far Eastern applied arts and Korean ceramics.

The **Upper Galleries** concentrate on painting and sculpture with three of the first five rooms holding an eclectic assortment of mostly nineteenth- and early twentieth-century European paintings. Among many, there are works by Picasso, Matisse, Monet, Renoir, Delacroix, Cézanne and Degas. The other two rooms concentrate on British painting, with works by William Blake, Constable and Turner, Hogarth, Reynolds, Gainsborough and Stubbs. Moving on, the Italian section boasts works by Fra Filippo Lippi and Simone Martini, Titian and Veronese, while Frans Hals and Ruisdael feature in the Flemish section. The twentieth-century gallery is packed with a fascinating selection including pieces by the likes of Lucian Freud, David Hockney, Henry Moore, Ivon Hitchens, Ben Nicholson and Barbara Hepworth.

To the Botanic Garden

Past the Fitzwilliam Museum, turn left along busy Lensfield Road for the **Scott Polar Research Institute** (Mon–Sat 2.30–4pm; free), founded in 1920 in memory of the explorer, Captain Scott, with displays from the expeditions of various polar adventurers, plus exhibitions on native cultures of the Arctic. There's more general interest near at hand in the shape of the **University Botanic Garden** on Bateman Street, to the south (daily 10am–4pm; £1.50), founded as early as 1846 and providing a quiet end to a day's sightseeing.

Newnham and the Sidgwick Site

Over the last hundred years, the university has spread its tentacles across the west bank of the Cam, beyond the Backs. The first institution established here was

Newnham College on Sidgwick Ave (☎01223/335700), built in redbrick Dutch style in the 1870s for women undergraduates. Opposite Newnham is the **Sidgwick Site**, where the arts faculties have been based since 1954, and where Cambridge's most notorious modern building, James Stirling's glass-skinned **History Faculty**, was erected in 1968. The critics loved it at the time, though the students and university authorities were somewhat less amused with a building which was like a hothouse in summer and leaked throughout the winter. The equally brutal brick tower, visible to the north, belongs to the **University Library**. Built in the 1930s and looking like something out of *1984*, it's one of the country's five copyright libraries, which receives a free copy of every book published; it now holds over five million books.

Eating and drinking

Students are not the world's greatest customers for restaurateurs, so although the **takeaway** and **café** scene is good in the centre, decent **restaurants** are a little thin on the ground. On any kind of budget, the myriad Italian places – courtesy of Cambridge's large Italian population – will stand you in good stead; otherwise, choose carefully, particularly in the more touristy areas, where quality isn't always all it should be. Happily, Cambridge abounds in excellent **pubs**, and our list rounds up the best of the traditional student and local drinking haunts.

Cafés

Café 31, 2 Quay Side. Bustling, modern coffee house beside the punt rental point at Magdalene Bridge.

Caffé Uno, 32 Bridge St. Popular, gleamingly new café-bar beside the punt rental point at Magdalene Bridge. Outside seating available.

Clowns, 54 King St. Italian-style cappuccino and cakes, sandwiches and snacks, and plenty of newspapers are available in this popular student café.

Copper Kettle, 4 King's Parade. Generations of students have whiled away time in this resolutely old-fashioned café opposite King's College, sipping coffee, eating pastries and putting the world to rights.

Roof Garden, Cambridge Arts Theatre, 6 St Edward's Passage. Conservatory-style rooftop café serving home-made snacks and sandwiches, as well as main meals and pre-theatre dinners. Closed Sun.

Nadia's, 11 St John's St. Good sandwich and cake takeaway in the centre, opposite St John's. One of several outlets.

Prêt-à-Manger, 19 Petty Cury. Designer coffee and sandwiches from the trendy London chain.

Restaurants

Brown's, 23 Trumpington St. Breezy brasserie with a wide-ranging menu housed in a former hospital outpatients department. The grand setting – all plants and fans – sets the meal off a treat. Inordinately popular, but no reservations – wait in line or at the bar. Moderate.

Caffé Piazza, 83 Regent St. Brick-and-tile pizza joint where you can also share dips, meatballs, salads and other snacky food, or just call in for a drink. Inexpensive.

Clowns Two, 8 Market Passage (☎01223/322312). The coffee bar's sister outlet, next to the Arts Cinema, makes its mark with pizza and pasta as well as the coffee and cakes it's best known for. Moderate.

Don Pasquale, 12 Market Hill (☎01223/367063). Great location, with seats on the square for lunchtime diners. Tasty food and an especially good place for a quick pick-me-up espresso and slice of pizza. Moderate.

Efes, 80 King St (☎01223/500005). Intimate Turkish restaurant, with chargrilled meats prepared under your nose and a decent *meze* selection. Moderate.

Eraina Taverna, 2 Free School Lane (☎01223/368786). Packed Greek taverna which satisfies the hungry hordes with huge platefuls of stews and grills, as well as pizzas, curries and a whole host of other menu madness. Try to avoid getting stuck in the basement, though at weekends (when you'll probably have to queue) you'll be lucky to get a seat anywhere. Inexpensive.

La Margherita, 15 Magdalene St (☎01223/315232). Cheapish and cheerful Italian outfit offering pizzas and pastas as well as standard meat and fish dishes. Inexpensive to Moderate.

Midsummer House, Midsummer Common (☎01223/369299). Lovely riverside restaurant with conservatory, specializing in top-notch French-Mediterranean cuisine. Reservations essential. Expensive.

Panos, 154 Hills Rd (☎01223/212958). Best Greek restaurant in town – try the scotch steak or any of the other charcoal grills. Closed Sun. Moderate.

Pizza Express, 28 St Andrew's St and 7a Jesus Lane. Superior pizza chain with an intimate branch at the first address and a grander, marbled hall at the second (in the former Pitt Club). Inexpensive.

Rainbow Vegetarian Bistro, 9a King's Parade (☎01223/321551). The only vegetarian restaurant in Cambridge, with main courses – ranging from couscous to lasagne and Indonesian *gado-gado* – all under £6. Good-value breakfasts, and organic wines served with meals. Inexpensive.

Twenty-Two, 22 Chesterton Rd (☎01223/351880). Consistently the best restaurant in Cambridge, a candlelit townhouse in which the good-value fixed-price menu touches all the modern bases. Closed Sun & Mon. Expensive.

Pubs and bars

Anchor, Silver St. Very popular riverside tourist haunt with views of the Backs, adjacent punt rental and an outdoor deck.

Champion of the Thames, 68 King St. Gratifyingly old-fashioned central pub with decent beer and a student/academic clientele.

Dadie's, Cambridge Arts Theatre, 6 St Edward's Passage. The ground-floor wine bar at the theatre makes a civilized meeting spot, though it's only open until 9pm – and closed Mon eve.

Eagle, Bene't St. An ancient inn with a cobbled courtyard where Crick and Watson sought inspiration in the 1950s, at the time of their discovery of DNA. It's been tarted up since and gets horribly crowded, but is still worth a pint of anyone's time.

Elm Tree, 42 Orchard St. Cosy local with frequent live music, mainly jazz. Just to the north of Parker's Piece and full of furiously smoking refugees from the nearby *Free Press*.

Free Press, 7 Prospect Row. Classic backstreet local with an admirable no-smoking policy, good beer, fine food and a clientele often made up of the university's rowing fraternity.

Fort St George, Midsummer Common. Pleasant riverside location, overlooking the boathouses, and with a series of cosy rooms – shame about the beer, though.

Maypole, 20a Park St. Small pub near the ADC serving world-class cocktails to student thespians.

Portland Arms, 129 Chesterton Rd. A real locals' pub near river and green, with Greene King beer, jazz every other Sunday night and few pretensions.

Rat & Parrot, Thompson's Lane, Jesus Green. The latest incarnation of this riverside pub sees it reinvented as a themed café-bar, with courtyard seating and heavy-duty bouncers.

Arts, entertainment and festivals

The arts scene is at its best during term time, with numerous student **drama** productions, **classical concerts** and **gigs** culminating in the traditional orgy of excess following the exam season, though the more firmly town-based venues, like the Corn Exchange, put on events throughout the year. Apart from the places highlighted below, each college and several churches contribute too – the **King's College choir** is of course the main attraction (see p.496), but the choral scholars who perform at the chapels of St John's and Trinity are also exceptionally good. For all the week's events, check the listings section of the student weekly, *Varsity*, or Adhoc's pocket *What's On?*, both of which are widely available from bookshops and newsagents. For advance information, call into the Corn Exchange (see below), which sells tickets for various venues, or at the tourist office.

June and July are the busiest times in Cambridge's calendar of **events**. The fortnight of post-exam celebrations, which take place in the first two weeks of June and are confusingly known as **May Week**, herald the ball and garden-party season, and include boat races, known as the "May Bumps", on the Cam by Midsummer Common. The vaguely hippified **Midsummer Fair**, descendant of the town's famous medieval Stourbridge Fair, discontinued in 1934, takes place in mid-June on Midsummer Common, with bands, theatre and much more besides – all for free. By contrast, you'll have to pay out around £50 for a tent pitch and entry into the three-day **Cambridge Folk Festival**, held annually at the end of July at Cherry Hinton, and attracting a wide variety of loosely folk-based acts.

Boat Race, 170 East Rd (☎01223/508533). Lively pub venue for all kinds of music, with gigs every night.

Cambridge Arts Cinema, 8 Market Passage, off Market St (☎01223/504444), has an excellent, wide-ranging programme.

Cambridge Arts Theatre, 6 St Edward's Passage, off King's Parade (☎01223/503333). The city's main repertory theatre, founded by John Maynard Keynes, and launching pad of a thousand-and-one famous careers, from Derek Jacobi to Stephen Fry, offers a top-notch range of cutting-edge and classic productions.

Corn Exchange, Wheeler St (☎01223/357851). Revamped nineteenth-century trading hall, now the main city-centre venue for opera, ballet, musicals and comedy as well as regular rock and folk gigs.

Junction, Clifton Rd (☎01223/511511). Rock, Indie, jazz, reggae or soul gigs, plus occasional comedy acts and dance groups at this popular arts and entertainments venue.

Listings

Airport Stansted Airport flight enquiries (☎01279/680500); late availability (☎0345/118118).

Banks and exchanges There are banks all over the city centre, and you can exchange traveller's cheques at the main post office (see below); at American Express, 25 Sidney St (☎01223/461410); and Thomas Cook, in the Grafton Centre (☎01223/322611) and at 18 Market Hill (☎01223/366141).

Bike rental Cambridge Recycles, 61 Newnham Rd at Fen Causeway (☎01223/506035) plus a summer stall at the train station; Geoffs Bike Hire, 65 Devonshire Rd (☎01223/365629); Mikes Bikes, 28 Mill Rd (☎01223/312591). Rates start at around £7 a day.

Bookshops Heffers is the biggest outfit in town with the main branch at 20 Trinity St. Cambridge University Press has a shop at 1 Trinity St. For secondhand books try the shops down St Edward's Passage off King's Parade: G. David, at no.3, is an antiquarian's and hard-back hunter's paradise; the Haunted Bookshop, at no. 9, is better for first editions, travel and illustrated books.

Buses Most departures are from Drummer Street bus station. Stagecoach Cambus (☎01223/423554) is the main city and regional operator and has a call-in information office at the Premier Travel Agency, Drummer Street. Cambridge Coach Services (☎01223/423900) operates direct services to Oxford, Norwich, Great Yarmouth and the London airports; National Express (☎0990/808080) runs services to London and other major cities.

Car rental Avis, 245 Mill Rd (☎01223/212551); Budget, 303–305 Newmarket Rd (☎01223/323838); Thrifty, 2a Elizabeth Way (☎01223/321321); Wilhire, Barnwell Rd (☎01223/414600).

Dentist ☎01223/415126

Hospitals Addenbrooke's Hospital, Hills Road (☎01223/217118).

Left luggage 24-hour lockers at the train station only.

Pharmacies Boots, 28 Petty Cury and 65 Sidney St (☎01223/350213); Lloyds, 54 Burleigh St (☎01223/352917) and 30 Trumpington St (☎01223/359449).

Police The main station is on Parkside (☎01223/358966).

Post office The main office is at 9–11 St Andrew's St (Mon–Fri 9am–5.30pm, Sat 9am–7pm).

Taxis There are ranks at the train station, Drummer Street bus station, King's Parade/Market Hill, and St Andrew's St near the post office. To book, call Intercity (☎01223/312233) or Panther (☎01223/715715).

Trains ☎0345/484950

Travel agent STA, 38 Sidney St (☎01223/366966).

Around Cambridge

Within easy reach of Cambridge, across the flat fen landscapes, are several absorbing, day-trip destinations. South of the city is **Grantchester**, a smart little place that's
typical of the villages hereabouts – though the real draw is that you can cycle or punt
there through open countryside. To the southwest is **Wimpole Hall**, a rambling
eighteenth-century country house, and to the northeast is **Anglesey Abbey**, a handsome old mansion that holds an outstanding collection of fine and applied art. A little
further afield, south along the M11, comes **Duxford Imperial War Museum** and
then, among the rolling hills of northwest Essex, the straggling market town of
Saffron Walden. Horse-racing aficionados will, however, have little truck with all of
this, heading straight for **Newmarket**.

All the places discussed below are accessible by bus or train from Cambridge.

Grantchester

The pretty little village of **GRANTCHESTER**, replete with thatched cottages and chestnut trees, is just a couple of miles up the Cam from Cambridge, and a popular destination on sunny days since it's an easy bike or punt ride away through **Grantchester
Meadows** – the signposted route starts at the southern end of Newnham Road. The
poet Rupert Brooke, who died in the First World War, lodged in the old vicarage here
as an undergraduate, penning the much-quoted lines "Stands the Church clock at ten
to three? And is there honey still for tea?" The clock in the pub named after Brooke
stands permanently at ten to three, though of the three village **pubs**, you're better off
heading for the *Red Lion* or the *Green Man*, both sited where the path from Cambridge
emerges on the village's main street.

Wimpole Hall

Wimpole Hall (mid-March to July, Sept & Oct Tues–Thurs, Sat & Sun 1–5pm; Aug
Tues–Sun 1–5pm; £5.70; garden only £2.50; NT), once the home of Rudyard Kipling's
daughter, is a huge eighteenth-century pile ten miles southwest of Cambridge. The
interior contains a library by James Gibbs, stunning trompe l'oeil decor by James
Thornhill in the chapel and several rooms by the celebrated Neoclassical architect, Sir
John Soane. The vast 360-acre grounds were landscaped by the likes of Capability
Brown and Humphrey Repton, and contain several follies including a Chinese bridge.
Soane also designed **Wimpole Home Farm** (mid-March to June, Sept & Oct
Tues–Thurs, Sat & Sun 10.30am–5pm; July & Aug Tues–Sun 10.30am–5pm; Nov to
mid-March Sat & Sun 11am–4pm; £2.30; NT), now a rare breeds farm with Suffolk
Punch horses in the stables and an exhibition of agricultural tools in the great barn.
Bus #175 (not Sun) from Cambridge comes out this way.

Anglesey Abbey

Anglesey Abbey (April to mid-Oct Wed–Sun 1–5pm; house & garden £6, £7 on Sun
when entry is by timed ticket; garden only £3.50; NT), six miles northeast of
Cambridge near the village of Lode, was actually never an abbey at all, but a priory (of
which only the chapter house and monks' parlour now survive). For once, the house,
dating from 1600, is of less interest than its contents, which feature the Fairhaven collection of paintings and furniture. There's everything here from an Egyptian bronze cat
to Ming vases, works by Lorrain, Constable, Cuyp and Gainsborough, all gathered
together this century by the house's last, very wealthy owner, Lord Fairhaven, who also
transformed the surrounding fenland into a glorious hundred-acre **garden** (April to

early July & mid-Sept to mid-Oct Wed–Sun 11am–5pm; early July to mid-Sept daily 11am–5.30pm), dotted with sculptures and urns from his collection. At the far end of the gardens, an old watermill has been restored and now grinds flour on the first Saturday of each month. To get to the abbey from Cambridge, take either **bus** #111 (Newmarket), #122 (Ely).

Duxford: Imperial War Museum

Eight miles south of Cambridge, and visible from the M11 (it's next to junction 10), are the giant hangars of the **Imperial War Museum** (daily mid-March to mid-Oct 10am–6pm; mid-Oct to mid-March 10am–4pm; £7.20), based at Duxford airfield. Throughout World War II, East Anglia was the centre of operations for the RAF and this flat, unobstructed landscape was dotted with dozens of airfields. Duxford itself was a Battle of Britain station, equipped with Spitfires, and there's a reconstructed Operations Room in one of the control towers. In total, Duxford holds over 150 historic aircraft, a wide-ranging collection of civil and military planes from the Sunderland flying boat to Concorde and the Vulcan B2 bombers, which were used for the first and last time in the Falklands; the Spitfires remain the most enduringly popular. Most of the planes are kept in full working order and are taken out for a spin several times a year at **Duxford Air Shows**, which attract thousands of visitors. There are usually four Air Shows a year and tickets cost around £12–15. For further details on these and on the free courtesy bus service linking Duxford with Cambridge, call ☎01223/835000.

Saffron Walden and Audley End

Some ten miles south of Cambridge, the fenlands are left behind for the hillier landscapes of Uttlesford, the district council's euphemism for the northwest corner of Essex. The main event here is **SAFFRON WALDEN**, a good-looking town that possesses dozens of antique timber-framed houses. There are several particularly fine examples on the main road, but the nicest areas of town to explore are away from the thundering traffic in the network of alleyways around the Market Place and the book and antique shops of Church Street. Many of these old houses sport fancy decorative plasterwork, known as pargeting – the last word on which is provided by the stepped gables of the **Old Sun Inn**, on Church Street, which Cromwell once used as his headquarters. The town's prefix was coined in medieval times when saffron crocuses were cultivated here for their dye and medicinal qualities. You can learn more about this and other aspects of the town's history at the **museum** on Museum Street, off Church Street (March–Oct Mon–Sat 10am–5pm, Sun 2.30–5pm; Nov–Feb Mon–Sat 10am–4pm, Sun 2.30–4.30pm; £1). Behind the museum are the scant ruins of the twelfth-century **castle**.

A mile or so to the west of town – beyond the village that bears its name – the palatial Jacobean mansion of **Audley End** (April–Sept Wed–Sun 11am–6pm, Oct Wed–Sun 10am–3pm; house & grounds £5.75; grounds only £3.50; EH) was built for the Earl of Suffolk at the start of the seventeenth century. A spectacularly lavish building, it was soon the talk of the aristocracy, so much so that Charles II purchased it in 1668, staying here whenever he went to the races at Newmarket. Returned to the Suffolks after the king's death, Audley End was modified on several later occasions, most notably when one of the Suffolks demolished the east wing in 1735 to reduce his overheads. Highlights of the guided tours include the striking wood panelling and plasterwork of the Great Hall and, less ostentatiously, the subtle elegance of Robert Adam's two Drawing Rooms. English Heritage has worked hard on renovating the **grounds**, which were first laid out by Capability Brown and contain a river, a lake and a splendid flower garden.

Buses to Saffron Walden stop near the Market Place, where the **tourist office** (April–Oct Mon–Sat 9.30am–5.30pm; Nov–March Mon–Sat 10am–5pm; ☎01799/510 444) has plenty of leaflets on local attractions. The nearest **train station**, is in Audley End village, a mile to the west of town off the B1383 and a long walk from Audley End house. In Saffron Walden, Castle and Church streets are just to the north of the Market Place, to the west is the High Street and its continuation Bridge Street. The only access to Audley End is off the B1383 – take Audley End Road out of Saffron Walden and follow the signs.

Saffron Walden is probably best enjoyed on a day-trip, but there are several **B&Bs** – try the *Archway Guest House*, Church St (☎01799/501500; ②), which – oddly enough – has a working 1960s' Juke Box in the breakfast room. The best **hotel** in town is the sixteenth-century *Saffron Hotel*, 10 High St (☎01799/522676; ⑤), which has seventeen comfortable bedrooms. The **youth hostel**, 1 Myddylton Place (☎01799/523117; closed Nov–Feb), occupies a converted, half-timbered medieval maltings, footsteps from the junction of Bridge and Castle streets. The best **pub** in town is the ancient *Eight Bells*, on Bridge Street.

Thaxted

THAXTED, nine miles southeast of Saffron Walden, enjoyed its heyday in the fourteenth and fifteenth centuries, when it prospered on the profits of the local cutlery industry. It was during this period that the town's splendid three-tiered, half-timbered **Guildhall** (April–Sept Sun 2–6pm; free) was erected – it now leans drunkenly on its ground-floor open arcading at the head of the marketplace. Another collection of half-timbered buildings can be seen up nearby Stony Lane, which leads to the town's gargantuan **parish church**, completed in 1500, its landmark spire reaching 181ft into the sky. Gustav Holst was organist here during his twelve-year sojourn in Thaxted, during which time he wrote much of *The Planets*, and initiated the annual music festival, held here in June (call ☎01371/831421 for details). Head down Mill Lane from the church's west door, past a neat little row of almshouses, to Thaxted's other principal sight, its **windmill** (May–Sept Sat & Sun 2–6pm; £1), which has been restored to full working order, though it hasn't ground flour since 1907.

Newmarket

NEWMARKET, twelve miles east of Cambridge, on springy heathland just over the county border in Suffolk, is famous for just one thing – **horse-racing**. According to legend, Boudicca's tribe were keen on Ben-Hur style chariot-racing, but history gives James I the honour of founding modern horse-racing here. James may have started it off, but Charles II brought the sport to prominence, visiting twice a year and bringing the entire royal court – and Nell Gwyn – with him. Two of the country's five flat-racing classics are held at Newmarket, the One Thousand Guineas and the Two Thousand Guineas, both held early in the season, which runs from the middle of April to October.

Coming from Cambridge, you'll pass the Rowley Mile Racecourse – named after one of Charles's own steeds – on your way into town. The approach roads are flanked by bridleways, and in the morning there are hundreds of racehorses being exercised along them. Newmarket itself is a one-horse town, with the Georgian Jockey Club, founded in 1752, occupying pride of place on the High Street. Next door is the **National Horse Racing Museum** (April–June, Sept & Oct Tues–Sun 10am–5pm; July & Aug daily 10am–5pm; £3.50), telling you more than you'll ever want to know about the sport. It also offers a variety of guided tours, including trips to the equine pool, the National Stud and the adjacent Jockey Club (for further details, call ☎01638/560622). Several **buses** make the half-hour journey to town from Cambridge and there's also a regular **train** service.

travel details

Trains

Cambridge to: Audley End (2 hourly; 15min); Birmingham (hourly; 2hr 50min); Bury St Edmunds (8 daily; 40min); Ely (hourly; 15min); Ipswich (6 daily; 1hr 20min); King's Lynn (hourly; 45min); Leicester (hourly; 1hr 50min); London (2 hourly; 1hr); Newmarket (8 daily; 20min); Norwich (hourly; 1hr); Peterborough (hourly; 50min); Stansted (10 daily; 40min); Thetford (hourly; 20–30min).

Colchester to: Clacton-on-Sea (hourly; 40min); Ipswich (2 hourly; 25min); London (2 hourly; 30min); Norwich (hourly; 1hr).

Ely to: King's Lynn (hourly; 30min); Liverpool (hourly 4hr 30min); Manchester (hourly; 3hr 30min); Nottingham (hourly 1hr 45min); Peterborough (hourly; 30min); Thetford (hourly; 30min).

Ipswich to: Bury St Edmunds (10 daily; 30min); Ely (7 daily; 1hr); Felixstowe (every 1–2hr; 25min); London (2 hourly; 1hr 10min); Lowestoft (every 1–2hr; 1hr 30min); Norwich (hourly; 45min); Peterborough (7 daily; 1hr 50min); Woodbridge (every 1–2hr; 15min).

Norwich to: Ely (hourly; 50min); Cromer (every 1–2hr; 50min); Great Yarmouth (hourly; 30min); Liverpool (hourly; 5hr 30min); London (hourly; 2hr); Lowestoft (hourly; 30–45min); Manchester (hourly 4hr 30min); Nottingham (hourly 2hr 30min); Peterborough (hourly; 1hr 30min); Sheringham (every 1–2hr; 1hr); Thetford (hourly; 30min).

Peterborough to: Bury St Edmunds (6 daily; 1hr); Cambridge (hourly; 50min); Liverpool (hourly; 4hr); London (2 hourly; 1hr); Manchester (hourly; 3hr); Norwich (hourly; 1hr 30min); Nottingham (hourly; 1hr 10min).

Buses

Bury St Edmunds to: Colchester (8 daily; 2hr); Lavenham (10 daily; 30min); Long Melford (10 daily; 45min); Sudbury (10 daily; 1hr); Thetford (7 daily; 40min).

Cambridge to: Bury St Edmunds (5 daily; 50min); Huntingdon (6 daily; 1hr); London (hourly; 2hr); Newmarket (6 daily; 30min); Oxford (9 daily; 3hr); Peterborough (6 daily; 1hr 50min); Stansted Airport (9 daily; 45min); Saffron Walden (5 daily; 1hr).

Colchester to: Coggeshall (hourly; 40min); Dedham (4 daily; 30min); Lavenham (8 daily; 1hr 30min); Long Melford (every 1–2hr; 1hr); St Osyth (hourly; 45min); Sudbury (every 1–2hr; 50min); Walton-on-the-Naze (3 daily; 50min).

Ely to: Cambridge (6 daily; 40min); Newmarket (5 daily; 1hr).

Ipswich to: Aldeburgh (2–6 daily; 1hr 45min); Colchester (6 daily; 30min); Framlingham (Mon–Sat 2–6 daily; 1hr 10min); Leiston (2–6 daily; 1hr 20min); Orford (1–2 daily; 1hr 15min).

King's Lynn to: Castle Rising (hourly; 15min); Hunstanton (every 30min; 50min); Norwich (every 2hr; 1hr 30min); Peterborough (every 2hr; 1hr); Sandringham (8 daily; 30min); Wisbech (every 2hr; 30min).

Norwich: to Bury St Edmunds (3 daily; 1hr 30min); Cromer (hourly; 50min); Great Yarmouth (hourly; 1hr 30min); King's Lynn (every 2hr; 1hr 30min); Little Walsingham (Mon–Sat 4–5 daily; 1hr 20min); Sheringham (hourly; 1hr 20min); Thetford (3 daily; 50min); Wells-Next-The-Sea (Mon–Sat 4–5 daily; 1hr 45min); Wroxham (2–4 hourly; 30min).

Saffron Walden to: Duxford (every 2hr; 20min); Thaxted (Mon–Sat 3–5 daily; 45min).

Sheringham to: Blakeney (Tues–Fri & Sun 3–5 daily; 20min); Wells-next-the-Sea (Tues–Fri & Sun 1–5 daily; 50min); Hunstanton (Tues–Fri & Sun 1–4 daily; 1hr 40min).

Sudbury to: Hadleigh (hourly; 30min–1hr); Long Melford (hourly; 5min); Lavenham (Mon–Sat hourly; 30min); Bury St Edmunds (hourly; 50min).

Wells-next-the-Sea to: Hunstanton (1–5 daily; 1hr); Kings Lynn (Mon–Sat 1–3 daily; 1hr 30min).

CHAPTER SEVEN

CENTRAL ENGLAND

Central England is the most diffuse region of the country, bracketed to the west by the Welsh border and to the east by the North Sea, but otherwise difficult to define geographically. At least there can be no doubt about the location of its economic and demographic focus – **Birmingham**, Britain's second city and once the world's greatest industrial metropolis. Long saddled with a reputation as a culture-hating, car-loving backwater, Birmingham has redefined its image in recent years with some bold artistic and redevelopment projects, most notably the construction of the complex that houses the country's best concert hall. Although it may still be few people's idea of a good-looking town, it's certainly one of the liveliest spots in the region, with nightlife encompassing everything from Royal Ballet productions to all-night raves, and a great spread of restaurants and pubs.

The conurbation clinging to the western side of Birmingham, known as the **Black Country**, more amply fulfils the negative stereotypes, although even here you'll find a few pleasant surprises, in the shape of several excellent museums and galleries. The region to the south of this giant West Midlands conurbation is very different, crossed as it is by the wide and fertile vales of the rivers **Severn** and **Avon** and holding central England's biggest tourist draws – **Stratford-upon-Avon**, a place now overburdened with Shakespeare-related paraphernalia, and the castle of nearby **Warwick**. However, the crowds and commercialism of these two towns fade away in neighbouring **Worcestershire**, a predominantly pastoral county typified by the handsome hills around the spa town of **Great Malvern** and by the low-key old cathedral city of **Worcester** itself.

Further west still is **Herefordshire**, a large and sparsely populated county that's home to several charming market towns, most notably the cathedral city of **Hereford**, pocket-sized **Ross-on-Wye** and **Hay-on-Wye**, where there's the largest concentration of secondhand bookshops in the world. Next door, rural **Shropshire** weighs in with **Ludlow**, one of the region's prettiest towns, awash with antique half-timbered buildings, and the amiable county town of **Shrewsbury**. Shropshire has a fascinating industrial history too, for it was here in the **Ironbridge Gorge** that British industrialists built the first iron bridge and pioneered the use of coal as a smelting fuel – two key events of the Industrial Revolution. To the north lies **Staffordshire**, where the halcyon days when the potteries of **Stoke-on-Trent** dominated the world market are recalled by an outstanding museum or two, and **Derbyshire**, whose northern reaches incorporate the region's finest scenery in the rough landscapes of the **Peak District**.

ACCOMMODATION PRICE CODES

Throughout this guide, hotel and B&B accommodation is priced on a scale of ① to ⑨, the number indicating the **lowest price** you could expect to pay per night in that establishment for a **double room** in high season. The prices indicated by the codes are as follows:

① under £40	④ £60–70	⑦ £110–150
② £40–50	⑤ £70–90	⑧ £150–200
③ £50–60	⑥ £90–110	⑨ over £200

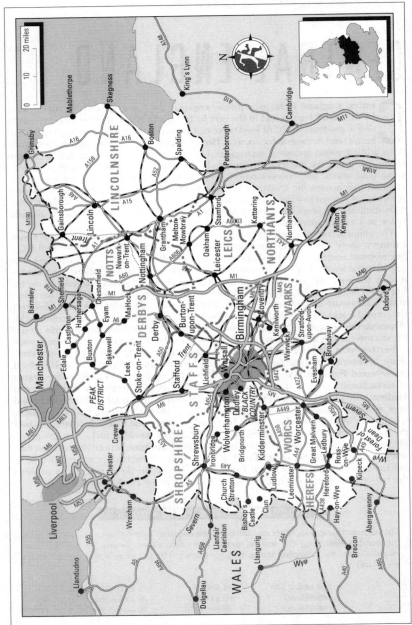

Most tourists bypass the counties of the East Midlands – **Nottinghamshire**, **Leicestershire**, **Northamptonshire** and **Lincolnshire** – on their way to more obvious destinations. It's true they miss little of overriding interest, though **Nottingham** and **Leicester** are boisterous cities and the rural charms of much of **Northamptonshire** hold some appeal. **Lincolnshire** is an agricultural backwater in comparison to its neighbours, but its sights – as distinct from the mostly dreary landscape – are far more diverting, most remarkably the cathedral at **Lincoln**, the alluring stone-built town of **Stamford** and the superb parish **churches** that are spread out across the county.

Travel in this region is simple. Birmingham sits at the heart of central England's rail and coach networks, with most of the region's main towns and cities enjoying easy links from there, as well as from London, Bristol, Manchester and points farther north. It is only really when you get into the outbacks of Shropshire, Herefordshire or Lincolnshire that public transport can be problematic.

THE WEST MIDLANDS AND THE PEAK DISTRICT

The factories of central England were the powerhouses of the Industrial Revolution, and the knot of towns at the very heart of the West Midlands – the **Black Country** – still carries a name redolent of a period that has long gone. Post-recession dereliction is the principal problem now facing an area that has taken the brunt of Britain's decline as a manufacturing power – **Birmingham**, for example, lost over a third of its manufacturing jobs between 1974 and 1983. In recent years many of the area's moribund towns have undergone something of a transformation, as the economy has been realigned with a new emphasis on service industries, a process exemplified by Birmingham itself, a city that's now making money from the business convention and exhibition trades. England's second city has also initiated some ambitious architectural and environmental schemes, jazzed up its museums and industrial heritage sites and given itself a higher profile on the British cultural scene than it's ever had before. Though there are signs that the investment in prestige projects is waning, in favour of schemes aimed at the creation of long-term employment, tourists will continue to benefit from the legacies of Birmingham's high-cost revamp.

The counties to the south and west of Birmingham and the Black Country –**Warwickshire**, **Worcestershire**, **Herefordshire** and **Shropshire** – comprise a rural stronghold that maintains an emotional and political distance from the conurbation: the left-wing politics of the big city seem remote indeed when you're in Shrewsbury, but in fact it's only seventy miles from Birmingham. For the most part, the four counties constitute a quiet, unassuming stretch of pastoral England whose beauty is rarely dramatic, but whose charms become more evident the longer you stay. Of the four counties, **Warwickshire** is the least obviously scenic, but draws by far the biggest number of visitors, for – as the huge road-signs declare at every entry point – this is "Shakespeare's County". Too many visitors spend a couple of hours wedged into the crowded streets of **Stratford**, and then take in **Warwick Castle** before heading on, but there is plenty more to this area than this. In the vicinity of Stratford and Warwick, for instance, are the grand stately homes of **Charlecote** and **Coughton Court** and the great medieval castle at **Kenilworth**, and even the gritty city of **Coventry** is worth a call for its magnificent modern cathedral.

Neighbouring **Worcestershire** and **Herefordshire** cover a vast area stretching from the urban fringes of the West Midlands and the mellow Cotswolds to the stark mountains along the Welsh border. Both contain ancient towns bursting with picture-postcard images, although, as in much of rural England, nightlife and entertainment can be less than thrilling. The main centres are the twin cathedral cities of **Worcester** and its smaller sibling, **Hereford**, both within easy reach of the picturesque villages and lush hills that characterize the two counties. Between the two cities lies **Great Malvern**, a mannered inland resort spread along the rolling contours of the **Malvern Hills**, while the rivers Wye and Severn meander southwards past the **Forest of Dean**, one of England's most extensive ancient woodlands.

Shropshire and **Staffordshire** are also mainly rural, albeit with zones of still-productive industry and several reminders of the manufacturing heyday. At **Ironbridge Gorge** a phalanx of museums commemorates the pioneering work of the Darby dynasty of engineers and of Thomas Telford, while the potteries of **Stoke-on-Trent** and the breweries of **Burton-on-Trent** remain large-scale employers in a part of the country that has been badly dented by the decline in British manufacturing. Both counties boast some appealing historic towns as well: in Shropshire there's a glut of old settlements to enjoy – from the county town of **Shrewsbury**, to the tiny cluster of streets that is **Much Wenlock** and the extraordinarily pretty **Ludlow**, dripping with rickety half-timbered buildings. In Staffordshire, the main attraction is **Lichfield**, which takes its tone from its spectacular cathedral and the legacies of its Regency high times. As for the countryside, little in central England can match the borderlands of Shropshire, where the ancient ridges of the **Long Mynd** and **Wenlock Edge** offer some of the region's wildest walks, but Staffordshire does contribute with windswept moorlands around **Leek**. These moors are the southern peripheries of the **Peak District National Park**, whose soft contours offer great opportunities for moderately strenuous walks, as well as the diversions of the former spa town of **Buxton**, the limestone caverns of **Castleton** and a couple of fine country houses, grandiose **Chatsworth** and fascinating **Haddon Hall**.

Birmingham, the nucleus of the region, is easily accessible by **rail** from London Euston, Liverpool, Manchester, Leeds, York and a score of other towns. It is also well served by the National Express **bus** network, with scores of buses leaving every hour for destinations all over Britain. Local **bus** services are excellent around the West Midlands conurbation – mostly run by West Midlands Travel (WMT) – but tend to dwindle the farther you move from Birmingham.

Stratford-upon-Avon and around

Despite its worldwide fame, **STRATFORD-UPON-AVON** is, at heart, an unassuming market town with an unexceptional pedigree. Its first settlers forded, and later bridged, the River Avon, developing commercial links with the inhabitants of the rich local farmland and the Forest of Arden. A charter for Stratford's weekly market was granted in the twelfth century, a tradition continued to this day, and the town later became an important stopping-off point for stagecoaches between London, Oxford and the north. Like all such places, Stratford had its clearly defined class system and within this typical milieu John and Mary **Shakespeare** occupied the middle rank, and would have been forgotten long ago had their first son, **William**, not turned out to be the greatest writer ever to use the English language. A consequence of their good fortune is that this ordinary little place is nowadays all but smothered by package-tourist hype and its central streets groan under the weight of thousands of tourists. Try not to let that deter you: dodging the multitudes is possible by avoiding the busiest attractions – principally the Birthplace Museum – and the Royal Shakespeare Company offers superb theatre. Moreover, Stratford still has the ability to surprise and delight, whether in the excellence of some of its restaurants or by the river views at the Holy Trinity Church.

Arrival and information

Stratford's **train station** is on the northwestern edge of town, ten minutes' walk from the centre. Now the end of the line, it receives hourly shuttles from Birmingham (Moor

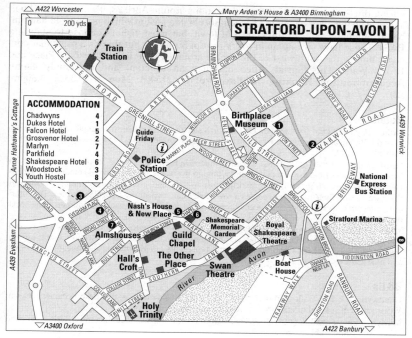

© Crown copyright

Street or Snow Hill stations) and frequent trains from Warwick (for connections to London Paddington or London Marylebone) except on Sundays, when there are only a couple of services all day. Local **bus services**, arrive and depart from the central Bridge Street; National Express services pull into the Riverside station on the east side of the town centre, off Bridgeway.

The **tourist office** (April–Oct Mon–Sat 9am–6pm, Sun 11am–5pm; Nov–March Mon–Sat 9am–5pm; ☎01789/293127) is located a couple of minutes' walk from the bus station by the bridge at the junction of Bridgeway and Bridgefoot. They have oodles of information on local attractions and operate an accommodation booking service (see below), which is very useful during the height of the summer when rooms can be in very short supply. It also issues bus timetables and sells bus tickets. General tourist information is also available from the Guide Friday office in the centre at 14 Rother St (☎01789/294466), but they basically exist to flog tickets for their bus tours of the town and environs (£8 excluding admission to properties). The tourist office will sell you an all-in ticket for all five **Shakespeare Birthplace Trust** properties (£11), or a **Three In-Town Shakespeare Property Ticket** (£7.50) for the three Trust properties in Stratford – both tickets are also available from any of the sites themselves.

Accommodation

As one of the most popular tourist destinations in England, Stratford's **accommodation** is distinctly pricey and gets booked up well in advance. In peak months, and during the Shakespeare birthday celebrations around April 23, it's essential to book ahead. The town has a couple of dozen **hotels**, the pick of which occupy old half-timbered buildings right in the centre of town, but most visitors choose to stay in a **B&B**. These have sprung up in every part of Stratford, but there's a particular concentration to the southwest of the centre around Grove Road, Evesham Place and Broad Walk. The tourist office operates an efficient and extremely useful **Accommodation Booking Hotline** (☎01789/415061; Mon–Fri 9.30am–4.30pm; £3).

Hotels

Dukes, Payton St (☎01789/269300). On the north side of the town centre, a couple of minutes' walk from the Birthplace Museum, this comfortable, privately owned hotel has a pleasant interior dotted with antiques. ⑤.

Falcon, Chapel St (☎01789/279953). Handily situated in the middle of the town centre, the half-timbered facade dates from the sixteenth century, though the rest is an unremarkable modern rebuild. ④.

Grosvenor, Warwick Rd (☎01789/269213). Close to the canal, just a couple of minutes' walk from the town centre, the *Grosvenor* occupies a row of pleasant, two-storey Georgian houses. The interior is done out in a crisp modern style and there's ample parking at the back. Discounted short break deals available. ⑤.

The Shakespeare, Chapel St (☎01789/294771). Right in the centre of town. Now part of a chain, this old hotel, with its mullion windows and half-timbered facade, is one of Stratford's best known. The interior has low beams and open fires and represents a fairly successful amalgamation of old and new features. ⑦.

B&Bs

Chadwyns, 6 Broad Walk (☎01789/269077). Just off Evesham Place, this B&B occupies pleasant Victorian premises and offers three en-suite rooms. ①.

Marlyn, 3 Chestnut Walk (☎01789/293752). More central and secluded than most B&Bs, and good value, with comfortable rooms. ②.

Parkfield, 3 Broad Walk (☎01789/293313). Very pleasant, accommodating B&B in a rambling Victorian house down a residential street off Evesham Place. They have a private car park – a useful facility in crowded Stratford – and most of the rooms are en suite. Less than ten minutes' walk from the centre. ②.

Woodstock, 30 Grove Rd (☎01789/299881). A smart and neatly kept B&B ten minutes' walk from the centre, by the start of the path to Anne Hathaway's Cottage. It has five extremely comfortable bedrooms, most en suite. No credit cards. ②.

Hostels and camping

Stratford Youth Hostel, Hemmingford House, Alveston (☎01789/297093). Two and a half miles east of town on the B4086 and served by Stagecoach Midland Red bus #18 and #X18, which runs every one or two hours from Wood Street. The hostel occupies a rambling Georgian mansion on the edge of the pretty village of Alveston and has dormitories and family rooms with en-suite facilities. Bike rental available too.

Stratford Racecourse Camp Site, Luddington Rd (☎01789/267949). One mile southwest of the town centre; hourly bus #218 (not Sun) passes the site. Closed Nov–Feb.

The Town

Spreading back from the River Avon, Stratford's **town centre** is fairly flat and compact, its mostly modern buildings filling out a simple gridiron just two blocks deep and four blocks long. Running along the northern edge of the centre is **Bridge Street**, the main thoroughfare lined with shops and chock-a-block with local buses. At its west end, Bridge Street divides into Henley Street, home of the **Birthplace Museum**, and Wood Street, which leads up to the market place. It also intersects with High Street. This, and its continuation Chapel and Church streets, cuts south to pass most of the old buildings that the town still possesses, most notably **Nash's House** and, on neighbouring Old Town Street, **Hall's Croft**. From here, it's a short hop to the charming **Holy Trinity Church**, where Shakespeare lies buried, and then only a few minutes back along the river past the **theatres** to the foot of Bridge Street. In itself, this circular walk only takes about fifteen minutes, but it takes all day if you potter around the attractions. In addition, there are two outlying Shakespearean properties, **Anne Hathaway's Cottage** in Shottery and **Mary Arden's House** in Wilmcote – though you have to be a really serious sightseer to want to see them all.

The Birthplace Museum

Top of everyone's Bardic itinerary is the **Birthplace Museum**, an ugly modern visitor centre attached to the heavily restored half-timbered building on Henley Street (late March to mid-Oct Mon–Sat 9am–5pm, Sun 9.30am–5pm; mid-Oct to late March Mon–Sat 9.30am–4pm, Sun 10am–4pm; £4.90). The visitor centre pokes into every corner of Shakespeare's life and times, making the most of what little hard evidence there is. His will is interesting in so far as he passed all sorts of goodies to his daughter, but precious little to his wife – the museum commentary tries to gainsay this apparent meanness, but fails to convince. Next door, the half-timbered dwelling is actually two buildings knocked into one. The west half, now fitted out in the style of a sixteenth-century domestic interior, was the business premises of the poet's father, who is thought to have worked as a glover, though some argue that he was a wool merchant or a butcher. Neither is it certain that Shakespeare was born in this building nor that he was born on April 23, 1564 – it's just known that he was baptized on April 26, and it's an irresistible temptation to place the birth of the national poet three days earlier, on St George's Day. However, both suppositions are now treated as fact at this shrine, where the east half of the building – bought by John Shakespeare in 1556 – displays a modest range of period artefacts designed to illuminate a life which remains distinctly enigmatic.

Nash's House and New Place

Follow the High Street south from the junction of Bridge and Henley streets, and you'll soon come to another Birthplace Trust property, **Nash's House** on Chapel Street (late March to mid-Oct Mon–Sat 9.30am–5pm, Sun 10am–5pm; mid-Oct to late March Mon–Sat 10am–4pm, Sun 10.30am–4pm; £3.30, includes New Place). The house was the property of Thomas Nash, first husband of Shakespeare's granddaughter, Elizabeth Hall, and is mostly taken up by a very dry history of Stratford. The adjacent gardens contain the foundations of **New Place** (same hours), Shakespeare's last residence, which was demolished in 1759 by its owner, the Reverend Francis Gastrell. It was quite deliberate: Gastrell was so plagued by Shakespeare pilgrims that he began by chopping down a mulberry tree that Shakespeare himself was reputed to have planted and, when this didn't work, he knocked down the house as well. An alleged descendant of the notorious mulberry is to be seen in the adjacent **Great Garden of New Place**, a formal affair of topiary and flowerbeds whose entrance is on Chapel Lane (March–Oct Mon–Sat 9am–dusk, Sun 10am–dusk; Nov–Feb Mon–Fri 9am–4pm, Sun noon–4pm; free).

On the other side of Chapel Lane stands the **Guild Chapel**, with its chunky tower and plain interior, containing some rather kitsch stained-glass windows. The adjoining King Edward VI **Grammar School**, where it's assumed Shakespeare was educated, incorporates a creaky line of fifteenth-century almshouses, just round the corner on Church Street.

SHAKESPEARE: WHAT'S IN A NAME?

Over the past hundred years or so, the deification of **William Shakespeare** (1564–1616) has been dogged by a loony backlash among a fringe of revisionist scholars and literary figures known as "**Anti-Stratfordians**". According to these heretics, the famous plays and sonnets were not written by a wool merchant's son from Stratford at all, but by someone else, and William Shakespeare was merely a *nom de plume*. The American novelist Henry James, among the most notorious arch-sceptics, once claimed that he was "haunted by the conviction that the divine William is the biggest and most successful fraud ever practised on a patient world".

A variety of candidates have been proposed for the authorship of Shakespeare's works, and they range from the faintly plausible (Christopher Marlowe, Ben Johnson, and the Earls of Rutland, Southampton and Oxford) to the manifestly whacko (Queen Elizabeth I, King James I and Daniel Defoe, author of *Robinson Crusoe*, who was born six years after publication of the first Folio). The wildest theories, however, have been reserved for Francis Bacon. In his book *The Great Cryptogram*, American congressman Ignatius Donnelly postulates that the word "honorificabilitudinitatibus", which crops up in *Love's Labours Lost*, was actually an anagram for the Latin "Hi ludi F Baconis nati tuiti orbi" ("These plays, F. Bacon's offspring, are preserved for the world"). Others have rallied around the Earl of Oxford's banner; Sigmund Freud maintained that Oxford wrote the plays, and Orson Welles agreed, saying that otherwise there were ". . . some awfully funny coincidences to explain away".

Lying at the root of the authorship debate are several unresolved questions that have puzzled scholars for years. How could a man of modest background from the provinces have such an intimate knowledge of royal protocol? How could he know so much about Italy without ever having travelled there? Why was he allowed to write potentially embarrassing love poems to one of England's most powerful aristocrats? Why did he not leave a library in his will, when the author of the plays clearly possessed an intimate knowledge of classical literature? Why, given that Shakespeare was supposedly a well-known dramatist, did no death notice or obituary appear in publications of the day?

The speculation surrounding Shakespeare's life stems from the fact that far less is known about the man himself than about his work. The few details that have been pre-

Hall's Croft

Chapel Street continues south as Church Street. At the end, turn left along Old Town Street for Stratford's most impressive medieval house, the Birthplace Trust's **Hall's Croft** (late March to mid-Oct Mon–Sat 9.30am–5pm, Sun 10am–5pm; mid-Oct to late March Mon–Sat 10am–4pm, Sun 10.30am–4pm; £3.30). The former home of Shakespeare's elder daughter, Susanna, and her doctor husband, John Hall, the immaculately maintained Croft, with its creaking wooden floors, beamed ceilings and fine kitchen range, holds a scattering of period furniture and a fascinating display on Elizabethan medicine. Hall established something of a reputation for his medical know-how and published some of his case notes in a volume entitled *Select Observations on English Bodies*. You can peruse Hall's casebook – noting that Joan Chidkin of Southam "gave two vomits and two stools" after being "troubled with trembling of the arms and thighs" – and then suffer vicariously at the displays of eye-watering forceps and other implements. The best view of the building itself is at the back, in the neat walled garden.

Holy Trinity Church

Beyond Hall's Croft, Old Town Street veers right to reach the handsome **Holy Trinity Church** (March–Oct Mon–Sat 8.30am–6pm, Sun 2–5pm; Nov–Feb Mon–Sat 9am–4pm, Sun 2–5pm; free), whose mellow, honey-coloured stonework dates from the thirteenth century. Enhanced by its riverside setting and flanked by the yews and weeping willows of its graveyard, the dignified proportions of this quintessentially

·ved come mostly from official archives – birth, marriage and death certificates and court
·ords. From these we know that on April 22 or 23, 1564, a certain John Shakespeare, various-
·described as a glove-maker, butcher, wool merchant and corn trader, and his wife, Mary, had
·ir first son, William; that the boy attended a local grammar school until financial problems
·ced him into his father's business; and that at the age of eighteen he married a local woman,
·ne Hathaway, seven years his senior, who five months later bore a daughter, Susanna, the first
·three children. Several years later, probably around 1587, the young Shakespeare was forced
· flee Stratford after being caught poaching on the estate of Sir Thomas Lucy at nearby
·arlecote (see p.521). Five companies of players passed through the town on tour that year,
·d it is believed he absconded with one of them to London, where a theatre boom was in full
·ing. *Henry VI*, Shakespeare's first play, appeared soon after, followed by the hugely success-
·*Richard III*. Over the next decade, Shakespeare's output was prodigious. Thirty-eight plays
·peared, most of them performed by his own theatre troupes based in the **Globe**, a large tim-
·r-framed theatre overlooking the south bank of the River Thames, in which he had a one-tenth
·are.
·uccess secured Shakespeare the patronage of London's fashionable set, among them the
·shing young courtier, Henry Wriothesley, Earl of Southampton, with whom the playwright is
·lieved to have had a passionate affair (Southampton is thought to have been the "golden
·uth" of the Sonnets). The ageing Queen Elizabeth I, bewigged and decked in opulent jew-
·ery, regularly attended the Globe, as did her successor, James I, whose Scottish ancestry and
·cination with the occult accounts for the subject matter of *Macbeth*. Shakespeare realized the
·mmercial importance of appealing to the rich and powerful. This, as much as his extraordi-
·ry talent, ensured his plays were the most acclaimed of the day, earning him enough money
·retire comfortably to Stratford, where he largely abandoned literature in the last years of his
· to concentrate on business and family affairs.
·Ultimately, the sketchy details of Shakespeare's life are of far less importance than the plays,
·nnets and songs he left behind. Whoever wrote them – and despite all the conjecture, William
·akespeare almost certainly did – the body of work attributed to this shadowy historical figure
·mprises some of the most inspired and exquisite English ever written. The greatest irony is
·t that *King Lear* and *The Tempest* were penned by a provincial middle-class merchant's son,
·t that of all the millions of visitors who pass through Stratford each year, the majority appear
·be more interested in the writer himself than in what he wrote.

English church are the result of several centuries of chopping and changing, culminating in the replacement of the original wooden spire with today's stone version in
1763. At the entrance, the **Sanctuary Knocker** is a reminder of medieval times when
local criminals could seek refuge from the law here, but only for thirty-seven days.
This, so local custom dictated, was long enough for them to negotiate a deal with their
persecutors. Inside, the nave is bathed in light from the **stained glass windows**,
some of which (predominantly along the south aisle) date from the fourteenth century. Quite unusually, you'll see that the nave is built on a slight skew from the line of
the chancel – supposedly to represent Christ's inclined head on the cross. Beside the
north transept is the **Clopton Chapel**, where the tomb of George Carew is a superbly
carved Renaissance extravagance decorated with military insignia appropriate to
George's job as master in ordnance to James I. But poor old George is long forgotten,
unlike William Shakespeare, who lies buried in the **chancel** (60p), his remains overseen by a sedate memorial plaque and effigy added just seven years after his death.

The theatres
Strolling north along the riverbank from the church, you'll soon reach Southern Lane
and its continuation, Waterside, home to the town's three Royal Shakespeare Company
theatres – The Other Place, the Swan Theatre and the Royal Shakespeare Theatre.
There was no theatre in Stratford in Shakespeare's day and indeed the first home-town
festival in his honour was only held in 1769 at the behest of London-based David

---

TICKETS FOR THE RSC

As the Royal Shakespeare Company works on a repertory system, you could stay in Stratford for a few days and see four or five different plays. Tickets for the **Royal Shakespeare Theatre** start at around £5 for standing room and a restricted view, rising to £39 for the best seats in the house. However, very popular shows get booked up months in advance. **Swan** tickets are generally between £5 and £36, with tickets for **The Other Place** hovering between £10 and £20.

The RSC's **box office** (Mon–Sat from 9am; ☎01789/403403) serves as the central booking agent for all three houses, although you collect your tickets from the theatre in question. At the Royal Shakespeare Theatre, one hundred tickets are kept back for that evening's performance and sold at just £10 each; for a real blockbuster, arriving to queue at 5am will not be too early. Stand-by tickets (for unsold seats) are also available on the day of performance, but only concessionary groups (OAPs, students, etc) are eligible. If all else fails, turn up about an hour before the performance and try your luck – though last-minute **returns** are quite rare. The RSC runs a **ticket availability information line** (☎01789/403404) and has a **Web site**, *www.rsc.org.uk*.

Garrick. Thereafter, the idea of building a permanent home in which to perform Shakespeare's works slowly gained momentum, and finally, in 1879, the first Memorial Theatre was opened on land donated by local beer baron Charles Flower. A fire in 1926 necessitated the construction of a new theatre, and the ensuing architectural competition was won by Elisabeth Scott. Her theatre is today's **Royal Shakespeare Theatre**. In the 1980s, the burnt-out original theatre round the back was turned into a replica "in-the-round" Elizabethan stage – the **Swan**; it's used for works by Shakespeare's contemporaries, classics from all eras and one annual piece by the man himself. The third auditorium, **The Other Place**, showcases modern and experimental pieces. The RSC also organizes a number of behind-the-scenes tours – ask at the box office for details.

Anne Hathaway's Cottage and Mary Arden's House

Anne Hathaway's Cottage (late March to mid-Oct Mon–Sat 9am–5pm, Sun 9.30am–5pm; late Oct to mid-March Mon–Sat 9.30am–4pm, Sun 10am–4pm; £3.90), also operated by the Birthplace Trust, is located just over a mile west of the town centre in **Shottery**. The most agreeable way to get there is on the signposted footpath from Evesham Place, at the south end of Rother Street. The cottage, complete with its dinky wooden beams and thatching, was the home of Anne Hathaway before she married Shakespeare in 1582. A few yards away, the **Shakespeare Tree Garden** has a patch that is planted with species mentioned in the plays.

The Birthplace Trust also keeps **Mary Arden's House**, three miles northwest of the town centre in Wilmcote (late March to mid-Oct Mon–Sat 9.30am–5pm, Sun 10am–5pm; late Oct to mid-March Mon–Sat 10am–4pm, Sun 10.30am–4pm; £4.40). Mary Arden was Shakespeare's mother, the only unmarried daughter when her father, Robert, died in 1556. Unusually for the time, she inherited the house and land, thus becoming one of the neighbourhood's most eligible women – John Shakespeare, eager for self-improvement, married her within a year. The house is a well-furnished example of an Elizabethan farmhouse and, though the labelling is rather scant, a platoon of guides fills in the details of family life and traditions.

Eating and drinking

Stratford is used to feeding and watering thousands of visitors, so finding refreshment is never difficult. The problem is that many places are geared to serving the day-tripper as rapidly as possible – not a recipe for much gastronomic delight. That said, there is a scattering of very good **restaurants**, several of which have been catering to theatregoers for many years, and a handful of **pubs** and **cafés** offer good food too. The best restaurants are concentrated along Sheep Street, running up from Waterside near the theatres.

Restaurants and cafés

Kingfisher Fish Bar, 13 Ely St. The best fish-and-chip shop in town. A five-minute walk from the theatres. Takeaway only. Closed Sun.

Lamb's Café Bistro, 12 Sheep St (☎01789/292554). Smart restaurant serving a mouth-watering range of stylish English and continental dishes. A good option for pasta lovers. Moderate.

Number 6, 6 Union St (☎01789/269106). Stratford's one and only specialist seafood restaurant. Moderate.

The Opposition, 13 Sheep St (☎01789/269980). Top-quality, imaginative international cuisine in a busy but amiable atmosphere. The dishes of the day, chalked up on a board inside, are excellent value. Moderate.

Pubs

Dirty Duck, 53 Waterside. The archetypal actors' pub, stuffed to the gunwales every night with a vocal entourage of RSC employees and hangers-on. Essential viewing.

The Garrick Inn, 25 High St. Arguably the town's most photogenic and best-preserved old ale house: exposed beams, real ales and good food.

Queen's Head, 54 Ely St. Attracts a mixed straight and gay crowd, and has a good range of ales.

Windmill Inn, Chapel St. Popular, youthful pub with a quirky, olde-worlde interior.

Listings

Banks and exchanges There are lots of banks in the town centre and all of them will change foreign currency and travellers' cheques. American Express has a bureau in the tourist office.

Bike rental Clarke's Cycles, 3 Guild St (☎01789/205057); Dawes & Lee Cooper, Greenhill St (☎01789/298333). Mountain bikes cost around £10 per day plus deposit.

Boat rental In the summertime, row boats (£4.50 an hour) and motor boats (£6 for 30min) can be rented at Stratford Marina, close to the tourist office in between the north end of Clopton Bridge (Bridgefoot) and the Moat House Hotel.

Books Waterstones, 18 High Street (☎01789/414418).

Buses Stagecoach Midland Red (☎01788/535555).

Car rental Ford, Arden Garages, Arden St (☎01789/267446); Hertz, at the train station (☎01789/298827).

Hospital Stratford General Hospital, Alcester Road – on the west side of the town centre (☎01789/205831).

Laundry Sparklean, 74 Bull St, off Old Town (daily 8am–9pm).

Pharmacy Boots, 11 Bridge St (Mon–Sat 9am–5.30pm; late opening rosta posted on the door).

Police Rother Street near the junction with Ely Street (☎01789/414111).

Post office Henley Street, on the town side of the Birthplace Museum (Mon–Fri 8.30am–5.30pm, Sat 8.30am–6pm)

Taxis Stratford Taxis ☎01789/415888.

Trains ☎0345/484950.

Charlecote Park and Coughton Court

Five miles east of Stratford off the B4086, **Charlecote Park** (April–Oct Mon, Tues & Fri–Sun noon–5pm; £4.90; NT) is a huge country estate centred on an ornate Elizabethan mansion. The house, refurbished in a rather heavy Victorian interpretation of Elizabethan style, is awash with souvenirs of the British empire, paintings of the estate and portraits of the Lucy family, who have lived here since 1247. The real pleasures of Charlecote, however, are the vast park and gardens, watered by the rivers Avon and Dene. Views over the surrounding villages are delightful, as are the formal lawns, the borders of plants and flowers from Shakespeare's plays and the croquet lawn – you can rent equipment from the gatehouse. Grazing throughout the estate are herds of fallow deer, whose ancestors are supposed to have been poached by the young William Shakespeare. Stagecoach Midland Red **buses** #18 and #X18 run to Charlecote village on the edge of the park (not Sun).

Eight miles east of Stratford, just beyond the small town of Alcester (pronounced "Ulster"), stands one of the finest Tudor houses in the region, **Coughton Court** (April–Sept Wed–Sun 11.30am–5pm; £6.25, grounds only £4.50; NT; hours vary, call to check ☎01789/762435), which boasts a particularly impressive central gatehouse and a courtyard framed by charming half-timbered houses. The Throckmortons have lived here since the beginning of the fifteenth century and now manage the property in conjunction with the National Trust, overseeing a large collection of antique furnishings and porcelain. The grounds offer a walled garden, a lake and gentle riverside walks.

Warwick

WARWICK, just eight miles northeast of Stratford and easily reached by bus and train, is famous for its massive castle, but it also possesses several charming streetscapes erected in the aftermath of a great fire in 1694, and a couple of particularly interesting buildings. An hour or two is quite enough time to nose around the compact town centre, but you'll need the whole day if, braving the crowds, you're set on exploring the castle too. Either way, Warwick is the perfect day-trip from Stratford.

Towering above the River Avon at the foot of the town centre, **Warwick Castle** (daily: April–Oct 10am–6pm; Nov–March 10am–5pm; £10.50) is locally proclaimed the "greatest medieval castle in Britain" and, if bulk equals greatness, then the claim is certainly valid, although much of the existing structure is the result of extensive nineteenth-century restoration. It's likely that the first fortress here was raised by Ethelfleda, daughter of Alfred the Great, in about 915 AD, but things really took off with the Normans, who built a motte and bailey towards the end of the eleventh century. Almost three hundred years later, the eleventh Earl of Warwick turned the stronghold into a formidable stone castle, complete with elaborate gatehouses, multiple turrets and a keep. The earl and his descendants played a prominent part in the Hundred Years' War. One of their number was the executioner of Joan of Arc and they all brought prisoners back to Warwick and incarcerated them in the dingy dungeons of Caesar's Tower pending ransom negotiations.

The entrance to the castle is through the old stable block, beyond which a footpath leads round to the imposing east gate. Over the footbridge and beyond the protective towers is the main courtyard. You can stroll along the ramparts and climb the towers, but most visitors head straight for one or other of the special displays installed inside by the present owners, Madame Tussauds. Among several displays, one of the most popular is the "Royal Weekend Party, 1898", an extravaganza of waxwork nobility hobnobbing in the private apartments which were rebuilt in the 1870s after fire damage. Another display, "Kingmaker – a preparation for Battle", adds smells and atmospheric sounds to a lifelike waxwork scene of the preparations for Richard Earl of Warwick's – as in "Warwick the Kingmaker" – final battle in 1471.

Re-emerging from the castle at the stables, Castle Street leads up the hill for a few yards to its junction with the High Street. Turn left and it's a brief stroll to another outstanding monument, the **Lord Leycester Hospital** (June–Sept Tues–Sun 10am–5pm; Oct–May Tues–Sun 10am–4pm; £2.75), a tangle of half-timbered buildings that lean at

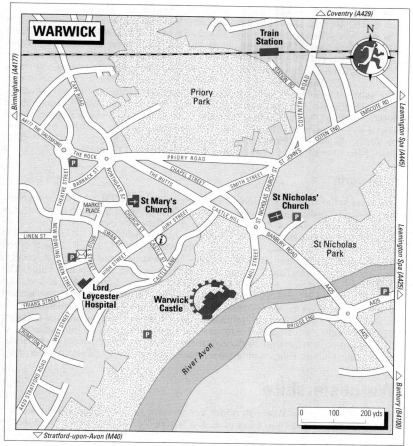

fairytale angles against the old West Gate. The complex represents one of Britain's best-preserved examples of domestic Elizabethan architecture. It was established as a hostel for old soldiers by the Earl of Leicester, a favourite of Queen Elizabeth I, and incorporates several beamed buildings, principally the Great Hall and the Guildhall, as well as a wonderful galleried courtyard and an intimate chantry chapel. There's a modest regimental museum here too – appropriately enough as retired servicemen (and their wives) still live here. Known as "Brethren", the veterans are distinguished by their black cloaks and silver boar pendants, which they don for ceremonial occasions and to receive visitors to the hospital.

Doubling back along the High Street, turn left up Church Street – opposite Castle Street – for the **Church of St Mary** (daily 10am–4pm), which was rebuilt in a weird Gothic-Renaissance amalgam after the fire of 1694. One part remained untouched, however – the **chancel**, a glorious specimen of the Perpendicular style with splendid flying ribs in the roof. On the right-hand side of the chancel, the **Beauchamp chapel** contains several beautiful tombs, exquisite works of art beginning with that of Richard Beauchamp, Earl of Warwick, who is depicted in an elaborate suit of armour of Italian design from the tip of his swan helmet down. The adjacent tomb of Ambrose Dudley is of finely carved alabaster, as is that of Robert Dudley, Earl of Leicester, one of Elizabeth I's most influential advisers.

Warwick's **train station** is on the northern edge of the centre, about ten minutes' walk from the castle. **Buses** stop beside the Market Place, from where it's a couple of minutes' walk east to St Mary's and a couple more along Church Street to the **tourist office**, in the Courthouse at the corner of Church and Jury streets (daily 9.30am–4.30pm; ☎01926/492212). The tourist office has a list of local hotels and B&Bs, but with Stratford so near and easy to reach, there's no special reason to stay here. For a bite to **eat**, head for the inexpensive *Charlotte's Restaurant and Tearoom*, 6 Jury St (☎01926/498930; closed Mon). For a drink, try the traditional *Zetland Arms*, 11 Church St.

Kenilworth

Five miles to the north of Warwick is workaday **KENILWORTH**, a town that received something of a boost when Sir Walter Scott wrote his novel of the same name, but has become little more than an upmarket dormitory to Coventry (see p.561). It does, however, have one remarkable sight – the **Castle** from which Scott took his inspiration (April–Oct daily 10am–6pm; Nov–March daily 10am–4pm; £3.10; EH). Begun in the twelfth century – the keep dates from then – the castle was one of the key strategic strongholds in the Midlands, alternately held by the king or a leading noble. The Dudleys acquired the castle in the sixteenth century and one of the family, Robert, Earl of Leicester, pleased Elizabeth I no end by turning the draughty fortress into an elegant palace in preparation for her visit. Kenilworth then became one of England's most fashionable country houses, hosting spectacular pageants and entertainments, but following Dudley's death the castle slid into gradual decay, hastened by the attention of Cromwell's troops in the Civil War. Today, the substantial red sandstone ruins still maintain a tremendous presence, with large remnants from each era still easily discernible.

Worcestershire

In geographical terms, **Worcestershire** can be compared to a huge saucer, with the low-lying plains of the Vale of Evesham and Severn Valley rising to a lip of hills: the Malverns in the west, the Cotswolds in the south, the Abberley and Clee hills to the northwest and the Clents and Lickeys in the northeast. In character, the county divides into two broad belts. To the north lie the industrial and overspill towns – Droitwich and Redditch for instance – that have much in common with the Birmingham conurbation, while the south is predominantly rural. Marking the transition between the two is **Worcester** itself, where the main event is the splendid cathedral. The south holds the county's finest scenery in the **Malvern Hills**, excellent walking territory and home to the amiable little spa town of **Great Malvern**. South Worcestershire's rural lifestyle is famously portrayed in *The Archers*, the BBC's never-ending radio soap, which attracts a massive and extraordinarily dedicated audience. Steam train enthusiasts will be keen to ride the Severn Valley Railway, which chugs north from Worcestershire's **Kidderminster** terminus to Bridgnorth; for more on the railway, see p.539.

The proximity of Birmingham ensures Worcestershire has a good network of **trains** and **buses**, though services do become less frequent to the villages in the south of the county. Worcestershire's **bus timetable information line** is ☎0345/125436.

Worcester

Right at the heart of the county, both geographically and politically, **WORCESTER** is a robust, slightly schizophrenic city, where timbered Tudor and refined Georgian buildings are overshadowed by charmless modern developments. The chief offender is the award-winning, £85-million Crowngate shopping mall, which obliterates a large swathe of the city centre. Postwar clumsiness apart, the biggest single influence on the city has always been the River Severn, which flows along Worcester's west flank. Because the Severn is prone to flood, building is prohibited in the meadows flanking the river, leaving clear space by the cathedral, which rises high above the muddy brown river on the eastern bank.

The City

Worcester's skyline is dominated by the squat sandstone bulk of its **Cathedral** (daily 7.30am–6pm; £2 suggested donation), a rich stew of architectural styles, and best approached from the path that runs along the river's edge and through a gate bearing marks of the city's flood levels. The oldest section of the cathedral is its multi-columned **crypt**: built underneath the Saxon monastery founded here by Saint Oswald in 983, it's the largest Norman crypt in the country. The large circular **Chapter House**, off the cloisters, is the other main Norman portion, and has the distinction of being the first such building constructed without the use of a central supporting pillar. Inside the main part of the cathedral, the western end of the twelfth-century **nave** displays the transition between the rounded Norman and pointed Gothic arches. The pillars of the nave are decorated with bunches of fruit, carved by stonemasons from Lincoln, most of whom succumbed to the Black Death, leaving inferior successors to finish the job. Built in the mid-twelfth century, the Early English **east end** is one of the most elaborate sections, with the choir's forest of slender pillars soaring over the intricately worked choir stalls. In front of the **high altar** is the tomb of England's most reviled monarch, King John. Before he died in 1216, the ailing John explicitly instructed that he was to be buried between the tombs of Saint Wulstan and Saint Oswald. Close by is the cathedral's richest monument: **Prince Arthur's Chantry**, a delicate lacy confection of carved stonework built as a memorial in 1504 by King Henry VII for his young son, Arthur, who died on his honeymoon with Catherine of Aragon – later to become the first wife of his younger brother, Henry VIII. The chantry is liberally plastered with heraldic and symbolic depictions of the houses of York and Lancaster, united by the Lancastrian Henry VII after his victory at Bosworth Field and subsequent marriage to Elizabeth, daughter of the Yorkist king Edward IV.

Tucked behind the cathedral in Severn Street, alongside the canal, the **Royal Worcester Porcelain** complex (Mon–Sat 9am–5.30pm, Sun 11am–4pm; £7, including factory tour Mon–Fri) contains a factory shop, a museum, where a large sample of old Worcester porcelain is displayed in period settings, and the factory itself. Beginning in the mid-eighteenth century, porcelain manufacture was long the city's main industry. Up behind the Royal Worcester complex, on the busy Sidbury dual carriageway, is the oldest building in the city, the timber-framed **Commandery**, which now holds the **Civil War Centre** (Mon–Sat 10am–5pm, Sun 1.30–5.30pm; £3.40). The Commandery was Charles II's headquarters leading up to the Battle of Worcester in 1651 and has also served as a college for the blind. It now contains a sequence of Tudor and Stuart period rooms plus exhibits on the role of religion in the seventeenth century and the events of the Civil War, focusing on the trial of Charles I and the background to Cromwell's victory. Most of the building is half-timbered and smartly panelled, with one small room sporting wall paintings dating from around 1500. Look out for the plaintive, glowing soul perched in the scales of judgement, at the mercy of a sly devil and virginal Madonna, who are each trying to force the scales in their favour.

Friar Street, which forks off Sidbury just west of the Commandery, by the *Olde Talbot Hotel*, is blighted by some garish 1960s developments, but these quickly give way to Worcester's most complete thoroughfare of Elizabethan and Tudor buildings. Sited inside one of these old timber-framed buildings is the **Museum of Local Life** (daily Mon–Wed, Fri & Sat 10.30am–5pm; free). The museum starts with an examination of Worcester during World War II, interesting chiefly because it's a typical picture of ordinary life throughout the war years. The photographs are fascinating, but thereafter the remainder of the museum is given over to anodyne reconstructions of Edwardian and Victorian shops, offices and domestic settings. Almost opposite is **The Greyfriars** (April–Oct Wed & Thurs 2–5pm; £2.60; NT), a largely fifteenth-century town house, whose principal attraction is the rambling walled garden at the back.

Right on the other side of town, in the Tything, almost a mile up the main street from the cathedral, is the **Worcester Museum & Art Gallery** (Mon–Wed & Fri 9.30am–6pm, Sat 9.30am–5pm; free), which offers a lively programme of temporary exhibitions and events. The permanent collections are less riveting, though the attractively displayed section on the River Severn warrants a few minutes and there are several charmingly Romantic paintings from the late nineteenth century.

Lower Broadheath

One of Worcestershire's most famous sons was the composer **Sir Edward Elgar**, whose statue faces the cathedral back at the bottom of the High Street. Inevitably, there's an Elgar Trail meandering round the county and its focus is his **birthplace** – a tiny, rustic brick cottage in **LOWER BROADHEATH**, a couple of miles west of Worcester on the B4204 (May–Sept Mon, Tues & Thurs–Sun 10.30am–6pm; Oct to mid-Jan & mid-Feb to April 1.30–4.30pm; £3). Inside, the crowded rooms contain Elgar's musical manuscripts, personal correspondence in his spidery handwriting, press cuttings, photographs and miscellaneous mementoes centred on the desk at which he worked. Regular buses #311 and #317 go directly to Broadheath Common and the cottage is a short walk from there.

Practicalities

Of Worcester's two **train stations**, Foregate Street, at the northern end of the High Street, is the more central, although some express services stop only at Shrub Hill, a fifteen-minute walk to the east of the city centre. The **bus station** is on the city side of the main river bridge, off The Butts behind the Crowngate shopping mall. From here, it's a brief stroll south to the **tourist office** (mid-March to Oct Mon–Sat 10.30am–5.30pm; Nov to mid-March Mon–Sat 10.30am–4pm; ☎01905/726311), in the Georgian Guildhall, towards the cathedral end of the High Street. **Bike rental** is available from Peddlers, 46 Barbourne Rd (☎01905/24238).

The best **hotel** options are the *Fownes' Hotel*, in an old glove factory at the cathedral end of City Walls Road ☎01905/613151; ⑤); the nearby *Loch Ryan*, 119 Sidbury (☎01905/351143; ④), which is noted for its food and terraced garden; and the *Star*, almost next to Foregate Street station (☎01905/24308; ⑤). Recommended central **B&Bs** include *Osborne House*, in a traditional Victorian villa at 17 Chestnut Walk (☎01905/22296; no credit cards; ②), and the excellent *Burgage House*, 4 College Precincts (☎01905/25396; no credit cards; ②), which occupies a Georgian town house with views over to the cathedral.

A few popular café-bars and restaurants serve **meals** all day along Friar Street – try *Osteria* at no. 21, a moderately priced Mediterranean restaurant offering tasty *tapas* (☎01905/745902). Friar Street continues north to become New Street, along which you'll find the pricier *King Charles II* (☎01905/22449), with a rather contrived seventeenth-century ambience but an outstanding traditional English menu. Alternatively, there's *Saffron's*, 15 New St (☎01905/610505), an unpretentious bistro serving mainly chargrilled steaks and chicken at around £10 per main course. A short walk further north, the friendly Worcester Arts Workshop in Sansome Street contains gallery space, an innovative theatre and an enjoyable café, making it a useful place to find out about local events.

You'll find a bunch of pleasant old **pubs** in the city centre, among them the *Cardinal's Hat*, 31 Friar St, a sixteenth-century building complete with half-timbered interior; it serves good-value lunches. *The Plough*, tucked away on the corner of Fish Street and Deansway, is among the liveliest places to drink, with a barrel-strewn patio that gets packed out on warm summer evenings. Less touristy are the *Horn & Trumpet* in Angel Street, which has live music, and the minuscule *Lamb & Flag* at 30 The Tything, one of the city's most popular pubs, and a must for Guinness drinkers.

The Malverns

One of the most exclusive and well-heeled areas of the Midlands, **The Malverns** is the generic name for a string of towns stretched along the lower slopes of the **Malvern Hills**, which rise spectacularly out of the flat plains and offer expansive views. The main centre of the region is **GREAT MALVERN**, a pretty little place served by rail from Worcester, Birmingham, Oxford and London. The town's medicinal waters became popular towards the end of the eighteenth century, but it was the Victorians who came here in droves, making the steep hike up to **St Anne's Well** on the hill behind town, where you can still try the stuff yourself. The peculiarities of Great Malvern's spa waters are explained in the town **museum**, housed in the delicately proportioned Abbey Gateway, plum in the centre on Abbey Road (Easter–Oct Mon, Tues & Thurs–Sun, also Wed in school holidays 10.30am–5pm; £1.50). Nineteenth-century cartoons show patients packed into cold wet sheets before hopping gaily away from their crutches and wheelchairs – exaggerated claims perhaps, but poor hygiene did bring on a multitude of skin complaints and the relief the spa waters brought was real enough.

The main sight in town is the **Priory Church**, adjacent to the museum, its patchwork exterior contrasting with the ordered interior, which is notable for its stained glass and hundreds of detailed wall tiles, all added to the building in the mid-fifteenth century. The window of the north transept is especially fine and contains a portrait of Prince Arthur, Henry VII's son – the same Arthur who is commemorated in Worcester cathedral (see p.525). Among the priory's graves is that of Darwin's granddaughter, who died here as a child despite being bathed with Malvern water. From the church, it's a short walk to the **Winter Gardens pavilion**, one of the key venues for the wide range of special events the town puts on each year, including the excellent **Almeida Drama Festival** held in August.

Great Malvern has two other claims to fame: one is the Morgan motor car, which is still handmade in a small factory here; the other is the composer **Edward Elgar**, who lived in the adjacent village of **MALVERN LINK** at the turn of the century. The views from his house on Alexandra Road formed a backdrop for Elgar while he composed his most enduring work, including the famous *Enigma Variations*, whose more lyrical passages have become anthems of the English countryside. Stare out across the Severn Valley from the flank of the Malverns on a fine summer's evening and it's not hard to see why England's most celebrated composer found such inspiration here.

For **walkers**, the Malvern Hills offer splendid day-hikes and a number of historical landmarks, including the remains of an Iron Age fort high on the ridge to the south of town. The panorama from here takes in the contrasts of the Malvern valley: plains to the east, and gentle hills rolling towards the gloomy Black Mountains in the west. The hike along the ridge and back takes about four-and-a-half hours. Start from the southern end at **Chase End Hill**, which is reachable by bus (depart Church St, Great Malvern Wed & Sat at around 9am) and work your way north; alternatively, take the same bus to **British Camp**, midway along the route, and begin there.

Great Malvern practicalities

Great Malvern **train station** is on the east edge of town, a mile or so from the centre along Avenue Road and Church Street. A range of inexpensive hiking leaflets are sold at the town's **tourist office**, right in the centre across from the priory church at 21 Church St (April–Nov daily 10am–5pm; Dec–March Mon–Sat 10am–5pm, Sun 10am–4pm; ☎01684/892289). They also sell the three excellent large-scale **maps** (£3.75) which are indispensable if you're planning on walking the length of the Malverns. This is also a rewarding, though physically demanding, area to explore by **bike** – you can rent cycles from Spokes & Saddles, 164 Worcester Rd, Malvern Link (☎01684/576141), less than a mile from the centre of town or one stop up the rail line.

Accommodation is plentiful. Right in the heart of town is the rambling old *Great Malvern Hotel*, 7 Graham Rd (☎01684/563411; ⑤) and, just along the street, at no. 23, are the Georgian symmetries of the charming *Montrose Hotel* (☎01684/572335; ⑥). Great Malvern **B&Bs** include the inexpensive *Kylemore*, 30 Avenue Rd (☎01684/563753; no credit cards; ①); the *Chalet House*, an impressive Edwardian house with garden access to the hills at 24 Wyche Rd (☎01684/572995; no credit cards; ②); and *Elm Bank*, an elegant Regency town house with en-suite rooms at 52 Worcester Rd (☎01684/566051; ②). The homely **youth hostel**, serving simple meals, is a couple of miles south of Great Malvern, off the main A449 at 18 Peachfield Rd, Malvern Wells (☎01684/569131; closed Nov–March). The nearest **campsite** is at *Odd Fellows Pub*, four miles southwest in Colwall (☎01684/540084) – the infrequent bus to Ledbury passes by.

For **food**, Great Malvern has oodles of cafés and tearooms – one of the more distinctive is *St Anne's Well*, a cosy vegetarian café serving inexpensive wholefood snacks, salads and cakes from its Victorian premises at the Well; just follow the signs up through the park from the centre. They'll also give you a glass to sample the spring water that babbles into a basin outside the door. The town's other café with character lies downhill from the tourist office at the train station. Known as the *Lady Foley Tea Room* during the day, and *Passionata* in the evening (☎01684/893033; Fri & Sat only), it's actually on one of the station platforms and makes the most of its Victorian surroundings. Finally, *Cridlans' Brasserie* (☎01684/562676), a French-style brasserie just outside the abbey gates, is a slightly pricier, but good-value place to eat, serving light lunches and tasty continental dishes on red-and-white-check tablecloths; try their delicious home-made sausage sandwich.

The Vale of Evesham

Lying southeast of Worcester, the **Vale of Evesham** is Britain's foremost fruit-growing area, a conservative rural stronghold of market gardens and orchards. **EVESHAM**, a slow-moving market town rapidly losing its character amid modern construction work, is the major centre of the Vale, served by regular trains from Worcester. It's built in a protective loop of the River Avon, which flows by the beautiful but scanty ruins of the Benedictine **abbey** and its flamboyant sixteenth-century **bell tower**. One of the abbey buildings now houses the **Almonry Museum and Heritage Centre** (Mon–Sat 10am–5pm, Sun 2–5pm; £2), a fairly routine civic collection enlivened by some interesting exhibits on the Battle of Evesham of 1265, at which Simon de Montfort, rebel against King Henry III, was killed by the troops of Prince Edward, later Edward I. The Heritage Centre also houses the **tourist office** (Mon–Sat 10am–5pm, Sun 2–5pm; ☎01386/446944).

There's no compelling reason to stay in Evesham, but there are several good **B&Bs**, notably *Agebury House*, a neat and tidy Victorian terrace opposite the tourist office at 42

Merstow Green (☎01386/41664; ①), and the comparable *Church House*, close to the town centre on Greenhill Park Road (☎01386/40498; no credit cards; ①). Alternatively, there's the *Evesham Hotel*, Coopers Lane (☎01386/765566; ⑥), an elegant hotel with scenic gardens and top-flight cuisine.

One especially popular excursion from Evesham is the short hop southeast along the A44 to the Cotswold gateway village of **BROADWAY** (buses from Evesham), an astoundingly pretty place but often overrun with tourists. Above the village sits **Broadway Tower Country Park**, dominated by the eighteenth-century folly of Broadway Tower (April–Oct daily 10.30am–5pm; Nov–March Sat & Sun 11am–3pm; £3.20), which houses exhibitions on subjects varying from William Morris and the Pre-Raphaelite movement to sheep farming. The park gives excellent views over the Cotswolds and has signposted walks and farmyard animal enclosures.

Herefordshire and the Forest of Dean

The rolling agricultural landscapes of **Herefordshire** have an easy-going charm, but the finest scenery hereabouts is along the banks of the **River Wye**, which wriggles and worms its way across the county linking most of the places of interest. Plonked in the middle of the county on the Wye is **Hereford**, a sleepy, rather old-fashioned sort of place whose proudest possession, the remarkable Mappa Mundi map, was almost flogged off in a round of ecclesiastical budget cuts back in the 1980s. To the west of Hereford, hard by the Welsh border, the key attraction is **Hay-on-Wye**, which – thanks to the purposeful industry of Richard Booth – has become the world's largest repository of second-hand books, on sale in a score of second-hand bookshops. Elsewhere, tiny **Kilpeck** to the southwest of Hereford has a superb Norman church, whilst **Leominster** to the north and **Ledbury** to the east are amiable market towns distinguished by their Tudor and Stuart half-timbered buildings – sometimes called "Black and Whites". In the southeast corner of the county is **Ross-on-Wye**, a genial little town with a picturesque river setting which is the ideal base for explorations into the **Forest of Dean**, nestling in between the rivers Wye and Severn, across the county boundary in Gloucestershire.

Herefordshire possesses one **rail line**, linking Ledbury, Hereford and Leominster, but otherwise you'll be restricted to the county's **buses**, which provide a reasonable service between the villages and towns (not Sun). For information on services, telephone the **County Bus Line** (☎0345/125436).

Hereford

Once a border garrison town against the Welsh, **HEREFORD** owed its military importance to its strategic position beside the River Wye. To the Saxons it was also a religious centre. One of their kings, Ethelbert, was murdered by the Welsh and legend has his ghost insisting his remains be interred here in Hereford cathedral. The fortifications that once girdled the city have all but vanished, but the cathedral has survived to form the main focus of architectural interest. Otherwise, Hereford is a drowsy market town set amid some of the least spoilt rural landscapes in England. Indeed, the town remains dependent on its agricultural base – the local **cider** industry is one of the city's biggest trades. The Wye meanders around the southern side of the city centre, with the medieval **Wye Bridge** and its twentieth-century neighbour, **Greyfriars Bridge**, connecting the two banks. The **cathedral** and its well-proportioned close sit on the northern bank, at the heart of the city centre, with the main shopping streets spreading out around them.

The City

The **Cathedral** is a curious building, an uncomfortable amalgamation of architectural styles, beginning with the dumpy red sandstone **tower**, constructed in the early fourteenth century to eclipse the western tower built by the Normans, which collapsed under its own weight in 1786. As a result of the accident, a great section of the **nave** was destroyed, leaving architects with a problem that was never satisfactorily resolved. The replacement nave lacks the grandeur of most other English cathedrals, though at least the Norman arches at its eastern end are impressive. The **north transept**, however, is a flawless exercise in thirteenth-century taste; designed by Bishop Aquablanca, probably to house his own tomb, it has soaring windows that are among the finest extant examples of Early English architecture. On the opposite side of the church, in the Norman **south transept**, unusual features include a German *Adoration of the Magi* that dates from the sixteenth century and an early fireplace, one of the few still surviving within an English church.

In the late 1980s, dire financial difficulties prompted the cathedral authorities to plan the sale of their most treasured possession, the **Mappa Mundi**. This parchment map was drawn in 1289, and at 65 by 53 inches it is the largest known example of such a work from that period. Its detail is astonishing, showing the complete world from its centre at Jerusalem, with Britain and Ireland sitting on the edge of the void. Eventually, a scheme was hatched to keep the map in Hereford by raising funds from shareholders, visitors and wealthy patrons, including oil tycoon John Paul Getty Jnr, who donated nearly half of the £2.6 million needed to construct a splendid new building at the southeast corner of Cathedral Close. Entered via the cloisters, the ground floor of this **Mappa Mundi Centre** (Easter–Oct Mon–Sat 10am–4.15pm, Sun 11am–3.15pm; Nov–Easter Mon–Sat 11am–3.15pm; £4) features a state-of-the-art interpretative exhibition that's an ideal primer for the Mappa, displayed in a dimly lit air-conditioned chamber along with the cathedral's other main treasures. Among the latter is an exquisitely enamelled casket alleged to contain relics of Thomas à Becket and a remarkable twelve-hundred-year-old Saxon gospel written on calf vellum. Also housed in the new building is the world's largest **Chained Library**, a collection of some 1400 books and manuscripts dating from the eighth to the fifteenth century.

The **City Museum and Art Gallery**, opposite the cathedral in a colourful Victorian building in Broad Street (April–Sept Tues–Sat 10am–5pm, Sun 10am–4pm; rest of year closed Sun; free), is a modest collection of wildlife, geological remains, local history and mawkish Victorian art. Broad Street continues up and round into the main square, **High Town**, which is fringed by some fine Georgian buildings and **The Old House**, sole remnant of the seventeenth-century timber-framed Butchers' Row and now a mildly diverting museum with period interiors and bric-a-brac (April–Sept Tues–Sat 10am–5pm, Sun 10am–4pm; rest of year closed Sun; free).

Cider enthusiasts should make their way to the **Cider Museum and King Offa Distillery**, over the ring road to the west of the city centre, a thirty-minute walk from the train station off the A438 at 21 Ryelands St (April–Oct daily 10am–5.30pm; Nov–March Tues–Sun 11am–3pm; £2.20). The museum tracks through the history of cider-making and you can view the distillation process and sample King Offa ciders, including a particularly tasty Cider Brandy. If this whets your appetite, there are guided tours of the more commercial **Bulmers' Cider Factory** on Plough Lane (Mon–Fri; £2.95; ☎01432/352000); tours must be booked at least one week in advance.

Practicalities

Hereford's **train station** is about half a mile northeast of the town centre and its **bus station** is nearby, just off Commercial Road. The **tourist office** is almost directly opposite the cathedral, at 1 King St (May–Sept Mon–Sat 9am–5pm & Sun 10am–4pm;

Oct–April Mon–Sat 9am–5pm; ☎01432/268430). **Bike rental** is available from Coombes Cycles, 94 Widemarsh St (☎01432/354373).

Recommended central **B&Bs** include the *Collins House*, in a Georgian villa at 19 St Owen St (☎01432/272416; ②) and *Charades*, 34 Southbank Rd (☎01432/269444; no credit cards; ①); further out in the countryside, about two miles south of town off the A49, *Grafton Villa Farm* (☎01432/268689; no credit cards; ②; closed Nov–Jan), offers three tastefully decorated bedrooms in the Georgian farmhouse of a working farm. As for **hotels**, the *Green Dragon*, Broad St (☎01432/272506; ⑤), occupies a grand Neoclassical building right in the centre; it's now one of the Forte Heritage chain.

For **food**, two good options are the inexpensive *Firenze*, 21 Commercial Rd, a pasta and pizza place, and the *Aroon Rai*, 50 Widemarsh St (☎01432/279971), a moderately priced Thai restaurant. In a town where the **cider** industry is so important, you should at least sample some of the finished product. There are shops at both Bulmers' and the Cider Museum, or you could head straight for one of Hereford's many **pubs**. Appealing choices include the *Black Lion*, down near the cathedral in Bridge Street, and *The Barrels* in St Owen Street, which serves Hereford's widest selection of real ales.

Hay-on-Wye

Straddling the Welsh/English border some twenty miles west of Hereford, the sleepy little town of **HAY-ON-WYE** is known to most people for one thing – books. Hay saw its first bookshop open in 1961 and has since become a bibliophile's paradise, with just about every spare inch of the town being given over to the trade, including the old cinema and the ramshackle stone castle. Most of Hay's inhabitants are outsiders, which means that it has little indigenous feel, but its setting, against the spectacular backdrop of Hay Bluff and the Black Mountains, together with its creaky little streets, is delightful. In summer, the town bursts with life as it plays host to a succession of riverside parties and travelling fairs, the pick of which is the **Hay Literary Festival** in the last week of May, when London's literary world decamps here.

Before you start browsing, pick up one of the free leaflets from the tourist office giving a rundown of the various shops and their specialities, along with a handy street plan. A

THE KING OF THE HAY

Richard Booth, whose family originates from the area, opened the first of his Hay-on-Wye second-hand bookshops in 1961. Since then, he has built an astonishing empire and attracted other booksellers to the town, turning it into the greatest market of used books in the world. There are now over twenty such shops in this minuscule town, the largest of which – Booth's own flagship – contains around half a million volumes.

Whereas so many rural and border towns have seen populations ebb away over the past fifty years, Hay is booming on the strength of its bibliophilic connections. Booth views this transformation of a hitherto ordinary little market town as a prototype for reviving an agrarian economy, depending on local initiatives and unusual specialisms. He is unequivocal in his condemnation of bulky government organizations, which, he asserts, have done little to stem the flow of jobs and people out of the region. This healthy distaste for bureaucracy, coupled with Hay's geographical location slap on the Welsh/English border and Booth's own self-promotional skills, led him to declare Hay independent of the UK in 1977, with himself, naturally, as **King**. He appoints his own ministers and offers "official" government scrolls, passports and car stickers to bewitched visitors. Although such a proclamation of independence carries no weight officially, most of the people of Hay seem to have rallied behind King Richard and are delighted with the publicity, and visitors, that the town's continuing high profile attracts.

CANOEING IN HAY-ON-WYE

Scores of visitors come to Hay-on-Wye to hike and cycle, but the surrounding countryside is just as pleasantly explored by **kayak** or **canoe** on the River Wye. In four to six days, it's possible to paddle your way downriver from Hay to Monmouth, overnighting in tents on isolated stretches of river bank, or holing up in comfortable B&Bs and pubs along the way. With regard to **kayak and canoe hire**, Paddles & Peddles, 15 Castle St (☎01497/820604), are a reputable outfit, who also have a boathouse on the river at the bottom end of town. Rental of life jackets and other essential equipment (such as waterproof canisters to carry your gear) is generally included in the price (around £35 per canoe for a full 24 hours, with discounts for longer trips), while transport to and from both the departure and finishing points by minibus can be arranged with the rental company.

good place to start is **Richard Booth's Bookshop**, 44 Lion St (☎01497/820322), the largest second-hand bookshop in Europe: a huge, draughty warehouse of almost unlimited browsing potential. It's owned – like just about everything in Hay – by Richard Booth, who lives in part of the castle, a fire-damaged Jacobean mansion built into the walls of a thirteenth-century fortress right in the centre of Hay. In another part of the mansion, Booth's wife runs the **Hay Castle Booth Books** (☎01497/820503), a sedate collection of fine-art, antiquarian and photography books.

On Castle Street, **H.R. Grant & Son** at no. 6 (☎01497/820309) and **Castle Street Books** at no. 23 (☎01497/820160) are two of the prime bookshops in town for historical guides and maps. Nearby Broad Street holds **Y Gelli Auctions** (☎01497/821179), with regular sales of books, maps and prints. Also on Broad Street is **West House Books** (☎01497/821225), best for Celtic and women's works.

Practicalities

Buses from Hereford stop in the car park in the town centre off Oxford Road. The adjacent **tourist office** (daily: Easter–Oct 10am–5pm; Nov–Easter 11am–1pm & 2–4pm; ☎01497/820144) stocks an exhaustive range of hiking books and maps, and can help arrange accommodation in the area. **Bike rental** is available from Paddles & Peddles, 15 Castle St (☎01497/820604).

Accommodation in town is plentiful, although things get booked up long in advance for the Hay Literary Festival. Arguably the best option is the *Old Black Lion*, Lion St (☎01497/820841; ③), a captivating inn dating back to medieval times with beamed ceilings and a penchant for candlelight in the evenings; try also *Belmont House*, Belmont Rd (☎01497/820718; no credit cards; ①), a classy guest house crammed with antiques inside an appealing Georgian villa; or the *Old Post Office*, Llanigon (☎01497/820008; no credit cards; ①), a wonderful seventeenth-century B&B two miles south of Hay. The last is well placed for local walks and serves up delicious vegetarian breakfasts. The nearest **campsite** is *Radnors End* (☎01497/820780 or 820233) in a beautiful setting, five minutes' walk from town across the Wye bridge on the Clyro road; washing and toilet facilities here are rudimentary, but pitches are cheap (£3) and the views over Hay and the Black Mountains are great.

Several of Hay's **pubs** offer top-quality bar food and meals, but you'll be hard pushed to find anywhere better than the *Old Black Lion* on Lion Street. Another favourite is *Pinocchio's*, an intimate, mid-priced Italian **restaurant** on Broad Street where you can pick up freshly cut *panini* at lunchtime for £3, while the *Granary*, also on Broad Street is the vegetarian's choice, specializing in wholefood snacks, soups and filling main meals made mostly with organic produce; it also has a roadside terrace that is a great place to kick off your boots and relax over a pint if you've been hiking.

Leominster and Croft Castle

LEOMINSTER (pronounced "Lemster"), thirteen miles north of the county town on the Hereford–Shrewsbury rail line, is Herefordshire's second town, and an increasingly important centre for the **antiques** trade. Worth an hour or two of exploration, the town's attractive centre is a largely half-timbered patchwork of medieval streets with overhanging gables, fanning out from the cramped confines of Corn Square. On the northeast edge of the centre, the chunky **Priory Church** has preserved several original Norman features, from the rounded windows in the clerestory and the sturdy pillars in the nave to the carved "green man" fertility symbol by the west door. The church also possesses a rare example of a **ducking stool**, used to dunk dishonest tradesmen, scolds and the odd "wayward" wife up until 1809.

The **tourist office**, on Corn Square (April–Sept Mon–Sat 9.30am–5pm; Oct–March Mon–Sat 10am–4pm; ☎01568/616460), hands out brochures listing local **accommodation** and, although there's no special reason to hang around, the *Copper Hall*, a large old building with its own walled garden at 134 South St (☎01568/611622; ②) is a pleasant enough spot to hang your hat.

From Leominster, it's just five miles northwest to **Croft Castle** (May–Sept Wed–Sun 1.30–5.30pm; April & Oct Sat & Sun 1.30–4.30pm; £3.40; NT) via the B4361. Here, the sturdy pink stone towers and walls of the original medieval fortress have been embellished by a string of subsequent owners. Mock-Gothic castellated bays lie each side of the gabled front and inside there's an exuberant Georgian-Gothic staircase as well as a kitschy Blue and Gold Room, complete with a vast gaudy chimney piece.

Ledbury

If you're heading east from Hereford to the Malverns (see p.527), then drop by **LEDBURY**, a busy little town whose Market Place is home to the dinky **Market House**, a Tudor beamed building raised on oak columns and with herringbone pattern beams. Running off the Market Place is Church Lane, which possesses a particularly fine ensemble of Tudor and Stuart buildings. Among them is a Heritage Centre, the Butchers' Row Folk Museum and, pick of the bunch, the so-called **Painted Room** (June–Sept Mon–Fri 11am–3pm, Sat & Sun 2–5pm; rest of year closed Sat & Sun; £2 donation requested), featuring a set of bold symmetrical floral frescoes painted on wattle-and-daub walls sometime in the sixteenth century. At the far end of Church Lane is **St Michael's parish church**, whose strong and slender spire pokes high into the sky. The nucleus of the church is Norman – note the round pillars and zigzag stonework – but the most interesting features are the funerary monuments inside, including the spectacular seventeenth-century **Skynner Tomb**, where five sons and five daughters kneel beneath the canopied slab on which their parents also kneel.

Ledbury **train station** is inconveniently situated on the northern edge of town, but **buses** stop on the High Street, metres from both the Market House and the **tourist office** (daily 10am–5pm; ☎01531/636147).

Kilpeck

The lonely hamlet of **KILPECK**, nine miles southwest of Hereford off the A465 Abergavenny Road, boasts the **Church of St Mary and David**, one of the most exquisitely preserved Norman churches in Britain. Here, the true vitality of Norman sculpture is revealed, beginning with the south door where the tympanum's Tree of Life is hooped by birds, dragons, a phoenix and all sorts of mythical monsters. Up above, the corbel displays over seventy grotesques with barely a saint or religious figure in sight. The sculptures may well have been inspired by pagan Viking carving, reminders of the Normans' Scandinavian ancestry – William the Conqueror was the descendant of a Viking chief who seized Normandy in the tenth century. The Victorians restored the corbel sculptures, but removed the more sexually explicit, with the exception of the genital-splaying sheila-na-gig – food for thought. Beyond the church graveyard are the battered remains of Kilpeck's medieval **castle**. There are five **buses** daily (Mon–Fri) from Hereford to Kilpeck.

Ross-on-Wye

ROSS-ON-WYE, perched high above a loop of the river sixteen miles southeast of Hereford, is the obvious base for exploring the Forest of Dean (see opposite) and makes an agreeable stop if you're heading for Gloucester and the Cotswolds (see pp.306–323). It's a relaxed town with a pleasing sense of proportion, thanks mainly to the efforts of pioneering seventeenth-century town planner, John Kyrle, also responsible for laying out **The Prospect**, the cliff-top public garden whose Mock-Gothic walls overlook the slender, tapering spire of the parish **Church of St Mary's**. Dating from the early thirteenth century, the church was clumsily renovated by the Victorians, but the interior contains – in the tomb of a certain William Rudhall – one of the last great alabaster sculptures from the specialist masons of Nottingham, whose work was prized right across medieval Europe. Look out also for a rare **Plague Cross** in the churchyard, commemorating the three hundred or so townsfolk who were buried here by night without coffins during a savage outbreak of the plague in 1637. The other item of architectural interest is the seventeenth-century **Market Hall**, a sturdy two-storey sandstone structure bang in the middle of town on the Market Place.

If you've strolled long enough around town but still have time to spare, strike out along one of the many well-defined **footpaths** that thread their way through the riverine fields and woodland bordering the Wye. A collection of leaflets giving detailed descriptions of several circular routes is available at the tourist office.

Practicalities

There are no trains to Ross, but the **bus station** is handily located on Cantilupe Road, a couple of minutes' walk from the Market Place and the **tourist office**, on the corner of High and Edde Cross streets (Easter–Sept Mon–Sat 9am–5pm, Sun 10am–4pm; rest of year closed Sun ☎01989/562768). Ross is strong on **B&Bs** with one of the best being the *Linden House*, next to a gnarled row of old Tudor almshouses opposite St Mary's on Church Street (☎01989/565373; no credit cards; ③), and offering tasty vegetarian breakfasts. Another first-rate choice is *Vaga House*, an immaculately maintained Georgian building just below the tourist office on Wye Street (☎01989/563024; no credit cards; ③). If you're **camping**, your only option is the *Broadmeadow Caravan Park*, occupying a field beside an artificial lake on the northeast edge of Ross (☎01989/768076; closed Nov–March). **Bikes** can be rented from Revolutions on Broad Street (☎01989/562639).

Restaurants range from the *Oat Cuisine*, a straightforward daytime wholefood café in Broad Street, to *Cloisters Wine Bar*, 24 High St (☎01989/567717; evenings only), the best mid-range place to eat, serving copious meat and fish dishes in an attractive wood, stone and candle-lit interior. In a similar mould is the moderately priced *Meader's* (☎01989/562803), at the bottom of Copse Cross Street near the Market Place, where you can try Hungarian specialities. Of the **pubs**, the ancient, oak-beamed *King Charles II* on Broad Street is the most appealing.

Around Ross: Goodrich and Symond's Yat Rock

Amid dramatic scenery some five miles south of Ross off the A40, the sullen sandstone mass of **Goodrich Castle** (daily: April–Oct 10am–6pm; Oct–March 10am–4pm; £3.10;

EH) commands clear views beyond the encircling river to the hills and forests of Wales. Its position guaranteed its importance as a border stronghold from the twelfth century, and the substantial ruins incorporate a Norman keep, a maze of later rooms and passageways and walkable ramparts, complete with murder holes, slits through which boiling oil or water was poured onto the attackers down below. During the Civil War, a determined Royalist garrison held on until the Parliamentarians built themselves a special cannon, "Roaring Meg", which soon brought victory – a considerable achievement considering the unreliability of the technology: large cannons had the unfortunate habit of blowing up as soon as anyone fired them.

Bus #34 (not Sun) from Ross to Monmouth stops at **GOODRICH VILLAGE**, from where it's an easy fifteen-minute walk north to the castle. There's a riverside **youth hostel** (☎01594/860300; closed Nov–March) just a mile or so south of the village in a former Victorian rectory at tiny Welsh Bicknor. From the hostel, it's a three-mile hike along the river to **Symond's Yat Rock**, which rises high above a loop in the Wye. It's one of the region's most celebrated views – and you can also get there by car from Goodrich village: head west along the B4229 and watch for the signs that direct you down a narrow country lane. Beyond the rock, the road continues (as the B4432) on into the Forest of Dean (see below).

The Forest of Dean

Wedged between the Rivers Wye and Severn to the south of Ross-on-Wye, the **Forest of Dean** is among the oldest and most extensive tracts of broadleaf woodland in Britain. It was designated a Royal Forest by the Normans in the early eleventh century, but as timber and metal extraction gathered pace during the Tudor era, it was thinned to the brink of extinction, forcing Henry VIII to embark on a massive replanting programme. This was intensified by Charles II, who also ordered the wholesale destruction of the region's iron mines in order to reduce the massive consumption of charcoal essential for the smelting process. Yet it was not until the early nineteenth century, when some thirty million acorns were planted by the government, that the forest's decline was finally reversed. Today, an estimated twenty million trees, predominantly silver birch, huge oaks and ash, cloak the area's winding river valleys, while greenery and wild flowers have largely reclaimed the ruined coal and iron mines, slag heaps and foundries that formerly flourished here.

With so many large towns and cities less than an hour away by road, it's not surprising that tens of thousands of visitors congregate here every year, most of them to picnic at sites set aside by the Forestry Commission. However, the central core – the part of the forest between Coleford and Cinderford – is still large enough to absorb even the heavy bank holiday crowds. A network of marked trails enables you to penetrate this area, both on foot and by bicycle, while bus services connect the major towns and cities. For timetable information, check with the Gloucestershire public transport line (☎01452/527516).

A good primer if you've just arrived in the region is the **Dean Heritage Centre**, at Soudley near Cinderford, in the northeast corner of the forest (daily: April–Sept 10am–6pm; March–Oct 10am–4pm; £3.30), which covers local history with exhibitions on mining, forestry and local crafts. From here, bypass soulless **CINDERFORD**, an incongruously grey town surrounded by industrial estates, and head straight through the heart of the forest on the B4226 towards Coleford. No buses cover this route, but the road passes within a stone's throw of **Beechenhurst Inclosure**, a picnic site and park information centre that's a good starting point for nature walks and the famous **Forest of Dean Sculpture Trail**. An easy walk (3.5miles), the trail is dotted with contemporary artwork and sculptures, including a giant chair on the crest of a hill.

This part of the forest is also a great area for **cycling**: Pedalabikeaway, 500 yards west of Beechenhurst (☎01594/860065), rents hybrid trail bikes, Victorian trikes, wheelchair tandems and mountain bikes at very reasonable rates; they also hand out maps showing the best routes.

Coleford and St Briavels

Four miles further west, the B4226 emerges from the woods at **COLEFORD**, bereft of trees but the most attractive of the larger forest towns and home of the area's main **tourist office**, on the High Street (July & Aug Mon–Sat 10am–4pm, Sun 10am–1.30pm; rest of year closed Sun; ☎01594/812388). Coleford, along with the surrounding villages, is the principal **accommodation** base for the forest. Two good **B&Bs** hereabouts are *Rookery Farmhouse*, a tastefully converted stable just over a mile west of town in Newland (☎01594/832432; no credit cards; ②); and the inexpensive *Allary House*, occupying a Victorian town house in Coleford at 14 Boxbush Rd (☎01594/835306; no credit cards; ①).

A couple of miles south of Coleford, off the B4228 Chepstow road, the much-visited **Clearwell Caves** (March–Oct daily 10am–5pm; £3.50) comprise a natural cave system enlarged by generations of miners. Nine caverns can be explored on foot and without a guide; you can also don a boiler suit, lamp and hard hat for trips to the deeper parts of the mines (£8), still worked to supply tinted pigments to the cosmetics and paints industries. Once each year at Hallowe'en, the mines host an underground "Rave in the Cave", complete with sound and light system and DJs.

Pushing on south along the B4228, it's a short hop to the pretty rose-stone village of **ST BRIAVELS**, perched on a ridge overlooking the Wye. A forbidding Norman **castle** (April–Sept daily 1–4pm) crowns a bluff in the centre of the village, its weathered stonework encircled by a dry moat. Formerly used by King John as a hunting lodge, and the region's administrative centre since medieval times, it now accommodates one of England's most impressive **youth hostels** (☎01594/530272; closed Nov–Jan). Beneath the keep extends a network of tunnels originally excavated in the thirteenth century by local miners. As a reward for their work, men over the age of 21 and born within one hundred miles of St Briavels were granted the right to mine for coal and iron ore anywhere in the Forest. This law is still in place, and within living memory a significant number of foresters made their living as **"Free Miners"**, paying a royalty each year from their earnings to the Crown. Today only a couple of commercial Free Miners survive, but some locals continue to exercise their ancient right to extract coal for household consumption from disused surface mines, known as "scowle holes".

If you're tempted to **stay**, the hostel is the obvious choice, though there are also a handful of en-suite rooms upstairs in *The George*, a friendly old pub beside the castle (☎01594/530228; ②). The pub also serves good food – mostly tasty local fish, meat and game – inside and on the rear terrace overlooking the castle moat.

Shropshire

One of England's largest and least populated counties, **Shropshire** stretches from its long and winding border with Wales to the very edge of the urban West Midlands. Its most unique attraction is industrial: it was here that the Industrial Revolution made a huge stride forward with the spanning of the River Severn by the very first **iron bridge**. The assorted industries that subsequently squeezed into the gorge are long gone, but a series of **museums** celebrate their craftsmanship – from tiles and iron through to porcelain and even clay pipes. The River Severn also flows through the county town of **Shrewsbury**, whose antique centre holds dozens of old half-timbered buildings, though **Ludlow**, further to the south, has the edge when it comes to handsome Tudor and Jacobean houses. Some of the most beautiful parts of Shropshire are

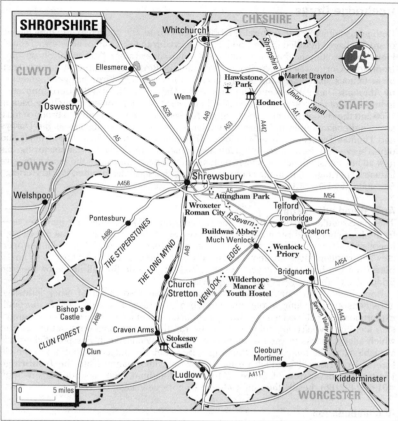

© Crown copyright

to the south and east of Shrewsbury in the twin ridges of **Wenlock Edge** and the **Long Mynd**, both of which are prime hiking areas, best explored from the attractive little towns of **Much Wenlock** and **Church Stretton** respectively. Out west, the hills become increasingly barren and dramatic as they approach the Welsh border. This is one of the remotest parts of England, a solitary landscape dusted with tiny hamlets and the occasional town, amongst which **Bishop's Castle** and **Clun** are perhaps the most appealing.

Yet, for all its attractions, Shropshire remains well off the main tourist routes, one factor protecting the county's remoteness being the paucity of its **public transport**. Shrewsbury and Telford are connected to Birmingham, and Ludlow, Craven Arms and Church Stretton are connected to Shrewsbury on the Hereford line, but that's about the limit of the **train** services, whilst rural **buses** tend to connect outlying villages on just a few days of the week. Precise bus timetable details are available on either the **Shropshire Traveline** (☎0345/056785) or for Telford, Ironbridge and Much Wenlock, the **Telford Traveline** (☎01952/200005).

Ironbridge Gorge

Both geographically and culturally, **Ironbridge Gorge**, the collective title for a cluster of small villages huddled in the wooded Severn valley to the south of new-town Telford, looks to the cities of the West Midlands conurbation rather than rural Shropshire. Ironbridge Gorge was the crucible of the Industrial Revolution, a process encapsulated by its famous span across the Severn gorge – the world's first iron bridge, engineered by Abraham Darby and opened on New Year's Day, 1781. He was the third innovative industrialist of that name – the first Abraham Darby started iron-smelting here back in 1709 and the second invented the forging process that made it possible to produce massive single beams in iron. Under the guidance of such creative figures as the Darbys and Thomas Telford, the area's factories once churned out engines, rails, wheels and other heavy-duty iron pieces in quantities unmatched in England. Manufacturing has now all but vanished, but the surviving monuments make the gorge the most extensive industrial heritage sight in the country – and one that has been granted World Heritage Site status by UNESCO.

Arrival and information

There are regular **buses** to Ironbridge Gorge from Telford and less frequent services from Shrewsbury and Birmingham, but travelling round the gorge by bus is well-nigh impossible – the shuttle that used to transport visitors between sights no longer operates and regular buses are few and far between. The best bet, therefore, is to hire a **bike** from Ironbridge by Bicycle (☎01952/884391), beside the toll house on the iron bridge itself: advance reservations are advised.

Ironbridge Gorge contains five museums and an assortment of other industrial attractions spread along a four-mile stretch of the River Severn Valley. A thorough exploration takes at least a day – two for comfort. Each museum charges its own admission fee, but if you're intending to visit several, then buy a **passport ticket** (£9.50), which allows access to each of them once in any calendar year. Passport tickets are available at all the main sights. **Parking** is free at all the museums, but not in the village of Ironbridge itself. Pick up local maps and information from the **Ironbridge Visitor Information Centre** (Mon–Fri 9am–5pm, Sat & Sun 10am–5pm; ☎01952/432166), beside the iron bridge in Ironbridge village.

Accommodation

Most visitors to the gorge come for the day, but there are several pleasant **B&Bs** in Ironbridge village, which is where you'll want to be. Two of the best are *The Library House*, which occupies a charming Georgian villa just yards from the iron bridge at 11 Severn Bank (☎01952/432299; no credit cards; ②), and *Eley's Bridge View*, whose spick and span rooms are also a stone's throw from the bridge at 10 Tontine Hill (☎01952/432541; ②). Alternatively, *Coalbrookdale Villa* is an attractive Victorian Gothic ironmasters' house up the hill from the bridge in tiny Paradise (☎01952/433450; no credit cards; ②). The gorge also boasts two **youth hostels**: one in the old Workers' Institute opposite the Coalbrookdale Museum of Iron, the other in the old Coalport China factory. They share the same telephone number (☎01952/588755) and are open all year.

Ironbridge village

There must have been an awful lot of nervous sweat during the construction of the **iron bridge** over the River Severn in the late 1770s. The first of its kind, no one was quite sure how the new material would wear and although the single span design looked sound, the fear was the bridge would tumble into the river. To compensate, Abraham

Darby used more iron than was strictly necessary, but the end result still manages to appear graceful, arching between the steep banks with the river way down below. The settlement at the north end of the span was promptly renamed **IRONBRIDGE**, and today its brown-brick houses climb prettily up the river bank. The village is also home to the **Ironbridge Visitor Information Centre** (Mon–Fri 9am–5pm, Sat & Sun 10am–5pm; free), which introduces you to the site and its history with a short audio-visual show and small exhibition.

Coalbrookdale's Museum of Iron

Just to the west of Ironbridge village, the gorge's big industrial deal was once **COALBROOKDALE**'s iron foundry, which boomed throughout the nineteenth century and employed up to 4000 men and boys. The foundry has been imaginatively converted into the **Museum of Iron** (daily 10am–5pm; £4.50), with a wide range of displays on ironmaking in general and the history of the company in particular. There are superb examples of Victorian and Edwardian ironwork including art castings – stags, dogs and water fountains for instance – that became the house speciality. In the complex too is the restored **furnace** where Abraham Darby pioneered the use of coke as a smelting fuel in place of charcoal. From the furnace, it's about 100 yards up to a pair of old ironmaster's homes, **Dale House** and **Rosehill** (admission included with Coalbrookdale museum), which contains items that once belonged to the Darby family.

The Tar Tunnel and Coalport China Museum

From Ironbridge, it's a couple of miles east along the river's edge to the **Tar Tunnel** (April–Oct daily 10am–5pm; £1), where bitumen oozes naturally from the walls. Close by, the **Coalport China Museum** (daily 10am–5pm; £3.80) occupies the restored factory where Coalport porcelain and china was manufactured from 1792 until the works transferred to Stoke-on-Trent in 1926. The complex has several well-preserved examples of the conical bottle-kilns that were long the hallmark of the pottery industry, and inside the museum there's an engrossing assortment of the gaudy crockery for which the company was famous.

Jackfield Tile Museum

On the opposite bank of the river, accessible either by footbridge from near the Tar Tunnel or the road bridge a mile upstream, is the **Jackfield Tile Museum** (daily 10am–5pm; £3.80). Housed in an old tile factory, the museum features a superb collection of brightly coloured tiles, from the fancy, flowery patterns of washstand splashbacks through to intricate Victorian fireplace tiles and a folksy *Punch and Judy* panel from the 1920s.

Broseley Clay Tobacco Pipe Museum

Heading west from Jackfield, along the south bank of the River Severn, follow the signs to the enjoyable **Broseley Clay Tobacco Pipe Museum** (April–Oct daily 10am–5pm; £2.50). During the late seventeenth and early eighteenth centuries, the satellite settlement of Broseley, formerly a source of raw materials for the foundries across the river, became a boom town in its own right, producing clay pipes for the swelling ranks of tobacco smokers in Britain. Occupying one of three factories that once existed here, the museum charts the history of smoking with a lively exhibition that culminates with some priceless film footage showing how the arm-length "Church Warden" pipes were made. After the rise of the cigarette eventually brought about the factory's closure, the building and its contents were left exactly as they were the day the workers downed tools. To their credit, the museum's creators have done their best to preserve this time-capsule effect, shunning actors in period costume in favour of informative panels.

Blists Hill Victorian Town

Doubling back to the north bank of the River Severn, **Blists Hill Victorian Town** (daily 10am–5pm; £6.80), lies a mile or so up the hill from the riverbank. Staffed by period-dressed employees, the rambling site encloses various reconstructed Victorian buildings – among them a school, a candlemakers, a doctor's surgery complete with horrific instruments, a gas-lit pub, a wrought-iron works and a slaughterhouse. Jam-packed on most summer days, it's especially popular with school parties.

Eating and drinking

For **food** in the Ironbridge Gorge, try the excellent *Meadow Inn* pub (☎01952/433193), down by the river on Buildwas Road about a mile west of the bridge, or the equally renowned *Horse and Jockey*, 15 Jockey Bank (☎01952/433798), just north of Coalport, whose legendary steak and kidney pie draws punters from miles away. If you're looking for something other than a pub meal, a good bet is the moderately priced *Oliver's Vegetarian Bistro* (☎01952/433086; closed Mon), on the High Street by the bridge. Anyone on a tight budget should head for the youth hostel in Coalport, where you can sit down to a filling three-course meal for under a fiver; they also offer healthy vegetarian options. **Real-ale** buffs will enjoy the *Coalbrookdale Inn*, past the Museum of Iron, which has the CAMRA stamp of approval for its excellent selection of beers.

Much Wenlock and the Wenlock Edge

Heading west from Ironbridge village along the northern bank of the River Severn, it's only a couple of miles along the A4169 to **Buildwas Abbey** (April–Oct daily 10am–6pm; £1.75; EH), a roofless but otherwise well-preserved twelfth-century structure in meadowland by the River Severn. In many ways its setting and isolation lend it more atmosphere than the skeletal ruin of the eleventh-century **priory** (April–Oct daily 10am–6pm; Nov–March Wed–Sun 10am–4pm; £2.30; EH) at **MUCH WENLOCK**, five miles to the south. With some solid Norman carving in its chapter house and lavatorium, the priory stands amid fine topiary in a dipped basin of green fields on the edge of the tiny town. Unfailingly quaint, Much Wenlock itself is a patchwork of Tudor, Jacobean and Georgian buildings, their style captured perfectly by the **Guildhall**, sitting pretty on sturdy oak columns in the middle of the Butter Market. The town is well stocked with accommodation, most of it listed by the **tourist office** on The Square (June–Aug daily 10.30am–1pm & 2–5pm; April–May & Sept–Oct Mon–Sat 10.30am–1pm & 2–5pm, Sun 2–5pm; ☎01952/727679). Pick of the **hotels** hereabouts has to be the charming *Talbot Inn* (☎01952/727077; ⑥), an old coaching inn that was formerly part of the abbey, with exposed beams, fresh flowers in summer and open fires during the winter. Of the **B&Bs**, one place in Sheinton Street at the top of town stands out – the *Old Police Station*, which offers two comfortable en-suite rooms and delicious breakfasts (☎01952/727056; no credit cards; ②).

A good reason to base yourself in this area for a night or two is to walk the beautiful **Wenlock Edge**, a limestone escarpment running twenty-odd miles southwest from the Ironbridge Gorge to Craven Arms (see p.546). Its south side is a gently shelving slope of exposed farmland, while the thickly wooded north face scarps steeply to the Shropshire plains, affording superb views across a sea of patchwork fields to the hills of the Welsh border. Much of the Edge is today owned by the National Trust, and a network of waymarked trails, graded by colour according to length and difficulty, winds through the woodland from a string of car parks along the B4371, which hugs the ridge from Much Wenlock to **Longville-in-the-Dale**. The paths are easy to follow and panels erected at the car parks outline the routes, but it's still a good idea to pick a copy of Ian

R. Jones's *Wenlock Edge* leaflet from the tourist office in Much Wenlock, which describes the trails in detail with the help of a hand-drawn map.

Two excellent **hostels** provide inexpensive accommodation for walkers and cyclists in the area, although neither is easily accessible by public transport. At Newton House Farm, one mile west of Much Wenlock on the main Shrewsbury road, the *Stokes Barn Bunkhouse* offers beds in a converted barn (☎01952/727293), while the YHA have one of their flagship properties at **Wilderhope Manor** (mid-Feb to Oct; ☎01694/771363). This magnificent Elizabethan mansion is set deep in idyllic countryside one and a half miles south of the B4371. Wilderhope tends to be block-booked by school groups during the summer term, but usually has vacancies at other times, although reservations are recommended throughout the year. Midland Red West **bus** #712 runs to within striking distance of the youth hostel from Ludlow on Mondays and Fridays, or you can catch one of the more frequent services from Ludlow and Bridgnorth to nearby Shipton, a couple of miles across the fields, and walk from there.

Bridgnorth

BRIDGNORTH, nine miles southeast of Much Wenlock along the A458, may be in Shropshire, but – with Wolverhampton just thirty minutes' drive away – it has all the bustle of the West Midlands. Spilling down a sheer-sided bluff beside the River Severn, the town prospered throughout the medieval era as a bridging point for the river, but was badly mauled and its economy dislocated by the Parliamentary army during the Civil War. Today, Bridgnorth is at its prettiest on top of the bluff in the **High Town**, where the High Street is interrupted by the seventeenth-century **Town Hall**, a half-tim-bered building perched on an arcaded base. At its southern end, High Street runs into West Coast Street. This soon leads to the domed **St Mary's church**, a solemn-looking edifice designed by Thomas Telford, and the shattered thirty-foot **tower** which is all that remains of the medieval castle: the ruin leans at a precarious angle of seventeen degrees. From here, a short but pleasant walkway tracks along the bluff above the river, ending up at the century-old **cliff railway** (Mon–Sat 8am–8pm, Sun noon–8pm; 50p), which clanks up the steepest rail gradient in Britain to connect Bank Street (off West Coast Street) to the Low Town below.

Bridgnorth is also the northern terminus of the **Severn Valley Railway**, whose trains steam down the valley to Kidderminster, some thirteen miles away. Trains oper-ate all year on a minimum of three days a week (Jan & Feb), increasing to a daily ser-vice for most of the summer (2–9 times daily). It takes a little over an hour for the train to travel from Bridgnorth to Kidderminster with the return fare costing between £9 and £20 (further details on ☎01299/403816). In Bridgnorth, the SVR station is in High Town across the footbridge from West Coast Street.

It only takes an hour or two to look round Bridgnorth and afterwards there are reg-ular **bus** services on to Shrewsbury and Ludlow amongst many possible destinations. Most countywide services arrive and depart from the bus stops on the High Street. If you do decide to stay, the **tourist office**, in the library on Listley Street off the south end of High Street (April–Oct Mon–Wed & Fri–Sat 9.30am–5pm, Thurs 10am–1pm & 2–5pm, Sun 11am–1pm & 2–4pm; Nov–March Mon–Wed & Fri–Sat 9.30am–5pm; ☎01746/763257), has a list of local **B&Bs**. For **food**, try *Quaints*, a neat and inexpen-sive vegetarian bistro on St Mary's Street, just off the High Street near the Town Hall.

Shrewsbury and around

SHREWSBURY, the county town of Shropshire, sits in a narrow loop of the River Severn, a three-hundred-yard spit of land being all that keeps the town centre from becoming an island. It would be difficult to design a better defensive site, and fortifications were first built on this narrow neck in the fifth century, after the departure of the Roman legions from the nearby garrison town of Wroxeter. The Normans were swift to realize the strategic potential of the site too, building the first stone castle, which was expanded and strengthened by Edward I in the late thirteenth century. As the town grew prosperous on the back of the Welsh wool trade its importance grew, reaching its apogee when Shrewsbury briefly became capital-in-exile for King Charles I during the early years of the Civil War. The eighteenth century saw the town evolve as a staging post on the busy London to Holyhead route and, although this traffic withered with the arrival of the railways, the town had by then become the host of a lively social season, patronized by the sort of people who could afford to send their offspring to the famous Shrewsbury School. The top-notch gatherings are, however, long gone and nowadays Shrewsbury is an easy-going, middling market town, albeit with several especially fine Tudor and Jacobean streetscapes.

Arrival, information and accommodation

Shrewsbury is well connected by **train** to the rest of the country, and its station, at the northeast edge of the centre, is a popular departure point for scenic rail journeys into mid-Wales. **Buses** from London, Birmingham and beyond pull into the National Express stand at the Raven Meadows bus station, off the Smithfield Road, five minutes' walk west of the train station. The **tourist office** is up the hill from the two stations, on The Square (May–Sept Mon–Sat 10am–6pm, Sun 10am–4pm; Oct–April Mon–Sat 10am–5pm; ☎01743/350761). The labyrinthine lanes and alleys of Shrewsbury's centre can be baffling, but fortunately it's too small an area to be lost in for long. As a general guide, Castle Gates/Castle Street runs from the train station up to Pride Hill, a short pedestrianized street that meets St Mary's Street/Dogpole at one end and High Street/Wyle Cop at the other. The Square off the High Street is at the heart of the city centre.

Shrewsbury has one particularly good **hotel**, the *Prince Rupert*, which occupies a tastefully converted old building, right in the centre of town off Pride Hill on Butcher Row (☎01743/499955; ⑤). Less expensive options in the centre include *The Lion*, a classic Georgian coaching inn on the Wyle Cop (☎01743/353107; ④) and the *College Hill Guest House*, a pleasant **B&B** in an old listed building at 11 College Hill, near The Square (☎01743/365744; no credit cards; ②). Most of the town's B&Bs are beyond the centre, with several dotted along Abbey Foregate, which runs east from the English Bridge at the foot of Wyle Cop: try the unassuming, neat and tidy *Abbey Court Guest House*, at no. 134 (☎01743/364416; no credit cards; ①). The **youth hostel**, housed in a former Victorian ironmaster's house, is about one mile east of the centre, at the far end of Abbey Foregate (☎01743/360179); it's near Lord Hill's Column, the monument erected in memory of Wellington's sidekick at the Battle of Waterloo. Take bus #8 or #26 from the bus station.

The Town

The sandstone **Castle**, sitting high above the castellated train station, rests on the site of fortifications that go back a millennium and a half. Today's buildings date mainly from the thirteenth century, although the great architect and engineer Thomas Telford was brought in during the 1780s to shore up the remains and turn the castle into an extravagant private home for local bigwig Sir William Pulteney. It is now home to the dull **Shropshire Regimental Museum** (Tues–Sat plus Easter–Sept Sun 10am–4.30pm; £2), a far less interesting attraction than the annual World Music Day (☎01743/231142), which takes place here in July and makes the most of the castle's dramatic setting.

Castle Gates winds up the hill from the station into the heart of the river loop where the medieval town took root. Off Pride Hill, there are several especially appealing half-timbered buildings dotted along **Butcher Row**, which leads into the quiet precincts of St Alkmund's church, where there's a charming view of the fine old buildings of **Fish Street**. From the church, Bear Steps clambers down to the High Street, on the far side of which, in the narrow Georgian confines of The Square, is the **Old Market Hall**, a heavy-duty stone structure built in 1596. To the south of The Square is College Hill, home of the lacklustre **Clive House Museum** (Tues–Sat plus mid-May to Sept Sun 10am–4pm; £2). Occupying the Georgian town house of Robert Clive of India (1725–1774), the museum focuses on period Georgian and Victorian interiors rather than plumping for an examination of Clive's extraordinary career. The conqueror of a vast chunk of India, locally born Clive was elevated to the peerage following his defeat of the ruler of Bengal, but was later the subject of a full-scale parliamentary enquiry into his conduct; though acquitted, he ended up committing suicide shortly afterwards.

A short stroll to the west, on Barker Street near the Welsh Bridge, is Shrewsbury's best museum and the main showpiece for both the town and its county, **Rowley's House** (Tues–Sat plus mid-May to Sept Sun 10am–5pm; £2). An ostentatious 1590s town house with a seventeenth-century brick residence tacked on, it houses a wide range of displays relating to local life, with the most interesting exhibits coming from the nearby Roman city of **Wroxeter** (see p.545), including a unique silver mirror from the third century AD.

On the western side of town, the pristine **Quarry Park**, home of the celebrated annual August **flower festival**, runs gently down to the river's edge, overlooked by the wedding-cake tower of the town's most celebrated church, **St Chad's** (daily: April–Oct 8am–5pm; Nov–Easter 10.30am–3.30pm; free). England's largest round church, St Chad's was consecrated in 1792 as a replacement for the parish church that had collapsed as the clock struck four one morning in 1788.

Back on The Square, High Street snakes down the hill to become **Wyle Cop**, lined with elegant Georgian buildings and leading to the **English Bridge**, which provides a handsome view of the town as it crosses the Severn. Beyond the bridge is Shrewsbury's most important ecclesiastical building, the **Abbey** (daily: Easter–Oct 9.30am–5.30pm; Nov–Easter 10.30am–3pm; free), now locked in the middle of a traffic intersection on Abbey Foregate. Founded in the 1080s by Roger de Montgomery, who was also responsible for the first stone castle here, the abbey was a Benedictine monastery that became a major political and religious force in Shropshire until the Dissolution. Unusually, the church and monastery buildings were not destroyed by the king's henchmen – indeed, the abbey church continued life as a parish church. Inside, the best feature is the huge west window of heraldic glass, dating from the fourteenth century. Underneath it is the original Norman door, and four of the nave pillars and their connecting arches also date from the original church. The monastery stood largely intact until the 1830s when a new road swept away most of the buildings. More recently, the remaining monastic outhouses have been converted into a new heritage centre, **The Shrewsbury Quest** (daily: April–Oct 10am–6.30pm; Nov–March 10am–5.30pm; £4.25), which re-creates the living conditions of medieval monks, basing the whole thing around Ellis Peters' *Brother Cadfael* stories. For Cadfael fans there's a mystery to be solved through clues hidden in barrels of corn, clothes chests and haunted bedrooms, as well as a replica of the author's study. For the more historically inquisitive the scriptorium, complete with quills, natural pigments and calligraphic stamps, and the garden planted with herbs used by medieval medics, will prove more inspiring.

Eating and drinking

For daytime **food**, try the *Goodlife Wholefood Restaurant* in the antique surroundings of Barrack's Passage, off Wyle Cop, or snack at *Philpotts Quality Sandwiches*, which deserves its name and is located at 15 Butcher Row. In the evening, there's the *Sol*, 82 Wyle Cop (☎01743/340560; closed Sun), an outstanding if pricey restaurant featuring local ingredients like Shropshire lamb cooked in a broadly Mediterranean style, and tasty tandoori at *Shalimar*, by the abbey at 23 Abbey Foregate (☎01743/366658). Some of the best **pub food** in the centre is served at *Loggerheads*, in St Alkmud's Place, with wood-panelled walls and exposed beams; try their filling "Big Head Pie" – steak pieces topped with puff pastry and served with chips, salad and a pint for around £5. Other good **pubs** are the *Severn Stars* on Coleham Head, just over the English Bridge from the town centre; the smoke-free *Three Fishes*, in an ancient building on Fish Street; and the lively *Coach & Horses*, on Swan Hill just south of The Square. The *Music Hall* **cinema** next door to the tourist office on The Square, screens art-house as well as mainstream releases (☎01743/244255).

Hawkstone Park

A common activity for eighteenth- and nineteenth-century gentry was to convert their estates into pleasure parks for strolling, hunting and contemplating nature. **Hawkstone Park** (Easter–Oct 10am–4/5pm, Nov–Easter Sat & Sun only 10am–dusk; £4.75), which lies about ten miles north of Shrewsbury between Hodnet and Weston, is an outstanding example of this. The park, which consists of a maze of tree-lined avenues, high ridges and sandstone cliffs, has lain undisturbed by all but a few locals for almost a hundred years. It was designed by the Hill family, who owned the estate from 1748 until 1895, and made good use of the lie of the land – rocky outcrops and two roughly parallel ridges in an otherwise flat land. On one ridge is a tall monument, a tower with 150 spiral steps leading to its windswept balcony. More unusual features along the one- or two-hour circular walk around the park include Swiss Bridge – two tree trunks spanning a deep gully – a hermit's cave and a curious set of dim and eerie grottos on Grotto Hill, from the top of which the views stretch for miles across the plains to the Welsh hills. Parts of the path are a little tricky underfoot, especially towards Foxes Knob, a sandstone outcrop reached via dark passageways snaking through the rock. Bus #572 runs from Shrewsbury to Hodnet (30min) on Tuesdays and Sundays, from where it's a two-mile walk to the park.

Attingham Park

In a more ostentatious mould is **Attingham Park** (April–Oct Mon, Tues & Fri–Sun 1.30–5pm; £4; NT), four miles southeast of Shrewsbury near the village of Atcham. Originally the stately pile of Noel Hill, the first Lord Berwick, this imposing Georgian mansion was designed in 1782 by George Steuart, with later additions by John Nash. The nearby bridge across the Severn was already completed when Hill decided to build here, and if his house was to be visible from the major thoroughfare, then it had to be appropriately impressive – hence the grand scale of the Neoclassical facade, with its four giant pillars and colossal portico. Crammed with luxurious furniture and souvenirs from successive Grand Tours of Europe, the interior typifies the Regency period's predilection for all things French and Italian. Thomas Hill, the second lord, was an ardent collector of Renaissance art, and his picture gallery, added in 1805 and spanned by the world's first cast-iron-rib ceiling (a product of the Coalbrookdale Company; see p.539), is Attingham's chief attraction. However, the mad spending spree in Naples during which most of the paintings exhibited here were acquired nearly bankrupted the estate, and Hill was forced to sell off many of his finest pieces to pay for building work on the house. These days, what remains, along with Attingham's collections of Regency silver and Staffordshire ceramics, are the property of the National Trust.

The surrounding **park** (March–Oct 8am–9pm, Nov–Feb 8am–5pm; grounds only £1.80; NT) was landscaped by Repton and offers pleasant riverside and woodland walks. From Shrewsbury, there are several **bus** services a day to Atcham, half a mile from the house.

Wroxeter Roman City

From Atcham, the B4380 heads east along the course of Watling Street, the former Roman military route that once linked central England and the wild Welsh borders with St Albans, London, Canterbury, Dover, and eventually the trans-European road network. A little under two thousand years ago, this now sleepy area of open farmland, a stone's throw from where Watling Street met the River Severn, was Britain's fourth largest city, Viroconium. The site, initially occupied by Cornovii tribespeople (traces of their fort are still visible atop the conical hill dominating the southern horizon), was first developed by Emperor Nero in 58 AD as part of his drive to conquer Wales. When Hadrian visited sixty years later, he ordered that Viroconium should be doubled in size to further his policy of strengthening the empire by expanding its frontier settlements. A collection of grand buildings was duly erected, and although some were destroyed in a fire around 160 AD, the ruins of the civic centre, dubbed **Wroxeter Roman City** by English Heritage (April–Oct daily 10am–6pm; Nov–March Wed–Sun 10am–4pm; £3; EH), are still impressive, particularly the large chunk of masonry that once formed part of the wall surrounding the central bath complex. You'll need a vivid imagination to picture the ruined grid plan as a teeming Roman metropolis, but the site's modest museum, together with English Heritage's informative accompanying booklet (£1.50), help fill in the gaps, while a complementary walkman tour, complete with stirring musical soundtrack and breathless voice-over, will keep any kids you might be travelling with happy for half an hour.

The Long Mynd and Church Stretton

Beginning about ten miles south of Shrewsbury, the upland heaths of the **Long Mynd**, ten miles long and between two to four miles wide, run parallel to and just to the west of the A49. This is prime walking territory and the heathlands are latticed with footpaths, the best of which offer sweeping views over the border to the Black Mountains of Wales. Nestled at the foot of the Mynd beside the A49 is **CHURCH STRETTON**, a tidy little place and one-time fashionable Victorian resort that makes the best base for hiking the area. The village also possesses the dinky parish church of St Lawrence, parts of which – especially the nave – are Norman. Look out also for the fertility symbol over the north doorway – it's a Sheila-na-gig comparable to the one in Kilpeck (see p.533). In the centre of the village near the church is the **tourist office** (Easter–Sept Mon–Sat 10am–1pm & 2–5pm; ☎01694/723133), which stocks a wide range of leaflets detailing local walks, hikes and mountain bike routes. Perhaps the most obvious hike is the short, half-mile stroll west up along the National Trust's **Carding Mill Valley** to the **Chalet Pavilion** tearoom and information centre (April–Oct daily 11am–5pm; Nov–March Sat & Sun 11am–4pm). Alternatively, strike up **Caer Caradoc**, the steep hill that looms directly east of the village; crowned by an extensive iron-age hill fort, its summit affords superb views of the Mynd and the rolling pasture land that extends east towards Birmingham. Waymarked trails lead to the top and down the other side to the picturesque hamlet of **CARDINGTON**, whose cosy village pub serves filling bar meals and fine pints of *Shropshire Lad* bitter. You can do the round walk in three to four hours.

Church Stretton is accessible from Shrewsbury and Ludlow by **train** and **bus**. Most buses stop in the centre of the village; the train station is a short walk from the tourist office just off the A49. There's no shortage of good-value accommodation in and around Church Stretton, much of it on lovely farms overlooking the Mynd. Recommended **B&Bs** include *Acton Scott Farm*, a seventeenth-century building one mile out of Stretton on the A49 with log fires and a choice of standard or en-suite rooms (☎01694/781260; no credit cards; ①), and *Dalesford*, on the western edge of town at the mouth of the Carding Mill Valley (☎01694/723228; no credit cards; ①). For a little more luxury, try *Jinlye*, on Castle Hill in All Stretton, one mile north, which backs onto the

Long Mynd and has great views (☎01694/723243; ③). **Campers** have a choice of several sites. These include *Small Batch* (☎01694/723358; closed Oct–Easter), one mile south at Little Stretton, which enjoys a gorgeous situation but is pretty simple, and the pricier and better equipped *Ley Hill Farm* (☎01694/771366; closed Nov–Feb), deep in the countryside near Cardington, with panoramic views of the surrounding hills. **Bike rental** is available from Terry's, 6 Castle Hill, All Stretton (☎01694/724334).

The **youth hostel** at **Bridges Long Mynd** (☎01588/650656), five miles' hike west from Church Stretton near Ratlinghope, is a splendid base for walks, sitting between the Long Mynd and the **Stiperstones**, a remote range of boggy heather dotted with ancient cairns and earthworks. Marooned amid gentler country east of the town on the B4371, near Longville-in-the-Dale, **Wilderhope Manor** is this area's other hotel; it's featured on p.541, along with an account of the Wenlock Edge.

Craven Arms and Stokesay Castle

CRAVEN ARMS, the next stop down the rail line from Church Stretton, lies half a mile or so north of the hamlet of **STOKESAY**, site of one of England's most appealing manor houses. **Stokesay Castle** (April–Oct daily 10am–6pm; Nov–March Wed–Sun 10am–4pm; £2.95; EH), as it's known, comprises a collection of leaning, half-timbered buildings that span a range of over three hundred years, gathered around a neat grassy courtyard. The main block is a thirteenth-century fortified manor, originally built by a prosperous wool merchant for the princely price of a sparrowhawk. Beautifully restored by English Heritage, it contains a vast banqueting hall that retains its central fireplace, vaulted timbers and large windows. The size of the windows is actually very significant: Edward I's suppression of the Welsh had made border life a good deal more secure for the English, so they could afford to weaken the walls to let more light in. Across the central courtyard is the black and yellow gatehouse, built over three hundred years after the manor house yet forming a harmonious group with the main building and the tiny parish church next door. The church was largely rebuilt in the mid-seventeenth century, but some of the original Norman features remain.

From Stokesay, it's just seven miles south to Ludlow or you can double back up the A49 for a mile or two and take the A489 west to Bishop's Castle and Clun.

Bishop's Castle and Clun

BISHOP'S CASTLE, midway between Offa's Dyke and the southern edge of the Long Mynd, is a real treat – uncluttered, very pretty and full of fine secondhand bookshops and junk stores. **Buses** from Shrewsbury and from Montgomery, Knighton, Clun and Ludlow, drop you at the bottom of the High Street, which winds past half-timbered frontages to the miniature Georgian **Town Hall** – this was England's smallest borough until 1967 – and the lurching **House on Crutches**. Stroll up past the town hall and veer to the right to reach the most renowned building in Bishop's Castle, the seventeenth-century **Three Tuns brewery** and its time-warped pub in Salop Street, which serves up traditional home-brew – a pale cider-coloured concoction that's deceptively potent; they also do excellent and imaginative bar meals here. What must be England's most eccentric **tourist office** is housed in a second-hand shop called *Old Time*, at 29 High St (daily 10am–10pm; ☎01588/638467; no credit cards; ①) – staff here can sort out accommodation, and offer rooms of their own.

Five miles south of Bishop's Castle, the modest village of **CLUN** is an excellent base for forest walks and jaunts out across the surrounding hills that roll west over the Welsh border. The village also embraces the battered ruins of a medieval **castle** (dawn–dusk; free), built by the Normans but abandoned in the sixteenth century. The castle's only noteworthy feature today is the chunky masonry of the ruined keep, but the setting more than compensates – the keep is raised on an earthen mound cradled by the river below. In and around Clun are several excellent **B&Bs**. Amongst them is the *Old Farmhouse* (☎01588/640695; no credit cards; ①), an eighteenth-century farmhouse with a pretty garden one mile from – and 300 feet above – Clun. The small **youth hostel** (☎01588/640582) is in a converted watermill, on the northern edge of Clun, about ten minutes' walk from the nearest bus stop. As regards **pubs**, Clun has two good ones – the *Buffalo Inn*, which offers excellent bar food, and the *Sun Inn* (☎01588/640559), whose à la carte restaurant is first-rate. There are **buses** to Clun from Shrewsbury, Ludlow and Bishop's Castle.

Ludlow

LUDLOW, perched on a hill nearly thirty miles south of Shrewsbury, is one of the most picturesque towns in the Midlands, if not in England – a cluster of beautifully preserved black-and-white half-timbered buildings packed around a craggy stone castle, with rural Shropshire forming a dreamy backdrop. Close to the Welsh border, the defensive qualities of the site were recognized by the Saxons, but it was the Normans who got down to business when Roger Montgomery turned up here with his men in 1085. Over the next decades, Montgomery's fortifications were elaborated into an immense **Castle** (May–July & Sept daily 10am–5pm, Aug daily 10am–7pm; rest of year daily 10am–4pm, but closed Jan weekdays; £3), strong enough to keep the Welsh at bay and the natural headquarters for the Council of Wales and the Marches, as the borders were then known. Slighted by Parliamentary troops in the Civil War, the rambling ruins of today include towers and turrets, gatehouses and concentric walls as well as the remains of the 110-foot Norman keep and an unusual Round Chapel built in 1120. With its spectacular setting above the River Teme, the castle also makes a fine open-air theatre during the **Ludlow Festival** every June and July.

The castle entrance opens out onto the main marketplace, home to the intriguing **Castle Lodge** (daily 10am–5pm; £2), predominantly Elizabethan in style. In the ground-floor oak-panelled rooms, stained-glass windows depict the coats of arms of Germans summoned by Henry VIII to help sack England's monasteries. In low-beamed chambers upstairs, there's a display of Ludlow's chequered history, which omits the popular rumour that Mary, Queen of Scots hid from Elizabeth's henchmen in the lodge's basement.

To the south and east of the marketplace, the gridiron of streets laid out by the Normans has survived intact, though most of the buildings date from the eighteenth century. It's the general appearance that appeals rather than any special sight, but steeply sloping **Broad Street**, running south from the marketplace, is particularly attractive, flanked by many of Ludlow's five hundred half-timbered Tudor and redbrick Georgian listed buildings. At its east end, the marketplace pushes into the Buttercross, off which the magnificently proportioned, fifteenth-century interior of the **church of St Laurence** (daily 10am–5pm; free) boasts vast stained-glass windows and some of the country's finest misericords. In its turn the Buttercross nudges King Street which intersects with the **Bull Ring**, home of the *Feathers Hotel*, an extraordinary Jacobean building with the fanciest wooden facade imaginable.

Practicalities

On the Shrewsbury–Hereford line, Ludlow **train station** is on the north side of town, a five-minute walk from the centre – just follow the signs. Most **buses** stop on Mill Street, across the marketplace from the castle entrance. Ludlow's **tourist office**, on the marketplace (Mon–Sat 10am–5pm, plus summer Sun 10.30am–5pm; ☎01584/875053), has a wide range of maps and books for walkers, and a selection of inexpensive leaflets detailing day hikes in the area. **Accommodation** is plentiful, though rooms can get scarce

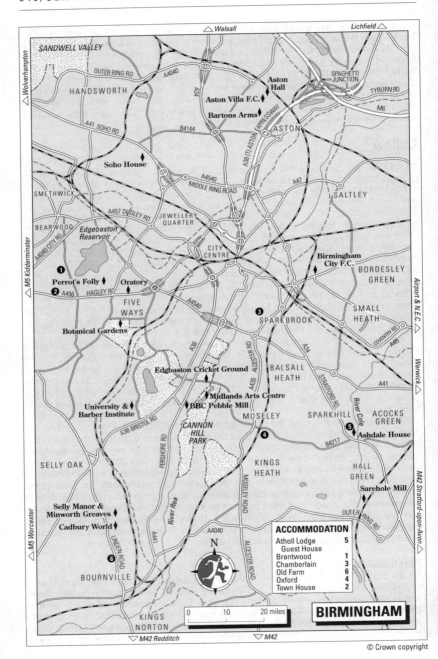

△ Walsall   Lichfield △

SANDWELL VALLEY

Wolverhampton ◁

OUTER RING RD
A4040
SPAGHETTI
JUNCTION
TYBURN RD

HANDSWORTH

A34
Aston
Hall
Aston Villa F.C.
Bartons Arms
A38 (T) ASTON EXPRESSWAY
M6

A41 SOHO RD
B4144
ASTON

Soho House
A4540
MIDDLE RING ROAD
A47
SALTLEY

SMETHWICK
A457 DUDLEY RD
JEWELLERY
QUARTER

BEARWOOD
Edgbaston
Reservoir
CITY
CENTRE

M5 Kidderminster ◁

A4040 CITY RD
Birmingham
City F.C.
BORDESLEY
GREEN

Airport & N.E.C. ▷

❶
Perrot's Folly
❷ A456 HAGLEY RD
Oratory

FIVE
WAYS
A4540
❸ SPARKBROOK
SMALL
HEATH

COVENTRY RD
A45

Botanical Gardens
A38
A435 ALCESTER RD
BALSALL
HEATH
A34
STRATFORD RD

Warwick ▷

A41

Edgbaston Cricket Ground
Midlands Arts Centre
BBC Pebble Mill
MOSELEY
SPARKHILL
River Cole
ACOCKS
GREEN

University &
Barber Institute
A38 BRISTOL RD
CANNON
HILL
PARK
❺
Ashdale House

SELLY OAK
KINGS
HEATH
HALL
GREEN
Sarehole Mill

PERSHORE RD
MOSELEY ROAD
❹
B4217
OUTER RING RD

M42 Stratford-upon-Avon ▷

Selly Manor &
Minworth Greaves
Cadbury World
LINDEN ROAD
River Rea
A441
A4040
ALCESTER ROAD

M5 Worcester ◁

❻
BOURNVILLE
N

ACCOMMODATION
Atholl Lodge   5
  Guest House
Brentwood   1
Chamberlain   3
Old Farm   6
Oxford   4
Town House   2

KINGS
NORTON
0   10   20 miles

BIRMINGHAM

▽ M42 Redditch   ▽ M42

© Crown copyright

during the festival. First choice if you can afford it has to be the beautiful *Feathers Hotel* on the Bull Ring (☎01584/875261; ⑤), an intricately decorated Jacobean town house with luxury rooms and period furnishings to match. Two other, less expensive **B&B** options are the *Wheatsheaf Inn*, a quaint little pub next to the town gate at the foot of Broad Street (☎01584/872980; ②); and the excellent *Number Twenty Eight*, in a couple of old properties beyond the town gate at 28 Lower Broad St (☎01584/876996; ④). Ludlow's **youth hostel** (advance bookings essential; ☎01584/872472) is at the bottom of Lower Broad Street by the River Teme in Ludford Lodge.

For **food and drink**, the *Feathers* serves up excellent snacks and meals at its café-bar; the popular *Olive Branch*, on the Bull Ring (daily 10am–3pm), specializes in inexpensive light meals and salads; and the *Rose and Crown*, off the marketplace, serves up a good range of beers and delicious bar food and has a sheltered courtyard.

Birmingham

If anywhere can be described as the first purely industrial conurbation, it is **BIRMING-HAM**. Unlike the more specialist industrial towns that grew up across the north and Midlands, "Brum" turned its hand to every kind of manufacturing, gaining the epithet "the city of 1001 trades". It was here that the pioneers of the Industrial Revolution – James Watt, Matthew Boulton, William Murdock, Josiah Wedgwood, Joseph Priestley and Erasmus Darwin (grandfather of Charles) – formed the Lunar Society, a melting-pot of scientific and industrial ideas that spawned the world's first purpose-built factory, the distillation of oxygen, the invention of gas lighting and the mass production of the steam engine. A Midlands market town swiftly mushroomed into the nation's economic dynamo – in the fifty years up to 1830 the population more than trebled to 130,000.

Now the second largest city in Britain, with a population of over one million, Birmingham has long outgrown the squalor and misery of its boom years. Nowadays, its industrial legacy is chiefly to be seen in a crop of excellent heritage museums, an extensive network of canals and a multiracial population that makes this one of Britain's more cosmopolitan cities. The shift to a post-manufacturing economy is symbolized by the new conference centre and by the enormous National Exhibition Centre on the outskirts, while Birmingham's cultural initiatives – enticing a division of the Royal Ballet to take up residence here, and building a fabulous new concert hall for the City of Birmingham Symphony Orchestra – have no equal outside the capital.

Arrival, information and city transport

Birmingham's **airport** is eight miles east of the city centre at Elmdon; the main terminal is connected to Birmingham International train station, from where there are regular services into the centre. **New Street train station**, to which all InterCity and the vast majority of local services go, is right in the heart of the city. However, trains on the Stratford-upon-Avon, Warwick, Worcester and Malvern lines usually use **Snow Hill** and **Moor Street** stations, both about ten minutes' signposted walk from New Street. National Express **coach** travellers are dumped in the grim surroundings of **Digbeth coach station**, from where it is a ten-minute uphill walk to the centre.

Free accommodation booking, maps and transport information are provided by all the city's **tourist offices**. The main office is located opposite the Council House on Victoria Square at 130 Colmore Row (Mon–Sat 9.30am–6pm, Sun 10am–4pm; ☎0121/693 6300). Five minutes' walk from New Street station in the other direction, there's a smaller branch and useful city ticket shop at 2 City Arcade, off New Street (Mon–Sat 9.30am–5.30pm; ☎0121/643 2514). There are also offices open Monday to Friday 9am to 5pm and during major conferences in the International Convention

Centre (ICC) in Centenary Square and in the National Exhibition Centre (NEC), next to the airport. The city council runs its own office in the Central Library, Chamberlain Square (Mon–Fri 9am–8pm, Sat 9am–5pm; ☎0121/236 5622).

With much of the cheaper accommodation located out of the city centre, you are likely to be using local **buses** at some point. West Midlands Travel (WMT) is the largest operator (the blue and silver buses), although vehicles of every hue can be seen jostling for custom on the city's streets. The off-peak day pass for WMT buses (also valid on most other operators and the metro) is good value for money (£2.50) and can be bought on the first bus used. If you're using local **trains** as well, it makes sense to buy a Centro Daytripper (£4). For information on all local public transport, call the Centro Hotline (☎0121/200 2700).

Accommodation

B&Bs and cheaper **hotels** are concentrated two miles west of the centre along the A456 **Hagley Road** (buses #9, #19, #120, #123–4, #126, #136–8, #192, #193, #292 from Centenary Square) and in **Acocks Green**, four miles southeast of the centre (trains from Moor Street or Snow Hill, or buses #1, #11, #37–8). In general, central hotels are geared up for the expense-account trade, although a few new cheaper places have made staying centrally more viable. The NEC tourist office co-ordinates cut-price weekend short stays (☎0121/780 4321) in most of the city-centre hotels, with prices starting at around £19 per person per night. These are available for Friday, Saturday and Sunday nights all year round and every night in July and August. In the centre of town there are also a couple of places offering B&B for gay and lesbian visitors – see the "Lesbian and Gay Birmingham" section on p.558.

Hotels and B&Bs

Atholl Lodge Guest House, 16 Elmdon Rd, Acocks Green (☎0121/707 4417). Comfortable guest house in a southeastern suburb, handy for the airport and NEC. ①.

Ashdale House, 39 Broad Rd, Acocks Green (☎0121/706 3598). Well-situated B&B, serving good vegetarian and organic food. ②.

Brentwood Hotel, 127 Portland Road, Edgbaston (☎0121/454 4079). Good-value small hotel near the Hagley Road, also offering self-catering apartments (☎0121/420 2301) on a weekly basis for £245. ②.

Birmingham Hotel, 55 Irving St (☎0121/622 4925). Medium-size, slightly downbeat hotel, handily placed just off Bristol Street, in the city centre. ③.

Chamberlain Hotel, Alcester St, Highgate (☎0121/606 9000). Splendid conversion of a magnificent Victorian workhouse within easy walking distance of the city centre, offering excellent value doubles. ③.

Holiday Inn Crowne Plaza, Central Square, Broad St (☎0121/631 2000). Large, anonymous central hotel with good health and fitness facilities. ⑦.

Hotel Ibis, Ladywell Walk, Arcadian Centre (☎0121/622 6010). Rather characterless, but well-situated hotel, bang in the Chinese Quarter, near the major theatres and nightclubs. ②.

Old Farm Hotel, 108 Linden Rd, Bournville (☎0121/458 3146). Friendly hotel, just 250 yards from Cadbury World museum. ③.

Oxford Hotel, 21 Oxford Rd, Moseley (☎0121/449 3298). Decent, comfortable place in this trendy southerly suburb. ⑤.

Travelodge, 230 Broad St (☎0121/644 5266). Ultra-anonymous central chain hotel (in the thick of bars and clubs), but worth trying for good-value doubles, all en suite. ②.

The City

The focus of Birmingham's city centre is where the main shopping thoroughfares of New Street and Corporation Street meet at right angles, just outside the shopping

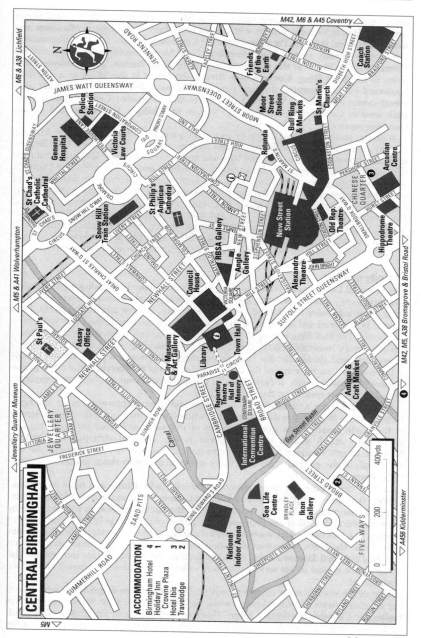

CENTRAL BIRMINGHAM

ACCOMMODATION
Birmingham Hotel 4
Holiday Inn 1
Crowne Plaza 3
Hotel Ibis 2
Travelodge

© Crown copyright

complex that houses New Street station. **New Street** runs west to the Council House and Town Hall in Victoria Square, with access from there to the central **Museum and Art Gallery** and through Paradise Forum to Centenary Square and the International Convention Centre. In the other direction, New Street heads towards the circular **Rotunda** office block, at the intersection with the **High Street**, where subways lead down to the **Bull Ring**. **Corporation Street** – planned in the 1870s as a mile-long boulevard cutting a swathe through congested slums – leads to the exuberant nine-teenth-century terracotta Victoria Law Courts and Methodist Central Hall; a short walk west of Corporation Street brings you to **St Philip's Cathedral** and its surrounding square.

With the scaling down of the inner ring road, pleasant old districts on the fringe of the city centre are being reintegrated into its framework – these include the **Chinese Quarter**, home of many of the best bars and clubs, the **Jewellery Quarter**, complete with an excellent museum and hundreds of workshops and retail outlets, and **Digbeth**, where the city first began. Farther out, to the southwest of the centre, is the well-heeled area of **Edgbaston**, home of the county cricket ground, the principal university and many of the city's best parks. To the south is the planned workers' village of **Bournville**, established in 1879 by the Cadbury family and, true to their Quaker beliefs, still without a pub. On the north side of the city, **Aston** is notable for the Villa football club and its stunning Jacobean Hall, while multicultural **Handsworth** is home to Matthew Boulton's old **Soho House**, where the Lunar Society used to meet.

The city centre

The principal Corporation, New and High streets are flanked by chainstores and shopping precincts – more interesting are the multifarious **markets** in and around the **Bull Ring**, yawning under the Rotunda at the intersection of New and High streets. Bulls used to be tethered and baited here, in the belief that if the animal died angry, the meat was better. The Bull Ring indoor shopping centre is scarcely a more edifying spectacle, fulfilling every miserable cliché about 1960s town planning – it's cheap, tatty, hugely disorienting and, thankfully, due to be demolished in the next few years. On the far side of the complex, on the edge of the market stalls, stands **St Martin's**, the city's grime-blackened parish church. It dates back to the fourteenth century, but was completely rebuilt in the last quarter of the nineteenth.

From St Martin's, **Digbeth** – the old main thoroughfare through medieval Birmingham – falls away to the southeast. It's now a busy, main road, though the streets to the north house some great examples of imposing industrial architecture. Just beyond the coach station on Gibb Street is the blue-and-white-painted **Custard Factory**, an arts complex fashioned out of the old Alfred Bird custard works. As well as a couple of chic poolside café-bars, there are small arts workshops and galleries within the complex.

Back in the centre, the finest church in the city is **St Philip's**, a bijou example of English Baroque, occupying a grassy knoll on Colmore Row, to the west of Corporation Street. Consecrated in 1715 as an overspill for the packed St Martin's, it became the city's cathedral in 1905 at the expense of the parish church, largely due to its superior position in a less congested, more upmarket corner of the city centre. The church was extended in the 1880s, when four new stained-glass windows were commissioned from local boy **Edward Burne-Jones**, a leading light of the Pre-Raphaelite movement. The windows are typical of his style – intensely coloured, fastidiously detailed and rather sentimental.

One of the world's most comprehensive collections of **Pre-Raphaelite art**, including an entire room of Burne-Jones's work, is housed in the **City Museum and Art Gallery** in Chamberlain Square (Mon–Thurs & Sat 10am–5pm, Fri 10.30am–5pm, Sun 12.30–5pm; free), 200 yards along Colmore Row. Founded in 1848, the Pre-Raphaelite

Brotherhood consisted of seven young artists, of whom Rossetti, Holman Hunt, Millais and Madox Brown are best known. The name of the group was selected to express their commitment to honest observation, which they thought lost with the Renaissance. Many of the Brotherhood's most important paintings are displayed here, including Brown's powerful image of emigration, *The Last of England*, and Rossetti's seminal *First Anniversary of the Death of Beatrice* (1849), inspired by Dante. Such was the group's dedication to realism (as they conceived it) that Hunt visited the Holy Land to prepare a series of religious paintings including his extravagant "The Finding of the Saviour in the Temple". It's a splendid collection, and one that richly deserves at least a couple of hours, but the museum has much more to offer. To begin with, there's a first-rate sample of eighteenth- to twentieth-century British art including an extensive collection of watercolour landscapes from 1750 to 1850 and numerous works by David Cox, Constable's Birmingham contemporary. Moving on, the **international collection** has its main strengths in seventeenth-century Italian paintings and sculpture, and a small showing of Impressionists.

Birmingham's industrial prowess is amply demonstrated throughout the museum. The ground-floor **Industrial Gallery**, housed in the original Victorian building complete with ornate skylights and huge gas lights, contains beautiful stained glass and local ceramics – and leads to the genteel **Edwardian tea room**, one of the most pleasant places in Birmingham for a midday break. Elsewhere in the building you'll find galleries devoted to **silver**, base metalwork and **jewellery**. Upstairs is a large and rather old-fashioned **natural history** collection, linked to a couple of rooms looking at ancient worlds. Tucked down by the back entrance off Great Charles Street are two interesting **local history** galleries, which focus mainly on the industrial beginnings and development of the city. The adjoining **Gas Hall** (same times; £4.95) is one of the country's most impressive venues for touring art exhibitions.

Chamberlain Square is also bounded by the huge municipal monolith of the domed **Council House**, and the classical **Town Hall** (1832–46), which is based on the Roman temple in Nîmes, whereas the glum **Central Library** looks like it's been modelled on a multistorey car park. The central focus is a fountain commemorating **Joseph Chamberlain** (1836–1914), whose political career took him from the Birmingham mayor's office to national prominence as leader of the Liberal Unionists and figurehead of the resistance to Irish home rule. On the steps is a statue of the city's first MP, Thomas Attwood, his coat-tails tumbling down the concrete.

On its south side Chamberlain Square opens onto the beautifully refurbished **Victoria Square**, whose centrepiece is a stunning fountain designed by Dhruva Mistry. Just across the raised flowerbeds you'll see a far less popular piece of contemporary sculpture – Anthony Gormley's rusting, thrusting *Iron Man*. On the corner of Victoria Square and New Street is the gallery of the **Royal Birmingham Society of Artists** (Mon–Sat 10.30am–5pm; £1), which hosts some enjoyable temporary exhibitions. Nearby, just along New Street, on the fourth floor of the Piccadilly arcade, is the **Angle Gallery** (Mon–Sat 11am–6pm, Sun 11am–5pm; prices vary), a good bet for radical art and installations. Retracing your steps to the far side of Chamberlain Square, walk through the hideously kitsch **Paradise Forum** – entered through the library complex – to get to **Centenary Square**, laid out as a complement to the showpiece **International Convention Centre** (ICC) and the **Birmingham Repertory Theatre**. Centre-stage on the wide paving is a butter-coloured sculpture called *Forward*, a rousing image of the city's history by Birmingham–born Raymond Mason.

On the **canals** at the back of the ICC, turn left for the bright, boat-filled **Gas Street Basin** (regular public boat trips operate from here and the ICC quayside), or turn right for a canalside wander up to the huge dome of the National Indoor Arena, where the canal forks. This whole area has been the focus of Birmingham's recent redevelopment, principally in the waterside bars, shops and clubs of **Brindley Place**, named after the eighteenth-century Birmingham town engineer who was responsible for many of Britain's early canals. Beside the main canal junction, the shell-like **National Sea Life Centre** (daily 10am–5pm; £7.50) can't help but raise a few eyebrows, given the city's inland location. Nevertheless, it's an enterprising educational venture, giving Birmingham's landlubbers an opportunity to view and even touch many unusual varieties of fish and sea life, even, at one point, from within a 360° glass tunnel. A couple of blocks back, in the heart of the Brindley Place complex, an imposing old Victorian school has now become the home of the city's celebrated **Ikon Gallery** (Tues–Fri 11am–7pm, Sat & Sun 11am–5pm; free), one of the most imaginative British galleries for touring exhibitions of contemporary art.

Where the canals fork at the Sea Life Centre, if you take the right turn along the Birmingham and Fazeley Canal, you'll pass by (and even under) everything from Victorian warehouses to the 500ft Telecom Tower. After about half a mile, you'll reach St Chad's Circus and the twin steeples of the Pugin-designed **St Chad's Catholic Cathedral** (1839–41), the first Catholic cathedral to be built in England since the Reformation. Perhaps more rewarding is Birmingham's long-established **Jewellery Quarter**, immediately northwest of the city centre, and well signposted from it. Bucklemakers and toymakers first colonized the area in the 1750s, opening the way for hundreds of silversmiths, jewellers and goldsmiths. There are still around five hundred jewellery-related companies in the area and most of the jewellery shops are now concentrated along Vitoria Street, Warstone Lane and Frederick Street. A short walk north of the Frederick Street/Warstone Lane intersection, the engrossing **Museum of the Jewellery Quarter**, 75–79 Vyse St (Mon–Fri 10am–4pm; Sat 11am–5pm; £2.50), is built around a factory that was abandoned in 1980 but had remained virtually unchanged since the 1950s. A visitor centre starts proceedings, detailing the growth and decline of the trade in Birmingham, but it's the old factory that steals the show. Here, the atmosphere and conditions of the old works are superbly re-created – the jewellers were wedged into tiny, hot and noisy spaces to churn out hundreds of earrings, brooches and rings. Their modern counterparts use the old machines to show how some of the most common designs were produced. Incidentally, the museum is only a couple of minutes' walk from the new Jewellery Quarter station, on the train line from Moor Street and Snow Hill stations to points west.

Bournville

The most noteworthy of Birmingham's suburbs is the planned village of **BOURNVILLE**, four miles southwest of the city centre (train from New Street or buses #61, #62 & #63 from Corporation Street), founded by the **Cadbury** family in 1879. The first of this Quaker dynasty, John Cadbury, opened a grocery store in Birmingham in 1824 and from it he sold his home-produced "Cocoa Nibs," part soothing nightcap, part a way of weaning the working class from alcohol by providing a cheap and tempting alternative to beer. The popularity of this sweet concoction exceeded John's wildest dreams and just over fifty years later his sons, George and Richard, were able to move the family business out of the city centre to Bournville, a purpose-built "factory in a garden". Much influenced by the utopian ideas of William Morris and the Arts and Crafts movement, the Cadburys' Bournville scheme included gardens for every worker's house, a village green and a half-timbered parade of shops. The brothers also uprooted a pair of Tudor houses, **Selly Manor** and **Minworth Greaves**, and plonked them on Maple Road – they are now open as a museum of Tudor and Jacobean furniture (Tues–Fri 10am–5pm, plus April–Sept Sat & Sun 2–5pm; £1.50). The Bournville Village Trust still operates today, laying down basic rules (no unkempt gardens, for example) to which all inhabitants, even those who own their property, must subscribe.

Cadbury World, tacked onto the huge factory off Linden Road (daily 10am–4pm; booking advised on ☎0121/451 4159; £6.50), takes visitors through the histories of the cocoa bean and the Cadbury dynasty – with excellent displays on advertising. But for chocoholics the point of the tour is the opportunity to gorge on free samples from the production line and stock up on the cut-price finished product.

Edgbaston

Leafy and prosperous, the suburb of **EDGBASTON**, just to the southwest of the city centre, was developed in the 1790s by the Calthorpe family as a genteel residential estate from which industry and commerce were explicitly banned. It's here, on Westbourne Road, you'll find the **Birmingham Botanical Gardens** (Mon–Sat 9am–7pm or dusk, Sun 10am–7pm or dusk; £4.20, Sun £4.50), whose ornamental gardens and glasshouses extend over fifteen acres. The gardens are parcelled up into a number of distinct areas, everything from a rhododendron garden, brilliant herbaceous borders and a rock garden to an Alpine yard. Buses #10, #21, #22, #23, #29 and #103 from the city centre pass close by.

Arguably the most agreeable of Birmingham's many public parks is **Cannon Hill Park**, off the Pershore and Edgbaston roads two miles south of central Birmingham – buses #45 and #47 from the city centre stop nearby. There are boating lakes and bowling greens, tennis courts and woodland, and the greenhouses hold a national collection of tropical plants. Cannon Hill is also home to the excellent **Midland Arts Centre** (see p.558), which has a good bar, café, cinema and bookshop and hosts an imaginative programme of art, craft and photography exhibitions.

Birmingham University, on the southern fringe of Edgbaston (trains from New Street or buses #61–63), is visible for miles around, thanks to the 328ft clock tower that dominates the campus. For the casual visitor, the university campus has one big draw, the **Barber Institute of Fine Arts**, at the east gate off Edgbaston Park Road (Mon–Sat 10am–5pm, Sun 2–5pm; free). Opened in 1939, this superb gallery contains a world-class collection of European paintings from the thirteenth century onwards. Notable pieces include a fine collection of Rembrandt studies, an unusual Rubens – *Landscape near Malines* – and Degas' *Jockeys Before the Race*, a characteristically audacious piece of off-centre composition. The Barber also houses a good collection of Impressionists, including Monet, Pissarro and Boudin, as well as works by Magritte, Bellini, Whistler, Van Gogh, Gainsborough, Gauguin and Turner.

Aston and Handsworth

Long before it was swallowed up by Birmingham, the suburb of **ASTON**, just over a mile to the north of the city centre, was a wealthy manorial estate, its heyday recalled by **Aston Hall** on Trinity Road (March–Oct daily 2–5pm; free), reached by bus #7 from the bottom of Corporation Street. A handsome Jacobean mansion, all turrets and high gables, the hall was built for the Holte family, whose Royalist loyalties brought them into conflict with the Parliamentarian stronghold of Birmingham during the English Civil War. The Roundheads ended up besieging the Holtes and were responsible for the still-visible gunshot marks in the balustraded staircase. About twenty rooms are open to the public, including the beautiful panelled Long Gallery, running the entire width of the house. Aston is also home to the **Bartons Arms**, one of Birmingham's grandest pubs, a Victorian riot of smoked glass, snob screens, mahogany surrounds and the city's most ornate toilets. The pub is located about three-quarters of a mile southwest of the Hall on Aston High Street (the A34).

To the west of Aston is **HANDSWORTH**, whose principal thoroughfare, the Soho Road (the A41), is flanked by Balti houses, Caribbean eateries, exotic vegetable shops and sari stores. On Soho Avenue, a side road off the west side of Soho Road, the council have refurbished Matthew Boulton's elegant home, **Soho House** (Tues–Sat 10am–5pm, Sun noon–5pm; £2.50; buses #70, #74, #78–9), in period style and have even managed to track down some of Boulton's own furniture. A kingpin amongst the city's early industrialists, Boulton ran his own factory, manufacturing clocks and vases, buckles and buttons, and developed the steam engine in partnership with James Watt. The Lunar Society (see p.547) met here regularly – as various displays explain in detail. Other exhibitions dip into the pedigree of Handsworth's ethnic stew, which is most vividly seen in the annual **Handsworth Carnival**, held in mid-August.

The Tolkien Trail

An extraordinary number of visitors to Birmingham come here to follow the trail of **J.R.R. Tolkien**, author of *The Hobbit* and *The Lord of the Rings*, who lived in many different parts of Birmingham between the ages of three and nineteen – a **Tolkien Trail** leaflet is available from the tourist offices. One prime Tolkien site lies four miles southeast of the city centre at **Sarehole Mill** on Cole Bank Road, Hall Green (March–Oct daily 2–5pm; free), reached by bus #4. The writer spent four years of his early childhood in a house opposite this eighteenth-century brick corn mill, and many of his literary ideas were inspired by the building and its gloomy lake – his drawing of Hobbiton and Sandyman's Mill in *The Hobbit* allegedly bears a striking resemblance to the then rural hamlet of Sarehole. Other places that influenced his whimsical yarns can still be visited – notably the spectacularly ornate Catholic **Oratory church**, just beyond Five Ways on the Hagley Road (open mornings) and the nearby **Perrot's Folly**, Monument Road (Easter–Sept Sun 2–5pm; £1.50), a curious 98-foot castellated tower built by the local landowner in 1758.

Eating and drinking

Birmingham's central **restaurants** have long had a reputation as soulless places which empty quickly, but this is changing rapidly, with new venues opening up in the slipstream of the growth in the conference and trade-fair business, particularly along Broad Street, near the ICC. There's also a concentration of decent, reasonably priced restaurants around the Chinese Quarter, at the top of Hurst Street – also the focus of the gay scene. Birmingham's gastronomic speciality is the **balti**, a delicious and astoundingly cheap Kashmiri stew cooked and served in a small wok-like dish called a *karahi*, with nan bread instead of cutlery. Although balti houses have opened up within the city centre, the original and arguably the best balti houses are in the inner-city southern suburbs of **Balsall Heath** and **Sparkhill**. Some of these are listed here – all are unlicensed, so take your own booze.

The city centre **pubs** vary as much as you'd expect: those on Broad Street, in the immediate vicinity of the Convention Centre, are garish places aimed at the delegates and weekend lager-lovers, but more traditional pubs abound throughout the centre and out into the livelier suburbs, such as Bearwood, Handsworth, Moseley and Balsall Heath.

Restaurants

Chez Jules, 5a Ethel St, off New Street (☎0121/633 4664). Best medium-priced French restaurant in the city centre, with especially good lunchtime offers. Moderate.

Chung Ying, 16–18 Wrottesley St (☎0121/622 1793). The best Cantonese dishes in the Chinese Quarter, and always busy. Moderate.

Grand Tandoori, 345 Stratford Rd, Sparkhill (☎0121/773 9244). Extensive balti menu in a concentration of other balti houses. Buses #4, #31, or #41. Inexpensive.

Green Room Café-Bar, Hurst St. Popular and relaxed café-bar opposite the Hippodrome Theatre for anything from a cup of tea or glass of wine through to a full meal. Inexpensive.

I Am The King Balti, 230–232 Ladypool Rd, Balsall Heath (☎0121/449 1170). The name may be ridiculous, but this really is one of the best in the city's main "balti belt". Inexpensive.

Kushi, 558 Moseley Rd, Balsall Heath (☎0121/449 7678). Excellent, award-winning balti house that's unlicensed, dirt cheap and deservedly popular. Inexpensive.

Left Bank, 79 Broad St (☎0121/643 4464). Swish and classy French and continental restaurant that mops up its fair share of ICC delegates. Moderate.

Mongolian Bar, 24 Ludgate Hill, off St Paul's Square (☎0121/236 3849). Lively and enjoyable restaurant, where you choose your ingredients and see them flash-fried before you. Moderate.

Punjab Paradise, 377 Ladypool Rd, Balsall Heath (☎0121/449 4110). One of the city's classic balti houses, specializing in milder dishes. Bus to the Moseley Dance Centre, then a ten-minute walk. Inexpensive.

Ronnie Scott's Café Bar, 258 Broad St (☎0121/643 4525). Serves an imaginative selection of snacks and meals, with jazz sounds and memorabilia as background. Late licence. Inexpensive.

San Carlo, 4 Temple St (☎0121/633 0251). Best all-round Italian restaurant in the centre, although somewhat lacking in atmosphere. It's near St Philip's Cathedral, just up from the pizza and pasta chain restaurants on New Street. Moderate.

Shah Faisal, 348–50 Stratford Rd, Sparkhill (☎0121/753 0607). Large and very tasty baltis in traditional surroundings. Buses #4, #31, or #41. Inexpensive.

Teppanyaki, Arcadian Centre, Hurst Street (☎0121/622 5183). Birmingham's first Japanese restaurant, swiftly gaining a top reputation. Expensive.

Warehouse Café, 54 Allison St, Digbeth (☎0121/633 0261). Imaginative vegan and vegetarian café open daytimes and evenings, above Friends of the Earth. Bring your own wine. Inexpensive.

Pubs and bars

Circo, 6–8 Holloway Circus. Serious pre-club posing palace, offering pricey designer beers, pastas and salads.

The Cube, Brindley Place. In the centre of fashionable Brindley Place, the terrace of this lively bar teems with drinkers on summer evenings.

The Dubliner, 57 Digbeth. Rather overdone Irish theme pub just up from the coach station, but serves excellent Guinness and has nightly live bands.

Fiddle and Bone, 4 Sheepcote St (☎0121/200 2223). Canalside pub-cum-restaurant owned by members of the City of Birmingham Symphony Orchestra, hence its musical name and theme. Has become very popular very quickly. Live music nightly.

James Brindley, next to the *Hyatt* off Bridge St. Frequented by businesspeople in the week, but at weekends the jazz brunches give this place a relaxed air. Great canalside location.

Medicine Bar and **Café des Artistes**, Custard Factory, Gibb Street, Digbeth. Popular pre-club haunts in a cheerful arts complex (see p.552).

Ministry bar, 55 Broad St. Second home to the Ministry of Sound, this bar boasts the best underground house and garage on the best sound system outside of their London base.

Old Contemptibles, 176 Edmund St. Real old spit-and-sawdust saloon, packed with business folk at lunch and in the early evening. Excellent lunchtime food.

The Old Fox, Arcadian Centre, Hurst Street. Over-modernized but popular pub, with an excellent selection of beer and amiable atmosphere.

Prince of Wales, Cambridge Street. Old-fashioned haunt with longstanding custom from the Repertory Theatre, now pulling them in from the neighbouring ICC.

The Victoria, John Bright Street. Elaborately tiled and smoky Irish pub, next to the Alexandra Theatre; best-value lunchtime food in the city centre.

Nightlife and entertainment

Nightlife in Birmingham is thriving, and the club scene is recognized as one of Britain's best, spanning everything from word-of-mouth underground parties to meat-market clubs. Live music, theatre and comedy surface in pubs and larger venues, including a strong Irish scene around Digbeth.

Birmingham's showpiece **Symphony Hall** and the Birmingham Royal Ballet are the spearheads of the city's resurgent high-cultural scene, and the social calendar gets an added boost from the range of new **festivals**, all of which offer many events for free. These include the **Readers' and Writers' Festival** in May and November, the **Jazz Festival** in the first two weeks in July, and the **Film and TV Festival** in November.

For current information on all events, performances and exhibitions, pick up a free copy of *What's On Birmingham and Midlands* (not to be confused with the inferior *What's On West Midlands*) from tourist offices, galleries or public venues.

Clubs

Baker's, 163 Broad St (☎0121/633 3839). Small, artily designed disco-club with a wide range of speciality evenings.

Bobby Brown's, 52 Gas St (☎0121/643 2573). Chart and retro sounds for the over-25s.

House of God, various venues. Birmingham's ever-popular techno night is still going strong and loud. This is the sound of the city.

Pulse, Hurst Street. Charts and drink promotions most of the week, but on Sunday the all-day "Sundissential" (☎0121/643 4715) is a wild dance party to finish the weekend off.

Que Club (and **The Chapel**), Central Hall, Corporation Street (☎0121/212 0550). Brum's premier "superclub", a conversion of the old Methodist Central Hall into a full-on, 2000-capacity groove. All-nighters every weekend.

Ronnie Scott's, 258 Broad St (☎0121/643 4525). Second of the late maestro's jazz clubs, good also for big names in blues and world music.

Sanctuary, Digbeth High Street (☎0160/447 4591). Opposite the coach station, the old Civic Hall now thumps to some big house tunes during a variety of one-nighters.

Lesbian and gay Birmingham

Angels café-bar, 127–131 Hurst St. Enormously popular gay and lesbian bar, with all-day snacks and meals.

Fountain Inn, 102 Wrentham St (☎0121/622 1452). A mainly male real-ale pub with B&B accommodation (②) and occasional cabaret.

The Fox, 17 Lower Essex St. Mostly women at this pub with an excellent atmosphere and a courtyard garden.

Brooks, 92–95 Smallbrook Queensway. Glammy pre-club bar.

The Nightingale, Essex House, Kent St (☎0121/622 1718). Birmingham's foremost gay club: fun, unpretentious and open every night except Mon & Thurs.

Subway City, Livery St, Snow Hill (☎0121/233 0310). Out of the Hurst Street "gay village", but worth the trek. Great weekend club, with dance music and groovy times.

The Village, 152 Hurst St (☎0121/622 4742). Mainly male and enjoyably stylish bar, with a camp garden and B&B accommodation (②).

Classical music, theatre, comedy and dance

Alexandra Theatre, Suffolk Street, Queensway (☎0870/607 7544). Mainstream pop concerts, musicals and plays.

City Tavern, Bishopsgate St, Five Ways (☎0121/643 4394). Pub theatre and live music in a cheerful backstreet local.

The Crescent Theatre, Sheepcote Street, Brindley Place (☎0121/643 5858). Adventurous theatre group and venue for visiting companies.

Glee Club, Arcadian Centre, Hurst Street (☎0121/693 2248). Dedicated comedy club, with top national names and up-and-coming stars.

Hippodrome Theatre, Hurst Street (☎0121/622 7486). Home of the Birmingham Royal Ballet and regular hosts of the Welsh National Opera. Also touring plays and big pre- and post-West End productions, plus "Britain's biggest pantomime" every Christmas.

Midland Arts Centre, Cannon Hill Park, Edgbaston (☎0121/440 3838). Venue for touring theatre companies and some local groups.

Old Rep Theatre, Station Street (☎0121/616 1519). Britain's oldest repertory theatre, now home to the imaginative Birmingham Stage Company.

Repertory Theatre, Centenary Square (☎0121/236 4455). Mixed diet of classics and new work, including some local and experimental writing in the Studio.

Symphony Hall, International Convention Centre, Centenary Square (☎0121/212 3333). Acoustically one of the most advanced concert halls in Europe, home of the acclaimed City of Birmingham Symphony Orchestra (CBSO), as well as a venue for touring music and opera.

Listings

Airport enquiries ☎0121/767 5511.

Banks Lloyds, 125 Colmore Row; HSBC, 130 New St; NatWest, 103 Colmore Row.

Bookshops Dillons, 128 New St; Bookscene, 35 Pallasades Shopping Centre; Waterstone's, 24 High St.

Bike rental In the city centre at On Yer Bike, 10 Priory Queensway (☎0121/627 1590).

Bus enquiries Local services ☎0121/200 2700; National Express ☎0990/808080.

Car rental Avis, 71a Park St and at the airport (both ☎0870/606 0100); Budget, 95 Station St (☎0121/643 0493).

Cricket Warwickshire County Cricket Ground, Edgbaston Rd, Edgbaston (☎0121/446 4422).

Exchange American Express, Bank House, Cherry St (☎0121/644 5533); Thomas Cook, 130 New St (☎0121/643 5057).

Football Aston Villa, based at Villa Park (☎0121/327 5353) is the city's big club. One-time equal, Birmingham City, based at St Andrews (☎0121/772 0101), is always threatening a revival – so they say.

Hospital Heartlands Hospital, Bordesley Green East (☎0121/766 6611) or Selly Oak Hospital, Raddlebarn Road, Selly Oak (☎0121/627 1627).

Laundry Nearest to the city centre is Clean & Care, 758 Alum Rock Road. Convenient for the hotels and B&Bs listed above is the Laundry & Dry Cleaning Centre, 236 Warwick Road.

Left luggage New Street station (Mon–Sat 6.45am–9.45pm, Sun 11.15am–6.45pm).

Lesbian and Gay Switchboard Daily 7–10pm ☎0121/622 6589.

Lost property At the police station.

Pharmacies Boots, 67 High Street (☎0121/236 6027).

Police Main city centre stations in Steelhouse Lane and on the corner of Digbeth and Allison St (both ☎0121/626 6000).

Post office Main post office at 1 Pinfold St, on the corner with Victoria Square (Mon–Fri 9am–5.30pm, Sat 9am–6pm).

Taxis Toa Taxis ☎0121/427 8888.

Train enquiries Long-distance services ☎0345/484950; local services ☎0121/200 2700.

Women's advice and information centre 191 Corporation Street (☎0121/212 1881).

The Black Country

To outsiders the area known as the **Black Country** appears to be an undifferentiated mass sprawling away from the western side of Birmingham, but in fact it's composed of several tightly-knit industrial communities, which have gradually expanded until each is touching its neighbours. The region earned its name in the mid-nineteenth century when smoke from hundreds of ironworkings choked the air and sooted the buildings – the environment is much cleaner today. Some of these towns grew on the basis of one or two staple products – leather in Walsall, locks in Willenhall, glass in Stourbridge – whilst the rest exploited the abundant local resources (chiefly coal and limestone) to develop a range of industries, with heavy engineering predominant. Although many of the older trades have long gone, this is still an area where manufacturing is regarded as the only real work, so it's unsurprising that the Black Country's industrial heritage is the main reason for visiting the area – best achieved by day-tripping from Birmingham. The Black Country Museum in **Dudley** is the chief tourist sight, while factories producing more decorative goods – such as the glassworks in Stourbridge and Brierley Hill – are often open to shoppers.

Dudley and around

Nine miles west of Birmingham, **DUDLEY** (from Birmingham, take bus #87 from New Street or #126 from Corporation Street) lays fair claim to being the capital of the Black Country as it was here in the seventeenth century that coal was first used for smelting iron. The town is actually much older – as evidenced by its ruined Norman **castle**, perched on the hill above town with grounds that now contain a zoo (Easter to mid-Sept daily 10am–4.30pm; mid Sept–Easter closes 3pm; £6.50) – but the main attraction is the **Black Country Museum** on the Tipton Road, over the far side of Castle Hill from the town centre (March–Oct daily 10am–5pm; Nov–Feb Wed–Sun 10am–4pm; £7.50). Buildings from the surrounding district – shops, a chapel, a pub, workshops, forges and homes – have been re-erected here and populated with local people in period costume, mimicking forms of labour that once employed thousands in these parts. For added authenticity you can take a trip down an underground coal seam, watch a silent movie in the cinema, or enjoy a canal trip into a tunnel under Castle Hill, through some flood-lit limestone caverns – but note this adds £2.70 to the admission fee.

At the centre of Dudley, the shopping area surrounding the wedge-shaped **Market Place** has suffered badly from the opening of the gargantuan Merry Hill Shopping Centre at **BRIERLEY HILL**, two miles to the southwest. Brierley Hill is also noted for its **beer** – if you only try one Black Country pub, make it the *Vine* (known locally as *"The Bull and Bladder"*), the Batham's brewery outlet on Delph Road, at the top of a run of excellent pubs that wind down the hill to the bottom of the **Delph Nine Locks** on the Dudley no. 1 canal.

Both Brierley Hill and **STOURBRIDGE** (train from Birmingham) thrived on the production of glass and crystal, industries still very evident today. The **Broadfield House Glass Museum** in Kingswinford, near Stourbridge (Tues–Sun 2–5pm; free) explains the history of the industry in this area, and gives details of local free factory tours.

Walsall

Some ten miles north of Birmingham, and readily reached by train or bus, **WALSALL** is a pleasantly stoic town, now attempting to diversify into tourism after years as a centre of the leather industry. Its prime attraction is the **Walsall Museum and Art Gallery**, currently on Lichfield Street (Tues–Sat 10am–5pm, Sun 2–5pm; free), but due to move to new premises on Wolverhampton Street in the near future. The gallery contains a wide-ranging collection of paintings, drawings, prints and sculpture assembled by Kathleen Epstein, the widow of Jacob Epstein, and her friend Sally Ryan. Among the paintings, there are works by Blake, Degas, Modigliani, Van Gogh, Picasso, Ruskin, Turner and – of course – Jacob Epstein. American-born, Epstein (1880–1959) was a controversial figure whose bold and audacious public sculptures were regularly criticized for indecency. In Paris, his *Tomb of Oscar Wilde* created such a stink that a bronze plaque was eventually fixed over the angel's genitals, whilst the aggressiveness of his robot-like *Rock Drill* of 1913 had the art establishment howling with horror. The museum displays Epstein's original drawings for both – and one of his most impressive sculptures adorns Coventry Cathedral (see p.563).

Of more local significance, the **Walsall Leather Museum** (April–Oct Tues–Sat 10am–5pm, Sun noon–5pm; Nov–March Tues–Sat 10am–4pm, Sun noon–4pm; free), on the ring road (A4148 – Littleton Street West), provides a surprisingly interesting look at the industry's development and its effect on the town. In particular, there are excellent displays examining the relentless working conditions of the early leather workers, and practical demonstrations of traditional skills. There's also a shop selling locally made leather goods. Walsall was the birthplace of *Three Men in a Boat* author **Jerome K. Jerome**, and although his family moved away in 1861, when Jerome was two, the town has striven to honour their most famous literary son – a tiny **Birthplace Museum** has opened in Belsize House, Bradford Street (Mon–Fri 9am–12.30pm & 1.30–5pm, Sat 8.30am–12.30pm & 1.30–4pm; free).

Wolverhampton and around

WOLVERHAMPTON, around fourteen miles northwest of Birmingham, doesn't win any beauty contests, but it does possess the excellent **Wolverhampton Art Gallery and Museum**, on Lichfield Street (Mon–Sat 10am–5pm; free). There's a healthy sample of English paintings here, featuring the likes of Gainsborough, Paul Nash, Stanley Spencer and Landseer, but the gallery is best known for its extensive collection of American and British Pop Art. Amongst many, Hamilton, Hockney, Warhol, Allen Jones and Lichtenstein are all featured, and there are also purposeful temporary exhibitions plus an eclectic selection of contemporary art.

Two fine houses sit on the edge of town. Three miles west is the mock-half-timbered **Wightwick Manor** – pronounced "Witick" – at Wightwick Bank, off the A454 (March–Dec Thurs & Sat 2.30–5.30pm; £5.40 for house and garden; NT). Built in 1887, it was designed by Edward Ould, a devotee of William Morris, and the extravagant furnishings, fittings and paintings all reflect the Pre-Raphaelite influence. The garden (Wed & Thurs 11am–6pm, Sat 1–6pm; £2.40) is maintained in its Victorian form, complete with lush orchards and ostentatious topiary. Buses #516 (Midland Red) and #890 (Green Bus) from Wolverhampton stop at the bottom of the road.

Located four miles to the north of Wolverhampton, off the A460 – and painfully near the M54 – **Moseley Old Hall** (mid-March to May Sat & Sun 1.30–5.30pm; June, Sept & Oct Wed, Sat & Sun 1.30–5.30pm; July–Aug Tues, Wed, Sat & Sun 1.30–5.30pm; £3.90; NT) is a much-modified Elizabethan country mansion famous for its association with Charles II. The king took refuge here after the Battle of Worcester in 1651 and you can see the bed he slept in and the hole in which he sheltered for the best part of two days as Parliamentarian troops scoured the area. An exhibition in the barn fills out the history. Buses #870–2 and #613 from Wolverhampton pass nearby, leaving a fifteen-minute walk.

Coventry

In medieval times, **COVENTRY**, twenty miles east of Birmingham, was one of England's most prosperous cities, its wealth founded on the cloth, thread and dyeing industries, precursors of the engineering plants that were to become the staple of the city's economy during the nineteenth century. It was here in 1898 that the Daimler Company manufactured the first British motor car, and thereafter the city rapidly became a major centre of car production. As a sign of the good times, the population quadrupled between 1900 and 1930 – from 70,000 to 250,000 – and the future looked rosy. However, Coventry's industrial success attracted the attentions of the Luftwaffe and, on November 14, 1940, in one of the biggest bombing raids of World War II, the Germans destroyed most of the city. The postwar period has not been easy for Coventry. Heavy industry has been on the skids and the motor production lines have waned to near-extinction. Neither has the new Coventry built to replace the old been an architectural success and – with the exception of the splendid **cathedral** – the city is lumbered with more than its fair share of unsightly buildings.

Arrival, information and accommodation

Coventry is an important rail junction and its **train station**, just south of the central ring road near Warwick Road, has direct services to and from London, Birmingham, and many major British cities. The recently revamped Pool Meadow **bus station** lies a short way north of the cathedral, and is served by National Express coaches to London, Birmingham, Bath and Bristol, and many other destinations. The bus station is also the hub of the local bus network, with regular connections to Warwick, Warwick University, Leamington and Stratford on Stagecoach Midland Red.

For free town maps and glossy local brochures, head for the **tourist office** on Bayley Lane, right in the centre of town opposite the old Cathedral (June–Aug Mon–Fri 9.30am–5pm, Sat & Sun 10am–4.30pm; rest of year Mon–Fri 9.30am–4.30pm, Sat & Sun 10am–4.30pm; ☎01203/832303). Their main city guidebook has a list of all the town's **accommodation** and they will also book a room on your behalf at no cost – though comparatively few casual visitors choose to stay here. One particularly pleasant **B&B** is the *Abigail Guest House*, 39 St Patrick's Rd (☎01203/221378; ①), whose five spick-and-span guest rooms occupy a Victorian terraced house a short walk south of the cathedral, close to the central ring road.

The City

The city centre is dominated by Sir Basil Spence's **St Michael's Cathedral** (daily Easter–Oct 9.30am–6pm, Nov–Easter 9.30am–5.30pm; £2 donation requested), raised alongside the shell of the blitzed old cathedral and dedicated with a performance of Benjamin Britten's specially written *War Requiem* in 1962. Easily the most successful of Coventry's postwar buildings, the cathedral's pink sandstone is light and graceful, the main entrance adorned by a stunningly forceful *St Michael Defeating the Devil* by Jacob Epstein (see p.560). Inside, Spence's high and slender nave is bathed in light from the soaring stained-glass windows, a perfect setting for the magnificent and immense **tapestry** of *Christ in Glory* by Graham Sutherland. The choice of artist could not have been more appropriate. A painter, graphic artist and designer, Sutherland (1903–1980) had been one of Britain's official war artists, his particular job being to record the effects of German bombing. A canopied walkway links the new cathedral with the ruins of the old, used every three years as an atmospheric venue for the **Coventry Mystery Plays** – the next cycle is due to be held in 2000. Finally, the cathedral's visitor centre (Easter–Oct Mon–Sat 10am–4pm, Nov–Easter Mon–Sat 11am–3pm; £1.25) features a historical exhibition on the city and cathedral with showings of a short video, *The Spirit of Coventry*.

A stone's throw southeast of the Cathedral on Jordan Well stands the **Herbert Art Gallery and Museum** (Mon–Sat 10am–5.30pm, Sun noon–5pm; free). The most outstanding exhibits here are Luca della Robbia's gigantic *Bacchus and Ariadne*, which fills an entire wall on the first floor, a famous portrait of King George III by Sir Thomas Lawrence, and a row of Lady Godivas that includes John Collier's much photographed pre-Raphelite version. Also of interest here are Sutherland's sketch studies for the cathedral tapestry, followed up with a trial piece made by French weavers. Downstairs on the ground floor, the go-ahead *Godiva City* exhibition covers one thousand years of local history with a succession of lively interactive displays. Among the original artefacts on show are a large bronze Saxon bowl, known as the Bagington Bowl, sundry

---

TELEPHONE NUMBERS

On April 22, 2000, all **telephone numbers** in Coventry will change. There will be a **new area code, 024**, and all local numbers will be prefixed with **76**, making the new local numbers eight digits long. For further information on the changes to the telephone numbering system in the UK, see the box on p.36.

LADY GODIVA

The story of **Lady Godiva** riding naked on horseback through the streets of Coventry is one of England's favourite folk tales – and the city milks the connection with postcards, key rings and statues. According to the most popular version of the story, Lady Godiva, the beautiful wife of the local lord, Leofric, the earl of Mercia, was appalled by the poverty she saw around her, and begged her husband to abolish the crippling taxes he levied on his people. Wearying of his wife's philanthropy, Leofric said he would do as she asked on condition that she ride naked through the town, never suspecting that a woman of her rank would agree to such a proposal. Lady Godiva, however, got around the dilemma by ordering the townsfolk to lock themselves in their houses and bolt their windows on the appointed day. Only one local lad, the original **"Peeping Tom"**, dared disobey the Countess's command, and he was struck blind before he had a chance to see Godiva, her long hair covering her body like a cape as she rode through the city, eyes lowered. The ordeal over, Godiva returned to her husband, who kept his word and repealed the taxes.

The story first appeared in 1188, but the historical figures it depicted lived nearly a century and a half before. Leofric was the Anglo-Saxon earl who, in 1043, built the Benedictine priory that helped transform Coventry from a small settlement into medieval England's fourth-largest town. His wife, Godgifu, outlived him by ten years, and may have been a powerful ruler in her own right after her husband's death; she was also pious and donated land and money to the Church. Beyond this, little is known about the couple. The Godiva story probably evolved from some kind of pagan fertility ritual, and was popularized in the writings of the Norman chronicler, Roger of Wendover, during the thirteenth century. "Peeping Tom" was a later embellishment, seemingly inspired by a particularly odd chain of events. In 1586, Coventry council asked a certain Adam van Noort (1562–1641) to paint the Godiva legend. He did so, but he placed Leofric in a window looking down at Godiva on her horse. For reasons that remain obscure, the city fathers exhibited the painting outside on Coventry's main square and, mistakenly, the populace took Leofric to be a peeper – and the sub-plot stuck. Researchers in the Herbert Art Gallery (where this painting now hangs) have sorted all this out and also believe that the notion of Godiva's nudity may have been a fanciful elaboration too. It seems more likely that Leofric, if he challenged his wife at all, dared her to ride through the city stripped of her jewellery and finery.

Whatever the truth of the matter, locals kept the story going and "Godiva Processions" kicked off Coventry's annual summer fair from its introduction in the seventeenth century until the 1800s, when all this public flaunting proved too much for the Victorians. More recently, the tradition has been revived in the form of a canny PR exercise to mark the start of the Spirit of Coventry Festival in June, when a local woman rides through the streets dressed in a body stocking.

items of pristine medieval leatherwork, and drawers of ornate ribbons, including one, woven for the Great Exhibition of 1851, that is allegedly the most complicated ever made.

Coventry has been home to dozens of carmakers, including such almost-forgotten names as Singer, Riley, Humber and Hillman. These connections are celebrated at the **Museum of British Road Transport** (daily 10am–5pm; free), on Hales Street, opposite Pool Meadow bus station, which contains the world's largest collection of British vehicles. Inevitably, the older vehicles attract most of the attention – there's a 1908 Riley, a bull-nosed Morris of 1922 and lots more – but there are more modern cars too, including the XJ6 Jaguar and the phallus-like "Thrust 2," in which Richard Noble set the world land speed record of 633.468mph. The museum also has a display devoted to the Coventry Blitz and a gift shop selling motor memorabilia.

A short walk to the west of the Road Transport Museum, off Corporation Street, **Spon Street** has several restored medieval houses, mostly moved here from other parts of the city. It's hardly an inspiring streetscape, but the red stone church of **Saint John's** has played an interesting part in linguistic history. During the English Civil War, Puritan Coventry sided squarely with Parliament, and Royalist prisoners from the surrounding districts were rounded up and incarcerated here in the church – hence the expression "sent to Coventry", meaning shunned or ostracized. But not everyone goes along with this version of events. Some claim the phrase derives from Shakespeare's Henry IV Part I, when Falstaff says of his motley band of foot soldiers: "*I'll not march through Coventry with them*".

Eating and drinking

Coventry hardly heaves with great places to **eat**, but *Pizza Express*, near the cathedral at 10A Hay Lane, is a safe bet for moderately priced, quality pizza and pasta, and they have a congenial rear terrace opening onto Castle Yard. Alternatively, for a snack or light meal, head for the *Bar Coast*, over in the shopping mall on Broadgate, where you can tuck into tasty Tex-Mex dishes, ciabattas, and healthy salads, or the *Tête à Tête* (Mon–Fri 8am–3pm, Sat 8am–4pm), a flowery tearoom at 188 Spon Street. The *Old Windmill*, also on Spon Street, at no. 22, has an attractive interior with flagstones and exposed wooden beams, serves a good range of brews and provides inexpensive bar food. Otherwise, Coventry's pub scene is rather too rough and ready for most tastes and many retreat to the campus of Warwick University, four miles to the south of the city. Here the **Warwick Arts Centre** is the largest arts complex outside London, with two theatres, a cinema, an art gallery, a bar and restaurant. For details of what's on, telephone the box office (☎01203/524524).

Staffordshire

Spreading north from the Birmingham conurbation, the miscellaneous and low-key landscapes of **Staffordshire** don't enthral too many people. Nonetheless, the county packs in coachloads of visitors owing to the presence of **Alton Towers** (☎0990/204060) – Britain's answer to Disney glitter, and the nation's most popular tourist attraction, with several million visitors annually. The white-knuckle rides take much more money than do the hoteliers in the cathedral city of **Lichfield**, at the southern end of Staffordshire, both the main historic attraction and the county's prettiest town. Lichfield also makes a handy base for visiting two towns of specific (day-tripping) interest, **Stoke-on-Trent**, famous for its pottery – and factory shops – and the old brewing capital of **Burton-upon-Trent**. Finally, beyond the county's industrial heartland, the northern reaches of Staffordshire hold the moorland town of **Leek**, one possible base for dipping into the Peak District National Park (see p.569).

Mainline **rail** services pass through Lichfield, Stafford and Stoke en route between London, Birmingham and the northwest, and through Burton-upon-Trent on the way from Birmingham to Yorkshire and the northeast. Wedged in between the major urban centres of the West Midlands and northwest England, the area is also well served by **coaches** and has a decent network of local **buses** and trains.

Lichfield

Just eighteen miles from the centre of Birmingham, the pocket-sized town of **LICHFIELD** is a slow-moving but amiable place that demands a visit for one reason – its magnificent sandstone **Cathedral** (daily 7.40am–6.30pm; £3 donation requested). Begun in 1085, but substantially rebuilt in the thirteenth and fourteenth centuries, the cathedral is unique in possessing three spires – an appropriate distinction for a bishopric that once extended over virtually all of the Midlands. The church stands on the site of a shrine built for the relics of St Chad, an English bishop noted for his humility who died here in Lichfield in 672.

The cathedral's **west front** is adorned by over one hundred statues of biblical figures, English kings and the supposed ancestors of Christ, some of them dating back to the thirteenth century but mostly Victorian replacements of originals destroyed by Cromwell's troops. Even the central spire was demolished during the skirmishes – Lichfield justly claims to be the cathedral that was most damaged during the Civil War. Extensive and painstaking rebuilding and restoration work, which was begun immediately on the restoration of the monarchy in 1660, has gone on ever since, although the bulk of it was only completed at the end of the nineteenth century.

The **interior** is no less impressive, even if the dimensions are surprisingly modest. The finest part of the main body of the church is the east end, where the choir is set at an angle of ten degrees to the line of the nave. The first three bays of the choir are the oldest part of the church, completed in the Early English style of the twelfth century, but the rest of the choir is middle Gothic – or Decorated. On the south side of the choir nave stands a two-storey thirteenth-century extension whose upper level, with its fine minstrels' gallery, was where the head of St Chad used to be displayed to the faithful. Most impressive of all, however, is the **Lady Chapel**, at the far end of the choir, which boasts a set of magnificent sixteenth-century windows, purchased from the Cistercian abbey at Herkenrode in southern Belgium in 1802.

SAMUEL JOHNSON

Eighteenth-century England's most celebrated wit and critic, **Samuel Johnson** was born above his father's bookshop in Lichfield's market square in 1709. From Lichfield he went to Pembroke College, Oxford, which he left in 1731 without having completed his degree. Disgruntled with academia, Johnson returned to Staffordshire as a teacher, before settling in Birmingham for three years, a period that saw his first pieces published in the *Birmingham Journal*.

In 1735 Johnson married Elizabeth Porter, a Birmingham friend's widow twenty years his senior, returning to his home district to open a private school in the village of Edial, three miles southwest of Lichfield. The school was no great success, so after two years the Johnsons abandoned the project and went to London with the young David Garrick, their star pupil. Journalism and essays were the mainstay of the Johnsons' penurious existence until publisher Robert Dodsley asked Samuel to consider compiling a **Dictionary of the English Language**, a project that nobody had undertaken before, and which was to occupy him for eight years prior to its publication in 1755. Massively learned and full of mordant wit ("lexicographer: a writer of dictionaries; a harmless drudge"), the Dictionary is one of Johnson's greatest legacies, although he was financially and emotionally stretched to breaking point by the workload it imposed upon him. Money problems continued to dog the writer – in 1759 he wrote the novel *Rasselas* in one week, in order to raise money for his mother's funeral – but a degree of financial stability came at last in the early 1760s, when the new king, George III, granted him a bursary of £300 per year.

In 1763 Johnson met James Boswell, a pushy young Scot who clung tenaciously to the cantankerous older man until he learned to like him. Their journey to Scotland resulted in one of the finest travel books ever written, **A Journey to the Western Isles of Scotland** (1775), in which Johnson's fascinated incredulity at the native way of life makes for utterly absorbing reading. Other publications from his final decade included a preface to Shakespeare's plays, a series of political tracts and the magnificent **Lives of the English Poets**. However, the work by which he is now best known is not one that he himself wrote – it is Boswell's **The Life of Samuel Johnson**, commenced on its subject's death in 1784, published in 1791 and still the English language's most full-blooded biography.

The cathedral's greatest treasure, the **Lichfield Gospels**, is displayed in the beautiful chapter house. One of the most exquisite and valuable surviving Anglo-Saxon artefacts in the country, this 1250-year-old illuminated manuscript contains the complete gospels of Matthew and Mark, and a fragment of the gospel of Luke, written in Latin and embellished with elaborate decoration. No one knows who wrote it, but experts believe it was produced locally and records certainly show it was stolen in a raid and carried off to Wales, from where it was eventually returned in medieval times. The page on display is the gorgeous Carpet Page, showing a decorative cross whose blend of Coptic, Celtic and Oriental influences make it the equal of the more famous Irish Book of Kells and Lindisfarne Gospels (see p.905). The fact that the book ends midway through St Luke means it's almost certainly one of a pair – and rare book specialists have long been on the look-out for the matching volume.

The south transept contains a bust of the city's most famous son, **Samuel Johnson**, and if you walk a couple of hundred yards south from the cathedral to Breadmarket Street, on the corner of the market place, you'll come to the **Samuel Johnson Birthplace Museum** (daily 10.30am–4.30pm; £2 or £3.20 joint ticket with Heritage Exhibition). Crammed with books, manuscripts and pictures, the museum pays handsome tribute to the great man, and produces a useful leaflet on the "Johnson Trail", for those who want to retrace his footsteps round his home patch. Opposite Johnson's house, in the middle of the market square, the twelfth-century parish church of **St Mary** is now home to the **Lichfield Heritage Centre** (daily 10am–5pm; £2), an over-designed but comprehensive presentation of the city's history, with illuminating sections on the Civil War and Regency periods. Outside the church, on either side of the market square, stand ponderous statues of Samuel Johnson and his biographer, James Boswell. Near the latter is a memorial to Edward Wightman, who was burnt at the stake for heresy on this very spot in 1612. It was dashed hard luck – he was the last Englishman to be so punished for this particular crime.

As for the rest of the centre, Lichfield is graced by dozens of elegant Georgian houses, with an especially handsome ensemble flanking **The Close**, by the cathedral. Another Georgian property to look for is **Donegal House**, a warm redbrick building tucked in the southwestern corner of the market square on Bore Street. It's now home to both the tourist office, on the ground floor, and the uninspiring **Lichfield Sketchbook** of local history up above (Mon–Sat 9am–5pm; free).

Practicalities

Frequent **trains** from Birmingham call at the Lichfield City central station before continuing to Lichfield Trent Valley station, on the northern fringe of the city and served by main-line trains from London Euston and the northwest. The **tourist office** is in Donegal House on Bore Street, just off the market square (Mon–Sat 9am–5pm; ☎01543/252109).

Lichfield has a reasonable range of **accommodation**. Best value among the hotels is *Oakleigh House*, 25 St Chad's Rd (☎01543/262688; ③), a large Victorian building overlooking the cathedral pool – or pond – with a popular conservatory restaurant (open to non-residents). **B&Bs** within easy reach of the cathedral include the excellent *Gaialands*, 9 Gaiafields Rd (☎01543/263764; no credit cards; ③), whose bright and cheerful rooms occupy part of a large and attractive Victorian home, and Mrs Jones's appealing B&B, in a listed nineteenth-century town house by the cathedral at 8 The Close (☎01543/418483; ③).

Most of the better-value **restaurants** are around Bore Street and St John Street, including a few Indian and Chinese places – the inexpensive *Prince of India*, 9 Bore St, is as good as anywhere. Alternatively, the *Olive Tree*, 34 Tamworth St, is a fashionable bistro serving up tasty Mediterranean-style dishes at reasonable prices.

Stoke-on-Trent

The inhabitants of **STOKE-ON-TRENT**, some thirty miles northwest of Lichfield, have been making pottery since Roman times, but mass production only began in the eighteenth century. Then, in the space of forty years, the development of local coalfields, the securing of a regular supply of fine-quality clay from Devon and Cornwall and the digging of the Trent-Mersey canal transformed the town and its environs into the biggest centre of pottery production in the world – known, logically enough, as **The Potteries**. It was all a terrible eyesore and the district, with its belching smoke stacks and fuming bottle kilns, became synonymous with industrial squalor, but the profits were enormous – quite enough to attract a string of talented entrepreneur-designers. The first of them, and still the most renowned, was Josiah Wedgwood, who opened a factory here in 1769. More recently, the industry has been in decline, hit hard by cheap foreign imports, but Britain's department stores are still stacked with The Potteries' products and local companies – such as Royal Doulton, Spode, Royal Worcester and Wedgwood – are making a fight of it. All this industrial activity doesn't spell much in the way of tourist delight, but Stoke-on-Trent's heritage museums and factory shops are enough to keep most visitors happy for a few hours at least.

The city of Stoke-on-Trent is, in fact, an amalgam of **six towns** – confusing for fans of locally born Arnold Bennett, who wrote about the five towns in novels such as *Clayhanger* and *Anna of the Five Towns*, ignoring the smallest of the six, **Fenton**. Of the other five, the major two are **Stoke** itself, which feels as if it has been left to wither to the benefit of **Hanley**, a mile to the north, which has all the main shops and the main civic museum. **Tunstall** and **Burslem** to the north and **Longton** to the southeast are the remaining Stoke towns, all largely autonomous communities. Trains arrive at **Stoke** station, whereas buses use the **Lichfield Street bus station** in central Hanley.

The **Potteries Museum and Art Gallery** in Bethesda Street, Hanley (Mon–Sat 10am–5pm, Sun 2–5pm; free), holds a magnificent and colossal collection of English pottery and ceramics. The museum tracks through the industry's eighteenth-century artistic heyday and the boom of the nineteenth with examples from all the leading manufacturers. There is also a section of Art Deco pieces – look out for the work of Clarice Cliff – and examples of present-day production. An excellent social history department includes a poignant memorial to three local people who died in the 1984–85 miners' strike – two men on picket duty and one boy scavenging for coal in the winter. For an introduction to the industry itself, head for the excellent **Gladstone Pottery Museum** in Uttoxeter Road, Longton (daily 10am–5pm; £3.95). Distinguished by the large bottle-kilns that used to dominate the entire city, the museum employs craftspeople to demonstrate the skills of pottery production, and details the evolution of the six towns and the social conditions of their people.

Dozens of pottery workshops and factories are open to visitors – the **tourist office** in the Potteries Shopping Centre on Quadrant Road in Hanley (Mon–Sat 9.15am–5.15pm; ☎01782/236000), can supply details. One of the better known companies is Royal Doulton, who have a factory shop at the Regent Works, Lawley Street, Longton (Mon–Sat 9am–5.30pm, Sun 11am–5pm; ☎01782/291172). Without a car, the most convenient way to get around all the main sites is with a China Day Rider bus ticket (£4), timetables for which are also available at the tourist office.

Leek

The sturdy town of **LEEK**, ten miles northeast of Stoke (from where there are frequent buses), is short of specific sights, but it is a lively and cheerful place from which to explore the barren moorlands that comprise the western peripheries of the Peak

District. The **tourist office**, 1 Market Place (April–Oct Mon–Sat 9.30am–5pm; Nov–March Mon–Fri 9.30am–5pm, Sat 10am–4pm; ☎01538/483741) is well stocked with information on walking, riding and cycling in the area, as well as on Leek's flourishing antiques and fine-art trade. **Accommodation** in Leek includes B&B at *Peak Weavers Hotel* on King Street, off Broad Street (☎01538/383729; ②), and the *Beechfield* on Park Road (☎01538/372825; ①). The nearest **youth hostel** is at Meerbrook Old School (☎01538/300148; April–June & Sept–Oct Fri & Sat only), three miles north on the banks of the Tittesworth reservoir. Best **pubs** are the *Swan* and *Bull's Head* in St Edward Street, the former with good food.

To the south and east of Leek are the roughly parallel **Churnet** and **Manifold valleys**, cutting green channels through the bleak moors, offering superb contrasts within very short distances. Both can be reached from **WATERHOUSES**, a tiny town about seven miles from Leek on the A523, and also on the fast and frequent bus route to Ashbourne. In Waterhouses, you can **rent bikes** from Peak Cycle Hire (☎01538/308609), who sell local cycling maps and will advise on local routes. If you want to stay in the Manifold valley, the best base is the **youth hostel** in the splendid surroundings of **Ilam Hall**, three miles east of Waterhouses (☎01335/350212; closed Dec & Jan). Ten miles southwest of Waterhouses, the **hostel** at Dimmingsdale, near Oakamoor (☎01538/702304) is ideally placed for the Churnet valley – and just two miles from **Alton Towers** (mid-March to early Nov 9.30am–7pm or dusk; £19.50; ☎0990/204060; *www.alton-towers.co.uk*). Britain's largest amusement park, Alton Towers preserves its number-one ranking by introducing more terrifying rides each season, with names like Nemesis and Oblivion. If the white-knuckle stuff is too strong for you, there are endless food outlets to escape into, along with landscaped and themed gardens and an array of less stressful fairground attractions. There's a "family friendly" **hotel** on site (☎0990/001100; ⑦ for four-person family rooms). The Alton experience doesn't come cheap; as well as the hefty entry fee (which covers all rides), be prepared to pay over the odds for food and drink.

Burton-upon-Trent

"One no sooner enters the town of Burton than he begins to be oppressed by a sense of brewery on the brain," wrote one nineteenth-century traveller, and for all the intersections and ring roads that today surround the place, little has changed in **BURTON-UPON-TRENT**, twelve miles northeast of Lichfield. Steel stacks belching steam and the all-pervasive aroma of stewed barley characterize a town that remains largely dependent on the Bass company, whose breweries have been Burton's raison d'être for the past hundred years or more. This is Britain's major brewing centre, but, unless you're an ale enthusiast, you'll find little to detain you. Devotees of the hop, however, can follow their noses to the **Bass Museum Brewery**, Horninglow Street (daily 10am–5pm; £4.50), where displays about the brewing process, the history of the industry in Burton and even the Bass company's drayhorses, culminate in a sample from the bar. You can also extend your visit to include a tour of the **brewery** (pre-book on ☎01283/511000; £3 extra), if there's enough demand. Group bookings are preferred – if you're alone, they'll add you in with a visiting party.

Practicalities

Burton is easily accessible by train from Birmingham and Derby, as well as by bus from Lichfield. The **train station** is on the west side of the town centre, a short walk along Station Street from the **tourist office**, at 183 High Street (Mon–Fri 9am–5.30pm, Sat 9am–4pm; ☎01283/516609). The **bus station** is in the Octagon Shopping Centre, one block from the tourist office along New Street. The latter operates a **room** reservation service in Burton and its environs, though there's no particular reason to stay unless – of course – you intend to research the local brews in depth.

Burton is stuffed with good **pubs**, all of which are detailed in the tourist office's handy booklet. The tap pub of the *Burton Bridge Brewery* on Bridge Street serves excellent beer in cosy surroundings, and round the corner in the High Street is a good Bass pub, the *Blue Posts*. Farther down the High Street, there are two fine Marston's pubs, the *Anchor* (New Street) and the *Leopard* (Lichfield Street). In *Coopers Tavern* on Cross Street, off Station Street, you can get a range of beers straight from the kegs stored in the back room. As for **food**, a fine range of après-booze curry can be consumed at either *George's Tandoori Restaurant*, 48 Station St (☎01283/533424), or the *Curry Centre*, 133 High St (☎01283/567362), both moderately priced.

Derby and the Peak District

In 1951, the hills and dales of the **PEAK DISTRICT**, at the southern tip of the Pennine range, became Britain's first national park. Wedged between **Derby**, Manchester and Sheffield, it is effectively the backyard for the fifteen million people who live within an hour's drive of its boundaries, though somehow it accommodates the huge influx with the minimum of fuss.

Landscapes in the Peak District come in two forms. The brooding high moorland tops of **Dark Peak**, fifteen miles east of central Manchester, take their name from the underlying gritstone, known as millstone grit for its former use – a function commemorated in the millstones demarcating the park boundary. Windswept, mist-shrouded and inhospitable, the flat tops of these peaks are nevertheless a firm favourite with walkers on the **Pennine Way**, which meanders north from the tiny village of **Edale** to the Scottish border (see box on p.576). Altogether more forgiving, the southern limestone hills of the **White Peak** have been eroded into deep forested dales populated by small stone villages and often threaded by walking trails along former rail routes. The limestone is riddled with complex cave systems around **Castleton** and under the region's largest centre, **Buxton**, a former spa town just outside the park's boundaries, at the end of an industrialized corridor reaching out from Manchester. Two of the country's most distinctive manorial piles, **Chatsworth House** and **Haddon Hall**, stand near **Bakewell**, a town famed locally not just for its cakes but also for its **well-dressing**, a possibly pagan ritual of thanksgiving for water that is observed in about twenty Peak villages throughout the summer.

Access and accommodation

Trains penetrate only as far as Buxton from the north and cut through Edale on the Manchester to Sheffield route. The main **bus access** is via the Trent bus company's TransPeak service from Nottingham to Manchester via Derby, Matlock, Bakewell and Buxton; otherwise bus #272 runs regularly from Sheffield to Castleton, via Hathersage and Hope, and the Peak Express connects Sheffield to Buxton. If you're not planning on walking between towns and villages, you'll need the essential, encyclopaedic *Peak District Timetable* (published twice-yearly; 60p), from local tourist and national park information offices, which lists all the local **public transport** services. Buses are more widespread than you might imagine, though there are limited winter and Sunday services throughout the region, and often only sporadic links between the major centres. Various one-day **transport passes** allow unlimited travel to and within specified zones. It's a complicated system, but broadly speaking the Peak Explorer (£8) covers the chunk of the park in Yorkshire, the Peak Wayfarer Manchester (£6.60), and the Derbyshire Wayfarer (£7.25) covers the rest. For all Peak District bus information call **Busline** on ☎01298/23098 (daily 7am–8pm).

A joint Derbyshire County Council/National Park venture provides for a series of **Peak Cycle Hire Centres**, which rent out **bikes** for £8 per day (plus a £20 deposit; discounts for YHA members). There's a full network of dedicated cycle lanes, tracks and old railway lines and the centres are located at: Ashbourne (Mapleton Lane, ☎01335/343156), Derwent (Fairholmes, ☎01433/651261), Hayfield (Information Centre, Station Rd, ☎01663/746222), Middleton Top (Visitor Centre, Middleton-by-Wirksworth, ☎01629/823204), Parsley Hay (☎01298/84493), and Waterhouses (Old Station Car Park, ☎01538/308609).

There's plenty of **accommodation** in and around the park, mostly in B&Bs, with a dozen youth hostels and numerous campsites scattered among them. A network of YHA-operated **camping barns** is also available. These are located in converted farm buildings and provide simple and inexpensive self-catering accommodation for between 6 and 24 people. For further details contact the YHA Camping Barns Reservation Office, 16 Shawbridge St, Clitheroe, Lancashire BB7 1LY (☎01200/428366). The Peak District National Park Authority office is at Aldern House, Baslow Road, Bakewell, DE45 1AE (☎01629/816200). They have an excellent **Web site** (*www.peakdistrict.org*) and also operate a string of **information centres**. These are supplemented by village tourist offices and in some smaller places by local stores doubling up as information points. Maps and trail guides are widely available (OS Outdoor Leisure maps 1 and 24 cover the Peak District) and guided countryside walks are commonplace – sign up locally. Finally, make sure to pick up a copy of the free *Peakland Post*, crammed with useful information.

Derby

The proximity of the Peak District might lead you to think that **DERBY**, eleven miles northeast of Burton, could prove to be an interesting stopping-off point. Sadly, the city – a status conferred as recently as 1977 – is an unexciting place, though its workaday centre is partly redeemed by several long and handsome nineteenth-century terraces and its **cathedral**, whose pinnacled tower soars high above its modest surroundings on Queen Street. Of the city's several museums, easily the best is the **Derby Museum and Art Gallery** on the Strand (Mon 11am–5pm, Tues–Sat 10am–5pm, Sun 2–5pm; free), a five-minute walk from the central marketplace. The museum exhibits a splendid collection of Derby porcelain, three thousand pieces tracking through the different phases and styles from the late eighteenth century until today: the painted scenes created by John Brewer during the Crown Derby period of 1784–1811 are especially charming. The museum also holds far and away the most comprehensive collection of the work of **Joseph Wright** (1734–1797), a local artist generally regarded as one of the most talented English painters of his century. Wright's bread and butter came from portraiture, though his attempt to fill the boots of Gainsborough, when the latter moved from Bath to London, came unstuck – his more forceful style did not satisfy his genteel customers and Wright soon hightailed it back to Derby. Wright was one of the few artists of his period to find inspiration in technology and his depictions of the scientific world were hugely influential.

The train station, on the lines between London and Sheffield and between Birmingham and the northeast, is a mile to the southeast of the city centre. Right in the heart of town, on the marketplace, is the city's **tourist office** (Mon–Fri 9.30am–5.30pm, Sat 9.30am–5pm, Sun 10.30am–2.30pm; ☎01332/255802) – worth a call if you're on your way into the Peaks.

Buxton

BUXTON was founded in 79 AD by the Romans, who happened upon a spring from which 1500 gallons of pure water gushed every hour at a constant 28°C. So famous did the spring become that Mary, Queen of Scots was allowed by her captors to come here for treatment of her rheumatism. Its heyday came in the last two decades of the eighteenth century, with the fifth duke of Devonshire's grand design to create a northern answer to Bath or Cheltenham, a plan thwarted by the climate, but not before some distinguished eighteenth-century buildings had formed the gracious Lower Buxton.

Like many former British spas, the town's heritage has been marred by a lack of money to refurbish ageing properties, though a belated attempt has been made to rescue some of the finer buildings. The thermal baths were closed in 1972, though the sweep of the **Crescent**, incorporating the former *St Ann's Hotel* – its grandest architectural feature, modelled on the Royal Crescent in Bath – has been preserved thanks to a hefty government grant. It's hoped that some of the public rooms will reopen in the future, but no firm plans have yet been made. The little street fountain in front of the Crescent, supplied by **St Ann's Well**, is still used to fill local water bottles and the nearby **Pump Room**, first erected in 1894, provides space for temporary art exhibitions in the summer. At the eastern end of the Crescent, a glass and cast-iron canopy hides the entrance to the Cavendish Arcade shopping centre, which makes a hash of preserving the original eighteenth-century bath houses.

The spa remnants apart, the town is at its best in the nearby landscaped **Pavilion Gardens**, just to the southwest of the Crescent, where the thousand-seat **Opera House** (tours most Sats at 11am; £1; call ☎01298/72190 to check), facing Water Street, is the main venue for the **Buxton Opera Festival** held during the last two weeks of July. The glasshouse gardens next to the Opera House shelter an array of exotic foliage and you can walk through to the double-decker glass-and-iron pavilion itself, overlooking the formal gardens, where there's a bar, coffee shop and restaurant with nice views.

Fronting the Crescent, an attractive park known as **The Slopes** – laid out in 1818 in the last flush of municipal enthusiasm – leads up to the traffic-choked Market Place. The top of The Slopes offers the best prospect over the Crescent to the *Palace Hotel* (see below) and the **Devonshire Hospital**; the latter, built in 1790 as a riding school, is covered by what for a long time was the world's widest domed roof. Just down Terrace Road from Market Place, the **Buxton Museum and Art Gallery** (Tues–Fri 9.30am–5.30pm, Sat 9.30am–5pm, Sun in summer only 10.30am–5pm; £1) houses a collection of ancient fossils, rocks and pots found in the Peak District, among them jawbones from Neolithic lions and bears. The displays on the first floor document the history of the region from the Bronze Age through to more recent times.

As rewarding as any of Buxton's architectural attractions is **Poole's Cavern** (Easter–Oct daily 10am–5pm; £4.50; ☎01298/26978), a mile to the south of town: follow the Broadwalk through the Pavilion Gardens and then take Temple Road. The guided-tour patter is irksome, but the orange and blue-grey stalactite formations are amazingly complex and the chambers impressively large; one marks the underground source of the River Wye. A twenty-minute walk up through the Grinlow Woods from the mouth of the cave leads to **Solomon's Temple**, a Victorian folly with great views across Buxton and the hills to the west.

Practicalities

There's an hourly train service from Manchester Piccadilly to Buxton, terminating two minutes' walk from the centre at the **train station** on Station Road. The TransPeak **bus** runs every two hours between Manchester (Chorlton Street Coach Station) and Nottingham, and stops in Buxton's Market Place, as do the regular buses from Sheffield Interchange. Although the town isn't actually in the National Park, its **tourist office** in the old Natural Mineral Baths on the Crescent (March–Oct daily 9.30am–5pm; Nov–Feb daily 10am–4pm; ☎01298/25106) covers the whole of the Peak District.

Accommodation is plentiful, but at the cheaper end of the market it is none too inspiring, many of the cheaper guest houses being located in dreary backstreets away from the centre. *Lakenham Guest House*, 11 Burlington Rd (☎01298/79209; no credit cards; ③), is a good first choice, overlooking Pavilion Gardens. *Hartington Hotel*, 18 Broad Walk (☎01298/22638; ③), also has a nice parkside location and reasonable facilities. For cheaper beds, try the streets off Market Place, where Grange Road and South Avenue provide several budget choices. At the upper end of the market, start with the friendly *Grosvenor House Hotel*, 1 Broad Walk (☎01298/72439; ③), near The Slopes, which has a variety of rooms and its own coffee shop. The historic associations of the *Old Hall Hotel*, in The Square, near the Opera House (☎01298/22841; ⑤), resonate with some – Mary, Queen of Scots stayed here in 1573 – while parts of the old spa was the *Palace Hotel* on Palace Road (☎01298/22001; ⑦, includes dinner), still sitting pretty above the town and with fantastic views. It is a twenty-minute walk to the *Sherbrook Lodge* **youth hostel**, set in wooded grounds on Harpur Hill Road, at the end of London Road (☎01298/22287); and a further five from there up Dukes Drive to the nearest **campsite**, *Lime Tree Park* (☎01298/22988; closed Dec–Feb).

The town's **eating** options are all fairly down-to-earth, typified by the bakeries and cafés along Spring Gardens, the main pedestrianized street. *Hargreave's Coffee Shop*, 18 Spring Gardens, has a bit more about it than most, an Edwardian tearoom above a china and knick-knack emporium. The *Wild Carrot*, 5 Bridge St (closed Mon & Tues), at the end of Spring Gardens, is an adventurous (mostly vegetarian) café offering Friday-night dinners. Otherwise, you're left with a motley collection of restaurants and a couple of pubs around Market Place, with *Firenze Pizzeria Ristorante*, 3 Eagle Parade (closed Mon; dinner only), about the best of the bunch. The annual **Buxton Festival** takes place every July, featuring a full programme of classical music, opera and drama, with supporting fringe events, including a film festival. Details from the Festival Office (%01298/70395), the Opera House, where many events are staged, or from the tourist office.

Castleton

The limestone hills of the White Peaks are riddled with water-worn cave systems, best explored in the four show caves within walking distance of **CASTLETON**, ten miles northeast of Buxton. It's an agreeable small town, overlooked by Mam Tor (see box opposite), ringed by hills and cut through by a babbling river lined with stone cottages: as a base for local walks it's hard to beat, and the hikers resting up in the quiet Market Place near the church have the choice of a fine spread of local accommodation and services. Overseeing the whole ensemble is **Peveril Castle** (April–Oct daily 10am–6pm; Nov–March Wed–Sun 10am–4pm; £2; ☎01433/620613), from which the village gets its name. Its construction was started by William I's illegitimate son William Peveril to protect the king's rights to the forest that then covered vast areas of the Peak District. After a stiff climb up to the keep, you can trace much of the surviving curtain wall, which commands great views of the Hope Valley.

The closest cavern to town, the **Peak Cavern** (Easter–Oct daily 10am–5pm; Nov–Easter weekends 10am–4pm; £4.75) is tucked in a gully at the back of the town, its gaping mouth once providing shelter for a rope factory and a small village, of which a vague floorplan remains. Daniel Defoe, visiting in the eighteenth century, noted the cavern's colourful local name, the "Devil's Arse", after the fiendish fashion in which the interior contours twisted and turned. Twenty minutes' walk out of town along the road to Winnat's Pass (there's a parallel route, across the fields) lies **Speedwell Cavern** (daily 9.30am–4.30pm; summer till 5.30pm; last entry 30min before closing; £5.25); at 600-feet below ground, it's the deepest cave accessible to the public in Britain. That said, there's precious little to see, with the main drama coming with the means of access itself – down a hundred dripping steps and then by boat through a quarter-mile-long claustrophobic tunnel that was blasted out in search of lead. At the end lies the

Bottomless Pit, a pool where 40,000 tons of mining rubble were dumped without raising the water level.

The other two caves are the world's only source of the sparkling fluorspar known as **Blue John**. Highly prized for ornaments and jewellery for the past 250 years, this semi-precious stone comes in a multitude of hues from blue through deep red to yellow, depending on its hydrocarbon impurities. Before being cut and polished it must be soaked in pine resin, a process originally carried out in France, where the term *bleu-jaune* (after its primary colours) provided the source of its English name. The **Treak Cliff Cavern** (March–Oct daily 9.30am–5.30pm; Nov–Feb daily 10am–4pm, last entry 40min before closing; £4.50; ☎01433/620571), a few hundred yards along the hillside from Speedwell, contains the best examples of the stone in situ and a good deal more in the shop. This is also the best cave to visit in its own right, dripping – literally – with stalactites (some up to 100,000 years old), flowstone and bizarre rock formations, all visible on an entertaining forty-minute walking tour through the main cave system. Water collected in one of the caves is used to make tea in the café at the entrance since it's much purer than the stuff that pours from the local taps. Tours of the **Blue John Cavern** (daily 9.30am–5.30pm; reduced hours in winter; £5; ☎01433/620638) dive deeper into the rock, with narrow steps and sloping paths following an ancient watercourse through whirlpool-hollowed chambers down to the Dining Room Cavern, where a former owner once held a banquet. Blue John Cavern is another fifteen minutes' sign-posted walk beyond Treak Cliff, or there's direct access off the A625, just west of Castleton.

Practicalities

The A625 runs through the centre of Castleton as the high street, with approaches from the west sidetracking down B roads and descending the steep Winnats Pass into town. From the east it's a clear run along the A625 from Sheffield. The main approach by public transport is by **bus** from Sheffield on the (roughly) hourly #272, though there are also limited local services from Bakewell and Buxton. The regular Manchester Piccadilly–Hope Valley–Sheffield trains stop at **Hope train station** two miles east of town, which is linked

---

WALKS AROUND CASTLETON

Several routes take you up from the Hope Valley onto the tops which ring Castleton, some taking in the show caves along the way and most being easy to follow in good weather: you'll need OS map *Outdoor Leisure 1*, or one of the trail leaflets from the information office.

A path runs west from town, climbing past Peak, Speedwell and Treak Cliff caverns before bending around a bluff to reach the Blue John Cavern: if you're sightseeing, you can complete the short circular walk here by following the minor road back down the precipitous **Whinnats Pass**, emerging again at Speedwell Cavern. For the best views, though, keep following the signposted path from Blue John for the slow climb up the National-Trust-owned **Mam Tor** (1696ft) and its barely discernible Iron Age hillfort (3km from Castleton, 1hr 30min). It's the Peak District's second-highest peak and the NT's most tramped upon outdoor site, attracting over 250,000 visitors a year – hence the flagstoned path up to the top and along the ridge, whose stone was helicoptered in. This channels the summer crowds along something of a hikers' motorway, but it has allowed the hillside to regenerate itself and the nesting birds to return. The views – to Kinder Scout, Castleton, Edale and down the Hope valley – remain unsurpassed.

From the peak the ridge rolls along to the northeast and opportunities to drop back down to Castleton can be taken at either Hollins Cross, Back Tor or from Losehill Pike, making the complete walk anything from three to six hours. Hollins Cross is also the lowest crossing-point on the two-hour walk from Castleton to Edale, which could also form part of a circuit involving scaling Mam Tor.

to Castleton by the #272 bus and other local services. The **Peak District National Park Information Centre** is on Castle Street, near the church (Easter–Oct daily 10am–1pm & 2–5.30pm; Nov–Easter daily 10am–1pm & 2–5pm; ☎01433/620679).

Accommodation is plentiful, but should be booked in advance at popular holiday times; the information office can help if you're stuck. The lively **youth hostel** (☎01433/620235, *castleton@yha.org.uk*) is housed in eighteenth-century Castleton Hall and the adjacent old vicarage on Market Place, just up past the church from the information office. The most welcoming **B&B** is the slightly eccentric *Bargate Cottage*, also on Market Place (☎01433/620201; no credit cards; ②), whose frilly rooms are overseen by a friendly proprietor who offers conversation, good breakfasts and welcome extras like drying baskets for hiking boots. Two or three other B&Bs are sited just over the road from here. *Cryer House*, a little way back down Castle Street (☎01433/620244; no credit cards; ②), opposite the church, has a lovely conservatory, or try for space at the popular *Kelseys Swiss House* on How Lane (☎01433/621098; no credit cards; ②), the eastern continuation of the main road through town. All the local pubs have rooms, such as *Ye Olde Cheshire Cheese*, How Lane (☎01433/620330; ③). The best lodgings are at *Ye Olde Nag's Head* at Cross Street on the main road (☎01433/620248; ⑤), a comfortable, if slightly sniffy, seventeenth-century coaching inn with some good weekend – and dinner, room and breakfast – deals. The nearest **campsite** is in Hope, two miles east of Castleton, where the *Laneside Caravan Park* (☎01433/620215; closed Nov–Easter) lies five minutes from Hope's pubs and shops.

The pubs are the mainstay for **eating out** in Castleton, and aren't bad to boot. *Ye Olde Cheshire Cheese* welcomes muddy boots and fills their owners with generous portions, while the *Castle* on Castle Street has an appealing series of rooms warmed by open fires. Best of all are the bar meals at *Ye Olde Nag's Head*, boasting treats like *bruschetta* and wild mushrooms; you can eat more expensively, and equally well, in their restaurant too.

Edale

There's almost nothing to **EDALE** except for a couple of pubs, a scattering of local B&Bs and a train station, and it's this isolation which is immediately appealing. Walkers arrive in droves throughout the year to set off on the 250-mile **Pennine Way** (see box on p.576) across England's backbone to Kirk Yetholm on the Scottish border; its starting-point is signposted from outside the *Old Nag's Head* at the head of the village.

An excellent **circular walk** (9 miles; 1300ft; 5hr) uses the first part of the Pennine Way, leading up onto the bleak gritstone table-top of **Kinder Scout** (2088ft), below which the village cowers. The route cuts west from the *Nag's Head* along a packhorse route once used by Cheshire's salt exporters. From the campsite and camping barn at *Upper Booth Farm* (☎01433/670250), you climb the Jacob's Ladder path continuing half a mile west to the carved medieval **Edale Cross**. Backtracking a couple of hundred yards, the Pennine Way branches north along the broken plateau edge to **Kinder Downfall**, Derbyshire's highest cascade. This was the site of the **Kinder Scout Trespass** of 1932, when dozens of protesters walked onto unused but private land, five subsequently receiving prison sentences. It was the turning-point in the fight for public access to open moorland, leading, three years later, to the formation of the Ramblers' Association. At Kinder Downfall turn east then southeast across the often boggy peat towards the wind-sculpted **Wool Pack** rocks, then across to the eastern rim, where a path to the south along Grindslow Knoll and down into Edale avoids Grindsbrook Clough, the highly eroded route of the original Pennine Way. It can be extremely wet up here among the bare furrows of peat – long-distance walker John Hillaby, on his *Journey Through Britain*, had to resort to removing his footwear to make his way across the sodden top of Kinder Scout, which to his appalled mind looked as if it were "entirely covered in the droppings of dinosaurs".

Edale is around four miles northwest of Castleton by road, slightly more direct by path. Hourly **trains** from Manchester or Sheffield (stopping in Hathersage, too; see p.579–580) provide surprisingly easy access; the only **bus** is a summer-only Sunday service from Castleton. Walking straight up the road 400 yards from the train station takes you to the **National Park Information Centre** (Easter–Oct daily 9am–1pm & 2–5.30pm; rest of the year closes at 5pm; ☎01433/670207) at Fieldhead. This sells all manner of trail leaflets and hiking guides and can advise about local **accommodation** options. The nearest **youth hostel**, the highly popular *Edale YHA Activity Centre* (☎01433/670302, *edale@yha.org.uk*) is a mile and a half northeast of Edale station, at Rowland Cote, Nether Booth. It's accessible along the road to Nether Booth or through the *Fieldhead* **campsite** (which may, or may not, still be in operation) behind the information centre. However, there is also camping at *Cooper's* at Newfold Farm (☎01433/670372), in the centre of Edale near the *Old Nag's Head*. Other options used by Pennine Way walkers include the **camping barns** at Upper Booth and at *Cotefield Farm*, Ollerbrook (☎01433/670273), which lies on the path to the youth hostel.

Those without hair shirts, or with more money, will do better at the **B&Bs**, starting with the *Old Parsonage*, behind the *Nag's Head* (☎01433/670232; no credit cards; ①; closed Oct–Easter). *Stonecroft*, a detached Victorian house on the village road near the church (☎01433/670262; no credit cards; ③) is good, too, while other private home and farmhouse options lie scattered out along the Nether Booth road: attractive *Edale House* (☎01433/670399; ①) is typical, a twenty-minute walk from the pub. The *Ramblers' Inn* (☎01433/670268; ③), close to the train station at the bottom of the village, has rooms, and is one of only two places to **eat** and drink. Those things, though, are best done at the hiker-friendly *Old Nag's Head* (☎01433/670291), at the top of the village, though you'll be forced down to the *Ramblers'* a couple of times a week in winter when the *Old Nag's Head* is closed.

Bakewell

BAKEWELL, flanking the banks of the River Wye twelve miles east of Buxton, is famous for its **Bakewell Pudding**. Known throughout the rest of the country as a Bakewell tart, this is a wonderful flaky, almond-flavoured confection invented here around 1860 when a cook botched a recipe for strawberry tart. Almost a century before this fortuitous mishap, the duke of Rutland set out to develop a spa here to surpass the work his rival, the duke of Devonshire, was doing at Buxton. The frigidity of the water made failure inevitable, leaving only Bath Gardens beside Rutland Square as a reminder of the venture.

Today, there's little reason to linger in town, though it makes a useful base for the surrounding countryside. Stone houses cling to the handful of surviving old lanes near the river, but the heavily trafficked market town (market day is Monday) does itself few other favours. Pop in at least to the **parish church**, All Saints, which sits on a rise at the top of town. Here you'll find a Saxon cross in the churchyard and handsome sixteenth-century tombs inside. One is of local bigwig Sir George Vernon, the other of his daughter Dorothy Manners and her husband John Manners (see Haddon Hall, p.577). Signs behind the churchyard point you up the lane to the **Old House Museum** in Cunningham Place (April–Oct daily 1.30–4pm; July & Aug daily 11am–4pm; £2), a Tudor house once owned by Richard Arkwright, now housing rustic tools and costumes from Bakewell's past. The energetic can head off along the **Monsal Trail**, which cuts eight miles north through some of Derbyshire's finest limestone valleys to Wyedale, three miles east of Buxton.

Practicalities

The nearest **train** stations are at Matlock and Buxton, leaving **bus** services such as the TransPeak Manchester to Nottingham service, the Peak Express from Sheffield, the

---

THE PENNINE WAY

The 250-mile-long **Pennine Way** was the country's first long-distance footpath, officially opened in 1965 and stretching north from the boggy plateau of Kinder Scout, through the Yorkshire Dales and Teesdale, crossing Hadrian's Wall and the Northumberland National Park, before entering Scotland to fizzle out at the village of Kirk Yetholm. People had been using a similar route for over thirty years before the official opening, inspired by Tom Stephenson, secretary of the Ramblers' Association, who had first identified the need for such a long-distance path in the 1930s. His idea was to stick to the crest of the Pennines where practicable and link up existing tracks, bridleways and footpaths, only descending to the valleys for overnight accommodation and services. The problem was that much of the route lay on private land, so years of negotiation and rerouteing were necessary before the Pennine Way could be officially declared open.

Now it's one of the most popular walks in the country, either taken in sections or completed in two to three weeks, depending on your level of fitness and experience. It's a challenge in the best of weather, since it passes through some of the most remote countryside in England – you must be properly equipped, able to use a map and compass and be prepared to follow local advice about current diversions and rerouteing; changes are often made to avoid erosion of the existing path. The National Trail Guides, *Pennine Way: South* and *Pennine Way: North* (Aurum Press) are essential, though some still prefer to stick to Wainwright's *Pennine Way Companion* (Michael Joseph). National park **information** centres along the route – particularly the one at Edale – stock a full selection of guides and associated trail leaflets and can offer advice. The YHA also operates a Pennine Way **room-booking service** (☎01629/581061) for its hostels. Finally, on reaching the end, you can get your certificate stamped at Edale's *Old Nag's Head* in the south or Kirk Yetholm's *Border Hotel* in the north.

---

infrequent bus from Castleton, and the #R32/32A from Derby/Matlock as the main routes into town. All services stop in central Rutland Square, with the **tourist office** in the restored, seventeenth-century Old Market Hall (Easter–Oct daily 9.30am–5.30pm; Nov–Easter daily 9.30am–5pm, closed Thurs afternoon; ☎01629/813227), just a couple of hundred yards down the road. This is very well equipped with local biking and hiking leaflets and guides.

For **B&B**, try the *Avenue House*, whose three attractively furnished rooms occupy part of a spacious Victorian house on Haddon Road, near the river (☎01629/812467; no credit cards; ②; closed Nov–Jan). Alternatively, the homely *Castle Inn*, on Castle Street (☎01629/812103; ①) is a sympathetic old inn by the bridge over the Wye with four straightforward, comfortable rooms. The town's **youth hostel**, at Fly Hill (☎01629/812313), north of the church off the Buxton road, is pretty central, while the closest **campsite**, *Greenhills Caravan Park* (☎01629/813052), lies a mile and a half north on the Buxton road. More upmarket is the luxurious *Hassop Hall Hotel* (☎01629/640488; ⑤), a cannily refurbished old manor house with beautiful bedrooms set in charming parkland just 2.5 miles north of Bakewell along the A619 and then the B6001.

There are several good **restaurants** in town, especially *Aitch's Wine Bar & Bistro*, 4 Buxton Rd, near North Church Street, which serves Mediterranean-style dishes, and the French *Renaissance* (closed Sun evening & Mon) on nearby Bath Street, which has a set three-course dinner for around £15. **Bar meals** at the *Castle Inn* are of a good standard too. Excellent **bakeries** all over town claim to bake Bakewell Pudding to the original recipe, with the favourite being the *Old Original Bakewell Pudding Shop* on Rutland Square – open until 9pm in summer and with a full restaurant menu as well as gargantuan, family-sized puddings for a fiver. *Bloomer's* on Water Lane is a fine deli and bakery, known for its home-made sweet and savoury pies.

For a walk or ride to a **country pub**, the wonderfully sited *Lathkil Hotel* (☎01629/812501; ⑨) in Over Haddon, two miles southwest of Bakewell, takes some beating. Its picture windows look out over Lathkil Dale, down into which footpaths meander, while there's reasonable bar food and a more adventurous evening menu in the restaurant.

Haddon Hall

The simple, understated **Haddon Hall** (April–Sept daily 11am–5pm; £5.50; parking 50p), two miles south of Bakewell on the banks of the Wye (by the A6 and on the TransPeak bus route), is one of the finest medieval manor houses in England. In the mid-twelfth century it passed from its Norman founders, the Avenells, to the Vernons, who owned it for four hundred years until 1558 when the sole heir, **Dorothy Vernon**, married John Manners, scion of another powerful family who later became dukes of Rutland. Their union is commemorated on their joint tomb in Bakewell church, but the romantic story of their elopement is probably apocryphal. At the start of the eighteenth century, when the Devonshires outdid the Rutlands by building nearby Chatsworth, the hall fell into two hundred years of neglect, thereby sparing it from Georgian and Victorian meddling.

Restoration at the beginning of this century revealed the **chapel**'s wall paintings of exotic plants and animals, plastered over at the Reformation. Across the courtyard, the fourteenth-century kitchens – originally detached from the house for fear of fire – are now connected by a passage to the banqueting hall, complete with a beautifully restored roof. A couple of less interesting domestic rooms lead to the house's highlight, the **Long Gallery**, built by John Manners for indoor promenades during inclement weather. The **gardens**, too, are gorgeous, and the whole heady ensemble turned up to great effect as Mr Rochester's Thornfield in Zeffirelli's *Jane Eyre*.

Chatsworth House

Chatsworth House (Easter–Oct daily 11am–5.30pm; last admission 4.30pm; house & grounds £6.25, grounds only £3.60, parking £1), four miles east of Bakewell via the A619, was built in the seventeenth century by the first duke of Devonshire, and has been in the family ever since. The monumental Palladian frontage beautifully sets off the hundred acres of formal gardens, but they are tiny in comparison to the vast **park**, redesigned in the 1750s by Capability Brown. In the 1820s, the sixth duke instigated more substantial changes when he added the north wing and set Joseph Paxton (designer of London's Crystal Palace) to work on the gardens, creating the **Emperor Fountain**. At 296ft, the fountain was the world's highest gravity-fed jet, but it now attains a meagre third of that. Inside the house, a maze of balconies and grand staircases lead, eventually, to the **State Apartments**, their ceilings daubed with overblown cherubic figures. None of the rooms is finer than the **Dining Room** in the north wing, its table set as it was for the visit of George V and Queen Mary in 1933, and its wall hung with seven Van Dycks. Vases of the semiprecious Blue John stone (see p.573) flank the door through to the **Sculpture Gallery**, where you can admire a Rembrandt and a Frans Hals before exploring the gardens, restaurant, estate shop or children's playground.

The principal approach to Chatsworth leads through the immaculately maintained estate village of **Edensor**, remodelled by the sixth duke for his employees, and well worth a few minutes in its own right. There's an infrequent bus service from both Bakewell and Baslow to Edensor, but otherwise the best bet is to catch any Bakewell to Baslow bus and walk from the bus stop through the park to the house – a distance of around a mile. Walking back to Bakewell from Chatsworth is also enjoyable, and Bakewell tourist office has a leaflet outlining a possible route.

If you are looking for **accommodation**, try *Fischer's Baslow Hall* on Calver Road (☎01246/583259; ⑥), on the outskirts of the village of **BASLOW**, a mile or so north of Chatsworth. The hall is one of the Peak's greatest luxuries, an Edwardian "restaurant-with-rooms" – there are just half a dozen – with superb food, both in the expensive restaurant and less formal café. There are some more economical **B&Bs** in the village too – the Bakewell tourist office has the list and will make reservations.

Eyam and around

Within a year of September 7, 1665, the attractive hillside lead-mining settlement of **EYAM** (pronounced "Eem"), seven miles north of Bakewell, had lost almost half of its population of 750 to the bubonic plague, a calamity that earned it the enduring epithet "The Plague Village". The first victim was one George Viccars, a journeyman tailor who is said to have released some infected fleas from a package of cloth brought from London into one of the so-called **plague cottages** next to the church. The ensuing epidemic was prevented from spreading to other villages by a self-imposed quarantine led by the rector, William Mompesson, who arranged for food to be left at places on the parish boundary – such as **Mompesson's Well**, half a mile up the hill to the north and still accessible by footpath from the village. Payment was made with coins left in pools of disinfecting vinegar – the stone bowls in which they were immersed can still be seen. The rector closed the church and held services in the open air at a natural rock arch to the south of the village – and every year since 1906 (on the last Sunday in August), a commemorative service has been held here, at Cucklet Delph. Mompesson himself survived the plague, though his wife succumbed; she lies buried in the shadow of a richly carved eighth-century Celtic cross in the churchyard (red roses are placed on her tomb on remembrance day). Informative panels inside the **parish church** (Easter–Sept Mon–Sat 9am–6pm, Sun 1–5.30pm; Oct–Easter Mon–Sat 9am–4pm, Sun 1–5.30pm) tell more of the village's history, highlighting a number of plague sites dotted around the town. The most harrowing of these are the **Riley Graves**, half a mile east of the village in open country, where a Mrs Hancock buried her husband, three sons and three daughters within eight days in August 1666.

Six years after the plague ended, **Eyam Hall** (April–Oct Wed, Thurs, Sun & bank hols, guided tours 11am–5.30pm, last entry 4.30pm; £4) was built for Thomas Wright a hundred yards west of the church, possibly in an attempt to install his son as the squire of the depleted village. Wright's heirs have lived in it ever since, building up a fine collection of furnishings that can be seen on an intriguingly anecdotal hour-long guided tour. Make time, too, for the **Eyam Museum** up Hawkshill Road (March–Oct Tues–Sun 10am–4.30pm; £1.50), beyond the hall, signposted off the main street. This goes into fascinating detail about the history, transmission and effect on society of the bubonic plague – still carried by rats in national parks in certain parts of the western United States.

Practicalities

Eyam makes a great overnight stop, though you should try and book accommodation in advance, since facilities are limited. There are **buses** to the village from Sheffield, Manchester, Buxton and Baslow. All run to the village, stopping outside the *Royal Oak* on the long, main Church Street.

First choice among the handful of **B&Bs** is the luxurious *Delf View House* (☎01433/631533; no credit cards; ③), a beautifully kept Georgian house set in its own grounds just along from the church; breakfast is served in a superb old dining room with its flagstone floor, imposing fireplace and beamed ceiling. Nearby *Aughton House* (☎01433/630381; ②) is of a similar age and appeal but a tad less grand in its outlook. Otherwise, both the *Royal Oak*, at the top of the village, and the *Bull's Head*, opposite the church, are pubs with rooms, though the finest inn is the *Miner's Arms* on Water

---

THE PLAGUE

Ring a ring o' roses
A pocket full of posies
Atishoo, atishoo
We all fall down

As the residents of Eyam began to drop like flies in the autumn of 1665, the locals resorted to home remedies and desperate snatches from folkloric memory to stave off the inevitable. There was little understanding in the seventeenth century of why or how the disease spread: Daniel Defoe, in his later journal of London's plague, recorded how the lord mayor ordered the destruction of all the city's pets, believing them to be responsible. Others, thinking it to be a miasma, kept coal braziers alight day and night in the hope that the smoke would push the infection back into the sky from where it was thought it had come. In isolated Eyam, with the plague among them and no way out through the self-imposed cordon, the locals improvised to little effect. Applications of cold water, herb infusions and draughts of brine or lemon juice were tried; poultices applied; bleeding by leeches was commonplace; and when all else failed, charms and spells were wheeled out – the plucked tail of a pigeon laid against the sore supposedly drew out the poison. All, of course, failed and the death toll mounted, though occasionally there was coincidental success: one fourteen-year-old girl mistakenly drank a pitcher of discarded bacon fat, left by her bedside; the fever passed and she recovered.

Centuries later, the horrifying events lie recorded in, of all things, a children's nursery game, whose rhyme became popular in plague-ridden England. The "roses" are the patches which developed on the victim's chest soon after contracting the disease; the "posies" are herbs or flowers, carried as charms; as the fever took hold, sneezing ("atishoo, atishoo") was a common symptom; until, chillingly, at death's door, "we all fall down".

Lane (☎01433/630853; ③), off the main square. This has nice modern rooms, some of them self-contained in a separate building next to the pub. Eyam **youth hostel**, a large Victorian house on Hawkhill Road (☎01433/630335; closed Dec–March), is a steep twenty-minute walk out of the village, past the museum. The best place **to eat** is the *Miner's Arms* which serves bar meals at lunch (Tues–Sat) and more formal, but very enjoyable, traditional British dinners and Sunday lunch in its restaurant.

Foolow and Bretton

A mile-and-a-half walk west through the fields from Eyam, the hamlet of **FOOLOW** has the excellent *Bull's Head* (☎01433/630873; no credit cards; ⑤) serving decent beer, bar meals and with live music once a week – local buses make the trip too. Just to the north of here, on a wild road up to a windswept ridge, the *Barrel* at **BRETTON** is another fine country pub, with amazing views from its terrace seats. A hundred yards down the road from the pub, a very basic **youth hostel** (reservations on ☎0114/288 4541; open weekends only, but daily for parts of July & Aug) plies its lonely trade: you can reach this and the pub by a path from Eyam, just two (steep) miles away.

Hathersage

The busy little town of **HATHERSAGE** on the A625, nine miles north of Bakewell and just eleven from Sheffield, has a hard time persuading people not to pass straight through into the heart of the national park. It's worth at least an hour though, particularly in its quieter reaches on the heights around the much restored village **church of St Michael and All Angels**, where a prominent grave site is said to be that of Sherwood outlaw Little John. The footpath up to the church starts by the side of the

Hathersage Inn on the main road. Hathersage's other claim to fame is as the "Morton" of Charlotte Brontë's **Jane Eyre** – a village name borrowed by the author from the landlord of the *George* in Hathersage, who met Charlotte off the stagecoach from Haworth when she came to stay here in 1845. She was visiting a friend, whose brother was the local vicar and, in the church, Charlotte doubtless was shown the memorial "Eyre brasses". She also used several other local names and buildings for her novel, notably North Lees Hall (Rochester's Thornfield Hall) and Moorseats (St John Rivers' Moor House) – all of which can be taken in on a four-mile circular walk around the town.

Hathersage also boasts its share of craft and cottage industries, most notably the impressive **Round Building**, just outside town on the B6001 (Mon–Sat 10am–5pm, Sun 11am–5pm; ☎01433/650220), where Sheffield designer David Mellor produces wonderful cutlery, tableware and kitchenware. There are several first-rate B&Bs – like *Moorgate*, on Castleton Road (☎01433/650293; no credit cards; ①) – and rooms in half a dozen pubs, including the fancy *George* itself (☎01433/650436; ⑤) or the *Scotsman's Pack* (☎01433/650253; ③), a flagstoned, eighteenth-century inn on School Lane, the way to the church. Real Brontë fans will be delighted to know that two apartments in the beautifully restored *North Lees Hall* can be rented – contact the *Vivat Trust* (☎0171/930 8030); prices run between £340 and £435 a week for the two-person and £440–570 for the larger five-person apartment. All the **pubs** serve bar meals, while the restaurant at the *George* is probably the best in town. Otherwise, *Longland's Eating House* on Main Road is a laid-back, licensed, mainly vegetarian, café above a good hiking/outdoors shop. The local **youth hostel** (☎01433/650493) is on the edge of the village, on the Castleton road, a hundred yards past the *George*. The #272 Sheffield–Castleton **bus** stops right outside the *George* and Hathersage is also on the Manchester–Sheffield **train** line.

THE EAST MIDLANDS

The four major counties of the East Midlands – **Nottinghamshire**, **Leicestershire**, **Northamptonshire** and **Lincolnshire** – have much in common. Their county towns, each with a long and eventful history, have been badly bruised by twentieth-century town planning and industrial development, but have soldiered on, becoming busy, bustling places with a positive, sometimes adventurous outlook. Embedded in the modernity are a few historical landmarks – a particularly fine church in Northampton, the castle in Nottingham, traces of Roman baths in Leicester and the magnificent cathedral at Lincoln – but by and large these are the frills rather than the substance. With the exception of Lincoln, few would describe the region's cities as especially good-looking, whereas the countryside around about them can be absolutely delightful.

Leicestershire is probably the most scenic of the counties, with the rocky, forested landscapes around Ashby and Calke Abbey in the western part of the county. Not far behind comes Northamptonshire, with its beautifully preserved villages and country towns, such as **Fotheringhay** and **Oundle**, plus rolling country estates, the best known of which is **Althorp**, the final resting place of Princess Diana. Elsewhere, tiny Rutland, the region's fifth and final county, weighs in with the little old town of **Oakham**, close to the watersports centre of Rutland Water reservoir. North of Oakham, the eastern reaches of Leicestershire and Nottinghamshire are dotted with antique market towns – the pick of which are **Southwell** and **Newark** – set within fine agricultural landscape that rolls over the county borders to form the western part of Lincolnshire. The majestic cathedral city of **Lincoln** and the splendidly intact stone town of Stamford are the chief urban attractions in this county, but Lincolnshire's most distinctive zone is **The Fens**, whose pancake-flat fields have taken centuries to reclaim from the marshes and the sea. Fenland villages and towns are generally short of charm, but the **churches**, whose spires regularly interrupt the wide-skied landscape, are simply stunning, the most impressive of the lot being St Botolph's in **Boston**. In north Lincolnshire, the low-lying chalky hills of the **Lincolnshire Wolds** contain the county's most diverse scenery, including woodland clustered round **Woodhall Spa**, and a string of sheltered valleys concentrated in the vicinity of **Louth**, the prettiest of the region's towns. To the east of the Wolds, the coast comprises miles of bungalows, campsites and caravan parks beside a sandy beach which extends, with a few marshy interruptions, from Mablethorpe to **Skegness**, the main resort.

Nottinghamshire

With a population of over 270,000, **Nottingham** is one of England's big cities, a long-time manufacturing centre for bikes, cigarettes, pharmaceuticals and lace. It is, however, more famous for Nottingham Forest football team (or rather, for its mercurial ex-manager, Brian Clough), for the Trent Bridge cricket ground and for its association with **Robin Hood**, the legendary thirteenth-century outlaw. Unfortunately the fortress-lair of Hood's bitter enemy, the Sheriff of Nottingham, is long gone, and today the city is at its most diverting in the Lace Market, whose cramped streets are crowded with the mansion-like warehouses of the Victorian lacemakers.

The county town is flanked to the north by the gritty towns and villages of what was, until Thatcher and her cronies decimated it, the Nottinghamshire coalfield, and to the south by the commuter villages of the Nottinghamshire Wolds, neither of which will hold your attention. Moving east, the thin remains of **Sherwood Forest** form **The Dukeries**, named after the five dukes who owned most of this area and preserved at least part of the ancient broad-leaved forest. Three of the four remaining estates – Thoresby, Worksop and Welbeck – are still in private hands, but **Clumber Park** is now owned by the National Trust and offers charming woodland walks. Beyond lie the market towns of eastern Nottinghamshire – **Newark** is the most important town here but nearby **Southwell** has the main attraction, the fine Norman church of Southwell Minster.

Fast and frequent **trains** connect Nottingham with, among many destinations, London, Birmingham, Newark, Lincoln and Leicester. County-wide bus services radiate out from the city too, making Nottingham the obvious base for a visit, though Newark is a palatable alternative except during the Newark International Antiques Fair, Europe's biggest such event, held six times a year, when accommodation here is all but impossible to find.

Nottingham and around

Controlling a strategic crossing over the Trent, the Saxon town of **NOTTINGHAM** was built on one of a pair of sandstone hills whose 130-foot cliffs look out over the river valley. In 1068, William the Conqueror built a castle on the other hill, and the Saxon and Norman communities traded on the low ground in between, the Market Square. The castle was a military stronghold and royal palace, the equal of the great castles of Windsor and Dover, and every medieval king of England paid regular visits. In August 1642, Charles I stayed here too, riding out of the castle to raise his standard and start the Civil War – not that the locals were overly sympathetic. Hardly anyone joined up, even though the king had the ceremony repeated for the next three days.

After the Civil War, the Parliamentarians slighted the castle and, in the 1670s, the ruins were cleared by the duke of Newcastle to make way for a palace, whose continental – and,

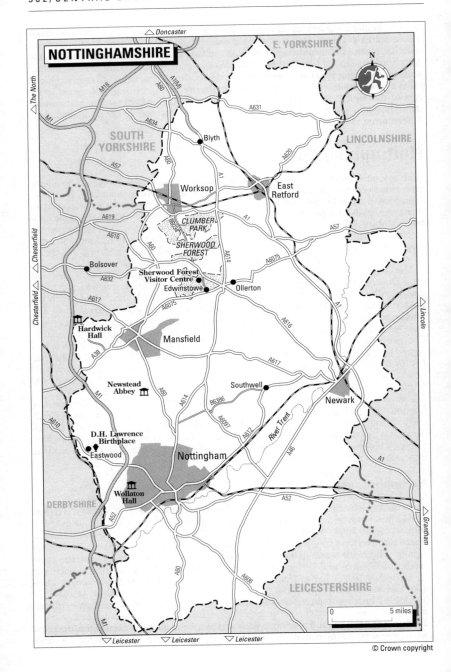

in English terms, novel – design he chose from a pattern book, probably by Rubens. Beneath the castle lay a market town which, according to contemporaries, was handsome and well kept – "One of the most beautiful towns in England", commented Daniel Defoe. But in the second half of the eighteenth century, the town was transformed by the expansion of the lace and hosiery industries. Within the space of fifty years, Nottingham's population increased from ten thousand to fifty thousand, the resulting slum becoming a hotbed of radicalism. In the 1810s, a recession provoked the hard-pressed workers into action. They struck against the employers and, calling themselves **Luddites**, after an apprentice-protester by the name of Ned Ludd, raided the factories to smash the knitting machines. This was but the first of several troubled periods. During the Reform Bill riots of 1831, the workers set fire to the duke's home in response to his opposition to parliamentary reform and, in the following decade, they flocked to the Chartist movement.

The worst of Nottingham's slums were cleared in the late nineteenth century, when the city centre assumed its present structure, with the main commercial area ringed by alternating industrial and residential districts. Crass postwar development, adding tower blocks, shopping centres and a ring road, has embedded the remnants of the city's past in a townscape that will be dishearteningly familiar if you've seen a few other English commercial centres.

Arrival and information

Nottingham train station is on the south side of the city centre, a five- to ten-minute walk from the Market Square – just follow the signs. Long-distance buses arrive at the Broad Marsh bus station down the street from the train station. Details of bus services across Nottinghamshire are available on the excellent Buses Hotline (daily 7am–8pm; ☎0115/924 0000). The city's tourist office is on the ground floor of the Council House, 1 Smithy Row (Easter to Oct Mon–Fri 9am–5.30pm, Sat 9am–5pm, Sun 10am–3pm; Nov–Easter Mon–Sat 9am–5.30pm; ☎0115/915 5330).

Accommodation

As you might expect of a big city, Nottingham has a good range of accommodation, with the more expensive **hotels** concentrated in the centre, the cheaper places and the **B&Bs** mostly located on the outskirts and the main approach roads. Finding a room is rarely difficult, but the tourist office will assist if required.

Cotswold Hotel, 330 Mansfield Road (☎0115/955 1070). Comfortable popular mid-range hotel with cheery half-timbered facade. On a main road about one mile north of the city centre. ②.

Greenwood City Lodge, 5 Third Ave, off Sherwood Rise (☎0115/962 1206). Attractive five-bedroomed guest house in a quiet corner of the city, down a narrow lane about a mile north of the city centre. Highly recommended. ②.

The Igloo Tourist Hotel, 110 Mansfield Rd (☎0115/947 5250). Backpackers' haven in the town centre, opposite the *Golden Fleece* pub, with a convivial atmosphere, good showers and free tea and coffee. Bunk-beds in mixed or single-sex dorms for £9 per person.

Royal Moat House Hotel, in the Royal Centre on Wollaton Street (☎0115/936 9988). Impressively plush, modern hotel in the city centre, with all facilities. ⑥.

Rutland Square Hotel, Rutland St, off St James' Street (☎0115/941 1114). Attractive and tastefully furnished modern hotel in a great location, just by the castle. ⑤.

YMCA, 4 Shakespeare St (☎0115/956 7600). In a handy location, with clean and frugal rooms, but fills up fast. Single rooms are a real bargain at £16 a night.

The Town

The **Old Market Square** is still the heart of the city, an airy open area, its shops, offices and fountains watched over by the neo-Baroque **Council House**, completed in 1928. From here, it's a five-minute walk west up Friar Lane to **Nottingham Castle** (daily 10am–5pm, but closed Fri Nov–Feb; free except Sat & Sun £2), whose heavily restored gateway stands above a folkloric bronze of Robin Hood, with plaques depicting his Merry Men on the wall behind. Beyond the gateway, lawns slope up to the squat ducal **palace**, which – after remaining a charred shell for forty years – was opened as the country's first provincial museum in 1878. The mansion occupies the site of the castle's upper bailey and, just outside the main entrance, two sets of steps (guided tours only) lead down into the maze of ancient caves that honeycomb the cliff beneath. One set leads into **Mortimer's Hole**, a three-hundred-foot shaft along which, so the story goes, the young Edward III and his chums crept in October 1330 to capture the queen mother, Isabella, and her lover, Roger Mortimer – his would-be usurpers and the murderers of his father, Edward II. Although the incident certainly took place, it's unlikely that this was the secret tunnel Edward used.

The interior of the ducal mansion boasts the **Story of Nottingham Gallery**, a lively and entertaining account of the city's development – in particular, look out for a small but exquisite collection of late medieval **alabaster carvings**, an art form for which Nottingham once had an international reputation. It's worth walking up to the top floor too, for a turn round the main **picture gallery**, a curious assortment of nineteenth-century romantic paintings in which the works of Richard Parkes Bonington are the most distinguished.

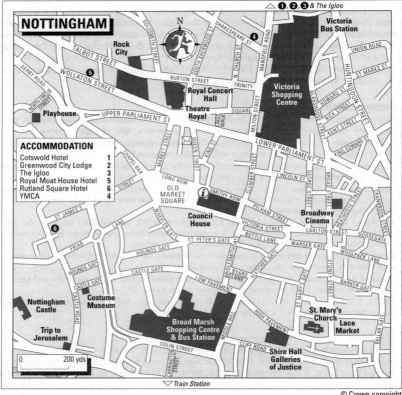

A couple of minutes' walk east of the castle is the **Museum of Costume and Textiles**, 51 Castle Gate (Wed–Sun 10am–4pm; free), the best of the city's other museums. In the 1760s, Nottingham saw the earliest experiments to produce machine-made lace, but it was not until the 1840s that the city produced the world's first fully machined lace garments. After that the industry boomed until its collapse after World War I when lace, a symbol of an old and discredited order, suddenly had no place in the wardrobe of most women. The museum's lace-trimmed dresses, accessories and underclothes are displayed on two floors, the changing fashions illustrated by a sequence of dioramas. At the bottom of the stairs there's also an intriguing collection of **samplers**, try-outs made on linen scraps before work on the handmade garments began. A few minutes' walk away, on the east side of the Market Square up along Victoria Street, is the **Lace Market**, whose narrow lanes and alleys surround the church of **St Mary**, a handsome, mostly fifteenth-century structure built on top of the hill that was once the Saxon town. The church abuts High Pavement, the administrative centre of Nottingham in Georgian times, and here you'll find the **Shire Hall**, whose Neoclassical columns and dome date from 1770. Now housing the **Galleries of Justice** (Tues–Sun 10am–4pm; £7.95), the building boasts two superbly preserved Victorian courtrooms as well as some spectacularly unpleasant old cells, a women's prison with bath house and a prisoners' exercise yard. A tour of the whole complex takes around four hours, but note that the interactive nature of a visit (on arrival you are issued with a criminal identity number, and so it continues) is not to everyone's liking. The surrounding sandstone-trimmed Victorian warehouses are at their most striking along **Broadway** and adjacent **Stoney Street**, where – at the corner of Woolpack Lane – a particularly fine warehouse boasts an extravagant stone doorway and slender windows, as well as long attic windows to light the mending and inspection rooms. Nearby, on Byard Lane, is the first shop of local lad **Paul Smith**, the great success story of recent British fashion.

Eating

Nottingham's **restaurant** scene has improved immeasurably in the last five years. French and Mediterranean cuisine are in vogue at present, but the Asian places continue to prosper. In the last couple of years, **cafés** have sprung up all over the city centre. Almost without exception, they've adopted the same formula – angular and ultramodern furnishings and fittings and a wide range of bottled beers. Many offer tasty, broadly Mediterranean food as well.

Bentons Café Bar, corner of Heathcote Street and Lower Parliament Street. Pleasant café-bar offering tasty dishes from an imaginative menu – salads and pastas through to steaks. Inexpensive.

Café De Paris, 2 Kings Walk, off Upper Parliament Street near the Theatre Royal (☎0115/947 3767). Arguably the best restaurant of its type in town, offering delicious bistro-style French cuisine in neat and informal surroundings. Moderate.

The Indian, 5 Bentinck Road (☎0115/942 4922). Outstanding Indian restaurant – the best in the city – a mile or so northwest of the centre. Lively and wide-ranging menu and attractive decor too. Moderate.

Pizza Express, 20 King St (☎0115/952 9095). Fashionable pizza and pasta spot serving the chain's usual delicious pizzas. Also at 24 Goose Gate, Hockley (☎0115/912 7888). Moderate.

Saagar Tandoori Restaurant, 473 Mansfield Rd (☎0115/962 2014). Excellent and very popular Indian restaurant, a mile or so north of the city centre. A local favourite. Moderate.

Salamander Vegetarian Restaurant, 23 Heathcote St (☎0115/941 0710). Nottingham's best vegetarian restaurant, with a sound menu. Inexpensive.

Sonny's Restaurant, 3 Carlton St (☎0115/947 3041). Well-prepared, unpretentious food in smart café-style surroundings. Main courses start at around £12.

Wax Café Bar, 27 Broad Street. Amongst the city's burgeoning band of café-bars, this is perhaps the trendiest. The food here is especially good – all light Mediterranean dishes at very reasonable prices. Inexpensive.

Pubs and nightlife

Nottingham's **nightclub** scene is boisterous and fast-moving, with clubs regularly opening and closing. The **pubs** around Market Square have a tough edge to them, especially at the weekends, but within a few minutes' walk there's a selection of lively and more enjoyable drinking-holes. For **live music**, both popular and classical, most big names play at the Royal Centre Concert Hall on Wollaton Street, and nearby **Rock City** pulls in some star turns too. The Broadway, 14 Broad St (☎0115/952 6611), is the best **cinema** in town, featuring the pick of mainstream and avant-garde films.

The Bomb, 45 Bridlesmith Gate. The frontrunner in the club scene with regular house, techno and jungle nights.

Broadway Cinema Bar, Broadway Cinema, 14 Broad St. Informal, fashionable bar serving an eclectic assortment of bottled beers to a cinema-keen clientele; can get too smoky for comfort.

Deluxe, 22 St James', St. Heaving and huge nightclub featuring dance and indie. Gay nights too.

Essance, Wollaton Street. This cavernous and immensely popular club is the city's best mainstream nightspot. The emphasis is on house, but the programme is lively and varied.

Gatsbys, Huntingdon Street. One of the more established of the city's gay bars, with a busy active scene.

The Limelight, Wellington Circus. The bar of the Nottingham Playhouse is a popular, easy-going spot with courtyard seating on summer nights. Good supply of real ales.

Lincolnshire Poacher, 161 Mansfield Rd. Very popular and relaxed pub, with a wide selection of bottled and real ales. Boorish, beer-swilling rugby players can rattle the equilibrium at the weekend. The *Forest Tavern*, just up the street, is a comparable pub, with a particularly good range of unusual draught beers.

Pitcher & Piano, High Pavement. Lively, fashionable pub in an imaginatively converted Victorian church on the edge of the Lace Market. Good fun.

Rock City, Talbot Street. Giant-sized, crowded nightclub/music venue, with different sounds and crowds each night, from Goth to metal to indie. Regularly hosts name bands on UK tours.

Ye Olde Trip to Jerusalem Inn, below the castle in Brewhouse Yard. Carved into the castle rock, this ancient inn may well have been a meeting point for soldiers gathering for the Third Crusade. Its cave-like bars, with their rough sandstone ceilings, are delightfully secretive.

Wollaton Hall and Eastwood

Leaving hourly from the Victoria bus station in the city centre, bus #31a or #31 runs four miles west to **Wollaton Hall**, a flamboyant Elizabethan mansion built for Sir Francis Willoughby in the 1580s by the architect of Longleat, Robert Smythson. Perched on top of a grassy knoll, the hall presents a grand facade of chimneys, turrets and tiers to the surrounding parkland (9am–dusk; free, cars £1), but the interior, clumsily refashioned in the nineteenth century, can only muster a workaday natural history museum (daily 11am–4/5pm, but closed Fri Nov–Feb; Mon–Fri free, Sat & Sun £2), while the Stable Block, just below the house, holds an equally routine Industrial Museum. Many visitors – and there are a lot of them – prefer to stroll the woodland around the park's lake.

D.H. Lawrence was born in the coalmining village of **EASTWOOD**, about six miles west of Nottingham. The mine closed years ago, and Eastwood is something of a post-industrial eyesore, but Lawrence's childhood home, a tiny two-up, two-down terraced house, has survived, refurbished as the **D.H. Lawrence Birthplace Museum**, 8a Victoria St (daily: April–Oct 10am–5pm; Nov–March closes 4pm; £1.75), though none of the original furnishings and fittings have lasted. Rainbow bus #1 departs for the thirty-minute trip to Eastwood from Nottingham's Victoria bus station every half-hour.

Newstead Abbey and Hardwick Hall

In 1539, Henry VIII granted **Newstead Abbey** (house April–Sept daily noon–5pm, £2; grounds daily 9am–dusk, £2), eleven miles north of Nottingham, to Sir John Byron, who demolished most of the church and converted the monastic buildings into a family home. In 1798, **Lord Byron** inherited Newstead, then little more than a ruin. He restored part of the complex, but most of the present structure dates from later renovations, which maintained much of the shape and feel of the medieval original while creating the warren-like mansion that exists today. Inside, a string of intriguing period rooms includes everything from a neo-Gothic Great Hall to the Henry VII Bedroom, fitted with carved panels and painted house screens imported from Japan. Some of the rooms are pretty much as they were when Byron lived here – notably his bedroom and dressing room – and in the Library is a small collection of the poet's possessions, from letters and manuscripts through to his pistols and boxing gloves. In the West Gallery, look out also for the painting of Byron's favourite dog, Boatswain, a perky beast who was buried just outside the house – the conspicuous memorial, with its absurdly extravagant inscription, marks the spot. The surrounding **gardens** are simply delightful, a secretive and subtle combination of walled garden, lake, Gothic waterfalls, yew tunnels and Japanese-style rockeries, complete with eccentric pagodas. There's a fast and frequent **bus** service from Nottingham's Victoria bus station to the gates of Newstead Abbey, a mile from the house, every twenty minutes or so; the journey takes about twenty-five minutes.

Some nine miles northwest of Newstead Abbey, just over the Derbyshire border, lies **Hardwick Hall** (house April–Oct Wed, Thurs, Sat & Sun 12.30–5pm; gardens same months daily noon–5.30pm; house & gardens £6, gardens only £3; NT), a startling sixteenth-century house whose walls comprise more glass than stone. Inside, there's a magnificent show of furniture and tapestries, many of which were listed in an inventory taken in 1601; outside, Longhorn cattle roam the grounds, mingling with a flock of Whiteface Woodland sheep.

Sherwood Forest and Clumber Park

Most of **Sherwood Forest**, once a vast royal forest of oak, birch and bracken covering all of west Nottinghamshire, was cleared in the eighteenth century, and nowadays it's difficult to imagine the protection it provided for generations of outlaws, the most famous of whom was **Robin Hood**. There's no "true story" of Robin's life – the earliest reference to him, in Langland's *Piers Plowman* of 1377, treats him as a fiction – but to the balladeers of fifteenth-century England, who invented most of the folklore, this was hardly the point. For them, Robin was a symbol of yeoman decency, a semi-mythological opponent of corrupt clergymen and evil officers of the law; in the early tales, although Robin shows sympathy for the peasant, he has rather more respect for the decent nobleman, and he's never credited with robbing the rich to give to the poor. This and other parts of the legend, such as Maid Marion and Friar Tuck, were added later.

Robin Hood may lack historical authenticity, but it hasn't discouraged the county council from spending thousands of pounds sustaining the **Major Oak**, the creaky tree where Maid Marion and Robin are supposed to have "plighted their troth". The Major Oak is a few minutes' walk from the visitor centre at the main entrance to **Sherwood Forest Country Park** (daily dawn–dusk; free), which comprises 450 acres of oak and silver birch crisscrossed with footpaths. The visitor centre is half a mile north of the village of Edwinstowe, itself twenty-odd miles north of Nottingham.

North of Ollerton, Edwinstowe's immediate neighbour, the A614 trims the edge of Thoresby Park to reach, after six miles, the eastern entrance to **Clumber Park** (daily dawn–dusk; NT), four thousand acres of park and woodland lying to the south of Worksop. The estate was once the country seat of the dukes of Newcastle, and it was here in the 1770s that they constructed a grand mansion overlooking Clumber Lake. The house was dismantled in 1938, when the duke sold the estate, and today all that remains of the lakeside buildings are the Gothic Revival **Chapel** (daily April–Oct

10.30am–6pm, Nov–March 10.30am–4pm), built for the seventh duke in the 1880s, and the adjacent stable block, which now houses a National Trust office (April–Oct daily 10.30am–5pm, Nov–March Sat & Sun only 10.30am–4pm), shop and **café** – located about two and a half miles from the A614. The woods around the lake offer some delightful strolls through planted woodland interspersed with the occasional patch of original forest, or you can go for an easy cycle ride by hiring a bike here.

Stagecoach East Midlands **bus** #33 leaves Nottingham's Victoria bus station hourly for the fifty-minute trip to Edwinstowe, before travelling on up the west side of Clumber Park en route to Worksop – get off at Carburton for the two-mile walk to the NT office in Clumber Park. The excursion is best done as a day-trip from Nottingham, but there is a **campsite** (☎01909/482303; closed Oct–March) in Clumber Park's walled garden, a few minutes' walk north of the chapel.

Southwell and Newark

SOUTHWELL, some fourteen miles northeast of Nottingham, is a sedate backwater distinguished by **Southwell Minster**, whose twin towers are visible for miles around, and the fine Georgian mansions facing it along Church Street. The Normans built the minster at the beginning of the twelfth century and, although some elements were added later, the Norman design predominates, from the imposing west towers through to the forceful, dog-tooth-decorated doorways. Inside, the nave's heavy stonework ends abruptly with the clumsy mass of the fourteenth-century screen, beyond which lies the Early English **choir** and the extraordinary **chapter house**. The latter is embellished with naturalistic foliage dating from the late thirteenth century, among the earliest carving of its type in England.

From Southwell, it's eight miles east to **NEWARK**, an amiable, low-key river port and market town that was once a major staging point on the Great North Road. Fronting the town as you approach from the west are the gaunt riverside ruins of **Newark Castle**, all that's left of the mighty medieval fortress that was pounded to pieces during the Civil War. A brief but pleasant riverside walk takes you from the castle past ancient houses to the old town lock, and a couple of minutes' walk away from the river lies the expansive **Market Place**. This square, surrounded by alleys of old-fashioned shops, is framed by a sequence of attractive Georgian and Victorian facades, as well as the mostly thirteenth-century church of **St Mary Magdalene**, whose massive spire, at 252ft, towers over the town centre.

There's a regular **bus** service from South Parade, on Nottingham's Old Market Square to Newark via Southwell, and Newark is also on the Nottingham–Lincoln **train** line. The Newark Castle **train station** is on the west side of the River Trent, a five-minute walk from both the castle and the adjacent **tourist office**, on Castlegate (daily 9am–5/6pm; currently ☎01636/678962). The **bus station** is on Lombard Street, a couple of minutes' walk south from the tourist office along Castlegate. Newark has a reasonable range of **hotels** and **B&Bs**, with one good option being the trim *Millgate House Hotel*, a short walk south along the river from the castle at 53 Millgate (☎01636/704445; ⑤). For **food**, make for the excellent *Gannets*, 35 Castlegate (☎01636/702066), which has a downstairs coffee bar serving daytime snacks and a smashing restaurant upstairs in the evenings, or the superb *Café Bleu* (☎01636/610141), a pricey French restaurant serving top-class meals from an inventive menu; it's one of the best restaurants in the county.

Leicestershire and Rutland

The compact county of **Leicestershire** is one of the more anonymous of the English shires, though **Leicester** itself is saved from mediocrity by its role as a focal point for Britain's Asian community, and by the closeness of the rugged terrain of **Charnwood**

Forest. To the west of Leicester, the rolling landscape is blemished by a series of industrial settlements, but things pick up markedly at **Ashby-de-la-Zouch**, a pleasing little town graced by the substantial remains of its medieval castle. Close by is **Calke Abbey**, where a dishevelled country house is surrounded by some of the region's most beguiling scenery. Near here too are the trim charms of **Market Bosworth**, where the main item of interest is the site of the Battle of Bosworth Field, the climactic engagement of the Wars of the Roses. To the east of Leicester, the farmland is studded with long-established market towns. None of them are particularly enthralling, but genial **Market Harborough** holds several attractive old buildings and an interesting museum, whilst **Melton Mowbray** is the pork pie capital of the world. Nearby, **Belvoir Castle** exhibits the art collection of the duke and duchess of Rutland.

To the east of Leicestershire lies England's smallest county, **Rutland**, reinstated in 1997 following twenty-three unpopular years of merger with its larger neighbour. As part of their spirited publicity campaign to revive their ancient county, Rutland's well-heeled burghers issued "passports" to locals and created quite a stir, breaking through the profound apathy which characterizes the English attitude to local government. Rutland has two places of note, **Oakham**, the county town, and nearby **Uppingham**, both handsome rural centres with elegant Georgian architecture.

Getting around Leicestershire and Rutland can be problematic. **Train** lines radiate out from Leicester, most usefully to Market Harborough and Oakham, and there's a good network of **bus** services between the market towns, but these fade away in the villages where, if there is a bus at all, it only runs once or twice a day. For all bus timetable enquiries, ring the **Busline** (☎0116/251 1411).

Leicester and around

On first impression, **LEICESTER** is a resolutely modern city, but further inspection reveals traces of its medieval and Roman past, situated immediately to the west of the centre, near the River Soar. The Romans, choosing this site in the middle of the territory of the rebellious Coritani, developed Leicester's precursor, Ratae Coritanorum, as a fortified town on the Fosse Way, the military road running from Lincoln to Cirencester, and Emperor Hadrian kitted it out with huge public buildings. Subsequently, in the eighth century, the Danes colonized the town and later still its medieval castle became the base of the earls of Leicester, the most distinguished of whom was Simon de Montfort, who forced Henry III to convene the first English Parliament in 1265. Since the late seventeenth century, Leicester has been a centre of the hosiery trade and it was this industry that attracted hundreds of Asian immigrants to settle here in the 1950s and 1960s. Today, about one third of Leicester's population is Asian and the city elected the country's first Asian MP, Keith Vaz, in 1987. Leicester's Hindus put on a massive and internationally famous **Diwali**, Festival of Light, in October or November, while the city's sizable Afro-Caribbean community celebrates its culture in a whirl of colour and music on the first weekend in August. The latter is the country's second biggest street festival after the Notting Hill Carnival (see p.113).

Arrival and information

On the northern line from London's St Pancras station, Leicester **train station** is situated on London Road just to the southeast of the city centre, and ten minutes' walk from **St Margaret's bus station**, which is on the north side of the centre, just off Gravel Street. The **tourist office** is in between the two at 7/9 Every St, on Town Hall Square (Mon–Wed & Fri 9am–5.30pm, Thurs 10am–5.30pm & Sat 9am–5pm; ☎0116/299 8888).

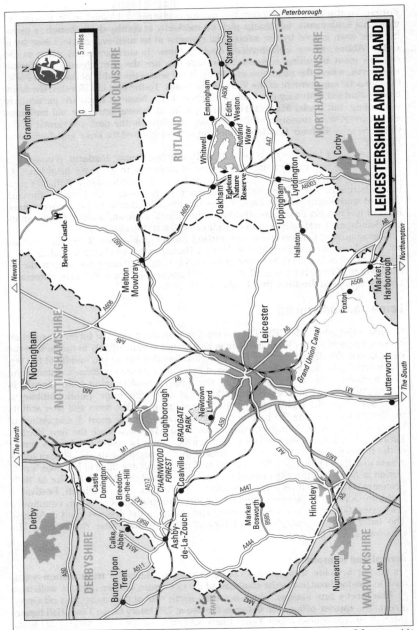

LEICESTERSHIRE AND RUTLAND

© Crown copyright

Accommodation

Most of Leicester's best **hotels** are grouped close to the centre, within walking distance of the train station. For **B&Bs**, start hunting around the Narborough Road (the A46), a mile or so west of the centre on the far side of the river. Leicester's B&Bs are very competitively priced, but for something even cheaper try the YMCA, the YWCA or the unofficial **youth hostel**. The tourist office operates a room reservation service.

Beaumaris, 18 Westcotes Drive (☎0116/254 0261). A small and unassuming family-run hotel sited about a mile west of the city centre, off the Narborough Road. ①.

Belmont House Hotel, De Montfort St (☎0116/254 4773). Comfortable lodgings here in this Georgian property which is very convenient for the centre – about 500 yards south of the train station. ⑤.

Holiday Inn, 129 St Nicholas Circle (☎0116/253 1161). Plush chain hotel in the centre with extensive leisure facilities including a swimming pool. ④.

Richards Students and Backpackers Lodge, 157 Wanlip Lane, Birstall (☎0116/267 3107). A self-styled backpackers' hostel on the northern edge of town, this place is a tiny suburban semi, with patio and summerhouse. It features just five beds at £8.50 per night and is restricted to those under 26. The owner serves copious, inexpensive meals. ①.

Scotia, 10 Westcotes Drive (☎0116/254 9200). There are eleven bedrooms – four en suite – in this efficient guest house which occupies rambling premises about a mile west of the city centre, off the Narborough Rd. ②.

Spindle Lodge, 2 West Walk (☎0116/233 8801). Located about 600 yards south of the train station off New Walk, this attractively converted Victorian house is in a conservation area. ②.

YMCA, 7 East St (☎0116/255 6507). Almost directly opposite the train station, the YMCA offers simple rooms for either sex. ①.

YWCA, 236 London Rd (☎0116/270 5083). A short walk from the train station, the YWCA provides spartan rooms for either sex. ①.

The Town

Leicester's landmark Victorian **clock tower** stands right in the heart of the city centre at East Gates, midway between the bus and train stations. From here, the old High Street runs west past the Shires shopping centre with Silver Street (subsequently Guildhall Lane) branching off it to reach **St Martin's Cathedral**, a much modified eleventh-century structure that incorporates a fine medieval wooden roof in the north porch. Next door is the **Guildhall** (Mon–Sat 10am–5.30pm, Sun 2–5.30pm; free), a half-timbered building which has served, variously, as the town hall and police station, and now contains a small museum. Several items from the old cells are on display – fearsome-looking manacles and the like.

From the Guildhall, it's a short walk west to the ring road and, just beyond, the Saxon church of **St Nicholas**, reached by keeping to the right of the *Holiday Inn*. Footsteps away, the **Jewry Wall** is a chunk of Roman masonry some eighteen feet high and seventy-three feet long that was originally part of Hadrian's public baths. The project was a real irritation to the emperor. Hadrian's grand scheme was spoilt by the engineers, who miscalculated the line of the aqueduct that was to pipe in the water, and so bathers had to rely on a hand-filled cistern replenished from the river – which wasn't what he had in mind at all. The adjacent **Jewry Wall and Archaeology Museum** (Mon–Sat 10am–5.30pm, Sun 2–5.30pm; free) charts Leicester's history from prehistoric to medieval times. Highlights include a fine assortment of Roman relics – from Fosse Way milestones to the splendid Peacock mosaic pavement – and some beautiful medieval glass.

Dodging the traffic, cross St Augustine Road to the south to arrive at the **Castle Gardens**, which, running alongside a canalized portion of the Soar, incorporate the castle motte, the mound where Leicester's Norman fortifications once stood. Walking through the gardens, you re-emerge on The Newarke, the location of the **Newarke Houses Museum** (Mon–Sat 10am–5.30pm, Sun 2–5.30pm; free), two Jacobean houses that make a delightful setting for an extensive exploration of the town's social history. In particular, look out for the display of Victorian toilets in the delicately titled "Hygiene Gallery" and some early twentieth-century furniture designed by a local man, Ernest Gimson, who was much influenced by William Morris. Behind the museum, in Castle View, is the attractive church of **St Mary de Castro** (summer Sat only 2–5pm), whose mixture of architectural styles incorporates several Norman features, notably a five-seater sedilia in the chancel. In the vicinity of the church lie the scant remains of the medieval castle, including the ruined Turret Gateway of 1423 and the twelfth-century Great Hall (no access) tucked behind the brick facade of the courthouse.

Nearby, stranded between the carriageways of the ring road stands the distinctive **Magazine Gateway**, once the medieval entrance to the Newarke. From here, it's a short walk south via the pedestrian underpass to the **Jain Centre**, on Oxford Street. The rites and beliefs of the Jains, a long-established Indian religious sect, focus on an extreme reverence for all living things – traditional customs include the wearing of gauze masks to prevent the inhalation of passing insects. The centre's splendid marble-fronted main building contains one of the few Jain temples in western Europe, and visitors may enter the lobby or, better, view the interior (Mon–Fri 2–5pm; call first if visiting outside these hours ☎0116/254 3091; donation requested).

From the Jain Centre, it's about ten minutes' walk southeast to New Walk, a tree-lined promenade that's the home of the **Leicester City Museum and Art Gallery**, at no. 53 (Mon–Sat 10am–5.30pm, Sun 2–5.30pm; free). Upstairs you'll find the country's largest collection of German Expressionists, as well as works by Walter Sickert, Jacob Epstein, Laura Knight and Stanley Spencer. On the ground floor, a collection of mummies, brought from Egypt as souvenirs in the 1880s, fills the Egyptian Gallery, which is next door to a display of crystals and minerals.

About half a mile north of the city centre, **Abbey Park** is a pleasant place to take a stroll, though nothing remains of the Augustinian abbey where Cardinal Wolsey died in 1530, on his way to London to face charges of high treason. The purported plan of the abbey is laid out on the lawns. Further out still, to the northeast, is **Belgrave**, the focus of Leicester's Asian community. Both Belgrave Road and its northerly continuation, Melton Road, are lined with Indian and Pakistani goldsmiths and jewellers, sari shops, Hindi music stores and curry houses; there's even a large cinema, the Bollywood, screening the latest releases from Bombay. It's never dull down here, but Sunday afternoons are particularly enjoyable, when locals have time to stroll the streets in their finest gear. Belgrave celebrates two major Hindu festivals – **Diwali**, the Festival of Light, held in October or November, when six thousand lamps are strung out along the Belgrave Road and 20,000 come to watch the switch-on alone, and **Navrati**, a nine-day celebration in October held in honour of the goddess Ambaji. During these two festivals there are all sorts of events held across the city – further information on ☎0116/266 8266.

Eating, drinking, nightlife and entertainment

With every justification, people come from miles around to browse Leicester's massive open-air **market** (Mon–Sat), right in the centre on the Market Place, and to eat in the **Indian restaurants** on the Belgrave Road – though the opening of lots of Balti places in the Highfields area has provided some intense competition. The most famous of the Belgrave Road restaurants is *Bobbys*, no. 154–156 (☎0116/266 0106). Run by Gujaratis, this moderately priced place is strictly vegetarian and uses no garlic or onions; if you're here on a weekend, try their delicious house speciality, *undhyu*, or the multi-flavoured *Bobbys Special Chaat*. Excellent alternatives include the *Sayonara Thali*, at no. 49 (☎0116/266 5888), which specializes in set *thali* meals, where several different dishes, breads and pickles are served together on large steel plates, and the *Chaat House* (☎0116/266 0513), south of *Bobby's* on the same side of the road. The latter does wonderful *masala dosas* and other south Indian snacks – legendary cricket captain Kapil Dev and his Indian team ate here when they were on tour. In the city centre, the *Case*, 4 Hotel St (☎0116/251 7675), is a chic place to eat with an imaginative, moderately priced menu, while the *Alhambra*, 70 High St (☎0116/253 2448), offers moderately priced and authentic Arabic cuisine – try the Maghreb Couscous.

As for **pubs**, the *Rainbow and Dove*, on Charles Street, attracts real-ale enthusiasts, the *Charlotte*, on Oxford Street, features bands most nights and the *Magazine*, Newarke Street, is a favourite student haunt. Amongst a deluge of new city-centre café-bars, two of the trendier, clubbier spots are *Left Bank*, just west of the river on Braunston Gate, and *Tabasco Jaz* on Albion Street. The excellent Phoenix Arts Centre, Newarke Street (☎0116/255 4854), is Leicester's top venue for the performing arts and doubles up as an independent cinema. The city's main concert hall is De Montfort Hall, Granville Road (☎0116/233 3111).

Charnwood Forest

Long bereft of most of its trees, what's left of the wild and stern landscapes of **Charnwood Forest** begin to the northwest of Leicester and extend intermittently as far as Loughborough and Coalville. In total, the "forest" covers fifteen thousand acres, but, with significant portions built upon and otherwise developed, the largest remaining section can be found six miles from the city in **Bradgate Park**, which was originally set aside as a hunting ground in the twelfth century. The park, now a favourite picnic spot, comprises a sizable chunk of semi-wilderness, where the heath- and bracken-covered scrubland, populated with red and fallow deer, is dotted with the rocky outcrops of Swithland slate that are Charnwood Forest's most distinctive feature. There are lots of easy walking trails within the park too, and one specific sight, lying roughly in the middle near **NEWTOWN LINFORD** – the sprawling ruins of **Bradgate House** (April–Oct Wed–Thurs, Sat–Sun 2–5pm; free), dating from the late fifteenth century. The house was built by Sir Thomas Grey and his son, Henry, whose three daughters were direct descendants of Henry VII, through their mother. The eldest of the three, **Lady Jane Grey**, was pushed into becoming Queen of England following the death of her cousin, Edward VI, in 1553. Her reign, however, only lasted nine days before she was ousted by Mary Tudor and promptly beheaded. A signposted five-minute walk away from the house is the **visitor centre** (April–Oct Tues–Fri 1–5pm, Sat & Sun 1–6pm; Nov & March Sat & Sun only 1–5pm; £1.20), which tracks through this history to great effect.

There are occasional **buses** (#121, #122, #123, #124) from Charles Street, by the Haymarket in Leicester, to Newtown Linford. Get off by the church, walk through the car park and follow the only tarmac road for the three-quarters-of-a-mile stroll through the park to the house.

Ashby-de-la-Zouch, Calke Abbey and around

ASHBY-DE-LA-ZOUCH, fourteen miles from Leicester, takes its fanciful name from two sources – the town's first Norman overlord was Alain de Parrhoet la Souche and the rest means "place by the ash trees". Nowadays Ashby is far from rustic, not least because its wide main drag, Market Street, serves as the main road between Leicester and Burton-upon-Trent (see p.568). Nevertheless, it's an amiable little place and just off Market Street stands its main attraction, the **Castle** (April–Sept daily 10am–6pm; Nov–March Wed–Sun 10am–4pm; £2.50; EH). Originally a Norman manor house, the stronghold was the work of Edward IV's chancellor, Lord Hastings, who received his "licence to crenellate" in 1474. But Hastings didn't enjoy his new home for long. Just nine years later, he was dragged from a Privy Council meeting to have his head hacked off on a log by the order of Richard III, his crime being his lacklustre support for the

Yorkist cause. Today, there's little left of the castle's external walls, but the hundred-foot-high **Hastings Tower**, a self-contained four-storey stronghold, has survived pretty much intact and incorporates a room where Mary, Queen of Scots was once imprisoned. The climb up the tower's well-worn spiral staircase leads to a grand view. For much of the nineteenth century, Ashby was a spa town, popularized by Thomas Cook's tours to its extensive Grecian-style baths. None remain now, but the steaming open-air swimming pool at Hood Park Leisure Centre, behind the tourist office, makes for a refreshing diversion (May–Sept Mon–Fri 9am–8pm, Sat & Sun 9am–1pm & 2–6pm; £2.20).

Another potential outing is to **Staunton Harold Church** (April–Sept Sat–Wed 1–5pm; Oct Sat & Sun 1–5pm only; £1; NT), a rare example of Commonwealth ecclesiastical architecture, complete with delightful painted ceilings, wood panelling and even the original seventeenth-century prayer cushions. The church is located in parkland five miles north of Ashby along the B587 – and just twenty minutes' walk (or a short drive) from **Calke Abbey** (April–Oct Sat–Wed 1–5.30pm; £5; NT), an enchanting early eighteenth-century mansion, whose rambling rooms are kept in a partial state of disrepair – just as they were when the house was recently donated to the National Trust. Footpaths crisscross the surrounding estate, whose sharp rocky contours prefigure the harsher topography of the Peak District to the northwest (see p.569).

There are fast and frequent **buses** from Leicester to Ashby and, if you're tempted to stay, the **tourist office** (Mon–Fri 10am–5pm, Sat 10am–3pm; ☎01530/411767), across Market Street from the castle, can help you find **accommodation**. Alternatively, you could try the comfortable *Cedars Guest House*, five minutes' walk north of the castle at 60 Burton Rd (☎01530/412017; ①), or the central *Queen's Head Hotel*, 79 Market St (☎01530/412780; ②), which also serves excellent traditional pub food.

Breedon-on-the-Hill

It's five miles northeast from Ashby to the village of **BREEDON-ON-THE-HILL**, which sits in the shadow of the massive but partly quarried hill from which it takes its name. A steep footpath and a winding road lead up from the village to the summit, where the thirteenth-century church of **St Mary and St Hardulph** occupies the site of an Iron Age hillfort and an eighth-century Anglo-Saxon monastery. The church contains numerous fragments from the old abbey, notably several fine sculptured friezes; the sixteenth-century tomb of the Shirley family is worth a look too, a bizarre alabaster affair decorated with a macabre skeleton.

Market Bosworth

The thatched cottages and Georgian houses of **MARKET BOSWORTH**, ten miles south of Ashby and eleven miles west of Leicester, fan out from a cobbled market square that was an important trading centre throughout the Middle Ages. From the sixteenth to the nineteenth century, the dominant family hereabouts were the Dixies, merchant-landlords whose memorials cram the local church of **St Peter**. The Dixies were not universally admired. The young Samuel Johnson taught at the town grammar school, but disliked the founder, Sir Wolstan Dixie, so much that he recollected his time there "with the strongest aversion and even a sense of horror".

Market Bosworth is best known for the **Battle of Bosworth Field**, fought on Redmoor Plain a couple of miles south of town in 1485. This was the last and decisive battle of the Wars of the Roses, an interminably long-winded and bitterly violent conflict amongst the nobility for control of the English crown. The victor was Henry Tudor, subsequently Henry VII, the vanquished was Richard III, who famously died on the battlefield. In desperation, Shakespeare's villainous Richard cried out "A horse, a horse, my kingdom for a horse," but in fact the defeated king seems to have been a much

more phlegmatic character. Taking a glass of water before the fighting started, he actually said "I live a king: if I die, I die a king." The battlefield is now set up as a tourist
attraction where the events of the battle can be pictured with the help of explanatory
plaques set along a trail through the fields. The site is open all year during daylight
hours and the attached **visitor centre** (April–Oct daily 11am–5/6pm; £2.80) provides a
lively account of the battle and its historical context.

There are hourly **buses** from Leicester to Market Bosworth, from where it's a three-
mile walk to the visitor centre. For local **accommodation**, head for the pleasant, family-run *Dixie Arms Hotel*, 6 Main St, Market Bosworth (☎01455/290218; ③).

Southeast of Leicester: Market Harborough and around

MARKET HARBOROUGH, fifteen miles southeast of Leicester, is an amiable
provincial town that once prospered from its position at the junction of the turnpike
roads to Leicester, Derby, Nottingham and London. The predominantly Georgian
High Street's *Three Swans* and *Angel* hotels were originally coaching inns, and the
handsome old **Town Hall** was designed to help local traders sell their wares – with
butchers on the ground floor and cloth merchants up above. Just off the High Street,
the triangular market place has long been the focus of town life. It's overlooked by the
medieval church of **St Dionysius**, with its striking limestone spire, and the **Old
Grammar School**, an early seventeenth-century, half-timbered structure mounted on
stilts to protect locals from the rain. From 1908 to 1974, the Victorian building standing directly behind the church on Adam & Eve Street was a factory owned by the
Symington family, who designed the world's best-selling corsets. The factory has been
redeveloped and now houses both the council offices and the town **museum**
(Mon–Sat 10am–4.30pm, Sun 2–5pm; free), which has an intriguing display of
Symington corsetry. The **tourist office** (Mon–Fri 9am–5pm & Sat 9.30am–12.30pm;
☎01858/821270) is here too.

There are frequent services from Nottingham, London and Leicester to Market
Harborough's **train station**, ten minutes' walk east of the town centre. The **bus sta-
tion** is on Northampton Road, just south of the High Street; from here there are regu-
lar services to the locks at Foxton. An hour or two is all most people need in Market
Harborough, but there are several good places to stay including the Georgian *Three
Swans*, a smart hotel on the High Street (☎01858/466644; ⑤).

Foxton

Separating the river systems of the Soar and Trent, the steep hill at **FOXTON**, a couple of miles northwest of Market Harborough, presented the canal owners of early
nineteenth-century England with a difficult technical problem, but one that was well
worth solving: if they could find a way to cross the obstacle by barge, then goods could
be transported across the Midlands without a time-consuming portage. They called
upon the leading engineer of the day, Thomas Telford, who designed a **flight of ten
locks**, with just one passing place, to climb the seventy-foot-high slope – and by 1814
the extended waterway system, the **Grand Union Canal**, reached as far north as the
Humber and south to the Thames.

The locks remain an impressive sight, incongruously busy in the midst of quiet
hills. Halfway down the flight is the **Canal Museum** (Easter–Sept daily 10am–5pm;
Oct–Easter Wed–Sun 11am–4pm; £2), where a modest exhibition outlines the history of the locks and the Grand Union, as well as that of the **Foxton Inclined Plane**.
This was a steam-powered boat lift that winched boats over Foxton Hill at the rate of
one every three minutes, compared to the normal 45-minute trip up the locks.
Completed in 1900, the lift was made uneconomic by competition from the railways
and was largely dismantled, though parts can still be seen.

Another good reason to come to Foxton is the *Bridge 61* **pub**, at the foot of the locks. Hemmed in by piles of narrow-boat junk, this is a major landmark on the canal system, a meeting place and servicing point for the hundreds of tourists and full-time "bargies" that pass through during the summer. As you might expect, the ale is excellent. For **B&B**, try the Old Manse (☎01858/545456; ②), a handsome ivy-covered Victorian house, a short walk from the locks on Swingbridge Street.

Melton Mowbray and Belvoir

MELTON MOWBRAY, fifteen miles northeast of Leicester, is famous for pork pies, an unaccountably popular English snack made of compressed balls of meat and gristle encased in wobbly jelly and thick pastry. The pie is the traditional repast of the fox-hunting fraternity, for whom the town of Melton, lying on the boundary of the region's most important hunts – Belvoir, Cottesmore and Quorn – has long been a favourite spot. The antics of some of the aristocratic huntsmen are legend – in 1837 the Marquis of Waterford literally painted the town's buildings red, hence the saying – but with the snowballing opposition to blood sports, the days of the tally-ho brigade may well be numbered. If you want to sample the genuine traditional hunters' pie, it is available in Melton only at Dickinson & Morris, on Nottingham Street.

Most of Melton Mowbray is Victorian, but a short walk south from the central market place is the medieval church of **St Mary**, distinguished by its impressive size (150ft long and the tower soaring to over 100ft) and by some of its detail. The clerestory is an especially fine illustration of the Perpendicular style, its 48 windows encircling the church and bathing the interior with great shafts of light. You could also drop by the town's **museum** (Mon–Fri 10am–5pm, Sat 10am–4pm, Sun 2–5pm; free), five minutes' walk from the market place down Sherrard Street, which features the work of John Ferneley, a local artist who made a small fortune selling hunting scenes to the gentry. There are plans for another museum too – this one dedicated to hunting.

Central **trains** runs frequent services from Leicester to Oakham via Melton Mowbray and Barton **buses** link Nottingham, Melton and Oakham.

Belvoir Castle

Heading northeast from Melton Mowbray along the A607, it's about ten miles to the lip of the escarpment overlooking the Vale of Belvoir (pronounced "beaver"). William the Conqueror gave the rich farmland of the valley to his standard-bearer Robert de Todeni, who built a castle down below on the largest hill he could find. In successive centuries the castle was destroyed and rebuilt several times, and the present **Belvoir Castle** (April–Sept Tues–Thurs & Sat–Sun 11am–5pm; £5), an incoherent castellated pile, dates from 1816. The exterior of the castle may not be much to look at, but inside, the duke and duchess of Rutland's hoard of art is another story. Particular highlights of the collection include the enormous Gobelin tapestries in the Regent's Gallery and the paintings in the Picture Gallery, notably Jan Steen's *Grace before Meat*, *Proverbs* by David Teniers the Younger and Hans Holbein's portrait of Henry VIII. German-born Holbein was introduced to the king on his second visit to England, in 1532, and Henry was so pleased by his first portraits, which picked a delicate line between flattery and honesty, that he kept him employed until the artist's death in 1543. Belvoir attracts day-trippers in their hundreds for its weekend "medieval" jousts and other special events. **Buses** from Melton, operated by Vale Runner (☎0116/251 1411), leave twice daily, at 10.10am and 11.30am.

Oakham and around

Some twenty miles east from Leicester, well-heeled **OAKHAM**, Rutland's county town, has a long history as a commercial centre, its prosperity bolstered by Oakham School, a late sixteenth-century foundation that's become one of the country's more exclusive private schools. The town's stone terraces and Georgian villas are too often interrupted by the mundanely modern to assume any grace, but the town has its architectural moments – particularly in the L-shaped **Market Place**, where the sturdy awnings of the octagonal Butter Cross shelter the old town stocks. On the north side of the Market Place stands **Oakham Castle** (April–Oct Tues–Sat 10am–1pm & 2–5.30pm, Sun 2–5.30pm; Nov–March Tues–Sat 10am–1pm & 2–4pm, Sun 2–4pm; free), a fortified house dating from 1191 of which the banqueting hall is pretty much all that remains. The hall is a good example of Norman domestic architecture and, inside, the whitewashed walls are covered with horseshoes, the result of an ancient custom by which every lord or lady, king or queen, is obliged to present an ornamental horseshoe when they first set foot in the house.

Close by, Oakham School is housed in a series of impressive ironstone buildings along the west edge of the Market Place. On the right-hand side of the school, a narrow lane allows you to see more of the buildings on the way to **All Saints'** church, whose heavy tower and spire rise high above the town. Dating from the thirteenth century, the church is an architectural hybrid, but the light and airy interior is distinguished by the medieval carvings along the piers beside the chancel, with Christian scenes and symbols set opposite dragons, grotesques, devils and demons. Finally, you could also spare a few minutes for the sizable **Rutland County Museum**, on Catmose Street (Easter–Oct Mon–Sat 10am–5pm, Sun 2–5pm; Oct–March Mon–Sat 10am–4pm, Sun 2–4pm; free), a brief signposted walk from the Market Place via the High Street. Here, an assortment of agricultural tools and Rutland County mementoes is enlivened by a lithograph of a disconcertingly huge prize-winning heifer.

Practicalities

With regular services from Leicester, Melton Mowbray and Peterborough, Oakham **train station** lies on the west side of town, five minutes' walk from the centre. **Buses** connect the town with Leicester, Nottingham and Melton Mowbray and these arrive at St John Street, close to the Market Place. A thorough exploration of Oakham only takes a couple of hours, but, should you decide to stay, the **tourist office**, at Flore's House, 34 High St (Mon–Sat 9.30am–5pm, Sun 10.30am–3.30pm; Nov–March Mon–Sat 10am–4pm; ☎01572/724329), will book accommodation. Alternatively, there are a couple of handy **B&Bs** near the High Street: *Angel House*, 20 Northgate (☎01572/756153; ③), and *Serpentine House*, 8 Lodge Gardens (☎01572/757878; ③), a quiet place with a spacious walled garden. Otherwise, the *Whipper-In Hotel*, on the Market Place (☎01572/756971; ④), has smartly decorated modern rooms behind its old facade. For **food**, the *Whipper-In* also serves excellent bar snacks, as does the *Rutland Angler*, nearby on Mill Street.

Rutland Water

Rutland Water, the horseshoe-shaped reservoir immediately to the east of Oakham, was created by the damming of the River Gwash in 1976. With a shoreline over twenty miles long, it's the second largest artificial lake in England and although few would say it's especially beautiful, it's a pleasant enough area – and a string of leisure complexes have developed along its periphery. On the north side of the water, beside the A606 about three miles east of town, lies the **Whitwell** site (buses from Oakham), where the emphasis is on watersports, especially windsurfing, canoeing and sailing. Here also is Rutland Water Cycling (☎07000/292546), which rents out standard range bikes from around £10.50 a day, £7.50 for four hours – a popular cycle path runs right round the lake. A mile or so to the east of Whitwell, the **Butterfly Farm and Aquatic Centre** (daily April–Aug 10.30am–5pm, Sept & Oct 10.30am–4.30pm; £3), on Sykes Lane in **Empingham**, exhibits Blue Emperors and Paris Peacocks among many species of butterfly, and these share a hothouse with tarantulas and giant stick insects. On the west side of the lake, just south of Oakham, the **Egleton nature reserve** is noted for its wildfowl, has hides, and is attached to the **Anglian Water Birdwatching Centre** (daily 9am–4/5pm; £3), with a viewing gallery and a video remote camera. Finally, on the south side of the lake, just beyond the dinky little village of **Edith Weston**, is Rutland Water's main landmark-cum-trademark **Normanton Church**, a good-looking mix of Georgian and Victorian features that now houses a small **museum** of local history (March–Oct daily 11am–4/5pm; 80p).

The reservoir's most opulent hotel is *Hambleton Hall* (☎01572/756991; ⑦), a vast Victorian pile of luxury on the peninsula jutting into the western end of Rutland Water. If you fancy the view, but not the cost, try the excellent food at the neighbouring *Finch's Arms* pub.

Uppingham and Lyddington

The town of **UPPINGHAM**, six miles south of Oakham, has the uniformity of style Oakham lacks, its wide, sloping High Street flanked by bow-fronted shops and iron-stone houses which mostly date from the eighteenth century. It's the general appear-ance that pleases, rather than any individual sight, but the town is mainly famous as the home of **Uppingham School**, a bastion of privilege whose imposing fortress-like building stands at the west end of the High Street. Founded in 1587, the school was distinctly second-rate until the middle of the nineteenth century, when a dynamic headmaster, the Reverend Edward Thring, grabbed enough land to give the school some of the biggest playing-fields in England – fitness being, of course, an essential attribute of the rulers of the British Empire. It's doubtful you'll want to stay, but Uppingham does have one especially good **hotel**, the *Lake Isle*, in an eighteenth-cen-tury town house at 16 High St East (☎01572/822951; ③). For **B&B**, the spick-and-span *Rutland House*, on High Street East (☎01572/822497; ①), occupies a spacious, double-fronted sandstone house.

One mile southeast of Uppingham, **LYDDINGTON** is a sleepy village of honey-hued cottages and pubs lining a straight main street, set against a backdrop of plump hills and broken broadleaf woodland. Early in the twelfth century, the Bishop of Lincoln, whose lands once extended south as far as the Thames, chose this as the site of a small palace – one of thirteen he erected to accommodate himself and his retinue while away on Episcopal business. Confiscated during the Reformation, **Lyddington Bede House**, on Blue Coat Lane (April–Oct daily 10am–6pm; £2.50; EH), was later converted into alms houses by Lord Burghley, and has since been beautifully restored by english Heritage. The highlight is the light and airy Great Chamber on the first floor, whose oak cornices are exquisitely carved. Careful lighting in the attic sets off the building's sturdy medieval timber frame to best advantage, while the ground floor harbours the tiny rooms that were for centuries occupied by local pensioners and the poor.

Accommodation in Lyddington is limited to the *Marquis of Exeter Hotel* on the main street (☎01572/822477; ③). Gutted by fire and completely restored a few years back, this former coaching inn has sixteen comfortable en-suite rooms and comes complete with a good restaurant serving a classy à la carte menu or less expensive bar meals.

Hallaton

HALLATON, some ten miles southwest of Oakham along steep and winding country lanes, is one of the region's most attractive villages, its postcard prettiness composed of neat ironstone cottages around a well-kept village green, embellished by a medieval church, a conical Butter Cross and a duck pond. Every Easter Monday, this tranquil scene is disturbed by the **Hare Pie Scramble and Bottle Kicking** contest, when the inhabitants of Hallaton fight for pieces of pie with the people of nearby Medbourne. The participants gather at the *Fox Inn* by the village pond, then proceed to kick small barrels of ale around a hill and across a stream, as has been the custom for several hundred years – though no one has the faintest idea why. The village **museum** (May–Oct Sat & Sun 2.30–5pm; donation requested) does its best to shed some light on the business. For a pint and a ploughman's, head for the green, where the *Bewicke Arms* is one of Leicestershire's oldest-established and most characterful pubs.

Northamptonshire

Northamptonshire is one of the region's less visited counties, generally regarded as somewhere you pass through on the way to somewhere else. Part of the problem is that three of the county's four big towns – Wellingborough, Corby and Kettering – are primarily industrial and whatever charms they offer to their inhabitants, there's not much to attract the casual visitor. The fourth town, **Northampton**, is, however, a good deal more interesting, possessed of several fine old buildings and an excellent museum devoted to shoe-making, the industry that has long made the place tick. Northampton is also just five miles from **Althorp**, family home of the Spencers and the burial place of Princess Diana.

Away from the towns, Northamptonshire comprises a wedge of gentle hills and patchy woodland dotted with villages, stately homes and country estates. The M1 forms an easy if arbitrary dividing line with **west Northamptonshire** on one side and the larger **east Northamptonshire** on the other. The prime target in the former is the canalside village of **Stoke Bruerne**, whereas the east boasts the good-looking country town of **Oundle**, which makes the best base for visiting the charming hamlet of **Fotheringhay** and, at a pinch, the overbearing pomp and circumstance of **Boughton House**.

Getting to Northampton by **public transport** is no problem, but to reach the villages and stately homes, you'll mostly need your own vehicle – or some careful planning around infrequent bus services. That said, the County Council now fund the Saunterbus service which links key attractions on specified days from April to September. A day ticket costs £3.70 and is available from the driver; timetable details from any Northamptonshire tourist office or Stagecoach buses (☎01604/620077).

Northampton and around

Spreading north from the banks of the River Nene, **NORTHAMPTON** is a workaday modern town whose appearance largely belies its ancient past. Throughout the Middle Ages, this was one of central England's most important towns, a flourishing commercial centre whose now demolished castle was a popular stopping-off point for travelling royalty. A fire in 1675 burnt most of the medieval city to a cinder and the Georgian town that grew up in its stead was itself swamped by the industrial revolution when Northampton swarmed with boot and shoe manufacturers. The town continues to grow, making room for London's overflow population, and light industries are settling on the outskirts, but the centre does hold several diverting old buildings and is the obvious place to gather information before checking out the rest of the county. Half a day is enough for a quick gambol round the sights, but if you're tempted to stay the night there's a reasonable supply of hotel accommodation and a light scattering of B&Bs. The only times of the year when finding a room here can be difficult are during the annual **Balloon Festival** in August, which attracts 200,000 visitors, and over the weekend of the British Grand Prix, held in mid-July at the nearby **Silverstone** race track. Northampton has one other claim to fame: it was here that Errol Flynn got his start in repertory in 1933, though he hightailed it out of town the following year leaving a whopping tailor's debt behind him.

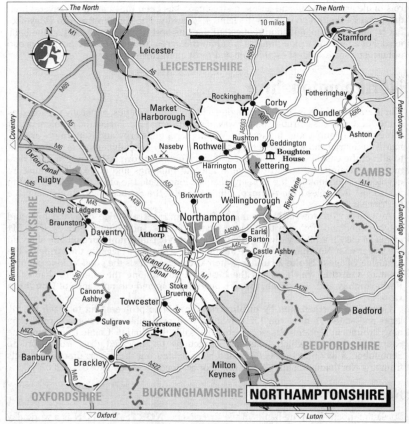

Arrival, information and accommodation

A tiny section of the castle remains beside Northampton's **train station**, which has regular services to London Euston and Birmingham, and is ten minutes' walk west of the town centre. Buses pull into the **bus station** on Lady's Lane, right in the centre behind the Grosvenor Shopping Centre. From here, it's just five minutes' walk south to the **tourist office** (Mon–Fri 9.30am–5pm, Sat 9.30am–4pm; late May to Aug also Sun noon–4pm; ☎01604/622677), opposite the Guildhall on St Giles Square. They operate an accommodation service, have oodles of information on the county and issue bus timetables.

The smartest **hotel** in the centre is the *Northampton Moat House*, a dependable chain hotel in a large modern block on Silver Street (☎01604/739988; ⑤). More distinctive is the *Lime Trees Hotel*, 8 Langham Place, Barrack Road (☎01604/632188; ④), in pleasant Georgian premises half a mile north from the centre. The pick of the more central

B&Bs is the *St Georges Private Hotel*, 128 St Georges Ave (☎01604/792755; ②). This attractive place has spacious, comfortable guest rooms and occupies a large Edwardian house about a mile and a half from the centre, overlooking Racecourse Park.

The Town

Northampton's finest building is **All Saints** church (daily 9am–3pm), just south of the main Market Square on George Row. Crowned by a heavy clock tower and a lavish glass dome, it was rebuilt after being destroyed in the Great Fire of 1675. The pillared portico is reminiscent of St Paul's Cathedral, but this one is topped by a statue of Charles II in a toga, raised to commemorate his donation of a thousand tons of timber after the fire and dressed with oak leaves each year on Oakapple Day (29 May). Inside, the breezy interior looks more like a ballroom than a church, its high ceiling coated in delicately sculpted plasterwork designed around a central rose, the shire's motif.

In front of the west end of the church, a patchwork of flower beds surrounds one of Lutyens's less inspiring monuments, a plain, blunt **war memorial** dating from 1926. In the opposite direction, round the back of the church, is the **Guildhall** (tours Thurs 2.15pm; £2.50), a flamboyant Victorian edifice constructed in the 1860s to a design by Edward Godwin, one of the period's most inventive architects. The Gothic exterior, with its high-pointed windows and dinky balustrade, sports kings and queens as well as scenes central to the county's history – look out for Mary, Queen of Scots with her head on the block, the Battle of Naseby and the fire of 1675.

The **Central Museum and Art Gallery** (Mon–Sat 10am–5pm, Sun 2–5pm; free), a hundred yards south on Guildhall Road, celebrates the town's industrial heritage with an extensive and surprisingly interesting display of shoes. Along with silk slippers, clogs and high-heeled nineteenth-century court shoes, there's one of the four boots worn by an elephant during the British Expedition of 1959, which retraced Hannibal's putative route over the Alps into Italy. There's celebrity footwear too – almost inevitably, a pair of Elton John shoes: the boots he wore in *Tommy* – but perhaps the most original gear is a *kadaitcha*, made by Australian aborigines from emu feathers and women's hair, and used to fool trackers. The rest of the museum is given over to an excellent display charting the town's history from its Roman days to the present, paying particular attention to the significance of the shoe industry, which employed half the town's population in 1920.

Back at All Saints, a narrow alley leads the few paces north to the vast cobbled **Market Square**, whose stalls brim with produce and bargains every day except Sunday. From the north side of the square, a lane leads through to Sheep Street, where the **Church of the Holy Sepulchre** (May–Sept Mon, Tues & Thurs 2–4pm, Wed & alternate Fri noon–4pm; free) is Northampton's oldest building and one of only five Norman round churches extant in the country. As its name suggests, the church's design was inspired by contact with the Holy Land – in this case, the founder, Simon de Senlis, was a veteran of the First Crusade. The only disturbance to the original circular plan is the eastern portion, which was added in 1860.

Eating and drinking

A good spot for daytime **snacks** is the *Corner House Coffee Bar*, at the corner of George Row and Bridge Street, or *Morelli's Cappuccino*, on Princes Walk. For more substantial **meals**, head for the moderately priced *Sorrentino Don Giovanni*, 64 Gold St (☎01604/602222), the town's most popular pizza and pasta joint, or treat yourself to a slap-up dinner at the smart and pricey *Lime Trees Hotel*, 8 Langham Place, Barrack Road (☎01604/632188). For a **drink**, the *Malt Shovel*, down by the Carlsberg brewery at 121 Bridge St, is a recently refurbished Edwardian pub with a wide range of bottled and draught beers plus inexpensive bar food.

Althorp

Some five miles northwest of Northampton off the A428, the ritzy mansion of **Althorp** is the focus of the Spencer estate. The Spencers have lived here for centuries, but this was no big deal until one of the tribe, **Diana**, married Prince Charles in 1981. The disintegration of the marriage and Diana's elevation to sainthood/stardom is a story known to millions – and most perceptively analysed by B. (for Beatrix) Campbell in her *Diana Princess of Wales: How Sexual Politics Shook the Monarchy*. The public grief following Diana's death in 1997 was quite astounding and Althorp became the focus of massive media attention as the coffin was brought up the M1 motorway from London to be buried on an island in the grounds of the family estate. The estate is open to visitors on timed-entry tickets in July and August only (9am–5pm; £9.50). Tickets must be purchased in advance (bookings on ☎01604/592020; *www.althorp.com*) and they give access to the **Diana exhibition**, in the old stable block, as well as the adjacent Althorp house, where there's a large collection of priceless paintings, including works by Gainsborough, Van Dyck and Rubens. From the house, a footpath leads round a lake in the middle of which is the islet (no access) on which Diana is buried.

Brixworth

Crowning a low rise above **BRIXWORTH** village, just off the A508 about six miles north of Northampton, **All Saints church** (usually open daily 10am–5pm, call ☎01604/880286 to check; bus #62 or #61) is one of England's finest surviving Anglo-Saxon churches, dating from around 680 AD. From a distance, its most striking feature is its unusual cylindrical stair-turret, added to the western tower in the ninth century as part of a plan to fortify the church against Viking raids. Closer inspection reveals something even rarer – Roman tiles, probably salvaged from a nearby villa, are stuck into the church, often at irregular angles, and form part of the fabric of the building. Inside, the uncluttered nave's whitewashed walls set off the stonework, notably in the triple archway set high up on the west wall. In 1400, a second, larger triple archway – which once lead into the presbytery – was replaced by a single arch, thereby opening the church up to the congregation. At the east end, the rounded apse, modelled on a Roman basilica, has been modified, but still incorporates three eighth-century pillars. To its right (as you face the altar), a curtained archway leads from the presbytery into the Lady Chapel, built in the thirteenth century by a local baron, Sir John de Verdun. His carved stone effigy lies in a recess in the south wall, with legs crossed and his finely carved suit of chain mail still visible. Further along the wall, look out for a small niche fronted with glass; this was where Brixworth's famous **reliquary**, two boxes containing fragments of bone thought to be Saint Boniface's larynx, was rediscovered in the nineteenth century. The relic was probably hidden here for safekeeping when Viking raids were at their peak.

Naseby

About six miles to the northwest of Brixworth, on a sloping field beside the A5199 immediately to the north of the A14 at **NASEBY**, stands a **monument** commemorating the battle of June 1645 in which Charles I was defeated by Parliament's troops. It was a crucial engagement – the Royalists were never likely to win the Civil War thereafter – and it was also the first time Parliament's (later Cromwell's) New Model Army saw action. Inexperienced, the New Model Army had a difficult time, but this was a different breed of soldier, driven by religious conviction rather than money, and within the space of a few months it had become the best in Europe – as Cromwell's enemies would find out to their cost. The commemoration of this critical battle is decidedly low-key – besides the lonely battlefield memorial, the only sight worth investigating is the **obelisk** and interpretation panel just outside Naseby beside the minor road to Clipston.

West Northamptonshire

The slice of easy countryside that comprises **west Northamptonshire**, across the M1 from Northampton, contains the attractive hamlet of **Stoke Bruerne**, pushed tight against the Grand Union Canal, and several stately homes, of which Elizabethan **Canons Ashby House** is the most appealing.

Towcester and Stoke Bruerne

Beyond the M1, just ten miles from Northampton, the old coaching town of **TOWCES-TER** (pronounced "Toaster") hardly sets the pulse racing, despite the best efforts of Dickens, who made the *Saracen's Head* famous in *Pickwick Papers*. However, things improve just three miles east of town at the village of **STOKE BRUERNE**, where the Grand Union Canal enters England's longest navigable tunnel, the 3075-yard Blisworth Tunnel, constructed at the beginning of the nineteenth century. Before the advent of steam tugs in the 1870s, boats were pushed through the tunnel by "legging" – two or more men would push with their legs against the tunnel walls until they emerged to hand over to waiting teams of horses. This exhausting task is fully explained in the excellent **Canal Museum** (daily: April–Oct 10am–6pm; Nov–March Tues–Sun 10am–4pm; £3), housed in a converted corn mill half a mile from the tunnel at the top of the flight of five locks. The museum records two hundred years of canal history with models, exhibits of canal art and spit-and-polish engines. It also houses the cabin of a butty boat, a showcase for the painted crockery and embroidery of canal families. Outside, the *Boat Inn* pub is stocked with narrow-boat trinkets, and there are two good places to **eat** – the moderately priced *Bruernes Lock Restaurant* (☎01604/863654) and the delightful *Old Chapel Tea Rooms*, which has a display of local art work. On the canal front, *Wharf Cottage* offers very cosy **B&B** (☎01604/862174; ①). Finally, the Stoke Bruerne Boat Company, in the village at 2 Stoke Plain Cottages, Bridge Road (☎01604/862107), rents a narrowboat out for the day for £90; advance reservations are recommended.

Canons Ashby and Sulgrave Manor

To the west of Towcester, a lattice of narrow roads drifts across the rolling countryside as far as the M40. Roughly in the middle, about eight miles away from either Towcester or Daventry, is one of the region's finest Elizabethan manor houses, **Canons Ashby House** (April–Oct Sat–Wed 1–5.30pm; £3.70; NT), which has been owned by the Drydens (as in John Dryden) since its construction. The lines of the exterior are somewhat spoiled by an incongruous peel tower, but the main event is the interior, which sports rare Elizabethan wall paintings and decorative Jacobean plasterwork. The **church** in the manor grounds is all that remains of the twelfth-century Augustinian priory after which the house is named.

From here, it's just a couple of miles south along country lanes to **Sulgrave Manor**, a neat stone Tudor house built by an ancestor of George Washington – his seven times great-grandfather to be precise (April–Oct Mon, Tues, Thurs & Fri 2–5.30pm, but opens 10.30am in Aug, Sat & Sun 10.30am–1pm & 2–5.30pm; March, Nov & Dec Sat & Sun only 10.30am–1pm & 2–4.30pm; £3.75). The house remained in the family until 1656, when Colonel John, great-grandfather of the American president, set sail for the New World and settled in Virginia (now Mount Vernon). George Washington never visited Sulgrave, but nevertheless the place has taken on the air of a shrine to American democracy and the interior holds a small museum charting George's remarkable career. The best features of the building are the Great Hall, with its low-beamed ceiling, flagstones and huge fireplace, and the kitchen, set around an ancient hearth hung with copper pots and pans. **Accommodation** is available in the village of Sulgrave at the excellent *Star Inn* (☎01295/760389; ③), which also does tasty bar meals.

East Northamptonshire

The River Nene wriggles its way across **east Northamptonshire** passing through a string of little villages and towns, amongst which **Oundle** is by far the most diverting. Within easy striking distance of Oundle is the historic hamlet of **Fotheringhay** and several country houses – hilltop **Rockingham Castle** is the most dramatic, **Boughton House** the richest. Spare time also for the eccentric Catholicism of the Triangular Lodge in **Rushton**.

Oundle

OUNDLE'S most conspicuous building is the parish church of St Peter's, right in the centre, with a magnificent two-hundred-foot Decorated spire, but the town's real appeal is the overall effect of pale limestone houses clinging to streets, whose layout has changed little over several centuries. Indeed, Oundle boasts some of the finest seventeenth- and eighteenth-century streetscapes in the Midlands, and provides a suitably exclusive setting for one of England's better-known private schools, **Oundle School**, which has been running since 1556 and owns many of the town's most prized buildings.

If you have your own transport, Oundle makes a good base for exploring the rural nooks and crannies of this part of the county. **Buses** from Peterborough, Stamford and Northampton stop in Oundle Market Place, a short walk from the **tourist office**, at 14 West St (Mon–Sat 9am–5pm, plus April to mid-Oct Sun noon–3pm; ☎01832/274333). They issue maps and bus timetables, have comprehensive details of local attractions and operate an **accommodation** service. The best place to stay is the *Talbot Hotel*, on New Street (☎01832/273621; ⑤). This charming hotel looks much the same today as it did when it was rebuilt in 1626, complete with what is thought to be the very oak staircase Mary, Queen of Scots used on her way to her execution at Fotheringhay Castle (see below). Apparently the queen's executioner stayed at the *Talbot* and both his and Mary's ghost are said to wander the upper floor. For somewhere less expensive, head for the comfortable *Ship Inn*, 18 West St (☎01832/273918; ①).

Fotheringhay

Nestling the River Nene just four miles northeast of Oundle, the tiny hamlet of **FOTHERINGHAY** once boasted an imposing medieval castle which witnessed two key events – the birth of Richard III in 1452 and the beheading of Mary, Queen of Scots in 1587. On the orders of Elizabeth I, Mary was executed in the castle's Great Hall with no one to stand in her defence – apart, that is, from her dog, who is said to have rushed from beneath her skirts as her head fell. Not long afterwards, the castle fell into disrepair and nowadays only a thistle-covered mound remains to mark its position; it's down a narrow lane on the bend of the road near the east end of the village.

Fotheringhay is itself distinguished by its old thatched cottages and the **church of St Mary and All Saints**, whose octagonal lantern tower soars high above the meadows flanking the river. Dating from 1415, the church is supported by a long series of flying buttresses and the interior holds two fancily carved medieval pieces – a pulpit and a fine stone font. On either side of the altar are the tombs of Elizabeth I's ancestors the dukes of York, Edward and Richard. Elizabeth found the tombs in disarray in 1573, and promptly had them rebuilt in a smooth white limestone that still looks like new.

Bus #6 links Oundle and Fotheringhay once daily (except Sun) in each direction.

Rockingham Castle

Some eleven miles west of Oundle, on the outskirts of Corby, **Rockingham Castle** (Easter to mid-Oct Thurs, Sun and Bank hol Mon, plus Tues in Aug, 1–5pm; £4.20) stands high above the Welland River valley in the heart of Rockingham Forest, which once stretched all the way to Northampton. A favoured hunting retreat of England's monarchs, from William Rufus and King John through to Edward I, the castle incorporates the original fortifications built by the Normans, but is mostly Tudor, a handsome, honey-coloured brick-and-stone complex designed by Edward Watson, ancestor of the present owners. The highlight is the timber-beamed **Great Hall**, the kernel of the original Norman castle, with grand fireplaces and trellised windows added by Edward I.

Geddington and Boughton House

When Queen Eleanor, cherished wife of Edward I, died in 1290 at Harby, near Lincoln, her embalmed body was carried in state to Westminster Abbey, and a memorial built at each resting point of the cortège. The most complete of the three surviving monuments graces the centre of **GEDDINGTON**, a sprawling village about twelve miles from Oundle beside the road to Kettering (the A43). Mounted on a stepped platform, this **Eleanor Cross** stands like a spire, culminating in a cluster of sumptuously carved points above three figures of Eleanor, overlooking the village she had stayed in when accompanying Edward on his royal hunting trips.

From Geddington, a country road leads the one mile southeast to the grandest of Northamptonshire's stately homes, **Boughton House** (house Aug daily 2–5pm; £4.50; grounds May to Aug Sat–Thurs 1–5pm; £1.50 for grounds only; free for disabled visitors). This pompous pile is the centre of an eleven-thousand-acre estate that incorporates five villages and has been owned by the dukes of Buccleuch and their ancestors, the Montagus, for five hundred years. The core of the house was originally a monastery, bought by Sir Edward Montagu in 1528 and enlarged by successive generations. Ralph, First Duke of Montagu, who claimed descent from William the Conqueror, made the grandest extensions in the 1690s when he added the arcaded north front. Ambassador to France, Ralph borrowed freely from French design and employed French artists and architects to glorify his mansion, earning the house the nickname "the English Versailles"; he also bought London's Mortlake tapestry factory so he could have the best works for his home. The present duke, Europe's largest private landowner, with assets worth an estimated £200,000,000, uses the house only periodically, spending much of his time on the family estates in Scotland.

The house is stuffed with the baubles and bangles of the landed aristocracy. Highlights include paintings by Gainsborough, Raphael and El Greco, a wonderful set of Baroque painted ceilings by Louis Chéron, no less than forty delicate oil sketches by Van Dyck, an extensive collection of swords, pistols and armour, and fine silverware, antique furniture, tapestries and porcelain.

Kettering to Corby **buses** pass through Geddington every couple of hours Monday to Saturday.

Rushton

Some four miles west of Geddington, reached along country roads, the pretty little village of **RUSHTON**, with its humped back bridge and ironstone cottages, lies just one mile to the east of the solitary **Triangular Lodge** (April–Oct daily 10am–6pm; £1.40; EH), an eccentric structure dating to 1597. It was built by Thomas Tresham, a determined Catholic whose refusal to accept England's Protestant reforms got him fined and banged up in prison. After his release, Tresham expressed his religious fervour architecturally with this ingenious building, whose triangular construction celebrates the Trinity – Father, Son and Holy Ghost. Made of limestone and ironstone to give a striped effect, each of the three sides is 33ft long, with three windows and three gables, and even the central chimney topping the three storeys is triangular. Only two of the date stones around the lodge are "true" – his release from prison in 1593, and the construction of the lodge in 1595. The rest form an outlandish arithmetical puzzle: subtracting 1593 from the other figures gives the dates of the Crucifixion, the Virgin Mary's death, the Great Flood and the traditional date of the world's creation, 3962 BC. The entrance on "God's" side leads inside, where the white-washed walls are interrupted only by triangular windows and fireplaces.

Harrington: the Carpet Baggers Aviation Museum

Approximately five miles west of Rushton, off the A14 just outside the tiny village of **HARRINGTON**, the **Carpet Baggers Aviation Museum** (March–Oct Sat & Sun 10am–5pm; £2; ☎01604/686608) occupies the site of a World War II intelligence base, taken off the military "secret" list in 1993. This is a specialist interest museum, well off the beaten track, set up by ex-"carpet baggers", intelligence personnel who were instrumental in sending secret agents to the continent. Part of the museum contains crushed remains of planes, mangled engine parts, bombs and bullets collected from the surrounding area by a dedicated member of the Carpet Baggers Association. A second building, where Colonel Colby devised the CIA, is stocked with 1940s photographs and newspapers, leaflets dropped into Europe by the Americans and a selection of weapons. The café, in the original intelligence room, has a video showing the making of PLUTO, an eighty-mile-long pipeline built in Corby to carry fuel under the Channel to the continent in time for D-Day in 1944.

Lincolnshire

The obvious place to start a visit to **Lincolnshire** is **Lincoln** itself, where the cathedral, the third largest church in England, remains the region's outstanding attraction. North and east of the city, the Lincolnshire **Wolds** band the county, their gentle green hills harbouring the pleasant old market town of **Louth**, where conscientious objectors were sent to dig potatoes during World War II. Here also is the faded gentility of **Woodhall Spa**, an Edwardian resort that served as the base of the Dambusters as they prepared for their Ruhr raid in 1943. The Wolds are flanked by the coast, so different from the rest of the county, its brashness encapsulated by **Skegness**.

Delightful **Stamford**, in the southwest corner of the county, is an alternative base, an attractive town boasting one of the great monuments of Elizabethan England, **Burghley House**. It also stands not too far away from **The Fens**, whose most appealing villages lie along the A17, a road that runs close to the old fenland port of **Boston**, now Lincolnshire's second town. On any tour of the Fens you'll pass some of the county's most imposing medieval **churches**. Several are worth a special visit, especially **St Botolph's** in Boston, **St Andrew's** in Heckington and **St Mary Magdalen's** in Gedney – seen to best advantage, like all the other churches of this area, in the pale, watery sunlight of the fenland evening. The other chief town of southern Lincolnshire is **Grantham**, birthplace of Margaret Thatcher and the site of its own splendid medieval church.

Getting around Lincolnshire by public transport can be difficult, but there are reasonable **bus** services between Lincoln and the larger market towns, like Louth, and **trains** connect Lincoln with Gainsborough and Skegness via Boston. Covering the whole of the county, the **bus timetable hotline** number is ☎01522/553135.

Lincoln

Reaching high into the sky from the top of a steep hill, the triple towers of the mighty cathedral of **LINCOLN** are visible for miles across the flatlands. This conspicuous spot was first fortified by the Celts, who called their settlement Lindon, "hillfort by the lake", a reference to the pools formed by the River Witham in the marshy ground below. In 47 AD the Romans occupied Lindon and built a fortified town which subsequently became, as Lindum Colonia, one of the four regional capitals of Roman Britain.

Today, only fragments of the Roman city survive, mostly pieces of the third-century town wall, and these are outdone by reminders of Lincoln's medieval heyday, which began during the reign of William the Conqueror with the building of the castle and cathedral. Lincoln flourished, first as a Norman power-base and then as a centre of the wool trade with Flanders, until 1369, when the wool market was transferred to neighbouring Boston. It was almost five hundred years before the town revived, the recovery based upon its manufacture of agricultural machinery and drainage equipment for the fenlands. As the nineteenth-century town spread south down the hill and out along the old Roman road – the Fosse Way – so Lincoln became a place of precise class distinctions: the "Up hill" area, sloping north from the cathedral, became synonymous with middle-class respectability, "Down hill" with the proletariat. It's a distinction that remains – locals selling anything from secondhand cars to settees still put "Up hill" in brackets to signify a better quality of merchandise.

For the visitor, almost everything of interest is confined to the "Up hill" part of town, and it's here also you'll find the best pubs and restaurants. In addition, within easy striking distance of Lincoln by car stand several fascinating churches: to the northeast, there's Snarford church, to the northwest two more, one at Coates-by-Stow, the other at Stow. In this direction too is the rare Old Hall at Gainsborough.

Arrival and information

Both Lincoln's **train station**, on St Mary's Street, and its **bus station**, close by off Norman Street, are located "Down hill" in the city centre. From either, it's a steep, twenty-minute walk to the cathedral, which can also be reached by city buses #1A, #7A and #8. There are two **tourist offices**. One is in the shopping centre on The Cornhill, close

---

LINCOLNSHIRE CHURCHES

The more important of Lincolnshire's famously diverse **churches** are described in the main text, but there are many others of interest, some of the most notable of which are listed below. For further information, almost all the county's tourist offices have details of the more significant local churches and will direct you to them.

Bicker, off the A52 near its junction with the A17. **St Swithin's** is noted for its Early English chancel and Norman nave.

Brant Broughton, eleven miles west of Sleaford on the A17. Fourteenth-century church of **St Helen**, notable for its massive spire and gargoyle-decorated nave.

Crowland, seven miles north of Peterborough on the A1073. The remains of **Croyland Abbey**, once the region's largest monastery, provide some idea of its splendour, with the ruinous west front and the fifteenth-century bell tower the best-preserved portions.

Kirkstead, southwest of Woodhall Spa off the B1191. Remote thirteenth-century **St Leonard's** is an excellent illustration of the Early English style. Built as the chapel of a long-gone Cistercian abbey.

Nocton, eight miles southeast of Lincoln off the B1188. **All Saints**, completed in 1872, was built to commemorate the First Earl of Ripon, local landowner and, briefly, prime minister. Wall paintings, stained glass and almost all the fittings are original.

Pickworth, off the A15 south of Sleaford. The outstanding wall paintings of **St Andrew's** date from the church's construction in the fourteenth century.

Raithby, off the A153 about a mile southwest of Louth. Gothic Revival church of **St Peter**, built in 1839.

Whaplode, six miles east of Spalding on the A151. **St Mary's** is a fascinating hybrid, the original Norman work supplemented by Early English, Tudor, Stuart and Georgian bits and pieces.

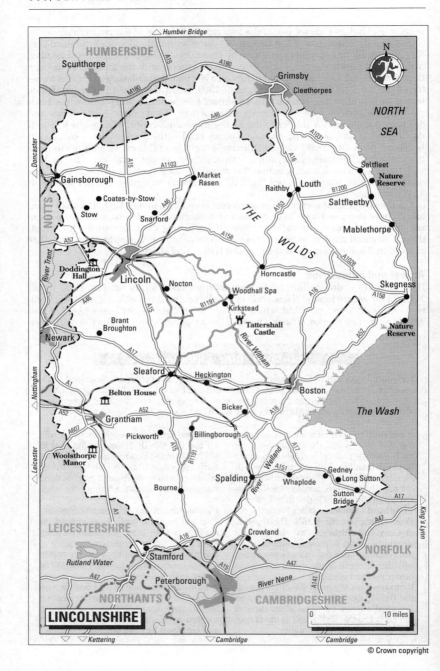

© Crown copyright

to the train and bus stations (Easter–Sept Mon–Thurs 9am–5.30pm, Fri 9am–5pm, Sat 10am–5pm; Oct–Easter same hours, but only till 4pm; ☎01522/873703), the other is at 9 Castle Hill, between the cathedral and the castle (Easter–Sept Mon–Thurs 9am–5.30pm, Fri 9am–5pm, Sat & Sun 10am–5pm; Oct–Easter same hours, but only till 4pm; ☎01522/873700). Both have a useful range of literature on Lincoln and its surroundings, take bookings for guided tours of the city, and operate an accommodation service.

Accommodation

Lincoln has a good supply of competitively priced **hotels** and **B&Bs**, though surprisingly few of them are in the vicinity of the Cathedral – "Up hill" – and this is precisely where you want to be. All the places below are "Up hill," unless otherwise indicated. On occasion, demand can exceed supply, in which case head for the tourist office, who operate an efficient accommodation service.

Carline Guest House, 1–3 Carline Rd (☎01522/530422). One of the best B&Bs in the city, *Carline* occupies a spick-and-span Edwardian house just five minutes' walk down from the cathedral – take Drury Lane from the top of Steep Hill and keep straight. Breakfasts are first-rate, the rooms smart and tastefully furnished. No credit cards. ②.

D'isney Place Hotel, Eastgate (☎01522/538881). This delightful hotel occupies a lovely eighteenth-century building close to the cathedral. Breakfast is served in the bedrooms, some of which have four-poster beds and spa baths. Highly recommended. ⑤.

Edward King House, The Old Palace, Minster Yard (☎01522/528778). For something a little different, head for this unusual B&B in a former residence of the Bishops of Lincoln. The exterior is a good bit grander than the rooms, but these are perfectly adequate and some have fine views over the city. Next to the cathedral. ①.

Lincoln youth hostel, 77 South Park (☎01522/522076). The town's HI hostel occupies a Victorian villa opposite South Common park, half a mile south of the train station. To get there, walk over Pelham Bridge, keep going down Canwick Road, straight over the island (past South Park Avenue) and it's the first turning on the right opposite the cemetery. Closed Jan. ①.

St Clements Lodge, 21 Langworth Gate (☎01522/521532). In a modest side street a short walk from the cathedral, this comfortable B&B offers a handful of pleasant guest rooms. To get there, follow Eastgate east from beside the cathedral. ②.

White Hart Hotel, on Bailgate (☎01522/526222). This is one of Lincoln's plushest hotels, a crisply refurbished old coaching inn next to the castle. Many of the bedrooms overlook the cathedral. One of the Forte Heritage chain. Weekend deals can half the normal price. ⑥.

The City

Approached through the arch of medieval Exchequergate, the west front of **Lincoln Cathedral** (June–Aug Mon–Sat 7.15am–8pm, Sun 7.15am–6pm; Sept–May Mon–Sat 7.15am–6pm, Sun 7.15am–5pm; £3 donation) is a glorious sight, a cliff-face of blind arcading mobbed by decorative carving. Most striking of all is the extraordinary band of twelfth-century carved panels which depict biblical themes with a passionate intimacy, their inspiration being a similar frieze at Modena cathedral in Italy. The west front's apparent homogeneity is deceptive, and further inspection reveals two phases of construction – the small stones and thick mortar of much of the facade belong to the original church, completed in 1092, whereas the longer stones and finer courses date from the early thirteenth century. These were enforced modifications, for in 1185 an earthquake shattered much of the Norman church, which was then rebuilt under the auspices of **Bishop Hugh of Avalon**, the man responsible for most of the present cathedral, with the notable exception of the fourteenth-century towers.

The cavernous **interior** is a fine example of Early English architecture, with the nave's pillars conforming to the same general design yet differing slightly, their varied columns and bands of dark Purbeck marble contrasting with the oolitic limestone that is the building's main material. Looking back up the nave from beneath the central tower, you can also observe a major medieval cock-up: Bishop Hugh's roof is out of alignment with the earlier west front, and the point where they meet has all the wrong angles. It's possible to pick out other irregularities too – the pillars have bases of different heights, and there are ten windows in the north wall and nine in the south – but these are deliberate features, reflecting a medieval aversion to the vanity of symmetry. Pre-Christian images are still visible around the cathedral; above the doorway to the left of the decorative stone rood screen at the head of the nave, the "cheeky green man" (an early fertility symbol) peers out from behind some foliage, watched by the beady eye of a stealthy dragon.

Beyond the central tower lies **St Hugh's Choir**, its fourteenth-century misericords carrying an eccentric range of carvings, with scenes from the life of Alexander the Great and King Arthur mixed up with biblical characters and folkloric parables. Farther on is the Gothic **Angel Choir**, completed in 1280, its roof embellished by dozens of finely carved statuettes, including the tiny Lincoln Imp (see opposite). Finally, a corridor off the choir's north aisle leads to the wooden-roofed **cloisters** and the ten-sided **chapter house**, where Edward I convened some of the first English Parliaments.

Hidden behind a high wall immediately below (and to the south of) the cathedral on Minster Yard are the ruins of what would, in its day, have been among the city's most impressive buildings. This, the medieval **Bishop's Palace** (April–Oct daily 10am–6pm, Nov–March Sat & Sun 10am–1pm & 2–4pm; £1.30; EH), once consisted of two grand halls, a lavish chapel, kitchens and ritzy private chambers, but today the only significant survivor is the battered and bruised Alnwick Tower and the undercroft. The damage was done during the Civil War when a troupe of Roundheads occupied the palace until they themselves had to evacuate the place after a fierce fire. Incidentally, a small **vineyard** has recently been established here – one of the most northerly in the world.

From the west front of the cathedral, it's a quick stroll across to **Lincoln Castle** (summer Mon–Sat 9.30am–5.30pm, Sun 11am–5.30pm; winter closes 4pm; £2.50). The castle walls incorporate bits and pieces from the twelfth to the nineteenth century and the wall walkway offers great views over town. The earliest remains are those of the **Lucy Tower**, built on the mound of the first Norman keep. Behind the walls, in the spacious castle grounds, is the dour redbrick old jail, now housing one of the four surviving copies of the **Magna Carta** and a remarkable **prison chapel**. Here, prisoners were locked in high-sided cubicles where they could see the preacher and his pulpit but not their fellow internees, an arrangement founded on the pseudo-scientific theory that defined crime as a contagious disease. Unfortunately for the theorists, their system of "Separation and Silence" drove many prisoners crazy, and it had to be abandoned, though nobody bothered to dismantle the chapel.

Leaving the castle via the west gate, you reach **The Lawn**, formerly a lunatic asylum and now a leisure complex incorporating a modest exhibition on mental health in the **Charlesworth Suite** (Mon–Fri 9am–4.30/5pm, Sat & Sun 10am–4/5pm; free), in the grandly porticoed building at the front. Adjoining the Charlesworth Suite is a display devoted to now-disbanded No. 50 and No. 61 squadrons, both active in bombing raids during World War II and both based in Lincolnshire. Close by, and also part of The Lawn, is the **Sir Joseph Banks Conservatory** (same hours; free), a large tropical glasshouse named after the local botanist who travelled with Cook on his first voyage to Australia.

As for the rest of **"Up hill" Lincoln**, it's scattered with historic remains, notably several slabs of Roman wall, the most prominent of which is the second-century **Newport Arch** straddling Bailgate, once the main north gate into the city. It's in fine condition, despite being crunched by a truck in the 1970s, and remains the only Roman arch in Britain that's still used by traffic. There's also a bevy of medieval stone houses, at their best on and around the aptly named Steep Hill as it cuts down to the city centre. In particular, look out for the tidily restored twelfth-century **Jew's House**, a reminder of the

Jewish community that flourished in medieval Lincoln – a rare and superb example of domestic Norman architecture, it now houses the *Jew's House Restaurant* (see below).

The **Usher Gallery**, Lindum Road (Mon–Sat 10am–5.30pm, Sun 2.30–5pm; £2), is on the hillside too, its well-presented displays featuring some fine watercolours of the cathedral and its environs, a pleasing sample of seventeenth-century Dutch and Italian paintings, and memorabilia celebrating Lincolnshire's own Alfred Tennyson (1809–92), one of Victorian England's favourite poets. There's also an eclectic collection of coins, porcelain, and watches and clocks dating from the seventeenth century. The timepieces were given to the gallery by its benefactor, James Ward Usher, a local jeweller and watchmaker who made a fortune by devising the legend of the **Lincoln Imp**, which he turned into the city's emblem in the 1880s. His story has a couple of imps hopping around the cathedral, until one of them is turned to stone for trying to talk to the angels carved into the roof of the choir. His chum made a hasty exit on the back of a witch, but the wind is still supposed to haunt the cathedral awaiting their return.

Eating and drinking

Lincoln's **café** and **restaurant** scene is a little patchy – too many places offer mundane food geared to the day-tripping trade – but there are excellent places too, mostly within shouting distance of the Cathedral. First stop must be *Browns Pie Shop*, 33 Steep Hill, which has a lively menu where the emphasis is on British ingredients; a main course here will cost you about £10. Next door, and similarly enticing, is the *Wig and Mitre* pub-restaurant, where a wide-ranging, moderately priced menu lists everything from sandwiches through to fillet steak. Another recommendable spot on Steep Hill is the more expensive – and more formal – *Jew's House Restaurant* (☎01522/524851). As for **pubs**, the obvious target is the *Victoria*, opposite the Lawn at 6 Union Rd, an amiable, traditional and long-established local that serves great-value down-to-earth food along with a vast array of guest beers.

Around Lincoln

Almost hidden by a clump of trees, half a mile down a country lane off the A46, about seven miles northeast of Lincoln at tiny **SNARFORD**, stands the solitary, square-towered church of **St Lawrence**. The church is dedicated to a Roman saint who was roasted to death on a gridiron, a fate that's made him the patron saint of cooks. For several centuries, the church was the family mausoleum of the St Pauls, the lords of the manor, and its cramped interior is dominated by the Elizabethan tomb of Sir Thomas and his wife, Faith, whose alabaster figures lie on an elaborately carved, six-poster bed. The brightly painted carving is superb, with finely crafted detail such as the flower-embroidered cushion at Sir Thomas's feet, Faith's ruff and open gown and the figures of the couple's eight kneeling children carved round the canopy. Opposite is the tomb of their son, Sir George, and his wife Frances, who lie propped up on their elbows looking back towards Sir Thomas. Once again, the carving is magnificent, with Frances decked out in Jacobean finery, a dark gown and a wide ruff beneath the frizzed hairstyle then fashionable. Behind the couple and the effigy of their child are the emblems of death – coffins and gravediggers' tools – together with the lily of purity and the rose of eternity.

A series of obscure byroads lead the eight miles west from Snarford to the remote farmstead and adjacent church of **St Edith's** that together constitute **COATES-BY-STOW**. Entered through a narrow Norman doorway, tiny St Edith's boasts a rare and partly painted wooden rood screen dating from the fifteenth century. Round about are the residue of several hundred years of worship: medieval pews and pulpit, a holy water stoup and a Norman font.

The village of **STOW**, on the B1241 some three miles west of St Edith's, embraces the fortress-like church of **St Mary**, whose austere rubble walls date from the beginning of the eleventh century, though the Normans refashioned the nave and the Victorians restored the church in the 1850s. The imposing interior is dominated by the magnificent Saxon arches of the central tower, the tallest of their period in England, whose simple elegance contrasts with the clumsy Norman arches inserted behind them. But some of the Norman work is excellent too, especially the ornate vaulted ribbing of the chancel and the dogtooth carving around the doorways – and look out for a scratched drawing of a Viking longship and some crude thirteenth-century wall paintings.

From Stow, it's about seven miles south to **Doddington Hall** (May–Sept Wed & Sun 2–6pm; house & gardens £4.20), a privately owned Elizabethan manor house built of locally manufactured bricks trimmed with stone. The house is surrounded by five acres of well-tended gardens (same hours plus March & April Sun 2–6pm; gardens only £2.10) and the interior, extensively remodelled in the 1760s, features a substantial collection of early English furniture and Chinese porcelain.

Alternatively, you could strike north to the old river-port of **GAINSBOROUGH**, a dreary place but for two outstanding buildings. These are the church of **All Saints** (closed Wed), whose spacious pastel-painted interior is a fine example of Georgian style, and **Gainsborough Old Hall** (Mon–Sat 10am–5pm, plus Easter–Oct Sun 2–5.30pm; £2.50; EH), a sprawling manor house with a magnificent Great Hall. Built in the 1460s, the timber-framed hall, bending and buckling from the contractions of the oak, has a huge hoop-shaped roof where the grain of the wood skilfully follows the lines of the arches. At the back of the hall, tiny doors lead to the well-preserved kitchen, and the timbered bedrooms of the first floor are worth inspecting too, though the exhibition on the Mayflower Pilgrims, some of whom worshipped here, is uninspiring. Gainsborough is thought to have been the setting for St Oggs in George Eliot's *Mill on the Floss*, whose tragic events result from a particularly ferocious tidal bore. Fortunately for the locals, the bore – or eagre – which rolls up the River Trent through Gainsborough fifty minutes after high tide in the Humber estuary doesn't often do much damage, but it still raises the river level between 8 and 13 feet; times are given in the local press.

The Wolds and the coast

The rolling hills and gentle valleys of the **Lincolnshire Wolds**, a narrow band of chalky land running north from near **Horncastle**, stand out amidst the more mundane agricultural landscapes of north Lincolnshire. A string of particularly appealing valleys is concentrated in the vicinity of **Louth**, which, with its striking church steeple and old centre, is easily the most enticing of the region's towns. South of Horncastle, as the Wolds shelve into the northern peripheries of the pancake-flat fenland, you'll find stretches of woodland clustered round the once fashionable hamlet of **Woodhall Spa** and the imposing redbrick **Tattershall Castle**, north Lincolnshire's main historical attraction. The coast comprises miles of bungalows, campsites and caravans parked beside a sandy beach that extends, with a few marshy interruptions, from Mablethorpe to **Skegness**, the main resort. Near Skegness, the **Gibraltar Point Nature Reserve** is a welcome diversion from the crass commercialism of the coast.

Horncastle, Woodhall Spa and Tattershall Castle

The market town of **HORNCASTLE**, twenty miles east of Lincoln, stands beside the confluence of the rivers Bain and Waring at the foot of the Wolds. It's a dozy little place of redbrick cottages and narrow streets that fan out from a tidy main square, adorned by a self-important market cross. Aside from a bumper crop of antique shops, Horncastle has little else to offer, but it was once famous for its horse fairs – George Borrow described one of them in *Romany Rye* – and remains a major crossroads.

One road, the B1191, cuts the seven miles southwest to **WOODHALL SPA**, an elongated village surrounded by a generous chunk of woodland. Here, the main street is lined with Victorian and Edwardian villas, reminders of the time when the spring water of this isolated place, rich in iodine and bromine, was a favourite tipple of the great and the good. A modest **museum** (Easter–Oct Mon–Sat 10am–5pm, Sun 11am–5pm), on Iddesleigh Road off the Broadway, outlines the development of the spa, but, nowadays, with the springs abandoned, the village feels marooned. It does, however, possess a particularly interesting hotel, the **Petwood Hotel**, on Stixwould Road (☎01526/352411; ⑥), whose half-timbered gables and stone facades shelter a fine panelled interior, built in 1905 for the furniture millionaires, the Maples. In World War II, long after the family had moved out, the house was requisitioned by the RAF and turned into the Officers' Mess of 617 Squadron, the **Dambusters**, famous for their bombing raid of May 16, 1943. The raid was planned to deprive German industry of water and electricity by breaching several Ruhrland dams, a mission made possible by Barnes Wallis's **bouncing bomb**. A rusting specimen stands outside the hotel, which also contains the old **Officers' Bar**, kitted out with memorabilia from bits of aircraft engines to newspaper cuttings. Another unexpected delight of Woodhall Spa is its **Kinema**, deep in the woods, yet only five minutes' walk from the town's main road. Its one of England's few remaining picture houses which projects a film from behind the screen, and at weekend showings a 1930s organ rises in front of the screen to play you through the ice-cream break. For details of what's on at the Kinema, call the tourist office (Easter to Sept Mon–Sat 10am–5pm, Sun 11am–5pm; ☎01526/353775).

From Woodhall Spa, it's about three miles southeast to **Tattershall Castle** (April–Oct Sat–Wed 10.30am–5.30pm; Nov to mid-Dec Sat & Sun noon–4pm; £3; NT), whose massive redbrick keep dominates the fenland from a lonely spot beside the road to Sleaford. There's been a castle here since Norman times, but it was Ralph Cromwell, the Lord High Treasurer, who built the present quadrangled tower in the 1440s. Cromwell, a veteran of Agincourt, was familiar with contemporary French architecture and it was to France that he looked for his basic design – in England, keeps had been out of fashion since the thirteenth century. Cromwell's quest for style explains Tattershall's contradictions. The castle walls are sixteen feet thick and rise to a height of one hundred feet, but there are no fewer than three ground-floor doorways with low-level windows to match. It's a medieval keep as fashion accessory, a theatricality that's continued inside the castle with the grand chimneypieces, the only highlight of the bare interior.

Louth

Henry VIII described the county of Lincolnshire as "one of the most brutal and beestlie of the whole realm", his contempt based on the events of 1536, when thousands of northern peasants rebelled against his religious reforms. In Lincolnshire, this insurrection, the **Pilgrimage of Grace**, began in the northeast corner of the county at **LOUTH**, under the leadership of the local vicar, who was subsequently hanged, drawn and quartered. There's a commemorative plaque in honour of the rebels beside Louth's church of **St James**, which is the town's one outstanding building, its Perpendicular buttresses, battlements and pinnacles set on a grassy knoll just to the west of the centre. The interior, clumsily renovated in the 1820s, is a disappointment, but it does contain the curious Sudbury Hutch, a portable cupboard used for displaying plate. Bearing a portrait of Henry VII and Elizabeth of York, the hutch purports to be medieval, but it may well be a fake.

Next to the church, the well-tended gardens and Georgian doorways of **Westgate** make it Louth's prettiest street and you can grab a drink here – down an alley off its north side – at the *Wheatsheaf Inn*. Afterwards, it doesn't take long to explore the rest of the town centre, whose cramped lanes and alleys are lined with redbrick buildings dating from the seventeenth century. If you're in Louth on a Wednesday morning, take a look at the lively antique auction that takes place in the central marketplace.

Louth's **tourist office**, in the New Market Hall off Cornmarket (Mon–Sat 9am–5pm; ☎01507/609289), has a competent range of local information including accommodation details. The best **hotel** is the *Priory*, on Eastgate (☎01507/602930; ③), a family-run place in a Victorian house with extensive gardens, about ten minutes' walk from the town centre. There's also an excellent **B&B**, *Keddington House*, in a pleasant Victorian house with its own heated pool a short walk from the centre at 5 Keddington Rd (☎01507/603973; ②). If you have your own transport, a third good choice is the *Gordon House B&B*, a pretty redbrick property with stylish rooms and a large landscaped garden, three miles southeast on the B1373 at Legbourne (☎01507/607568; ①). Back in Louth, the *Priory* serves moderately priced dinners, while the miscellaneous snack bars dotted round the market offer cheaper alternatives. The town **bus station**, on Eastgate, has reasonably regular weekday services arriving from Lincoln and Skegness.

The Saltfleetby and Theddlethorpe dunes

A worthwhile short excursion from Louth takes you east along the B1200 across six or seven miles of monotonous fen farmland to the coast. This byroad is built on an old Roman road used to transport salt inland from the salt pans of the coast. At the point where the road meets the main A1031, just south of tiny Saltfleet, a chalky track heads straight through the dunes to the small **Saltfleetby and Theddlethorpe Nature Reserve**, one of the few stretches of shoreline hereabouts where you can escape the crowds in summer. The dunes are at their prettiest in midsummer, when buckthorn bushes and sea heather flowers form a carpet of violet, spreading to the narrow band of surf on the horizon. You can reach the sea via an unmarked path that crosses the marshes from the car park, fishing for crabs in the creeks and watching the reserve's wader and wildfowl population on the flats. Be sure to check the tide times before you set out and keep a close eye on the water level.

Skegness and around

SKEGNESS has been a busy resort ever since the railways reached the Lincolnshire coast in 1875. Its heyday was before the 1960s, when the Brits began to take themselves off to sunnier climes, but it still attracts tens of thousands of city-dwellers each year, who come for the wide, sandy beaches and for a host of attractions ranging from nightclubs to bowling greens. Every inch the traditional English seaside town, Skegness gets the edge over many of its rivals by keeping its beaches clean and its parks spick-and-span, whilst a massive leisure complex in neighbouring Ingoldmells has Europe's largest indoor "fun pool". Indeed, Skegness has a tradition of keeping ahead of its competitors: in 1908 it came up with the ground-breaking "Skegness is So Bracing" slogan beneath a picture of a "Jolly Fisherman" and it was here in 1936 that ex-showman Billy Butlin opened the first "Butlin's Holiday Camp." All that said, the seafront, with its rows of tacky souvenir shops and amusement arcades, can be dismal, especially on rainy days, and you may well decide to sidestep the whole caboodle by heading south along the coastal road to **Gibraltar Point Nature Reserve** (daily dawn to dusk), where a series of footpaths crisscross a narrow strip of salt marsh, sand dune and beach.

The **tourist office** (April–Sept daily 9am–6pm; Oct–March Mon–Fri 9am–5pm, Sat 10am–4pm, Sun noon–4pm; ☎01754/764821), behind the beach in the Embassy Centre on Grand Parade, can provide a colossal list of accommodation, including scores of **B&Bs** and **guest houses**. A series of convenient choices is strung out along South Parade and Drummond Road, a few minutes' walk from the Embassy Centre: try the *Belle View Hotel*, 12 South Parade (☎01754/765274; ②), the *Singlecote Hotel*, 34 Drummond Rd (☎01754/764698; ②), or *Scarborough House*, 54 South Parade (☎01754/764453; ②). For something a little more original, there's the *Old Mill Guest House*, an old and imaginatively converted windmill five miles inland at Westend, Burgh Le Marsh (☎01754/810081; ②). Skegness **bus** and **train** stations are ten minutes' walk inland from the clock tower beside the tourist office, straight up Lumley Road.

The Lincolnshire Fens

The Lincolnshire section of **The Fens**, the great chunk of eastern England extending from Cambridge to Boston, encompasses some of the most productive farmland in Europe. With the exception of the occasional hillock, this pancake-flat, treeless terrain has been painstakingly reclaimed from the marshes and swamps that once drained into the Wash, a process that has taken almost two thousand years. In earlier times, outsiders were often amazed by the dreadful conditions hereabouts – as one medieval chronicler put it: "There is in the middle part of Britain a hideous fen which [is] oft times clouded with moist and dark vapours having within it divers islands and woods as also crooked and winding rivers." These dire conditions spawned the distinctive culture of the so-called **fen slodgers**, who embanked small portions of marsh to create pastureland and fields, supplementing their diets by catching fish and fowl, and gathering reed and sedge for thatching and fuel. Their economy was threatened by the large-scale land reclamation schemes of the late fifteenth and sixteenth centuries, and time and again the fenlanders sabotaged progress by breaking down the banks and dams. But the odds were stacked against the saboteurs, and a succession of great landowners eventually drained huge tracts of the fenland; by the end of the eighteenth century the fen slodgers' way of life had all but disappeared. Nonetheless, the Lincolnshire fens remain a distinctive area of introverted little villages, with just one major settlement, the old port of **Boston**.

Boston

Bisected by the muddy River Witham as it nears the Wash, **BOSTON** (a corruption of Botolf's stone, or Botolph's town), was named after the Anglo-Saxon monk-saint who first established a monastery here, overlooking the estuary and main river crossing point, in 645 AD. In the thirteenth and fourteenth centuries, the settlement expanded to become England's second largest seaport, its flourishing economy dependent on the wool trade with Flanders. Local merchants, revelling in their success, built the magnificent medieval church of St Botolph, whose 272-foot tower still presides over the town and surrounding fenland. The church was completed in the early sixteenth century, but by then Boston was in decline as trade drifted west towards the Atlantic and the Witham silted up. The town's fortunes only revived in the late eighteenth century when, after the nearby fens had been drained, it became a minor agricultural centre with a modest port that has, in recent times, been modernized for trade with the EU. A handsome town with a distinctive fenland feel, Boston is an appealing place to break a journey along England's east coast between Lincoln and Norfolk. On Saturdays and Wednesdays, a busy market livens up the main square, and the surrounding flatlands are peppered with pubs that make ideal targets for forays into the fens.

Mostly edged by Victorian redbrick buildings, the narrow streets of Boston's cramped centre radiate out from the massive bulk of **St Botolph** (Mon–Sat 8.30am–4.30pm, Sun 8.30am–4pm; winter closes Sun noon). Most of the church's exterior masonry, embellished by the high-pointed windows of the Decorated style, dates from the fourteenth century, but the huge and distinctive tower, whose lack of a spire earned the church the nickname "**Stump**", is of later construction. The octagonal lantern, added in the early sixteenth century, is visible from twenty miles away and once sheltered a beacon that guided travellers in from the fens and the North Sea. A tortuous spiral staircase leads to a balcony near the top, from where the views over Boston and the fens amply repay the price of the ticket (£2) and stiff climb.

Down below, St Botolph's light and airy interior contains some intriguing fourteenth-century **misericords**, bearing a lively mixture of vernacular scenes, such as organ-playing bears, a pair of medieval jesters squeezing cats in imitation of bagpipes and a schoolmaster birching a boy, watched by three more awaiting the same fate. There's also the **Cotton Chapel**, dedicated to John Cotton, vicar here in 1612 and later a leading light among the Puritans of Boston, Massachusetts. In the early seventeenth century, Lincolnshire's Boston became a centre of Nonconformism, providing a stream of emigrants for the colonies of New England.

It was here too, in 1607, that several of the **Pilgrim Fathers** were incarcerated after their failed attempt to escape religious persecution by slipping across to Holland. They were imprisoned for thirty days in the **Guildhall** (Mon–Sat 10am–5pm, plus April–Sept Sun 1.30–5pm; £1.20, free on Thurs), on South Street near St Botolph, and this now accommodates a small museum containing several old cells, one of which has been returned to its seventeenth-century appearance.

A small **memorial** to the Pilgrim Fathers has been erected about two miles southeast of the town beyond the village of **Fishtoft**, supposedly at the point on the river bank where the ship in which they were travelling to Holland was stopped. No one knows for sure exactly where this happened, so the granite monument is somewhat bogus, but the car park marks the start of an enjoyable **walk** along the Witham to the sea. From the riverside, the views over the dykes and fens are backdropped by the truncated profile of the Stump.

PRACTICALITIES

It's ten minutes' walk east from Boston **train station** to the town centre via West Street, where the back of the Regal cinema overlooks the **bus station**. Close to St Botolph, in the Market Place beneath the Assembly Rooms, is the **tourist office** (Mon–Sat 9am–5pm; ☎01205/356656), where you can pick up details of several **B&Bs**. Among them is the likeable *Ailsa Villa*, 16 Sleaford Rd (☎01205/352253; ③), just west of the train station, and the *Bramley House*, a converted eighteenth-century farmhouse one mile further down Sleaford Road at no. 267 (☎01205/354538; ③). With your own transport, it's worth considering the six-mile drive south of town to the village of Sutterton, where *Georgian House*, a beautiful period building with its own landscaped garden on Station Road, is among the best-value places to stay in the area (☎01205/460048; ②).

For **food**, try *Goodbarn's*, beneath the north side of the Stump on Wormgate, which serves copious pub meals inside or out in a relaxing back garden overlooking the river. Tucked away in the corner of Church Close, *Monsuda* (☎01205/355671) is an authentic Thai restaurant, with a bona fide Thai chef, where a three-course meal will set you back around £15. Vegetarians should head for *Maud Foster Windmill*, at the west edge of town on Willoughby Road (Wed & Sat 11am–5pm, Sun 1–5pm, plus July & Aug Thurs & Fri 11am–5pm; ☎01205/352188), whose tearoom serves a range of vegetarian and vegan meals, as well as a good selection of delicious cakes.

Heckington

The village of **HECKINGTON**, twelve miles west of Boston and five east of Sleaford, is a tidy little place draped around the church of **St Andrew**, a splendid example of the Decorated style, with a pinnacled spire and elaborate canopied buttresses framing the flowing tracery of the windows. Inside, the original fourteenth-century chancel fittings have survived, including the tomb of the founder, Richard de Potesgrave, and an **Easter Sepulchre**, whose exquisitely carved figures are set against a dense undergrowth of foliage. The sepulchre, one of the finest in England, was built to accommodate the host between Good Friday and Easter morning. The **sedilia** is intriguing too, boasting a cartoon strip of domestic scenes on the subject of food – a man eating fruit, a woman feeding the birds and suchlike. Heckington has one other attraction, its unique eight-sailed **windmill**, near the train station on Station Street, which is worth visiting when it's in operation (Easter to mid-July Thurs–Sun noon–5pm; mid-July to mid-Sept daily noon–5pm; mid-Sept to Easter Sun 2–5pm; £1.50). Afterwards, pop over to the *Nags Head*, 34 High St (☎01529/460218; ②), where the **food** is excellent.

Spalding

Built beside the muddy banks of the River Welland sixteen miles south of Boston, the agricultural town of **SPALDING** is encrusted with the dust blown off the surrounding farmland. The grime coats the portentous warehouses and mansions that line the Welland, though one of them, **Ayscoughfee** (pronounced "Ascuffee") **Hall**, a much modified medieval wool merchant's house on Churchgate, has been cleaned up to accommodate an excellent **museum** on the history of the Fens and the culture of its people (Mon–Fri 10am–5pm, plus March–Oct Sat 10am–5pm & Sun 11am–5pm; free). The hall also contains the **tourist office** (Mon–Fri 9am–5pm, plus March–Oct Sat 10am–5pm, Sun 11am–5pm; ☎01775/725468), who will provide the complicated directions to Spalding's only other noteworthy attraction, the **Romany Museum** (March–Oct Wed–Sun 10.30am–5pm; full guided tour & slide show £4, museum only £2.75), tucked away on the eastern outskirts of town close to the A16. Hemmed in by a scrap metal yard and Gypsy site, its prize pieces are several beautifully painted *vardos*, or horse-drawn caravans, displayed beside their shining metal modern counterparts. There's little in the way of written information about the exhibits, but one Gypsy or another is invariably on hand to talk you through the collection and you can usually get your palm read too.

Spalding is at its liveliest during the three-day **flower festival**, held at the beginning of May, but even then you're unlikely to want to stay. If, however, you do take to the place, the tourist office has a short list of **B&Bs**, amongst which is the excellent *Bedford Court*, which occupies a handsome old house close to the Welland at 10 London Rd (☎01775/722377; no credit cards; ②); four of the five commodious bedrooms are en suite.

Gedney and Long Sutton

Travelling east from Spalding, it's eleven miles to the scattered hamlet of **GEDNEY**, where the massive church of **St Mary Magdalen** intercepts the fenland landscape. The church is rather the worse for wear, with various sections sinking into the ground at different angles, but it's still an impressive building, chiefly on account of its tower – a blend of Early English and Perpendicular – and the alabaster effigies of Adlard and Cassandra Welby, facing each other on the south wall near the chancel.

LONG SUTTON, a modest farming centre about a mile east from Gedney, spreads out from a trim Market Place and the church of **St Mary**, whose arcaded tower supports the oldest lead spire in the country, dating from around 1200. Long Sutton once lay on the edge of the five-mile-wide mouth of the River Nene. This was the most treacherous part of the road from Lincoln to Norfolk, and locals had to guide travellers across the obstacle on horseback, though not always without mishap. In 1205, King John was caught by the rising tide here, losing his jewels and baggage train in the quicksands somewhere between Long Sutton and Terrington St Clement in Norfolk. In 1831, the River Nene was embanked and then spanned with a wooden bridge at **SUTTON BRIDGE**, a hamlet just to the east of Long Sutton. The present swing bridge, with its nifty central tower, was completed in 1894.

Stamford

STAMFORD is delightful, a handsome little limestone town of yellow-grey seventeenth- and eighteenth-century buildings edging narrow streets that slope up from the River Welland. It was here that the Romans forded this important river, establishing a fortified outpost that the Danes subsequently selected for one of their regional capitals. Later the town became a centre of the medieval wool and cloth trade, its wealthy merchants funding a series of almshouses known as "callises", after Calais, the English-occupied port through which most of them traded. Indeed, Stamford cloth became famous throughout

Europe for its quality and durability, a reputation confirmed when Cardinal Wolsey used it for the tents of the "Field of the Cloth of Gold", the conference of Henry VIII and Francis I of France outside Calais in 1520. Stamford was also the home of William Cecil, Elizabeth's chief minister, who built his splendid mansion, Burghley House, close by. The town survived the collapse of the wool trade, prospering as an inland port after the Welland was made navigable to the sea in 1570, and, in the eighteenth century, as a staging point on the Great North Road from London. More recently, Stamford escaped the three main threats to old English towns – the Industrial Revolution, wartime bombing and postwar development – and was designated the country's first Conservation Area in 1967. Thanks to this, its unspoilt streets lent themselves perfectly to the filming of the TV adaptation of George Eliot's *Middlemarch* in 1993.

The Town

Above all, it's the harmony of Stamford's architecture that pleases, rather than any specific sight. There are, nevertheless, a handful of buildings of some special interest in the compact centre, beginning with the church of **St Mary**, set beside a mixed Georgian and medieval close on St Mary's Street. The church, with its splendid spire, has a small, airy interior that incorporates the Corpus Christi chapel, whose intricately embossed, painted and panelled roof dates from the 1480s.

From St Mary's, several lanes thread through to the carefully maintained High Street, where Ironmonger Street leads north to Broad Street, the site of **Browne's Hospital** (May–Sept Sat & Sun 11am–4pm), the most extensive of the town's almshouses. This paupers' hospital was inelegantly remodelled by the Victorians, but the chapel preserves much of its fifteenth-century stained glass, as does the nearby church of **St John**, just to the west on Red Lion Square. Back on Broad Street, the **Stamford Museum** (April–Sept Mon–Sat 10am–5pm, Sun 2–5pm; Oct–March Mon–Sat 10am–5pm; free) features a tasteless exhibit comparing the American midget Tom Thumb with **Daniel Lambert**, the Leicester fat man who died at Stamford in 1809, aged 39 and weighing 52st 11lb (336kg). After Lambert's death his clothes were displayed in a local inn which Tom Thumb, otherwise Charles Stratton, visited several times to perform a few party tricks, like standing in Lambert's waistcoat armhole.

Down the hill from St Mary's, on the other side of the Welland, is the **George Hotel**, on High Street St Martin's, a splendid old coaching inn whose Georgian facade supports one end of the gallows that span the street – not a warning to criminals, but an advertising hoarding. Close by, the late fifteenth-century church of **St Martin** shelters the magnificent tombs of the lords Burghley, with a recumbent William Cecil carved beneath twin canopies. Just behind, the early eighteenth-century effigies of John Cecil and his wife show the couple as Roman aristocrats, propped up on their elbows to gaze across at their distinguished ancestor.

From St Martin's church, it's a fifteen-minute stroll south along High Street St Martin's to **Burghley** (pronounced "Burlee") **House** (April–Sept daily 11am–4.30pm; £6.10; guided tours Mon–Fri), an extravagant Elizabethan mansion standing in parkland landscaped by Capability Brown. Completed in 1587 after 22 years' work, the house sports a mellow-yellow ragstone exterior, embellished by dainty cupolas, a pyramidal clock tower and skeletal balustrading, all to a plan by **William Cecil**, the long-serving adviser to Elizabeth I. A shrewd and cautious man, Cecil steered his queen through all sorts of difficulties, from the wars against Spain to the execution of Mary, Queen of Scots, vindicating Elizabeth's assessment of his character when she appointed him secretary of state in 1558: "You will not be corrupted with any manner of gifts, and will be faithful to the state."

With the notable exception of the Tudor kitchen, little remains of Burghley's Elizabethan interior. Instead, the house bears the heavy hand of John, Fifth Lord Burghley, who toured France and Italy in the late seventeenth century, commissioning furniture, statuary and tapestries, as well as buying up old Florentine and Venetian paintings, such as Paolo Veronese's *Zebedee's Wife Petitioning our Lord*. To provide a suitable setting for his old masters, John brought in Antonio Verrio and his assistant Louis Laguerre, who between them covered many of Burghley's walls and ceilings with frolicking gods and goddesses. These gaudy and gargantuan murals are at their best in the Heaven Room, an artfully painted classical temple that adjoins the Hell Staircase, where the entrance to the inferno is through the gaping mouth of a cat. Have a close look also at the fine portraits in the Pagoda Room, in particular the querulous Elizabeth I and a sublimely self-confident Henry VIII by Joos van Cleve.

Finally, if you're in Stamford in June, July or August, head out to **Tolethorpe Hall**, a graceful Elizabethan mansion that's home to Stamford Shakespeare Company. The troupe gives outdoor performances, but the audience is safely covered by a vast open-fronted marquee; call ☎01780/754381 for details.

Practicalities

With frequent services from Peterborough and Oakham, Stamford **train station** is five minutes' walk from the town centre, which is just to the north across the river. The **bus station** is in the centre off All Saints' Street, a short stroll from the **tourist office**, inside Stamford Arts Centre at 27 St Mary's St (Mon–Sat 9.30am–5pm, plus April–Oct Sun 10am–3pm; ☎01780/755611).

Stamford has several charming **hotels**, the most celebrated of which is the delightful *George Hotel*, High Street St Martin's (☎01780/755171, *www.stamford.co.uk/george*; ⑦), an old and cleverly remodelled coaching inn with flagstone floors and antique furnishings, where the most appealing rooms overlook the cobbled courtyard. Just along the street is the attractive *Garden House Hotel* (☎01780/763359, *www.stamford.co.uk/gardenh*; ⑤), which occupies a tastefully modernized eighteenth-century building with twenty smart bedrooms. Stamford also possesses lots of first-rate **B&Bs**. As ever, the tourist office has the full list, but one especially good place is *Martins*, 20 High St St Martin's (☎01780/752106, *www.stamford.co.uk/bb/martins.htm*; ③), a Georgian house whose three spacious guest rooms are immaculately maintained and tastefully decorated. Breakfasts are delicious, guests have access to the walled garden and dinner is served by prior request. Another less expensive, but highly recommendable option is *Mrs Swithinbank's B&B*, 16 St George's Square (☎01780/482099, *www.stamford.co.uk/bb/16stgeor.htm*; ①), in a pleasant Victorian house overlooking St George's church and with a walled garden and a tiled and beamed main hall.

For **food**, it has to be the *George Hotel* – either in the formal and expensive restaurant, where the emphasis is on British ingredients served in imaginative ways, or in the moderately priced and informal Garden Lounge. There's delicious and inexpensive bar food too, served in the York Bar at lunchtimes.

Grantham and around

GRANTHAM, midway between Stamford and Lincoln, was once a major staging point on the Great North Road from London, but today its lengthy high street is no more than a provincial thoroughfare flanked by an unappetizing combination of modern offices and Victorian redbrick. The town's more successful days are recalled by two ancient inns, the stone-fronted *Angel and Royal*, founded by the Knights Templar in the twelfth century, and the *George*, where Charles Dickens's Nicholas Nickleby stopped on his way to Dotheboys Hall – and now guzzled up into a shopping centre. Grantham's present pride and joy is the church of **St Wulfram** (Mon–Sat 10.30am–3.30pm, Sun 7.30am–noon & 6–8pm; free), set within its own close on Swinegate, close – and to the left of – the Guildhall, standing halfway along the main drag.

St Wulfram's most obvious feature is its 282ft central spire, a fourteenth-century construction whose angular lines are emphasized by pointed blind arcading, slim window openings and the narrowest of columns. Inside, highlights are the sinuous window tracery in and around the south chancel aisle, and the late-sixteenth-century, 150-volume **chained library** (Mon 10am–noon & 2–4pm, Thurs & Fri 2–4pm) above the south porch. The high altar is of interest too, not for itself, but because its position prompted a bitter wrangle in 1627. Believing the altar should be more conspicuous, the High Church party turned it round to look down the nave, but the Puritans objected and came to move it back again. The resulting brawl, something of a cause célèbre, hardened attitudes in the run-up to the Civil War.

Beside the church is King's private school, whose original sixteenth-century classroom, with its mullioned windows and high-pitched stone roof, fronts Church Street. This was where **Isaac Newton** received his initial education in the 1650s. There's a statue of the great physicist and mathematician outside the Guildhall and a room of mementoes, including a plaster-cast death mask, in the adjacent **museum** (Mon–Sat 10am–5pm; free), which also has a display on **Margaret Thatcher**, who was born in Grantham in 1925. In a moment of gay abandon, Mrs Thatcher gave several of her dresses to the museum, though her absurdist handbags and threatening hairstyle were always more memorable. Her childhood home is up along the main street at 2 North Street: originally a grocer's store, it's been turned into a chiropractic clinic.

Grantham **train station** is ten minutes' walk from the Guildhall: follow Station Road to the four-way junction and turn right along Wharf Road, where you'll also find the **bus station**. Next door to the Guildhall is the **tourist office** (Mon–Sat 9.30am–5pm; ☎01476/406166). Grantham's smartest **hotel** is the *Angel and Royal*, down the road on the High Street (☎01476/565816; ④), and another establishment claiming to be England's oldest inn; more certain is that King John held court here, and that Richard III signed the Duke of Buckingham's death warrant in one of its rooms. The handiest **B&B** is the *Archway House*, by St Wulfram's at 15 Swinegate (☎01476/561807; ③), in an attractive old house with an oak-panelled dining room. The *Beehive Inn*, close by on Castlegate, serves tasty **bar snacks**; it also boasts its own hive of South African bees, fixed to the tree outside the pub.

Belton House

The honey-coloured limestone facade of **Belton House** (April–Oct Wed–Sun 1–5pm; gardens & park 11am–5.30pm; combined ticket £5.20; NT), three miles northeast of Grantham beside the A607, is Restoration design at its finest, its delicate symmetry enhanced by formal gardens and by a later landscaped park. Belton was built in the 1680s for a local family of lawyer-landowners, the Brownlows, whose subsequent climb up the aristocratic ladder prompted them to remodel the interior of their home in the sumptuous Neoclassical style of the late eighteenth century. Entry is through the Marble Hall, where a sequence of family portraits, including three by Reynolds, are framed by the intricate limewood carvings that remain Belton's most distinctive feature. Several of them, both here and in the **saloon**, are thought to be the work of **Grinling Gibbons**, the great Rotterdam-born woodcarver and sculptor. Belton is also noted for its pastel-shaded, Adam-style plasterwork ceilings and, on display in the Chapel Drawing Room, a pair of splendid tapestries, which, despite their Indian and Japanese themes, were made in John Vanderbank's workshop in Soho, London. In the park is one of the region's best adventure playgrounds, complete with a railway ride through the woods.

It's easy to reach Belton by **bus** from Grantham: service #601 makes the ten-minute trip roughly every hour from Monday to Saturday.

Woolsthorpe Manor

The birthplace and family home of Sir Isaac Newton, **Woolsthorpe Manor** (April–Oct Wed–Sun 1–5.30pm; £2.70; NT) lies seven miles south of Grantham, just off the A1 in the hamlet of **WOOLSTHORPE-BY-COLSTERWORTH**. The house is a pleasantly modest affair of mullioned windows and heavy-beamed ceilings and was where Newton (1642–1727) sat out the plague years of 1665–7 working on all manner of scientific theories. The apple orchard in front of the house contains a descendant of the illustrious tree whose apple dropped on Newton's head to such great, gravitational effect.

travel details

Trains

Birmingham New Street to: Birmingham International (every 15–30min; 15min); Burton-upon-Trent (hourly; 35min); Coventry (every 15–30min; 25min); Derby (hourly; 45min); Great Malvern (every 30min; 1hr); Hereford (10 daily; 1hr 50min); Kidderminster (every 30min; 30min); Leicester (hourly; 50min); Lichfield (every 15min; 45min); London (every 30min; 1hr 40min); Shrewsbury (hourly; 1hr 20min); Stoke-on-Trent (hourly; 55min); Stourbridge (every 15min; 20min); Walsall (every 30min Mon–Sat; 25min); Wolverhampton (every 30min; 20min); Worcester (every 30min; 55min).

Birmingham Snow Hill to: Stratford-upon-Avon (Mon–Sat hourly; 50min); Warwick (Mon–Sat hourly; 40min).

Derby to: Birmingham (every 20min; 45min); Burton (every 30min; 12min); Leicester (hourly; 30min); London (hourly; 1hr 50min); Nottingham (every 20min; 35min).

Grantham to: Derby (hourly; 1hr); Lincoln (every 30min; 45min); London (hourly; 1hr 15min); Nottingham (every 30min; 35min); Skegness (hourly; 1hr 20min).

Hereford to: Birmingham (hourly; 1hr 40min); Great Malvern (hourly; 30min); Leominster (hourly; 12min); London (5 daily; 2hr 45min); Ludlow (hourly; 25min); Shrewsbury (hourly; 55min); Worcester (every 1hr 30min; 40min).

Leicester to: Birmingham (every 30min; 1hr); Coventry (hourly; 45min); Derby (hourly; 35min); Lincoln (hourly; 1hr 40min); London (every 30min; 1hr 30min); Market Harborough (every 90min; 15min); Melton Mowbray (hourly; 15min); Nottingham (every 30min; 20min); Oakham (hourly; 30min); Stamford (hourly; 50min).

Lincoln to: Birmingham (hourly; 3hr); Boston (hourly; 1hr); Cambridge (hourly; 1hr); Gainsborough (hourly; 20min); Grantham (every 30min; 45min); London (hourly; 2hr 15min); Leicester (hourly; 1hr 30min); London (hourly; 2hr 15min); Newark (hourly; 25min); Nottingham (hourly; 45min); Peterborough (hourly; 1hr 20min); Skegness (hourly; 1hr 40min); Spalding (13 daily; 1hr).

Northampton to: Birmingham (every 30min; 1hr); Coventry (hourly; 40min); London Euston (every 30min; 1hr 10min–1hr 40min).

Nottingham to: Leicester (every 30min; 30min); Lincoln (hourly; 1hr 15min); London (hourly; 1hr 50min); Newark (hourly; 30min).

Shrewsbury to: Birmingham (2–4 hourly; 1hr 10min); Church Stretton (every 30min; 15min); Craven Arms (hourly; 25min); Hereford (2–3 hourly; 55min); Ludlow (hourly; 30min); Leominster (hourly; 40min); Telford (every 30min; 20min).

Stamford to: Cambridge (hourly; 1hr 20min); Leicester (hourly; 40min); Oakham (hourly; 10min); Peterborough (hourly; 15min).

Stoke-on-Trent to: Birmingham (hourly; 1hr).

Stratford-upon-Avon to: Birmingham (Mon–Sat hourly; 55min); Oxford (4 daily; 1hr 10min); Warwick (Mon–Sat 8 daily; 25min).

Worcester to: Birmingham (every 30min; 40min–1hr); Hereford (13 daily; 40min).

Buses

Birmingham to: Burton-upon-Trent (Mon–Sat hourly; 1hr 30min); Derby (5 daily; 1hr); Dudley (every 30min; 50min); Evesham (hourly Mon–Sat; 2hr); Hereford (Mon–Sat 6 daily; 3hr); Ironbridge (5 daily; 1hr); Kidderminster (hourly; 1hr); Leicester (5 daily; 1hr); Leominster (Mon–Sat 6 daily; 2hr 30min); Lichfield (hourly Mon–Sat; 1hr); London (hourly; 2hr 30min); Ludlow (Mon–Sat hourly; 2hr); Nottingham (5 daily; 1hr 20min); Shrewsbury (5 daily; 1hr 45min); Stoke-on-Trent (10 daily; 1hr); Stratford-upon-Avon (hourly; 1hr); Wolverhampton (every 30min; 1hr); Worcester (every 30 min; 1hr 30min).

Boston to: Skegness (hourly; 45min–1hr); Spalding (hourly; 35min).

Bridgnorth to: Ironbridge (Mon–Sat 6 daily; 35min); Kidderminster (Mon–Sat 8 daily; 45min); Ludlow (Mon–Fri 2 daily; 1hr 15min); Much Wenlock (Mon–Sat 8 daily; 20min); Shrewsbury (Mon–Sat 6–8 daily; 1hr); Wolverhampton (hourly; 50min).

Burton-upon-Trent to: Birmingham (Mon–Sat hourly; 45min–1hr 30min); Lichfield (Mon–Sat hourly; 30min).

Coventry to: Kenilworth (Mon–Sat hourly; 25min); Stratford-upon-Avon (Mon–Sat hourly; 1hr 15min); Oxford (3 daily; 1hr 30min); Warwick (Mon–Sat hourly; 40min).

Derby to: Ashbourne (5 daily; 30min); Birmingham (5 daily; 1hr); Leek (5 daily; 1hr); Leicester (7 daily; 1hr); Lichfield (2 daily; 35min).

Grantham to: Lincoln (hourly; 1hr); Nottingham (2 daily; 45min–1hr 10min); Stamford (3 daily Mon–Sat; 30min).

Hereford to: Birmingham (2 daily; 2hr); Great Malvern (1 daily; 40min); Leominster (Mon–Sat 2 hourly; 45min); Worcester (Mon–Sat 8 daily; 1hr–1hr 25min).

Leicester to: Ashby-de-la-Zouch (hourly; 1hr); Birmingham (6 daily; 1hr); Bristol (5 daily; 4hr); Foxton (2 daily; 30min); Market Bosworth (hourly; 50min); Market Harborough (hourly; 45min); Melton Mowbray (hourly; 50min); Northampton (6 daily; 1hr 20min); Nottingham (9 daily; 45min); Oxford (2 daily; 2hr 20min); Uppingham (6 daily; 50min).

Lincoln to: Boston (3 weekly; 1hr 30min); Grantham (hourly; 1hr); Louth (4 daily; 1hr 10min); Peterborough (1 daily; 2hr); Skegness (Mon–Sat 5 daily, Sun 1 daily; 1hr 45min); Sleaford (5 daily; 1hr 15min); Stamford (1 daily; 1hr 30min); Woodhall Spa (2 weekly; 50min).

Louth to: Grimsby (3 daily; 40min); Horncastle (2 daily; 25min); Skegness (1 daily; 50min); Lincoln (hourly; 50min).

Ludlow to: Birmingham (Mon–Sat hourly; 2hr); Bishop's Castle (Mon–Sat 3 daily; 55min); Bridgnorth (Mon–Fri 1 daily; 1hr 15min); Church Stretton (Mon–Sat 6 daily; 30min); Hereford (Mon–Sat 7 daily; 55min); Kidderminster (Mon–Sat hourly; 1hr); Leominster (Mon–Sat 7 daily; 25min); Shrewsbury (Mon–Sat 5 daily; 1hr 20min).

Northampton to: Birmingham (2 daily; 1hr 30min); Brixworth (7 daily; 15min); Coventry (2 daily; 55min); Leicester (10 daily; 45min–1hr); Lincoln, via Birmingham (1 daily; 5hr); Milton Keynes (5 daily; 25min); Nottingham (1 daily; 2hr 30min).

Nottingham to: Leicester (hourly; 45min); Northampton (1 daily; 2hr 25min); Newark (hourly; 1hr 20min).

Shrewsbury to: Birmingham (3–4 daily; 1hr 50min); Bishop's Castle (Mon–Sat 3 daily; 1hr 45min); Bridgnorth (Mon–Sat 6–8 daily; 1hr); Church Stretton (Mon–Sat 5–8 daily; 45min); Ironbridge (6 daily; 45min); Ludlow (Mon–Sat 5 daily; 1hr 20min); Much Wenlock (Mon–Sat 6 daily; 40min); Stoke-on-Trent (Mon–Sat 6 daily; 1hr 50min).

Stamford to: Nottingham (1 daily; 1hr 15min).

Stoke-on-Trent (Hanley) to: Alton Towers (1 daily; 1hr); Birmingham (9 daily; 1hr); Buxton (3 daily; 1hr); Coventry (7 daily; 2hr 20min); Leek (3 daily; 25min); Shrewsbury (6 daily; 1hr 50min); Stratford-upon-Avon (2 daily; 2hr 30min).

Stratford-upon-Avon to: Alcester (Mon–Sat 6 daily; 35min); Birmingham (hourly; 1hr); Blenheim Palace (3 daily; 1hr 10min); Coventry (Mon–Sat hourly, 5 on Sun; 1hr 15min); Evesham (Mon–Sat hourly; 50min); Kenilworth (hourly; 55min); Oxford (3 daily; 1hr 30min); Warwick (hourly; 20min); Worcester (3 daily; 45min).

Worcester to: Birmingham (every 30min; 1hr–1hr 30min); Evesham (Mon–Sat 7 daily, Sun 1 daily; 40min–1hr); Great Malvern (every 30min; 30min); Hereford (Mon–Sat 8 daily; 1hr 30min); Tewkesbury (Mon–Sat 6 daily, Sun 2 daily; 1hr 10min).

CHAPTER EIGHT

THE NORTHWEST

Within the **northwest** of England lie some of the ugliest and some of the most beautiful parts of the country. The least attractive zones of this region are to be found in the inchoate sprawl connecting the country's third and sixth largest conurbations, Manchester and Liverpool, but even here the picture isn't unrelievedly bleak, as the cities themselves have an ingratiating appeal. **Manchester**, in particular, surprises many who don't expect to see beyond its dour, industrial heritage. Where once only a handful of Victorian Gothic buildings lent any grace to the cityscape, Manchester today is rapidly building on its past with an eye firmly on the 2002 Commonwealth Games, which it is hosting. Quite apart from a clutch of top-class museums, where Manchester really scores is in the buzz of its thriving café and club scene, which places it at the leading edge of the country's youth culture. **Liverpool**, set on the Mersey estuary, is maybe less appealing at first glance, though Georgian town houses, grand civic buildings, its twin cathedrals and a burgeoning café scene soon change perceptions. At the redundant docks that once made the city's fortune, many of the old warehouses and buildings have been redeveloped as part of the Albert Dock scheme, housing a fine swathe of museums, including the Tate.

The hills, which form the southern tip of the Pennine range, melt away to the west into undulating, pastoral **Cheshire**, a county of rolling green countryside and country manor houses, interspersed with dairy farms from whose churns emerge tons of crumbly white Cheshire cheese. The county town, **Chester**, with its complete circuit of town walls and partly Tudor centre, is as alluring as any of the country's northern towns, capturing the essence of what has always been one of England's wealthiest rural counties. It's easily the main place of interest in the region, though the villages of the **Cheshire Plain** are set in a landscape that conjures archetypal images of pastoral England.

Lancashire, which historically lay directly to the north of Cheshire, reached industrial prominence in the last century primarily due to the cotton-mill towns around Manchester and to the thriving port of Liverpool. Today, neither of those cities is part of the county, having been excised when England's first substantial county boundary changes since the Domesday Book were enacted in 1974. The urban counties of Merseyside and Greater Manchester chopped off the southern section of Lancashire while Cumbria grabbed a substantial northern chunk leaving Lancashire little more

---

ACCOMMODATION PRICE CODES

Throughout this guide, hotel and B&B accommodation is priced on a scale of ① to ⑨, the number indicating the **lowest price** you could expect to pay per night in that establishment for a **double room** in high season. The prices indicated by the codes are as follows:

① under £40	④ £60–70	⑦ £110–150
② £40–50	⑤ £70–90	⑧ £150–200
③ £50–60	⑥ £90–110	⑨ over £200

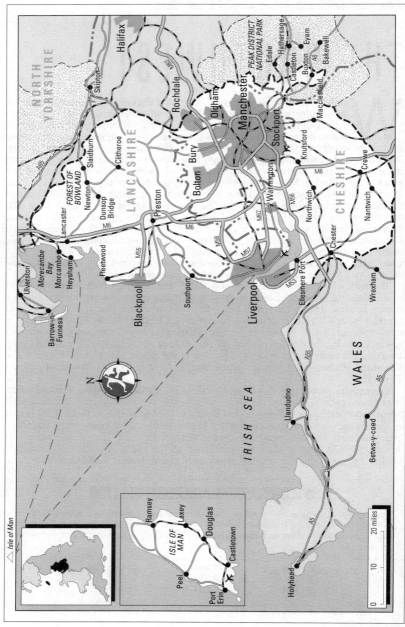

© Crown copyright

than half its former size. Still, it retains the charming towns and villages of the **Ribble Valley**, while along the coast to the north of the major cities stretches a line of **resorts** – from Southport to **Morecambe** – which once formed the mainstay of the northern British holiday trade. Today, not one beach along here meets EU water-quality standards and, as with the ageing Yorkshire resorts, there's something of a desperation about many of the towns as they watch their client base disappear on cheaper, sunnier holidays to Florida and the Mediterranean. Only **Blackpool** is worth visiting for its own sake, a rip-roaring resort which has stayed at the top of its game by supplying undemanding entertainment with more panache than its neighbours. For anything more culturally invigorating you'll have to continue north to the historically important city of **Lancaster**, with its Tudor castle. Finally, the semi-autonomous **Isle of Man**, only twenty-five miles off the coast and served by ferries from Liverpool and Heysham (or short flights from Liverpool), provides a terrain almost as rewarding as that of the Lake District but without the seasonal overcrowding.

Getting around

Manchester's international **airport** picks the city out as a major point of arrival in England, and there are direct train services from the airport to Liverpool, Blackpool, Lancaster, Leeds and York, as well as to Manchester itself. Both Manchester and Liverpool are well served by **trains**, with plentiful connections to the Midlands and London, and up the west coast to Scotland. There's also a frequent rail and bus service between both cities, and from each to Chester, allowing an easy triangular loop between Greater Manchester, Merseyside and Cheshire. The major east–west rail lines in the region are the direct routes between Manchester, Leeds and York, and between Blackpool, Bradford, Leeds and York. In addition, the Morecambe/Lancaster–Leeds line slips through the Yorkshire Dales (with possible connections at Skipton for the famous Settle–Carlisle line; see p.768); further south, the Manchester–Sheffield line provides a rail approach to the Peak District (see p.569). Regional **rover tickets** (£49) are available for a week's unlimited travel in the northwest or in the "coast and peaks" region (basically between Liverpool, Manchester, the Peak District and North Wales).

Manchester

Whether you approach from the north or south, your first glimpse of **MANCHESTER** takes in the monuments to a history of prosperity, decline and revival that is still unfolding. Stoic tower blocks and empty shells of mills and factories reach for the skyline beside rows of back-to-back houses whose slate roofs and cobbled back alleys glisten in the seemingly ever-present rain. All this reinforces traditional images of the struggling post-industrial city, but Manchester is being treated to an urban facelift unequalled in Britain as old buildings are being cleaned, new ones built, the canals tidied up and inner-city estates revamped in a concerted effort to pull Manchester out of the doldrums of the 1960s and 1970s. In part these efforts were prompted by high crime rates in ugly, peripheral housing estates, and by the city's selection as the venue for the **Commonwealth Games** in the year 2002, following a succession of failed bids to host the Olympics. But in the city centre, the main engine of change was the devastating IRA bomb, which exploded in June 1996 and wiped out much of the city's commercial infrastructure. The subsequent redesign and rebuilding of the city centre was quick and impressive, and millennium projects have given further impetus to Manchester's contemporary renaissance (see box on p.631). The city today boasts a thriving **social and cultural scene** that few, if any, English rivals can match: its cutting-edge sports facilities, concert halls, theatres, clubs and café society are boosted by

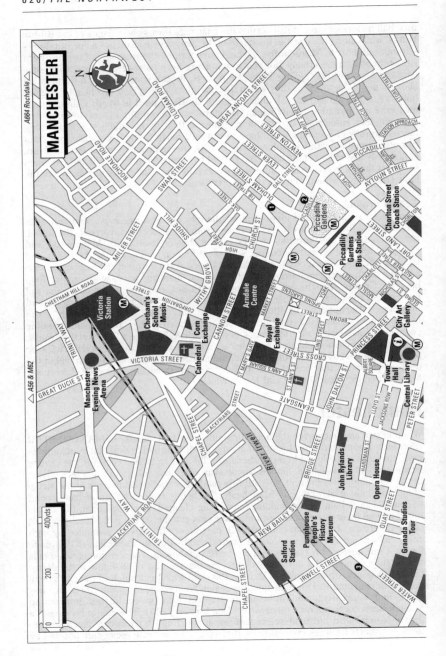

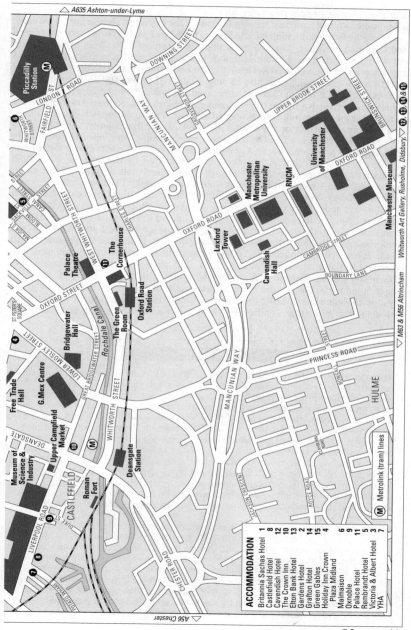

ACCOMMODATION

Britannia Sachas Hotel	1
Castlefield Hotel	8
Cavendish Hotel	12
The Crown Inn	10
Elton Bank Hotel	13
Gardens Hotel	2
Grafton Hotel	14
Green Gables	15
Holiday Inn Crown Plaza Midland	4
Malmaison	6
Oxnoble	9
Palace Hotel	11
Rembrandt Hotel	5
Victoria & Albert Hotel	3
YHA	7

© Crown copyright

England's largest student population and a blossoming gay community whose spending-power has transformed a once-derelict part of the city into a pioneering Gay Village.

Despite a history stretching back to Roman times, and pockets of surviving medieval and Georgian influence, Manchester is first and foremost a Victorian manufacturing city with the imposing streets and buildings to match. Its rapid growth was the equal of any flowering of the Industrial Revolution – from little more than a village in 1750 to the world's major cotton-milling centre in only a hundred years. The spectacular rise of **Cottonopolis**, as it became known, came from the production of competitively priced imitations of expensive Indian calicoes, using machines evolved from Arkwright's first steam-powered cotton mill, which opened in 1783. The rapid industrialization of the area brought prosperity for a few but a life of misery for the majority, and the discontent of the poor came to a head in 1819 when eleven people were killed at **Peterloo**, in what began as a peaceful workers' demonstration against the oppressive Corn Laws (see box below). Exploitation had worsened still further by the time the 23-year-old Friedrich Engels came here in 1842 to work in his father's cotton plant, and the suffering he witnessed – recorded in his *Condition of the Working Class in England* – was a seminal influence on his later collaboration with Karl Marx, the *Communist Manifesto*.

Waterways and railway viaducts form the matrix into which the city's principal buildings have been bedded – as early as 1772 the Duke of Bridgewater had a canal cut to connect the city to the coal mines at Worsley, and the world's first passenger rail line, connecting Manchester with Liverpool, was opened in 1830. The **Manchester Ship Canal**, constructed to entice ocean-going vessels into Manchester and away from burgeoning Liverpool, was completed in 1894, and played a crucial part in reviving Manchester's competitiveness. A century later, with the docks, mills and canals no longer in industrial use, it's the splendid behemoths of Victorian Gothic that echo the city's past. Meanwhile, looking towards a brighter future, Manchester's planners are embracing the millennium: entire new city-centre districts are taking shape as once-

---

PETERLOO

Agitation for social and parliamentary reform in the early nineteenth century was concentrated in the booming industrial cities, led by radical orators like Henry Hunt, who addressed massed rallies of working men and women. Such a meeting was planned for **St Peter's Fields** in Manchester for August 16, 1819, with Hunt as main speaker, and though rumours spread throughout the city about the possibility of trouble, the local magistrates seemed content to let the rally take place. In the weeks before the event, many local people practised marching in orderly file so as to look respectable on the day; on the day itself, a crowd of almost 80,000 turned up in its Sunday best, with women and children much in evidence – hardly the revolutionary rabble feared by the government critics of the reform movement. But as Hunt began to speak the magistrates decided to stop him, sending in their special constables (mostly recruited from the ranks of local businessmen) to arrest him. As pandemonium erupted, Hunt gave himself up to avoid further trouble, but with the special constables now under siege from the crowd, the yeomanry were sent in.

Panic broke out as people tried to escape from the swords of the mounted soldiers, who cleared the fields in ten minutes. In what the press dubbed "**Peterloo**", 400 people were wounded, over a hundred by sword cuts, the rest by the stampeding crowd, and the final reckoning saw eleven dead, including two women and one child. Home Secretary Lord Sidmouth later congratulated the Manchester authorities on their handling of the situation; the government passed the draconian Six Acts, restricting the right of public meeting; while Hunt was released on bail. Protests were widespread, even among the government's own supporters, and Peterloo became the catalyst for yet more agitation, culminating in the 1832 Reform Act and the subsequent rise of the Chartist movement.

blighted areas are reclaimed for retail and residential use, while inner-city suburbs such as Hulme and Moss Side, both scarred by gang violence and drug dealing, are at last giving tenants a say in the design of new estates and shopping centres, and encouraging the development of local businesses.

Arrival, information and city transport

A direct rail link into the city makes **Manchester Airport**, ten miles south of the city, an increasingly popular point of entry into Britain. Trains to Piccadilly (every 15min 5.15am–10.15pm, reduced service through the night; 25min) cost £2.25, £2.65 before 9.30am. It's slightly cheaper (£2.15) to take one of the buses from the airport to Piccadilly Gardens or Chorlton Street (every 15–30min, 6am–10.45pm), though these take almost twice as long as trains to reach the centre in the rush hour. A taxi from the airport to the centre costs around £12.

Manchester's three main **train stations** form the points of a triangle that encloses much of the city centre. National mainline trains all pull into **Piccadilly Station**, facing London Road, on the east side, from where you can walk a few hundred yards west into the city's core, via Piccadilly Gardens. Regional routes to points south, east and west call both here and at **Oxford Road Station**, south of the centre, while **Victoria Station**, in the north, services the northern hinterland and Bradford. The city's Metrolink tram service connects Piccadilly station (the platform is underneath the train station) to Victoria and G-Mex – the latter being the best stop if you're heading straight for Castlefield. National Express and most long-distance buses use **Chorlton Street Coach Station**, a few hundred yards west of Piccadilly train station. Local and some regional buses might drop you instead in nearby Piccadilly Gardens.

The **Manchester Visitor Centre** in the town hall extension on Lloyd Street, facing central St Peter's Square (Mon–Sat 10am–5.30pm, Sun 11am–4pm; ☎0161/234 3157), offers a free map of the city centre, sells the handy *City Guide* (£1.50) and dishes out various other useful leaflets and brochures. You can also buy National Express bus tickets, check rail timetables, and book guided tours and accommodation (see p.630). There are direct trams to the Visitor Centre (St Peter's Square stop) from Piccadilly and Victoria stations. To find out **what's on** in the city, buy the fortnightly *City Life* listings and reviews magazine, from any newsstand.

For bus, train and airport enquiry numbers for **departures from the city**, see "Listings", p.643.

City transport

The city centre is compact enough to cover on foot, though buses will be needed for Oxford Road and its continuation Wilmslow Road, which runs to the curry restaurants of Rusholme. Deregulation has caused an explosion in the number of city-centre bus services: Stagecoach is the main operator, though several more ply the same routes and undercut each other furiously on fares, particularly down the heavily trafficked Wilmslow Road corridor.

Piccadilly Gardens Bus Station is the hub of the urban bus network, though a new transport interchange at **Shudehill** (north of the Arndale Centre; due for completion by 2001) may affect the location of some routes. For Oxford and Wilmslow roads, use the stops at the bottom of Oxford Road by the Palace Hotel. **Information** about all services is available from the Travel Shop, on the southern side of Piccadilly Gardens in the parade of shops (Mon–Sat 7am–6pm, Sun 10am–6pm); or call the GMPTE bus enquiry line (☎0161/228 7811 daily 8am–8pm). You're unlikely to get enough use out of the various **travel passes** on offer, except perhaps for the seven-day Stagecoach Mega-Rider (£6.50), which gives unlimited travel on Stagecoach's city and local buses, or the Wayfarer (£6.60), which allows 24 hours' unlimited travel throughout Greater Manchester and into the Peak District.

Metrolink (☎0161/205 2000) – the electric tram service – whisks through the city centre and out to the suburbs, linking Bury with Altrincham (every 6–15min 6am–11.30pm). An extension to the service now runs to Salford Quays, with new stations planned for the Shudehill transport interchange, the Eastlands Commonwealth Games stadium and the airport. Tickets for short hops start at 80p, though you're unlikely to use the system for getting around, unless you simply fancy the ride. There are stations at Piccadilly Station, Piccadilly Gardens, St Peter's Square, G-Mex and Victoria Station.

Accommodation

Central Manchester is full of **hotels** that cater to expense-account clients, but is not over-burdened with budget places, though almost all the plusher hotels offer weekend reductions – note that, during the week, breakfast isn't included at most of the pricier hotels. Cheaper **guest-house** accommodation is concentrated some way out of the centre, mainly on the southern routes out of the city, where reasonably convenient places can be found and the bus services are good. **B&B** accommodation in private houses is easy to arrange, too, though again it won't be particularly central, which makes the city's well-located **youth hostel**, in Castlefield, a first-choice for most budget travellers – book it well in advance. If you use the Visitor Centre's **accommodation booking service**, you'll pay a fee, though their free *Accommodation Guide* lists most of the city's possibilities.

Hotels, guest houses and B&Bs

Britannia Sachas Hotel, Tib St, Piccadilly (☎0161/228 1234). The decor, hardly any less restrained inside than out, does at least settle down in the rooms themselves. Handy location, good facilities, including a pool, and decent weekend prices. Midweek ⑤, weekend ③.

Castlefield Hotel, Liverpool Rd (☎0161/832 7073). Redbrick, warehouse-style development in the Castlefield basin, opposite the Science and Industry museum. Nicely appointed rooms, and boasting attached leisure club and pool. Midweek ⑤, weekend ③.

Cavendish Hotel, 402 Wilbraham Rd, Chorlton (☎0161/881 1911). Edwardian guest house three miles south of the centre. Decent rooms with TV and tea- and coffee-making facilities. ②.

The Crown Inn, 321 Deansgate (☎0161/834 1930). Very central B&B accommodation above a traditional pub. No credit cards. ③.

Elton Bank Hotel, 62 Platt Lane, Rusholme (☎0161/224 6449). Two miles from the city centre, overlooking Platt Fields Park and convenient for the curry houses of Rusholme. No credit cards. ②.

Gardens Hotel, 55 Piccadilly (☎0161/236 5155). Right on Piccadilly Gardens, but it doesn't suffer too much from the noise. This accommodating three-star place has an en-suite bathroom and TV with each room. Midweek ⑤, weekend ③.

Grafton Hotel, 56–58 Grafton St (☎0161/273 3092). Six knocked-through terraced houses by the medical school, south of the university. En-suite rooms fall into the next category up. No credit cards. ①.

Green Gables, 152 Barlow Moor Rd, West Didsbury (☎0161/445 5365). Traditional guest house in a residential area, with regular bus service into town. ①.

Holiday Inn Crowne Plaza Midland Hotel, Peter St (☎0161/236 3333). Once the terminus hotel for Central Station (now G-Mex) and the place where Rolls met Royce for the first time, this building is the apotheosis of Edwardian style. The bars and public rooms impress most, though there's a full raft of leisure facilities and substantial weekend reductions available – which is the only time breakfast is included in the room rate. Midweek ⑧, weekend ⑦.

Malmaison, Piccadilly (☎0161/278 1000, *manchester@malmaison.com*). An ornate Edwardian facade given sleek interior lines and contemporary design from the Malmaison group. It's just a couple of minutes from the train station. Breakfast costs extra, though there is a good bar and brasserie. Midweek ⑥, weekend ⑤.

The Oxnoble, 71 Liverpool Rd (☎0161/839 7740). Rooms above a popular pub opposite the Science and Industry Museum and very handy for the Castlefield bars. The food is good too; breakfast is extra (£2–6, depending what you have). ②.

The Palace Hotel, Oxford St (☎0161/288 1111). An Alfred Waterhouse glazed-tile extravaganza (formerly the Refuge Assurance HQ), opposite the Cornerhouse arts centre. Midweek ⑧, weekends ⑦.

Rembrandt Hotel, 33 Sackville St (☎0161/236 1311). Comfortable, friendly, central pub-hotel in the heart of the Gay Village, and popular with a gay clientele, though it's a noisy, late-night location. A few cheaper rooms without bathroom are available. ②.

Victoria & Albert Hotel, Water St, Castlefield (☎0161/832 1188). Superb restoration job for a canalside warehouse, with exposed beams, pipes and brickwork part of the interior fabric. Facilities, bars and restaurant are excellent, and it's just across from Granada Studio Tours. ⑦, ⑥ at weekends.

Hostels and university accommodation

International Backpackers Hostel, 41–43 Greatstone Rd, Stretford; 64 Cromwell Rd, Stretford (☎0161/872 3499 or 865 9296; mobile ☎0411/556157, *manchester.backpacker@good.co.uk*). A friendly welcome is on offer in these two converted houses, with laundry facilities and kitchen provided. They're three miles out of the centre but on the Metrolink line (to Old Trafford stop). Dorms provide the cheapest accommodation; twins/doubles also available. No credit cards.

Manchester YHA, Potato Wharf, Castlefield (☎0161/839 9960, *manchester@yha.org.uk*). Excellent hostel, overlooking the canal, opposite the Museum of Science and Industry. The en-suite rooms sleep one to four people (you can pay more to have the room to yourself) and the bunks convert into double beds; facilities for disabled people are available.

University accommodation, University of Manchester/UMIST Central Accommodation Office (Mon–Fri 9.30am–5pm; ☎0161/275 2888). Call for information about vacancies at the various university hostels (available during summer vacations).

THE REDEVELOPMENT OF MANCHESTER

On 15 June 1996 the IRA exploded a 3300lb bomb in the centre of Manchester causing the largest explosion on the mainland since the war: amazingly, no one was killed, though over two hundred people were injured and nearly seven hundred businesses were put out of action, most in the devastated area around the Arndale Centre and the Royal Exchange. Within a year much of the superficial damage had been made good, but rather than simply patch up the rest of the buildings, the planning authorities embarked on an ambitious £500,000,000 **rebuilding scheme**.

At its heart is a plan to create a pedestrian boulevard ("New Cathedral Street") from the cathedral to St Ann's Church, which will incorporate a new **Exchange Square** awash with water features and public sculpture, a restored Arndale Centre, and relocated historic buildings within its perimeters. The *Old Wellington Inn* and *Sinclair's Oyster Bar*, both traditional pubs on medieval foundations, have been moved brick-by-brick from their former berth on Shambles Square to a new landscaped site in front of the cathedral. The Sixties' eyesore that was the **Arndale Centre** is being enlarged, stripped of its awful tiles, modernized and clad in glass; while what is now the largest Marks & Spencer's store in the world sports a gigantic glazed wall down one side of Exchange Square. The historic **Corn Exchange** across from the cathedral (also badly damaged by the bomb) has been refurbished completely, retaining its facade and glass dome, with its triangular interior transformed into a high-tech leisure and retail centre.

Most of the above developments are now largely complete, though a second wave of building through to 2001 intends to refashion the area around the cathedral as a **Millennium Quarter**. A new traffic-free **City Park** will feature **Urbis** at its core – a high-tech visitor centre with cafés, shops, a "Wonderwall" of city information, and various new virtual and technological attractions. The former Mirror Building nearby is already being turned into the futuristic **Printworks Entertainment Centre**, with an IMAX screen, cinema megaplex and various retail units and themed restaurants. Later, Cannon Street will be enclosed to form a **Winter Garden**.

The City

If Manchester can be said to have a centre, it's **St Peter's Square** and the cluster of buildings focused on it – the Town Hall (with the Visitor Centre in its modern extension), Central Library and the Midland Hotel, originally built in the railway age for visitors to Britain's greatest industrial city. South of here, the huge vault of the former Central Station now functions as the **G-Mex** exhibition centre, with the Hallé orchestra's home, Bridgewater Hall, opposite. There's been a general spruce-up spreading west to the **Castlefield** district, site of the city's two most popular tourist attractions – the **Museum of Science and Industry** and **Granada Studio Tours**. Many of the city's remaining attractions, museums and galleries, and the majority of eating and drinking spots, are scattered over a broad expanse to the north along the central spine of **Deansgate** and east towards **Piccadilly Gardens** (from where most city bus routes originate). Other diversions string out along the main southern artery **Oxford Road**, strictly Oxford Street until a quarter of a mile out but always referred to by the former name.

Year-round **guided walks** (£3) can be booked at the Visitor Centre in St Peter's Square. There are usually two or three departures a week, concentrating on various themes – from city burial grounds to industrial archeology.

The Town Hall and around

Manchester could claim little architectural merit without its Victorian neo-Gothic buildings. One of its boldest, Alfred Waterhouse's **Town Hall** (Mon–Fri 9am–5pm; free), finished in 1877, divides the plain expanse of St Peter's Square from the more harmonious Albert Square to the north (whose memorial to Prince Albert is flanked by statues of John Bright and a perky William Gladstone). You're free to wander inside the Town Hall – enter from Albert Square or Lloyd Street into the echoing stone-vaulted interior and climb one of the grand staircases to the **Great Hall**, with its iron candelabras, stained glass windows, double hammer-beam roof and paintings by Ford Madox Brown depicting decisive moments from Manchester's past. Elsewhere in the building, the mosaic floors are littered with statues and busts of civic worthies, from Anti Corn-Law leaders to Sir Charles Hallé. **Guided tours** of the building set off from Albert Square (Easter–Sept Sat & every other Wed 2pm; Oct–Dec Sat 2pm; times vary, call 0161/274 3157 to check; £3).

On the south side of the Town Hall, the circular **Central Library** (Mon–Thurs 10am–8pm, Fri & Sat 10am–5pm) faces St Peter's Square. Built in 1934 as the largest municipal library in the world, it's an elegant Classical construction with a domed reading room. The library building is still an impressive sight, but modern building has dwarfed adjacent landmarks: Lutyens' **Cenotaph** in St Peter's Square passes virtually unnoticed these days amid the swooshing trams; while around the back of the library (head through Library Walk), on Mount Street, the historic **Friends Meeting House** has managed to see off various attempts to knock it down.

Over on Peter Street, the late-Victorian **Midland Hotel** – now the *Holiday Inn Crowne Plaza Midland* – has worn well, and might tempt you in for tea and cakes in its lavish Edwardian interior. The exterior is no less beguiling: witness the exterior dragon-relief tiling. The hotel's earlier visitors ventured out for an evening's entertainment at the **Free Trade Hall** further up Peter Street, which sponsored concerts by the city's own Hallé Orchestra for over a century, until Bridgewater Hall was completed in 1996. The Italianate facade survived wartime – and IRA – bombing and will be retained as part of any future development on the site. The Free Trade Hall was originally built on the site of St Peter's Fields, where in 1819 eleven demonstrators were killed by the local militia during an event known as the "Peterloo Massacre" (see box on p.628).

South of St Peter's Square, Lower Mosley Street runs past the **G-Mex Centre** (see p.643), opposite which rises the **Bridgewater Hall** (guided tours £2.50, call ☎0161/907

9000 to book), at the junction of Bridgewater Street. This – Britain's finest purpose-built concert hall – displays enough post-modern architectural angles and curves to fit in with the fairly bleak surroundings and, uniquely, is balanced on shock-absorbing springs to guarantee clarity of sound. It's said that when the IRA bomb exploded, staff and patrons at Bridgewater Hall were the only ones in the city centre not to feel the blast. The *Stalls* café-bar inside makes a good drinks stop.

The other way up Mosley Street, north of St Peter's Square, rises Charles Barry's porticoed **City Art Gallery**, where the array of high Victorian art includes the country's finest public collection of works by the Pre-Raphaelite Brotherhood. Unfortunately, the gallery is now closed for major renovations which won't be completed until 2001.

Castlefield

Fifteen minutes' walk southwest of the town hall lies the rapidly developing area of **Castlefield**. The country's first man-made canal, the Bridgewater Canal, brought coal and other goods to the warehouses here in the late eighteenth century; the railway followed fifty years later, cementing Castlefield's pre-eminent position, which only declined after World War II. Since the early 1980s, an influx of money allied to a fair amount of speculative vision has resulted in a cobbled canalside, cleaned-up water, outdoor events arena, new bars and a snazzy hotel or two. It was Britain's first "urban heritage park" and you can find out about its various festivals, the September carnival, bank-holiday street markets, walkable towpaths and canal cruises at the **Castlefield Visitor Centre** at 101 Liverpool Rd (Mon–Fri 10am–4pm, Sat & Sun noon–4pm; free; ☎0161/834 4026).

The castle-in-the-field itself is a **Roman fort** – finally abandoned around 410 AD – whose reconstructed north gate and the foundations of a few houses can be seen on Liverpool Road. This is just a hundred yards from the considerably more diverting **Museum of Science and Industry** (daily 10am–5pm; last admission 4pm; £5), one of the most impressive museums of its type in the country, mixing technological displays and special blockbuster exhibitions with trenchant analysis of the social impact of industrialization. The entry ticket is valid all day, thus allowing for a decent lunch break – and you need it, especially if you want to catch any of the huge array of Lancashire-made steam engines progressively fired throughout the day in the Power Hall. Beyond the smoothly spinning flywheels and hissing pistons of the house-sized Haydock beam engine comes the locomotives section, where pride of place goes to a working replica of Robert Stephenson's *Planet* – for which his father George's *Rocket* was the prototype. Built in 1830, the *Planet* reliably attained a scorching 30mph but had no brakes; the museum's version does, and uses them at weekends (Easter–Nov Sat & Sun noon–4pm; Dec–Easter Sun only), dropping passengers a quarter-mile away at the **world's oldest passenger railway station**. It was here that the *Rocket* arrived on a rainy September 15, 1830, after fatally injuring Liverpool MP William Huskisson at the start of the inaugural passenger journey from Liverpool.

A reconstructed Victorian sewer below the station illustrates the problems of sanitation in the 1870s, when poor areas were still using street-end standpipes and John Ruskin was vociferously opposing the Manchester Corporation's plan to dam Thirlmere in the Lake District. The improvements brought about by domestic electrification are brought home in a suite of rooms that includes a wonderfully kitsch Fifties living room. There's also a hands-on science centre, where the kids hog all the best experiments and a new gallery dealing with fibres, fabrics and fashion, while the museum's comprehensive selection of carding machines, bobbin threaders and cotton looms crash into action at weekends in the Textile Gallery. The **Air and Space Gallery**, housed across the road, is an anomaly in that it barely touches on Manchester at all. If the cut-away engines, passenger-carrying kite and lightweight treatment of space exploration aren't your thing, you can always pay to get pitched about for a few minutes in the flight simulator.

Good though the Museum of Science and Industry is, as a tourist attraction it can't compete with the nearby **Granada Studios Tour**, entered around the corner on Water Street (Easter–Sept daily 9.45am–6pm; Oct–Easter Mon–Fri 9.45am–4.30pm, Sat & Sun 9.45am–5.30pm; last admission 2hr before closing; £14.99). Each year 700,000 people file through the studio doors into an American-style street scene, complete with cops and friendly baseball players, and then undergo various different "experiences", ranging from motion simulator rides to special effects shows and a smoothly orchestrated backstage tour. The indoor TV show sets – Sherlock Holmes's Baker Street, the House of Commons, Blind Date – provide more entertainment, but it's the allure of Britain's longest-running soap opera that keeps the turnstiles moving, even though most of the footage for *Coronation Street* is now shot elsewhere. Nonetheless, most punters are happy enough to marvel at the stars on celluloid prior to wandering around the set used for outdoor sequences and into the *Rovers Return* for a pint.

Along Deansgate

Central **Deansgate** cuts through the city from the canal to the cathedral, its architectural reference points ranging from Victorian industrialism to Sixties' functionalism. There's massive development afoot south of Peter Street, where work is currently under way on transforming the magnificent sweep of late-nineteenth-century warehousing known as the **Great Northern Railway Company's Warehouse** into a new commercial and leisure complex. Further north (just south of Bridge Street) is the second of Deansgate's great buildings, the beautifully detailed **John Rylands Library** (Mon–Fri 10am–5.30pm, Sat 10am–1pm; free; guided tours Wed noon; £1), the city's supreme example of Victorian Gothic. Now part of Manchester University, it was founded in 1890 by Enriqueta Ryland to house the theological works collected by her late husband, and now displays Bibles in more than three hundred languages among its million-strong general collection. Temporary exhibitions highlight the library's other assets, though you should venture inside whatever's showing to see the superb interior – carved and burnished wood, Art Nouveau metalwork, delicately crafted stone and stained glass.

From the library, continue up Deansgate and left into Bridge Street to reach the **Pumphouse People's History Museum** (Tues–Sun 11am–4.30pm; £1, free on Fri), an exhibition recording the lives and protests of England's working class over the last two hundred years. Posters, press reports, charters and anti-Government cartoons show the struggles of suffragettes, reformers and radicals, fighting for equal representation, votes and fair pay; trade unionism is also well documented, with one of the country's best historic collections of marching banners; and there are displays devoted to social and cultural life, including coverage of local football and music.

St Ann's Square

St Ann's Square, tucked away off the eastern side of Deansgate, was severely damaged by the IRA bomb in 1996 but since its restoration has emerged to provide an anchor for the remarkable transformation taking place between here and the cathedral to the north (see box on p.631). Squat **St Ann's Church** (daily 8am–6pm) – baptismal church of Thomas De Quincey – flanks its southern side. Built in 1712, its lovely Renaissance interior was restored under the masterful direction of Alfred Waterhouse at the end of the nineteenth century, from when dates the eye-catching stained glass. The church is fronted by a statue of nineteenth-century Free Trader Richard Cobden, joint-leader with John Bright of the Anti-Corn-Law League which finally forced the repeal in 1846 of the restrictive Corn Laws. On the western side of the square, keep an eye out for the entrance to the **Barton Arcade**, a stunning Victorian shopping gallery which runs through to Deansgate.

However, crowning glory of St Ann's Square is the restored **Royal Exchange**, which houses the famous **Royal Exchange Theatre** (see p.643), the country's largest theatre-in-the-round, whose steel-and-glass cat's cradle sits plonked under the building's immense glass-domed roof. Formerly the Cotton Exchange, this building employed seven thousand people until trading finished on December 31, 1968 – the old trading board still shows the last day's prices for American and Egyptian cotton. Also inside there's a good bookshop and crafts gallery, a terrific café/restaurant plus bar, while the associated Royal Exchange Shopping Centre – three floors of shops and cafés – wraps around the building.

The pedestrianized area around St Ann's Square and **King Street** to the south provides Manchester's best shopping, boasting most of the popular designer and high street outlets. To the north, the **Arndale Centre** – a concrete horror of which the Sixties could be truly proud – is also slowly emerging a better place during its protracted post-bomb refit.

The Cathedral and Chetham's Library

At the far end of Deansgate stands the small, Perpendicular **Cathedral** (daily 7.30am–6pm; free organ recitals Thurs at 1pm), the third church on this site since its foundation in the ninth century. A fragment of stone by the choir and a fourteenth-century arch by the tower are all that remain of the earlier structures, and in truth it's been hacked about too much to have any real coherence – the famed widest nave in England (114ft, as opposed to York Minster's 106ft) is entirely a result of rich families adding side chapels to the fifteenth-century church, which were later opened out to provide space for Manchester's burgeoning nineteenth-century population of worshippers. However, it's surprising it's still here at all: a 1000lb bomb in 1940 all but destroyed the interior, knocked out most of the stained glass (which is why it's so light inside) and necessitated the complete restoration of the fine misericords, which depict dragon-slaying as well as more mundane scenes – backgammon players and a calf butcher among them. The 1996 bomb did another £250,000 worth of (relatively minor) damage, now largely restored, while there's been more upheaval associated with the planned City Park development (see box on p.631), which, among other things, will give the cathedral a new visitor centre.

The cathedral's choristers are trained in **Chetham's Hospital School**, across the way on Long Millgate (ask at the porter's lodge for entrance). This fifteenth-century manor house became a school and a free public library in 1653, then was transformed into a music school in 1969. There are **free recitals** (Mon–Fri 1.30pm; ☎0161/834 9644) during term time and a half-hour tour following the concert on Wednesdays – call for details. The oak-panelled **library** (Mon–Fri 9am–12.30pm & 1.30–4.30pm) itself – with its carved eighteenth-century bookcases – is a real delight. Someone is usually on hand to show you the restored reading room, with the windowed alcove where, it's claimed, Marx and Engels used to study.

East of the Town Hall: Chinatown, the Northern Quarter and the Gay Village

The grid of streets east of the Town Hall, between Princess and Charlotte streets, marks the boundaries of Britain's largest **Chinatown**, heralded by the inevitable Dragon Arch. North of here, across **Piccadilly Gardens**, the still shabby but improving Oldham Street was once lined with expensive shops, though the area has suffered wholesale decay in modern times. It's recently been adopted by "alternative" entrepreneurs who have dubbed it the **"Northern Quarter"** and helped populate the area with trendy clothes and shoe boutiques, record shops and cafés – notably in The Emporium, the five floors of Affleck's Palace at the junction with Church Street and in the Coliseum on Church Street itself. There are rather more lasting skills and crafts on display in the excellent **Manchester Craft Centre**, 17 Oak St (Mon–Sat 10am–5.30pm; free) – a great place to pick up ceramics, fabrics, earthenware, jewellery and decorative art. There's a good café inside, too. Loft apartments now on the market suggest that developers have got their sights on reinventing this whole district, but its unfortunate location – between the busy Great Ancoats Road and Piccadilly Gardens – make this a tall order. However, the renovated **Smithfield Buildings** on Oldham Street, is proving a popular loft-style residential and retail development, and a proposed marina and leisure complex on the Rochdale Canal, near Great Ancoats Road, should help matters.

To the southeast, the roads off Portland Street lead down to the Rochdale Canal, heart of Manchester's thriving **Gay Village**. The pink pound has transformed this part of the city and canalside cafés, clubs, bars and businesses have turned a formerly abandoned warehouse district into something with the verve of San Francisco. There's Britain's first gay shopping centre here, the Phoenix on Hart Street (off Portland St), while on a warm summer's day outside *Metz*, *Manto* and others (see p.639), there's an unhurried atmosphere that reeks of cappuccino cool.

Oxford Road and points south

From St Peter's Square, **Oxford Road** – initially Oxford Street – stretches through a ragged mile of faculty buildings to Rusholme and the leafy suburbs beyond. Oxford Road Station lurks behind the **Cornerhouse** (see p.643), the dynamo of the Manchester arts scene. In addition to screening art-house films – sometimes with introductions by their directors – the Cornerhouse has three floors of gallery space (Tues–Sat 11am–6pm, Sun 2–6pm; free) devoted to contemporary and local artists' work. The café and bar are popular, too. Across the road, Alfred Waterhouse's majestic **Refuge Assurance** building of 1891 is one of Manchester's joys, its soaring clock-tower, dome and terracotta facade now hiding the bulk of the *Palace Hotel* (see p.631). An endless stream of buses runs from here down Oxford Road: #40, #41, #42, #43, #44, #47, #48 and #49 (among others) all pass the buildings and sights detailed below.

A Gothic Revival building, half a mile south along Oxford Road, houses the **Manchester Museum** (Mon–Sat 10am–5pm; free), one of the city's great unsung treats, which makes a fine display of its superb Egyptian exhibits. The museum has been at the centre of the Egyptology world since the 1890s and has done pioneering work on mummy dissection; captivating displays enlarge upon the burial practices and techniques that their work has revealed. Upstairs, an amazing three-tiered mammal gallery presents a multitude of stuffed specimens alongside an aquarium whose star exhibit is a ten-foot-long boa constrictor. There are full ethnographical collections, too, given a novel slant by placing a case full of "People of Manchester" items next to the traditional Maori and Ethiopian artefacts – a bus ticket, a Take That CD and a clothing fetish "symbolising a particular association" (a Manchester United scarf) providing an instructive view of how others might see our lives. The museum is undergoing long-term refurbishment until 2001, which means certain galleries and exhibitions may be closed from time to time. But when it's complete, the museum will have new geology and ethnology galleries, an interactive "Science for Life" exhibit and Discovery Centre, plus a new café.

Another half-mile away is the city's modern art collection, housed in the redbrick **Whitworth Gallery** (Mon–Sat 10am–5pm, Sun 2–5pm; free). As you walk in you confront Jacob Epstein's African-influenced nude, *Genesis*, which caused mass protest at its unveiling and later became part of a Modern Art freak show in Blackpool. The gallery forms two distinct halves, "historic" and modern, with its pre-1880 historic collection incorporating a strong assembly of watercolours by Turner, Constable, Cox and Blake as well as Gillray engravings, Hogarth prints and oddities like Ford Madox Brown's *Execution of Mary Queen of Scots* – his first, and not entirely successful, attempt at a large-scale historical work. The modern collection concentrates on post-1880 British staples, with Moore, Frink and Hepworth setting off contributions from lesser-known artists. Look for works by Paul Nash (one of the organizers of the London Surrealist exhibition of 1936), the World War II artist John Piper, or those of Stephen Conroy, a contemporary figurative painter whose subjects resonate with Victorian images. With Manchester's cotton connections it is perhaps not surprising that the gallery also displays the country's widest range of textiles outside London's Victoria and Albert Museum.

Walk just two hundred yards south of the Whitworth Gallery and you'll catch the pungent spicy smell of **Rusholme**'s Wilmslow Road, a "golden mile" of curry houses, sari shops and grocers stocked with all manner of exotic vegetables, halal meats and sticky sweets. A couple of times a year, particularly during the Eid festival at the end of Ramadan, this section of the Wilmslow Road erupts into horn-blowing, car-revving celebration as young Muslims come from across Britain to parade themselves and their high-performance cars up and down the main road throughout the night. In Platt Fields Park, at the south end of the curry mile (just past Hardy's Well pub), the **Gallery of English Costume** (March–Oct Tues–Sat 10am–5.30pm; Nov–Feb Tues–Sat 10am–4pm; free) fills Georgian Platt Hall. Its collection spans fashion through the ages, giving particular emphasis to Manchester's former role as a textile centre and the clothes of the working class – you're more likely to see a pair of Nike trainers and an anorak than designer shoes and silk jackets.

Most of the buses that head down Oxford Road continue through Rusholme and the student areas of Fallowfield and Withington to Didsbury, Manchester's most prestigious and leafy suburb. There are some great pubs and restaurants here, and a large park containing **Didsbury Botanical Gardens** (dawn–dusk; free), a landscaped patch of ponds, shrubs, rare pines and firs and an imaginative array of cacti and flowers. A pleasant hour's walk follows the river from Didsbury to **Chorlton Water Park** (daily 8am–dusk; free), an attractive slice of the country squeezed into the concrete metropolis. Watersports are available between April and September; in the winter, ducks and other wildfowl visit the lake. From the park, a short walk will take you to Barlow Moor Road, served by frequent buses returning to the city centre.

Salford Quays

The new Metrolink extension to **Salford Quays** provides easy access to one of the city's first urban development projects, which transformed the run-down quays on the western edge of the city centre into a waterfront residential and leisure complex. The Quays will host the country's New Imperial War Museum, though that isn't expected to open until 2002. For now, apartments and quayside promenades aside, the major attraction is the spectacular new **Lowry Centre** (☎0161/995 2000) which opens for business in 2000. No artist is more closely linked with an English city than Lowry is with Manchester, and the centre will house the most extensive Lowry exhibition in the country. It's based on the collections formerly held in both the City Art Gallery and the Salford Museum and Art Gallery, and wide-ranging exhibits illustrate Lowry's early views on the desolation and sadness of Manchester's mill workers and his changing outlook in later life when he repeated earlier paintings changing the greys and sullen browns for lively reds and pinks. Lowry also expanded his repertoire as he grew older, capturing mountain scenes and seascapes in broad sweeps of his brush, and painting full-bodied realistic portraits which are far less known than his matchstick crowds.

Old Trafford and Maine Road

Manchester United, arguably the most famous team in the world, play at **Old Trafford** – the self-styled "Theatre of Dreams" – around three miles from the city centre. The club's following is such that only season ticket holders can ever attend games, but tours of Old Trafford and its museum (April–Oct daily 9.30am–9pm;

Nov–March daily 9.30am–5pm; museum and tour £7.50, museum only £4.50; advance booking essential, call ☎0161/877 4002) might placate out-of-town fans who want to gawp at the silverware, sit in the dug-out and visit the *Red Café*. In recent years, the city's poorer soccer cousins, Manchester City, have struggled in the lower leagues, and though their support remains high you're more likely to get in to see a game. The ground, **Maine Road** in inner-city Moss Side, also hosts a rather humbler tour (call for times; £3; ☎0161/226 1782).

Eating and drinking

The bulk of Manchester's eating and drinking places are scattered around the city centre and in the areas bordering Oxford Road all the way to Rusholme – a narrow band from which few Mancunians stray. The greatest central concentration of **restaurants** is around Portland Street, especially in and around **Chinatown**, while out at Rusholme you'll find the best range of **curries** this side of the Pennines. Most city **pubs** dish up something filling at lunchtime, but for a more modish snack or drink, European-style **café-bars** are burgeoning around the centre of town, in the Northern Quarter, and especially in the Gay Village on the Rochdale Canal.

Cafés and café-bars

Manchester's café-bar scene is its pride and joy, with most of the places below fielding a very definite crowd and atmosphere. Lots of places have outdoor seating, and take advantage of relaxed licensing laws to offer drinks without food – though the food at many café-bars is, in fact, worth a special visit. As a general rule, the places listed below are open daily from 11am or noon until around 11pm or midnight, unless otherwise stated.

Affleck's Palace, 52 Church St, at the junction with Oldham Street. Five floors of boutiques, with the best of the cafés on the top floor. Closes 6pm, & all day Sun.

Atlas, 376 Deansgate. Part of the first wave of café-bars in the city, *Atlas* still turns over a good business, with regulars attracted by the Italian food, roomy interior and back patio looking out over the canal.

Barça, Arch 8 & 9, Catalan Square. Trendy Castlefield bar/restaurant tucked into the restored railway arches, boasting Mick Hucknall as part-owner and excellent, if pricey, Spanish food.

Café Pop, 34–36 Oldham St. Retro café with Scooby Snax sandwiches, comic-book decor and a yesteryear soundtrack. Closes 5.30pm, 7pm Thurs–Sat.

Citrus, 2 Mount St. Mellow café-bar behind the Central Library with plenty of room to sprawl and chow down on the Mediterranean food. Open until 2am Fri, Sat & Sun.

Cornerhouse, 70 Oxford St. The place to sip a cappuccino after viewing the galleries or catching a movie. The first-floor café dishes up soups, dips, sandwiches and baked spuds until 8.30pm; downstairs in the bar, arty types preen and pontificate.

Cyberia, 12 Oxford St, opposite the Odeon cinema. The city's first dedicated Internet café, with PC access from £5 an hour. Also big sandwiches, DJ nights, and a fully licensed bar, which stays open until 2am Fri, Sat & Sun.

Dry 201, 28–30 Oldham St. The earliest of the designer café-bars on the scene, *Dry* is still as cool as they come, with tapas-like snacks and an Internet café.

Green Room, 54–56 Whitworth St West. Attractively styled vegetarian café-bar attached to the city's main fringe theatre.

The Grinch, 5–7 Chapel Walks. Amiable wine bar in the Victorian Old Half Moon Chambers, with pavement tables, a decent Mediterranean-style menu and live music at the weekend.

Java Bar Espresso, Station Approach, Oxford Rd; Smithfield Building, 55 Oldham St. Coffee vendors, serving up terrific cappuccinos, lattes and all the variants, plus biscotti and sandwiches. Oxford Road branch closes 9pm, Oldham Street 7pm.

J.W. Johnson's, 78 Deansgate. The place to be seen with the city's rich kids, wannabes and the Man United youth team. Streetside tables and all-day food.

Manto, 46 Canal St. Gay Village stalwart whose chic crowd laps up the contemporary art exhibitions and fashion shows. A canalside Sunday brunch is a treat here, or hog one of the sought-after balcony tables.

Metz, 3 Brazil St. Classy converted warehouse bar and restaurant, with deck seating, opposite *Manto* and with a similar gay/straight mix. It's great for a pre-club drink or two and its Eastern European food's not bad either.

Night & Day, 26 Oldham St. Unpretentious café-bar with a late licence until 2am Fri, Sat & Sun, excellent food and live music – jazz, blues, Latin and funk – from local musicians. Closed Sun.

On The Eighth Day, 109 Oxford Rd. Worthy veggie café next to the Metropolitan University, serving a changing menu of soups, stews and salads. Closes 7pm, 4.30pm on Sat, & all Sun.

Prague V, 40 Chorlton St. Gay-friendly hangout on the Canal Street corner, with Czech beer, Mediterranean-inspired meals and snacks, and a drinks licence until 1am Thurs–Sat.

TeN, 10 Tariff St. More informal and cosy than the other café-bars, with sounds ranging from techno to Latin. Closes 2am, 10.30pm on Sun.

Velvet, 2 Canal St. The redbrick facade hides a stylish, laid-back basement cavern, with good food, outrageous staff, campy clientele, late-night sounds (Thurs–Sat until 1am) and Sunday jazz.

Restaurants

There's been a revolution in Manchester's dining scene in recent years, with the long-standing city-centre **restaurants** being joined by a host of trendy super-brasseries like *Mash & Air, Simply Heathcotes* and *Nico Central*. If you've got the cash and are in the city for any length of time, you should go to at least one of them to see what all the fuss is about. It also pays to make the bus or cab ride out to the suburbs, particularly those of south Manchester, where Asian (Rusholme) and Mediterranean/Modern-British (West Didsbury, Chorlton) restaurants are all the rage. Rusholme's curry houses (buses #11, #40, #41, #42, #43, #44, #45, #47, #48 or #49) will be of particular interest to those on a tight budget.

CITY CENTRE

Abbaye, 44 Canal St (☎0161/236 5566).The city's pioneering Belgian mussels-and-beer joint, with mussels served five ways (including smoked garlic) and a stack of speciality beers. It's all very Gay Village, with exposed brickwork and a huge Canal Street frontage. Bar licensed until 2am Fri, Sat & Sun. Moderate.

Beaujolais, 70 Portland St (☎0161/236 7260). One of the better French places with a menu (and a good-value set lunch) that covers all the classics. Closed Mon & Sat lunch, plus all Sun. Moderate.

Brasserie St Pierre, 57–63 Princess St (☎0161/228 0231). Wonderful French restaurant with a traditional feel and welcoming service. Set meals keep the prices manageable at lunch. Closed all Sun, & Mon eve. Expensive.

Café Istanbul, 79 Bridge St (☎0161/833 9942). An open-fronted restaurant with delicious Turkish dishes, including a great *meze* selection, and an extensive wine list. Closed Sun. Inexpensive to Moderate.

Cocotoo's, 57 Whitworth St West (☎0161/237 5458). Busy Italian restaurant that makes full use of its echoing railway arch location by splashing Renaissance murals right across the ceiling. For food, stick to the pizzas and pastas to make it a generally cheap night out. Moderate.

Dimitri's, 1 Campfield Arcade (☎0161/839 3319). Pick and mix from the Greek/Spanish/Italian menu (there's lots of choice for vegetarians), or grab a sandwich, an arcade table and sip a drink (Greek coffee to Lebanese wine). Moderate.

Dome, Lloyd House, 24 Lloyd St (☎0161/819 1990). A great building conversion makes a sympathetic space for this agreeable brasserie. Try and get a table in the circular entrance lobby, overlooking Albert Square. Moderate.

Koreana, 40 King St (☎0161/832 4330). Popular Korean restaurant with excellent set menus and cook-your-own barbecue (*bulgogi*) meals. Closed Sat lunch & Sun. Moderate to Expensive.

Little Yang Sing, 17 George St (☎0161/228 7722). The basement forerunner of its bigger Cantonese brother (see below) has had a cheery facelift, and the same great food keeps on coming – lunchtime *dim sum* and rice or noodle dishes, and down-to-earth Cantonese cooking, with lots of choice under £8. Moderate.

The Market Restaurant, 104 High St (☎0161/834 3743). One of the city's hidden treasures, this is a very relaxing spot for dinner. The regularly changing menu throws its Modern-British weight around in adventurous, eclectic fashion. Also a very good wine and beer list. Reservations essential. Wed–Sat eve. Expensive.

Mash & Air, 40 Chorlton St (_Mash_ ☎0161/661 6161; _Air_ 0161/661 1111). Oliver Peyton's converted cotton mill on three floors is named after a stage in the brewing process and brews its own beer on the premises. It's flashy and crowded and the cutting-edge food is superb, but you'll have to queue for hours to get table space in the cheaper _Mash_ (for chargrill/pizza/pasta dishes) and reserve well in advance for the more intimate _Air_ on the top floor. Moderate to Expensive.

Nico Central, Mount St (☎0161/236 6488). Nico Ladenis' Manchester brasserie (inside the Midland Hotel) is a real winner, if just a tad snooty for such a working city. Check out the Modern-French cuisine or simply call in for a drink in the amazingly well-stocked, amazingly beautiful bar. Expensive.

Pearl City, 33 George St (☎0161/228 7683). Likeable Cantonese diner with a menu of stupifying vastness and at least a nod to authenticity. Lunch deals are particularly good. Inexpensive to Moderate.

Pizza Express, 6–8 South King St (☎0161/834 0145). The centre's most reliable pizzas, served in familiar surroundings. Inexpensive to Moderate.

Simply Heathcote's, Jackson Row (☎0161/835 3536). Massive, minimalist dining rooms operated by Michelin-starred (though not yet for this restaurant) Lancastrian chef Paul Heathcote. Mixes Mediterranean and local flavours, so expect updated working-class dishes alongside the parmesan shavings. The set lunch/early-bird menu is one of the city's best deals. Moderate to Expensive.

Tampopo, 16 Albert Square (no phone). Basement noodle bar with long benches and no lingering. Noodle dishes are Japanese, Thai or Indonesian with most dishes under £6. Closed Sun. Inexpensive.

Yang Sing, 34 Princess St (☎0161/236 2200). Now back in its refurbished original premises after a devastating fire, this is still one of the best Cantonese restaurants in the country, with thoroughly authentic food, whether it be a lunchtime plate of fried noodles or the full works. Moderate to Expensive.

OUT OF THE CENTRE

Café Primavera, 48 Beech Rd, Chorlton (☎0161/862 9934). Stylish surroundings for a stylish Mediterranean menu – fish of the day is usually a good choice. Dinner only. Moderate.

Darbar, 65–67 Wilmslow Rd, Rusholme (☎0161/224 4392). Award-winning Asian food in plain but friendly surroundings. The chef's special (he's been voted Manchester's Curry Chef of the Year twice) is _nihari_, a slow-cooked lamb dish, while other homestyle choices appear on Sundays. Take your own booze. Inexpensive.

Felix, 156 Burton Rd, West Didsbury (☎0161/445 1921). Food full of Mediterranean flavour in a hip south Manchester haunt. Good for fish, early-bird menu deals and long Sunday brunches. Closed Mon lunch. Moderate.

Greens, 43 Lapwing Lane, West Didsbury (☎0161/434 4259). Imaginative gourmet vegetarian meals from the owners of _Felix_, with the same good early-bird deals; you can bring your own wine. Closed Mon & Sat lunch. Moderate.

Kosmos Taverna, 248 Wilmslow Rd, Fallowfield (☎0161/225 9106). Highly rated Greek restaurant with real country specials alongside the more mainstream favourites. Great for Sunday lunch; otherwise dinner only. Moderate to Expensive.

Lime Tree, 8 Lapwing Lane, West Didsbury (☎0161/445 1217). Bundles of Modern-British joy, with a menu that chargrills and roasts as if its life depended on it. Very fashionable, and not terribly pricey for what you get. Closed all Sat, & Mon lunch. Moderate to Expensive.

Punjab Sweet House, 177 Wilmslow Rd, Rusholme (☎0161/225 2960). Superb all-vegetarian Indian restaurant, specializing in _dosas_, _thalis_ and special sweets. Inexpensive.

Sanam, 145–151 Wilmslow Rd, Rusholme (☎0161/224 8824). One of Rusholme's earliest arrivals, now thirty years old, the Sanam serves all the usual dishes plus award-winning _gulab juman_. Drop by the take-away sweet and snack centre on the way home. No alcohol allowed. Inexpensive to Moderate.

Sangam, 13–15 Wilmslow Rd, Rusholme (☎0161/257 3922). The ever-expanding _Sangam_ can do no wrong – great curry-house classics, every time, and a fine place for a relaxed Sunday lunch or a drink in its café-bar. Moderate.

THE GAY SCENE

Manchester has one of Britain's most vibrant gay scenes, centred along the Rochdale Canal between Princess and Sackville streets, in the so-called **Gay Village**. The café-bars and clubs here are among the city's best, while the area hosts the annual gay **carnival** (August bank holiday) and the bi-annual lesbian and gay arts **festival**, "It's Queer Up North", to be held next in 2000 and 2002 (information on ☎0161/228 1998).

Early evenings kick off by the lock at one of the café-bars along Canal Street – try *Manto, Metz, Bar 38* or *Velvet* – at the extravagant *Via Fossa* pub or at the more macho *New Union*, 111 Princess St, just off Canal Street (☎0161/228 1492). An older crowd drinks in the *Rembrandt Hotel*. A camp neon Liberty beckons you into *New York, New York*, 98 Bloom St (☎0161/236 6556), for live Djs. And there are regular **club nights** for gays and lesbians at *Cruz 101*, 101 Princess St (☎0161/237 1554), the main party place in town; *Follies*, 6 Whitworth St (☎0161/236 8149), a lesbian favourite; and *Glide*, on Charles St (☎0161/273 3722).

For further **information**, try the Manchester Lesbian and Gay Switchboard (☎0161/274 3999 daily 4–10pm) which can put you in touch with the dozen or so other organizations and services operating out of the Gay Village.

Shere Khan, IFCO Centre, 52 Wilmslow Rd, Rusholme (☎0161/256 2624). Big brash Indian brasserie with stylish (ie, uncomfortable) chairs and a wide-ranging menu strong on karahi and biryani dishes. Moderate.

Tandoori Kitchen, 131 Wilmslow Rd, Rusholme (☎0161/224 2329). Interesting Persian specialities – grilled meats a speciality – among the usual curry-house offerings; take your own booze. Inexpensive.

Pubs

Quite apart from its café-bars, Manchester has a full complement of great pubs, including several Victorian classics that have stood the test of time. Off-the-shelf contemporary pubs include the usual Irish theme-bars as well as some rather better conversions of old warehouse buildings. Several splendid historic city-centre buildings have also been converted into pubs: the *Forgery & Firkin* in former Portico Library on Mosley Street; the *Square Albert* in the former Memorial Hall, a Victorian Gothic beauty on Albert Square; and the *Athenaeum*, on York Street, and *Rothwell's* – both former banks – on Spring Gardens. It's also worth noting that the two historic pubs lost to the city when the Shambles Square was destroyed by the 1996 bomb – *Sinclair's Oyster Bar* and the *Old Wellington Inn* – have now been repaired and relocated 200 yards north to a site on New Cathedral Street.

The Beer House, 6 Angel St. The best place for ale-tasting, with a constant stock of more than thirty brands of beer.

Britons Protection, 50 Great Bridgewater St. Elegantly decorated traditional pub opposite Bridgewater Hall, with a couple of cosy rooms, a brickyard beer garden, and a mixed crowd.

The Castle Hotel, Oldham St. An old-fashioned workers' pub which comes as a welcome break from the Northern Quarter's relentless trendiness.

Circus Tavern, 86 Portland St. Manchester's smallest pub – a Victorian drinking-hole that's many peoples' favourite city-centre pit-stop. You may have to knock on the door to get in.

Dukes '92, Castle St. Huge old warehouse on the duke of Bridgewater's canal in Castlefield, classily revamped with art on the walls. Serves great-value food including a wide range of pâtés and cheeses.

Footage and Firkin, 137 Grosvenor St. Predominantly student filled-beer-hall-style pub, with brewery on site, gigs and big-screen sports coverage.

Joshua Brooks, 106 Princess St. Its canalside balcony and large flagstoned basement is popular with local students for a pre-club drink; also a good selection of guest and bottled beers.

The Lass o' Gowrie, 1 Charles St. Outside, glazed tiles and Victorian styling; inside, stripped floors and a micro-brewery. All in all, one of the city's better studenty pubs.

Marble Arch, 73 Rochdale Rd. Curious real-ale house with a sloping floor, some fine internal decor and – more importantly – scores of bottled beers and a great atmosphere.

The Mark Addy, 2 Stanley St. A popular pub serving a choice of fifty cheeses and eight pâtés (including vegetarian). Eat inside, or outside by the River Irwell.

Mr Thomas' Chop House, 52 Cross St. Victorian classic with a Dickensian feel to its nooks and crannies. Office workers, hardcore daytime drinkers, old goats and students all call it home. There's good-value food served in the ornate dining room, too.

O' Shea's, 80 Princess St. Packed, student-filled Irish pub, with live music nights and filling food.

Peveril of the Peak, 127 Great Bridgewater St. The pub that time forgot – one of Manchester's best real-ale houses, with a youthful crowd and some superb Victorian glazed tilework outside.

Via Fossa, Canal St. The elaborate mock-Gothic rooms pack in a high-energy (largely gay) crowd – just the place to ratchet up the atmosphere after the laid-back café-bar antics down the road.

Nightlife

For the best part of two decades now, Manchester has been vying with London as Britain's capital of **youth culture**, spearheaded by the success of its musical exports, from the saintly Morrissey and The Smiths to Joy Division, New Order, Simply Red and Oasis, by way of the clubbie-druggie wave fronted by The Happy Mondays and The Stone Roses. Banks of fly posters advertise what's going on in the numerous **clubs** which, as elsewhere, frequently change names and styles on different nights of the week; the most enduring are listed below and you can expect to pay £3–15 cover depending on what's on. Many of the city's grooviest café-bars also host regular club nights, particularly places like *Dry 201, Atlas, Citrus, Cyberia, Prague V* and *TeN* (for more on all of these, see p.638-639). Manchester has an excellent **live music** scene in pubs and clubs, with tickets for local bands (and Oasis were a local band once) ranging from £2 to £5. Mega-star gigs take place either at the G-Mex Centre or one of the major stadiums, all listed below. For the broadest coverage of Manchester's musical happenings, check the fortnightly *City Life* magazine, Friday's *Manchester Evening News* and the monthly freesheet *Alive*.

Academy, Oxford Rd, on the university campus (☎0161/275 2930). Box-like venue for new and established bands.

The Attic, above the *Thirsty Scholar*, 50 New Wakefield St (☎0161/236 6071). Regular weekend blasts of funk, soul and dance for a cool, collected student crowd.

Band on the Wall, 25 Swan St (☎0161/832 6625). Cosy joint with a great reputation for its live bands – from world and folk to jazz and reggae – and club nights.

The Boardwalk, 15 Little Peter St (☎0161/228 3555). One of the hot venues for new bands – a nervy Oasis played their first gig here. There are good club nights here, too.

The Brickhouse, 6 Whitworth St West (☎0161/236 4418). Indie, techno, Seventies or glam, depending on the night.

Discotheque Royale, Peter St (☎0161/839 1112). Mainstream dance and chart sounds at the weekends, for an older, over 20s, crowd; midweek it's student and Seventies nights.

Generation X, 11–13 New Wakefield St (☎0161/236 4899). Stylish café-bar known for its club nights, spinning house, soul, and drum'n'bass.

Manchester Roadhouse, 8–10 Newton St (☎0161/237 9789). Regular and varied gigs by local bands seeking glory, and a succession of fine club nights, too.

Manchester University Students Union, Oxford Road (☎0161/275 2930). Ring for details of live bands throughout the academic year.

Paradise Factory, 112–116 Princess St (☎0161/228 2966). One of the hottest clubs on the scene, occupying the old Factory Records building. There's a gay night on Fridays, with a women's den upstairs. Closed Sun & Mon.

The Ritz, Whitworth St West (☎0161/236 4355). A one-time ballroom where they still spread talc on the floor some nights of the week. Suits and stilettos disco Fri & Sat; student nights Mon & Wed.

South, 4a South King St (☎0161/831 7756). Could be playing anything, depending on the night, from funk and house to Northern Soul.

Star & Garter, Fairfield St (☎0161/273 6726). Thrash/punk pub venue for loud, young bands; late bar until 2am.

5th Avenue, 121 Princess St (☎0161/236 2754). Student indie/retro scene Mon & Thurs–Sat.

STADIUM VENUES

G-Mex Centre, Windmill St (☎0161/832 9000). Mid-sized city-centre indoor stadium.

The Manchester Apollo, Ardwick Green (☎0161/242 2560). Huge theatre auditorium.

Manchester Evening News Arena (formerly the NYNEX), Victoria Station, Hunts Bank (☎0161/930 8000). Indoor stadium that seats 20,000.

Arts and culture

Manchester is blessed with the North's most highly regarded **orchestra**, the Hallé (under principal conductor, Kent Nagano). Based at the Bridgewater Hall, and several other venues, including the city's churches and its cathedral, the orchestra stages classical **concerts** throughout the year. The Cornerhouse is the local **arts** mainstay, while a full range of mainstream and fringe **theatres** produce a year-round programme of events. The biggest annual fest is autumn's **Manchester Festival**, an arts and TV extravaganza, with events in the city's clubs, theatres and open spaces.

Bridgewater Hall, Lower Mosley St (☎0161/907 9000). Home of the Hallé (founded 1857) and the Manchester Camerata (the acclaimed chamber orchestra); also sponsors a full programme of chamber, classical and jazz concerts.

Contact Theatre, 15 Oxford Rd (☎0161/274 4400). One of the most innovative theatre companies in provocative new premises. Puts on predominantly modern works and has a good café-bar.

Cornerhouse, 70 Oxford St (☎0161/200 1500). Engaging arts centre with three cinema screens, changing art exhibitions, recitals, talks, bookshop, café and bar.

Dancehouse Theatre, 10 Oxford Rd (☎0161/237 9753). Home of the Northern Ballet School, and venue for dance, drama and comedy. Also has a café-bar.

Green Room, 54–56 Whitworth St West (☎0161/950 5900). Rapidly changing fringe programme which includes dance, mime and cabaret.

Library Theatre, St Peter's Square (☎0161/236 7110). Classic drama and new writing, in a theatre beneath the Central Library.

Odeon, 1 Oxford St (☎0870/505 0007). Seven-screen city-centre cinema showing mainstream movies.

Opera House, Quay St (☎0161/242 2509). Major venue for touring West End musicals, drama and concerts.

Royal Exchange Theatre, St Ann's Square (☎0161/833 9833). The theatre-in-the-round in the Royal Exchange has been thoroughly refurbished, and a Studio Theatre (for works by new writers) added alongside the main stage.

Royal Northern College of Music (RNCM), 124 Oxford Rd (☎0161/273 4504). Stages top-quality classical and modern-jazz concerts, including performances by Manchester Camerata.

Virgin Cinemas, Salford Quays (☎0161/873 7155). Showing the latest mainstream releases.

Listings

Airport General enquiries ☎0161/489 3000; flight enquiries ☎0839/888747.

Banks and exchange There are branches of all the major banks in the city centre: Barclays, 51 Mosley St, 12 Piccadilly, 133 Deansgate; NatWest, 55 King St, 33 Piccadilly, 115 Deansgate; Midland, 100 King St, 22 Cross St, 8 High St; Lloyds, 67 Piccadilly, Market St, King St. The only late-night exchanges, other than the big hotels, are at the airport (6am–midnight) and at the Castlefield YHA (daily 7am–11pm); at other times head for American Express 10–12 St Mary's Gate (☎0161/833 0121); or Thomas Cook (☎0161/236 8575) 23 Cross St, 2 Oxford St.

Bookshops The main chains have outlets on Deansgate and around St Ann's Square. Frontline Books, Wilmslow Rd, Rusholme, is Manchester's foremost outlet for radical literature. Gibb's Bookshop, 10 Charlotte St, is great for secondhand books and classical music.

Bus information For all city services, call GMPTE (☎0161/228 7811); for intercity services, call National Express (☎0990/808 080).

Car rental Avis, 1 Ducie St (☎0161/236 6716) and at the airport (☎0161/436 2020); Budget, 660 Chester Rd, Old Trafford (☎0161/877 5555) and at the airport (☎0161/499 3042); Europcar/InterRent, York St, Piccadilly Plaza (☎0161/832 4114) and at the airport (☎0161/436 2200); Hertz, 31 Aytoun St, near Piccadilly Station (☎0161/236 2747) and at the airport (☎0161/437 8208).

Dentist Dental Hospital of Manchester, Higher Cambridge St (☎0161/275 6666).

Hospital Manchester Royal Infirmary, 13 Oxford Rd (☎0161/276 1234).

Internet *Cyberia* (see Cafés and café-bars, p.638); Net-Works Centre at the Central Library (Tues & Thurs 10am–7.30pm, Wed 1–7.30pm, Fri & Sat 10am–4.30pm).

Laundry There are several launderettes along Wilmslow Road in Rusholme, or you could use the facilities at the YHA hostel.

Left Luggage Chorlton Street coach station (daily 9.30am–5.30pm; £1 per bag); Piccadilly train station (Mon–Sat 7am–7pm, Sun 11am–7pm; from £2).

Pharmacy Cameolord Ltd, 7 Oxford St (daily 8am–midnight; ☎0161/236 1445).

Police Greater Manchester Police, Bootle St (☎0161/872 5050).

Post Office 26 Spring Gardens; 63 Newton St. The Spring Gardens office has a *bureau de change* and poste-restante section.

Taxis Mantax (☎0161/236 5133); Taxifone (☎0161/236 9974); and, for cabs to the airport, Airtax (☎0161/499 9000).

Train information Local rail information from GMPTE (☎0161/228 7811). National Rail Enquiries (☎0345/484950) for all other services. Piccadilly Station has a walk-in Travel Centre (Mon–Sat 8am–8.30pm, Sun 11am–7pm) for national and international train enquiries.

Travel Agents USIT Campus in the YHA shop, 166 Deansgate (☎0161/273 1721); and branches at UMIST, Manchester Metropolitan University, Manchester Academy and the University of Manchester. STA Travel, 75 Deansgate (☎0161/834 0668).

Chester

In 1779 Boswell wrote to Samuel Johnson: "Chester pleases me more than any town I ever saw." **CHESTER**, forty miles southwest of Manchester, has changed since then, but not so much. A glorious two-mile ring of medieval and Roman walls encircle a neat kernel of Tudor and Victorian buildings, including the unique raised arcades called the "Rows". Very much the commercial hub of its county, Chester has enough in the way of sights, restaurants and atmosphere to make it an enjoyable base for a couple of days, though it can get very crowded.

The fabric of the town is run through with two thousand years of history. In 79 AD the Romans built Deva Castra here, their largest known fortress in Britain. Later, Ethelfleda, the daughter of King Alfred the Great, extended and refortified the place, only to have it brutally sacked by William the Conqueror's armies. Trade routes to Ireland made Chester the most prosperous port in the northwest, a status it recovered after the English Civil War, which saw a two-year-long siege of the town at the hands of the Parliamentarians. By the middle of the eighteenth century, however, silting of the port had forced the Irish trade to be rerouted first through Parkgate on the Dee estuary, and then to Liverpool. Things improved a little with the Industrial Revolution, as the canal and railway networks made Chester an important regional trading centre, a function it still retains. More recent improvements in the town's infrastructure have left an almost impenetrable ring of bypasses which hardly relieve the congested centre.

Arrival, information and accommodation

National Express and most regional bus services (including the hourly #X8 from Liverpool) arrive at **Chester bus station**, between Delamere and George streets. Close by are the northern city walls and Northgate Street, down which you'll find the

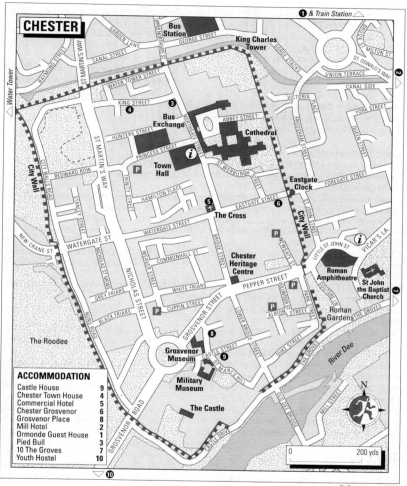

© Crown copyright

main **tourist office** in the town hall (May–Oct Mon–Sat 9am–5.30pm, Sun 10am–4pm; Nov–April Mon–Sat 9am–5.30pm; ☎01244/402111). Most other local buses use the **bus exchange** just behind the town hall, off Princess Street. Merseyrail **trains** from Liverpool (every 20–30min 6am–11pm; 45min) and all other regional and national services call at the **train station**, northeast of the centre, from where it's a ten-minute walk down City Road and along Foregate Street to the central Eastgate Clock. The City-Rail Link bus from the station to the centre (every 12min, 30min on Sun) is free to anyone with a valid train ticket, otherwise it's 35p.

The **Chester Visitor Centre**, on Vicars Lane opposite the amphitheatre (May–Oct Mon–Sat 9am–6.30pm, Sun 10am–5pm; Nov–April Mon–Sat 10am–5pm, Sun

10am–4pm; ☎01244/402111), books **accommodation**, sells tickets for ferries to Ireland, and has a seven-day *bureau de change*. Its upper storey houses a mock-nineteenth-century street with period shops, where locally made crafts are on sale, and there's a café here too. Central city **parking** is scarce, so drivers should use the Park and Ride scheme, catching a bus from one of the car parks scattered around the ring road.

Chester's popularity is apparent as soon as you arrive, and in high summer **B&B accommodation** can be in short supply, as can space in the more characterful old inns. The places reviewed below are the best of the central choices: if you arrive late, or strike out in the centre, there are lots of budget-rated B&Bs along Brook Street, just a couple of minutes from the train station, and several moderate but bland hotels down City Road, also near the station.

Accommodation

10 The Groves (☎01244/317907).There's just one double (en suite) in this riverside B&B, so get your phone call in early. There's TV, tea- and coffee-making facilities, and parking available. No credit cards. ①.

Castle House, 23 Castle St (☎01244/350354). B&B in a sixteenth-century house with good facilities; bang in the centre and excellent value for money. No credit cards. ②.

The Chester Grosvenor, Eastgate St (☎01244/324024). Superbly appointed luxury hotel bristling with liveried staff, very comfortable bedrooms and a whole host of facilities, not least two fine restaurants. ⑨, ⑧ at weekends.

Chester Town House, 23 King St (☎01244/350021). A very high-standard B&B in a comfortably furnished seventeenth-century town house, on a curving, cobbled central street off Northgate Street. No credit cards. ③.

Commercial Hotel, St Peters Church Yard (☎01244/320749). Friendly inn with good beer and half-a-dozen pleasant rooms in a brick-walled churchyard. ②.

Grosvenor Place Guest House, 2–4 Grosvenor Place (☎01244/324455). Pleasant town house B&B in a good, if noisy, location near the museum. ②.

Mill Hotel, Milton St (☎01244/350035). Sensitive warehouse conversion on the canal, between St Oswald's Way and Hooley Way, not far from the train station. Has its own car park and a nice waterside bar; rooms with balcony attract a £10 supplement. ④.

Ormonde Guesthouse, 126 Brook St (☎01244/328816). One of the best of a string of similarly priced B&Bs along this street, two minutes from the train station. No credit cards. ②.

Pied Bull, Northgate St (☎01244/325829). Characterful old coaching inn, close to the walls and cathedral. ②.

Youth Hostel, Hough Green House, 40 Hough Green (☎01244/680056, *yhachester@compuserve.com*). Twenty-minutes' walk from the centre, this Victorian house has a cafeteria, games room, and coin-op laundry facilities; family rooms available.

The City

Walking tours – assorted Roman, historic and ghost trails – from the Town Hall tourist office and from the Vicar Lane Visitor Centre (May–Oct twice daily; Nov–April once daily; £3) aren't a bad way to orient yourself. The main thoroughfares of Chester's Roman grid plan meet at **the Cross**, where the town crier welcomes visitors to the city (May–Aug Tues–Sat at noon). Both sides of all four streets are lined by **the Rows**, unique galleried arcades running on top of the ground-floor shops. The engaging black-and-white tableau is a blend of genuine Tudor houses and Victorian half-timbered imitations, with the finest Tudor buildings on Watergate Street – though Eastgate Street is perhaps the most picturesque, leading to the filigree **Eastgate Clock**, erected atop a sandstone arch to commemorate Victoria's Diamond Jubilee. There's no clear explanation of the origin of the Rows – they were first recorded soon after the fire that wrecked Chester in 1278, and may well originally have been built on top of the heaped rubble left after the blaze.

You can get the best insight into Chester's Roman heritage at **Dewa Roman Experience** tucked away up Pierpoint Lane, off Bridge Street (daily 9am–5pm; £3.80). You're free to touch the archeological finds on show after following an armoured soldier through Roman street scenes and an excavation of Roman, Saxon and Medieval buildings. Most of the Roman city lies buried beneath Chester, though remnants have occasionally surfaced during rebuilding: *Spud-u-like*, across the way at 43 Bridge St, warrants a moment's diversion for the well-preserved Roman hypocaust (early central heating), part of a bathhouse visible in the basement. There's a more general introduction to the town in the **Chester Heritage Centre** at the bottom of Bridge Street (March–Oct Mon–Sat 11am–5pm, Sun noon–5pm; £1.25), housed in what used to be St Michael's church.

The Cathedral

North of the Cross, the neo-Gothic town hall dominates its square at the end of Northgate Street across from the heavily restored **Cathedral** (daily 9.30am–6pm; free tours Mon–Sat 2.30pm), whose entrance is through the archway into the peaceful, Georgian Abbey Square. Taking the role of cathedral in 1541 after the Dissolution of the Monasteries, this Benedictine church is dedicated to St Werburgh, a seventh-century Anglo-Saxon princess who became Chester's patron saint. Parts of the eleventh-century structure can still be seen in the north transept but the highlights in an otherwise simple interior are the fourteenth-century choir stalls, with their intricately carved misericords. Doors in the north wall of the nave lead into the shady sixteenth-century cloisters, encircling a small garden whose focal point is an imaginative and striking bronze sculpture by Stephen Broadbent of the woman of Samaria offering water to Jesus at the well.

Around the walls

East of the cathedral, steps provide access to the top of the two-mile girdle of the medieval and Roman **city walls** – the most complete set in Britain, though in places the wall is barely above street level. You can walk past all its turrets and gateways in an hour or two, calling first at the fifteenth-century **King Charles Tower** (April–Oct Sat 10am–5pm, Sun 2–5pm; 50p), in the northeast corner. So named because Charles I is said to have stood here in 1645 watching his troops being beaten on Rowton Moor, it now houses a small but interesting exhibition on the siege of Chester, immediately after the Royalist defeat. The **Water Tower** (same hours as King Charles Tower; 50p), at the northwest corner, houses a display charting, among other aspects of the city's trading past, the changes brought about by the gradual silting of the River Dee. South from the tower you'll see the **Roodee**, England's oldest racecourse, laid out on a silted tidal pool where Roman ships once unloaded wine, figs and olive oil from the Mediterranean and slate, lead and silver from their mines in North Wales. Races are still held here in May, June and July; the tourist office has further details.

Until nineteenth-century excavation work, much of the wall near the Water Tower was propped up by scores of sculpted tomb panels and engraved headstones, items probably used to rebuild the walls in a hurry in the turbulent fourth century. Many are now on display at the **Grosvenor Museum**, 27 Grosvenor St (Mon–Sat 10.30am–5pm, Sun 2–5pm; free), just inside the city walls near the southern end of the Roodee. This is the best investigation of Roman Chester, with good displays about the legionary system, city buildings, grave sites, defences, daily life and culture. The tombstones themselves form the largest collection from a single Roman site in Britain, the finest being the carving of a wounded barbarian – the surviving piece of a memorial to a Roman cavalryman. The back of the museum opens into a preserved Georgian house complete with furnished kitchen, parlour, bedrooms, rickety floors and sloping stairs.

Across the traffic roundabout on Castle Street, the dull **Cheshire Military Museum** (daily 10am–5pm; 50p) inhabits part of the same complex as the Norman **Chester Castle** (Easter–Sept daily 10am–6pm; Oct–Easter daily 10am–4pm; free; EH). Though the castle was founded by William the Conqueror, most of what you see today is little older than the eighteenth-century Greek Revival Assize Courts and council offices on the same site, the building of which led to the demolition of much of the medieval structure. The castle's history is explained in a couple of cells in the guard room (across the car park), but the gracefully simple St Mary de Castro chapel in the surviving Agricola Tower is the main attraction here.

South of the castle, the wall is buried under the street, but it rises again alongside the **Roman Gardens** (unrestricted access) on Souters Lane at Little John Street, where Roman foundations dug up during redevelopment are on display. Across the road stands the half-excavated remains of the **Roman Amphitheatre** (Easter–Sept daily 10am–6pm; Oct–Easter daily 10am–1pm & 2–4pm; free; EH); it is estimated to have held seven thousand spectators, making it the largest amphitheatre in Britain, but the stonework is barely head-high now.

The partly ruined pink-stone **Church of St John the Baptist** (daily 9.15am–6pm), a little to the east in Grosvenor Park, was founded by the Saxon king Ethelred in 689 and briefly served as the cathedral of Mercia. Rebuilt in its entirety by the Normans, although smaller than St Werburgh's it is considerably more impressive, the solid Norman pillars of the nave rising to a Transitional triforium and Early English clerestory. Outside are the romantic eastern ruins – left to deteriorate having been cut off from the rest of the church after the Reformation – and the stones of the northwest tower, which collapsed in 1881, possibly weakened by its use as a Parliamentary gun emplacement during the Civil War. What's claimed to be a thirteenth-century coffin – emblazoned with the inscription "Dust to Dust" is set into an arch at the eastern end of the ruins.

Steps from the church gardens and from the southern edge of the city walls lead to the tree-shaded **Groves**, on the banks of the Dee, with its bandstand, slender iron footbridge and villas overlooking the willows draped along the opposite bank. Bithells Boats runs half-hour **cruises** on the river (every 15min; April–Nov 10am–6.30pm; Dec–March Sat & Sun 11am–4pm; £3) and two-hour trips in the summer (Wed & Sat 11am & 8.15pm, rest of week 11am only).

Eating, drinking and entertainment

You can't walk more than a few paces in Chester without coming across somewhere good to **eat and drink**, as often as not housed in a medieval crypt or Tudor building. Places below are open for lunch and dinner unless otherwise stated. Some of the **pubs** are highly atmospheric and most serve bar meals, though the quality isn't always up to much. For something different, reserve for the *Mill Hotel*'s one-hour bar-meal **cruise** (£2.50 plus lunch; ☎01244/350035); they also run evening and champagne cruises.

A batch of annual **festivals** keeps the town's concert halls and churches busy: the Folk Festival in May, Young Musician's Festival in June and the renowned **Summer Music Festival** every July, which sees outdoor concerts and fireworks in Grosvenor Park, as well as a simultaneous Fringe Festival.

Cafés and restaurants

Arkle, *Chester Grosvenor Hotel*, Eastgate St (☎01244/324024). Traditional English food served to the highest standards in a very formal setting. The £25 set lunch is the best value. Very Expensive.

Boulevard de la Bastille, Bridge St Row. One of the nicest of the arcade cafés, with tables looking over the street, doing a roaring trade in breakfasts, pastries and sandwiches.

The Brasserie, *Chester Grosvenor Hotel*, Eastgate St (☎01244/324024). The *Grosvenor*'s informal brasserie is a great place for a coffee and pastry, or come for the inventive French and fusion cooking.

Cathedral Refectory, Chester Cathedral, St Werburgh St. Bistro-style dishes served in the thirteenth-century monks' dining room. Closed Sun. Inexpensive.

Chez Jules, 69 Northgate St (☎01244/400014). Classic brasserie menu, including a terrific value £6 set lunch. Inexpensive.

Espresso Bar, 60 Northgate St. A couple of friendly Italian guys froth up a great cappuccino and serve mouth-watering sandwiches. Closed Sun.

Francs, 14 Cuppin St (☎01244/317952). An excellent and very French bistro with good-value set meals. You can also just drop in for a coffee and cake. Moderate.

The Garden House, 1 Rufus Court, off Northgate St (☎01244/320004). A highly praised bistro in a Georgian house by the walls, with a sunny courtyard garden. Moderate to Expensive.

Mamma Mia, 87 St Werburgh St (☎01244/314663). Popular with a party crowd, this pizzeria-restaurant serves speciality fish and vegetarian dishes along with the pizzas. Moderate.

Ruan Orchid, 14 Lower Bridge St (☎01244/400661). Their huge menu ranges across all the Thai regions – good for red and green curries, duck dishes and noodles. Moderate.

Vincent's, Lower Bridge St (☎01244/310854). When it's time to ring the changes try this bright and breezy Caribbean restaurant. Moderate.

Pubs and bars

Alexander's Jazz Theatre and Café Bar, 2 Rufus Court (☎01244/340005). Continental-style café-bar with *tapas* from the counter and live music or comedy nightly.

The Albion, corner of Albion and Park streets. Victorian terraced pub in the shadow of the walls with renowned bar food.

The Boat House, The Groves. An intimate pub by the river, decked out with black and white prints of nineteenth-century fishing families, and serving a great selection of ales.

Boot Inn, Eastgate Row. A characterful pub in the upper gallery with a back room where fourteen Roundheads were killed, and a highbacked seat once used by soliciting prostitutes; the rest is less successfully maintained, ruined by piped music and slot machines.

The Falcon, Lower Bridge St. This half-timbered Samuel Smith's pub was once a town house built by the Grosvenor family by enclosing part of a Row.

Fortress & Firkin, Frodsham St. Modern canalside pub with outdoor seats and regular live bands.

Old Harkers Arms, 1 Russell St, below the City Road bridge. Canalside real-ale boozer imaginatively sited in a former warehouse.

Telford's Warehouse, Tower Wharf, Raymond St (☎01244/390090). Warehouse-style wine-bar pub with regular live music. It's just off the city walls by the Water Tower, built partly over the turning basin of the Shropshire Union Canal.

Watergates, Watergate St. A cosy wine bar in a crypt formerly used as a wine merchants. Real ales, plus good bar and restaurant meals.

Around Chester

There are four attractions in the environs of Chester: the **zoo**, **Beeston** and **Peckforton castles** and the **boat museum** at Ellesmere Port. On a Sunday (and bank holidays) you can get a Cheshire Bus Adventure Ticket (£3.50 on the bus), which gives unlimited bus travel throughout the county and a discount on entry charges to the zoo and museum.

Chester zoo

Chester's most popular attraction, **Chester Zoo** (daily: April–Sept 10am–6pm; Oct–March 10am–4pm; last admission 2hr before closing; £9), is one of the best in Europe. It is also the second largest in Britain (after London), spreading over 110 landscaped acres, with new attractions opening all the time. The zoo is well known for its conservation projects and has had notable success with a pair of Asiatic lions who, within four months of their introduction from north India in 1994, became the parents of three healthy cubs. Ten more have subsequently been born. Animals are grouped by region in large paddocks viewed from a maze of pathways or from the creeping monorail, with main attractions being the baby animals (elephants, giraffes and orang-utans), the new rainforest habitat, complete with jaguars, and the Twilight Zone bat cave. Kids enjoy the Animal Discovery Centre, where they're encouraged by the staff to touch and learn. The zoo entrance is signposted off the A41 to the north of town and reached by bus #4, #14 or #40 (Mon–Sat; every 30min) from Chester's bus exchange, or the #11c and #12c (every 30min, Sun & public holidays) to Liverpool's Albert Dock. Merseyrail stations sell a combined train, bus and zoo-admission ticket, using the #40 bus link from Bache Merseyrail station, one stop north of Chester.

Beeston and Peckforton castles
For the best views over the Cheshire Plain, head out to the ruins of **Beeston Castle** (daily: Easter–Oct 10am–6pm; Nov–Easter 10am–4pm; £2.80; EH), which sits high on an isolated sandstone crag twelve miles southeast of Chester. Built by the Earl of Chester in 1220, it changed hands several times during the Civil War, the Royalists finally surrendering to the Parliamentarians in 1646, when it was promptly dismantled.

A mile south of Beeston you'll find **Peckforton Castle** (Easter–Sept daily 10am–6pm; £2.50), as well placed as Beeston for views. At little over 150 years old, the red sandstone castle, designed by Anthony Salvin, boasts a resident ghost and has a singing minstrel to amuse visitors.

To get to either castle you really need a car, since local bus services don't really give you any time at the castles before the afternoon return journey.

Ellesmere Port Boat Museum
It's claimed that the **Ellesmere Port Boat Museum** (April–Oct daily 10am–5pm; Nov–March Mon–Wed, Sat & Sun 11am–4pm; £5.50), seven miles north of Chester, has Britain's largest collection of floating canal vessels, a contention that seems completely plausible when you see the flotilla. Scores of barges are scattered throughout the canal basin and staircase of locks where the Shropshire Union Canal meets the refinery-lined River Mersey at the head of the Manchester Ship Canal. Indoor exhibits trace the history of canals and their construction, and you can take a short ride on a narrow boat (£2.30). The museum is five minutes' walk from Ellesmere Port train station (change at Hooton from Chester) or take bus #3 (every 30min) or the hourly #X8 (Liverpool bus) from Chester bus station on Delamere Street.

The Cheshire Plain

The bustle of Chester is no measure of the rest of the county, a region of lush pastureland and unflustered little towns strung together by hedgerowed lanes. Perhaps because of the familiarity of the landscape, the Danes took a liking to the **Cheshire Plain**, leaving the names of the River Dane and **Knutsford** (Canute's ford) as evidence of their occupation. Since that time farming has continued to be the mainstay of the county's economy, but salt mining around **Northwich** and silk manufacturing in **Macclesfield** have contributed in their day. Once the main centre of southern Cheshire, **Nantwich** has benefited from the rise of nearby Crewe and is today a sleepy town packed with four-hundred-year-old houses and shops. It's really the only place you might want to consider staying in; otherwise, all the various attractions are best seen as a stop on the way between Chester and Manchester. Call the Cheshire Bus Enquiry Office (☎01244/602666) for all bus timetable enquiries.

Northwich

Like several towns on the Cheshire plain, **NORTHWICH**, seventeen miles east of Chester, owes its existence to the underground pockets of rock salt laid down here when the area was an inland sea. Salt was a crucial commodity to the Romans, who began sluicing it to the surface as brine, then evaporating it in lead pans. Methods of salt extraction changed little into this century but brine is now pumped from under the town to chemical plants on the Mersey as the raw material for chlorine and alkali manufacture. The extraction of the underlying strata has caused considerable subsidence, with the result that a number of mock-Tudor buildings in the centre are now shored up. All this and a lot more is explained at **The Salt Museum**, 162 London Rd (Tues–Fri 10am–5pm, Sat & Sun 2–5pm; £2), twenty minutes' walk from the **train station**. The **Lion Salt Works** on the Trent and Mersey Canal on Ollershaw Lane in nearby Marston (daily 1.30–4.30pm), maintains a series of traditional open salt pans, and has its own exhibitions about the industry.

Knutsford and around

While conquering the greater part of England between 1015 and 1018, the Danish king Knut (Canute) is said to have crossed Lily Stream at the spot where the winding streets and eighteenth-century houses of **KNUTSFORD** now stand. From medieval times the town was important locally for its market and coaching inns, but today is a quiet wealthy community that makes much of its role as the model for Cranford in the book of the same name by **Elizabeth Gaskell**. Gaskell spent her childhood years here, living for a while in Heathwaite House, 18 Gaskell Ave (not open to the public), and getting married in **St John's** parish church. A small permanent exhibition in the **Knutsford Heritage Centre**, 90a King St (Mon–Fri 1.30–4pm, Sat noon–4pm, Sun 2–4.30pm; free), explains more about her connection with the town, while admirers will want to complete their Gaskell tour by visiting the **Unitarian** church, behind the train station, where she is buried. A map posted outside the tourist office can help you track down all these sights.

Even without the lure of Mrs Gaskell, Knutsford makes a handsome place for a stroll, not least down narrow King Street in the centre, lined with old inns, antique shops and cafés, and still featuring several cobbled yards and side-alleys. The buildings raised by Manchester glove-maker and philanthropist **Richard Watt** also catch the eye, though their loosely Mediterranean style may not be to everyone's taste. The most visible of these are the terracotta-roofed **Ruskin Rooms** on Drury Lane, built as a reading and recreation place for the townspeople, and **The King's Coffee House**, 60 King St, which now houses *La Belle Epoque* brasserie, with its Art Nouveau interior.

Knutsford lies on the Chester–Manchester **train** line. The **tourist office** is opposite the train station in the council offices on Toft Road (Mon–Thurs 8.45am–5pm, Fri 8.45am–4.30pm, Sat 9am–1pm; ☎01565/632611). To reach King Street, walk along Toft Road from the tourist office and turn right down Church Hill at the parish church. You might want to **stay the night** at the *Royal George Hotel*, on King St (☎01565/634151; ③), breakfast not included) which features in several of Gaskell's novels – or contact the tourist office for a list of local B&Bs. King Street also has all the **eating** options, notably the well-regarded *La Belle Epoque* brasserie (☎01565/633060; closed Sun), with its moderately priced menu, as well as several pubs, a couple of wine bars and cafés, and branches of *Pierre Victoire* and *Café Rouge* (both brasseries) and *Est Est Est* (Italian).

Tatton Park

Knutsford's King Street ends at the southern gates of thousand-acre **Tatton Park** (Easter–Oct daily 10am–7pm; Nov–Easter Tues–Sun 11am–5pm; free; parking £3), from where it is another mile past herds of deer to the vast Regency **mansion** (April–Oct Tues–Sun noon–4pm; £3), built at the end of the eighteenth century. A couple of Canalettos lurk among the period furniture, and regular guided tours (on the hour) will point out many other treasures. There's also a working farm and stables (£3) and historic exhibits in the Tudor Old Hall to keep you occupied, though the extensive formal **gardens** (closes 1hr earlier than the park; £3; NT) are probably the most pleasurable part of the estate. If you plan on seeing everything – which would take the best part of a day – then buy a saver ticket (£4.50) which is valid for any two attractions. Groundwork Cycle Hire (Mon–Fri 10.30am–6pm, Sat noon–6pm; ☎01625/560050) in the park grounds can rent you a bike to explore the surroundings.

Macclesfield

In the late eighteenth and early nineteenth centuries **MACCLESFIELD** was one of Britain's main silk spinning and weaving centres, its trade booming when French silks became unavailable during the Napoleonic Wars. The mills declined rapidly after the 1940s, when artificial fibres became available, leaving just a few manufacturers and two museums as testimony. The **Heritage Centre**, housed in a former Sunday School on Roe Street (Mon–Sat 11am–5pm, Sun 1pm–5pm; £2.70, joint ticket with Paradise Mill £4.75), puts the industry and its interaction with the community into perspective through an audiovisual presentation, archaic equipment and a World War II silk map of Northern Europe. After that, take a trip down to **Paradise Mill**, on Park Lane (Tues–Sun 1–5pm; £2.70), where the top floor is devoted to rows of ageing Jacquard looms and spinning machines that are set in action by the tour guides, many of them ex-weavers. Both museums are within ten minutes' walk of the **bus station** on Sunderland Street and the **train station** across the road, a major stop on the London–Manchester line. The **tourist office** is in the town hall on Market Place (Mon–Thurs 9am–5pm, Fri 9am–4.30pm, Sat 9am–4pm; ☎01625/504114).

Nantwich

In 1583 **NANTWICH** was almost entirely destroyed by fire. Such was the town's importance for its salt production that Elizabeth I donated £1000 and ordered a nationwide appeal to help with rebuilding, a gesture commemorated by a plaque on **Queen's Aid House** on the High Street. A largely pedestrianized centre makes Nantwich a good place to amble around and see Cheshire's second-best set of timber-framed buildings, with an essential stop being the predominantly fourteenth-century **Church of St Mary**, where the ribbed vaulting in the chancel has bosses depicting the life of the Virgin. The church and neighbouring **Sweetbriar Hall** are two of the three buildings to have survived the fire – the other is the timber-framed Elizabethan **Churche's Mansion** in Hospital Street.

The *Crown Hotel* on the High Street is perhaps the most striking of the black-and-white buildings, the gallery on the top floor now converted into separate rooms. It's also one of the most atmospheric and lively spots in town for a drink. Elements of the town's former cottage industries of cheese-, salt- and shoemaking are showcased in the small **Nantwich Museum** on Pillory Street (April–Sept Mon–Sat 10.30am–4.30pm; Oct–March Tues–Sat 10.30am–4.30pm; free), 150 yards from the church.

The **train station** sees hourly traffic on the Manchester–Crewe–Cardiff line and is only five minutes' walk from the **tourist office** in Church House, Church Walk (Mon–Fri 9.30am–5pm, Sat 10am–4pm; bank holidays & Sun in Aug 11am–3pm; ☎01270/610983). Pick of the **accommodation** is the *Crown Hotel*, High St (☎01270/625283; ④, breakfast not included), a half-timbered sixteenth-century coaching inn, followed by the *Lamb Hotel*, Hospital St (☎01270/625286; ③), which also serves good bar meals. Local B&Bs are plentiful: *Kiltearn House*, 33 Hospital St (☎01270/628892; no credit cards; ②) is a nice central choice, while anyone with their own transport could plump for *Stoke Grange Farm*, three miles north on the Chester Road (☎01270/625525; no credit cards ②), a friendly canalside farmhouse.

Liverpool

Once the country's main transatlantic port and the empire's second city, **LIVERPOOL** spent too many of the twentieth-century postwar years struggling against adversity. Things are looking up at last, as economic and social regeneration brightens the centre and old docks. Yet – even as any short-term visitor to the city could tell you – nothing ever broke Liverpool's extraordinary spirit of community, a spirit that emerged strongly in the aftermath of the Hillsborough football stadium disaster of 1989, when the deaths of 95 Liverpool supporters seemed to unite the whole city. Indeed, acerbic wit and loyalty to one of the city's two football teams are the linchpins of Scouse culture – though Liverpool makes great play of its musical heritage, which is reasonable enough from the city that produced The Beatles.

Although it gained its charter from King John in 1207, Liverpool remained a humble fishing village for half a millennium until the silting-up of Chester and the booming slave trade prompted the building of the first dock in 1715. From then until the abolition of slavery in Britain in 1807, Liverpool was the apex of the **slaving triangle** in which firearms, alcohol and textiles were traded for African slaves, who were then shipped to the Caribbean and America. The holds were filled with tobacco, raw cotton and sugar for the return journey. After the abolition of the trade, the port continued to grow into a seven-mile chain of docks, not only for freight but also to cope with wholesale European **emigration**, which saw nine million people from half of Europe leave for the Americas and Australasia between 1830 and 1930. Some never made it further than Liverpool and contributed to a five-fold increase in population in fifty years. An even larger boost came with immigration from the Caribbean and China, and especially Ireland in the wake of the potato famine in 1845. The resulting mix became one of Britain's earliest multi-ethnic communities, described by Carl Jung as "the pool of life".

The docks were busy until the middle of this century when a number of factors led to the port's decline: cheap air fares saw off the lucrative liner business; trade with the dwindling empire declined, while European traffic boosted southeastern ports at Tilbury, Harwich and Southampton; and containerization meant reduced demand for handling and warehousing. The arrival of car manufacturing plants in the 1960s, like Ford at Halewood, stemmed the decline for a while, but Liverpool never really recovered from the bodyblow of losing its fundamental business. Successive city councils have tried to alleviate the depressed economy, most notably during the 1980s when local jobs and services were maintained at the cost of a massive budget deficit and in the face of determined opposition by a central government obsessed with restricting local government spending. EU development funds have been forthcoming since Liverpool was classified as one of Europe's poorest areas, and millennium money has kick-started other projects, though – compared to the wholesale redevelopment of neighbouring Manchester – the city still has a fair hill to climb.

Yet, like Manchester, Liverpool has a legacy of magnificent municipal buildings – best seen en masse from across the river or on the Mersey ferry – and these are the chief attractions of the cityscape, along with its two famous **cathedrals**. The city's mercantile past and aspects of its recent history are well covered in a number of museums and galleries, especially in the rejuvenated warehouses of **Albert Dock**, site of the **Tate Gallery**. These sights can easily sustain a day or two – and make time to drop into one of Liverpool's many late-closing bars, the surest way to get the feel of the place.

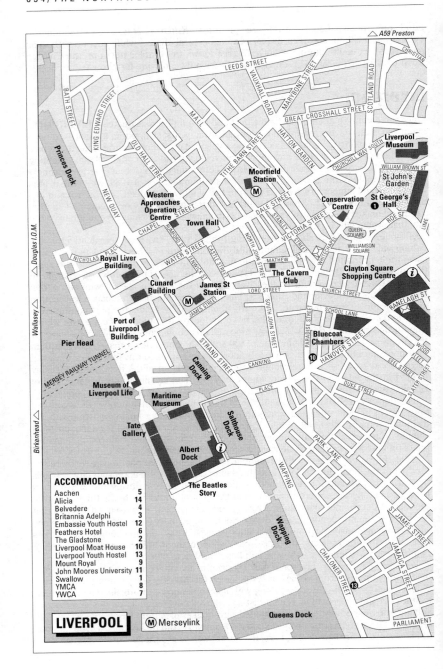

ACCOMMODATION

Aachen	5
Alicia	14
Belvedere	4
Britannia Adelphi	3
Embassie Youth Hostel	12
Feathers Hotel	6
The Gladstone	2
Liverpool Moat House	10
Liverpool Youth Hostel	13
Mount Royal	9
John Moores University	11
Swallow	1
YMCA	8
YWCA	7

LIVERPOOL   Ⓜ Merseylink

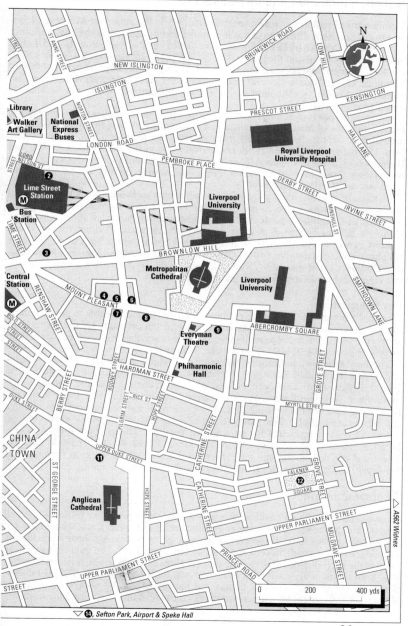

Library
Walker Art Gallery
National Express Buses
London Road
Lord Nelson St
Lime Street Station
M
Bus Station
Central Station
M
Bold Street
Street
Duke Street
CHINA TOWN
St George Street
Anglican Cathedral

NEW ISLINGTON
Islington
St Anne Street
Street
Norton Street
Pembroke Place
Brownlow Hill
Mount Pleasant
Renshaw Street
Berry Street
Rodney Street
Pilgrim Street
Upper Duke Street
Hope Street
Hardman Street
Rice St
Hope Street
Upper Parliament Street
Upper Parliament Street
Street

Brunswick Road
Low Hill
N
Kensington
Prescot Street
Royal Liverpool University Hospital
Derby Street
Hall Lane
Irvine Street
Minshull St
Liverpool University
Liverpool University
Smithdown Lane
Metropolitan Cathedral
Abercromby Square
Everyman Theatre
Philharmonic Hall
Catherine Street
Myrtle Street
Grove Street
Catherine Street
Falkner Square
Grove Street
Upper Parliament Street
Princes Road
Mulgrave Street
△ A562 Widnes

2
3
4 5 6
7
8
9
11
12

0   200   400 yds

▽ 14, Sefton Park, Airport & Speke Hall

© Crown copyright

Arrival, information and city transport

Mainline trains pull in to **Lime Street** station, while the suburban **Merseyrail** system (for trains from Chester) calls at four underground stations in the city, including Lime Street, Central (under the main post office on Ranelagh Street) and James Street (for Pier Head and the Albert Dock). National Express **buses** use the station on Norton Street, just northeast of Lime Street. Local buses depart from a variety of terminals: Queen Square (for eastbound, cross-river and Chester services); Paradise Street Bus Station (southbound and a few northbound services); and St Thomas Street (northbound).

Liverpool **airport**, eight miles southeast of the city centre, handles flights for Belfast, Dublin, the Isle of Man, Nice, Malaga and Amsterdam. A **taxi** to Lime Street costs around £10, or take bus #80/180 from outside the main entrance (every 30min 6am–11pm) into the city centre. **Ferry** arrivals – from the Isle of Man, Dublin and Belfast – dock at the terminals just north of Pier Head, close to Albert Dock and not far from James Street Merseyrail station. For all **departure details** and travel enquiry numbers, see "Listings" on p.666.

All the tourist information you could possibly want – including timetables, maps and the comprehensive *Liverpool and Merseyside Visitor Guide* – are available from two handy offices: the **Merseyside Welcome Centre** centrally located in Queen Square (Mon–Sat 9.30am–5.30pm, Sun 10am–5pm) and the **Atlantic Pavilion tourist information centre** at the Albert Dock (daily 10am–5.30pm), which both share the same telephone enquiries number (☎0151/708 8838). Both also sell the **National Museums and Galleries on Merseyside** (NMGM) Eight Pass (£3) which gives unlimited access into eight local museums for twelve months.

City transport

Liverpool city centre is surprisingly compact and you'll easily be able to get around on foot, though the odd bus route may come in useful and everyone should take a ferry across the Mersey at some point, if only to be able to say that they've sung *that* song in its proper environment. Mersey ferry ticket information is given on p.661.

The local transport authority is **Merseytravel**, which co-ordinates all buses, trains and ferries. Their main office is at 24 Hatton Gardens (Merseytravel Line ☎0151/236 7676 daily 8am–8pm), and there are also information centres at Queen Square, at the Merseyside Welcome Centre, Paradise Street Bus Station and Pier Head. Daily off-peak, zonal Saveaway tickets (£2.10–4.30) for unlimited use on most city buses, trains and ferries are available from post offices, newsagents and the Merseytravel offices, but aren't really worthwhile for most tourist ventures. **Useful bus routes** include Smart buses #1 (linking Queen Square and Albert Dock), #4 (Albert Dock, Paradise Street and the cathedrals) and #5 (Queen Square and Albert Dock on evenings and Sundays). The #222 links Pier Head, Albert Dock and Queen Square.

Accommodation

Liverpool has very limited central **accommodation**, with just a few business-oriented four-stars at the top end of the range and a clutch of budget hotels along Mount Pleasant. What the city does have, however, is a wide range of hostels and halls of residence, including a terrific youth hostel a short walk from Albert Dock. You might snag a cheap B&B in the surrounding suburbs – the tourist offices can help. There is no useful campsite. Both tourist offices will book rooms for you for free; call ☎0345/585291 for their details of special-offer weekend breaks and packages. It's also always worth asking about weekend rates at the bigger hotels, which can turn up some surprising deals.

Hotels and B&Bs

Aachen, 89–91 Mount Pleasant (☎0151/709 3477). The best and most popular of the Mount Pleasant budget choices, with friendly staff, a range of value-for-money rooms, big breakfasts and a bar. ②.

Alicia, 3 Aigburth Drive, Sefton Park (☎0151/727 4411). Restored townhouse in the *Feathers* mold, with pleasant park views and a variety of rooms. ③–④.

Belvedere, 83 Mount Pleasant (☎0151/709 2356). A convenient and cheap central hotel with few frills. ①.

Britannia Adelphi Hotel, Ranelagh Place (☎0151/709 7200). Liverpool's *Adelphi* catered to passenger-liner customers in its heyday, but it's lost its lustre since then. But for its location, one block from Lime Street station, and fame (star, if that's the right word, of TV's fly-on-the-wall series *Hotel*), it remains a relatively good deal (though breakfast isn't included). You should be able to negotiate a weekend discount. ⑤.

Feathers Hotel, 117–125 Mount Pleasant (☎0151/709 9655). A converted and modernized terrace of Georgian houses, with nicely presented en-suite rooms and a help-yourself buffet breakfast included in the price. ⑤.

The Gladstone, Lord Nelson St (☎0151/709 7050). Standard accommodation, just behind Lime Street station, with summer and weekend deals knocking a tenner off the room rate. ③.

Holiday Inn Express, Britannia Pavilion, Albert Dock (☎0151/709 1133, *liverpool@premierhotel.co.uk*). Giving the rest of the city-centre accommodation a run for its money, all the 170 dockside rooms go for the same bargain price, and are en suite, with continental breakfast included. ③.

Liverpool Moat House, Paradise St (☎0151/471 9988). Well-equipped, modern hotel a short walk from the Albert Dock, with comfortable rooms and good sports facilities including a fine indoor pool and spa. The midweek rate doesn't include breakfast. Midweek ⑦, weekend ⑥.

Mount Royal, 28 Mount Pleasant (☎0151/709 4421). A refit has smartened up the rooms and facilities at this Mount Pleasant favourite – used, incidentally, as the backdrop for the lovers' tryst in *Letter to Brezhnev*. The price drops at weekends if you stay two or more nights. ⑤.

Swallow Hotel, 1 Queen Square (☎0151/476 8000). Stylish new city-centre hotel, handy for Lime Street and the museums, and featuring a leisure club (with indoor pool and hot tub), restaurant and bar. ⑦.

Hostels and halls of residence

Embassie Youth Hostel, 1 Falkner Square (☎0151/707 1089). Twenty minutes' walk from Lime Street station (bus #80), in a Georgian terrace west of the Anglican cathedral, this relaxed hostel has dorm beds, a self-catering kitchen, TV lounge and laundry facilities. Free showers, tea, toast and coffee included in the price.

John Moores University, Cathedral Park, St James Rd (☎0151/709 3197). Self-catering accommodation in the shadow of the metropolitan cathedral. Available with and without continental breakfast. July to early Sept only.

Liverpool Youth Hostel, Wapping (☎0151/709 8888, *liverpool@yha.org.uk*). One of the YHA's best, just south of Albert Dock, a new building decorated with Beatles memoribilia. Accommodation is in smart two-, three-, four- or six-bed rooms (with private bathroom and heated towel rail). There's also a kitchen, licensed café, lobby lounge, luggage storage and laundry facilities. The price includes breakfast; premium twin rooms (small surcharge) also have TV and tea/coffee facilities.

University of Liverpool Halls of Residence, Roscoe & Gladstone Hall, Greenbank Lane (☎0151/794 6405). Inconveniently situated four miles out of the centre (bus #80) and only open June to Aug, but a useful fall-back.

YMCA, 56 Mount Pleasant (☎0151/709 9516). Separate floors of basic accommodation for men and women; singles and twins available. Breakfast included. The restaurant has bargain meals.

YWCA, 1 Rodney St (☎0151/709 7791). Cheap rooms for women only. Centrally heated and with communal kitchens and laundry facilities.

The City

The main sights are fairly widely scattered throughout the centre of Liverpool but you can easily walk between most of them, through cityscapes ranging from soulless shopping arcades to the surviving regal Georgian terraces around Rodney and Hope streets. Even the walk from the Anglican cathedral through the shops to Albert Dock will only take half an hour or so. The tourist offices can book you onto a variety of **guided walks and tours** (from £2.50), or make your own way using the themed trail leaflets on sale in the offices. **Public sculpture** abounds, from the statues of Victoria, Albert, Disraeli and Gladstone around St George's Hall to contemporary groupings like the assortment of suitcases and trunks at the Hope Street end of Mount Street.

Around Lime Street

Emerging from **Lime Street Station** – whose cast-iron train shed was the largest in the world on its completion in 1867 – you can't miss **St George's Hall**, one of Britain's finest Greek Revival buildings and a testament to the wealth generated from transatlantic trade. Once Liverpool's concert hall and crown courts, its tunnel-vaulted Great Hall is open to the public for monthly craft and antique fairs and for daily **guided tours** in summer (late-July & Aug Mon–Sat 11am–4pm; £1.50), when the exquisite floor, tiled

---

THE BEATLES IN LIVERPOOL

Liverpool has sustained its musical impetus ever since the Sixties and is still turning out some excellent bands, but none is ever likely to eclipse **The Beatles**. **Mathew Street**, ten minutes' walk west of Lime Street station, is where *The Cavern* used to be – once the womb of Merseybeat, it's become a little enclave of Beatles nostalgia, most of it bogus and typified by the Cavern Walks Shopping Arcade, with an awful bronze statue of the boys in the atrium. *The Cavern* itself saw 275 Beatles gigs between 1961 and 1963 and was where the band was first spotted by Brian Epstein; the club closed in 1966 and was partly demolished in 1973, though a latterday successor, the *Cavern Club* at 10 Mathew St, complete with souvenir shop, was rebuilt on half of the original site, using, it's claimed, the original bricks. The *Cavern Pub*, immediately across the way, is also a musical *arriviste*, boasting a coiffed Lennon lounging against the wall and an exterior "Cavern Wall of Fame", highlighting the names of all the bands who appeared at the club between 1957 and 1973. A few pubs, like *Rubber Soul* and *Lennon's Bar*, raise no more than a token toast to the soul of Beatlemania, embodied better at *The Beatles Shop*, 31 Mathew St, with the "largest range of Beatles gear in the world".

For the above, you'll have to head to the Albert Dock for **The Beatles Story** in the Britannia Vaults (daily: April–Sept 10am–6pm; Oct–March 10am–5pm; £6.45), tracing The Beatles' rise from the early days at *The Cavern* (re-created here) to their disparate solo careers, ending with John's death. Dedicated pilgrims will get more from the two-hour Beatles **Magical Mystery Tour** (July & Aug Mon–Fri & Sun 2.20pm, Sat 11.50am & 2.20pm; rest of year 2.20pm; book through Mersey Tourism, ☎0151/709 3285; £9.50), on board a customized double-decker bus staffed by guides with – in some cases – first-hand acquaintance with The Beatles. It leaves Albert Dock, visiting Strawberry Fields (a Salvation Army home), Penny Lane (an ordinary suburban street) and the terraced houses where the lads grew up. One of these, **20 Forthlin Road**, home of the McCartney family from 1955–1964, has been preserved by the National Trust and is now open to visitors who duly tramp round the 1950s terraced house where John and Paul wrote songs and where Paul's mother Mary died. The house is only accessible on a pre-booked minibus tour (June–Oct Wed–Sat; £4.50; £1.50; NT), which leaves half-a-dozen times daily from Speke Hall (see p.662) – the price includes the tour, the minibus to Forthlin Road and free access to Speke Hall grounds.

Beatlemania is wholeheartedly celebrated on August Bank Holiday Monday (the last Monday of the month) at the culmination of the annual Beatles Week and **Mathew Street Festival**, filling the town centre with wannabe moptops, jiving to the sounds of tunes that have been hummed and strummed in Liverpool since the first concert rocked *The Cavern*.

with thirty thousand precious Minton tiles, is on show. The hall's Willis organ, the third largest in Europe, is played during occasional recitals. Check on forthcoming events, lectures and other tours with Civic Halls (☎0151/707 2391). Beyond St George's Hall, the civic buildings along **William Brown Street** – the Walker Art Gallery, Central Library and Liverpool Museum – make their mark.

Walker Art Gallery

Liverpool's **Walker Art Gallery** on William Brown Street (Mon–Sat 10am–5pm, Sun noon–5pm; £3; free with NMGM Eight Pass) houses one of the country's finest provincial art collections, with pieces dating from the fourteenth century to the present day. A rolling refurbishment programme occasionally closes some galleries, or moves pictures from one to another. Pick up a floor plan on your way in, and watch out for the excellent series of explanatory leaflets in the various rooms which highlight schools of painting and explore artistic themes. There's a good range of Italian work on show, with Simone Martini's expressive *Christ Discovered in the Temple* (1342) forming a prelude to an array of mostly second-rank Renaissance art. An assertive Rembrandt self-portrait from 1630 is displayed alongside works by Poussin, Rubens and other seventeenth-century masters, but here, as in Manchester, British painting occupies centre stage. George Stubbs, England's greatest animal painter – and native Liverpudlian – shows off his preoccupation with horse anatomy in his painting of *Molly Longlegs* (1762), while Turner's maturing style is captured in the romantic *Linlithgo Palace* and the much later *Landscape*, its subject barely discernible in the washes of colour. Nothing could contrast more strongly than the contemporaneous work of the Pre-Raphaelites, whose nostalgic fastidiousness is typified by Millais' *Lorenzo and Isabella*. A group of Impressionists and Post-Impressionists including Degas, Cézanne and Monet drag the collection into the twentieth century, leading to pieces by Lucian Freud and an archetypal Hockney, *Peter Getting Out of Nick's Pool*. A twentieth-century gallery sees a changing selection of paintings and sculptures, while the museum also displays exhibits from its large applied-art collection – glassware, ceramics, precious metals, and sculpted furniture, largely retrieved from the homes of the city's early industrial businessmen. Contemporary work floods the building during the John Moores Exhibition, held here from October of odd-numbered years to the following January.

Liverpool Museum

The collections at the **Liverpool Museum**, William Brown Street (Mon–Sat 10am–5pm, Sun noon–5pm; £3; free with NMGM Eight Pass), are eclectic to say the least, from tarantulas in its basement "Vivarium" to a space research rocket on the top floor, and it's an appealing diversity which grows on you the longer you stay. The museum had its origins in the natural history collections bequeathed by the Earl of Derby in the mid-nineteenth century, and these have subsequently been augmented by some superior fossil, natural habitat and evolution exhibits. There's also a full dinosaur section, starring a set of dinosaur footprints found on the Wirral. Ethnographical collections from the Americas, Egypt, the Pacific Islands and West Africa contain much of interest too, while the tarantulas and other creepy-crawlies share the basement with the millionth Ford Escort to come off the Halewood assembly line. Another handy benefactor was Henry Blundell, eighteenth-century gentleman-collector and well-travelled Catholic, who gathered together Roman antiquities, busts, sculpture and funerary monuments and then built a replica of the Parthenon to house his private collection. The museum shows off a large selection of his antiquities; others are in the Walker Art Gallery. Make time too for the top-floor Space and Time galleries, and the Planetarium (Tues–Sun pm; £1); there's also a café, which has a summer terrace and views of the Liverpool skyline.

The cathedrals

On the hill behind Lime Street, off Mount Pleasant, rises the funnel-shaped Catholic **Metropolitan Cathedral of Christ the King** (Mon–Sat 8am–6pm, Sun 8am–5pm; free), denigratingly known as "Paddy's Wigwam" or the "Mersey Funnel". Built in the 1960s in the wake of the revitalizing Second Vatican Council, it was raised on top of the tentative beginnings of Sir Edwin Lutyens's grandiose project to outdo St Peter's in Rome. Bits of Lutyens's cathedral can be seen in the crypt. At the other end of the aptly named Hope Street, the Anglican **Liverpool Cathedral** (daily 8am–6pm; £1 donation requested) looks much more ancient but was actually completed eleven years later, in 1978, after 74 years in construction. The last of the great Neo-Gothic structures, Sir Giles Gilbert Scott's masterwork claims a smattering of superlatives: Britain's largest and the world's fifth largest cathedral, the world's tallest Gothic arches and the highest and heaviest bells. Not enough important people have died to fill out the stark pillarless interior, but a visit to see the beautiful stone tracery in the finely detailed Lady Chapel – the first part of the cathedral to be completed, in 1910 – and a look at Elizabeth Frink's last work, a bronze of Christ, pad out the free **guided tours** (times vary, call ☎0151/709 6271 for details). On a clear day, a trip up the 330ft **tower** (11am–4pm; £2) through the cavernous belfry is rewarded by views to the Welsh hills. In the southern arcade the **Elizabeth Hoare Embroidery Collection** (included in tower ticket) contains a manageable display of sumptuous ecclesiastical vestments and traces the art's history from the thirteenth century.

The city centre: Bold Street to the Pier Head

Having seen the Walker Art Gallery, Liverpool Museum and the cathedrals, you've seen the central showpiece attractions, but you may as well trace a route back through the city centre, stirring after years of neglect. **Bold Street** and its backstreet offshoots – Slater Street, Wood Street, Fleet Street – are busy reinventing themselves as café-land, with an increasing number of places opening in which you can sip a latte, neck a late-night beer or shop for punk records and vintage clothing. Concert Square, just off Bold Street, its space once occupied by a factory, was levelled to provide room for a warehouse-style bar development, whose outdoor seats are at a real premium in the summer. On neighbouring Wood Street, the **Open Eye Gallery**, at no. 28–32 (Tues–Fri 10.30am–5.30pm, Sat 10.30am–5pm; free) features renowned temporary exhibitions of photography and the media arts.

Bold Steet ends at Hanover Street, with the pedestrianized shopping street, Church Street continuing beyond. To the left, School Lane throws up the beautifully proportioned **Bluecoat Chambers**, built in 1717 as an Anglican boarding school for orphans and now a contemporary art gallery (Tues–Sat 10.30am–5pm; free) with a decent café and bookstore (Mon–Sat 9.30am–5pm) and arts centre (see p.665). The **Quiggins Centre** (Mon–Sat 10am–6pm), a bit further along at 12–16 School Lane, is a converted warehouse packed with ever-changing shoplets hawking records, posters, jewellery, clubwear and skateboards, plus a cheap café.

From School Lane turn right on Paradise St and walk down Whitechapel to **Queen Square** which has seen a lot of recent redevelopment. One of the neighbourhood's surviving Victorian warehouses, on the corner of Whitechapel, has re-emerged as the **Conservation Centre** (daily 10am–5pm; £3, free with NMGM Eight Pass; ☎0151/478 4999). This is where Merseyside's museums and galleries undertake their restoration work and give visitors a hands-on, behind-the-scenes look, and fascinating it is – you (and the touring school parties) will soon learn to identify fabrics and furniture beetles and how to get the rust off a gold disc. The centre's *Café Eros* is a light-filled space, well-suited for temporary art and photography exhibitions.

Heading on towards Pier Head, Mathew Street and the Cavern Quarter (see box on p.658) loom large, but rather than taking the most direct route to the ferry, don't pass up the opportunity to walk down Water Street. The Georgian **Town Hall** is a beauty and is open to the public in the summer (late-July & Aug Mon–Sat 11am–4pm; £1.50), while behind here, at 1 Rumford St, the **Western Approaches Operations Centre** (Mon–Thurs & Sat 10.30am–4.30pm, last admission 3.30pm; £4.75) fills about a third of the hundred-room underground complex where, from spring 1941 until the end of the war, the Anglo-American air-sea campaign was orchestrated. Sticking with Water Street for the final approach to Pier Head gives you a flavour of the city's nineteenth- and early-twentieth-century mercantile heyday, passing gems like the **Martins Bank Building** (now Barclays) with its lavish lobby, and the deeply resonant India Buildings and West Africa House.

The Pier Head

Though the tumult of shipping which once fought the current here has gone, the **Pier Head** landing stage remains the embarkation point for the **Mersey Ferries** to Woodside (for Birkenhead) and Seacombe (Wallasey). Ride one if only for the magnificent views of the Liverpool skyline and the prominent, 322-feet high **Royal Liver Building** (tours April–Sept by appointment only; call ☎0151/236 2748) – it's topped by the "Liver Birds", a couple of cormorants which have become the symbol of the city.

Straightforward ferry shuttles operate every thirty minutes during morning and evening rush hours (95p each way); at other times the boats run circular **heritage cruises** (hourly: Mon–Fri 10am–3pm, Sat & Sun 10am–6pm; £3.30; ☎0151/630 1030), complete with sappy commentary and repeated renditions of Gerry Marsden's *Ferry 'cross the Mersey*. If you're going to stop off at the **Seacombe Aquarium** (daily: summer 10am–6pm; winter 10am–4pm; £1.55), buy the joint ticket (£4.30).

It's all a long way from the simple rowboat crossing pioneered by medieval Benedictine monks who first wanted to cross the Mersey at this point. Even when Daniel Defoe visited Liverpool in the eighteenth century – when the city was first booming – he was taken by the rusticity of the river crossing "over the Mersee": having reached the city side he was surprised to find himself hoisted "on the shoulders of some honest Lancashire clown" and bundled through the shallows to the shore.

Albert Dock

Albert Dock, five minutes' walk south of the Pier Head, was built in 1846 when Liverpool's port was a world leader. It started to decline at the beginning of this century, as the new deep-draught ships were unable to berth here, and last saw service in 1972. A decade later the site was given a complete scrubdown and refit, with much of the space in the former warehouses being turned over to speciality shops and to monuments of the more meaningful economic activities that used to take place here. Billed as "Liverpool's Historic Waterfront" it's a type of rescued urban heritage that's been copied throughout the country, but rarely as successfully as here. There's free **parking** – follow the city-centre signs – and **buses** every twenty minutes during the day from Queen Square bus station. All the museums have admission charges: the Maritime Museum, HM Customs Museum and Museum of Liverpool Life are part of the NMGM Eight Pass scheme (see p.654), while the **Waterfront Pass** (£9.50) saves you money if you want to see the lot. Passes are available at the individual museums or at the Albert Dock tourist office, itself a useful source of information about what's on at the dock.

The **Merseyside Maritime Museum** (daily 10am–5pm; £3; free with NMGM Eight Pass) fills one wing of the Albert Dock and in summer also takes over part of Canning Dock for floating displays. A trip through the museum can easily take two hours. Spread over four floors, it has sections on the history of Liverpool's evolution as a port and shipbuilding centre, and models of seacraft – from Samoan rafts to opulent passenger liners. An illuminating display details Liverpool's pivotal role as a springboard for over nine million emigrants – the Irish potato famine and a multiplicity of European wars, combined with the lure of gold and free land, brought people scurrying here to buy their passage to North America or Australia. To cater for them, short-stay lodging houses sprang up all over the centre, as illustrated in an 1854 street scene. On board the ships – there's a walk-through example – people were packed into dark, noisy ranks of bunks where they "puffed, groaned, swore, vomited, prayed, moaned and cried". Meanwhile, the **HM Customs and Excise Museum**, inside the Maritime Museum, gives the lowdown on smuggling and revenue collection.

The Maritime Museum, though, is at its best in its "Transatlantic Slavery" exhibit, which manages to be enlightening, shocking and refreshingly honest, and banishes years of Eurocentric excuses to expose the true horror of the exploitation of African slaves who were kidnapped, abused and sold as property. The slave trade continued for four hundred years up to 1900; even after official abolition in 1807 the number of slaves shipped to sugar plantations in the Americas ran into millions. The conditions they endured on the transatlantic voyage are illustrated by a reconstruction of a slave ship, echoing with haunting voices reading from diaries of slaves and slavers, telling of rape, torture and death. The exhibition winds up with a video of Africans resident in Britain airing their views on the impact of slavery and the legacy of racism, after which you'll probably be ready to mull over what you've seen in the museum's excellent top-floor **café**, approached through a hall hung with nineteenth-century racist propaganda, countered by protest cartoons from the abolitionist camp.

The neighbouring **Tate Gallery Liverpool** (Tues–Sun 10am–6pm; free; special exhibitions usually £2.50–5) is the country's foremost twentieth-century art showcase outside the capital, drawing from the same pool of paintings and sculpture as its London cousin, and often displaying them more successfully in its spacious and well-lit rooms. Popular retrospectives and an ever-changing display of individual works are its bread-and-butter – break up visits to the gallery and the dock with espressos in the Tate's dockside café-bar/bistro.

The **Museum of Liverpool Life** (daily 10am–5pm; £3, free with NMGM Eight Pass) lies across the dock. Particularly revealing about the hardships that have moulded the resilient Scouse character, it has excellent sections on the city's traditional work, with investigations of the lives of ordinary shipwrights, stevedores, carters and seamen. The role of trade unions is traced, from protests in the eighteenth century to the 1981 and 1983 Peoples' March for Jobs, and there's space too for coverage of topics as diverse as the women's suffrage movement and the social unrest that led to the Toxteth riots in the 1980s. It is not all doom and gloom though – in the popular-culture sections, Merseyside football gets good coverage (though there's no mention of poor old Tranmere Rovers), as does Aintree's Grand National, music from the Sixties to the Nineties (with a working jukebox), the homegrown soap *Brookside* and local writers like Alan Bleasdale, Willy Russell, Beryl Bainbridge and Carla Lane.

The outskirts

Located near Liverpool's airport, six miles southeast of the centre, **Speke Hall** (Easter–Oct Tues–Sun 1–5.30pm; Nov to mid-Dec Sat & Sun 1–4.30pm; gardens Easter–Oct same times as house, Nov–Easter Tues–Sun 1–4.30pm; house & gardens £4.10; gardens only £1.50; NT) is one of the country's finest examples of Elizabethan timbered architecture. Sitting in an oasis of rhododendrons, the house encloses a beautifully proportioned courtyard overlooked by myriad diamond panes. Highlights of the interior are the Jacobean plasterwork in the Great Parlour and the Great Hall's carved oak panel. Bus #80/180 from Paradise Street in the city centre to the airport runs within half a mile of the entrance.

For a glimpse of one of the more benign aspects of Merseyside's industrial past, take the Merseyrail under the river to **Port Sunlight**, a garden village created in 1888 by industrialist William Hesketh Lever for the workers at his soap factory. The project, similar in scope to those of Titus Salt at Saltaire near Bradford (see p.751) and John Cadbury at Bournville in Birmingham (see p.554), is explained at the **Port Sunlight Heritage Centre**, 95 Greendale Rd (April–Oct daily 10am–4pm; Nov–March Sat & Sun 10am–4pm; 40p), set amid the open-planned housing estates. Off Greendale Road, a little further from Port Sunlight station, the **Lady Lever Art Gallery** (Mon–Sat 10am–5pm; Sun noon–5pm; £3; free with NMGM Eight Pass) houses a small collection of English eighteenth-century furniture, Pre-Raphaelite paintings by artists such as Rossetti and Ford Madox Brown, Wedgwood china, porcelain and assorted Greek and Roman artefacts. There's also a nice café.

Eating, drinking and nightlife

Liverpool's dining scene is slowly shifting up a gear and there's now a fair choice of classy **restaurants** alongside a great selection of cafés and budget places. Most are around Hardman and Bold streets, at Albert Dock, and along spruced-up Nelson Street, heart of Liverpool's **Chinatown**, which stretches around the corner onto Berry Street. **Café-bars** have made a belated appearance, both down at the Albert Dock and in the central streets off Bold Street: Concert Square, especially, has three of them, where you can hog the pavement tables until 2am at the weekends. Most café-bars also serve creditable food: we pick out the best of the bunch in the listings below.

Liverpool's **pubs** stay open later than most, with many now serving until 1am or 2am. Several act as **live music** venues for up-and-coming bands, who tend to disappear from the local circuit as soon as they achieve fame. The **Liverpool Now** festival (every October) sees local bands playing in various venues around the city for a fortnight. The rise of late-opening bars has stolen a good deal of trade from the **clubs**, which are mainly notable for their lack of pretence, fashion playing second string to dancing and drinking. The evening paper, the *Liverpool Echo*, has listings of what's going on, or pick up flyers in the shops, bars and cafés.

Cafés

Bluecoat Café Bar, Bluecoat Chambers, School Lane. Mainly vegetarian food – salad bar, baked potatoes and dips – served throughout the day. Closed Sun.

Brook Café, Quiggins Centre, 12–16 School Lane. Hipster hangout on the top floor for breakfast (10am–noon) and all-day café meals. Closed Sun.

Café Tabac, 126 Bold St. Popular licensed café with veggie bohemian leanings. Mon–Sat till 11pm, Sun till 5pm.

Coopers Food Hall, 63–67 Bold St. A deli/butcher/bakery with eat-in "brasserie" section for breakfasts, sandwiches and sushi. Closed Sun.

Everyman Bistro, 9–11 Hope St. Cool theatre-basement hangout with great quiche, pizza and salad-type meals for around a fiver. It's licensed, too, so it's not a bad place for a late-night drink. Mon–Sat noon–midnight.

The Refectory, Liverpool Anglican Cathedral, St James' Mount. Appetizing snacks and lunches under the Gothic arches, and with terrace seating, too.

Starbuck's, 2 Castle St. Liverpool's branch of the American chain. Real coffee in all its guises, and some comfy seats in which to enjoy it. Closed Sun.

Walker Art Gallery Tea Room, William Brown St. Gallery café with daily specials, drinks and snacks.

Cafés-bars

Beluga Bar, 40 Wood St. Cool basement space that's great for just a drink, or come to eat – there's a changing, seasonal menu. Mon–Sat 11am–2am.

Café Blue, Albert Dock. Brick-vaulted café-bar with upstairs grill – a useful stop for a cheap lunch (hotpot, salad niçoise or chilli for under a fiver), cappuccino, a pasta or tapas dinner or a late-night drink. Mon–Thurs & Sun noon–11pm, Fri & Sat noon–1am.

Life Café, 1a Bold St. The eighteenth-century Lyceum Library makes a grand backdrop for this late-opening café-bar, serving pasta, pizza, salads, Thai curries and sandwiches. Live music and comedy some nights; also home to *Voodooroom* club nights. Mon–Wed 10am–1am, Thurs–Sat 10am–2am, Sun 10am–10pm.

Metz, Baker House, Rainford Gardens, off Mathew St. Great sounds, food and drink in the Cavern Quarter. Mon–Thurs & Sun noon–11pm, Fri & Sat noon–midnight.

Taste, Tate Gallery, Albert Dock. Industrial-lite café-bar at the Tate serves bangers and mash, nachos, burgers, salads and sandwiches during the day. In the evening the Mediterranean comes out to play, with varied tapas, paella and roast vegetable dishes. Sun, Tues & Wed 10am–6pm, Thurs–Sat 10am–11pm.

Restaurants

Armadillo Restaurant, 31 Mathew St (☎0151/236 4123). Mediterranean-style dishes with a vegetarian bias. The menu is more extensive in the evening, but you can eat for half the price if you arrive before 6.45pm (Tues–Fri). Closed Sun & Mon. Moderate to Expensive.

Becher's Brook, 29a Hope St (☎0151/707 0005). The city's best restaurant. Seasonal Modern-British dishes served with panache in a classic Georgian house. Closed Sat lunch & all Sun. Expensive.

Casa Italia, 40 Stanley St (☎0151/227 5774). Lively trattoria with better than average pasta and pizza dishes. Inexpensive.

Est Est Est, Unit 6, Edward Pavilion, Albert Dock (☎0151/708 6969). Authentic pizza and pasta – you may have to wait in line at weekends. Inexpensive.

Far East, 27–35 Berry St (☎0151/709 6072). One of the longest-serving and most reliable of Liverpool's Cantonese eating houses: a fairly no-frills operation, but with authentic *dim sum* (noon–6pm), noodles, casseroles, rice plates and other classics. Moderate.

The Lower Place, Philharmonic Hall, Hope St (☎0151/210 1955). Fast winning friends with its char-grilling, oven-roasting, sun-drying ways. Not cheap, but always enjoyable. Closed Sun. Expensive.

Not Sushi, Imperial Court, Exchange St East (☎0151/709 8894); and at Bar XS, 80 Bold St (☎0151/707 8777). Japanese noodle bar also branching out into grilled chicken, gyoza dumplings and – despite the name – sushi. Inexpensive to Moderate.

Number Seven Café, 7 Falkner St (☎0151/709 9633). Highly popular, laid-back restaurant with a daily changing blackboard menu of contemporary flavours – soups, salads, fish and meat. Kitchen closes at 9pm. The next-door deli is a treat too. Moderate.

Valparaíso, 4 Hardman St (☎0151/708 6036). Chilean and other Latin-American dishes. Early evening specials served Tues–Thurs 5–7pm. Closed Sun & Mon. Moderate.

Ziba, 15–19 Berry St (☎0151/708 8870). Stylish space (formerly a car showroom) now serving cutting-edge Modern-British food along with risottos, Oriental flourishes and vegetarian specialities. Closed Sun eve. Expensive.

Pubs

The Baltic Fleet, 33a Wapping. Restored pub with age-old shipping connections – opposite Albert Dock and across from the youth hostel. It's got a great period feel and is known for its fine food and local beer.

The Dispensary, 87 Renshaw St. Entirely synthetic but highly sympathetic re-creation of a Victorian pub using rescued and antique wood, glass and tiles. A real-ale choice.

The Flying Picket, 24 Hardman St. A friendly local tucked in behind the Trade Union centre. *The Picket*, upstairs, is one of the best venues for local bands.

The Grapes, 25 Mathew St. Busy city-centre pub in the Cavern Quarter, where John, Paul, George and Ringo once downed pints between sets at *The Cavern*.

Guinan's, 15 Slater St. The best of several Irish-themed pubs to have sprung up in recent years. Open until 2am, often with live bands and no cover charge.

The Lisbon, 35 Victoria St. Traditional pub with mixed gay and straight clientele; disco Mon & Wed.

The Philharmonic, 36 Hope St. A superb, traditional watering-hole where the main attractions – the beer aside – are the mosaic floors, tiling, gilded wrought-iron gates and the marble decor in the gents.

White Star, Rainford Gardens, off Mathew St. Enjoyable drinking haunt that's one of the better locals in the city centre; The Beatles certainly used to think so.

Ye Cracke, 13 Rice St. Crusty backstreet pub off Hope Street, much loved by the young Lennon, and with a great jukebox.

Clubs

The Blue Angel, 108 Seel St (☎0151/428 1213). A long-standing student club known locally as "The Razz". In their earlier incarnation as The Silver Beatles, the Fab Four appeared here.

Cream, Wolstenholme Square, off Hanover St (☎0151/709 1693). One of Liverpool's most popular clubs, often featuring big DJ names (when the cover charge will be steep). A varied round of club nights and all-nighters attracts coachloads from across the country; call for details.

The Lomax, 34 Cumberland St (☎0151/707 9977). Indie band venue with nightly gigs. Cover £3–10.

Arts, sport and entertainment

The Royal Liverpool Philharmonic Orchestra, up with Manchester's Hallé as the north-west's best, dominates the city's **classical music scene** and often plays at the Philharmonic Hall and the Everyman Theatre. The Anglican cathedral is also a favourite spot for classical concerts, with its good acoustics and inexpensive tickets. **Theatre** is well entrenched in the city, at a variety of venues. Annual **festivals** include the Hope Street Art Festival (June); a celebration of African arts and music in Africa Oye (June); the Summer Pops (July), when the Royal Philharmonic sets itself up beneath a huge marquee on King's Dock to perform a series of classical concerts; the **Brouhaha Street Theatre Festival** (August), which involves performances by a host of European theatre groups; and the **Mathew Street Festival** (August), a free shindig, with local and national street performers playing the best of The Beatles.

Liverpool's most popular recreational activity, however is **football**. Liverpool football club has never quite recovered its glory days of the Seventies and Eighties, but its supporters are counted among the nation's best and most loyal. Everton, the city's less glamorous and recently far less successful side, command equally intense devotion but rather smaller crowds, so there's more chance of getting in to see them. Liverpool play at Anfield (ticket office ☎0151/260 8680) and offer a tour around the well-stocked museum, trophy room and dressing rooms (daily 10am–5pm; museum and tour £8, museum only £5; booking essential ☎0151/260 6677). Everton play at Goodison Park (ticket office ☎0151/330 2300; tours Mon, Wed, Fri & Sun 11am & 2pm; £4; booking advised).

The first Saturday in April is **Grand National Day** at Aintree – the "World's Greatest Steeplechase". The race is the culmination of a meeting that starts on the previous Thursday, with prices for entry into the grounds ranging from £7 to £65. Catch the Merseyrail to Aintree and buy a ticket on the gate or book on ☎0151/523 2600. A new Visitor Centre (☎0151/522 2922) lets you ride the National on a race simulator.

Bluecoat Arts Centre, School Lane (☎0151/709 5297). Eclectic mix of events – drama, dance, poetry, comedy, music and art exhibitions; always worth a look.

Cinemas: Odeon, London Rd (☎0870/505 0007); the Virgin 8 Edge Lane Retail Park (☎0151/252 055).

Everyman Theatre, Hope St (☎0151/709 4776). Presents everything from Shakespeare to Jarman, as well as concerts, exhibitions, dance and musical performances.

Liverpool Empire Theatre, Lime St (☎0151/709 1555). The city's largest theatre, a venue for touring West End shows, opera, ballet and music. The Beatles' first major gig was here in 1962.

Philharmonic Hall, Hope St (☎0151/709 3789). Home of the Royal Liverpool Philharmonic Orchestra, and with a full programme of other concerts. Shows classic films once a month.

Royal Court Theatre, Roe St (☎0151/709 4321). Refurbished Art Deco theatre and concert hall, which sees regular pop and rock concerts among other events.

Unity Theatre, Hope Place (☎0151/709 4988). Puts on the city's most adventurous range of contemporary works.

Listings

Airport ☎0151/486 8877 or 448 1234.

Banks and exchanges American Express, 54 Lord St (☎0151/708 9202); Thomas Cook, 55 Lord St (☎0151/236 1951). You can also change money at the two tourist offices, the two main post offices (see below) and at the airport.

Bookshops Most of the bookshops are along Bold Street: Dillons at no. 14, Waterstones at no. 52 and the more radical News from Nowhere at no. 112.

Buses National Express (☎0990/808080); Merseytravel (☎0151/236 7676).

Car rental Avis, 113 Mulberry St (☎0151/709 4737); Budget, 418 Scotland Rd (☎0151/298 1888); Europcar, St Vincent St (☎0151/708 9150); Hertz, 8 Brownlow Hill (☎0151/709 3337).

Ferries Isle of Man Steam Packet Company (☎08705/523523); Norse Irish Ferries (☎0151/944 1010); Sea Cat (☎08705/523523).

Hospital Royal Liverpool University Hospital, Prescot Street (☎0151/706 2000).

Laundry Liver Launderette, 2b Princess Rd (Mon–Fri 9am–6pm, Sun 9am–4pm).

Left luggage Lime Street Station, daily 7am–10pm; £2.

Pharmacy Moss Chemists, 68–70 London Rd. Open daily until 11pm.

Police The Cop Shop, Church St (☎0151/709 6010).

Post offices City-centre offices at 23–33 Whitechapel, and The Lyceum, 1 Bold St.

Taxis Mersey Cabs (☎0151/298 2222); Davy Liver (☎0151/709 4646); Computer Cabs (☎0151/709 5553).

Travel agent Discounted and student tickets from USIT Campus, at YHA shop, 25 Bold St (☎0151/709 9200), plus branches at both universities.

Trains for all enquiries, call ☎0345/484950.

Blackpool

Shamelessly brash **BLACKPOOL** is the archetypal British seaside resort, its "Golden Mile" of piers, fortune-tellers, amusement arcades, tram and donkey rides, fish-and-chip shops, candyfloss stalls, fun pubs and bingo halls making no concessions to anything but low-brow fun-seeking of the finest kind. From ukelele-strumming George Formby and his "little stick of Blackpool rock" to today's predatory, half-dressed gangs of stag and hen parties, few visitors, then or now, are in any doubt about the point of a holiday here. There are seven miles of wide sandy beach backed by an unbroken chain of hotels and guest houses, and though the sea-water quality is still highly debatable, even after heavy investment in a new sewage system, there's nothing wrong with the beach itself – except for the crowds packing the central stretches on hot summer days. Sixteen million people come here each year. If you want a bit more isolation than those numbers allow, come in winter when there's nothing more bracing than a lonely tramp along the windswept sands – "bracing", of course, as Paul Theroux points out, being "the northern euphemism for stinging cold".

Wealthy visitors were already summer holidaying in Blackpool at the end of the eighteenth century, and while it took a day to get there from Manchester by carriage and two days from Yorkshire, the town remained a select destination. The coming of the railway in 1846 made Blackpool what it is today: within thirty years, there were piers, promenades and theatres for the thousands who descended. The **Winter Gardens**, with its barrel-vaulted ballroom, the Baroque **Grand Theatre** on Church Street, Blackpool's own "Eiffel Tower" on the seafront and other refined diversions were built to cater to the tastes of the first influx, but it was the Central Pier's "open air dancing for the working classes" that heralded the crucial change of accent. Suddenly Blackpool was favoured destination for the "Wakes Weeks", when whole Lancashire mill towns descended for their annual seven days' holiday.

Attention to the accents tells you that Lancashire, Yorkshire and Scotland still provide the bulk of the resort's visitors, who show no signs of drying up. Where other British holiday resorts have suffered from the rivalry of cheap foreign packages, Blackpool has simply gone from strength to strength by shrewdly providing exactly what its visitors want. Underneath the populist veneer there's a sophisticated marketing approach which balances ever more elaborate rides and attractions with well-grounded traditional entertainment. The best example of this is the way the town has cleverly extended its season: when other resorts begin to close up for the winter, Blackpool's main season is just beginning, as over half a million light bulbs are used to create **the Illuminations** which decorate the promenade from the beginning of September to early November. The first static display took place in 1912, was re-created periodically between the wars and has been an annual event since 1949, "switched on" each year by publicity-hungry TV and pop stars.

Arrival and accommodation

Blackpool's main **train station** is Blackpool North (direct trains from Manchester, Preston and London), half a dozen blocks up Talbot Road from North Pier. A few steps down Talbot Road, towards the sea, stands the combined National Express and local **bus station**; town buses run from here direct to the Pleasure Beach, though it's more fun to walk down to the front, take a tram and get your bearings. Blackpool's **airport** – which handles regular flights to and from the Isle of Man – lies two miles south of the centre; bus #22/22a will take you there from the bus station. The main **tourist office** at 1 Clifton St (Easter to early Nov Mon–Sat 9am–5pm, Sun 10am–3.45pm; rest of year Mon–Thurs & Sat 8.45am–4.45pm, Fri 8.45am–4.15pm; ☎01253/478222) is on the corner of Talbot Road, five minutes' walk from the stations; a seasonal office sits on the prom opposite Blackpool Tower. You can pick up maps and hefty accommodation brochures at the tourist office; it also sells Travel Cards (one-day, £4.50; three-day £12; five-day £15; seven-day £16) for use on all local buses and trams.

Blackpool claims to have more **hotel beds** than Portugal, a plausible boast when whole blocks of streets, particularly those set back from the promenade between North and Central piers, are devoted to guest houses. Prices are generally low (from £15 per person, even less out of season), but rise at weekends during the Illuminations. In peak season, it's simply a matter of looking for vacancy signs or asking the tourist office for help – anything cheap between North and Central piers is guaranteed to be noisy; for more peace and quiet (an unusual request in Blackpool, it has to be said), look for places along the more restful North Shore, beyond North Pier. You could also contact one of the umbrella organizations representing scores of central hotels, like the Blackpool Hotel and Guest House Association (☎01253/621891), which can match your requirements with a particular hotel. There are local **campsites**, but none are particularly near the town and, with B&B prices being as they are, no great savings are to be made by spending the night under canvas.

Accommodation

The Garfield, 22 Springfield Rd (☎01253/628060; no credit cards; ①), two blocks west of Talbot Road, is welcoming, central and convenient for station and town; slightly pricier en-suite rooms are available too. *Boltonia*, 124–126 Albert Rd (☎01253/620248; no credit cards; ②) marks a qualitative step up. For those wanting a vegan guest house, there is the non-smoking *Wildlife Hotel*, 39 Woodfield Rd (☎01253/346143; no credit cards; ①), situated off the promenade halfway between Central and South piers. Along North Shore, a mile or so from the action, the grid west of Warbreck Hill Road has hundreds more options. Rooms are generally larger and better equipped here in detached properties like *Grosvenor View*, 7–9 King Edward Ave (☎01253/352 851; ③).

In the end, you get what you pay for, and if you can afford it Blackpool is the place to splash out on some swankier digs, insulated from hoi polloi: the *Clifton Hotel*, on the North Pier prom at Talbot Square (☎01253/621481; ⑤) is a beauty with fine sea views, while the superior *Imperial*, further up North Promenade (☎01253/623971, *imperialblackpool@paramount-hotels.co.uk*; ⑧), is the politician's conference favourite, with a good bar and restaurant. A couple of miles inland, near the zoo and across from Stanley Park, the *De Vere* on East Park Drive (☎01253/838866; ⑦) is a reclusive retreat set in its own grounds, with a fine indoor pool.

The Town

With seven miles of beach – the tide ebb is a full half a mile, leaving plenty of sand at low tide – and accompanying promenade, you'll want to jump on and off the electric **trams** if you plan to get up and down much between the piers. South Pier to North Pier – between which lies most of what there is to see and do – costs 80p, though Travel Cards are available, too. Most of the town-centre shops, bars and cafés lie between Central and North piers.

Blackpool Pleasure Beach

The major event in town is Blackpool's **Pleasure Beach** on the South Promenade (March–Easter Sat & Sun 10am–8pm; Easter–June Mon–Fri 2–8pm, Sat & Sun 10am–10pm; July–Nov 5 daily 10am–11pm; hours can vary, call ☎01253/341033), just south of South Pier – complete with its own train station to help funnel over seven million annual visitors directly into what's billed as "Britain's biggest tourist attraction". Entrance to the amusement park is free, but you'll have to fork out for the superb array of "white knuckle" rides including "The Big One", the world's fastest roller coaster (85mph) which involves a terrifying near-vertical drop from 235ft. This is bad enough, though the "PlayStation", whooshes you up a 200ft steel tower at 80mph and then drops you back down in free-fall. After these, the Pleasure Beach's wonderful array of antique wooden rollercoasters – "woodies" to aficionados – seem like kids' stuff, but each is unique. The original "Big Dipper" was invented at Blackpool in 1923 and still thrills; the "Wild Mouse" (1958) and, best of all, the "Grand National" (1935) – whose 3300ft twin track races you against a parallel car – are both equally, excitingly, rattly. Before each one sets off, the public-service announcement intones "Please do not wave your hands in the air" – when any self-respecting woodie rider knows that's exactly what you have to do. If you're not leaving until you've been on everything – a sensible course of action – buy one of the ticket books (£20), which saves you paying a pound or two a time to ride (£4.20 for "The Big One").

The seafront and the tower

Across the road, the **Sandcastle** (June–Oct daily 10am–5.30pm; Nov–May Sat & Sun only; £5) is the only place you are likely to want to swim. With every aquatic diversion kept at a constant 29°C it can be a welcome respite from the biting sea air. Jump a tram for the ride up to **Central Pier** with its 108-feet high revolving Big Wheel. The **Sea-Life Centre** (daily 10am–6pm; to 10pm Fri & Sat in summer; £5.50) here is one of the country's best, with eight-foot sharks looming at you as you march through a glass tunnel. For a taste of what Blackpool attractions used to be like, you could then hit **Louis Tussauds Waxworks** (daily 10am–10pm; £3.50) – exactly as you would expect, plus a "highly educational" adults-only anatomy section for an extra pound.

Blackpool's cast-iron **piers** also strike a traditional note, the first one (North Pier), opened in 1863, is now a listed building. Elegant structures themselves, they've been covered ever since with arcades and amusements, while much of what passes for evening family entertainment – TV comics and variety shows – takes place in the various pier theatres. Between Central and North piers stands the 518-feet **Blackpool Tower** – the skyline's only real touch of grace – erected in 1894 when it was thought that the Northwest really ought not to be outdone by Paris. It's now marketed as "Tower World" (Easter to early Nov daily 10am–11pm; rest of year Sat 10am–11pm, Sun 10am–6pm; £6.50; times and prices can vary, call ☎01253/622242) which offers a ride up to the top (where there's a postbox), an unnerving walk on the see-through glass floor, plus a visit to the Edwardian ballroom and various other attractions. From the very early days, there's been a Moorish-inspired **circus** (June–Oct 2 shows daily except Fri; £6.50; combined ticket with Tower £9) between the tower's legs, which still functions, though in the spirit of the times it's now animal-free.

If you've seen and been on everything mentioned so far you'll have been here for days, spent a fortune and thoroughly enjoyed yourself. These, it has to be said, are just the A-list attractions – indefatigable holidaymakers also take in Blackpool's zoo and model village on East Park Drive, the summer circus at the Pleasure Beach, or any one of a number of pleasure flights, go-kart rinks, children's play areas, ten-pin bowling alleys or other jollifications.

Eating, drinking and nightlife

Eating revolves around the typical British seaside fare of fish and chips, available all over town, but at its supreme best in *Harry Ramsden's*, 60–63 The Promenade, on the corner of Church Street near the Tower; the celebrated Yorkshire chippie chain has a takeaway counter too. Even more traditional seaside food is available from the glorious, wood-panelled, 120-year-old *Robert's Oyster Bar*, 92 The Promenade, near the base of the Tower, where you can buy oysters, cockles and mussels, or fish platters then wash them down with a Guinness from the *Mitre* pub around the corner. Given the sheer volume of customers, other restaurants don't have to try too hard: you'll have no trouble finding cheap roasts, pizzas, Chinese or Indian food, but might struggle if you're seeking a bit more sophistication. *Lagoonda*, 37 Queen St (☎01253/293 837), off Talbot Square, is a

---

GAY BLACKPOOL

Blackpool has become one of the most popular gay resorts in the country, with around forty hotels and guest houses that welcome, or cater specifically for, a gay clientele. Blackpool tourist office can supply a full gay **accommodation** list, but good places to try first include *Raffles Hotel*, set back from Central Pier at 73–75 Hornby Rd (☎01253/294713; ②); *Mardi Gras*, 41–43 Lord St (☎01253/751087; ②), the all-male *Trades Hotel*, 51–55 Lord St (☎01253/294812; ②), and the *Amalfi Guest House*, for women, at 19–21 Eaves St (☎01253/622971; ①).

There's **nightlife** to match, with *Funny Girls* the most high-profile venue. *Flamingos*, opposite the train station at the top of Talbot Road (☎01253/624901), is the largest and liveliest gay club outside London, with four storeys of dance floors. Gay **bars** include the *Flying Handbag*, 170 Talbot Rd (☎01253/625522); *Basil's on the Strand*, 9 The Strand (☎01253/294109); *Lucy's Bar*, beneath *Rumours* in Talbot Square (☎01253/293204), and the *Cow Bar*, inland at Cookson and Church streets (☎01253/623537).

party-time Afro-Caribbean restaurant with surprisingly good food and service given that the staff have to spend their time negotiating the limbo bar. If you really want a blowout, head for the expensive *September Brasserie*, 15–17 Queen St (☎01253/623282; closed Sun & Mon), or the refined *Palm Court Restaurant* at the *Imperial*.

If you like your **nightlife** late, loud and libidinous, summertime Blackpool has few English peers. In all the pubs and clubs, young men can expect to have their attire and demeanour given the once-over by the hired hulks at the door; "girls" and "ladies" can expect free drinks and entry and a lot of largely good-natured amorous jousting. *Yates' Wine Lodge* has two popular branches, in Talbot Square and between Central and South piers where you can sip an amontillado sherry or champagne on draught. There's a rowdy bar in the *Clifton Hotel*, at North Pier; and a plethora of Irish theme bars, notably *O'Neill's* on the corner of Talbot Road and Abingdon Street, and *Finn's* on Talbot Square. The *Pump and Truncheon*, 13 Bonny St, behind the Sea Life Centre, is a real-ale pub, while the *Raikes*, half a mile inland on Liverpool Road, also has good beer, occasionally decent jazz/blues bands, and a place in local history – the Great Blondin once performed his tightrope act here.

For **dancing**, local opinion favours *Main Entrance*, at the Central Promenade, 100 yards south of the Tower, whose *Federation* club nights bring in star DJs. *Funny Girls*, a transvestite-run bar on Queen St (☎01253/291144), at Queen Square, has nightly shows which attract long (gay and straight) queues (see box on p.669 for more on the gay scene). Specific **music** spots to look out for include the *Tache* in Cookson Street, behind the Talbot Road bus station, which has live rock, pop and indie bands, plus house and chart sounds in its *Barny's* club. *Blackpool Opry*, 181–189 Church St, is the place for country music and line dancing. Otherwise, **entertainment** is based very heavily on family shows, musicals, veteran TV comedians, crooners and stage spectaculars put on at a variety of end-of-pier and Pleasure Beach theatres or historic venues like the *Grand Theatre* (☎01253/290190) and *Opera House* on Church St (☎01253/627786).

The Ribble Valley

When the nineteenth-century cotton weavers of Preston enjoyed a rare break from their industry they took to the bucolic retreats of the **Ribble Valley**, which cuts through the heart of northern Lancashire to the River Ribble's source in the Yorkshire Dales. In stark contrast to the conurbations to the south, the valley – then, as now – paraded a stream of small market towns and isolated villages set among verdant fields and rolling hills. Much of the northwestern part of the region is occupied by thinly populated grouse moorland known as the **Forest of Bowland** – the name "forest" is used in its traditional sense of "a royal hunting ground", and much of the land still belongs to the Crown. What few trees do grow here are clustered in the valleys, which are accessible only by unclassified roads that follow former cattle droving tracks. **Public transport** is limited to the train service from Manchester and Blackburn, or buses from Preston, to the market town of **Clitheroe** on the forest's southern fringes; from there, buses run out to Dunsop Bridge, Newton and **Slaidburn** (with connections on to Settle in Yorkshire), the three tiny villages in the heart of the region. Hikers can follow the course of the river from its source to the estuary along the seventy-mile **Ribble Way**, which passes through Clitheroe: route guides are available from local bookshops and tourist offices.

Clitheroe

A tidy little market town on the banks of the River Ribble, **CLITHEROE** is best seen from the terrace of its empty **Norman Keep** which towers above the Ribble Valley floor. From here, the small centre is laid out before you and, if there's little else specific to see

– save a **Castle Museum** (May–Sept daily 11am–5pm; rest of the year closed Thurs & Fri; £1.50) in the extensive grounds – you can at least spend an hour or two browsing around the shops and old pubs. There's been a **market** in town since the thirteenth century: the current affair is held off King Street every Tuesday, Thursday and Saturday.

An obvious target is Pendle Hill, a couple of miles to the east, where the ten **Pendle Witches** allegedly held the diabolic rites that led to their hanging in 1612. The evidence against them came mainly from one small child, but nonetheless a considerable mythology has grown up around the witches, whose memory is perpetuated by a hilltop gathering each Halloween. With a car, you could also run out to the ruined Cistercian abbey at Whalley (a few miles south of Clitheroe) or the Roman museum at Ribchester (southwest).

Ribble Way walkers might be glad of the town's accommodation options – full details from the **tourist office**, at 14 Market Place (Mon–Sat 9am–5pm; ☎01200/425566) – but you're unlikely to stop otherwise. There are superior café **meals** at *Mansells* in Swan Courtyard (closed Sun), off the main street. Pedal Power on Waddington Road (☎01200/422066) can sort you out with a **mountain bike** for in-depth exploration of the Forest of Bowland or nearby Gisburn Forest.

The Forest of Bowland

Heading northwest from Clitheroe on the B6478, brings you to the **Forest of Bowland** just beyond Waddington, with a short run over the fells to **NEWTON**, a village centred on the excellent *Parkers Arms* pub. It's two miles west of here to **DUNSOP BRIDGE**, a duck-riddled riverside hamlet from where an old drover's track (now a very minor road) known as the Trough of Bowland begins its twenty-mile slog across the tops to Lancaster. Those in the know make their way the couple of miles south from here to the splendid *Inn at Whitewell* (☎01200/448222; ⑤), which serves fabulous food and has a welcoming, old-fashioned bar.

Keep to the B road past Newton and it's a couple of miles northeast to **SLAIDBURN**, the most substantial and attractive of the Forest's settlements. Hoary stone cottages fronted by a strip of aged cobbles set the tone – a truly ancient **inn**, the *Hark to Bounty* (☎01200/446246; ③), and a popular **youth hostel** (☎01200/446656; closed Oct–March), itself a former inn, complete the picture. There's also accommodation at *Pages Farm* on Woodhouse Lane (☎01200/446205; no credit cards; ①), half a mile from the pub, and snacks and drinks at the *Riverbank Tearooms* next to the car park.

Lancaster and around

LANCASTER, Lancashire's county town, dates back at least as far as the Roman occupation, though only the scant remains of a bath-house and traces of the fort wall survive from that period. It became an important port on the slave triangle, and it's the legacy of predominantly Georgian buildings from that time that gives the town its character. It's no surprise that many people choose to spend a night here on the way to the Lakes or Dales to the north, and it's an easy side-trip the few miles west to the resort of **Morecambe** if the lure of the beach becomes too strong.

Arrival

Lancaster is a frequent stop on the West Coast rail line from London to Scotland and on the north–south coach routes. From the combined local bus and National Express station on Cable Street it's a five-minute walk to the **tourist office** at 29 Castle Hill (April–June &

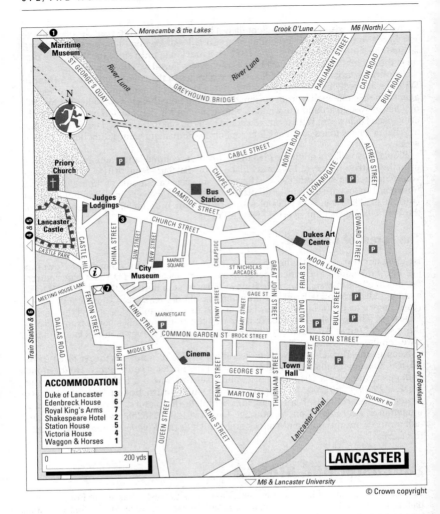

© Crown copyright

Oct Mon–Sat 10am–5pm; July–Sept Mon–Sat 10am–6pm, Sun noon–4pm; Nov–March Mon–Sat 10am–4pm; ☎01524/32878), in front of the castle, which is well signposted from the **train station**, a couple of hundred yards away in Meeting House Lane. You can change money at the office, book accommodation, and check on space on the Old Calendar Walks – seasonal, "olde-worlde" strolls through the city streets with costumed guides.

Accommodation

Duke of Lancaster Hotel, 75 Church St (☎01524/66909). A family-run pub with standard rooms above a busy road, close to the castle. No credit cards. ②.

Edenbreck House, Sunnyside Lane (☎01524/32464). For peace and quiet head for this large Victorian house out of the centre, at the end of Ashfield Avenue, ten minutes' walk up Meeting House Lane. No credit cards. ①.

Royal King's Arms, Market St (☎01524/32451). Lancaster's best-sited hotel, opposite the castle, has some comfortable rooms. Rates are negotiable during the week, and always a little lower at the weekend (when breakfast is included in the price). ⑤.

Shakespeare Hotel, 96 St Leonardsgate (☎01524/841041). Popular town-house hotel on a central street near several long-stay car parks. All rooms are en suite and non-smoking. Advance reservations advised. ②.

Station House, 25 Meeting House Lane (☎01524/381060). On a busy road, opposite the train station, but providing budget accommodation just two minutes' from the centre. No credit cards. ①.

Victoria House, 35 West Rd (☎01524/381489). Castle Park, which runs beside the castle, turns into West Rd, where you'll find this amiable B&B in a restored Victorian house. No credit cards. ②.

Waggon & Horses, St George's Quay (☎01524/846094). Pleasant new rooms above a riverside pub, just past the Maritime Museum. No credit cards. ②.

The City

Lancaster Castle (tours: Easter–Oct daily 10.30am–5pm; last tour at 4pm; £3.50) has been the city's focal point since Roman times, when there was a fort on this site. The Normans built the first castle here in around 1093 in an attempt to protect the region from marauding Scots armies, and it was added to throughout medieval times, becoming a crown court and prison in the eighteenth century, a role it still fulfils today. Currently, about a quarter of the building can be visited on an hour's tour beginning around the back in the Shire Hall, though as the prison is due to close in the next few years it's hoped that more of the building should eventually be open to the public. For now, you'll have to content yourself with the eight-foot-thick walls of the thirteenth-century Adrian's Tower, which encircle a room hung with instruments of torture. These were used on the prisoners who were slammed up in the lightless cells next door, which you are invited to experience briefly. The castle's neighbour, the former Benedictine **Priory Church of St Mary** (Easter–Oct daily 9.30am–5pm; free), has a Saxon doorway at the west end and some finely carved fourteenth-century choir stalls, the only features that predate its fifteenth-century reconstruction. Standing in front of the church's porch is the best place to view the castle's Norman keep.

A two-minute walk down the steps between the castle and church brings you to the seventeenth-century **Judges' Lodging** (Easter–June & Oct Mon–Sat 2–5pm; July–Sept Mon–Fri 10am–1pm & 2–5pm, Sat & Sun 2–5pm; £2), once used by visiting magistrates and now home to two museums. The ground and first floors house furniture by Gillows of Lancaster, one-time boat builders who, in the eighteenth century, took to cabinet-making with the tropical timber which came back as ballast in their boats. Their high-quality work eventually earned them contracts to fit the great Cunard transatlantic liners, the *Queen Mary* and *Queen Elizabeth*. The finely worked pieces on display mainly come from the earlier period, with an especially beautiful Regency writing desk and a magnificent billiard table – Gillows are credited with first putting the slate under the baize. The top floor is given over to a **Museum of Childhood**.

Continuing down the hill and left onto Dameside you arrive on the riverbank, where the top floor of one of the eighteenth-century warehouses is taken up by part of the **Maritime Museum**, St George's Quay (daily: Easter–Oct 11am–5pm; Nov–Easter 12.30–4pm; £2), entered through the Old Custom House. The museum's ample coverage of life on the sea and inland waterways of Lancashire is complemented by the **City Museum** on Market St (Mon–Sat 10am–5pm; free), based in the former Town Hall, built in 1781, five minutes' walk east of the Judges' Lodging. This explores the city's history through Neolithic, Roman, medieval and Georgian Lancaster.

For a panorama of Morecambe Bay and the Cumbrian fells, take a bus from the bus station (or a 25-minute walk) and haul yourself up to the 220ft **Ashton Memorial** (Easter–Sept daily 10am–5pm; Oct–Easter Mon–Fri 11am–4pm, Sat & Sun 10am–4pm), a lavish self-celebration raised in 1807 in **Williamson Park**, Lancaster's highest point, by local statesman and lino magnate Lord Ashton. The *Pavilion Tea Room* (daily: summer 10am–5pm; winter closes 4pm) at the memorial is a nice spot. The grounds, which include a **butterfly and palm house** (same hours as the memorial; £2.95, includes entry to the memorial), were given to the town by Ashton's father, who employed cotton workers to landscape it when the American Civil War caused a cotton famine. The other local excursion is to the **Crook O'Lune**, a beauty spot made famous by J.M.W. Turner. It's four miles northeast of the city reached by a path/cycle-way along the River Lune, and there's a picnic site and snack bar at the other end.

Cafés and Restaurants

Il Bistro Morini, 26 Sun St (☎01524/846252). The best Italian in town, with regional specialities emphasizing seafood, duck and pork. Best to book in advance. Closed Tues. Expensive.

Fortune Star, Thurnham St (☎01524/842828). Cheap and cheerful Cantonese restaurant. No great nod to authenticity, but at these prices, a meal's a steal. Inexpensive.

Lancastrian Antiques Tea Rooms, Penny St. Chi-chi antique-shop tearooms, just the place to peruse the morning paper.

Navigation Bistro, Penny St (☎01524/849484). Canalside wine bar (signposted off the top of Thurnham St) with outdoor tables and a varied menu. Moderate.

Pizza Margherita, 2 Moor Lane. Good-natured pizza restaurant, where you can fill up for around £8. Inexpensive.

Reds Café Bar, 11 Church St. Minimalist café-bar with espresso machine, baguette sandwiches and a Fifties' style jukebox.

Simply French, 27 St George's Quay (☎01524/843199). Riverside brasserie in a converted warehouse close to the Maritime Museum. Cheap lunch deals (around £6) are the main attraction, but dinner isn't particularly pricey. Inexpensive to Moderate.

The Whale Tail, 78a Penny St. Veggie and wholefood café serving good breakfasts. Closes 5pm, 3pm on Sundays.

Drinking and entertainment

Dukes, Moor Lane (☎01524/66645). The city's main arts centre, with cinema, theatre and other events.

Friary & Firkin, corner of St Leonardsgate and Rosemary Lane. A former church, now a real ale pub with a booming student presence.

George & Dragon, St George's Quay. For a riverside drink, either here or the *Waggon & Horses* up the road (see accommodation, p.673) are the best pubs.

Ye Olde John O'Gaunt, Market St, near the City Museum. Terrific city-centre local concentrating on the good things – home-cooked food, large range of whiskies and vodkas, special beers, tea and coffee on request, live trad jazz and R&B, and a beer garden.

Water Witch, Aldcliffe Rd. Canalside pub named after an old canal packet boat. A student crowd munches burgers, shoots pool and hogs the canalside tables.

Morecambe

Although the name **MORECAMBE**, meaning "Great Bay", dates from Celtic times, the seaside town five miles west of Lancaster only took it in the nineteenth century when it rapidly expanded from a small fishing village into a full-blown resort. The catalyst, as with Blackpool, was the arrival of the railway, which not only brought in the northern mill workers on holiday, but also enabled the quick transport of the bay's shrimps and mussels to the towns they had come from. Across the bay, Grange-Over-Sands (see p.718) was always the more refined resort and with Blackpool to the south hoovering up the rest of the local demand for bucket-and-spade holidays, Morecambe went into decline after the war. There's been some recent regeneration – notably the restored Stone Jetty, a new arts centre and revamped promenade amusements – but the sweep of the bay is still the major attraction, with the local sunsets a renowned phenomenon. The Stone Jetty, remodelled by sculptors and stonemasons, now features bird sculptures and a statue of one of Britain's most treasured comedians – Eric Bartholomew, who took the stage name Morecambe when he met his comedy partner, Ernie Wise.

Any information you need can be had from the **tourist office** in the Station Buildings on the Central Promenade (Mon–Fri 9.30am–4pm, Sat 9.30am–4pm, Sun 11am–4pm; ☎01524/582808). The **Platform arts centre** (☎01524/582803) shares the same building. There's a regular **bus service** from Lancaster bus station, and it's a fifteen-minute ride.

The Isle of Man

The **Isle of Man**, almost equidistant from Ireland, England, Wales and Scotland, is one of the most beautiful spots in Britain, a mountainous, cliff-fringed island just thirty-one miles by thirteen, into which are shoehorned austere moorlands and wooded glens, sandy beaches, fine castles, beguiling narrow-gauge railways and scores of standing stones and Celtic crosses. It takes some effort to reach, and the weather is hardly reliable, factors which have seen tourist numbers fall since its Victorian heyday, when the island developed as rapidly as the other northwestern coastal resorts. This means, though, that the Isle of Man has been spared the worst excesses of the British tourist trade: there's peace and quiet in abundance, walks around the unspoilt hundred-mile coastline, picket fences and picnic spots, rural villages straight out of a 1950s' picture-book, steam trains and cream teas – a yesteryear ensemble only slightly marred by the island's reputation of being a tax haven for greedy Brits and a refuge for the sort of people who think that even Victorian values were a bit on the lax side.

The capital, Douglas is atypical of an island which prides itself on its Celtic and Norse heritage, and it's the vestiges of the distant past – the castles at the former capital **Castletown** and the west coast port of **Peel** – that make the most obvious destinations. Elsewhere, **Port Erin** has one of the island's best beaches, while to the north **Laxey** is an attractive proposition for its huge **waterwheel** and the meandering train ride to the barren summit of **Snaefell**, the island's highest peak. From its summit you get an idea of the range of the Manx scenery, the finest parts of which are to be found in the seventeen officially designated National Glens, most of them linked by the **Raad Ny Foillan** (Road of the Gull) coastal footpath (see box on p.677, which passes several of the island's numerous hillforts, Viking burial ships and Celtic crosses.

Though the landscapes are wonderful, the island's main tourist draw is the **TT (Tourist Trophy) motorcycle races** in the first two weeks in June, a frenzy of speed and burning rubber that's shattered the island's peace annually since 1907. Thousands of bikers swamp the place to watch a nonstop parade of maniacs hurtling round the roads on a 37-mile circuit at speeds approaching 120mph. This is only the most famous of a summer-long list of **rallies and races** on the island's roads, from the Manx Rally (May), International Rally and Manx Classic (both September) to the Kart Racing Festival (July), when go-carts buzz through the streets of Peel. If you want to stay on the island at these times, you must book your accommodation well in advance.

Some history

The island may have already been populated when it became a separate land mass at the end of the last Ice Age around 8000 BC, but the earliest substantial human traces are Mesolithic flint workings from about 6000 BC, predating the Neolithic farming settlements by around three millennia. Saint Patrick is said to have come here in the fifth century bringing Christianity, which struggled for a while when the **Vikings** established garrisons here in the eleventh century, though they converted while they reigned as **Kings of Mann**. The Scots under Alexander wrested power from the Norsemen in 1275, the beginning of an ultimately unsuccessful 130-year struggle with the English for control of the island. During the English **Civil War**, James Stanley, Seventh earl of Derby and lord of Man, raised an army to support Charles II, but in his absence a local militia offered the island to Cromwell, provided the traditional rights of the islanders – long infringed upon by English overlords – were maintained. It was a shortlived insurrection: with the restoration of the monarchy, the leaders of the militia were executed and the island returned to Crown control.

The distinct identity of the island remained intact, however, and many true Manx inhabitants, who comprise a shade under fifty percent of the island's 72,000 population, insist that the Isle of Man is not part of England, nor even of the UK. Indeed, the island has its own government, **Tynwald**, arguably the world's oldest democratic parliament, which has run continuously since 979 AD. Tynwald consists of two chambers, the 24-member House of Keys and the smaller, more elite Legislative Council, both presided over by a lieutenant-governor who is appointed by the British monarch, the lord of Man, and the island remains a crown dependency. To further complicate matters, the island maintains a unique associate status in the EU, neither contributing nor receiving funds but enjoying the same trading rights. The island has its own sterling currency, worth the same as the mainland currency; its own laws, though they generally follow Westminster's; an independent postal service; and a Gaelic-based language which nearly died out but is once again being taught in schools. It also, of course, produces its own tailless version of the domestic cat, as well as famously good kippers and queenies (scallops).

For most of its history, crofting and fishing, interspersed with a good bit of smuggling, have formed the basis of the economy. The first regular steamship service from England commenced in 1819, and **tourism** began to flourish during the late-Victorian and Edwardian eras with the influx of northwestern factory workers. At its turn-of-the-century height, tourism was bringing in half a million visitors a year, but in recent times the real money-spinner has been the **offshore finance industry**, exploiting the island's low income tax and absence of capital gains tax and death duties. More than fifty banks have been established on the island since 1991, whole streets in **Douglas**, the capital, are taken up by consultancies and the island is dotted with the houses and swanky cars of British tax exiles. This hasn't helped the island's image problem, which largely stems from its archaic human rights legislation. Homosexuality was illegal here until 1992, while the death penalty and corporal punishment were only abolished in 1993, in response to pressure from Westminster and the European Union. With such a record, it might seem perverse that in 1881 Tynwald became the first government to see fit to grant women a vote, although this was limited to property owners and empowered very few.

Getting to the island

Most visitors from England arrive at Douglas, the main port, on **ferries** or the quicker **Sea Cats**, both run by The Isle of Man Steam Packet Company (☎08705/523523 Mon–Sat 7am–8pm, Sun 9am–8pm), from either Heysham (near Lancaster; ferries only) or Liverpool (ferries and Sea Cat). **Heysham** (3hr 30min) has the most frequent service, with two or three sailings a day in July and August dropping to one or two daily during the rest of the year. **Liverpool** manages two to three Sea Cat services a day (2hr 30min) between April and September, with a much-reduced ferry service (4hr) at other times (between October and March, down to 1 daily at weekends).

One-way **fares** start at £16 for foot passengers and £95 for drivers (covers the car, driver and one passenger), with five-day deals costing from £55/£152; but advance-purchase tickets, special offers and night-time sailings offer substantial savings – call for the latest deals, or contact a travel agent, who may be able to provide a well-priced transport-plus-accommodation package.

The best **flight** deals are from Liverpool, with Manx Airlines (☎0345/256256) charging from £60–90 return for the 40-minute flight (up to 6 flights daily). Manx Airlines also has flights from Manchester (from £99; 2–3 flights daily; 50min) and several of the UK's other regional airports. Jersey European (☎0870/567 6676) flies from Blackpool (from £70–125; 2 daily; 35min).

Getting around the island

With a car you could see almost everything in a couple of days; even on foot, it only takes around five days to circumnavigate the entire island. But however you get around, don't miss a trip on one of the two century-old **rail services** which still provide the best public transport to all the major towns and sights except for Peel. The carriages of the **Steam Railway** (Easter–Oct daily 10am–5pm; £7.60 return to Port Erin) rock their fifteen-mile course from Douglas to Castletown, Port St Mary and Port Erin at a spirited pace, making up in character for what they lack in comfort. The rolling terrain due north of Douglas was too steep for conventional trains, but by 1893 fledgling technology was available to construct the **Manx Electric Railway** (Easter–May, Sept & Oct daily 10am–5pm; June–Aug 10am–7.30pm; £6.20 return) which runs for seventeen miles from Douglas's Derby Castle Station to Ramsey via Laxey. Normally operating a single wooden carriage, it resembles a tramway more than a train, particularly since it follows the road most of the way to Laxey before peeling off into the countryside beyond. The **trains** are the most enjoyable way to get to Laxey, Ramsey, Castletown and Port Erin but **buses** are often quicker – bus routes are given in the text where appropriate.

WALKING ON THE ISLE OF MAN

Quite apart from the local walking opportunities that the glens, coastline and hills offer, there are a number of established day hikes and long-distance walks open to anyone in a reasonable state of fitness. OS Landranger map 95 covers the entire island, while the free small guide *Walks & Wildlife on the Isle of Man*, available from Douglas tourist office, spells out all the options and indicates what you're likely to see en route at any particular time of the year.

Short sections of **disused railway line** provide some of the gentlest introductions to the scenery: notably the Heritage Trail (10 miles), from the Quarterbridge in Douglas to Peel, and the 16-mile route from Peel north to Ramsey, via Kirk Michael. A good route to combine with an outward journey or return by steam train is the 12-mile **Port Erin to Castletown** hike along the cliff tops and beaches, with a possible detour to Cregneash village (p.684). From the summit of **Snaefell**, various descents are possible, the easiest of which is the direct route back down the Laxey Valley to Laxey.

There are two main long-distance footpaths, the shortest being the 28-mile **Millennium Way**, from Castle Rushen in Castletown to Ramsey, following the old medieval "Royal Way". It splits into three day hikes (though serious hikers do it in one day), with the second half of the walk, from Baldwin to Ramsey, across the most remote terrain. The greatest challenge, however, is the round-island **Raad ny Foillan (Road of the Gull)**, a well-signposted (white gull on a blue background) 95-mile coastal walk which takes most people around five days to complete. The path follows the coast wherever possible, and only on the northern stretch – north and west of Ramsey – are you ever within anything but easy reach of accommodation and facilities.

If you plan to do much gadding about, it may be worth buying a **day-rover ticket** (£10.70), which covers the electric and steam train routes as well as the trip to Snaefell summit (see p.681). There's also an "Island Freedom" ticket – which gives seven days' unlimited travel on these routes, plus free bus and horse-tram rides (£29.40) – and separate one-day (£5.20) and three-day (£11.90) **bus rover** tickets. Tickets are available from the Travel Shop (see below), main train and tram stations, and the tourist office in Douglas.

Outside race times, the roads are a joy to **drive** – there's relatively little traffic, even in summer, and on the TT stretches, the straights and gentle curves tempt you all too easily into Michael Schümacher mode, encouraged by the fact that there's no speed limit on the Isle of Man outside the towns and villages.

Douglas

DOUGLAS, heart of the offshore finance industry, also has the vast majority of the island's hotels and good restaurants, and it makes as good a base as any, since all roads lead here. A mere market town as late as 1850, with one pier and an undeveloped seafront, Douglas was a product of Victorian mass tourism and displays many similarities to Blackpool, just across the water: five-storey terraces back the mile-and-a-half-long curve of the promenade and its tram tracks, and the town even makes a paltry attempt to emulate the illuminations. However, whereas Blackpool thrives, Douglas – despite its financial acumen – has that permanent end-of-season feel, with peeling terraces, rusty seafront railings and cafés and hotels which, for the most part, share a bleak insistence on providing budget-rated services and entertainment. It's not really Douglas's fault – where once half a million people a year sported on the sands, package tourism to hotter climates has long since burst the bubble. You can still have a thoroughly enjoyable – and remarkably inexpensive – time in town, but put aside thoughts of state-of-the-art entertainment and sophisticated nightlife. Instead, pull up a candy-striped deckchair and enjoy the extensive sands. When it rains, stroll the covered arcades, ride the trams or attend the afternoon tea dances.

Arrival, orientation and information

All air arrivals are at **Ronaldsway airport** (☎01624/821600 or 826000) at Ballasalla, around ten miles southwest of Douglas, close to Castletown. Buses (every 30min–1hr 7am–11pm) connect the airport with Castletown/Port St Mary or Douglas.

Ferries and Sea Cats dock by the **Sea Terminal** at the southern end of the Douglas waterfront. Fifty yards beyond the forecourt taxi rank, the Lord Street **bus station** is the hub of the island's dozen or so bus routes; the **Travel Shop** (Mon–Sat 8am–5.40pm; ☎01624/662525), a little way beyond the station at the bottom of Lord Street, has timetable information and sells various islandwide **discount travel tickets** for buses and trains – see "Getting around the island" on p.677 for details.

North Quay runs 300 yards west from the bus station alongside the river and fishing port to Douglas Station, the northern terminus of the **steam railway** to Port Erin. The waterfront (progressively Loch, Central and Queen's promenades) runs a mile and a half north to Derby Castle Station for the **electric railway** to Laxey and Ramsey – take the horse-drawn tram along the promenade or bus #23, #24, #25 or #26 from Douglas bus station. Between April and September, bus #30 connects the steam railway station directly with the electric railway station every couple of hours.

The **tourist office** is in the Sea Terminal building (Easter & mid-May to Sept daily 9am–7.30pm; April & Oct daily 9am–5pm; Nov–Easter Mon–Thurs 9am–5.30pm, Fri 9am–5pm, Sat 9.30am–12.30pm; ☎01624/686766). There's a smaller office at the airport, open to meet flight arrivals.

All the local **car rental** outfits have offices at the airport and in town: try Athol (☎01624/623232), Hertz/National (☎01624/825855), Mylchreests (☎0500/823533) or Ocean Ford (☎01624/662211). Eurocycles at 8a Victoria Rd, off Broadway (☎01624/624909), rents out reliable **bikes**.

Accommodation

B&Bs are packed in along Douglas's front and up the roads immediately off Harris Promenade, particularly along Broadway, Castle Mona Avenue, Empress Drive and Empire Terrace. Prices start at as little as £20 for a double (in admittedly small rooms) and a sea-view room can be had for £40. The sheer number of choices, most with just a few rooms, precludes any real recommendations at the bottom end of the scale – you'll have to stroll along and look for vacancy signs – but flower-draped *Blossoms*, 4 The Esplanade (☎01624/673360; no credit cards; ①), and *Seafield*, 14 Empire Terrace (☎01624/674372; no credit cards; ①), are typical of what's on offer. If you're prepared to spend a bit more for comfort and proper **hotel** facilities, then again, comparative bargains abound. The distinctively styled *Edelweiss Hotel*, Switzerland Rd (☎01624/675115; ③) is set slightly back from Queen's Promenade; while top choices include the classy *Empress Hotel*, Central Promenade (☎01624/661155; no credit cards; ⑤), the *Sefton Hotel* next to the Gaiety Theatre on Harris Promenade (☎01624/626011; ⑤), and the fine castellated mansion that is the *Castle Mona Hotel*, Central Promenade (☎01624/624540; ④) – originally built in 1801 for the Duke of Athol. The best lodgings, though, are at a smaller luxury hotel very near the Sea Terminal: *Admiral House Hotel*, on Loch Promenade (☎01624/629551; ⑤), a lovingly restored, club-like retreat with just a dozen rooms and an excellent restaurant.

The nearest **campsite** backs onto Nobles Park Grandstand on Glencrutchery Road, a mile north of the tourist office (☎01624/621132; closed Oct–May and during TT and Manx Grand Prix races). Otherwise, you'll have to head out to *Glenlough Farm*, three miles west at Union Mills on the Peel road (☎01624/851326; closed Oct–April), or to *Glendhoo International Campsite*, two miles north at the Cronk ny Mona crossroads on the A18 (☎01624/621254; closed Oct–Easter).

The Town

The seafront vista has changed little since Victorian times, and is still trodden by heavy-footed carthorses pulling **trams** (jump on for a few pence). On Harris Promenade the opulent **Gaiety Theatre**, fronted by a stained glass canopy, is unique among the nine theatres designed by Frank Matcham, which includes the Grand in Blackpool. The lush, lapis-blue interior, paintings and decorated stage backdrop have been restored with precision. Hour-long tours of the theatre take place each Saturday (10.30am; donations welcome).

The town is at its oldest, and most interesting, in the streets near the harbour, where an attempt has been made to preserve Douglas's "historic quayside". There's not much to it, save a few old pubs and the odd teetering building, and you're soon pushed up Victoria Street, past the Manx Legislative Building, to the **Manx Museum**, on the corner of Kingswood Grove and Crellins Hill (Mon–Sat 10am–5pm; free). The museum makes a good start for anyone wanting to get to grips with Manx culture and heritage before setting off around the island, kicking off with a National Gallery of Manx painters – from Alfred James Collister and his friend Archibald Knox to the contemporary abstract artist Bryan Kneale. Other rooms provide an absorbing synopsis of the island's history, packed with Neolithic standing stones, Celtic grave markers and other artefacts, notably some excellent displays relating to Viking burials and runic crosses. Much of the current understanding of Manx culture was pieced together from digs at Peel Castle in the 1980s, which turned up a cache of silver coins minted in Dublin in

1030, and evidence of a pagan sacrifice, in the form of a woman's severed scalp, on display next to the trove. More recent activities get the full treatment, too, with collections of smutty postcards from the 1930s, displays about the TT races and information boards explaining the capital's financial wheeling and dealing.

Eating, drinking and entertainment

For their setting alone, the *Bay Room Restaurant* (closed Sun), in the Manx Museum, and *Greens Vegetarian Restaurant*, in the ticket office at the steam railway station, both demand a look, and also dish up great inexpensive food – though both close at 5pm. *Scotts Bistro*, 7 John St (☎01624/623764; closed Sun), near the old town hall, is housed in Douglas's oldest (seventeenth-century) building and has queenies in garlic sauce alongside its other Anglo-French choices. The formal *Waterfront Restaurant*, at the top of North Quay (☎01624/673222; closed Sat lunch & all Sun), across from the train station, offers the island's finest and most expensive dining experience – fish, obviously, is the speciality, with meals a cool £40 a head. The moderate *Blazers Wine Bar* next door (same phone number; closed Sat lunch & all Sun) is run by the same people and is a more relaxing spot to sample a few of the same dishes at a fraction of the price. *La Tasca*, in the basement of the *Admiral House Hotel* on Loch Promenade (☎01624/629551), has great tapas and Spanish dishes, including a rich paella; meals from around £15–20 a head.

For **drinking**, the funky *Bushy's Brew Pub* on Victoria Street at the harbour has a boisterous clientele, a jukebox built into the back of an old Ford Anglia and serves own-brewed "Old Bushy Tail", which will soon revive flagging spirits. The *Rovers Return*, behind the town hall, around the corner from *Scott's Bistro*, is a real locals' pub with more Manx-brewed beer. *Tramshunters* on Harris Promenade, is a cavernous real-ale bar, short on anything approaching atmosphere but noted for its beef sandwiches.

Laxey and around

Filling a narrow valley, the straggling town of **LAXEY**, seven miles north of Douglas, spills down from its train station to a small harbour and long, pebbly beach, squeezed between two bulky headlands. The Manx Electric Railway from Douglas drops you at the station used by the **Snaefell Mountain Railway**. Shops and a couple of cafés here attempt to divert the crowds who disembark and then head inland and uphill to Laxey's pride, the **"Lady Isabella" Great Laxey Wheel** (Easter–Oct daily 10am–5pm; £2.75), smartly painted in red and white. With a diameter of over 72ft it's said to be the largest working waterwheel in the world – a slightly bogus claim as it doesn't drive anything. Until 1929 the wheel was used to pump water from the local lead mines which, with their silver-rich ore, were a major money-spinner. The mechanism and its relation to the mine are all well explained. Otherwise Laxey is at its best down in **Old Laxey**, around the harbour, half a mile below the station, where large car parks attest to the popularity of the beach and river.

Hourly **buses** #15, #15A and #15C run to Laxey from Douglas; the #15C runs directly to Old Laxey four times a day (not Sun). Old Laxey has several **guest houses** to choose from, but most have only one or two rooms, so it's advisable to book in advance – you can check on space at Douglas tourist office. The nearest **campsite** is a rather basic affair on Quarry Road (☎01624/861241; closed Oct–April), behind the school, signposted off Minorca Hill which runs down to the harbour and Old Laxey from the Ramsey road.

The *Mines Tavern*, by the station, has some shaded outdoor seats and serves **lunch**, or you can try the *Riverside Studio* close to the waterwheel (☎01624/862121; closed Mon), which serves rich main courses and sumptuous sweets, accompanied by live jazz and blues on Wednesdays and at weekends. Down at the harbour, drinking is done at the *Shore Hotel*, a nice **pub** by the bridge which brews its own bitter.

Snaefell, Tholt-y-Will Glen and Sulby Glen

Every few minutes, the tramcars of the **Snaefell Mountain Railway** (Easter–Oct daily 10.30am–3.30pm; £6.40 return) begin their thirty-minute wind from Laxey through increasingly denuded moorland to the island's highest point, the top of **Snaefell** (2036ft) – the Vikings' "Snow Mountain" – from where you can see England, Wales, Scotland and Ireland on a clear day. The four-and-a-half miles of track were built in seven months over the winter of 1895 by two hundred men; one gang worked down from the summit, the other up from Laxey, an unimaginable effort in bitter conditions. At the summit, most people are content to pop into the inelegant café and bar and then soak up the views for the few minutes until the return journey.

The road route up, the A18 from Ramsey, also makes for a super ride, since it forms part of the TT course. Where the A18 and A14 (Snaefell–Sulby) meet, just below the summit, there's an isolated railway halt where drivers and hikers can pick up the mountain railway for a truncated ride to the summit and back. Three miles below the summit, down the A14, which sweeps past **Sulby Reservoir**, the road drops into **Tholt-y-Will Glen**, one of the island's more picturesque corners, with its gushing river and walks through the verdant plantations. There's a car park at the *Tholt-y-Will* inn, a Swiss-style chalet with gardens in a lovely location – a magnet for coach tours.

The A14 continues north to join the A3 Ramsey road, along a fine route – above the river – through **Sulby Glen**, with bracken-clad hills flanking the road. A signposted turn, just before the A3, cuts east to **Cronk Sumark**, a Celtic hill-top fort close to a large picnic area.

Maughold

The Manx Electric Railway trains stop within a mile and a half of **MAUGHOLD**, seven miles northeast of Laxey, a tiny hamlet just inland from the cliffside lighthouse at **Maughold Head**. It's an isolated spot which only adds to the attraction of Maughold's parish church, in whose grounds is maintained an outstanding collection of early Christian and Norse **carved crosses** – 44 pieces, dating from the sixth to the thirteenth century, and ranging from fragments of runic carving to a six-foot-high rectangular slab. Look inside the church, too, at the old parish cross, fourteenth century in date and sporting the earliest known picture of the Three Legs of Mann apart from that on the twelfth-century Sword of State. Bus #16 comes direct to Maughold from Ramsey, four or five times a day (not Sun).

Ramsey

RAMSEY marks the northern terminus of the Electric Railway, 45 minutes beyond Laxey. The Victorian tourist boom left behind the island's only iron pier and a solitary grand terrace along the front, but the bulk of the town, by the harbour – once more important than that in Douglas – is a dispiriting swatch of build-by-numbers modernity. The beach really isn't worth hanging around for and the only sight, the **Grove Rural Life Museum** (Easter–Sept daily 10am–5pm; £2.75), is a mile north on the A9. This, once the summer home of a Merseyside shipping magnet, is crammed with Victorian country-house furniture.

There's limited local accommodation in Ramsey, but no cause to use it. The best part of town, the harbour, is overlooked by several **pubs**, of which the *Trafalgar*, near the swing bridge, is the most alluring.

St Johns

The trans-island A1 (and hourly bus #5 or #6 from Douglas) follows a deep twelve-mile-long furrow between the northern and southern ranges from Douglas to Peel. A hill at the crossroads settlement of **ST JOHNS**, nine miles along it, is the original site of

Tynwald, the ancient Manx government, which derives its name from the Norse *Thing Völlr*, meaning "Assembly Field". Nowadays the word refers to the Douglas-based House of Keys and Legislative Council, but acts passed in the capital only become law once they have been proclaimed here on July 5 (ancient Midsummer's Day) in an annual open-air parliament that also hears the grievances of the islanders. Tynwald's four-tiered grass mound – made from soil collected from each of the island's parishes – stands at the other end of a processional path from the stone **St John Chapel**, which traditionally doubled as the courthouse. Early accounts of the ceremony indicate that the king sat at the top of the mound, facing east and brandishing his sword; the barons to his side, judges in front of him, and the representatives of the Keys, clergy and squires on the terraces below – with the rabble kept outside the enclosure. Until the nineteenth century the local people arrived with their livestock and stayed a week or more – in true Viking fashion – to thrash out local issues, play sports, make marriages and hold a fair. Now Tynwald Day begins with a service in the chapel, followed by a procession to the mound where the offices of state are carried out, after which a fair and concerts begin.

There's not much else at St Johns save a local craft centre and the *Tynwald Hill Inn*, which has some outdoor tables overlooking the mound.

Peel and around

The main settlement on the west coast, **PEEL** immediately captivates, with its fine castle rising across the harbour and a popular sandy beach running the length of its eastern promenade. It's a town of some antiquity and its enduring appeal is as one of the most "Manx" of all the island's towns, a character that is manifested in various ways – from an age-old Tuesday market in the marketplace above the harbour to the line of smoke-belching kipper factories along the harbourside.

Archeological evidence indicates that **St Patrick's Isle**, which guards the harbour, has had a significant population since Mesolithic times. What probably started out as a flint-working village on a naturally protected spot gained significance with the foundation of a monastery in the seventh or eighth century, parts of which remain inside the ramparts of the red sandstone **Peel Castle** (Easter–Sept daily 10am–5pm; £3; NT & EH). The Vikings built the first fortifications and the site became the residence of the Kings of Mann until 1220, when they moved to Castle Rushen in Castletown. The English continued strengthening the fortress, eventually completing a fifteen-foot curtain wall around the islet. Only this is in good repair, leaving the huge ward dotted with miscellaneous remains, including the Gothic vaults of St Germain's Cathedral, whose fourteenth-century crypt was later used as a prison. An annual Shakespeare festival and concerts take place within the castle walls, while below the ramparts on the west side there's a tiny sand beach.

It's a fifteen-minute walk from the town around the river harbour and over the bridge to the castle. On the way, you'll have passed the excellent harbourside House of Mannannan **heritage centre** (daily 10am–5pm; £5, £7 joint ticket with castle; NT & EH) named after the island's ancient sea-god. You'll should allow at least two hours to get around the museum, which concentrates strongly on participatory exhibits – whether it's listening to Celtic legends in a replica longhouse, examining the contents and occupants of a life-sized Viking ship, walking through a kipper factory or steering a steamer. There are dozens of other diversions throughout, illuminating the island's history and culture by way of dioramas, video presentations, hands-on exhibits and re-created street and domestic scenes – all in all, an essential counterpoint to the more traditional approach of Douglas's Manx Museum.

Practicalities

The most regular **bus** service to Peel is the hourly #5 or #6 from Douglas, which runs into town along the promenade to Crown Street; this service continues to Ramsey via

Kirk Michael and Sulby. The much less frequent #8 (not Sun) connects Peel to Port Erin, via St Johns and Castletown. Central **accommodation** includes the Georgian *Merchant's House*, 18 Castle St (☎01624/842541; no credit card; ②), and a couple of B&Bs on Bridge Street, just off the seafront Marine Parade. For sea views, try one of the guest houses which huddle together at the end of Marine Parade; *Fernleigh* (☎01624/842435; no credit card; ②) and *Waldick Hotel* (☎01624/842410; no credit card; ③). The *Peel Camping Park*, on Derby Road (☎01624/842341; closed mid-Sept to mid-May), is signposted about half a mile out on the Douglas road.

When it comes to **eating**, if you are looking for something more than the seafront cafés and fish-and-chip shops, then *Chez Cousteau* at Castle Court on the promenade (☎01624/844761) is as good as anything on the island, a wonderful seafood café and oyster bar serving queenie chowder, smoked fish platters, fish pâtés and fresh fish at moderate prices. The **pub** opposite the House of Mannannan, the *Creek Inn*, also serves a delicious array of fish pâtés and other reasonable food at its outdoor tables.

Niarbyl

Five miles south of Peel, off the A27, just after Dalby, a minor road runs down to the grassy car park above **Niarbyl**, a little headland of jutting rock, framed by clear water and steep banks and fronted by a flat pebbled beach, above which sits a picture-perfect thatched cottage. On clear days, the Calf of Man (see below) is visible in the distance; on even better days, seals can be seen on the rocks. South of the headland, the moorland road (A27, then A36) is one of the most dramatic on the island, forming a high-level switchback route to Port Erin, providing sweeping views both southwest across the cliffs and southeast across the plain to Castletown.

Port Erin and around

Plans for the southern branch of the steam railway beyond Castletown included the speculative construction of the new resort of **PORT ERIN**, at the southwestern tip of the island, a 1hr 15min ride from Douglas. The aspect certainly demanded a resort: a wide, fine sand beach backing a deeply indented bay sits beneath green hills, which climb to the tower-topped headland of Bradda Head to the northwest.

A century on, an arm of holiday apartments stretches out towards the headland, while the far side of town is marked by the breakwater and small harbour. Families relish the beach here, and the timewarped atmosphere, which appears to have altered little in forty years. The town's elegant redbrick train station is still here, with one of its engine sheds converted into a small **railway museum** (currently undergoing restoration). When you tire of the sand, it's time to take one of the **cruises** (April–Oct daily; £6–8) to the **Calf of Man** bird sanctuary, half a mile off the southwest coast. Prices for the cruises (which depart from the pier) vary depending on whether you make a simple return trip, land on the island, or opt for a full cruise. If you're going to make a day of it, take a picnic.

Practicalities

The **train station** is on Station Road, a couple of hundred yards above and back from the beach. **Buses** #1 and #2 from Douglas/Castletown, and #8 from Peel/St Johns, stop on Bridson Street, across Station Road and opposite the *Cherry Orchard* hotel. Rooms are pretty hard to come by since most **accommodation** is in holiday apartments or long-stay hotels, booked by the week. Still, you could try one of the large hotels on the cliff-top promenade, like the *Royal*, *Imperial* or *Countess* (all part of the same group; ☎01624/833116; ④), whose aspect is generally better than their interiors, and which offer out-of-season discounts. The *Balmoral Hotel*, further down the Promenade (☎01624/833126; ③), and the nearby *Falcon's Nest*, at the seafront end of Station Road

(☎01624/834077; ③), are cheaper options; while the best rooms are at the *Cherry Orchard Hotel* on Bridson Street (☎01624/833811; ⑤), a couple of hundred yards back from the promenade, a motel with its own pool, sauna, restaurant and bar.

The couple of beachfront **cafés** serve the usual daytime snacks and meals – you're better off heading instead for *La Patisserie* on Church Road between the *Cherry Orchard* and the promenade, a good deli-bakery which will make up sandwiches to take away. Come the evening, your choice is between *Da Vinci's* in the *Grosvenor Hotel* on the promenade – moderately priced pizza and pasta, but not as the Italians know it – or the overpriced restaurant in the *Falcon's Nest*. The bar in the *Royal Erin Hotel* on the promenade has bay views in abundance from its picture windows.

Around the coast to Port St Mary

The harbour at Port Erin marks the start of a six-mile loop around Meayll Hill on the coastal path past **Spanish Head**, the island's southern tip, to **Port St Mary**. It's one of the best short walks on the island, giving the opportunity of a detour to **Cregneash Village Folk Museum** (Easter–Sept daily 10am–5pm; £2.75), a picturesque cluster of nineteenth-century thatched crofts on the slopes above Spanish Head. This was a real Gaelic-speaking village until well into this century, though the advent of postwar tourism turned it into a tourist attraction. It's now peopled at weekends with spinners, weavers, turners and smiths dressed in period costumes; there's an information centre with introductory video, demonstrations of thatching and dry-stone walling, and a chance to walk through the seasonal crops in the field and watch the horses at work. The local views are stunning and it's only a short walk south to **The Chasms**, a headland of gaping rock cliffs swarming with gulls and razorbills.

The fishing harbour still dominates little **PORT ST MARY**, with its houses strung out in a chain above the busy dockside. The best beach is away to the northeast, reached from the harbour along a well-worked Victorian path which clings to the bay's rocky edge. High above the harbour, on Bay View Road, the *Bay View Hotel* (☎01624/832234; ②) has a skinny garden over the road tucked on top of the cliff. Regular steam **trains** run to Port Erin or back to Douglas from Port St Mary, with the station a ten-minute walk along High Street, Bay View Road and Station Road; hourly **buses** from the harbour serve the same places.

Castletown

From the twelfth century until 1869, **CASTLETOWN** was the island's capital, but then the influx of tourists and the increase in trade required a bigger harbour, so Douglas took over. So much the better for Castletown, which is a much more pleasant place than it might otherwise have been. Its sleepy harbour and low-roofed cottages are all dominated by **Castle Rushen** (Easter–Sept daily 10am–5pm; £4), one of the most complete and compact medieval castles in Britain. Formerly home to the island's legislature and still the site of the investiture of new lieutenant-governors, the present structure was probably started in the thirteenth century, its limestone walls well under way by the time the last Viking monarch, Magnus, died here in 1256. The heavy defences, comprising three concentric rings of stone-clad ramparts, fosses and a complex series of doors and portcullises, must have made entry a forbidding objective. Today, a mannequin archer guards access to displays on the castle's history, a prelude to five floors of rooms furnished in medieval and seventeenth-century styles, the most evocative being the tapestry-draped banqueting hall. The rooms may seem unending, but it is worth pressing on to the rooftop viewpoint to admire the town below, it's somnolent streets centred on a dinky marketplace with an unfinished memorial column – the "candlestick" – commemorating a nineteenth-century governor.

The **Old Grammar School** was the former capital's first church, built around 1200, and used as a school from 1570. There's not a lot to see, but it does house a handy **tourist office** (Easter–Sept daily 10am–5pm). Below the castle boats and yachts bob about in the harbour, while something of the island's nautical heritage can be gleaned from the little **Nautical Museum** on Douglas Street (daily 10am–5pm; £2.75), just across the harbour footbridge, which displays an armed eighteenth-century schooner among other exhibits.

The **steam train station** is five minutes' walk from the centre of Castletown, out along Victoria Road from the harbour; **buses** #8 (from Peel/Port Erin) and #1 (from Douglas) stop in the main square. You may find signs advertising local B&Bs, but otherwise the only **accommodation** is the swanky *Castletown Golf Links Hotel* at Derbyhaven (☎01624/822201; ⑤, room only), on the Langness peninsula, east of town. There's a clutch of **cafés** around the marketplace, though for an outdoor view of the harbour head for the *Chablis Cellar*, 21 Bank St (☎01624/823527; closed Sun eve), which does inexpensive **bistro** lunches and evening meals. The *Castle Arms*, across on the quayside, also serves food.

If you're in no hurry to get back to Douglas, stop off at **Port Soderick**, halfway along the train route between Castletown and Douglas, where you can walk down the glen to a cliff-backed bay with a stony beach and the nicely sited *Anchor Inn*.

travel details

Trains

Blackpool to: Manchester (hourly; 1hr 10min); Preston (hourly; 30min).

Chester to: Birmingham (5 daily; 2hr); Crewe (hourly; 20min); Knutsford (hourly; 50min); Liverpool (2 hourly; 45min); London (3 daily; 3hr 30min); Manchester (2 hourly; 1hr–1hr 20min); Northwich (hourly; 30min).

Crewe to: Birmingham (16 daily; 1hr); Bournemouth (3 daily; 5hr); Brighton (2 daily; 5hr 20min); Chester (hourly; 20min); Carlisle (11 daily; 2hr 10min); Liverpool (18 daily; 45min); London (2 hourly; 2hr); Manchester (2 hourly; 50min); Nantwich (8 daily; 10min); Oxenholme (11 daily; 2hr 10min).

Lancaster to: Barrow-in-Furness (17 daily; 1hr); Carlisle (hourly; 1hr); Heysham (1 daily; 30min); Morecambe (every 40min; 10min).

Liverpool to: Birmingham (hourly; 1hr 40min); Chester (2 hourly; 45min); Crewe (18 daily; 45min); Leeds (hourly; 2hr); London (hourly; 2hr 40min); Manchester (hourly; 50min); Newcastle (8 daily; 4–5hr); Oxford (12 daily; 3–4hr); Preston (14 daily; 1hr 5min); Sheffield (hourly; 1hr 45min); York (hourly; 2hr 20min).

Manchester to: Barrow-in-Furness (Mon–Sat 7 daily, 3 on Sun; 2hr 15min); Birmingham (hourly; 1hr 30min); Blackpool (hourly; 1hr 10min); Buxton

(hourly; 50min); Cardiff (10 daily; 3hr 10min); Carlisle (2 daily; 2hr 30min); Chester (2 hourly; 1hr–1hr 20min); Crewe (2 hourly; 50min); Leeds (hourly; 1hr); Liverpool (every 30min; 50min); London (hourly; 2hr 40min); Newcastle (10 daily; 3hr); Northwich (hourly; 30min); Oxenholme (4–6 daily; 40min–1hr 10min); Penrith (2–4 daily; 2hr); Preston (15 daily; 55min); Sheffield (hourly; 1hr); York (hourly; 1hr 35min).

Buses

Blackpool to: Birmingham (4 daily; 3hr 40min); London (4 daily; 6hr); Manchester (every 2hr; 1hr 50min); Preston (every 2hr; 40min); Windermere (2 daily; 1hr 40min).

Chester to: Bristol (1 daily; 3hr); Liverpool (hourly; 1hr); London (5 daily; 4hr 45min); Manchester (4 daily; 1hr 15min).

Lancaster to: Barrow-in-Furness (1 daily; 2hr); Carlisle (4–5 daily; 1hr 10min–4hr 30min); Kendal (hourly; 1hr); Keswick (5–10 daily; 2hr 50min); Kirkby Lonsdale (6 daily; 1hr); Leeds (1 daily; 3hr 30min); London (2–3 daily; 5hr 40min); Manchester (2 daily; 2hr); Whitehaven (2 daily; 3hr); Windermere (hourly; 1hr 45min).

Liverpool to: Birmingham (6 daily; 2hr 30min); Blackpool (Mon & Fri–Sun 1 daily; 2hr); Bristol (1 daily; 4hr); Chester (hourly; 1hr); Leeds (2 hourly;

2hr 40min); London (5 daily; 4hr 15min); Manchester (hourly; 1hr); Oxford (2 daily; 5–6hr); Preston (2 daily; 1hr).

Manchester to: Birmingham (8 daily; 2hr 15min); Blackpool (every 2hr; 1hr 50min); Bristol (4 daily; 4hr); Buxton (6–7 daily; 1hr 15min); Cambridge (2–3 daily; 6hr 30min); Carlisle (2–3 daily; 2hr 30min); Chester (4 daily; 1hr 15min); Kendal (1–3 daily; 2hr 45min); Keswick (1–3 daily; 3hr 50min); Lancaster (2 daily; 2hr); Leeds (hourly; 1hr 40min); Liverpool (hourly; 1hr); London (6 daily; 4hr); Newcastle-upon-Tyne (3 daily; 4hr); Preston (9 daily; 1hr 10min); Sheffield (2 hourly; 1hr 30min); Windermere (1–3 daily; 3hr); York (1 daily; 3hr).

CHAPTER NINE

CUMBRIA AND THE LAKES

The **Lake District** is England's most hyped scenic area, and for good reasons. Within an area a mere thirty miles across, sixteen major lakes are squeezed between the steeply pitched faces of England's highest mountains, an almost alpine landscape that's augmented by waterfalls and picturesque stone-built villages packed into the valleys. Most of what people refer to as the Lake District – or simply the Lakes – lies within the **Lake District National Park**, England's largest national park, established in 1951. This, in turn, falls entirely within the northwestern county of **Cumbria**, formed in 1974 from the historic counties of Cumberland and Westmorland, and the northern part of Lancashire. Consequently Cumbria contains more than just its lakes, stretching south and west to the **coast**, and north to its county town of **Carlisle**, a place that bears only few traces of a pedigree that stretches back beyond the construction of Hadrian's Wall. To the east, **Penrith** and the **Eden Valley** separate the lakes from the near wilderness of the northern Pennines.

The heart of the region is Scafell, a volcanic dome that had already been weathered into its present shape before the last Ice Age, when glaciers flowed off its flanks to gouge their characteristic U-shaped valleys. As the ice withdrew, terminal moraines of sediment dammed the meltwater, so that the main lakes now radiate like immense spokes from the hub of Scafell. Human interaction has also played a significant part in the shaping of the Lake District. Before Neolithic peoples began to colonize the region around five thousand years ago, most of the now bare uplands were forested with pine and birch, while the valleys were blanketed with thickets of oak and alder. As these first settlers learned to shape flints into axes, they began to clear the upland forests, a process accelerated by the road-building Romans. An even greater impact was made by the Norse Vikings in the ninth and tenth centuries, who farmed the land extensively and left their mark on the local dialect: a mountain here is referred to as a "fell", a waterfall is a "force", streams are "becks", a mountain lake is a "tarn", while the suffix

ACCOMMODATION PRICE CODES

Throughout this guide, hotel and B&B accommodation is priced on a scale of ① to ⑨, the number indicating the **lowest price** you could expect to pay per night in that establishment for a **double room** in high season. The prices indicated by the codes are as follows:

① under £40	④ £60–70	⑦ £110–150
② £40–50	⑤ £70–90	⑧ £150–200
③ £50–60	⑥ £90–110	⑨ over £200

"-thwaite" indicates a clearing. In later centuries grazing flocks of sheep cropped the hills of their wild flowers, while charcoal-making and the mining of copper and graphite further altered the contours and vegetation.

The region remained a land apart for centuries, its features – rugged and isolated – mirrored in the characteristics of its inhabitants. Daniel Defoe thought it "eminent only for being the wildest, most barren and frightful of any that I have passed over" – and, as he went on to point out, he'd been to Wales so he knew what he was talking about. Two factors spurred the first waves of **tourism**: the reappraisal of landscape brought about by such painters as Constable and the writings of Wordsworth and his contemporaries, and the outbreak of the French Revolution and its subsequent turmoil, which put paid to the idea of the continental Grand Tour. At the same time, as the war pushed food prices higher, farmers began to reclaim the hillsides, a tendency sanctioned by the General Enclosure Act of 1801. Most of the characteristic dry-stone walls were built at this time, a development that alarmed Wordsworth, who wrote in his *Guide to the Lakes* that he desired "a sort of national property, in which every man has a right and interest who has an eye to perceive and a heart to enjoy". His wish finally came to fruition in 1951 when the government designated 880 square miles of the Lake District as England's largest national park.

Arrival and information

Too many people bring cars to the Lake District and, as a consequence, once-quiet valleys and unspoilt villages have disappeared under the weight of traffic. But people arrive by car for a reason – simply that, if you're not intent on walking between places, getting around by **public transport** is time-consuming and, in the winter months, restrictive. However, the central and northern lakes and towns are at least relatively easy to see without your own transport. **National Express buses** connect London and Manchester with Windermere, Ambleside, Grasmere and Keswick. **Trains** leave the West Coast main line at **Oxenholme**, north of Lancaster, for the branch line service to Kendal and Windermere. The only other places directly accessible by train are Penrith, further north, also on the West Coast line, and the towns along the Cumbrian coast, from Grange-over-Sands to Whitehaven (though there's a limited service here on Sundays). A couple of private **narrow-gauge and steam train lines** connect various rural points. Of the lakes themselves, Windermere, Coniston Water, Derwent Water and Ullswater have **ferry** services of varying degrees of usefulness.

Everywhere else in the Lakes is connected by local **bus**, with Stagecoach Cumberland the biggest operator; their **Explorer Tickets** (one-day £5.50, four-day £13.60) are valid on the entire network. The dozens of routes are all spelled out in detail in the free Lakeland Explorer timetable, available from tourist offices; or call Stagecoach Cumberland's **timetable information line** (☎01946/63222 Mon–Sat 7am–7pm, Sun 9am–5.30pm). **Cumbria County Council's** Journey Planner department (☎01228/606000 Mon–Fri 9am–5pm, Sat 9am–noon) can advise about all the region's bus, coach, rail and ferry services. Finally, the **YHA** operates a shuttle-bus service between its most popular hostels (Easter–Oct; £2 a journey; ☎015394/32304).

As a rule you can escape the crowds by getting around on foot – some of the country's most celebrated **walks** run through the Lake District, often forming circuits or "horseshoe" routes around various peaks and valleys. Of the long-distance paths, Wainwright's Coast-to-Coast, which starts in St Bees, near Whitehaven, spends its first few sections in the northern Lakes, while the Dales Way finishes in Windermere, but the only true Lake District hike is the 70-mile **Cumbria Way** between **Ulverston** and **Carlisle**. Cyclists have the choice of shadowing walkers on Sustrans' **Sea to Sea (C2C) cycle route**, a 140-mile trip between Whitehaven/Workington and Sunderland/Newcastle, or using the **Cumbria Cycle Way**, which circles the region.

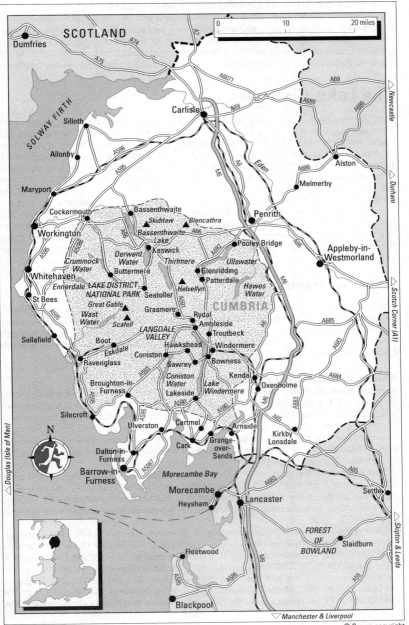

© Crown copyright

High summer isn't the ideal time to visit the Lakes – April and October are the best, as the crowds are thinner, the sights are still open and the high walks unlikely to be snowbound. In high season, **accommodation** – including abundant B&Bs, excellent country guest houses and 27 youth hostels – can be stretched to capacity. The widely scattered campsites usually just about manage, or you could check out the Lake District National Park Authority's **camping barn** network – ask for a brochure at tourist offices.

The Lake District

Eighteen million visitors a year now pour into the Lake District, making some of the villages even busier than the cities the tourists have come from. Given a week you could see most of the famous settlements and lakes – a circuit taking in the towns of Ambleside, Windermere and Bowness, all on **Windermere**, the Wordsworth houses and sites in pretty villages like **Hawkshead** and **Grasmere**, and the more dramatic northern scenery near **Keswick** and **Ullswater** would give you a fair sample of the whole. But it's away from the crowds that the Lakes really begin to pay dividends, so aim if you can to steer by central valleys like **Langdale** and **Eskdale**, and the lesser visited lakes of **Wast Water** and **Buttermere**. Of course, it's only when you start to walk and climb around the Lakes that you can really say you've explored the region. Four peaks top out at over 3000 feet – including **Scafell Pike**, the highest in England – but there are literally hundreds of other mountains, crags and fells to roam.

Kendal and around

The limestone-grey town of **KENDAL** might be billed as the "Gateway to the Lakes", but it's nearly ten miles from Windermere – the true start of the lakes – and has more in common with the market towns to the east. It's a pleasant stop, though, cut through by an attractive river and boasting two of Cumbria's grandest stately homes – **Sizergh Castle** and **Levens Hall** – both within easy reach of the town.

Arrival, information and accommodation

Kendal's **train station** is the first stop on the Windermere branch line, just five minutes from the **Oxenholme** main-line station. By catching bus #41 or #41A to the town hall from Oxenholme (Mon–Sat, every 20min) you can avoid the wait for the connecting train. Otherwise, head across the river and up Stramongate and Finkle Street to reach Highgate, a ten-minute walk. National Express buses stop opposite the **bus station** on Blackhall Rd (off Stramongate) on their way south, but opposite the post office on Stricklandgate going north.

The **tourist office** (Easter–Oct Mon–Sat 9am–5pm, Sun 10am–4pm; Nov–Easter Mon–Sat 9am–5pm; ☎01539/725758) is in the town hall on Highgate, and as well as supplying all the usual accommodation guides and local information, sells National Express tickets. You can book space here on the weekly summer guided walks (July & Aug Wed; £2).

Most of the local **B&Bs** lie along the road to Windermere, north of the centre, though there are a couple of places close to the train station, like *Bridge House*, 65 Castle St (☎01539/722041; no credit cards; ②). In the centre itself are the *Hillside Guest House*, 4 Beast Banks (☎01539/722836; no credit cards; ②; closed Dec–Feb), just off All Hallows Lane opposite the town hall, and *Da Franco's Hotel and Restaurant*, 101 Highgate (☎01539/722430; ②). *Lakeland Natural Vegetarian Guesthouse* at Low Slack, Queen's Rd (☎01539/733011; no credit cards; ③) backs onto woods five minutes' walk west of the centre. There's a **youth hostel** at 118 Highgate (☎01539/724066), which is attached to The Brewery arts centre (see p.692), while the most convenient **campsite** is *Ashes Lane* at Staveley, four miles northwest of town, off the Windermere Road (☎01539/821119; closed mid-Jan to mid-March), reached by bus #555 from the bus station.

The town

As the largest of the southern Cumbrian towns Kendal can be a congested place, but it offers rewarding rambles around the "yards" and "ginnels" which make an engaging maze on both sides of Highgate and Stricklandgate, the main streets. The old **Market Place** has long since succumbed to development, with the market hall now converted to the Westmorland Shopping Centre, but traditional stalls still do business outside every Wednesday and Saturday.

Strolling around or following one of the summer walks organized through the tourist office will take you down to the riverside walk and past restored almshouses, mullioned shopfronts and trade signs like the pipe-smoking Turk outside the snuff factory on Lowther Street. The "Kendal green" cotton cloth, actually yellow wool, was worn by English archers and earned Kendal a mention in Shakespeare's *Henry IV*, but today the town's most visible product is **Kendal Mintcake**, a solid block of sugar and peppermint oil, an energy-giving confection that has been hoisted to the top of the world's highest mountains.

The first of the town's three museums, the **Kendal Museum**, stands on Station Road (April–Oct daily 10.30am–5pm; Nov–March daily 10.30am–4pm; £2.50; £1 with a ticket for one of the other museums). Probably the least captivating of the three, it houses a fairly run-of-the-mill study of Cumbria's natural history and archeological finds, redeemed by reverential displays on the life of **Alfred Wainwright**. In 1952 this one-time borough treasurer, dissatisfied with the accuracy of existing maps of the paths and ancient tracks across the fells, embarked on what became a series of 47 walking guides, all but two of them painstakingly handwritten with mapped routes and delicately drawn views. Ironically, the popularity of his purple-prosed pocket guides has led to the ravaging of the land he so adored, especially on his most trekked route, the Coast-to-Coast from St Bees in Cumbria to Yorkshire's Robin Hood's Bay, much of which is not on designated rights of way and often crosses sensitive wildlife areas and archeological sites.

The other two museums are in the Georgian **Abbot Hall** and its stable block, by the river to the south. The main hall, painstakingly restored to its 1760s town-house origins, houses the **Art Gallery** (times and prices as Kendal Museum), where cherubic portraits by society painter George Romney line the walls, along with works by Constable, Ruskin, Turner, Edward Lear and lesser local artists. Few can compete with the furniture designed and built by Gillows of Lancaster, whose chairs, writing desks and games tables have all survived in excellent condition. The small modern art collection upstairs is rounded out with Barbara Hepworth's *Oval Form*, gracing the grass between the hall and the stables which house the **Museum of Lakeland Life and Industry** (times and prices as Kendal Museum). Here, reconstructed seventeenth-, eighteenth- and nineteenth-century house interiors stand alongside workshops which make a fairly vivid presentation of rural trades and crafts, from spinning and weaving to tanning – medieval Kendal was on the main north–south cattle-trade routes and leather production was once an important local industry. The mock-up study of **Arthur Ransome**, author of the children's classic *Swallows and Amazons*, is enlivened by an innocently hilarious commentary – "1904: enters into his Bohemian period" – as well as by memorabilia from his stint as *Manchester Guardian* reporter during the Russian Revolution: he urged support for the Bolsheviks throughout the period and, after the break-up of his first marriage, married Eugenia, Leon Trotsky's personal secretary. John Cunliffe, creator of *Postman Pat*, whose adventures are set just north of Kendal, gets more laid-back treatment next door, with a welter of original drawings and the author's desk and typewriter on show.

WALKING IN THE LAKE DISTRICT

An almost unchartable network of Lake District paths connects the lakes themselves, tracks the broken knife-edge ridges of the fells and mountains or weaves easier courses around the flanks and onto the tops. The various walks detailed in this section are largely aimed at the moderate walker with half a day or so on their hands and require no real experience. Even so, you should always be **properly equipped**: wear strong-soled, supportive shoes or boots, carry water, and take a map (and know how to use it). Bad weather can move in quickly, even in the height of summer, so before starting out you should check the weather forecast – many hotels and outdoor shops post a daily forecast – call ☎017687/75757 (24-hour line).

The best general **map** of the area is the Ordnance Survey inch-to-the-mile (1:63,360) Touring Map and Guide 3, with hill shading and illustrated text on the back. Essential for **walking** are the 1:50,000 OS Landranger maps 89, 90, 96 and 97, or even the yellow 1:25,000 OS Outdoor Leisure series, which cover the whole Lake District except the northern flanks of Skiddaw, and are detailed enough to show fences. Many shops and tourist offices also sell local walk leaflets, and regional trail and hiking guides, of which Wainwright's (see p.690) are the best known.

Just behind Abbott Hall, the wide aisles of the Early English **parish church** (daily: Easter–Oct 9.20am–4.30pm; Nov–Easter 9.20am–noon) house a number of family chapels, including that of the Parr family, who once owned **Kendal Castle**, on a hillock to the east across the river. First erected in the early thirteenth century, it's claimed as the birthplace of Catherine Parr, Henry VIII's sixth wife, but the story is probably apocryphal – she was born in 1512, at which time the building – now a ruin – was already in an advanced state of decay. If you fancy the climb up for the views, follow the footpath from the end of Parr Street, across the footbridge just north of the church and hall.

Eating and drinking

Kendal certainly doesn't lack decent **cafés**, starting with the wood-beamed *Farrers Tea & Coffee Merchants*, 13 Stricklandgate (closed Sun), and the *1657 Chocolate House*, on Branthwaite Brow, an olde-worlde spot which sells little other than hot chocolate (in dozens of guises) and cakes. There's also a good café at the Abbott Hall Art Gallery. For inexpensive veggie wholefood lunches and riverside seating, visit the *Waterside Café* on Gulfs Road, by the river at the bottom of Lowther Street. The **restaurant** in *Da Franco's Hotel* serves pizzas and moderately priced Italian dishes, while there's a qualitative jump upwards with meals at the highly regarded *Moon*, 129 Highgate (☎01539/729254; dinner only, closed Mon in winter), an easy-going bistro.

For evening entertainment the **Brewery Arts Centre**, on Highgate (☎01539/725133), with its café, bar, cinema, theatre and concert hall, is a good bet. There's live music throughout the year and a renowned annual jazz and blues festival each November. There are several characterful old **pubs** worth trying: the *Cask House*, just up All Hallows Lane from the town hall, and the *Ring o' Bells* by the church.

Sizergh Castle

Three miles to the south of Kendal stands **Sizergh Castle** (April–Oct Mon–Thurs & Sun 1.30–5.30pm; gardens open 12.30pm; £4.50; gardens only £2.20; EH), tucked away off the A591 amid acres of parkland and reached on bus #555. Home of the Strickland family for eight centuries, Sizergh is more of a grand manor house than a castle, but owes its epithet to the fourteenth-century peel tower (which you'll often see spelled "pele" tower in the north of England) at its core, one of the best examples of the towers built throughout the region as safe havens during the protracted border raids of the Middle Ages. Like much of the rest of the house, the Great Hall underwent significant changes in Elizabethan times, when extensions were added to the house and most of its rooms were panelled in oak with their ceilings layered in elaborate plasterwork. Each room is hung with portraits of the family and their royal acquaintances and stocked with exquisite furniture, including an extraordinary bedstead made from a pew that once stood in Kendal parish church. Little has changed in the Banqueting Hall since the fourteenth century, save for the loss of an upper storey and the addition of a partition at the east end, added to provide more private sleeping quarters for the heads of the family.

Levens Hall

Two miles south of Sizergh, just of the A590, **Levens Hall** (April to mid-Oct Mon–Thurs & Sun noon–5pm; gardens open 10am; £5.30; gardens only £3.90; ☎015395/60321), also built around an early peel tower, is more uniform in style than Sizergh, since the bulk of it was built or refurbished in classic Elizabethan style between 1570 and 1640 by James Bellingham. The house did not stay in the Bellingham family; a descendant lost the whole estate in a hedonistic spate of gambling, and it was later bought by the privy purse to James II and ancestor of the present owners, the Bagots.

The main entrance opens into the spacious Great Hall, its panelled walls lined with coats of arms; to the left of the hall are the large and small drawing rooms. The other end of the Great Hall leads to the most splendid apartment, the dining room, panelled not with oak but with goat's leather, printed with a deep green floral design – one goat was needed for every forty or so squares. Upstairs, the bedrooms offer glimpses of the beautifully trimmed **topiary gardens** below, where yews in the shape of pyramids, peacocks and top hats stand between blooming bedding plants. There's also a steam-engine collection and café.

A mile away, across the A590, **buses** (#555 from Kendal) drop you in the village of Levens, at the bottom of which stands the welcoming *Hare & Hounds*, a cosy pub with bar meals and good beer.

Windermere, Bowness and around

WINDERMERE town was all but non-existent until 1847 when a railway terminal was built here, making England's longest lake (after which the town is named) an easily accessible resort. Most of the guest houses and amenities built for the Victorians still stand, and Windermere remains the transport hub for the southern lakes, but there's precious little else to keep you in the slate-grey streets. Instead, all the traffic pours a mile down hill to its older twin town, Bowness.

Bus #599 leaves Windermere train station for the ten-minute run down to the lakeside piers of **BOWNESS**. This is undoubtedly the more attractive of the two settlements, spilling back from the lake, though as Cumbria's most popular resort – packed with trinket shops, second-rate cafés and souvenir-hunting tourists – it's a victim of its own popularity and is overrun for much of the year. Assuming you don't take one look at the crowds and turn tail, Bowness itself has enough scattered attractions to fill a morning. Just back from the lake, **St Martin's Church** (Easter–Sept daily 10am–4pm) is notable for its stained glass, particularly that in the east window which sports the fifteenth-century arms of John Washington, an ancestor of first American president George Washington. Most tourists, though, bypass the church and everything else in Bowness bar the lake for the chance to visit **The World of Beatrix Potter** in the Old Laundry on Crag Brow (daily: Easter–Sept 10am–6.30pm; Oct–Easter 10am–4pm; £3.25), whose conveyor-belt approach will soon rid you of any enthusiasm you might have had for the children's story writer. Five hundred yards north of Bowness, on Rayrigg Road, the **Windermere Steamboat Museum** (Easter–Oct daily 10am–5pm;

£3.25) has as its star exhibit the 1850 *Dolly*, claimed to be the world's oldest mechanically driven boat, and extremely well preserved after spending 65 years in the mud at the bottom of Ullswater.

All, however, come second-best to a trip on **Windermere** itself – according to Wordsworth's *Guide to the Lakes*, "None of the other Lakes unfold so many fresh beauties." Rowing boats are available for rent at the pier while Windermere Lake Cruises (☎015394/43360) operates stylish steamers and vintage cruisers to Lakeside at the southern tip (£4 one-way; £5.90 return) or to Waterhead (for Ambleside) at the northern end (£3.80 one-way; £5.70 return). There's also a shuttle service between Bowness piers and Sawrey (£1.20 one-way, £2 return), saving pedestrians the walk down to the car-ferry (see below). A 24-hour **Freedom-of-the-Lake ticket** costs £9.50. Services on both routes are frequent between Easter and October (every 30–60min at peak times and weekends), but much reduced during the winter.

There's also a **ferry service** across the water to Sawrey (Mon–Sat 7am–10pm, Sun 9am–10pm; departures every 20min; 40p; cars £2) from just south of Bowness, which provides access to Beatrix Potter's former home at Hill Top and to Hawkshead beyond. The ferry pier is a ten-minute walk south of the cruise piers, through the parkland of Cockshott Point.

Arrival and information

National Express and most local **buses** stop outside Windermere **train station** (luggage storage available here), itself only a few yards from the **tourist office** on Victoria Street (daily: July & Aug 9am–7.30pm; rest of the year 9am–5pm; ☎015394/46499), one of the most useful in the region. There's a second information office down in Bowness, by the piers on Glebe Road (Easter–Oct Mon–Thurs & Sun 9.30am–6pm, Fri & Sat 9.30am–6.30pm; Nov–Easter Fri–Sun 9.30am–5pm; ☎015394/42895). Both offices have **money-exchange** and room-booking services; you can also change money inside Windermere's post office on Crescent Road. For **bike rental**, contact Country Lanes, The Railway Station, Windermere (☎015394/44544), which provides route maps for local rides.

Accommodation

Windermere doesn't have the waterside advantages of Bowness, but it does have a lot more **accommodation** – wherever you plan to stay, you should book well in advance from Easter onwards. The nearest **youth hostel** is at Troutbeck (see p.696), while the only close **campsite** is *Braithwaite Fold* (☎015394/42177; closed Nov–March) near the ferry to Sawrey, half a mile from Bowness.

The cheapest **rooms in Windermere** are at the slightly shambolic *Backpackers Hostel* in the Old Bakery at the top of the High St (☎015394/46374; no credit cards; ①), across from the tourist office, where a motley assortment of international travellers hang out. Otherwise, there's no shortage of accommodation on the High Street and neighbouring Victoria Street, with plenty of other **B&Bs** on College Road, Oak and Broad streets. Top choices include *Ashleigh Guesthouse* at 11 College Rd (☎015394/42292; no credit cards; ②), and the *Archway* at no. 13 (☎015394/45613; ②), both non-smoking and the latter serving great breakfasts, with specials like pancakes, kippers and home-made yoghurt. *Brendan Chase*, 1–3 College Rd (☎015394/45638; ②), also has some cheaper rooms available, while the rather grander *Applegarth Hotel*, College Rd (☎015394/43206; ③), retains its ornate Victorian interior and terraced garden. Elsewhere, particularly friendly and comfortable B&Bs include: the non-smoking *Haven*, 10 Birch St (☎015394/44017; no credit cards; ①); *Broadlands Guest House*, 19 Broad St (☎015394/46532, *broadlands@clara.co.uk*; no credit cards; ①); *Yorkshire House*, 1 Upper Oak St (☎015394/44689; no credit cards; ①); and the non-smoking

Village House, 5 Victoria St (☎015394/46041; no credit cards; ①). Best hotel choice in Windermere – and a candidate for best in the Lakes – is *Miller Howe*, on Rayrigg Road, the A592 (☎015394/42536, *lakeview@millerhowe.com*; ⑨; closed Jan), whose terrifically expensive rooms (the best with lake- views) come with supremely theatrical dinners and breakfasts.

In **Bowness**, *Montclare House* on Crag Brow (☎015394/42723; no credit cards; ①), the main street, is as cheap as the **B&Bs** get, but you may want to spend a little more – and you'll have to if you want even the chance of a lake view. Try *Above The Bay*, 5 Brackenfield (☎015394/88658; no credit cards; ③), an elevated stone house with lake views, just off the Kendal road a little way south of the centre; or, by far the best central option, *The Old England*, Church St (☎015394/42444; ⑦), a relaxed grande-dame hotel opposite the church, with heated outdoor pool and terraced lakeside gardens. Alternatively, seek out the seventeenth-century *Laurel Cottage* in St Martin's Square (☎015394/45594; no credit cards; ②), right in the thick of things; or *Gilpin Lodge*, Crook Rd (☎015394/88818, *hotel@gilpin-lodge.co.uk*; ⑥), a country-house retreat a couple of miles east on the Kendal road (B5284).

Eating, drinking and entertainment
Eating and drinking is generally better done down in Bowness, but look out for Windermere's *Renoir's Coffee Shop*, on Main Road, for daytime sandwiches and frothy coffees, and the *Miller Howe Café* inside Lakeland Ltd by the train station, which serves up moderately priced bistro meals. Also worth trying is *High Street Restaurant*, at 4 High St (☎015394/44954; dinner only, closed Sun), a reliable Anglo-French restaurant, where three courses might run to £20–25 or so, cheaper if you stick to the *table d'hôte*. In Bowness there's a huge range of **cafés and restaurants**, but you'll have to exercise quality control. The *Hedgerow Teashop* on Lake Road serves an all-day breakfast and a decent range of teas and fruit infusions. Budget pizza and pasta is on offer at *Rastelli's*, also on Lake Road, while *Stefan's Bistro* in Queen's Square (closed Wed) is the place for light meals, meat and pasta dishes. The most rewarding – and most expensive – restaurant is the excellent, upmarket Anglo-Italian *Porthole Eating House*, 3 Ash St (☎015394/42793; closed Tues), with operatic warbling and open fires in winter.

For a **drink**, try *The Hole in't Wall* pub, the town's oldest hostelry, in Falbarrow Road behind Bowness church. *The Royalty* on Lake Road (☎015394/43364) is that rare lakeland beast, a **cinema**, with a repertory programme alongside the more commercial screenings.

Around Windermere
Three miles northwest of Windermere, the Lake District National Park has its headquarters and main information point at **Brockhole Visitor Centre** (Easter–Oct daily 10am–5pm; grounds & gardens open all year; free; parking £2), a fine mansion set in landscaped grounds on the shores of the lake. Besides the permanent natural history and geological displays, the centre hosts a full programme of guided walks, children's activities, garden tours, special exhibitions, lectures and film shows. The book shop is one of the best in the region for local guides and maps, and there's a café with an outdoor terrace overlooking the lake. Buses between Windermere and Ambleside run past the visitor centre, or you can get there by Windermere Lake Cruises launch from Waterhead, Ambleside (hourly 10.45am–4.45pm; £4.30 return).

From Bowness piers **cruises** head south down the lake the five or so miles to **Lakeside**, on Windermere's quieter southern reaches. Lakeside is also the terminus of the **Lakeside and Haverthwaite Railway** (Easter–Oct 6 daily; £3.40 return; ☎015395/31594), whose steam-powered engines chuff along four miles of track through the forests of Backbarrow Gorge. The boat arrivals at Lakeside connect with train departures throughout the day and you can buy a joint boat-and-train ticket (£8.80 return) at Bowness if you fancy the extended tour. Also on the quay at Lakeside is the **Aquarium of the Lakes** (daily 9am–5.30pm; £4.95), an entertaining natural history exhibit centred on the fish and animals found in and along a lakeland river, including a pair of captive otters and a walk-through-tunnel aquarium. Again, there's a joint ticket available with the boat ride from Bowness (£9.10 return).

Troutbeck

Troutbeck Bridge, a mile northwest of Windermere along the A591, heralds the start of a gentle valley below Wansfell, where you'll find Windermere's local **youth hostel**, *High Cross* at Bridge Lane (☎015394/43543), almost a mile uphill from the bridge. A YHA shuttle-bus service operates to the hostel from Windermere train station (meeting arriving trains) and from Ambleside youth hostel, or there's a fine cross-country walking route (3 miles, 1hr 30min) via **Orrest Head** (784ft), whose summit gives a 360° panorama from the Yorkshire fells to the Langdales and Troutbeck Valley – the path branches off the main road a hundred yards south of Windermere train station.

TROUTBECK's main attraction lies at the southern end of the village, a little further up the minor valley road from the hostel. **Townend** (Easter–Oct Tues–Fri & Sun 1–5pm; £3; NT) has been preserved as a seventeenth-century yeoman-farmer's house, complete with original furniture and decorative woodwork. There's not much more to the village itself than a road crossing at the village green, but it marks the starting point for the energetic five-hour walk along **High Street**, a nine-mile range running north to Brougham near Penrith. The course of a Roman road follows the ridge, probably once linking the forts at Brougham and Galava in Waterhead.

Troutbeck's expensive **inn**, the *Mortal Man* (☎015394/33193; ⑦; closed mid-Nov to mid-Feb) has terrific valley views from its rooms and beer-garden; the room rate includes breakfast and dinner. For non-residents, coffee and biscuits on the terrace is a great way to soak up the seventeenth-century atmosphere, if not a bar meal (not Mon). Cheaper **B&Bs** in the village offer less exalted lodgings – Windermere and Ambleside tourist offices can help – while Troutbeck's other old inn, the *Queen's Head*, down on the main A592 (☎015394/32174; ④; minimum two-night stay at weekends) serves good food.

Ambleside

AMBLESIDE, five miles northwest of Windermere, is at the heart of the southern lakes region, making it a first-class base for walkers, but also ensuring it high-season crowds second only to Windermere's. The town centre consists of a cluster of grey-green stone houses, shops and B&Bs hugging a circular one-way system, which loops round just south of the narrow gully of stony Stock Ghyll. The rest of town lies a mile south at **Waterhead** (referred to as Ambleside on ferry timetables), a harbour on the shores of Windermere that's filled with ducks, swans and rowing boats and overlooked by the landscaped gardens of several plush hotels. There are quieter shores a few minutes' walk further south for picnics or, if the weather's good, a bracing dip in the lake.

There's precious little to look at in Ambleside itself, but you could spare a few minutes for the mural of the rush-bearing ceremony in **St Mary's Church**, whose spire is visible from all over town. A couple of hundred yards north, **Bridge House** (Easter–Oct daily 10am–5pm; free), now a National Trust information centre, straddles Stock Ghyll – legend has it that a Scotsman built the two-storey, two-roomed house to evade land taxes. Behind this is **Adrian Sankey's Glass Works** (daily 9am–5.30pm; 30p), where you can watch glass being blown, then splash out on one of the unique finished products. For more on Ambleside's history, stroll a couple of minutes' along

Rydal Road to **The Armitt** (daily 10am–5pm; £2.50), whose collection catalogues the very distinct contribution to lakeland society made by John Ruskin, Beatrix Potter and longtime Ambleside resident, writer Harriet Martineau.

Practicalities

Buses (including National Express) all stop on Kelsick Road, opposite the library. The **tourist office** is just up the road, in Central Buildings on Market Cross (daily 9am–5pm; ☎015394/32582). You can **change money** at the post office in Market Place. For **bike rental**, try Biketreks on Compston Rd (☎015394/31505), or Ghyllside Cycles on The Slack (☎015394/33592).

Lake Road, running between Waterhead and Ambleside, is lined with dozens of **B&Bs**, but other options are scattered all over town, with particular concentrations on central Church Street and Compston Road. The cheapest rates are at *Linda's B&B and Bunkhouse* at *Shirland,* Compston Rd (☎015394/32999; no credit cards; ①), closely followed by *Iveing Cottage,* Old Lake Rd (☎015394/32340; no credit cards; ①), just south of the centre, where dorm space, singles and doubles all cost the same per person. The amiable, three-roomed *Waterwheel Guesthouse,* Bridge St (☎015394/33286; no credit cards; ①), fills quickly; it's up the cobbled alley off Rydal Road right by the bridge across Stock Ghyll. Another popular choice is *3 Cambridge Villas,* Church St (☎015394/32307; no credit cards; ②). Or move up a notch to *Cherry Garth*, Old Lake Rd (☎015394/33128; ④), a roomy Victorian house with gardens and good winter discounts. One of the Lake District's most agreeably sited **youth hostels** is at Waterhead on the A591 (☎015394/32304), a huge lakeside affair with doubles and family rooms available, bike rental and various other useful services; the drawbacks are that it's a twenty-minute walk from Ambleside itself, usually filled to capacity with school parties, and the crowded dining room serves poor cafeteria food. The nearest **campsite** is the *Low Wray National Trust Campsite* (☎015394/32810; closed Nov–Easter) three miles south of town by the lake at Wray – hourly bus #505/506 on the Ambleside to Hawkshead/Coniston route passes within a mile.

Pippins, at 10 Lake Rd, is great for all-day breakfasts, burgers and night-time pizzas, while *Zeffirelli's,* Compston Rd (☎015394/33845) specializes in inexpensive vegetarian pizzas and pasta and offers a three-course -dinner with cinema-ticket special. There's a

---

WALKS FROM AMBLESIDE

The Rothay valley north of Ambleside is largely taken up by the fast A591, which means that Rydal Water and Rydal Mount – the closest attractions – are best seen by bus or on the circular walk from Grasmere (see p.699). Where Ambleside scores is in its proximity to the fells immediately east and west of town, and a couple of good walks are possible straight from the town centre.

The first walk heads west past Ambleside church, through Rothay Park and down to the footbridge across the river. From here you tack past Brow Head Farm, following the path to Lily Tarn and then striking up and northwest across **Loughrigg Fell** (1099ft). Dropping down to Loughrigg Terrace (2hr) overlooking Grasmere, you can then join the Grasmere circular walk at this point, before cutting south at Rydal on the A591 and following the minor road back along the River Rothay to Ambleside – a total of 6 miles (4hr).

The walk over **Wansfell** to **Troutbeck** and back (6 miles, around 4hr) has more extensive views and is a little tougher. Stock Ghyll Lane runs up the left bank of the tumbling stream to one of the more attractive waterfalls in the region, **Stock Ghyll Force**. The path then rises steeply to **Wansfell Pike** (1581ft) and down into Troutbeck village, with the *Mortal Man* inn a short detour to the left. Head south down the minor road through the village, towards Townend, just before which a track leads west onto the flanks of Wansfell and around past the viewpoint at **Jenkin Crag** back to Ambleside.

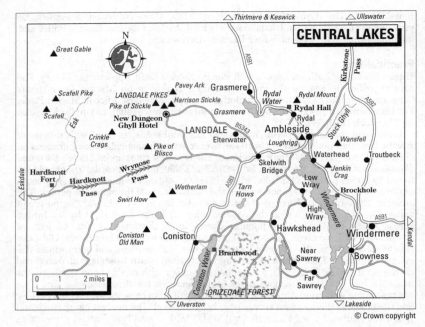

© Crown copyright

pricier, classic Italian menu at *Luigi's,* Kelsick Rd (☎015394/33676; dinner only, closed Sun), near the bus stops. However, easily the best **restaurant** in town is the *Glass House* (☎015394/32137; closed Mon in winter), a renovated, split-level fulling mill with waterwheel on Rydal Road – expect accomplished Mediterranean/Modern-British cooking, for around £25–30 a head; book in advance for dinner or just come for coffee or a light lunch. There are lots of **pubs**, but few worth the effort of tracking down – even the long-standing beer-lover's and climbers' favourite, the *Golden Rule*, on Smithy Brow by Stock Ghyll, is a half-hearted affair, though the *Royal Oak* on Church St does have some popular outdoor tables.

Langdale Valley

Three miles west of Ambleside along the A593, **Skelwith Bridge** marks the start of **Great Langdale**, a U-shaped glacial valley overlooked by the prominent rocky summits of the **Langdale Pikes**, the most popular of the central Lakeland fells. A couple of classic inns and campsites further along the B5343 provide accommodation for most of the serious valley hikers and climbers, but **Elterwater** village, a mile or so west of Skelwith Bridge makes an extremely pretty stopover, too.

The #516 Langdale Rambler **bus** from Ambleside's Kelsick Road runs to Skelwith Bridge, Elterwater and the *Old Dungeon Ghyll Hotel* (see opposite) at the head of the valley between April and October.

Skelwith Bridge

A cluster of houses and businesses huddle along either side of the river at **SKELWITH BRIDGE**, prime among them Kirkstone Galleries (daily: April–Oct 10–6pm,

Nov–March 10am–5pm), an ornamental stonemasons' showroom specializing in Westmorland green slate, with a crowded souvenir store and *Chesters* coffee shop. Once you've splashed in the water by the bridgeside picnic area, you can set off on the rustic stroll along a signposted footpath to Elterwater, just a mile away; the route forms a short section of the Cumbria Way. Drivers should note the minor road south from Skelwith Bridge, up to the *Drunken Duck Inn* (see "Tarn Hows", p.706) and on to Tarn Hows.

Elterwater

ELTERWATER village lies half a mile northwest of its namesake water, an attractive settlement fringed by sheep-filled commonland and centred on a tiny village green. It sees its fair share of Langdale-bound hikers, not least because of its two local **youth hostels**. Both are reasonable spots: *Elterwater Langdale,* just across the bridge from the village (☎015394/37245), is the most convenient; *Langdale High Close*, a mile from Elterwater (☎015394/37313), has a more spectacular setting, high on the road over Red Bank from Skelwith Bridge to Grasmere. There's traditional hospitality at the *Britannia Inn* (☎015394/37210, *britinn@edi.co.uk*; ④), a solid old lakeland pub on the green, with comfortable rooms, and good food in the bar; rates are a few pounds cheaper in the *Maple Tree Corner* annexe. If you're moving on, stock up in the village shop, as it's the last place for supplies this side of the hiking trails.

The Langdale Pikes

Rather than following the B5343 (minor road though it is) west of Elterwater up the valley, stick with the riverside Cumbria Way footpath as far as the *New Dungeon Ghyll Hotel*, three miles from Elterwater. A path indicated by the "Stickle Ghyll" sign (starting point 4 on the Central Lakes map; see opposite) follows the beck straight up to **Stickle Tarn**, around to the right then left up to Pavey Ark. Two more adventurous routes to the top of **Pavey Ark** (2297ft) can be easily seen on the crags above Stickle Tarn: **Jack's Rake** trail ascends the face right to left, and is the hardest commonly used route in the Lake District, requiring a head for heights and steady footing. From near its base, an easier route rises to the right. It is fairly easy from then on to **Harrison Stickle** (2414ft), down to the stream forming the headwaters of Dungeon Ghyll and slowly up to **Pike of Stickle** (2326ft). Backtracking a short distance, a path leads to the right almost parallel with Dungeon Ghyll, back to the start (4 miles; 2400ft ascent; 4hr).

The traditional **accommodation** for anyone visiting the valley is the peerless *Old Dungeon Ghyll Hotel* (☎015394/37272; ⑤, ⑥ with dinner), superbly isolated at the end of the B5343, seven miles northeast of Ambleside; it offers great three-course dinners in its restaurant (book in advance) and also has a stone-flagged hikers' bar with roaring range and filling food. Every British climber of note has stayed at the hotel at some time or other. In the evening, the bar fills up with refugees from the nearby *Great Langdale* campsite (☎015394/37668). A mile or so back down the road, the *New Dungeon Ghyll Hotel* (☎015394/37213; ⑤, ⑥ with dinner) is similarly equipped though a shade smarter than the *Old Ghyll*. You can also eat here, or at the adjacent *Sticklebarn Tavern* (☎015394/37356; ①), which has very popular bunk-barn accommodation; while the *Greenhowe Caravan Park* (☎015394/37231; ②; closed Nov–Feb), just to the south, has a range of static caravans for rent for groups of two and upwards.

Grasmere and around

Four miles northwest of Ambleside, the village of **GRASMERE** consists of an intimate cluster of grey-stone houses on the old packhorse road which runs beside the babbling River Rothay. It's an eminently pleasing ensemble, set back from one of the most alluring of the region's small lakes, but it loses much of its charm in summer thanks to the hordes who descend on the trail of the village's most famous former resident, **William Wordsworth** (1770–1850). The poet, his wife Mary, sister Dorothy and other members of his family are buried beneath the yews in **St Oswald's churchyard** (Mon–Sat 10am–4pm, plus Sun services), in whose interior you can admire the unique twin naves, split by a solid arched partition. At the rear entrance to the churchyard stands **Sarah Nelson's Gingerbread Shop** (Mon–Sat 9.30am–5.30pm, Sun 12.30–5.30pm), converted from the schoolhouse where Wordsworth once taught.

Practicalities

Grasmere is on the main #555 **bus** route between Kendal and Keswick; this and other services stop on the village green. The **tourist office** (April–Oct daily 9.30am–5pm; some winter weekends; ☎015394/35245), five minutes' away down Langdale Road, is tucked in by the main **car park** on Red Bank Road at the southern end of the village.

Accommodation can be hard to come by in summer – book well in advance, especially for popular central places like the *Harwood*, Red Lion Square (☎015394/35248; no credit cards; ③). Some of the nicest places are a little way out of the centre: *Banerigg Guest House* (☎015394/35204; no smoking; no credit cards; ②), is a lakeside property ten minutes' walk out on the Ambleside road (A591) – guests are free to take boats out onto the water; or there's *Titteringdales Guesthouse*, on Pye Lane (☎015394/35439, *Titteringdales@grasmere.net*; no credit cards; ②; closed Jan), to the north, just off the A591. There's a gamut of fancier places, too: Georgian *St Oswald's*, set in its own grounds, off Red Bank Rd (☎015394/35705; ②); *Rothay Lodge* at White Bridge (☎015394/35341; ③), five minutes' walk from the centre; and the *Red Lion* in central Red Lion Square (☎015394/35456; ⑤), which is a sympathetically styled eighteenth-century coaching inn.

Of course, there's no shortage of local places with Wordsworthian connections. Top of the pile is *White Moss House* (☎015394/35295, *dixon@whitemoss.demon.co.uk*; ⑧, with dinner; closed Dec–Feb), a house once owned by Wordsworth, a mile south on the A591, at the northern end of Rydal Water. It's a glorious spot, and the food is wonderful. *The Swan* (☎015394/35551; ⑦, ⑧ at weekends) on the A591 just outside Grasmere rated a mention in Wordsworth's "The Waggoner" and remodelling hasn't robbed it of its essential eighteenth-century character. Lesser budgets are required for *How Foot Lodge*, at Town End (☎015394/35366; ③; closed Jan), a Victorian house owned by the National Trust, just yards from Dove Cottage (see below).

Grasmere has no campsite but two very popular **youth hostels**: *Butterlip How*, a Victorian house 150 yards north of the green on Easedale Road (☎015394/35316), and *Thorney How*, a characterful former farmhouse, just under a mile further along the unlit road (☎015394/35591) – bring a torch.

Picnic fixings are best from Langman's Delicatessen & Bakery in Red Lion Square, while Baldry's (closed Tues–Thur in winter) – also in the square – is a wholefood tea rooms with home-made bread, pies and quiche. Bar **meals** are available in the village pubs, or try the *Rowan Tree Licensed Restaurant*, on Church Bridge, Stock Lane, opposite the churchyard, for vegetarian dishes on a terrace overlooking the river. The fanciest local **restaurants** are those at *White Moss House* and *The Swan* (see above). The only enjoyable **pub** in the village is the *Red Lion* – whose public bar is called the *Lamb Inn*. Otherwise, you'll need to walk out to the *Traveller's Rest*, half a mile north along the A591, a popular place for bar meals, though the thundering main road does its outdoor tables no favours.

Dove Cottage

On the southeastern outskirts of the village, on the main A591, stands **Dove Cottage** (daily 9.30am–5.30pm; closed mid-Jan to mid-Feb; £4.80), home to William and Dorothy Wordsworth from 1799 to 1808 and where Wordsworth wrote some of his best poetry.

Guides bursting with anecdotes lead you around rooms which reflect Wordsworth's guiding principle of "plain living but high thinking" and are little changed now but for the addition of electricity and internal plumbing. This maxim, however, was only temporary, as Wordsworth was raised in comfortable surroundings and returned to a relatively high standard of living when he moved to Rydal Mount. If you visit the cottage, you've already paid for the **museum** full of paintings, manuscripts and bric-a-brac once belonging to the Wordsworths, Southey, Coleridge and Thomas De Quincey. In good weather, the garden is open for visits as well (hours as house).

Rydal Mount

Another mile and a half southeast along the A591 from Grasmere, the hamlet of **RYDAL** consists of an inn, a few houses and **Rydal Mount** (March–Oct daily 9.30am–5pm; Nov–Feb Wed–Mon 10am–4pm; £3.50), home of William Wordsworth from 1813 until his death in 1850. Parts of the house have been redecorated, but furniture and portraits give a good sense of its former occupants, as does Wordsworth's airy attic study. For many, the highlight is the garden, which has been preserved as Wordsworth designed it. Bus #555 passes the house on the way to Grasmere from Windermere/Ambleside.

Coniston Water

At five miles long and half a mile across at its widest point, **Coniston Water** is not one of the most immediately imposing of the lakes, yet it has a quiet beauty which sets it apart from the more popular destinations. The nineteenth-century art critic and social reformer **John Ruskin** made the lake his home and his isolated house today provides the most obvious target for a day-trip, but the plain village grows on visitors after a while, especially those who base themselves at Coniston for some of the central Lakes' most rewarding walking.

In the mid-1960s, the long uninterruptedly glass-like surface of Coniston Water attracted the attention of national hero **Donald Campbell**, who in 1955 had set a world water speed record of 202mph on Ullswater, bumping it up to 276mph nine years later in Australia. On January 4, 1967 he set out to better his own mark on Coniston Water, but just as his jet-powered *Bluebird* hit an estimated 320mph, a patch of turbulence sent it into a somersault. Campbell's shoes, helmet, oxygen mask and teddy bear mascot were recovered from the water, but his body and boat were destroyed completely – the tragic moment was recorded by photographs and newspaper accounts, now on display at the *Sun Inn* in the village.

A CIRCULAR WALK FROM GRASMERE

One of the lakes' easier circuits is the trip **around Grasmere and Rydal Water** from Grasmere village, a shade over four miles. It can be completed in two hours or so, though as it passes Wordsworth haunts Rydal Mount and Dove Cottage, it could be turned into an all-day sightseeing venture.

From the tourist office in Grasmere, follow Red Bank Road along the western edge of the lake, climbing up a track through Redbank Woods after a mile (signposted "Loughrigg Terrace and YHA"). Signposts soon lead you out onto **Loughrigg Terrace** itself, where tremendous views of the lake unfold. The terrace skirts Loughrigg Fell as it heads east and then you switch ridges to follow that above **Rydal Water**, where you'll pass the dripping, water-filled maw of **Rydal Cave**, a disused slate quarry. Rounding the eastern edge of Rydal, you cross and climb off the A591, past the church, to **Rydal Mount**, above which a bridleway runs back above the northern shore of Rydal Water. It emerges at Dove Cottage, on the outskirts of Grasmere.

WRITERS IN THE LAKE DISTRICT

William Wordsworth was not the first to praise the Lake District – Thomas Gray wrote appreciatively of his visit in 1769 – but he dominates its literary landscape, not solely through his poetry but also through his still useful *Guide to the Lakes* (1810). Born in Cockermouth in 1770, he was sent to school in Hawkshead before a stint at Cambridge, a year in France and two in Somerset. In 1799 he returned to the Lake District, settling in the Grasmere district, where he spent the last two-thirds of his life with his sister Dorothy, who not only transcribed his poems but was an accomplished diarist as well.

Wordsworth and fellow poets **Samuel Taylor Coleridge** and **Robert Southey** formed a clique that became known as the "Lake Poets", a label based more on their fluctuating friendships and their shared passion for the region than on any common subject matter in their writings. A fourth member of the Cumbrian literary elite was the critic and essayist **Thomas De Quincey**, chiefly known today for his *Confessions of an English Opium-Eater*. One of the first to fully appreciate the revolutionary nature of Wordsworth's and Coleridge's collaborative *Lyrical Ballads*, De Quincey became a long-term guest of the Wordsworths in 1807, taking over Dove Cottage from them in 1809. He stayed there until 1820, but it was only in the 1830s that he started writing his *Lake Reminiscences*, offending Wordsworth and Coleridge in the process.

Meanwhile, after short spells at Allan Bank and The Vicarage, both in Grasmere, the Wordsworths made Rydal Mount their home, supported largely by William's position as Distributor of Stamps for Westmorland and his later stipend as Poet Laureate. After his death in 1850, William's body was interred in St Oswald's churchyard in Grasmere, to be joined five years later by Dorothy and by his wife Mary four years after that.

Inspired by Wordsworth's writings and by the terrain itself, the social philosopher and art critic **John Ruskin** also made the Lake District his home, settling at Brantwood outside Coniston in 1872. His letters and watercolours reflect a deep love of the area, also demonstrated by his unsuccessful fight to prevent the damming of Thirlmere. Much of Ruskin's feeling for the countryside permeated through to two other literary immigrants, **Arthur Ransome**, also a Coniston resident and writer of the children's classic *Swallows and Amazons*, and **Beatrix Potter**, whose favourite Lakeland spots feature in her children's stories. Potter, in fact, is the only serious lakeland rival to Wordsworthian dominance, with her former home at Hill Top in Near Sawrey, her husband's office in Hawkshead and a museum in Bowness all packed with international visitors throughout the year. Whatever you think of her work, every visitor to the Lakes has at least some cause to be grateful to Beatrix Potter, who donated several parcels of land to the National Trust.

Other famous Lake District literary names must number **Sir Hugh Walpole**, who lived at Derwentwater and set his Herries novels in Borrowdale; **Harriet Martineau**, who lived in Ambleside for thirty years and received most of literary England in her drawing room; poet **Norman Nicholson**; and professional Cumbrian, writer and broadcaster **Melvyn Bragg**.

Practicalities

Buses – principally the #505/506 from Kendal, Windermere, Ambleside or Hawkshead – stop on the main road through the village, outside the **tourist office** (April–Oct daily 9.30am–5.30pm; limited weekend hours in winter; ☎015394/41533). Coniston is something of an outdoors centre and you can **rent bikes** from Meadowdore (☎015394/41638) on the main road near the *Crown*, as well as from Summitreks, 14 Yewdale Rd (☎015394/41212) – the latter also organizes adventurous days out on water and land.

B&Bs are plentiful. The most comfortable are *Shepherds Villa*, Tilberthwaite Ave (☎015394/41337; no credit cards; ③) – the B5285 into the village – and the vegetarian *Beech Tree Guesthouse*, Yewdale Rd (☎015394/41717; no credit cards; ③) – the Ambleside road; both have more expensive en-suite rooms available. *Orchard Cottage*, also on Yewdale Rd (☎015394/41373; no credit cards; ②), but nearer the centre, is a large modern bungalow, but all the spacious rooms are en suite. The fall-back choice is *Lakeland House* on Tilberthwaite Avenue (☎015394/41303; no credit cards; ①), opposite the Campbell memorial – a slightly shabby but friendly enough place, accustomed to walkers and their ways and with an attached café. All the pubs have rooms, but the best are those at the *Sun Hotel* (☎015394/41248; ④, minimum two-night stay at weekends), a fine old inn 200 yards uphill from the bridge in the centre of Coniston. Out of the centre at Waterhead, a slate-flagged farmhouse has been turned into *Thwaite Cottage* (☎015394/41367; no credit cards; ②), half a mile away on the Hawkshead road.

Of the two **youth hostels**, *Coniston Holly How* (☎015394/41323) is the closer, just a few minutes' walk north of Coniston on the Ambleside road, but *Coniston Coppermines* (☎015394/41261) is more peaceful, in a dramatic mountain setting a steep mile or so from the village – either follow the "Old Man" signs past the *Sun Hotel* or strike off up the small road between the *Black Bull* and the Co-op; both routes lead to the hostel. The nearest **campsite** is the *Coniston Hall Campsite*, Haws Bank (☎015394/41223; booking essential; closed Nov–March), a mile south of town by the lake.

Eating opportunities outside the pubs are limited, but in any case you shouldn't look much further than the *Sun Hotel*, whose cosy bar has filling meals. You can get sandwiches made up at *Meadowdore* (see opposite) for your day's walking. The *Sun* is also the cheeriest place for a **drink**, though the *Black Bull* in the centre brews its own *Bluebird* beer.

Coniston village and water

A memorial plaque to Campbell decorates the green in the slate-grey village of **CONISTON** (a derivation of "King's Town"), hunkered below the craggy and copper-mine-riddled bulk of **The Old Man of Coniston** (see box on p.704). Having studied this and Ruskin's grave, which lies in the churchyard beneath a beautifully worked Celtic cross, you've seen all that Coniston has to offer, save for the excellent **Ruskin Museum** on Yewdale Road (Easter to mid-Nov daily 10am–5.30pm; £3), which combines local history exhibits with a fascinating look at Ruskin's life and work through his watercolours, manuscripts and personal memorabilia. The village is a functional kind of place, with plenty of accommodation and cafés, and keeps itself to itself to such an extent that first-time visitors are surprised to find it has a lake – **Coniston Water** is hidden out of sight, half a mile southeast of the village. Here, the *Bluebird Café* sells ices and drinks, while the adjacent Coniston Boating Centre can provide the wherewithal for fooling around on the water – rowing boats, sailing dinghies, canoes, electric launches and motorboats. Boat speeds are now limited to 10mph, a graceful pace for the sumptuously upholstered **Steam Yacht Gondola** (Easter–Oct 4 daily; £4.75 round trip; ☎015394/36003), built in 1859, which leaves Coniston Pier for hour-long circuits, calling at Park-a-moor landing stage then Ruskin's Brantwood. The wooden Coniston **motor launches** (Easter–Oct hourly; Nov–Easter 4 daily depending on the weather; ☎015394/36216) operate a year-round service to Brantwood on two routes, north (£3.40 return) or south (£5.40) around the lake.

Brantwood

Both steam yacht and motor launches dock beneath the magnificently sited **Brantwood** (mid-March to mid-Nov daily 11am–5.30pm; mid-Nov to mid-March Wed–Sun 11am–4pm; house, gardens & launch £7; house only £4; gardens only £2), two and a half miles by road from Coniston, where art critic and moralist **John Ruskin** lived from 1872 until his death in 1900.

Champion of J.M.W. Turner and the Pre-Raphaelites and proponent of the supremacy of Gothic architecture, Ruskin insisted upon the indivisibility of ethics and aesthetics, and was appalled by the conditions in which the captains of industry made their labourers work and live, while expecting him to applaud their patronage of the arts. "There is no wealth but life", he wrote in his study of capitalist economics, *Unto the Last*, elaborating with the observation: "that country is richest which nourishes the greatest number of noble and happy human beings". A twenty-minute video expands on his philosophy and whets the appetite for rooms full of his watercolours, doing justice to a man who greatly influenced such disparate figures as Proust, Tolstoy, Frank Lloyd Wright and Gandhi. Nonetheless, not all Ruskin's projects were a success, partly because of his refusal to compromise his principles. A London teashop, established to provide employment for a former servant, failed since Ruskin refused to advertise; meanwhile, his street-cleaning and road-building schemes, designed to instil into his students (including Arnold Toynbee and Oscar Wilde) a respect for the dignity of manual labour, simply accrued ridicule.

Ruskin bought Brantwood in 1871, sight unseen, from engraver and Radical William James Linton, complaining when he saw it that it was "a mere shed". The views, however, captivated him and Ruskin spent the next twenty years adding to the house and laying out its gardens. His study – hung with handmade paper to his own design – and dining room boast superlative lake views, bettered only by those from the Turret Room where he used to sit in later life in his bathchair, itself on display downstairs, along with his mahogany desk and Blue John wine goblet, among other memorabilia. Various other exhibition rooms and galleries display Ruskin-related arts and crafts, while the *Jumping Jenny Tearooms* – named after Ruskin's boat – has outdoor terrace seating for meals and drinks. There's also a well-stocked book shop if you want to bone up on the Pre-Raphaelites or the Arts and Crafts Movement.

Hawkshead and around

Greystone **HAWKSHEAD**, between Coniston and Ambleside, wears its beauty well, its patchwork of cottages and cobbles backed by woods and fells and barely affected by twentieth-century intrusions. This is partly due to the enlightened policy of banning traffic in the centre – huge car parks at the village edge take the strain and when the crowds of day-trippers leave, Hawkshead regains its natural tranquility.

The Vikings were the first to settle the land here, the village probably founded by and named for one Haukr, a Norse warrior. It was an important wool market at the time Wordsworth was studying at **Hawkshead Grammar School** (Easter–Oct Mon–Sat 10am–12.30pm & 1.30–4.30pm, Sun 1–5pm; £2), founded in 1585, whose entrance lies opposite the tourist office – pride of place is given to the desk on which William carved his signature. While there he attended the fifteenth-century **Church** (daily 9am–6pm) above the school, which harks back to Norman designs in its

---

THE OLD MAN OF CONISTON

The walk from Coniston village to the top of the **Old Man of Coniston** (2628ft) is one of the Cumbrian classics, tiring but not overly difficult. Staying at *Coniston Coppermines* youth hostel gives you an early start. Otherwise, from the bridge in the village, follow the path to the *Coppermines* hostel up past the *Sun Hotel*. At Church Beck, with the hostel in the distance ahead, a sign on the gated bridge puts you on the path, with the stream to your right. The path gradually swings to the left, taking a steep and twisting route through abandoned quarry works and their detritus, including several fallen heavy-duty pulley systems. Cairns keep you on the right route, up past a gorgeous glassy tarn, and then there's a final scramble to the massive cairn at the **summit** (under 2hr for most walkers). The views from here are tremendous – to the Cumbrian coast, and across to Langdale, Windermere and Coniston itself.

rounded pillars and patterned arches. Its chief interest is in the 26 pithy psalms and biblical extracts illuminated with cherubs and flowers, painted on the walls during the seventeenth and eighteenth centuries.

From its knoll the churchyard gives a good view over the village's twin central squares, and of Main Street, housing the **Beatrix Potter Gallery** (Easter–Oct Sun–Thurs 10.30am–4.30pm; £2.90; NT), occupying rooms once used by her solicitor husband. With their timed-entry ticket, fans get bustled into rooms full of Potter's original illustrations, though the less devoted might find displays on her life as keen naturalist, conservationist and early supporter of the National Trust more diverting – Potter bequeathed her farms and land in the Lake District to the Trust on her death.

Practicalities

The main **bus service** to Hawkshead is the #505/506 between Bowness, Ambleside and Coniston; on reaching Hawkshead it loops down to Hill Top and back for the Beatrix Potter house at Near Sawrey. The **tourist office** is at the main car park (Easter–Oct daily 9.30am–5.30pm; rest of year limited weekend hours; ☎015394/36525) and can change money, book you on free local guided walks and assist with finding **accommodation**. Some contend that Wordsworth briefly boarded at what is now *Ann Tyson's Cottage*, Wordsworth St (☎015394/36405; no credit cards; ②), behind the fifteenth-century Minstrels Gallery on the main square. There are also two adjacent self-catering cottages available for rent. *Ivy House*, Main St (☎015394/36204; ④) makes a characterful base with its eighteenth-century elegance; and *Greenbank House Hotel*, fifty yards further along Main St (☎015394/36497; ②), at the edge of the village, is also good. Dinner is available at both places. All four of the village's **pubs** also have accommodation, with the sixteenth-century *Queen's Head* on Main Street (☎015394/36271; ④) the pick of the bunch: off-season and multi-day stays bring the price down a few pounds. The **youth hostel**, *Esthwaite Lodge* (☎015394/36293), is a mile to the south down the Newby Bridge road, housed in a Regency mansion with good-sized family rooms. **Camping** is available in the heart of Grizedale Forest (see below), which will be more relaxed than at Hawkshead's busy *Croft Caravan and Campsite* (☎015394/36374; closed Nov to mid-March), on North Lonsdale Road, right by the village. There's a second local site, *Hawkshead Hall Farm* (☎015394/36221; closed Dec–Feb), half a mile north of the village – bus #505/506 passes it on the way into Hawkshead.

Pubs provide the main **eating** options, not bad at either the *Queen's Head* or *King's Arms*, both of which have bar meals as well as a more formal restaurant. Of the tearooms, *Whig's* on The Square (closed Thurs) serves its eponymous speciality baked rolls; while *Room With a View* in Laburnam House, immediately below the church, is a rated vegetarian restaurant.

Grizedale Forest

If the weather looks promising, time is well spent among the remarkable sculptures in **Grizedale Forest**, southwest of Hawkshead, which drapes over the Furness Fells separating Coniston Water from Windermere. There's a summer bus service (#515, from Ambleside and Hawkshead or Ulverston and Newby Bridge) to **Grizedale Forest Centre** (Feb–Dec daily 10am–5pm; free; parking £2; ☎01229/860010), three miles southwest of Hawkshead; otherwise you'll have to **rent a bike** from the *Croft* campsite in Hawkshead. Grizedale Mountain Bikes at the centre (daily 9am–5pm; call ☎01229/860369 to reserve in advance) also has (slightly more expensive) bikes available, or just head out on foot along ten miles of the Silurian Way, which links the majority of the eighty-odd stone and wood sculptures scattered among the trees. Since 1977 artists have been invited to come here, often for six months at a time, to create a sculptural response to their surroundings using natural materials. Some of the resulting works are startling, as you round a bend to find a hundred-foot-long wave of bent logs or a dry-stone wall slaloming the conifers. Pick up a map from the centre and take a picnic. If you're planning to use the **campsite** (☎01229/860257; closed Oct–Feb), just past the visitor centre, call ahead as it's very popular.

Hill Top

It's two miles from Hawkshead, down the eastern side of Esthwaite Water on the B5285 to the pretty twin hamlets of Near and Far Sawrey, the first the site of Beatrix Potter's beloved **Hill Top** (Easter–Oct Sat–Wed 11am–5pm; £4; NT). A Londoner by birth, Potter bought the farmhouse here with the proceeds from her first book, *The Tale of Peter Rabbit*, and retained it as her study long after she moved out following her marriage in 1913. Its furnishings and contents have been kept as they were during her occupancy – a condition of Potter's will – and the small house is always busy with visitors; so much so that numbers are often limited. In summer, expect to have to queue.

The *Tower Bank Arms* in the village is the place to muse on your next move. You'd be lucky to get a room in one of the local B&Bs, but another mile down the road brings you to the **ferry crossing** across Windermere to Bowness (see p.693). A signposted "hilltop to the lake" path connects the ferry terminal with the Potter house.

Tarn Hows

A minor road off the Hawkshead–Coniston B5285 winds the couple of miles northwest to the highly popular **Tarn Hows**, a body of water surrounded by spruce and pine and circled by paths and picnic spots. The land was donated by Beatrix Potter in 1930 – one of several such grants – since when the National Trust has carefully maintained it. It takes an hour to walk around the tarn, during which you can ponder on the fact that this miniature idyll is in fact almost entirely artificial – the original owners enlarged two small tarns to make the one you see today, planted and landscaped the surroundings and dug the footpaths. It's now a Site of Special Scientific Interest – keep an eye out for some of the Lakes' (and England's) few surviving native red squirrels.

A special, free, National Trust Tarn Hows **bus service** runs between Hawkshead and Coniston on Sundays between Easter and the end of October, linking with the regular #505/506. Otherwise, you'll have to pay to use the designated car park. Drivers, though, then have the option of following the signs north to Ambleside along the minor road, reaching the *Drunken Duck Inn* (☎015394/36347, *drunkenduckinn@demon.co.uk*; ⑤) after three miles, at the **Barngates** crossroads. There's a cheery welcome, fine rooms, deservedly popular bar food and occasional folk/jazz gigs. From here, the road descends in two improbably steep and narrow miles to Skelwith Bridge (see p.698).

Keswick and Derwent Water

Standing on the shores of **Derwent Water** at the junction of the main north–south and east–west routes through the Lake District, **KESWICK** makes a good base for exploring delightful Borrowdale – the start of many walking routes to the central peaks around Scafell Pike – or Skiddaw and Blencathra, which loom over the town. There's plenty of accommodation and some good cafés aimed at walkers, while several bus routes radiate from the town, getting you to the start of even the most challenging hikes. For those not up to a day on the fells, the town remains a popular place throughout the year, with a big enough population (around five thousand) to warrant a bevy of local museums and sights.

Arrival and information

Most **buses**, including National Express services, use the terminal behind Lakes Foodstore, off Main St. The joint **tourist office** and **National Park Information**

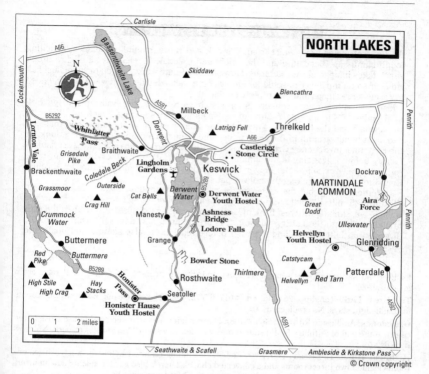

© Crown copyright

Centre is in the Moot Hall on Market Square (daily: April–June & Sept–Oct 9.30am–5.30pm; July & Aug 9.30am–7pm; Nov–March 10am–4pm; ☎017687/72645). George Fisher, at 2 Borrowdale Rd (☎017687/72178), is one of the most celebrated **outdoors stores** on the Lakes, with a full range of equipment and maps, a daily weather information service and café. For **bike rental**, try Keswick Mountain Bikes on Southey Hill (☎017687/75202). Daily **guided walks** – from lakeside rambles to mountain climbs – depart daily (Easter–Oct 10.15am; £4) from the Moot Hall; just turn up with a packed lunch.

B&Bs and hotels

You should have no trouble finding accommodation, and competition at the lower end of the market keeps the prices keen. B&Bs cluster along Bank Street and Stanger Street, near the post office, and around Southey, Blencathra and Eskin streets, in the grid near the start of the A591 Penrith road. Smarter places line *The Heads*, overlooking Hope Park, a couple of minutes' south of the centre on the way to the lake.

Bluestones, 7 Southey St (☎017687/74237). Well-kept guest house used to walkers; big breakfasts and on-street parking. No credit cards. ①.

Bridgedale Guesthouse, 101 Main St (☎017687/73914). The cheapest central rooms, just around the corner from the bus station; options range from a bed-only rate to an en-suite room. No credit cards. ①.

Derwentwater Hotel, at Portinscale, off the A66 (☎017687/72538, *derwentwater.hotel@dial.pipex.com*). Superior lakeside retreat (two miles west of Keswick) with comfortable rooms – some deluxe, with

---

WALKS FORM KESWICK

All sorts of major walks start from Keswick and the surrounding villages, including tough climbs up Blencathra and the celebrated Coledale Horseshoe, an all-day circuit which takes in up to eleven summits. However, moderate walkers keen to spend just half a day or so on the fells can settle for either of the walks detailed below – you'll still need to carry decent maps and be properly equipped.

Rising sharply through coniferous forests above Keswick, the walk up **Latrigg Fell** (4–6 miles; 900ft ascent; 2–3hr) gives splendid views across Derwent Water to Borrowdale and the high fells. Follow Station Road past the youth hostel and museum and, as it bends around to the right to become Brundholme Road/Briar Rigg, look for the right turn up Spooney Green Lane across the A66. From here skirt the west flank of Latrigg before zigzagging to the summit from the north. Return either directly down the southern gully or follow the longer eastern ridge to Brundholme, returning through Brundholme wood or along the railway path.

More demanding, but the easiest of the region's true mountain walks, is the hike up **Skiddaw** (5 miles; 3000ft ascent; 5hr), a smooth mound of splintery slate. Follow the walk above, skirting the west flank of Latrigg, but continue straight ahead when the path branches right to the Latrigg summit. It is pretty much a steady walk (with a possible diversion up Little Man along the way) before reaching a false summit and finally the 3054ft High Man.

---

lounges and sweeping views – a conservatory and rated restaurant. Two-night B&B rates are a good deal. ⑦.

The Great Little Teashop, 26 Lake Rd (☎017687/73545). Relaxed teashop B&B, with discounts for multi-night stays. No credit cards. ②.

Greystones, Ambleside Rd (☎017687/73108). Non-smoking Victorian terraced house close to the centre at the end of St John's St. En-suite rooms with fell views and TVs; guests car park. No credit cards. ②.

Highfield Hotel, The Heads (☎017687/72508). Beautifully restored hotel whose stylish feature rooms include two turret rooms and a converted chapel. There's also garden seating and an inventive restaurant with some of the best food in town. ③, ④ for feature rooms.

Howe Keld, 5–7 The Heads (☎017687/72417). Welcoming, non-smoking, mid-sized hotel with a reputation for great breakfasts (vegetarian specialities included) and cosy rooms. Car park. ③.

Keswick Country House Hotel, Station Rd (☎017687/72020). Grand Victorian hotel, built for the nineteenth-century railway trade and sitting in landscaped grounds, with dinner.

Lane's End, 4 High St (☎017687/74436). Delightful flower-clad cottage with just three rooms, tucked away off St John's St. No credit cards. ①.

Lyzzick Hall, Under Skiddaw, A591 (☎017687/72277). A couple of miles northwest of town, this is a relaxed country-house hotel set in its own grounds, with an indoor pool and very good restaurant. ⑤, ⑥ with dinner.

CAMPSITES AND YOUTH HOSTELS

Castlerigg Hall, Castlerigg (☎017687/72437; closed Nov–Easter). Out-of-town campsite, southeast of Keswick; you can reach the nearby stone circle by footpath.

Derwentwater Caravan Club and Camping Site (☎017687/72392; closed Dec & Jan). Less than ten minutes' walk from the centre, down by the lake, off Main St beside the supermarket.

Derwentwater Youth Hostel, Borrowdale (☎017687/77246). Based in an old mansion with fifteen acres of grounds sloping down to the lake, a couple of miles south of Keswick along the B5289.

Keswick Youth Hostel, Station Rd (☎017687/72484). A converted woollen mill by the river in town; good location, and free tea and coffee on arrival.

Skiddaw House Youth Hostel (phone *Carrock Fell* hostel: ☎016974/78325). One of the most remote buildings in England, 1500ft above sea level and with no motor vehicle access; it's on the Cumbria Way, six miles from Keswick by path. Bunk beds, log fires and limited food supplies; bring your own.

The town and around

Granted its market charter by Edward I in 1276 – **market day** is Saturday – Keswick was an important wool and leather centre until around 1500, when these trades were supplanted by the discovery of local graphite. **The Cumberland Pencil Museum**, west of the centre at Greta Bridge, on Main St (daily 9.30am–4pm; £2.50), tells the story, beginning with its early application as moulds for cannon balls. With the Italian idea of putting graphite into wooden holders, Keswick became an important pencil-making town, and remained one until the late eighteenth century, when the French discovered how to make pencil graphite cheaply by binding the common amorphous graphite with clay. Keswick's monopoly was quickly broken, and only the factory which owns the museum still survives. Inside, a mock-up of the long-defunct Borrowdale mine leads through a potted history of graphite use, with multifarious examples of the finished product and a video of the modern process.

On the edge of Fitz Park, on Station Road, you'll find the **Keswick Park Museum and Art Gallery** (Easter–Oct daily 10am–4pm; £1), a quirky Victorian collection of ancient dental tools, fossils and some prized manuscripts and letters written by the Lakeland Poets. Less relevant, but perhaps more entertaining, is the **Cars of the Stars Motor Museum**, Standish St (Easter to early Jan daily 10am–5pm; £3), showcasing The Saint's Volvo, James Bond's Lotus, Lady Penelope's Rolls Royce, and Chitty Chitty Bang Bang among others.

Keswick's most celebrated landmark, the nearby **Castlerigg Stone Circle**, is made especially resonant by its magnificent mountain backdrop. From the end of Station Road, take the Threlkeld rail line path (signposted by the *Keswick Country House Hotel*) for half a mile, then turn onto the minor road to the right where the path runs under the road – the site's a mile further on atop a sweeping plateau. Thirty-eight hunks of Borrowdale volcanic stone, the largest almost eight feet tall, form a circle a hundred feet in diameter; another ten blocks delineating a rectangular enclosure within. The array probably had an astronomical or timekeeping function when it was erected four or five thousand years ago. Back on the rail path, you can easily continue all the way to **Threlkeld** itself, three miles from town, on a delightful riverside walk with the promise of a drink in one of Threlkeld's old pubs at the end. Keener hikers use Threlkeld as the starting point for the gut-busting climb up **Blencathra**, whose five great ridges loom above the A66: you'll need to be well prepared to tackle this.

Eating, drinking and entertainment

Many of the **places to eat** cater to a walking crowd, which means large portions and few airs. Several of the **pubs** also have meals worth investigating, while there's a fair amount of entertainment in Keswick throughout the year: a **cinema** on St John's St (closed Dec–Feb), the annual **jazz festival** each May, **beer festival** in June, and traditional country shows in the locality during the summer.

Abraham's Tea Rooms, in George Fisher's outdoor store, 2 Borrowdale Rd. The top-floor tearoom comes to your aid with warming mugs of *glühwein*, home-made soups, big breakfasts and daily specials. No credit cards. Inexpensive.

Brysons, 42 Main St. Top-notch bakery and tearooms with breakfasts, traditional main dishes and cream teas. No credit cards. Inexpensive.

The Four in Hand, Lake Rd, opposite George Fisher's. Popular pub for its food – grilled Cumberland ham and eggs, local trout and other Lakeland specialities. Inexpensive to Moderate.

The Great Little Tea Shop, 26 Lake Rd. Daytime jacket potatoes and sandwiches give way to evening meals of vegetarian bakes, seafood specials and local duck; it's open until 9pm. No credit cards. Moderate.

Loose Box Pizzeria, King's Arms Courtyard, Main St (☎017687/72083). Popular pizza-and-pasta joint – the house special is *spaghetti rustica* (tomato, garlic, chilli and prawns). Moderate.

Mayson's, 33 Lake Rd. Licensed, self-service café serving bakes, pies and stir-fries (until 8.45pm in summer). No credit cards. Inexpensive.

La Primavera, Greta Bridge (☎017687/74621).The town's top restaurant, with classic pastas, meats and fish; closed Mon. Moderate to Expensive.

Around Derwent Water

On any reasonably decent day, the best move in Keswick is down to the shores of **Derwent Water**, five minutes' walk south of the centre along Lake Road and through the pedestrian underpass. It's among the most attractive of the lakes, ringed by crags and studded with islets, and is most easily seen by hopping on the **Keswick Launch** (Easter–Nov daily 10am–6pm, until 7.30pm in summer; £4.85 round-trip, or 75p per stage; ☎017687/72263), which runs right around the lake calling at several points en route.

Departures are frequent enough to combine a cruise with a lakeside walk; or you can make the entire lake loop on foot from Keswick on the **Derwent Water Circuit** (around 10 miles; 3–4hr), outlined in a leaflet available from the tourist office. The closest and most popular hike is to **Friars' Crag**, from where medieval pilgrims left for St Herbert's Island in the middle of the lake, to seek the hermit's blessing. Ruskin's childhood visit to Friars' Crag inspired "intense joy, mingled with awe", feelings likely to be duplicated if you return to Keswick via the 530ft Castlehead view point – a three-mile round-trip in all. Other ports of call as you make your way around Derwent Water on foot or by launch include the dry-stone **Ashness Bridge** and **Lodore Falls** (see "Borrowdale", below, for both) and the woodlands and moulded landscapes of **Lingholm Gardens**. Best climb is up **Cat Bells** (launch to Hawes End), a renowned vantage-point (1481ft) above the lake's western shore – allow two -and -a -half hours for the scramble to the top and a return along the wooded lake shore.

Borrowdale and Scafell

It is difficult to overstate the beauty of **Borrowdale**, with its river flats and yew trees, lying at the head of Derwent Water and overshadowed by the peaks of **Scafell** and **Scafell Pike**, the highest in England. Climbs up these, as well as up Great Gable, one of the finest-looking mountains in England, start from the head of the valley, accessible on the #77/77a and #79 **buses** from Keswick, which run south along the B5289.

Just before the *Derwentwater* youth hostel, a narrow road branches left for a steep climb to the photogenic **Ashness Bridge**. The minor road ends two miles further south at **Watendlath**, an idyllic little tarn and tearooms which can be hopelessly overrun at times in summer – the National Trust's free Watendlath Wanderer bus runs here every couple of hours from Keswick on summer Sundays, via Ashness. A path from Watendlath continues on to Rosthwaite, a mile and a half southwest – an easy hour's walk.

Back on the B5289, a path at the agreeable *Stakis Lodore Hotel* (☎017687/77285; ⑧, with dinner) heads to the **Lodore Falls**. This diversion is only really worth it after sustained wet weather, when you'll be able to appreciate Robert Southey's magnificent, alliterative evocation of the falls in *The Cataract of Lodore*: "Collecting, projecting, receding and speeding, and shocking and rocking, and darting and parting", and so on, for line after memorable line.

Further south, past the wonderfully sited *Borrowdale Hotel* (☎017687/77224; ⑦, with dinner), which has an excellent restaurant, there's a slight detour across an old packhorse bridge to **GRANGE**, a peaceful riverside hamlet, peered down upon by Borrowdale's forested crags. *Grange Bridge Cottage* (☎017687/77201; no credit cards; ①) has just one double room available and it's in a great spot, right by the bridge with an attached tea garden. There are a couple of other local B&Bs, too, while a very minor road (and the Cumbria Way) meanders up the west side of Derwent Water from here to Keswick, with a diversion at Manesty to climb Cat Bells (see opposite).

At Grange, it's under a mile south to the 1900-ton **Bowder Stone**, a house-sized lump of rock scaled by way of a wooden ladder and worn to a shine on top by thousands of pairs of feet. Controversy surrounds the origin of the rock. Some say it came from the fells above, others contend it was brought by the last Ice Age from Scotland.

Shaded paths through the wood, and the B5289, lead in around a mile to the straggling hamlet of **ROSTHWAITE**, which sustains the most concentrated batch of accommodation in the valley. As well as two or three B&Bs, there are comfortable rooms at the hiker-friendly *Royal Oak Hotel* (☎017687/77214; ⑤, with dinner) and the smarter, neighbouring *Scafell Hotel* (☎017687/77208; ⑤). Tea and scones served in the *Royal Oak*'s firelit sitting room are a treat. For something more substantial, the *Scafell Hotel*'s attached *Riverside Inn* – the only local pub – serves popular bar meals, while the set dinner in either hotel's restaurant is a good deal, too. At the general store – the only one in the valley – you'll be able to put together a basic picnic. A nice **youth hostel**, *Borrowdale Longthwaite* (☎017687/77257), is a mile south of Rosthwaite, on the riverside footpath to Seatoller, opposite *Chapel House Farm* **campsite** (☎017687/77602).

Another mile on, **SEATOLLER** and the **Seatoller Barn National Park Information Centre** (Easter–Nov daily 10am–5pm; ☎017687/77294) marks the end of the #79 bus route from Keswick. There are regular events, craft displays, talks and walks based at the information centre; there's also a car park and a few slate-roofed houses clustered around the moderately priced *Yew Tree Restaurant* (☎017687/77634; closed Mon in winter & all Jan), a cosy place fashioned from seventeenth-century cottages. *Seatoller House* (☎017687/77218; no credit cards; ③; closed Dec–Feb) next door has **rooms** (and dinner available), and there's an informal **campsite** in a small field by the beck along the minor road south to **SEATHWAITE**, twenty minutes' walk away. This is a popular base for walks up the likes of Great Gable and Scafell Pike (see below): the trout farm at the foot of the valley has a fine **café** (Easter–Sept daily 10am–6.30pm), serving fresh grilled trout or sandwiches, and there's another basic **campsite** used extensively by Great Gable climbers.

Scafell, Scafell Pike and Great Gable

In good weather, the minor road to Seathwaite is lined with parked cars by 9am as hikers take to the paths for the rugged climbs up the three major peaks of Scafell, Scafell Pike and Great Gable. Technically, the climbs are not too difficult, though, as always, you should be well-prepared and reasonably fit.

The summit of **Scafell Pike** (3205ft), the highest point in England, is close to the second highest point in the Lakes, **Scafell** (3163ft), and an eight-mile, six-hour, loop walk taking in both leaves Seathwaite via Stockley Bridge to the south, branching up Styhead Ghyll to **Styhead Tarn**. This is as far as many get, and on those all-too-rare glorious summer days the tarn is a fine place for a picnic. A direct, but very steep approach to **Great Gable** (2949ft) is also possible from Styhead Tarn, though most people cut west at Seathwaite campsite up Sourmilk Ghyll and approach via **Green Gable** (2628ft), also an eight-mile, six-hour return walk. However, the easiest Great Gable climb is actually from Honister Pass.

Buttermere, Crummock Water, Lorton Vale and Loweswater

Overlooked by the steep Borrowdale Fells, the B5289 cuts west at Seatoller, up and over the dramatic **Honister Pass**. Bus #77/77A comes this way, making the initial, steep mile-and-a-quarter grind to the car park at the top of Honister Pass, by the *Honister Hause* **youth hostel** (☎017687/77267). Great Gable climbers start from here and follow a path (6 miles; 4hr) past Grey Knotts and Brandreth to Green Gable, before rounding Great Gable and returning along an almost parallel path to the west.

Back at the pass, the B5289 follows Gatesgarthdale Beck for three miles and makes a dramatic descent into the **Buttermere valley** by *Gatesgarth Farm* campsite (☎017687/70256), then runs another mile beside the lake – past more camping at *Dalegarth* (☎017687/70233; closed Nov–March) – to the **youth hostel** (☎017687/70245) just before **BUTTERMERE** village. The village has two hotels: the *Bridge Hotel* (☎017687/70252; ⑥, ⑦ with dinner) and the smaller *Fish Hotel* (☎017687/70253; ③) – both serve reasonable meals, while the *Bridge* has a popular, traditional flagstoned, bar. There's **camping** at *Syke Farm* right by the lake.

The village itself – set between the two expanses of Buttermere and neighbouring **Crummock Water** – makes a good walking base, with a particularly easy two-mile hike out along Crummock Water's southwestern edge to the 125ft **Scale Force** falls. The four-mile, **round-lake** stroll circling Buttermere itself shouldn't take more than a couple of hours; you can always detour up Scarth Gap to Haystacks if you want more of a climb and some views. The much longer classic walkers' circuit (8 miles; 6hr 30min) climbs from the village up **Red Pike** and then runs along the ridge, via High Stile, High Crag and Haystacks, before descending Scarth Gap or Warnscale Bottom back to the lake.

The scenery flattens out as the road heads north from Crummock Water and into the pastoral **Lorton vale**, with Cockermouth just a few miles beyond. A minor road south just beyond Brackenthwaite leads directly to minuscule **Loweswater**, one of the less frequented lakes, around which there's a gentle, four-mile (2hr) walk. En route, you'll pass the *Kirkstile Inn* (☎01900/85219; no credit cards; ③), a welcoming sixteenth-century inn with decent bar meals.

The #77/77A bus leaves Lorton vale just shy of Cockermouth at Lorton, turning east along the B5292 to tackle the **Whinlatter Pass** on the way back to Keswick. It's an easy ascent – no relation to the hardier passes to the south – dominated by the woodland plantations of the **Whinlatter Forest Park**, whose visitor centre (daily: summer 10am–5pm; winter 11am–4pm; ☎017687/78469) has a café, exhibitions, waymarked trails for hikers and cyclists (bike rental available), and a permanent orienteering course.

Wast Water and Eskdale

Great Gable and Scafell stand as a formidable last-gasp boundary between the mountains of the central lakes and the gentler land to the southwest, which smooths out its wrinkles as it descends to the Cumbrian coast. **Wast Water**, which points its slender finger towards the pass between both ranges, remains one of the most isolated of the region's lakes; at its southern end, forested valleys fall away into **Eskdale**, perhaps the prettiest of the unsung Lakeland valleys. **Public transport** is very limited; in fact, there's none to Wast Water, which makes it one to savour if you fancy getting right off

---

A RIVERSIDE WALK FROM ESKDALE

An easy riverside walk (2 miles; 1hr) starts 200 yards east of Dalegarth station down a track to St Catherine's church opposite the road to Boot. In low water you can cross the river below the church by stepping stones; you turn right, then left, up a path beside a stream to **Stanley Ghyll Waterfall**. Returning along the path beside the stream, a branch on the left leads back to Dalegarth station via a bridge over a swimming hole. If you don't cross the stepping stones, you can take a path following the right bank to Doctor Bridge where you can cross and double back for Stanley Ghyll or continue to the road and the *Woolpack Inn*.

the beaten track. Eskdale is accessed either by the Ravenglass and Eskdale Railway (see p.724), which drops you right in the heart of superb walking country around the hamlet of Boot; or by the east–west minor road route between the coast, via Eskdale Green, and Little Langdale, just west of Skelwith Bridge.

Wast Water

The awesome sight of the peaks crowding slim, deep **Wast Water**, impresses most visitors who venture to this remote lake. The highest slopes in England frame the northern shores, while on the wild southeastern banks rise the impassable screes which separate the lake from Eskdale to the south. The only road winds from the main coastal A595, through remote settlements, before meeting the lake at its southwestern tip, at the *Wasdale Hall* **youth hostel** (☎019467/26222), a country house set in its own lakeside grounds – the nearest other hostels are Black Sail (7 miles), Eskdale (10 miles) and Borrowdale (9 miles), all a day's hike away.

The minor road then hugs the shore of the lake, ending four miles away at **Wasdale Head**, a Shangri-la-like clearing between the mountain ranges, where you'll find the marvellous *Wasdale Head Inn* (☎019467/26229; ⑤), with good food and rooms. Nearby, there's the National Trust's *Wasdale Head* **campsite** (☎019467/26220; closed Nov–March). Scafell Pike and Great Gable are both popular hiking targets from here, as is the route over the pass into Borrowdale. Hikers can also head south, via Wasdale Head Hall Farm and Burnmoor Tarn, over the fells into Eskdale (5 miles; 3hr).

Eskdale

The attractive rural ride by road or train through **Eskdale** from the west begins to peter out as you approach Dalegarth station (terminus of the Ravenglass and Eskdale Railway), just beyond which nestles the dead-end hamlet of **BOOT**. The few stone houses cowering beneath the fells mark the last remnant of civilization before the road turns serious. Three miles beyond Boot and 800-feet up, the remains of granaries, bath houses and the commandant's quarters for **Hardknott Roman Fort** command a strategic and panoramic position. After negotiating the appalling, narrow switchbacks of **Hardknott Pass**, the road drops to Cockley Beck, before making the equally alarming ascent of **Wrynose Pass**; at the col, the **Three Shire Stone** marks the old boundary of Cumberland, Westmorland and Lancashire. Beyond, it's a seven-mile descent past the foot of the Langdale valley to Ambleside – by the time you reach the *Three Shires* pub in Little Langdale you'll need a stiff drink.

Boot has a fair smattering of **accommodation and services**, which makes it the obvious base for extended walks in the valley, though there are B&Bs and the occasional pub in pretty nearby hamlets like Eskdale Green and Santon Bridge, back down the valley. The nearest place to Dalegarth station, and one of the nicest, is *Brook House Hotel* (☎019467/23288; ③), which serves meals in its *Poachers Bar* and has a separate restaurant, too. Further up, in Boot itself, the *Burnmoor Inn* (☎019467/23224, *burnmoor@montrose.demon.co.uk*; ③) is the traditional hikers' choice, with decent en-suite rooms, lashings of hot water and hearty Cumbrian food – there's *glühwein* served in the bar and a peaceful beer garden.

Further up the road past the hamlet it's 500 yards to *Hollins Farm* **campsite** (☎019467/23253) and another three-quarters of a mile to the *Woolpack Inn* (☎019467/23230; ③). This is also a hikers' favourite, serving filling food, and doubling as a common starting point for the **Woolpack Round** (16 miles; 8–10hr), a tough circuit topping the two highest mountains in England and several others which aren't much lower. It is not easy going and a certain amount of scrambling is required, but the views and the varied terrain make this one of the finest Lakeland walks. Another 400 yards beyond the pub you'll find *Eskdale* **youth hostel** (☎019467/23219).

Cockermouth

The farming community of **COCKERMOUTH**, midway between the coast and Keswick at the confluence of the Cocker and Derwent rivers, is yet another station on the Wordsworth trail: the **Wordsworth House** on Main St (Easter–June Mon–Fri, 11am–5pm; July & Aug Mon–Sat, 11am–5pm; £2.80; NT) is where William and Dorothy were born and spent their first few years. The terracotta-hued eighteenth-century building was nearly replaced by a bus station in the 1930s, but was saved and given to the National Trust who have furnished it with imports from their vaults. Some of the original features remain and there are occasional Wordsworthian relics – a chest of drawers here, a pair of candlesticks there – but despite the best endeavours of the enthusiastic staff it's disappointingly lifeless. The kitchen has been put to good use as a café, but on a warm day the walled garden beside the river is more pleasurable than the house.

Cockermouth tries hard to please, with its tree-lined streets and riverside setting, but after the dramatic fellside approaches from the south and east the town itself falls a little flat. However, there's certainly no shortage of local attractions, even if they're all resolutely minor in scale and appeal. Next door to the Wordsworth House, you can get your hands dirty at **The Printing House**, 102 Main St (Easter–Oct Mon–Sat 10am–4pm; £2.50), where visitors are invited to tackle some of the seventy-odd printing machines ranging from wood-block to Linotype. Otherwise it's a toss-up on a rainy day between **The Cumberland Toy and Model Museum**, Banks Court (Feb–Nov daily 10am–5pm; £2), and the 90-minute-long **Jenning's Brewery Tour**, on Brewery Lane nearer the river (Easter–June & Oct Mon–Fri 11am & 2pm; July–Sept Mon–Fri 11am & 2pm, Sat 11am; £3; booking advisable; ☎01900/823214), which culminates with a tasting. Things improve somewhat inside **Castlegate House** (March–Dec Mon, Tues, Fri & Sat 10.30am–5pm, Wed 10.30am–7pm; free), a Georgian mansion on Castlegate, opposite the entrance to Cockermouth Castle – itself a private residence and closed to the public. The house supports a changing programme of contemporary art displays, specializing in the work of some very accomplished local artists.

Finally, you may derive some entertainment from the **Lakeland Sheep and Wool Centre** (Easter to mid-Nov daily; call for times; £3), south of town on the Egremont road, where indoor sheepdog trials, sheep-shearing displays and related exhibits introduce visitors to the complexities of country life. Access to the visitor centre and café is free.

Practicalities

All **buses**, including National Express services, stop on Main Street, from where you follow the signs east to the **tourist office** in the Town Hall, off Market Place (April–June & Oct Mon–Sat 10.30am–4.30pm; July–Sept Mon–Sat 10am–6pm, Sun 2–5pm; Nov–March Mon–Sat 10.30am–4pm; ☎01900/822634). Two of the best **B&Bs** are fairly central: the biker- and hiker-friendly *Castlegate Guest House*, 6 Castlegate (☎01900/826749; no credit cards; ②), and *Manor House*, 23 St Helen's St (☎01900/822416; no credit cards; ①), beyond the end of Market Place. The *Trout Hotel* on Crown Street (☎01900/823591; ⑤), by the river, is the top choice, and there are also nice, modern rooms available in the *Shepherd's Hotel*, out at the Lakeland Sheep and Wool Centre (☎01900/822673; ②). Ten minutes' walk south along Station Road, then Fern Bank brings you to the *Double Mills* **youth hostel** (☎01900/822561) in a seventeenth-century watermill. *Wyndham Holiday Park* (☎01900/822571; closed Dec–Feb) lies a similar distance east along St Helen's Street and St Helen's Road.

Eating well, at least during the day, requires a little perseverance. All the pubs along Main Street compete to sell the same poor bar meals at rock-bottom prices, which leaves you with the *Norham Coffee House*, 73 Main St (closed Sun), which trades on its history – formerly the home of John Christian, grandfather of *Mutiny on the Bounty's*

Fletcher Christian – and its courtyard seating. *Beatfords* (closed Sun), further along Main Street in the Lowther Went Shopping Centre, is actually much better, a bit on the chintzy side but with proper coffee and good home-made dishes. In the evening, choose between the *Riverside Restaurant*, at 2 Main St, on the bridge at the eastern end (☎01900/823871; closed Tues), offering a moderately priced mixed menu, and the *Quince and Medlar*, 12 Castlegate (☎01900/823579; closed Sun & Mon), serving excellent vegetarian dishes. The *Trout Hotel* has bar meals, fine beer and a riverside garden. **Market day** in Cockermouth is Monday.

Ullswater

Wordsworth declared **Ullswater** "the happiest combination of beauty and grandeur, which any of the Lakes affords", a judgement that still holds good. At over seven miles long, Ullswater is the second longest lake in Cumbria and much of its appeal derives from its serpentine shape, a result of the complex geology of this area: the glacier that formed the trench in which the lake now lies had to cut across a couple of geological boundaries, from granite in the south, through a band of Skiddaw slate, to softer sandstone and limestone in the north.

The only **public transport to Ullswater** is the #108 bus service (May–Oct) from Penrith, which runs via Pooley Bridge, Gowbarrow and Glenridding to Patterdale. On summer weekends, three daily buses continue south over the Kirkstone Pass to Bowness.

Patterdale and Glenridding

The chief lakeside settlements, Patterdale and Glenridding, are less than a mile apart at the southern tip of Ullswater, each with a smattering of cafés and B&Bs but not otherwise notable except as a base for one of the most popular scrambling routes in the country – up the considerable heights of Helvellyn (see p.716).

Accommodation is abundant. In **GLENRIDDING** the best place is the lakeside *Glenridding Hotel* (☎017684/82228; ⑥) – complete with indoor pool, pub, restaurant

---

ULLSWATER WALKS

While Helvellyn (see p.716) dominates the southwest side of Ullswater, the fells flanking the east side of the lake offer some invigorating hikes, too.

Using the Ullswater Steamer to travel from Glenridding to **Howtown**, the easiest walk back (5 miles; 3hr) follows the shore of Ullswater around Hallin Fell (or over, climbing 263ft) to **Sandwick**, then crosses fields before rejoining the shore at **Long Crag** for the final two miles to the south end of the lake at Patterdale.

A considerably more strenuous route (8 miles; 4–5hr) from Howtown cuts past the *Howtown Hotel* and then heads up lovely **Fusedale**, at the head of which there's a sharp and unrelenting climb up to the **High Street**, a broad-backed ridge that was once a Roman road. Once on top the path is clearly visible for miles, and following the ridge south you meet the highest point, **High Raise** (2632ft) – 2hr from Howtown – where there's a cairn and glorious views. The route then runs south and west, via the stone outcrops of **Satura Crag**, past **Angle Tarn** and finally down to the A592, just shy of Patterdale's pub and post office.

Either of these walks can be combined with an initial stretch **between Pooley Bridge and Howtown**. The most popular haul (7 miles; 3–4hr) leaves Pooley Bridge pier, heads through the village and follows the road up to **Roehead**. A path then runs up to the **Stone Circle** on the Roman road and down the side of the fell, south of Sharrow Bay, to Howtown pier.

and coffee shop – though there are plenty of cheaper spots, like the *Fairlight Guest House* (☎017684/82397; no credit cards; ①), by Glenridding's main car park; *Cherry Holme* (☎017684/82512; no credit cards; ②), a little way north of the village on the A592, just beyond the petrol station; or *Moss Crag Guest House* (☎017684/82500; no credit cards; ②; closed Dec), near the shops, which has its own tearooms. *Gillside Caravan & Camping* (☎017684/82346; closed Nov–Feb) lurks a little way up the valley behind the helpful **tourist office** (Easter–June, Sept & Oct daily 9am–5.30pm; July & Aug 9am–6pm; Nov–Easter Fri–Sun 10am–4pm; ☎017684/82414) in the main car park. Climbers wanting an early start on Helvellyn stay at the *Helvellyn Youth Hostel*, two miles west up the valley from Glenridding.

In **PATTERDALE**, the cheapest and most popular bed is at the rustic, pine **youth hostel** (☎017684/82394), just south of the hamlet on the A592. B&Bs are strung out along the A592 as far south as Hartsop, but for central lodgings try *Barco House* (☎017684/82474; no credit cards; ②; closed Nov to mid-March), *Home Farm* (☎017684/82370; no credit cards; ①; closed Nov–Feb) or the *White Lion* (☎017684/82214; ③), a pub which also serves bar meals. *Side Farm* (☎017684/82337), in the centre, is open all year for **camping**; the only other service is a small post office/village **shop** opposite the pub.

Around the lake

On busy summer days the A592 up the western side of the lake is packed with traffic, all looking for space in one of the few designated car parks. Busiest is usually that below **Gowbarrow Park**, three miles north of Glenridding, where the A5091 meets the A592; the hillside still blazes green and gold in spring, as it was doing when the Wordsworths visited; it's thought that Dorothy's recollections of the visit in her diary inspired William to write his famous "Daffodils" poem. The car park at Gowbarrow is also the start of an easy, brief walk up to **Aira Force**, a bush-cloaked seventy-foot fall that's spectacular in spate and can be viewed from bridges spanning the top and bottom of the drop.

It's best, if you have time, to get out on the lake itself, traversed by the **Ullswater Steamer** (☎01539/721626), which – as well as its round-the-lake cruises (£5.50) – has services from Glenridding to Howtown, halfway up the lake's eastern side (Easter–Oct daily; £2.75 one way; 35min) and from Howtown to Pooley Bridge, at the northern end of the lake (Easter–Oct daily; £3.30; 20min). There's a bar on board the steamer.

HOWTOWN is tucked into a little clearing at the foot of beautiful Fusedale, where the *Howtown Hotel* makes a great spot for lunch. A minor road from here hugs the eastern shore of the lake the four miles to **POOLEY BRIDGE**, passing the incomparable *Sharrow Bay* (☎017684/86301; ⑨, with dinner) on the way, one of England's finest hotel-restaurants (the full experience will set you back around £250 for a double). Pooley Bridge itself has more basic pleasures. It's a cute retreat – packed to distraction in summer – with a church and three pubs, most notably the *Pooley Bridge Inn* (☎017684/86215; ④), whose balcony rooms (⑤) provide a fine vantage point. There is also a smattering of local B&Bs, including *Ullswater House* (☎017684/86259; no credit cards; ②), opposite the inn, and a summer-only **tourist office** in The Square (daily 10am–5pm; ☎017684/86530).

Climbing Helvellyn

The climb to the summit of **Helvellyn** (3114ft), the most popular of the four 3000ft mountains in Cumbria, is challenging enough for most visitors, who tend to make a day-long circuit from either Glenridding or Patterdale. You are unlikely to be alone or get lost on the yard-wide approaches – on summer weekends and bank holidays the car parks below and paths above are full by 10am – but the variety of routes up and down at least offers a chance of escaping the crowds.

Indeed, if you are hoping to escape the crowds, avoid the most frequently chosen approach via the infamous **Striding Edge**, an alarming, undulating rocky ridge offering the most direct access to the summit. Paths from Ullswater meet at the beginning of Striding Edge: a steep one from Glenridding car park and a slightly less taxing one from the broad-bottomed Grisedale valley (road access just north of Patterdale), half a mile south of Glenridding. With **Red Tarn** – the highest Lake District tarn – a dizzying drop below, purists negotiate the very ridge top of Striding Edge; slightly safer, but no less precipitous tracks follow the line of the ridge, just off the crest. However you get across (and some refuse to go any further when push comes to shove) there's a final, sheer, hands-and-feet scramble to the flat **summit** (2hr 30min from Ullswater). As rockside memorials (and the occasional hovering rescue helicopter) attest, people do get into trouble on Striding Edge: if you're at all nervous of heights you'll find it a challenge to say the least; in poor weather, it's madness even to contemplate it.

The good news is that once you're up the various descents all seem like child's play. The classic return is to the northeast via the less demanding **Swirral Edge**, where a route leads down to Red Tarn, then follows the beck to the disused slate quarry workings and the dramatically sited **Helvellyn youth hostel** (☎017684/82269), two miles from Glenridding. Another route, of equal duration, climbs back up to **Catstye Cam** and drops down the northern ridge path into Keppel Cove, where you cross the dam and continue to the hostel. Either of these Helvellyn approaches and descents makes for around a seven-mile (5–6hr) walk.

Northwest from the summit, a path (2.5 miles; 1hr 30min) runs down to **Thirlmere reservoir** (a straight up-and-down route which provides the easiest walk to Helvellyn's summit); bus #555 between Keswick and Grasmere/Ambleside runs along Thirlmere's eastern shore.

Most enjoyable of all, though, is the path south from Helvellyn, following the flat ridge past **Nethermost Pike and Dollywagon Pike**. Looking back to Striding Edge as you go reveals its sheer awfulness – on clear days the line of walkers negotiating the edge stands out in silhouette, resembling a Stone Age rollercoaster. After Dollywagon Pike, there's a long scree scramble down to **Grisedale Tarn** and then the gentlest of descents down **Grisedale Valley**, past Ruthwaite Lodge hut, alongside the babbling beck, emerging on the Patterdale–Glenridding road – a good six hours all told for the entire circuit.

The Cumbrian coast

South and west of the national park, the **Cumbrian coast** attracts much less attention than the spectacular scenery inland, but it would be a mistake to write it off. It splits into two distinct sections, the most accessible being the **Furness peninsulas** area, just a few miles from Windermere's Lakeside, where varied attractions include the resort of **Grange-over-Sands**, the monastic priory at **Cartmel**, and market towns like **Ulverston** and **Broughton-in-Furness**. Parts of this region share nearby Lancashire's industrial heritage and in the ship-building port of **Barrow-in-Furness** it's possible to see a slow revival that's only just starting to pay dividends in terms of tourism – though the dramatic ruins of nearby **Furness Abbey** have been attracting visitors for almost two hundred years.

The **Cumbrian coast** itself is generally judged to begin at **Silecroft** near Millom and stretches for more than sixty miles to the small resort of **Silloth**, on the shores of the Solway Firth. In between lie isolated beaches and the headland of **St Bees** as well as the delights of the **Ravenglass and Eskdale Railway** and the Georgian port of **Whitehaven**.

Grange-over-Sands

Before the coming of the railways, the main route to the Lake District was the "road across the sands" from near Lancaster to **GRANGE-OVER-SANDS**, travellers being led by monks from Cartmel Priory, then from the sixteenth century by a royally appointed guide. The tradition continues today with one guide left, who can be hired by groups to lead the way around the slip sands and hidden channels which claimed so many lives between the fourteenth and nineteenth centuries. The eight-mile walk takes the best part of a day; ask at the Grange tourist office for further details.

Otherwise, genteel Grange is a bit of a let-down, despite its solid Victorian buildings and formal gardens. Having been attracted here by the mild climate (supposedly the warmest in the north of England), and after tramping along the mile-long esplanade with its fine views of the marshy bay, you've just about covered all it's got to offer, other than the walk to the top of **Hampsfell** (750ft; 3hr; 4 miles). On a clear day the view from the crinkled limestone summit is spectacular; a well-marked pointer on the roof of a nineteenth-century hospice will help you identify peaks as far away as Skiddaw.

Grange **tourist office** is in Victoria Hall, on Main St (mid-March to Oct daily 10am–5pm; ☎015395/34026), four hundred yards left from the **train station** and National Express stop. Keep walking up Main Street to the top of town to reach Kents Bank Road, which has plenty of **accommodation** lining both sides on the way out of town. *Thornfield House* (☎015395/32512; ②; closed Nov–Feb) and *Methven Hotel* (☎015395/32031; ③) are typical of places in their price ranges, offering variously sized en-suite rooms with TV; the tourist office can make other enquiries for you. For something a bit more in keeping with the Victorian surroundings, the *Grange Hotel* (☎015395/33666; ⑤), across from the train station at Station Square, sits high among the trees with bay views from its front rooms. The nearest **youth hostel** is a ten-minute train ride away at the smaller resort of Arnside, on Redhills Road (☎01524/761781). **Eating** options aren't great in Grange, though you can fill up in the cafés along Main Street. *Tomlinson's Café* is good for fish and chips, sticky toffee pudding and decent coffee. *Hazelmere Café*, in a Victorian parade closer to the station, has more varied choices, including veggie and ethnic combinations.

Cartmel

Sheltered several miles inland from Morecambe Bay, **CARTMEL** grew up around its twelfth-century Augustinian priory and is still dominated by the proud **Church of St Mary and St Michael** (daily: summer 9am–5.30pm; winter 9am–3.30pm; tours Easter–Oct Wed 11am & 2pm; free), the only substantial remnant to survive the Dissolution. A diagonally crowned tower is the most distinctive feature outside, while the light and spacious Norman-transitional interior climaxes at a splendid chancel, illuminated by the 45-foot-high **East Window**. You can spend a good half-hour scanning the immaculate misericords and numerous tombs, chief among them the **Harrington Tomb** in the Town Choir, to the south of the chancel – the weathered figure is that of John Harrington, who rebuilt this section in 1340. The choir went on to act as the parish church when the rest of the building was abandoned following the Reformation, the nave only regaining its cover in the 1620s, thanks to the munificence of local landowner, George Preston. Another patron of the church was one Rowland Briggs who paid for a shelf on a pier near the north door and for a supply of bread to be distributed from it every Sunday in perpetuity "to the most indigent housekeepers of this Parish". Before you leave, peruse the grave stones on the church floor, reminders of men and women swept away by the tide while crossing the sands.

Everything else in the village is modest in scale, centred on the attractive **market square**, beyond the church, with its Elizabethan cobbles, water pump and fish slabs. Refreshment is at hand at any of the village's four pubs, all on, or close to, the square, and you can then walk down to the **racecourse** whose delightful setting by the River Eea deserves a look even if the races (held on the last weekend in May and August) aren't in action. Given Cartmel's rather twee attraction, you'll not be surprised to find a couple of antique shops, though better browsing is done at Peter Bain Smith's **book shop** on the square – with a huge selection of local books and guides – and at the Cartmel Village Shop, known to aficionados for the quality of its sticky toffee pudding.

Practicalities

Trains stop at Cark-in-Cartmel, two miles southwest of the village proper; the #530/#531 **bus** from there or from Grange train station (originating in Kendal) runs to the village. Alternatively, an hour-long walk across the low hills from Grange up Grange Fell Road and across the breast of Hampsfell into the pastoral Eea valley makes a more interesting approach.

The only time you'll need to book **accommodation** well in advance is during race weeks. On Market Square, *Market Cross Cottage* (☎015395/36143; no credit cards; ③) is a cosy, seventeenth-century B&B with oak-beamed dining room, serving a good breakfast and evening meals. *Blue Bell House* in Devonshire Square (☎015395/36658; no credit cards; ③), down towards the church, is of a similar age and hue, while the cheapest rooms are at *Bank Court Cottage* (☎015395/36593; no credit cards; ①), through the arch in Market Square by the book shop. Up a notch, rooms at the celebrated *Cavendish* on Cavendish St (☎015395/36240, *thecavendish@compuserve.com*; ⑤), just off the square, have been refurbished while retaining their original sixteenth-century features; all have en-suite bathrooms. Swanky *Uplands* on Haggs Lane (☎015395/36248; ⑦, with dinner; closed Jan & Feb), a mile out of the village on the Grange road, has loads of country-house cachet. If you fancy staying a little longer, *Longlands at Cartmel*, at the base of Hampsfell just a mile north of the village (☎015395/36475, *longlands@cartmel.com*; weekly rates from £250) lets some delightful cottages on a self-catering basis, with an optional repertoire of delicious evening meals on offer; the dining room also opens as a restaurant on summer weekends. There's **camping** at *Wells House Farm* (☎015395/36270), just a couple of minutes' walk from the square.

The village **pubs** form the basis of the evening's eating and entertainment. The *King's Arms* on the square has outdoor tables and bar meals, with daily chalk-board specials that ring the changes. The *Cavendish*, though, is the real winner, the oldest and most characterful of the pubs, sitting on the site of a monastic guest house and offering good (if pricey) food and its own award-winning beer.

Holker Hall

One of Cumbria's most interesting and well-presented country estates, **Holker Hall** (Easter–Oct Mon–Fri & Sun 10am–6pm; last admission 4.30pm; various combination tickets available; hall, gardens, grounds & motor museum £7.25) lies just over a mile north of Cark-in-Cartmel station. The vast, red sandstone hall, which is made up of a pleasing combination of Victorian, Elizabethan and older styles, overlooks acres of beautifully designed gardens, woods and nature trails. Only the New Wing of the house, rebuilt following a fire in 1871, is open to the public, displaying silk wall coverings, Louis XV furniture and a bedroom where Queen Mary slept in 1937. Its opulent rooms are still in use by the Cavendish family who've owned the hall since the late seventeenth century, but you can wander freely around them. The real showpieces are the cantilevered staircase and the library, which is stocked with more than 3000 leather-bound books, some of whose spines are fakes, constructed to hide electric light switches added later.

The 25-acre **gardens** incorporate a variety of water features, including a limestone cascade and fountain, while next to the house, the **Lakeland Motor Museum** (Easter–Oct Sun–Fri 10am–4.45pm) displays more than a hundred vehicles, from 1880s tricycles and wartime ambulances to funky 1920s bubble cars and 1980s MGs. A special exhibition concentrates on the speed-freak Campbells – Sir Malcolm and son Donald – whose exploits shattered the Lakeland calm for thirty years until Donald was killed in 1967.

There's also an annual **garden and countryside festival** (day ticket, £7) held over three days at the end of May/beginning of June, when the garden's floral displays are at their best, backed by a whole host of craft displays and musical events. A summer **bus** service, the #534, from Grange to Newby Bridge/Lakeside, runs past the hall.

Ulverston and around

The railway line winds westwards from Cartmel to **ULVERSTON**, a close-knit market town, which formerly prospered on the cotton, tanning and iron-ore industries. It's an attractive place, enhanced by its dappled grey limestone cottages and a jumble of cobbled alleys and traditional shops zigzagging off the central **Market Place**. Stalls still set up here and in the surrounding streets every Thursday and Saturday; on other days (not Wed) the **market hall** on New Market Street is the centre of commercial life.

The first thing you'll notice on the approach to Ulverston is what looks like a lighthouse high on a hill to the north of town. This is the **Hoad Monument**, built in 1850 to honour locally born Sir John Barrow, a former secretary of the admiralty. It's open in the summer (if the flag's flying) and the walk to the top grants fine views of the bay and fells. However, Ulverston's most famous son is Stan Laurel (born Arthur Stanley Jefferson), the whimpering, head-scratching half of Laurel and Hardy who are celebrated in a mind-boggling collection of memorabilia at the **Laurel and Hardy Museum** up an alley at 4c Upper Brook St (daily 10am–4.30pm; £2; closed Jan), near Market Place. The copy of Stan's birth certificate (16 June 1890, in Foundry Cottages, Ulverston) lists his father's occupation as "comedian" – young Arthur Stanley could hardly have become anything else. The eccentric showcase of hats, beer bottles, photos, models, puppets, press cuttings and props is mixed with copies of letters from the pair: one from Stan, in retirement in Santa Monica (where he's buried), complains that, since his incapacitating stroke, he can't pursue his favourite sport – shark fishing. You're ushered into a Twenties-style cinema, with almost constant screenings of the duo's films, by an overzealous curator whose party piece – automatically doffing the bowler hat to the lifesized model of Stan – is for his own evident amusement rather than for any children who happen to be present.

Down from the museum, in Lower Brook Street, Ulverston's **Heritage Centre** (Mon, Tues & Thurs–Sat 9.30am–4.30pm; £2) is a little bland, but gives a good overview of the town's history and its various industrial achievements. The other main attraction is the **glass factory**, Cumbria Crystal, on Lightburn Road, close to the railway bridge (Mon–Thurs 9am–4pm, Fri 9am–3pm; £1), where you can watch the crystal-making process from blowing to painstaking carving. There's more glass manufacturing at Heron Glass, at The Gill, at the top of Upper Brook Street, whose site marks the start of the seventy-mile **Cumbria Way** to Carlisle.

Practicalities

Ulverston train **station**, serving the Cumbrian coast railway, is only a few minutes' walk from the town centre – head up Princess Street and turn right at the main road for County Square. **Buses** arrive on nearby Victoria Road from Cartmel, Grange-over-Sands, Barrow, Bowness, Windermere and Kendal. The **tourist office** is in Coronation Hall on County Square (Mon–Sat 10am–5pm; ☎01229/587120).

Pick of the **B&Bs** is the *White House*, a three-hundred-year-old beamed cottage at the bottom of Market Street (☎01229/583340; no credit cards; ①; closed Nov–Easter). There's also a great *Walker's Hostel* on Oubas Hill (☎01229/585588; no credit cards; ①), on the A590 as you come into town: thirty beds in small shared rooms, with vegetarian breakfasts and evening meals available – bed, breakfast and dinner costs just £15. **Cafés** include the *Ship's Wheel Café*, King St, renowned for its frothy coffees and traditional cooking. Most of the **pubs** serve lunches, too: the *Rose & Crown*, on King Street, has live music on Wednesday nights, though the *Farmers Arms* in Market Place is a nicer pub.

Out of town, follow the A590 briefly and then turn off at the signpost for **Canal Foot**, running through an industrial estate to reach the beautifully sited *Bay Horse Inn* (☎01229/583972, *reservations@bayhorse.furness.co.uk*; ⑦, ⑧ with dinner), by the last lock on the Ulverston canal. The cooking here is celebrated far and wide and even if you can't run to lunch or dinner in the waterside conservatory, you can order a coffee, soup or sandwich at one of the outdoor tables.

Around Ulverston: Bardsea and Conishead Priory

To the south of Ulverston, the Barrow peninsula slopes down to its sandy east and west coasts from a raised backbone dotted with villages and scattered with cairns and ancient fort sites. The village of **BARDSEA**, overlooking the coast from a modest hillside two miles south of Ulverston, is an ideal base for short jaunts to the pebbly beach at **Wadhead Scar**, or uphill to **Birkrigg Common** (436ft). From this grassy parkland cut through by limestone outcrops, the views north include a ripple of fells and many of Cumbria's higher peaks, while to the east you can watch the shallow waters lapping over Morecambe sands. The common boasts two stone circles, one of which is easy to spot – a neat cluster of lichen-clad rocks brushed by high grasses that's been standing for over two thousand years. There are two pubs serving the village, the *Bradylls Arms* which has a suntrap beer-garden and conservatory restaurant, while down on the road by the beach the *Old Mill* (Wed–Sun 11am–5pm) serves drinks, teas and meals.

Half a mile north of Bardsea, the high turrets of **Conishead Priory**, an extravagant Gothic mansion, push through a canopy of woodland. More like a palace than a religious retreat, it was built over the remains of an Augustinian priory destroyed during the Dissolution, and now houses Manjushri, a Buddhist institute ringed by prayer flags (Easter–Sept Sat & Sun 2–5pm; ☎01229/584029). Most visitors come for meditation courses, but guided tours (Easter–July, Sept & Oct Sat & Sun 2–5pm; £2) of the ornate halls and cloisters are also available, and there are free tours on Saturdays (Easter–Sept 2–5pm) of the Buddhist temple in the grounds, which incorporates the largest bronze Buddha statue in Europe.

Barrow-in-Furness

With shipyard cranes piercing the skyline, **BARROW-IN-FURNESS** has a distinctly industrial feel that's been the town's hallmark since it grew up around a booming iron industry in the mid-nineteenth century. Steelworks and shipbuilding followed, making Barrow one of England's busiest ports, and the town still makes a handsome living from orders for military hardware. Yet even Barrow's most enthusiastic supporters could hardly claim the town as attractive: recession in the 1980s emptied many of the proud Victorian buildings and left the centre rough at the edges. However, some of the buildings still retain the capacity to surprise – the splendid red-sandstone Gothic Town Hall for one – while recent regeneration is attempting to put the heart back into Barrow.

For visitors, the best move is straight to the **Dock Museum** (Easter–Oct Wed–Fri 10am–5pm, Sat & Sun 11am–5pm; Nov–Easter Wed–Fri 10.30am–4pm, Sat & Sun noon–4pm; free), on North Road, half a mile from the centre; it's signposted from all over town. Located in the dried-out graving dock where ships were once repaired, the museum tells the history of Barrow – which is also the history of modern shipbuilding. The creation of the Furness railway in 1846 to carry iron ore to the coast led to Barrow's growth from a village of less than 200 people to a thriving port within 25 years. Steel-making and shipbuilding went hand in hand, and boomed between the wars. Later, as the steelworks declined (the last one finally closed in 1983) and the Cold War intensified, the emphasis shifted to submarine building. Today, VSEL – the privatized successor to the historic firm of Vickers – builds nuclear subs in the town's Devonshire Dock Hall. Even if the history leaves you cold, the museum exhibits (on the shipbuilding process, local railways, iron- and steel-making) are well-presented.

Few lake-bound tourists stay the night, though Barrow's **tourist office**, located in the theatre-arts centre, Forum 28, on Duke Street, opposite the town hall (Mon–Fri 9.30am–5pm, Sat 10–4pm; ☎01229/870156), can help with accommodation if necessary. You can also get information here on visiting the nearby nature reserves on **Walney Island**, a six-mile strip of land accessed from Barrow's Jubilee Bridge.

Furness Abbey

Furness Abbey (April–Sept daily 10am–6pm; Oct daily 10am–4pm; Nov–March Wed–Sun 10am–4pm; £2.50; EH), a set of roofless red-sandstone arcades and pillars hidden in a wooded vale – the so-called "Valley of Deadly Nightshade" – lies a mile and a half out of Barrow on the Ulverston road (local buses to Dalton-in-Furness and Ulverston pass close by). Now one of Cumbria's finest ruins, it was once the most powerful abbey in the northwest, possessing much of southern Cumbria as well as land in Ireland and the Isle of Man. Founded in 1124, the abbey's industry was remarkably diverse – it owned sheep on the local fells, controlled fishing rights, produced grain and leather, smelted iron, dug peat for fuel and manufactured salt. By the fourteenth century it had become such a prize that the Scots raided it twice, though it survived until April 1536, when Henry VIII chose it to be the first of the large abbeys to be dissolved; the Abbot and 29 of his monks, who had hitherto resisted (and indeed, had encouraged the locals to resist Dissolution – a treasonable offence), were pensioned off for the sum of two pounds each.

The abbey has been a popular tourist diversion since the early nineteenth century, when a train station was built to bring in visitors, among them Wordsworth who was very taken with the "mouldering pile". Borrow a portable tape-player from the reception desk to get the best out of the site since there are no maps or explanatory signs. The transepts stand virtually at their original height, while the massive slabs of stone-ribbed vaulting, richly embellished arcades and intricately carved *sedilia* in the presbytery are the equal of any of Yorkshire's far busier abbey ruins. A small museum houses some of the best carvings, including rare examples of effigies of armed knights with closed helmets and – as medieval custom dictated – crossed legs. Only seven others have ever been found intact. The *Abbey Tavern* at the entrance serves drinks at tables scattered about some of the ruined outbuildings.

Piel Castle

The attacks by the Scots goaded Furness Abbey into protecting itself with **Piel Castle** on **Piel Island**, guarding the approaches south of the town. This is reached from Roa Island, three miles southeast of Barrow down the A5087 (bus #11 or #12); turn off at Rampside (signposted "Lifeboat station"). At **ROA**, which has a pub and a small café, you can debate the prospects of the infrequent, weather- and tide-dependent **ferry** (Easter–Sept Mon–Fri 11am–5pm, Sat & Sun 11am–6pm; winter on request; £1.50 each way; ☎01229/835809) across to Piel Island. Apart from the ruins of a massive keep, it is the island's only commercial building, the *Ship Inn*, which draws people over here. This serves bar meals and allows camping.

Dalton and Broughton-in-Furness

North of Barrow, the A590 runs the four miles to the straggling town of **DALTON-IN-FURNESS**, old enough to have been mentioned in the Domesday Book but retaining little of interest today save the surviving fourteenth-century keep of **Dalton Castle** (Easter–Sept 2–5pm; free) at the top of the old market square. If you've stopped for this, you may as well walk past the keep to the churchyard of **St Mary's**, where the eighteenth-century artist George Romney is buried.

Fairly regular buses run up to Dalton from Barrow (and on to Ulverston), but for the area's largest attraction – the nearby animal park – you'll really need your own transport, though there is a summer service from Barrow, Dalton, Bowness and Ulverston (#X18; mid-July to Aug 2–3 daily). Whatever you feel about zoos, you're likely to be positively surprised by the **South Lakes Animal Park** (daily: summer 10am–6pm; winter 10am–dusk; £6.50), half a mile or so outside Dalton. An award-winning "conservation" zoo, it relies on ditches and trenches (not cages) for the most part to contain its animals and is split into separate habitat areas, ranging from the Australian bush to a tropical rainforest. It's quite something to encounter free-roaming kangaroos in rural Cumbria. Call for feeding times to see the park at its best – the tiger-feeding (encouraging them to climb and jump for their meal) is unique in Europe.

Beyond Dalton, it's ten miles up the A595 to the small market town of **BROUGHTON-IN-FURNESS** which, unlike its near namesake, has retained much of its Georgian beauty. Tall houses surround a charming square, complete with obelisk, stone fish slabs and stocks. From the square, follow Church Street to the edge of town and you'll reach **St Mary Magdalene**, originally twelfth-century, though much restored in the nineteenth century.

Nestling in the Duddon Valley, the town makes a handy local walking or touring base (Coniston is only eight miles away) and the **tourist office** in the old Town Hall on the square (Easter–Oct Mon–Fri 10am–4pm, Sat 9am–4pm, Sun 10am–1pm; ☎01229/716115) can help with **accommodation**. There are several B&Bs, like *Garner House* on Church St (☎01229/716462; no credit cards; ②), or pub rooms, among others at the *Manor Arms*, The Square (☎01229/716286; ②). The *Coffee Bean* on the square has the nicest tearooms, while *Beswick's*, also on the square, at the corner of Griffin St (☎01229/716285; dinner all year, plus lunch & teas in summer), is a bistro with good food and a great wine list

Along the coast to St Bees

Road (A595) and rail routes follow the **Cumbrian coast** from Broughton-in-Furness to St Bees, with diversions to a series of small villages and lengthy beaches that, for the most part, live a quiet existence outside the short summer season. The first decent stretch of sand is at **Silecroft**, a few miles northwest of Millom; the Cumbria Coastal Way runs along the back of the beach and there's a train station back in Silecroft village. However, it's **Ravenglass** that's the principal stop before the headland of St Bees – a sleepy little estuary village overshadowed by the nearby nuclear reprocessing plant, **Sellafield**.

Ravenglass and the Ravenglass and Eskdale Railway

The single main street of **RAVENGLASS**, fifteen miles or so up the coast, preserves a row of characterful nineteenth-century cottages, facing out across the mud flats and dunes. Despite appearances, the village dates back to the arrival of the Romans who established a supply post here in the first century AD for the northern legions manning Hadrian's Wall. Look for the sign to the "Roman Bath House", just past the station: 500 yards up a single-track lane lie the fairly extensive remains of a fort which survived in Ravenglass until the fourth century.

Local **accommodation** includes *Rose Garth* (☎01229/717275; no credit cards; ②), a guest house on the main street, and the *Holly House Hotel* (☎01229/717230; ②), further up, which also has a public bar. Ravenglass station is the starting point for the toy-like **Ravenglass & Eskdale Railway** (summer daily; winter Sat & Sun; £6.50 return; ☎01229/717171), known affectionately as La'al Ratty. Opened in 1875 to carry ore from the Eskdale mines to the coastal railway, the tiny train, running on a 15-inch gauge track, takes forty minutes to wind its way through seven miles of forests and fields between the fell sides of the Eskdale Valley to Dalegarth station. Dalegarth station (and the nearby hamlet of Boot, see p.713) is a popular starting point for walks on and up into the central lakeland peaks, and consequently the railway makes for a fine approach to Eskdale itself (see p.713). You can also break your journey at various stations en route, with the earliest stop at **Muncaster Mill** (Easter–Oct daily 10am–5pm; £1.60), a restored, working eighteenth-century mill where the machinery turns every day, milling organic flour which then ends up in breads and cakes in the teashop. From here, and from the other stations, there are gentle fellside and woodland **walks**; equip yourself with a map and timetable and you can easily complete a circuit and catch a return train back down to the coast.

Sellafield

The main blot on the Cumbrian coast looms large after Ravenglass, namely British Nuclear Fuels' (BNFL) **Sellafield** nuclear reprocessing plant, sited midway between Ravenglass and Whitehaven. Its Thermal Oxide Reprocessing (Thorp) plant handles spent fuel from BNFL's own reactors and from those of countries as diverse as Japan and Switzerland. It's a significant local employer – thousands of jobs currently depend on BNFL's presence in Cumbria – which enjoys high-level bipartisan political support, and as nuclear power supplies something like thirty percent of the country's electricity needs, BNFL clearly is proud of its technical expertise. This much, at least, you'll glean from the multi-million-pound **Sellafield Visitors Centre** (daily: April–Oct 10am–6pm; Nov–March 10am–4pm; free), a popular public relations exercise involving "all the excitement you can handle" during a guided coach tour of the site and various hands-on exhibits dealing with all things nuclear. You'll learn all about the safe recycling of nuclear fuel and how radiation is part of everyday life. What you're less likely to come away with is a balanced view of the entire process, or indeed any knowledge of why reprocessing was deemed necessary in the first place – it's still the only way to produce the plutonium needed for nuclear weapons, while depleted uranium is widely used in otherwise conventional anti-tank weapons and missiles. Critics question the entire reprocessing system at Sellafield and elsewhere, pointing to the lethal maritime and atmospheric discharges (virtually all European radioactive pollution comes from reprocessing) and the manifest dangers of waste transportation. Not that the only current alternative – underground or undersea dumping – is any more attractive, certainly not for Cumbria which already has a low-level nuclear waste dump near Sellafield and may host another now that the British government has decided to reconsider long-term undergound dumping.

The visitor centre is tricky to reach without your own **transport**: the best you can do is get off the train at Sellafield station and walk the few minutes up to the main gate, to where a bus will be sent to pick you up.

St Bees

The close-knit central streets in the coastal village of **ST BEES** give it the feel of a retirement colony. It's a suitably elderly settlement, with a nunnery established here as early as the seventh century, succeeded by **St Bees Priory**, just north of today's train station, in the twelfth century. This was slightly damaged in the Dissolution, but retains huge Norman arches above its entrance porch; it also houses a small exhibition of Celtic crosses and headstones in the nave. The long sands lie a few hundred yards west of the village, while the steep, red-sandstone cliffs of **St Bees Head** to the north are good for windy walks and bird-watching. The headland's lighthouse marks the start of Wainwright's 190-mile **Coast-to-Coast Walk** to Robin Hood's Bay (see p.834).

St Bees is on the Cumbrian coast train line and lies just five miles south of Whitehaven, from where there's a regular bus service. **Accommodation** needs advance reservations in high season, though at other times of the year there should be no problem finding somewhere to stay. *Tomlin Guest House*, out of the centre on Beach Rd (☎01946/822284; no credit cards; ①), is a good first choice; the *Queen's Hotel*, Main St (☎01946/822287; ③) is a nice old pub with a beer garden.

Whitehaven

Some fine Georgian houses mark out the centre of **WHITEHAVEN**, one of the few grid-planned towns in England. The economic expansion that forced this planning was as much due to the booming slave trade as to the more widely recognized coal traffic. Whitehaven spent a brief period during the eighteenth century as Britain's third busiest port (after London and Bristol), making it a prime target for an abortive raid led by Scottish-born American lieutenant **John Paul Jones**. Disgusted with the slave trade he witnessed while ship's mate in America, Jones returned to the port of his apprenticeship to rebel, but, let down by a drunk and potentially mutinous crew, he damaged only one of the two hundred boats in dock and his mini-crusade fell flat. All this and more is explained in the **Beacon** (Easter–Oct Tues–Sun 10am–5.30pm; Nov–Easter 10am–4.30pm; £3.80), an enterprising heritage centre on the harbour. The **harbour** itself sits at the heart of a millennium renaissance project which, by 2001, should have spruced up the quayside and provided new promenades, a heritage trail, an information centre, and other varied attractions including a museum based in a former rum warehouse. The 140-mile Sea-to-Sea (C2C) cycle route to Sunderland/Newcastle currently starts its first leg (the 31 miles to Keswick) from the harbour: once the millennium project is complete, there'll be an official starting-point and registration office.

For all the changes round the harbour, it's Whitehaven's Georgian streets and neatly painted houses that make up one of Cumbria's most distinguished towns. There's a **market** held here every Thursday and Saturday, which adds a bit of colour. Otherwise, stroll up to the seventeenth-century church of **St Nicholas** on Lowther Street, where all that stands is its tower; the rest succumbed to a fire in 1971, but there's a lovely garden now surrounding the former nave. Also on Lowther Street, don't miss Michael Moon's second-hand **book shop** at no. 19 (closed Sun), a bookworm's treasure trove.

Practicalities

The #X5 **bus** links Whitehaven with Cockermouth, Keswick and Penrith, while **trains** follow the coastal route south to Barrow and north via Maryport to Carlisle. The **tourist office** is in the Market Hall on Market Place (Easter–Oct Mon–Sat 9.30am–5pm, Sun 10am–4.30pm; Nov–Easter Mon–Sat 10am–4.30pm; ☎01946/852939) and can help with accommodation. There's very little choice of **places to eat**: best spots are the *Westminster Café*, opposite St Nicholas' on Lowther Street, for light lunches, sandwiches and espresso, and *Bruno's*, 9–11 Church St, where a full Italian meal can be had for under £20.

Maryport to Silloth

North of Whitehaven it's undistinguished country for the most part, at least until you're past Workington. **MARYPORT**, fifteen miles from Whitehaven, makes the first bid for your attention, with views of the Solway Firth and the Scottish hills across the water and a history going back to Roman times. That's taken care of in the **Senhouse Roman Museum** (July–Sept daily 10am–5pm; April–June & Oct Tues & Thurs–Sun 10am–5pm; £1.50), high on a hill above the harbour, which collates sculpture, altars and inscriptions from the Roman fort of Alauna. The town's modern history dates from its eighteenth-century heyday as an industrial port – named after the wife, Mary, of local lord and entrepreneur Humphrey Senhouse. The best part of Maryport is still its harbour and marina, now smartly landscaped and featuring the **Maryport Aquaria** (daily: March–Oct 10am–5pm; Nov–Feb 11am–4pm; £3.80), with its underwater Cumbrian world. But walk into the streets behind the harbour and Maryport's long decline since the Great Depression of the 1930s is still all too apparent: local coal -mining reduced drastically in the 1950s, the port closed for business in the 1960s and was then silted up for the best part of twenty years until the recent regeneration. For a glimpse of better days, walk uphill to Fleming Square (on the way to the Roman museum), whose surviving cobbles are still surrounded by Georgian houses. The **tourist office** is at the bottom of Senhouse Street, across from the harbour (Mon–Thurs 10am–5pm, Fri & Sat 10am–1pm & 2–5pm, Sun 2–5pm; ☎01900/813738); it shares the premises, an old inn, with the town's small museum of local history.

North to Silloth

Five miles further up the coast, the B5300 road runs right through **ALLONBY**, a former weaving village with a long shingle and sand beach, and the *Ship Inn*, where Dickens once slept. Both beach and road continue north as far as **SILLOTH-ON-SOLWAY**, another eight miles away and perhaps the Solway Firth's nicest spot, though its pleasures are all modest – a Victorian resort with wide cobbled streets, a large seafront green and promenade, and wildlife-rich local salt marshes and dunes. The name, incidentally, is a corruption of the "sea-lathes", or seaside grain silos, established by Cistercian monks who farmed the area in medieval times.

Buses run here from Maryport and from Carlisle, just 21 miles away. There's a seasonal **tourist office** on the green (May–Sept Fri–Sun 10am–4pm, Mon 10am–2pm; ☎016973/31944) where you can debate the possibility of a room and pick up a leaflet on local walks.

East Cumbria: the Eden Valley and Penrith

The Lake District might end abruptly with the market town and transport hub of **Penrith**, ten miles northeast of Ullswater, but Cumbria doesn't. To the east, the **Eden Valley** splits the Pennines from the Lake District fells, and boasts a succession of hardy market towns, prime among which is the former county town of **Appleby-in-Westmorland**. This lies on the magnificent **Settle to Carlisle railway**, connecting Cumbria with the Yorkshire Dales (see p.768). The other great local feat of engineering – the M6, following the main London–Penrith–Glasgow rail line – misses the best of the valley, yet remains one of the most attractive sections of motorway in the country. Northeast of Penrith, the A686 leads you imperceptibly from Cumbria into Teesdale, via the high town of **Alston**, providing a superb if lonely approach to Hexham and Hadrian's Wall.

Penrith

Once a thriving market town on the main north–south trading route, **PENRITH** today suffers from undue comparisons with the improbably pretty settlements of the nearby Lakes. The brisk streets, filled with no-nonsense shops and shoppers, have more in common with the towns of the North Pennines than the stone villages of south Cumbria, and even the local building materials emphasize the geographic shift. Its deep-red buildings were erected from the same rust-red sandstone used to construct **Penrith Castle** (daily: June–Sept 8am–9pm; Oct–May 8am–4.30pm; free) in the fourteenth century, as a bastion against raids from the north; it's now a crumbling ruin, opposite the train station. The town is at its best in the narrow streets, arcades and alleys off **Market Square**, and around St Andrew's churchyard, while if you call into the tourist office on Middlegate, you'll find it shares its seventeenth-century school-house premises with a small local **museum** (April–Sept Mon–Sat 10am–6pm, Sun 1–6pm; Oct–March Mon–Sat 10am–5pm; free).

Trains from Manchester, London, Glasgow and Edinburgh pull into Penrith station, five minutes' walk south of Market Square and Middlegate. The **bus station** is on Albert Street, behind Middlegate, and has regular services to Patterdale, Keswick, Cockermouth, Carlisle and Alston. The **tourist office** on Middlegate (April–Oct daily 10am–6pm; Nov–March Mon–Sat 10am–5pm; ☎01768/867466) can help you find **accommodation**. The bulk of the B&Bs line Victoria Road, the continuation of King Street running south from Market Square: *Victoria Guest House*, at no. 3 (☎01768/863823; no credit cards; ①), and *Blue Swallow*, at no. 11 (☎01768/866335; no credit cards; ②), are both comfortable and convenient. The *George Hotel*, on Devonshire Street by Market Square (☎01768/862696; ④), is a central old coaching inn with attractive prices, cosy wood-panelled lounges and a decent bar. For **picnic** food, the fantastically -stocked J. & J. Graham's deli-grocery in Market Square can't be beaten, though for a sit-down **meal** you should head for *Chataways Bistro* (closed all Mon & Sun eve), whose imaginative food is enhanced by its setting on the edge of St Andrew's churchyard. Across the churchyard in Bishop's Yard, *Dolce Vita* (closed Sun) serves reasonable pizza and pasta.

Around Penrith

A couple of impressive attractions lie close to town, the nearest being **Brougham Castle** (April–Sept daily 10am–6pm; Oct daily 10am–dusk; £1.90; EH), a mile and a half south of Penrith by the River Eamont. Passed down through the influential Clifford family to Lady Anne, the castle overlaps the site of a Roman fort and contains a collection of tombstones commemorating Britons who adopted Roman customs and the Latin language.

Even more spectacular is **Dalemain** (Easter–Sept Mon–Thurs & Sun 11.15am–5pm; £5; gardens only £3), three miles southwest of town, reached from either the A66 or A592. This country house, set in ample grounds, started life in the twelfth century as a fortified tower, but has subsequently been added to by every generation, culminating with a Georgian facade grafted onto a largely Elizabethan house. There's the usual run of imposing public rooms, while the medieval courtyard and Elizabethan great barn doubled as the grim schoolroom and dormitory of Lowood School in the TV adaptation of Charlotte Brontë's *Jane Eyre*.

Appleby-in-Westmorland

One-time county town of Westmorland, **APPLEBY-IN-WESTMORLAND** is protected on three sides by a loop in the River Eden. The fourth was defended by the now privately owned **Appleby Castle** (Easter–Sept daily 10am–5pm; Oct daily 10am–4pm; £4), where rare species of farm animals are bred on the grounds. You can climb to the top of the Norman keep, which was restored by **Lady Anne Clifford**, who, after her father's death in 1605, spent 45 years trying to claim her rightful inheritance. A triptych known as *The Great Painting*, which she commissioned to commemorate her eventual success, is displayed in the Great Hall along with other fine paintings and porcelain.

Lady Anne also founded the **almshouses** on Boroughgate, the town's backbone, which runs from High Cross, former site of the cheese market outside the castle, to Low Cross, previously a butter market but now site of the general Saturday market. **St Lawrence's Church**, at Low Cross, holds the tombs of Lady Anne Clifford and her mother.

The town is usually peaceful, but changes its character completely in June when the **Appleby Horse Fair** takes over nearby Gallows' Hill, as it has done since 1750. Britain's most important gypsy gathering, it draws hundreds of chrome-plated caravans and more traditional horse-drawn "bow-tops", as well as the vehicles of tinkers, New-Age travellers and sightseers. Historically, the main day of the fair was the second Wednesday of June (the official day for horse trading), but today most of the action (including road racing, hair-raising stunts and fortune-telling) and trading takes place between the previous Sunday and the Tuesday, culminating on the Tuesday evening with trotting races at Holme Farm field. The whole week gets the full support of the local council but only some of the residents, many complaining about the disruption and the boisterous revelry.

Practicalities

The **Settle to Carlisle railway** is the best way to get to Appleby, although **bus services** from Penrith are frequent enough. The **tourist office**, in the Moot Hall on Boroughgate (April–Oct Mon–Sat 10am–5pm, Sun noon–4pm; Oct–March Mon–Thurs 10am–noon, Fri & Sat 10am–noon & 2–4pm; ☎017683/51177), is ten minutes' walk from the station. **Bike rental** is available from Eden Bikes, The Sands (☎017683/53533), next to the river.

During the horse fair, **accommodation** is scarce; if you're planning to visit at this time, book well in advance. There's a clutch of places on Bongate, five hundred yards from town, over the bridge from Low Cross, then south along the B6260: try *Arbury House* (☎017683/53419; no credit cards; ②; closed Nov–March) or nearby *Old Hall Farm* (☎017683/51773; no credit cards; ③) – both signposted off the road and very friendly places. The top hotel in town is the *Tufton Arms Hotel* on Market Square (☎017683/51593; ⑥). The closest **campsite** is the *Wild Rose* (with swimming pool) three miles south at Ormside (☎017683/51077); a similar distance to the north, the quiet hamlet of Dufton has the nearest **youth hostel** (☎017683/51236).

There is no shortage of **places to eat** and the old pubs tend to be the most atmospheric places: the *Tufton Arms Hotel* dishes up generous bar meals and the *Royal Oak* on Bongate is renowned for its Cumberland sausages; the *Tufton Arms* also has a restaurant, serving things like grilled goats' cheese and fresh fish. Otherwise *Lady Anne's Pantry*, 9 Bridge St (closed Sun in winter), is a good café, and there's tea and cakes too in the Courtyard Gallery, an arts and crafts store at 32 Boroughgate. The *Stag Inn* at Dufton (where the hostel is) is an enjoyable country inn with a beer garden, and it's worth the five-mile drive south to Sandford to the *Sandford Arms* for its excellent bar meals and more formal restaurant.

Northeast: the route to Alston

The main routes north from Penrith are the M6 and the rail line to Carlisle, but if you're heading for Hadrian's Wall the A686 provides an alternative trans-moor route, via

Alston. Various bus services follow the route – the #888, #X89 and the #X88 all pass through Alston from Penrith – from where there are onward services to Teesdale, Durham and Newcastle. The #681 starts in Alston, running ten miles north to Haltwhistle to join the A69 Carlisle–Newcastle road.

Having your own transport gives you the opportunity to make a couple of detours along the way, with the first diversion to the prehistoric stone circle known as **Long Meg and her Daughters**. Standing outside a ring of stones nearly four hundred feet in diameter, Long Meg is the tallest stone at eighteen feet and has a profile like the face of an austere old lady. The stone family, said by some to be a coven of witches turned to stone by a magician, is just outside Little Salkeld, off the A686, six miles north of Penrith and just over a mile's walk from Langwathby on the Settle to Carlisle railway.

Back on the main road, at **MELMERBY**, make a point of stopping at the Village Bakery (daily until 5pm), whose proprietor's enthusiasm for his wood-fired brick oven has sparked interest in such matters in some of the most fashionable restaurants in the country. Wonderful breakfasts, lunches and teas are served.

Having covered an initial stretch of smooth vales and aromatic pine woods, the road then winds steeply up the bracken-strewn slopes of **Hartside Top**. This 1900-feet-high bulk marks the western edge of the Pennines and has a welcome café at its summit (open daily in summer).

Alston

Seven miles beyond Hartside Top, **ALSTON** commands the head of the South Tyne Valley. It no longer has a market to back up its claim to being the highest market-town in England but still has its market cross, beside the cobbled curve of the steep main street, which is lined with charming tearooms and cosy pubs. Alston's **parish church** of **St Augustine**, on the main street, is of some interest for the history of the **Derwentwater Clock** inside. It belonged to the local landowner and Jacobite rebel James Radcliffe who was beheaded for treason in 1716, followed 48 years later by his brother Charles Radcliffe – the last traitor to be decapitated – after which his heirs bequeathed the clock to the church.

The town's also of note for the narrow-gauge **South Tynedale Railway** (Easter week, July & Aug daily; rest of year Sat & Sun only; £3.50 return; talking timetable ☎01434/382828) whose steam engines start from a station downhill from the church then follow the route of an old coal-carrying branch of the Carlisle to Newcastle line. The line runs a mile and a half north to Gilderdale, with an extension for a similar distance on to Kirkhough on the Pennine Way, a handy starting point for the twelve-mile walk north to Greenhead on Hadrian's Wall (45-minute round-trip from Alston).

Leaflets on local walks are doled out at the **tourist office** inside the station (Easter–Oct daily 10am–5pm; ☎01434/381696), where you can also book **accommodation**. In Alston itself, *Nentholme House*, two hundred yards east of the cross at the Butts (☎01434/381523; no credit cards; ①) is one of the best B&Bs, while a couple of miles out of town out on the Nenthead Road the *Lovelady Shield Country House* (☎01434/381203; ⑥, with dinner) serves excellent food. Alston's **youth hostel**, the *Firs* (☎01434/381509), is just south of the centre, overlooking the South Tyne river valley; and you can **camp** centrally at *Tyne Willows* (☎01434/381318; closed Nov–Easter) by the station behind the Texaco garage. The *Angel Inn* on Front Street (☎01434/381363; no credit cards; ①), is a nice old seventeenth-century pub serving good bar **meals** all day. *Blueberry's Tea Shop* on the Market Square (☎01434/381928; no credit cards; ①) can also provide snacks and rooms. Other good pubs include the *Turk's Head* in the Market Square and the nearby *Blue Bell*.

Carlisle and around

CARLISLE, the county town of Cumbria and its only city, is also the repository of much of the region's history. Its strategic location has been fought over for more than 2000 years. The original Celtic settlement was superseded by a Roman town, whose first fort was raised here in AD72. Carlisle thrived during the construction of Hadrian's Wall and then, long after the Romans had gone, the Saxon settlement was repeatedly fought over by the Danes and the Scots – the latter losing it eventually to the Normans. The struggle with the Scots defined the very nature of Carlisle as a border city: William Wallace was repelled in 1297 and Robert the Bruce eighteen years later, but Bonnie Prince Charlie's troops took Carlisle in 1745 after a six-day siege, holding it for only six weeks before surrendering to the Duke of Cumberland, who bombarded the city with cannon dragged from Whitehaven.

It's not surprising then that Carlisle still trumpets itself as the "great border city" and it's well worth a day of anyone's time to explore its compact centre and visit the trio of top-class sights: cathedral, castle and Tullie House Museum. The only surviving bit of Hadrian's Wall in Cumbria, at Birdoswald Fort, fifteen miles east of Carlisle, is also worth a stop.

The town

Directly opposite the train station stands the **Citadel**, its twin drum towers and battlemented gatehouses framing the main thoroughfare of English Street. The original Citadel was erected on the orders of Henry VIII as he revamped the city defences – today's is a nineteenth-century pastiche, housing council offices, but effective nonetheless as a symbolic entrance to the city centre. English Street is pedestrianized as far as the expansive **Green Market** square, formerly heart of the medieval city, though a huge fire in 1392 destroyed its buildings and layout. The Lanes shopping centre on the east side of the square – its "alleys" lit through a cast-iron-and-glass roof – stands where the medieval city's lanes once ran. Otherwise, the only historic survivors are the market cross (1682), the Elizabethan former town hall behind it, which now houses the tourist office (see opposite) and the timber-framed Guildhall beyond that (at the southern end of Fisher Street). The much-restored Guildhall now contains a small **museum** (Easter–Sept Thurs–Sun 1–4pm; 50p) of guild and civic artefacts – Carlisle's eight historical trade guilds each had a meeting room in the hall.

The rest of the sites lie up Castle Street, which runs between Green Market and the castle itself. It's only a few steps along to **Carlisle Cathedral** (Mon–Sat 7.30am–6.15pm, Sun 7.30am–5pm; £2 donation requested), founded in 1122 but embracing a considerably older heritage. Christianity was established in sixth-century Carlisle by St Kentigern (often known as St Mungo), who became the first bishop and patron saint of Glasgow. The cathedral's sandstone bulk has endured the ravages of time and siege: Parliamentarian troops during the Civil War destroyed all but two powerful arches of the original eight bays of the Norman nave, but there's still much to admire in the ornate fifteenth-century choir stalls and the glorious **East Window**, which features some of the finest pieces of fourteenth-century stained glass in the country, although two-thirds of it is a faithful nineteenth-century restoration. In the northwest corner of the nave, steps lead down to the **Treasury**, containing glittering chalices and communion sets, and Henry VIII's charter of the foundation of the Dean and Chapter in 1541. Opposite the main entrance the reconstructed **Fratry**, or monastic building, houses the cathedral library, while its undercroft doubles as the Prior's Kitchen, a daytime café aptly using space that was once the monks' dining hall.

For more on Carlisle's history, head for the **Tullie House Museum and Art Gallery** (Mon–Sat 10am–5pm, Sun noon–5pm; £3.75), reached up Castle Street or through the cathedral grounds, via Abbey Street. This takes a highly imaginative approach to Carlisle's turbulent past, with special emphasis put on life on the edge of the Roman Empire – climbing a reconstruction of part of Hadrian's Wall you learn about catapults and stone-throwers, while other sections elaborate on domestic life, work and burial practices. There's also plenty on the Jacobite siege of 1745, as well as a dramatic attempt to convey the intensity of the feuds between the "Reivers" border families who lived beyond the jurisdiction of the Scottish and English authorities from the fourteenth to the seventeenth century in the so-called "Debatable Lands". The art gallery shows changing exhibitions of contemporary arts and crafts, and the adjacent **Tullie Old House** (daily noon–4pm; free), site of the original city museum, now contains assorted paintings, china and other exhibits.

A new extension to Tullie House – the heritage and educational facility – has combined with various projects to provide a bridge across the fast Castle Way road, which used to cut the castle off from the rest of the city centre. A new footbridge uses design elements from the city's former medieval Irish Gate, while a 24-hour public walkway reaches beneath Castle Way to **Carlisle Castle** (daily Easter–Oct 9.30am–6pm; Nov–Easter 10am–4pm; £3; EH), originally built by William Rufus on the site of a Celtic hillfort. Having clocked up over nine hundred years of continuous military use, the castle has undergone considerable changes, most evident in its outer bailey, which is filled with fairly modern buildings named after battles from the Napoleonic Wars and World War I. Apart from the gatehouse, with its reconstructed warden's quarters, it's the **inner bailey** surrounding the keep that's the real draw. It was here, in 1568, that Elizabeth I kept Mary Queen of Scots as her "guest". There's a **Military Museum** located in the former armoury, but much more interesting are the excellent displays in the **Keep** and the elegant heraldic carvings made by prisoners in a second-floor alcove. The castle was recaptured from Bonnie Prince Charlie's troops in 1745, but the story of "the licking stone" in the dungeon providing moisture for the parched Scottish prisoners is probably apocryphal. More credible is the claim that they were the first to sing "You'll take the high road and I'll take the low road", referring to their poor prospects of returning to Scotland alive. Don't leave without climbing to the battlements for a view of the Carlisle rooftops.

Practicalities

From the **train station**, just off Botchergate, outside the Citadel, it's a five-minute walk to the **tourist office** in the Old Town Hall on Green Market (June–Aug Mon–Sat 9.30am–6pm, Sun 10.30am–4pm; Sept, Oct & March–May Mon–Sat 9.30am–5pm, Sun 10.30am–4pm; Nov–Feb Mon–Sat 10am–4pm; ☎01228/625600), which can book accommodation and provide a map.

The **bus station** is off Lowther Street, parallel to English Street, and most of the budget **accommodation** is east of here, concentrated on the streets between Victoria Place and Warwick Road. Most places are less than ten minutes' walk from the centre. Good choices – all of them Victorian town houses in a conservation area – include *Ashleigh House*, 46 Victoria Place (☎01228/521631; no credit cards; ②); *Cornerways Guest House*, 107 Warwick Rd (☎01228/521733; no credit cards; ①); *Courtfield House*, 169 Warwick Rd (☎01228/522767; no credit cards; ②); *Langleigh House*, 6 Howard Place (☎01228/530440; no credit cards; ②); and *Howard House*, 27 Howard Place (☎01228/529159; no credit cards; ②). More expensive central options include, the *Cumbrian Hotel*, Court Square (☎01228/531951; ⑥, ⑤ at weekends), right by the train station, and the nearby *County Hotel*, round the corner at 9 Botchergate (☎01228/531316, *cohot@enterprise.net*; ③) – there are good weekend discounts here. The nearest **campsite** is *Orton Grange* caravan park (☎01228/710252) on the Wigton road (A595) four miles southwest of the city – take bus #300. The outdoor pool is open in summer.

For daytime **meals** head for *Café Courtyard*, Treasury Court (enter through the gates on Scotch Street or Fisher Street) or *Delifrance*, behind the tourist office at the southern end of Fisher Street – both have outdoor tables in the summer. *Watts Victorian Coffee Shop*, 11 Bank St, is a pleasant choice too. In the evening, choose between *Franco's*, the pizzeria-restaurant occupying the ground floor of the Guildhall on Fisher Street, or *Fat Fingers* on Abbey St (☎01228/511774), near Tullie House and the cathedral, a café-bar whose menu trawls the world for inspiration. Off Warwick Road, *Cecil's Treat* at 36 Cecil St (☎01228/514868; closed Mon–Thurs eve & all Sun), offers a menu ranging from roast lamb to vegetable bake.

Around Carlisle: Birdoswald Fort and Lanercost Priory

Birdoswald Fort (Easter–Oct daily 10am–5.30pm; Nov daily 10am–4pm; £2.50; EH) is fifteen miles east of Carlisle (signposted off the A69) and five miles beyond Brampton, which has the nearest train station, a mile and a half south of the village. The Hadrian's Wall Bus (see p.884) connects Carlisle with the site. This is the only place along the wall where all tiers of the Roman structure are found intact, the defences comprising an earth ditch, a large section of masonry wall, and the trench and mound foundations behind it. A visitor centre fleshes out the historic background, and you can walk to the nearby Harrow's Scar Milecastle for some spectacular views.

If you're driving, you may as well combine a trip to the Wall with a visit to the highly attractive ruins of **Lanercost Priory** (Easter–Sept daily 10am–6pm; Oct daily 10am–5pm; £2), three miles northeast of Brampton. The Augustinian priory dates from 1166 and lies in a lovely spot: carved stones found here date back to Roman times, and the priory church is still used as the local parish church.

travel details

Trains

Appleby-in-Westmorland to: Carlisle (6 daily; 40min).

Carlisle to: Appleby (6 daily; 40min); Barrow-in-Furness (5 daily; 2hr 20min); Edinburgh (8 daily; 1hr 40min); Lancaster (hourly; 1hr); Leeds (6 daily; 2hr 50min); London (8 daily; 4hr 20min); Manchester (2 daily; 2hr 30min); Newcastle (hourly; 1hr 20min–1hr 40min); Preston (21 daily; 1hr 20min–1hr 40min); Whitehaven (hourly; 1hr 10min).

Oxenholme (Lake District) to: Birmingham (6 daily; 2hr 30min–3hr); Carlisle (14 daily; 40–50min); London (5 daily; 3hr 30min–5hr); Manchester (3–9 daily; 1hr 40min); Penrith (14 daily; 30min); Preston (hourly; 30–40 min).

Buses

Carlisle to: Appleby (1 daily; 1hr 15min); Keswick (Mon–Sat 4 daily, 1 on Sun; 1hr 30min–2hr); Lancaster (4 daily; express services 1hr 10min, some services up to 4hr 30min); London (3 daily;

5hr 30min); Manchester (2 daily; 2hr 30min); Newcastle (Mon–Sat 13 daily, 4 on Sun; 2hr 30min); Whitehaven (hourly; 1hr 30min); Windermere/Bowness (3 daily; 2hr 20min).

Kendal to: Ambleside (hourly; 40min); Cartmel (7 daily; 1hr); Grasmere (hourly; 1hr); Keswick (1 hourly 1–2hr; 1hr 30min); Lancaster (hourly; 1hr); Manchester (Mon–Sat 3 daily, 1 on Sun; 2hr 45min); Windermere/Bowness (hourly; 30min).

Keswick to: Ambleside (hourly; 1hr); Buttermere (2 daily; 30min); Carlisle (Mon–Sat 4 daily, 1 on Sun; 1hr 30min–2hr); Cockermouth (7 daily; 35min); Grasmere (hourly; 40min); Kendal (hourly; 1hr 30min); Lancaster (5–10 daily; 2hr 50min); Manchester (1–3 daily; 3hr 50min); Seatoller (Mon–Sat 9 daily, 5 on Sun; 30min); Whitehaven (5 daily; 1hr 40min); Windermere (hourly; 1hr).

Windermere to: Ambleside (up to 3 hourly; 15min); Barrow-in-Furness (Mon–Sat 3 daily, 1 on Sun; 1hr 40min); Carlisle (3 daily; 2hr 20min); Grasmere (hourly; 30min); Kendal (hourly; 30min); Keswick (hourly; 1hr); Lancaster (hourly; 1hr 45min); Manchester (Mon–Sat 3 daily, 1 on Sun; 3hr).

CHAPTER TEN

YORKSHIRE

ew visitors pass through **Yorkshire**, England's largest county, without spending time in history-soaked **York**, for centuries England's second city until the Industrial Revolution created new centres of power and influence. Famed primarily for its minster, the city is a comprehensive, if somewhat over-restored, ensemble of tiny medieval alleys, castle ruins, tucked-away churches, riverside gardens and topnotch museums. York's mixture of medieval, Georgian and Victorian architecture is mirrored in miniature in the prosperous north and east of the county by towns such as **Beverley**, centred on another soaring minster; **Richmond**, banked under a crag-bound castle; and **Ripon**, gathered around its honey-stoned cathedral. **Knaresborough** shares similar attributes, but is overshadowed by the faded gentility of neighbouring **Harrogate**, a spa town geared these days towards the conference trade rather than health-seeking visitors. The Yorkshire coast, too, retains something of the grandeur of the days when its towns were the first to promote themselves as resorts: places like **Bridlington** and **Scarborough** boomed in the nineteenth century and again in the postwar period, though these days they're living on past glories. Instead, it's in characterful places like **Whitby** and **Robin Hood's Bay** – busy, smaller resorts with unspoiled historic centres – that the best of the coast is to be found.

The engine of growth during the Industrial Revolution was not in the north of the county, but in the south and west. By the nineteenth century, Leeds, Bradford, Sheffield and their satellites were the world's mightiest producers of **textiles** (an industry first nurtured by the monastic houses of the moors and dales) and of **steel**. Ruthless economic logic devastated the area this century, leaving only disused textile mills, abandoned steel- and heavy-engineering works, and great soot-covered civic buildings in cities battered by depression. However, a new vigour has infused South and West Yorkshire during the last decade, and the city-centre transformations of **Leeds** and **Sheffield** in particular have been remarkable. Both are now making open play for tourists with a series of high-profile attractions, from the Royal Armouries to the National Centre for Popular Music, while **Bradford** and its **National Museum of Photography, Film and Television** waylays people on their way to **Haworth** – birthplace of the Brontë sisters, and wretchedly over-visited.

During even the worst of times, broad swathes of moorland survived above the slum- and factory-choked valleys, and it can come as a surprise to discover the amount of open countryside on Leeds' and Bradford's doorsteps. The **Yorkshire Dales**, to the northwest, form a lovely patchwork of limestone hills and serene valleys, ranging from

---

ACCOMMODATION PRICE CODES

Throughout this guide, hotel and B&B accommodation is priced on a scale of ① to ⑨, the number indicating the **lowest price** you could expect to pay per night in that establishment for a **double room** in high season. The prices indicated by the codes are as follows:

① under £40	④ £60–70	⑦ £110–150
② £40–50	⑤ £70–90	⑧ £150–200
③ £50–60	⑥ £90–110	⑨ over £200

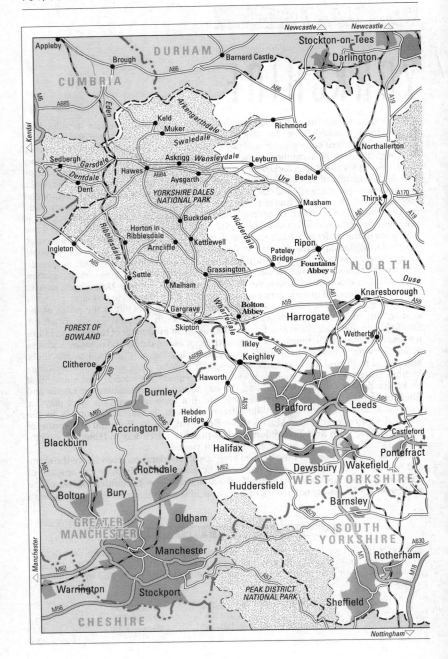

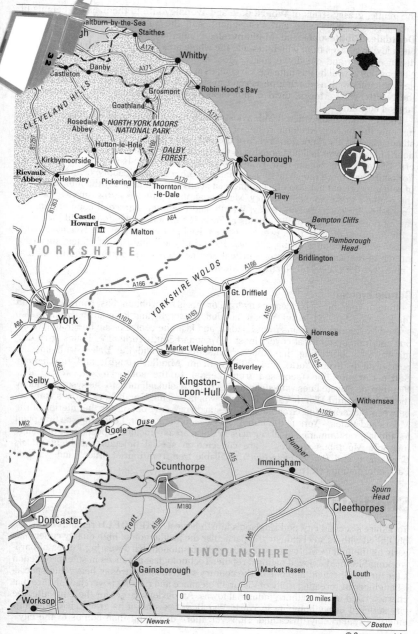

© Crown copyright

the gentle, grassy spans of **Wharfedale** and **Wensleydale** to the majestic heights of Ingleborough, Whernside and Pen-y-ghent, and the wilder valleys of **Swaledale, Dentdale, Ribblesdale** and **Malhamdale**. Numerous stone-built villages provide often idyllic centres from which to walk, the whole area being covered by tracks, long-distance paths and old drove roads. Most are waymarked by the Yorkshire Dales National Park, which runs information centres and smaller information points. Less visited, but still worth as much time as you can spare, is the county's other National Park, the **North York Moors**, divided into bleak upland moors and with a tremendous rugged coastline.

The region is also scattered with a host of historic sites and buildings. These include not only the more predictable roster of stately homes, among which **Castle Howard** stands out, but also imperious relics of the Industrial Revolution, from the civic splendour of Leeds' town hall and arcades to the Italianate pastiche of **Saltaire**, a millwork-ers' village on the outskirts of Bradford. In an earlier age, before the Reformation, Yorkshire had more monastic houses than any other English county, centres not only of religious retreat but also of a commercial acumen that was to lay the foundations of the region's great woollen industry. Many beautifully situated **ruins** survive today at Fountains, Rievaulx, Bolton Abbey, Whitby and elsewhere, graceful counterpoints to the more solid remains of the **castles** at York, Richmond, Scarborough and Pickering – the foremost of more than twenty castles raised in Yorkshire by the Normans. York boasts some **Roman** remains, and near Pickering you'll find Britain's finest surviving stretch of Roman road; still more ancient are the prehistoric barrows and dykes that ripple over the Dales and North York Moors.

Getting around

Getting to Yorkshire's big centres by train or bus is no problem. Fast **train** services on the East Coast main line link York to London, Newcastle and Edinburgh. Leeds is also served by regular fast trains from London, and is at the centre of the integrated Metro bus and train system that covers most of West and South Yorkshire. Trains are a useful way of approaching the Moors, Yorkshire coast and the Dales, with lines to Scarborough (from York) and Whitby (from Middlesbrough), and the famous **Settle–Carlisle** line (accessed from Leeds) to the southern and west Dales. Picturesque private lines with steam trains make useful adjuncts to the system, notably the **Keighley and Worth Valley** line to Haworth and the **North York Moors Railway** between Pickering and Grosmont. **Buses** are your only option for the interior of the Moors and Dales – York is the hub of services to the former, Leeds the starting point for the latter. Summaries of all services in these areas – including post buses and sum-mer-only Moorsbus shuttles – are collected in special timetable booklets (*Moors Connections* and *Dales Connections*), available free from tourist offices and National Park information centres.

Sheffield

Yorkshire's second city, and England's fourth-largest, **SHEFFIELD** remains inextrica-bly linked with its steel industry, in particular the production of high-quality cutlery. As early as the fourteenth century, the carefully fashioned, hard-wearing knives of hard-working Sheffield enjoyed national repute. Technological advances in steel production later turned Sheffield into one of the country's foremost centres of heavy and special-ist engineering, creating a city of Victorian elegance and racking poverty, a mixture that characterized most northern industrial towns. An obvious target for the Luftwaffe, the city suffered heavy bombing in World War II, yet several of its grand civic buildings emerged remarkably unscathed. However, more damaging than bombs to the city's pre-eminence was the steel industry's subsequent downturn, which by the 1980s had tipped parts of Sheffield into dispiriting decline.

As with Leeds, the economic and cultural revival has been marked and rapid, spurred on by dogged local business incentives, an enthusiastic council and bundles of lottery money. In the last fifteen years, Sheffield steel production has risen to its highest ever level, while the arrival of new high-tech industries has cemented the revival. Meanwhile, **Meadowhall** shopping centre, in a resurrected steel works and billed as Europe's most successful mall, attracts thirty million visitors a year. Urban regeneration is in full swing: the "Heart of the City" project is fast transforming the centre; a glut of **sports facilities** (including the Ski Village, Europe's largest artificial ski resort) backs Sheffield's claim to be considered "National City of Sport"; while the city that gave the world the iconoclastic Jarvis Cocker of Pulp now houses the **National Centre for Popular Music**, one of the country's most enterprising visitor attractions.

Consequently, tourism is booming and with the Peak District so close – in fact, over a third of the city lies within the boundary of the **Peak District National Park** (see p.569) – you may well decide to allot it a night or two. The city's two universities and large student population (around 45,000) lends the café and **nightlife** scene a welcome edge.

Arrival, information and accommodation

Sheffield's **train station** is just east of the city centre off Sheaf Square. The **bus station**, known as the Sheffield Interchange, is on Pond Street about two hundred yards to the north; this is also where the National Express services pick up and drop off. The Destination Sheffield **tourist office** on Surrey Street (Mon–Fri 9.30am–5.15pm, Sat 9.30am–4.15pm; ☎0114/273 4671) is just five minutes' walk from the stations, near the town hall, and is well-equipped with brochures, leaflets and guides to the city.

Sheffield city centre is easy to make your way around on foot, and you will only need to use the **local public transport** system to reach some of the outlying museums and galleries or the Botanical Gardens. Most local buses depart from the High Street, while the sleek, cheap **Supertram** system (info on ☎0114/272 8282) connects the city centre with Meadowhall (northeast), Middlewood (northwest) and Halfway (southeast). For fare and timetable **information**, visit the Travel Information Centre at the Interchange (Mon–Sat 8am–5pm, Sun 9am–5pm) or call the Travel Line on ☎01709/515151. A one-day TravelMaster Pass (£4.95) gives unlimited travel on buses, trains and trams throughout South Yorkshire. Otherwise, there's a day-rider (£1.70) and a seven-day Mega-rider (£5.50) pass just for the Supertram.

Sheffield isn't blessed with many good-value central **accommodation** options, so the tourist office's room-booking service can come in handy. There's no youth hostel, though the university has accommodation available during the summer vacation.

Bristol, Blonk St (☎0114/220 4000, *sheffield@bhg.co.uk*). Breezy business hotel near the river, quays and markets. All rooms are en suite. ⑤, ④ at weekends.

Cutlers, George St (☎0114/273 9939). City-centre inn with budget en-suite rooms, all with TV and tea -and -coffee-making facilities. You may get a few pounds shaved off at weekends. ④.

Priory Lodge, 40 Wolstenholme Rd (☎0114/258 4670). Suburban accommodation, a mile south-west of the centre. ②.

Rutland Arms, 86 Brown St (☎0114/272 9003). Victorian pub with pleasant beer garden and a few standard rooms, just seconds from the music centre. No credit cards. ②.

Stakis, Victoria Quays (☎0114/252 5500). Makes superb use of its revitalized canalside site, with a range of leisure facilities. The standard midweek rate is room only; special and weekend deals (two-night minimum) bring the price down considerably and usually include breakfast. ⑦.

University of Sheffield, Halifax Hall, Endcliffe Vale Rd (☎0114/222 8811). A couple of miles west of the city centre, but linked to it by a regular bus service (#M60, from Flat St). Variety of single rooms – either with washbasin or en-suite facilities – in the student hall of residence. Available mid-June to mid-Sept only; small discount for stays of more than three nights. ①.

The City

Millions of pounds have been earmarked to turn Sheffield city centre away from the twin legacies of Victorian solidity and late-twentieth-century sterility. New squares, pedestrianized precincts and designated retail and cultural "quarters" all form part of the plan, and despite unavoidable millennium posturing, there's been a pleasing coherence to the various schemes recently put under way.

There's been most progress in the revamped post-industrial area near the train station – rather grandly known as the **Cultural Industries Quarter** – where clubs and galleries exist alongside high-tech arts and media businesses. The major player here is the **National Centre for Popular Music** on Paternoster Row (daily 10am–6pm, last admission 3.30pm; £5.95, £7.25 at weekends, on bank holidays and throughout July & Aug), a landmark attraction designed by Nigel Coates, whose main exhibition areas are set within four giant stainless-steel drums – a nod to the city's most prominent industry. You should allow at least two hours for a visit, and be prepared for the fact that it's an interactive arts and education centre and not a traditional museum. Instead of viewing spangly guitars, gold discs and stage costumes, you're encouraged to make, record and mix music, have a go at designing an album sleeve, investigate the global impact of popular music, check the Guinness-sponsored interactive databases and sit in on the specially commissioned works being aired in the world's first 3-D surround-sound auditorium. The hip ground-floor café-bar shows signs of rivalling the **Showroom** cinema-and-bar complex across the road, and you can probably find someone to debate the relative merits of famous Sheffield popsters and rocksters, from Def Leppard and the Human League through to Jarvis Cocker and Babybird. The renowned **Site Gallery**, just up the road on Brown Street (Tues–Sat 11am–5pm; free) specializes in photography and multimedia exhibitions.

To the north of town, near the River Don, **Castlegate** and its traditional **markets** are still undergoing ambitious redevelopment, while the spruced-up warehouses and cobbled towpaths in the neighbouring canal basin, **Victoria Quays**, now house high-tech businesses, a hotel, and leisure facilities. In the centre itself, the main development is around the impressive **Town Hall**, at the junction of Pinstone and Surrey streets. Completed in 1897, it's topped by the figure of Vulcan, the Roman god of fire and metalworking, and the facade sports a fine frieze depicting traditional Sheffield industries. A mid-Seventies extension to the town hall had few friends during its life – its recent demolition has allowed room for the city's new centrepiece, the **Millennium Gallery and Winter Garden**, whose completion is expected during the year 2000. As well as semipermanent displays loaned by London's Victoria and Albert Museum, the gallery is also destined to hold the Hawley collection of Sheffield hand tools and, of more general interest, the city's Ruskin collection, founded by John Ruskin in 1875 to "improve" the working people of Sheffield. Their education must have been wonderfully eclectic if the collection is anything to go by – a bulging library is complemented by an intriguing potpourri of watercolours, minerals, paintings and medieval illuminated manuscripts.

North of the town hall, **Fargate** meets Church Street, where the city's **Cathedral of St Peter and St Paul** retains elements of its fifteenth-century origins, though it's been restored on many occasions since. Across Cathedral Square sits the **Cutler's Hall** of 1832, an imposing reminder of Sheffield's traditions. The Company of Cutlers was first established in 1624 to regulate the affairs of the cutlery industry, and this is the third hall on the site. Its silver collection is unrivalled, though you may need to be part of a group to view it: call ☎0114/272 8456 for details. South of the town hall and the fountain-splashed **Peace Gardens** piazza, the pedestrianized **Moor Quarter** draws in shoppers, though the nearby **Devonshire Quarter**, centred on Division Street, is the trendiest shopping area. At The Forum by Devonshire Green, thirty-odd retail outlets flog club- and skate-wear, retro clothing, music, applied art and baubles, while the café-bar here is a popular spot for hanging out.

The city's traditional sights include the **Graves Art Gallery** (Tues–Sat 10am–5pm; free), located on the top floor of the City Library (entrance on Surrey Street). It leans most heavily towards nineteenth- and twentieth-century British artists like Turner, Nash, Gwen John and the Pre-Raphaelites. Parts of the city's nineteenth-century collection are also held at the **Mappin Art Gallery** in Weston Park (Wed–Sat 10am–5pm, Sun 11am–5pm; free), a mile west of the city centre (bus #52 from the High Street). Sheffield's most instructive museums, however, are those devoted to its industrial past. The **City Museum** (Wed–Sat 10am–5pm, Sun 11am–5pm; free), adjacent to the Mappin, contains the definitive collection of cutlery and Sheffield ware, but it's eclipsed by the **Kelham Island Museum**, Alma Street (Mon–Thurs 10am–4pm, Sun 11am–4.45pm; £3), on Kelham Island, one mile north of the city centre (bus #47 or #48 from Flat Street). Exhibits here reveal the breadth of the city's industrial output, ranging from a colossal twelve-thousand horsepower steam engine to a silver-plated penny-farthing made for the tsar of Russia. Many of the old machines are still working, arranged in period workshops where craftspeople demonstrate some of the finer points of cutlery production.

Finally, Sheffield's **Botanical Gardens** (daily 10am–dusk; free), a couple of miles southwest of the centre, provide a restful spot on a hot day – nineteen acres of Victorian landscaping, as well as the impressive glass Paxton Pavilions and a café-bar. There are two entrances, on Clarkehouse Road (bus #50 or #59 from the High Street) and Thompson Road (buses #81–86 from the High Street).

Eating and drinking

Sheffield has plenty of great **café-bars** and good-value **restaurants**, all pretty adept at making a play for the student pound. The **pubs** listed below are those with a bit of character and staying power, but for the best insight into what makes Sheffield tick as a party destination take a night-time walk along **West Street** where competing theme and retro bars go in and out of fashion (and business). Students also frequent the bars and pubs of Broomhill and Ecclesall Road, but neither area is particularly central.

Café-bars

All Bar One, 15 Leopold St. Roomy chain café-bar with a blackboard menu, plenty of decent wine (racked above the long bar), pine tables, stripped floors and fans. A nice place to sit outside in the sun.

Casablanca, 150–154 Devonshire St. Easygoing bar-bistro with live jazz most nights and a reasonably priced mainstream menu.

The Forum, 127–129 Division St. Long the mainstay of the Devonshire Quarter, the Forum has a great menu and laid-back clientele. Closed Sun.

Halcyon, 113–117 Division St. Designer bar with cosy sofas and a touch of class.

Lloyd's No.1, Waterworks Building, 2 Division St. Split-level café-bar in a beauty of a building, with decent food and, during the day at least, a quieter feel than its rivals.

Nonna's 2, Brown St. Lovely little Italian deli-café, serving *frittata* or scrambled eggs and smoked salmon for breakfast, and ciabatta sandwiches, salads and coffee until 8pm. Closed Sun.

Showroom, 7 Paternoster Row. Part of the independent cinema complex opposite the National Centre for Popular Music, the relaxed *Showroom* has a café on one side serving Mediterranean-style snacks and sandwiches, and a great bar on the other with a couple of sofas and a long see-and-be-seen window.

Restaurants

Antonio's Flying Pizza, 255 Glossop Rd (☎0114/273 9056). Long-established and rumbustious Italian pasta and pizza place. Inexpensive.

Blue Room Café, 22a Norfolk Row. Cheap and cheerful daytime vegetarian/wholefood café, with a few outdoor seats in the summer. Soccer fans can revel in the proximity of the nearby Reed Employment Centre, a terraced house where Sheffield United first came into being in 1889.

Encore, Crucible Theatre, Tudor Square (☎0114/275 0724). Accomplished Modern-British cooking in the theatre restaurant; pre-show dinner and meal-and-ticket deals offer the best value. Moderate.

Nirmals, 189–193 Glossop Rd (☎0114/272 4054). The most highly rated Indian restaurant in town, open until 1am at the weekend. Inexpensive.

Trippet's Wine Bar, 89 Trippets Lane (☎0114/278 0198). There's always a nice atmosphere in this unstuffy wine bar behind West Street. The bistro food is popular and there's live jazz and blues on occasion. Moderate.

Pubs

Bath Hotel, 66 Victoria St. Timeless Victorian classic off Glossop Road – no frills, but well-kept real ale and handsome original features.

Broomhill, 484 Glossop Rd. In one of the city's leafier areas, lively and popular with students.

Fat Cat, 23 Alma St. Cosy, old-fashioned and famed for its umpteen real ales. It's in old steel-land, about a quarter of an hour's walk north from the city centre.

Frog & Parrot, Division St. A boisterous pub with some dark little nooks and crannies, lots of beers and a good jukebox. Decent mix of locals and students.

The Washington, 79 Fitzwilliam St. A good pub with good beer that's a favoured muso's hangout. Just two minutes from Division Street.

Nightlife and the arts

Friday's *Sheffield Telegraph* lists the week's performances, events, concerts and films; look out also for the highly useful and entertaining *Dirty Stop Out's Guide*, a comprehensive listings' booklet, available at the tourist office.

Clubs and live music venues

Arena, Broughton Lane (☎0114/256 5656) and **Don Valley Stadium**, on Worksop Road (☎0114/278 9199). Stadium venues on the edge of town, on the Supertram route out to Meadowhall.

The Boardwalk, Snig Hill (☎0114/279 9090). Popular venue for indie bands, rock, folk and comedy.

Capitol, 14–16 Matilda St (☎0114/276 3523). A converted warehouse where the night's clubbing continues until well into the following day.

Josephine's, Fountain Precinct, Barker's Pool (☎0114/273 9810). Upmarket, glitzy club.

Leadmill, 6–7 Leadmill Rd (☎0114/275 4500), in the Cultural Industries Quarter, hosting live bands and DJs most nights of the week.

Nelson Mandela Building, Pond Street (☎0114/253 4122). Part of Sheffield Hallam University; hosts regular gigs and club nights..

Niche, 87–91 Sydney St (☎0114/275 1414). Sheffield's finest all-nighter, staying open until 8am – a free minibus service takes people on to the *Capitol* (see above).

Republic, 112 Arundel St (☎0114/249 2210). Club housed in an old steel and engineering works.

Tin Pan Alley, 8–10 Fitzwilliam St (☎0114/272 0070). Live bands most nights of the week.

University of Sheffield, on Western Bank (☎0114/222 8777). Hosts regular gigs and club nights.

Pulse (over-18s) and **Vogue** (for over-25s), both part of the Arena Leisure Park on Terry Street (☎0114/243 4531), near the Sheffield Arena.

Theatres and cinemas

The Crucible, Lyceum and Studio **theatres** in Tudor Square (☎0114/276 9922) put on a full programme of theatre, dance, comedy and concerts. The Crucible also hosts the annual Music in the Round festival of chamber music (May), and the Sheffield Children's Festival (late June, or July), whose events are performed entirely by children. There are mainscreen **cinemas** at Meadowhall (☎0114/256 9444) and Arundel Gate (☎0114/272 3981). The Showroom, 7 Paternoster Row (☎0114/275 7727), is the art-house alternative, the biggest independent cinema outside London.

Leeds and around

Yorkshire's commercial capital, and one of the fastest-growing cities in the country, **LEEDS** has undergone a radical transformation in recent years. There's still a true northern grit to its character, and in many of its dilapidated suburbs, but the grime has been removed from the Victorian centre and the city is revelling in its renaissance as a financial, administrative and cultural boomtown. An early market town, wool was traded here in medieval times by the monks of nearby Kirkstall Abbey. By the eighteenth century, the advent of canals and technical innovations such as the harnessing of steam power turned what had been a cottage industry into a dynamic large-scale economy. Leeds quickly boomed beyond its capacity to support its burgeoning population, and while the textile barons prospered, the city acquired a reputation for grimness that proved hard to shake off. In 1847 Charles Dickens described Leeds as "the beastliest place, one of the nastiest I know", an observation that many visitors might have applied to the city until comparatively recently.

Now, however, improved communications, a major clean-up and urban rejuvenation schemes have been the making of modern Leeds. The most obvious manifestation of change has been the advent of late-opening cafés, bars, clubs and eclectic restaurants, and the arrival of the swanky department store, Harvey Nichols. The formerly run-down city quarters have been revitalized and have made Leeds a noted **nightlife** destination. It's long been the region's **cultural** centre, home to Opera North, the noted West Yorkshire Playhouse and a triennial international piano competition that ranks among the world's top musical events. The **Royal Armouries** aside, the **City Art Gallery** has the best collection of British twentieth-century art outside London; **Leeds City Museum** and **Armley Mills Museum** take care of the city's historical legacy; while further from the city you might try to see the ruins of **Kirkstall Abbey** and one of the country's great Georgian piles, **Harewood House**.

Arrival, transport and accommodation

National and local Metro trains use **Leeds City Station** off City Square on the southern flank of the city centre, which also houses the impressive Gateway Yorkshire **tourist office** in the Arcade (Mon–Sat 9.30am–6pm, Sun 10am–4pm; ☎0113/242 5242), stuffed with leaflets and information about Leeds and the rest of West Yorkshire. The **bus and coach station** occupies a sprawling site to the east, behind Kirkgate Market, on St Peter's Street, close to the West Yorkshire Playhouse – as well as for National Express and all regional services, this is also the depot for buses from York, the coast, the Dales and Manchester.

City transport

Leeds city centre is easily walked around and you'll have little use for the extensive bus network unless you're staying at a far-flung B&B or planning to use the city as a base for visiting destinations like Bradford or Haworth. Buses depart from stops all over the city, including the **bus station** on St Peter's Street, but ongoing roadworks, pedestrianization and other developments mean that departure points occasionally change. The **Metro Travel Centre** at the bus station has up-to-date service details (Mon–Fri

8.30am–5.30pm, Sat 9am–4.30pm), and you can also ask in the tourist office, which has timetables for every conceivable local service; or call **Metroline** (Mon–Sat 8am–7pm, Sun 9am–5.30pm; ☎0113/245 7676) which advises on current routes and fares throughout the city and region. If you're planning to see a slice of West Yorkshire over a day or two, consider one of the available **passes** for use on local buses and trains – there's the bus/train day rover (£4.50), separate bus or train day rovers (£3.80 each) and a family day rover (£6).

Accommodation

There's a good mix of **accommodation** in Leeds, including some fairly central places near the university campus that shouldn't break the bank as well as business hotels that do a steady trade. Plenty of other cheaper B&Bs lie out to the northwest in Headingley, though these are all a bus ride away. The tourist office can **book you a room**; call their booking line on ☎0800/808050.

Other options include well-equipped rooms and self-catering apartments in a number of halls of residence, rented out during university holidays by the **University of Leeds** (☎0113/233 6100; ①) – call well in advance and expect a two-night minimum stay. There's a **YWCA** at 22 Lovell Park House, Lovell Park Hill (☎0113/245 7840), which is open to men as well as women, but it rarely has rooms available for single-night or short stays. The nearest **youth hostel** is in Haworth (see p.755). The nearest **campsite** is near Roundhay Park on Elmete Lane (☎0113/265 2354), three miles northeast of the city – buses #10 and #12 (#19 or #19a Sun) make the journey; get off at the Oakwood clock, from where it's a five-minute walk.

42 The Calls, 42 The Calls (☎0113/244 0099, *hotel@42thecalls.co.uk*). Stunning designer hotel – Leeds' top choice – converted from an old grain mill on the canal, with public rooms and bedrooms flaunting stripped oak beams, iron piping, metallic facing and CD players. Weekend rates sometimes available. ⑦.

Avalon Guest House, 132 Woodsley Rd (☎0113/243 2545). Decent budget B&B near the university in a large Victorian house; en-suite rooms creep into the next price category. ③.

Glengarth, 162 Woodsley Rd (☎0113/245 7940). Homely B&B, with good rates and a variety of single and double rooms; the cheapest don't have en-suite facilities. No credit cards. ③.

The Griffin, 31 Boar Lane (☎0113/242 2555). Central Victorian hotel, handily placed for shopping and café life. Weekend rates are an especially good deal, when prices drop by £20 or so. ⑤.

Malmaison, Sovereign Quay (☎0113/398 1000). The arrival of *Malmaison* in Leeds has given *42 The Calls* (see above) something to think about. Designer waterside premises (behind Swinegate), with the signature *Malmaison* style. Breakfast isn't included. ⑥, ⑤ at weekends.

Moorlea, 146 Woodsley Rd (☎0113/243 2653). Amiable place near the university, with comfortable singles and doubles; those with en-suite showers fall into the next category up. No credit cards. ③.

Queen's Hotel, City Square (☎0113/243 1323). Refurbished Art Deco landmark, right in front of the station, with period *Palm Court Lounge*, bar, restaurant and free car parking. During the week, steep room-only rates are paid by a business clientele; weekend rates include breakfast (and special deals throw in dinner too). ⑦, ⑤ at weekends.

Wellesley, Wellington St (☎0113/243 0431). Severe Victorian hotel – plain but comfortable inside – with bargain rates for the city-centre location, and including some cheaper rooms without en-suite facilities. ④.

The city

Leeds city centre splits itself into three reasonably distinct areas, starting with the **universities** on the heights to the northwest, arranged around some pleasant green swathes but framed by the more brutal excrescences of Sixties planning. The city's revitalized commercial life is most apparent in the packed pedestrianized streets south of the **Headrow**, where the Victorian and Edwardian buildings, arcades and markets glitter with brand names and designer labels, while down along the **Leeds–Liverpool**

Canal a kind of post-industrial chic has infused the converted warehouses and railway arches. If you want some purpose to your wanderings, take one of the themed **guided walks** that depart from the tourist office at 2pm on most Wednesdays and Sundays between April and October (£2.50).

City Square opposite the train station hasn't been much of an introduction to Leeds for years, though that's set to change as the surrounding buildings (including the Queen's Hotel and the train station's North Concourse) are renovated and smartened up, and the square pedestrianized. Pavement cafés are planned, and while the statues might get moved around, the prancing Edward, the Black Prince, and the bronze nymph gas-lamps should all survive.

From the square it's a short walk up to the main Headrow where you can't miss **Leeds Town Hall**, one of the finest expressions of nineteenth-century civic pride in the country. The masterpiece of local architect Cuthbert Broderick, it's a classical colossus of great skill, colonnaded on all sides, guarded by white lions and topped by a perky clocktower and sculptures embodying Industry, Art, Music and Science. Venture at least as far as the *Victoria Tearooms* (Mon–Fri 10am–4pm; entrance on Calverley St side) for a cup of tea with a nice view.

The City Museum and Art Gallery (for both, see below) line up next door, along the Headrow, though most people make a beeline for the brimming, shop-filled **arcades** further along on either side of pedestrianized **Briggate**. These nineteenth-century palaces of marble, mahogany, stained glass and mosaics have been magnificently restored to house the shops and businesses which are at the heart of Leeds' revival. Perhaps the most splendidly decorated of all is the light-flooded **Victoria Quarter**, with Harvey Nichols as its designer lodestone – you'll need to suspend financial disbelief before plonking yourself down in its fashionable *Espresso Bar* or *Fourth Floor Café-Bar* (see pp.746–747).

Across Vicar Lane, the restored **Kirkgate Market** (closed Wed afternoon & Sun) is the largest market in the north of England. Housed in a superb Edwardian building, it's a descendant of the medieval woollen markets that were instrumental in making Leeds the early focus of the region's textile industry. The **outdoor market** behind here (Tues, Fri & Sat), incidentally, is where Michael Marks set up stall in 1884 with the slogan "don't ask the price, it's a penny" – an enterprise that blossomed into the present-day retail giant Marks & Spencer. Visible at the bottom of the street, on the corner of Vicar Lane and Duncan Street, the elliptical, domed **Corn Exchange** (open daily) was built in 1863, also by Cuthbert Broderick, whose design leaned heavily on his studies of Paris's corn exchange. It's now a hip market for jewellery, clothes, furnishings, music and other bits and bobs – extra craft stores open up at weekends. Behind here, under the railway arches on Assembley Street and along Call Lane, Leeds' **Exchange Quarter** flexes its fashionable muscles in a series of hip cafés and restaurants, many housed in beautifully restored buildings.

City Museum and City Art Gallery

Since the 1960s, **Leeds City Museum** (Tues–Sat 10am–5pm; free) has been unsatisfactorily housed on the second floor of the Central Library on the Headrow; its first home, built on Park Row by the Leeds Philosophical and Literary Society, was irreparably damaged during the war. Rather dark galleries dutifully run through local history from prehistoric times, highlighting fossils, Roman finds, a puzzling ethnographical section and, most startling of all, an unusually large array of stuffed animals, including a fearsome specimen of the Bengal Tiger, shot in 1860, and the illicitly bagged "Leeds Yak", potted the same year in Tibet. If and when the museum does move into new premises, as is often proposed, visitors would miss the real attraction of its current home – the Victorian mosaic floors, marble pillars, sculpted capitals and stained glass.

The adjacent **Leeds City Art Gallery** (Mon–Sat 10am–5pm, Wed 10am–8pm, Sun 1–5pm; free) comprises one of the best arrays outside London of twentieth-century

British art. Changing selections from the permanent collection of nineteenth- and twentieth-century art and sculpture are presented, with an understandable bias towards pieces by Henry Moore and Barbara Hepworth, both former students at the Leeds School of Art; Moore's *Reclining Woman* lounges at the top of the steps outside the gallery. There's Victorian painting and sculpture on the ground floor, with notable chunks of work by local landscapist John Atkinson Grimshaw, while the upper floor merges French Impressionists with the English artists they influenced. Prime amongst these was the founder of the Camden Town Group, Walter Sickert, and his younger disciples Spencer Frederick Gore and Harold Gilman; later artists like Matthew Smith, Stanley Spencer and Wyndham Lewis are also represented. In addition, there are some outstanding pieces by names with greater recognition – busts by Jacob Epstein, paintings by L.S. Lowry, a David Hockney etching here, a Francis Bacon snarl there. The **café** (Mon–Sat 10am–4pm, Sun 1–4pm) is a quiet place to unwind, and there's direct access to the **Craft Centre and Design Gallery** below (Tues–Fri 10am–5pm, Sat 10am–4pm; free), where changing displays of contemporary jewellery, ceramics and applied art are on show.

From the City Art Gallery, a slender bridge connects to the adjacent **Henry Moore Institute** (daily 10am–5.30pm, Wed until 9pm; free), which has its own entrance on the Headrow. Housed in a former Victorian merchant's warehouse, now faced in black marble, the Institute is devoted to showcasing temporary exhibitions of sculpture from all periods and nationalities, and not, as you might imagine, pieces by the masterful Moore. For the best selection of Moore's works (and Barbara Hepworths, too) you need to visit nearby **Wakefield's City Art Gallery** on Wentworth Terrace (Mon–Sat 10.30am–5pm, Sun 2.30–5pm; free) or the **Yorkshire Sculpture Park** (daily 10am–dusk; free) at Bretton Hall, West Bretton, south of Wakefield.

Along the canal: Granary Wharf to the Royal Armouries

The biggest transformation in Leeds has been along the **Leeds–Liverpool Canal**, formerly a stagnant relic of industrial decline. New businesses, sought-after balconied apartments and trendy restaurants line both sides, while a slew of attractions stretch along a mile or so of the waterside, connected by a pleasant footpath. At **Granary Wharf**, a couple of minutes' walk from the train station, stores and craftshops fill the extensive cobbled, vaulted arches (the "Dark Arches"), while every weekend (and bank holiday) a market with stalls, bands and entertainers spills out onto the canal basin.

Further up on the south side, past Victoria and Leeds bridges, **Tetley's Brewery Wharf** (daily 10.30am–5pm; brewery tours at noon, 1pm & 3pm; £3.95, full brewery tour only for over-14s) stands in front of one of the region's oldest, and most favoured, breweries. The entrance price gets you a run through the history of pubs and brewing, a chance to stroke the shire horses (which used to pull the beer wagons), a tour of the brewery, and a free tasting to follow – entrance to just the museum and shire horses part of the complex is £2 and open to all ages. There's a waterside restaurant and bar at the Brewery Wharf, but it's usually packed.

Sticking with the south side, five minutes further along the canal footpath is the glass turret and gun-metal grey bulk of the **Royal Armouries** (daily: April–Oct 10.30am–5.30pm; Nov–March 10.30am to 4.30pm; £7.95, discount tickets available at the Gateway Yorkshire tourist office). Purpose-built to house the arms and armour collection from the Tower of London, it's a hugely adventurous museum which requires a leap of faith – discard the notion that all you'll see are casefuls of weapons, and you're in for a treat. Themed galleries cover concepts like "War" and "Hunting", while there are enough demonstrations (jousting to falconry), interactive displays, hands-on exhibits and computer simulations to keep everyone interested. Bus #63B runs every fifteen minutes direct to the Armouries from Leeds City Square, a five-minute ride.

Out of the city

The nearest of the surrounding sights is the **Thackray Medical Museum**, on Beckett Street (Tues–Sun 10am–5.30pm; daily during school holidays; £4.40), next to the well-known St James' Hospital ("Jimmy's" from the TV series). Sited in a former workhouse, it's a mile east of the city centre, with buses #5a, #13, #17, #41, #42, #43, #50 and #88 all running past. Essentially a medical history museum, it's a hugely popular and entertaining place – ghoulish too at times when it delves into topics like surgery before anaesthetics, and the workings of the human intestine. Needless to say, kids love it.

For Leeds' industrial past, visit the vast **Armley Mills Museum**, two miles west of the centre off Canal Road (Tues–Sat 10am–5pm, Sun 1–5pm; £2), which runs between Armley and Kirkstall Road – take bus #5a, #14, #66 or #67. There's been a mill on the site since at least the seventeenth century, and the present building was one of the world's largest woollen mills until its closure in 1969. Displays recount the whole story of Leeds' industrial history, with plenty of working machinery, together with a definitive account of how cloth was made, starting from the fleece off the sheep's back to great rolls of finished cloth. A new Printing Gallery is devoted to the story of the city's printing trade.

You can also visit the ruins of **Kirkstall Abbey** (dawn to dusk; free), the city's most important medieval relic, built between 1152 and 1182 by Cistercian monks from Fountains Abbey (see p.788). It lies about three miles northwest of the city centre on Abbey Road; take bus #732, #733, #734, #735 or #736. Despite the urban huddle close at hand, the site's still evocatively bucolic, with plenty of signed footpaths around, and the cloisters in particular are a nice spot to while away some quiet time. The former gatehouse now provides the setting for the **Abbey House Museum**, a good presentation of local folk history.

Four miles east of the city, the Jacobean house of **Temple Newsam** (April–Oct Tues–Sat 10am–5pm, Sun 1–5pm; £2) contains many of the paintings and much of the decorative art owned by Leeds City Art Gallery, including one of the largest collections of Chippendale furniture in the country; bus #27 runs here from the centre. The splendid park (daily 10am–dusk; free) was laid out by Capability Brown in 1762, and it's this rather than the art which brings many locals to picnic in the grounds. Further east still, about ten miles from Leeds, the rest of the city's art collection is housed in **Lotherton Hall** (Tues–Sat 10am–5pm, Sun 1–5pm; £2), off the B1217 near Aberford, once the home of a local industrialist, and endowed with fine gardens and a deer park. Buses #64 and #64a run to the village, from where it's a twenty-minute walk to the hall (there are direct buses on summer Sundays).

If you were to see just one stately home within the area, however, it should probably be **Harewood House**, seven miles north of Leeds (Easter–Oct daily 11am–4.30pm, grounds & bird garden 10am–6pm; Nov–Easter Sat & Sun only; £6.95, bird garden & grounds only £5.75). The house was designed and decorated by one of the greatest architectural teams ever assembled: conceived in 1759 by York architect John Carr, the building was finished by Robert Adam, the furniture made by Thomas Chippendale and the landscaped gardens laid out by Capability Brown. To cap it all a sweeping terrace designed by Sir Charles Barry (architect of the Houses of Parliament) overlooks the garden. Georgian purists might lament some of the later Victorian additions but the ensemble is still outstanding, and is further enhanced by **paintings** by artists of such mettle as Turner, Gainsborough, Reynolds, El Greco and a whole host of Italian masters. There are guided tours of the house and galleries throughout the summer every Tuesday and Thursday at 2pm. One of the more unusual features outside is the **Bird Garden**, four acres of aviaries caging over 150 species – the penguins get fed at 2pm. There are frequent buses to Harewood from Leeds (including the #36, #781 and #X35); the house is near the junction of the A659 and the A61 Leeds to Harrogate road.

Eating, drinking and nightlife

Eating out in Leeds has been transformed in recent years, with a plethora of conversions of warehouses and grain mills into up-to-the-minute British **restaurants** and brasseries. Michelin stars are not unknown, but there's a down-to-earth approach to prices, with even the fanciest places offering special lunch or early-bird deals. It's all a long way from when the big name in local cooking was *Harry Ramsden's*, a byword for "proper" fish and chips, but now franchised all over England and even as far away as Hong Kong – the original restaurant is in Guiseley, northwest of the city. Along with its restaurants, Leeds rivals Manchester in the number of late-opening, continental-style **café-bars** which dot the centre and exploit the city's relaxed licensing laws to the full. Many put tables out year round, and most serve good food too. Given the wealth of other options, the city's **pubs** seem a distinct second-best, though some sterling spruced-up Victorian (and older) examples still pull in the punters, most of whom move on to one of the city's **clubs,** many of which have a nationwide reputation – not least because Leeds lets you dance until 5 or 6am most weekends.

For information about what's on and local **listings**, the *Yorkshire Evening Post* is your best bet, or look out for the free *Leeds Weekly News*. Other free listings magazines and papers come and go – the monthly *Alive* is probably the most reliable.

Cafés and café-bars

Bagel Factory, Swan St and Thornton Arcade, Briggate. Inventive fillings and good coffee, near the City Varieties (see p.748).

Carpe Diem, Basement, Civic Court, Calverley St. Hidden down some steps around the back of the Art Gallery, this neo-Victorian wine bar is tops for good-value food, wine by the glass and decent beer. A resident DJ hits the decks every Saturday until 1am. Closed Sun.

Cornucopia, Corn Exchange, Call Lane. Long-standing favourite in the bowels of the Corn Exchange. Self-service croissants, coffee and lunch specials.

The Courtyard, 25–37 Cookridge St. Huge, airy café-bar that gets a bit too packed at night, but slip in during the day for snacks, coffee and drinks in the brick-paved courtyard (heated in winter). Fresh and funky club sounds until 2am at weekends.

Cuban Heels, The Arches, Assembley St, in a salsa café under the railway arches, opposite the Corn Exchange. Skip the food and come for the bottled beers and cool sounds. Live jazz Wednesdays, funk and soul at weekends.

Espresso Bar, Harvey Nichols, Victoria Quarter Arcade, Briggate. Domain of the high-fashion shopper, the arcade espresso bar is a pleasant, if overpriced, place to muse on exactly how much those shoes will set you back.

The Fat Cat, South Parade, junction with East Parade. The former Pearl Assurance Building gets the 1930s treatment – high ceilings, burnished wood, fans and panelling. Serves veggie and regular breakfasts, plus food all day. The **Slug & Lettuce** occupies the other (Headrow) side of the building but has gone for a more up-to-date look.

Norman, Call Lane. The industrial-chic background of scuffed floor and cast-iron girders is lightened by sinuous plastic lights, tables and chairs. Add the juice bar, the Asian noodle-and-satay menu and the Saturday-night club sounds, and you've got one of the city's more unique browsing and sluicing spots.

Pasta Romagna, 26 Albion Place. One of a clutch of places along this pedestrianized street – outdoor tables, pizza slices, cappuccino and a mixed crowd of shoppers and slackers.

Pitcher & Piano, Assembley St. Exchange Quarter magnet for city hipsters, drinking at the outdoor tables or chowing down on Modern-British food and snacks in the gargantuan interior.

Shear's Yard, The Calls. More a tapas bar than café, but a nice spot for an outdoor coffee or glass of wine with nibbles, and with live jazz during the week.

Townhouse, Assembley St. Café-bar grill and restaurant, serving fashionable food, all-day drinks, cocktails, and weekend club nights. There's a fairly brisk circuit between here and the *Pitcher & Piano*, and other local hangouts.

Restaurants

Art's Café, 42 Call Lane (☎0113/243 8243). Bare-bones, stripped-floor café-restaurant in the Exchange Quarter, that grills goat's cheese, sears tuna and roasts onions like there's no tomorrow. Moderate.

Bibi's, Minerva House, 16 Greek St (☎0113/243 0905). Classic old-time Italian, busy at lunch and weekends, with the full range of pizzas and pasta alongside pricier mainstream meat and fish concoctions. Moderate.

Brasserie 44, 44 The Calls (☎0113/234 3232). Informal but trendy Modern-British brasserie, with some temptingly priced lunch and early-bird deals, serving everything from Whitby cod to Middle Eastern *meze*. Closed Sat lunch & Sun. Moderate to Expensive.

Bryan's, 9 Weetwood Lane, Headingley (☎0113/278 5679). The local rival to *Harry Ramsden's* – order the fish and chips and judge for yourself. Inexpensive.

Café Rouge, Assembley St (☎0113/245 1551). This French chain establishment is getting terrific use out of the old Assembley Rooms, where Leeds' gentry once schmoozed and gambled. Breakfast, lunch or dinner, inside or out, or just stop by for a coffee or a beer. Moderate.

Est Est Est, 31–33 East Parade (☎0113/246 0669). The usual classy pizzas and plate-glass windows from this chain – not that there's a whole lot to look out on in this part of town. Moderate.

Fourth Floor Café, Harvey Nichols, Briggate (☎0113/204 8000). Light lunches, souped-up British classics (grilled steak, fish and chips, bangers and mash) and exotic flavours (Thai spices are common) at dinner. And great views over the rooftops of central Leeds. Closed Mon–Wed eve & Sun. Moderate (lunch) to Expensive (dinner).

Harry Ramsden's, White Cross, Guiseley (☎01943/879531). If you feel like making the pilgrimage (bus #732, #733, #734 or #736 from the bus station) the original fish-and-chip restaurant is out in Guiseley – expect to wait in line before entering the portals of gastronomic heaven itself. Moderate.

Leodis, Victoria Mill, Sovereign St (☎0113/242 1010). Former mill with a rescued cast-iron and wood interior and river views, serving English and French brasserie classics. Closed Sat lunch and Sun. Moderate to Expensive.

Oporto, 31–33 Call Lane (☎0113/245 4444). Funky Exchange Quarter bistro-bar where the flavours mix and match: *pissaladiere* (Provençal tart) and *crostini* during the day, Asian-influenced, Mediterranean and Modern-British meals at night. Moderate.

Pizza Express, White Cloth Hall, Crown St. No menu surprises from the chain, but a great building (behind the Corn Exchange) with soaring conservatory. Jazz on Sundays. Inexpensive to Moderate.

Pool Court at 42, 42–44 The Calls (☎0113/244 4242). Shares a kitchen and ownership with the adjacent *Brasserie 44*. This is the sharp end of the business – cutting-edge Modern-British cuisine, and with a sought-after balcony overlooking the canal. Closed Sat lunch & Sun. Expensive to Very Expensive.

Rascasse, Canal Wharf, Water Lane (☎0113/244 6611). Yet another canalside warehouse development which pushes all the right Modern-British buttons – if it's not seared, it's roasted or chargrilled. Very stylish, with a great interior and canal views. Closed Sat lunch & Sun. Moderate to Expensive.

Souz le Nez en Ville, Basement, Quebec House, Quebec St (☎0113/244 0108). Housed in the splendid red-brick building of the former Liberal Club, this basement wine bar/restaurant is strong on fish and packs in a local business clientele. Closed Sun. Moderate to Expensive.

Thai Siam, 68 New Briggate (☎0113/245 1608). Little local dinner-only Thai place with reliable food and service. Closed Mon. Inexpensive to Moderate.

Pubs

Dry Dock, Woodhouse Lane. Converted coal-barge with rooftop seating and vodka bar, near Leeds Metropolitan University – one of the more bizarre drinking-holes in the city.

Duck & Drake, Kirkgate, by the railway bridge. Real-ale pub with a changing selection, and local bands performing for free two or three nights a week.

The Ship, Ship Inn Yard, off Briggate. Less well known than *Whitelocks* but almost as appealing, and serving lunchtime snacks. The yard tables – crammed into a space about three feet wide – take the city's obsession with continental outdoor ways to extremes.

Victoria, Great George St. Ornate Victorian pub, restored to its former glory.

The Whip, Duncan St at Briggate. Unchanged Victorian courtyard pub serving great Tetley's beer.

Whitelocks, Turk's Head Yard, off Briggate. Up an alley opposite Littlewoods, Leeds' oldest and most atmospheric pub retains its traditional decor, though you'll be hard pushed to see any of it at peak times.

Clubs and live music

Club Uropa, 54 New Briggate (☎0113/242 2224). Immensely popular club nights, with a good line in guest DJs.

Cockpit, Bridge House, Swinegate (☎0113/244 1573). Weekend Mod revival nights underneath the railway arches; indie sounds and bands, Britpop, and drum 'n' bass nights at other times.

Duchess of York, 71 Vicar Lane (☎0113/245 3929). Great pub venue for indie bands and stand-up comedy.

The Fruit Cupboard, 52–54 Call Lane (☎0113/243 8666). Gay-friendly bar and club (and attached café), open Thurs, Fri & Sat nights for funk, disco, soul and house. Friday is very funky disco night.

Irish Centre, York Rd (☎0113/248 0887). Long-standing venue for rock bands of all hues, though a bit short on atmosphere.

Liquid, 2 Central Rd (☎0113/246 9595). Smart and stylish, ultra-fashionable Exchange Quarter club, playing everything from funk and soul to drum 'n' bass. Friday gets the local vote. You'll want your best club gear.

NATO, 66–69 Boar Lane (☎0113/244 5144). Hip happenings at one of Leeds' most enjoyable clubs. Thursday is the locals' night out; watch for flyers.

Observatory, 40 Boar Lane. Loud and late, ravey chart dance bar housed in an old, domed bank building opposite the train station.

Planet Earth, City Square (☎0113/243 4733). Swish and studenty club (next to the Queen's Hotel) with midweek cheap-drinks promotions.

The Pleasure Rooms, 9 Lower Merrion St (☎0113/245 0923). House, disco, dance and trance on various nights of the week, with top-name DJs on the list.

Queen's Court, Queen's Court (☎0113/245 9449). The city's newest, and most enjoyable, gay club and bar, with midweek cabaret nights and weekend dance parties. Call for schedules.

Town & Country Club, 55 Cookridge St (☎0113/280 0100). Most reliable venue for high-profile live bands; also hosts regular weekend retro club nights.

The Underground, Portland Crescent (☎0113/244 3403). Sleek place around the back of the *Town and Country* for highly popular Latin, salsa, funk, Motown and soul nights. Sunday sees cool jazz and bebop bands playing all day.

The Warehouse, 19–21 Somers St (☎0113/246 8287). One of the biggest clubs in the city, with house, garage and techno sounds bringing in clubbers from all over the country.

Arts, festivals and entertainment

The city supports an enterprising **arts scene**, not just confined to the showpiece theatres and halls mentioned here. **Opera North**, based at the Grand Theatre, gives a free performance each summer at Temple Newsam, as does the **Northern Ballet Theatre** – details from the tourist office. Temple Newsam also hosts other concerts and events, from Shakespearean performances to major rock gigs. **Roundhay Park** is the other large outdoor venue for concerts. The **Grand Theatre and Opera House**, 46 New Briggate (☎0113/222 6222) is the regular base of Opera North and also puts on a full range of theatrical productions. Further classical music can be heard at the **Leeds Town Hall**, The Headrow (☎0113/247 6962), which supports an annual international concert season of great distinction and is the venue for Leeds' internationally renowned piano competition. The city's most innovative playhouse, the **West Yorkshire Playhouse**, Quarry Hill Mount (☎0113/213 7700), has two theatres and hosts a wide range of productions and premieres of local works. The **City Varieties**, Swan St, off

Briggate (☎0113/243 0808), is one of the country's last surviving music halls, though it's less music-hall fare these days and more tribute bands, middle-of-the-road comedians and cabaret – great building and bar though. For **cinemas** the main screens are at the Odeon, Headrow (☎0870/505 0007) and ABC, Vicar Lane (☎0113/245 2665). Hyde Park Picture House, Brudenell Road, Headingley (☎0113/275 2045), is a classic vintage cinema with **independent and art-house shows** alongside more mainstream films; take bus #56, #57 or #63 from the city centre. An **international film festival** is held each October (programmes from the tourist office); August heralds another festival in the **West Indian Carnival** (only beaten in size by Notting Hill).

Bradford and around

Lost in its smoky valley among the Pennine hills . . . Bruddersford is generally held to be an ugly city . . . but it always seemed to me to have the kind of ugliness that could not only be tolerated but often enjoyed.

J.B. Priestley, *Bright Day*, 1940.

Priestley was writing about a thinly-disguised **BRADFORD**, his home town, and the sentiment – from a writer who championed Bradford at every possible opportunity – though typically blunt, is not unduly harsh. Even today's civic authority seems content to accept the judgement: the quotation, after all, is emblazoned on the plinth of the statue of the city's favourite, if cantankerous, son. For first and foremost, Bradford – now England's fourth largest metropolitan area – has always been a working town, booming in tandem with the Industrial Revolution, when it changed in decades from a rural seat of woollen manufacture to a polluted metropolis. In its Victorian heyday it was the world's biggest producer of worsted cloth, its skyline etched black with mill chimneys, and its hills clogged with some of the foulest back-to-back houses of any northern city. "Every other factory town in England is a paradise compared to this hole," wrote the German poet Weerth in 1840. "In Manchester the air lies like lead upon you; in Birmingham it's as if you're sitting with your nose in a stove; in Leeds you splutter with the filth as if you had swallowed a pound of Cayenne pepper – but you can put up with all this. In Bradford, however, you are lodged with the devil incarnate… If anyone wishes to feel how a sinner is tormented in Purgatory, let him travel to Bradford."

The city has left this nether world behind and is valiantly laying on tourist attractions to rinse away its associations with urban decrepitude. A few spruced-up buildings and the rejuvenation of the late-Victorian woollen warehouse quarter, Little Germany, signify an attempt to beautify the city centre, but in truth Bradford itself no longer has the architectural heritage or the cultural interest with which to wage a tourist war. Although there are the unexpected pleasures of the **National Museum of Photography, Film and Television** and the nearby model village of **Saltaire**, with its David Hockney Gallery, you couldn't make out a case for seeing much else. Most visitors hang around at least long enough to sample one of Bradford's famous **curry houses**, but with Haworth (see p.753) the indisputable local draw, and York and the heart of the Yorkshire Dales only an hour away, few stay longer.

The city

The focal point of the city centre is **Centenary Square**, commemorating not the founding of the original town – the "broad ford" was known before the arrival of the

Romans – but the hundredth anniversary of the granting of its city charter by Queen Victoria in 1897; Elizabeth II turned up to snip the ribbon. The **City Hall** behind shouts its Victorian credentials; the Gothic extension at the back was the work of Richard Norman Shaw, architect of, among other things, the more fantastical Northumbrian country house of Cragside (see p.895). The City Hall's original architects, local boys Lockwood and Mawson, also provided Bradford with **St George's Hall**, a Neoclassical extravaganza on Bridge Street still in use as a concert hall. Edwardian audiences later flocked to the minaret-topped **Alhambra Theatre**, across Princes Way, again splendidly restored and boasting a full programme of events.

Just across from here, on the rise, is the superb **National Museum of Photography, Film and Television** (Tues–Sun & public holidays 10am–6pm; free), which since its foundation in 1983 has become one of the most visited national museums outside London. It has recently emerged from a major refit, but still wraps itself around Britain's largest cinema screen (52ft by 64ft), whose daily **IMAX** and 3-D film screenings (£5.80) are billed as "so real you'll think you're there". When you arrive it's as well to buy your cinema ticket for a later showing since this is one of the most popular attractions. There's also a ground-floor **café-restaurant**, *Intermission* (open until 9pm), two good **shops** – including a separate children's shop – stuffed full of movie posters, videos, and related knick-knacks.

The museum's ground floor kicks off with the Kodak Gallery, a museum-within-a-museum which houses the contents of Kodak's private collection and traces the story of popular photography. Like the floors which follow, it's crammed with memorabilia and hundreds of cameras, but also contains the world's biggest lens and other superlatives. Successive floors are devoted to every nuance of film and television, including some emphasis on state-of-the-art topics like digital imaging and computer animation, and detours into subjects like advertising and news-gathering. The place is a revelation to anyone with any technical or professional interest, and in the unlikely event that the endless gizmos don't appeal there are all sorts of nostalgic nuggets to grab the attention. Outside the museum a statue of playwright and author **J.B. Priestley** looks out over his native city, coat-tails flying, "as if he has a very bad case of wind" according to the travel writer Bill Bryson.

A walk past the Venetian-Gothic **Wool Exchange** building on Market Street – designed by Lockwood and Mawson – provides ample evidence of the wealth of nineteenth-century Bradford. The building has been splendidly restored, its arcades filled with modern shops and restaurants, and its main hall presided over by a statue of Richard Cobden, the statesman and economist who led the 1838–1846 campaign of the Anti-Corn Law League. Over to the east, north of Leeds Road, the tight grid of streets that is **Little Germany** retains an enclave of warehouse and office buildings in which transplanted German and Jewish merchants once plied their wool trade. The buildings have enticed in new businesses and community ventures, and at the **Design Exchange**, 34 Peckover St (Mon–Fri 9am–5pm; free), the temporary art and design exhibitions are usually worth a look. Priestley is honoured again at the **Priestley Centre for the Arts** (formerly the Bradford Playhouse and Film Theatre), over on Chapel Street, whose cellar bar (open from 5.30pm) is a useful retreat.

For further insights into what once made the city tick, visit the **Bradford Industrial Museum** (Tues–Sat 10am–5pm, Sun noon–5pm; free) in the old Victorian Moorside Mills, on Moorside Road in Eccleshill, three miles northeast of town. Exhibitions and special events document the city's industrial heritage, alongside working textile machinery, surviving examples of the former workers' cottages, historic transport collection and working shire horses, who haul around a selection of trams and buses.

Buses #608 and #609 from Bank Street run here, stopping on Moorside Road, or take #612 from the Interchange.

Practicalities

Trains and buses both arrive at **Bradford Interchange** on Croft Street, a little to the south of the city-centre grid. There's also a much smaller station at **Forster Square**, across the city, for trains to Keighley. The **tourist office** (Mon–Fri 9am–5.30pm, Sat 9am–5pm; ☎01274/753678) is located in the Central Library on Prince's Way and has all the usual leaflets and brochures, plus free city-centre maps and a useful *Guide to Mill Shopping*, which takes you around the discount outlets of the surviving local woollen mills.

The best-value **accommodation** within half a mile of the centre is at the *Ivy*, 3 Melbourne Place (☎01274/727060; no credit cards; ①), and the *New Beehive Inn*, Westgate (☎01274/721784; no credit cards; ①). You could splash out on more central, luxurious digs: the Victorian-era *Pennington Midland Hotel*, by the station on Forster Square (☎01274/735735; ⑤), has large rooms and good weekend rates; while the equally venerable *Quality Victoria Hotel*, on Bridge Street (☎01274/728706; ⑤) has similar prices, but a deal more style, since it was revamped by the team responsible for Leeds' *42 The Calls*. The nearest youth hostel is at Haworth (see p.753).

Bradford's large Asian and Indian population has made the city famous for its **curry houses**, which are scattered all over the city. General opinion still favours the *Kashmir*, 27 Morley St (☎01274/726513), Bradford's first-ever curry house, which lies two minutes up the road that runs west from the Alhambra and the National Museum. Once a simple café-style place, it's been expanded and upgraded, though it still sports formica tables and rock-bottom prices: it claims to bake over two thousand chapattis a day, and the chicken, spinach and dhal dishes are particularly fine. Nearby, the *International*, at 40–42 Mannville Terrace (☎01274/721449) also has its long-standing adherents. Both of these are very cheap and open until 2am every day (3am at weekends), and – like many others in town – are unlicensed, though you can take your own booze. Vegetarians will enjoy *Hansa's*, just up from the Alhambra at 44 Great Horton Rd (☎01274/730433; closed Mon), which specializes in Gujerati food. In the centre, the upmarket *Bombay Brasserie* (☎01274/737564), in a converted church on Simes Street, off Westgate, packs diners in for more refined, musically accompanied meals. Further afield, a short drive away up Great Horton Road, past the university, more excellent curries are to be found at the Muslim *Mumtaz Paan House*, 386–392 Great Horton Rd (☎01274/571861; no alcohol allowed), where the food is sold by weight – a half-pound dish feeds two and the sweet lassi is legendary. The *Bharat*, 496–502 Great Horton Rd (☎01274/521200), is noted for its *thalis* and vegetable side dishes. Out east on the Leeds Road in Thornbury, again a drive away, *Akbar's*, 1276–1278 Leeds Rd (☎01274/773311), is a buzzing balti house whose huge family naan breads are draped over a hook placed on the table so you can tear off strips at will.

The **Pictureville** cinema at the National Museum of Photography, Film and Television (see opposite) has a year-round repertory programme and hosts three major annual **festivals**: the Bradford Film Festival (March), the Animation Festival (June) and the Black and Asian Film-Makers' Festival (September). A new auditorium, the Cubby Broccoli Cinema, has expanded the museum's film programme.

Saltaire

Heading out of Bradford towards Keighley (along the A650) to the north, no one should pass up the chance to drop in on **SALTAIRE**, three miles out, a model industrial village and textile mill built by the industrialist Sir Titus Salt. You can catch trains to Saltaire station (right by Salt's Mill; see below) from Bradford Forster Square, or take bus #679 from the Interchange, which stops in Saltaire village. Buses #662–665, also from the Interchange, drop you at the top of Victoria Road from where it's a half-mile walk to Salt's Mill. Drivers should follow the signs to Keighley (along the A650) from the city centre and then look for the signs to Saltaire and the car parks.

The village is a perfectly preserved 25-acre realization of one man's vision of an industrial utopia. Having built his fortune on the innovative use of alpaca and mohair, Salt found that by 1850 his factory was too small to meet demand for his new textiles. While economic imperatives demanded a new factory, Salt's spell as mayor of Bradford in 1849 during a cholera epidemic had also awakened a mixture of old-world paternalism and hyper-strict Congregational Christianity. "Cholera," he said, "is God's voice to people," adding that he had been confronted with "disclosures too frequently made of immorality and vice prevalent among a large class of the population". Saltaire was built between 1851 and 1876, modelled on buildings of the Italian Renaissance, a period evoked because it was perceived as an era when cultural and social advancement were a direct consequence of the commercial acumen of textile barons. It was built, moreover, in open countryside – impossible to imagine now from the urban surroundings – so that Salt's employees would reap the benefits of the unpolluted, uplifting fresh air.

Salt's Mill, built to emulate an Italian palazzo and larger than St Paul's Cathedral in London, was the biggest factory in the world when it opened in 1853 (on Salt's 50th birthday). Its 1200 looms produced over 30,000 yards of cloth a day, and the mill was surrounded by schools, hospitals, a train station, parks, baths and wash-houses, plus 45 almshouses and around 850 houses. The style and size of each dwelling was designed to reflect the place of the head of that family in the factory hierarchy, one example – for all Salt's philanthropic vigour – of his rigid adherence to the prevailing class orthodoxy. Nor was Salt in any doubt of his own position in the scheme of things: of the village's 22 streets, for example, all – bar Victoria and Albert streets – were named after members of his family. Further to the master's whim, the church was the first public building finished, and was strategically placed directly outside the factory gates. Most tellingly of all, the village contained not a single pub. Saltaire's **tourist office**, 2 Victoria Rd (daily 10am–5pm; ☎01274/774993), is housed in one of the original shops and offers hour-long **guided walks** of the village throughout the year (Sat at 2pm, Sun & public holidays at 11am & 2pm; £2).

Salt's Mill itself is the fulcrum of the village, its several floors now housing glitzy art, craft and furniture shops, and a craft centre. But its enterprising centrepiece is

THE KEIGHLEY AND WORTH VALLEY RAILWAY

The **Keighley and Worth Valley Railway** runs steam trains (summer daily; rest of the year Sat & Sun) along a five-mile stretch of track between Keighley and Oxenhope, stopping at Haworth en route. The restored stations are a delight, with sections of the line etched into the memory of those who recall the film of E. Nesbit's *The Railway Children*, which was shot here in 1970. Valley footpaths run between the stations at Oakworth, Haworth and Oxenhope, allowing you to make a day of your reminiscences. Regular trains from Leeds or Bradford's Forster Square run to Keighley, where you change onto the branch line for the **steam services** (mid-June to Aug Mon–Fri 4 daily, Sat & Sun 7–12 daily; Sept to mid-June Sat & Sun and school holidays reduced services; £6 return, day rover ticket £8). Call the station at Haworth (☎01535/645214) for current fares and timetables; 24-hour recorded information is available on ☎01535/647777.

the **1853 Gallery** (daily 10am–6pm; free; ☎01274/531163), an entire floor of the old spinning shed given over to the world's largest retrospective collection of the works of Bradford-born **David Hockney**. Changing exhibitions cover all phases of the artist's career, from his student days through his Californian-swimming-pool period and up to his more recent experiments with faxes, Xerox machines and Polaroids. *Salt's Diner* (☎01274/530533) on the same floor has a Hockney-designed logo, menu and crockery, and serves tasty Mediterranean-inspired meals amid the original cast-iron pillars.

To enjoy the area further take the short signposted walk, across the Leeds–Liverpool Canal and River Aire at the bottom of Victoria Road, and through the bluebell woods, to **Shipley Glen**, where there's a Victorian funicular **tramway** (May–Sept daily; rest of the year Sat & Sun; 50p return) up to the family pleasure grounds and funfair. Or there's a **waterbus** service along the canal (between Shipley and Bingley) which stops at Saltaire, allowing you to cruise the waterway at leisure or make the return journey to Bradford by train from stations at either Shipley or Bingley (timetable information on ☎01274/595914; 75p per stage, day -rover £5.75).

Haworth

Of English literary shrines, probably only Stratford sees more visitors than the quarter of a million who swarm annually into **HAWORTH** to tramp the cobbles once trodden by the Brontë sisters. Quite why the sheltered life of the Brontës should exert such a powerful fascination is a puzzle, though the contrast of their pinched provincial existences with the brooding moors and tumultuous passions of *Wuthering Heights* probably forms part of the answer. Whatever the reasons, during the summer the village's steep, cobbled **Main Street** is lost under huge crowds, herded by multilingual signs around the various stations on the Brontë trail.

Of these, the **Brontë Parsonage Museum**, at the top of the main street (April–July & Sept daily 10am–5.30pm; Aug Wed 10am–7pm, rest of the week 10am–5.30pm; Oct to mid-Jan & early Feb to March daily 11am–5pm; £4.20), is the obvious focus, a modest Georgian house bought by Patrick Brontë in 1820 to bring up his family. After the tragic early loss of his wife and two eldest daughters (see p.751), the surviving four children – Anne, Emily, Charlotte and their dissipated brother, Branwell – spent most of their short lives in the place, which is furnished as it was in their day, and filled with the sisters' pictures, books, manuscripts and personal treasures. You can see the sofa on which Emily is said to have died in 1848, aged just 28, for example, and the footstool on which she sat outside on fine days writing *Wuthering Heights*. In Charlotte's room are displayed her tiny shoes and wedding clothes, while other rooms contain mementoes of the rest of the family, including a copy of Branwell's portrait of his three sisters which hangs on the staircase. An exhibition room tells the family history in exhaustive detail, bolstered by personal letters, childhood writings, sketches, diaries, documents and other interesting archive material.

Not surprisingly, it can all be a bit of a scrum inside the house, though it's scarcely any less crowded at the other stops. The bluff **parish church** in front of the parsonage – substantially rebuilt since the Brontës lived here – contains the family vault; Charlotte was married here in 1854. At the **Sunday School**, between parsonage and church, Charlotte, Anne and even Branwell did weekly teaching stints; Branwell, however, was undoubtedly more at home in the **Black Bull**, a pub within staggering distance of the parsonage near the top of Main Street. He got his opium at the pharmacist's over the road (now a gift shop).

THE BRONTËS AT HAWORTH

Patrick Prunty or Bronty (it's unclear which) was born in Ireland and became a schoolmaster at the age of sixteen. He later won a place at St John's, Cambridge, where he changed his name to **Brontë**, perhaps influenced by naval hero Lord Nelson, who was made the Duke of Brontë. Later ordained, the Reverend Brontë, and his Cornish wife Maria, took up living at Thornton, just outside Bradford, where the four youngest of their six children – Maria, Elizabeth, Charlotte, Branwell, Emily and Anne – were born between 1816 and 1820. The house, at 72–74 Market St, still stands. Later that year, the Brontë family moved into the draughty parsonage in nearby Haworth.

It could hardly be called an auspicious start to life in a new home. Mrs Brontë died within the year and her sister was despatched to help look after the children. The four oldest girls were sent away to school, but withdrawn after first Maria, then Elizabeth, died after falling ill. The surviving daughters, and smothered Branwell, were kept at home, where they amused themselves by making up convoluted stories and writing miniature books. As they successively came of age, the girls took up short-lived jobs as governesses at various local schools; Charlotte and Emily even spent a year in Brussels, learning French. **Branwell**, meanwhile, was already sowing the dissolute seeds of his disappointing future: he acquired an interest and certain talent for art, but failed to apply to study at the Royal Academy, got into debt, and then spent two years as a junior stationmaster near Halifax but was later dismissed in disgrace. He then took a tutor's job but was dismissed again after developing what was darkly referred to as an "unwise passion" for his employer's wife. He retreated to Haworth, made himself overly familiar with the beer in the *Black Bull* and began experimenting with drugs.

Charlotte's, Emily's and Anne's continuing attempts to amuse themselves with their writings led to the private publication, in 1846, of a series of poems, paid for using part of a legacy from their aunt. They used the (male) pseudonyms Currer, Ellis and Acton Bell – corresponding to their own initials – and though few copies of the collection were ever sold, the little volume acted as a catalyst. Using the same name, **Charlotte** wrote a novel the same year, which was rejected by various publishers; but her *Jane Eyre*, submitted in 1847, was an instant success. **Emily**'s *Wuthering Heights* and **Anne**'s *Agnes Grey* received similar acclaim the same year; Anne's second novel, the better-known *Tenant of Wildfell Hall*, was published in 1848. As far as the public was concerned, the brilliant Bell brothers were a publishing sensation.

But the next two years destroyed the family, as it was ravaged by consumption. First Branwell, who had sunk ever deeper into addictive misery and ill-health, died in September 1848, followed by Emily in December of that year, and Anne in May of the following year. Charlotte lived on for another six years, writing two more novels – *Shirley* (1849) and *Villette* (1853) – and becoming something of a literary figure once she had revealed her identity, making friends with fellow author Elizabeth Gaskell, who later wrote Charlotte's biography. Charlotte finally married Reverend Brontë's curate, Arthur Bell Nicholls, who moved into the parsonage, but she died after nine months of marriage in the early stages of pregnancy. The Reverend Brontë lived on until 1861 – the entire family, except Anne (who is buried in Scarborough; see p.831) lies in the Brontë vault in the village church, next to the house.

Local walks

A century and a half of academic sleuthing has pinned down many of the local houses and locations the sisters incorporated into their work. However, more than any other locale, it's the wild moorland surrounding Haworth which best captures the Brontë spirit. If you've come this far you should try some of the well-signed and much-travelled **walks**, many described by the sisters themselves, particularly those to the spots which are popularly – but in most cases wrongly – said to have been the inspiration for various locations in the novels. A leaflet available from the tourist office describes the routes.

The most popular walk runs to **Brontë Falls** and **Bridge**, reached via West Lane and a track from the village, and to **Top Withens**, a mile beyond, a ruin fancifully thought to be the model for Wuthering Heights (allow 3hr for the round trip). A plaque here bluntly points out that "the buildings, even when complete, bore no resemblance to the house she [Emily] described". The moorland setting, however, beautifully evokes the flavour of the book, and to enjoy it further you could walk on another two and a half miles to **Ponden Hall**, perhaps the Thrushcross Grange of *Wuthering Heights* (this section of path, incidentally, forms part of the Pennine Way).

Practicalities

There are frequent **buses** to Haworth from Bradford Interchange, just eight miles away, with services every hour during the day. Buses #663, #664, #665 and #699 run to Haworth, stopping at various points in the streets immediately at the bottom of the cobbled Main Street. However, perhaps the nicest way of getting here is by **train**, using the private steam trains of the **Keighley and Worth Valley Railway** (see p.752); the station is half a mile from the village centre – walk up Bridgehouse Lane to the bottom of Main Street. The busy Haworth **tourist office** is at 2–4 West Lane, at the top of Main Street (daily 9.30am–5pm; ☎01535/642329), and will book rooms for you.

Main Street and its continuation, **West Lane**, form one long run of gift and tea shops, cafés and guest houses, those on the east side staring across the bare valley beyond. If you want to stay, you'll need to book ahead at most times of the year – even in winter special events (like the Christmas fair) fill the available **accommodation** at the drop of a hat. The tourist office has a full list of hotels and guest houses. You can join Branwell's ghost in the *Black Bull Hotel* in Main Street (☎01535/642249; ②); the *Old White Lion Hotel*, a little further up (☎01535/642313; ③), is a more comfortable old inn. The best guest house is the *Apothecary*, 86 Main St (☎01535/643642, *apot@sisley86.freeserve.co.uk*; ②), opposite the church, whose breakfast room and attached café have splendid views. *Heather Cottage*, 25–27 Main St (☎01535/644511; no credit cards; ①), is less dramatically sited but has its own tearooms. Victorian *Moorfield Guest House*, 80 West Lane (☎01535/643689; ②), makes the most of its elevated position. The **youth hostel**, *Longlands Hall* (☎01535/642234), is housed in the mansion of a Victorian mill owner, a mile from the centre at Longlands Drive, Lees Lane, off the Keighley road, and overlooks the village. The Bradford buses stop on the main road nearby. For something a bit more luxurious, try *Weaver's*, 15 West Lane (☎01535/643822; ⑤), a converted row of weavers' cottages stuffed with period furniture.

Weaver's (dinner only, closed Sun & Mon) is also one of the best **restaurants** in the county, serving good traditional northern cuisine using local ingredients from around £25 a head – it's essential to book ahead. Otherwise, you're looking at bar meals in the pubs or a choice of one of a score of teashops and cafés. The *Fleece Inn* near the bottom of Main Street offers a changing selection of real ales, including one usually on sale for a pound or so a pint. Down in the lower part of Haworth there are several Indian restaurants and fish-and-chip shops, most concentrated on Mill Hey.

The Yorkshire Dales

The **Yorkshire Dales** – "dales" from the Viking word *dalr* (valley) – form a lovely and varied upland area of limestone hills and pastoral valleys at the heart of the Pennines, wedged between the Lake District to the west and the North York Moors to the east. Protected as a **National Park**, the region is crammed with opportunities for outdoor activities: the area is crisscrossed by several long-distance footpaths; there's a specially designated circular cycle way, and a host of centres are geared up for caving and other more specialist pursuits.

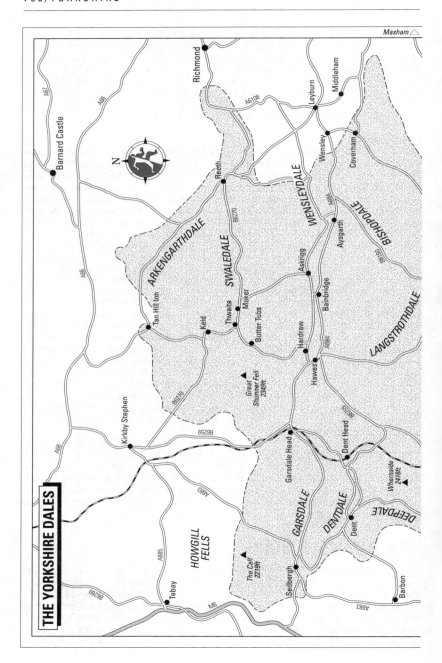

THE YORKSHIRE DALES

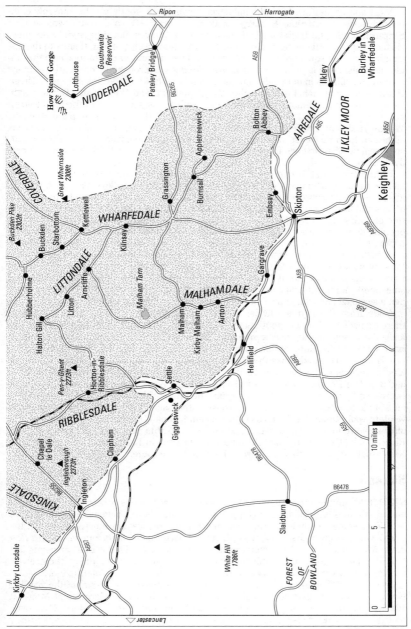

© Crown copyright

Most approaches are from the industrial towns to the south, via the superbly engineered **Settle to Carlisle Railway**, or along the main A65 road from towns such as **Skipton**, **Settle** and **Ingleton**. This makes southern dales like **Wharfedale** the most visited, while neighbouring **Malhamdale** is also immensely popular, thanks to the fascinating scenery squeezed into its narrow confines around **Malham**, perhaps the single most visited village in the region. **Ribblesdale**, approached from Settle, is more sombre, its villages in demand from hikers intent on tackling the Dales' famous **Three Peaks** – the mountains of Pen-y-ghent, Ingleborough and Whernside. To the northwest lies the more remote **Dentdale**, which with **Garsdale** is one of the least known but most beautiful of the valleys. Moving north, there are two parallel dales, **Wensleydale** and **Swaledale**, the latter pushing Dentdale as the most rewarding overall target. Both flow east, with Swaledale's lower stretches encompassing **Richmond**, an appealing historic town from which Ripon, York and the North York Moors are easily reached.

Public transport throughout the Dales is surprisingly good, though there are limited bus services on Sundays, in winter and to the more remote valleys. Pick up the invaluable, free *Dales Connection* bus timetable (published twice a year), available from tourist offices and from the various **National Park information centres**. There are main centres at Grassington, Aysgarth Falls, Malham, Reeth, Hawes and Clapham, for which opening hours and other details are given in the text below; all can help with accommodation, sell excellent walk and trail leaflets, and organize year-round hikes and events, from nature trails to photography workshops. In addition, there are numerous National Park **information points** in shops, post offices and cafés throughout the region, which tend to open during local business hours throughout the year (usually Mon–Fri 9am–5pm). At information centres and points, pick up a copy of the free *Visitor* newspaper, a seasonal publication packed with useful listings, information and adverts.

Aside from the myriad B&Bs, hotels and farmhouses offering accommodation, there's a useful network of youth hostels as well as a series of **bunkhouse barns** – typically, basic self-catering accommodation for around £7 a night per person; **camping barns** are usually more rudimentary versions. For either, book well in advance if it's crucial to secure a bed, since they're very popular with long-distance walkers. For any kind of serious hiking, you'll need the *OS Outdoor Leisure* series of **maps** (nos. 2, 10 and 30). The **Pennine Way** cuts right through the heart of the Dales, and the region is crossed by the Coast-to-Coast Walk, but the principal local route is the **Dales Way**, an 84-mile footpath from Ilkley to Bowness in the Lake District, which takes around a week to walk. Colin Speakman's *Dales Way* guidebook (Dalesman Press) is useful. An alternative route is the less-walked, seventy-mile **Ribble Way** from the estuary of the River Ribble, between Lytham St Anne's and Preston in Lancashire, to Ribblehead in Ribblesdale; there's a National Park guidebook to the route.

Skipton

SKIPTON, southernmost town of the Dales, rightly belongs to Airedale, but almost any trip to the southern dales is going to pass through here, particularly if you want to see Wharfedale, five miles to the east. Apart from practical advantages, however, the town's worth a few hours in its own right, particularly on one of its four weekly **market** days (Mon, Wed, Fri & Sat), when the streets and pubs are filled with what seems like half the Dales population, milling around and determined to enjoy themselves. Similarly lively Christmas markets in December are an enjoyable feature, too.

Sceptone, or "Sheeptown", was a settlement long before the arrival of the battling Normans, whose **Castle**, located at the top of the High Street (March–Sept Mon–Sat 10am–6pm, Sun noon–6pm; Oct–Feb Mon–Sat 10am–4pm, Sun noon–4pm; £4) provided the basis for the present fortress, among England's best preserved, thanks mainly to the efforts of Lady Anne Clifford, who rebuilt much of her family seat between 1650 and 1675 following the pillage of the Civil War. The castle withstood a three-and-a-half-year Parliamentary siege – at one point it was the last remaining Royalist stronghold in the north – and when its surrender was finally negotiated, the Royal garrison marched out through the gates "with colours flying, trumpets sounding, drums beating". Little survives in the way of furniture or fittings, but starting with the proud battlements – emblazoned with the Clifford cry, *Desormais* ("Henceforth"!) – the castle very much looks the part. A self-guided tour leads you through the original Norman gateway into the beautiful Conduit Court, whose yew tree was supposedly planted by Lady Anne. Beyond lie the banqueting hall, spacious kitchens and storerooms (giving a clue as to how the castle withstood such a long siege), bedchambers and six towers with their slit windows. The walls are up to twelve feet thick, yet in places it's possible to see the breaches made by Cromwell's men. The castle roofs were later removed on the Lord Protector's orders, but Lady Anne was allowed to replace them provided they weren't sufficiently strong to bear the weight of cannon.

Lady Anne also displayed her restorative skills on the **Church of the Holy Trinity**, which stands in front of the castle at the top of the High Street (summer daily 8.15am–5.30pm; winter daily 8.15am–dusk; £1 donation requested), and has a fine bossed fifteenth-century roof, beautiful chancel screen (dating from 1533) and a twelfth-century font crowned with a towering wooden Jacobean cover. The church also retains a medieval anchorite's cell, a rare find.

Down the High Street, on the first floor of the town hall, drop into the entertaining **Craven Museum** (April–Sept Mon & Wed–Sat 10am–5pm, Sun 2–5pm; Oct–March Mon & Wed–Fri 1.30–5pm, Sat 10am–noon & 1–4pm; free), a brief introduction to the geology, flora, fauna, folk history and archeology of Craven, the region cradled between Wharfedale and the Lancashire border. The collection runs the gamut from boneshaker bicycles to policemen's helmets, by way of flints, fossils, snuff boxes, grandfather clocks and a hippopotamus skull, all seemingly last labelled and laid out in the 1950s.

After that, all that remains is to stroll through the oldest part of town, over and around Mill Bridge (left at the top of the High Street). The **High Corn Mill** here is a working watermill that's stood since the Domesday Book, now converted into shops. Steps from the bridge lead down to **Springs Canal**, along which a path runs under the sheer walls of the castle, bears left over a footbridge and then returns on high ground for more castle views, emerging back at the mill twenty minutes later.

Practicalities

Skipton is a vital transportation hub, with direct **trains** from Leeds, Bradford, Keighley, Carlisle, Lancaster and Morecambe. The station is on Broughton Road, a ten-minute walk from the centre. Note that if you're heading for the Settle–Carlisle Railway (p.768), most trains **from Skipton** are direct – you shouldn't need to change at Settle unless you want to break your journey. The **bus station** is closer in, on Keighley Road, just shy of Devonshire Place at the bottom of the High Street. There are National Express coaches from London, and buses from Bradford via Keighley, as well as from Leeds, Ilkley, Harrogate and York; a useful summer service (#X9; Wed, Fri & Sat only) links the Lake District with Skipton. Local services run from Skipton to Settle (not Sun hourly) for connections on to Ingleton and Horton; Malham (not Sat or Sun 3–4 daily); and Grassington (not Sun hourly). You can **rent bikes** from Eric Burgess Cycles on Water Street (☎01756/794386), or from Dave Ferguson Cycles, 1 Brook St, off Gargrave Road (☎01756/795367) – from around £10 a day at both. For **walking and camping supplies**, the celebrated Lake District firm George Fisher has an outlet at 1 Coach St, with the similarly endowed Dales Outdoor Centre back down the road.

The alleys on the western side of the High Street emerge onto the banks of the **Leeds–Liverpool Canal**, which runs right through the centre of Skipton. You can rent boats from the Canal Basin, off Coach Street: Pennine Boat Trips at Waterside Court (☎01756/790829), next to the George Fisher outdoor store, runs daily **canal cruises** (April–Oct; £3); while Pennine Marine Ltd, The Boat Shop, 19 Coach St (☎01756/795478) can provide self-steered **narrowboats** (from £60 a day).

If the Keighley and Worth Valley Railway (see p.752) hasn't satisfied your need for steam, the **Yorkshire Dales Railway Society** runs an impressive range of locomotives from the station at **Embsay**, two miles east of the town on the A59 (trains Sun all year, and up to 5 days a week in summer, from 11am–4pm). Trains run the four miles to Bolton Abbey station; ☎01756/795189 or 794727 for information; £5 return). There are hourly buses from Skipton to Embsay (the #214; not Sun).

The **tourist office** is on narrow Sheep Street, parallel with the bottom of High Street (April–Oct Mon–Sat 10am–5pm; Nov–March Mon–Sat 10am–4pm; ☎01756/792809). **Accommodation** is plentiful, with a host of central pubs offering rooms. Best choice is the *Woolly Sheep Inn*, 38 Sheep St (☎01756/700966; ②), a restored seventeenth-century inn which fills quickly. Otherwise, there are rooms at the *Red Lion*, on the High Street (☎01756/790718; ③) or at the fairly shabby *Devonshire Hotel*, on Newmarket Street (☎01756/793078; ①). B&Bs tend to lie on the outskirts, ten minutes or so out of the centre, on Gargrave (west) and Keighley (south) roads. *Peace Villas*, 69 Gargrave Rd (☎01756/790672; no credit cards; ①), and the *Skipton Park Guest 'Otel*, virtually opposite at 2 Salisbury St (☎01756/700640; no credit cards; ②), are the best places on Gargrave Road; the *Highfield Hotel*, 58 Keighley Rd (☎01756/793182; no credit cards; ②) is one of a clutch on that road.

Eating is better in Skipton than in most Dales towns. *Claire's Kitchen*, next to the *Devonshire* on Newmarket Street, is good for large breakfasts, while *Herbs*, 10 High St (closed Tues & Sun), is a veggie place serving savoury crumbles, salads and quiche for around a fiver. At night, make for the *Woolly Sheep Inn* which has inventive bar food, decent beer and a garden. The *Aagrah*, on Keighley Road near the bus station, might be decked out like a snake-charmer's boudoir, but has a loyal local following for its fresh, tasty Indian dishes. *Le Caveau*, 86 High St (closed Sun & Mon), a pricey Anglo-French restaurant, is the town's top spot. Other than the *Woolly Sheep*, the only other **pub** worth drinking in is the *Royal Shepherd* in Canal Street, a backstreet local with good beer.

Wharfedale

The lower reaches of **Wharfedale** extend way to the east, embracing towns as distant as Wetherby before joining the Ouse south of York, but for most people the dale really starts just south and east of Skipton, with **Ilkley** and **Bolton Abbey**, and then continues north in a broad, pastoral swathe scattered with villages as picture-perfect as any in northern England. **Grassington** is the main village, a popular walking centre, packed to capacity in summer; lesser hamlets in Upper Wharfedale, like **Kettlewell** and **Buckden**, make less frenetic bases. Upland roads lead from the head of the valley up minor dales to cross the watershed into Wensleydale, though the most attractive itinerary would take you up lonely Littondale to **Arncliffe**, a village almost too good to be true, and then over the tops to either Malham or Ribblesdale.

Throughout the year, the #71 **bus** runs roughly hourly (not Sun) to Grassington and Hebden from Skipton (via Cracoe and Threshfield), and less frequently on up the B6160 to Kettlewell, Starbotton and Buckden. This is augmented by two seasonal services: the **Dalesbus** (Easter–May & Oct Sun; June–Sept Sat & Sun; Aug Tues, Sat & Sun), from Leeds, Bradford and Ilkley to Buckden, travelling on to Wensleydale; and the Sunday-only **Wharfedale Wanderer** (late May to Aug), which leaves Ilkley hourly for Grassington via Bolton Abbey, and then travels on to Kettlewell, Starbotton and Buckden.

Ilkley

Approaching Wharfedale from Leeds and the southeast, along the A65, it's a gentle climb to the approaching moorland, with barely a hint of the coming grandeur even by the time you reach the small, stone town of **ILKLEY**, gamely claiming to be the gateway to the Dales. It's really no such thing, though it was once a spa town of some repute and still boasts a handsome centre of Victorian buildings and landscaped gardens. Its history can be traced right back to the Romans, who built the fort of Olicana here in AD79, the foundations of which lie under the grassy knoll behind All Saints parish church on Church Street. Sundry Roman relics and other local finds are displayed in the adjacent, sixteenth-century **Manor House Museum** (Wed–Sat 11am–5pm, Sun 1–4pm; free).

To the south, encroaching upon the very town, broods **Ilkley Moor**, littered with ancient stone circles and weathered rocks – and, if the more lurid tales are to be believed, site of numerous UFO appearances and alien abductions. In the words of a round known to many Yorkshire schoolchildren, the windswept moor is also where "tha's been a-courtin' Mary Jane, on Ilkley Moor baht-'at [without a hat]" – a foolish sartorial omission since, according to the round, you'll catch your death of cold, die, be buried, eaten by worms, which are eaten by ducks, which are eaten by people, until "then we shall all 'ave etten thee". With hat firmly in place you can follow the numerous tracks which cut across the highest part of the moor, seeking out Bronze Age stone circles like the Twelve Apostles or the weathered rocks known as the Cow and the Calf, before heading south to Keighley, six miles away.

The **bus** and **train** stations are next to each other on Station Road – aside from regular train and bus connections with Leeds/Bradford, the #X84/784 bus runs hourly between Leeds, Ilkley and Skipton, while the town is also on the route of the Dalesbus and the Wharfedale Wanderer. Opposite the station in the Town Hall is the **tourist office** (Mon–Sat 9.30am–5.30pm, Sun 1–4pm; ☎01943/602319), outside which is pinned a local accommodation list. You're unlikely to stay, but you might find time to **eat**. *Broadbent's Café-Bistro*, 16 The Grove – a continuation of Station Road – has good coffee, sandwiches and daily specials at teashop prices, while at no. 32 is a branch of the Harrogate tea-and-cake stalwart *Betty's*. The foodie choice is the *Box Tree*, 37 Church St (☎01943/608484; closed Mon), an outstanding French restaurant with meals at around £30 a head, excluding drinks. Ilkley's annual **literature festival** (Sept/Oct) attracts top names to its events and readings.

Bolton Abbey and the Strid

BOLTON ABBEY, five miles east of Skipton, is the name of a whole village rather than an abbey, a confusion compounded by the fact that the place's main monastic ruin is known as **Bolton Priory** (Mon–Sat 8.30am–7pm, or dusk if earlier; Fri 8.30am–4pm; free). The priory formed part of an Augustinian community founded at nearby Embsay by Cecily de Romille in 1120, and moved here in the 1150s by her daughter, Alice, to commemorate the drowning of her son in the Strid (see below). Turner painted the site, and Ruskin described it as the most beautiful in England, though the priory is now mostly ruined, a consequence of the Dissolution; only the nave, which was incorporated into the village church in 1170, has survived in almost its original state. A £10 bribe sent by the last prior to Thomas Cromwell, Henry VIII's lieutenant, unsurprisingly failed to change the course of history.

The priory is also the starting point for several highly popular riverside walks, including a section of the **Dales Way** footpath that follows the river's west bank to take in Bolton Woods and the **Strid** (from "stride"), an extraordinary piece of white water two miles north of the abbey, where softer rock has allowed the river to funnel into a cleft just a few feet wide. Numerous people have drowned trying to make the leap (the river here is 30ft deep), and the quite obvious dangers are underlined by the lifebelts hung nearby. Beyond the Strid, the path – a designated nature trail – emerges at **Barden Bridge**, four miles from the priory, where the fortified **Barden Tower** was another little restoration job for Lady Anne Clifford; there's a tearoom here. You can then return to Bolton Abbey either by doubling back the same way, or by taking the country lanes and tracks on the other (east) bank, perhaps incorporating a lovely short detour past the becks and waterfalls of the **Valley of Desolation** midway between Barden and Bolton.

To get here without your own transport, you're reliant upon the Wharfedale Wanderer summer bus service, or a taxi from Skipton – the journey will set you back around £8 each way. Embsay and Bolton Abbey Steam Railway (see p.760) is a mile and a half from the priory ruins. Drivers have to stump up £3 to park in one of the estate **car parks**. There's local information from the estate office (☎01756/710533) and an information point at **Cavendish Pavilion**, a mile north of the priory, where there's also a riverside restaurant and café (April–Oct daily; Nov–March weekends only).

Accommodation hereabouts is limited. At Bolton Abbey the main hotel is the sumptuous *Devonshire Arms* (☎01756/710441; ⑧), just south of the village, owned by the duke and duchess of Devonshire and furnished with antiques from their ancestral pile at Chatsworth – its brasserie and bar are open to the public. Considerably easier on the pocket is B&B at *Hesketh Farm*, a mile west of the village (☎01756/710541; no credit cards; ①), and at *Holme House Farm*, a quarter of a mile south of Barden, overlooking the river (☎01756/720661; no credit cards; ①). Skipton tourist office has details of several other local farmhouse B&Bs. *Barden Tower Barn*, right by the tower and just 300 yards off the Dales Way (☎01756/720330) is a useful bunkhouse stop for long-distance hikers; it's reserved for groups only at weekends.

Grassington and around

You might follow the Dales Way up the River Wharfe at least as far as **GRASSINGTON**, the dale's popular main village, located nine miles from Bolton Abbey. It's fairly dreary on its outskirts but has a good Georgian centre, albeit one tempered by dollops of fake rusticity. The surroundings are at their best by the river, where the shallow Linton Falls thunder after rain; a waterside path leads a mile upstream to the Grass Wood nature reserve. Back in the village, the cobbled Market Square is home to several inns and to the **Upper Wharfedale Museum** (Easter–Sept daily 2–4.30pm; Oct–Easter Sat & Sun 2–4.30pm; 50p), an occasionally eccentric collection of minerals, farming implements and local miscellanea. Other traditional rural pursuits, as well as music and arts events, are celebrated in the annual **Grassington Festival** held every June.

The **National Park information centre** on Hebden Road (April–Oct daily 10am–4pm; Nov–March most weekends 10am–4pm; ☎01756/752774), across from the **bus stop**, books accommodation and provides wide-ranging information, particularly on the region's long lead-mining tradition. You might grab a **parking** space in the Market Square; otherwise, there's a pay-and-display car park at the information centre. For hiking boots and **camping gear**, visit Mountaineer on Garrs Lane (☎01756/752266), up past the *Black Horse* pub.

In summer you should book **accommodation** in advance. Good B&Bs include *Kirkfield*, a detached house in its own grounds on Hebden Road (☎01756/752385; no credit cards; ①), just past the National Park Centre; and the more central *Town Head Guest House*, 1 Low Lane (☎01756/752811; no credit cards; ②), next to the Town Hall off Main Street. Costlier, but with a good reputation, is seventeenth-century *Ashfield House* on Summers Fold (☎01756/752584; ④; closed Dec & Jan), fifty yards off the square (behind the *Devonshire Hotel*), which boasts a walled garden and good breakfasts. If you want to stay right on the square, there's the Georgian *Grassington House Hotel* (☎01756/752406; ④), or the welcoming *Black Horse*, Garrs Lane

(☎01756/752770; ④). The local hostel is at Linton (see below), while the nearest **campsite** is the small *Bell Bank*, Skirethorns Lane, in Threshfield (☎01756/752321), a little over a mile to the west – milk and eggs are available to buy.

Grassington has plenty of **cafés** and a few **restaurants**. The *Dales Kitchen*, 51 Main St, serves traditional and Mediterranean dishes during the day and has monthly themed evening menus. All the **pubs** serve bar meals, the *Black Horse* having the best and also being the nicest place to down a pint. The *Devonshire Hotel*, also on the square, has a more expensive and refined menu. Otherwise, head over to Threshfield where the stone-flagged *Old Hall Inn* (☎01756/752441; closed Sun eve & Mon) wins plaudits for its great food: expect to have to wait for a table before tucking into salmon with tomato and coriander sauce, local sausages and the like.

At busy times you may have to look further afield for accommodation and services, but Grassington is surrounded by tiny scenic **villages**. The closest, **Linton**, a mile to the southwest across the river, sports a **youth hostel** (☎01756/752400) housed in a sevententh-century rectory. The rooms are musty and a bit basic, but you can eat well across the green at the *Fountaine Inn*. To the southeast, back down the Dales Way, the three superb hamlets of Appletreewick, Burnsall and Hebden each have accommodation of one sort or another. At **Appletreewick**, as well as the odd B&B, there's a campsite, *Mason's*, at Ainhams farm (☎01756/720236; closed Nov–Easter), while the cosy *Craven Arms* doles out filling meals to walkers. **Burnsall's** wonderful *Red Lion* (☎01756/720204; ⑤, ⑦ with dinner) has river views from its comfortable rooms and features inventive meals using local ingredients; the *Wharfe View Tearooms* also overlooks the river. There are cheaper B&Bs here, usually displaying vacancy signs. The Skipton bus runs up the B6265 through **Cracoe**, a couple of miles south of Grassington, whose beamed *Devonshire Arms* (☎01756/730237; ③) makes another comfortable base. Best of all is the renowned *Angel Inn*, in the hamlet of Hetton (☎01756/730263), a mile southwest from Cracoe along a country lane. It serves some of the best food and wine in the region, including a wide range of perfectly judged fish dishes – gratifyingly full meals run to around £25, though you can eat for less.

Kilnsey

Wharfedale's scenery above Grassington grows still more impressive, starting a mile north with a tract of ancient woodland, **Grass Wood**, and followed two miles later by **Kilnsey Crag**, a dramatic, glacially carved overhang which attracts its fair share of climbers. Information on the crag and its surroundings can be gleaned from the **National Park information point** at Kilnsey Park on the southern edge of **KILNSEY** village. There's a **trout farm** in the park (daily 9am–5.30pm or dusk in winter), which aside from its fishing (rods available to rent) provides a whole host of children's activities as well as a café; the deli-shop is worth a visit if you're self-catering, selling everything from eggs and honey to game and gravadlax. You can stay in Kilnsey at the *Tennant Arms* (☎01756/752301; ③), whose restaurant overlooks the crag, or at a couple of local farmhouse B&Bs. Half a mile further north, at the junction of the Littondale road, there's a **bunkhouse barn**, *Skirfare Bridge Barn* (☎01756/752465), with a drying room and kitchen.

Littondale

Just beyond the Kilnsey Crag, a minor road branches off left into **Littondale**, an empty, pristine dale with stunning scenery and views, especially at Hesleden Bergh, around six miles up the dale, where a road climbs south over the moors – with Pen-y-ghent looming to the west – to Stainforth in Ribblesdale. A daily school bus (which the public can use) from Grassington runs up Littondale as far as Halton Gill, but otherwise there's no public transport.

   ARNCLIFFE, halfway up the dale, is as idyllic a village as you'll find. The ivy-covered *Falcon* (☎01756/770205; ③, ④ with dinner) on the village green attracts walkers from far and wide; the dinner, bed and breakfast deal is good value, and the beer's good. There's a campsite back down the road, a mile and a half southeast of Arncliffe, at *Hawkswick Cote Farm* (☎01756/770226; closed Nov–Feb). The minor moorland road south to Malham from Arncliffe can be treacherous in winter; check the weather reports before setting off. *Raikes Cottage*, just out of Arncliffe on the Malham road, is a nice riverside tearoom (weekends only in winter).

   On foot, the ideal way to see the dale is to follow the valley-floor **footpath** from Arncliffe to **LITTON** (2–3 miles), where the ancient and unspoilt *Queen's Arms* (☎01756/770208; ②) could serve as a base for climbing Pen-y-ghent; a steep track also cuts north across the fells to Buckden. There's B&B accommodation available too; try *Litton Hall* (☎01756/770238; no credit cards; ①), look for local vacancy signs or contact the **National Park information point** at Litton post office.

   The path (and road) then continues the three miles up to **Halton Gill**, where just outside the hamlet there's the self-catering *Halton Gill Bunk Barn* (☎01756/770241), and beyond to **FOXUP** and **COSH** (two miles from Halton Gill) – possibly the most remote settlements in the Dales, though B&B is available at Foxup's *Bridge Farm* (☎01756/770249; no credit cards; ①; closed Nov–March).

Kettlewell

The landscapes in the last six miles of Wharfedale and its continuation, **Langstrothdale**, hardly suffer by comparison with Littondale, a large proportion of their moors and valleys forming part of the National Trust's vast Upper Wharfedale Estate. **KETTLEWELL** (Norse for "bubbling spring"), three miles north of Kilnsey, is the main centre for the upper dale, a far more attractive proposition for a weekend's walking or relaxing than Grassington, with an informal **National Park information point** in the Over and Under outdoor shop, a **campsite** (☎01756/760886) just to the north at Fold Farm, and the *Whernside House* **youth hostel** (☎01765/760232) in the centre of the village. There's plenty of other **accommodation** in the village, notably the very agreeable *Langcliffe Country House* (☎01756/760243; ④), a few hundred yards up a road opposite the *King's Head* pub. The rooms are all en suite and a home-made four-course dinner (£16) is served in the valley-facing conservatory. Other village choices include the *Elms* on Middle Lane (☎01756/760380; no credit cards; ②) and *Chestnut Cottage* by the stream (☎01756/760804; no credit cards; ②). The village **pubs**, the *Bluebell* and the *King's Head*, are both cosy places for a drink.

Starbotton, Buckden and Hubberholme

It's lovely country north of Kettlewell, accessed either via the dale's single lonely road (B6160) or the Dales Way path, both of which push to the dale's upper limit. At **STARBOTTON**, two miles away, the *Fox & Hounds* (☎01756/760269; ③; closed Mon in winter & all Jan) has three rooms for rent, ancient flagged floors, a huge fire and popular food. Topnotch pub accommodation is also available in **BUCKDEN**, another couple of miles to the north, this time at the superbly sited *Buck Inn* (☎01756/760228; ⑤, ⑥ with dinner). For information on Buckden's other half-dozen cheaper B&B options (many on outlying farms), contact the **National Park information point** at the village's Riverside Gallery. Beyond Buckden, the road winds up and down Bishopdale the ten miles or so to Aysgarth in Wensleydale (see p.775).

   A mile upstream, the river flows through Langstrothdale to **HUBBERHOLME** and the stone-flagged, whitewashed *George* (☎01756/760223; ②), the favourite pub of archetypal Yorkshireman J.B. Priestley, who revelled in visiting a hamlet he thought "one of the smallest and pleasantest places in the world". He's buried in the churchyard of the small chapel of St Michael and All Angels, over the stone bridge from the pub. There's a year-round bunkhouse barn in Hubberholme at *Grange Farm* (☎01756/760259), just five minutes' walk from the pub on the route back to Buckden. The Dales Way marches on up the valley, with the next halt over in Dent (see p.772), a superb cross-dales hike.

Malhamdale

A few miles west of Wharfedale lies **Malhamdale**, the uppermost reaches of Airedale and one of the National Park's most heavily visited regions, thanks to its three outstanding natural features: Malham Cove, Malham Tarn and Gordale Scar. It's classic limestone country, dominated by a mighty escarpment topped by a fractured pavement, and cut through with sheer walls, tumbling waterfalls and dry valleys – in short, a place to feed the soul while exercising the body. Unfortunately for those seeking solitude, all three main attractions are within easy hiking distance of **Malham village**, so any walking you do locally is likely to be in company, with the Pennine Way further adding to the column of walkers processing through the area.

The approach by **public transport** is on the #210 bus or post bus from Skipton (not Sat or Sun), a thirty- to sixty-minute ride depending on the service. You may simply choose to **walk** in across country: Malham is only around six miles from Gargrave (a station on the Skipton–Settle train line, and on the Pennine Way) to the south, and a similar distance from Settle to the west – a particularly fine approach – or from Grassington to the east.

Malham village

Unless you're here off-season, some idea of what to expect in **MALHAM** comes at the vast peripheral car park, likely to be packed solid with hikers and day-trippers. The village is home to barely more than a couple of hundred people, who inhabit the huddled stone houses on either side of a bubbling river, but this microscopic gem attracts perhaps half a million visitors a year. Provided you're prepared to do some walking you can escape the worst of the crowds, and something of the village's off-peak charm can be enjoyed in the evening when most of the trippers have gone home, but if you're planning on staying, note that competition is stiff for rooms.

Unless you already have maps and accommodation sorted out, your first stop should be the **National Park information centre** on the southern edge of the village (Easter–Oct daily 9.30am–5pm; Nov–Easter Sat & Sun 10am–4pm; ☎01729/830363). It sells a range of local walking guides and can help with finding a room. In summer, you'll need to book ahead to get a bed at the **youth hostel** (☎01729/830321, *malham@yha.org.uk*). However, there's also a (centrally-heated) **bunkhouse barn** at *Hill Top Farm* (☎01729/830320), immediately north of the National Park information centre, and several good village **B&Bs**, among them rambling *Beck Hall* (☎01729/830332; ②), set in its own streamside gardens a couple of hundred yards from the fork in the village centre; and the excellent *Miresfield Farm* (☎01729/830414; ②), on the edge of the village near the information centre. The comfortable *Riverhouse Hotel* (☎01729/830315; ③), on the road through the village, serves great evening meals, and you can sit in the little front garden for tea and sandwiches. The *Buck Inn* (☎01729/830317; ③) is almost next door, and also has rooms. You can **camp** at *Townhead Farm* (☎01729/830287; reservations advised), near the cove, and under Gordale Scar at *Gordale Scar House Campsite* (☎01729/830333; closed Nov–March). There's a tearoom or two in the village, and a basic shop. Meals are served in the **pubs**, notably at the *Buck*, with a popular walkers' back bar, but also at the fancier *Lister Arms*, over the bridge.

You might also put up in any of Malhamdale's three other villages to the south: pretty **Kirkby Malham**, **Hanlith** and **Airton**, all within three miles of Malham itself. The information centre can advise on vacancies, but try the *Lindon House Guest House* (☎01729/830418; no credit cards; ①) in Airton. Closer to Malham, in Hanlith, the *Coachman's Cottage* (☎01729/830538; no credit cards; ②) is a nice seventeenth-century house, while Kirby Malham's *Victoria Inn* (☎01729/830213; ③) is a friendly spot and has reasonable food.

Malham Cove, Malham Tarn and Gordale Scar

Malham Cove appears in spectacular fashion a mile north of Malham, a white-walled limestone amphitheatre rising three hundred feet above its surroundings. Like Gordale Scar's ramparts to the east, it was formed by a shear along the Mid-Craven Fault, a geological tear that runs 22 miles from Wharfedale to Kirkby Lonsdale in Cumbria. Still visible on the cliff-top are the black stains left by an earlier waterfall, once higher than Niagara, which dried up during the eighteenth century. Now it's merely a stream of bubbles at the base. It is not, as is often claimed, the source of the Aire, which has more humble beginnings at Aire Head springs, half a mile south of Malham village.

A broad track leads to the cove, passing some of England's most visible prehistoric field banks en route. Fewer people make the breath-sapping haul to the top, where the rewards are fine views and the famous **limestone pavement**, an expanse of clints (slabs) and grykes (clefts) created by water seeping through weaker lines in the limestone rock. Unusual plants and ferns such as dog's mercury and hart's tongue shelter in the crevices, making this a favoured spot for botanists.

To the northwest rises the great bulk of Fountains Fell, its name a link with Fountains Abbey many miles to the east, erstwhile owner of huge estates in Craven. A simple walk over the moors, either via the Pennine Way or the more interesting dry valley to the west, abruptly brings **Malham Tarn** into sight, a lake created by an impervious layer of glacial debris. This, too, is an area of outstanding natural interest, its numerous waterfowl protected by a nature reserve on the west bank, visible from a nature trail which forms part of the Pennine Way on the east bank.

Unless your interests are ornithological, however, it's best to make do with the view from the cliff-top and avoid the long hike round the lake; you can then turn south for **Gordale Scar**, which is also easily approached direct from Malham village. Here the cliffs are if anything more spectacular than at Malham Cove, complemented by a deep ravine to the rear caused by the collapse of a cavern roof. A little to the south of the scar, off the road, lies **Janet's Foss**, a gem of a waterfall set amidst green-damp rocks and overarching trees.

There's a classic circuit which takes in Malham's trio of sights in a clockwise **walk from Malham** (8 miles; 3hr 30min), the only problem being at Gordale Scar, where it may be difficult to scramble down the stream-cut gorge after heavy rain for the last leg back to Malham. If you don't want to see the Tarn and open moorland, the walk is easily cut short by taking a waymarked track from the northern edge of the pavement, above Malham Cove, down to Gordale Bridge and thus on to Gordale Scar (5 miles; 2hr 30min). From Gordale Scar you could simply follow the Gordale lane back into the village, though the longer path via Janet's Foss, along the beck and across the fields, is more pleasant.

Ribblesdale

The scenery of **Ribblesdale**, to the west of Malhamdale, is more dour and brooding than the bucolic valleys to the east. It's entered from Settle, starting point of the superbly engineered **Settle–Carlisle Railway**, among the most scenic rail routes in the country (see p.768). After Stainforth, close to one of the more noted of the Dales' many waterfalls (or "forces"), the valley's only village of any size is **Horton in Ribblesdale**, a focus not only for the Ribble Way and Pennine Way, but also where most people start the **Three Peaks Walk**, an arduous hike around the Dales' highest peaks.

Settle is the **transport** junction for Ribblesdale, with daily **trains** heading north through Horton to Carlisle and south to Skipton, Keighley and Leeds; a limited service operates on Sundays. The hourly #580 **bus** (not Sun) also connects Skipton with Settle, from where a useful service runs three or four times daily (not Sun) north through Stainforth to Horton but no further, and northwest via Giggleswick and Clapham to Ingleton in the western dales (see p.770). Coming from Malham, you could **walk** the six miles along an old pack road via Kirkby Fell and Attermire Scar, the latter being grandiose cliffs on the Mid-Craven Fault.

Settle

Nestled under the wooded knoll of Castleberg, **SETTLE** is well -placed for upper Ribblesdale to the north and a pleasant enough base if you haven't the time to find a more intimate overnight stop within the National Park. The village has a typical seventeenth-century market square, top-heavy with tearooms but still sporting its split-level arcaded shambles, which once housed butchers' shops. Other than on Tuesdays, when the **market** is in full swing, there's not much to see in the few streets behind the square. Aim instead for the **Watershed Mill Visitor Centre**, on Langliffe Road (Mon–Sat 10am–5pm, Sun 11am–5pm; free), north of the centre by the river, an early nineteenth-century cotton mill transformed into a market selling Dales goods; there are craft demonstrations throughout the year and a coffee shop.

All other local diversions involve a good **walk**. The shortest is the slog up the path to the top of Castleberg for views over the town. The **Ribble Way** footpath, which passes through town, continues to Stainforth (see below), or there's the well-signposted four-mile round-trip hike northeast to **Victoria Cave**, a gaping maw in the Mid-Craven Fault in which archeologists found the bones of prehistoric beasts.

The friendly **tourist office** in the town hall on Cheapside, just off Market Place (daily 10am–5pm; ☎01729/825192), is the place to seek out onward routes and hiking itineraries; local walks are all detailed in leaflets. The **train station** is less than five sign-posted minutes from Market Place. Two comfortable old town inns, the *Royal Oak* on Market Place (☎01729/822561; ④), and the *Golden Lion*, just off Market Place along Duke Street (☎01729/822203; ③), are the best **places to stay**. Central B&B accommodation is at the *Liverpool Guest House* on Chapel Square (☎01729/822247; no credit cards; ①), whose old-fashioned rooms are handy for the pubs and restaurants. Other choices include the *Yorkshire Rose* (☎01729/822032; no credit cards; ②), situated along Duke St from the Golden Lion, and – further up Duke St, at the edge of town – *Penmar Court Guest House* (☎01729/823258; no credit cards; ①) and the vegetarian *Sansbury Place* (☎01729/823840; no credit cards; ②). The *Oast Guest House*, 5 Penyghent View, Church Street (☎01729/822989; no credit cards; ①), is on the Giggleswick Road. The nearest campsite is at Stainforth.

Both the inns serve good **food** and decent beer. The *Royal Oak* gets the nod by virtue of its extraordinary carved oak-panelled bar and dining room. The *Little House*, a wine bar on Duke St (☎01729/823963; closed Mon), next to the police station, is moderately priced, or there's an amiable trattoria, *Peppe's Place* (☎01729/822277; summer closed Sun, Mon, & Wed lunch; winter closed Mon–Wed, & Sun lunch), on the Market Place, for pizza and pasta. During the day it's hard to see anyone resisting the lure of *Ye Olde Naked Man Café* (closed Wed), serving breakfasts, proper coffee and good home-made food – the name, apparently, is a reference to an eighteenth-century landlord's disgust at clothing fashions.

Stainforth

STAINFORTH, two miles north of Settle, makes a good base for walks in the lower part of the Ribble valley, with several B&Bs; a pub, the *Craven Heiffer* (☎01729/822599; ③);

THE SETTLE-CARLISLE RAILWAY

With the nineteenth-century railway boom at its height, the Midland Railway company – eager to muscle in on the profits made by its rival, the London and North Western Railway on its successful west coast route – applied to Parliament to build a line which would link the industrial heartlands of West Yorkshire with Carlisle and the Scottish borders beyond. In the six years between 1869 and 1875, when the 72-mile **Settle–Carlisle** line opened, herculean efforts were made by thousands of navvies to blast a route through the unforgiving Dales mountainsides. Living in squalid shanty towns by the sides of the track, and even in the newly opened railway tunnels themselves, six thousand men built twenty viaducts and bored fourteen tunnels in a feat of Victorian engineering that has few equals in Britain. Over two hundred of the workers died, some of smallpox and other diseases, others in horrific accidents; many now lie buried in the village churches that line the route.

The railway itself was an immediate success, forming a popular route to Scotland and later used as a freight and troop carrier during World War II. By the 1970s, though, services had been severely reduced as British Rail "rationalized" its operations and in 1983 it was announced that the line was to close. After a vociferous campaign, local groups kept the line open and as tourist interest has picked up, the route seems set to have an assured future, at least in the medium term. Stations have been restored to their nineteenth-century glory and special steam train services sometimes operate.

The attraction in riding the line is the chance to experience what the operators – with no hint of hype – dub "England's most scenic railway". From Settle, the drag up Ribblesdale brings ever more spectacular views – between Horton and Ribblehead the line climbs two hundred feet in five miles, before crossing the famous 24-arched Ribblehead viaduct. Dent is the highest, and bleakest, main-line station in England. Further on, the route heads through Ais Gill, 1100 feet above sea level, before it finally drops into the gentler Eden Valley and on to Carlisle.

The journey from Settle to Carlisle takes just under an hour and forty minutes, so it's easy to make a **return trip** (£18 day-ranger for unlimited travel) along the whole length of the line if you wish. There are connections from Skipton and Leeds (2hr 40min); full **timetable** details are available from National Rail Enquiries, ☎0345/484950, or from the Web site (*www.settle-carlisle.co.uk*). If you only have time for a short trip, the **best section** is that between Settle and Garsdale (30min), though note that you'll typically have a very short or very long wait for the return train. It's best to combine a trip with a hike. You can access the Pennine Way or Coast-to-Coast walk from the line; use it to link places like Settle, Dent and Ingleton in a loop walk, or sign up for one of the **free guided walks** organized by the Friends of the Settle–Carlisle Line (☎01729/822007). These walks can be joined from stations along the route; local tourist offices also have more details.

a **youth hostel** set in extensive grounds about a quarter of mile south of the centre (☎01729/823577, *stainforth@yha.org.uk*); and a **campsite** at *Knight Stainforth Hall*, Little Stainforth (☎01729/822200). Stone-built *Husbands Barn* (☎01729/822240; ②), a farm B&B south of the village on the main road, near the youth hostel, also has a well-equipped **bunkhouse barn**.

The nicest route to the village is by the **footpath from Settle**, part of the Ribble Way, which runs gently alongside the river, reaching Stainforth Force waterfall in around an hour, the village itself ten minutes later. The path starts in Settle just across the bridge to Giggleswick and, though poorly signposted, is easy to follow. **Stainforth Force** is hardly in the Niagara league, but there's some splashing around to be done in the shallow pools, and you might like to peer over the seventeenth-century **Stainforth Bridge**, a packhorse bridge just a stone's throw away. The best of the area's short walks climbs up to another waterfall, **Catrigg Force**, a mile east of the village, easily reached by an unsurfaced lane. Meanwhile, the Ribble Way presses on northwards, avoiding the river at first, but eventually following it into Horton; a couple of miles north of Stainforth you'll pass through **Helwith Bridge** where *Helwith Bridge Hotel* (☎01729/860220; ②) has the only rooms and food en route.

Horton in Ribblesdale

The noted walking centre of **HORTON IN RIBBLESDALE** dates from Norman times – its church, St Oswald's, retains its original proportions in the fine nave – but the village gained a new lease of life in the nineteenth century when the arrival of the Settle–Carlisle Railway allowed it to expand its age-old quarrying operations. Mine workings old and new slightly spoil the west side of the village, but it's of no consequence whatsoever for some of the Dales' finest hiking opportunities. Walks west of the village can be planned to clamber over vast tracts of limestone pavement, scars, gills, potholes, becks and dry valleys, while old "green roads" (shepherd's trackways) surround Horton, providing plenty of scope for gentle pottering.

The celebrated **Pen-y-ghent Café** (also known as the *Three Peaks Café*) in the village is a National Park **information point** (summer Wed–Fri & Mon 9am–6pm, Sat & Sun 9am–8pm; rest of the year Wed–Mon 9am–6pm; ☎01729/860333) and an unofficial headquarters for the famous **Three Peaks Walk**, a 25-mile, 12-hour circuit of Pen-y-ghent (2273ft), Whernside (2414ft) and Ingleborough (2376ft). The village is most convenient for the ascent of sphinx-shaped **Pen-y-ghent** (3–4hr round trip), arguably the most dramatic of the three summits, just to the east on the Pennine Way; the other peaks are more easily climbed from Ingleton (see p.770), Chapel-le-Dale or Dentdale. The last Sunday of April sees lunatics running over the three peaks in the gruelling "Three Peaks Race" – what takes normal people the best part of a day to walk takes the winner under three hours. As well as providing huge mugs of tea and coffee, warming platefuls of food, maps, guides and weather reports, the *Pen-y-ghent Café* operates a "safety service" for **walkers**, enabling anyone undertaking a long hike (including the Three Peaks) to register in and out.

Horton straggles along an L-shaped mile of the Settle–Ribblehead road (B6479), with the **train station** at the northern end and the church at the southern end. In between are the café, a post office/store and a campsite. **Accommodation** in Horton is much in demand and should be booked in advance. B&Bs include the *Willows* (☎01729/860373; no credit cards; ②) and the more elegant *Rowe House* (☎01729/860212; no credit cards; ②), both left out of the station and a little way up the Ribblehead road. There's also the *Knoll* (☎01729/860283; no credit cards; ①), by the post office. Of the two **pubs**, the *Crown Hotel* (☎01729/860209; ②), by the bridge, is the clear winner, a popular walkers' haunt with plain but cosy rooms and good bar food served until 8.30pm. *Dub Cote* (☎01729/860238) is a useful **bunkhouse barn** at Brackenbottom, just out of the village on the Settle road, in the direction of Pen-y-Ghent, and there's also a central tents-only **campsite** at *Holme Farm* (☎01729/860281), near the church.

If all these options fall through, or you've got transport and can look further afield, then head the mile or so south down the road to **Studfold**, where *Middle Studfold Farm* (☎01729/860236; no credit cards; ①) or nearby *Studfold House* (☎01729/860200; no credit cards; ①) both do B&B. Two miles to the north at **Selside**, *South House* (☎01729/860271; no credit cards; ①) is another useful standby, a working farm which produces evening meals on request.

Up to Ribblehead

However you get there – walk, cycle, drive or take a train – you shouldn't miss a trip to the head of the valley, where the **Ribblehead Viaduct** cuts a superb profile, backed by some of the most uncompromising moors in the entire National Park. It's a wonderfully bleak spot, the viaduct towering a hundred feet overhead, supporting the railway line which then disappears into the 2629 yards of the Blea Tunnel, no less dramatic a feat of engineering. You can access the Dales, Ribble and Pennine Ways from points east of the line, or walk from Ribblehead station the five miles down the windswept B6255 towards Ingleton, past White Scar Caves (see opposite). Should you miss the last train, salvation is at hand in the shape of the *Station Inn* (☎01524/241274; ②; irregular opening times in winter) right by the rail bridge. There's nothing else near the station, and the next stop on the line is at Dent, similarly isolated (see p.772), so it pays to study timetables carefully.

The Western Dales

The **Western Dales** is a term of convenience for a couple of tiny dales running north from **Ingleton**, a village perfectly poised for walks up **Ingleborough** and **Whernside**, and for **Dentdale** and **Garsdale**, two of the loveliest and least-known valleys in the National Park. (Much of this region has been hived off into Cumbria, to the disgust of its erstwhile Yorkshire population.) Unless you have a car or are hiking from stop to stop, any extensive exploration is difficult, though Ingleton is linked by **bus** to Clapham, Settle (for Skipton) and Horton, and the Settle–Carlisle Railway offers access to upper Dentdale and Garsdale, with fine walks possible virtually off the station platforms. There's also a very useful cross-country summer bus service (the Cumberland #X9) between York and the Lake District, calling in Ingleton en route. Ingleton has the most accommodation, but **Dent** is by far the best target for a quiet night's retreat, with a cobbled centre barely altered in centuries.

Clapham and its caves

CLAPHAM, a seductive little village at the southern foot of Ingleborough, makes a fine introduction to the region. Pop into the **National Park information centre** (April–Oct daily 10am–5pm; Nov–March occasional Sat & Sun; ☎01524/251419), alongside the car park, for a leaflet on the nature trail through Clapdale Woods to **Ingleborough Cave** (March–Oct daily 10am–5pm; Nov–Feb Sat & Sun 10.30am–dusk; £4), the Pennines' oldest show cave. The trail footpath – the only access – was laid out with numerous exotic trees and flora, most brought to Britain by Reginald Farrer, a scion of the family which owns Ingleborough Hall and the surrounding estate. Farrer was one of the fathers of alpine botany and his obsession was such that on returning from expeditions he would refuse to greet friends or family until his specimens were safely potted and planted. Follow the footpath beyond the caves, and after a little over a mile you reach **Gaping Ghyll**, 365ft deep and 450ft long, probably the most famous of the Dales' many potholes; carry on another two miles northwest from here and the summit of Ingleborough looms – a more interesting approach than the haul up from Ingleton.

Clapham is equidistant from Settle and Ingleton, just off the A65, around four miles from either; its **train station** (on the Leeds/Skipton–Lancaster line) offers another entry to the Dales, but lies over a mile south of the village. There's a post office, general store, a café or two, and a good if pricey **hotel**, the riverside *New Inn* (☎01524/251203; ④). Cheaper rooms are available at *Arbutus House*, on Riverside (☎01524/251240; ②, no credit cards), and by the station at the *Flying Horseshoe* pub, (☎01524/251229; ②), which also serves meals.

Ingleton

INGLETON caters for a fair share of tourists, together with a reasonable number of cavers and climbers, but while the straggling slate-grey village is pleasant enough there's little specific to see, save a substantially rebuilt Norman church. The village sits at the confluence of two streams, the Twiss and the Doe, whose beautifully wooded valleys are easily the area's best features. The White Scar Caves aside (see below), the four-and-a-half mile **Falls' Walk** (entrance fee £1.50, parking – including fee – £5) is the main local attraction, a lovely circular walk up the tree-hung Twiss Valley, past viewing points over the Pecca Falls and Thornton Force, turning east at Ray Bridge to reach the head of the Doe at Beezley Farm (refreshments available), where a signed path takes you back down the Doe Valley to Ingleton by way of Beezley, Rival and Snow falls. The walk entrance is through the car park, beyond the small bridge in Ingleton. Reckon on two and a half hours to complete the circuit, and take care in wet weather.

More serious hikers tackle **Ingleborough**, one of the Three Peaks, whose flat plateau is reached by a slightly laborious route to the east (3 miles; 2hr 30min). There are splendid views from here on a clear day, and for anyone fit, equipped and experienced enough the option arises to move on to **Whernside** to the north, the third peak and Yorkshire's highest point.

Inglesport, a **hiking store** on Main Street in the village, is the place for maps, equipment and weather forecasts. Otherwise, various leaflets and town maps are available from Ingleton's **tourist office** in the community centre car park, just off Main Street (May–Oct daily 10am–4.30pm; ☎015242/41049), and with a **bus** stop outside. The tourist office also doles out lists of the village's accommodation, among which there's a **youth hostel**, *Greta Tower* (☎015242/41444), an old stone house in its own gardens located centrally in a lane between the market square and the swimming pool. There are a dozen other overnight options, many strewn along Main Street; the best **guest houses** include the no-smoking *Seed Hill* on Main Street, near the church and square (☎015242/41799; no credit cards; ②), a sixteenth-century house with en-suite rooms and lovely cottage garden; *Ingleborough View*, much further down Main Street past the tourist office (☎015242/41523; no credit cards; ②); and the *Bridge End Guest House* on Mill Lane (☎015242/41413; ①), close to the Falls Walk entrance. There are also two good Victorian-era hotels: the *Springfield*, on Main Street beyond *Ingleborough View* (☎015242/41280; ②), and *Moorgarth Hall*, New Road (☎015242/41946; ③), a mile or so south of the village on the A65. You can **camp** at nearby *Moorgarth Farm* (☎015242/41428), while *Stacksteads Farm*, also a mile south but off the minor road to High Bentham (☎015242/41386; ②), has tent space and a **bunkhouse barn**.

Ingleton has its fair share of **services** – bank, shops, bakers and grocery stores – making it a good place to stock up for the hiking to come, but it fails to make much impact when it comes to **eating**. The *Inglesport Café* on the first floor of the store on Main Street (daily 9am–6pm) at least knows what its customers want – hearty soups and chips with everything. None of the **pubs** in the village is up to much, though with your own transport you can drive three miles down the A65 towards Clapham to the *Goat Gap* (☎015242/41230; ③), a seventeenth-century inn and restaurant with decent food.

White Scar Caves and Chapel-le-Dale

Northeast of Ingleton, the Hawes road (B6255) offers some exhilarating views of the peak. It's around five miles to Ribblehead station, making this route one method of switching dales, but there's no public transport except a ridiculously early school bus. Just one and a half miles out of Ingleton – an easy walk – is the entrance to the **White Scar Caves** (daily 10am–5pm; £5.95), the longest show cave in England. Don't be put off by the steep price – it's worth every penny for the eighty-minute tour of dank underground chambers, contorted cave formations and glistening stalactites. The system was discovered in 1923 by a student, one Christopher Long, who crawled into a fissure in the hillside pushing a candle wedged in a bowler hat ahead of him to light his way. Within two years a tunnel had been blasted out to accommodate visitors – it's now lined with steel-grid walkways along which you edge, the thundering of the internal waterfall becoming ever louder the further in you venture. The 200,000-year-old Battlefield Cavern, only open to the public since 1990, is a remarkable 330 feet long and 100 feet high, and to get this far you've had to negotiate natural features like the "Squeeze" (where the walkway between two rock faces is little over a foot wide) and the "Gorilla Walk" (several hundred yards where you need to hunch your way along a low-roofed tunnel). With water underfoot for the entire trip, the caves are most impressive (and scariest) after heavy rain when the water level rises rapidly – on occasion tours are suspended (so call to check if in doubt). **Tours** run every hour or so, and there's a café on site.

Three miles farther up the road, a path strikes southeast from the hamlet of **Chapel-le-Dale** for the **Souther Scales Nature Reserve**, a fine limestone pavement with associated flowers and ferns. The summit of Ingleborough is less than two miles beyond. Of perhaps broader appeal is the flagstoned **Hill Inn** (☎015242/41256; ①) near Chapel-le-Dale itself. Built in 1615 – J.M.W. Turner and John Buchan are listed among its drinkers – it's one of the lonelier pubs in England, but a lively, unpredictable place, with occasional live music and lots of climbers and cavers. Bunkhouse and standard double and twin rooms are available and there's a related **campsite** nearby – ask at the bar. Take a look inside the local **church** (daily 9am–5pm), too, a tiny and remote seventeenth-century chapel where many of the workers who died building the Settle–Carlisle Railway are buried.

A little way beyond Chapel-le-Dale, the road passes under the Settle–Carlisle Railway at Ribblehead (see p.769), start of a bleakly beautiful few miles of road.

Deepdale, Dentdale and Garsdale

Any rail or road route to Dentdale has plenty of scenic rewards, but the most breathtaking is the minor-road route from Ingleton up **Kingsdale** and down **Deepdale**, with the vast whalebacks of Gragareth and Whernside rising to each side of the windswept little road. Deepdale is a superb and intimate little dale, among the best in the National Park, closely rivalled by **Barbondale**, which feeds into Dentdale a couple of miles to the west. The road is minor enough (gated in parts) for walkers to feel reasonably secure in **walking** its ten-mile length to Dent, but to avoid the road altogether, at least for a while, you can hike the first couple of miles up the Falls Walk from Ingleton (see p.770) to Ray Bridge. Across on the east side a path continues north to the farmhouse at Braida Garth, following which there's an unavoidable couple of miles' road walking to reach the path around High Pike, which winds northwest to Barbondale, with a side path taking you into the centre of Dent – perhaps four hours from Ingleton.

As you might expect, there's next to nothing to do locally except walk or revel in the scenery, but there are few better spots to do either, with **DENT** village an unbeatable base. When travel writers turn out clichés like "stepping back in time", they mean to describe places like this – the main road gives way to grassy cobbles, while the huddled stone cottages sport blooming window-boxes trailing over ancient lintels, and have tiny windows to keep in the warmth. In the seventeenth and eighteenth centuries, Dent supported a flourishing hand-knitting industry, later ruined by mechanization. These days, the hill-farming community supplements its income through tourism and craft ventures, most notably the independent Dent Brewery, a little way up the dale, which produces excellent beer for the local pubs.

Accommodation is surprisingly plentiful. You can stay at either of the village's two pubs, the *Sun Inn* (☎01539/625208; ①) and the *George & Dragon* (☎01539/625256; ②), which are next to each other in the centre and under the same management. The *Sun* is the nicer, truly welcoming to walkers and with a great traditional feel; that said, the en-suite rooms at the *George and Dragon* are a tad more comfortable. There are a handful of other overnight possibilities, most notably the non-smoking *Stone Close Guest House* (☎01539/625231; ①; closed Jan), which has a good café (10.30am–5.30pm) doubling as a **National Park information point**. If you ask around, you'll also find B&B in local private houses, while there's a **campsite** on the western edge of the village, at *High Laning Farm* (☎01539/625239). Steak dinners, pies, and Dent Brewery beers are specialities at the *Sun*, where you can eat and drink in front of a log fire. An evening meal (£11; not Tues) is served at the *Stone Close Guest House* at 7.30pm, provided you reserve in advance. The only other facilities in the village are a post office/store and a couple of little craft shops.

Confusion – and not a few sore feet – is caused by Dent's **train station** (on the Settle to Carlisle line) not being in Dent at all, but five miles to the east. Between mid-May and mid-October a **bus** runs between station and village twice a day on Sundays only (currently from the station at 11am and 6.35pm, to the station at 10.44am and 6.09pm). Otherwise the only bus service to and from Dent is that to Sedburgh to the west (schooldays only, 4 daily), from where you can reach Kirkby Stephen, or Kendal in the Lakes. If you get stuck, the hamlet of **Cowgill**, half a mile below the station, has the *Sportsman's Inn* (☎01539/625282; ②) to hand. **Dentdale youth hostel** at *Dee Side House* (☎01539/625251) is a couple of miles south of here down the Dales Way.

Train is the best way to reach **Garsdale**, a dale so untrammelled by the modern world it doesn't even have a town or village within its ten-mile span, simply a scattering of farm hamlets, most of Norse origin, as names like Thursgill, Dandra Garth and Knudsman Ing suggest. Aye Gill Pike to the south and Baugh Fell to the north rise incredibly steeply from the valley floor, creating two of the most monolithic-looking mountains in the Dales. Get off the train at **Garsdale Head**, the easternmost point in the dale – it's five miles down the A684 to Hawes (see p.774) and Wensleydale from here, but again, there's no regular bus, just a summer National Park service (June to mid-Sept 1 daily).

Wensleydale

That's it Gromit... cheese. We'll go somewhere where there's cheese!

A Grand Day Out, Nick Park.

Best known of the Dales to outsiders, if only for its cheese – though what cracking cheese it is, as Wallace often attests – **Wensleydale** is the largest, least varied and most serene of the National Park's dales. Known in medieval times as Yoredale, after its river (the Ure), the dale today takes its name after a now-inconsequential village, and while there are towns to detain you – including one of the area's biggest in Hawes – it's Wenselydale's rural attractions that linger longest in the mind. Many will be familiar to devotees of the **James Herriott** books and TV series (see p.775), set and filmed in the dale; elsewhere, there are several well-known waterfalls – notably **Aysgarth Falls** – and, as the dale opens into the Vale of York, a variety of historic buildings that range from **castles** at Bolton and Middleham to **abbeys** at Jervaulx and Coverham.

The dale is traversed by the National Park's only east–west **main road** (A684), and linked by high moor roads to virtually all the park's other dales of note. Although the scenery is less spectacular than in other valleys, hiking possibilities are as plentiful as elsewhere, with the **Pennine Way** crossing the valley at Hawes. Year-round **public transport** is limited to a post bus from Hawes on varied routes (Mon–Fri 2–3 daily, Sat 1 daily) via Bainbridge, Askrigg, Aysgarth and Castle Bolton to Leyburn (for Richmond); and the Arriva services (#156, #157, #159) along the same route between Hawes and Richmond. There are also seasonal connections between Garsdale Head station and Hawes (June–Aug Tues, Fri & Sat 2–3 daily), as well as the useful

Wensleydale Tourer which runs daily in summer (late July to Sept; day-tourer ticket £4.95) – it meets morning and evening trains at Garsdale and otherwise runs on a circular route throughout the day between Aysgarth and Hawes.

Hawes

HAWES – from the Anglo-Saxon *haus*, a mountain pass – is head of Wensleydale in all respects: it is its chief town, main hiking centre, and home to its tourism, cheese and rope-making industries. Hawes also claims to be Yorkshire's highest market town, and received its market charter in 1699; the weekly **Tuesday market** – crammed with farmers and market traders – is still going strong. If you haven't yet bought any cheese, the groaning stalls will doubtless persuade you otherwise. The cheese trail invariably leads to the **Wensleydale Creamery** on Gayle Lane (Mon–Sat 9.30am–5pm, Sun 10am–4.30pm; £2), a few hundred yards (signposted) south of the centre. The first cheese in Wensleydale was made by medieval Cistercian monks from ewes' milk, and after the Dissolution local farmers made a version from cows' milk which, by the 1840s, was being marketed as "Wensleydale" cheese. The first commercial creamery was founded in Hawes at the turn of the twentieth century, and production continues again today, after the industry was rescued in the 1990s from recession and neglect. The Creamery's "Cheese Experience" tours tell you all this and more, with plenty of opportunity to see the stuff being made, to sample and purchase in the shop, or tuck in at the *Buttery* restaurant.

All three of Wensleydale's industries come together in the **Dales Countryside Museum** (Easter–Oct daily 10am–5pm; Nov–Easter Wed, Fri, Sat & Sun 11am–4pm; £2.50), housed in Station Yard's former train station and warehouses, on the Aysgarth side of town. The comprehensive and well-presented collection, garnered by Dales chroniclers Marie and Joan Ingilby, embraces lead-mining, farming, peat-cutting, knitting (hand-knitted hosiery was a speciality) and all manner of rustic minutiae. Alongside it, in a long shed, the **Hawes Ropemakers Museum** (Mon–Fri 9am–5.30pm; also Sat July–Oct 10am–5.30pm; free) presents popular demonstrations of traditional rope-making.

Another local attraction is a mile and a half out of town to the north, where people cough up the 70p toll at the *Green Dragon* pub (☎01969/667392; ②) to walk to **Hardraw Force**. It's about all the fall is worth for much of the year, for though this is the highest above-ground waterfall in the country (Gaping Ghyll and other potholes have longer underground drops) there's often barely a trickle dribbling over the edge. Summer brass-band recitals in the natural amphitheatre of Hardraw Scar – an old tradition, recently revived – make for a more surreal attraction.

One of the best but toughest local walks follows the Pennine Way, immediately west of the *Green Dragon*, to **Great Shunner Fell** (five miles one way; 2hr 30min). Most people, however, find it more rewarding to drive along the parallel road over to Thwaite in Swaledale (see p.779) for the views. The road heads past the **Butter Tubs**, a series of deeply eroded natural wells five miles north of Hawes.

Services and accommodation in Hawes are gathered together along and just off the main A684, which runs through town. The **National Park information centre** shares the same buildings as the Hawes Ropemakers Museum (Mon–Fri 9am–5.30pm; also Sat July–Oct 10am–5.30pm; ☎01969/667450). **Buses** stop in Market Place (except for the post buses which depart from outside the post office), over the road from the information office car park. There's central, comfortable B&B **accommodation** at the *Steppe Haugh Guest House*, Town Head (☎01969/667645; no credit cards; ①); the *Old Station House*, on Hardraw Road, opposite the museum (☎01969/667785; ②); and at *Laburnam House*, The Holme (☎01969/667717; no credit cards; ①); at the turn-off from the main road to the museum. All the **pubs** in and around the market square – the *Board, Crown, Fountain* and *Bull's Head* – have rooms, too, so you shouldn't be stuck for choice; best are those at the *Board* (☎01969/667223; ②) and the *White Hart Inn* (☎01969/667259; ②), an eighteenth-century coaching inn on the cobbled Main Street, which – confusingly – lies just off the main road through town. Fanciest place is *Cocketts Hotel*, on Market Place (☎01969/667312; ④), with eight fine en-suite rooms in a seventeenth-century building. Finally, there's a smart **youth hostel** (☎01969/667368) at Lancaster Terrace, at the junction of the main A684 and B6255. **Campers** need to head for the *Bainbridge Ings* site (☎01969/667354), half a mile east of the centre, just off the A684 (Aysgarth road).

Pub **food** aside, you can pick from proper fish -and -chips at *The Chippie* on Market Place (closed Mon & Thurs lunch, & all Sun); coffees, snacks and lunches at the first-floor *Wensleydale Pantry* on the main road through town; pricier French-influenced meals at *Herriot's Hotel*, Main Street, opposite the *White Hart Inn*; and traditional English dinners in the *Cocketts Hotel* restaurant. *Laburnam House* has a nice tearoom attached.

Bainbridge and Countersett

BAINBRIDGE, five miles east of Hawes, centres on an emerald village green (complete with stocks), with an unearthly looking glacial mound behind, once the site of a Roman fort. Nightly at 9pm from Holyrood (late Sept) to Shrove Tuesday, a horn is blown three times on the green, continuing a tradition that dates back to Norman times, when the horn was sounded to guide travellers through the dense woodlands that once encircled the village. Paths (follow the River Bain) and minor roads to the south lead to **Semer Water** (2 miles), one of the Dales' few lakes, formed behind a dam of glacial material – there's not a scrap of evidence to support the traditional story that a lost city sits under the lake. All sorts of walks are possible from **Countersett**, a hamlet (with a B&B or two) near its shore, the best leading into Bardale and Raydale.

In Bainbridge, overlooking the green, there's the popular *Rose & Crown Hotel* (☎01969/650225; ④), a fifteenth-century coaching inn with a restaurant, bar meals and a decent wine list – the Bainbridge horn hangs in the hall when not in use. Other local B&Bs put out signs, or try the *Riverdale Country House Hotel*, also on the green (☎01969/650311; ③), where you can also take afternoon tea.

Askrigg

The mantle of "Herriot country" lies heavy on **ASKRIGG**, a mile across the valley from Bainbridge, the TV series *All Creatures Great and Small* having been filmed in and around the village. There's little to see or do, though the pubs and Georgian houses have their charms, and you might stroll to a couple of nearby falls, **Whitfield Force** and **Mill Gill Force**, both a mile or so to the west of the village. To the east, there are well-signed paths along high ground via Carperby to Aysgarth or Castle Bolton, around a five-mile pull to either.

The market at Askrigg has its origins in medieval times, and predates that of Hawes – notice the bull-ring set outside the church here, a relic of bull-baiting days. There's an **information point** in the village shop in the Market Place and plenty of **accommodation**, too, starting with the *King's Arms* in Market Place (☎01969/650258; ⑤), a cosy old haunt with plush rooms, wood panelling, good beer, local cheese platters and crusty locals. B&Bs include the *Apothecary's House* (☎01969/650626; no credit cards; ②), a fine-looking period house in Market Place, on the main street. For a rural retreat, you can't beat *Helm Country House* (☎01969/650443; no credit cards; ④), a seventeenth-century farmhouse a mile west with magnificent views, open fires, oak beams and a cast-iron Aga oven – an Aga-cooked dinner at £16 a head is served in the stone-flagged dining room.

Aysgarth and around

The ribbon-village of **AYSGARTH**, straggling along and off the A684, is the vortex that sucks in Wensleydale's largest number of visitors, courtesy of the twin **Aysgarth Falls**, half a mile below the village (there's a path through the fields). Water crashes down a series of limestone steps (impressive in full spate), while in summer the riverbanks alongside are choked with picnicking families. A marked nature trail runs through the surrounding woodlands and there's a big car park and excellent **information centre** on the north bank (Easter–Oct daily 10am–5pm; Nov–Easter occasional Sat & Sun; ☎01969/663424). The **Upper Falls** and picnic grounds lie just back from here, by the bridge and church; the more spectacular **Lower Falls** are a half-mile stroll to the east through shaded woodland. Don't leave without calling at the church of St **Andrew**, worth a look for its carved pews and one of Yorkshire's finest rood screens, dating from 1500 and possibly removed from nearby Jervaulx Abbey. Immediately below the church is an old water-driven mill, now the idiosyncratic **Yorkshire Carriage Museum** (daily 9.30am–dusk; £2), housing fifty plus coaches, hearses, fire engines and estate vehicles; the adjacent *Mill Race* tearooms occupy another of the old buildings. The mill produced one of history's more famous sartorial job lots: the red flannel shirts worn by the Italian soldiers of Garibaldi's 1860 army of unification.

Aysgarth has a superb aspect, with glorious views across the valley from several points, a setting spoiled only by the fast A684 through the village which precludes any quiet contemplation. **B&Bs** along the main road include *Marlbeck* (☎01969/663610; no credit cards; ①), while the village's only **pub**, the *George & Dragon* (☎01969/663358; ③), has pleasant en-suite rooms and a bar-meal menu with plenty of choice. Otherwise, *Low Gill Farm* (☎01969/663554; no credit cards; ①; closed Nov–Easter) is particularly beautifully sited, in lovely country a mile or so west on the minor road to Thornton Rust. Other local choices are all down by the falls, where the *Wensleydale Farmhouse* (☎01969/663534; no credit cards; ②) is on the main road at the turn-off for the falls, with the well-regarded **youth hostel** (☎01969/663260) just behind. Bar **meals** are served at the *Palmer Flatt* pub on the main road. There's a **campsite**, *Westholme Caravan Park* (☎01969/663268; closed Nov–Easter), half a mile east on the A684.

Castle Bolton

There's a superb **circular walk** northeast from Aysgarth via Castle Bolton (6 miles; 4hr), a route detailed in a National Park pamphlet available from the information centres in Hawes or Aysgarth – or you can simply drive to the castle in about ten minutes. The walk starts at the falls themselves and climbs up through Thoresby, with the foursquare battlements of **Castle Bolton** (March–Oct daily 10am–5pm; restricted winter opening, call ☎01969/623981 for details; £3) themselves a magnetic lure from miles away across the fields. Built in 1379 by Richard le Scrope, Lord Chancellor to Richard II, it's a massive defensive structure in which Mary, Queen of Scots was imprisoned for six months in 1568. The Great Hall, a few adjacent rooms, and the castle gardens have been restored, though the owners seem more keen to get you into the café that's incorporated into the castle – a welcome spot if you've just trudged up from Aysgarth (and free to enter). The only other facility hereabouts is the village post office, housed in what could pass for Goldilocks' cottage; the nearest **pub** is just over a mile to the east, the *King's Arms* at Redmire.

Leyburn and Wensley

A few miles east of Aysgarth, Wensleydale broadens into a low-hilled pastoral valley, the border of the National Park marking the end of classic Dales scenery and the start of the Vale of York's more mundane flats. **WENSLEY** is a beguiling place wound around a green village square. The church of the **Holy Trinity** ranks as one of the Dales' finest, founded in the thirteenth century but with fabric dating from the five centuries that followed, the most impressive being an extravagant box pew and a sixteenth-century rood screen removed from Richmond's Easby Abbey.

The market town of **LEYBURN** occupies almost the last piece of straggling high ground on the valley's north edge, a handsome place set around three open squares, replete with buildings from its eighteenth-century heyday. Market day is Friday, when Market Place puts out its fruit, veg, hard goods and bric-a-brac stalls; this is where the local **buses** stop too. There's a **tourist office** just off Market Place at 4 Central Chambers on Railway St (April–Oct daily 9.30am–5.30pm; Nov–March Mon–Sat 9.30am–4.30pm; ☎01969/623069), and plenty of places to **stay and eat**. There are agreeable rooms at the *Secret Garden House* in Grove Square (☎01969/623589; ②), a Georgian house with a garden; the *Posthorn* on the edge of Market Place dishes up all-day breakfasts and other meals; for a traditional inn, try the *Golden Lion* in Market Place (☎01969/622161; ③). For decent Masham beer visit the *Sandpiper Inn*, a little seventeeth-century **pub** on the road at the bottom of Market Place.

Middleham and Jervaulx Abbey

Two miles southeast of Leyburn, the tiny town of **MIDDLEHAM** is approached over an impressive early-nineteenth-century castellated bridge – a morning bus (not Sun) comes this way from Leyburn. A well-to-do place set around a sloping cobbled square, it's dominated by the imposing ruins of **Middleham Castle** (April–Oct daily 10am–6pm; Nov–Easter Wed–Sun 10am–4pm; £2.20; EH). Built by the Normans to guard the route from Skipton to Richmond, it gained added historical resonance when it passed by marriage to the future Richard III in 1471 and became his favourite home; his son, Edward, died here. The keep is one of England's largest, despite being badly damaged after Richard's defeat at Bosworth Field. Castle aside, Middleham captivates for at least long enough to have a coffee in one of its pubs or tearooms. Racehorses clip-clopping through the centre are a common sight, with over five hundred trained locally – on Good Friday each year there's free access to all the racing stables.

The best moderately priced place to stay is at the *Castle Keep* on Castle Hill (☎01969/623665, *castle.keep@argonet.co.uk*; ③), a walker-friendly tearoom and **guest house** with two en-suite rooms; the tearoom doubles as an evening bistro with creative local cooking. Otherwise, several **pubs** and a couple of other hotels vie for custom around the square – the *White Swan*, *Black Swan*, *Richard III* and *Black Bull* all have rooms available.

Wensleydale all but peters out with the overgrown and privately owned ruins of **Jervaulx Abbey** (dawn–dusk; £1.50 donation requested), four miles southeast of Middleham on the A6108 road to Ripon. Founded in 1156, it is the least prepossessing of the great trio of Cistercian abbeys completed by Fountains and Rievaulx (see p.790 & 821), but makes an enjoyable stop for a ramble amid the bramble-covered stones. A conservatory-style tearoom over the road (closed Jan & Feb) has snacks and lunches. On Tuesday, Thursday, Friday and Saturday, one **bus** a day from Leyburn and Middleham passes the abbey.

Masham

If you're a beer fan, the market town of **MASHAM**, another four miles along the road, is an essential point of pilgrimage – if you're not, there's little point in visiting. Home of **Theakston's** brewery, sited here since 1827, tours are offered (call in advance ☎01765/689057; £3) in which you'll learn the arcane intricacies of the brewer's art and become familiar with the legendary *Old Peculier* (sic) ale. The tour price includes a free pint and there's a visitor centre and bar on site too, though the most atmospheric place for a drink is the brewery pub, the *White Bear*. Following Theakston's huge marketing success, which has seen its beers made available all over Britain, one of the family brewing team left to set up the smaller, independent **Black Sheep Brewery**, also based in Masham and offering daily tours (☎01765/689227; £3.75) – to many minds Black Sheep bitter is even better than Theakston's. Both breweries are just a few minutes' signposted walk out of the centre. There's a car park at Black Sheep, though not at Theakston's, but there's usually plenty of space to park in Masham's central squares. You may need to soak up the alcohol with something more substantial than pub food: there's a bistro and bar inside the Black Sheep Brewery, as well as *Floodlite*, 7 Silver St (the main road through town), a well-regarded Anglo-French **restaurant**, with a good-value set lunch, and dinners at around £25. **Buses** from Masham's Market Place depart a couple of times a day for Ripon, and on summer Sundays a service runs on to Leeds and Bradford. Market days are Wednesday and Saturday.

Swaledale

The National Park's northernmost dale, **Swaledale** is rivalled only by Dentdale and Garsdale for the lonely grandeur of its landscapes. Narrow and steep-sided in its upper reaches, it emerges rocky and rugged in its central tract, which takes in the remote villages of **Keld**, **Thwaite** and **Muker**, before more typically pastoral scenery cuts in at **Reeth**. On any extended tour of the Dales the obvious approach is from Wensleydale and the south (on minor roads from Hawes or Askrigg), though the proximity of Richmond (see p.780) to the A1 makes it a dale you could easily take in as a quick aside if you're heading north. Indeed, this is one dale where it really pays to have your own transport. From Richmond, **bus** #30 runs up the valley along the B6270 as far as Keld, but it's a limited service (Mon–Sat 3–4 daily), and the only other access is with the summer-only **Swaledale Roamer** (Sun only, June to mid-Sept), which meets trains at Garsdale and then stops at Hawes, Keld, Muker and Reeth.

Keld and around

KELD, eight miles north of Hawes, and eleven from Kirkby Stephen, is at the crossroads of the Pennine Way and the Coast-to-Coast path, making it an ideal hiking centre. No more than a straggle of hardy buildings, it is surrounded by relics of the lead-mining industry that once brought a prosperity of sorts to much of the valley (though at a price – the average life expectancy of a nineteenth-century Swaledale miner was 46 years). Here you'll also see the incredible profusion of ancient field barns, or **laithes**, for which the dale is renowned, the legacy of a system of husbandry that dates back to Norse times. Keld's busy **youth hostel** is *Keld Lodge*, an old shooting lodge near the telephone kiosk (☎01748/886259); B&B at *Butt House* (☎01748/886374; no credit cards; ①; closed Sept–Easter), is a more tempting proposition. There's also a **campsite** at *Park Lodge* (☎01748/886274; closed Oct–Easter), but no pub, nor any other facilities, in Keld.

Any number of local walks are possible, the shortest being to **Kisdon Force**'s triple-stacked waterfall and its wooded gorge half a mile east of Keld, though the best is the hike southeast along the River Swale to Muker, below the circular bulk of Kisdon hill (2–3 miles; 1hr 30min). The valley road cuts round Kisdon to the south, following part of the so-called **Corpse Way**, a lane used by those paying their last respects when the nearest church was ten miles away at Grinton – footpaths follow its still obvious route down the valley.

North and west of Keld, the upper reaches of Swaledale are wild indeed, with an atmosphere bordering on desolate even in summer. The Kirkby Stephen road (B6270) gives access to short side-valleys such as Stonesdale, Whitsun Dale and Birkdale where you can spend a lonely hour or two, while the Pennine Way shadows the very minor Stonesdale road for the three or four miles across Stonesdale Moor to the splendid **Tan Hill Inn** (☎01833/628246; ②). Reputedly the highest pub in Britain (1732ft above sea level), the *Tan Hill* was built to serve the coal mines that fed the lead mines and smelting mills of the lower dale. The wind blows hard year-round up here, and in winter snow drifts up to the windows – but there's an open fire lit daily in the stone-flagged interior, Theakston and Black Sheep bitter on draught, bar meals, and camping outside for the truly dedicated.

Thwaite to Low Row

One of Swaledale's attractions is the possibility of walking the footpaths that link villages all the way down the valley. **THWAITE**, another Norse-founded settlement, is the first hamlet south of Keld, just a two-mile walk away and with accommodation and meals at *Kearton Guest House* (☎01748/886277; no credit cards; ②). Some of the loveliest scenery follows beyond the little village of **MUKER** (the name derives from the Norse for "meadow"), a mile or so to the east, distinguished by tiny side-valleys such as Oxnop Beck, south of Oxnop. Muker has a **National Park information point** in the village store and a couple of B&Bs, including *Hylands* (☎01748/886003; no credit cards; ②), an immaculate seventeenth-century cottage off the main road, near the church. There are also a couple of teashops, a nice Dales pub, the *Farmers Arms*, serving good food, and a **campsite** at *Usha Gap*, half a mile from the village in the direction of Thwaite (☎01748/886214), set alongside a stream.

Beyond Muker, there's not much to tempt you away from the bucolic riverside, save perhaps for the **Gunnerside Gill**, a little valley which contains the best of the area's old lead mines. These are all easily seen on a circular six-mile walk from **GUNNERSIDE** itself, and are covered in a special trail leaflet available from the village post office's **National Park information point**. Further east at Low Row, there's a **bunkhouse barn** at the *Punch Bowl Inn* (☎01748/886233; ①), with inexpensive B&B and basic bar meals also available. This makes as nice a stop as any, with fine valley views from the pub tables, a choice of almost 150 malt whiskies, and the unmissable opportunity to walk along country roads to the intriguingly named hamlet of **Crackpot**, a mile to the south.

Reeth and around

A couple of miles east lies **REETH**, set in a bowl of bleak moorland. It's the dale's main village and market centre – market day is Friday – and its desirable cottages are gathered around a triangular green. Reeth has the biggest range of facilities in the whole dale, including a petrol station, a post office and the only bank, and it also has several local craft workshops making everything from cabinets to guitars. The **National Park information centre** on the green (daily 10am–5pm; ☎01748/884059) has local maps and brochures. If the area's lead-mining heritage appeals, drop into Reeth's **Swaledale Folk Museum** (Easter–Oct daily 10am–5.30pm; £1.75), signposted just off the green.

Some cottages around the green post **B&B** signs in their windows. Other choices for accommodation include two places on the Grinton Road at the edge of the village: the house at 2 Bridge Terrace (☎01748/884572; no credit cards; ①; closed Nov–Easter), which offers breakfast made from local ingredients and has lots of books to read; and *Hackney House*, also on Bridge Terrace (☎01748/884302; no credit cards; ①). Further out, on the Arkengarthdale road, is *Elder Peak* (☎01748/884770; no credit cards; ①; closed Nov–March). There are also several good **pubs** offering rooms and food, most obviously the *Black Bull* (☎01748/884213; ②) and the *King's Arms* (☎01748/884259; ③), opposite the green. Many of the cottages around the green double as a **cafés**. The *Olde Temperance* serves breakfast to hikers from 8am, the *Copper Kettle* (summer daily 10am–8.30pm; winter times vary) has big platefuls of filling food. For picnic supplies try *Reeth Bakery*, known for its great chocolate cake.

To escape Reeth's crowds, walk or drive three miles east to **Marrick Priory**, a ruined twelfth-century Benedictine nunnery set among trees on the north bank of the

Swale. A mile farther east, approached from the B6270 road, are the tower and ruined nave of **Ellerton Priory**, a fifteenth-century Cistercian foundation. There are also numerous paths across the fields on the south side of the river, letting you complete a circular walk from Reeth via Grinton, whose attractive bridge, church and riverside inn, *The Bridge*, are just a mile away by road. The local **youth hostel**, *Grinton Lodge*, is housed in a former shooting lodge spectacularly sited in the hills above (☎01748/884206), ten minutes' walk from Grinton. You can rent mountain bikes here, and the hostel can provide route details for local rides – book in advance.

Many people come to this area to make a television-inspired pilgrimage up **Arkengarthdale** to **Langthwaite**, three miles to the northwest, a cute village used in the opening credits of *All Creatures Great and Small*; a handful of local B&Bs and the atmospheric *Red Lion* pub soak up the passing trade there.

Richmond

Although marginalized on the National Park's northeasternmost borders, **RICHMOND** is the Dales' single most tempting historical town, thanks mainly to its magnificent castle, whose extensive walls and colossal keep cling to a precipice above the River Swale. Indeed, the entire town is an absolute gem, centred on a huge cobbled market square backed onto by hidden alleys and gardens housing mainly Georgian buildings of great refinement. The town itself is much older, having been dubbed *Riche-Mont* ("noble hill") by the Normans who first built a castle here in 1071. That heritage is also celebrated in local street names like Frenchgate and Lombard's Wynd (a "wynd" being a narrow alley).

The Town

There's no better place to start than **Richmond Castle** (daily: April–Sept 10am–6pm; Oct 10am–1pm & 2–6pm; Nov–March 10am–1pm & 2–4pm; £3; EH), reached by signposted alleys from the market square. Originally built by Alan Rufus, first Norman Earl of Richmond, it retains many features from its earliest incarnation, principally the gatehouse, curtain wall and Scolland's Hall, the oldest Norman great hall in the country. Legend, however, links it to earlier times, notably to King Arthur, who's reputed to lie in a local cave awaiting England's hour of need. The castle was roofed with Swaledale lead, and its building and upkeep was paid for over the centuries with a levy of two pence per mule-load of lead brought down the dale. There are prodigious views from the splendidly preserved fortified keep, which is over a hundred feet high, and from the Great Court, now an open lawn which ends in a sheer fall to the river below. Outside the main entrance a Georgian terrace, the **Castle Walk**, wraps around the skirts of the castle, offering more views of the river and hills beyond.

Most of medieval Richmond – all cobbled streets and narrow wynds – sprouted around the castle, but much of the town now radiates from the vast **Market Place**, with the Market Hall alongside (market days are Thursday, Friday and Saturday). It's difficult to get a good view of things now the square is overwhelmed by traffic, but the Victorian and Georgian buildings which border the square still have some appeal. The most unusual structure is the defunct **Holy Trinity** church, built in 1135 and now serving as the **Green Howards Museum** (Feb Mon–Fri 10am–4.30pm; March & Nov Mon–Sat 10am–4.30pm; April–Oct Mon–Sat 9.30am–4.30pm, Sun 2–4.30pm; £2), honouring North Yorkshire's Green Howards regiment. The **Richmondshire Museum**, reached down Ryder's Wynd, off King Street on the northern side of the square (Easter–Oct daily 11am–5pm; £1.50), is of more general interest. It has displays relating to lead-mining and local crafts, and contains a brick-by-brick reconstruction of a local fifteenth-century "cruck" house, built using a curved timber frame.

The keenest interest of all, however, is in the town's **Theatre Royal** (Easter–Oct Mon–Sat 10.30am–4.30pm, Sun 11am–2pm; £1.50), dating from 1788, making it one of England's oldest extant theatres. The theatre is on the corner of Friar's Wynd (a narrow alley running north of the Market Place) and Victoria Road, opposite the **tourist office**. Unassuming from the outside, the theatre's tiny interior is one of England's finest pieces of Georgian architecture. Built by one Samuel Butler – an actor-manager who owned several regional theatres in the north, and third husband of the splendidly named actress Tryphosa Brockell – the theatre hosted the greats of eighteenth-century theatre, Edmund Kean among them, before packed houses of over 400 people, each person paying a shilling a time. The theatre now seats just 214, a figure which still seems remarkable given the shoebox size of the building. After years of neglect, during which time it was used variously as wine cellars and as a warehouse, the theatre re-opened in 1962, both for performances (call ☎01748/823021 for details) and **tours**, which leave roughly every 45 minutes during the day (last tour 45min before closing). A museum at the rear gives an insight into eighteenth-century theatrical life, allowing visitors to have a go at scene-shifting, use the thunderbox prop or try on the various masks and costumes.

The river and Easby Abbey

Below the castle, the **River Swale** cuts a pastoral swathe through the surrounding countryside, with the banks immediately east of town popular for picnics. A lovely sign-posted walk runs along the north bank out to the beautifully situated church of St Agatha and adjacent **Easby Abbey** (daily: April–Sept 10am–6pm; Oct 10am–1pm & 2–6pm; Nov–March 10am–1pm & 2–4pm; EH; free), whose golden stone walls stand a mile southeast of the town centre. Founded in 1152 by Premonstratensian canons – the so-called White Monks – the abbey is now ruined, the greatest damage having been caused in 1346 when the English army was billeted here on its way to the battle of Neville's Cross. However, the evocative remains are extensive, and in places – notably the thirteenth-century refectory – still remarkably intact. You can vary your return to town by crossing the bridge a little further down from the abbey and walking back along the old railway track.

Practicalities

Buses all stop in the Market Place; there are regular services into Wensleydale and Swaledale, to Barnard Castle in County Durham (p.855), and to Darlington (p.862), just ten miles to the northeast, which is on the main East Coast train line. Free **parking** is available in and around Market Place for two hours – pick up a parking disc from any local shop. The **tourist office**, at Friary Gardens, Victoria Road (summer daily 9.30am–5.30pm; winter Mon–Sat 9.30am–4.30pm; ☎01748/850252), is helpful in finding accommodation, and also organizes free **guided walking tours** (April–Sept, 1–2 weekly) around the town.

Recommended **accommodation** includes the *Old Brewery Guest House*, 29 The Green (☎01748/822460; ②), a former inn and now a highly tempting spot on a quiet green west of (and below) the castle. The nearby *Restaurant on the Green*, on the corner at 5–7 Bridge St (☎01748/826229; ①) also has a couple of rooms available. Central Frenchgate features the characterful seventeenth-century *Willance House*, at no. 24 (☎01748/824467; no credit cards; ②); *Carlin House* at no. 6 (☎01748/826771; no credit cards; ①); and the adjacent *Channel House* at no. 8 (☎01748/823844; no credit cards; ②) – though they only have a couple of rooms each. The tatty but genial *Windsor House*, 9 Castle Hill (☎01748/823285; no credit cards; ①), is about as cheap as you'll find, and is right next to the castle, just off the Market Place. Slightly out of town, the excellent *West End Guest House*, 45 Reeth Rd, along and beyond Victoria Road (☎01748/824783; ②), gets consistently good reports. Several of the town-centre pubs have rooms, too, though none can beat the luxury of the *King's Head Hotel*, on Market Place (☎01748/850220; ⑤). The nearest **campsite** is three miles west of town on the Reeth Road at *Swaleview Caravan Park* (☎01748/823106; closed Nov–Easter).

For **meals**, *The Bistro*, a pleasant place with an indoor patio on Chantry Wynd (☎01748/850792), off Finkle Street, serves filled croissants, ciabatta sandwiches, and Mediterranean lunches at around the £5 mark, and stays open for dinner from Wednesday to Saturday (6–9.30pm). There are more Mediterranean flavours at the *Frenchgate Café*, 29 Frenchgate (☎01748/824949), which posts its dinner menu daily at 6pm, while down on The Green, *Restaurant on the Green*, at 5–7 Bridge St (Thurs–Sat dinner; ☎01748/826229), makes a mark with its inventive bistro food. Otherwise you could always push the boat out at the *King's Head*, whose ritzy *à la carte* menu lets you eat for around £25; there's a cheaper bar menu too.

Richmond's **pubs** – there are half a dozen around the market square alone – are all rather grim, surprisingly, though the *Black Lion* on Finkle Street has its moments. The *Unicorn*, on Georgian tree-lined Newbiggin (at the end of Finkle St) is a quieter spot. The proximity of Catterick Garrison, a few miles south of town, means that loud, aggressive young men with short hair tend to ruin any chance of a peaceful drink at weekends.

Harrogate to Ripon

Somewhat off the beaten track unless you're driving between York and the Dales, **Ripon** – despite its ancient cathedral – would hardly merit a visit on its own were it not for nearby **Fountains Abbey**, Britain's largest and most beautiful monastic ruin. Easily seen from Ripon, it has the added bonus of being the focal point of **Studley Royal**, an eighteenth-century landscaped garden complete with lake, temples, water garden and deer park. With time and transport you could take in a handful of other historic buildings nearby, though better excursions are perhaps made from the refined spa town of **Harrogate**: either to **Knaresborough** for its castle, or to **Nidderdale**, an often overlooked adjunct to the Dales proper – for which Harrogate's bus and train connections make the town a perfect gateway.

Harrogate

HARROGATE – the very picture of genteel Yorkshire respectability – owes its airy, planned appearance and early prosperity to the discovery of Tewit Well in 1571. This was the first of over eighty ferrous and sulphurous springs that, by the nineteenth century, were to turn the town into one of the country's leading spas. By the mid-twentieth century, however, taking the waters had become a less popular pastime, and since the early 1970s Harrogate has instead concentrated on hosting a year-round panoply of conferences, exhibitions and festivals. Monuments to its past splendours still stand dotted around town and, despite the jarring efforts of contemporary architects, Harrogate manages to retain its essential Victorian and Edwardian character. Much of its appeal lies in the splendid parks and gardens – "England's floral town" keeps admirable pace with the changing seasons, and if you pick up a "Floral Trail" leaflet from the tourist office you'll be guided around the best of the current blooms.

Harrogate's spa heritage begins with the **Royal Baths Assembly Rooms** on Crescent Road, built in 1897, where you can still take a **Turkish bath** in the plush, tiled Victorian surroundings (call ☎01423/556746 for hours; from £8 a session); the public entrance is on

Parliament Street. The contemporaneous **Royal Hall**, built as a concert hall, stands across the way (corner of Ripon Road and King's Road), while just around the corner from the Assembly Rooms stands the **Royal Pump Room** (built 1842) in Crown Place, built over the sulphur well that feeds the Royal Baths. The **museum** here (April–Oct Mon–Sat 10am–5pm, Sun 2–5pm; Nov–March closes at 4pm; £1.75) re-creates something of the town's health-fixated past and also lets you sample the water; free **guided walks** leave here several times a week between Easter and October (information from the tourist office). The town's earliest surviving spa building, the old Promenade Room of 1806, is just 100 yards from the Pump Room on Swan Road – now restored and housing the **Mercer Art Gallery** (Tues–Sat 10am–5pm, Sun 2–5pm; free), which hosts regularly changing fine-art exhibitions. The main **Conference and Exhibition Centre** along King's Road – an example of empty 1980s pretension – doesn't fit at all with the rest of town. Harrogate deserves much credit, however, for the preservation of its green spaces, most prominent of which is **The Stray**, a jealously guarded green belt that curves around the south of the town centre. To the southwest, the 120-acre **Valley Gardens** are the venue for the annual Spring Flower Show and Sunday band concerts in summer, while many visitors also make for the **Harlow Carr Botanical Gardens** (daily 9am–6pm or dusk if earlier; £3.50), the main showpiece of the Northern Horticultural Society. These lie one -and -a -half miles out, on the town's western edge; take the B6162 Otley road, or walk beyond the Valley Gardens, through the Pine Woods. Although laid out with a scientific purpose – breeding fruit and vegetable stock suited to northern climates – the gardens are a year-round floral extravaganza, with especially wonderful rose displays. A specialist **Museum of Gardening** in the grounds (daily 9.30am–4pm; included in the gardens entry fee) gathers together gardening tools and historical material, while the *Garden Room Restaurant* and a refreshment kiosk (April–Sept) provide meals and drinks – or you can bring your own picnic.

Practicalities

National Express buses drop you on Victoria Avenue, near the library; local and regional services (from Knaresborough, York, Skipton, Pateley Bridge, Ripon and Leeds) use the **bus station** on Station Parade. The **train station** (for services from Leeds and York) is on the same road, just a few minutes from all the central sights. There's limited-hours **parking** along and around West Park, on the way into town, and there are central car parks on Oxford Street and near the train station. Harrogate's **tourist office** (May–Sept Mon–Sat 9am–6pm, Sun noon–3pm; Oct–April Mon–Fri 9am–5.15pm, Sat 9am–12.30pm; ☎01423/537300) is in the Royal Baths Assembly Rooms (Crown Place entrance).

ACCOMMODATION

There are scores of **accommodation** options, starting with the B&Bs on King's Road and Franklin Road, north of the centre. Side streets like Studley Road, off King's Road beyond the conference centre, are quieter. You shouldn't have any problem finding somewhere to stay, other than during one of Harrogate's many **festivals**. Of these the most famous are the **flower shows** (second weeks of April and Sept); but there's also the Great Yorkshire Show (second week in July), the Northern Antiques Fair (second half of Sept), and various book fairs, music festivals and craft shows.

Alaine Guest House, 56–58 King's Rd (☎01423/560424). Terraced house opposite the conference centre, with some en-suite rooms. No credit cards. ①.

Alexander Guest House, 88 Franklin Rd (☎01423/503348). Recommended Victorian-era guest house on a residential street, under ten minutes' walk from the centre. No credit cards. ②.

Cavendish Hotel, 3 Valley Drive (☎01423/509637). A comfortable, friendly place. The best rooms here (all en-suite) overlook the Valley Gardens. ③.

Fountains Hotel, 27 King's Rd (☎01423/530483). Family-run venture just up from the conference centre, with a nice rose garden out front. No credit cards. ②.

The Imperial, Prospect Place (☎01423/565071). The doyen of spa-era hotels, the *Imperial* can't be bettered for location. It was once the home of Lord Carnarvon, discoverer of the tomb of Tutankhamen. ⑦.

Lynton House, 42 Studley Rd (☎01423/504715). A relaxed B&B on a quiet side road. No credit cards. ①.

Old Swan Hotel, Swan Rd (☎01423/500055). Large ivy-covered inn set in its own grounds, much rebuilt in Victorian times. Agatha Christie hid out here during her disappearance in 1926; today's comforts are suitably country-house style. ⑦.

Rudding Park Hotel, Rudding Park, Follifoot (☎01423/871350). Stylish country-house hotel located three miles southeast of town (down the A661). Terrifically relaxing with a fine bar and brasserie, and attached gardens and golf course. ⑦.

Ruskin Hotel, 1 Swan Rd (☎01423/502045). Appealing Victorian villa with six characterful en-suite rooms, terraced bar and charming gardens. ⑤.

The White House, 10 Park Parade (☎01423/501388). Classy place overlooking The Stray on the Knaresborough road. A delightfully furnished country-house-style villa with a good restaurant. ⑦.

EATING AND DRINKING

There are eating places to suit every budget in Harrogate, though, given the conference trade, there's an understandable emphasis on restaurants that are classy but predictable. There's also a plethora of new-wave café-bars, complete with espresso machines and fashionable food, but there are precious few town-centre pubs.

La Bergerie, 11–13 Mount Parade (☎01423/500089). The town's best French restaurant, with well-priced three- and four-course traditional menus – you'll need to book in advance. Dinner only; closed Sun. Moderate.

Betty's, 1 Parliament St (☎01423/502746). The Harrogate branch, founded in the 1920s by the Swiss Frederic Belmont, is the original of this famous tea-shop chain – Yorkshire teas and cakes, Alpine dishes and lunch specials, served daily until 9pm. Inexpensive to Moderate.

The Bistro, 1 Montpellier Mews (☎01423/530708). Fashionable food – polenta, roast scallops, pan-seared salmon and the like – served in a cosy mews cottage. Lighter lunches are good value. Closed Sun & Mon. Expensive.

Café Rouge, 21–29 Beulah St (☎01423/500043). Reliable French food, from breakfast croissant to steak-frites dinner. Moderate.

Court's, 1 Crown Place (☎01423/536336). Spacious wine bar with up-to-the-minute food, comfortable sofas to lounge in, and outdoor tables on the cobbles. Closed Sun evening. Moderate.

Drum and Monkey, 5 Montpellier Gardens (☎01423/502650). Long-standing fish and seafood restaurant, a firm favourite with locals and out-of-towners alike. Closed Sun. Moderate to Expensive.

Garden Room Restaurant, Harlow Carr Botanical Gardens, Crag Lane (☎01423/505604). Handy garden spot with patio seating for lunches and snacks; dinner served Thurs–Sat. Moderate.

Est Est Est, 16 Cheltenham Crescent (☎01423/566453). Harrogate's best Italian, a stylish place with classy pizzas, and interesting fish and meat dishes. Moderate to Expensive.

Lloyd's No. 1, Parliament St (☎01423/538701). Typical of the town-centre café-bars; you can sink in the armchairs here and sip an espresso any time. Inexpensive.

Montey's, 3 Corn Exchange Buildings, The Ginnel (☎01423/526652). Café-cum-music bar with inexpensive lunches and live music most evenings. Inexpensive.

Rick's Just for Starters, 7 Bower Rd (☎01423/502700). Amiable mix-and-match bistro where, a few main courses aside, nothing much costs more than £3–5. Closed Sun lunch. Inexpensive to Moderate.

Salsa Posada, 4 Mayfield Grove (☎01423/565151). Funky but cramped Mexican restaurant with good-natured staff churning out reasonably authentic *nachos, burritos, fajitas* and the rest. Closed Sun lunch. Moderate.

Knaresborough

A four-mile hop east from Harrogate, **KNARESBOROUGH** rises spectacularly above the River Nidd's limestone gorge, its old town houses, pubs, shops and gardens clustered together on the wooded northern bank, with the river itself crossed by two bridges ("High" and "Low") and an eye-opener of a rail viaduct. The rocky crag above the town is crowned by the stump of a **Castle** (Easter–Sept daily 10.30am–5pm; £1.75) dating back to Norman times. Built on the site of Roman and Anglo-Saxon fortifications, it's now little more than a fourteenth-century keep in landscaped grounds, thanks to Cromwell's wrecking tactics during the Civil War. It was here that Henry II's knights fled after the murder of Thomas à Becket in Canterbury Cathedral; here, too, that Richard II was held before being removed to Pontefract, where he was murdered in 1400. In Castle Yard, close to the castle entrance, stands the **Old Court House Museum** (same hours & ticket as castle), with an original Tudor court and displays on local history and the Civil War; you're also allowed into the spooky **sallyport**, the old escape tunnel from the castle.

These historic sites aside, there's not much to the town, but it is a very appealing place nonetheless, with a central **Market Place** (markets every Wednesday) claiming the oldest pharmacist's shop in England, in business since 1720, and a pub named after local boy "Blind Jack" (John) Metcalfe, the celebrated eighteenth-century civil engineer, who, despite his lack of sight, managed to build roads and bridges all over Britain during the Industrial Revolution. Below town, the enjoyable **riverside** is the other focus, with wooded walks along both banks; at the *Marigold* café, there's outdoor seating, hour-long river cruises in summer, as well as boats and bikes for hire.

The town's two novelty acts are to be found on the west side of the river. **Mother Shipton's Cave** (daily: Easter–Oct 9.30am–5.45pm; Nov–Easter 10am–4.45pm; £4.55) was home to a sixteenth-century soothsayer who predicted the defeat of the Armada, the Great Fire of London, world wars, cars, planes, iron ships – falling short, however, in the most important oracular chestnut of them all, of the End of the World: "The world to an end will come," she prophesied, "in eighteen hundred and eighty one." Close by is an equally tourist-thronged spot, the **Petrifying Well**, where dripping, lime-soaked waters coat everyday objects – gloves, hats, coats, toys – in a brownish veneer that sets rock-hard in a few weeks. Both cave and well are contained within a riverside estate, reached along a fine eighteenth-century wooded "Long Walk", studded with picnic areas; the main entrance is just over the High Bridge, north of the town, which you can reach by walking along the river from below the castle.

Practicalities

The **bus station** is on the High Street, with services to and from Harrogate, Ripon, York and Leeds. **Trains** (from the same destinations) pull up at the station just off the High Street, in the backstreets high above the river. The **tourist office** is close by at 35 Market Place (Easter–Oct Mon–Sat 10am–5.30pm, Sun 2–5pm; ☎01423/866886), and there's a list of accommodation and other services in the window. Free **guided walks** around the town leave from the Castle Yard outside the Old Court House Museum (June–Sept, 2 weekly; call ☎01423/500600 for information); while summer ghost walks depart from the Market Cross (☎01423/860162 for reservations; £3).

Best sited of the central **places to stay** is the half-timbered *Villa Hotel*, 47 Kirkgate (☎01423/865370; no credit cards; ②), opposite the train station, with fine views over river and valley from its front rooms and from its attached tearoom. B&Bs are plentiful: try *Ebor Mount*, 18 York Place (☎01423/863315; no credit cards; ②) or, a little way out of the centre, down the High Street and turn right, the recommended *Grove House*, 14 Boroughbridge Rd (☎01423/868857; no credit cards; ①), a tasteful old house with a large garden. The town's best spot is the *Dower House Hotel*, an ivy-covered Georgian mansion at Bond End, near the High Bridge (☎01423/863302; ⑤), on the way (by road) to Mother Shipton's Cave entrance. There are also rooms (and not bad food and beer) at the *Yorkshire Lass* on High Bridge (☎01423/862962; ③), an eclectically decorated pub right opposite the entrance. Nearest **campsite** is the *Lido Leisure Park*, on the Wetherby road south of the centre (☎01423/865169; closed Dec–Easter), with space for tents.

Pollyanna's Tearooms up Jockey Lane, off the High Street, is the best **café**, while a couple of **pizzerias** offer value for money – the *Bella Rosa*, 25 Castlegate (closed Sun), opposite the tourist office, and *Da Mario's* at 15 Waterside (evenings only, closed Tues), down by the boat rental place. Drink in *Blind Jack's* **pub** in the Market Place or in the *Mother Shipton Inn* at Low Bridge, a fine, traditional stone building with a maze of rooms, snugs and alcoves, and a great garden looking over the river to the town's famous rail viaduct.

Nidderdale

The rumours claim **Nidderdale** was excluded from the Yorkshire Dales National Park so that reservoirs and other landscape-scarring features could go ahead unencumbered by planning restrictions. Despite these developments, the dale's beautiful upper reaches stand comparison with its more famous neighbours, yet remain relatively unknown and undervisited. Onward itineraries are pretty limited, however: the main approach is along the east–west B6265 between Grassington in Wharfedale and Ripon, with the only available route north the wild road from **Pateley Bridge**, the dale's main village, to Masham and, ultimately, Wensleydale. The **bus** service is pretty much restricted to the regular Harrogate & District #24 from Harrogate to Pateley Bridge, which on summer Sundays continues on to Grassington; another summer Sunday service runs between Bradford/Leeds and Ripon via Pateley Bridge and Brimham Rocks. A long-distance footpath, the **Nidderdale Way** runs in a circular 53-mile loop around the dale from Hampsthwaite village car park, three miles west of Harrogate. Dalesman Publishing produces a guide, *The Nidderdale Way*, and the route is indicated on OS maps nos. 99 and 104.

Ripley

The lower vale is a patchwork of farming land, its first obvious distraction coming at **RIPLEY** (bus #36 from Ripon or Harrogate), four miles north of Harrogate, an impeccably kept village whose bizarre appearance is due to a whim of the Ingilby family, who between 1827 and 1854 rebuilt it in the manner of an Alsace-Lorraine village, for no other reason than they liked the style. (The project was financed by selling an outlying farm on the Ingilby estate, now Harrogate's town centre.) Summer crowds pile in for the cobbled square, original stocks and the twee cottages and shops, not to mention the Ingilby house, parkland and **Castle** (gardens March–Dec daily 10am–5pm, Jan & Feb weekends only; castle April, May & Oct Sat, Sun & bank hols 10am–3pm; June–Sept Thurs & Fri 11.30am–4.30pm, Sat & Sun 10am–3pm; gardens only £2.25; castle and gardens £4.50; ☎01423/770152), with its museum of armour, weapons, furniture and suchlike. You don't have to pay to enter the castle forecourt, where there's an excellent deli and a separate café, *Cromwell's Eating House*. Close to the bridge over the village beck, look in on **All Saints'** church, whose stonework bears the indentations of musket balls, said to be caused by the execution of Royalist soldiers after the Battle of Marston Moor. The graveyard also contains the "Kneeling" or "Weeping" cross, a stone with eight niches to receive the knees of penitents. It's believed to be the only one of its kind in the country.

The highly attractive *Boar's Head* (☎01423/771888; ⑦), part of the estate, has pricey **rooms**, but there's a lovely bar and beer garden, too, and a high-class **restaurant** with prices to match.

Pateley Bridge and around

The little town of **PATELEY BRIDGE** serves as the dale's focus, housing the **tourist office** at 14 High St (Easter–Sept daily 10am–5pm; ☎01423/711147) and acting as a

China Town, Manchester

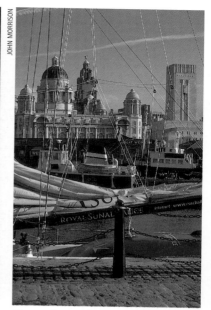

Liverpool waterfront

Blackpool beach, Lancashire

PETER WILSON

York Minster

JOHN MORRISON

Whitby, North Yorkshire

JOHN MORRISON

Judging sheep, Swaledale, Yorkshire Dales

Castle Howard, Yorkshire

Petrifying Well, Knaresborough, North Yorkshire

EDMUND NÄGELE

Hadrian's Wall, Northumberland

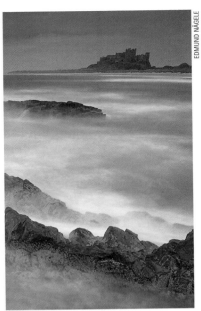
EDMUND NÄGELE

Bamburgh Castle, Northumberland

NEIL SETCHFIELD

Tyne and Swing bridges, Newcastle upon Tyne

base for campers, cavers and visitors of every shade. Its **Nidderdale Museum** (Easter–Sept daily 2–5pm; winter weekends only 2–5pm; £1; ☎01423/711225), in the old council offices opposite the church on the edge of the village, provides a run-through of dale life in days gone by, with a re-created village shop, office and house interior to poke around. After that, you could stroll the **Panorama Walk** (2 miles; 1hr), signposted from the top of the High Street, or refuel in one of the tea rooms, pubs and restaurants along the High Street. Several local guest houses and hotels provide **accommodation**, one of the nicest places being the *Sportsmans Arms* (☎01423/711306; ④), a couple of miles out off the Nidderdale road at Wath-in-Nidderdale – there's really good food served here too.

Five miles west of the village on the Grassington road lie the **Stump Cross Caverns** (Easter–Oct daily 10am–5.30pm; winter Sat & Sun 10.30am–4pm; £4), one of England's premier show caves, though only one massive stalagmite-filled cavern of the three-mile complex is open to the public.

About the same distance east of the village, signposted off the B6265, are the extraordinary **Brimham Rocks**, nearly four hundred acres of strangely eroded millstone grit outcrops scattered over one-thousand-foot high moors. The land at Brimham was once part of the wealthy Fountains Abbey estate, whose monks grazed their sheep between the weatherbeaten tors. Today, it's all under the protection of the National Trust, which maintains the paths between the rocks and safeguards the nesting jackdaws. It costs £2 to park your car, and after a clamber on the rocks, you can follow the path up to the **information centre** at Brimham House (April–Oct daily 9am–6pm; free). Views from the terrace here are superlative, stretching over the Vale of York, with York Minster visible on clear days. A refreshment kiosk (June–Aug daily, winter weekends only) serves drinks and cakes.

North of Pateley Bridge, above the **Gouthwaite Reservoir**, Nidderdale closes in and the scenery is superb. Part of the reservoir is a restricted-access nature reserve, but plenty of geese, waders and waterfowl can be seen all year round from the surrounding roads and tracks. In the upper valley, seven miles from Pateley Bridge, there's also the **How Stean Gorge** (daily 10am–6pm; £2), a terrific ice-gouged ravine of surging waters and overhanging rocks. Take a torch and you can explore Tom Taylor's Cave, a dark, narrow squeeze through an underground cavern. There's summer camping (call ☎01423/755666) behind the gorge café (café closed Mon & Tues in Jan & Feb). At the gorge, the minor road takes a turn to the northeast for the moorland crossing to Masham. A minibus service runs from Pateley Bridge past the reservoir (15min) to the gorge (30min), but only on summer Sundays and bank holiday Mondays (end May–Sept).

Ripon

The unassuming market town of **RIPON**, eleven miles north of Harrogate, only really diverts by virtue of its relatively small but vital **Cathedral** (daily 8am–6.30pm; £2 donation requested), which can trace its ancestry back to foundation in 672 by Saint Wilfrid; the original crypt is still extant below the central tower. The rest of the building was destroyed by the Danes in the ninth century, then a second church fell foul of the Normans, part of whose replacement remains, though the bulk of the present building dates from the reign of Archbishop Roger of York (1154–81). Although having a rather plain exterior there's plenty that pleases here, from the subtle, twin-towered, thirteenth-century west front to the choir's misericords, full of painted figures of miserable clergymen, executed by the same team that carved the impressive stalls at Beverley.

The town's other focus is its **marketplace**, "...the finest and most beautiful square...in England", according to Defoe, linked by Kirkgate to the cathedral; market day is Thursday. A ninety-foot obelisk built in 1780 dominates the square, a blustering conceit in stone, raised by William Aislabie to celebrate his sixty years as the local MP. At its apex stands a horned weather vane, an allusion to the "Blowing of the Wakeman's Horn", a ceremony – now something of a tourist attraction – which may date from 886, when Alfred the Great reputedly granted Ripon a charter (which would make it England's oldest chartered town) and an ox's horn was presented for the setting of the town's watch. The last official Wakeman died in 1637 – his half-timbered **Wakeman's House** stands on the square – but the horn is still blown nightly at 9pm in the square's four corners and outside the house of the incumbent mayor.

Two restored buildings show a different side of Ripon's heritage. At the **Prison and Police Museum,** on St Marygate (July & Aug daily 11am–5pm; May, June & Sept daily 1–5pm; April & Oct daily 1–4pm; free) behind the cathedral, the old cells serve as the backdrop for an exhibition on the evils of previous punishments. It's questionable whether conditions in the nineteenth century were worse here or in the nearby **Ripon Workhouse,** on Allhallowgate (same hours as museum), where the "undeserving" poor were incarcerated for such heinous crimes as being unable to pay their bills.

Practicalities

The **bus station** is dead central, just off the Market Place, while the town's **tourist office** is on Minster Road opposite the cathedral (April–Oct Mon–Sat 10am–5.30pm, Sun 1–4pm; ☎01765/604625). There's no huge reason to stay the night, though Ripon is the nearest base from which to visit Newby Hall and Fountains Abbey. The range of **accommodation** options includes the *Riverside Guest House*, 20 Iddesleigh Terrace (☎01765/602707; no credit cards; ②); the *Coopers*, 36 College Rd (☎01765/603708; no credit cards; ①), a quiet spot overlooking countryside; *Bishopton Grove House*, Bishopton (☎01765/600888; no credit cards; ①), a Georgian house in a peaceful corner of the town; and the *Unicorn Hotel*, the Market Place (☎01765/602202; ④), an old coaching inn and central Ripon's finest. There are several small **restaurants** along Kirkgate, though the best place to eat is at the *Old Deanery* (☎01765/603518; closed Sun dinner, & Mon; ⑦, includes dinner), across from the cathedral, with its formal set two- and three-course dinners, cheaper brasserie lunches and couple of guest rooms. The *Water Rat* on Bridge Lane is a nice riverside pub – head out of town down Bondgate.

Newby Hall

One of England's most splendid Queen Anne houses, **Newby Hall** (Easter–Oct Tues–Sun noon–5pm, gardens open at 11am; £6; gardens only £4.30; ☎01423/322583), stands just five miles southeast of the town near Skelton, south of the B6265. Completely overhauled by Robert Adam for his patron William Weddell, it contains some outstanding decorative plasterwork, and is further adorned by lashings of Chippendale furniture and rich eighteenth-century tapestries. The grounds and gardens, too, are a delight, with parts sectioned off for the entertainment of kids – there's an adventure playground, miniature railway and paddling pool, as well as a tearoom and picnic area.

Fountains Abbey and Studley Royal

It's tantalizing to imagine how the English landscape might have appeared had Henry VIII not dissolved the monasteries, with all the artistic ruin and impoverishment precipitated by that act. **Fountains Abbey,** four miles southwest of Ripon, gives a good idea of what might have been, and is the one ruin amongst Yorkshire's many monastic fragments you should make a point of seeing. Linked to it are the elegant water -gardens of **Studley Royal,** landscaped in the eighteenth century to form a setting for the abbey, but only reunited as a single 680-acre National Trust estate in 1983.

THE CISTERCIANS

England's monastic tradition received a boost in the middle of the twelfth century when Norman landlords, seeking to secure spiritual salvation and raise a bit of cash, handed over portions of their estates to various religious orders, often to dissident offshoots of the Benedictines such as the **Cistercians**. Inevitably the poorest and least promising part of an estate, these parcels of land were well suited to the Cistercians, who were bent on removing themselves from the world and a Benedictine orthodoxy which in their eyes had become insufficiently strict. Committed to toil, self-sufficiency and prayer, the movement was founded at Cîteaux in Burgundy, in reaction to the arrogant affluence of the Cluniacs, who themselves had earlier reacted against the same perceived fault in the Benedictines. Fountains found itself in the vanguard of the movement, founded just five years after Waverley, the first Cistercian foundation in England.

Dressed in rough habits of undyed sheeps' wool, the so-called "White Monks" lived a frugal and mostly silent existence. Besides this core of priest-monks common to all Benedictine communities, whose obligatory presence at choir seven times daily, starting with matins at 2.30am, left little time for work outside the cloister, the Cistercians uniquely had a second tier of lay brethren known as **conversi**, or "bearded ones". At Fountains, around forty monks were complemented by two hundred such *conversi*. At Rievaulx the imbalance was equally marked, its community comprising of over five hundred *conversi* and only 150 monks. Not ordained, and with fewer religious demands, the new recruits – often skilled farmers and masons – could venture far from the mother house, returning only for major festivals and feast days. They were organized into **granges** (farms) to run flocks of sheep, drain land (hence Yorkshire's many "Friar's Ditches"), clear pasture, mine stone, lead or iron – even, in a couple of cases, to run a stud farm and sea-fishing business. Fountains' holdings in the Craven area of the Dales alone totalled over a million acres.

The Cistercians' success prompted the Augustinians (Kirkham and Guisborough) and Benedictines (York and Whitby) to follow suit, though within a hundred years much of their early vigour had been lost, partly as a result of an economic downturn which followed the Black Death. Granges were broken into smaller units and leased to a new class of tenant farmer, as the Cistercians joined the older orders in living off rents rather than actively developing their own estates.

The site is signposted off the B6265 Ripon to Pateley Bridge road, ten miles north of Harrogate. **Parking** at the visitor centre is free, but costs £2 at Studley Royal. Getting there by **public transport** is relatively straightforward, at least during the summer. The closest rail link is Harrogate, with a bus connection on to Ripon; buses also run to Ripon from York train station. In addition, summer bus services connect the abbey visitor centre with Ripon, Harrogate, York and Leeds – call (Mon–Fri ☎01765/608888, Sat & Sun ☎01765/601005) for details, since services and routes change occasionally.

The **abbey, gardens** and **visitor centre** are open daily – except Friday in November, December and January – for the following hours: April to September 10am to 7pm, October to March 10am to 5pm, or dusk if earlier; Fountains Hall is open daily from April to October from noon to 3pm. **Admission** is £4.30, though you don't have to pay to get into Studley's deer park (all year in daylight hours) or St Mary's Church (Easter & May–Sept daily 1–5pm).

The visitor centre has a full programme of year-round **activities and events** at both Fountains Abbey and Studley Royal, and also offers **free guided tours** of the abbey (Easter–Oct 1–3 daily) and water gardens (Easter–Oct daily at 2pm). You get a sketch **map** of the entire estate on entry, but the National Trust's *Fountains Abbey* brochure (70p) is a good additional investment. Finally, there's a restaurant at the visitor centre and a lakeside tearoom (April–Sept only).

The abbey

Beautifully set in a narrow, wooded valley, through which the River Skell flows to join the Ure at Ripon, **Fountains Abbey** was founded in 1133 by thirteen dissident Benedictine monks from the wealthy abbey of St Mary's in York (perhaps encouraged by the success of Rievaulx, founded a year earlier) and formally adopted by the Cistercians two years later (see box on p.789). Within a hundred years, it had become the wealthiest Cistercian foundation in England, a century which saw the three main phases of the abbey's structural development: the church's nave and transepts, the domestic buildings, and the church's east end. Only the church's domineering tower belongs to a later period. At the Dissolution the abbey was sold to Sir Richard Gresham, and ultimately became a source of building stone for the nearby Fountains Hall (see below). Further desecration was avoided when in 1768 it became part of Studley Royal under William Aislabie, who extended the landscaping exploits of his father to bring the ruined abbey within the estate's orbit.

Most immediately eye-catching is the abbey church, in particular the **Chapel of the Nine Altars** at its eastern end, whose delicacy is in marked contrast to the austerity of the rest of the nave. A great sixty-foot-high window rises over the chapel, complemented by a similar window at the nave's western doorway, over 370ft away. The **Perpendicular Tower**, almost 180ft high, looms over the whole ensemble, added by the eminent early sixteenth-century Abbot Marmaduke Huby, who presided over perhaps the abbey's greatest period of prosperity. Equally grandiose in scale is the undercroft of the **Lay Brothers' Dormitory** off the cloister, a stunningly vaulted space over three hundred feet long that was used to store the monastery's annual harvest of fleeces. Its sheer size gives some idea of the abbey's entrepreneurial scope, some thirteen tons of wool a year being turned over, most of it sold to Venetian and Florentine merchants who toured the monasteries. The monks soon became speculators, buying wool from local farmers to sell in addition to their own production.

The size of the lay buildings – including a substantial **Lay Brothers' Infirmary** – give an idea of the number of lay brothers at the abbey: all are considerably larger than the corresponding monks' buildings, of which the most prepossessing are the **Chapter House** and **Refectory** – notice the huge fireplace of the tiny **Warming Room** alongside the refectory, the only heated space in the entire complex. Outside the abbey perimeter, between the gatehouse and bridge, are the Abbey Mill and **Fountains Hall**, the latter a fine example of early seventeenth-century domestic architecture.

Studley Royal

A bucolic riverside walk, marked from the visitor centre car park, takes you through the abbey and past Fountains Hall to a series of ponds and ornamental gardens, harbingers of **Studley Royal** (which can also be entered via the village of Studley Roger, where there's a separate car park). This lush medley of lawns, lake, woodland and **Deer Park** was laid out in 1720 by John Aislabie, MP for Ripon and Chancellor of the Exchequer until his involvement with the South Sea Company – one of the great financial scandals of the century – led to his resignation. There are some scintillating views of the abbey from the gardens, though it's the cascades and **water gardens**, fed by canals from the Skell, which command most attention, framed by several small temples positioned for their aesthetic effect. Just within the park stands the church of **St Mary** (1871), neatly approached by an avenue of limes that frame the distant towers of Ripon cathedral. Organ recitals are held here most weekends (May–Sept 2.30pm). You could easily spend an afternoon whiling away time in the gardens: the full circuit, from visitor centre to abbey and gardens and then back is a good couple of miles' walk.

he north's most compelling city, a place whose history, said George VI, "is
of England". This is perhaps overstating things a little, but it reflects the
e of a metropolis that until the Industrial Revolution was second only to
population and importance, not only at the heart of the country's religious
so a key player in some of the major events that have shaped the nation.
s a more provincial air hangs over the city, except in summer when York
heritage site for the benefit of tourists. That said, no trip to this part of the
complete without a visit to York, and the city's former importance has
sy to get to, with plenty of road and rail connections. Heavy tourist traffic
roduced plenty of accommodation, with the emphasis on small B&B places
sidential districts near the city centre. And if you want more than museums
ments, York's university and colleges provide the spur for a reasonably
ghtlife.

is well placed for any number of **day-trips**: the coast is only an hour away
ger by bus), and Harrogate, Knaresborough and Ripon are all easily acces-
However, these are all places that – with the time – you could profitably spend
n, and the only essential day-trip is northeast to **Castle Howard**, the gem
nglish stately homes.

story of York

ns chose York's swampy position, at the confluence of two minor rivers, as
a military camp during their campaigns against the Brigantes in 71 AD, and
is fortress became a city – **Eboracum**, capital of the empire's northern
territories and one of its most important administrative centres. The base for
northern campaigns, it was also ruled for three years by Septimius Severus,
emperors to die in the city. The other, Constantine Chlorus, was the father
tine the Great, first Christian emperor and founder of Constantinople; at
eath, his son was proclaimed Roman Emperor here – the only occasion an
as enthroned in Britain.

ught over after the decline of Rome, the city emerged as a **Saxon** vassal,
and later became the fulcrum of Christianity in northern England. It was here,
Day in 627, that Bishop Paulinus, on a mission to establish the Roman Church,
ing Edwin of Northumbria in a small timber chapel built for the purpose. Six
the church became the first minster and Paulinus the first archbishop of
7 the city fell to the **Danes**, who renamed it **Jorvik**, and later made it the cap-
ern England (Danelaw), following a treaty in 886 between Alfred the Great and
he Dane. Later Viking raids culminated in the decisive **Battle of Stamford
**066) six miles east of the city, where English King Harold defeated Norse King
a Pyrrhic victory in the event, for his weakened army was defeated by the
ust a few days later at the Battle of Hastings, with well-known consequences
cerned. In York, aside from the physical remains left by the Vikings on show
of the museums, the very street names tell of their profound influence – the
e" is derived from an old Norse word for street.

rmans devastated much of York's hinterland in their infamous "Harrying of
", building two castles astride the Ouse in the city itself. Stone walls were
during the thirteenth century, when the city became a favoured Plantagenet
l commercial capital of the north, its importance reflected in the new title of
rk, bestowed ever since on the monarch's second son. The 48 **York Mystery**
of only four surviving such cycles, date from this era, created by the powerful
ch rose with the city's woollen industry.

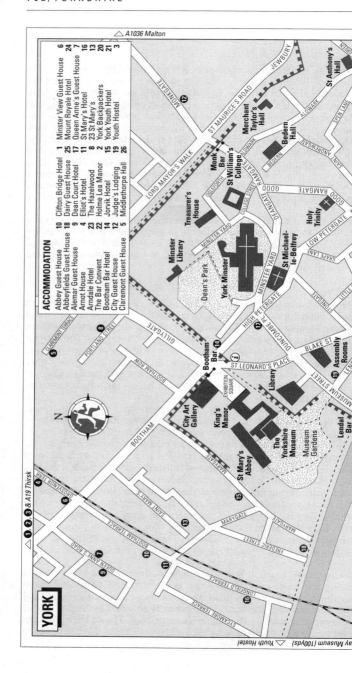

YORK

△ A1036 Malton

ACCOMMODATION

Abbey Guest House	6
Abbeyfields Guest House	24
Alemar Guest House	7
Arnot House	16
Arndale Hotel	13
The Bar Convent	20
Bootham Bar Hotel	21
City Guest House	3
Claremont Guest House	
Clifton Bridge Hotel	10
Dairy Guest House	18
Dean Court Hotel	9
Eliot's Hotel	4
The Hazelwood	23
Holme Lea Manor	22
Jorvik Hotel	14
Judge's Lodging	15
Middlethorpe Hall	12
Minster View Guest House	1
Mount Royale Hotel	25
Queen Anne's Guest House	17
St Mary's Hotel	11
23 St Mary's	8
York Backpackers	2
York Youth Hotel	19
Youth Hostel	26

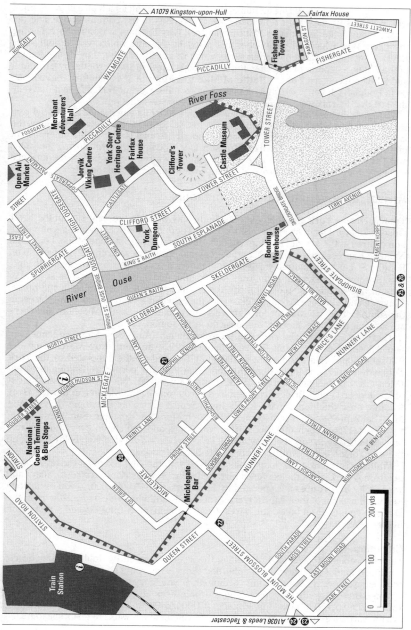

© Crown copyright

Although Henry VIII's Dissolution of the Monasteries took its toll on a city crammed with religious houses, York remained strongly wedded to the Catholic cause, and the most famous of the Gunpowder Plot conspirators, **Guy Fawkes**, was born here. During the **Civil War** Charles I established his court in the city, which was strongly pro-Royalist, inviting a Parliamentarian siege which was eventually lifted by Prince Rupert of the Rhine, a nephew of the King. Rupert's troops, however, were routed by Cromwell and Sir Thomas Fairfax at the **Battle of Marston Moor** in 1644, another seminal battle in England's history, which took place just six miles west of York. It's said that only the fact that Fairfax was a local man saved York from destruction.

The city's eighteenth-century history was marked by its emergence as a social centre for Yorkshire's landed elite. Whilst the Industrial Revolution largely passed it by, the arrival of the **railways** brought renewed prosperity, thanks largely to the enterprise of pioneering "Railway King" **George Hudson** (see p.803), lord mayor during the 1830s and 1840s. Chocolate, in the shape of Terry and Rowntree-Nestlé, is now the financial mainstay, together with the proceeds from several million annual tourists.

Arrival, information, transport and tours

Trains arrive at **York Station**, just outside the city walls on the west side of the River Ouse, a 750-yard walk from the historic core. There are information and accommodation centres at the station, left-luggage lockers and a luggage-storage office. Long-haul National Express **buses** and most other regional bus services drop off and pick up on Rougier Street, two hundred yards north of the train station, just before Lendal Bridge, though some services call at the train station, too. Arriving by car you'd be advised to park in one of the **car parks** on the roads shadowing the city walls: in the north, Gillygate and Clarence Street are closest to the Minster; Piccadilly and Tower Street in the southeast are convenient for Clifford's Tower and the Castle Museum; and there are also car parks on Queen Street near the train station.

There's a useful **tourist office** at the train station (April–Sept Mon–Sat 9am–8pm, Sun 9.30am–5pm; Oct Mon–Sat 9am–6pm, Sun 9.30am–5pm; Nov–March Mon–Sat 9.30am–5.30pm, Sun 10am–4pm; ☎01904/621756); and another, operated by the **York Tourism Bureau**, at 20 George Hudson St, around the corner from Rougier Street (Mon–Sat 9am–5.30pm, Sun July–Sept 10am–4pm; ☎01904/554488). The main tourist office is over Lendal Bridge, two hundred yards west of the Minster in the **De Grey Rooms**, on Exhibition Square (April–June, Sept & Oct daily 9am–6pm; July & Aug Mon–Sat 9am–7pm, Sun 9am–6pm; Nov–March Mon–Sat 9am–5pm, Sun 9.30am–3pm; ☎01904/621756). Each office is stuffed with maps and leaflets on every conceivable tour and attraction, and also provides an accommodation service (see below). Pick up the free **York Visitor Guide**, an invaluable listings magazine.

Walking is the best way to acquaint yourself with the city, and often the only way to get from A to B, given the confused historic layout of pedestrianized streets, alleys and yards. City **bus routes** are operated by First York (☎01904/435600) – you're unlikely to get full use out of their Minstercard (weekly, £9, unlimited rides), available from the De Grey rooms or on board the buses. Consider **renting a bike** instead – rental outfits are given on p.806.

City tours

York is probably tour capital of Britain, the streets clogged by double-decker buses, costumed guides and carefully shepherded sightseers. Doing it yourself is, frankly, the most enjoyable way, though if time is limited, or you fancy some of the more inventive options, there's plenty of choice. The tourist offices all push the Guide Friday **bus tours** (£7.50, £5.50 if booked in advance; ☎01904/640896), but much more interesting are the various **guided walks** on offer, from evening ghost walks to historical tours led by the York Association of Voluntary Guides (☎01904/640780) – most cost £3–4 and the tourist offices have all the information. It's also pleasant to get out on the river, either on a **cruise** (with several similar operators) or by renting your own **boat** – try York Marine Services Ltd on King's Staithe (☎01904/704442), near Skeldergate Bridge.

Accommodation

York is a busy tourist town, with the range of **accommodation** you'd expect, from countless cheap B&Bs to a clutch of topnotch luxury hotels. The main B&B concentrations are in the sidestreets off **Bootham and Clifton** (immediately west of Exhibition Square), as well as in the **Mount** area (turn right out of the station and head down Blossom Street), and, less conveniently, along **Haxby Road** (north of town; take bus #1, #2a or #3). True city-centre places are thin on the ground and obviously in great demand; booking's definitely a good idea from June to August. If you're stuck for a bed, make straight for the tourist offices, who'll **book you a room**. They also put out a list of guest houses if you want to hunt on your own, and there's a useful board of places posted in the station office window. Thomas Cook also has an accommodation booking office at the train station (daily 8am–10pm; ☎01904/673411). It's worth noting that, in a reversal of policy in most cities, larger hotels in York tend to charge slightly less during the week than at weekends.

York's nearest **campsites** are all a fair way out of the centre: nearest is the *Riverside Caravan and Camping Park* (☎01904/705812; closed Nov–March) in Bishopsthorpe, off the A64, a couple of miles south, which you can reach by ferry from King's Staithe (£3.95 return); the campsite is right by the landing stage. Otherwise, the *Poplar Farm Caravan Park* at Acaster Malbis (☎01904/706548; closed Nov–March), about four miles south, has tent sites and can be reached by bus #192 (4 daily) from Skeldergate Bridge, by the river.

Hotels and B&Bs

Abbey Guest House, 14 Earlsborough Terrace, Marygate (☎01904/627782). Riverside terraced guest house in a great location with bright, pretty, bargain-priced rooms, two of which, overlooking the river, are en suite. ②.

Abbeyfields Guest House, 19 Bootham Terrace (☎01904/636471). B&B in an elegant and sensitively furnished Victorian house; all rooms have bathrooms and TV. No credit cards. ②.

Alemar Guest House, 19 Queen Anne's Rd (☎01904/652367). On a Bootham sidestreet where houses tend to favour the mock-Elizabethan pebble-dash frontage, this very well-kept, non-smoking B&B is about the best of the bunch, with clean and comfortable rooms. No credit cards. ①.

Arnot House, 17 Grosvenor Terrace, Bootham (☎01904/641966). Victorian family house preserving many of its original features, offering well-furnished and equipped no-smoking rooms with distant views of the Minster. Vegetarian breakfasts on request. ③.

Arndale Hotel, 290 Tadcaster Rd (☎01904/702424). Pleasant, welcoming hotel with walled garden overlooking the racecourse a mile south of the centre; many rooms have four-posters and whirlpool baths, and there's secure parking. Midweek and winter rates are a few pounds less than usual. ⑤.

The Bar Convent, 17 Blossom St (☎01904/643238). Grand Georgian building next to Micklegate Bar, housing a museum and café as well as single and double rooms with separate bathrooms and access to a self-catering kitchen. Breakfast buffet included, though bed-only rates are available. No credit cards. ②.

Bootham Bar Hotel, 4 High Petergate (☎01904/658516). A refined eighteenth-century hotel with en-suite rooms, just 100 yards from the Minster. ④.

City Guest House, 68 Monkgate (☎01904/622483). Central, non-smoking, family-run guest house with budget rates, not far from the Minster. Off-season prices are around £5 a night less; most rooms have en-suite showers and there's a useful car park. ②.

Claremount Guest House, 18 Claremount Terrace, Gillygate (☎01904/625158). Fine and friendly B&B with just two rooms (one en-suite, one with separate bathroom) in a quiet Victorian cul-de-sac about 200 yards from the Minster, at the Lord Mayor's Walk end of Gillygate. ②.

Clifton Bridge Hotel, Water End, Clifton (☎01904/610510). A mile northwest of the Minster beyond Bootham, but close to a riverside walk to the city centre. Nicely situated in its own grounds. ④.

Dairy Guest House, 3 Scarcroft Rd (☎01904/639367). Victorian house half a mile south of the station, with rooms heavy on stripped pine and flowery furnishings. Offers a choice of traditional or wholefood/vegetarian breakfasts. Closed mid-Dec to Jan. ②.

Dean Court Hotel, Duncombe Place (☎01904/625082). Perfectly sited neo-Victorian hotel with views of the Minster from the front rooms, which means it's pricey, but the facilities come up to scratch. There's garage parking nearby. Ask about special-break prices. ⑦.

Elliott's Hotel, Sycamore Place, Bootham Terrace (☎01904/623333). A surprising find – a large detached Victorian house tucked away in a peaceful and convenient spot, with comfortable rooms, big breakfasts, bar snacks and a restaurant. ③.

The Hazelwood, 24–25 Portland St, Gillygate (☎01904/626548). Good variety of rooms – all with private bath – in a central residential area, also with a pleasant garden. ④.

Holme Lea Manor, 18 St Peter's Grove, Clifton (☎01904/623529). Comfortable en-suite rooms with period touches (some have four-posters) in a quiet, tree-lined Victorian cul-de-sac just ten minutes from the centre. ②.

Jorvik Hotel, 52 Marygate, Bootham (☎01904/653511). In an extremely good position opposite the western entrance to St Mary's Abbey, this family-run-town house hotel has a variety of rooms and some private parking – you'll pay more to overlook the abbey gardens. ③.

Judge's Lodging, 9 Lendal (☎01904/638733). One of the top central, historic choices, located in the lovely eighteenth-century Georgian residence of the former assize court judges, a few minutes from the Minster. There's secure parking and a good cellar-bar. ⑥–⑦.

Middlethorpe Hall, Bishopsthorpe Rd (☎01904/641241). York's most celebrated spot, a grand eighteenth-century mansion a couple of miles south of the city, next to the racecourse. Antiques, wood panelling, superb rooms (some set in a private courtyard), gardens, parkland, pool and spa, and a fine restaurant, all at stratospheric prices. ⑧.

Minster View Guest House, 2 Grosvenor Terrace, Bootham (☎01904/655034). The touted views are of the Minster tower across the rail line and park beyond, but it's still a nice place on a relatively quiet road just off Bootham. No credit cards. ②.

Mount Royale Hotel, The Mount (☎01904/628856). Luxurious, antique-filled retreat south of the station with superb garden-suites set around a private garden, together with a heated pool and other facilities. It's family-owned and run, too, which gives it the edge over similarly endowed spots. ⑥.

Queen Anne's Guest House, 24 Queen Anne's Rd (☎01904/629389). Budget-rated Bootham B&B with just a couple of rooms with their own bathroom. No credit cards. ②.

St Mary's Hotel, 17 Longfield Terrace (☎01904/626972). Homely and flower-hung hotel in a peaceful railway cutting backstreet south of Bootham, with the river (and a pleasant walk into the centre) just a hundred yards away. Rooms with and without bathroom; cheaper rates in winter. ②.

23 St Mary's, 23 St Mary's, Bootham (☎01904/622738). Very pleasant and amiable family-house hotel just west of St Mary's Abbey and gardens. No credit cards. ③.

Hostels and student accommodation

Fairfax House, 99 Heslington Rd (☎01904/432095). University of York Georgian housing, containing well-equipped single rooms, available at Easter and during summer vacations for short stays or week-long breaks. Call in advance (Mon–Fri 9.30am–4.30pm). It's ten minutes east of the centre, off Barbican Road.

York Backpackers Hostel, 88–90 Micklegate (☎01904/627720). Dorm space, doubles and family rooms in a Grade 1 listed building, the 1752 former home of the High Sheriff of Yorkshire. There's a self-catering kitchen, laundry, Internet facilities, TV and games room, and licensed bar. Self-service breakfast costs extra.

York International Youth Hostel, Water End, Clifton (☎01904/653147). Large Victorian mansion about a 20min walk along Bootham from the tourist office and then a left turn at Clifton Green. A nicer and quicker approach from the station is to follow the riverside footpath west. Pricey beds mostly in four-bedded dorms; also a café with licence for alcohol with meals. Book well ahead in summer.

York Youth Hotel, 11–13 Bishophill Senior (☎01904/625904). Centrally located, on the west side of the river, off Micklegate, and attracting a mixed international crowd – dorm, single and twin rooms available, with a pound off for multi-night stays; breakfast extra. Also a late-night bar, kitchen, laundry and bike rental.

The City

Take a look at one of the maps dotted around the city centre and you're confronted with a baffling and intimidating prospect. If the city council and tourist office are to be believed, there are around sixty churches, museums and historic buildings crammed within York's walls. In fact the tally of things you really want to see is surprisingly limited, with most sights within easy walking distance of one another. Even so, it's hard to get round everything in less than two days, and equally difficult to stick to any rigid itinerary. The **Minster** is the obvious place to start, followed by the cluster of buildings that circle it; then you might cut south to the **Shambles**, central to the city's old centre and pedestrianized grid, or walk around **the walls** from the Minster to Exhibition Square and Museum Street for the **City Art Gallery**, **Yorkshire Museum** and **St Mary's Abbey**, evocative ruins surrounded by the city's loveliest gardens. Thereafter you could walk through the main shopping streets to take in the **Merchant Adventurers' Hall**, most striking of the city's smaller medieval buildings, then deal with **Clifford's Tower** and the nearby **Jorvik Viking Centre** and **Castle Museum**. Lastly, be sure to leave time to take in the **National Railway Museum**, a superb museum whose appeal goes way beyond railway memorabilia.

York Minster

York Minster (daily June–Sept 7am–8pm; Oct–May 7am–5pm; £2 donation requested; ☎01904/624426) ranks as one of the country's most important sights, a fact not lost on the thousands who throng its colossal and, it must be said, strangely unatmospheric interior – this must be the only great church in the country where people are employed to vacuum the floor in the wake of the tourists. Seat of the archbishop of York, it is Britain's largest Gothic building and home to countless treasures, not least of which is the world's largest medieval **stained-glass** window and an estimated half of all the medieval stained glass in England. Samuel Johnson, visiting in 1773, was overwhelmed, but not, of course, lost for words, thinking it "an edifice of loftiness and elegance equal to the highest hopes of architecture". In addition to the main body of the church, any complete tour of the building, which took 250 years to complete, should also include the **foundations, crypt, chapter house** and an ascent of the great **central tower**. Once inside, be sure to pick up the *Welcome to York Minster* leaflet, a detailed account of the building. Voluntary guides are also on hand (at the reception desk by the entrance) to offer free **tours** of the interior.

In its earliest incarnation the Minster was probably the wooden chapel used to baptize King Edwin of Northumbria in 627. After its stone successors were destroyed by the Danes, the first significant foundations were laid around 1080 by the first Norman archbishop, Thomas of Bayeux. Subsequent incumbents, notably Archbishop Roger (1154–81), added to the building, and it was from the germ of this Norman church that the present structure emerged. The oldest surviving fabric, in the south transept, dates from 1220 and the reign of Archbishop Walter de Grey, who also began work on a new north transept in 1260. A new chapter house, in the Decorated style, appeared in 1300, and a new nave in the same style was completed in 1338. The Perpendicular choir was realized in 1450 and the western towers in 1472. In 1480, the thirteenth-century central tower, which had collapsed in 1407, was rebuilt, thereby bringing the Minster to more or less its present state.

In the 1960s, in the course of investigating subsidence that had begun to affect the building, it was found that the 20,000-ton, 234ft central tower was resting on only a shallow bed of loose stones, a discovery which prompted a £2-million project that was to involve packing the foundations with thousands of tons of concrete and over six miles of reinforced steel rods. That wasn't the end of the church's troubles, though. In 1984 lightning struck the Minster, unleashing a disastrous fire which raged through the south transept, destroying the timber-framed central vault and all but two of its extraordinary roof bosses.

THE WINDOWS

Nothing else in the Minster can match the magnificence of the stained glass in the nave and transepts. The **West Window** (1338) contains distinctive heart-shaped upper tracery (the "Heart of Yorkshire"), whilst in the nave's north aisle, the second bay window (1155) contains slivers of the oldest stained glass in the country. In the fifth bay, notice the window showing St Peter attended by pilgrims (1312), with the funeral of a monkey among the fascinating details in its lower scenes. Moving down to the crossing, the north transept's **Five Sisters Window** is named after the five fifty-foot lancets, each glazed with thirteenth-century *grisaille*, a distinctive frosted, silvery-grey glass. Opposite, the south transept contains a sixteenth-century, 17,000-piece **Rose Window**, commemorating the 1486 marriage of Henry VII and Elizabeth of York, an alliance which marked the end of the Wars of the Roses.

The greatest of the church's 128 windows, however, is the majestic **East Window** (1405), at 78ft by 31ft the world's largest area of medieval stained glass in a single window. Its themes are the beginning and the end of the world, the upper panels showing scenes from the Old Testament, the lower sections mainly episodes from the book of Revelation. Notice also the glass of the transeptal bays, midway down the south wall of the choir, with their scenes from the lives of saints Cuthbert and William of York. The tombs of William, a twelfth-century archbishop of York, and of Cuthbert, ordained bishop in 685, stood near the high altar until the Reformation, and were credited with numerous miracles.

THE REST OF THE INTERIOR

Before leaving the main body of the interior, give some time to the north transept's four-hundred-year-old wooden clock with its oak knights, and the stone **choir screen**, knotted with incredibly intricate carvings and decorated with life-size figures of English monarchs from William I to Henry VI – all except the latter carved in the last quarter of the fifteenth century. Most of the choir dates from restorations following a fire in 1829. The painted **stone shields** round much of the nave and choir are those of Edward II and the barons who in 1309–10 held a "parliament" in York. Amongst the many tombs, those of most interest are the monument in the south transept to Walter de Grey, a beautiful grey-green canopy protecting a recumbent stone figure, and the tomb of the ten-year-old William, second son of Edward III, in the choir aisle.

Be sure also to go down to the **crypt** (60p), the spot that transmits the most powerful sense of antiquity, as it contains portions of Archbishop Roger's choir and sections of the 1080 church, including pillars with fine Romanesque capitals. The font stands over the supposed site of Paulinus's timber chapel, while a small illuminated doorway opens onto the base of a pillar belonging to the guardhouse of the original Roman camp.

The foundations, or **undercroft** (£1.80), are more intriguing still. Most of the area's seven separate chambers have been turned into a museum, fitted into a space excavated during the restorations in the 1960s, whose concrete consequences contrast with capitals, sculpture and fabric from the present Minster, its Norman predecessor and the ancient Roman fort. Fragments of the last include the tribune where Constantine the Great was probably proclaimed emperor, the basis of the museum's claim that you can "Walk Where World History Was Made". Amongst precious church relics in the adjoining treasury are silver plate found in Walter de Grey's tomb and the eleventh-century *Horn of Ulf*, presented to the Minster by a relative of the tide-turning King Canute.

Access to the foundations is from the south transept, also the entrance to the **central tower** (£2), which you can climb for rooftop views over the city. Finally pop into the **Chapter House** (70p), an architectural novelty whose buttressed octagonal walls remove the need for a central pillar, otherwise a common feature of this type of building.

Around the Minster

Past the Minster's west front a gateway leads into **Dean's Park**, a quiet green oasis bordered by a seven-arched fragment of arcade from the Norman archbishop's palace and by **York Minster Library** (Mon–Fri 9am–5pm; free), housed in the thirteenth-century chapel of the same palace. Among its more interesting exhibits is the baptismal entry for Guy Fawkes (dated April 16, 1570), removed from **St Michael-le-Belfrey** on High Petergate (open for Sunday services only), immediately south of the Minster. The church was built in 1536 and is bursting with seventeenth-century brasses and medieval stained glass.

Walk through Dean's Park with the Minster on your right, then through the gate at the top to reach the **Treasurer's House** in Chapter House Street (Easter–Oct daily except Fri 10.30am–4.30pm; £3.50; NT), a glorious seventeenth-century town house that stands on the site of houses used by the Minster's treasurers until the Dissolution. Now owned by the National Trust, it offers exhibitions and videos which trace the site's changing fortunes, together with the paintings and furniture of industrialist Frank Green, who lived here from 1895 to 1930. There's a nice café on site, too.

Just around the corner in College Street stands **St William's College** (daily 10am–5pm; 60p), an eye-catching half-timbered building studded with oriel windows, initially dedicated to the great-grandson of William the Conqueror (first archbishop of York) and built in its present guise in 1467 for the Minster's chantry priests. During Charles I's three-year residence it served time as the Royal Mint and the king's printing press. These days it serves as a visitor centre for the Minster and a conference hall and banqueting centre, though three of the medieval rooms are open for viewing provided they're not in use.

The walls

Although much restored, the city's superb **walls** date mainly from the fourteenth century, though fragments of Norman work survive, particularly in the gates (or "bars"), whilst the northern sections still follow the line of the Roman ramparts. The only break in the walls is east of Monk Bar, where the city was first protected by the marshes of the River Foss and later by the deliberately flooded area known as King's Pool.

Monk Bar at the northern end of Goodramgate is as good a point of access as any, tallest of the city's four main gates and host to a small **Richard III Museum** (daily March–Oct 9am–5pm, Nov–Feb 9am–4pm; £1), where you're invited to decide on the guilt or innocence of England's most maligned king. For just a taste of the walls' best section – with great views of the Minster and swathes of idyllic-looking gardens – take the ten-minute stroll west from Monk Bar to Exhibition Square (see below) and **Bootham Bar**, the only gate on the site of a Roman gateway and marking the traditional northern entrance to the city. A stroll round the walls' entire two-and-a-half-mile length will take you past the southwestern **Micklegate Bar**, long considered the most important of the gates since it, in turn, marked the start of the road to London. It was built to a Norman design reputedly using ancient stone coffins as building stone, and was later used to exhibit the heads of executed criminals and rebels. The engaging **Micklegate Bar Museum** (daily 10am–dusk; £1.50) occupies a surviving fortified tower and tells the story by way of old lithographs, models, paintings and the odd gruesome skull. **Walmgate Bar** in the east is the best preserved and has traditionally been the city's strongest bar. It was unsuccessfully undermined by the Roundheads during the Civil War, its present slight sag said to be a consequence of that episode.

Goodramgate and the Shambles

East of Goodramgate, in a labyrinth of quiet residential streets centred on Aldwark, is clustered a series of good-looking historic buildings. **Bedern Hall**, a medieval lodging and refectory for the Minster's priests, and the plain-faced **St Anthony's Hall**, can be walked past pretty quickly, though the half-timbered **Black Swan Inn** down on Peasholme Green beckons for a drink (see p.805), while the **Merchant Taylors' Hall** (April–Oct Tues only 10am–4pm; free) is a similar picture of late-medieval perfection. The Merchant Taylors' guild took upon itself the job of establishing a weaving work-house to prevent "laytering and ydleness of vacabunds and poor follc"; a small upstairs museum explains their good work. At the south end of Goodramgate, **Our Lady's Row**, the oldest houses in the city (1316), stands hard against **Holy Trinity** (March–Oct Tues–Sat 9.30am–5.30pm; Nov–April Tues–Sat 9.30am–4pm; free), a much altered fifteenth-century church known for its east window, jumbled box pews and saddle-back tower, an unusual feature in English churches.

The Shambles, off King's Square at the southern end of Goodramgate, could be taken as the epitome of medieval York, though the crowds and self-conscious quaint-ness take the edge off what would otherwise be a perfect medieval thoroughfare. Flagstoned, almost impossibly narrow and lined with perilously leaning timber-framed houses, it was the home of York's butchers, its erstwhile stench and squalor now diffi-cult to imagine, though old meat hooks still adorn the odd house. At no. 35, there's a **shrine** (closed to the public) to Margaret Clitherow, the Catholic wife of a butcher, mar-tyred in 1586 for allegedly sheltering priests; she was pressed to death with rocks piled on top of a board on the city's Ouse Bridge. Newgate **market** (daily 8am–5pm) lies off the Shambles, together with the core of the city's shopping streets; **Parliament Street** sees a couple of outdoor markets a year, usually in high summer and a month before Christmas.

Exhibition Square

Exhibition Square, outside Bootham Bar, holds the city's main tourist office in the De Grey Rooms, opposite which stands the **City Art Gallery** (Mon–Sat 10am–5pm, Sun 2.30–5pm; free), an extensive collection of British, early Italian and northern European paintings. Most are decidedly second-division, but the gallery puts on a year-round series of excellent special exhibitions, and is noted for its collections of British studio pottery and twentieth-century British painters like Gwen John, Stanley Spencer and Walter Sickert.

Left of the gallery as you face it stands **King's Manor**, founded in 1270 and enlarged in 1490 to provide lodgings for the abbot of nearby St Mary's Abbey. After the Dissolution it was ceded to the lord president of the Council of the North, effectively making it northern England's royal headquarters: Henry VIII, James I and Charles I all stayed here. It's now owned by the university, but the courtyard is usually open if you want a peek inside.

The Yorkshire Museum and St Mary's Abbey

South of Exhibition Square on Museum Street stands the entrance to the **Yorkshire Museum** (April–Oct daily 10am–5pm; Nov–March Mon–Sat 10am–5pm, Sun 1–5pm; £3.60), which lies within the beautifully laid-out grounds of St Mary's Abbey, itself now in ruins. It's one of York's better museums, with changing temporary exhibitions aimed largely at kids, but otherwise strong on archeological remains which it presents in a series of rooms examining the Roman presence in the city – grave effects, cooking utensils in a reconstructed Roman kitchen, glassware, farming equipment and jew-ellery all illustrate the sophistication of life in the provincial capital of "Lower Britain". There are impressive displays of Viking and Anglo-Saxon artefacts, too, though chief exhibit is the fifteenth-century Middleham Jewel, found near Middleham Castle (see p.777) in 1985 – a diamond-shaped jewel with an oblong sapphire, claimed as the finest piece of Gothic jewellery in England.

Part of the museum basement incorporates the fireplace and chapter house of **St Mary's Abbey**, whose ruins lie around the Museum Gardens, the abbey's former grounds (abbey and gardens free). Founded around 1080, the abbey later became an important Benedictine foundation, additionally significant as it was from here that disenchanted monks fled to found Fountains Abbey (see p.788). The fact that the abbey controlled the city's brothels at the time can hardly have helped the Benedictine cause. The church (1259) and gatehouse are both reasonably well preserved, but this is really a spot to come for time out from the sightseeing. For a good extended stroll drop down to the river at Lendal Bridge for a quiet walk to Water End Bridge.

Lendal and St Helen's Square

The street called **Lendal** cuts down from Museum Street to **St Helen's Square** – marking the entrance to the Roman city – and the York institution that is **Betty's** tearooms (see p.804), where you're close to a brace of impressive historic buildings. The Georgian **Mansion House** (1725), in St Helen's Square, is the private home of the city's mayor, and is consequently open only to guided tours by prior arrangement (call ☎01904/552012). However, you can visit the six-hundred-year-old **Guildhall** (May–Oct Mon–Fri 9am–5pm, Sat 10am–5pm, Sun 2–5pm; Nov–April Mon–Fri 9am–5pm; free) behind, which was almost totally destroyed by bombing in 1942, but has since been restored to an almost mirror image of its original, timber-roofed state, though only one of the fourteen magnificent Victorian stained-glass windows remains. Back up Blake Street from the square, have a look too inside the **Grand Assembly Rooms**, built between 1732 and 1736 by the third earl of Burlington. An epicentre of chic during York's eighteenth-century social heyday, the building attempted to emulate London's grander salons; its 52-columned Central Hall is a tribute to the Egyptian Hall of the capital's Mansion House. The Rooms are now occupied by a smart café/restaurant (usually daily 10am–5pm and some evenings; occasionally closed for functions; call ☎01904/637254 for details), so for the price of a cup of coffee you can peruse the ornate marbled interior. Be sure to search the rotunda's mural of Roman York, in which Burlington had himself painted as Constantine the Great.

Back at St Helen's Square, **Stonegate** leads northeast towards the Minster, a street as ancient as the city itself. Originally the Via Praetoria of Roman York, it's now paved with thick flags of York stone, which were once carried along here to build the Minster, hence the street name. Guy Fawkes' parents lived on Stonegate (there's a plaque opposite *Mulberry Hall*) and its Tudor houses retain their considerable charm – an alley at no. 52A leads to the scant remains of a twelfth-century Norman stone house, a rarity in England.

South to the Jorvik Viking Centre

Coney Street, Davygate, Parliament Street and all the alleys and streets off and in between heave shoulder-to-shoulder most of the year with shoppers. There's not much to stop for until you reach the entrance to the **Merchant Adventurers' Hall**, off Fossgate (mid-March to mid-Nov daily 8.30am–5pm; mid-Nov to mid-March Mon–Sat 8.30am–3.30pm; £1.90), where the overpowering whiff of wood polish prepares you for one of the finest medieval timber-framed halls in Europe. The beautiful building was raised by the city's most powerful guild, dealers in wool from the Wolds, woollens from the Dales and lead from the Pennines, commodities that were traded for exotica from far and wide. An icon brought back from Russia gives some idea of the organization's commercial scope. Antique fairs are held in the undercroft most Saturdays throughout the year.

The last clutch of historic attractions and sights fills the streets between the hall, castle and river. Castlegate throws up the **York Story**, a heritage centre housed in the former St Mary's Church (Mon–Sat 10am–5pm, Sun 1–5pm; £1.90; joint ticket with Castle Museum £5.95), with a video introduction to the city among other less than gripping exhibits. You may get more out of the adjacent **Fairfax House**, also on Castlegate (Mon–Thurs & Sat 11am–5pm, Sun 1.30–5pm; open Fri too in Aug & Sept; £3.75), an elegant Georgian town house restored to take an eighteenth-century collection of fine arts left by Noel Terry, scion of one of the city's chocolate dynasties.

These though are all small -fry compared to the blockbuster exhibit that is Coppergate's horrendously over-visited **Jorvik Viking Centre** (daily April–Oct 9am–7pm; Nov–March 9am–5.30pm; last admission 2hr before closing; £4.99), a multi-million-pound affair that takes you on a twenty-minute "time-car" ride back through time to experience the sights, smells and sounds of a riverside Viking village – with the voice of Magnus Magnusson for company. It's actually not bad, given its populist slant, and kids certainly get their money's worth with the contents of Viking toilets to examine and a costume box for dressing up. You need to get here bang on opening time to have any chance of beating the queues (though a timed-ticket system means you can always come back later at a pre-arranged time), and leave time to potter around the museum, devoted to artefacts found during excavations of Coppergate's real Viking village, now lost beneath the shopping centre outside.

It's worth noting that the museum organizes York's annual **Viking Festival** every February when themed events take place throughout the city – details from the Festival Office at the centre. You may also want to move on to the associated Archeological Resource Centre, or **ARC**, housed in the medieval church of St Saviour, St Savioursgate (Mon–Fri 10am–3.30pm, Sat 1–3.30pm; £3.60), close to the Shambles, a hands-on archeology centre – the only one of its kind in the country – where you can grapple with everything from old bones to computers to build up a picture of Viking and Roman life.

York Castle and the Castle Museum

Despite the rich architectural heritage elsewhere in the city, there's precious little left of **York Castle**, one of two established by William the Conqueror. Only the perilously leaning **Clifford's Tower** (daily Easter–Sept 10am–6pm, July & Aug open until 7.30pm; Oct–Easter 10am–4pm or dusk; £1.80; EH) remains, as evocative a piece of military engineering as you could wish for: a stark and isolated stone keep built on one of William's mottes between 1245 and 1262. The old Norman keep was destroyed in 1109 during one of the city's more shameful historical episodes, when 150 Jews were put inside the tower for their own protection during an outburst of anti-Semitic rioting. The move did little to appease the mob, however, and faced with starvation or slaughter the Jews committed mass suicide by setting the tower on fire.

Immediately east of the tower lies the excellent **Castle Museum** (April–Oct Mon–Sat 9.30am–5.30pm, Sun 10am–5.30pm; Nov–March Mon–Sat 9.30am–4pm, Sun 10am–4pm; £4.75), a remarkable collection founded by a Dr Kirk of Pickering, who realized, even eighty years ago, that many of the everyday items used in rural areas were in danger of disappearing. He took the unusual step of accepting bric-a-brac from his patients in lieu of fees. When the pile of miscellanea grew too large for his own home it was housed in the old Debtors' Prison and Female Prison, the former, incidentally, where the famous highwayman Dick Turpin spent his last night on earth. A whole range of early craft, folk and agricultural ephemera is complemented by costumes, militaria, workshops, two entire reconstructed streets and special exhibitions on subjects as diverse as chocolate and fire engines. In particular, look for the lovely corridor of old hearths and fireplaces, Kirk's fetishistic collections of truncheons and biscuit moulds – surely unsurpassed – and some magnificently archaic televisions and washing machines. Be certain to follow the museum's marked itinerary, though note that it's easy to miss the guiding arrows near the museum shop that take you upstairs for the military displays and the rambling dungeons and period rooms, all of which are well worth seeing. Pride of place is given to a dazzling Viking helmet, discovered during the Coppergate excavations and the only one of its kind ever found.

The National Railway Museum

The **National Railway Museum** on Leeman Road (daily 10am–6pm; £5; ☎01904/621261), ten minutes' walk from the station, is a must if you have even the slightest interest in railways, history, engineering or Victoriana. It was the first national museum to open outside London and contains a stunning collection. The Great Hall alone features some fifty restored locomotives dating from 1829 onwards, among them the *Mallard*, at 126mph the world's fastest steam engine; its record-speed run wrecked the engine, and it had to be towed back to base. The South Hall, a former goods station, complete with tracks and platforms, holds the major permanent exhibitions, where you can see the plush splendour of the royal carriages ("Palaces on Wheels") and the bleak segregation of classes in the Victorian coaches. Take a walk through the 1938 dining car and then take a break on the platform at the *Brief Encounter* café. Dotted around the hall is a welter of miscellaneous memorabilia: posters, models, paintings and period photographs, even a lock of George Stephenson's hair. Elsewhere, the interactive Magician's Road gallery teaches you how to shunt, brake, drive and signal, and there are free loco rides in the school holidays for kids. New projects include a walk-round backstage storage area of the museum's reserve collection, and visits to the engineering workshop and a track-and-signal viewing area which has been established over the East Coast main line.

GEORGE HUDSON

It would be hard to find a better caricature of a Victorian business baron than the portly and bewhiskered "Railway King" **George Hudson** (1800–71), a perfect symbol of all the fortitude and failings of Victorian capitalism. Starting out as he meant to go on, Hudson was sent away from home in disgrace at the age of fifteen. Soon afterwards he became apprenticed to a York draper, married the boss's daughter and then quickly inherited the business when his father-in-law was found drowned in the Ouse in mysterious circumstances. Another £30,000 came his way from a great-uncle in 1827, Hudson having spent many days at his relative's deathbed, during which time the will was altered in his favour. The windfall was ploughed into North Midland Railway shares, the basis of his subsequent empire, and a stepping stone to a career in local politics which saw him become councillor, alderman and ultimately – in 1837 – Lord Mayor of York.

He seized the main chance in 1833, as the rail network crept closer to York, offering local landowners huge tranches of cut-price shares to allow the railways to cross their land. With the gentry in his pockets his business boomed, and by 1844 he controlled 1016 miles of track – the largest network under single ownership until rail nationalization – and was elected MP for Sunderland a year later. In one typical move he managed to buy the Whitby and Pickering Railway in 1845 for £80,000 – £25,000 less than it had cost to build.

Hudson's empire continued to expand, but only by paying artificially high dividends to his shareholders. When his stocks, which had made countless paper fortunes, failed to go on rising, nemesis was just round the corner. Investigations and law suits brought by disgruntled investors revealed untold dubious business deals and in 1849 Hudson was forced to resign the directorship of his six companies. A ruined man, he was committed to York's Debtors' Prison, able to afford only one meal a day, before being rescued by a small pension offered by a hard core of loyal shareholders. York, for its part, chose to forget the undoubted wealth Hudson's railways had brought the city, shunning its former hero until 1968, when a street and offices near the station were given his name.

Eating and drinking

It's impossible to walk more than about fifty yards in central York without coming across either a pub, teashop, café or restaurant – Defoe put it down to the "abundance of good company . . . and good families", though these days it's the tourist and student pound which fires the commercial engines. In keeping with much else in the city, many establishments are relentlessly and self-consciously old-fashioned, though there are some real highlights – truly historic **pubs**, the remarkable *Betty's*, the ultimate **teashop** experience, and a scattering of well-regarded **restaurants**. There's a sense of solid Yorkshire worth in most establishments – no trendy Mediterranean Leeds café society here – and provided you pick and choose carefully, you can avoid much of the tourist-aimed dross that passes for budget eating and drinking.

Tearooms and cafés

The Bar Convent, Blossom Street, at Nunnery Lane. Beautiful Georgian surroundings for a combined museum of early Christianity and an airy café with a lovely garden serving sandwiches and inventive lunches. Mon–Sat 9.30am–5pm.

Betty's, 6–8 St Helen's Square. If there are tea shops in heaven they'll be like *Betty's*, a York institution founded in 1919, with an Art Nouveau cladding and a permanent queue waiting for seats, despite the (relatively) high prices. There are a dozen or so fish and meat hot dishes, some extraordinary puddings, and a shop where you can buy fine-grade teas and coffees, and some of the teashop staples – like pikelets and Yorkshire fat rascals. Daily 9am–9pm.

Blake Head Vegetarian Café, 104 Micklegate. Bookstore-café with patio for freshly baked cakes, pâtés, quiche, brunch, salads and soups – a favoured student hangout. Mon–Fri 10am–4.30pm, Sat 10am–5pm.

Mulberry Hall Coffee Shop, Stonegate. Wend through the fifteenth-century house, now York's poshest china and glassware shop, for fine snacks in snazzy surroundings. Mon–Sat 10am–5pm.

National Trust York Tearooms, 30 Goodramgate. A slickly run place just 200 yards from the Minster, serving snacks and light meals; sample one of Yorkshire's noted "fruit wines" while you're here. Mon–Sat 10am–5pm.

Petergate Fisheries, Low Petergate, at Church St. You can get fish and chips in most York cafés, but this spot – in business for 85 years – has the best, sit-down or takeaway. Mon–Sat noon–10pm.

The Rockwell Rooms, Stonegate Walk, Stonegate. Atrium pavement café and brasserie, within a heritage shopping development built on the site of the city's medieval stained-glass works. Daily: summer 9am–9pm, winter 9am–5pm.

Spurriergate Centre, St Michael's Church, Spurriergate. Quiche, salads and baked potatoes served in the impressive interior of twelfth-century St Michael's. Closed Sun.

Taylor's, 46 Stonegate. Owned by *Betty's* and in the same league; over 100 years old, it's the picture of a classic tea shop, serving more substantial dishes, too, like fish and chips and a grilled breakfast. Daily 9am–5.30pm.

Treasurer's House, Minster Yard. Superior tearoom in the cellars of a National Trust property. Easter–Oct daily except Fri 10.30am–4.30pm

Restaurants

Café Rouge, 52 Low Petergate (☎01904/673293). French snacks and meals, from breakfast to dinner, in a relaxed city-centre location. Moderate.

Melton's, 7 Scarcroft Rd (☎01904/634341). Simple, classy cooking, including very good fish dishes, and imaginative vegetarian food – Tuesdays and Thursdays have the best non-meat choices. Set lunch and early-bird deals too. Closed Mon lunch & Sun dinner. Expensive.

Oscar's, 8 Little Stonegate (☎01904/652002). Bustling bar-bistro with a nice courtyard for alfresco eating, which is about its best feature since the food (grills, pasta, burgers and the like) rarely reaches the heights. Inexpensive to Moderate.

La Piazza, 45 Goodramgate (☎01904/642641). Authentic Italian coffee bar out front, courtyard restaurant out back, tucked into a nice Tudor building. Proper pizzas, Italian pop music and friendly family staff. Inexpensive to Moderate.

Pierre Victoire, 2 Lendal (☎01904/655222). You know what to expect in this chain brasserie, but it delivers every time – especially with the unbeatable two-course lunch for six quid. Moderate.

Pizza Express, River House, 17 Museum St. Grand old riverside club rooms with sought-after balcony, the venue for *Pizza Express*'s usual menu of good-quality pizzas. Inexpensive to Moderate.

The Rubicon, 5–7 Little Stonegate (☎01904/676076). All the veggie classics – nut roast among them – in a laid-back wholefood restaurant. Closed Sun lunch. Inexpensive to Moderate.

St William's College Restaurant, 3 College St (☎01904/634830). Candlelight and jazz in a historic building bang next door to the Minster: the food has Mediterranean hankerings, with the restaurant part of the operation closing at 9.30pm, and on Sundays; otherwise a superior café during the day. Moderate.

19 Grape Lane, 19 Grape Lane (☎01904/636366). Cramped but renowned town-house restaurant serving top-quality modern British dishes, including some great puddings. Lunch deals bring the price into most people's range. Closed Sun. Expensive.

Pubs

Bay Horse, 55 Blossom St. Unspoilt pub, full of hideaway corners and bric-a-brac, situated out through Micklegate Bar.

Black Swan, Peasholme Green. York's oldest (sixteenth-century) pub and a Grade II listed building with some superb stone -flagging and wood panelling. Home of the city's folk club.

Golden Ball, Cromwell Rd, Bishophill. Perhaps the city centre's nicest and most archetypal "local", with an attractive beer garden tucked away at the back. It's just two minutes from the river and the *Bonding Warehouse*.

Hole in the Wall, High Petergate. Very close to the Minster, yet rarely crowded, this pleasant, stripped-down retreat is something of a find in the city centre.

Judge's Lodging Cellar Bar, 9 Lendal. Cosy drinking hole with good beer, in the eighteenth-century cellars of the *Judge's Lodging*, now a smart hotel.

King's Arms, King's Staithe. Close to the Ouse Bridge, this pub has a fine riverside setting with outdoor tables – and accordingly gets very busy in summer.

Royal Oak, 18 Goodramgate. Good beer in a touristy sixteenth-century pub conveniently situated between the Minster and Monk's Bar.

Spread Eagle, 98 Walmgate. One of the city's most popular old-fashioned pubs, known for its good beer and live bands.

Tap & Spile, Monkgate. Traditional bare-bones pub with a great range of real ales.

Ye Olde Starre, Stonegate. Vies with the *Black Swan* for historic precedence, but although there's good beer, a cramped beer garden and plenty of atmosphere it's too central and thus too crowded for prolonged enjoyment.

Nightlife and entertainment

There are healthy helpings of **live music** and **nightlife**, much of it detailed in free weekly handouts like *York What's On* and *YourKmusic*. Most bigger bands bypass the city in favour of Leeds, though the Barbican Centre pulls in its fair share of major mainstream artists, while the pub **music scene** flourishes; the best places are listed below. The themed Irish pubs like *O'Neill's* on Low Ousegate and *Scruffy Murphy's* at Micklegate Bar can also usually be relied upon for some weekend faux-folk high-jinks. **Clubbing** is a bit of a disaster in York – you know, with names like *Toffs* and *Ziggy's*, that the northern club revolution has yet to hit the city – but there are one-offs at the York Arts Centre and elsewhere worth keeping an eye on the listings magazines for.

Cultural entertainment is wide and varied, with the city supporting a couple of arts centres and theatres, cinemas and regular classical music recitals, often in the city's churches and the York Minster itself. The annual **Early Music Festival**, held in July, is perhaps the best of its kind in Britain, with dozens of events spread over ten days – details are available on ☎01904/658338 or from the tourist offices. The famous **York Mystery Plays** are held every four years – next performances are in 2004.

Live music

Barbican Centre, Barbican Road (☎01904/656688). Country, rock, folk and MOR stalwarts all appear here sooner or later.

Black Swan, Peasholme Green (☎01904/632922). Regular Thursday folk nights with a full range of quality bands and singer-songwriters.

Bonding Warehouse, Skeldergate, by the bridge (☎01904/622527). Live bands several times a week in a fine riverside venue – and good for a drink at other times.

The Cells, 32 Parliament St (☎01904/679993). The city's old police cells now in business as an atmospheric café-bar, with acoustic music and jazz several nights a week.

Fibbers, Stonebow (☎01904/651250). A sister venue to the *Duchess* in Leeds, with indie bands playing most nights of the week.

Punch Bowl Inn, Stonegate (☎01904/622305). Pub venue for jazz and blues, a couple of nights a week.

Cinema, theatre and the arts

Cinema: the city-centre screens are at the Odeon, Blossom St (☎01904/623287, info line ☎01426/954742), but the best venue is the out-of-town Warner Brothers multiplex at Clifton Moor (☎01904/691199).

Grand Opera House, Cumberland Street, at Clifford Street (☎01904/671818). Musicals, ballet and family entertainment in all its guises.

Theatre Royal, St Leonard's Place (☎01904/623568). Musicals, pantos and mainstream theatre, as well as a nice café-bar.

York Arts Centre, Micklegate (☎01904/627129). Independent theatre productions, as well as gigs, poetry, and dance.

Listings

Banks and exchange Most main banks are in and around St Helen's Square. American Express, 6 Stonegate (☎01904/670030); Thomas Cook, 31 Stonegate (☎01904/644344), 4 Nessgate (☎01904/639928) and inside Midland Bank on Parliament St (☎01904/626770). You can also change money at the tourist offices.

Bike rental Bob Trotter, 13–15 Lord Mayor's Walk, at Monkgate (☎01904/622868); Cycle Scene, 2 Ratcliffe St (☎01904/653286); and York Cycleworks, 14–16 Lawrence St (☎01904/626664). Rates from around £10 per day, plus a £50 deposit.

Bus information National Express (☎0990/808080); East Yorkshire (☎01482/327146) for Hull, Beverley and Bridlington; Harrogate & District (☎01423/566061) for Knaresborough, Harrogate, Ilkley and Skipton; Stagecoach Cumberland (☎01946/63222) to the Lake District; Yorkshire Coastliner for Leeds, Castle Howard, Pickering, Scarborough and Whitby (☎01653/692556).

Car rental Avis (☎01904/610460); Budget (☎01904/644919); Eurodollar (☎01904/612141); Hertz (☎01904/612586); Kenning (☎01904/659328); Peugeot Car Rental (☎01904/638032).

Hospital York District Hospital, Wigginton Road (24hr emergency number ☎01904/631313; bus #1, #2 or #3.

Police Fulford Rd (☎01904/631321).

Post Office The main office is at 22 Lendal (☎01904/617285).

Taxis Station Taxis (☎01904/623332); York Taxis (☎01904/631161).

Train information National Rail Enquiries ☎0345/484950.

Castle Howard

Immersed in the deep countryside of the Howardian Hills, fifteen miles northeast of York, off the A64, **Castle Howard** (March–Oct daily 11am–5pm; gardens open at 10am; £7; grounds only £4.50; ☎01904/648333) is the seat of one of England's leading aristocratic families and among the country's grandest stately homes. Since providing the setting for the television version of *Brideshead Revisited*, the house's car parks have been packed every weekend, but fitting it into a public transport itinerary is something of a problem. In summer there are just two Yorkshire Coastliner buses a day (1 on Sun) from York, and three (1 on Sun) from Malton and Pickering, but various bus tours from York can bring you out and back, too.

The colossal main house was designed by **Sir John Vanbrugh** in 1699 and was almost forty years in the making – remarkable enough, were it not for the fact that Vanbrugh was, at the start of the commission at least, best known as a playwright. He had no formal architectural training and seems to have been chosen by Charles Howard, third Earl of Carlisle, for whom the house was built, purely on the strength of his membership of the same London gentlemen's club. Shrewdly, Vanbrugh recognized his limitations and called upon the assistance of Nicholas Hawksmoor, who had a major part in the house's structural design – the pair later worked successfully together on Blenheim Palace. If Hawksmoor's guiding hand can be seen throughout, Vanbrugh's influence is clear in the very theatricality of the building, notably in the palatial **Great Hall**. This was gutted by fire in the 1940s, but has subsequently been restored from old etchings and photographs to something approaching its original state. The rest of the house is full of furniture by Sheraton and Chippendale, paintings by the likes of Gainsborough, Veronese, Rubens and Van Dyck, and room after room of decorative excess – all trinkety objets d'art, gaudy friezes and monumental pilasters.

Vanbrugh soon turned his attention to the estate's thousand-acre **grounds** where he could indulge his playful inclinations to excess, and the formal gardens, clipped parkland, towers, obelisks and blunt sandstone follies stretch in all directions, sloping gently to a large artifical lake. He completed the **Temple of the Four Winds** before his death in 1726, leaving Hawskmoor to design the Howard family **Mausoleum**, which is taller than the house itself. Take a look, too, at the fine **stables** which have been converted into the Costume and Regalia Gallery, Britain's largest private collection of period clothes. There's a **café** here, and another by the lake, as well as a children's playground, nature trails and all the modern paraphernalia of an English stately home.

Eden Camp

Further along the A64 from the Castle Howard turn-off, **Eden Camp** (daily 10am–5pm, last admission 4pm; £3.50; ☎01653/697777), a World War II museum sited within a former POW camp, is the winner of a recent Museum of the Year award, and makes for another good day out from York. It's eighteen miles northeast of the city at Malton, at the junction of the A169 to Pickering. Originally built in 1942 to house Italian and, later, German POWs captured in the North Africa campaigns, the barracks and buildings have been re-equipped to tell the story of what it dubs "The Peoples' War". Walk-through exhibits and tableaux deal with topics like rationing, air raids, evacuees, the Home Guard, the Land Army, munitions and the various branches of the services. Most visitors need around three hours to get around everything.

Hull, the Humber and the East Yorkshire coast

Generations of Yorkshire people, born and bred in the historic **East Riding**, were outraged to wake up one morning and find themselves part of "Humberside", just one of the notorious local government conveniences created by the 1974 bastardization of the English counties. Consequently, there was almost universal rejoicing when the Lincolnshire adjuncts from across the **River Humber** were dropped in 1996 and towns like **Hull** could once again revel in their Yorkshire ancestry. The region's character has been shaped by a strong seafaring tradition, boosted by Hull's advantageous position on the Humber estuary. Northeast, up the **East Yorkshire coast**, lonely beaches, wild foreshores and forgotten seafront villages draw curious tourists keen to get off the beaten track a little. The bucket-and-spade resorts of **Bridlington** and **Filey** have gently declined over the years and are now rather melancholy places, but there's nothing disappointing about the cliffs of **Flamborough Head**, one of the best places in Britain for birdwatching. Inland, this part of the county is defined by the flatlands that stretch northwards from Hull to meet the **Yorkshire Wolds**, a crescent-shaped ridge of hills that falls to the sea at Flamborough. Historic **Beverley**, with its marvellous Minster, can be easily reached by **buses** from Hull (or York), while Hull is also linked to Doncaster by the main London–York **train** line; a branch line links Hull and Beverley with Bridlington, Filey and Scarborough, further up the coast. Drivers approaching from Lincolnshire and the south will cross the famous **Humber Bridge**, opened in 1981, the world's longest single-span suspension bridge; a viewing area allows you stop and gasp. Hull also makes the start of Sustrans' National Cycle Network **Hull to Harwich** east coast route, a 370-mile cycle route, detailed in two separate route maps available from Sustrans (see p.44).

Hull

HULL's most famous adopted son, the poet and university librarian Philip Larkin, wrote "I wish I could think of just one nice thing to tell you about Hull, oh yes . . . *it's very nice and flat for cycling,*" capturing something of the character of a town which reaches few heights, physical or otherwise. The town – rarely known by its full grandiose title of **Kingston-upon-Hull** – undoubtedly suited the poet's curmudgeonly temperament, but he might have mentioned Hull's self-reliant and no-nonsense atmosphere (qualities reflected in abundance in the contemporary town's most famous resident, local MP and Deputy Prime Minister John Prescott), or that the restored docks and old town centre are surprisingly appealing.

Hull's **maritime** pre-eminence dates back to 1299, when it was laid out as a seaport by Edward I. It quickly became England's leading harbour, and was still a vital garrison when the gates were closed against Charles I in 1642, the first serious act of rebellion of what was to become the English Civil War. Daniel Defoe visited the town several times in the early eighteenth century, part of the travels that were later to spawn his encyclopedic *Tour Through the Whole Island of Britain*; despite thinking it "second rate", he remembered Hull well enough to have Robinson Crusoe set sail from here on his fateful voyage. A commemorative plaque to the shipwrecked mariner stands in the town's Queen's Gardens.

The central **Princes Dock** sets the tone for Hull's modern refurbishment, the once abandoned waters now lined by landscaped brick promenades and overlooked by Princes Quay, a multi-tier, glass-spangled shopping centre, with the revamped **marina** beyond. To reach the marina, you'll need to cross busy Castle Street, where the decommissioned **Spurn Lightship**, once moored off Spurn Head (see p.812), is docked.

The town's maritime legacy is exhaustively detailed in the excellent **Town Docks Museum** (Mon–Sat 10am–5pm, Sun 1.30–4.30pm; free), housed in the Neoclassical headquarters of the former Hull Docks Company, flanking the east side of Queen Victoria Square, immediately north of Princes Quay. The main boost to the town's coffers in the eighteenth and nineteenth centuries was whaling, and the museum tells the story well, displaying gruesome whaling equipment, such as a blubber pot cauldron, alongside model ships, old photographs, Inuit relics and a whale skeleton; Hull whalers pursued the right whale in their thousands, so known because it was the "right" whale to catch for commercial purposes. There are also displays about whale species and conservation, examples of the maritime art of "scrimshandering" – the ornate carving of whale bone and walrus tusk by bored sailors – and yet more rooms detailing trawling methods, and Hull's long relationship with the Humber. More marine art lurks across the square in the **Ferens Art Gallery** (Mon–Sat 10am–5pm, Sun 1.30–4.30pm; free), distinguished by twentieth-century British pieces and the odd Constable, Frans Hals and Canaletto. Temporary exhibitions highlight various themes throughout the year.

Leave Queen Victoria Square on its east side by pedestrianized Whitefriar Gate, turn right on Trinity House Lane after two hundred yards, and you're in front of **Holy Trinity** (Tues & Fri 10am–4pm, Sat 9.30am–4pm; plus Wed & Thurs noon–4pm Easter–Sept; free), among the largest and most pleasing parish churches in the country, notable for its brick transepts and chancel. This area is traditionally home to Hull's market traders: there's an indoor **market hall** (Mon–Sat 7.30am–5pm) across from the church, with another entrance on Trinity House Lane, and an **open market** held next to the church (Tues, Fri & Sat 9am–4pm). Across Market Place is perhaps Hull's most revered relic – the **Old Grammar School**, a redbrick edifice built in 1583 and which for 120 years doubled as the town's Merchant Adventurers' Hall. As a school, it numbered amongst its pupils William Wilberforce, instigator of the abolition of slavery in the British Empire, and seventeenth-century poet Andrew Marvell, also MP for Hull. (Hull-born Stevie Smith, incidentally, completes the town's poetic triumvirate.) The building now incorporates an educational resource centre called **Hands On History** (Sat 10am–5pm, Sun 1.30–4.30pm; school holidays daily 10am–5pm; free), which is aimed at schoolchildren, though the public is free to pop in to see the displays and archives.

Two blocks east you hit the **High Street**, whose crop of older buildings and narrow cobbled alleys have seen it designated an "Old Town Conservation Area". At its northern end stands **Wilberforce House** (Mon–Sat 10am–5pm, Sun 1.30–4.30pm; free), containing some useful exhibits on slavery and its abolition. The Georgian houses next door have also been restored to house various period collections from the local archives, in particular the town's celebrated silver collection. The **Streetlife Transport Museum** (Mon–Sat 10am–5pm, Sun 1.30–4.30pm; free) is here on the High Street too, re iving the days of horse-drawn carriages, trams and steam engines. Just behind it, on the River Hull, a reconditioned fishing vessel, the **Arctic Corsair** is open for guided tours (Easter–Oct Wed 10am–4pm, Sun 1.30–4.30pm; guided tours on the hour; £1.50). All of Hull's **museums** have the same telephone information number (☎01482/613902).

Guided tours around the old town (April–Oct, Mon, Wed, Thurs, Fri & Sat at 2pm; £2.50) depart from the tourist office (see below), or you can pick up one of the self-guided trail leaflets which, in the case of the "Fish Pavement" tour, can raise a wry smile – an A-to-Z of fish plaques set in the pavements of the old town.

Practicalities

The **train station** is on the west side of town, on the main drag of Ferensway, with the **bus station** a couple of blocks north. Drivers might as well aim straight for the **car park** in the Princes Quay shopping centre, signposted on every road into town. The main **tourist office** is on Paragon Street at Victoria Square (Mon 10am–6pm, Tues–Sat 9.30am–6pm, Sun noon–4pm; ☎01482/223559), and there's another at King George Dock (daily 7.30–10.30am; ☎01482/702118), open to coincide with the early-morning arrival of the North Sea **ferries** from Rotterdam and Zeebrugge – a bus at 8am leaves from the dock for the centre of town.

Few touring visitors stay the night, which means you'll have no trouble finding **accommodation**, except perhaps during the various festivals and fairs – the biggest events are the Jazz Festival (July/Aug), Sea Shanty Festival (Sept), Hull Fair (Oct) and the Hull Literature Festival (Nov). The tourist office has full lists, but the most central B&B options include the *Clyde House Hotel*, 13 John St, Kingston Square

(☎01482/214981; ②) and the family-run *Pines Hotel*, 138 Spring Bank (☎01482/215480; no credit cards; ①). There are loads of other options on and off this latter road, a little way northwest of the centre, at the end of Ferensway. The *Comfort Inn*, south of the train station at 11 Anlaby Rd (☎01482/323299; ②) marks a step up; while considerably more upmarket is the handsome *Quality Hotel Royal*, 170 Ferensway (☎01482/325087; ⑥), right by the station, or – best-sited of all – the *Forte Marina* on Castle Street overlooking Hull Marina (☎01482/225221; ⑥), which has an indoor pool.

For **food**, Hull's best includes the expensive *Cerutti's* (☎01482/328501; closed Sat lunch & Sun), on dockside Nelson Street, and the moderately priced *Operetta*, 56–58 Bond St (☎01482/218687; closed Sun lunch), which nestles in one of the least charming central streets but serves quality pizzas and pasta. There's also a food court in the Princes Quay shopping centre at Princes Dock, while Studio 10$^{1}/_{2}$ on King Street (closed Sun), opposite Holy Trinity, serves snacks, veggie specials and dozens of teas and coffees. Next door, *Fiddleheads*, 10 King St (☎01482/224749; closed Sun & Mon), is a well-thought-of vegetarian and vegan restaurant. Of Hull's many **pubs**, the *Olde White Harte*, 25 Silver St, has a pleasant courtyard and a history going back to the seventeenth century; *Green Bricks* on Humber Dock Street overlooks the marina; the *Olde Black Boy* on the High Street specializes in real ales; while at the dockside *Minerva* on Nelson Street they brew their own (Pilot's Pride) and serve reasonable bar meals. The renowned Hull Truck Theatre Company, Spring Street (☎01482/323638), is worth a call if you're in town, producer of many of the **plays** of award-winning John Godber among others – incidentally, British thesps John Alderton and Tom Courtney are also natives of Hull.

Beverley

BEVERLEY ranks as one of northern England's premier towns, its Minster the superior of many an English cathedral, its tangle of old streets, cobbled lanes and elegant Georgian and Victorian terraces the very picture of a traditional market town. Over 350 buildings are listed as possessing historical or architectural merit, and though you could see its first-rank offerings in a morning, this is one of a handful of places in this part of the world that you might want to stay in for its own sake.

Approaches to the town are dominated by the twin towers of **Beverley Minster** (Mon–Sat 9am–dusk, Sun 2.30am–5pm; £1 donation requested), visible for miles across the wolds and airy flatlands. Initiated as a modest chapel, the minster became a monastery under John of Beverley. Trained at Whitby and later ordained bishop of York, he was buried here in 721 and canonized in 1037 – his body lies under the crossing at the top of the nave. Fires and the collapse of the central tower in 1213 paved the way for two centuries of rebuilding, funded by bequests from pilgrims paying homage to the saint, and the result was one of the finest Gothic creations in the country. The **west front**, which crowned the work in 1420, is widely considered without equal, its survival due in large part to Baroque architect Nicholas Hawksmoor, who restored much of the church in the eighteenth century. Similar outstanding work awaits in the interior, most notably the fourteenth-century **Percy Tomb** on the north side of the altar, its sumptuously carved canopy one of the masterpieces of medieval European ecclesiastical art. Nearby stands the **Fridstol**, a Saxon "sanctuary chair" dating from Athelstan's reign (924–39) which provided safe haven for men on the run. Athelstan himself is said to have deposited a dagger on the altar in 934, vowing to return to Beverley if he defeated the Vikings and Scots in battle, which he duly did, carrying the banner of St John before him. The north transept – aisled, like the transepts at York Minster – harbours another remarkable tomb, behind the second column on the right as you stand with your back to the main altar, bearing the effigy of an unknown fourteenth-century priest. Other incidental carving throughout the church is magnificent, particularly the 68 misericords of the oak **choir** (1520–24), one of the largest and most accomplished in England. Much of the decorative work here and elsewhere is on a musical theme. Beverley had a renowned guild of itinerant minstrels, which provided funds in the sixteenth century for the carvings on the transept aisle capitals, where you'll be able to pick out players of lutes, bagpipes, horns and tambourines.

Cobbled Highgate runs from the Minster through town, along the pedestrianized shopping streets of Butcher Row and Toll Gavel and past the main Market Square, to Beverley's other great church, **St Mary's**, a chapel once attached to the Minster. On the corner of Hengate and North Bar Within, it nestles alongside the **North Bar**, sole survivor of the town's five medieval gates. The church is a tantalizing amalgam of styles, from the south porch's Norman arch to the thirteenth-century chancel and fifteenth-century Perpendicular elements of the tower and nave. Inside, the chancel's painted panelled ceiling (1445) contains portraits of English kings from Sigebert (623–37) to Henry VI, from about the same time as the eye-catching rood screen and misericords. Amidst the carvings, the favourite novelty is the so-called "Pilgrim's Rabbit", said to have been the inspiration for the White Rabbit in Lewis Carroll's *Alice in Wonderland*.

Practicalities

Beverley is most easily reached by regular **train** or **bus** (every 30min; #121, #122, #X46, #246) from Hull, though there are also several daily buses from York (1hr 20min; #X46). Station Square is just a couple of minutes' walk from the Minster. The **tourist office** is at 34 Butcher Row in the main shopping area (Mon–Fri 9.30am–5.30pm, Sat 10am–5pm; plus June–Aug Sun 10am–2pm; ☎01482/867430).

There's plenty of local **accommodation**, including a recommended guest house, the *Eastgate*, 7 Eastgate (☎01482/868464; no credit cards; ②), very close to the Minster, with a couple of cheaper rooms without a shower. Among the hotels, the top town-centre choices are the nicely situated *King's Head*, 38 Market Place (☎01482/868103; ③), the *Beverley Arms*, North Bar Within (☎01482/869241; ⑥) or the *North Bar Hotel*, 28 North Bar Without (☎01482/881375; ③), though all are eclipsed by the *Manor House*, Northlands, Walkington (☎01482/881645; ⑤; breakfast not included), three miles south of Beverley. Of the pubs, try the *Windmill Inn*, 53 Lairgate (☎01482/862817; ②), which has a dozen rooms for rent. The **youth hostel** (☎01482/881751) occupies one of the town's finer buildings, a restored Dominican friary that was mentioned in the Canterbury Tales. It's located in Friar's Lane, off Eastgate, just a hundred yards southeast of the Minster.

For **food**, *Cerutti 2* in Station Square (closed Sun) is a sister brasserie to that in Hull, though not as pricey and serving good fresh fish. Otherwise, there's a full complement of tearooms and cafés, or you can eat in the **pubs** – the celebrated *White Horse* on Hengate, near St Mary's, is a thoroughly atmospheric traditional drinking den with folk music nights; there's also the *Queen's Head* in Wednesday Market; or the real-ale haunt, the *Tap & Spile* on Flemingate, immediately behind the Minster. More expensive meals are on offer in the restaurant of the *Beverley Arms*, though its wood-panelled bar is open to all for drinks. The **Beverley and East Riding Folk Festival** takes place each June, featuring an international roster of music, song, dance and comedy.

The East Yorkshire coast

The **East Yorkshire coast** curves in a gentle arc between the cliffs of Flamborough Head in the north before bending inland at Spurn Head in the south, a finger-thin isthmus formed by the constant erosion and shifting currents that scour much of England's eastern shores. Between the two lie a handful of tranquil villages and miles of windswept dunes and mudflats, noted bird sanctuaries, and superbly lonely retreats accessible to anyone prepared to cycle or walk the paths and lanes that fan out amidst the dunes. **Buses** run out to a few points, mostly from Hull and Bridlington, but you'll need your own transport to make the most of the region. However, the two main resorts, Bridlington and Filey, are linked by the regular **train** service between Hull and Scarborough. There's also an hourly bus service between Bridlington, Filey and Scarborough.

Hikers also converge on Filey from a couple of **long-distance footpaths**. The **Wolds Way** links the resort to the River Humber by way of a 79-mile path through the gently rolling chalk hills to Hessle, in the shadow of the Humber Bridge, west of Hull. More challenging still, Filey is the traditional end of the 110-mile moor-and-coast **Cleveland Way** (see p.821), which loops from Helmsley to Saltburn and then heads south down the coast. Leaflets and information on the hikes are available from Filey's tourist office, and there are useful trail guides to both, published by Aurum Press.

Spurn Head

Few parts of the British coast are as dangerous as **Spurn Head**, a sand and pebble peninsula that hardly suggests the imminence of maritime catastrophe, but whose lifeboat station is the only one in Britain permanently staffed by a professional crew. Access is via the village of **Easingham** (at the end of the B1445), beyond which a four-mile toll road runs through a Yorkshire Wildlife Trust nature reserve known for its seals, butterflies, dunal flora and seabirds – this is one of the best spots in the country to observe spring and autumn bird migrations. **Sunk Island**, a few miles to the west on the fringes of the Humber estuary is also a birdwatchers' haven.

Hornsea and Burton Constable Hall

Some twenty miles of empty and unspoilt beaches line the coast from Spurn Head to **HORNSEA**, largest of the coast's villages and synonymous with the pottery that's made in a park-set factory on its outskirts on the B1242. There's free access and parking at the factory site, **Hornsea Freeport** (daily 9.30am–5pm; July & Aug 9.30am–6pm), where there are guided tours and the opportunity to buy, though most people stump up the extra cash (£1 a time) for the veritable fleet of add-on distractions like a model village, butterfly world and play area for kids. In the centre of town, the **Hornsea Museum**, at 11 Newbegin (Easter–Oct Mon–Sat 11am–5pm, Sun 2–5pm; £2), gives a run-through of local history. Hornsea **tourist office** is at 120 Newbegin (Easter–Sept Mon–Sat 10.30am–4.20pm; ☎01964/536404).

A quarter of a mile inland lies **Hornsea Mere**, Yorkshire's largest freshwater lake, scooped out by glacial action and now an RSPB sanctuary for herons and other nesting wildfowl. The other attraction hereabouts is **Burton Constable Hall** (Easter–Sept Sat–Thurs 1–5pm; £4; grounds open same days noon–5pm; free), an Elizabethan stately home redesigned in the eighteenth century; it's about seven miles to the southwest, off the B1238 from Aldbrough. On show inside are Chippendale furniture, the Long Gallery's five thousand books, and paintings by Renoir, Gainsborough and Pissarro – after which you can stroll in the two hundred acres of parkland landscaped by Capability Brown.

Bridlington and Filey

The southernmost major resort on the Yorkshire coast, **BRIDLINGTON** has maintained its harbour for almost a thousand years, though for much of that time it remained a small-scale place of little consequence: Defoe noted it only because of its use to the eighteenth-century coastal coal ships who sought shelter here in bad weather. Like many coastal stations, it flourished in Edwardian times as a resort, but spent recent decades in the same decline as the traditional English bucket-and-spade holiday. Renovations have smartened up the seafront promenade, which looks down upon the town's best asset – its sweeping sandy **beach**. It's an out-and-out family resort, which means plenty of candy-floss, amusement arcades, rides, diversions and shops full of tat, and in truth there's little to delay your progress northwards once you've paddled in the sea and eaten fish and chips on the milling harbourfront. The **tourist office**, 25 Prince St (Easter–Oct Mon–Sat 9.30am–5.30pm, Sun 9am–5pm; Nov–Easter Mon–Sat 9.30am–5.30pm; ☎01262/673474), might be able to persuade you otherwise, and has full lists of local accommodation – the Flamborough Road has a fair choice, with places like *The Ryburn* at no. 31 (☎01262/674098; no credit cards; ②) a fair bet. Among the endless **cafés and restaurants** serving the same seaside food, *Jerome's*, Royal Prince's Parade (☎01262/671881) on the prom, stands out, a Greek café with *meze* and vegetarian platters, decent coffee and sea views from the outdoor tables; it's open until 10pm in summer.

FILEY, half a dozen miles further north up the coast – and at the very edge of the Yorkshire Wolds – has a deal more class as a resort, retaining many of its Edwardian features, including some splendid panoramic gardens. It, too, claims miles of wide sandy beach, stretching most of the way south to Flamborough Head and north the mile or so to the jutting rocks of **Filey Brigg**, where a nature trail wends for a couple of miles through the surroundings. If you're going to clamber around on the Brigg, check the tide tables first since people get caught unawares by the incoming waters at times. **Bus and train** stations are just west of the centre on Station Road. Walk down Station Avenue and Murray Street to Filey's **tourist office** in the Borough Council offices on John Street, at the top of the foreshore road (May–Sept daily 9.30am–5.30pm; Oct–April Sat & Sun 10am–12.30pm & 1–4.30pm; ☎01723/512204). You'll find a clutch of standard **B&Bs** on Rutland Street, off West Avenue, which runs from the church in the centre of town. A couple of pricier hotels sit amongst the holiday flats down on the beachfront. *Downcliffe House* (☎01723/513310; ④) is the pick of them, with a seaview restaurant with outdoor terrace serving a decent menu of fresh fish.

Flamborough Head and Bempton Cliffs

Around fourteen miles of precipitous four-hundred-foot cliffs gird **Flamborough Head**, just to the northeast of Bridlington, a chalky knuckle whose 1979 designation as a Heritage Coast has guaranteed a degree of protection not only for a multitude of breeding seabirds, but also for a wealth of geological and archeological features. The best of the seascapes are visible on the peninsula's north side, accessible by road from **FLAMBOROUGH** village. The lighthouse beyond is closed to the public, the latest in a line of warning beacons here that date back to the seventeenth century, but which, in earlier times at least, manifestly failed to do their job: between 1770 and 1806, 174 ships went down in the hazardous waters off the headland. Ancient tumuli ripple over much of the headland, while the tip of the peninsula is almost cut off by the famous **Danes' Dyke**, a two-mile wooded ditch that runs from Cat Nab in the north to Sewerby Rocks in the south. Some believe it was a formal boundary built during the Viking invasions, though the chances are that it's an earthwork of pre-Roman vintage.

To see the best of Flamborough Head's coastline, try to walk at least part of the grassy cliff-top track, a signposted Heritage Coast path. From **BEMPTON**, two miles north of Bridlington, a quiet lane leads to **Bempton Cliffs**, an RSPB sanctuary and the best single place to see the area's thousands of cliff-nesting birds; parking costs £2.50. This is the only mainland gannetry in England; you'll see gannets diving from fifty feet in the air to catch mackerel and herring. Bempton also boasts the second-largest **puffin colony** in the country, with around 7000 returning to the cliffs between March and August – they spend the winter on the open seas. Late-March and April is the best time to see the puffins, when they display before nesting in the cliff's deep crevices, but the **Visitor Centre** (March–Oct daily 10am–5pm; Nov & Feb weekends only 9.30am–4pm;

☎01262/851179) can advise on other breeds' activities (best between May and July) and rent you a pair of binoculars (£2) – there are also kittiwakes, guillemots, razorbills and the largest colony of fulmars in England. Not surprisingly, an egg-collecting industry once thrived here, the eggs' albumen being used in the tanneries of Leeds – you can still see the pulleys used by the local "climmers", as they were called. RSPB puffin and seabird **cruises** (most Saturdays, June–Sept; £7.50; reserve on ☎0191/212 0353) are a spectacular way to see the Bempton and Flamborough Head cliffs. They last three to four hours and depart from Bridlington.

Beyond Bempton runs the Heritage Coast path, which you can follow all the way round to Flamborough Head or curtail by cutting up paths to Flamborough village. Sporadic buses link Flamborough and Bempton villages. The *Seabirds*, at the junction of the roads to the two villages, is a nice **pub** with a good line in fresh fish bar meals.

The North York Moors

Virtually the whole of the **North York Moors**, from the Hambleton and Cleveland hills in the west to the cliff-edged coastline to the east, is protected by one of the country's finest National Parks. The moors are lonely, heather-covered, flat-topped hills cut by deep, steep-sided valleys, and views here stretch for miles, interrupted only by giant cultivated forests, pale shadows of the woodland that covered the region before it was cleared by Neolithic and later peoples. Barrows and ancient forts provide memorials of these early settlers, mingling on the high moorland with the **Roman remains** of Wades Causeway, the battered stone crosses of the first Christian inhabitants and the ruins of great monastic houses such as Rievaulx.

Two pivotal centres, both market towns, in the park's southern reaches provide the main approaches: **Helmsley**, best starting point for any exploration of the western and central moors, and **Pickering** (actually just outside the National Park), for the eastern moors and northern Esk Valley. The central moors offer the best walking and the most noted landscapes, with **Hutton le Hole** perhaps the most picture-perfect village in the region. Any exploration of the district should also include the religious ruins of **Rievaulx Abbey** and possibly Byland Abbey or Mount Grace Priory; the views from **Sutton Bank** or from the windows of the trains of the North York Moors Railway; the gentle landscapes of the **Esk Valley**, blessed with its own small train line; and any one of countless deep-rural pubs, isolated hamlets or woodland walks. Popular long-distance paths cross the park, notably the Cleveland Way, which follows the coast and northern moors, and the Lyke Wake Walk, both of which are covered in more detail in the following section.

Help and information is available from a number of **National Park information centres**, where you can pick up local trail guides and accommodation listings – most also organize special events and guided walks throughout the year. The seasonal *Moors Visitor* newspaper details local attractions, while the best hiking **maps** are the Outdoor Leisure OS series, nos. 26 and 27.

The main southern artery linking the western, central and eastern divisions is the A170, which runs from Thirsk, through Helmsley and Pickering to Scarborough. Two trans-moor roads, the Helmsley–Stokesley B1257 (west side) and the Pickering–Whitby A169 (east), offer access into the very heart of the moors, with minor (often extremely minor) roads and tracks branching off in all directions: in winter, check the forecast first before setting off on any minor route, since this part of the country is always one of the first to be cut off in bad weather.

A big local draw are the **steam trains** of the North York Moors Railway between Pickering and Grosmont. At Grosmont you can connect with the regular trains on the Esk Valley line, running either six miles east to Whitby and the coast, or west through

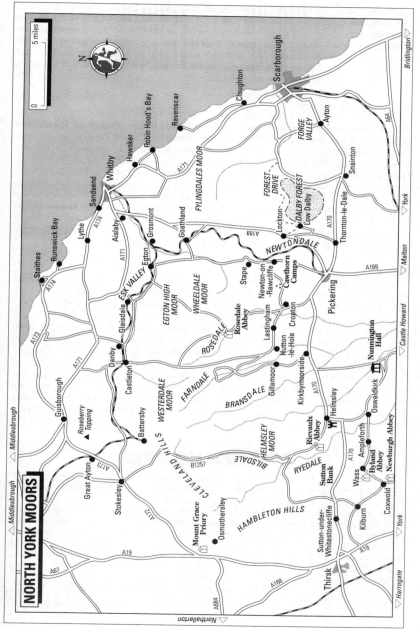

NORTH YORK MOORS

© Crown copyright

scintillating countryside to more remote settlements (and ultimately to Middlesbrough). The main **bus** approaches to the moors are from Scarborough and York to Helmsley and Pickering, though beyond these towns local services are limited. You'll need the free *Moors Connections* booklet, a summary of all rail and bus routes on and around the moors, available from tourist offices and park information centres. There are also special summer Moorsbus services, running between points not usually served by public transport; see the box below for more details.

The western moors

The **western moors** are marked on their western edge by the scarp of the **Hambleton Hills** – crowned by the Cleveland Way – and the ruler-straight line of the A19 road between York, **Thirsk** (just outside the park, but a useful gateway) and Middlesbrough. To the east they are closed by Rye Dale, one of the region's more bucolic valleys, and the B1267 from **Helmsley**, by far the area's nicest town and its best base for explorations. Most outings are likely to centre less on the scenery – except for the walks and staggering views from **Sutton Bank** on the A170 – than on a cluster of historic buildings, of which the most prepossessing is **Rievaulx Abbey**, easily seen from Helmsley. It's closely followed by **Mount Grace Priory**, to the north of Thirsk, and then by Shandy Hall, Byland Abbey and Newburgh Priory at the pretty village of **Coxwold**, and **Nunnington Hall** to the east, grouped conveniently close together on a minor road loop from Thirsk to Helmsley.

Thirsk

The small market town of **THIRSK**, 23 miles north of York, made the most of its strategic crossroads position on the ancient drove road between Scotland and York and on the historic east–west route from dales to coast. Its medieval prosperity is clear from the large, cobbled **Market Place** (market days are Monday and Saturday), now overrun by traffic, while later well-to-do citizens endowed the town with a bevy of commendable Georgian houses and halls, like those still standing on Kirkgate, which runs off the square. The **Thirsk Museum** at 16 Kirkgate (Easter–Oct Mon–Sat 10am–5pm, Sun 2–4pm; £1) – incidentally, the birthplace of eighteenth-century cricketer Thomas Lord, who founded the eponymous London cricket ground – does its best to fill in the background. However, Thirsk's main draw is its attachment to the legacy of local vet Alf Wight, better known as **James Herriott**. Despite the confusing claims of various Yorkshire Dales villages, Thirsk was the "Darrowby" of the Herriott books, not least because the town was where the

---

THE MOORSBUS

The National Park Authority is making sterling efforts to reduce traffic congestion in the region by promoting public transport, in particular its bus service, the **Moorsbus** (☎01439/770657), which runs every Sunday and bank holiday Monday from the end of May to the end of October, and daily in the summer school holidays (late July–late Aug). All local tourist and National Park information offices have timetables, but the various **services** basically connect Helmsley to Sutton Bank, Rievaulx, Coxwold and Kilburn; Pickering to Hutton le Hole, Castleton and Danby, to Rosedale Abbey and to Dalby Forest; and Helmsley and Pickering to each other. Departures are usually four times daily (hourly on the main routes), and timed so that day-trips are possible to the various sights; all-day **tickets** cost £2.50. Long-distance services (£5) from York (1hr 10min), Hull (1hr 40min), Beverley (1hr), Darlington (2hr) and Middlesbrough (1hr) let you commute into the park for a day's moorland sightseeing.

vet had his actual surgery, just across the road from the Thirsk Museum. Following a £1.5m refurbishment, this building at 23 Kirkgate has emerged as the hugely popular **World of James Herriott** (daily: Easter–Oct 10am–5.30pm; Nov–Easter 10am–5pm, last admission 1hr before closing; £4), an entertaining re-creation of the vet's 1940s surgery, dispensary, operating theatre, sitting room and kitchen, each crammed with period pieces and Herriott memorabilia. Countryside exhibits, veterinary science displays and an investigation of how the Herriott books were adapted for film and TV complete the experience.

Buses stop in the Market Place: there are two National Express services from York a day and local services between Thirsk, Kilburn, Coxwold and Helmsley on Mondays, Fridays and Saturdays. The **train station** (services from York and Middlesbrough) is a mile west of town on the A61 (Ripon road); minibuses connect station to town centre. The **tourist office** is inside the World of James Herriott, 23 Kirkgate (daily: Easter–Oct 10am–5.30pm; Nov–Easter 10am–5pm; ☎01845/522755) and can help with **accommodation**. *Lavender House*, 27 Kirkgate (☎01845/522224; no credit cards; ①), and *Kirkgate House*, 35 Kirkgate (☎01845/525015; ③), are both well sited on the road up to the impressive parish church, and the **pubs** in the Market Place offer rooms as well. The *Golden Fleece* and *Three Tuns* both serve **meals**, while the nicest daytime choice is the *Yorks Tearooms*, next to the clocktower on Market Place, a genteel café with enterprising lunches, speciality coffees and its own deli around the back. *Charles' Bistro* (☎01845/527444; closed Sun night), a moderately priced place on Bakers Alley (off Market Place, behind NatWest), has daily lunch deals and continental-style dinners and pastas.

Osmotherley

Eleven miles north of Thirsk, the little village of **OSMOTHERLEY** huddles around its green, proud of its ancient market cross and curious adjacent stone table from on top of which it's said John Wesley preached during one of his sermon tours. Having seen agriculture and industry come and go, the pretty settlement now gets by as a hiking centre, since it's a key stop on the Cleveland Way as well as starting-point for the infamous Lyke Wake Walk (see box on p.818). Its proximity to Mount Grace Priory is another reason to stop by – it's around a two-mile walk from the village, via Chapel Wood Farm, with a short detour to the nearby **Lady Chapel** on the way there or back. A more strenuous local hike involves following the Cleveland Way beyond the farm to the 982ft summit of Scarth Wood Moor and then down to Cod Beck Reservoir (3 miles; 1hr 30min).

There's a popular **youth hostel** at Cote Ghyll (☎01609/883575), half a mile north of the village, and an adjacent campsite too – you should really book in advance. For more comfort make straight for the *Three Tuns* (☎01609/883301; ④) on the village green, a lovely **pub** brimming with awards and serving fresh seafood meals. A couple of tea shops and cottage B&Bs complete the picture.

Mount Grace Priory

The fourteenth-century **Mount Grace Priory** (Easter–Oct daily 10am–6pm; Nov–March Wed–Sun 10am–1pm & 2–4pm; £2.70; NT & EH), the most important of England's nine Carthusian ruins and the only one in Yorkshire, provides a striking contrast to its more grandiose and worldly Cistercian counterparts. The Carthusians took a vow of silence and lived, ate and prayed alone in their two-storey cells, each separated from its neighbour by a privy, small garden and high walls. The incumbents were given their meals through a hatch, specially angled to prevent the monks from seeing their waiters. The foundations of the cells are still clearly visible, together with one which has been reconstructed to suggest its original layout and the monks' way of life. Other substantial remains include the ruins of the gatehouse and the walls and tower of the priory church, which divides the site's two main courtyards.

THE LYKE WAKE WALK

One of England's more macho long-distance paths, the **Lyke Wake Walk** was founded in 1955 as a light-hearted idea: anyone who completed the 42-mile walk in less than 24 hours became a member of the Lyke Wake Club and qualified for a badge in the shape of a coffin. As word spread it became something of a cult, the net result being deeply eroded paths and mountains of litter – to the extent that the National Park authority now discourages large groups. The path isn't marked on most maps for the same reason. Although still the most popular walk on the moors, it has recently become less choked with groups, and is complemented by another trans-moors route, Wainwright's similarly controversial Coast to Coast walk.

The Lyke Wake starts at **Osmotherley**, eleven miles north of Thirsk, and shadows the Cleveland Way for a while along the northern edge of the Cleveland Hills before reaching **Ravenscar**, near Robin Hood's Bay, by way of Fylingdales and the notorious Jugger Howes. It links numerous prehistoric sites, following the age-old tracks of monks, miners and smugglers. The path's name, incidentally, comes from a dialect poem, the *Lyke Wake Dirge*, the story of a journey across one of the "burial routes" that linked the moors' ancient burial mounds. It recalls the ancient practice of waking (keeping vigil) over a dead body (the lyke). Provided you're completely fit, used to long-distance walking, have been in training and have back-up, first-timers can complete the walk in around sixteen hours – some people have *run* it in less than five, though they are, of course, completely mad.

Road access to the priory is straight up the busy A19 from Thirsk, eleven miles to the south; it's reached off a signposted minor road just after the Osmotherley turn-off. Heading onwards into the National Park, it's much more enjoyable to bear east afterwards, through Osmotherley and Hawnby, along the very minor roads across the Cleveland Hills to join the B1257 for Helmsley. By **public transport**, take the train from Thirsk to Northallerton, six miles southwest of the priory, and then any of the regular Northallerton–Osmotherley buses (hourly, not Sun).

Sutton Bank and Kilburn

The main A170 road enters the National Park from Thirsk as it climbs five hundred feet in half a mile to **Sutton Bank** (960ft), a phenomenal viewpoint whose panorama extends across the Vale of York to the Pennines on the far horizon. At the top of the climb stands a huge car park and a lavish North York Moors National Park **Visitor Centre** (Easter–Oct daily 10am–5pm; Nov–March daily 11am–4pm; ☎01845/597426), full of background on the short waymarked walks you can make from here, and with a café too.

To the south of the A170, the marked **White Horse Nature Trail** (2–3 miles; 1hr 30min) skirts the crags of Roulston Scar, passing the Yorkshire Gliding Club en route to the **Kilburn White Horse**, northern England's only turf-cut figure, at 314 feet long and 228 feet high. Unlike its ancient southern counterparts, it's a rather sham affair cut by a local schoolmaster in 1857 and only white because it's covered in imported chalk chippings. You could make a real walk of it by dropping a couple of miles down to **KILBURN** village – a minor road also runs from the A170, passing the White Horse – synonymous with woodcarving since the days of "Mouse Man" Robert Thompson (1876–1955), whose woodcarvings – marked by his distinctive mouse motif – are found in York Minster and Westminster Abbey. The **Mouseman Visitor Centre** (Easter–Oct daily 10am–5pm; closed Mon April, May & Oct; £1.50) in Thompson's restored workshop has woodworking demonstrations most days, while the village's *Forresters Arms* – a good place to recuperate – sports locally made furniture.

Coxwold

The first serious diversion off the A170 is **COXWOLD**, as attractive a little village as they come. The majority of its many visitors come to pay homage to the novelist **Laurence Sterne**, who is buried by the south wall (close to the porch) in the churchyard of **St Michael's**, where he was vicar from 1760 until his death in 1768; the gravestone is badly damaged, though that which marked the place of his original grave in London (see below) hangs in the porch, complete with an inscription by enthusiastic eighteenth-century masons who admired him. The church, with its odd octagonal tower, is worth closer scrutiny – particularly the three-decker pulpit and medieval stained glass – before heading for **Shandy Hall**, 150 yards further up the road past the church (house June–Sept Wed 2–4.30pm, Sun 2.30–4.30pm; gardens June–Sept Sun–Fri 11am–4.30pm; house and gardens £3; gardens only £1.50), Sterne's home, now a museum crammed with literary memorabilia. It was here that he wrote *A Sentimental Journey through France and Italy* and the wonderfully eccentric *The Life and Opinions of Tristram Shandy, Gentleman*, which prompted Samuel Johnson loftily and misguidedly to declare "nothing odd will last".

Of the village's many lovely, ivy-covered stone buildings, the *Fauconburg Arms* (☎01347/868214; ③), a superb old **pub** on Main Street, has the most to recommend it, with a cosy bar with good food, a more formal restaurant and pleasant rooms. Cheaper accommodation is available at the *School House* (☎01347/868356; no credit cards; ①; closed Dec & Jan), a welcoming cottage tea-house.

The pub is named after the viscount who married Mary, daughter of Oliver Cromwell, whom he brought to live in **Newburgh Priory**, half a mile south of the village (April–June Wed & Sun 2–6pm, also Easter & Aug bank hols; £4, grounds only £2.50). Raised on the site of an Augustinian monastery founded in 1150, the house is famous for reputedly containing a tomb with the headless body of Oliver Cromwell. The story claims that Mary brought her father's body here after it was exhumed from Westminster Abbey in readiness to be "executed" at Tyburn in revenge for Cromwell's part in the Civil War. Resourceful Mary is supposed to have exchanged Oliver's corpse with that of some ordinary Joe, but it's not quite clear how this tale can be made to tally with the fact that Oliver's body had been mummified before its burial, and thus would have been expected to resemble the recently deceased leader.

THE MYSTERIOUS CORPSE OF LAURENCE STERNE

Irish-born **Laurence Sterne** (1713–68) took Holy Orders after receiving his Cambridge degree, married in 1741 and by 1760 was living in Coxwold, officiating at St Michael's Church. The first two volumes of his great novel, the rambling and brilliant *Tristram Shandy*, published in 1760, catapulted him to fame and he became a controversial figure in literary London. Further volumes of *Tristram Shandy* enhanced his reputation, and Sterne began to travel in the 1760s, partly in an attempt to improve his poor health. His sojourn in France and Italy provided material for *A Sentimental Journey* (1768), but the journey proved too much for him and he died of pleurisy in London, where he was buried. Immediate rumours surfaced that Sterne's body had been unknowingly appropriated by body-snatchers and sold to doctors for medical experimentation – a story given credence when Sterne's body was finally exhumed from its London graveyard in 1969 for reburial in Coxwold. Various bones and no fewer than five skulls were uncovered in the grave, one of which – after comparison with contemporary busts – is thought to have been Sterne's. Presumably, the eighteenth-century doctors who illegally bought the body were horrified to learn of its identity and hurriedly reburied it in its grave together with other human bits and pieces they had lying around. Sterne – or at least part of him – now lies at rest in Coxwold churchyard.

Buses run to Coxwold from Thirsk on Mondays, Fridays and Saturdays (and on to Helmsley), and the Moorsbus runs here from Helmsley in summer. By car, turn off the A170 at Sutton-under-Whitestonecliffe, five miles east of Thirsk, or come south down the A19 and follow the signs through the country lanes – either approach lets you take in Kilburn and the White Horse on the way to or from Coxwold.

Byland Abbey

Laurence Sterne talked of "A delicious Walk of Romance" from Coxwold to twelfth-century **Byland Abbey** (Easter–Sept daily 10am–6pm; Oct daily 10am–4pm; Nov–Easter Wed–Sun 10am–1pm & 2–4pm; £1.70; EH), a mile and a half northeast of the village; the summer Moorsbus runs here. His description captures the appeal of the ruins – seen from the distance as a mere finger of stone – which though larger in ground area than the Cistercian houses at Fountains and Rievaulx, are far less well preserved, leaving the haunting location and stark west front as the abbey's most memorable aspects. Other colossal but skeletal remains include the lay brothers' "lane", a rare example of the corridor which kept abbey servants at a remove from the cloister and the ordained monks. Equally unusual are some fine thirteenth-century green-and-yellow tiled floors, seen to best effect in the south transept chapels. The *Abbey Inn* (closed Sun evening & Mon), opposite the priory entrance, serves coffee and excellent meals.

Nunnington Hall

Moving eight miles due east from Byland through Ampleforth (famous for its Catholic public school) and Oswaldkirk brings you to **Nunnington Hall** (June–Aug daily except Mon 1.30–6pm; April, May, Sept & Oct Wed–Sun 1.30–5.30pm; £4; garden only £1; NT), a part-Tudor manor house stranded in the flats of lower Rye Dale about five miles southeast of Helmsley. The panelled bedrooms and vast main hall are impressive, but the principal diversion is the famous Carlisle Collection, 22 miniature rooms all furnished and decorated in different styles. The house, woods and gardens are all supposed to be haunted, though the most notable presence are peacocks strutting the garden lawns. There's also a tearoom. Bus #94 from Helmsley (Mon–Sat 2 daily) runs to Nunnington, from where it's a short walk to the hall.

Helmsley

One of the moors' most appealing towns, **HELMSLEY** makes a perfect base for visiting the western moors and Rievaulx Abbey. Local life revolves around a large cobbled market square (market day is Friday), dominated by a vaunting monument to the second earl of Feversham, whose family were responsible for rebuilding most of the village in the last century. The old **market cross** marks the start of the 110-mile Cleveland Way (see box opposite), and the town hall on the western edge of the square houses the tourist office and National Park information centre.

Close to the square, on the village's western fringe, is **Helmsley Castle** (April–Sept daily 10am–6pm; Nov–March Wed–Sun 10am–1pm & 2–4pm; £2.20; EH), its unique twelfth-century D-shaped keep ringed by massive earthworks. After a three-month siege during the Civil War it was "slighted" by Sir Thomas Fairfax, the Parliamentary commander, and much of its stone was plundered by townspeople for local houses.

To the southwest of the town, overlooking a wooded meander of the Rye, stands the Fevershams' country seat, **Duncombe Park** (May–Sept Sun–Fri, April & Oct Sun–Thurs; house and gardens 11am–5.30pm, parkland and visitor centre 10.30am–6pm; house, gardens and parkland £5.50; gardens and parkland £3.50; parkland only £2), built for the Fevershams' ancestor Sir Thomas Duncombe in 1713. The

---

THE CLEVELAND WAY

The 110-mile **Cleveland Way**, one of England's premier long-distance National Trails, starts at Helmsley in the North York Moors and follows a route that embraces both the northern rim of the moors and Cleveland Hills and the cliff scenery of the North Yorkshire coast. The path hits the coast at Saltburn and then runs south down the coast, terminating at Filey (p.813), south of Scarborough – though an unofficial "Missing Link" joins Scarborough to Helmsley, through the Tabular Hills, thus completing a circular walk.

Most people complete the Cleveland Way in around nine or ten days, though it's easy to walk short stages instead, particularly on the **coastal section**, where towns, villages and services are closer together. The outstanding high cliff sections are (from south to north): Hayburn Wyke to Robin Hood's Bay (7 miles); Robin Hood's Bay to Whitby (6 miles); Sandsend to Runswick Bay to Staithes (7 miles); and Staithes to Skinningrove, the section with the highest cliffs (5 miles).

The **Cleveland Way Project** (The Old Vicarage, Bondgate, Helmsley, YO6 5BP; ☎01439/770657) produces an annual *Accommodation and Information Guide*, an invaluable route-planning aid. Local information offices in Helmsley, Whitby, Sutton Bank, Scarborough and Filey can also advise you. As well as B&Bs, hotels and campsites en route, there are **youth hostels** at Helmsley, Osmotherley, Whitby, Robin Hood's Bay and Scarborough – all should be booked well in advance.

You'll need the OS Outdoor Leisure **maps** nos. 26 and 27 and Landranger sheet 101, though the *National Trail Guide: Cleveland Way* by Ian Sampson (Aurum Press) and *Walking the Cleveland Way and The Missing Link* by Malcolm Boyes (Cicerone Press) cover the ground in detail, too.

---

building is by gentleman-architect William Wakefield, though he was probably influenced by Vanbrugh who was working on Castle Howard at about the same time. The **grounds** are perhaps more appealing than the house (which was extensively rebuilt after a fire in 1879), boasting swathes of landscaped gardens which include Britain's tallest ash and lime trees, and a brace of artfully sited temples. Keen gardeners will also want to visit the **Helmsley Walled Garden**, within the Duncombe Park Estate (April–Oct daily 10.30am–5pm; rest of the year Fri–Sun only same hours; £2), whose five carefully tended acres are slowly emerging from a wholesale renovation after years of neglect.

Rievaulx Abbey

From Helmsley you can easily hike across country to **Rievaulx Abbey** (daily April–Sept 10am–6pm; Oct–March 10am–1pm & 2–4pm; £2.90; EH), once one of England's greatest Cistercian abbeys, and these days the most heavily visited historic building on the moors. The signposted path follows the opening two miles of the Cleveland Way, plus a mile's diversion off the Way, and takes around an hour and a half – a trail leaflet is available from the tourist office in Helmsley. If you don't fancy the walk, the summer-only Moorsbus has a shuttle service out here.

Founded in 1132, the abbey became the mother church of the Cistercians in England (see p.789), quickly developing from a series of rough shelters on the deeply wooded banks of the Rye to become a flourishing community with interests in fishing, mining, agriculture and the woollen industry, the latter supported by a chain of associated moorland farms. At its height, 140 monks and up to 500 lay brothers lived and worked at the abbey, though numbers fell dramatically once the Black Death (1348–49) had done its worst. Nemesis came with the Dissolution, when many of the walls were razed and the roof lead stripped – the beautiful ruins, however, still suggest the abbey's former splendour. They are at their best in the triple-arched nave, oriented from north to south instead of the conventional west–east axis because of the valley's sloping site.

The Chapter House retains an original shrine to the first abbot, William. A **visitor centre** mounts exhibitions pertaining to the ruins and to monastic life in the valley.

Rievaulx Terrace

Although they form some sort of ensemble with the abbey, there's no access between the ruins and **Rievaulx Terrace and Temples** (Easter–Oct daily 10.30am–6pm, or dusk if earlier; £2.80; NT), a site entered from the B1257, a couple of miles northwest of town. This pleasing half-mile stretch of grass-covered terraces and woodland was laid out as part of Duncombe Park in the 1750s, and as with Studley Royal at Fountains Abbey, the Terrace was engineered partly to enhance the views of the abbey. The resulting panorama over the ruins and the valley below is superb, and this makes a great spot for a picnic or simply for strolls along the lawns and woodland trail. Tuscan and Ionic temples lie at opposing ends of the Terrace, the latter with a fine painted ceiling, excellent furniture and a permanent exhibition on eighteenth-century English landscape design.

Helmsley practicalities

Helmsley is connected by **bus** to Pickering and Scarborough (#128), Malton (#94), York (#57) and Thirsk (#58), which makes it a fairly handy base. It's also a hub for the Moorsbus, which takes trippers out to Sutton Bank, Rievaulx, Byland Abbey, Coxwold and Kilburn – see the box on p.816 for more details. Make sense of all the connections in the useful **tourist office** in the town hall on Market Place (Easter–Oct daily 9.30am–6pm; Nov–Easter Sat & Sun 10am–4pm; ☎01439/770173), which sells local trail leaflets and has information on the two **long-distance footpaths**: the Cleveland Way and the Ebor Way, a gentle seventy-mile route to Ilkley that links with the Dales Way. There's mountain **bike rental** from Footloose on Borogate (☎01439/770886).

There's plenty of **accommodation**, starting with the *Castle View Guest House*, behind *Monet's* restaurant at 19 Bridge St, just off the square (☎01439/770618; no credit cards; ①). Slightly more expensive is *Stilworth House*, 1 Church St, behind the tourist office and square (☎01439/771072; no credit cards; ②), with a pleasant lounge and garden. Other modest B&Bs are scattered along Ashdale Road, a few hundred yards up Bondgate from the Market Place and on the right. Pricier hotels include the classy *Feversham Arms*, 1 High St, behind the church (☎01439/770766; ⑤), which also has some good dinner, bed and breakfast deals; and the *Feathers Hotel*, 1 Market Place (☎01439/770275; ④). Finest of all is the *Black Swan*, also on Market Place (☎01439/770466; ⑦), a gorgeous Elizabethan-Georgian hybrid with splendid gardens and some good off-season deals. The purpose-built **youth hostel** (☎01439/770433) is a few hundred yards east of Market Place – follow Bondgate to Carlton Road and turn left.

The old **pubs** in the Market Place – the *Royal Oak* and the *Feathers* – are both atmospheric places for a drink and a bite to eat. Best place for a snack or **meal** is *Monet's* on Bridge Street, while the *Black Swan* is the place for drinks in its panelled bar, afternoon teas and good, if pricey, lunches and dinners. *Hunters*, at 13 Borogate, just by the Market Place, is an overstuffed **deli**, excellent for putting together a picnic. Borogate itself has several fine little **shops** in ancient houses, including a working smithy and a good second-hand bookshop in the old fire station.

For a drive out into the country, and a fine meal, you can't do better than the invariably packed *Star Inn* (☎01439/770397; no food Sun eve & Mon) at **Harome**, a thatched pub a couple of miles south of the A170, where superior food and good beer are the norm. You can either wait for a table in the bar or book ahead for the dining room.

The central moors

The highest and wildest terrain in the North York Moors is in the **central moors**, bounded by Rye Dale in the west and by **Rosedale** in the east. Purple swathes of summer heather carpet the tops, where ancient crosses and standing stones provide hints of the moorland's distant past. Stunning villages like **Hutton le Hole** and **Lastingham** give way to higher, isolated valleys, connected by steep minor roads and rough tracks – it's the one part of the National Park where having your own transport is vital if you don't plan to hang around too long. The Moorsbus connects most of the better-known destinations, but really this is an area for walking and taking in the scenery. Drivers could base themselves virtually anywhere to see these dales, though Helmsley suggests itself; if you're using the Moorsbus, then Pickering, across to the east (see p.825), is the transport hub. Moving onwards, it's just a 13-mile drive (or Moorsbus journey) from Hutton le Hole across the highest part of the moors to Castleton in the Esk Valley (see p.829).

Hutton le Hole

Lying around eight miles northeast of Helmsley, one of Yorkshire's quaintest villages, **HUTTON LE HOLE**, has become so great a tourist attraction that you'll have to come off-season to get much pleasure from its tidy gardens, its stream-crossed village green and the sight of sheep wandering freely through the lanes. On warm summer days, the stream banks are covered with splashing picnickers. Apart from the sheer photogenic quality of the place, the big draw is the **Ryedale Folk Museum** (Easter–Oct daily 10am–5.30pm; £3), an ever-expanding set of displays over a two-acre site. Local life is documented from the era of prehistoric flint tools, through Romano-British artefacts and pottery, to a series of reconstructed buildings, notably a sixteenth-century house, a glass furnace, a crofter's cottage and a nineteenth-century blacksmith's shop. Special events and displays throughout the season mean there's always something going on.

The museum also houses a National Park **information centre** (☎01751/417367), where you can buy leaflets detailing local hikes. The nearby car park fills very quickly in summer as walkers disperse from the village. **Accommodation** is zealously fought for, too: try the *Barn Hotel* (☎01751/417311; ②), on the through road just down from the museum, or the Georgian *Hammer and Hand* (☎01751/417300; ②), a comfortable period B&B on the village green next to the pub, or fall back on the mercy of the information office, which holds lists of other local B&Bs. Both the *Barn* and *Hammer and Hand* have associated tearooms, the latter serving evening meals too, while the *Forge Tea Shop* (weekends only Nov–Feb) – a renowned stop for tea and cakes – completes the set. If you stay the night you'll have plenty of time to become acquainted with the *Crown*, the friendly local **pub**.

Lastingham

About a mile and a half east of Hutton le Hole is **LASTINGHAM**, its rose-fronted stone cottages gathered in a dell near its bubbling beck. Here stands **St Mary's** (daily 9am–dusk), a superb little church, built over Lastingham Abbey, a Benedictine house founded in 654 by monks Cedd and Chad from Lindisfarne, both of whom were later canonized. The monastery was destroyed by the Danes and then partly rebuilt by monks from Whitby, who left in 1087 to found St Mary's in York without finishing their work here. The present church, however, preserves the early Norman crypt, one of Yorkshire's great ecclesiastical treasures. Burial place of Saint Cedd, the crypt was once a sacred point of pilgrimage. Today its heavy vaults and carved columns still shelter the head of an eighth-century Anglo-Saxon cross, a Viking "hogback" tombstone and the original doorposts of the Saxon monastery.

The hamlet is tiny, with just one cosy **pub**, the *Blacksmiths Arms* opposite the church, which doubles as the local post office. *Holywell House* (☎01751/417624; no credit cards; ①) is a lovely eighteenth-century cottage at Spaunton Bank Foot, between Hutton le Hole and Lastingham.

Farndale

Farndale is entered from the south by a minor road from **Gillamoor**, a little to the west of Hutton le Hole. Further up the vale the country lanes are packed in spring with tourists come to see the area's wild daffodils, protected by the two-thousand-acre **Farndale nature reserve**. The flowers grow in several parts of the dale, but the best area is north of **Low Mill**, where roads from Gillamoor and Hutton le Hole meet, about four miles north of the latter. Take the path beside the car park (signposted "High Mill") over the bridge and follow the track alongside the somnolent River Dove. As well as the thousands of daffodils, notice the alder trees, whose Gaelic name, *ferna*, may well have given Farndale its name. At High Mill, *Poppy's Pantry* (closed Wed) can serve you a refreshing glass of home-made lemonade in the garden, just beyond which, at **Church Houses**, you regain the road (and find the tiny, stone *Feversham Arms*). Turn right on the tarmac here for about three-quarters of a mile and you can follow the route back south to Low Mill via High Wold House (3.25 miles; 2hr–2hr 30min). There's a B&B in these quiet surroundings at *Oak House*, at Dale End (☎01751/433053; no credit cards; ①), northwest of Church Houses, the road being signposted from the *Feversham Arms* (☎01751/433206; ②), which also has a few rooms. It's worth noting that the **Moorsbus** runs a special "Daffodil" service every Sunday in April and over Easter, shuttling visitors from Hutton le Hole to Farndale.

The onwards road route cuts east from Church Houses up onto **Farndale Moor** to meet the high moor road from Hutton le Hole that passes the *Lion* on Blakey Ridge (see below) and curves around the head of Rosedale before dropping down to Rosedale Abbey.

Rosedale and Blakey Ridge

Rosedale, just a couple of miles east of Farndale, is slightly wilder and steeper, and has a good network of wild upland roads ranging over its moors, which are densely studded with prehistoric tumuli and ancient stone crosses, like **Ralph Cross** standing sentinel at the isolated crossroads at the top of the dale.

The largest of its communities, trim and tidy **ROSEDALE ABBEY**, four miles northeast of Hutton le Hole, preserves only a few fragments of the Cistercian priory (1158) which gave it its name, most of them incorporated into **St Lawrence's** parish church. It's hard to believe now, but in the last century the village had a population of over five thousand, most employed in the ironstone workings whose remnants lie scattered all over the lonely high moors round about. The first mine opened in 1851, some three million tons of ore being excavated between 1856 and 1885. Horse-drawn wagons dragged the stone by pack road to Pickering until the opening of a remarkable moorland railway which connected with the main Esk Valley line at Battersby to carry ore north to the ironworks of Teesside.

You can pick up the still clearly distinct line, now a panoramic footpath, at several points near the high road on Blakey Ridge, on the west of the dale, but for a fine circular walk join it at **Hill Cottages**, one and half miles northwest of Rosedale Abbey and follow it all the way round the head of the valley, returning either via Dale Head Farm, the valley bottom and Thorgill, or the broad track that runs south down Blakey Ridge above Thorgill (10 miles; 3hr 30min).

Rosedale village itself gets packed on summer weekends and it can be tough finding a parking space on the grass verges. A fair proportion of visitors are here to sit outside the *Milburn Arms* (☎01751/417312; ⑤; closed Jan), overlooking the small green, which makes a peaceful base: its **rooms** are pricey for what you get, but there are views over the hills, a beer garden out front, and above-average cooking in the bar and restaurant. Otherwise, there are teas and snacks to be had in the *Abbey Tearooms* (closed Wed plus closed all Nov–Easter), and a popular **campsite** at *Rosedale Caravan Park* (☎01751/417272) down by the river. There's a very good restaurant and bar meals, too, at the *Blacksmiths Arms* (☎01751/417331; ⑤) at **Hartoft End**, a couple of miles south of Rosedale Abbey.

North of Rosedale Abbey, you can reach the *Lion Inn* (☎01751/417320; ③) on **Blakey Ridge**, a couple of miles south of the junction with the Hutton le Hole–Castleton road (along which the Moorsbus travels). A truly windswept local, with a sixteenth-century core, the inn has fairly standard bar meals, but good beer and an unbeatable location for an isolated night's stay – though come Sunday lunchtime the car park soon fills up. Some make the slight detour from the Lyke Wake Walk, since the pub roughly marks the halfway spot.

Pickering and the eastern moors

The biggest centre for miles around, **Pickering** takes for itself the title "Gateway to the Moors", which is pushing it a bit, though it's certainly a handy place to stay if you're touring the villages and dales of the **eastern moors**. Its undoubted big pull, and biggest plus if you're using public transport, is the **North Yorkshire Moors Railway** (NYMR; see box on p.827), which provides a beautiful way of travelling up (and walking from) **Newtondale**, the Moors' most immediately spectacular dale, and of connecting with the Esk Valley line in Esk Dale and, ultimately, Whitby and the Yorkshire coast. Otherwise, Moorsbus services radiate from Pickering and there are regular bus services to and from Helmsley, Scarborough, York and Leeds.

Few people pay much attention to the countryside east of Pickering, which consists for the most part of apparently unending ranks of conifers and characterless moorland. **Dalby Forest**, however, the most accessible of the woodlands, is redeemed by a superb forest drive and a large number of specially marked trails. Villages are few and far between, though in **Thornton-le-Dale** the region has a high-ranking contender for prettiest village in Yorkshire. By far the best itinerary here is to see Thornton-le-Dale and then drive or bike through Dalby Forest to rejoin the main A170 Pickering–Scarborough road at one of several points just outside Scarborough. Without your own transport you're stuck as far as touring around is concerned, though there is a Moorsbus service into the forest from Pickering.

Pickering

A thriving market town at the junction of the A170 and the transmoor A169 (Whitby road), **PICKERING** rather fancies itself, yet a couple of hours is enough to show you its charms, certainly if you've already seen the best of the North York Moors to the west. Its most attractive feature is its motte and bailey **Castle** on the hill north of the market place (Easter–Oct daily 10am–6pm; Nov–March Wed–Sun 10am–4pm; £2.50; EH), reputedly used by every English monarch up to 1400 as a base for hunting in nearby Blandsby Park. Eight monarchs certainly put up here, including Edward II after his trouncing by the Scots at the Battle of Byland Abbey in 1322, and possibly a ninth, Richard II, was kept here as a prisoner shortly before his murder in Pontefract. The ruins are in pretty good shape, with much of the walls, keep and original towers intact, and some good views over the town and countryside. A simple chapel in the grounds dates back to 1227 and is dedicated to St Nicholas, the fourth-century Bishop of Myra – Santa Claus by any other name.

Back down in the village, you could also happily potter around the informal **Beck Isle Museum of Rural Life** on Bridge Street, behind the train station (Easter–Oct daily 10am–5pm; £2), or the central church of **St Peter and St Paul**, famed for a Norman font and extensive fifteenth-century frescoes, discovered in 1851 but painted over again by the local vicar who feared they'd provoke idolatry. Although crude and rather heavy-handedly restored, the scenes are still compelling, including Herod's feast, St George and the dragon and the martyrdom of Thomas à Becket.

The **tourist office**, on Eastgate car park (Easter–Oct Mon–Sat 9.30am–6pm, Sun 9.30am–5.30pm; Nov–Easter Mon–Sat 10am–4.30pm; ☎01751/473791), just above the Malton/Whitby/Scarborough roundabout, can provide full timetables for the **NYMR** (see box opposite) and sell you a map of town, which you won't need. More useful are their **accommodation** lists: if you haven't made a reservation in summer, you may as well call here first to see what's still available. Tree-lined Eastgate (the Scarborough road) has the tastefully presented *Eden House* at no. 120 (☎01751/472289; no credit cards; ②) and *Heathcote House* at no. 100 (☎01751/476991; no credit cards; ②); there are more modest places on the same road. *Bramwood*, 19 Hallgarth (☎01751/474066; no credit cards; ②) lies through an arch off the Whitby road, a lovely eighteenth-century house with walled garden. A couple of the pubs also have rooms, top choice the *White Swan*, on the Market Place (☎01751/472288; ⑤), whose weekend rates are typically around £10 less. A less ritzy pub B&B is available at the *Black Swan*, 18 Birdgate (☎01751/472286; ②). The nearest **youth hostel** is at the *Old School*, Lockton (☎01751/460376), five miles northeast off the A169 – about two miles' cross-country walk from the NYMR station at Levisham (see opposite), or ask to be dropped at the turn-off by the Whitby bus. The local **campsite** is at the award-winning *Upper Carr* (☎01751/473115; closed Nov–Feb), a mile and half south of town on the Malton Road. It also has on-site chalets available and, probably a first for a campsite, Internet facilities.

Best place to **eat and drink** in Pickering is the *White Swan*, with small, cosy beamed rooms and nice box windows in the bar from which to survey the passing scene. There's good beer, lunchtime bar snacks and a fine restaurant with a French-tinged menu. None of the cafés are up to much bar the *Tea Shop*, 26 Hungate, which uses local ceramic crockery and has a good range of teas, coffees and cakes. The *India Garden*, 7 Eastgate Square, is that rare moorland thing, an Indian restaurant – no surprises, except that it's there in the first place. Out of town, opposite the campground entrance, is the *Black Bull*, which serves breakfast, lunch and dinner.

Walks from the North Yorkshire Moors Railway

Most people make a full return journey for the superb scenery of the roadless **Newtondale**, but if you want to combine some walking with the train rides, stop en route at one of the minor stations.

The first is **Levisham**, perfect for walks to **LEVISHAM** village, a mile and a half to the east, where the *Horseshoe Inn* (☎01751/460240; ②) is a favourite target, especially for Sunday lunch. A steep winding road continues another mile beyond Levisham, down across the beck and then up to **LOCKTON**, where there's a youth hostel and a path due north to the **Hole of Horcum**, a bizarre natural hollow gouged by the glacial meltwaters that carved out Newtondale – the paths run back to Levisham station from here, and the entire seven-mile circuit is one of the Moors' best short walks. In the other direction, a couple of miles west of the station – and reached along a minor road – the fascinating **Cawthorn Camps** (always open; free) are the only Roman camps of their kind in the world. The site's jumbled collection of earthworks, spreading over 103 acres, puzzled archeologists for years, as all the previously discovered Roman marching camps in Europe were built on precise geometrical plans. It's now known that this was a military training area, troops from York's Ninth Legion garrison being sent here on exercises, many of which obviously involved building camps. Local tribes had been assimilated easily, unlike the Picts to the north, making this a safe area for such exercises. A one-mile trail skirts the perimeter, offering grand views over the dale beyond.

THE NORTH YORKSHIRE MOORS RAILWAY

One of the northeast's big tourist draws, the volunteer-run **North Yorkshire Moors Railway** connects **Pickering** with the Esk Valley (Middlesbrough–Whitby) line at **Grosmont**, eighteen miles to the north. The line was completed by George Stephenson in 1835, just nine years after the opening of the Stockton and Darlington Railway, making it one of the earliest lines in the country. Even by the standards of later projects it was a remarkable feat of engineering, navigating 1-in-15 gradients and using thousands of tons of brushwood and heather-stuffed sheepskins to provide bedding for the track through the dale's extensive bogs. For twelve years carriages were pulled by horse, with steam locomotives only arriving in 1847. The line closed in 1965 and was formally reopened in 1973.

Scheduled **services** operate between late March and early November (plus Christmas specials), with trains running hourly to three times daily depending on the time of year; for timetable information ring ☎01751/472508 or pick up a leaflet from local tourist offices. A day-return **fare** along the whole line costs £9.20. Part of the line's attraction, of course, are the **steam trains**, though be warned that diesels are pulled into service when the fire risk in the forests is high.

The easy way here, incidentally, is direct by Moorsbus from Pickering, which then runs on to Rosedale Abbey.

The second stop, **Newtondale Halt**, is only a couple of miles northwest of the Hole of Horcum, or you can head off through the extensive woods of **Cropton Forest** to the west on trails specially marked by the Forestry Commission. Comprising just a few farms and isolated houses, **STAPE** – three miles southwest through the forest – is an archetypal high moors community, perfectly placed to act as a base for local walks. *Grange Farm* (☎01751/473805; no credit cards; ②) is typical of farmhouse B&Bs in the vicinity, and Pickering's tourist office can provide details of others. At Stape you're just two miles south from the best-preserved stretch of Roman road in Europe, **Wheeldale Roman Road**, a mile of Wade's Causeway that ran from York to bases on the coast: the remains show a twenty-foot-wide stretch of sand and gravel studded by sandstone slabs and edged with kerbs and ditches, and the fact that it's plumb in the middle of open moorland only adds to its appeal. It's signposted off the untarred road from Stape to Goathland, perhaps the wildest and most adventurous north–south route over the moors – though anyone equipped with a decent map will also be able to find their way to the Roman road direct by track from Newtondale Halt, again around a three-mile walk.

Just to the east of the road, down in Wheeldale Beck, **Wheeldale youth hostel** (☎01947/896350), housed in a former shooting lodge, is one of the most isolated and basic in England – exterior washrooms, no showers and no heating except for an open fire. Booking in advance is essential. From the hostel, clearly marked paths and a minor road drop down the three miles into **Goathland**, the third stop on the railway line and another excellent walking spot – all the details on this village are included in the Esk Valley section.

Thornton-le-Dale

THORNTON-LE-DALE, just two miles east of Pickering, hangs onto its considerable charm despite the main A170 Scarborough road scything through its centre. Most of the houses, pubs and shops are fairly alluring, none more so than the thatched cottage near the parish church, which features in so many ads, magazine covers, chocolate boxes and calendars that it's been described as the most photographed house in Britain. There are too many cafés, gift shops and other people around for most tastes, but the old market cross, stocks and various stream-side strolls are well worth half an hour if you can get here off-season.

Various of the local **B&Bs** might entice, like *Bridgefoot House* (☎01751/474749; no credit cards; ②), in a prime position on the beck. There are a couple of cheaper places, too, and both the **pubs** – the *New Inn* and *Buck Inn* – also have rooms. Tearooms and bar meals aside, food in the village isn't up to much. Consider instead the four-mile diversion to the east, along the A170, to the village of **Ebberston**, where the *Grapes* pub serves large home-cooked meals. Wardill Brothers in the Square (☎01751/474335) **rents bikes**, an eminently sensible way to see Dalby Forest (see below).

Dalby Forest

Minor roads from Thornton-le-Dale and from the A169 (Whitby road) lead into the monumental expanse of **Dalby Forest**: drivers pay a toll (£2.50; road closed 9pm–7am) to join the start of a nine-mile forest drive that emerges close to Hackness, just four miles from Scarborough. It's best to make first for the **visitor centre** (daily April & Oct 11am–4pm; May, June & Sept 10am–5pm; July & Aug 10am–5.30pm; ☎01751/460295) at **Low Dalby**, which has information not only on the forest, one of the first to be planted after the foundation of the Forestry Commission in 1919, but also on wildlife, picnic spots and the range of marked trails scattered around the woods, varying in length from one to sixteen miles. A kiosk here sells drinks, snacks and ices. The Moorsbus calls at the centre in summer.

The best hikes are from a car park about three miles north of Low Dalby at Low Staindale, which include the Cross Cliff View Walk and the marvellous **Bridestones Trail** (1.5 miles; 1hr) – a trail leaflet is available for the latter walk, which is of added interest for the bridestones themselves, great sandstone tors rising out of the heather that have been eroded into unearthly shapes. Similarly named outcrops are found all over the moors, and may be named for their connections with ancient fertility rites, or derive from a Norse word meaning "brink", or "boundary" stones. Another extremely popular walk or drive – trail leaflet available – takes in the **Forge Valley**, a deep-cut gorge scoured by glacial meltwaters during the last Ice Age. Start the walk (4 miles; 2hr–2hr 30min) from the Green Gate car park at the vale's northern end, three miles south of Hackness. For off-road driving adventures in the forest, contact **Langdale Quest** (Easter & May–Oct weekends and bank holidays; mid-July to Aug daily except Fri; ☎01723/882335), which rents out fully equipped vehicles for treasure-hunt-type activities using fifty miles of forest track.

Drivers or hikers looking for refreshment could do worse than aim for Hackness: a couple of miles before the village, the pub at **Langdale End**, the *Moorcock Inn*, is a real delight, traditionally furnished and attracting a steady stream of locals who drive out for the food and beer.

The Esk Valley

The northernmost reaches of the National Park are crossed by the east–west **Esk Valley**, whose pretty river flows into the sea at Whitby (p.836). It's a part of the North York Moors overlooked by many visitors – partly, one suspects, because its very attractions, at least in the eastern stretches, are its valley characteristics: there's not much moorland tramping to be done until you reach **Danby**, one of the finest of all moorland villages. Access is easy, either by road from Whitby via the A169 through Sleights, or more attractively by **train**: the North York Moors Railway connects at **Grosmont**, where you're on the **Esk Valley line** which runs between Middlesbrough and Whitby (4–5 daily, including Sunday).

Grosmont to Danby

GROSMONT, little more than a level-crossing, station and a couple of tearooms, sees plenty of summer traffic. Walkers pile off the trains to head north up the appealing rail and riverside path to Goathland (see below), three miles away, but if you're sticking with the train wait until the next stop west at **EGTON BRIDGE**. It's similarly tiny but has the bonus of a beautifully sited riverside pub, the *Horse Shoe*, while half a mile north, up the steep road from the station, there's a second pub, the *Wheatsheaf*, at **EGTON** itself, serving fine meals in its restaurant. Don't confuse the other pub here, also a *Horseshoe*, with the one down by the river. At **GLAISDALE**, with its old packhorse bridge, the nearest pubs to the station are also tempting, with valley views from the *Arncliffe Arms* and the *Anglers Rest* (camping here, too); again, the village itself is a steep climb away from the track.

Further west, the scenery becomes tinged by the looming moors until at the isolated stone village of **DANBY**, you're once again within striking distance of some excellent walks, all detailed on trail leaflets available from the **Moors Centre** (Easter–Oct daily 10am–5pm; Nov–Easter weekends only 11am–4pm; ☎01287/660654). The centre, a converted sixteenth-century farmhouse and former shooting lodge, also houses exhibitions about the local flora and fauna as well as a good tearoom. Whitby tourist office (☎01947/602674) can help with **accommodation** in local farmhouse B&Bs scattered up the sheep-laden side dales, and there's certainly much to be said for a quiet night away from the crowds. The *Duke of Wellington* (☎01287/660351; ②), at the crossroads, has a few rooms, and it's a nice pub even if the bar food isn't anything special. Just around the corner, the *Stonehouse Bakery & Tea Shop* is great for daytime snacks, serving olive bread or ciabatta sandwiches alongside coffee, scrumptious peanut brittle and other treats. A mile out of the village at **Ainthorpe**, the *Fox & Hounds* (☎01287/660218; ②) looks out over the moors, its refurbished rooms and tasty homecooked food both good reasons to stop.

At **CASTLETON**, the next stop and much the largest centre hereabouts, a minor moorland road cuts south across Danby High Moor to Hutton le Hole, past the *Lion Inn* at Blakey, and since the Moorsbus runs this way in summer, it's a handy jumping-off point to reach the southern sections of the National Park. From Castleton, it's 45 minutes on to Middlesbrough, or about the same back to Whitby.

Great Ayton

On reaching **GREAT AYTON**, the North York Moors gives way to the **Cleveland Hills**, whose scattered peaks provide the buffer between the rural east of the region and the encroaching industry of Teesside to the west. The town makes a handsome enough stop, with the River Leven flowing through the middle connecting the pretty High Green and Low Green at either end of the long High Street. It's Great Ayton's **Captain Cook** connections, though, that draw most visitors: the town was the boyhood home of James Cook between 1736 (when he was eight) and 1745. The young Cook lived at Aireyholme Farm (no public access) on the outskirts of town, though after James left to go to sea his father built a family **cottage** on Bridge Street, which was later dismantled and shipped to Melbourne, Australia in 1934; its site is marked by an obelisk of Australian granite near Low Green. Other Cook-related sights include **All Saints' Church**, also at Low Green, which the family attended and where Cook's mother Grace is buried; Cook's school, now the **Schoolroom Museum** at 47 High Street (Easter–Oct daily 2–4.30pm, also July & Aug Mon–Sat 10.30am–12.30pm & 2–4.30pm; £2); and a **sculpture** of a youthful Cook on High Green which depicts him – bare-chested, long-locked – in Leonardo DiCaprio mode. For an afternoon's leg-stretching, a waymarked path runs northeast out of Great Ayton, past Aireyholme Farm and up to the summit of **Roseberry Topping** (1050 ft), the queerly shaped conical peak visible from all over the locality – beacons were lit on top of here during the threat by the Spanish Armada. It's a reasonably stiff climb, followed by a tramp across Easby Moor to the south to the fifty-foot-high **Cook Monument** (1827) for more amazing views, before circling back to Great Ayton.

The Esk Valley **train station** lies half a mile northeast of town. **Buses** from Middlesbrough and Guisborough stop on the High Green, just back from which, in the car park, is the **tourist office** (Easter–Oct Mon–Sat 10am–4pm, Sun 1–4pm; ☎01642/722835), which has all the relevant Cook brochures and trail guides. Great Ayton has two nice **pubs**: the *Buck* at Low Green by the river and the *Royal Oak* on High Green.

Beck Hole and Goathland

South of Grosmont, train, footpath and beck climb out of the Esk Valley towards Goathland. Only on foot will you be able to stop at **BECK HOLE**, after a couple of miles, an idyllic bridgeside hamlet focused on the *Birch Hall Inn*, one of the finest rural pubs in all England – tiny to the point of claustrophobic, still doubling as a sweet shop and store as it has for a century, and serving great slabs of sandwiches with local ham and home-baked pies.

A gentle path from the hamlet runs the mile through the fields up to **GOATHLAND**, another highly attractive village, this time set in open moorland beneath the great expanses of Wheeldale and Goathland moors. If it seems oddly familiar – and if it seems unduly crowded – it's because it's widely known as "Aidensfield", the fictional village at the centre of the *Heartbeat* TV series. Pub, shop, garage and houses are all roped in to appear in most episodes: the large car parks tell of its popularity on the tourbus circuit. Real fans won't want to miss the exhibitions and TV props contained within the **Goathland Exhibition Centre** (daily 10am–5.30pm; £2.10), a local history centre sited near St Mary's Church. Outside summer weekends, when it's packed to distraction, Goathland can still be a joy to wander, with signposts pointing you to the local sight, the **Mallyan Spout**, a seventy-foot-high waterfall. This lies half a mile or so from the imposing, stone *Mallyan Spout Hotel* on the common (☎01947/896486; ⑤), itself the best place to stay, and certainly the best place to eat and drink; there are bar meals and a recommended restaurant. Plenty of other local B&Bs offer much cheaper rooms: keep an eye out for signs, or book through Whitby's tourist office.

At Goathland, you're handily poised for the hike up the moor to Wheeldale Lodge youth hostel and the Roman road (see p.827), while steam trains chunter back to Pickering from the station below the village.

The North Yorkshire coast

A bracing change after the flattened seascapes of East Anglia and much of East Yorkshire, the **North Yorkshire coast** is the southernmost stretch of a cliff-edged shore that stretches almost unbroken to the Scottish border. **Scarborough** is the biggest town and resort, and the terminus for bus and rail links from York and beyond. Like many places hereabouts it has tempting sands, though the vagaries of the northern climate and the chilly North Sea waters mean that you'll probably do little more than admire them from afar. Cute **Robin Hood's Bay** is the most popular of the many Yorkshire villages, with fishing and smuggling traditions, while bluff **Staithes** – a fishing harbour on the far edge of North Yorkshire – has yet to tip over into full-blown tourist mode. **Whitby**, in between the two, is the best stopover, its fine sands and resort facilities tempered by its abbey ruins, cobbled streets, Georgian buildings and maritime heritage – more than any other local place Whitby celebrates Captain Cook as one of its own. Heading to virtually any of the smaller coastal hamlets will bring you to similar-looking but far quieter spots, and for those who want to sample the most dizzying cliff-tops, the **Cleveland Way** provides a marked path along virtually the entire length of the coast.

Hourly **buses** (fewer on Sundays) run along the A171 between Scarborough and Whitby, and a similarly frequent service operates to Robin Hood's Bay, and north between Whitby and Staithes. The Yorkshire Coastliner service connects Leeds and York with Scarborough (hourly) or Whitby (2–4 daily). You can also reach Scarborough direct by **train** from York (1hr) or Hull (1hr 30min).

Scarborough

The oldest resort in the country, **SCARBOROUGH** first attracted early seventeenth-century visitors to its newly discovered mineral springs. By the 1730s, the more enterprising spa-goers were also venturing onto the sweeping local sands and dipping themselves in the bracing North Sea, popularizing the racy pastime of sea-bathing. Still fashionable in Victorian times – to whom it was "the Queen of the Watering Places" – Scarborough saw its biggest transformation after World War II, when it (and many other resorts) became a holiday haven for workers from the industrial heartlands. In the 1950s, three million visitors a year thronged the beaches, rode on the donkeys and paddled in the rock pools, enjoying the full-blooded facilities of a town that, in a memorable phrase of Paul Theroux's, "had the same ample contours as its landladies". The age of air travel changed the holiday demographics of all English resorts, but although numbers are down since its heyday, you wouldn't necessarily know it on a hot summer's day when there are long queues outside the seafront fish-and-chip shops and ice cream stalls. All the traditional ingredients of a beach resort are here in force, from superb, clean sands, kitsch amusement arcades and Kiss-Me-Quick hats to the more refined pleasures of its tightknit old-town streets and a genteel round of quiet parks and gardens.

The Town

There's no better place to acquaint yourself with the local layout than from the walls of **Scarborough Castle** (April–Oct daily 10am–6pm; Nov–March Wed–Sun 10am–1pm & 2–4pm; £2.30; EH), mounted on a jutting headland between two golden-sanded bays east of the town centre. Bronze and Iron Age relics have been found on the wooded castle crag, together with fragments of a fourth-century Roman signalling station, Saxon and Norman chapels and a Viking camp, reputedly built by a Viking with the nickname of *Scardi* (or "harelip"), from which the town's name derives. The present castle consists mainly of a three-storey keep (1158–64), a thirteenth-century barbican and raking buttressed walls which trace the cliff edge. Although besieged many times, the fortifications were never taken by assault, its only fall coming in the Civil War when the Parliamentarians starved the garrison into surrender. It took a further pounding from an infamous German naval bombardment of the town in 1914. As you leave the castle, drop into the church of **St Mary** (1180), immediately below on Castle Road, whose graveyard contains the tomb of Anne Brontë, who died here in 1849.

The town museums are clustered around Valley Road, south of the train station, most notably the Victorian **Wood End** on The Crescent (May–Sept Tues–Sun 10am–5pm; Oct–April Wed, Sat & Sun 11am–4pm; free), the holiday home of the Sitwell family of writers and aesthetes; there's a fine conservatory and various natural history collections. The nearby **Rotunda Museum** on Vernon Road (May–Sept Tues–Sun 10am–5pm; Oct–April Tues, Sat & Sun 11am–4pm; free), housed in a circular Georgian rotunda of great refinement, holds the local archeological and historic finds, including Gristhorpe Man, a 3500-year-old local found buried with his grave goods in a hollowed oak trunk; there's also a diverting exhibition on the famous **Scarborough Fair**, first granted a charter by Henry III in 1253. After this, the chief distraction is the unexpected concentration of Pre-Raphaelite art in the church of **St-Martin-on-the-Hill** (1863) further south on Albion Road. The Victorian-Gothic pile has a roof by William Morris, a triptych by Burne-Jones, a pulpit with four printed panels by Rossetti, stained glass by Morris, Burne-Jones and Ford Madox Brown, and an east wall whose tracery provides the frames for angels by Morris and *The Adoration of the Magi* by Burne-Jones.

The bays

Most of what passes for family entertainment takes place on the **North Bay** – massive water slides at Atlantis, the kids' amusements at Kinderland, and the miniature North Bay Railway (daily Easter–Sept), which runs up to the most educational of the lot, the **Sea Life Centre**, with its pools of flounders, rock-pool habitats and fishy exhibits. The most enjoyable **amusements and rides** are the old-fashioned ones on the harbour, under the castle, where creaky dodgems and shooting galleries compete for custom. From the harbourside here you'll be able to take one of the short **cruises and speed-boat trips** that shoot off throughout the day in the summer; or look over the *Hatherleigh*, a deep-sea trawler permanently moored on the Lighthouse Pier.

The **South Bay** is more refined, backed by the pleasant Valley Gardens and the Italianate meanderings of the South Cliff Gardens, and topped by an esplanade from which a **hydraulic lift** (continuous service until 4pm, summer 10pm; 30p) putters down to the beach. Here, Scarborough's Regency and Victorian glories are still evident in hotels like the *Crown* and, most impressively of all, the **Grand Hotel** built in 1867 by Cuthbert Broderick, the shaper of central Leeds. Its six million bricks and fifty-two chimneys dominate the cliff-top, an ensemble which drew high praise from architectural arbiter Nikolaus Pevsner, who thought it a "high Victorian gesture of assertion and confidence". For years now it's been operated as a pack-'em-in-cheap lodging house by *Butlin's* holiday company, which means no one will stop you if you stroll in through the still-grand interior, buy a drink at the bar and head out onto the gargantuan, neglected terrace from which the views of town, beach and castle are magnificent.

It's a fair hike from one end of Scarborough to the other; ease the strain by taking one of the **seafront buses** (60p) which run throughout the summer from the *Corner Café* in North Bay to the Spa Complex in South Bay.

Arrival and information

The **train station** is at the top of town facing Westborough; buses pull up outside or in the surrounding streets, though the National Express services (direct from London) stop in the car park behind the station. Scarborough's **tourist office** is in Pavilion House, Valley Bridge Road (daily May–Sept 9.30am–6pm; daily Oct–April 10am–4.30pm; ☎01723/373333), just over the road from the station, diagonally opposite the landmark Stephen Joseph Theatre (see below). To reach the harbour and castle, walk straight down Westborough, Newborough and Eastborough, through the main shopping streets.

Accommodation

Scarborough is crammed with inexpensive **hotels and guest houses**. In high season, if you arrive without a reservation, you'd do best to head straight for the tourist office and let them find something; at other times it's worth looking around for the best deals, since off-season prices often drop considerably. Happy hunting grounds include North Bay's Queen's Parade, where most of the guest houses have sweeping bay views and parking; to be closer to the castle head up its continuation, Blenheim Terrace, where a score more options await. The cheapest places in town are those without the sea views – try along central Aberdeen Walk (off Westborough), or on North Marine Road and Trafalgar Square, behind Queen's Parade. Above South Bay, hotels tend to be pricier, though there's a clutch of B&Bs along and around West Street.

The **youth hostel** occupies a converted watermill at the White House, Burniston Road, Scalby Mills (☎01723/361176); it's a mile or so north of the town centre on the A165 and ten minutes' walk from the Sea Life Centre and the sea; the Cleveland Way passes close by. Most of the town's huge **campsites** are in this area, too, handy for the North Bay: *Scalby Manor Caravan Park* (☎01723/366212; closed Nov–Easter) and *Scalby Close Park* (☎01723/365908; closed Nov–Easter), both on Burniston Road, have tent spaces.

Hotel Anatolia, 21 West St (☎01723/360864). Nice old Victorian redbrick, one block back from the Esplanade, on a street full of similar choices. No credit cards. ②.

Crown Hotel, Esplanade (☎01723/373491). Built in 1847 in a Regency terrace above South Bay, the *Crown* makes the most of its period features, views and genteel feel. Dinner, bed and breakfast rates offer the best deal. ⑥.

Interludes, 32 Princess St (☎01723/360513). Quiet Georgian town house in the old-town streets behind the harbour. Bay views from the upper floors, and theatre bills, photographs and traditional English decor throughout; call for details of Stephen Joseph Theatre breaks. ③.

Paragon Hotel, 123 Queen's Parade (☎01723/372676). Standard B&B rooms, though an above-average breakfast lifts the spirits. No credit cards. ②.

Red Lea Hotel, Prince of Wales Terrace (☎01723/362431). Part of a stylish terrace above South Bay, boasting sea-view rooms and a small indoor pool. ⑤.

Riviera, St Nicholas Cliff (☎01723/372277). Restored Victorian hotel opposite the Grand (down Bar Street, off Westborough) with super bay views and en-suite rooms. ③.

Whiteley Hotel, 99 Queen's Parade (☎01723/373514). Formerly a Victorian merchant's house (its best facade facing North Marine Rd, around the back), this is one of the best Queen's Parade options with good-value en-suite rooms. ②.

Cafés and restaurants

Cafés, fish-and-chip shops and **tearooms** are thick on the ground: those down by the harbour are of variable quality and popularity, serving up fried food as fast the punters can get it down. There's a more discerning selection when it comes to **restaurants**, not least because the town has a fair-sized Italian population – including the descendants of several POWs who were held at Malton's Eden Camp (see p.807) and settled in Scarborough after the war.

Bonnet, Huntriss Row, off Westborough (☎01723/361033). The Victorian-styled pedestrianized street has several coffee shops worth investigating: this one is also open for dinner (Wed–Sat until 9.30pm). Inexpensive.

Café Italia, 36 St Nicholas Cliff. Utterly charming, microscopic Italian coffee bar next to the *Grand Hotel*, where genuine coffee, foccaccia slices and ice cream keep a battery of regulars happy. Inexpensive.

Il Castello, 34–36 Castle Rd (☎01723/377312). The town's best pizzas, and some inventive home-made pastas and other Italian dishes, at slightly higher prices than usual. Closed Mon & Tues. Moderate.

Florio's, 37 Aberdeen Walk, off Westborough (☎01723/351124). Cheery pasta-and-pizza restaurant, popular with families and parties, open evenings only. Moderate.

Gianni's, 13 Victoria Rd (☎01723/507388). The most immediately welcoming of the town's Italian restaurants, housed in a Scarborough town house. The good-natured staff bustle up and down stairs, delivering quality pizzas, pastas and quaffable wine by the carafe. Moderate.

The Golden Grid, 4 Sandside (☎01723/360922). The harbourside's choicest fish-and-chip establishment, "catering for the promenader since 1883". Offers grilled fish, a *fruits-de-mer* platter and a wine list alongside the standard crispy-battered fry-up. Closed Mon–Thurs dinner in winter. Inexpensive–Moderate.

Lanterna, 33 Queen St (☎01723/363616). Long-established, special-night-out destination, featuring traditional, seasonal Italian cooking in quiet, formal surroundings. Closed Sun. Expensive.

Stephen Joseph Theatre Restaurant, Westborough (☎01723/368463). Fashionable food in the theatre restaurant including bangers and mash, French and Med-inspired mains, seasonal salads and desserts. Closed Sun, and other evenings when there's no performance. Moderate.

Drinking, nightlife and entertainment

Best **pub** by miles is the *Hole in the Wall* on Vernon Road, a cosy, real-ale haunt with beer-knowledgeable staff and good food (noon–2pm). The *Alma* on Alma Parade, at the top of Westborough, is a thoroughly decent local, as is the *Leeds Arms* on St Mary's Street below the church and castle. The *Highlander*, next to the Crown on the Esplanade, has a traditional lounge bar with beer garden, and its owner has a collection of over a thousand bottles of whisky – drams from around fifty of them are for sale.

The cultural heart of Scarborough is not the Spa Complex or Futurist Theatre and their end-of-pier summer shows but the **Stephen Joseph Theatre** (☎01723/370541), on the corner of Westborough and Valley Bridge Road, opposite the train station. Housed in a former Art Deco cinema, this premieres every new play of local playwright Alan Ayckbourn and promotes strong seasons of theatre and film; a good café/restaurant (see above) and bar is open daily except Sunday.

Hayburn Wyke and Ravenscar

At **Hayburn Wyke**, a tiny and tranquil bay mostly owned by the National Trust, Hayburn Beck runs through scrub and woodland before tumbling onto the rocky beach in a small waterfall. The waters have carved away layers of the surrounding boulder clay, making this a good spot to forage for fossils. The Cleveland Way cuts through from Scarborough, six miles to the south, but road access takes you only as far as the *Hayburn Wyke Hotel*, half a mile back from the beach, an arrangement which keeps the bay area and the adjoining 34-acre nature reserve remarkably unspoilt.

A back-lane drive, or – one of the Cleveland Way's more exhilarating passages – a four-mile hike over the five-hundred-foot ramparts of **Beast Cliff**, brings you to the village of **RAVENSCAR**, six hundred feet above the sea in the lee of tumuli-spotted Stoupe Brow (871ft). Views to the north around the sweep of Robin Hood's Bay are superb, particularly from the mock-battlemented *Raven Hall Hotel* (☎01723/870353; ⑥), constructed on the site of an old Roman signal station and used as a hideaway for George III when his bouts of madness kept him from the public gaze. There's a small charge for non-patrons to wander the hotel's panoramic cliff-edge terraces or to use the Yorkshire coast's most precariously sited and windswept swimming pool. The hotel marks the end of the Lyke Wake Walk (see p.818), so it's not uncommon to see hikers celebrating with a beer in front of the open fire.

Close by is a National Trust **Coastal Centre** (Easter–Sept daily 10.30am–5pm; ☎01723/870138), which has displays on the village's dead-end streets and isolated houses, part of an 1895 scheme to create "another Scarborough", an enterprise foiled by the cliffs' unstable geology. Also featured are the fossils that can be found on the coast immediately below; it's well worth scrambling down the path to the left of the hotel, but take great care on the foreshore, where the tide is fast-rising – explore on the ebb tide only and don't be tempted into swimming. The most detailed exhibits, however, relate to the area's **alum mines**. Quarries dot the Old Peak cliffs and the ridges of Stoupe Brow, where alum was mined between 1640 and 1862, the mineral being used in the leather and textile industry to fix dyes, and in the manufacture of candles and parchment. The industry declined in the nineteenth century, as chemical byproducts of the iron and steel foundries came to replace alum in many of the processes in which it had been used. The last mine closed in 1871, and a marked trail from the centre takes you past re-excavated workings.

B&B is available at *Smugglers Rock*, a Georgian country house with good views (☎01723/870044; no credit cards; ②; closed mid-Nov to Feb). There's a tearoom, too, *Foxcliffe* (☎01723/871028; closed Nov to mid-March), while *Bent Rigg Farm* (☎01723/870475), a little way southeast of the church, has a bunkhouse and space for camping (closed Nov–April).

Robin Hood's Bay

Although known as Robbyn Huddes Bay as early as Tudor times, there's nothing except half-remembered myth to link **ROBIN HOOD'S BAY** with Sherwood's legendary bowman – locals anyway prefer the old name, Bay Town or simply Bay. Perhaps the best-known and most heavily visited spot on the coast, the village fully lives up to its reputation, with narrow streets and pink-tiled cottages toppling down the cliff-edge site, evoking the romance of a time when this was both a hard-bitten fishing community and smugglers' den *par excellence*. So packed together are the houses, legend has it that ill-gotten booty could be passed up the hill from cottage to cottage without the pursuing king's men being any the wiser.

From the upper village, lined with Victorian villas, now mostly B&Bs, it's a 1-in-3 walk down the hill to the harbour. Here, Bay is little more than a couple of narrow streets lined with gift shops and cafés, and a steep slipway that leads down to the curving, rocky **shoreline**. When the tide is out, the massive rock beds are exposed, split by a geological fault line and studded with fossil remains. There's an easy walk to **Boggle Hole** and its youth hostel, a mile south, returning inland via South House Farm and the path along the old Scarborough–Whitby railway line (see below). Back in the old village, a rash of second-hand bookshops has appeared, the biggest and best being The Old Chapel, in the old hillside Wesleyan Chapel. Author **Leo Walmsley** (1892–1966), who spent his childhood in Bay, was educated in the chapel's schoolroom and later wrote several novels of seaside life coloured by his experiences. One, *Three Fevers*, was filmed in Robin Hood's Bay and Whitby as *Turn of the Tide* (1935), the first feature by the newly formed J. Arthur Rank organization.

Practicalities

The main approach, the B1447, comes in from the north off the A171, and you have to leave cars in the two **car parks** in the upper part of the village. **Buses** from Scarborough or Whitby, seven miles north, drop you here too. Whitby has the nearest train station, and the nearest tourist office (see p.839); **walkers**, along the coastal Cleveland Way, can make Whitby to Robin Hood's Bay in around three hours.

Accommodation is plentiful, but often in short supply during high season. Many people see the village as a day-trip from Whitby, and you can check on Bay accommodation in the tourist office there, or simply stroll the streets of the lower, old part of the village to see if any of the small cottage B&Bs have got vacancies. There are also three good **pubs** in the lower village, two of which have rooms: the tiny *Laurel*, on Main Street (☎01947/880400; ①; two-night minimum), whose small self-catering flat sleeps two; and the *Bay Hotel*, right on the harbour (☎01947/880278; ②), which is the traditional start or end of the Coast-to-Coast Walk. As well as a score of guest houses in the upper village, there's the late-Victorian *Victoria Hotel*, Station Road (☎01947/880205; ④), at the top of the hill, with fine views from some of its rooms, and a cliff-top beer garden. You'll probably end up **eating** in the pubs – food at the *Bay Horse* is the best – though the *Bramblewick Tearooms* near the harbour is open in the early evenings in summer and serves home-made meals and fresh fish. *The Old Chapel* bookshop has a vegetarian café, super coastal views from its terrace tables and weekly folk gigs; and *Bay Fisheries*, a wet-fish shop next to the *Laurel*, serves crab sandwiches to take away. The other pub, the eighteenth-century *Dolphin* in King Street, is the oldest in the village, and has folk nights every Friday.

Boggle Hole's **youth hostel** is one of Yorkshire's most popular, a former mill located in a wooded ravine about a mile south of Robin Hood's Bay at Mill Beck (☎01947/880352). Note that a torch is essential after dark, and that you can't access the hostel along the beach once the tide is up.

Hawsker

The twenty-mile Whitby to Scarborough railway line was a victim of the 1960s' cuts, though its length has been preserved as a bridleway which makes an alternative route to the Cleveland Way. The best section is undoubtedly that between Whitby and Ravenscar via Robin Hood's Bay, boasting huge views of the tumbling cliffs and sparkling sea. A couple of miles northwest of Robin Hood's Bay at **HAWSKER**, on the

BRAM STOKER AND DRACULA

For a moment or two I could see nothing, as the shadow of a cloud obscured St Mary's Church. Then as the cloud passed I could see the ruins of the Abbey coming into view; and as the edge of a narrow band of light as sharp as a sword-cut moved along, the church and churchyard became gradually visible. . . [It] seemed to me as though something dark stood behind the seat where the white figure shone, and bent over it. What it was, whether man or beast, I could not tell.

Dracula, Bram Stoker

It was, of course, the figure of the voracious Count, feasting upon the blood of Lucy. Her friend Mina Murray – despite "flying along the fish-market to the bridge" and "toiling" up the endless steps to the Abbey – failed to save her. The story of Dracula is well known, but it's this exact attention to the geographical detail of Whitby – little changed since Stoker first wrote the words – which has proved a huge attraction to visitors on the Dracula trail.

Bram Stoker (1847–1912) was born in Dublin and wrote his first stories while working in the Irish civil service. A meeting with Sir Henry Irving in 1877 led him to quit his job and move to London, where he became Irving's manager and close friend. Forgettable adventure novels followed, until in 1890, on holiday in Whitby, Stoker began to become interested in writing a story of vampires and the undead, already popularized in "Gothic" novels earlier that century. Using first-hand observation of a town he knew well – he stayed at a house on the West Cliff, now marked by a plaque – Stoker built a story which mixed real locations, legend, myth and historical fact: the grounding of Count Dracula's ship on Tate Hill Sands was based on an actual event reported in the local papers. The novel was published in 1897 and became synonymous with Stoker's name; it's been filmed, with varying degrees of faithfulness, dozens of times since, though no film version has yet used Whitby as a backdrop.

With many of the early chapters recognizably set in Whitby, it's hardly surprising that the town has cashed in on its **Dracula Trail** – ask at the tourist office for details. The various sites – Tate Hill Sands, the abbey, church and steps, the graveyard, Stoker's house – can all be visited, while down on the harbourside the Dracula Experience attempts to pull in punters to its rather lame horror-show antics. Keen interest has also been sparked amongst the **Goth** fraternity, who now come to town en masse a couple of times a year (usually in late spring and around Halloween) for a vampire's ball, concerts and readings; at these times the streets are overrun with pasty-faced characters in Regency dress, wedding gowns, top hats and capes, meeting and greeting at their unofficial headquarters, the otherwise sedate *Elsinore* pub on Flowergate. A kind of truce has been called with the authorities at St Mary's church, who understandably objected to the more lurid goings-on in the churchyard at midnight; these have largely been curtailed and now there's even a special Goths service held at the church.

A171, Trailways (☎01947/820207) is a bike rental outfit based in the old Hawsker train station, perfectly placed for day-trips along the largely flat railway line in either direction. They'll deliver or pick up from local addresses (including Boggle Hole youth hostel); there's also a refreshments kiosk at the station, a small campsite and bunkhouse.

Whitby

If there's one essential stop on the North Yorkshire coast it's **WHITBY**, whose historical associations, atmospheric ruins, fishing harbour and intrinsic charm make it many people's favourite northern resort. The seventh-century abbey here made Whitby one of the key foundations of the early Christian period, and a centre of great learning, though little interfered with the fishing community which scraped together a living on the harbour banks of the River Esk below. For a thousand years, the local herring boats landed their catch until the great whaling boom of the eighteenth century transformed the fortunes of the town. Melville's *Moby Dick* makes much of Whitby whalers like William Scoresby, while James Cook took his first seafaring steps from the town in 1746, on his way to becoming a national hero. All four of Captain Cook's ships of discovery – the *Endeavour, Resolution, Adventure* and *Discovery* – were built in Whitby: the return of the replica *Endeavour* in 1997, billed as the "homecoming", attracted a crowd of 100,000; there are also plans to moor a replica *Resolution* in town.

Hemmed in by steep cliffs and divided by the River Esk, the town splits into two distinct halves joined by a swing bridge: the **old town** to the east, centred on a curving cobbled street of great character, and the newer (though mostly eighteenth- and nineteenth-century) town across the bridge, generally known as **West Cliff**, which is home to the quayside, most of the hotels and shops, and the few arcades, amusements and souvenir stalls that have been allowed to proliferate. Virtually everything you want to see is in or above the old town on the east side, principally the glorious Abbey ruins and St Mary's church, and the Captain Cook Memorial Museum, though the town museum on the west side shouldn't be missed by anyone with a nostalgic bent.

Walkers should note that two of the best parts of the Cleveland Way depart from Whitby: southeast to Robin Hood's Bay (six miles) and northwest to Staithes (eleven miles), both along thrilling high-cliff sections.

The old town and abbey

Cobbled **Church Street** is the old town's main thoroughfare, barely changed in aspect since the eighteenth century, though now lined with tearooms and gift shops, many selling jewellery and ornaments made from **jet**. This hard, black natural carbon, found locally, was worn first by the Romans but received its greatest boost after being shown at the Great Exhibition of 1851, after which it was popularized as mourning wear. In nineteenth-century Whitby, the industry employed over a thousand people, many working in factories around Church Street; now just a handful of workshops remain. Parallel Sandgate has more of the same, the two streets meeting at the small marketplace where souvenirs and trinkets are sold. Off either side, impossibly skinny alleys ("yards") – once gated, to keep out thieves – lead to quiet courtyards and flower-decked cottages.

At the end of Church Street, you climb the famous **199 steps** of the Church Stairs – now paved, but originally a wide wooden staircase built for pallbearers carrying coffins to the church of St Mary above. Having made the climb, you've followed in the fictional footsteps of Bram Stoker's **Dracula**, who in the eponymous novel (see box opposite) takes the form of a large dog that bounds up the steps after the wreck of the ship bearing his coffin. In the precarious cliffside graveyard he claimed Lucy as his victim, taking refuge in the grave of a suicide victim, which he then used as a base for his nocturnal forays. On wild and windswept nights the atmosphere up here is still suitably ghoulish; during the day, the views over the harbour and town are magnificent, while a little searching reveals the grave of William Scoresby Snr, master whaler, and inventor of the crow's nest.

The bizarre parish church of **St Mary** at the top of the steps, loftily removed from the town it served, is an architectural dog's dinner dating back to 1110, boasting a Norman chancel arch, a profusion of eighteenth-century panelling, box pews unequalled in England and a triple-decker pulpit – note the built-in ear trumpets, added for the benefit of a nineteenth-century rector's deaf wife. The Cholmley family pew, in particular, almost obscuring the chancel, is superb, a capricious confection of twisting wooden columns. Notice also the galleries, arranged like a ship's decks, and the roof, constructed by seventeenth-century naval carpenters as if part of a ship's cabin.

The cliff-top ruins of **Whitby Abbey** (daily: April–Sept 10am–6pm; Oct–March 10am–4pm; £1.70; EH), beyond St Mary's, are some of the most evocative in England, the nave, soaring north transept and lancets of the east end giving a hint of the building's former delicacy and splendour. Its monastery was founded in 657 by Saint Hilda of Hartlepool, daughter of King Oswy of Northumberland, and by 664 had become important enough to host the **Synod of Whitby**, an event of seminal importance in the development of English Christianity. It settled once and for all the question of determining the date of Easter, and adopted the rites and authority of the Roman rather than the Celtic Church. One of the burning issues decided was whether priests should shave their tonsures in the shape of a ring or a crescent. **Caedmon**, one of the brothers at the abbey during its earliest years who was reputedly charged with looking after Hilda's pigs, has a twenty-foot cross in his memory which stands in front of St Mary's, at the top of the steps. His nine-line *Song of Creation* is the earliest surviving poem in English, making the abbey not only the cradle of English Christianity, but also the birthplace of English literature. The original abbey was destroyed by the Danes in 867 and refounded by the Benedictines in 1078, though most of the present ruins – built slightly south of the site of the Saxon original – date from between 1220 and 1539.

Whitby likes to make a fuss of Captain Cook who served an apprenticeship here from 1746–49 under John Walker, a Quaker shipowner. The **Captain Cook Memorial Museum** (Easter–Oct daily 9.45am–5pm; March Sat & Sun 11am–3pm; £2.60), housed in Walker's rickety old house in Grape Lane (just over the bridge on the east side, on the right), contains an impressive amount of memorabilia, including ships' models, letters and paintings by artists seconded to Cook's voyages. The eighteen-year-old Cook assisted on the coal runs between Newcastle and London, learning his seafaring skills in flat-bottomed craft called "cats". Designed for inshore and river work their specifications were to prove perfect for Cook's later surveys of the South Sea Islands and the Australian coast. When he wasn't at sea, Cook, together with the other apprentices, slept in Walker's attic.

West Cliff

Whitby developed as a holiday resort in the nineteenth century, partly under the influence of entrepreneur George Hudson, who had brought the railway to town. Wide streets, elegant crescents, boarding houses and hotels were laid on the heights of **West Cliff**, across the harbour from the old town, topped by a whalebone arch, commemorating Whitby's former industry, and a statue of Captain Cook. The small **harbour front** below, along Pier Road, sports an active fish market and a run of arcades and chip shops, leading to the twin, pincered piers and lighthouses: when the tide's out, the broad, clean sands to the west stretch for three miles to **Sandsend** (where the beer garden of the *Hart Inn* makes a tempting target).

More matters maritime are explored in the **Whitby Lifeboat Museum** (irregular hours; donation requested), on Pier Road, the best museum of its kind in the country. Whitby lifeboat crews over the years have won more RNLI gold medals for gallantry than any other crew in Britain; you'd envy none of them the job, particularly after seeing one exhibit, the last RNLI hand-rowed boat, a flimsy-looking craft used until well into this century. A more recent lifeboat now carries passengers out of the harbour on short **cruises**, leaving from the bandstand most summer days.

Final port of call should be the gloriously eccentric **Whitby Museum** in Pannett Park (May–Sept Mon–Sat 9.30am–5.30pm, Sun 2–5pm; Oct–April Mon–Tues 10.30am–1pm, Wed–Sat 10.30am–4pm, Sun 2–4pm; £1), at the back of West Cliff, back from the train station. There's more Cook memorabilia, including various of the ethnic objects and stuffed animals brought back as souvenirs by his crew, as well as casefuls of exhibits devoted to Whitby's seafaring tradition, its whaling industry in particular. Some of the best and largest fossils of Jurassic period reptiles unearthed on the east coast are also preserved here, while the rest of the museum is a fine jumble of local material, all carefully annotated in spidery handwriting and on clunky typed cards.

Practicalities

Trains on the Esk Valley line to Whitby from Middlesbrough, via Danby and Grosmont (for connections for the North Yorkshire Moors Railway), arrive at the station in Station Square, a couple of hundred yards south of the bridge to the old town. **Buses** from the adjacent bus station run hourly to Robin Hood's Bay, Scarborough, Middlesbrough and points between, and there's a regular summer bus service to Grosmont. Yorkshire Coastliner services from Leeds, York and Pickering drop here, too, as do National Express buses from London and York.

Whitby's **tourist office** (daily: May–Sept 9.30am–6pm; Oct–April 10am–4.30pm; ☎01947/602674) is a right turn outside the train station to the corner of Langborne Road and New Quay Road, opposite the Co-op, and will book accommodation.

ACCOMMODATION

The main B&B concentrations are on West Cliff, in the streets stretching back from the elegant Royal Crescent. Across the river in the old town, several pubs have rooms, while if you're prepared to travel a couple of miles out of Whitby you can find some pleasant inns and hotels in relaxed country surroundings.

The very popular **youth hostel**, East Cliff (☎01947/602878), is a converted stable a stone's throw from the abbey, with superb views over the town – book well in advance. There's a backpackers' hostel, *Harbour Grange*, at Spital Bridge, also on the eastern side of the river (☎01947/600817). The nearest **campsite** is a mile west of town on the Sandsend road, at *Sandfield House Caravan Park* (☎01947/602660; mid-March to Oct), though it only has a few tent sites.

Beehive, Newholm (☎01947/602703). Isolated country pub in a hamlet a couple of miles inland, reached down the Sandsend road, with a roaring log fire in winter and sunny space outside in summer. ②.

The Dolphin, Bridge St (☎01947/602197). The pub by the swing bridge has riverside views from some of its B&B rooms. ②.

Duke of York, Church St (☎01947/600324) At the bottom of the 199 steps, this popular pub has ensuite rooms overlooking the harbour, and is only a few steps from the harbour beach. ②.

Dunsley Hall, Dunsley (☎01947/893437). Quite the grandest retreat in the locality, this stately oak-panelled pile has all the trimmings, including a pool, sauna and leisure club, a good restaurant and very clubbable bar. It's a couple of miles inland of town. ⑥.

Estbek House, Sandsend (☎01947/893424). Georgian house with restaurant and tea garden, overlooking the stream at Sandsend, a couple of miles from Whitby and just yards from the beach. ②.

Lavinia House, 3 East Crescent, Khyber Pass (☎01947/602945). Comfortable family-run guest house with five rooms, the largest at the front boasting sea views. The restaurant's recommended too, though you need to book in advance. No credit cards. ②.

Middle Earth, 26 Church St (☎01947/606014). A nice pub with rooms, decent beer and outdoor seats overlooking the marina. It's the other way down Church Street from the 199 steps, back past the bridge and along the river. ②.

Number Five, 5 Havelock Place (☎01947/606361). Amiable West Cliff B&B which provides a good breakfast and has a good atmosphere. No credit cards. ①.

Shepherd's Purse, 95 Church St (☎01947/820228). Popular wholefood shop and restaurant with its best rooms set around a galleried courtyard; vegetarian breakfast available. ②.

White Horse & Griffin, Church St (☎01947/604857). Easily the most atmospheric place to stay in the old town – a welcoming eighteenth-century coaching inn with comfortable en-suite rooms, open fires and a good fish restaurant. ②.

CAFÉS AND RESTAURANTS

Unsurprisingly, Whitby is well known for its freshly caught fish. A multitude of cafés around town – especially along Pier Road and Bridge Street – serve **fish and chips**, bread and tea for around £4, the same thing in most of the **restaurants** costs a few pounds more.

Ditto, 26 Skinner St (☎01947/601404). Smashing Italian restaurant that's serious about its food – the blackboard menu changes daily and you really need to book in advance. Dinner only, closed Sun & Mon. Moderate to Expensive.

The Dolphin, Bridge St (☎01947/602197). Great fresh fish meals in the pub – from calamari with salsa to grilled tuna or paella – as well as a popular carvery.

Grapevine, 2 Grape Lane (☎01947/820275). Best café in town, whose tiny kitchen dishes up great breakfasts and tasty tapas-style lunches and dinners (dinners, weekends only in winter). Inexpensive to Moderate.

Hadley's, 11 Bridge St (☎01947/604153). Most salubrious of the cheaper fish-and-chipperies with most things under a fiver. Inexpensive.

Huntsman Inn, Aislaby (☎01947/810637). It's well worth driving (or cabbing) out the couple of miles to Aislaby for the home-cooked pub food here – steaks a speciality. Inexpensive to Moderate.

Magpie Cafe, 14 Pier Rd (☎01947/602058). The traditional fish-and-chip choice in town for over forty years, with a wide-ranging menu. In summer you'll have to wait in long queues to get through the doors. Closes 9pm. Moderate.

Shepherd's Purse, 95 Church St (☎01947/820228). Daytime wholefood café meals give way to pizza, pasta and fish dinners in hippy-rustic surroundings. Moderate.

Trenchers, New Quay Rd (☎01947/603212). Highly rated fish-and-chip restaurant, near the tourist office, with booth seating, snappy service and mountainous portions – nearly always a queue in summer. Closes 9pm & all Nov–March. Moderate.

White Horse & Griffin, Church St (☎01947/604857). When it's on top of its game, the restaurant here is a real winner – well-cooked local fish and game, served in cosy bistro surroundings. Moderate to Expensive.

DRINKING, MUSIC AND FESTIVALS

There are scores of **pubs** in Whitby, including the *Duke of York* on Church Street, at the bottom of the 199 steps, with harbour views and a mixed clientele of tourists and locals, and the *Middle Earth*, with regular music nights (see "Accommodation" for both). On the other side of the river, the mock-rustic *Tap & Spile*, on New Quay Road near *Trenchers*, is the real-ale haunt, with a changing selection of guest beers and live folk music nearly every night. The *Little Angel*, at 18 Flowergate, and the *Elsinore* opposite, are both decent locals known for their beer, while the *Dolphin*, right on the bridge, has river views and a few outdoor tables.

Whitby is at the centre of the local **music scene**, with especially good folk nights in some of its pubs – English folk's first family, the Waterson/Carthys, are from nearby Robin Hood's Bay. There are regular year-round rock gigs at the *Angel Hotel*, on New Quay Road near the bridge, while pubs like the idiosyncratic *Black Horse*, 91 Church St, the *Fleece* also on Church Street (the other way towards the marina), and the *Tap & Spile*, New Quay Road, put on regular folk gigs. It all comes to a head during the annual **Whitby Folk Week** in August (the week immediately preceding the bank holiday), when the town's streets, pubs and concert halls are filled day and night with singers, bands, traditional dancers, storytellers and music workshops. A special festival campsite is usually set up, but if you want regular accommodation for this week, book well in advance. Other festivals throughout the year also make a splash, some with a seafaring theme; the **Regatta** every August is a weekend of fairground rides, spectacular harbourside fireworks and boat races; and the Goths descend a couple of times a year (see box on p.836) for a good-natured vampiric vacation.

Staithes

Beyond the beach at Sandsend, a fine coastal walk through pretty Runswick Bay leads in around four hours to the fishing village of **STAITHES**; road access is along the A174. At first sight, it's an improbably beautiful grouping of huddled stone houses around a small harbour, backed by the severe outcrop of Cowbar Nab, a sheer cliff face which protects the northern flank of the village. There's much less tourism here than in Robin Hood's Bay, which means few if any gift shops and only a smattering of cafés and B&Bs. Any time spent here, especially out of season, soon reveals its gruffer side – crumbling houses on either side of the beck, the fierce winter wind whistling down the cobbled main street, and the tenacious last gasp of a declining fishing fleet which once employed 300 men in 120 boats. Storms and floods have battered Staithes for centuries: the *Cod and Lobster*, the pub at the harbour, has been rebuilt three times and is shuttered against the wind, while the draper's shop in which James Cook first worked before moving to Whitby collapsed completely in 1745 – its rebuilt successor is now marked by a plaque. Cook is remembered in the **Captain Cook and Staithes Heritage Centre**, on the High Street (daily 10am–5.30pm; £1.75), which re-creates an eighteenth-century street among other interesting exhibits. Other than this, you'll have to content yourself with pottering about the rocks near the harbour – there's no beach to speak of – or clambering the nearby cliffs for spectacular views; at **Boulby**, a mile and a half's trudge up the coastal path (45min), you're walking on the highest cliff (670ft) on England's east coast. You may also be interested to learn that the coast between Whitby and Staithes has some of the best **surf** waves in Britain and there's quite a little local community dedicated to riding them – details and gear from Zero Gravity (☎01947/820660), Whitby's surfshop at 14 Flowergate.

Practicalities

The road into Staithes, off the A174, puts drivers into a **car park** at the top of the hill leading down into the old village; don't ignore the signs and drive down, since there's nowhere to park, and it's hard work turning round again. You could stay at one of the B&Bs in the houses at the top of the village, but better **accommodation** is available down below, either at the *Endeavour Restaurant* (☎01947/840825; no credit cards; ③; closed Sun in winter) – itself the best place to eat for miles around, with superb fresh fish meals at around £25 a head – or at one of the pubs; the *Black Lion* (☎01947/841132; ②) has functional bedrooms, cosy fires and a decent bar menu. Walkers and surfers are welcome at *York House*, High Barrass (☎01947/841187; no credit cards; ②), up a flight of steps off the High Street, at the bottom of the village; veggie breakfasts on request. There's **camping** back up the road out of the village at *Staithes Caravan Park*, Warp Mill (☎01947/840291; closed Nov–Feb).

travel details

Trains

Main routes and services are given below. For more detailed information about specific lines, turn to the following pages: Settle to Carlisle Railway (p.768); North Yorkshire Moors Railway (p.827); Keighley and Worth Valley Railway (p.752).

Harrogate to: Knaresborough (every 30min; 15min); Leeds (every 30min; 45min); York (hourly; 30min).

Hull to: Beverley (Mon–Sat hourly, Sun 4 daily; 15min); Leeds (hourly; 1hr); London (hourly; 3hr); Scarborough (every 2hr; 1hr 30min); York (10 daily; 1hr 15min).

Knaresborough to: Harrogate (every 30min; 15min); Leeds (every 30min; 45min); York (hourly; 30min).

Leeds to: Birmingham (10 daily; 2hr); Bradford (every 15min; 20min); Carlisle (3–9 daily; 2hr 40min); Harrogate (every 30min; 45min); Hull (hourly; 1hr); Knaresborough (every 30min; 45min); Lancaster (3 daily; 2hr); Liverpool (hourly; 2hr); London (every 30min; 2hr); Manchester (every 30min; 35min); Settle (3–8 daily; 1hr); Sheffield (every 30min; 45min–1hr 15min); Skipton (hourly; 40min); York (every 30min; 40min).

Pickering to: Grosmont (April–Oct 5–8 daily, plus limited winter service; 1hr).

Scarborough to: Hull (every 2hr; 1hr 30min); York (8–15 daily; 45min).

Sheffield to: Leeds (every 30min; 45min–1hr 15min); London (every 45min; 2hr 30min); York (hourly; 1hr 20min).

Whitby to: Danby (June–Sept 4 daily; Oct–March Mon–Sat 4 daily; 35min); Grosmont (June–Sept 4 daily; Oct–March Mon–Sat 4 daily; 15min); Middlesbrough (June–Sept 4 daily; Oct–March Mon–Sat 4 daily; 1hr 30min).

York to: Birmingham (10 daily; 2hr 40min); Bristol (10 daily; 4hr); Bradford (every 45min; 1hr); Durham (every 30min; 40min); Edinburgh (hourly; 2hr); Exeter (5 daily; 5hr); Harrogate (hourly; 35min); Hull (hourly; 1hr 15min); Leeds (every 30min; 40min); London (every 30min; 2hr); Manchester (hourly; 1hr 45min); Newcastle (every 30min; 1hr); Penzance (4 daily; 7hr 30min); Scarborough (8–15 daily; 45min); Sheffield (hourly; 1hr 20min).

Buses

Only main routes are given below; for others, particularly minor local services, check the text. It's essential to pick up either the Dales Connections or Moors Connections timetable booklets from a local tourist office; for details of the Moorsbus in the North York Moors National Park see p.816.

Helmsley to: Pickering (hourly; 40min); Scarborough (hourly; 1hr 40min); York (Mon–Sat 3 daily; 1hr 30min).

Harrogate to: Knaresborough (every 10–15min; 20min); Leeds (every 30–60min; 40min); Pateley Bridge (Mon–Sat hourly, Sun 2 daily; 50min); Ripon (every 30min; 30min); York (Mon–Sat hourly; 1hr 15min).

Pickering to: Castle Howard (May–Sept 1–3 daily; 30min); Helmsley (3–7 daily; 40min); Scarborough (Mon–Sat hourly, Sun 6 daily; 1hr); Whitby (5 daily; 1hr); York (Mon–Sat hourly, Sun 3 daily; 1hr 20min).

Scarborough to: Helmsley (3–6 daily; 1hr 35min); Hull (1 daily; 2hr); Leeds (hourly; 3hr); Malton (hourly; 1hr); Middlesbrough (4–8 daily; 2hr); Pickering (hourly; 1hr); Robin Hood's Bay (hourly; 45min); Whitby (hourly; 1hr); York (hourly; 1hr 45min).

Settle to: Horton-in-Ribblesdale (Mon–Sat 3–5 daily; 15min); Ingleton (Mon–Sat 3–4 daily; 30min); Skipton (Mon–Sat hourly; 40min).

Skipton to: Buckden (Mon–Sat 1–2 daily; 1hr 5min); Grassington (Mon–Sat hourly; 30min); Harrogate (5–6 daily; 1hr); Ilkley (hourly; 20min); Keighley (hourly Mon–Sat; 30min); Kettlewell (Mon–Sat 1–2 daily; 55min); Knaresborough (4 daily; 1hr 30min); Malham (Mon–Fri 2–3 daily; 40min–1hr 15min); Settle (Mon–Sat hourly; 40min); York (Mon–Sat 4 daily; 1hr 50min).

Whitby to: Castle Howard (May–Oct 1 daily; 1hr 15min); Grosmont (July–Sept 7 daily; 25min); Goathland (Mon–Fri 2 daily; 30min); Hull (1 daily; 2hr 45min); Malton (5 daily; 1hr 25min); Middlesbrough (10 daily; 1hr); Pickering (5 daily; 1hr); Robin Hood's Bay (hourly; 25min); Staithes (hourly; 30min); York (Mon–Sat 4 daily, Sun 1 daily; 2hr).

York to: Beverley (4 daily; 1hr 15min); Birmingham (1 daily; 4hr 25min); Blackpool (1 daily; 5hr); Bradford (5 daily; 1hr 45min); Cardiff (1 daily; 7hr 30min); Castle Howard (1–2 daily; 1hr); Derby (1 daily; 3hr 30min); Harrogate (Mon–Sat hourly; 1hr 15min); Hull (5 daily; 1hr 30min); Leeds (10 daily; 45min); London (4 daily; 4hr 20min); Manchester (1 daily; 4hr 25min); Newcastle (3 daily; 2hr 25min); Nottingham (2 daily; 3hr 35min); Pickering (Mon–Sat hourly, Sun 4 daily; 1hr 20min); Sheffield (4 daily; 2hr 15min); Skipton (5 daily; 1hr 50min); Whitby (Mon–Sat 4 daily, Sun 1 daily; 2hr).

CHAPTER ELEVEN

THE NORTHEAST

F or England's northeastern region – in particular the counties of **Northumberland** and **Durham** – the centuries between the Roman invasion and the 1603 union of England and Scotland were a period of almost incessant turbulence. To mark the empire's limit and to contain the troublesome tribes of the far north, **Hadrian's Wall** was built along the seventy-odd miles between the North Sea and the west coast, an extraordinary military structure that is now one of the country's most evocative ruins. When the Romans departed, the northeast was plunged into chaos and divided into unstable Saxon principalities until order was restored by the kings of Northumbria, who dominated the region from 600 until the 870s. It was they who nourished the region's early Christian tradition, which achieved its finest flowering with the creation of the **Lindisfarne Gospels** on what is now known as Holy Island. The monks abandoned their island at the end of the ninth century, in advance of the Vikings' destruction of the Northumbrian kingdom, and only after the Norman Conquest did the northeast again become part of a greater England.

The Norman kings and their immediate successors repeatedly attempted to subdue Scotland, passing effective regional control to powerful local lords. Their authority is recalled by a sequence of formidable coastal fortresses, most impressively those at **Bamburgh**, **Alnwick** and **Warkworth**, and also by **Durham Cathedral**, the magnificent twelfth-century church of the prince bishops of Durham, who ruled the whole of County Durham. Long after the northeast had ceased to be a critical military zone, its character and appearance were transformed by the **Industrial Revolution**. Coal had been mined here for hundreds of years, but exploitation only began in earnest towards the end of the eighteenth century, when two main coalfields were established – one dominating County Durham from the Pennines to the sea, the other stretching north along the Northumberland coast from the Tyne. The world's first **railway**, the **Darlington and Stockton** line, was opened in 1825 to move coal to the nearest port for export, while local coal and ore also fuelled the foundries of **Middlesbrough** and Consett, which in turn supplied the shipbuilding and heavy-engineering companies of Tyneside. The region boomed, creating a score of sizable towns, amongst which Newcastle was pre-eminent – as it remains today.

Most visitors dodge the industrial areas, bypassing the unsightly towns along the **Tees Valley** – Darlington, Stockton, Middlesbrough and Hartlepool – on the way to **Durham**. From Durham it's a short hop to **Newcastle**, an earthy city distinguished by some fine Victorian buildings and a vibrant cultural scene and nightlife. North, past the

ACCOMMODATION PRICE CODES

Throughout this guide, hotel and B&B accommodation is priced on a scale of ① to ⑨, the number indicating the **lowest price** you could expect to pay per night in that establishment for a **double room** in high season. The prices indicated by the codes are as follows:

① under £40	④ £60–70	⑦ £110–150
② £40–50	⑤ £70–90	⑧ £150–200
③ £50–60	⑥ £90–110	⑨ over £200

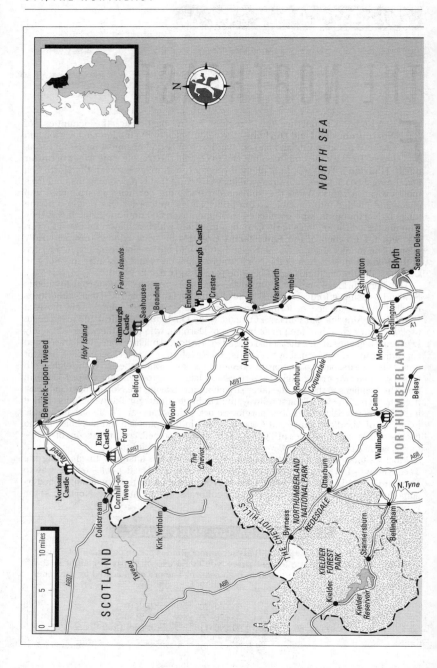

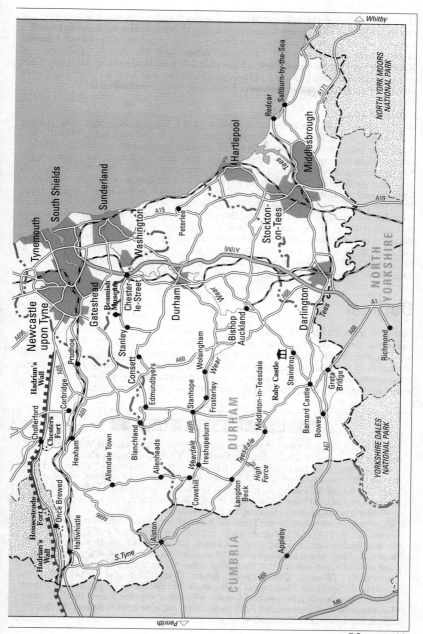

old colliery villages, the brighter parts of the Northumberland coast boast some fine castles, as well as **Holy Island**, the extravagant ramparts of **Berwick-upon-Tweed**, a string of superb, if chilly, beaches, and the desolate archipelago of the **Farne Islands**. Inland there are the scenic Durham **dales** and the harsh landscapes of **Northumberland National Park**, a huge chunk of moorland and tree plantations that edges the most dramatic portion of Hadrian's Wall. The wall itself is easily visited from the appealing abbey-town of **Hexham**, just half an hour from Newcastle.

Getting around

With frequent trains running up the coast on the London–Scotland route (calling principally at Darlington, Durham, Newcastle and Berwick-upon-Tweed), and numerous buses between the main towns, **getting around** the northeast without a car is usually not a problem, though it's more difficult to explore the Northumberland National Park. Durham, Newcastle, Hexham and Alnwick are the main transport hubs, while Hadrian's Wall has its own bus service, operating out of Carlisle and Hexham (see p.886). You might consider investing in a **travel pass**. The Northeast Explorer Pass (1-day, £4.95) gives unlimited travel on local buses from Berwick-upon-Tweed as far south as Scarborough in North Yorkshire or west to Carlisle – buy it on board any bus. Useful train passes include the Northeast Regional Rover (7 days; £65) and the wide-ranging North Country Rover (any 4 days out of 8; £55), which is valid as far south as Leeds and Hull and west as far as Preston. If you're relying on public transport, you'll find the *Northumberland Public Transport Guide* (£1) very useful – it's sold at most local tourist offices.

Durham

The view from **DURHAM** train station is one of the finest in northern England – a panoramic prospect of Durham Cathedral, its towers dominating the skyline from the top of a steep sandstone bluff within a narrow bend of the River Wear. This dramatic site has been the resting place of St Cuthbert since 995, when his body was moved here from nearby Chester-le-Street, over one hundred years after his fellow monks had fled from Lindisfarne in fear of the Vikings, carrying his coffin before them. Cuthbert's hal-

---

HIKING AND BIKING ROUTES

The main long-distance footpath through the Northeast is the **Pennine Way**, which cuts up from the Yorkshire Dales through the North Pennines, crosses Hadrian's Wall at Greenhead and then climaxes in a climb through the Northumberland National Park and Cheviot Hills. Less demanding is the 63-mile pilgrim's route, **St Cuthbert's Way**, which links Holy Island with Melrose, just across the border in Scotland, via Kirk Yetholm – northern end of the Pennine Way – and Wooler. Tourist offices in Berwick-upon-Tweed or Wooler have route and accommodation information.

Other major routes include the **Teesdale Way**, 90 miles from Middleton-in-Teesdale to Teesmouth (just beyond Middlesbrough), via Barnard Castle and Darlington (information and leaflets from Durham County Council, call ☎0191/386 4411); and the 78-mile **Weardale Way**, which follows the river from Cowshill at the head of the valley to the coast at Sunderland (information from Wear Valley and Sunderland tourist offices).

Sustrans's 140-mile **C2C cycle route** from Whitehaven/Workington to Sunderland/Newcastle ("Sea to Sea") also drops into the northeast just beyond Alston and links Allenheads, Stanhope and Consett with either city. You'll need the *C2C Route Map* and possibly the associated *B&B Guide*, both available from Sustrans, PO Box 21, Bristol, BS99 2HA (☎0117/929 0888).

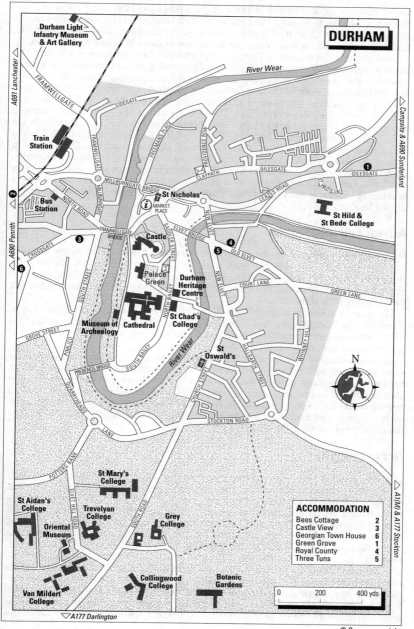

DURHAM

Durham Light Infantry Museum & Art Gallery

River Wear

A691 Lanchester

Campsite & A690 Sunderland

FRAMWELLGATE

SIDEGATE

Train Station

FREEMANS PLACE

PROVIDENCE ROW

CLAYPATH

GILESGATE

GILESGATE

ST CHILD'S LN

A690 Penrith

Bus Station

NORTH ROAD

MILLBURNGATE BRIDGE

St Nicholas'

MARKET PLACE

LEAZES ROAD

St Hild & St Bede College

CROSSGATE

FRAMWELLGATE BRIDGE

Castle

SADDLER STREET

ELVET BRIDGE

NEW ELVET

OLD ELVET

SOUTH STREET

Palace Green

Durham Heritage Centre

NORTH BAILEY

COURT LANE

GREEN LANE

GROVE STREET

Museum of Archeology

Cathedral

St Chad's College

NEW ELVET

HALLGARTH STREET

WHINNEY HILL

PIMLICO

SOUTH BAILEY

St Oswald's

River Wear

PREBENDS BRIDGE

CHURCH STREET

N

QUARRYHEADS LANE

STOCKTON ROAD

POTTERS BANK

St Mary's College

St Aidan's College

ELVET HILL ROAD

Trevelyan College

Oriental Museum

SOUTH ROAD

Grey College

Van Mildert College

Collingwood College

Botanic Gardens

ACCOMMODATION

Bees Cottage	2
Castle View	3
Georgian Town House	6
Green Grove	1
Royal County	4
Three Tuns	5

A177 Darlington

A1(M) & A177 Stockton

0   200   400 yds

© Crown copyright

lowed remains made Durham a place of pilgrimage for both the Saxons and the Normans, who began work on the present cathedral at the end of the eleventh century. In the meantime, William the Conqueror, aware of the defensive possibilities of the site, had built a castle that was to be the precursor of ever more elaborate fortifications.

Subsequently, the bishops of Durham were granted extensive powers to control the troublesome northern marches of the kingdom, ruling as semi-independent **prince bishops**, with their own army, mint and courts of law. The first, William de Carileph, laid the foundation stone of the new cathedral in 1093; his successors provided glorious chapels and treasures which owed as much to the prince bishops' confident sense of self-worth as to their devotion to God. The bishops were at the peak of their power in the fourteenth century, but thereafter their office went into decline, especially in the wake of the Reformation, yet they clung to the vestiges of their powers until 1836, when they ceded them to the Crown. They abandoned Durham Castle for their palace in Bishop Auckland and transferred their old home to the fledgling **Durham University**, England's third oldest seat of learning after Oxford and Cambridge. And so matters rest today, cathedral and university monopolizing a city centre which remains an island of privilege in what is otherwise a moderately sized, working-class town at the heart of the old Durham coalfield.

Arrival and information

Durham **train station** – on the main East Coast line from London Kings Cross to Scotland – is about ten minutes' walk from the city centre, either via Millburngate Bridge or via North Road – the site of the **bus station** – then the pedestrianized Framwellgate Bridge. If you don't fancy the walk, use one of the **minibuses** that link the cathedral with both stations.

The **tourist office**, in Market Place (June & Sept Mon–Sat 9.30am–5.30pm; July & Aug Mon–Sat 9.30am–6pm, Sun 2–5pm; Oct–May Mon–Sat 10am–5pm; ☎0191/384 3720), will book accommodation, hand you a free map and supply the usual range of leaflets plus *What's on in Durham*, listing local events.

You can **walk** around the whole of the city centre, though a couple of outlying attractions can be reached by local bus (details given in the text where appropriate). Ask at the tourist office about **guided walks**, if you'd like a little more historical direction to your ramblings. In addition, you may want to get out onto the river, either by renting **rowing boats** (£2.50 per person an hour) from Brown's Boathouse, Elvet Bridge or by taking the one-hour **cruise** aboard the *Prince Bishop* (☎0191/386 9525; £3), which has regular summer departures, again from Elvet Bridge.

Accommodation

Durham has a long list of **guest houses** and **B&Bs**, with particular concentrations on Gilesgate, northeast of Market Place, and around Crossgate, south of the bus station. Gilesgate and its side streets are the places to head for if you need to keep costs down. Good budget B&Bs include *Green Grove*, 99 Gilesgate (☎0191/384 4361; no credit cards; ①), with a mix of standard and en-suite rooms, and *Bees Cottage Guest House*, Bridge St, off Sutton Street, not far from the train station (☎0191/384 5775; no credit cards; ③). *Castle View Guest House*, 4 Crossgate (☎0191/386 8852; ③) is a recommended central choice (next to St Margaret's Church), since it has a great castle view. The *Georgian Town House*, 10 Crossgate (☎0191/386 8070; no credit cards; ③) boasts more character than most, serves up good breakfasts and has some rooms with cathedral views. Moving swiftly up the price bracket, the *Royal County*, Old Elvet, just across Elvet Bridge (☎0191/386 6821; ⑦), is Durham's top hotel, and has its own riverside leisure centre with indoor swimming pool, sauna and solarium. Its sister hotel, the

Three Tuns, New Elvet (☎0191/386 4326; ⑦), is a former sixteenth-century coaching inn with slightly cheaper rates and access to the *Royal County's* leisure centre. Both hotels discount their prices out of season.

The cheapest beds in town are at the various colleges of **Durham University**, which welcome visitors at Christmas, Easter and between July and September. Between them, the colleges provide a pool of inexpensive dormitory-style accommodation and private rooms (②, including breakfast). The best colleges are University College (☎0191/374 3863), whose rooms are inside the castle, and St Hild and St Bede on Leazes Road (☎0191/374 3069); the tourist office has a full list. The nearest **campsite**, the *Grange Camping and Caravan Site* (☎0191/384 4778), lies beside the junction of the A1(M) and the A690, about two miles northeast of the city on Meadow Lane, Carrville. To get there from the bus station take bus #220 or #222 for Sunderland.

The City

Surrounded on three sides by the River Wear, Durham's surprisingly compact centre is readily approached by two small bridges which lead from the western, modern part of town across the river to the spur containing castle and cathedral. The commercial heart of this "old town" area is the triangular **Market Place**, inappropriately dominated by an equestrian statue of the third marquis of Londonderry, a much-hated nineteenth-century colliery owner – in the words of John Doyle, a pitman from Horden: "His Lordship reached three score and ten / A very fine performance when / One thinks how many did him scorn / And wished him dead 'ere he was born."

Flanking the square are the **Guildhall** and **St Nicholas' Church**, both now modernized beyond distinction. The **Market Hall**, which still holds a lively market (Thurs & Fri 9am–4pm, Sat 9am–4.30pm), is buried in the vaults of the buildings that line the west side of the square.

The Cathedral

From Market Place, it's a five-minute walk up the steep and cobbled Saddler Street to the majestic **Durham Cathedral** (daily May–Sept 9.30am–8pm; Oct–April Mon–Sat 9.30am–6pm, Sun 2.30–5pm; £2 suggested donation), facing the castle across the manicured Palace Green. Standing on the site of an early wooden Saxon cathedral, built to house the remains of St Cuthbert, the present cathedral – the work of French master masons – was completed in 1133, and has survived the centuries pretty much intact, a supreme example of the Norman-Romanesque style. Visiting in 1773, Samuel Johnson captured its overpowering essence well: "it rather awes than pleases, as it strikes with a kind of gigantick dignity, and aspires to no other praise than that of rocky solidity and indeterminate duration".

Entry is through the **northwest porch**, an eighteenth-century addition, where a replica of the lion-head **sanctuary knocker** is a reminder of the medieval distinction between secular and religious law. The church used to be ringed by wooden crosses and, once a fugitive reached them, he or she could claim sanctuary from the lay authorities for up to 35 days. In theory, this right to sanctuary was universal, but in practice it was mostly used by the rich to give them time to arrange their affairs before they went into exile. Rarely did anyone try to stop these wealthy runaways from reaching safety and, after the prescribed period, the monks gave their "guests" a robe of St Cuthbert and a white wooden cross, which extended the church's protection while they made their way to the nearest port.

The awe-inspiring **nave**, completed in 1128, is a bold and inventive structure that used pointed arches for the first time in England, raising the vaulted ceiling to new and dizzying heights. The weight of the stone is borne by massive pillars, their heaviness relieved by striking Moorish-influenced geometric patterns – chevrons, diamonds and vertical fluting. Most of the cathedral's/ early fixtures and fittings were destroyed by

Cromwell's Scottish prisoners, who were deposited inside the church after the battle of Dunbar in 1650. The Scots did not, however, damage the gaudily painted, sixteenth-century **Prior Castell's clock**, which now hangs in the south transept, because it sported their emblem, the thistle. A door here gives access to the **tower** (Easter–Sept Mon–Sat 9.30am–4pm; Oct–Easter 9.30am–3pm; £2), from the top of which are gut-wrenching views of the city.

Separated from the nave by a Victorian marble screen is the **choir**, where the dark-stained Restoration stalls are overshadowed by the vainglorious **bishop's throne**, reputedly the highest in medieval Christendom, built on the orders of the fourteenth-century Bishop Hatfield, whose militaristic alabaster tombstone lies just below. Beyond, the **Chapel of the Nine Altars** dates from the thirteenth century, its Early English stonework distinguished by its delicacy of detail. Here, and around the adjoining **Shrine of St Cuthbert**, much of the stonework is Frosterley marble, each dark shaft bearing its own fancy pattern of fossils. Cuthbert himself lies beneath a plain marble slab, his presence and shrine having gained a reputation over the centuries for their curative powers. The legend was given credence in 1104, when the saint's body was exhumed for reburial here, upon the completion of the eastern end of the new Norman cathedral, and was found to be completely uncorrupted, more than four hundred years after his death on Lindisfarne. Almost certainly, this was the result of his fellow monks having (unintentionally) preserved the body by laying it in sand containing salt crystals – though to medieval eyes, here was testament enough to the saint's potency.

Back near the entrance, stuck on the edge of the ravine at the west end of the church, the **Galilee Chapel** was begun in the 1170s, its light and exotic decoration in imitation of the Great Mosque of Cordoba, a contrast to the forcefulness of the nave. Subdivided by twelve slender columns, each surrounded by a medley of geometric patterns, the chapel contains the simple tombstone of the **Venerable Bede**, the Northumbrian monk credited with being England's first historian. Bede died at the monastery of Jarrow in 735 (see p.878), and his remains were transferred here in 1020.

An ancient wooden doorway opposite the main entrance leads into the spacious **cloisters**, which are flanked by what remains of the monastic buildings. These include the undercroft of the **monks' dormitory** (April–Sept Mon–Sat 10am–3.30pm, Sun 12.30–3pm; 80p) and, more potently, the **Treasury** (Mon–Sat 10am–4.30pm, Sun 2–4.30pm; £2), which is stuffed with ecclesiastical bric-a-brac, from altar plate, bishops' rings and seals to vestments, illuminated manuscripts and relics from the life and times of St Cuthbert – principally fragments of his much-travelled oak coffin. The original Sanctuary Knocker is here, too, dating from 1140. Also in the undercroft is the cathedral shop and café. You may want to turn up in time for one of the **guided tours** (May–July & Sept Mon–Sat 10.30am & 2pm; Aug Mon–Sat 10.30am, 11.30am & 2pm; £2.50), which operate on a first come, first served basis.

The Castle

Across Palace Green from the cathedral, **Durham Castle** (Easter & July–Sept Mon–Sat 10am–12.30pm & 2–4pm, Sun 10am–noon & 2–4pm; Oct–June Mon, Wed & Sat 2–4pm; £3; ☎0191/374 3800) lost its medieval appearance long ago, during refurbishments arranged by a succession of prince bishops, but the university went further by renovating the old keep as a hall of residence. It's only possible to visit the castle on a 45-minute guided tour, highlights of which include rapid visits to the fifteenth-century kitchen, a climb up the enormous hanging staircase and the jog down to the so-called "Norman chapel" – in fact the medieval treasure room. In the Great Hall, your guide will suggest that the miniature suits of armour above the Musicians' Gallery were issued to young boys by Cromwell, who sent them into battle ahead of his regular troops as a human shield. Treat this tale with caution – it may be Royalist propaganda. The castle is sometimes closed for official visits during its regular opening hours; call ahead to check.

River walks

Below the castle and the cathedral are the wooded banks of the **River Wear**, where a pleasant footpath runs right round the peninsula. It takes about thirty minutes to complete the circuit, passing a succession of elegant bridges with fine vantage points over town and cathedral. **Framwellgate Bridge** originally dates from the twelfth century, though it was widened to its present proportions in the mid-nineteenth century. Just along from here, on the riverbank, the university's **Museum of Archeology** (April–Oct daily 11am–4pm; Nov–March Mon, Thurs & Fri 12.30–3pm, Sat & Sun 11.30am–3.30pm; £1) occupies an old stone fulling mill, its displays a mixture of permanent archeological relics and temporary exhibitions. Eighteenth-century **Prebends Bridge** boasts celebrated views of the cathedral, and the path then continues round to handsome **Elvet Bridge**, again widened far beyond its medieval course, though still retaining traces of both its erstwhile bridge-houses and the chapel, St Andrew's, which once stood at its eastern end.

The alternate route from Prebends to Elvet Bridge is along South and North Bailey, a cobbled thoroughfare lined by well-worn Georgian houses, many of them occupied by university college buildings. The church of St Mary-le-Bow, on North Bailey, immediately below the cathedral, now does duty as the **Durham Heritage Centre** (Easter to late May Sat & Sun 2–4.30pm; late May to June & Sept daily 2–4.30pm; July & Aug daily 11.30am–4.30pm; £1), a pot-pourri of audiovisual displays, dioramas, exhibitions and activities such as brass-rubbing.

The rest of the city

Durham has a smattering of other attractions, the most noteworthy being the university's **Oriental Museum** (Mon–Fri 9.30am–5pm, Sat & Sun 2–5pm; £1.50), set among college buildings a couple of miles to the south of the city centre on Elvet Hill (off South Road), whose wide-ranging collection contains an outstanding display of Chinese ceramics. To get there from the bus station, take bus #5 or #6 (to Bishop Auckland) and ask to be put off on South Road for the museum. After the museum, you may as well continue on foot to the nearby **Botanic Gardens**, whose glasshouses (daily 9am–4pm; £1), café and visitor centre (March–Oct daily 10am–5pm; Nov–Feb daily 11am–4pm; £1) are set in eighteen wooded acres near Collingwood College; buses run back to the centre from either Elvet Hill Road or South Road.

North of the centre, a twenty-minute walk from the train station up Framwellgate takes you to the **Durham Light Infantry Museum and Art Gallery** (Tues–Sat 10am–5pm, Sun 2–5pm; £2), at Aykley Heads, whose eponymous regimental section – consisting of uniforms, weapons and medals – won't be to everyone's taste, though it's worth enquiring about the art gallery's current exhibitions and concert programme.

Eating

Sandwiches, pies and snacks are on sale at bakeries and takeaways all over the centre, while the **market** on Market Place is good for fruit. Of the **cafés**, *Vennel's*, Saddler's Yard – named after the skinny alley or "vennel" where it stands – serves light lunches in a little hidden courtyard; the entrance is next to Waterstone's, off Saddler Street at the junction with Elvet Bridge. Just over the way, on Elvet Bridge itself, *Lisann's* dispenses tea, coffee, cakes and sandwiches. Further up the hill, on Palace Green, to the side of the cathedral, the *Almshouse* conjures up mostly vegetarian meals for around £5 (open until 8pm in summer). Hot lunches are on offer at the *Undercroft*, inside the cathedral.

Most of Durham's **restaurants** are concentrated in the streets radiating from the Market Place. *Shaheens*, 48 North Bailey (closed Sun), serves the best curry in town, while for Italian food, the honours are shared between *Emilio's*, 96 Elvet Bridge, and *Pizzeria Venezia*, 4 Framwellgate Bridge (closed Sun). The latter is the very paradigm of an Italian restaurant, with red-checked tablecloths, bad Italian pop music and football posters – but it's reliable (as the coterie of dining Italian businessmen attest) and cheap, especially at lunchtime. The resolutely modern Med-British dishes at *Bistro 21*, a converted farmhouse at Aykley Heads (☎0191/384 4354; closed Sun), north of the centre, make for a good night out; it's just a bit further on from the museum and art gallery. For riverside views, you'll either have to put up with the mainstream pasta dishes at *Bella Pasta*, 21 Silver St, at the foot of Framwellgate Bridge, or eat a **pub** lunch at the *Coach & Eight* opposite or the *Swan & Three Cygnets* on the west side of Elvet Bridge.

Drinking, nightlife and entertainment

Durham's central **pubs** blow hot and cold, depending on whether or not the students are in town. Good bets at most times include the *Court Inn*, on Court Lane, and the lively *Hogshead*, 58 Saddler St, with its selection of real ales. The *Dun Cow*, a five-minute walk east of the bridge at 37 Old Elvet, is also a favourite. Bleary-eyed old socialists will want to make time for a quick pint in the *Market Tavern*, a nineteenth-century pub on Market Place, where the influential Durham Miners' Association was founded in 1871.

For more highbrow entertainment, the university sponsors an annual season of **classical concerts** at various venues around the city, while **Durham Art Gallery** (☎0191/384 2214 at Aykley Heads hosts lunchtime piano recitals and other events and concerts. Choral works are often performed in the cathedral. Durham Student's Union (☎0191/374 3310) puts on **gigs** during term time, with rock, jazz and comedy most regularly performed at Dunelm House, New Elvet. The local **cinema**, Robins Cinema on North Road (☎0191/384 0308), has a film club as well as showing mainstream releases.

Annual events and **festivals** come thick and fast in the summer. In June the **Durham Regatta** packs the riverbanks and river, and the same month usually sees the start of the university's revamped **arts week**. The **Miners' Gala** in July – when the traditional lodge banners are paraded through the streets – recalls the city's proud industrial past; sorrows about its demise are drowned at two respected annual **beer festivals**, one in February, one in September. For further details, pick up a programme of forthcoming events at the tourist office.

The rest of County Durham

In the 1910s, **County Durham** produced 41 million tons of coal each year, raised from three hundred pits by 170,000 miners. This was the heyday of an industry that since the 1830s had transformed the county's landscape, spawning scores of pit villages which matted the rolling hills from the Pennines to the North Sea, between Newcastle and Stockton-on-Tees. The miners' union, waging a long struggle against serf-like pay and conditions, achieved a gradual improvement of the miners' lot, but could not prevent the slow decline of the Durham coalfield from the 1920s: just 127 pits were left when the mines were nationalized in 1947, and only 34 in 1969. Today, only a mere handful of pits remain strung out along the coast to exploit the broader seams that run under the sea. As a consequence, the old colliery villages have lost their sense of purpose and structure, some becoming godforsaken terraces in the middle of nowhere, others being swallowed up by neighbouring towns. For a taste of the old days, most people troop off to the reconstructed colliery village (and much more) at the open-air **Beamish Museum**, north of Durham.

County Durham's other obvious tourist attractions are to the west of the coalfield. There's **Raby Castle**, a stately home to the east of the market town of **Barnard Castle**, itself the setting for the opulent art collection of the **Bowes Museum**. Farther west lie the Pennine valleys of **Teesdale** and **Weardale**, whose upper reaches boast some enjoyable moorland scenery, most dramatically at Teesdale's **High Force** waterfall, which adjoins the Pennine Way. These two dales are best toured in an anticlockwise direction, beginning at Barnard Castle and travelling up Teesdale to Langdon Beck and on to Alston, where you can cross over to Weardale and take the road back down the valley through Stanhope and into Bishop Auckland. Another option is to leave Weardale at Stanhope for the ten-mile trip north across the moors to the delightful stone village of **Blanchland**, tucked away in the valley of the Derwent River across the border in Northumberland.

Getting around County Durham by **bus** and **train** presents few problems. A comprehensive range of services links all the major towns and villages, although the bus network does peter out as you travel up the dales. Many services are also greatly reduced, or nonexistent, during the winter months. You may need to make use of Durham County Council's public transport **enquiry line** (☎0191/383 3337 Mon–Thurs 8.30am–5pm, Fri 8.30am–4.30pm); many County Durham bus routes are covered in their useful *Across the Rooftop of England* leaflet. If you want to get further off the beaten track, contact the Council's **Environment Department** (☎0191/383 4144) for details of its year-round programme of **guided walks**. These range from rural rambles to religious or industrial heritage trails, and most cost just £1; for more information contact Durham's tourist office, or any of the local tourist offices detailed below.

Beamish Museum

Established in 1970, the open-air **Beamish Museum** (April–June, Sept & Oct daily 10am–5pm; July & Aug 10am–6pm; Nov–March Tues–Thurs, Sat & Sun 10am–4pm; last admission 3pm, 4pm in summer; £3–10 depending on season; ☎01207/231811), spreading out across the fields beside the A693 about ten miles north of Durham, is extremely popular with local people, who come to chew the fat with the costumed guides, most of whom are recruited for their real-life experience. The collier who takes you down the reopened drift mine was once a miner, and the blokes driving the steam engine used to work for British Rail, adding a touch of authenticity and sadness to the proceedings, as those industries continue to deteriorate in tandem with the boom in heritage museums like this one.

Buildings from all over the region have been reassembled here and the museum divides into four main sections: a pint-sized colliery village as of 1913, complete with cottages, Methodist chapel, old stone winding house and drift mine; a train station and goods yard; an early nineteenth-century manor and farm with traditional breeds of livestock; and a large-scale re-creation of a 1920s north country town, its High Street lined by shops, bank, pub, dentist's surgery, printer's workshop, newspaper office, garage and solicitor's office – all painstakingly kitted out with period furnishings and fittings. There's a great deal to see and what with the tram rides, Victorian funfair, tearoom, the *Sun Inn* pub and picnic areas, most people make a day of it – reckon on around five hours to get round the lot in summer, much less in **winter** when only the town and train station are open (call ahead to check). Concerts and **special events** throughout the year – from craft displays to whippet racing – can bring out the crowds; the museum can let you have a programme of future events.

Practicalities

Drivers should follow signs to the museum off the A1(M) Chester-le-Street exit, then follow the signs along the A693 to Stanley. By **bus**, take the #720 from Durham bus station (hourly) or the #709 from Newcastle (hourly from Eldon Square), which drop you close to the main entrance. There are also hourly services from Sunderland. Calling the

Durham County Council transport line (☎0191/383 3337) or the museum itself is the quickest way to check current departure times. Hang on to your bus ticket and you should get a discount on entrance to the museum, too.

Most people visit from one of the major cities nearby, but if you wanted to stay closer to Beamish itself (and perhaps take advantage of the Next Day Return Visit Ticket; available April–Oct; £4), get hold of the accommodation list provided by the on-site **Beamish tourist office** (open same hours as the museum; ☎0191/370 2533), which lists B&Bs, hotels and campsites in the nearby village and around the park. There's also a good **pub** just outside the main gate, the *Shepherd & Shepherdess*, full of traditional food and fittings.

Bishop Auckland

Eleven miles southwest of Durham city, **BISHOP AUCKLAND** has been the country home of the bishops of Durham since the twelfth century and their official residence for more than a hundred years. Their palace, the gracious **Auckland Castle** (May, June & Sept Fri & Sun 2–5pm; July Thurs, Fri & Sun 2–5pm; Aug Wed–Sun 2–5pm; £3), standing in eight-hundred-acre grounds, is approached through an imposing gatehouse just off the town's Market Place. The palace has been extensively remodelled since its medieval incarnation, redesigned to satisfy the whims of such occupants as the seventeenth-century Bishop Cosin who refurbished the original banqueting hall to create today's splendid marble and limestone **chapel**. Here, the stained-glass windows relate the stories of early Christian saints familiar throughout the Northeast, especially Cuthbert, Bede and Aidan. The other rooms are rather sparse, though there's an outstanding exception in the long dining room, with its thirteen paintings of Jacob and his sons by Zurbarán, commissioned in the 1640s for a monastery in South America. The medieval kitchens contain an exhibition on the life of St Cuthbert. You can stroll into **Bishop's Park**, too (daily 7am–sunset; free), where an eighteenth-century deer house survives.

The town itself plays second fiddle to the castle, though the Market Place is handsome enough. However, you could follow the mile-long lane that leads north to the remains of **Binchester Roman Fort** (Easter & May–Sept daily 11am–5pm; £1.50). Only a small portion of the ten-acre site – Roman *Vinovia* – has been excavated (with most of the finds displayed in the Bowes Museum at Barnard Castle, but a stretch of cobbled Dere Street has been uncovered (a fortified supply route stretching from York to Hadrian's Wall) and, more remarkably, so has the country's best example of a **hypocaust**, built to warm the private bath suite of the garrison's commanding officer. There are events held at the site throughout the summer, including parades of Roman soldiers and open days depicting life in Roman Britain; call ☎01388/663089 for details.

The fort was abandoned in the fifth century and many of its stones, stamped with the inscription of the cavalry regiment stationed here, found their way to the hamlet of **ESCOMB**, three miles west of Bishop Auckland (bus #86 or #87 from town), where they were used to build a seventh-century **Saxon church** (daily: summer 9am–8pm; winter 9am–4pm; free). Now surrounded by modern houses, the church (key at 22 Saxon Green if closed) has a striking steep-roofed nave, only sixty by twenty feet. Opposite, you can get a bar **meal** at the sixteenth-century *Saxon Inn*.

Practicalities

Bishop Auckland is linked by **train** to Darlington and by regular **buses** to Weardale, Barnard Castle, Newcastle, Darlington, Middlesbrough and Saltburn. There's also a Tuesday bus service to Blanchland and Hexham. Buses drop you centrally, just a few minutes' west of the town hall, in Market Place, which houses the **tourist office**

(April–Sept Mon–Fri 10am–5pm, Sat 9am–4pm Sun 1–4pm; rest of year closed Sun ☎01388/604922).

Accommodation options include the handily positioned *Queen's Head Hotel*, 38 Market Place (☎01388/603477; ③), or cheaper rooms at the *Albion Cottage Guest House*, on Albion Terrace (☎01388/602 217; no credit cards; ①). For **food**, the *Laurel Room* in the Town Hall, Market Place, is open until 4pm for snacks and drinks (closed Sat & Sun), or try *Rossi's Tea Room*, also in Market Place (closes 3.30pm & all Sun). The *Bishop's Bistro*, 17 Cockton Hill Rd (☎01388/602462), has a good, moderately priced, lunch and dinner menu (closed Sun).

Raby Castle and Staindrop

The #8 bus between Bishop Auckland and Barnard Castle runs down the A688 to provide access to the splendid, sprawling battlements of **Raby Castle** (Easter week daily 1–5pm; May & June Wed & Sun 1–5pm; July–Sept Mon–Fri & Sun 1–5pm; castle & gardens £4, gardens only £1.50), roughly halfway between the two. The castle mostly dates from the fourteenth century, reflecting the power of the Neville family, who ruled the local roost until 1569. It was then that Charles Neville helped plan the "Rising of the North", the abortive attempt to replace Elizabeth I with Mary Queen of Scots. The revolt was a dismal failure, and Neville's estates were confiscated, with Raby subsequently passing to the Vane family in 1626. The Vanes held on to the castle despite some difficult times: the second owner, Sir Henry, a leading Puritan and briefly the governor of Massachusetts at the tender age of 23, was imprisoned by Cromwell for his criticism of the overzealous Protectorate, and then executed on the orders of Charles II for treason in 1662.

The Vanes, now the lords Barnard, still live in the castle, the **interior** of which was extensively renovated in the eighteenth and nineteenth centuries, though the medieval kitchen remains intact. Raby's focal point is the first-floor Baron's Hall, still of cathedral-like dimensions in spite of the floor being raised ten feet in 1787 to let carriages pass through the neo-Gothic entrance below. Also of note are the Palladian library and the octagonal drawing room, unchanged since its completion in the 1840s. The whole castle is stuffed with antiques, from the usual oligarchic family portraits and ranks of Meissen porcelain, to paintings by artists such as Joshua Reynolds and Luca Giordano.

Outside the castle, in the two-hundred-acre **deer park**, are the walled **gardens** (same days as castle 11am–5.30pm), where peaches, apricots and pineapples once flourished under the careful gaze of forty Victorian gardeners. Heated cavity walls and curtains protected the trees from frost – above the last remaining apricot tree you can still see the hooks for the curtain rail. The castle's coach houses contain a collection of horse-drawn carriages, admission to which is included in the castle or gardens ticket.

One mile south of the castle, lies the pretty little village of **STAINDROP**, whose fortunes have always depended on the lords of Raby, and whose church of **St Mary** contains their tombs, including the bruised alabaster memorial of Ralph Neville, grandfather of Edward IV and Richard III. The church – a large rambling construction of Saxon origin – also possesses an especially fine thirteenth-century sedilia. From Staindrop it's only five miles to Barnard Castle, with fairly regular services on the #8 or #75 buses.

Barnard Castle

Fifteen miles southwest of Bishop Auckland, the skeletal remains of **Barnard Castle** (Easter–Oct daily 10am–6pm; Nov–Easter Wed–Sun 10am–4pm; EH; £2.30), poking out from a cliff high above the River Tees, overlook the town which grew up in its shadow. First fortified in the eleventh century, the castle was long a stronghold of the Balliols, an Anglo-Scottish family interminably embroiled in the struggle for the

Scottish crown. It was one of this clan, Bernard, who built the circular tower which survives to this day, an impressive thirteenth-century fortification just to the right of the later Round Tower, where a beautiful oriel window carries the emblematic boar of Richard III, one of the subsequent owners. By the seventeenth century the castle had outlived its usefulness and the Vanes quarried its stone to repair their premises at Raby.

The **town**, however, continued to thrive as a market centre and it's quite pleasant to potter around the wide, well-kept streets of what the locals, using the typical regional diminutive, call "Barney". Wednesday is market day, while further up from Market Place, St Mary's church and the curious eighteenth-century colonnaded Market Cross building (used, variously, as butter market and jail) make up the official sights.

Castle aside, the prime attaction is the grand French-style chateau that constitutes the **Bowes Museum** (daily 11am–5pm; £3.90), just half a mile west of the centre, up Newgate. Begun in 1869, the chateau was commissioned by John and Josephine Bowes, a local businessman and MP and his French actress wife, who spent much of their time in Paris collecting the ostentatious treasures and antiques. They shipped the whole lot back to Durham and, in an early show of arts patronage, turned the house into a museum for the enlightenment of the Teesdale public (though neither lived to see its formal opening in 1892). It's a hugely rewarding collection, ranging from furniture, paintings, tapestries and ceramics to incidental curiosities, notably a late eighteenth-century mechanical silver swan in the lobby which still performs twice daily, preening to a brief forty-second melodic burst. Among the paintings, look out for El Greco's *The Tears of St Peter* and a couple of Goyas and Canalettos; elsewhere, there's varied interest in the French decorative and religious art, English period furniture, and an excellent toy collection – whose nineteenth-century lead soldiers were made possible by the new industry in nearby Stanhope. An archeological display on the ground floor rounds things off, tracing the history of County Durham from the Ice Age to the late-medieval period. There's a café, too, and a stroll in the grounds on a nice day is no bad thing.

Back in the town centre, it's a pleasant mile-and-a-half walk from the castle, southeast along the banks of the Tees, to the glorious shattered ruins of **Egglestone Abbey** (dawn–dusk; free), a minor Premonstratensian foundation dating from 1195. Turner painted here on one of his three visits to Teesdale, and also at nearby **Rokeby Hall** (June to mid-Sept Mon & Tues 2–5pm; £3.50), a Palladian country house where Walter Scott wrote his ballad *Rokeby*. The house is noted for its extensive collection of eighteenth-century needlework pictures. You can get to the hall directly on bus #79 from Barnard Castle, which also runs to Abbey Bridge End, for Egglestone Abbey.

Practicalities

Buses stop on either side of central Galgate – once the road out to the town gallows, hence the name. Barnard Castle has plenty of accommodation – the **tourist office**, in Woodleigh on Flatts Road, at the end of Galgate by the castle (daily: April–Oct 10am–6pm; Nov–March 11am–4pm; ☎01833/690909) has an extensive list, including several convenient **B&Bs**, such as *The Homelands*, 85 Galgate (☎01833/638757; no credit cards; ②), and the agreeable *Marwood View*, 98 Galgate (☎01833/637493; no credit cards; ②) – both also have single rooms. Of the pubs, the *Old Well Inn*, 21 The Bank (☎01833/690130; ③), has the best rooms. The town is also ringed by **campsites**, the nearest being two miles southwest of the centre at *West Roods Farm*, Boldron (☎01833/690116; closed Oct–March), on the way to Bowes.

For **food**, the *Hayloft*, in Horsemarket off Galgate (Nov–April closed Sun), has tasty and inexpensive home-baked snacks and meals during the day, and the *Market Place Teashop*, 29 Market Place, also gets the gastronomical thumbs-up. The *Golden Lion* in

Market Place or the *Old Well Inn*, a little farther along The Bank, both do decent bar meals. *Oldfield's*, at 7 The Bank (☎01833/630700; closed all Sun & Tues eve) serves light meals during the day, but also features blackboard specials, vegetarian dishes and à la carte dinners at moderate prices. The *Hole in the Wall*, Queen St (☎01833/630220), is a well-thought-of brasserie. For a quiet drink, best choice is the *White Swan* **pub**, set high up opposite the castle.

West to Bowes

The main A66 road heads west of Barnard Castle into Cumbria, towards Appleby, a fine moorland route along which the #X74 bus runs. Local buses from Barnard Castle (not the #X74) detour into **BOWES**, where the huge twelfth-century stone keep of **Bowes Castle** (dawn–dusk; free) overlooks the River Greta valley. Some come on the trail of Dickens (see box below), though without your own transport, it's not really worth the effort. However, if you're driving this way you could opt to **stay** at the *Bowes Moor Hotel* (☎01833/628331; ③), another four miles west of Bowes, in the middle of uncomfortably exposed moorland and supposedly England's highest hotel – there's bar food available and a restaurant. You could also call in at the Otter Trust's excellent **North Pennines Reserve** (Easter–Oct, daily 10.30am–6pm; £4) at Vale House Farm, just three miles west of Bowes, on the south side of the A66. A small valley of the River Greta cuts through the 230-acre farmland, and hides let you glimpse the wildlife; the otters are fed at noon and 3pm.

CHARLES DICKENS AND THE YORKSHIRE SCHOOLS

The precociously talented, 26-year-old **Charles Dickens**, already a hugely successful author with his *Pickwick Papers* and *Oliver Twist*, produced his third novel in serial form in 1838. **Nicholas Nickleby** presented the usual panoply of comic and grotesque figures, none more so than Wackford Squeers, the "villainous", one-eyed headmaster of Dotheboys Hall who, memorably, "appeared ill at ease in his clothes, and as if he were in a perpetual state of astonishment at finding himself so respectable". As throughout his career, Dickens did his homework assiduously. On a trip north in early 1838 he visited various of the so-called "Yorkshire Schools" in the area around Barnard Castle – established, more often than not, by unscrupulous businessmen who cared little for their charges. In these schools, illegitimate or awkward children, or simply those of unsuspecting parents, were destined for years of neglect, ill-abuse or worse. Dickens stayed at the *King's Head* on Market Place in **Barnard Castle** (no longer a hotel, though there is a coffee shop and bar), spied on a local watchmaker's shop (giving him the idea for *Master Humphrey's Clock*) and visited nearby **Bowes**, whose Bowes Academy was run by the notorious William Shaw, earlier prosecuted for neglect of his schoolboys, several of whom had gone blind in his care. Dickens took careful note and modelled Squeers on Shaw and Dotheboys Hall on Bowes' school; along with others in the locality, it closed in the wake of the success of the novel, with parents and authorities finally moved to action. The school building – "a long cold-looking house" – still stands at the west end of the village; Shaw is buried in the churchyard. As is the way with notoriety, several teachers soon claimed to be the original Wackford Squeers and Dickens himself, in print at least, remained vague about his identity, claiming in the novel's preface that Squeers was "representative of a class, and not of an individual". This was perhaps just as well, since the same preface reveals the reactions of those who believed themselves to be so slighted; one gentleman, according to Dickens, proposing coming to London "for the express purpose of committing an assault and battery upon his traducer".

Teesdale

Extending twenty-odd miles northwest from Barnard Castle, Teesdale begins calmly enough, though the pastoral landscapes of its lower reaches are soon replaced by wilder Pennine scenery. There's a regular **bus service** as far as Middleton-in-Teesdale, with less frequent (but still daily) services on to **High Force, Bowlees Country Park** and **Langdon Beck** (for the youth hostel). Beyond that, there's a bus once or twice a week during July and August on to **Alston** (in Cumbria; see p.729), from where you can either return east by bus along Weardale or cut north on services to Haltwhistle or Hexham for Hadrian's Wall. Your own transport makes Teesdale an easy day's sightseeing from Barnard Castle.

Middleton-in-Teesdale

MIDDLETON-IN-TEESDALE, the valley's main settlement, was once the archetypal "company town", owned lock, stock and barrel by the Quaker-run London Lead Company, which began mining here in 1753. The firm built substantial stone cottages for their workforce, who in return were obliged to observe a host of regulations, such as sending their children to Sunday school and keeping off the booze. Not that the Quakers were over-mindful of working conditions: lead miners here, as elsewhere, suffered bronchial complaints brought on by the contaminated air in the mines, illnesses compounded by long hours and an early start – "washerboys", who sorted the lead ore from the rock for ten hours a day and more, began at eight years old.

There are no specific sights in the village, but it's a quiet and remote spot to spend the night. A number of **B&Bs** advertise their services, including *Bluebell House* in the central Market Place (☎01833/640584; no credit cards; ①). Nearby *Teesdale Hotel* (☎01833/640264; ④), a seventeenth-century coaching inn, offers spick-and-span en-suite accommodation and a bar menu. The nearest **campsite** is the *Daleview Caravan Park* (☎01833/640233; closed Nov–Feb), half a mile south, down Bridge Street and across the river.

It's also worth knowing about the *Rose & Crown* (☎01833/650213; ⑤), a couple of miles or so back down the road towards Barnard Castle, in the pretty village of **Romaldkirk**, with its impressive church and village green. The eighteenth-century inn has accomplished local cooking and real ale.

Newbiggin to Langdon Beck

From Middleton, it's about three miles to tiny **NEWBIGGIN**, home to the world's oldest surviving **Methodist Chapel** (April–Sept Wed 2–4pm). Finished in 1759, the chapel houses a small display on the history of local Methodism, the faith of the majority of Durham's lead miners.

Past Newbiggin, the countryside becomes harsher and the Tees more vigorous as the B6277 travels the two miles on to **Bowlees Country Park and Visitor Centre** (April–Sept daily 10.30am–5.30pm; 50p), the halt for the short walk to the rapids of **Low Force**. Close by is the altogether more impressive **High Force**, a seventy-foot cascade which rumbles over an outcrop of the Whin Sill, a black dolerite ridge that pokes up in various parts of northern England. The waterfall is on private Raby land, and visitors must pay 50p to view the falls and £1 to use the nearby car park, by the B6277. From the road, it's a ten-minute walk through the woods to the viewing point, where daredevil visitors clamber on the rocks above the gushing waters – after rain, it's a thunderously impressive sight. You can avoid the entrance fee by walking up from Low Force on the opposite bank of the river along the **Pennine Way**, but the view of the falls isn't as spectacular. Back by the car park, the *High Force* pub and hotel (☎01833/622222; ③) brews its own beer (a Teesdale Bitter and the stronger, award-winning, Cauldron Snout) to accompany the bar meals.

The Pennine Way continues the six miles upstream to **Cauldron Snout**, near the source of the Tees, where the river rolls two hundred feet down a dolerite stairway as it leaves **Cow Green Reservoir**. It's also possible to reach the reservoir by car: turn off the main road at **Langdon Beck** – about a mile north of the stone-built **youth hostel** on the B6277 at Forest-in-Teesdale (☎01833/622228, *langdonbeck@yha.org.uk*) – and follow the three-mile-long lane to the car park, a mile's walk from the Snout. The B6277, meanwhile, climbs ever higher as it leaves Teesdale, peaking at just under 2000 feet before dropping into Cumbria for Alston.

Weardale

Seeing **Weardale** by **public transport** means relying on the hourly bus between Bishop Auckland and Alston (down the A689, via Frosterley, Stanhope, St John's Chapel, Ireshopeburn, Cowshill and Killhope), or the summer Saturday-only service from Durham to Alston, which also calls at Stanhope and Killhope. With your own transport, you can cut between the two valleys, Teesdale and Weardale, on one of the minor moorland roads, branching off either at Newbiggin or Langdon Beck. The account below runs west to east, starting at Alston – for more details on Alston, see p.729.

Killhope and Ireshopeburn

Lead and iron-ore mining flourished in and around Weardale from the 1840s to the 1880s, leaving today's landscape scarred with old workings. One of the bigger mines, situated about three miles west of Cowshill, up at the head of the valley and a chilly 1500 feet above sea level, has been turned into the **Killhope Lead Mining Centre** (April–Oct daily 10.30am–5pm; Nov Sun 10.30am–4pm; £3.40, £5 including mine visit), where all sorts of industrial debris lies scattered across a large open-air site, including a recently restored 34-foot-high waterwheel, built to power the crushing apparatus. It still turns, using six thousand gallons of water per minute from a string of diverted streams. You can also try your hand as a washerboy on the old washing floor, if you're prepared to compete with the schoolkids, while descending Park Level Mine with hard hat and lamp gives you a taste of the miserable mining life. Incidentally, if you're intending to take a trip on the South Tynedale railway, at nearby Alston (p.729), buy a combined ticket at the mine.

There's a turning north onto the B6295 for Allendale (see p.861), a little farther east down the main road, just past which tiny **IRESHOPEBURN** is the home of the **Weardale Museum** (Easter, May–July & Sept Wed–Sun 2–5pm; Aug daily 2–5pm; £1), which footnotes the history of the local lead-mining industry with a gruesome display of miners' ruined lungs.

Stanhope and Frosterley

About nine miles downstream from Ireshopeburn lies **STANHOPE**, the main village of the valley and a useful base for walks across the moors – the **tourist office** (Easter to mid-Nov daily 10am–5pm; mid-Nov to Easter Mon–Fri 10am–4pm, Sat & Sun 11am–4pm; ☎01388/527650), in the Durham Dales Centre, Castle Gardens, opposite Market Place, has all the trail details and a list of **B&Bs**. On summer Saturdays, there's a direct **bus** east to Bishop Auckland, Durham and Sunderland, or west to the Lake District.

From Stanhope, it's two miles to **FROSTERLEY**, where quarries once produced the exquisite, fossil-encrusted black limestone "marble" used to such effect in Durham Cathedral. Quarrying began here in the thirteenth century and reached its peak in the nineteenth century as the industrial revolution took hold; the quarry scars can be seen all around the village, while the parish church has a superb polished font. The *Black*

Bull Inn here (☎01388/527 784; no credit cards; ②) is a nice old pub, with an open fire-place, decent bar meals and a couple of rooms.

North across the moors

Two minor roads branch **north from Weardale**, over the border into Northumberland, heading towards Hexham and Hadrian's Wall and crossing some of the most glorious, isolated moorland in the north of England. With your own transport, it's well worth forsaking the main roads to follow either of these routes, to Allendale or Blanchland. **By bus**, the only possible approach is from the north, from Hexham.

The Allen Valley

The B6295 climbs out of Weardale and drops into the **Allen Valley**, where heather-covered moorland shelters small settlements that once made their living from lead mining. The River Allen itself can be extremely beautiful at times, widening as it tumbles north to join the River Tyne just east of Bardon Mill. It was from this valley that painter John Martin (p.873) drew much of his inspiration, and the dramatic surroundings are still easily viewed today from a series of river walks (see box below) accessible from either of the main settlements.

At **ALLENHEADS**, at the top of the valley, twelve miles from Stanhope, handsome stone buildings stand close to the river. The **Heritage Centre** (Easter–Nov daily 9am–5pm; £1.50) details the village's erstwhile industry, and incorporates an early Armstrong hydraulic engine used for driving the saw mill, while a series of nature trails and local walks guide you around the locality. An old barn at the centre, known in these parts as a *hemmel*, has been converted into the *Hemmel Café*, though for true idiosyncracy pop into the village's *Allenheads Inn* (☎01434/685200; ②), whose owners have stuffed it with every conceivable piece of junk-shop arcana. Lunch and dinner is served, and the owners also rent out a two-bedroom stone cottage. Allenheads, incidentally, is on the C2C cycle route (see box on p.846), and there's useful **bunkhouse** accommodation at *Allenheads Lodge Outdoor Centre*, in the village (☎01434/685 374; no credit cards).

WALKS IN AND AROUND THE ALLEN VALLEY

The **Allen Valley** offers some of the finest walking in the region. There are all manner of circular walks that can be undertaken from Allendale town, the best base hereabouts, most of which involve pottering up or down the banks of the river. A very good path takes you all the way from Allendale **south to Allenheads** (around nine miles one way), leaving or crossing the river on occasion, though connoisseurs rate higher the northern section, from Allendale to the River Tyne (eight miles one way), much of it passing through National Trust land. This is at its most dramatic when passing through beautiful **Allendale Gorge**; there's road access at **Plankey Mill**, around which the river becomes full of splashing families on summer weekends. Where the Allen flows into the Tyne, you're only a mile or so east of the train station at Bardon Mill and only another hour and a half's cross-country walk from **Hadrian's Wall** at Housesteads (p.889), enabling you to move on east or west by train, bus or on foot.

Alternatively, back at Allendale, there are glorious moorland routes east across **Hexhamshire Common**, descending either to Hexham itself (via Dipton Mill and its pub; see p.888) or, three miles further east, to Corbridge. Both towns are easily reached in a day from Allendale. From Allenheads, after a bit of initial clambering north or south, the cross-moorland routes east are to Blanchland (see opposite), a tiring day's walk but eminently worthwhile.

ALLENDALE TOWN, another four miles north, also goes about its quiet, rural way, and claims to be at the exact centre of the British Isles. This is a peaceful place to stay, with a small supermarket, a post office and several friendly pubs and small hotels, all centred on the main market square. The best **accommodation** here is at the welcoming *King's Head* (☎01434/683681; ②), right in the square, which has nice rooms (with and without shower), home-cooked meals and great live music nights. B&B is on offer in the *Allendale Tea Rooms* (☎01434/683575; no credit cards; ②), opposite the hotel, or in the welcoming *Old Hostel*, 1 Allen View, Catton (☎01434/683780; no credit cards; ②), on the road out, just to the north of town. Allendale's major curiosity is the **New Year's Eve** "tar barrels" ceremony, when a huge, spluttering bonfire is lit in the square around which the locals parade with barrels – more like trays – of burning pitch balanced on their heads to usher in the new year.

The #688 **bus** runs from Hexham to Allendale and Allenheads, but no further, four or five times a day (not Sun).

Blanchland

The other trans-moorland route is the B6278 which cuts north from Weardale at Stanhope for ten extraordinarily wild miles to tiny **BLANCHLAND**, a handful of ancient, lichen-stained stone cottages huddled round an L-shaped square that was once the outer court of a twelve-man Premonstratensian abbey, founded in the twelfth century. The village has been preserved and protected since 1721, when Lord Crewe, the childless bishop of Durham, bequeathed his estate to trustees on condition that they rebuilt the old conventual buildings, for Blanchland had slowly fallen into disrepair after the abbey's dissolution. The original trustees obliged and their successors have allowed but the faintest whiff of the twentieth century to intrude, their last concession being the construction of a pint-sized shelter in celebration of Queen Victoria's Diamond Jubilee.

Consequently, the village bears many reminders of its monastic past, from the sturdy gatehouse that now accommodates the post office to the L-shaped parish church where the medieval chancel and tower were all used to good effect during the rebuilding of 1752. But it's the **Lord Crewe Arms Hotel** (☎01434/675251; ⑦) that steals the show. Once the abbot's lodge, the hotel's nooks and crannies have all sorts of surprises, an enticing mixture of medieval and eighteenth-century Gothic features, like the dark vaulted basements, two big fireplaces left over from the canons' kitchen and a priest's hideaway stuck inside the chimney. It's a superb place to stay – two-night breaks bring the price down a little – with a delightful garden-cum-cloister and lavish rooms. The **restaurant** serves heavy table d'hôte dinners for around £30, and there's a fine public bar in the undercroft. Don't count on being able to get anything else locally, apart from limited supplies at the village shop (Nov–Easter closed Mon–Thurs & Sun).

There are two **bus routes** serving Blanchland: the #773 from Consett (not Sun), which is itself linked by hourly bus to Newcastle; or the more direct but very infrequent, once-weekly (currently Tues) #869 from Hexham, which runs on to Edmundbyers and Bishop Auckland.

East of Blanchland

Beyond **Blanchland**, drivers will probably be keen to make Hexham by the most direct route along the B6306, but consider taking a detour east to the main A68 and driving past the **Derwent Reservoir**. At the attractive village of **EDMUNDBYERS**, where B6306 meets B6278, is a (heavily restored) twelfth-century church and a simple **youth hostel** (☎01207/255651) in seventeenth-century Low House, just half a mile from the reservoir – bus #773 from Consett passes close by, while the village lies on the C2C cycle route (see p.846). You can camp at the hostel, too, and there are a couple of local B&Bs if you craved more comfort. A few miles farther east, at the junction with the A68, at

Carterway Heads, the *Manor House Inn* (☎01207/255268; ②) has four rooms over-looking the reservoir and some of the best **pub food** in northeastern England – wild mushroom soufflé, stilton tart, local fish, home-made desserts – at around £15 a head.

The Tees Valley: Darlington to the coast

In a region whose physical face was blighted first by industrial success and then by urban neglect, the towns along the **Tees Valley** take some beating. Driving north especially, from Yorkshire, it seems that from Middlesbrough onwards a view isn't considered a view unless it's blocked by towers and pipes, clouded by smoking chimneys and framed by rusting machinery. This, of course, is a harsh judgement and only half the story – the **River Tees**, along with the Tyne farther north, was one of the great engines of British economic power in the late nineteenth century. That it's so far off the tourist map as to be invisible is hardly the fault of towns whose livelihood disappeared once iron- and steel-making and shipbuilding became things of the past in Britain. But once there were rich pickings here, in places like **Darlington**, twenty miles south of Durham city, where the first steam train, George Stephenson's *Locomotion*, made its inaugural run and is now on permanent display. The line ran first to **Stockton-on-Tees** and was then extended to ports at **Middlesbrough** and **Hartlepool**, to enable ever-increasing amounts of Durham coal to be unloaded and exported. Iron from the local Cleveland Hills supported a shipbuilding industry, which in Hartlepool at least had been flourishing since the eighteenth century.

In truth, few people are going to stop at any of these towns. For those that do, Darlington is the most surprisingly attractive, and you'd have to be hard-hearted not to derive some pleasure from Hartlepool's historic quay. Drivers will find navigating the swirling ring-roads and bypasses something of a trial, but it's worth bearing in mind the route east as one possible **approach to North Yorkshire**. Once out on the coast at Saltburn, or inland beyond Guisborough, you're very quickly in the heart of the North York Moors. **Public transport** links are good, too, with regular services connecting the bus and train stations of all the towns in the area. In particular, note the Esk Valley train line from **Middlesbrough to Whitby** which runs via Grosmont, northern terminal point of the North York Moors Railway.

Darlington

DARLINGTON hit the big time in 1825, when George Stephenson's *Locomotion* hurtled from here to nearby Stockton-on-Tees, with the inventor at the controls and flag-carrying horsemen riding ahead to warn of the onrushing train, which reached a terrifying fifteen miles per hour. This novel form of transport soon proved popular with passengers, an unlooked-for bonus for Edward Pease, the line's instigator: he had simply wanted a fast and economical way to transport coal from the Durham pits to the docks at Stockton. Subsequently, Darlington grew into a rail-engineering centre, and didn't look back till the pruning of the network and the closure of the works in 1966.

It's little surprise, then, that all signs in town point to the **Darlington Railway Centre and Museum** (daily 10am–5pm; £2.20), housed in Darlington's North Road station, which was completed in 1842; it's a twenty-minute walk up Northgate from the central market place. The museum's pride and joy is the original *Locomotion*, actually built in Newcastle, which continued in service until 1841 – other locally made engines superseded it, and some of these are on show, too, but on the whole it's a disappointingly unspirited collection of railway memorabilia. Indeed, the museum feels strangely lifeless except on one of the half-dozen "steam weekends" held during the summer, when an engine hauls visitors up a quarter-mile stretch of track next door. The failure to make much of one of Britain's most iconic industrial relics doesn't fill the visitor full of confidence, but in fact the rest of Darlington (or at least the centre) shows itself off well. Its origins lie deep in Saxon times, following which it enjoyed a long history as an agricultural centre and staging post on the Great North Road. The monks carrying St Cuthbert's body from Ripon to Durham stopped in Darlington, the saint lending his name to the graceful central, riverside church of **St Cuthbert** (Easter–Sept daily 11am–2pm; weekends only in winter), where the needle-like spire and decorative turrets herald the delicate Early English stonework inside. One of England's largest market squares spreads beyond the church up to the restored Victorian covered **market** (Mon–Sat 8am–5pm), next to the clock tower, both designed by Alfred Waterhouse, the architect responsible for Manchester's grandiose town hall and London's Natural History Museum. The surrounding buildings are all solidly nineteenth-century, too, many paid for by the town's hardworking Quaker industrialists (of whom Pease was a leading light), who doubtless would have frowned upon the current civic authority's attempts to humanize the town centre. The pedestrianized Market Place has been given back to the people and while it may not be Rome, you can sip a cappuccino at one of several cafés and pubs which spill tables outside at the first hint of sunshine.

Practicalities

Darlington's **train station** is on the main line from London to Scotland (via Durham and Newcastle) and there are also train services to Middlesbrough and Bishop Auckland. From the station, walk up Victoria Road to the roundabout and turn right down Feethams for the central Market Place. You'll pass the new town hall on Feethams, behind which is the **bus station**; buses from here also call at the train station en route to Barnard Castle and Middleton-in-Teesdale.

The town's helpful **tourist office** on the south side of Market Place at 13 Horsemarket (Mon–Fri 9am–5pm, Sat 10am–4pm; ☎01325/388666), has a substantial list of B&Bs. Central **accommodation** options include the *King's Head*, on Priestgate (☎01325/380222; ⑤), and the more reasonable *Cricketers Hotel*, at 53 Parkgate (☎01325/384444; ③), next to the civic theatre. Cheap and basic board is available at the town's *Arts Centre* (☎01325/483271; ①), about half a mile west of the centre in Vane Terrace, where guests can use the kitchen as well as the centre's bar (usual pub hours) and bistro (closed Sun) – follow Duke Street from central Skinnergate.

There are several **cafés** on and around Market Place, while the *Hole in the Wall* pub on the square serves spicy Thai lunches (closed Sun) for a fiver. Across the river from the church, down Parkgate, the *Cottage Thai*, 94 Parkgate (☎01325/361717; closed Sun), is more authentic and more expensive. The **Arts Centre** has a full, year-round programme of theatre, exhibitions and gigs.

Piercebridge

Five miles west of Darlington, off the A67, the remains of a Roman fort are visible at the small village of **PIERCEBRIDGE**, on the River Tees. The **site** (free access) was first occupied in AD 70 and soon became a major strategic river crossing on the fortified Dere Street supply route; defensive ditches and sections of the fort wall are clearly visible, while various foundations have been identified as the remains of guard rooms, a temple and a row of houses. Amble out here late in the day and Piercebridge can make a decent **overnight stop**, provided you book ahead for the highly attractive eighteenth-century *George Hotel* (☎01325/374576; ④), whose ensuite rooms and restaurant look across the gentle banks of the river. The bar food is good, too. Buses run this way from Darlington or Barnard Castle.

Middlesbrough

MIDDLESBROUGH, the region's largest town, fifteen miles east of Darlington, is entirely a product of the early industrial age, with nineteenth-century iron and steel barons throwing up factories and housing almost as fast as they could ship their products out of the docks on the River Tees. What was a mere hamlet at the turn of the nineteenth century was a thriving industrial town of 100,000 people by the turn of the twentieth – "a vast dingy conjuring trick" to J.B. Priestley's mind. When iron and steel declined in importance and the local shipbuilding industry collapsed (the last shipyard closed in 1986), Middlesbrough took to the chemical industry, whose expansive, belching plants still surround the outskirts, making for an unsightly, forbidding approach to the town. Add to this a contemporary renaissance in light engineering and it seems that, compared to many of its neighbours, Middlesbrough can boast relative success in keeping its economic head above water. For visitors, however, none of these enterprises lend themselves easily to the celebration of industrial heritage so much in evidence further west, in the coalfields. The modern town centre is unremarkable in every way and only a pair of bridges recall earlier engineering feats. The **Transporter Bridge** (1911) at Ferry Road, just north of the centre, is the sole working example left in the country, its central section carting cars and pedestrians across the Tees (Mon–Sat 5am–11.05pm, Sun 2–11.05pm; cars 80p, pedestrians 30p) towards Hartlepool. Further southwest, the **Newport Bridge** (1934) was the first vertical lift bridge built in England.

The town prefers to trumpet its position as "Gateway to Captain Cook Country", fair enough given that he was born a mile and a half away in Marton in 1728. Here, the **Captain Cook Birthplace Museum** in Stewart Park (June–Sept Tues–Sun 10am–5.30pm; Oct–May Tues–Sun 9am–4pm; £2) covers the life and times of Captain James Cook, and does it very well by way of good interpretative and interactive displays. As well as displays of artefacts brought back from the South Seas on Cook's voyages, touch-screen terminals provide contemporary testimony by his botanist Sir Joseph Banks, while a series of short films fill in the background about Cook's life and a sailor's lot at sea. Buses #28, #29, #30, #66 and #90 from the bus station run every fifteen minutes or so to Marton – ask the driver for the stop – and while you're in the park you may as well call in at nearby **St Cuthbert's** church on Stokesley Road, where Cook was baptized. It's usually closed during the day but the key is available at the vicarage. In truth, though, despite best local efforts, the Captain Cook trail runs cold after this. There's a scale model of his *Endeavour* hanging from the ceiling in the Cleveland Shopping Centre, right in the middle of town, a bizarre commemorative public sculpture, the *Bottle of Notes*, further down Russell Street, and then that's it until you reach the far more attractive Yorkshire coastal towns where Cook first made his name.

Just a trio of museums to the south, along Linthorpe Road, offer any further reason to delay your onward journey. The **Middlesbrough Art Gallery**, 320 Linthorpe Rd (Tues–Sat 10am–5.30pm; free) houses temporary exhibitions by local and national artists. It's also worth checking out the modern art and temporary exhibitions in the **Cleveland Gallery**, too, a left turn off Linthorpe Road in Victoria Road (Tues–Sat 10am–5pm; free). A hundred yards up Linthorpe Road from the Middlesbrough Art Gallery is the **Dorman Museum** (Tues–Sat 10am–5.30pm; free), originally a nineteenth-century natural history museum though now expanded to cover the history of Middlesbrough. It's an interesting selection of exhibits with the most eye-catching being the collection of Linthorpe pottery – richly glazed, unusually shaped ceramics from a late-nineteenth-century workshop designed to combat local unemployment.

Practicalities

From the **train station** (direct services from Manchester, Leeds, York and Newcastle), it's just a short walk up Albert Road to the main Corporation Road. Turn right for the

bus station – five minutes further up on its continuation, Newport Road – and left for the **tourist office**, 51 Corporation Rd (Mon–Thurs 9am–5pm, Fri 9am–4.30pm, Sat 9am–1.30pm; ☎01642/243425), where you can pick up all manner of brochures, leaflets, accommodation and restaurant lists. Linthorpe Road, for the museums, runs south off Corporation Road, between tourist office and bus station.

It's difficult to see why you'd want to stay the night, with both Durham and the coast so close. To **eat**, the eccentrically decorated *Purple Onion*, 80 Corporation Rd (☎01642/222250), is the best place in town, serving bitingly trendy food at middling-to-high prices; you should book at the weekends. Otherwise, *Savini's*, 149 Linthorpe Rd (☎01642/250133), is a good-value Italian bistro, with happy-hour meals until 7pm.

Hartlepool

If there's one Teesside town trying hard to reinvent itself it's **HARTLEPOOL**, ten miles north of Middlesbrough, England's third largest port in the nineteenth century and a noted shipbuilding centre, but deprived of investment and hope for years following successive economic downturns. These days, though, its image is slowly being transformed by the renaissance of its once decaying dockland area, now spruced up as the popular **Hartlepool Historic Quay** off Marina Way (daily: summer 10am–7pm; rest of year 10am–5pm; last admission 2hr before closing; £4.95). The entrance fee gets you on to the bustling eighteenth-century quayside where active attractions based around press-gangs, the Royal Navy, seaport life and fighting ships stir the senses. There's also a replica eighteenth-century maritime pub, as well as coffee shop and market, while a separate fee is charged if you want to take a guided tour of the **Trincomalee** (Mon–Fri 10.30am–3.30pm, Sat & Sun 10.30am–4.30pm; £2.50), a navy training ship built in 1817. On the edge of the quay in the entertaining **Museum of Hartlepool** at Jackson Dock (daily 10am–5pm; free), you can trace the town's history and climb the port's original lighthouse. Back in the town centre, ten minutes' walk away, the restored nineteenth-century Christ Church, on Church Square, houses Hartlepool's accomplished **Art Gallery** (Tues–Sat 10am–5.30pm, Sun 2–5pm; free) and the **tourist office** (same hours; ☎01429/266522), which can help if you're seduced into staying.

The coast: Redcar and Saltburn

As the towns along the Tees estuary boomed in the nineteenth century, Victorian industrialists looked east to **the coast** for relaxation, creating a string of resorts to which thousands flocked on high days and holidays. The new railway from Darlington and Stockton soon reached Redcar and then Saltburn, both places still making a living today as resorts, albeit with very different characters. There are regular **train** services from Newcastle/Darlington and Middlesbrough to both Redcar and Saltburn, while **buses** from Middlesbrough bus station (with connections from Newcastle) run hourly to Redcar and Saltburn.

Redcar

REDCAR, ten miles northeast of Middlesbrough, started life as a fishing village, until the lengthy sands here attracted day-trippers and then development. The beach is still the best thing about the town, despite the industrial clutter marring the local views. The rest of Redcar is now subsumed within an almighty jumble of guest houses, cafés, donkey rides, chip shops, discos, fairground attractions and a racecourse. It's not sophisticated, but it can be fun for an afternoon or evening out. For a list of local accommodation, call in at the **tourist office**, 3 Dundas St (Easter–Sept daily 9am–5pm; Oct–Easter Mon–Sat 9am–5pm; ☎01642/471921) – you shouldn't have any trouble finding a place to stay.

Saltburn

SALTBURN, just three miles southeast of Redcar, at the end of the beach, is a completely different beast, a truly Victorian resort retaining much of its original character. The railway arrived in 1861; the station is still one of the town's most impressive nineteenth-century edifices. Saltburn soon became a rather fashionable spa town and boasted all the necessary accoutrements: ornate Italian Gardens; miniature railway; hydraulic **tramway** (May to mid-Sept daily 10am–1pm & 2–7pm; mid-Sept to Oct Sat & Sun 11am–1pm & 2–5pm; 45p), complete with stained glass windows, that connects upper town to pier and promenade; and prominent hotels, all of which continue to flourish today. Indeed, given the surviving buildings and rather genteel atmosphere, the town's annual Victorian Celebrations each August seem superfluous – a week during which the locals dress up in costume and live the Victorian life to the full.

Buses stop in the parade outside the train station. If you want to stay in summer, it's best to call first at the **tourist office** in the railway station buildings (Easter–Sept daily 9am–5pm; Oct–Easter Mon–Sat 9am–5pm; ☎01287/622422) and find out about accommodation vacancies. Out of season, you'll be able to pick and choose from a selection of good-value **guest houses** and **hotels**. For surroundings in keeping with the town, the *Rushpool Hall Hotel* on Saltburn Lane (☎01287/624111; ⑤) is a fine choice: a Victorian country house set in its own grounds about a mile from the centre, whose turrets, grand staircase and elegant public rooms are straight out of an Agatha Christie whodunnit. It's always worth asking about special offers here; rooms sometimes come down to around half the listed price.

Don't forget to have a **drink** in the *Ship Inn*, at the eastern end of the beach and promenade, an old smugglers' haunt from the time when banditry went hand-in-hand with the fishing and salt-panning (hence "Saltburn") that kept most of the locals employed during the eighteenth century. Steps behind here lead up the cliff to join the coastal section of the **Cleveland Way**, the path that starts deep in the North York Moors at Helmsley (see p.820). It hits the coast at Saltburn, from where it's nine miles across the high cliffs to the next stop at Staithes, and 54 miles in total to the end of the path at Filey.

Newcastle upon Tyne

At first glance **NEWCASTLE UPON TYNE** – virtual capital of the area between Yorkshire and Scotland – may appear to be just another grimy industrial conurbation, but the banks of the Tyne have been settled for nearly two thousand years and the city consequently has a greater breadth of attractions than many of its northern rivals. The Romans were the first to bridge the river here, and the "new castle" appeared as long ago as 1080. In Elizabethan times a regional monopoly on **coal** export brought wealth and power to Newcastle and – as well as giving a new expression to the English language – engendered its other great industry, shipbuilding. At one time, 25 percent of the world's shipping was built here, and the first steam train and steam turbine also emerged from Newcastle factories. In its Victorian heyday, Newcastle's engineers and builders gave the city an elegance which has survived the ravages of recent development, much of which was perpetrated by John Poulson, a mediocre architect whose name became a byword for civic corruption. Industrial decline hit Newcastle early, as highlighted by the **Jarrow March** of 1936 (see p.879), but this remains a vibrant place, with a commercial resilience that's symbolized by the hugely successful **MetroCentre** across the river at Gateshead. Although grandstand sights are few, there's an impressive energy about Newcastle's handsome city centre, while its revitalized **Quayside**, scene of much of the city's **nightlife**, continues to thrive. Indeed, there's a sharper edge to Newcastle's carousing these days, with new cafés, bars and clubs rivalling the tradi-

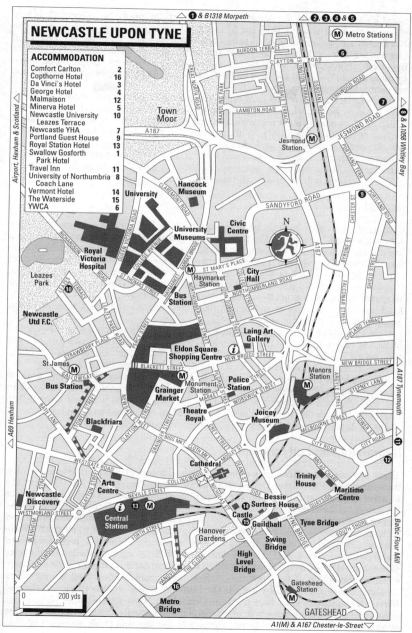

NEWCASTLE UPON TYNE

ACCOMMODATION

Comfort Carlton	2
Copthorne Hotel	16
Da Vinci's Hotel	3
George Hotel	4
Malmaison	12
Minerva Hotel	5
Newcastle University	
Leazes Terrace	10
Newcastle YHA	7
Portland Guest House	9
Royal Station Hotel	13
Swallow Gosforth	
Park Hotel	1
Travel Inn	11
University of Northumbria	8
Coach Lane	
Vermont Hotel	14
The Waterside	15
YWCA	6

© Crown copyright

tional knees-up antics of the notorious Bigg Market. Culturally, too, Newcastle is way ahead of its local rivals – Durham included – boasting the best art gallery in the Northeast, and a slew of good theatres and music venues. The new **International Centre for Life**, a biotechnology research centre and visitor attraction, is the city's main millennium project, while by 2001 work should have been completed on transforming the old **Baltic Flour Mill** on the Gateshead side of the river into a state-of-the-art centre for contemporary visual arts.

All these factors, as well as hard times and a sense of remoteness from the capital, have given Newcastle's inhabitants, known as **Geordies**, a partisan pride in their city, which finds its most evident expression in fanatical support for the **Newcastle United** football team (the "Magpies"). With the stadium still anchored in the city centre (despite periodic attempts to relocate it), and every other young (and not so young) supporter wearing the familiar black-and-white shirt, it's difficult to overstate the team's importance – the death a few years ago of United's most famous goalscorer, Jackie Milburn, brought thousands onto the streets for what was almost a state funeral.

Arrival

Coming to Newcastle by train gives a fantastic view of the city's trademark bridges across the steep Tyne valley. The train station, **Central Station**, on Neville Street, is a five-minute walk south of the city centre and has a useful tourist office and Metro station. National Express **coach** services arrive at Gallowgate station (St James Metro) opposite St James's Park football ground, while regional **bus** services from places like Bamburgh, Berwick, Alnwick and Darlington use the **Haymarket** bus station (Haymarket Metro), just north of the centre, close to the university. Most other city and local bus services arrive at and depart from the underground bus station at **Eldon Square** (not far from Monument Metro).

Newcastle also has an **airport**, six miles north of the city, which is linked to Central Station by Metro (5.50am–11.10pm every 8–15 min; 25min; £1.70). Buses #76, #77 and #78 run from outside the airport (8am–5pm every 20min–1hr; 50min; £1.40) to Eldon Square. Alternatively, you could take a taxi into the centre (around £12).

Ferry arrivals from Sweden, Denmark, Norway, Germany and Holland dock at Royal Quays, North Shields, seven miles east of the city. Connecting bus services run you into the centre, stopping at Central Station, while a taxi will cost around £10. Alternatively, walk the twenty minutes to Percy Main Metro and take the train.

For all **departure details** and enquiry numbers, see "Listings", p.877.

Information and city transport

There are **tourist offices** in **Central Station** (June–Sept Mon–Fri 10am–8pm, Sat 9am–5pm, Sun 10am–4pm; Oct–May Mon–Sat 10am–5pm; ☎0191/230 0030), in the **Central Library** on Princess Square, behind Northumberland Street (Mon & Thurs 9.30am–8pm, Tues, Wed & Fri 9.30am–5pm, Sat 9am–5pm; ☎0191/261 0610), and at the **airport** (information on ☎0191/214 4422). All hand out accommodation lists and a useful map, and have various brochures and booklets available, including self-guided walking-tour "heritage trails". You'll also be able to buy the invaluable *Northumberland Public Transport Guide* (£1). Theatre and cinema **listings** are contained in the *Evening Chronicle* and in the free *Northern Review*, an arts and entertainment review magazine covering the whole of the north of England that's available from the tourist office. Reading *The Crack* (monthly; free) is the best way to find out about gigs, clubs and bars: you can usually get a copy from the Central Library tourist office.

You can walk around the whole of central Newcastle easily enough, though if you're staying in Jesmond you'll need to get to grips with the excellent public transport system.

City and suburban **buses** depart in the main from Eldon Square, although the #33 to Jesmond in fact leaves from Bewick Street, near Central Station and runs along Grainger and Pilgrim streets. East of Eldon Square, **Monument** marks the city centre and site of the main interchange for the conurbation's efficient rail system, the **Metro** (6am–11.30pm every 4–15min). This runs on two lines: Greenline, connecting South Shields, Jarrow, Gateshead, Central Station, Monument and Jesmond with the airport; and the circular Yellowline connecting Monument with Jesmond, North Shields and Whitley Bay. One-way tickets for short hops start at 55p, though discount **passes** – many also valid on the buses and local ferries – are available. Most useful for visitors are the Day Rover (£3.50) or Weekend Rover (Fri 6pm to Sun midnight; £6.30), for unlimited travel in Tyne and Wear, and the Metro Day Saver (£2.80) for unlimited metro and ferry rides (after 9.30am); the Network tickets (valid for a week or more) are sold on a zonal basis. For all **public transport enquiries**, call Nexus (☎0191/232 5325 Mon–Sat 8am–8pm, Sun 9am–5pm) or visit one of its Travel Centres, located at Haymarket, Monument or South Shields Metro stations or at Gateshead Metro Centre Bus Station.

To get out on the Tyne, sign up for one of River Tyne Cruises' three-hour **sightseeing cruises**, which depart from the Quayside (June–Aug 2pm; £7; ☎0191/251 5920). The local public transport authority also operates summer Sunday afternoon cruises from North and South Shields, at the mouth of the river (information on ☎0191/203 3315). Guided, themed **walking tours** of the city centre (Easter–Oct; £2.50) are arranged by the Central Library tourist office.

Accommodation

Hotel expansion shows no signs of slowing in Newcastle, with the success of the Quayside area prompting plans for several new properties (including a large Hilton on the Gateshead waterfront, near the forthcoming Baltic arts centre). The biggest concentration of **hotels** and **guesthouses** is in Jesmond, along and around Osborne Road, a mile north of the city centre: take the Metro to Jesmond or the #33 bus from Bewick Street, opposite the train station. You shouldn't have difficulty finding a bed at any time of the year, though visiting business folk make weekdays busier than **weekends** for most of the year. Consequently, many hotels offer discounts for Friday- and Saturday-night stays, especially at the upper end of the scale where savings can be considerable. Save yourself time and effort by using the free **room-booking service** available at the tourist offices to personal callers. The very cheapest beds are at the **youth hostel** or in one of the **student residences** during the summer: book well in advance for these.

Hotels and guest houses

Comfort Carlton, 82–86 Osborne Rd (☎0191/281 3361). Excellent value, with tasteful en-suite rooms, bar and restaurant. ④.

Copthorne Hotel, The Close, Quayside (☎0191/222 0333). Superbly located bang on the riverside, this modern hotel – recently refurbished – has Tyne views from most of its rooms, a sunny atrium and good leisure facilities. Rooms come with modems and voicemail. It's expensive (and breakfast costs extra), but prices drop dramatically at the weekend. ⑨.

Da Vinci's Hotel, 73 Osborne Rd (☎0191/281 5284). Light, well-furnished rooms above a classy restaurant complete with piano and Leonardo prints. Weekends see a tenner knocked off the room rate. ④, ③ at weekends.

George Hotel, 88 Osborne Rd (☎0191/281 4442). Victorian town house hotel with some of the city's cheapest rooms. No credit cards. ②.

Malmaison, Quayside (☎0191/245 5000, newcastle@malmaison.com). Chic lodgings in the former Co-op building, right on the Quayside. Rooms come with great beds, CD players and modems. Jazzy sounds, crushed velvet sofas, brasserie, bar and gym round off the facilities. Weekend rates (when available) are typically around £25 off. ⑥.

Minerva Hotel, 105 Osborne Rd (☎0191/281 0190). Family-run place with pleasant rooms (ones with shower in the next price category), a cosy bar, inexpensive dinners, and secure parking. No credit cards. ①.

Portland Guest House, 134 Sandyford Rd (☎0191/232 7868). Simple, spotless rooms in a renovated Georgian house, a ten-minute walk from the city centre and close to Jesmond Metro station. No credit cards. ①.

Royal Station Hotel, Neville St (☎0191/232 0781). The city's original Victorian station hotel, built in 1858 and now fully modernized. Great central location and surprisingly low weekend prices. ⑤.

Swallow Gosforth Park Hotel, High Gosforth Park (☎0191/236 4111). One of Newcastle's best hotels, in a relaxed spot set in woodland five miles north of the centre off the A1(M), adjacent to the racecourse and golf course. There's a leisure complex, two restaurants and bars, and big weekend discounts, plus Internet access from all bedrooms. ⑦.

Travel Inn, City Rd (☎0191/232 6533). When all you want is a bed and a bath you can't beat the reliable Travel Inn chain, now installed near the Quayside. ②.

Vermont Hotel, Castle Garth (☎0191/233 1010). High-class business hotel next to the castle, with good views and facilities. ⑧.

The Waterside, 48–52 Sandhill (☎0191/230 0111). Small, luxury hotel right in the centre of the Quayside night-time action, and with its own decent bar. Very good weekend deals. ⑤.

Hostels and university accommodation

Newcastle University, Leazes Terrace Student House (☎0191/222 8150). Centrally located student accommodation near the football ground, available early July to late Sept. Singles and doubles available.

Newcastle YHA, 107 Jesmond Rd (☎0191/281 2570, *newcastle@yha.org.uk*). Popular town-house hostel with sixty beds near Jesmond Metro station – reserve in advance in summer. Breakfast and cheap meals served. Closed Dec and Jan.

University of Northumbria, Coach Lane Campus Halls of Residence, Coach Lane (☎0191/227 4024). Student hall of residence offering cheap B&B, available April & July–Sept.

YWCA, Jesmond House, Clayton Rd (☎0191/281 1233). Purpose-built B&B accommodation for both sexes (age limit 18–50), near the YHA. Weekly rates and evening meals available. Jesmond Metro.

The City

Anyone arriving by train from the north will get a sneak preview of the **Castle** (April–Sept Tues–Sun 9.30am–5.30pm; Oct–March Tues–Sun 9.30am–4pm; £1.50), as the rail line splits the keep from its gatehouse, the Black Gate, on St Nicholas' Street. A wooden fort was built here on the site of an Anglo-Saxon cemetery by Robert Curthose, illegitimate eldest son of William the Conquerer, but the present keep dates from the twelfth century and is everything a castle should be – thick, square and labyrinthine. Staircases and rooms, including a bare Norman chapel, lie off a draughty Great Hall, where displays relate to the Civil War siege of 1644 by a Scottish army supporting the Parliamentarian cause; a small museum room shows various archeological finds. Down in the garrison room, prisoners were incarcerated during the sixteenth to eighteenth centuries, while locals rushed to its deep shelter in World War II to sit out German bombing. There's also a great view from the rooftop over river and city. Little remains of the outer fortifications except the Black Gate, which was added in 1242 for £500, and is topped by a seventeenth-century house.

Further along St Nicholas' Street stands the **Cathedral** (Mon–Fri 7am–6pm, Sat 8am–4pm, Sun 9am–noon & 4–7pm; free), dating mainly from the fourteenth and fifteenth centuries and remarkable chiefly for its tower – erected in 1470, it is topped with a crown-like structure of turrets and arches supporting a lantern. Inside, behind the high altar, is one of the largest funerary brasses in England, commissioned by Roger Thornton, the Dick Whittington of Newcastle – he arrived penniless and died its richest merchant in 1430. The brass is etched with near life-size figures of Thornton and his wife. Much of the interior was given a neo-Gothic remodelling in the late nineteenth century under Sir George Gilbert Scott – the ornate reredos, depicting various Northumbrian saints, is from this period, as is the font canopy with its intricate pinnacles. In the northeast corner of the church you'll find a war memorial dedicated to Danish seamen – evidence of Tyneside's enduring links with Scandinavia. There are occasional **free tours** of the cathedral (Easter–Oct Wed 11.30am).

Quayside, the bridges and around

From between the castle and the cathedral a road known simply as Side, formerly the main road out of the city, descends to the **Quayside** and the area known as **Sandhill**, where the first bridges across the Tyne stood. There have been fixed river crossings here since Roman times and today the Tyne is spanned by six bridges in close proximity, the most prominent being the looming **Tyne Bridge** of 1929 – symbol of the city – which became the model for the Sydney Harbour bridge. To the west of it, road and rail lines cross the river on the **High Level Bridge**, built by Robert Stephenson in 1849 – Queen Victoria was one of the first passengers across, promoting the railway revolution. Further west, under the bridge and up the steep steps to Hanover Street, a section of the old encircling medieval city wall survives. The river views from the adjacent **Hanover Gardens** are magnificent.

Protected by the towering castle, the quayside district became the commercial heart of the city and in the sixteenth and seventeenth centuries its half-timbered houses were the homes of Newcastle's wealthiest merchants. One is **Bessie Surtees' House**, at 41–44 Sandhill (Mon–Fri 10am–4pm; free; EH), the residence of a well-heeled eighteenth-century woman who scandalously eloped to Scotland with a local yokel; all ended well and the groom in question went on to become Lord Eldon, Chancellor of England. The house has been renovated with materials, and even staircases and windows, appropriated from other buildings of the same era.

Opposite is the **Guildhall**, rebuilt many times since its foundation in 1316, where court sessions were held; John Wesley preached here in 1742 and had to be rescued from a volatile crowd by a hefty fishwife. On Sundays (9am–2.30pm) a busy **market** spreads around the nearby hydraulic **Swing Bridge**, which was erected in 1876 by Lord Armstrong to replace the old Tyne Bridge, so that larger vessels could reach his shipyards upriver.

Much of the Quayside was destroyed by a conflagration in 1854, which did for a large part of the medieval layout. There used to be, for example, many more narrow alleys, or "chares", than the half-dozen which survive today. East along the quay, the widest of them, Broad Chare, heads away from the river to the unspoiled ensemble of **Trinity House**, with its enclosed courtyard and own graciously carved chapel (by arrangement only; call ☎0191/261 4691), built in 1505 for the Mariners' Guild and still run by the Brethren of Master Mariners. Controllers of all shipping on the river, the guild had its own naval school whose alumni included Collingwood and Captain Cook. Next door, at no. 29, the **Trinity Maritime Centre** (April–Oct Mon–Fri 11am–4pm; £1.50), housed in an old ship chandler's warehouse, has a few rooms of maritime mementoes and some lovingly detailed model ships, as well as an illustrative model of eighteenth-century Quayside as it was before the fire.

Beyond Broad Chare, the modern-day regeneration of Quayside is in full swing. A landscaped promenade, public sculpture and pedestrianized squares have paved the way for a series of fashionable new bars and restaurants, while across on the other side of the river, the former **Baltic Flour Mill** is slowly being converted into a visual arts centre (due to open in 2001). There will be galleries, artists' studios, workshops and cinema, plus a concert hall for the Northern Sinfonia. A stylish pedestrian and cycle

Millennium Bridge, designed to pivot to allow ships to pass, will span the river at this point allowing direct access from Newcastle's Quayside.

Grey Street to the city walls

By the mid-nineteenth century, Newcastle's centre of balance had shifted away from the river, uphill to the rapidly expanding Victorian town. In a few short years, businessmen-builders and architects like Richard Grainger, Thomas Oliver and John Dobson fashioned what Nikolaus Pevsner later thought to be the best-designed Victorian town in England, with classical facades of stone lining splendid new streets, most notably **Grey Street** – "that descending, subtle curve", as John Betjeman described it. The street takes its name from the Northumberland dynasty of political heavyweights whose most illustrious member was the Second Earl Grey, prime minister from 1830 to 1834. In the middle of his term of office he carried the Reform Bill through parliament, an act commemorated by **Grey's Monument** at the top of the street.

Cleaning and restoration has rescued many of Newcastle's finer buildings: J.B. Priestley, visiting in the 1930s, thought that the city "might almost have been carved out of coal", so black was its stone. Today, Grey Street shows off much of its Victorian elegance, best exemplified by the **Theatre Royal**, halfway down. Other streets fell to the municipal butchers in the 1960s and 1970s – Eldon Square, once a model of Victorian balance, now a shopping centre, a case in point – though not all was lost: **Grainger Market** (Mon–Sat 8am–5pm), near Grey's Monument, maintains its style, once Europe's largest undercover market when built in the 1830s; while John Dobson's **Central Station**, facing Neville Street, trumpeted the confidence of the Railway Age with its soaring interior spaces and curved ironwork. And in Grainger Street and John Dobson Street survive the names, and something of the inspiration, of the two men who did most to reshape the nineteenth-century city.

West of here, behind Gallowgate, is the most complete stretch of the old **city walls**, leading down to Westgate Road. Once encircling the whole of medieval Newcastle, built six to ten feet thick and 25 feet high in parts, they remained in place until the sixteenth century, after which time many sections were plundered for building stone. Several towers remained in use by the city guilds as meeting houses and here, at the "West Walls", alongside Stowell Street, one, the **Morden Tower**, gained prestige as the haunt of poets such as Allen Ginsberg, Basil Bunting and Tom Pickard. Through the arch, the outer defensive ditch has been restored. Stowell Street, incidentally, is Newcastle's **Chinatown**, lined with restaurants and supermarkets. Across Stowell Street from the tower, at Friar's Green, is the tranquil courtyard of **Blackfriars** (usually Mon–Sat 10am–5pm, though times vary; closed Mon in winter; free), a thirteenth-century stone monastery with ruined cloistered grounds, now lovingly restored to house a crafts centre, series of workshops and café/restaurant.

Just to the south of here, off Blenheim Street, the **Discovery Museum** in Blandford House, Blandford Square (Mon–Sat 10am–5pm, Sun 2–5pm; free) attempts to put the city's history into context, with various galleries concentrating on Newcastle's maritime history, its pioneering inventors, armed forces, local costumes and fashion, and community groups. Temporary exhibitions run throughout the year, while the hands-on "Science Factory" gets rave reviews from kids.

The Laing Gallery

Newcastle's – indeed, the Northeast's – premier art collection is the **Laing Gallery** on New Bridge St (Mon–Sat 10am–5pm, Sun 2–5pm; free), off John Dobson Street, behind the library. It's a splendidly organized museum, in which local pottery, glassware, costume and sculpture play their part, while on permanent display is a sweep through

British art from Reynolds to John Hoyland, with a smattering of Pre-Raphaelites, so admired by English industrial barons.

William Bell Scott, a friend of Ruskin's and creator of the murals at Wallington (see p.881), is represented by a picture of mid-nineteenth-century Bigg Market, though the real treat here is the lashings of **John Martin** (1789–1854), a self-taught Northumberland painter with a penchant for massive biblical and mythical scenes. He came from a rather dysfunctional family – his elder brother wore a tortoiseshell hat, another brother set fire to York Minster – and with the benefit of twentieth-century psychological hindsight, it's easy to imagine what demons drove him in his work. Early studies are inoffensive topographical works of castles and landscapes, but the dramatic northeastern scenery was soon to influence him strangely. In *The Bard* (1817), depicting Thomas Gray's poem of the same name, the last surviving Welsh bard – resembling a biblical Charlton Heston on drugs – curses the English troops before jumping to his death from crags Martin conjured from his visits to Allendale Gorge. Much later, in *The Destruction of Sodom and Gomorrah* (1852), blazing buildings and violent colours were presumably influenced by the Tyne's industrial furnaces. Whatever you think of Martin's work – and it certainly provokes extreme reactions – it's hard not to be moved by a paranoiac who was convinced equally of his own genius and of everyone else's opposition to his talent. He regularly exhibited at London's Royal Academy, where in the early days his paintings either failed to sell or – in the case of *Clytie* (1814), which suffered an accidental varnish spill – were "deliberately" damaged.

Martin's histrionics aside, the other must-see in the gallery is the **Art on Tyneside** exhibition, which romps through the history of art and applied art in the region since the seventeenth century with considerable gusto. There's portraiture and landscapes of the city through the ages, as well as digressions on eighteenth-century coffee houses, clothes and materials, glassware and wood engraving – the latter, most famously, by Thomas Bewick (1753–1828), whose pastoral works were inspired by the surrounding countryside. The exhibition comes up to date with coverage of Sixties pop artists Richard Hamilton and Victor Pasmore, both of whom taught at Newcastle University, and of the architectural developments in the 1980s, including analysis of the award-winning Byker Wall project, on the outskirts of the city centre, pioneered by Ralph Erskine.

The university museums

Newcastle University, opposite Haymarket Metro, contains a knot of fine museums and galleries, located off King's Walk: the **Museum of Antiquities** (Mon–Sat 10am–5pm; free) makes a good place to get to grips with the history of Hadrian's Wall; the small **Greek Museum** (Mon–Fri 9.30am–12.30pm & 2–4.30pm; free) contains a valuable collection of armour, jewellery and pottery; while the celebrated **Hatton Gallery** (Mon–Sat 10am–5.30pm; free), attached to the Fine Art Department, features a collection of African sculpture, the only surviving example of Kurt Schwitters' *Merzbau* (a sort of architectural collage) and a variety of temporary exhibitions, often showcasing work by local students. Also attached to the university is the **Hancock Museum** on adjacent Claremont Road (Mon–Sat 10am–5pm, Sun 2–5pm; £2.25); based on an eighteenth-century natural history collection, it's grown to immense dimensions – with more than 150,000 insect specimens. Across to the east, over on the University of Northumbria campus on Sandyford Road (also Haymarket Metro), the **University Gallery** (Mon–Thurs 10am–5pm, Fri & Sat 10am–4pm; free) specializes in temporary exhibitions of twentieth-century art.

Beyond the University of Newcastle stretch the 1200 acres of the **Town Moor**, the city's green lung. It's the site of the annual "Hoppings" in June, a huge week-long **fair** of rides, stalls and other attractions which keeps going until well after dark.

Eating

Newcastle's tastes have moved a long way from traditional dishes, such as black pudding or the gargantuan bread rolls called "stottie cakes". At the budget end of the market Italian, Indian and Chinese food dominates the scene, while at the top end of the scale the city is beginning to attract some top-class chefs. The Quayside and the streets around it are where the most fashionable hang-outs are situated. For Chinese food, check out the Cantonese restaurants along Stowell Street in Chinatown. You'll need to book in advance at weekends at several places. If you're counting the pennies, aim to eat early – many city-centre restaurants offer **early bird/happy hours** deals before 7pm, while others serve **set lunches** at often ludicrously low prices.

Cafés and coffee shops

Blakes Coffee House, 53 Grey St. Near the *Theatre Royal*, this is one of the longest-standing coffee houses in town, serving sandwiches, mountainous ciabatta included. Closed Sun.

Café Churchill, corner of Mosley and Dean streets. Proper coffee, sandwiches, pasta, crepes and Brit-Med lunch specials in a gloriously tiled Victorian relic. Closed Sun.

Fenwick, Northumberland St. Give the department store a whirl – inside is a good second-floor coffee shop, as well as three restaurants, a wine bar and self-service café.

Pani's, High Bridge St, off Grey St. Just up a side street below the Theatre Royal, this little Italian coffee and sandwich bar has a loyal clientele.

The Side Café Bistro, 1–3 The Side. Pasta, salad, *bruschetta* and cappuccino in an amiable little place near the Quayside.

Tyneside Coffee Rooms, 2nd floor, Tyneside Cinema, 10–12 Pilgrim St. Coffee, snacks and arthouse movie talk in the cinema café.

Restaurants

21 Queen Street, 21 Queen St (☎0191/222 0755). Newcastle's premier restaurant serves inventive seafood and local meat dishes in tasteful, relaxed surroundings. Be prepared to fork out at least £40 a head for à la carte, though set lunches are a veritable bargain at under £20. Closed Sat lunch & Sun. Very Expensive.

Asha Raval, 27 Queen St (☎0191/232 7799). High-class Indian restaurant boasting some less travelled dishes on the menu. Moderate.

Barn Again, 21 Leazes Park Rd (☎0191/230 3338). Anglo-French cooking, in a bistro hidden away in a courtyard up an alley close to the football ground. Closed Sun & Mon. Expensive, Moderate at lunch.

Café 21, 33–35 The Broadway, Darras Hall, Ponteland (☎01661/820357). It's a taxi ride out of the city (just a couple of miles from the airport), but locals willingly make the journey for a highly appealing blackboard brasserie menu overseen by the owners of 21 Queen St (see above). Similarly informal operations are located in Sunderland and Durham. Closed Sun & Mon, dinner only Tues–Fri. Moderate to Expensive.

Café Sol, Pink Lane (☎0191/221 0122). Off-the-shelf tapas bar (checked tablecloths, bullfight posters, flamenco nights, *El Pais* to read) with food a cut above the average, ranging from open sandwiches to mussels, cured meats and salads. Closed Sun. Inexpensive.

Courtney's, 5–7 Side (☎0191/232 5537). Modern-British food of distinction, pressing all the right trendy buttons (oven-roasting, wok-frying). The set lunches (under £20) are one way to keep the cost down. Closed Sat lunch & all Sun. Expensive.

Da Vinci's, 73 Osborne Rd, Jesmond (☎0191/281 5284). Good to know about if you're staying in Jesmond, this is a pleasing town-house restaurant with great Italian food. Moderate.

Est Est Est, Quayside (☎0191/260 2291). Super-stylish Italian on the Quayside, with terrific pizzas (try the pizza Spago with red onions, sour cream and smoked salmon), plus a full menu of classic Italian dishes. Moderate to Expensive.

Fisherman's Lodge, Jesmond Dene (☎0191/281 3281). Classy, formal restaurant in Jesmond Dene Park, two miles from the centre, offering well-received modern and traditional British cuisine. Excellent vegetarian choices and the set lunches are a good deal. Closed Sat lunch all Sun. Very Expensive.

The Fox Talbot, 46 Dean St (☎0191/230 2229). Fashionable surroundings, fashionable food, fashionable bright young things eating it. Closed Sun. Inexpensive.

Heartbreak Soup, Baltic Chambers, 77 Quayside (☎0191/222 1701). Good-value Tex-Mex-Caribbean food (with inspiring veggie choices) in colour-splashed surroundings down by the river. Closed Sun. Moderate.

La Tasca, Quayside (☎0191/230 4006). A veritable tapas barn (next to *Est Est Est*) with Spanish tiling and cast-iron candelabras. The food's not bad, though the place really comes into its own in summer when you can sit out on the quayside, grazing, chatting and drinking. Moderate.

Leela's, 20 Dean St (☎0191/230 1261). A rare treat among the flock-wallpaper curry houses, *Leela's* serves high-quality South Indian cuisine, with plenty of vegetarian options. Closed Sun. Moderate to Expensive.

Metropolitan, 35 Grey St (☎0191/230 2306). City-centre brasserie that's great at all times of the day: sandwiches, snacks and an all-day bar, early bird suppers, or brasserie favourites like sausages and mash, fish cakes, seared tuna, or lamb and steak. Live music Mon night. Closed Sun. Moderate.

Rupali, 6 Bigg Market (☎0191/232 8629). Owned by the self-styled Asian Lord of Harpole, but otherwise few frills or surprises, just budget Indian food in the most boisterous part of town. Inexpensive.

Sabatini, 25 King St (☎0191/261 4415). Quayside Italian with Neo-Impressionist daubs on the wall, good pizzas and a full menu besides. Closed Sun. Moderate.

Drinking, nightlife and entertainment

Newcastle's boisterous **nightlife** centres on the pubs and clubs in the older parts of town: between Grainger Street and the cathedral in the area called the Bigg Market – spiritual home of Sid the Sexist and the Fat Slags, from the locally based *Viz* magazine – and around Sandhill and the Quayside, where the bars are smaller and more atmospheric. Expect to queue to get into the more popular bars and pubs, and to have someone scrutinize your clothes as you attempt to gain entry – jeans and trainers are best avoided. As with restaurants, **happy hour** is a big deal in Newcastle – early doors drinking is positively encouraged. Top brew is, of course, **Newcastle Brown Ale** – known locally as "Dog" – produced in this city since 1927.

Pubs, bars and clubs

There's not a great deal of point listing all the Bigg Market or Sandhill/Quayside **pubs** and **bars** – everyone swans in and out of each in the biggest (and largely good-natured) cattle market in western Europe. But try and make time for one or two of the places listed below, which each have their own particular attraction. Note most clubs (though not pubs) are closed on Sundays.

Bodega, 125 Westgate Rd. Restored Edwardian gin-palace with a good beer selection and a studenty crowd which packs in to watch the soccer on TV.

BieRRex, 2a Hancock St. Café-bar whose *raison d'être* is its long list of punishingly strong continental beers. There's decent food served here too.

Bridge Hotel, Castle Square, St Nicholas St. Right opposite the castle, by the High Level Bridge, this Victorian pub has a great view of the Tyne from its beer garden.

The Cooperage, 32 The Close, Quayside. Cosy Quayside pub, originally a sixteenth-century house, just along from the Tyne Bridge, with a good range of guest beers and, often, live bands.

Crown Posada, 31 Side. Local beers and guest ales in a highly attractive wood-and-glass-panelled Victorian pub down by the Quayside.

Frog & Firkin, 1 Sandgate. Open-plan, split-level, student-dominated joint with outdoor terrace, set back from the Quayside and river.

Head of Steam, Neville St. Dowdy in the extreme from the outside, but a real-ale crowd is attracted to this beer-lover's pub opposite Central Station.

Julie's, The Close, Quayside. Glitzy club that's a firm favourite with Newcastle United soccer players letting off steam. Disco and "Ladies Nights" give way to house, dance and garage come the weekend. Closed Sun.

Old George, Old George Yard, off Bigg Market. Rambling, former coaching inn with courtyard that's worth a drink at quieter times.

Pitcher & Piano, Quayside. The Quayside's most spectacular design – sinuous roof, huge plate-glass walls – is a great place to drink, but there's also fine contemporary cooking in the restaurant. Live jazz Sun eve.

Planet Earth, Low Friar St. Popular city dance club, hosting 60s, 70s and 80s music nights, plus the usual weekend house and dance shenanigans. Closed Sun.

Powerhouse, Waterloo St. The city's best gay club attracts a friendly crowd. Mon is cabaret night, Thurs is popular. Closed Tues, Wed & Sun.

Quayside Bar, 35 The Close, Quayside. Newcastle's only surviving medieval warehouse, now a quayside pub-restaurant (under the High Level Bridge) with outdoor tables.

Tuxedo Royale, Quayside, Gateshead. Floating nightclub, on the south side of the river below the Tyne Bridge, with a raucous 18–25-year-old set rolling back the pop years. Closed Sun.

Live music

There's **live music** most nights in the city, either at one of the venues listed below or organized by the **students' unions** at Newcastle University (☎0191/239 3926) and Northumbria University (☎0191/232 6002). It's also worth checking programmes at the various arts centres in and around the city (see below) for folk, rock, roots and jazz gigs. Two **festivals** to note are the annual Newcastle Jazz Festival every July, and the Newcastle Free Festival in August, when anything from flamenco to folk hits the streets.

The Archer, Archbold Terrace, Jesmond (☎0191/281 3010). Regular gigs by up-and-coming local and touring bands.

Newcastle Arena, Arena Way (☎0191/401 8000 or 260 5000). City-centre stadium which attracts all the big pop and rock names, but it's a lifeless venue, better suited to ice hockey and basketball, which also play here.

The Jazz Café, 23 Pink Lane (☎0191/232 6505). Intimate jazz club with a late licence, near the station. Closed Sun.

The Riverside, 57–59 Melbourne St (☎0191/261 4386). Best spot in the city for touring live bands and club nights.

Tyneside Irish Centre, 43–49 Gallowgate (☎0191/261 0384). Opposite the coach station. Regular Irish folk gigs and dances.

Theatre and the arts

There's a full **theatrical and cultural** life in the city and its surroundings, from the offerings at the splendid Victorian *Theatre Royal* and *Tyne Theatre and Opera House* to those of smaller contemporary theatre companies and local arts centres. Ask, too, about occasional summer theatrical performances at the Castle Keep, outdoor promenade productions of Shakespeare and the like. Main **cinema** screens are the Odeon, Pilgrim Street (☎0870/505 0007; Monument Metro), Warner Brothers (☎0191/221 0222; Manors Metro) and UCI in the MetroCentre, Gateshead (☎0191/460 8523), with more challenging films shown at the Tyneside Cinema (see below). And while the City Hall (below) is the main **classical music** concert venue, you'll also find performances throughout the year at Newcastle University's King's Hall, Newcastle Arts Centre and in St Nicholas' cathedral.

Buddle Arts Centre, 258 Station Rd, Wallsend (☎0191/200 7132). Friendly community arts centre with a fine range of events and concerts, and easy to reach from central Newcastle. Wallsend Metro.

City Hall, Northumberland Rd (☎0191/261 2606). The city's main concert venue; the Northern Sinfonia performs from October to May. Haymarket Metro.

Customs House, Mill Dam, South Shields (☎0191/454 1234). Arts centre on the banks of the Tyne, hosting gigs, films and theatre. There's also a bar and a restaurant. South Shields Metro.

Dance City, Peel Lane, off Waterloo St (☎0191/261 0505). Modern dance productions in a small city venue. Central Station Metro.

Live Theatre, 27 Broad Chare (☎0191/232 1232). Enterprising youthful theatre company with regular productions promoting local actors and writers. Also fine live folk, blues, roots and jazz at its weekly *Jumpin' Hot Club*. Central Station Metro.

Newcastle Arts Centre, Black Swan Court, Westgate Road (☎0191/261 5618). Art gallery, exhibition space, and concert and drama venue – always worth checking what's on. Central Station Metro.

Newcastle Playhouse, Barras Bridge (☎0191/230 5151). Modern theatre, home of Newcastle's own Northern Stage company. The Gulbenkian Studio here hosts theatre, dance and recitals. Good café-bar (closed Sun). Haymarket Metro.

Theatre Royal, Grey St (☎0191/232 2061). Drama, ballet, opera and dance; and the annual RSC season in Sept and Oct. Monument Metro.

Tyneside Cinema, Pilgrim St (☎0191/232 1507). The city's premier art-house cinema. Hosts an acclaimed annual International Film Festival in Nov. Monument Metro.

Tyne Theatre & Opera House, Westgate Rd (☎0191/232 0899). Beautifully restored Victorian theatre with a wide range of shows, including productions by the English Shakespeare Company and concerts by the Northern Sinfonia. Central Station Metro.

Listings

Airport and flight enquiries Call Newcastle International Airport (flight info ☎0191/214 3334; general & airline info ☎0191/286 0966). Direct scheduled services to regional British airports, as well as Dublin, Belfast, Scandinavia, Paris, Brussels and Düsseldorf.

Banks and exchanges Banks are concentrated around Grey and Northumberland streets. There's a bureau de change at the airport and in the main post office.

Books Waterstone's, 104 Grey St; Blackwells, Grand Hotel Buildings, Percy St.

Buses For all city and local bus enquiries, call Nexus (☎0191/232 5325). Northumberland County Council has a Transport Enquiries line (☎01670/533128). Otherwise call the various companies: National Express for long-distance routes (☎0990/808080); Arriva Northumbria for most regional services (☎0191/212 3000); Arriva Northeast (☎0345/124125) for services south to Teesside, Middlesbrough and North Yorkshire; Stagecoach for the Newcastle area (☎0191/276 1411) or for Carlisle and Cumbria (☎01946/592000).

Car rental Avis (☎0191/232 5283), Europcar (☎0191/286 5070), and Hertz (☎0191/286 6748) all have outlets at the airport. The best local rates are offered by Auto Hire, 79–81 Blenheim St (☎0191/232 7774).

Dentist In an emergency, contact the dental school at the Royal Victoria Infirmary, Queen Victoria Rd (☎0191/232 5131).

Ferries North Shields ferry terminal at Royal Quays, seven miles east of the city (follow signposts on A1058 and A19), has sailings to Scandinavia, Amsterdam and Germany. Contact Fjord Line (for Bergen, Haugesund and Stavanger; ☎0191/296 1313) or Scandinavian Seaways (Gothenberg/Kristiansand, Hamburg and Amsterdam; ☎0990/333000). Buses leave from Central Station to the terminal before each sailing; the nearest Metro station is Percy Main, from where it's a twenty-minute walk to the ferry terminal.

Hospital Royal Victoria Infirmary, Queen Victoria Rd (☎0191/232 5131), behind the university, just 400 yards from Haymarket bus station. Also, emergency doctor at the Saville Medical Centre, 7 Saville Place (☎0191/232 4274).

Internet Check email and get on line at McNulty's café, 26–30 Market St (☎0191/232 0922).

Left luggage Lockers available at the train station.

Lost property Contact Nexus (see Buses, above) for property left on a bus or the Metro; or the police (below) for general lost property enquiries.

Pharmacies Boots, Monument Mall, Grey St (☎0191/232 4423; open to 7pm). Local, late-opening pharmacies are listed in the local press.

Police Corner of Market and Pilgrim streets (☎0191/214 6555).

Post Office St Mary's Place, near the Civic Centre, at Haymarket (☎0345/223 344), for money exchange and poste restante.

Taxis There are ranks all over the centre, including those at Haymarket, Bigg Market, and outside Central Station. Weekend nights are the most difficult times to hail a cab; the queues at the Bigg Market ranks can be horrendous. Call Noda (☎0191/222 1888) at Central Station for advance bookings.

Trains For all enquiries, call ☎0345/484950.

Travel agents Usit Campus, Level 5, Student Union Building, King's Walk (☎0191/232 2881).

Around Newcastle

The Metro network connects most of the day-trip destinations along the Tyne, and a Day/Weekend Rover or Metro Day Saver ticket (see "Information and city transport", p.868) enables you to get the best out of the local transport systems. In addition to the Metro, the Day/Weekend Rover is valid for most buses in the county of Tyne and Wear, the train to Sunderland and the ferry between North and South Shields. For all **timetable** and **route information**, call Nexus on ☎0191/232 5325.

Along the Tyne

The Metro runs east along both banks of the **River Tyne**, connecting Newcastle with several historic attractions, and with the sandy beaches at Tynemouth and Whitley Bay – the beaches are fine if you just want to see the sea, though anyone intending to head further north up the Northumberland coast will find there's no comparison. You may also be interested to know that South Tyneside is officially designated **Catherine Cookson Country**: the prolific author was born in South Shields and although her childhood homes have since been demolished, South Shields tourist office (at the museum and art gallery, Ocean Rd, South Shields; Easter–Oct Mon–Sat 10am–1pm & 2–5.30pm, Sun 1–5.30pm; Nov–Easter Mon–Sat 10am–1pm & 2–5pm; ☎0191/454 6612) can provide details of the "Catherine Cookson Trail" – plaques, sites and buildings associated with her life and novels, which romanticize the grittier industrial corners of South Tyneside.

It's worth noting that to make a round trip of it, you can cross the river between **NORTH SHIELDS** and **SOUTH SHIELDS** on the Shields Ferry (Mon–Sat 6.30am–10.50pm, Sun 10.30am–6pm; every 15–30min; 7min; 65p one-way). There are Metro stations at either end.

Wallsend

As the name tells you, **WALLSEND**, four miles east of Newcastle, was the last outpost of Hadrian's great border defence, but the site doesn't really live up to its status. The remains of **Segedunum Fort**, the most completely excavated of the wall sites, are now crammed between the shipyards a couple of minutes' walk from Wallsend bus and Metro stations, and the remnants are unlikely to stir anyone who is not already a Roman fan.

Tynemouth

Pressing on through North Shields brings you to the coast at **TYNEMOUTH**, a pleasant village perched on the promontory between sea and river. Long considered a strategically important site, on the cliff-top stand the striking ruins of the **Benedictine priory** (April–Oct daily 10am–6pm; Nov–March Wed–Sun 10am–1pm & 2–4pm; £1.70; EH), later fortified with a **castle**, where early kings of Northumbria were buried. A church was first built here in the seventh century, but the oldest visible features, such as the beautiful chancel, are Norman. Further towards the river are the **Watch House** and **Museum** of the Tyneside Volunteer Life Brigade (Tues–Sat 10am–3pm, Sun 10am–noon; free), packing 130 years of maritime history into a creaky wooden building.

Jarrow

JARROW, five miles east of Newcastle, and south of the Tyne, has been ingrained on the national consciousness since the 1936 march (see box opposite), though the town made a mark earlier, as the seventh-century St Paul's church and monastery was one of the region's early cradles of Christianity. The first Saxon church here was built in 681 AD by monks from St Peter's at Monkwearmouth, and its monastic buildings soon attracted a reputation for scholastic learning. It was here that the **Venerable Bede** (673–735 AD) came to live as a boy, growing to become one of Europe's greatest scholars and England's first historian – his *History of the English Church and People,* describing the struggles of the island's early Christians, was completed at Jarrow in 731. His other writings were many and varied – scientific works on chronology and the calendar, lives of St Cuthbert, historical and geographical treatises – and his influence was immense, prompting a European-wide revival in monastic learning. Yet astonishingly Bede rarely left the monastery, and probably never travelled further than York, relying on visitors and friends for much of his information. After he died in 735, St Paul's soon became a site of pilgrimage, though church and monastery were later sacked by Viking raiding parties. Even after Bede's bones had been appropriated by a relic-collecting Durham priest in 1020 (they were eventually interred in Durham cathedral; see p.849), Jarrow remained high in the clerical consciousness, with monks eager to study at the monastery where Bede had once lived. The monastery was revived in 1074 and continued in existence until the Reformation.

The years have been kind to **St Paul's** (Mon–Sat 10am–4pm, Sun 2.30–4pm), a tranquil stone church framed by the industrial clutter of the Tyneside docks beyond. Once two separate Anglo-Saxon churches standing end-to-end (joined where the tower now stands), inside the original seventh-century dedication stone (dated 23 April, 685 AD, the earliest in England) can be seen, set in the arch above the chancel. Outside are the bare ruins of the buildings, cloister and burial ground of the **monastery**. Most of the standing walls and ruins date from the later eleventh-century re-foundation.

Access to the church and monastery ruins is free, although they stand within the wider development that is **Bede's World** (April–Oct Tues–Sat 10am–5.30pm, Sun noon–5.30pm; Nov–March Tues–Sat 10am–4.30pm, Sun noon–4.30pm; £3), a fascinating exploration of early medieval Northumbria, centred on two museums and an Anglo-Saxon farm site. The main **museum**, housed in a striking Mediterranean edifice with tiled courtyard and atrium, traces the development of Northumbria and England through the use of captivating extracts from Bede's *Ecclesiastical History* set alongside archeological finds and reconstructions. Over at the Georgian **Jarrow Hall** there are more Bede-related displays, a monastic herb garden, and a café. After this you can take

THE JARROW CRUSADE

Jarrow provides the perfect example of what happens to a company town when its company closes. It owed its growth in the last century to the success of the steelworks and shipyard owned by local MP Charles Palmer. Producer of the world's first oil tanker, the Jarrow production line was a phenomenal organization, employing at its zenith some ten thousand men. However, demand for steel and ships went into decline after World War I, and eighty percent of the workforce had been laid off by 1934, the year Palmers was sold off and broken up. From the consequent despair was born the Jarrow Crusade.

On October 5, 1936, led by the town's radical MP Ellen Wilkinson, two hundred men left Jarrow to walk the 290 miles to London under the "**Jarrow Crusade**" banner. Supported by all the town's politicians, the protesters gathered sympathy and support all along the road to the capital, becoming the most potent image of the hardships of 1930s Britain. Some charitable aid was forthcoming after the marchers presented their petition to Parliament, but real recovery only came about through the rearmament of Britain in the build-up to World War II. Palmers was resurrected at nearby Hebburn, and struggled through a series of takeovers into the 1970s, by which time the local economy was on the brink of a state nearly as bad as that of the 1930s. In 1986, with unemployment on Tyneside reaching 32 percent, the fiftieth anniversary of the Jarrow Crusade was marked by another march on the seat of government. The hardships of the 1930s were instrumental in the creation of the Welfare State; the hardships of the 1980s were all but ignored.

a turn through *Gyrwe*, the eleven-acre demonstration **farm** which features reconstructed timber buildings from the early Christian period, as well as demonstrating contemporary agricultural methods. Kids can feed the pigs and ducks and throughout the summer there are craft demonstrations, concerts and other activities (including themed feasts). Allow at least a couple of hours for church, museums and farm.

St Paul's and Bede's World are at Church Bank in Jarrow, a signposted fifteen-minute walk through an industrial estate from **Bede Metro station**. Alternatively, buses #526 or 527 from Neville Street (Central Station) in Newcastle or Jarrow Metro station stop close to the museum on Church Bank. Drivers will find the site a little way off the A185, at the south end of the Tyne tunnel; follow the signs at the A185/A19 roundabout junction.

North of Newcastle: the stately homes

North of the city, a bevy of **stately homes** vie for attention. You could see any of them as half-day trips out of Newcastle by bus, though those with their own transport have the best of things. You can see **Seaton Delaval** en route to the Northumberland coast, or **Belsay** and **Wallington** before heading into the Northumberland National Park.

Seaton Delaval Hall
One of Vanbrugh's great Baroque houses, **Seaton Delaval Hall**, lies eleven miles northeast of Newcastle, its gloomy north facade looking over the bleak terrain towards the port of Blyth. Fire badly damaged the hall in 1822, a century after it was built, but subsequent restorations have done ample justice to the sombre grandeur of a building that exemplifies the architect's desire to create country houses with "something of the castle air". It's been closed for renovations recently, but opens again for the 2000 season; latest details from the Newcastle tourist office (see p.868). Public transport is with the #363 (hourly) or #364 (hourly; not Sun) **bus** from Haymarket, a 35-minute ride to Seaton Delaval Avenue head, from where it's a twenty-minute walk to the hall.

Belsay and Wallington
Belsay Hall, Castle and Gardens (daily: April–Sept 10am–6pm; Oct 10am–5pm; Nov–March 10am–4pm; £3.80; EH), fourteen miles northwest of Newcastle, were inherited in 1795 by Sir Charles Monck, who eleven years later decided to build a brand new hall here after his return from a honeymoon-cum-Grand-Tour of Europe. Inspired by the Neoclassical buildings of Berlin and the Classical architecture of Athens, Sir Charles planned a majestic Doric house, an austere one-hundred-foot-square sandstone block raised on a podium of three steps. Built between 1807 and 1817, the **Hall** has now been impressively restored, though the equally severe interior, with the bedrooms and state rooms surrounding a multi-columned hall, is devoid of furnishings and fittings – instead, special exhibitions often adorn the main reception rooms.

To the west lie the **gardens**, where a footpath threads through the trim formality of the winter gardens to reach the **Quarry Gardens**. Here, in the quarry used for the building of the Hall, lush vegetation cascades over exposed rock faces, planned by Sir Charles as a Romantic antidote to the severity of the house. The track also leads to the substantial remains of the medieval **castle**, its battlements punctuated by four formidable corner turrets. **Belsay village**, on the main road about a mile from the Hall, is readily reached by **bus** from Newcastle; the #808 from Eldon Square (not Sun), or #508 from Haymarket (summer Sun only). There's a tearoom at the hall and, just off the main road near the village, the *Blacksmith's Coffee Shop* (closed Mon, except bank holidays), which makes its own scones.

Eight miles northwest of Belsay lies the tiny village of **Cambo**; the summer Sunday #508 service (twice a day) links the two. Just outside the village stands **Wallington**

House (April–Oct Mon & Wed–Sun 1–5pm; £5.20; NT) an ostentatious mansion rebuilt by Sir Walter Blackett, the coal- and lead-mine owner, in the 1740s. The interior's high-light is the Rococo plasterwork, though William Bell Scott's Pre-Raphaelite decorations in the central hall are good fun, too, and there are diverse attractions for kids, like the dolls' house collection and museum of curiosities. A tearoom and shop rounds off the facilities. There's a separate charge if you only want to see the **grounds** and walled gardens (daily: April–Oct 10am–7pm; Nov–March 10am–4pm; £3.80).

South of Newcastle: Wearside

There's been a long rivalry between Newcastle and Sunderland, twelve miles to the southeast: both cities outraged about being lumped together in the municipal appellation Tyne *and* Wear; both Geordies (from Newcastle) or Mackems (from Sunderland) indignant at being taken for the other by know-nothing southerners; with supporters of both passionately followed football teams cock-a-hoop at the old enemy's misfortunes. To an outsider it can seem at times to be a bewildering argument over nothing at all, but whisper in **Wearside** at your peril the obviously superior charms of Newcastle as a city. Yet **Sunderland** and the River Wear do have their attractions, and in the adjacent new town of **Washington** stands one of the more intriguing historic sites of the Northeast.

Sunderland

SUNDERLAND, bisected by the River Wear and elevated in 1992 to the ranks of Britain's cities, shares Newcastle's long history, river setting and industrial heritage but cannot match its architectural splendour. Formed from three medieval villages flanking the Wear, it was one of the wealthiest towns in England by 1500, and later supported the Parliamentary cause in the Civil War. The twentieth century made and broke the town: from being the largest shipbuilding town in the world, supporting a dozen ship-yards, Sunderland slumped after ferocious bombing during World War II. Depression and recession did the rest.

There's nothing much to turn the head in Sunderland's pedestrianized centre, although the advent of the millennium has prompted the building of a winter garden in Mowbray Park. Work on this closed the excellent **Sunderland Museum and Art Gallery** on Borough Road, at the top of Mowbray Park, for the duration, but it opens again for the 2000 season; call the tourist office for the latest information. It's certainly well worth checking to see, since the city's history is well told here, most effectively in the exhibition *And Ships Were Born*, which relates how Wearside ships once were sent the world over – a trade, incidentally, which gave the city inhabitants their "Mackem" nickname, derived from a stage in the shipbuilding process. In "Coal", which deals movingly with the local coal-mining industry, the roll call of closed collieries is sober-ing – one of the last to go, Wearmouth, has since been reclaimed as the site of Sunderland Football Club's new stadium, known hereabouts as the Stadium Of Light.

What real interest there is in Sunderland lies across the River Wear, whose remodelled, landscaped **Riverside** is actually the oldest settled part of the city. You can walk here eas-ily enough, up Bridge Street from the centre and across the Victorian Wearmouth Bridge (around 20min). Here, in front of the university campus buildings, the early Christian church of **St Peter** (Easter–Oct Mon–Fri 2–4.30pm; by arrangement at other times, call ☎0191/567 3726), built in 674 AD, is the elder sibling of St Paul's church at Jarrow. The tower and west wall are original Saxon features and the church displays fragments of the oldest stained glass in the country, the work of seventh-century European craftsmen. The extraordinary building further down on the waterside is the city's **National Glass Centre** (daily 10am–5pm; £5; ☎0191/515 5555), whose exhibition galleries tell the story of British glass and glass-making – a traditional industry in Sunderland since medieval times, when workshops turned out stained glass for the north's monastic houses and churches. There's plenty to get your teeth into, not least a glass roof you can walk on, a craft shop, and glass-making demonstrations in the on-site factory (call for times).

Further north, out in the beach resort of **Roker** (bus #E1, #E3, #17 or #19) the church of **St Andrew's** on Park Avenue (Mon–Fri 9.15–11.30am) is known as "the cathedral of the Arts and Crafts movement". The nave echoes the upturned hull of a ship, while the sanctuary has a beautiful painting depicting the heavens, with an electric light fitting at the centre of the sun. The tapestries and carpets are from the William Morris workshop, and like the church they date from the early 1900s. It's a mile or so north up the coast from Roker to the twin resort of **Seaburn**, again with a goodish stretch of sand.

The fifteen-mile **River Wear Trail** follows the course of the river from Sunderland, through Washington. The trail starts in town on the south side of the Wearmouth Bridge, the first stretch running through Festival Park before entering the green Wear valley. A few miles to the west, and visible from every road in the vicinity, the hilltop **Penshaw Monument** draws admiring glances – a nineteenth-century pseudo-Greek temple, 100 feet long and 70 feet high, erected in honour of John George Lambton, the first earl of Durham.

PRACTICALITIES
All buses use the **Park Lane Bus Station** in the city centre. The nearby **train station** is opposite the Bridges Shopping Centre, with the **tourist office** close by at 50 Fawcett St (Mon–Sat 9am–5pm; ☎0191/553 2000). For **food** in the city centre, try the *Ground Floor*, on Derwent Street, which serves open sandwiches and Mediterranean lunches. The best restaurant is *Brasserie 21*, Low St, Wylam Wharf (☎0191/567 6594; closed Sun), part of a mini-empire with branches in Newcastle and Durham. The reclaimed warehouse, on the riverside below West Wear Street, serves a fashionable menu, and prices aren't too steep. Across the river, there's *Trattoria Due* (☎0191/510 0600) in the North Dock of the Marine Activities Centre, on St Peter's Riverside, and a fine restaurant in the National Glass Centre, with riverside views.

Washington

Five miles west of Sunderland, the River Wear keeps to the south of the New Town of **WASHINGTON**, focus of much of the region's contemporary investment and manufacture. Split into planned, numbered districts, and organized on American lines, it's not an obvious stop, although the original **Old Village** has been zealously preserved as a conservation area and boasts a couple of pubs and tea rooms. Drivers should follow the signs for District 4 off the A1231 (Sunderland–Newcastle road).

Just off the village green, past the leafy churchyard on The Avenue, stands the ancestral home of the family which spawned the first **US president**. The "de Wessyngtons" – later the Washingtons – originally came over with William the Conqueror, and by 1183 were based at the **Old Hall** (April–Oct Sun–Wed 11am–5pm; £2.75; NT), where they lived until 1613. Carefully preserved as a Jacobean showpiece, the echoing, stone-flagged house has a fine kitchen and Great Hall, and some exemplary wood panelling, and although none of the furniture is original to the Washington family, it is contemporaneous. A breezy video tells the life of George Washington, and plenty of memorabilia pads things out – a notable John Singleton Copley portrait, commemorative spoons and coins, and even the silver spade with which President Jimmy Carter planted a tree during his 1977 visit. Every Fourth of July, the raising of the US flag at the house heralds a day of Independence celebrations; entry to the Old Hall is free that day. Washington himself probably knew little of his family's northeast English origins – the Old Hall had passed into other hands well before the future president's great-grandfather emigrated to

Virginia in 1656, an exile after the English Civil War. Yet it seems too much of a coincidence that the old Washington family coat-of-arms (three stars and three horizontal red-and-white stripes) found its echo more than a century later in the earliest version of the new country's Stars and Stripes.

The other main attraction in the area is the **Washington Wildfowl and Wetlands Centre** (daily: June–Sept 9.30am–5pm; Oct–May 9.30am–4pm; £4.50), east of town and north of the River Wear in District 15, its hundred acres designed by Sir Peter Scott and home to swans, geese, ducks and flamingos. Its trails, hides, play areas, visitor information centre and children's activities make for an enjoyable day out. It's signposted off most local roads, four miles from the A1(M), or see below for public transport.

For Washington Village and the Old Hall, the best service is on the #185 bus from Sunderland Central Bus Station (not Sun). The Wildfowl Centre is reached on the #189 from Newcastle's Eldon Square (not Sun) or the #X4 from either Newcastle's Eldon Square or Sunderland's Park Lane (not Sun). If disaster strikes, all these buses (and many others from Newcastle or Sunderland) call or terminate at **Washington Galleries Bus Station**, from where you'll be able to reach either site. Most buses prefixed with a "W" run to Washington Village from the Galleries.

Hadrian's Wall and Hexham

Some of the great monuments of antiquity are hard to take in at a glance. You need a guide, a knowledgable person to explain the significance of dilapidated stonework. The Wall is an exception. You can see exactly what the Romans were up to.

John Hillaby, *Journey Through Britain*, 1970.

In 55 and 54 BC, Julius Caesar launched two swift invasions of southeast England from his base in Gaul, his success proving that Britain lay within the Roman grasp. The full-scale assault began under Claudius in 43 AD and, within forty years, Roman troops had reached the Firth of Tay. In 83 AD, the Roman governor Agricola ventured farther north, but Rome subsequently transferred part of his army to the Danube, and the remaining legions withdrew to the frontier which was marked by the **Stanegate**, a military roadway linking Carlisle and Corbridge.

Emperor Hadrian, who toured Roman Britain in 122 AD, found this informal arrangement unsatisfactory. His imperial policy was quite straightforward – he wanted the empire to live at peace within stable frontiers, most of which were defined by geographical features. In northern Britain, however, there was no natural barrier and so Hadrian decided to create his own by constructing a 76-mile **wall** from the Tyne to the Solway Firth – "to separate the Romans from the barbarians", according to his biographer. It was not intended to be an impenetrable fortification, but rather a base for patrols that could push out into hostile territory and a barrier to inhibit movement. It was to be punctuated by **milecastles**, which were to serve as gates, depots and mini-barracks, and by observation **turrets**, two of which were to stand between each pair of milecastles. Before the Wall was even completed, major modifications were made: the bulk of the garrison had initially been stationed along the Stanegate, but they were now moved into the Wall, occupying a chain of new **forts**, which straddled the Wall at six- to nine-mile intervals. These new arrangements concentrated the Wall's garrison in a handful of key points and brought them nearer the enemy, making it possible to respond quickly to any threat. Simultaneously, a military zone was defined by the digging of a broad ditch, or **vallum**, on the south side of the Wall, crossed by causeways to each of the forts, turning them into the main points of access and rendering the milecastles, in this respect, largely redundant. The revised structure remained in operation until the last Roman soldiers left in 411 AD.

© Crown copyright

Most of Hadrian's Wall disappeared centuries ago, yet walking or driving its length remains a popular pastime. There are plans to complete a long-distance **footpath** along the entire course of the Wall, but disputes with landowners look set to make this a long-term project. Currently, only certain sections are accessible, but these are more than enough to give an idea of the whole. Approached from Newcastle along the valley of the Tyne, via the Roman museum and site at **Corbridge**, the prosperous-looking market town of **Hexham**, with its fine eleventh-century abbey, makes an ideal base. Most visitors stick to the best-preserved portions of the Wall, which are concentrated between the hamlet of **Chollerford**, three miles north of Hexham, and **Haltwhistle**, sixteen miles to the west. It is here, especially between **Housesteads** and **Steel Rigg**, that the Wall is at its most beautiful, as it clings to the edge of the Whin Sill, a precipitous line of dolerite crags towering above the austere Northumberland National Park moorland. Walking this part of the Wall couldn't be easier: a footpath runs along the top of the ridge, incorporating a short stretch of the **Pennine Way**, which meets the Wall at Greenhead and leaves at Housesteads, where it cuts off north for Bellingham. Scattered along this section are a variety of key archeological sites and museums, notably **Chesters Roman Fort and Museum**, near Chollerford, the remains of **Housesteads Fort** and that of **Vindolanda**, and the milecastle remains at **Cawfields**, north of Haltwhistle.

Visiting the Wall

Using **Hexham** as your base, you can see most of the Northumbrian section of the Wall by bus or car, with the B6318 following the line of the Wall from Chollerford to Greenhead.

There's a special **Hadrian's Wall Bus Service** which links Hexham bus and train stations with Chesters, Housesteads, Once Brewed Visitor Centre, Vindolanda, the Milecastle Inn, Cawfields car park, Haltwhistle town and train station, the Roman Army Museum and Greenhead, Birdoswald and Carlisle. This operates between late-May and late-September, three to four times a day in either direction; it's an hour from Hexham to Haltwhistle, with one-way tickets costing £2 (Day Rover tickets, from the driver or local tourist offices, £5); holders of Northeast Explorer/Stagecoach Cumberland Explorer passes get half-price travel. A reduced winter service (mid-Oct to late May) runs between Carlisle and Housesteads, via Brampton and Haltwhistle, with two to three departures a day (not Sun). Full timetables are available from Hexham, Carlisle or Haltwhistle tourist offices, or the Once Brewed Visitor Centre.

During the summer period, a connecting Sunday-morning bus service starts at Gateshead Metro, calling at Newcastle's Eldon Square before moving on to Hexham. There's also a year-round, hourly service (every 2hr on Sun), the #685, which runs along the A69 between Carlisle, Greenhead, Haltwhistle and Newcastle (Eldon Square). Finally, the #880 or #882 bus from Hexham to Bellingham runs via Chollerford, from where Chesters is just half a mile's walk along the road to the west. During the period May to mid-September, some of these services divert to Chesters itself. For further details on all these services, call Cumbria County Council Journey Planner (☎01228/606000) or the Northumberland County Council Transport Enquiries Line (☎01670/533128).

The nearest **train** stations are on the Newcastle–Carlisle line at Hexham, Bardon Mill and Haltwhistle, leaving you a fair walk to Chesters, Vindolanda and Cawfields/Greenhead respectively.

Hexham has a good range of **accommodation**, something that can't be said for most settlements along this section of the Wall. Only Corbridge, handy for Chesters, and Haltwhistle, three miles or so south of the Wall itself, have any real choice of accommodation; there are **youth hostels** at Once Brewed (see p.889), Greenhead (see p.891) and Acomb, near Hexham (see p.887), as well as the occasional pub or farmhouse B&B in the countryside between Greenhead and Hexham.

Corbridge

Buses from Newcastle and trains on the Newcastle–Hexham–Carlisle train line all stop at **CORBRIDGE**, a quiet and well-heeled town overlooking the River Tyne from the top of a steep ridge. This spur of land was first settled by the Saxons, and their handiwork survives in parts of the church of **St Andrew**, on the central Market Place, but it's the adjacent **Vicar's Pele** that catches the eye, an unusually well-preserved fortified tower-house dating to the fourteenth century. Other buildings are less striking but form a handsome ensemble, with tawny-coloured stone houses alternating with some surprisingly upmarket shops and eating places. Corbridge is the closest place of any real attraction west of Newcastle and consequently is something of a gentrified commuter town.

Arrival, information and accommodation

The **train station** is half a mile outside the town, across the river; from here it's an easy walk into the centre, with the *Angel Inn* on Main Street one of the first places you reach having crossed the bridge. Outside the inn is one place that **buses** stop; you might also be dropped near the post office on Hill Street, around the corner. Corbridge **tourist office** is also on Hill Street, at the library (Easter–Oct Mon–Sat 10am–1pm & 2–6pm, Sun 1–5pm; ☎01434/632815).

There's plenty of accommodation in and around Corbridge, with convenient **B&Bs** near the train station on Station Road – try *Holmlea* (☎01434/632486; no credit cards; ①) – and, more centrally, on Main Street – the *Riverside Guest House* (☎01434/632942; no credit cards; ②). You'll need to book in advance for the ivy-covered *Angel Inn* on Main Street (☎01434/632119; ⑤), opposite the Riverside Guest House, which has just five en-suite rooms, and there's even nicer accommodation and a fine riverside location at the *Lion of Corbridge Hotel*, Bridge End (☎01434/632504; ⑤), which is right by the bridge on the way in from the train station.

The Roman site

One mile to the west of the Market Place, accessible either by road or along the riverside footpath – take the street opposite the *Watling Coffee House* – lies **Corbridge Roman Site** (Easter–Oct daily 10am–6pm; Nov–Easter Wed–Sun 10am–1pm & 2–4pm; £2.80; EH), the location of the garrison town of Corstopitum. This is the oldest fortified site in the region, first established as a supply base for the Roman advance into Scotland in 80 AD (and thus predating the Wall itself). It remained in regular military use until the end of the second century, after which it became surrounded by a fast-developing town – most of the visible archeological remains date from this period, when

Corstopitum, the most northerly town in the empire, served as the nerve centre of Hadrian's Wall, guarding the bridge at the intersection of Stanegate and Dere Street. Clearly labelled, the extensive remains provide an insight into the layout of the civilian town, showing the foundations of temples, public baths, garrison headquarters, workshops and houses as well as the best-preserved Roman granaries in Britain – huge, buttressed buildings with a ventilation system enabling the grain to be stored for long periods.

The site **museum** boasts a good selection of Roman artefacts, from domestic items and imported ceramics to vivid temple friezes. The celebrated *Lion and Stag* fountainhead – the so-called "Corbridge Lion" – gets pride of place; to the Romans, the lion and its prey symbolized the triumph of life over death. The contents of an armourer's box discovered beneath the floor of the hospital revealed the existence of an underground strongroom, used to distribute the soldiers' pay.

Eating and drinking

The *Watling Coffee House*, on Watling Street just off the main square, and *Chadwick's* on Middle Street, not far from the church, both serve light **meals** throughout the day. Down Hill Street, the *Corbridge Larder* is a high-class deli that makes up good sandwiches, or there's the *Valley* (☎01434/633434; closed Sun), an amiable Indian restaurant in the Old Station House on Station Road, right by the train station. Further up the same road, the *Ramblers Country House Restaurant* (☎01434/632424) at Farnley (closed Sun eve & Mon) is precisely that, a comfortable place with gardens where set dinners are under £20 without drinks.

Back in town, for **bar meals** and beer, visit the *Wheatsheaf*, on Watling Street (visible at the end of the road, beyond the *Watling Coffee House*), an attractive seventeenth-century former farmhouse with a couple of Roman stones in the stableyard. Or – in the other direction – you could try the stone-built *Black Bull*, on Middle Street. Otherwise, the *Dyvels*, very close to the train station, is a nice, small local pub with a beer garden.

Hexham

In 671, on a bluff above the Tyne, four miles west of Corbridge, Saint Wilfrid founded a Benedictine monastery whose church was, according to contemporary accounts, the finest to be seen north of the Alps. Unfortunately, its gold and silver proved irresistible to the Vikings, who savaged the place in 876, but the church was rebuilt in the eleventh century as part of an Augustinian priory, and the town of **HEXHAM**, governed by the Archbishop of York, grew up in its shadow. It's a handsome market town of some interest – indeed, it's the only significant stop between Newcastle and Carlisle – and however keen you are to reach the Wall, you'd do well to give Hexham a night or even make it your base.

Arrival, information and accommodation

Well connected with Newcastle, Haltwhistle and Carlisle, Hexham's **train station** sits on the eastern edge of the town centre, a ten-minute walk from the abbey and the **tourist office** on Hallgate (Easter to mid-May & Oct Mon–Sat 9am–5pm, Sun 10am–5pm; mid-May to Sept Mon–Sat 9am–6pm, Sun 10am–5pm; Nov to Easter Mon–Sat 9am–5pm; ☎01434/605225), where you can pick up accommodation lists and Hadrian's Wall bus timetables. The **bus station** is situated off Priestpopple, a few minutes' stroll south of the tourist office.

The tourist office can point you in the right direction for **accommodation**. Good options include the Edwardian retreat that is the *Kitty Frisk House*, a few minutes from the centre on Corbridge Road (☎01434/601533; no credit cards; ②); the quiet and secluded *West Close House*, on Hextol Terrace off the B6305 Allendale Road (☎01434/603307; no credit card; ②), which is very friendly and offers wholefood continental breakfasts alongside the usual fry-ups; and the bright and breezy *Topsy Turvy*, 9 Leazes Lane (☎01434/603152; no credit cards; ①). The *Beaumont Hotel*, overlooking the abbey from Beaumont Street (☎01434/602331; ⑥), has spacious doubles at the bottom of its price category and two-night dinner, bed and breakfast deals; alternatively, try the sympathetically renovated *Royal Hotel* on Priestpopple (☎01434/602270; ④), topped by a gleaming gold dome, which has a dozen en-suite rooms, plus a great bar and brasserie.

The **youth hostel** (☎01434/602864) occupies converted stable buildings in the village of **Acomb**, two miles from Hexham – take bus #880 or #882, which both pass the train station. The **campsite** here, at *Fallowfield Dene Caravan Park* (☎01434/603553; closed Nov–Feb), is a nice place with proper laundry facilities. Closer to town, *Riverside Leisure* (☎01434/604705; closed Feb), beside the Tyne half a mile north of the abbey, forms part of the caravan and leisure park at the end of Tyne Green Road.

The Town

The stately exterior of **Hexham Abbey** (daily: May–Sept 9am–7pm; Oct–April 9am–5pm; £2 donation suggested), properly the Priory Church of St Andrew, still dominates the west side of the Market Place. Entry is through the south transept, where there's a bruised but impressive first-century tombstone honouring Flavinus, a standard-bearer in the Roman cavalry, who's shown riding down his bearded enemy. The memorial lies at the foot of the broad, well-worn steps of the canons' **night stair**, one of the few such staircases – providing access from the monastery to the church – to have survived the Dissolution. Beyond, most of the high-arched nave dates from an Edwardian restoration and it's here that you gain access to the **crypt**, a Saxon structure made out of old Roman stones, where pilgrims once viewed the abbey's reliquaries. The nave's architect also used Roman stonework, sticking various sculptural fragments in the Walls, many of which he had unearthed during the rebuilding.

At the end of the nave is the splendid sixteenth-century **rood screen**, whose complex tracery envelops the portraits of local bishops. Behind the screen, the chancel displays the inconsequential-looking **frith stool**, an eighth-century stone chair that was once believed to have been used by Saint Wilfrid, rendering it holy enough to serve as the medieval sanctuary stool. Nearby, close to the high altar, there are four panels from a fifteenth-century **Dance of Death**, a grim, darkly varnished painting.

The rest of Hexham's large and irregularly shaped **Market Place** (main market day is Tuesday) is peppered with remains of its medieval past. The massive walls of the fourteenth-century **Moot Hall** were built to serve as the gatehouse to "The Hall", a well-protected enclosure that was garrisoned against the Scots. Nearby, the archbishops also built their own prison, a formidable fortified tower dating from 1330 and constructed using stones plundered from the Roman ruins at Corbridge. Now, as the **Old Gaol**, this accommodates the tourist office and the **Border History Museum** (Easter–Oct Mon–Sat 10am–4.30pm; Feb–Easter & Nov Mon, Tues & Sat 10am–4.30pm; £1.80), which provides information and displays concerning the border-raiding Reivers (see p.891) as well as the building's use as a prison – a function it abandoned in 1824.

Down by Hexham Bridge, behind the railway line, a short trail runs through the riverside **Tyne Green Country Park**, a couple of miles upstream to Watersmeet, the spot where the North Tyne (from Kielder Water) and South Tyne (from the Pennines) rivers join. The *Boatside Inn* at Watersmeet has decent pub food, and the walk there and back is very pleasant on a summer's evening.

Eating and entertainment

There are several **coffee shops** and **tearooms** in town open during the day, of which *Mrs Miggins*, on St Mary's Wynd, just off Beaumont Street (opposite Queen's Hall), is among the best, serving inexpensive home-made meals and snacks. Off the Market Place, *O'Kane's*, 3 Old Church, St Mary's Chare, is a pleasant little bistro, while the *Hexham Tans*, further up at 11 St Mary's Chare, is a vegetarian café. *Corbridge Larder*, inside Robb's department store, is the place for picnic supplies.

Bar meals are served at most of the pubs, but top honours go to the *Priestpopple Brasserie* on Priestpopple, part of the Royal Hotel, serving an impressive French-inspired menu, good-value lunches and all-day coffee and drinks. Otherwise, try *Danielle's Bistro*, 12 Eastgate (☎01434/601122; closed Sun), or the *Diwan-e-Am*, on Priestpopple, an Indian restaurant with an eclectic menu. Out of town on Dipton Mill Road, a mile or so south of the centre, the *Black House* (closed Mon all year, plus Tues & Wed in winter) is set in an atmospheric old stable house – come for morning coffee, afternoon tea and home-cooked lunches. In the same direction is *Dipton Mill* itself, now a pub with good bar meals, real ale, streamside beer garden and a pleasant setting. It's a 45-minute walk from Hexham on lovely hilly footpaths; the tourist office will point you in the right direction.

The main focus of **entertainment** in town is the **Queen's Hall Arts Centre** on Beaumont Street (☎01434/607272), which puts on a year-round programme of theatre, dance, music and art exhibitions; it also has a café open until around 8.30pm. The centre has information about Hexham's annual **jazz festival**, held every June. There's often live music at various town-centre **pubs**, none of which, otherwise, are particularly enticing. For just a drink, the *Tap & Spile* on the corner of Battle Hill and Eastgate is probably the most welcoming, with a full range of guest beers.

Chollerford and Chesters Roman Fort

At **CHOLLERFORD**, around four miles north of Hexham, a bridge crosses the North Tyne river, overlooked by the swanky *George Hotel* (☎01434/681611; ⑨), whose renowned restaurant has a fine garden and river views.

Two thousand years ago, the main river crossing was a little way downstream, half a mile west of present-day Chollerford, where **Chesters Roman Fort** (daily: Easter–Oct 10am–6pm; Nov–Easter 10am–4pm; £2.80; EH), otherwise known as *Cilurnum*, was built to guard the erstwhile Roman bridge over the river, its six-acre plot accommodating a cavalry regiment roughly five hundred strong. Enough remains of the original structure to pick out the design of the fort, and each section has been clearly labelled, but the highlight is down by the river where the vestibule, changing room and steam range of the garrison's **bath-house** are still visible, along with the furnace and the latrines.

Back at the entrance, the **museum** has an excellent collection of Roman stonework, most of which was retrieved by the Victorian antiquarian John Clayton, who spent years attempting to preserve the Wall. In particular, look out for the sculpture of Mars from Housesteads, the relief depicting three water nymphs, several stone marker plaques recording the building work completed by the different legions and an incised representation of a strange phallus-like fish.

If you've got your own transport (it's probably not worth the walk), you can head another three miles west from Chesters along the B6318 to reach the site of **Brocolitia Fort** and its late third-century **temple** dedicated to Mithras, the god of sun and light (dawn–dusk; free).

Housesteads to Once Brewed

Overlooking the bleak and bare Northumbrian moors from the top of the Whin Sill, **Housesteads Roman Fort** (daily: Easter–Oct 10am–6pm; Nov–Easter 10am–4pm;

£2.80; EH & NT), eight miles west of Chesters – and a good ten-minute walk up from the car park – has long been the most popular site on the Wall. The fort was built in the second phase of the Hadrianic construction and is of standard design but for one enforced modification – forts were supposed to straddle the line of the Wall, but here the original stonework tracked along the very edge of the cliff, so Housesteads was built on the steeply sloping ridge to the south. Access is via the tiny **museum**, from where you stroll across to the south gate, beside which there are a few remains of the civilian settlement that was dependent on the one thousand infantrymen stationed within. Inside the perimeter, look out for the distinctive cubicles of the barrack blocks, the courtyard plan of the commanding officer's house and the tooth-like stone supports of the granaries.

You don't need to pay for entrance to Housesteads if you simply intend to walk west along the Wall from here. The three-mile hike past the lovely wooded **Crag Lough** to **Steel Rigg** (car park) offers the most fantastic views, especially when you spy the course of the Wall as it threads over the crags ahead.

Practicalities

Leaving the Wall at Steel Rigg, it's roughly half a mile south to the main road and the very informative **Once Brewed National Park Visitor Centre** (May–Oct daily 10am–6pm; much reduced hours in winter, call for details; ☎01434/344396), which has exhibitions and information on both the Wall and the national park. The side road beyond the centre continues for half a mile down to Vindolanda; note that the summer **Hadrian's Wall bus** calls at both the visitor centre and Vindolanda.

For local **accommodation**, there's the popular *Once Brewed Youth Hostel* (☎01434/344360, *oncebrewed@yha.org.uk*), next to the visitor centre, and the *Twice Brewed Inn* (☎01434/344534; ①), two hundred yards or so west down the main road from the visitor centre. This also has more expensive en-suite rooms available. Drivers could cut the three miles southeast across the back roads to the one-shop-one-pub village of **Bardon Mill** (also a stop on the Hexham–Carlisle train line), where the (originally at least) eighteenth-century *Bowes Hotel* (☎01434/344237; ②) has reasonable rooms and food. At slightly larger **Haydon Bridge**, another four miles or so to the east, the *General Havelock Inn* (☎01434/684376; closed Sun evening, Mon & Tues) is the best local place to **eat** hearty Northumbrian cooking, either in the bar or in the rear restaurant which overlooks the river.

There's also a very well-equipped **backpackers' hostel**, *Hadrian's Lodge*, on isolated North Road (☎01434/688688), just under two miles north of Haydon Bridge – from the Wall and the B6318 take the turning for Haydon Bridge about a mile east of Housesteads. Bunk rooms, five self-catering cottages (£120–150 for 3 nights, £250–300 a week), licensed bar and café, bike rental and drying room, make this a good alternative to the *Once Brewed Youth Hostel*.

Vindolanda

The excavated garrison fort of **Vindolanda** actually predates the Wall itself – as do several of the forts hereabouts – though most of what you see today dates from the second to third century AD, when the fort was a thriving metropolis of five hundred soldiers with its own civilian settlement attached. The **site** (May & June daily 10am–6pm; July & Aug daily 10am–6.30pm; April & Sept daily 10am–5.30pm; March & Oct daily 10am–5pm; Nov & Feb daily 10am–4pm; £3.80) is operated by the private Vindolanda Trust, which has done an excellent job of presenting its finds. Note that the Trust also administers the Roman Army Museum at Greenhead; if you're visiting both sites, be sure to request a discounted joint-admission ticket (£5.60).

The **excavations** at Vindolanda are spread over a wide area, with civilian houses, inn, guest quarters, administrative building, commander's house and main gates all clearly visible; a full-scale re-created section of the Wall gives an idea of what a mile-tower would have looked like.

The path through the excavations then descends to the café, shop and **museum** (same hours as site), the latter housing amongst other finds the largest collection of Roman leather items ever discovered on a single site – dozens of shoes, belts, even a pair of baby boots. Other cases illustrate daily life in the fort – with exhibitions about blacksmiths, potters and cooking – though the most intriguing sections are concerned with the excavated hoard of **writing tablets**. Between 1973 and 1992, two hundred significant texts were discovered on the site, dealing with subjects as diverse as clerical filing systems and children's schoolwork. Then, in 1993, final excavations from a bonfire site revealed more tablets, apparently discarded when the garrison received orders in 103–104 AD to move to the Danube to participate in Emperor Trajan's Second Dacian War. The writings depict graphically the realities of military life in Northumberland, under the prefecture of Flavius Cerialis: soldiers' requests for more beer, birthday party invitations, court reports on banishments for unspecified wrongdoings, even letters from home containing gifts of underwear for freezing frontline grunts.

Cawfields and Haltwhistle to Greenhead

Wall-walkers can continue west from Steel Rigg/Once Brewed to **Cawfields** (free access), a distance of around three miles. This was the site of a temporary Roman camp that again pre-dated the Wall, and there are also the remains of another milecastle, this one perched on one of the most rugged crags on this section. There's a car park and picnic site at Cawfields, too, while if you make your way the mile or so south to the main B6318 you'll find the splendid *Milecastle Inn*, the first decent **pub** for miles around and one which specializes in home-cooked pies. The Hadrian's Wall buses (see p.884) stop here, too.

The inn stands at a crossroads, with the small town of **HALTWHISTLE** just under a couple of miles away. There's not much to it – apart from what must be one of the longest main streets in Britain – but there is a **tourist office** (Easter–Sept Mon–Sat 10am–1pm & 2–6pm, Sun 1–5pm; Oct–Easter Mon–Fri 10am–1.30pm & 1–3.30pm; ☎01434/322002) in the **train station**, right at the western edge of town, close to the A69; from here, walk up to Westgate, which becomes Main Street. **Market day** in Haltwhistle is Thursday, while in summer you might coincide with either June's agricultural show – one of the biggest hereabouts – or July's town carnival.

Haltwhistle has a selection of **B&Bs**, including the attractive, stone *Hall Meadows*, right at the top of Main Street (☎01434/321021; no credit cards; ①). Alternatively, *Ashcroft* on Lantys Lonnen, very near the tourist office (☎01434/320213; ②), has nice rooms (including one with a four-poster), while at the eastern end of town, just a mile from the Wall, the *Ald White Craig Farm* on Shield Hill (☎01434/320565; ②; closed Oct–March), is a popular choice. Two or three pubs also offer accommodation, including the *Manor House Hotel* (☎01434/322588; ②) on Main Street. The *Haltwhistle Camping Site* is in Burnfoot Park (☎01434/320106; closed Nov–Feb), beside the Tyne on the southeast edge of town. There are several tearooms along and around Main Street, while for beer and **bar meals**, the *Spotted Cow Inn*, down on Castle Hill, the eastern extension of Main Street, is an agreeable spot. Just a couple of miles south of town, the *Wallace Arms* at Rowfoot, near Featherstone, is situated in fine surroundings, a nice place for a pub meal and a country walk.

Roman Army Museum

A further four-mile trek west from Cawfields takes you past the remains of **Great Chesters Fort** before reaching a spectacular section of the Wall, known as the

Walltown Crags, where a turret from a signal system predating the Wall still survives. The views from here are marvellous. Adjacent to the crags, at Carvoran, the Vindolanda Trust's **Roman Army Museum** (May & June daily 10am–6pm; July & Aug daily 10am–6.30pm; April & Sept daily 10am–5.30pm; March & Oct daily 10am–5pm; Nov & Feb daily 10am–4pm; £3; joint admission ticket with Vindolanda £5.60) does its best to inject some interest into its dioramas, reconstructions and exhibits, but it's rather tame stuff compared to the other sites.

Greenhead

Push on just a mile southwest, and you're soon in minuscule **GREENHEAD**, where the *Greenhead Hotel* (☎016977/47411; ②), which serves reasonable food, sits opposite the **youth hostel** (☎016977/47401), located in a converted Methodist chapel. If neither of these appeals, *Holmhead Guest House* (☎016977/47402; ③) probably will, an old stone farmhouse up a track behind the hostel. Sporting exposed beams, and partly built with stones taken from the Wall itself, it also serves an excellent set-menu dinner (£17) using local ingredients – book ahead, since there are only four rooms (as well as a self-catering cottage with its own walled garden).

The hamlet – served by the Hadrian's Wall bus – is where the **Pennine Way** cuts **east**, following the Wall as far as Housesteads before bearing north again. Heading **west**, the next section of Hadrian's Wall worth exploring is at Birdoswald (see p.732), a four-mile walk or ten-minute ride on the bus.

Northumberland National Park

Northwest Northumberland, the great triangular chunk of land between Hadrian's Wall and the coastal plain, is dominated by the wide-skied landscapes of the **Northumberland National Park**, whose four hundred windswept square miles rise to the **Cheviot Hills** on the Scottish border. These uplands are interrupted by great slabs of forest, mostly the conifer plantations of the Forestry Commission, and a string of river valleys, of which Coquetdale, Tynedale and Redesdale are the longest.

Remote from lowland law and order, these dales were once the homelands of the **Border reivers**, turbulent clans who ruled the local roost from the thirteenth to the sixteenth century. The reivers took advantage of the struggles between England and Scotland to engage in endless cross-border rustling and general brigandage, activities recalled by the ruined **bastles** (fortified farmhouses) and **peels** (defensive tower-houses) that lie dotted across the landscape.

Good walking country can be found right across the National Park and it's this activity that attracts thousands of visitors every year. The most popular trail is the **Pennine Way**, which, entering the National Park at Hadrian's Wall, cuts up through Bellingham on its way to The Cheviot, the park's highest peak at 2674ft, finishing at Kirk Yetholm, over the border in Scotland. This part of the Pennine Way is 64 miles long in total, but it's easy to break the hike up into manageable portions as the footpath passes through a variety of tiny settlements, several of which have youth hostels, B&B accommodation and campsites. As an introduction, it's hard to beat the lovely moorland scenery of the fifteen-mile stretch from Housesteads at Hadrian's Wall to **Bellingham**, a pleasant town on the banks of the North Tyne. Bellingham is also on the road to **Kielder Water**, a massive pine-surrounded reservoir which has been vigorously promoted as a water-sports centre and nature reserve since its creation in 1982. Further north, **Rothbury**, in Coquetdale, is close to both the Simonside Hills and **Cragside**, the nineteenth-century country home of Lord Armstrong, whilst at **Wooler** footpaths lead into the Cheviot Hills. North of Wooler, out of the park and en route to Berwick, a succession of battle sites and **ruined castles** attest to the erstwhile military significance of this border region.

To attempt a tour of the region by **bus** – there aren't any trains – is a time-consuming business. Most services go up or down the valleys, with few crossing the hills between them. But the park should really be explored on **foot** and, once you've selected your base, you won't have any difficulty in reaching it.

Bellingham

The stone terraces of **BELLINGHAM** (pronounced Bellinjum) slope up from the banks of the Tyne on the eastern edge of the Northumberland National Park. There's nothing outstanding about the place, but it is a restful spot set in splendid rural surroundings, and it does contain the much modified medieval church of **St Cuthbert**, which has an unusual stone-vaulted roof – designed (successfully) to prevent raiding Border reivers from burning the church to the ground. The volunteer-run **Heritage Centre** on Front Street (May–Sept Fri–Mon 1.30am–4.30pm; 50p) has more on this turbulent period and also offers changing exhibitions about traditional local life. For a local stroll, follow the two-and-a-half-mile round-trip trail through the woods to **Hareshaw Linn**, a comely waterfall with a thirty-foot drop.

Buses from Hexham (and, on summer Sundays, direct from Newcastle's Eldon Square) stop in the centre on Market Place, a few hundred yards down from the tourist office. There are onward services to Kielder or Otterburn most days; while the Pennine Way passes right through the village. The **tourist office** on Main Street (Easter–Oct Mon–Sat 10am–1pm & 2–6pm, Sun 1–5pm; Nov–Easter reduced hours, call for details; ☎01434/220616) is housed in Bellingham's former Poor House building and is well stocked with local information.

Despite its size, the village's proximity to the park and Pennine Way means that there's a fair choice when it comes to looking for **accommodation**. You may still want to book ahead in summer, particularly if you're coinciding with the last Saturday in August, when the Bellingham Show, the big agricultural event of the year, is staged. The **youth hostel** (☎01434/220313) has simple self-catering facilities in a primitive-looking hut some six hundred yards west of the centre, above the village on Woodburn Road (signposted from Main Street). Central **lodgings** are available at *Lyndale Guest House* (☎01434/220361; ②), just past the *Rose & Crown* pub. *Westfield House*, opposite the fire station (☎01434/220340; ③) is rather grander, and serves a good dinner to guests. Bellingham's pubs – the *Rose & Crown*, the *Black Bull* and the *Cheviot* – all have a few rooms, too; those at the *Cheviot* (☎01434/220696; ③) are the nicest. The local **campsite** is at *Demesne Farm* (☎01434/220258; closed Nov–Feb), right in the centre near the police station.

For **food**, you're dependent on the bar meals served at the pubs, best at the *Cheviot*. If you're buying supplies, note that the **shops** close early on Thursdays and Saturdays, while the **petrol station** is closed on Sundays.

West to Kielder Water

From Bellingham, narrow country roads fan west into the hills and forests surrounding **Kielder Water**, the eastern end of which is just eight miles away. A succession of ruined **bastle houses**, an architectural feature peculiar to the area, provides an early target; otherwise, the glorious open countryside offers few distractions and even fewer facilities – if you want to be sure of a room at any of the places mentioned below, you'd do best to book ahead. There's a limited daily **bus service** from Bellingham to Kielder (as well as a summer Sunday service which originates in Newcastle), but it's fine walking and cycling country.

Bastles on the Tarset

The constant cross-border skirmishing of the late medieval period had an immediate effect on the rural vernacular architecture of the northeast. Lonely farmhouses were fortified in an attempt to ward off attacks, and the area west of Bellingham is rich in the remains of these so-called **bastle houses**. The best preserved lies seven miles northwest of the village, beyond Greenhaugh, where the late sixteenth-century **Black Middens Bastle House** (free access; EH) sits above the waters of Tarset Burn. From a distance, it looks like any other ruined, roofless, stone farmhouse; indeed, close up, it looks like any other ruined, roofless, stone farmhouse, albeit one with extremely thick walls, strategic, narrow upper-floor windows and low surrounding walls. The main door and living quarters were on the upper floor, reached by an exterior staircase, which made it more difficult for attackers to batter their way in. From here, you can continue up the marked trail along the **Tarset Valley**, passing several more ruined bastles, though none as evocatively placed as Black Middens.

The hamlet of **Greenhaugh** has the only facilities hereabouts in the shape of a phonebox and the extremely basic *Holly Bush Inn*, where you can get a sandwich and a drink.

Kielder Water and Forest

Further west, the road follows the North Tyne River and skirts the forested edge of **Kielder Water**, passing the assorted visitor centres, waterside parks, picnic areas and anchorages that fringe its southern shore. First stop is the Visitor Centre at **Tower Knowe** (daily: May–Sept 10am–5pm; Oct–April 10am–4pm; ☎01434/240398), eight miles from Bellingham, with a café and an exhibition (£1) on the history of the valley and lake. Another four miles west, at **Leaplish**, the waterside park (daily: April & Oct 10am–4pm; May–Sept 10am–5pm; ☎01434/250312), lodge, bar and restaurant are the focus of most of Kielder's outdoor activities: watersports, bike rental on marked trails, pony trekking and fishing are all on offer, and there's a heated indoor pool. Leaplish now also has **bunk-barn accommodation**, with dorms and two double rooms (①) available, plus a drying room, kitchen and shower. A ten-mile, hour-and-a-half's **cruise** on the Osprey ferry (April–Oct 5 daily; £4) is always a pleasure; departures are from the piers at either Tower Knowe or Leaplish.

Eighteen miles from Bellingham, at the top of the reservoir, just three miles from the Scottish border, stands **Kielder Castle** (Easter–July & Sept daily 10am–5pm; Aug daily 10am–6pm; Oct–Easter Sat & Sun 11am–4pm; ☎01434/250209; free; parking £1), built in 1775 as the hunting lodge of the Duke of Northumberland, and now an information centre and exhibition area praising the work of the Forestry Commission. The castle is surrounded by the **Border Forest Park**, several million spruce trees subdivided into a number of approximately defined forest areas: Wark and Kielder are broadly to the south of the reservoir, Falstone and Redesdale to the north. Several easy and clearly marked **footpaths** lead from the castle into the forest – try the "Duke's Trail" through Ravenshill Wood, a slice of ancient and semi-natural woodland. There's **mountain bike rental** available from Kielder Bikes (☎01434/250392) at the castle, too, if you want a tougher introduction to the forest routes. Visitor centre facilities are rounded off by a gift shop and restaurant.

The **bus** from Hexham/Bellingham calls at Falstone, Tower Knowe, Leaplish and Kielder. The twice-daily post bus follows a similar route and also calls at Stannersburn, though it takes a lot longer to complete the journey.

If you want to **stay** in the area, options are limited. On the road in from Bellingham, a couple of miles before the water, the early seventeenth-century *Pheasant Inn* (☎01434/240382; ③) at **Stannersburn** has eight comfortable rooms in a modern extension and decent meals served in the bar or restaurant. The riverside hamlet of

Falstone, a mile to the north, boasts the smaller *Blackcock Inn* (☎01434/240200; ③), as well as a tearooms (in the former village school) that doubles as a national park information centre. There's also B&B in two rooms at *High Yarrow Farm* (☎01434/240264; ①; closed Nov–April) on the road to Kielder, plus a couple of B&Bs in **Kielder** village itself, close to the castle – ask at the information centre. *Kielder* campsite (☎01434/250291; closed Oct–Easter) is by the banks of the Tyne, about half a mile north of the castle.

Redesdale

From Bellingham, it's a fifteen-mile trek north along the Pennine Way to **BYRNESS** in **Redesdale**, which can also be reached direct from Kielder Castle via a rough, eleven-mile forestry road that snakes through the pine-clad hills of the northeast portion of the Border Forest Park. Set beside the main road, Byrness is a tiny place, but it is fairly well equipped for walkers, with both a simple **youth hostel** at 7 Otterburn Green (☎01830/520425; closed Oct–Feb), and a **hotel** with public bar, the *Byrness* on the main road (☎01830/520231; ②), right opposite the emergent Pennine Way path; the cheapest rooms share a shower. At the *Border Forest* **campsite** (☎01830/520259; closed Nov–Easter), a mile south of Byrness off the A68, there's a bunkhouse and small chalets available, too.

Redesdale has only one settlement of any size, **OTTERBURN**, ten miles southeast of Byrness down the A68. It's an undistinguished place today, surrounded by heather-clad, sheep-laden countryside, with little except the name of the local pub, the *Percy Arms*, to recall its most notable hour. It was at Otterburn in August 1388 that an English army led by Sir Henry Percy ("Hotspur") was defeated by the Scots under James, Earl of Douglas. Douglas was killed in battle, as were 1800 English troops, while Hotspur was taken prisoner – a chain of events later made the subject of the medieval ballad of *Chevy Chase*. The supposed battle site is about a mile northwest of the village, off the A68, marked by a stone cross set in a little pinewood – though you may as well pick virtually any large field in the vicinity, since historians not only dispute its exact location, but also argue about the site of the Scottish base camp and even the exact date of the battle itself.

There are several places **to stay**, including the *Butterchurn Guest House*, opposite the church on Main Street (☎01830/520585; ②), and the comfortable *Percy Arms* itself (☎01830/520261; ⑤), further down the road, where you can get coffee, bar meals and full dinners. B&B accommodation is also available on a couple of local farms – keep an eye out for signs. The *Border Reiver* (☎01830/520682) is an unusual place, part village shop, part coffee-house-restaurant, with just about every other service you could think of – from lottery tickets to dry-cleaning – thrown in to boot. If you're driving, you could always aim for the comforts of the en-suite rooms in the *Redesdale Arms* (☎01830/520668; ③), an old **coaching inn** on the A68, three miles west of the village.

From Byrness and Otterburn there are two **buses** a day to Newcastle (or north through the borders to Edinburgh) as well as less regular services to Bellingham (from where buses run to Hexham). After Byrness comes Northumberland's longest uninterrupted stretch of the Pennine Way, the 27-mile haul to the end of the hike at Kirk Yetholm (see p.897), though you can detour to Wooler (see p.897).

It's worth knowing that the highly scenic moorland region immediately north of Otterburn is a **military training area**, consisting of almost 60,000 acres of MoD land. Periodic squabbles break out between conservation groups, who rue the intrusion, and locals who welcome the investment the army brings. Visitors intent on walking the area's footpaths and bridleways must heed all signs and flags; better yet, take local advice before setting off.

Rothbury

ROTHBURY, straddling the River Coquet some eighteen miles northeast of Otterburn, prospered as a late Victorian resort because it gave ready access to the forests, burns and ridges of the Simonside Hills. In the centre, where the High Street widens to form a broad triangle, there are hints of past pretensions in the assertive facades overlooking the **Rothbury Cross**, erected in 1902. Rothbury remains a popular spot for walkers, and the Northumberland National Park **Visitor Centre**, near the Cross on Church Street (Easter–Oct daily 10am–5pm; July & Aug 10am–6pm; ☎01669/620887) offers advice on local trails, several of which begin in the Simonside Hills car park, a couple of miles southwest of town. The most appealing of these trails is the five-mile round trip along the Simonside ridge, with panoramic views out over Coquetdale. A renowned **traditional music festival** each July brings folkies and fans into town from all over the region for Northumbrian pipe music, dancing and story-telling.

Victorian Rothbury was dominated by Sir William, later the first **Lord Armstrong**, the immensely wealthy nineteenth-century engineer and arms manufacturer, who built his country home at **Cragside** (Easter–Oct Tues–Sun 1–5.30pm; £6.20; gardens only £3.95; NT), on the steep, forested slopes of Debdon Burn, a mile to the east of the village. At first, Armstrong was satisfied with his modest house, but in 1869 he decided to build something more substantial, and hired Richard Norman Shaw, one of the period's top architects, to do the job. Work continued until the mid-1880s, the final version being a grandiose, and utterly romantic, Tudor-style mansion, whose black and white timber-framed gables and upper storeys are entirely out of place in the Northumbrian countryside. The overly spick-and-span interior is stuffed with Armstrong's furnishings and fittings, heavy dark pieces enlivened by his art collection and by the William Morris stained glass in the library and the dining-room inglenook. Later extensions catered for Armstrong's numerous hobbies and diversions – in the Gallery was placed his natural history and shell collection, a billiard room was added, while the marble-decked drawing room was completed in time for the visit of the prince and princess of Wales in 1884. Doubtless, they were too well brought up to comment on Shaw's "masterpiece", the spectacularly hideous Renaissance-style marble chimneypiece, which uses ten tons of the stuff to overly sentimental effect.

Armstrong was an avid innovator, fascinated by hydraulic engineering and by hydro-electric power. At Cragside he could indulge himself, damming the Debdon Burn to power several domestic appliances, like the spit and the dumb waiter in the massive kitchen, as well as heating his personal Turkish-style plunge bath and steam room. In 1880, after several false starts, he also managed to supply Cragside with electricity, making this the first house in the world to be lit by hydroelectric power. The remains of the original system – including the powerhouse and pumping station – are still visible in the **grounds**, which, together with the splendid **formal gardens**, have longer opening hours (same days 10.30am–7pm or dusk).

Given the hefty admission price you'll probably want to make a day of it, and that's easily done, especially if you come clutching a picnic. Shaded, signposted trails run up hill and down dale through the grounds, past banks of bluebells and rhododendrons; the tallest tree in England (a 191-foot Douglas fir) pierces the pine grove. Over at the visitor centre there's a **café/restaurant**, and an explanatory video and other displays in the adjacent Armstrong Energy Centre.

Practicalities

Buses from Newcastle's Haymarket station stop on the High Street, outside the *Queen's Head*. You can get local **tourist information** from the nearby National Park

Visitor Centre. There are several convenient **B&Bs** – like the *Orchard Guest House*, at the top of the High Street (☎01669/620684; ②), which also serves dinner. The *Queen's Head Hotel* (☎01669/620470; ②), at the other end of the High Street, has en-suite rooms with TV, and carvery and restaurant; it also has a few cheaper rooms without shower. There are also rooms and bar meals at the town's two other pubs: the *Turk's Head* up the High Street and the *Newcastle Hotel*, across from the Queen's Head. Otherwise, you have to head further out of town for lodgings; *Silverton Lodge*, on Silverton Lane (☎01669/620144; ①; closed Dec & Jan) is about ten minutes' walk from the centre, up the main street. Most of the places to **eat** are strung out along the High Street: the *Vale Café* serves all-day breakfasts and basic meals, and the *Sun Kitchen* is an old-fashioned tearooms.

Brinkburn Priory and Longframlington

From Rothbury the B6344 runs four miles southeast through pretty **Coquetdale**, following the course of the river, to reach the splendid sight of **Brinkburn Priory** (Easter–Oct daily 10am–6pm; £1.60; EH), nestling in a loop of the Coquet. Founded as an Augustinian priory in 1135, its church – the only surviving building – was built fifty years later and it's this that provides the focus of interest today. Thoroughly but sympathetically restored in the nineteenth century, it's a superb example of northern Transitional architecture, featuring a fine Norman doorway and an echoing nave, empty save for a remarkable series of enormous contemporary wooden religious sculptures by Durham sculptor Fenwick Lawson. English Heritage is also responsible for the rambling manor house adjacent to the church. Built around 1810, but incorporating parts of the earlier monastic buildings, it was rebuilt by the great Newcastle architect John Dobson in the 1830s, and last lived in during the 1950s. It's now a rather forlorn ruin, though essential maintenance work has arrested its decline and the public is free to wander its beautifully proportioned halls.

A couple of miles north of the priory, up the A697, drivers could make their base at the village of **Longframlington**; there are also half a dozen buses a day from Rothbury. The eighteenth-century *Granby Inn* (☎01665/570228; ③), on the High Street, is renowned for its large breakfasts, excellent home-made food and a range of malt whiskies in the bar. Just north of the village, up the A697, *Embleton Hall* (☎01665/570249; ⑤) has its devotees, too, a peaceful country-house hotel set in five acres, and boasting a fine restaurant (evenings only) and bar meals.

Wooler and the Cheviot Hills

There's nothing immediately attractive about stone-terraced **WOOLER**, a grey one-street market town twenty miles north of Rothbury, though its hillside setting high above Harthope Burn and its proximity to the **Cheviot Hills** do much to lift the spirits. Local walks provide an introduction to the range, with a particular favourite being the one-mile hike to the top of Humbleton Hill, site of a battle in 1402 in which Hotspur (see p.894) inflicted heavy casualties on forces of the Douglas clan. But to get into the heart of the Cheviots you'll have to tackle the trek to The Cheviot itself, seven miles to the southwest. Wooler is also a staging-post on **St Cuthbert's Way**, the trans-Cheviot route, which runs west from the town to Kirk Yetholm and beyond or northeast to Holy Island.

Back in town, a two-mile **town trail** (covered by a 20p leaflet available from the tourist office) drags you around what are presumed to be points of interest; there's no denying that there are fine views en route though. Or pick up the leaflet on country **walks** of between five and nine miles from Wooler, accessible by local bus.

Practicalities

Fast and frequent **buses** link Wooler with Berwick-upon-Tweed and Alnwick, the two nearest towns. The bus station is set back off the High Street. Over the road, the **tourist office** at 16 Market Place (Easter–Oct Mon–Sat 10am–1pm & 2–5pm, Sun 10am–2pm; ☎01668/282123) can help with accommodation and walking information.

There are a couple of handy **B&Bs** on the High Street, including *Tilldale House*, at no. 34 (☎01668/281450; no credit cards; ①), which has spacious en-suite rooms. The *Black Bull*, *Wheatsheaf* and *Red Lion* pubs all have accommodation, too, though the nicest hostelry is the ivy-encrusted *Tankerville Arms* on Cottage Road (☎01668/281581, *enquiries@tankervillehotel.co.uk*; ⑤), a seventeenth-century coaching inn just off the A697 below town. Wooler also has a comfortable **youth hostel** – the most northerly in England – at 30 Cheviot St (☎01668/281365), a five-minute walk up the hill from the bus station, as well as a **campsite**, *Highburn House* on Burnhouse Road (☎01668/281344; closed Nov–Feb), just outside town, about half a mile from the bus station.

Most **eating** places are found along the High Street and in Market Place, where a couple of cafés serve breakfasts and lunches. For picnics, the *Delicatessen*, 24a Market Place, makes up good sandwiches and sells home-made pies. Of the **pubs**, the *Black Bull* on the High Street, serves undistinguished bar meals, as does the *Wheatsheaf*, further along by Market Place.

To Kirk Yetholm: the end of the Pennine Way

It's a fair hike from Wooler up the Harthope valley to **The Cheviot**, which at 2674ft is the highest point in the Cheviot Hills. Starting out from Wooler youth hostel, count on four hours up, a little less back. It helps if you can drive, or catch a lift, to Hawsen Burn, the nearest navigable point, which still leaves you two hours walking there and back – your reward, an utterly bleak spot with views, on a clear day, to the coast, the castles at Bamburgh and Dunstanburgh, and over to Holy Island.

If you're properly equipped, and prepared for a long day's walking, on the west side of the peak you can join the **Pennine Way** at Scotsman's cairn. Here, you're about seven miles south of the trail end at the Scottish village of **KIRK YETHOLM**, where there's a **youth hostel** (☎01573/420631; closed Sept to mid-March), down a lane off the village green, and several B&Bs. At this point, you're just over the border and just out of the national park; it's fourteen miles east by road back to Wooler.

North to Berwick

North of Wooler, the B6525 leads straight to Berwick-upon-Tweed, but if you're in no hurry you'd do well to meander northwestwards up the A697 towards Coldstream, a route which allows you a glimpse into the precarious fourteenth- to sixteenth-century history of the border region. You're soon into rich, flat farmland, watered by the tributaries of the River Tweed, which marks the border with Scotland at this point. The views behind you are of the Cheviots, while detours off the main roads put you on country lanes presided over here and there by stately mansions with gatehouses. The reasonably frequent #267 **bus** from Wooler (not Sun) calls at the places covered below.

Ford, Etal, Branxton and Crookham

Eight miles north of Wooler Follow, off the A697, is the village of **FORD**. The fourteenth-century castle isn't open to the public, but you can **stay** in the grounds: the *Estate House* (☎01890/820414, *burton@ford.ace.co.uk*; ③) is a delightful retreat serving a good breakfast. While here, you could take a look inside the former school, now **Lady Waterford Hall** (Easter–Oct daily 10.30am–12.30pm & 1.30–5.30pm), which features pictures and murals by Louisa Anne, Marchioness of Waterford, a pupil of Ruskin.

You'll need to backtrack slightly up the B6354 to reach the nearby **ETAL** (pronounced "Eetle"), whose **castle** (Easter–Sept daily 10am–6pm; Oct daily 10am–5pm; £2.60; EH) can be visited. Built in 1340 on the banks of the quiet River Till, only the well-preserved central keep and gatehouse still stand, but they make a handsome sight, especially when taken in conjunction with the pretty little village itself. The *Black Bull* here is the only thatched pub in Northumberland, and serves sandwiches and bar meals. If you've got children in tow, it's worth knowing that from Heatherslaw Mill, a couple of miles back down the road to Ford, the narrow-gauge **Heatherslaw Light Railway** (Easter–June & mid-Sept to Oct daily 10.30am–3.30pm; July to mid-Sept 10.30am–4.30pm; Santa Specials Dec, call ☎01890/820244 for details; £3.70 return) runs up the banks of the River Till to the foot of Etal Castle; the return journey takes about forty minutes. The railway's *Granary Café* keeps body and soul together.

Back on the A697, another minor road leads a mile or so west to the hamlet of **BRANXTON**, just above which, on the slopes of Branxton Hill, is the site of the English victory at the **Battle of Flodden** (1513). It was one of the most decisive of sixteenth-century conflicts: up to ten thousand Scots died in battle, including James IV – fighting at the head of his troops – and most of the contemporary Scottish nobility. The bodies were dumped in pits in Branxton churchyard, their passing now remembered by a simple granite memorial on the hill inscribed "To the brave of both nations". You can **stay** in nearby **CROOKHAM**, where the atmospheric *Coach House* (☎01890/820293; ③; closed Nov–March) has a range of rooms in converted farm buildings sporting exposed beams. Guests are pampered with tasty home-made breakfasts and dinners. The *Blue Bell* in the village serves bar meals.

The border and Norham Castle

The A697 runs four miles west of Branxton to reach the **border**, marked by Cornhill-on-Tweed on the English side and Coldstream in Scotland across the River Tweed. There's little point lingering in either with Berwick so close, but save time for the ruins of **Norham Castle** (Easter–Oct daily 10am–6pm; £1.70; EH), overlooking the tumbling Tweed, just six miles or so to the northeast (signposted off the A698). Its surviving pink sandstone walls and foursquare keep stand out above the flat farming country, the trees lining the green-grassed ramparts stripped bare by the winds in winter and providing a leafy curtain in summer. It was considered one of the strongest of the border castles, but James IV of Scotland nevertheless engineered its capture before meeting his nemesis at Flodden Field.

The Northumberland coast

The low-lying **Northumberland coast**, stretching 64 miles north from Newcastle to the Scottish border, boasts many of the region's principal attractions, but first you have to clear the disfigured landscape of the old Northumbrian coalfield, which extends up as far north as the port of Amble. In its heyday at the beginning of the twentieth century this area employed a quarter of Britain's colliers, but most of the mines closed years ago. Attempts have been made to clean up parts of this coast and its hinterland: at Ashington, once a huge pit village (birthplace of the footballing Charlton brothers and the great Jackie Milburn), a country park has been created from a former slag heap, while the marina at Amble and the prospect of summer jaunts to offshore Coquet Island and its nature reserve provide some relief.

Beyond Amble, however, you emerge into a pastoral, gently wooded landscape that spreads over the thirty-odd miles to Berwick-upon-Tweed. On the way there's a succession of mighty fortresses, beginning with **Warkworth Castle** and **Alnwick Castle**, the stronghold-cum-stately-home of the Percys, the county's biggest landowners.

Further along, there's the formidable fastness of **Bamburgh** and then, last of all, the magnificent Elizabethan ramparts surrounding **Berwick-upon-Tweed**. In between you'll find splendid sandy beaches – notably at Bamburgh and the tiny seaside resort of **Alnmouth** – as well as the site of the Lindisfarne monastery on **Holy Island** and the seabird and nature reserve of the **Farne Islands**, reached by boat from Seahouses.

An excellent network of **bus** services makes it easy to travel up and down the coast, and the main London to Edinburgh **train** line passes through Alnmouth and Berwick – though very few fast services stop at the former. Only Holy Island is tricky to reach by public transport, an infrequent bus from Berwick-upon-Tweed being the sole connection. **By car**, the A1 from Alnwick (and, before that, from Newcastle) provides the fastest route to Berwick, though it runs well inland of the major coastal attractions. For these, the B1340 from Alnwick and its offshoots – often signposted "Coastal Route" – is the one to follow.

Warkworth

WARKWORTH, a coastal hamlet set in a loop of the River Coquet a couple of miles from Amble, is best seen from the north, from where the grey stone terraces of the long main street slope up towards the commanding remains of **Warkworth Castle** (daily: April–Oct 10am–6pm; Nov–March 10am–1pm & 2–4pm; £2.40; EH), which perch on top of an immense grassy mound at the far end of the village. Enough remains of the outer wall to give a clear impression of the layout of the medieval bailey, but – apart from the well-preserved gatehouse through which the site is entered – nothing catches your attention as much as the **keep**. Mostly built in the fourteenth century, this three-storeyed structure, with its polygonal turrets and high central tower, has a honeycomb-like interior, a fine example of the designs developed by the castle-builders of Plantagenet England. It was here that most of the Percy family, earls of Northumberland, chose to live throughout the fourteenth and fifteenth centuries. The castle's cellars were used to good effect in the torture-chamber scenes in the Oscar-nominated film *Elizabeth* (1998), parts of which were also filmed in various other Northumbrian castles, from Raby to Alnwick.

The main Castle Street sweeps down into the attractive village, flattening out at Dial Place, beyond which stands the church of **St Laurence**, whose many Norman features include the impressive ribbed vaulting of the chancel. From the churchyard (or, further up, from below the castle), a delightful path – signposted "Mill Walk" – heads the half-mile inland along the peaceful right bank of the Coquet to the little boat that shuttles visitors across to **Warkworth Hermitage** (April–Sept Wed & Sun 11am–5pm; £1.60; EH), a series of simple rooms and a claustrophobic chapel that were hewn out of the cliff above the river sometime in the fourteenth century, but abandoned by 1567. The last resident hermit, one George Lancaster, was charged by the sixth earl of Northumberland to pray for his noble family, for which lonesome duty he received around £15 a year and a barrel of fish every Sunday.

Practicalities

Warkworth is on the route of the **bus service** linking Alnwick, Alnmouth and Newcastle, while other local services run to and from Alnwick and Amble. Buses stop in Dial Place, near the church. Alnmouth (see p.900) has the nearest **train station**, and is much better placed for the beach, so you probably won't want to **stay** in Warkworth. However the village does possess the splendid *Sun Hotel*, 6 Castle Terrace (☎01665/711259; ⑤), whose conservatory is a fine place for meals and teas with views of the castle and coast. There's a handful of **B&Bs**, too, including *Roxbro House*, 5 Castle Terrace (☎01665/711416; no credit cards; ①), also perfectly sited immediately below the castle walls.

If **meals** at the *Sun* are out of your league – French-inspired table d'hôte dinners from around £20 (or dinner, bed and breakfast deals with your room) – you'll need to eat down in the village itself. Superior meals and teas are available at the *Greenhouse*, Dial Place (closed Sun eve & Mon), near the church, where smoked salmon, cassoulet, and other bistro favourites are served on stripped pine tables. *Topsey Turvey's*, over the way at 1 Dial Place, is also open for bistro meals (closed Sun & Mon). Next door, the *Mason's Arms* has more traditional **pub food** and a beer garden.

Alnmouth

It's just three miles north from Warkworth to the seaside resort of **ALNMOUTH**, whose narrow, mostly nineteenth-century centre is strikingly situated on a steep spur of land between the sea and the estuary of the Aln. It's a lovely setting, and there's a wide sandy beach and rolling dunes. Alnmouth was a busy and prosperous port up until 1806, when the sea, driven by a freakish gale, broke through to the river and changed its course, moving the estuary from the south to the north side of Church Hill and rendering the original harbour useless. Alnmouth never really recovered, though it has been a low-key holiday spot since Victorian times, as attested by the elegant seaside villas at the south end of town. Many come for the golf: the village's splendid nine-hole course, right on the coast, was built as early as 1869 (it's claimed to be the second oldest in the country) and dune-strollers really do have to heed the "Danger – Flying Golf Balls" signs which adorn Marine Road.

Practicalities

There are local bus services from Alnwick and Warkworth, while the regular Newcastle to Alnwick **bus** also passes through Alnmouth and calls at its **train station** at Hipsburn, a mile and a half west of the centre. This makes the resort a convenient interlude on the journey up or down the coast, especially as it's well equipped with B&Bs – in summer, you'd do best to book ahead, particularly if you're planning to stay during Alnwick Fair in June (see opposite), when all local accommodation is scarce.

Most of the **accommodation** lies along or just off the main Northumberland Street. Best central B&B is *The Grange* opposite the church (☎01665/830401; no credit cards; ②), a reclusive stone house with garden, overlooking the river. A few yards further down Northumberland Street, at no. 56, the friendly *Copper Beach* (☎01665/830443; no credit cards; ②) has huge rooms in a period stone cottage above a good restaurant (see below). A string of **pubs** along Northumberland Street also offers accommodation; the most reasonable is the *Saddle Hotel*, at no. 25 (☎01665/830476; ③), whose spacious rooms have bath and TV, the top-floor ones enjoying (partial) sea views. Top choice is the fancy *Schooner Hotel* (☎01665/830216; ④) – it's only worth spending this much if you can secure a room with a sea view (though dinner, bed and breakfast deals and off-season rates bring the price down slightly). Sea views are guaranteed at the *Marine House Private Hotel* (☎01665/830349; ⑤, includes dinner), whose squeezed rooms all face the golf links and coast; bartering can get you a B&B rate, though they're keener to sell you a dinner package. There's an adjacent seafront cottage to rent, too.

There are a couple of coffee houses along the main street, while **lunches and dinners** are served in the bar-lounges and dining rooms of the pubs. The *Saddle Hotel* has a large menu; the restaurant at the *Red Lion*, an old coaching inn further up the street, is better and more expensive, serving fresh fish and other meals. The *Tea Cosy Tea Room*, at no. 23 (☎01665/830393), serves bistro dinners at weekends in summer, but the best choice is to eat at the oak-beamed *Beaches* (underneath *Copper Beach B&B*), where meals of local cod, filo-stuffed chicken, beef stir-fries and the like go for around £12 a head; you can take your own wine.

Alnwick

The unassuming town of **ALNWICK** (pronounced "Annick"), some thirty miles north of Newcastle and four miles inland from Alnmouth, is renowned for its castle – seat of the dukes of Northumberland – which overlooks the River Aln immediately to the north of the town centre. Alnwick itself is an appealing market town of cobbled streets and Georgian houses, centred on the old cross in Market Place, site of a weekly **market** (Saturdays) since the thirteenth century. Other than catching the market in full swing, the best time to visit is during the boisterous week-long **Alnwick Fair**, a medieval re-enactment which starts on the last Sunday in June. There's a costumed procession on that day, preceded by street entertainment, with stalls doing a roaring trade in roast ox sandwiches. During the week that follows, the Playhouse stages special concerts, pubs lure in punters with Yard-of-Ale contests and the like, and the Market Place is given over to a craft fair and a "Pie Court", where unfortunates suffer duckings and a spell in the stocks. Costumes are available for rent during the fair – ask at the tourist office.

Arrival, information and accommodation

Alnwick is a hub for much of the coastal and inland transport, and there are regular bus services to and from Alnmouth, Warkworth and Newcastle, as well as inland to Rothbury and summer routes to Craster, Seahouses and Bamburgh. Alnwick **bus station** is on Clayport Street, a couple of minutes' walk west of the Market Place, where you'll find the **tourist office**, in the arcaded Shambles (April–Sept Mon–Sat 9am–5pm, Sun 10am–4pm; Oct–March Mon–Fri 9am–5pm, Sat 10am–4pm; ☎01665/510665).

Several **B&Bs** lie just beyond the gatehouse at the end of Bondgate. Here, among others along Bondgate Without, you'll find the *Lindisfarne* at no. 6 (☎01665/603430; no credit cards; ①) and the *Oronsay Guest House*, a Victorian villa at no. 18 (☎01665/603559; no credit cards; ①). For a different architectural backdrop, head instead for the *Georgian Guest House*, a right turn through the arch up Hotspur Street (☎01665/602398; no credit cards; ①). Alnwick's main **hotel** is the *White Swan*, on Bondgate Within (☎01665/602109; ⑤), where you might want to pop in at least for coffee – there's a comfortable lounge, while the hotel's fine panelled dining room was swiped from an old ocean liner, the *Olympic*, the twin of the *Titanic*. Many prefer the more intimate *Bondgate House Hotel*, back outside the gate, at 20 Bondgate Without (☎01665/602025; ②), or even the accommodating *Oaks Hotel*, a couple of miles from the centre on South Road (☎01665/510014; ③). You can **camp** at *Alnwick Rugby Club* in Greensfield Park (☎01665/602987; closed Nov–March), a little way south of the centre but walkable.

The castle

The Percys – who were raised to the dukedom of Northumberland in 1750 – have owned the **Castle** (Easter–Sept daily 11am–5pm; £5.95) since 1309, when Henry de Percy reinforced the original Norman keep and remodelled its curtain wall. His successor, another Henry, built the imposing barbican and connecting gatehouse. In the eighteenth century, the castle was badly in need of a refit, so the first duke had the interior refurbished by Robert Adam in an extravagant Gothic style – which in turn was supplanted by the gaudy Italianate decoration preferred by the fourth duke in the 1850s.

Nowadays, the castle is part of a business empire based on the duke's extensive Northumbrian estates. Your stiff entry fee contributes to the company's coffers, which would be better justified if more of the castle were open to the public: most of Capability Brown's grounds remain out of bounds and so are the bulk of the rooms – only half a dozen or so can be visited out of around one hundred and sixty. Moves are afoot, however, to restore the nineteenth-century walled garden into a contemporary water garden, complete with fountains, waterfalls, canals and pavilion that should be opened to the public by 2001.

Entry to the castle is through the carriageway to the right of the fourteenth-century barbican, whose sturdy battlements sport a number of stone soldiers, a piece of eighteenth-century flummery replacing the figurines of medieval times, set up there to ward off the evil eye. Beyond, the broad lawns of the bailey surround the heavy walls of the **keep**, where the dark and drab **entrance hall** is covered with the armaments of the Percy Tenantry Volunteers, a private force raised by the second duke during the Napoleonic Wars. The hall leads to the **grand staircase**, a marble pomposity that climbs up to the guard chamber, whose Renaissance-style decor, from the mosaic floor to the stucco ceiling, is typical of the work of the Italian craftsmen hired by the fourth duke. The most lavish decoration is in the **red drawing room**, where the rich polygonal panels of the ceiling bear down on damask-covered walls and some magnificent ebony cabinets rescued from Versailles during the French Revolution. Each room displays part of the duke's extensive collection of paintings, including pieces by Canaletto, Titian, Tintoretto, Van Dyck and Turner. A couple of towers contain **museum** collections – the Regimental Museum of the Royal Northumberland Fusiliers in the Abbot's Tower, early British and Roman finds in the Postern Tower – but the bucolic garden walks and **grounds** are a more profitable use of time once you've seen the main rooms.

The rest of town

From outside the castle, it's a few minutes' walk north along Bailiffgate and then Ratten Row to the gates of **Hulne Park**, a substantial tract of hilly woodland to the northwest of Alnwick. Deep inside the park, a three-mile hike from the entrance, are the rusticated remains of **Hulne Priory**, a thirteenth-century Carmelite monastery built above the north bank of the River Aln. It's a lovely, peaceful spot and, although the greystone ruins are slight, they are enlivened by several whimsically carved stone monks, modern sculptures which have the place pretty much to themselves. The duke owns the park, and access is controlled – pedestrians and cyclists only, from 11am to sunset in summer.

The tiny town of Alnwick has a trim and tidy cobbled Market Place, but there's not much else to see, except for the **gatehouses** on Pottergate and Bondgate, the principal remains of the medieval town walls, and the grandiose **Percy Tenantry Column** just to the southeast of the centre along Bondgate Without. This 75-foot high column, surmounted by the Percy lion, was built by the tenants of the second duke in 1816 after he had reduced their rents by 25 percent. As it turned out, their humble gratitude was somewhat premature. The third duke promptly bumped the rents up again and locals wryly renamed their monument the "Farmers' Folly". A little further on, housed in the listed Victorian train station, **Barter Books**, one of the largest secondhand bookshops in England, is worth a call.

Eating, drinking and entertainment

Copperfields Coffee House, 11 Market St, opposite the tourist office, serves daytime snacks and **meals**, while various pubs offer bar meals, like the *Market Tavern Hotel* on Fenkle Street (off Market Place) and, further down, the *Oddfellows Arms*, on Narrowgate. For more atmosphere, visit the *Gate Bistro*, 14 Bondgate Within (closed Mon, & Tues & Sun eves in winter) – up a side alley between the *Swan Hotel* and the gatehouse – a licensed café/restaurant with some interesting specials. Narrowgate also has a couple of other bistro-cafés, at least one open in the evenings for dinner.

Few of the town's **pubs** offer much scope for a civilized drink: those along Narrowgate – *Ye Olde Cross* and the *Black Swan* – are crowded and boisterous at the weekend. The "Dirty Bottles" in *Ye Olde Cross*'s window have supposedly not been moved for two centuries, since the person who put them there dropped down dead immediately afterwards. The nicest local pub is the *Masons' Arms* at **Rennington**, four miles northeast of town on the Seahouses (B1340) road, an old coaching inn with good bar food. Back in town, check to see what's on at the **Alnwick Playhouse,** just through the arch on Bondgate Without (☎01665/510785), a venue for theatre, music and film throughout the year, and also host to concerts during the town's annual **International Music Festival** every August.

Craster, Dunstanburgh Castle and around

Heading northeast out of Alnwick along the B1340, it's a six-mile hop to the region's kipper capital, the tiny fishing village of **CRASTER,** perched above its minuscule harbour. There's not a great deal to make you stop long, but you can buy wonderful kippers here at Robson's factory and have a pot of tea in the *Bark Pots.* Even better is the *Jolly Fisherman,* the **pub** above the harbour, with sea views from its back window and famously good crab sandwiches and kipper pâté.

Most spectacularly, however, the village provides access to **Dunstanburgh Castle** (April–Oct daily 10am–6pm; Nov–March Wed–Sun 10am–4pm; £1.80; NT & EH), whose shattered medieval ruins occupy a magnificent promontory about thirty minutes' windy walk up the coast – there's a car park in Craster. Originally built in the fourteenth century, parts of the surrounding walls survive – offering heart-stopping views down to the crashing sea below – though the dominant feature is the massive keepgatehouse which stands out from miles around on the bare coastal spur. Mel Gibson's *Hamlet* used the walls and keep to impressive effect.

In summer, half a dozen **buses** a day (the #501/401) run to Craster from Alnwick, a half-hour journey; the service continues to Seahouses and Bamburgh.

Embleton, Newton-by-the-Sea and Beadnell

EMBLETON, on the other side of the promontory from the castle, has a fine sandy beach, windswept and deserted in winter, busier in summer though rarely overly so. A couple of pubs here, and in similarly attractive **NEWTON-BY-THE-SEA,** next beachside hamlet north, make good lunch stops. Newton's the *Ship* is the pick of the bunch, on a square of old cottages, just yards from the beach and serving fresh crab and salmon sandwiches. **BEADNELL,** too, has a pub, a fine beach and the excellent *Beach Court* on Harbour Rd (☎01665/720225, *russ@beachct.demon.co.uk*; ④), a distinctive **guest house** right next to the shore, with sea views and three lovely rooms – the most expensive of which is a "turret" suite (⑤) with its own observatory. Tourist offices in Alnwick and Seahouses can arrange other local B&B accommodation, and the #501 bus passes through both places. There are local **campsites** at *Dunstan Hill* (☎01665/576310; Nov–March), a mile inland from Dunstanburgh castle, close to the B1339.

Seahouses and the Farne Islands

From Craster, it's twelve miles north to **SEAHOUSES,** a desultory fishing-port-cum-resort that's the embarkation point for **boat trips** to the windswept and treeless **Farne Islands,** a rocky archipelago lying a few miles offshore. Owned by the National Trust and maintained as a nature reserve, the Farnes are the summer home of many species of migrating seabirds, especially puffins, guillemots, terns and kittiwakes. To protect the birds, only two of the islands are open to visitors: **Inner Farne** (April–Sept daily; landing fee £4) and **Staple Island** (same months & prices). The crossing can be rough, but the islands have a wild beauty that makes it all worthwhile, and on Inner Farne you can also visit a tiny, restored fourteenth-century chapel built in honour of St Cuthbert, who spent much of his life here. Of the islets you don't land on, but should see from the boat, a cottage on the Brownsman was the first home of **William Darling** and his family; when the Longstone lighthouse was lit in 1826, the family moved islands – twelve years later his daughter Grace became a national heroine after a daring sea rescue.

Weather permitting, several boat owners operate daily **excursions**, usually starting at around 10am: Billy Shiels (Easter–Oct; ☎01665/720308), the best of the bunch, runs a varied programme, from two-and-a-half-hour **cruises** round either island (£8), to all-day trips landing at both (£15); all trips also visit the grey seal colonies off the islands. Note that if you land on the islands, you'll have to pay the separate NT landing fee (members free). For more information, call the **National Trust Shop**, 16 Main St, Seahouses (☎01665/721099), across from the *Olde Ship* (see below).

Practicalities

It's unlikely you'd choose to stay the night in Seahouses, and there are regular **buses** to both Alnwick and Berwick-upon-Tweed, but, if you've returned from the Farnes late in the day, you may not want to go any further. Seahouses has a range of reasonably priced **B&Bs** – details from the **tourist office** (daily: April & Oct 10am–4pm; May–Sept 10am–6pm; ☎01665/720884), in the Seafield Road car park above the harbour.

The *Olde Ship*, 9 Main St (☎01665/720200; ④), quite apart from its pleasant rooms, is a great place to drink, full of nautical bits and pieces and serving good **food**. Otherwise, there's a whole host of fish-and-chip restaurants. If you want to take some of the local catch home, the *Fisherman's Kitchen,* 2 South St (May–Sept Mon–Fri 9am–5pm, Sat 9am–4pm; variable hours in winter) sells smoked kippers and salmon from its traditional **smokehouse**.

Bamburgh

Flanking a triangular green in the lee of its castle, three miles north of Seahouses, the tiny village of **BAMBURGH** is only a five-minute walk from two splendid sandy beaches, backed by rolling, tufted dunes. From the sands – in fact from everywhere – **Bamburgh Castle** (April–Oct daily 11am–5pm; £4) is a spectacular sight, its elongated battlements crowning a formidable basalt crag high above the beach. This beautiful spot was first for-tified by the Celts, but its heyday was as an Anglo-Saxon stronghold, one-time capital of Northumbria and the protector of the preserved head and hand of St Oswald, the sev-enth-century king who invited St Aidan over from Iona to convert his subjects. To the Normans, however, Bamburgh was just one of many border fortresses administered by second-rank vassals: as an eleventh-century monastic chronicler expressed it: "[Bamburgh], renowned formerly for the magnificent splendour of her high estate, has been burdened with tribute and reduced to the condition of a handmaiden."

Nonetheless, rotted by seaspray and buffeted by winter storms, Bamburgh Castle struggled on until 1894, when the new owner, Lord Armstrong (see p.895), demolished most of the structure to replace it with a cumbersome castle-mansion. The focal point of the new building was the Great Hall, a soulless teak-ceilinged affair of colossal dimensions, whose main redeeming feature is an exquisite collection of Fabergé stone animal carvings. In the adjacent Faire Chamber there's also a pastoral miniature by Jan Brueghel the Younger. In the basement of the keep, the stone-vaulted ceiling maintains its Norman appearance, making a suitable arena for a display of suits of armour and other antique militaria. There's some interest, too, in a display in the former laundry building, where exhibits trace Armstrong's career as inventor, shipbuilder and indus-trialist, a neat counterpoint to the displays at Cragside.

Bamburgh is also the home of the **Grace Darling Museum** (Easter to mid-Oct Mon–Sat 11am–7pm, Sun 2–6pm; donation requested), which celebrates the daring sea rescue accomplished by Grace and her lighthouseman father, William, in September, 1838. It began when a gale dashed the steamship *Forfarshire* against the rocks of the Farne Islands. Nine passengers struggled onto a reef, where they were subsequently saved by the Darlings, who left the safety of the lighthouse to row out to them. *The Times* trumpeted

Grace's bravery, offers of marriage and requests for locks of her hair streamed into the Darlings' lighthouse home and for the rest of her brief life Grace was plagued by unwanted visitors – she died of tuberculosis aged 26 in 1842. The museum details the rescue and displays the fragile boat the Darlings used; in the churchyard of thirteenth-century **St Aidan's** opposite is the pompous Gothic Revival memorial that covers Grace's body.

Practicalities

A regular **bus** service links Alnwick and Berwick-upon-Tweed with Bamburgh. You'll be dropped on Front Street by the green, opposite the *Castle Hotel*. There are several places **to stay**, including the highly appealing *Lord Crewe Arms Hotel*, Front St (☎01668/214243; ⑤; closed Nov–Feb), a comfortable old inn with oak beams, open fires (and cheaper rates) in winter, and a moderately priced restaurant. Nearby *Green Gates*, 34 Front St (☎01668/214535; no credit cards; ②), has a couple of rooms with castle views, and there are also pleasant rooms at the *Green House*, 5–6 Front St (☎01668/214513; ②; closed Jan), at the top of the village – rooms at the front just fall into the next category but have nice views of the green. If these are all full, try the *Glenander Guest House*, 27 Lucker Rd (☎01668/214336; no credit cards; ③), one of two or three places on the same road offering B&B.

For budget **meals**, the *Victoria Hotel*, at the top of Front Street, has a reasonably priced brasserie-restaurant, and serves substantial meals in its back-room bar. Otherwise, there are a couple of tearooms, a bucket-and-spade general store, and fancier meals in the *Green House* restaurant (closed Sun), serving meals of local meat and fish for around the £15 mark; you should book ahead on summer weekends.

Romantic big-spenders should head out of town, to **Waren Mill**, a couple of miles to the west on the B1342, where the *Waren House Hotel* (☎01668/214581; ⑦) is set in its own grounds on the edge of Budle Bay, overlooking Holy Island. Eating well here is no trouble whatsoever. At the other end of the scale, *Waren Caravan Park* (☎01668/214366; closed Nov–March) has the closest **camping** to Bamburgh; take the local #501 bus to Waren Mill.

Holy Island

There's something rather menacing about the approach to **Holy Island**, past the barnacle-encrusted marker poles that line the causeway. The danger of drowning is real enough if you ignore the safe crossing times posted at the start of the three-mile trip across the tidal flats. (The island is cut off for about five hours every day, so to avoid a tedious delay it's best to consult the tide timetables at one of the region's tourist offices.) Once on the island, the ancient remains of the priory and the brooding castle conjure yet more fantasies, not all pleasant. Small (just one and a half miles by one), sandy, flat and bare, it's easy to picture the furious Viking hordes sweeping across Holy Island, giving no quarter to the monks at this quiet outpost of early Christianity. Today's sole village is plain in the extreme, which doesn't deter summer day-trippers from clogging the car parks as soon as the causeway is open. But Holy Island has a distinctive and isolated atmosphere, especially out of season. Give the place time and, if you can, stay overnight, when you'll be able to see the historic remains without hundreds of others cluttering the views.

Once known as **Lindisfarne**, Holy Island has an illustrious history. It was here that St Aidan of Iona founded a monastery at the invitation of King Oswald of Northumbria in 634. The monks quickly evangelized the Northeast and established a reputation for scholarship and artistry, the latter exemplified by the **Lindisfarne Gospels**, the apotheosis of Celtic religious art, now kept in the British Museum. The monastery had sixteen bishops in all, the most celebrated being **St Cuthbert**, who only accepted the job after Ecgfrith, another Northumbrian king, pleaded with him. But Cuthbert never settled here and, within two years, he was back in his hermit's cell on the Farne

Islands, where he died in 687. His colleagues rowed the body back to Lindisfarne, which became a place of pilgrimage until 875, when the monks abandoned the island in fear of marauding Vikings, taking Cuthbert's remains with them – the first part of the saint's long posthumous journey to Durham (see p.850). In 1082 Lindisfarne, renamed Holy Island, was colonized by Benedictines from Durham, but the monastery was a shadow of its former self, a minor religious house with only a handful of attendant monks, the last of whom was evicted at the Dissolution.

The island

There's not much to the **village**, just a couple of streets radiating out from a small green and church cross, everything within a five-minute walk of everything else. If you've arrived by car, you'll have to **park** in one of the large signposted carparks – keep an eye on the time and tide if you're not intending to stay.

Just off the green, the pinkish sandstone ruins of **Lindisfarne Priory** (daily: Easter–Oct 10am–6pm; Nov–Easter 10am–4pm; £2.80; EH) are from the Benedictine foundation. Enough survives to provide a clear impression of the original structure, notably the tight Romanesque arches of the nave and the gravity-defying stonework of the central tower's last remaining arch. Behind lie the scant remains of the monastic buildings while adjacent is the mostly thirteenth-century church of **St Mary the Virgin**, whose delightful churchyard overlooks the ruins. The **museum** (same times as priory; entrance included in priory fee) features a collection of incised stones that constitute all that remains of the first monastery. The finest of them is a round-headed tombstone showing armed Northumbrians on one side, and kneeling figures before the Cross on the other – presumably a propagandist's view of the beneficial effects of Christianity. The priory, incidentally, marks the beginning (or end) of St Cuthbert's Way (p.896), the 63-mile cross-border hiking route to and from Melrose in Scotland.

Stuck on a small pyramid of rock half a mile away from the village, past the dock and along the seashore, **Lindisfarne Castle** (April–Oct Mon–Thurs, Sat & Sun 1–5.30pm; £4; NT) was built in the middle of the sixteenth century to protect the island's harbour from the Scots. It was, however, merely a decaying shell when Edward Hudson, the founder of *Country Life* magazine, stumbled across it in 1901. Hudson bought the castle and turned it into a holiday home to designs by Edwin Lutyens, who used the irregular levels of the building to create the L-shaped living quarters that survive today. Lutyens kept the austere spirit of the castle alive in the great fireplaces, stone walls, columns and rounded arches which dominate the main rooms.

The two historic sites are all that most people bother with, but a **walk** around the island's perimeter is a fine way to spend a couple of hours. From the grass banks above the harbour, there are views across to the two nineteenth-century obelisks, built on the distant sandbanks as navigational aids – boats line them up with the church tower to steer their way in. Most of the northwestern portion of the island is maintained as a **nature reserve**: from a bird hide you can spot ter s and plovers, and then plod through the dunes and grasses to your heart's content. The island even supports a seal colony, though sightings by visitors are rare – legend rather touchingly has it that the seals kept vigil with St Cuthbert as he prayed at the water's edge of his new domain.

Back in the village, two other attractions suck in the trippers. The **Museum of Island Life** (daily Easter–Oct) on Marygate occupies an eighteenth-century fisherman's cottage and gives an idea of former living and working conditions. Everyone then decants into **St Aidan's Winery**, just up from the green, sole producer of Lindisfarne Mead, a sickly concoction on sale all over the Northeast coast. You can sample the mead before you buy, which – given its rather challenging taste – seems a misguided marketing ploy.

Practicalities

The #477 **bus** from Berwick-upon-Tweed to Holy Island is something of a law unto itself given the interfering tides, but basically there's a twice-daily service (not Sun) from mid-July to the end of August; services two or three days a week on either side, between May and September; and a severely reduced service between October and March. Departure times vary with the tides, and the journey takes thirty minutes; local tourist offices can provide the latest details or call the Berwick Bus Shop (☎01289/307283). Throughout the year, you can also ask to be dropped off by the Berwick–Newcastle buses at Beal, though from here you face a four-mile walk to the island. All walkers and drivers must check the **tide tables** (at any local tourist office) to see when it's safe to cross.

The island is short on places **to stay** and you should make an advance booking, whenever you visit. Two good places are the *North View Guest House*, on Marygate (☎01289/389222; ③; closed Jan), which offers comfortable rooms in a sixteenth-century listed building; or the cheaper, and very friendly, *Britannia House* (☎01289/389218; no credit cards; ②; closed Nov–Feb), just by the green, which has bargain-rated en-suite rooms. Otherwise, you're looking at staying in one of the pubs, best the refurbished *Ship* on Marygate (☎01289/389311; ③). Camping isn't allowed anywhere on the island.

While the island's accommodation is reasonable, the prospects of a decent **meal** are slim. It can only be the islanders' descent from errant monks that explains why you can't get anything to eat anywhere after 8.30pm – it's no good enjoying yourself if you've got to get up at four in the morning to save souls. Guests at *North View* are lucky since they can partake of the good-value set dinner. Otherwise you have to take your chances in the *Ship* – pick of the **pubs**, with good Holy Island Bitter – the *Lindisfarne Hotel* or the *Manor House Hotel*, all of which have similarly uninspiring menus.

Berwick-upon-Tweed

Before the union of England and Scotland in 1603, **BERWICK-UPON-TWEED**, some twelve miles north of Holy Island, was the quintessential frontier town, changing hands no fewer than fourteen times between 1174 and 1482, when the Scots finally ceded the stronghold to the English. Interminable cross-border warfare ruined Berwick's economy, turning the prosperous Scottish port of the thirteenth century into an impoverished garrison town, which the English forcibly cut off from its natural trading hinterland up the River Tweed. By the late sixteenth century, Berwick's fortifications were in a dreadful state of repair and Elizabeth I, apprehensive of the resurgent alliance between France and Scotland, had the place rebuilt in line with the latest principles of military architecture.

The new design recognized the technological development of artillery, which had rendered the traditional high stone wall obsolete. Consequently, Berwick's **ramparts** – one and a half miles long and still in pristine condition – are no more than twenty feet high but incredibly thick: a facing of ashlared stone protects ten to twelve feet of rubble, which, in turn, backs up against a vast quantity of earth. Further protected by ditches on three sides and the Tweed on the fourth, the walls are strengthened by immense bastions, whose arrowhead-shape ensured that every part of the wall could be covered by fire. Begun in 1558, the defences were completed after eleven years at a cost of £128,000, more than Elizabeth paid for all her other fortifications put together. And, as it turned out, it was all a waste of time and money: the French didn't attack and, once England and Scotland were united, Berwick was stuck with a white elephant.

Arrival, information and accommodation

From Berwick **train station** it's about ten minutes' walk down Castlegate to the town centre. Most regional **buses** also stop in front of the station, though some may also stop closer in on Golden Square (where Castlegate meets Marygate), on the approach to the Royal Tweed Bridge. For all local bus information, call in at the **Berwick Bus Shop**, 125 Marygate (☎01289/307283). If you're heading into town from here, Eastern Lane runs off Marygate to the right, where you'll find the **tourist office** in the Maltings arts centre (July & Aug Mon–Wed 10am–6pm, Thurs–Sat 10am–8pm, Sun 10am–4pm; rest of year Mon–Wed 10am–6pm, Thurs–Sat 10am–8pm; ☎01289/330733). They sell weekly **parking** permits (useful since they're valid throughout the region) and can book you on to informative one-hour **walking tours** of town (Easter–Oct Mon–Fri; £2.50). For local **bike rental**, call Brilliant Bicycles, 17a Bridge St (☎01289/331476).

Berwick has plenty of **accommodation** and the tourist office offers a room-booking service. You need to decide whether you want to stay within the ramparts or across the river, either in Tweedmouth, just on the other side of the bridge, or near the beach at Spittal. **In the centre**, the best-value B&B is at *3 Scott's Place* (☎01289/305323, *scottsplace@btinternet.com*; ②), a Georgian town house off Castlegate – nice, large en-suite rooms, friendly hosts and a fine breakfast. Also highly recommended is *No.1 Sallyport*, 41 Bridge St (☎01289/308827; ③), a seventeenth-century house next to the city walls (above the Bridge Street Bookshop) with elegant en-suite rooms, fresh coffee and inventive home cooking. Reservations are essential. Other options include *Clovelly House*, 58 West St (☎01289/302337; ②), and the *Riverview Guest House*, 11 Quay Walls (☎01289/306295; ②; closed Jan & Feb). If these are full, try one of the other places ranged along Church Street and Ravensdowne; or head north up Castlegate, past the station, and on to North Road where there are several other places, including the recommended *Dervaig Guest House*, 1 North Rd (☎01289/307378, *dervaig@btinternet.com*; ③). The best central **hotel** is the *King's Arms*, Hide Hill (☎01289/307454; ⑤), one of the myriad English coaching inns that Charles Dickens is supposed to have slept and lectured in.

Across Berwick Bridge in **Tweedmouth**, you can't beat the delightful *Old Vicarage Guest House*, a spacious Victorian villa at 24 Church Rd (☎01289/306909; ③); book ahead as it's popular. The suburb of **Spittal** (bus #B1 from the bus station) has more guest houses located along Main Street, just a couple of minutes from the beach: try the *Roxburgh*, at no. 117 (☎01289/306266; ①). There are plenty of local **campsites**, though only *Marshalls Meadows Farm* (☎01289/307375) has space for tents.

The Town

Today, the easy **stroll** along the top of the ramparts offers a succession of fine views out to sea, across the Tweed and over the orange-tiled rooftops of a town that's distinguished by its elegant Georgian mansions. These, dating from Berwick's resurgence as a seaport between 1750 and 1820, are the town's most attractive feature, with the tapering **Lions' House**, on Windmill Hill, and the daintily decorated facades of **Quay Walls**, beside the river, of particular note. The three bridges spanning the Tweed are worth a second look too – the huge arches of the **Royal Border Railway Bridge**, built in the manner of a Roman aqueduct by Robert Stephenson in the 1840s, contrasting with the desultory concrete of the **Royal Tweed**, completed in 1928 and the modest seventeenth-century **Berwick Bridge**. This last was opened in 1624 and cost £15,000 to build, an enormous sum partly financed by James VI of Scotland, who is said to have been none too impressed with its rickety wooden predecessor which he crossed on his way to be crowned James I of England in 1603.

Within the ramparts, the Berwick skyline is punctured by the stumpy spire of the eighteenth-century **Town Hall** at the bottom of Marygate, right at the heart of the compact centre. This retains its original jailhouse, now housing the **Cell Block Museum** (Easter–Oct Mon–Fri tours at 10.30am & 2pm; £1) with its tales of crime and punishment in Berwick. From here, it's a couple of minutes' walk along Church Street to **Holy Trinity** church, one of the few churches built during the Commonwealth, the absence of a tower supposedly reflecting the wishes of Cromwell, who found them irreligious.

Opposite the church, the elongated **Barracks** (Easter–Oct daily 10am–6pm; Nov–Easter Wed–Sun 10am–4pm; £2.60; EH) date from the early eighteenth century and were in use until 1964, when the King's Own Scottish Borderers regiment decamped. Inside, there's a predictable regimental museum, as well as the *By Beat of Drum* exhibition which in a series of pictureboards traces the life of the British infantryman from the sixteenth to the nineteenth century. If all this sounds worthy but dull, it is – rescued only by the fine proportions of the barracks buildings themselves, and by a superior **Borough Museum and Art Gallery**, sited in the so-called Clock Block. Geared up for school parties, the museum features imaginative dioramas, recordings and displays of local traditional life, even a model of a local clergyman haranguing visitors from his pulpit. Upstairs is the kernel of the gallery's fine and applied art collection, the gift of the shipping magnate William Burrell. Highlights include examples of Bengali metalwork; ceramic Oriental jars displayed under glass floor panels in a sinuous, walk-in dragon; Roman glassware; church sculpture; and several Chinese bronzes.

Eating, drinking and entertainment

For daytime **snacks**, **coffee** and **lunches**, you're best off at *Popinjays* café on Hide Hill. Berwick's best **restaurant** is *Foxton's*, 26 Hide Hill (☎01289/303939), a brasserie serving a full menu (with chargrilled specialities) alongside its daytime menu of sandwiches and coffees. You should reserve in advance at the weekend. Other choices include the *Royal Garden*, a Chinese restaurant at 35 Marygate, and the *Magna Tandoori*, 39 Bridge Street.

In 1799, there were 59 **pubs** and three coaching inns in Berwick; strange, then, that today there's barely one worth drinking in. Two of the three inns remain, the *King's Arms* on Hide Hill and the *Hen & Chickens* on Sandgate, and you may as well call in at both at some point. Otherwise, the *Barrels Ale House*, 59–61 Bridge St at the foot of the Berwick Bridge, has guest beers, tapas lunches and an extraordinary back room with over-the-top sculpted tables and chairs. The Maltings on Eastern Lane is Berwick's **arts centre** (☎01289/330999), with a year-round programme of music, theatre, film and dance, and river views from its licensed café.

travel details

Trains

Darlington to: Bishop Auckland (every 1–2hr; 30min).

Durham to: Darlington (every 30min; 20min); London (hourly; 3hr); Newcastle (every 30min; 20min); York (hourly; 50min).

Hexham to: Carlisle (hourly; 1hr); Haltwhistle (hourly; 20min); Newcastle (hourly; 40min).

Middlesbrough to: Durham (hourly; 50min); Grosmont, for North York Moors Railway (see p.827: Mon–Sat 4 daily; 1hr); Newcastle (hourly; 1hr 10min); Redcar (hourly; 11min); Saltburn (hourly; 40min); Whitby (Mon–Sat 4 daily; 1hr 30min).

Newcastle to: Alnmouth (Mon–Sat 5 daily, Sun 3; 30min); Berwick-upon-Tweed (hourly; 45min); Carlisle (7 daily; 1hr 25min); Corbridge (Mon–Sat hourly, 4 on Sun; 40min); Durham (every 30min; 20min); Haltwhistle (hourly; 1hr); Hexham (hourly; 40min); London (hourly; 3hr 15min); Sunderland (every 30min; 30min).

Buses

Alnwick to: Bamburgh (4–6 daily; 1hr 5min); Berwick-upon-Tweed (3 daily; 2hr).

Bamburgh to: Alnwick (4–6 daily; 1hr 5min); Craster (4–5 daily; 30–40min); Seahouses (Mon–Sat 9 daily, Sun 4; 10min).

Barnard Castle to: Bishop Auckland (Mon–Sat 9 daily, Sun 6; 50min); Darlington (hourly; 35–45min); Middleton-in-Teesdale (hourly; 25–35min); Raby Castle (9 daily; 15min); Staindrop (Mon–Sat 9 daily, Sun 6; 15min).

Berwick-upon-Tweed to: Edinburgh (2 daily; 1hr 45min); Holy Island (2 daily, but see p.907; 30min); Newcastle (Mon–Sat 6 daily, 3 on Sun; 2hr 20min–3hr 10min); Wooler (Mon–Sat 4–7 daily; 50min).

Bishop Auckland to: Barnard Castle (Mon–Sat 9 daily, Sun 6; 50min); Cowshill (Mon–Sat 7 daily, Sun 4; 1hr 10min); Darlington (Mon–Sat hourly; 35min); Hexham (1 weekly; 1hr 50min); Newcastle (hourly; 1hr 15min); Stanhope (Mon–Sat 7 daily, Sun 4; 45min); Sunderland (Mon–Sat 4 daily; 2hr).

Blanchland to: Consett (Mon–Sat 4 daily; 40min); Hexham (1 weekly; 45min).

Darlington to: Barnard Castle (hourly; 35–45min); Bishop Auckland (every 20min; 45min); Carlisle (1 daily; 3hr 15min); Middleton-in-Teesdale (Mon–Sat 9 daily, Sun 3; 1hr 20min).

Durham to: Barnard Castle (1 daily; 1hr); Beamish (May–Sept 1–3 daily; 25min); Bishop Auckland (every 30min; 30min); Consett (hourly; 40min); Darlington (every 30min; 1hr); Newcastle (hourly; 1hr); Stanhope (June–Sept 1–2 weekly; 45min); Sunderland (every 15–30min; 50min).

Hadrian's Wall: for details of the complicated bus services along Hadrian's Wall, see p.884.

Haltwhistle to: Alston (Mon–Sat 4–5 daily; 45min); Greenhead (mid-July to early Sept Mon–Sat 4 daily, Sun 1; 5min); Hexham (hourly; 40min).

Hexham to: Allendale (Mon–Sat 4–6 daily; 25min); Allenheads (Mon–Sat 4–6 daily; 45min); Bellingham (Mon–Sat 5 daily; 40min); Bishop Auckland (1 weekly; 1hr 50min); Blanchland (1

weekly; 45min); Byrness (1 weekly; 1hr 15min); Chesters (mid-July to early Sept 1–4 daily; 15min); Edmundbyers (1 weekly; 55min); Haltwhistle (hourly; 40min); Housesteads (mid-July to early Sept Mon–Sat 4, Sun 1; 30min); Milecastle Inn (mid-July to early Sept Mon–Sat 4 daily, Sun 1; 50min); Once Brewed (mid-July to early Sept Mon–Sat 4 daily, Sun 1; 35min); Otterburn (1 weekly; 1hr); Vindolanda (mid-July to early Sept Mon–Sat 4 daily, Sun 1; 40min).

Middlesbrough to: Newcastle (hourly; 1hr); Redcar (hourly; 25min); Saltburn (hourly; 40min).

Middleton-in-Teesdale to: High Force (Tues, Wed, Fri, Sat & Sun 2–3 daily; 12min); Langdon Beck (Tues, Wed, Fri, Sat & Sun 2–3 daily; 18min).

Newcastle to: Alnmouth (hourly; 1hr 30min); Alnwick (Mon–Sat 6 daily, 3 on Sun; 1hr 10min–1hr 45min); Bamburgh (3 daily; 2hr 30min); Barnard Castle (1 daily; 1hr 25min); Berwick-upon-Tweed (Mon–Sat 6 daily, 3 on Sun; 2hr 20min–3hr 10min); Carlisle (hourly; 2hr); Corbridge (Mon–Sat every 30min, Sun every 2hr; 1hr); Craster (3 daily; 1hr 50min); Durham (hourly; 1hr); Hexham (Mon–Sat every 30min, Sun every 2hr; 1hr 15min); Leeds (1 daily; 3hr); Middlesbrough (hourly; 1hr); Otterburn (2 daily; 2hr); Prudhoe (Mon–Sat every 30min, Sun every 2hr; 40min); Rothbury (Mon–Sat 7 daily, 2 on Sun; 1hr 15min); Seahouses (3 daily; 2hr 10min); Stanhope (1–2 weekly; 1hr 10min); Warkworth (hourly; 1hr 20min); Wooler (Mon–Fri 1–2 daily, Sat 4; 2hr–2hr 20min).

Wooler to: Alnwick (Mon–Sat 4 daily; 45min); Berwick-upon-Tweed (Mon–Sat 4–7 daily; 50min); Craster (Mon–Fri 1 daily; 1hr 30min); Seahouses (Mon–Fri 1 daily; 1hr 10min).

A BRIEF HISTORY OF ENGLAND

THE BEGINNINGS

Off and on, people have lived in Britain for the best part of half a million years, though the earliest evidence of human life dates from about **250,000 BC**. These meagre remains, found near Swanscombe, east of London across the Thames from Tilbury, belong to one of the migrant communities whose comings and goings depended on the fluctuations of the Ice Ages. Renewed glaciation then made the area uninhabitable once more, and the next traces — mainly roughly worked flint implements — were left around 40,000 BC by cave-dwellers at Creswell Crags in Derbyshire, Kent's Cavern near Torquay and Cheddar Cave in Somerset. The last spell of intense cold began about 17,000 years ago, and it was the final thawing of this **last Ice Age** around 5000 BC that caused the British Isles to separate from the European mainland.

The sea barrier did nothing to stop further migrations of nomadic hunting communities, drawn by the rich forests that covered ancient Britain. In about 3500 BC a new wave of colonists arrived from the continent, probably via Ireland, bringing with them a **Neolithic** culture based on farming and the rearing of livestock. These tribes were the first to make some impact on the environment, clearing forests, enclosing fields, constructing defensive ditches around their villages and digging mines to obtain flint used for tools and weapons. Fragments of Neolithic pottery have been found

near Peterborough and at Windmill Hill, near Avebury in Wiltshire, but the most profuse relics of this culture are their graves, usually stone-chambered, turf-covered mounds (called **long barrows**), which are scattered throughout the country — the most impressive ones are at Belas Knap and Rodmarton in Gloucestershire and at Wayland's Smithy in Berkshire.

The transition from the Neolithic to the **Bronze Age** began around 2000 BC, with the immigration from northern Europe of the so-called **Beaker Folk** — named from the distinctive cups found at their burial sites. Originating in the Iberian peninsula and bringing with them bronze-workers from the Rhineland, these newcomers had a well-organized social structure with an established aristocracy, and quickly intermixed with the native tribes. Many of England's stone circles were completed at this time, including **Avebury** and **Stonehenge** in Wiltshire, while many others belong entirely to the Bronze Age — for example, the Hurlers and the Nine Maidens on Cornwall's Bodmin Moor. Large numbers of earthwork forts were also built in this period, suggesting a high level of tribal warfare, but none of these were able to withstand the waves of Celtic invaders who, spreading from a homeland in central Europe, began settling in Britain around 600 BC.

THE CELTS AND THE ROMANS

Highly skilled in battle, the **Celts** soon displaced the local inhabitants all over Britain, establishing a sophisticated farming economy and a social hierarchy that was dominated by a druidic priesthood. Familiar with Mediterranean artefacts through their far-flung trade routes, they introduced superior methods of metalworking that favoured iron rather than bronze, from which they forged not just weapons but also coins and ornamental works, thus creating the first recognizable British art. The principal Celtic contribution to the landscape was a network of hillforts and other defensive works stretching over the entire country, the greatest of them at **Maiden Castle** in Dorset, a site first fortified almost 2500 years earlier.

Maiden Castle was also one of the first Celtic fortifications to fall to the **Roman** legions in 43 AD. Coming at the end of a lengthy but low-level infusion of Roman ideas into the country, the Roman invasion had begun hesitantly, with small cross-Channel incursions by

Julius Caesar in 55 and 54 BC. Britain's rumoured mineral wealth was a primary motive behind these raids, but the immediate spur to the eventual conquest nearly a century later was the dangerous collaboration between British Celts and the fiercely anti-Roman tribesmen in France, and the need of the emperor **Claudius**, who owed his power to the army, for a great military triumph. The death of the British king Cunobelin, who ruled all southeast England and was the inspiration for Shakespeare's Cymbeline, offered the opportunity Claudius required, and in **August 43 AD**, a substantial force landed in Kent, from where it fanned out, soon establishing a base along the estuary of the Thames. Joined by Claudius and a menagerie of elephants and camels for the major battle of the campaign, the Romans soon reached Camulodunum (Colchester), and within four years were dug in on the frontier of south Wales.

The Catuvellauni chief, Caratacus, continued to conduct a guerrilla campaign from Wales until his eventual betrayal and capture in about 50 AD. About ten years later, a more serious challenge to the Romans arose when the East Anglian Iceni, under their queen **Boudicca** (or Boadicea), sacked Camulodunum and Verulamium (St Albans), and even reached the undefended port of Londinium, precursor of London. The uprising was soon quashed, and turned out to be an isolated act of resistance, with many of the already Romanized southeastern tribes of England probably welcoming absorption into the empire. However, it was not until 79 AD that Wales and the north of England were subdued, the latter process being sealed in 130 AD by the completion of **Hadrian's Wall**: running from the Tyne to the Solway, it marked the northern limit of the whole Roman Empire, and stands today the most impressive remnant of the Roman occupation.

The written history of England begins with the Romans, whose rule lasted nearly four centuries. For the first time the country was absorbed into a unified and peaceful political structure, in which commerce flourished and cities prospered, including the most northerly Roman town of Eboracum (York), the garrison of Isca Dumnoniorum (Exeter), the leisure resort of Aquae Sulis (Bath), and of course **Londinium**, which immediately assumed a pivotal role in the commercial and administrative life of the

province. Although Latin became the language of the Romano-British ruling elite, local traditions were allowed to coexist with imported customs, so that Celtic gods were often worshipped at the same time as the Roman, and sometimes merged with them. Perhaps the most important legacy of the Roman occupation, however, was the introduction of **Christianity** from the third century on, becoming firmly entrenched after its official recognition by the emperor Constantine in 313.

ANGLO-SAXON ENGLAND

As early as the reign of Constantine, Roman England was being raided by Germanic Saxon pirates, and by the middle of the fourth century Picts from Scotland and Scots from northern Ireland were harrying inland areas in the north and west. As economic life declined and rural areas became depopulated, individual military leaders began to usurp local authority, so that by the start of the fifth century England had become irrevocably detached from what remained of the Roman Empire. Within fifty years the **Saxons** were settling on the island, the start of a gradual conquest that – despite bitter resistance led by such semi-mythical figures as King Arthur – culminated in the defeat of the native Britons in 577 at the **Battle of Dyrham** (near Bath), at which three British kings were killed. Driving the few recalcitrant tribes deep into Cumbria, Wales and England's West Country, the invaders eliminated the Romano-British culture and by the end of the sixth century the rest of England was divided into the Anglo-Saxon kingdoms of Northumbria, Mercia, East Anglia, Kent and Wessex. So complete was the Anglo-Saxon domination of England, through conquest and intermarriage, that some ninety percent of English placenames today have an Anglo-Saxon derivation. Only in the westerly extremities of the country did the ancient Celtic traditions survive, as untouched by the new invaders as they had been by the Romans. Here also, Christian worship was kept alive, though the countrywide revival of Christianity was driven mainly by the arrival of **St Augustine**, who was despatched by Pope Gregory I and landed on the Kent coast in 597, accompanied by forty monks.

The missionaries were received by **Ethelbert**, the overlord of all the English south of the River Humber, whose marriage to a

Christian princess from France made him sympathetic to Augustine's message. Ethelbert gave Augustine permission to found a monastery at Canterbury (on the site of the present cathedral), where the king himself was then baptized, followed by ten thousand of his subjects at a grand Christmas ceremony. Despite some reversals in the years that followed, the Christianization of England proceeded quickly, so that by the middle of the seventh century all of the Anglo-Saxon kings had at least nominally adopted the faith. Tensions and clashes between the Augustinian missionaries and the more freebooting Celtic monks inevitably arose, to be resolved by the **Synod of Whitby in 663**, when it was settled that the English Church should follow the rule of Rome, thereby ensuring a realignment with the European cultural mainstream.

The central English region of **Mercia** became the dominant Anglo-Saxon kingdom in the eighth century under kings Ethelbald and Offa, the latter being responsible for the greatest public work of the Anglo-Saxon period: **Offa's Dyke**, an earthwork stretching from the River Dee to the Severn, marking the border with Wales. But after Offa's death **Wessex** gained the upper hand, and by 825 **Egbert** had conquered or taken allegiance from all the other English kingdoms. The supremacy of Wessex coincided with the first large-scale **Danish** (or Viking) invasions, which began with pirate raids, such as the one that destroyed the great monastery of Lindisfarne in 793, then gradually grew into a migration, prompted by unsettled conditions at home.

In 865 a substantial Danish army landed in East Anglia, and within six years they had conquered Northumbria, Mercia and East Anglia. The Danes then set their sights on Wessex, whose new king was **Alfred the Great**, a warrior whose dogged resistance was balanced by his desire to coexist with the Danes – a mixture that ensured the survival of his kingdom. Having established a border demarcating his domain from the northern **Danelaw**, the part of England in which the rule of the now-Christianized Danes was accepted (a border roughly coinciding with the Roman Watling Street), Alfred directed his resources into internal reforms and the strengthening of his defences.

Although Danish attacks had recommenced before the end of Alfred's reign in 899, his successor, **Edward the Elder**, still managed to establish Saxon supremacy over the Danelaw and was thus the de facto overlord of all England, acknowledged even by Scottish and Welsh chieftains. The relative calm continued under Edward's brother, **Edgar**, king of Mercia and Northumberland, who became the first ruler to be crowned **king of England** in 973. However, this was but a lull in the Viking storm. Returning in force, the Vikings milked Edgar's son **Ethelred the Unready** ("lacking counsel") for all the money they could, but the ransom (the Danegeld) paid brought only temporary relief. In 1016 Ethelred fled to Normandy, establishing links there which were to have a far-reaching effect on ensuing events.

The first and best king of the short-lived Danish dynasty was **Canute**, who was followed by his two unexceptional and disreputable sons, after whom the Saxons were restored under Ethelred's son, **Edward the Confessor**. It was said of Edward that he was better suited to have been a priest than a king, and most of his reign was dominated by Godwin, Earl of Wessex, and by Godwin's son Harold. On Edward's death, the Witan – a sort of council of elders – confirmed **Harold** as king, despite the claim of William, Duke of Normandy, that the exiled and childless Edward had sworn himself to be William's vassal, promising him the succession. Harold's brief reign was overshadowed by the events in the last two of its ten months, when he first marched north to fend off an invasion attempt by his brother Tostig (who had been deprived of his earldom of Northumbria) in league with King Harald of Norway. Having defeated their combined forces at Stamford Bridge in Yorkshire, Harold was immediately forced to return south to meet the invading William, who routed the Saxons at the **Battle of Hastings** in 1066. Harold was killed, and on Christmas Day of that year William the Conqueror was installed as king in Westminster Abbey.

THE NORMANS AND THE PLANTAGENETS

Making little attempt to reach any understanding with the indigenous Saxon culture, **William I** imposed a new military aristocracy on his subjects, enforcing his rule with a series of strongholds all over the country, the grandest of which was the Tower of London. The sporadic rebellions that broke out during the early years of his reign were ruthlessly suppressed – Yorkshire and the north were ravished and the fenland resistance of Hereward the Wake was brought to a brutal end – but perhaps the single most effective controlling measure was the compilation of the **Domesday Book** between 1085 and 1086. Recording land ownership, type of cultivation, the number of inhabitants and their social status, it afforded William an unprecedented body of information about his subjects, providing the framework for the administration of taxation, the judicial structure and feudal obligations.

In 1087, William was succeeded by his son William Rufus, an ineffectual ruler but a notable benefactor of the religious foundations that were springing up throughout the realm. Rufus died in mysterious circumstances – killed by an arrow while hunting in the New Forest – and the throne passed to William I's youngest son. The new king, Henry I, spent much of his reign in tussles with the country's barons, but at least he proved to be more conciliatory in his dealings with the Saxons, even marrying into one of their leading families. On his death in 1135, William I's grandson Stephen of Blois contested the accession of Henry's daughter Mathilda (also called Maud), with the consequence that the nineteen years of his reign were spent in civil war. Mathilda's son was eventually recognized as Stephen's heir, and the reign of **Henry II** (1154–89), the first of the **Plantagenet** branch of the Norman line, provided a welcome respite from baronial brawling. Asserting his authority throughout a domain that reached from the Cheviots to the Pyrenees, Henry presided over immense administrative reforms, including the introduction of trial by jury. However, his attempts to subordinate ecclesiastical authority to the Crown went terribly awry in 1170, when he sanctioned the murder in Canterbury Cathedral of his erstwhile drinking companion **Thomas à Becket**, whose canonization just three years later created an enduring Europe-wide cult.

The last years of Henry's reign were riven by quarrels with his sons, the eldest of whom, **Richard I** (or Lionheart), spent most of his ten-year reign crusading in the Holy Land. Neglected, England fell prey to the scheming of Richard's brother **John**, the villain of the Robin Hood tales, who became king in his own right after Richard was killed in battle in 1199. But John's inability to hold on to his French possessions and his rumbling dispute with the Vatican alienated the English barons, who eventually forced him to consent to a charter guaranteeing their rights and privileges, the **Magna Carta**, which was signed in 1215 at Runnymede, on the Thames.

The power-struggle with the barons continued into the reign of Henry III, who was defeated by their leader Simon de Montfort at Lewes in 1264, when both Henry and Prince Edward were taken prisoner. Edward escaped and promptly routed the barons' army at the battle of Evesham in 1265, killing de Montfort in the process. Inheriting the throne in 1272, **Edward I** was a great law-maker in the mould of William I and Henry II. He presided over the Model Parliament of 1295, a significant step in the evolution of consensual politics, though he was mostly absorbed in extending his kingdom within the island, annexing Wales and imposing English jurisdiction in Scotland. In 1314, however, **Edward II** suffered the worst-ever English defeat at the hands of the Scots, whom Robert the Bruce led to a huge victory at **Bannockburn**. This reversal added to the unpopularity already created by the king's dependence on upstart favourites, and Edward was eventually overthrown by his wife Isabella and her lover Roger Mortimer, by whom he was horribly put to death in Berkeley Castle, Gloucestershire.

Although **Edward III** was initially preoccupied by Scottish wars, his reign is chiefly remembered for his claim to the French throne, a feeble pretence considering he had earlier recognized the King of France and done homage to him, but one that launched the **Hundred Years' War** in 1337. Early English victories such as the Battle of Crécy in 1346, and the capture of Calais the following year, were interrupted by the outbreak of the **Black Death** in 1349, a plague which claimed about one and a half million lives – over a third of the entire English population. The resulting scarcity of labour produced economic turmoil at home, where attempts to restrict the rise of wages and to levy a poll-tax (a tax on each person irrespective of wealth) provoked widespread riots, which peaked with the **Peasants' Revolt** of 1381. After seizing Rochester Castle and sacking Canterbury, the rebels marched on London, where the boy-king **Richard II** met

Wat Tyler, the leader of the revolt, at Smithfield. The resulting scuffle led to Tyler's murder and the dispersal of the mob, and soon afterwards the Bishop of Norwich routed the Norfolk rebels, the prelude to a wave of repression and terrible retribution.

Parallel with this social unrest were the clerical reforms demanded by the scholar **John Wycliffe**, whose followers made the first translation of the Bible into English in 1380. Another sign of the elevation of the common language was the success enjoyed by **Geoffrey Chaucer** (c.1340–1400), a wine merchant's son, whose *Canterbury Tales* was the first major work written in the vernacular and one of the first English books to be printed.

THE HOUSES OF LANCASTER AND YORK

During the later years of Edward III's reign England had in effect been ruled by his son, **John of Gaunt**, Duke of Lancaster, whose influence remained paramount during the minority of Richard II. In 1399 the vacillating Richard II was overthrown by John of Gaunt's son, who took the title **Henry IV** and founded the **Lancastrian** dynasty. Fourteen years later, he in turn was succeeded by his son, the bellicose **Henry V**, who promptly renewed the war with France, which had been limping along ingloriously since a victory at Poitiers in 1356, and famously defeated the French at the battle of **Agincourt**. It was a stunning victory that forced the French king to sign the Treaty of Troyes in 1420, making the English king the heir to the French throne. However, when Henry died just two years later his son was still an infant and the regents who governed the country on his behalf were unable to resist the French rally under **Joan of Arc**. By 1454, only Calais was left in English hands.

Meanwhile **Henry VI**, who was temperamentally more inclined to the creation of such architectural coups as King's College Chapel in Cambridge than to warfare, had suffered lapses into insanity. Strongest of the rival contenders for the throne was Richard, Duke of York, by virtue of his direct descent from Edward III. It was no coincidence that the **Wars of the Roses** – named after the red rose which symbolized the Lancastrian cause and the white Yorkist rose – broke out just a year after the return of the last English garrisons from France.

The returning soldiers filled the country with footloose knights and archers accustomed to a life of plunder and war. The instability of the time was signalled by **Jack Cade's Rebellion** of 1450, when a disorganized rabble challenged the king's authority, winning a battle at Sevenoaks before being scattered. However, political disputes within the circle surrounding the mad king were to prove much more threatening to the regime. The Duke of York's authority over Henry was challenged by the king's accomplished and ambitious wife, Margaret of Anjou, whose forces defeated and slew Richard at Wakefield in 1460. She and Henry were in turn overwhelmed by Richard's son, who was crowned **Edward IV** in 1461 – the first king of the **Yorkist** line.

The civil strife entered a new stage when Edward attempted to shrug off the overbearing influence of Richard Neville, Earl of Warwick and Salisbury, or "Warwick the Kingmaker", as he became known. Warwick then performed a dramatic volte-face by allying himself with his old enemy Margaret of Anjou, forcing Edward into exile and proclaiming Henry king once more. Henry VI's second term was soon interrupted by Edward's unexpected return in 1471, when Warwick was defeated and killed at the Battle of Barnet and the rest of the Lancastrians were crushed at Tewkesbury three months later. Margaret was captured, Henry's heir was killed and Henry himself was soon afterwards dispatched in the Tower.

Edward IV proved to be a precursor of the great Tudor princes, licentious, cruel and despotic, but also a patron of Renaissance learning. In 1483, his twelve-year-old son succeeded as **Edward V**, but his reign was cut short after only two months, when he and his younger brother were murdered in the Tower of London – probably by their uncle, the Duke of Gloucester, who was crowned **Richard III**. Increasingly unpopular as rumours circulated of his part in the fate of the princes in the Tower, Richard was toppled at Bosworth Field in 1485 by Henry Tudor, Earl of Richmond, who took the throne as **Henry VII**.

THE TUDORS

The opening of the **Tudor** period brought radical transformations. A Lancastrian through his mother's descent from John of Gaunt, Henry VII reconciled the Yorkist faction by ·marrying

Edward IV's daughter Elizabeth, thereby putting an end to the internecine squabbling among the discredited gentry. The growth of the wool and cloth trades and the rise of a powerful merchant class brought a general increase in wealth, while England began to assume the status of a major European power partly as a result of Henry's alliances and political marriages – his daughter to James IV of Scotland and his son to Catherine, daughter of Ferdinand and Isabella of Spain.

The relatively easy suppression of the rebellions of Yorkist pretenders Lambert Simnel and Perkin Warbeck ensured a smooth succession for **Henry VIII** in 1509. Apart from his fast-moving love life, Henry is best remembered for his separation of the English Church from Rome and his establishment of an independent Protestant church – the Church of England. This is not without its ironies. Henry was not a Protestant himself and such was his early orthodoxy that the pope even gave him the title "Defender of the Faith" for a pamphlet he wrote attacking Luther's treatises. In fact, the schism between Henry and the pope was triggered not by doctrinal issues but by the failure of his wife Catherine of Aragon – widow of his elder brother – to provide Henry with male offspring. Failing to obtain a decree of nullity from Pope Clement VII, he dismissed his long-time chancellor Thomas Wolsey and followed the advice of Thomas Cromwell, forcing the English Church to recognize him as its head. The most far-reaching consequence of this step was the **Dissolution of the Monasteries**, a decision taken mainly to enjoy the profits of the ensuing land sales. The first phase of the Dissolution in 1536, involving the smaller religious houses, was a factor in the only significant rebellion of the reign, the **Pilgrimage of Grace**, a protest largely in the north of the country, which Henry put down with great cruelty, preparing the ground for the closure of the larger foundations in 1539.

In his later years Henry became a corpulent, syphilitic tyrant, six times married but at last furnished with an heir, **Edward VI**, who was only nine years old when he ascended the throne in 1547. His short reign saw Protestantism established on a firm footing, with churches stripped of their images and Catholic services banned, yet on Edward's death most of the country readily accepted his half-sister **Mary**, daughter of Catherine of Aragon and a fervent Catholic, as queen. She restored England to the papacy and married the future Philip II of Spain, forging an alliance whose immediate consequence was war with France and the loss of Calais, last of England's French possessions. The marriage was unpopular and so was Mary's rash decision to begin persecuting Protestants, executing the leading lights of the English Reformation, Hugh Latimer, Nicholas Ridley and Thomas Cranmer, the archbishop of Canterbury who was largely responsible for the first English prayer book, published in 1549.

The accession of the Protestant **Elizabeth I** in 1558 took place in a highly volatile atmosphere, with the country riven between opposing religious loyalties and threatened from abroad by Philip II. Heresy and treason were the twin preoccupations of the Elizabethan state, a society in which a sense of English nationhood was evolving on an almost mystical level in the vacuum created by the break with Rome. Aided by a team of exceptionally able ministers, the queen provided a focal point for national feeling, enthusiastically supported by a mercantile class that was opposed to foreign entanglements or clerical restrictions, and was represented in a Parliament made stronger by the constitutional decisions of the preceding decades.

The forty-five years of Elizabeth's reign saw the efflorescence of a specifically English Renaissance, especially in the field of literature, which reached its pinnacle in the brilliant career of **William Shakespeare** (1564–1616). It was also the age of the seafarers Walter Raleigh, Francis Drake, Martin Frobisher and John Hawkins, whose piratical exploits helped to map out the world for English commerce. English navigational skills were demonstrated by Drake's voyage round the world (1577–80), but it was the defeat of the mighty **Spanish Armada** in 1588 that established England as a major European sea power. The commander of the English fleet, Lord Howard of Effingham, was a practising Catholic, a fact that dashed Philip's hope of a Catholic insurrection in England – a hope in part founded on the widespread sympathy for Elizabeth's cousin **Mary Queen of Scots**, whose twenty-year imprisonment in England had ended with her beheading in 1587.

THE STUARTS AND THE COMMONWEALTH

On Elizabeth's death the heir to the throne was James VI of Scotland, son of Mary Queen of Scots, who became **James I** of England in 1603, thereby uniting the English and Scottish crowns. James quickly moved to end hostilities with Spain and adopted a policy of toleration to the country's Catholics. Inevitably, both initiatives offended many Protestants, whose worst fears were confirmed in 1605 when Guy Fawkes and a group of Catholic conspirators were discovered preparing to blow up king and Parliament in the so-called **Gunpowder Plot**. During the ensuing hue and cry, many Catholics met an untimely end and Fawkes himself was hung, drawn and quartered. At this time, also, certain Protestant groups collectively known as **Puritans** hoped to establish a "New Jerusalem", far from the impurities of the secular state. Their aspirations converged with commercial interests to prompt the foundation of several early colonies in North America. In 1608, the first permanent **colony in North America** was established in Virginia, followed in 1620 by the landing in New England of the Pilgrim Fathers, the nucleus of a colony that would absorb about a hundred thousand mainly Puritan immigrants by the middle of the century.

Meanwhile, a split was inevitable between James, who clung to the medieval notion of the divine right of kings, and the landed gentry who dominated the increasingly powerful Parliament. The gentry were largely Protestant and sympathetic to the Calvinist Puritans, who James foolishly persecuted. Recoiling from the rigours of his Parliament, the king relied heavily on court favourites, progressing from the skilful Robert Cecil, Earl of Salisbury, and the philosopher Francis Bacon, to the rash and unpopular George Villiers, Duke of Buckingham. The latter also had a close and baleful influence on the second Stuart king, **Charles I**.

From 1629 to 1640 Charles ruled without the services of parliament, but was forced to recall it after he had antagonized the Scots by trying to foist Archbishop Laud's Anglican prayer book on them. Charles's high-handed measures were overturned by Parliament and his chief ministers were impeached, notable among them being Thomas Wentworth, Earl of Strafford (executed in 1642), and Archbishop Laud himself (executed in 1645). Facing the concerted hostility of Parliament, the king withdrew to Nottingham where he raised his standard, the opening military act of the **Civil War**. The Royalist forces ("Cavaliers") were initially successful, winning the battle of Edgehill, but afterwards the Parliamentarian army ("Roundheads") was completely overhauled by **Oliver Cromwell**. The New Model Army Cromwell created was something quite unique: singing psalms as they went into battle and urged on by preachers and "agitators", this was an army of believers whose ideological commitment to the Parliamentary cause made it truly formidable. Cromwell's revamped army cut its teeth at the battle of Naseby and thereafter simply brushed the Royalists aside. Attempting to muddy the political waters, Charles surrendered himself to the Scots, but they finally handed him over to the English Parliament, by whom – after prolonged negotiations, endless royal shenanigans and more fighting – he was ultimately executed in January 1649.

For the next eleven years England was a **Commonwealth** – at first a true republic, then, after 1653, a **Protectorate** with Cromwell as the Lord Protector and commander in chief. Cromwell later reformed the government, secured advantageous commercial treaties with foreign nations and used his New Model Army to put the fear of God into his various enemies and with particular brutality in Catholic Ireland. After his death in 1658 his son Richard ruled briefly and ineffectually, and in 1660 Parliament voted to restore the monarchy in the person of **Charles II**, the exiled son of the previous king.

The turmoil of the previous twenty years had unleashed a furious debate on every strand of legalistic, theological and political thought, a milieu that spawned a host of leftist sects – such as the Levellers, who demanded wholesale constitutional reform, and the more radical Diggers, who proposed common ownership of all land. Nonconformist religious groups flourished, prominent among them the pacifistic **Quakers**, led by the much persecuted George Fox (1624–91), and the Dissenters, to whom the most famous writers of the day, John Milton (1608–74) and John Bunyan (1628–88), both belonged. With the **Restoration**, however, these philosophical and proto-communist eddies gave way to a new exuberance in the fields of art, literature and the theatre, a remarkable transition from the sombreness of the Puritan era, when secular drama and other such fripperies were banned outright. In the scientific arena, just six months after his accession Charles II founded the **Royal Society**, which numbered Isaac Newton (1642–1727) among its first fellows.

The low points of Charles's reign came with the **Great Plague** of 1665 and the **Great Fire of London** the following year, though the latter had the positive consequence of allowing Christopher Wren (1632–1723) and other great architects to redesign the capital along more contemporary classical lines. Moreover, the political scene was not entirely tranquil: tensions still existed between king and Parliament, where the traditional divisions of court and country began to coalesce into **Whig** and **Tory** parties, respectively representing the low-church gentry and the high-church aristocracy. A measure of vengeance was also wreaked on the regicides and other leading Parliamentarians, though its intensity was nothing like that of the anti-Catholic hysteria sparked off by the Popish Plot of 1678, the fabrication of the trickster Titus Oates.

The succession in 1685 of the Catholic **James II**, brother of Charles II, provoked much opposition, though – as one might expect from a country recently racked by civil war – there was an indifferent response when the **Duke of Monmouth**, the favourite among Charles II's illegitimate sons, landed at Lyme Regis to mount a challenge to the new king. His undisciplined forces were routed at Sedgemoor, Somerset, in July 1685; nine days later Monmouth was beheaded at Tower Hill, and in the subsequent **Bloody Assizes** of Judge Jeffreys, hundreds of rebels and suspected sympathizers – mainly in Somerset and Devon – were executed or deported.

When seven bishops protested against James's **Declaration of Indulgence** of 1687, removing anti-Catholic restrictions, the king showed something of his father's obstinacy by having them tried for seditious libel, though he was quickly forced to acquit them. When James's son was born, a child destined to be brought up in the Catholic faith, the Protestant opposition gathered momentum. Messengers were dispatched to **William of Orange**, the Dutch husband of Mary, the Protestant daughter of James II. William landed in Brixham in Devon, proceeding to London where he was acclaimed king in the so-called **Glorious Revolution** of 1688, the final postscript to the Civil War.

William and Mary were made joint sovereigns, having agreed to a **Bill of Rights** defining the limitations of the monarch's power and the rights of his or her subjects. This, together with the **Act of Settlement of 1701** – among other things, barring Catholics or anyone married to one from succession to the English throne – made Britain the first country to be governed by a **constitutional monarchy**, in which the roles of legislature and executive were separate and interdependent. The model was broadly consistent with that outlined by the philosopher and political thinker John Locke (1632–1704), whose essentially Whig doctrines of toleration and social contract were gradually embraced as the new orthodoxy.

Ruling alone after Mary's death in 1694, William regarded England as a prop in his defence of Holland against France, a stance that defined England's political alignment in Europe for the next sixty years. In the reign of **Anne**, second daughter of James II, English armies won a string of remarkable victories on the continent, beginning with the Duke of Marlborough's triumph at Blenheim in 1704, followed the next year by the capture of Gibraltar, establishing a British presence in the Mediterranean. The War of the Spanish Succession, the overall struggle within which these engagements occurred, was closed by the Treaty of Utrecht in 1713, which settled the European balance of power for some time. Otherwise Anne's reign was distinguished mainly for the 1707 **Act of Union**, uniting the English and Scottish parliaments.

When the queen died childless in 1714, the Stuart line of kings ended, though there were to be pro-Stuart, or Jacobite, challenges to the throne in years to come. In accordance with the terms of the Act of Settlement, the succession passed to a non-English-speaking German, the Duke of Hanover, who became George I of England.

THE HANOVERIANS

As power leaked away from the monarchy into the hands of the Whig oligarchy – many Tories having been discredited for suspected Jacobite sympathies – the king ceased to attend Cabinet meetings, his place being taken by his chief minister. Most prominent of these ministers was **Robert Walpole**, regarded as England's **first prime minister**. To all intents and purposes, Walpole ruled the country from 1721 to 1742. This was a tranquil period politically, with the country standing aloof from foreign affrays, but the financial world was prey to a mania for speculation. Of the numerous fraudulent or ill-conceived financial ventures of this time, the greatest was the fiasco of the **South Sea Company**, which in 1720 sold shares in its monopoly of trade in the Pacific and along the east coast of South America. The "bubble" burst when the shareholders took fright at the extent of their own investments and the value of the shares dropped to nothing, reducing many to penury, and almost wrecking the government, which was saved only by the astute intervention of Walpole.

Peace ended in the reign of **George II**, when in 1739 England declared war on Spain at the start of yet another dynastic squabble, the eight-year War of the Austrian Succession. Then in 1745 the country was invaded by the **Young Pretender**, Charles Stuart, in the second and most dangerous of the Jacobite Rebellions. So-called Bonnie Prince Charlie reached Derby, just 130 miles from London, before retreating to Scotland where he was defeated by the Duke of Cumberland at Culloden. The **Seven Years War** brought yet more overseas territory, as English armies wrested control of India and Canada from France, then in 1768 **Captain James Cook** departed from Plymouth on his voyage to New Zealand and Australia, further widening the scope of the colonial empire.

In 1760, **George III** succeeded his father. The early years of his sixty-year reign saw a revived struggle between king and Parliament, enlivened by the intervention of John Wilkes, first of a long and increasingly vociferous line of parliamentary radicals. The contest was exacerbated by the deteriorating relationship with the thirteen colonies of North America, a situation brought to a head by the American **Declaration of Independence** and England's defeat in the Revolutionary War. Chastened by this disaster, England chose not to interfere in the momentous events taking place across the Channel, where France, its most consistent foe in the eighteenth century, was convulsed by rev-

olution. Out of the turmoil emerged the country's most daunting enemy so far, Napoleon, whose progress was interrupted by Nelson at Trafalgar in 1805, and finally stopped ten years later by the duke of Wellington at Waterloo.

THE INDUSTRIAL REVOLUTION

England's triumph over Napoleon was largely due to its financial strength, itself a result of the switch from an agricultural to a manufacturing economy, a process generally referred to as the **Industrial Revolution**. The earliest mechanized production lines were constructed in the Lancashire cotton mills, where cotton-spinning was transformed from a cottage industry into a highly productive factory-based system. Initially, river water powered the mills, but the technology changed after James Watt patented his **steam engine** in 1781. Watt's engines needed coal, which made it convenient to locate mills and factories near coal mines, a tendency that was accelerated as **ironworks** took up coal as a smelting fuel, vastly increasing the output from their furnaces. Accordingly there was a shift of population towards the Midlands and north of England, where the great coal reserves were located, resulting in the rapid growth of the industrial towns and the expansion of Liverpool as a commercial port, importing raw materials from India and the Americas and exporting manufactured goods. Commerce and industry were served by steadily improving transport facilities, such as the building of a network of **canals** in the wake of the success of the Bridgewater Canal in 1765, which linked coal mines at Worsley with Manchester and the River Mersey. But the great leap forward occurred with the arrival of the **railway**, heralded by the opening of the Liverpool–Manchester line in 1830, with power provided by George Stephenson's *Rocket*.

Boosted by a vast influx of Jewish, Irish, French and Dutch immigrants, many of whom introduced new manufacturing techniques, the country's population rose from about seven and a half million at the beginning of George III's reign to more than fourteen million at its end, an increase whose major cause was the slowing-down of the death-rate owing to improvements in medical science. But while factories and their attendant towns expanded, the rural settlements of England suffered, inspiring the elegiac pastoral yearnings of Samuel Taylor

Coleridge and William Wordsworth, the first great names of the **Romantic** movement in English literature. Later Romantic poets such as Percy Bysshe Shelley and Lord Byron took a more socially engaged stance, inveighing against social injustices that were aggravated by the expenses of the Napoleonic Wars and their aftermath, when many returning soldiers found their jobs had been taken by machines. Discontent emerged in demands for parliamentary reform, and in 1819 demonstrators in Manchester — centre of the cotton industry and most important of the industrial boom towns still unrepresented in Parliament — were mown down by troops in what became known as the **Peterloo Massacre**.

The following year George III, by now weak, old, blind and insane, died and was succeeded by his grandson **George IV**. One of the hallmarks of the new reign was a greater degree of religious toleration with Catholics and Nonconformists now permitted to enter Parliament. Furthermore, after years of struggle, workers' associations were legalized, and a civilian police force was created, largely the work of **Robert Peel**, a reforming Tory who also outlined the basic ideology of modern Conservatism. More far-reaching changes came under **William IV**, with the passing of the **Reform Act** of 1832, whereby the principle of popular representation was acknowledged (though most adult males still had no vote); two years later, the revised **Poor Law** alleviated the condition of the destitute. Significant sections of the middle classes wanted far swifter democratic reform, as was expressed in public indignation over the **Tolpuddle Martyrs** — the Dorset labourers transported to Australia in 1834 for joining an agricultural trade union — and support for **Chartism**, a working-class movement demanding universal male suffrage. Poverty and injustice were the dominant theme of the novels of **Charles Dickens** (1812–70) and the preoccupation of the paternalistic reform movements that were a feature of the nineteenth century. This social concern had been anticipated in the previous century by the Methodism of John Wesley (1703–91) and the anti-slavery campaign promoted by evangelical Christians such as the Quakers and William Wilberforce. As a result of their efforts, slavery was banned in Britain in 1772 and throughout the colonies in 1833 — putting an end to what

had been a major factor in the prosperity of ports such as Bristol and Liverpool.

VICTORIAN ENGLAND

In 1837 William IV was succeeded by his niece **Victoria**, whose long reign witnessed the zenith of British power. For most of the period, the British economy boomed and typically the cloth manufacturers could boast that they supplied the domestic market before breakfast, the rest of the world thereafter. The British shipping fleet was easily the mightiest in the world and underpinned an empire on which "The sun never set" with Victoria herself becoming the symbol of both the nation's success and the imperial ideal. There were extraordinary intellectual achievements too — as typified by the publication of Charles Darwin's *The Origin of Species* in 1859 — and the country came to see itself as both a civilizing agent and, on occasion, the hand of (a very Protestant) God on earth. Britain's industrial and commercial prowess was best embodied by the great engineering feats of Isambard Kingdom Brunel and by the **Great Exhibition** of 1851, a display of manufacturing achievements from all over the world.

With trade at the forefront of the agenda, much of the political debate during this period crystallized into a conflict between the **Free Traders** — represented by an alliance of the Peelites and the Whigs, forming the Liberal Party — and the **Protectionists** under Bentinck and **Disraeli**, guiding light of the Tories. During the last third of the century, Parliament was dominated by the duel between Disraeli and the Liberal leader **Gladstone**. Although it was Disraeli who eventually passed the Second Reform Bill in 1867, further extending the electoral franchise, it was Gladstone who had first proposed it, and it was Gladstone's first ministry of 1868–74 that passed some of the century's most far-reaching legislation, including compulsory education, the full legalization of trade unions and an Irish Land Act.

There were foreign entanglements too. In 1854 troops were sent to protect the Turkish empire against the Russians in the **Crimea**, an inglorious debacle whose horrors were relayed to the public by the first ever press coverage of a military campaign and by the revelations of a shocked Florence Nightingale. The potential fragility of Britain's empire was exposed by the

Indian Mutiny of 1857, but reassuringly the imperial status quo was eventually restored and Victoria took the title Empress of India after 1876. Thereafter, the British army was flattered by a series of minor wars against poorly armed Asian and African opponents, but promptly came unstuck when it faced the Dutch settlers of South Africa in the **Boer War** (1899–1902). The British ultimately fought their way through to victory, but the discreditable conduct of the war prompted a military shake-up at home that was to be of significance in the coming European war.

FROM WORLD WAR I TO WORLD WAR II

Victoria died in the first month of 1901, to be succeeded by her son, **Edward VII**, whose leisurely and dissolute life could be seen as the epitome of the complacent era to which he gave his name. Edwardian England came to an end on August 4, 1914, when the Liberal government, honouring the Entente Cordiale signed with France in 1904, declared war on Germany. Hundreds of thousands volunteered for the army, but their enthusiastic nationalism was not enough to easily win **World War I**, which dragged on for four years and cost millions of lives. Britain and her allies eventually prevailed, but the number of dead beggared belief, undermining the English majority's respect for the ruling class, whose generals had shown a particularly vile combination of incompetence and indifference to the plight of their men. Many looked admiringly at the Soviet Union, where the communists had rid themselves of the Tsar and seized control in 1917.

At the war's end in 1918 the political fabric of England was changed dramatically when the sheer weight of public opinion pushed parliament into extending the **vote** to all men aged twenty-one or over and to women of thirty or over, subject to certain residential or business qualifications. This tardy liberalization of women's rights owed much to the efforts of the radical **Suffragettes**, led by Emmeline Pankhurst and her daughters Sylvia and Christabel, but the process was only completed in 1929 when women were at last granted the vote at twenty-one, on equal terms with men.

During this period, the **Labour Party** supplanted the Liberals as the main force on the left wing of British politics, its strength built on an alliance between the working-class trade unions and middle-class radicals. Labour formed its first government in 1923 under Ramsay MacDonald, but following the publication of the **Zinoviev Letter**, a forged document that seemed to prove Soviet encouragement of British socialist subversion, the Conservatives were returned with a large majority. In 1926, the tensions which had been building up since the end of the war, produced by a severe decline in manufacturing and attendant escalating unemployment, erupted with the **General Strike**. Spreading instantly from the coal mines to the railways, the newspapers and the iron and steel industries, the strike lasted nine days and involved half a million workers, provoking the government into draconian action – the army was called in, and the strike was broken. The economic situation deteriorated even further after the crash of the New York Stock Exchange in 1929, which precipitated a worldwide depression. Unemployment reached over 2.8 million in England in 1931, generating a series of mass demonstrations that reached a peak with the **Jarrow March** from the Northeast to London in 1936. The same year, economist John Maynard Keynes argued in his *General Theory of Employment, Interest and Money* for a greater degree of state intervention in the management of the economy, though the whole question was soon overshadowed by international events.

Abroad, the structure of the British Empire had undergone profound changes since World War I. The status of Ireland had been partly resolved after the electoral gains of the nationalist Sinn Fein in 1918 led to the establishment of the Irish Free State in 1922, from which the six counties of the mainly Protestant North "contracted out". Four years later, the **Imperial Conference** recognized the autonomy of the British dominions, an agreement formalized in the 1931 Statute of Westminster, whereby each dominion was given an equal footing in a Commonwealth of Nations, though each still recognized the British monarch. The royal family itself was shaken in 1936 by the **abdication of Edward VIII**, following his decision to marry a twice-divorced American, Wallis Simpson. Although the succession passed smoothly to his brother **George VI**, the scandal further reduced the standing of the royals, a process which has gathered pace in recent years.

Non-intervention in both the Spanish Civil War

and the Sino-Japanese War was paralleled by a policy of appeasement towards **Adolf Hitler**, who began to rearm Germany in earnest in the mid-1930s. This policy was epitomized by the antics of Prime Minister Neville Chamberlain, who returned from meeting Hitler and Mussolini at Munich in 1938 with an assurance of good intentions that he took at face value. Consequently, when **World War II** broke out in September 1939, Britain was seriously unprepared. In May 1940 the discredited Chamberlain stepped down in favour of a national coalition government headed by the charismatic **Winston Churchill**, whose bulldog persistence and heroic speeches provided the inspiration needed in the backs-against-the-wall mood of the time. Partly through Churchill's manoeuvrings, the United States became a supplier of foodstuffs and munitions to Britain. Given that the US had broken trade links with Japan in June (in protest at their attacks on China), this factor may have precipitated the Japanese bombing of Pearl Harbour on December 7, 1941 and thus the US's entry into the war as a combatant, an intervention which combined with the heroic resistance of the Russian Red Army, swung the balance. In terms of the number of casualties it caused, World War II was not as calamitous as the Great War (as World War I is often known), but its impact upon the civilian population of England was much greater. In its first wave of bombing, the *Luftwaffe* caused massive damage to industrial and supply centres such as London, Coventry, Manchester, Liverpool, Southampton and Plymouth; in later raids, intended to shatter morale rather than factories and docks, the cathedral cities of Canterbury, Exeter, Bath, Norwich and York were targeted. At the end of the fighting, nearly one in three of all the houses in the nation had been destroyed or damaged, nearly a quarter of a million members of the British armed forces had lost their lives and over 58,000 civilians were dead.

POSTWAR ENGLAND

The end of the war in 1945 was quickly followed by a general election. Hungry for change, the electorate displaced Churchill in favour of the Labour Party under **Clement Attlee**, who, with a large parliamentary majority, set about a radical programme to **nationalize** the coal, gas, electricity, iron and steel industries, as well as the inland transport services. Building on the plans for a social security system presented in

Sir William Beveridge's report of 1943, the **National Insurance Act** and the National **Health Service Act** were both passed early in the Labour administration, giving birth to what became known as the **welfare state**. But despite substantial American aid, the huge problems of rebuilding the economy made austerity the keynote, with the rationing of food and fuel remaining in force long after 1945.

In April 1949, Britain, the United States, Canada, France and the Benelux countries signed the **North Atlantic Treaty** as a counterbalance to Soviet power in eastern Europe, thereby defining the country's postwar international commitments. Yet confusion regarding Britain's post-imperial role was shown up by the **Suez Crisis** of 1956, when Anglo-French and Israeli forces invaded Egypt to secure control of the Suez Canal, only to be hastily recalled following international condemnation. Revealing severe limitations on the country's capacity for independent action, the Suez incident resulted in the resignation of the Conservative prime minister Anthony Eden, who was replaced by the more pragmatic **Harold Macmillan**. Nonetheless, Macmillan maintained a nuclear policy that suggested a continued desire for an international role, and nuclear testing went on against a background of widespread marches under the auspices of the Campaign for Nuclear Disarmament.

The 1960s, dominated by the Labour premiership of **Harold Wilson**, saw a boom in consumer spending and a corresponding cultural upswing, with London becoming the hippest city on the planet. The good times lasted barely a decade. Though Tory prime minister Edward Heath led Britain into the brave new world of the European Economic Community, the 1970s were a decade of recession and industrial strife. A succession of public-sector strikes and mis-timed decisions by James Callaghan's Labour government handed the 1979 general election to **Margaret Thatcher**, who four years earlier had ousted Heath to become the first woman to lead a major political party in Britain.

Thatcher went on to win three general elections, steering England into a period of ever greater social polarization. While taxation policies and easy credit fuelled a consumer boom for the professional classes, the erosion of manufacturing industry and the weakening of the welfare state created a calamitous number of people trapped in long-term impoverished unemployment. Despite the intense dislike of her regime among a substantial portion of the population, Thatcher won an increased majority in the 1983 election, partly because of the successful outcome of the 1981 war to regain control of the **Falkland Islands**, partly owing to the fragmentation of the Labour opposition, from which the short-lived Social Democratic Party had split in panic at what it perceived as the radicalization of the party.

Social and political tensions surfaced in sporadic urban rioting and the year-long **miners' strike** (1984–85) against pit closures, a bitter industrial dispute in which the police were given unprecedented powers to restrict the movement of citizens, while the media perpetrated some immensely misleading coverage of events. The violence in Northern Ireland

also intensified, and the bombing campaign of the IRA came close to killing the entire Cabinet when it blew up the Brighton hotel in which the Conservatives were staying for their 1984 annual conference.

The divisive politics of Thatcherism reached their apogee with the introduction of the Poll Tax, a lunatic scheme that led ultimately to Thatcher's overthrow by colleagues who feared annihilation should she lead them into another general election. The uninspiring new Tory leader, **John Major**, won the Conservatives a fourth term in office in 1992, albeit with a much reduced majority in Parliament. While his government presided over a steady growth in economic performance, they gained little credit amid allegations of mismanagement, feckless leadership and what became known as "sleaze" among Conservative MPs, with revelations of extramarital affairs, cover-ups and financial

CHRONOLOGY OF ENGLISH MONARCHS

HOUSE OF WESSEX
Egbert 802–39
Ethelwulf 839–55
Ethelbald 855–60
Ethelbert 860–66
Ethelred I 866–71
Alfred the Great 871–99
Edward the Elder 899–924
Athelstan 924–39
Edmund I 939–46
Eadred 946–55
Eadwig 955–59
Edgar 959–75
Edward the Martyr 975–79
Ethelred II (Ethelred the Unready) 979–1016
Edmund II (Edmund Ironside) 1016

HOUSE OF SKJOLDUNG
Canute 1016–35
Harold I 1035–40
Harthacanute 1040–42

HOUSE OF WESSEX
Edward the Confessor 1042–66
Harold II 1066

HOUSE OF NORMANDY
William I (William the Conqueror) 1066–87

William II (William Rufus) 1087–1100
Henry I 1100–35
Stephen 1135–54

HOUSE OF PLANTAGENET
Henry II 1154–89
Richard I (Richard the Lionheart) 1189–99
John 1199–1216
Henry III 1216–72
Edward I 1272–1307
Edward II 1307–27
Edward III 1327–77
Richard II 1377–99

HOUSE OF LANCASTER
Henry IV 1399–1413
Henry V 1413–22
Henry VI 1422–61 & 1470

HOUSE OF YORK
Edward IV 1461–70 & 1471–83
Edward V 1483
Richard III 1483–85

HOUSE OF TUDOR
Henry VII 1485–1509
Henry VIII 1509–47
Edward VI 1547–53

Mary I 1553–58
Elizabeth I 1558–1603

HOUSE OF STUART
James I 1603–25
Charles I 1625–49
Commonwealth and Protectorate 1649–60
Charles II 1660–85
James II 1685–88
William III and Mary II 1688–94
William III 1694–1702
Anne 1702–14

HOUSE OF HANOVER
George I 1714–27
George II 1727–60
George III 1760–1820
George IV 1820–30
William IV 1830–37
Victoria 1837–1901

HOUSE OF SAXE-COBURG
Edward VII 1901–10

HOUSE OF WINDSOR
George V 1910–36
Edward VIII 1936
George VI 1936–52
Elizabeth II 1952–

deceit seized upon with glee by an increasingly cynical British press. Major's unaggressive style was frequently called into question, not least among his own party, among whom vocal right-wing **Euro-sceptics** called for Britain to disassociate itself from the planned integration of the economies of the European Union and the introduction of a Europe-wide currency, the euro.

The government's noncommittal "wait-and-see" policy towards monetary union impressed neither its critics at home nor Britain's European partners, relations with whom plummeted further when it was revealed that a brain-wasting disease in cattle (bovine spongiform encephalopathy – **BSE** – or "mad cow disease") was widespread in British beef. Concerned about the threat of the disease spreading to humans as well as cows, the EU slapped an export ban on British beef, domestic sales of meat plunged (briefly), a programme of slaughter was introduced and amid the hysteria and confusion the government was, yet again, roundly blamed.

Sharing the malaise of the Conservative government in the early 1990s was the **Royal Family**, whose credibility fissured with the break-up of the marriage of Prince Charles and Diana. Revelations about the cruel and heartless treatment of Diana by both the prince and his family damaged the royals' reputation perhaps beyond repair and suddenly the institution itself seemed an anachronism, its members stiff, old-fashioned and dim-witted. By contrast, **Diana**, who was formally divorced from Charles in 1994, appeared warm-hearted and glamorous and her death in a car accident in Paris in 1997 may have saved the royal family as an institution. In the short term, Diana's death had a profound impact on the British, who joined in a media-orchestrated exercise in public grieving unprecedented in recent history.

The Labour party, itself in disarray through the 1980s, began to regroup in 1994 under a dynamic young leader, **Tony Blair**, who persuaded the party to distance itself from traditional left-wing socialism and take on a mantle of idealistic, media-friendly populism. The transformation worked to devastating effect, sweeping Blair to power in the general election of May 1997 on a wave of genuine popular optimism. There were immediate rewards in enhanced relations with Europe and progress in the Irish peace talks, whilst the long process of rebuilding the national health service and combating poverty started in earnest. Blair's electoral touch was repeated in Labour-sponsored referendums in both Scotland and Wales in favour of a devolved regional government, and the long-awaited reform of the House of Lords is pending. The drive and energy of the Labour government is indisputable and as yet they have not been snagged by any particular issue, though further difficulties in Northern Ireland, the need to improve the nation's public transportation and their failure to reduce hospital waiting lists are three major problems. Blair and the Labour Party remain streets ahead of their rivals in the opinion polls, but they might yet be undermined by a lack of a central defining principle.

THE MONUMENTS AND BUILDINGS OF ENGLAND

THE NEOLITHIC PERIOD AND THE BRONZE AGE

The oldest traces of building in England date from the **fourth millennium BC**, when **Neolithic** peoples, who practised rudimentary agriculture, succeeded the hunting-and-gathering Paleolithic and Mesolithic population, who had inhabited cave-dwellings and hide-covered camps. The remains of round stone huts have been excavated on Carn Brea, outside Redruth in Cornwall, but the major surviving habitations are entrenched sites found throughout southern England, consisting of concentric rings of ditches and banks. The largest of these is at Windmill Hill in Wiltshire, created by a civilization that was also responsible for numerous **long barrows** (burial mounds) all over England. These featureless, pear-shaped hummocks of earth are concentrated along the southern chalk downs from Sussex to Dorset, with others dotted around Lincolnshire, Yorkshire and the Cotswolds, where the barrows are noteworthy for holding stone chambers for collective family burials.

One of the largest and most elaborate Neolithic burial sites is **Woodhenge**, on Salisbury Plain, comprising a network of banks and ditches enclosing no fewer than six concentric ovals of wooden posts, arranged along the axis of the midsummer sunrise. The site lies not far from the most famous of all English prehistoric monuments, **Stonehenge**, started around 3000 BC and subsequently added to over the next thousand years by the so-called Beaker Folk, an early Bronze Age culture. This extraordinary megalithic stone circle probably had an astronomical and sacred significance, as did **Avebury**, on the other side of Salisbury Plain, which is even more extensive than Stonehenge, though less massive and less well preserved. The two sites represent communal, highly organized efforts, embellished over the years in much the same way as medieval cathedrals. Less grandiose **stone circles and rows** survive up and down the country, from Castlerigg, near Keswick in the Lake District, to the Hurlers of Cornwall's Bodmin Moor. Hut circles on the moors of the West Country bear testimony to the presence of later Bronze Age peoples; Grimspound, on Dartmoor, is one of the best examples – dating from around 1200 BC, its round stone houses with beehive roofs are ringed by a protective wall.

THE CELTIC AND ROMAN PERIODS

Five hundred years later, **Celtic** invaders brought the techniques of the Iron Age to the British Isles. Their chief contribution to the English landscape was a series of **hilltop forts** and other defensive works, often adapted from earlier constructions. At their simplest, these settlements consisted of a circular earthwork within which the inhabitants dwelt in timber-built round huts – a good example is Castle Dore, near Fowey in Cornwall. At **Maiden Castle**, in Dorset, a town was enclosed within a multiple system of ramparts, a formidable enlargement of what had been a modest and much more ancient hillfort. The best preserved of all Iron Age villages, however, is the stronghold of **Chysauster**, near Zennor in Cornwall, consisting of stone houses arranged in pairs, each with a courtyard and garden plot. The settlement was inhabited until well into the Roman era, preserved thanks to its distance from the most westerly Roman outpost.

The **Romans** were the first to impose rigorously systematized architecture on the English landscape, as their consolidation of peace permitted the erection of monumental public buildings: amphitheatres, like that at Chester in Cheshire; theatres, like the one at York; and baths, most famous of which were of course at **Bath**. Although no Roman temples remain standing, Colchester and St Albans have revealed impressive remains, as befits two of Roman Britain's principal centres. Other important towns such as London, Gloucester, Leicester and Lincoln – all planned according to the classic chessboard pattern favoured by the Romans – have yielded little, due chiefly to the extensive reuse of the ancient sites. In general, the architecture of this and other Roman provinces was less ambitious and sophisticated than that of Rome itself, yet the grandeur of such palaces as **Fishbourne** in West Sussex – built around 75 AD, probably for a Romanized British chieftain – was clearly intended to affirm the vast superiority of Roman civilization. Fishbourne's columned entrance prefaces an interior whose decorative details were as carefully elaborated as the ground plan, with lavish use of mosaics, a feature also exemplified by private houses excavated at St Albans and Cirencester. Most of the great Roman villas reached their peak of comfort and artistic excellence during the first half of the fourth century, when even relatively modest farmhouses were equipped with central heating.

ANGLO-SAXON ENGLAND

A hundred years later, the Romans had withdrawn from the islands and all traces of their culture were neglected and crumbling. The **Anglo-Saxons** who followed them had little interest in the achievements of the eclipsed civilization, neither were they inspired to rival them. Once they had progressed beyond the use of mud, wattle and thatch, the Anglo-Saxons mainly constructed in **timber**, a specialization in which the English were to excel throughout the Middle Ages, though its perishability has meant that little remains from the six hundred years preceding the Norman Conquest. What fragments have survived were the product of the new Christian ideology, expressed in **stone-built churches** that were intended to have an enduring monumental function. The conversion of the English kings at the end of the sixth century initiated a period lasting until the sixteenth-century Reformation, in which church construction was the chief medium of architectural innovation.

But even stone-built churches were vulnerable to the Viking raids from the eighth century onwards, and those that did survive were subject to constant modifications and accretions. Such was the case with two of the earliest

English churches, both in **Canterbury**: St Peter and St Paul, built in about 597, and the town's first cathedral, erected about five years later. In general terms, these Anglo-Saxon structures seem to have been modelled on churches in Rome, with round apses at the eastern end, unlike the more Celtic-inspired square ends that can be seen at the little church of St Laurence, in Bradford-on-Avon, Wiltshire, or in the churches constructed during the Christian revival in **Northumbria** towards the end of the seventh century. Here, the ascetic Celtic tradition of the Scottish and Irish monks who led the movement did not encourage refined architecture, and the three churches built by Benedict Biscop in County Durham – Monkwearmouth, Escomb and the Venerable Bede's own church at Jarrow – are small and roughly built. The most impressive of all Saxon churches, however, lies in the Midlands, at Brixworth in Northamptonshire, erected around 670, and distinguished by the systematic use of arches.

In the eighth and ninth centuries, church building was deflected by the increasing ferocity of the Viking raiders, who despoiled the richest of the country's churches. A revival came with the installation of Dunstan as bishop of Glastonbury around 940, which led to the foundation of monasteries all over the country, much of the work being undertaken by churchmen who had spent time in the great European houses. Far from showing the influence of continental styles, however, the sparse remains demonstrate instead a penchant for quirky decoration – for example the spiral columns in the crypt at Repton, Derbyshire.

THE NORMANS

English insularity came to an end when the influence of **Norman** architecture began to be felt in the years just before the Conquest of 1066. The finest pre-Conquest building to employ the Romanesque style was Edward the Confessor's rebuilt **Westminster Abbey** (1050–65), the design of which was an imitation of the great French abbey churches of Caen and Jumièges. Edward's work has since disappeared, but the capital still boasts a remarkable example of Norman architecture – the **Tower of London**, the most formidable of a chain of defence works thrown up throughout the country.

The earliest types of **castle** followed a "motte and bailey" design, consisting of a central tower (or keep) placed on a mound (the motte), and encircled by one or more courts (the baileys). Most were built of wood until the time of Henry II, though some of the more important sites were stone-constructed from the beginning, including **Rochester** and **Colchester** castles and the **White Tower** at the Tower of London. **Dover Castle** (1168–85), built by Henry II, introduced the refinement of a double row of outer walls with towers at intervals, a design probably influenced by the fortresses encountered by Crusaders in the Holy Land.

Once the country had been secured, the Normans set about transforming the English Church, filling the highest ecclesiastical offices with imported clergy, all of whom were keen to introduce the lofty architectural conceptions then current in Europe. Many of the major churches of the country – for example at **Canterbury**, **York**, **St Albans**, **Winchester**, **Worcester** and **Ely** – were rebuilt along Norman lines, with cruciform ground plans and massive cylindrical columns topped by semicircular arches. The summit of the Norman style was achieved at **Durham Cathedral**, begun in 1093, which has Europe's first example of large-scale ribbed vaulting, and spectacular zigzag and diamond patterns on its colossal piers, a strong and immediately influential contrast to the austerity of the first generation of Norman churches. An increasing love of decoration was also evident in the elaborately carved capitals and blind arcading in Canterbury Cathedral, the beakhead moulding in Lincoln Cathedral, and to a lesser extent in the ornamental features of the numerous parish churches surviving from this period, which often reveal greater evidence of Anglo-Saxon traditional craftwork.

In common with the rest of Europe, England witnessed the growing influence of the **monastic houses** in the twelfth century, a continuation of a process begun before the Conquest by the Benedictines. The **Cistercians** were responsible for some of the most splendid foundations, establishing an especially wealthy group of self-sufficient monasteries in Yorkshire – **Fountains**, **Rievaulx** and **Jervaulx** abbeys – which featured examples of the pointed arch, an idea imported from northern France, where it may have been introduced by Crusaders returning from the Middle East. The reforming Cistercians favoured a plain style, but the native penchant for decoration gradually infiltrated their buildings – for instance at Kirkstall Abbey (c.1152), near Leeds – while other orders had a preference for greater elaboration from the start. Amongst the latter was the **Cluniac** order, whose extravagantly ornate west front of Norfolk's Castle Acre priory (1140–50) is typical.

Incidentally, it's characteristic of the English Church that bishoprics were often given to the heads of monastic houses. Thus many English cathedrals were also monastic churches, which explains the prevalence of **cloisters**, **chapter houses** and other monastic structures within the precincts of English cathedrals, and the existence within the main body of the cathedral of areas that were set aside for the use of the monks rather than the laity.

THE TRANSITIONAL AND EARLY ENGLISH STYLES

Profuse carved decoration and **pointed arches** were distinctive elements in the evolution of a **transitional style** in the second half of the twelfth century, representing a shift away from purely Romanesque forms. The pointed arch permitted a far greater flexibility in the relation of the height of a building to its span than had the round arch. It also allowed the introduction of highly scientific systems of vaulting and buttressing, which in turn led to a significant increase of window area in the walls between the buttresses, since these walls no longer had to carry the main weight of the roof. Improvements in masonry techniques also meant that walls could be reduced in thickness, and the cylindrical columns of the Normans replaced by more slender piers.

The first phase of **Gothic** architecture in England began in earnest in the last quarter of the twelfth century, when Gothic motifs were used at Roche Abbey and **Byland**, both in Yorkshire. However, it was the French-designed **choir** at **Canterbury Cathedral**, built 1175–84, which really established the new style, even though it was compromised by the fact that Gothic themes had to be grafted onto the ruins of the Anglo-Norman building that had been destroyed by fire in 1174. This first phase, lasting through most of the thirteenth century, is known as **Early English** (or Pointed or Lancet), and was given its full expression in what is regarded as the first truly Gothic cathedral in

England, **Wells**, largely completed in 1190.

Begun shortly afterwards, **Lincoln Cathedral** takes the process of vertical emphasis further, substituting wall-shafts soaring all the way to the ceiling for Wells' three-tier nave subdivided horizontally, and using decoration more profuse than anything in France at the time. The influence of Lincoln remained strong in English architecture, though it was resisted by the builders of **Salisbury Cathedral**, which, despite later restoration work, is one of the most homogeneous of the Early English churches, most of it being built in the comparatively short period 1220–65.

A transitional phase in the evolution of Gothic architecture is represented by the rebuilding of **Westminster Abbey** in 1220, when the Abbey became the most French of English churches. There was a French influence at work in the flying buttresses that were added to support its greater height, and in the lavish use of **window tracery**, whereby geometric patterns were created by subdividing each window with moulded ribs (or mullions), a device first seen at Reims in 1211.

THE DECORATED AND PERPENDICULAR STYLES

The development of complicated tracery is one of the chief characteristics of the **Decorated** style, ushered in by Westminster Abbey and by the Angel Choir at Lincoln and the nave of Lichfield, both designed in the late 1250s. The fully blown Decorated style emerged around the end of the thirteenth century and the beginning of the fourteenth, when the cathedral at **Exeter** was almost completely rebuilt, with a dense exuberance of rib vaulting and multiple moulding on the arches and piers. **York Minster**, rebuilt from 1225 and the largest of all English Gothic churches, introduced another innovation associated with this period – **lierne vaulting**, whereby a subsidiary, mainly ornamental, rib is added to the roof complex. Intricately carved roof bosses and capitals are other common features of Decorated Gothic, as is the use of the organic **ogee curve** – ie a curve with a double bend in it. One-off experiments are also characteristic of this period, the most striking examples being the octagonal lantern tower at **Ely** (1320s) and the rebuilding of **Bristol** cathedral (1298–1330), which shows many of the features of the continental hall-church type of design, in which the

naves and aisle are roughly the same height.

The style that came to prevail in the second half of the fourteenth century, the severe **Perpendicular**, was the first post-Conquest architecture that was unique to England. This insularity was due partly to the loss of almost all the English possessions in France by the end of the Hundred Years' War, and partly to the Black Death, which had depleted the number of craftsmen capable of the elaborate carvings and mouldings characteristic of the Decorated style. Whereas France had progressed to an emphatically curvilinear or "Flamboyant" style, the emphasis in England was on rectilinear design, anticipated in the rebuilding of **Gloucester Cathedral** (1337–57). Here the cloister features the first fully developed **fan vault** while the massive east window is a good example of the new window design, in which the maximization of light is paramount and the tracery organized in vertical compartments. Edward II's tomb – the focal point of Gloucester cathedral – also exemplifies the wave of **memorial building** during the Perpendicular period.

The chantry tombs at **Winchester Cathedral** and **Tewkesbury Abbey** are resplendent monuments from this period, as is the tomb of the Black Prince in **Canterbury Cathedral**, where the Norman nave was rebuilt after 1379, though it was the addition of the Bell Harry Tower and tracery in the aisle windows that injected the most strongly Perpendicular elements. Henry Yevele, who was responsible for this work at Canterbury, and his contemporary at Winchester, William Wynford, were forerunners of the modern architect, reflecting the gradual elevation of the mastermason into an overall creative and supervisory role.

The turmoil of the Wars of the Roses meant that few new "prestige" buildings were commissioned in the half-century after 1425, though parish churches eagerly embraced the new style, most notably in East Anglia, Somerset and the Cotswolds. The restoration of strong government saw a resurgence of royal patronage and the realization of a triad of major architectural projects in **St George's Chapel**, Windsor, **King's College Chapel**, Cambridge, and **Henry VII's Chapel** in Westminster Abbey, all completed in the reign of Henry VII. By now, walls had become panelled screens filled mostly with stained glass, with the weight transmitted from stone ribs onto bold buttresses that were usually capped with tall pinnacles. King's College developed fan vaulting into an element that extended over the whole nave and harmonized with the windows and wall panelling, but it was the densely sculptured Henry VII's Chapel that took such vaulting to the limit, the complexity heightened by a lavish use of decorative pendants – a rare element in English design.

THE RENAISSANCE

Perpendicular motifs remained prominent throughout the Tudor era, with the impact of **Renaissance** architecture confined initially to small decorative features. Such were the terracotta busts of Roman emperors at the otherwise conventionally Tudor **Hampton Court Palace**, to which Henry VIII added a Great Hall with a superb hammer-beam roof similar to that in Westminster Hall (1397–99), albeit here embellished with Italianesque details.

The dissemination of the latest ideas in design and decoration came about chiefly through commissions from high-ranking courtiers and statesmen. These notables flamboyantly demonstrated their acquaintance with the sophisticated classical canons in such mansions as **Burghley House**, Lincolnshire (1552–87), and **Longleat**, Wiltshire (1568–80), projects which mingled the Gothic and the Renaissance while also heralding a taste for landscaped parklands in preference to enclosed courtyards. (With Henry VIII's Dissolution of the Monasteries some twenty to thirty percent of England's land was suddenly released into private hands.) The mason at Longleat, Robert Smythson, was probably also the designer of **Hardwick Hall** in Derbyshire (1591–96), celebrated in local rhyme as "Hardwick Hall, more glass than wall" – words which sum up the predilection for huge glazed areas displayed in Elizabethan great houses.

Hatfield House in Hertfordshire, rebuilt 1607–11 by the chief minister of Elizabeth and James I, Robert Cecil, represents a bridge between Elizabethan and Jacobean architecture, which is characterized by a greater infusion of classical ideas. Classicism at this time, however, was considered primarily decorative, as exemplified in the Tower of the Five Orders (1613–18) at the **Bodleian Library** in Oxford, where the Classical Orders as defined by Vitruvius were applied as appendages to a

building with mullioned windows, battlements and pinnacles. The unadulterated spirit of the Renaissance did not find full expression in England until **Inigo Jones** (1573–1652) began to apply the lessons learned from his visits to Italy, and in particular from his familiarity with Palladio's rules of proportion and symmetry, as laid out in the Quattro Libri dell'Architettura, published in 1570. Appointed Royal Surveyor to James I in 1615 (a position he held also under Charles I), Jones changed the direction of English architecture with only a handful of works, in which he brilliantly adapted Palladian ideals to English requirements. Three of his most prominent projects were built in London: the **Banqueting House** in Whitehall (1619–22), the first truly classical building to be completed in England since Roman times; the **Queen's House** at Greenwich (1617–35); and **St Paul's Church**, Covent Garden (1630s), the focal point of the first planned city square in England.

WREN AND BAROQUE

Despite Jones's promulgation of classical architecture, the Gothic endured into the seventeenth century, especially in Oxford, where Christ Church was given a magnificent fanvaulted staircase hall as late as 1640. Oxford's first classical construction, the **Sheldonian Theatre**, was also the first building designed by the artistic heir of Inigo Jones, **Christopher Wren** (1632–1723), who established himself as a brilliant mathematician and astronomer before turning to architecture shortly after the Restoration of 1660. As far as is known, Wren never visited Italy (though he met Bernini, the greatest architect of the day, in Paris), and his work was never so wholeheartedly Italianate as that of Inigo Jones, the influences of French and Dutch architecture contributing to an eclectic style that mingled orthodox classicism with **Baroque** inventiveness.

Wren's work in Oxford was quickly followed by Pembroke College Chapel, Cambridge, but the bulk of his achievement is to be seen in London, where the **Great Fire of 1666** led to a commission for the building of 53 churches. The most striking of these buildings display a remarkable elegance and harmony within the constraints of very cramped sites; they include **St Bride** in Fleet Street, **St Mary-le-Bow** in Cheapside, **St Vedast** in Foster Lane, and, perhaps the finest of all, the domed **St Stephen Walbrook** alongside Mansion House – all of which were rebuilt after partial destruction in World War II. Most monumental of all was Wren's rebuilding of **St Paul's Cathedral** (1675–1710), which was built in a cruciform shape very different from his original radical design, though its principal feature – the massive central dome – was retained.

As Surveyor-General, Wren also rebuilt, extended or altered several royal palaces, including the south and east wings of **Hampton Court** (1689–1700). Other secular works include **Chelsea Hospital** (1682–92), **Trinity College Library**, Cambridge (1676–84), the **Tom Tower** of Christ Church, Oxford (1681–82) – a rare work in the Gothic mode – and, grandest of all, **Greenwich Hospital** (1694–98), a magnificent foil to the Queen's House built by Inigo Jones, and to Wren's own **Royal Observatory** (1675).

Work at Greenwich Hospital was continued by Wren's only major pupil, **Nicholas Hawksmoor** (1661–1736), whose distinctively muscular form of the Baroque style is seen to best effect in his London churches. Most of these are in the East End with the best being **St George-in-the-East** (1715–23) and **Christ Church**, Spitalfields (1723–29). His exercises in Gothic pastiche included the western towers of **Westminster Abbey** (1734) and **All Souls College**, Oxford (1716–35), while the mausoleum at **Castle Howard** in Yorkshire (1729) shows close affinities with the Roman Baroque.

The third great English architect of the Baroque era was **John Vanbrugh** (1664–1726), who was famed as a dramatist but lacked any architectural training when he was commissioned by the Earl of Carlisle to design a new country seat at **Castle Howard** (1699–1726). More flamboyant than either Hawksmoor or Wren – with both of whom he worked – Vanbrugh went on to design numerous other grandiose houses, of which the outstanding examples are the gargantuan **Blenheim Palace** (1705–20), the culminating point of English Baroque, and the fortress-like **Seaton Delaval**, not far from Newcastle upon Tyne (1720–28), a building which harks back to the architecture of medieval England.

GIBBS AND PALLADIANISM

In the field of church architecture, the most influential architect of the eighteenth century

was **James Gibbs** (1682–1754), whose masterpiece, **St Martin-in-the-Fields** in London (1722–26), with its steeple sprouting above a pedimented portico, was widely imitated as a model of how to combine the classical with the Gothic. Gibbs was barred from royal commissions on account of his Catholic and Jacobite sympathies, but he worked at the two universities, designing Cambridge's **Senate House** (1722–30) and the **Fellows' Building** at King's College (1723–49), and Oxford's **Radcliffe Camera** (1737–49), a beautifully sited construction drawing heavily on Gibbs's knowledge of Roman styles. Gibbs was one of the very few architects of his generation to have studied in Italy, which had been cut off by war, but this situation changed when the Treaty of Utrecht (1713) opened up Europe to English aristocrats on the Grand Tour, as the self-educating long holiday on the continent became known. For architecture in England, the immediate result was a rebirth of the **Palladianism** introduced by Inigo Jones a century before, an orthodoxy that was to dominate secular architecture in eighteenth-century England.

The movement was championed by a Whig elite led by **Lord Burlington** (1694–1753), an enthusiastic patron of the arts whose own masterpiece was **Chiswick House** in London (1725), a domed villa closely modelled on Palladio's Villa Rotonda. Burlington collaborated with the decorator, garden designer and architect **William Kent** (1685–1748) in such stately piles as **Holkham Hall** in Norfolk (1734), whose imposing portico and ordered composition typify the break with Baroque dramatics. The third chief player in the return to Renaissance simplicity was **Colen Campbell** (1673–1729), author of the influential *Vitruvius Britannicus* (1715), a compilation of designs from which architects freely borrowed. Campbell worked closely with Burlington on such works as **Burlington House** in London (1718–19), though his best achievements were two country homes, Houghton Hall, Norfolk (1722), and Mereworth Castle, Kent (1723).

The Palladian idiom was further disseminated by such men as **John Wood** (1704–54), designer of Liverpool Town Hall (1749–54) but better known for the work he did in his native **Bath**, helping to transform the city into a paragon of town planning. His showpieces there are **Queen Square** (1729–36) and the

Circus (1754), the latter completed by his son, **John Wood the Younger** (1728–81), who went on to design Bath's **Royal Crescent** (1767–74). The embellishment of Georgian Bath was furthered also by **Robert Adam** (1728–92), a Palladian who designed the town's **Pulteney Bridge** (1769–74). Adam's forte, however, was in the field of domestic architecture, especially in the designing of decorative interiors, where he showed himself to be the most versatile and refined architect of his day. His elaborate concoctions are best displayed in **Syon House** (1762–69) and **Osterley Park** (1761–80), both on the western outskirts of London, and **Kenwood** (1767–79) on the edge of Hampstead Heath, all epitomizing his scrupulous attention to detail as well as his dexterity at large-scale planning. Adam's chief rival was the more fastidious **William Chambers** (1723–96), whose masterpiece, **Somerset House** on London's Aldwych (1776–98), is an academic counterpoint to Adam's dashing originality.

Adam and Chambers competed in a highly active market whose chief patrons regarded themselves as belonging to the most cultivated class in the island's history. Undoubtedly they were among the wealthiest, spending vast sums of money not just on their houses but also on the grounds in which these houses stood. **Landscape gardening** was the quintessential English contribution to European culture in the eighteenth century, and its greatest exponent was **Capability Brown** (1716–83) – so-called because of his custom of assessing the "capabilities" of a landscape. All over England, Brown and his acolytes modified the estates of the landed gentry into "Picturesque" landscapes, an idealization of nature along the lines of the paintings of Poussin and Lorrain, often enhancing the view with a romantic "ruin" or some exotic structure such as a Chinese pagoda or Indian temple.

THE NINETEENTH CENTURY

The greatest architect of the late eighteenth and early nineteenth centuries was **John Nash** (1752–1835), whose Picturesque country houses, built in collaboration with the landscapist Humphrey Repton (1752–1818), represented just one aspect of his diverse repertoire. In this versatility Nash was typical of his time, though he is associated above all with the style favoured during the **Regency** of his friend the Prince of Wales (afterwards George IV), a decorous style that owed much to Chambers and Adam, making plentiful use of stucco. His strangest and best-known building was also a commission from the Prince – the orientalized Gothic palace known as the **Brighton Pavilion**. A prolific worker, Nash was responsible for much of the present-day appearance of such **resorts** as Brighton, Weymouth, Cheltenham, Clifton and Tunbridge Wells, as well as for numerous parts of the central **London** cityscape, including the **Haymarket Theatre** (1820), the church of **All Souls**, Langham Place (1822–25), **Clarence House** (1825) and **Carlton House Terrace** (1827). He also planned the layout of **Regent's Park** and **Regent's Street** in London (from 1811), and remodelled **Buckingham Palace** (1826–30), a project that foundered at the death of his patron.

Nash's contemporary, **Sir John Soane** (1753–1837), was more of an inventive antiquarian, his pared-down classical experiments presenting a serious-minded contrast to Nash's extrovert creations. Very little remains of his greatest masterpiece, the **Bank of England** (1788–1833), but his idiosyncratic style is well illustrated by two other buildings in London – his own home on **Lincoln's Inn Fields** (1812–13) and **Dulwich Art Gallery** (1811–14).

Classicism was soon challenged by a style that had been heralded as early as 1753, when the diarist and connoisseur Horace Walpole built **Strawberry Hill** near Twickenham, an ornate Gothic villa created at a time when everything Gothic was despised by people of taste. Nash and other exponents of the Picturesque also dabbled in the Gothic, as a passion for romance and medievalism gained ground in literary and intellectual circles. In 1818, when Parliament voted a million pounds for the construction of new Anglican churches, the **Gothic Revival** got properly under way – two-thirds of the churches built under this Act were in a Gothic or near-Gothic style. Though many public buildings continued to draw on Renaissance, Greek or Roman architecture – eg the town halls of Birmingham and Leeds (1832–50 & 1853–58) – the status of neo-Gothic was confirmed when it was decided that the Houses of Parliament should be rebuilt in that style after the fire of 1834. The fact that the contract was given to **Sir Charles Barry** (1795–1860), designer of the classical Reform Club, shows how architects were expected to be masters of all fashions, although his collaborator on the project, **Augustus Welby Pugin** (1812–52), was to become the unswerving apostle of the neo-Gothic movement.

A crucial moment in the so-called "Battle of the Styles" came with the debate over the new government offices (now the Foreign Office) in **Whitehall** (1855–72), when the most eminent architect of the day, **Sir George Gilbert Scott** (1811–78), was instructed to replace his Gothic design with an Italian Renaissance one. On the other hand, Scott was able to give rein to his personal tastes in the extravaganzas of **St Pancras Station** (1868–74) and the **Albert Memorial** (1863–72), both based on his preferred Flemish and north Italian Gothic models. When the first English cathedral to be consecrated outside London since the Middle Ages was built at Truro (1880–1910), the approved design was a scholarly exercise in French-influenced Gothic; yet when it came to commissioning the Catholic **Westminster Cathedral** (1895–1903), what was chosen was a neo-Byzantine design.

Further enriching the variety of nineteenth-century architecture, numerous engineer-architects employed cast iron and other industrial materials in works as diverse as Isambard Kingdom Brunel's **Clifton Suspension Bridge** in Bristol (1829–64) and Joseph Paxton's glass and iron **Crystal Palace** (1851), erected in just six months and subsequently transferred from London's Hyde Park to the suburb of Sydenham, where it burned down in 1936. The potential of iron and glass was similarly exploited in **Newcastle Central Station** (1846–55), the first of a generation of monumental railway stations incorporating classical motifs and rib-vaulted iron roofs.

Rejection of these industrial technologies in favour of "traditional" materials such as brick, stone and timber was propounded by **John Ruskin** (1819–1900) and his disciple **William Morris** (1834–96), leader of the Arts and Crafts Movement, through which his ideas on the importance of honest handicraft and functionalism were put into practical effect. Morris was not himself an architect, but his work on the interior of his own home, the **Red House** in

Bexley, Kent (1854), which was built from designs by Philip Webb (1831–1915), was to be immensely influential in its emphasis on the architect's obligation to design every aspect of the building.

Morris's insistence on total responsibility for the interior details as well as exterior appearance was echoed in the work of **Richard Norman Shaw** (1831–1912), whose redbrick, heavily gabled constructions – in a Dutch style reminiscent of the Queen Anne period – were widely imitated in central London. His best work is displayed in Swan House, Chelsea (1875), Albert Hall Mansions, Kensington (1879) – one of England's earliest apartment blocks – and in Bedford Park, west London (1877), the first of the capital's "garden suburbs".

Another architect to fall under the sway of the Arts and Crafts Movement was **Charles Voysey** (1851–1941) whose clean-cut cottages and houses eschewed all ostentation, depending rather on the meticulous and subtle use of local materials for their effect. The originality of Voysey's work and that of his contemporaries M.H. Baillie Scott (1865–1945) and Ernest Newton (1856–1922) was later debased by scores of speculative suburban builders, though not before their refreshingly simple style had found recognition first in Germany and then across the rest of Europe.

THE TWENTIETH CENTURY

While the use of reinforced concrete and the modernist ideas of Le Corbusier, Walter Gropius and the Bauhaus were making ground on the Continent, and while the North American scene was being revolutionized by high-rise steel-frame buildings, England remained attached to a rather nostalgic aesthetic. The insularity of English architecture is typified by the career of **Sir Edwin Lutyens** (1869–1944), most of whose early works were country houses in the Arts and Crafts style. Later he moved through a succession of classicized styles, such as the elegantly Baroque mode that he dubbed "Wrenaissance" and a more sober neo-Georgianism that marked the beginning of a widespread Georgian Revival. However, perhaps his most striking achievements in England are the one-off **Castle Drogo** on Dartmoor (1910–30), the last of the great country houses, and the **Cenotaph** on London's Whitehall (1918), a masterpiece of stripped-down monumentalism.

The revivalist tendency prevailed throughout the early decades of the century, but an awareness of more radical architectural trends surfaced in isolated projects in the 1930s. One of these was **Senate House** in London's Bloomsbury (1932), designed by **Charles Holden** (1875–1960), who was also responsible for some of London's Underground stations, notably **Arnos Grove** (1932). Perhaps the most successful applications of the austere International Modern style were achieved by the **Tecton** group, led by the Russian immigrant Lubetkin, whose **Penguin Pool** in London Zoo (1934) is a witty demonstration of the plastic possibilities of concrete.

Yet general acceptance of modern style had to wait for the reforming atmosphere of the years immediately following World War II, and in particular for the 1951 **Festival of Britain** on London's South Bank, which showcased the latest technological marvels. Many of the festival pavilions were designed by **Basil Spence** (1907–76), whose best-known work was the replacement of the bombed **Coventry Cathedral**, incorporating defiantly modernist detail into a neo-Gothic structure (1951–59). The only architectural remnant of the Festival of Britain is the **Royal Festival Hall** (1949), an immensely practicable and handsome structure with a claim to be the best-loved modern building in the country. The site was later augmented by the addition of the far less attractive **National Theatre** (1967–77) by **Denys Lasdun** (b.1914), a Tecton architect who remained true to the principles of the group.

The massive postwar rebuilding programme was conditioned by an acute housing crisis and severe financial constraints, so the emphasis was on the utilization of prefabricated technologies to get as many units built as quickly and as cheaply as possible, with little overall planning or consideration for the environment. The unpopularity of the ubiquitous tower blocks was aggravated by the insensitivity shown by speculative developers, who were given almost free rein in the construction of office buildings and shopping centres throughout the country – Plymouth, Southampton and Birmingham have especially hideous examples.

Some of the more interesting architecture of the 1960s was created at the new "redbrick" universities, notable examples being Spence's **Sussex University** at Brighton (1961) and Lasdun's **University of East Anglia** at Norwich (1963). Among the younger generation who designed some of their first works for the universities were **James Stirling** (1926–92) and **Norman Foster** (b. 1935), architects who, along with **Richard Rogers** (b. 1933), have found greater scope working abroad than in Britain. That said, Stirling's Postmodern extension for London's **Tate Gallery** (1989) was one of the more controversial projects of recent times, and Rogers' **Lloyd's Building** (1978–86) in London is a bold hi-tech display along the lines of his Pompidou Centre in Paris. Factory sites have provided Foster with several English contracts, though the building with the highest profile is his glass-tent terminal at London's **Stansted Airport** (1991). Significantly, state-funded buildings hardly feature in a list of recent architectural highspots, reflecting the last Tory government's (1979–1997) emphasis on the primacy of private enterprise and its concomitant neglect of public building.

Give or take the occasional prestige project, the present scene is stranded between a popular dislike for the modern and a general reluctance amongst architects to return to the architectural past. In this regard, the interventions of Prince Charles have not been helpful. Posing as the voice of common sense and jumbling this up with his role as a major landowner, the Prince has campaigned against architectural modernism, one of the results being a countrywide rash of modern office buildings with peculiar pastel-painted gables and other retrospective accoutrements. The most obvious repercussion, however, was in regard to the **Sainsbury Wing** (1991) at London's National Gallery, a commission which was eventually handed to Postmodernist supremos Robert Venturi and Denise Scott-Brown, who produced a safe pastiche of Neoclassicism. One up-and-coming architect, whose recent works have found critical acclaim – without royal blessing – is **Michael Hopkins**, who rose to prominence with his eye-catching Mound Stand for the Lord's Cricket Ground. He also pulled off a delicate balancing act at the **Glyndebourne Opera House** (1994), producing a generally well-liked wood-panelled auditorium, and his latest work, the **Inland Revenue Headquarters** (1995) in Nottingham, has also found favour with most observers.

THE WILDLIFE OF ENGLAND

Almost every part of England has a history of human settlement, a history that has had a profound effect on the country's wildlife, bequeathing a patchwork of woodland, heathland, meadowland and a miscellany of other habitats. An inventory of England's wildlife would run on for hundreds of pages, and there are plenty of specialized publications for those who want to get to grips with the subject. What follows is a general overview of the species to be found in England, with an emphasis on the way in which their habitats have evolved.

THE HISTORY OF THE LAND

The English climate nowadays is mainly of the variety known as "Atlantic", being damp and relatively mild, although there are slight regional variations – the southwest has warmer summers for example, whereas Norfolk has a more "continental" climate, drier in summer, harsher in winter. The current climate is obviously a principal determinant of a country's wildlife, but it's essential to bear in mind that the history of its climate is every bit as important.

The crucial period was the easing of the last **Ice Age**, a process that began around 12,000 years ago, when trees from the warmer south – to which Britain was then attached by land – began to colonize the country. The first arrivals were **birches** and **Scots pine**, but hardwoods such as **oak**, **ash**, **lime** and **elm** eventually shaded them out, creating a tangled forest over all but the bleakest and wettest zones. Incidentally, the Scots pines that you see in England today are not wild specimens – they have all been planted. In certain upland areas some plants and animals survive as relics of the glacial period: an example is the mountain ringlet butterfly, which is found above the 1800ft contour in the Lake District and on some Scottish mountains but lives nowhere else in Britain.

The **beech** was the last of England's sixty or so native woody shrubs and trees to take root before the meltwater raised the sea level to form the English Channel. Other species, such as the sweet chestnut (introduced in Roman times), are by contrast evidence of the role that **human settlement** has played in changing the landscape. Indeed, no sooner was the Channel flooded than **Stone Age** farmers were crossing it with their domesticated animals. These first colonists created **grazing land** and fields for their corn crop by clearing the native woods, starting with the lighter wooded areas – the chalk downlands, gravel islands in river valleys, and the thinly wooded sandstones of the Pennines. The chalk downlands and the Pennines have been grazed ever since, with just the odd tree giving an indication that these open areas were once naturally wooded.

Clearance of the denser woodland on the heavier valley soils started in pre-Roman days and by medieval times most of the wildwood had gone, although some was maintained for supplies of heavy timber, firewood, poles and so on. These **working woodlands** were often relics of the original wildwood, but other woodlands quickly grew on areas that were once open land, abandoned when whole villages were annihilated by plagues or some other catastrophe. There are also large areas of what's known as **wood pasture**, areas of rough unploughed land, dotted with trees that were usually pollarded – that is their branches were cut at head height out of reach of grazing deer and cattle. Even such ancient trees as Robin Hood's Major Oak in **Sherwood Forest** and the Knightwood Oak in the **New Forest** are old pollards. (Note, however, that the word "forest" does not necessarily denote woodland. The word originally signified land set aside by the Norman kings for their royal hunts. These forests could include woodland, but were just as likely to contain heath, moor or marsh – the New Forest is still a marvellous example of a forest that is not primarily wooded.)

For centuries on each side of the Roman occupation, **ploughland** was kept open, but there were always some fenced, hedged or walled **grazing paddocks**. By Tudor times there were already a large number of such fields, a trend which culminated with the Georgian and Victorian "enclosures" when almost all the remaining open land – ploughland as well as grazing – was divided into fields. Providing a perfect combination of shelter and light, similar to a woodland clearing, the field **hedges** offer a habitat to numerous species: songbirds such as the blackbird and thrush are found more often in hedges than elsewhere.

The **wetlands** of England have also been refashioned, with the medieval abbeys in particular draining swampy land to create fields across the Norfolk Fens, the Somerset levels, Romney Marsh and other coastal areas. Today only a few patches of bogland remain undrained, while few rivers have remained free of interference.

MODERN PROBLEMS AND CONSERVATION

In the last forty years, the rural economy has been transformed by **intensive farming**, which has introduced a high degree of mechanization and chemical use. Many old woods, heaths and moors have been dug up and replanted with conifers, thereby eliminating their wild flowers and animal life. Most of the old pastures and meadows have been drained, ploughed and reseeded with vigorous hybrid grasses; the grass is then cut young as silage rather than being left to grow long for hay, so wild flowers no longer have time to set seed, and the birds that used to nest in the grass – such as lapwings and snipe – have been driven out. Ploughland is now regularly sprayed with insecticides, wiping out the food supply for numerous species – even rooks are far less common than they used to be. And of course thousands of acres have become factory sites, housing estates or transport routes, and although railway cuttings, canals, quarries and motorway verges can attract certain species, England's richest wildlife is now to be found in pockets of landscape that have escaped agribusiness.

Although many species have legal protection, this is difficult to police and there are numerous conditions to the protection offered, the main ones being the exclusion clauses for

the practice of "good farming or forestry". The choicest habitats are protected as **Sites of Special Scientific Interest** (SSSI), but even here the landowners simply have to inform English Nature (the national conservation agency) if they are about to do something damaging, whereupon EN must try to buy them off. Only specific **nature reserves**, managed solely for the benefit of rare species and old established flora and fauna, can guarantee their survival. Fortunately, England has many such reserves, run by organizations as diverse as English Nature, local councils, the Royal Society for the Protection of Birds and a plethora of county wildlife trusts.

WILD FLOWERS

It may seem paradoxical, but it was the traditional use of old habitats that created England's wealth of wild flowers. Chalk grassland, the habitat of yellow vetches, pinkish restharrow, blue bellflower and many wild orchids, is a typical example. This abundance of wild flowers is due partly to the lime in the soil, and partly to its impoverishment by centuries of **grazing** by sheep or rabbits – the poor soil prevents ranker plants from elbowing out the flowers, and any that do take root are quickly cropped short by the animals. The reason that many downland flanks are today developing patches of coarse grass and scrub is that grazing has ceased.

The artificial **fertilization** of downland and meadowland, by encouraging the growth of grasses, wipes out wild flowers almost as effectively as spraying a herbicide. Communities of pepper saxifrage, great burnet and adder's-tongue fern are all good indicators of old meadowland, but a consequence of modern high-tech farming is that many of the modest downland and meadowland flowers are now rare on farmland and are more likely to be observed on **roadside verges**. Indeed, the latter sometimes constitute a record of the botany lost from the ploughed and planted field on the other side of the fence. Sadly, these displaced species have no security here, their cramped populations being too small to guarantee survival after harsh summers or insect attacks. Hardly at risk, however, are the **cow parsleys** – in the plural since their massed ranks disguise a succession of different species. Originally growing in woodland glades, cow parsleys are now typical of English country lanes, and once again their presence is largely determined by human interference – ie by the intensity of trimming.

It's a similar story with **woodland flowers**, whose growth is encouraged by traditional **coppicing**, which regularly opens up the soil to the sun. Indeed the typical thick carpet of **bluebells** is as much due to coppicing as to the mild Atlantic climate, and masses of bluebells can often indicate an old wood, especially if backed by early purple orchids and wood anemones. **Snowdrop** woods are often indicative of the former presence of a monastery – a European flower with a natural range that ends in Normandy, the snowdrop was grown here to celebrate Candlemas in February, and quickly spread beyond the monastery walls. Of course, soil conditions and other natural factors are extremely influential too, resulting in different types of flower being found in different types of woodland. Thus some **beech woods** are famous for their white or purplish **helleborines** and other orchids; **ash woods**, which grow on limestone, are known for **lily of the valley** and the dusky red **bloody cranesbill**.

Ancient **ploughland** was distinguished by blue cornflower and yellow corn marigold, but only **poppies** seem able to survive modern farming. **Heathers** are characteristic of the bleak **moorlands**, where – in the very wet areas – you might also find the delicate flowers of **cranberry**, the brilliant yellow **bog asphodel** and the insect-trapping **sundew**. The higher zones of the Lake District and Pennine hills might be as colourful as the Alpine slopes were it not for centuries of hard grazing, but white **mountain avens**, dusky **saxifrage** and pink **moss campion** can still be found on rock faces out of the reach of sheep. On **heathland**, but not moorland, heathers are often accompanied by yellow **broom** and **gorse**; but both share yellow **tormentil**, pink **lousewort** and dainty blue **harebell**.

English **wetland** and **water** plants have evolved from land-growing species, a kinship that's evident from the close resemblance of the white **water crowfoots** and the buttercups – only the **water lilies** have no surviving relatives on dry land. Among the most attractive wild flowers of these habitats are the gold **kingcup** – popular with Victorian botanists and thus often found in the vicinity of granges and

rectories – and the **bogbean**, with its creamy pink-fringed petals. Pollution and disturbance are major threats to wetland plants, as is evident on the Norfolk Broads, where holiday craft have eradicated plants from all but a few lagoons.

Communities of wild flowers manage to flourish even in the seemingly harsh conditions of the **sea shore**, none of them more colourful than the blue-tinted **sea holly** and the yellow **horned-poppy**, which grow out on the bare sand. A host of flowers grows on the back shore, where the sand is harder and broken shells add lime to the ground, while on the edges of salt marshes you'll come across **sea lavender**, **sea aster** and **thrift**, among a variety of other species.

BIRDS

The destruction of the countryside has had a severe impact on England's 130 resident **bird** species – even the ubiquitous blackbird perhaps totals only three million pairs, and these numbers can plummet in a harsh winter. **Seabirds** such as gannets, gulls, fulmars and cormorants safe on their offshore bolt holes are virtually the only species unaffected by increasing urbanization. Nonetheless, an extraordinary variety of birds still thrives on mainland England.

Some birds are uniquely adapted to live with certain trees – such as the crossbill, which has a beak that has evolved to prise open fir cones – but in general, **woodland** birds select their habitat according to the profile of the wood rather than the actual species of tree it contains. Thus an acre of dense oak wood may hold more than a dozen types of songbird, while in the more open beech wood only the **wood warbler** is likely to nest. The **nightingale**, found only in the south of England, prefers the low bushy growth of recently coppiced woods, which it abandons seven years after the cut – another example of the link between land use and wildlife.

Over the centuries some species have become typical of the **farmed countryside**, such as the **rook**, **linnet**, **bunting** and the **barn owl**, which was encouraged to nest in barns as a rat catcher – often a hole was left in a side wall for the bird to enter. A recent arrival is the **collared dove**, which first nested in England in 1955, and is partial to the spills of grain from barley farms. The **pheasant**, originally raised and released for sport, now breeds wild in large numbers.

Game birds are a case apart, however, and their control can be an influence on the countryside. Shooting woods are often landscaped to steer pheasants into the line of fire, while belts of weed are now being left around fields to sustain **partridges**. The August **grouse** shoot has an effect on moorland, as large areas of heather are burnt to encourage fresh green growth to feed the birds.

Numerous species are adapted to specific environments, such as the **freshwater birds**, which split into two general groups – the **dipper** and a few other species that like the rushing upland streams, and the larger group that includes the "diving" and "dabbling" **ducks** found on lowland waters.

Birds that are found in every type of habitat are the opportunistic **scavengers** such as the **crow**, which is now so widespread that its "natural" home is not known. Persecution is sometimes a key factor in the distribution of scavengers and **raptors**. For instance, a couple of hundred years of shotguns and gamekeeping have forced the **golden eagle** back to one or two pairs in the Lake District, whilst the once common **red kite** has been pushed out to Wales. Similarly, **peregrines**, the bane of pigeon-racers' lives, are now found only on remote moors and sea cliffs and even **buzzards** are far from numerous.

Migrants are a key feature of English birdlife. **Swifts**, **swallows** and **martins** are easy to spot at the start of the summer, and of course the **cuckoo** has a distinctive call, as does the **chiffchaff**, an even earlier arrival from the south, with an unmistakable song that gives it its name. Many birds retreat from the cold of the Arctic to winter here, common examples including the **brent goose**, **barnacle goose**, **whooper swan** and **Bewick's swan**. Just as many species stop off on longer winter journeys to rest and feed, with English estuaries often safeguarding European stocks – the Dee for example regularly feeds hundred-thousand-strong flocks of **grey plover**, **oystercatcher** and numerous other waders.

Migration can be a relatively local affair, however. The **curlew**, a wader with a particularly plaintive cry, nests on the moors of the Pennines and elsewhere but in winter flies down to the seashore. The **kingfisher** similarly forsakes the frozen streams for the coast. English birds are surprisingly mobile in winter too, when hedgerow blackbirds often fly far afield in search of food and even blue tits, which might seem to have a range not much bigger than a back garden, may well fly daily miles across a county.

MAMMALS

Most of England's **mammals** are originally **woodland** species that moved into the territory during the period when the wildwood became established. There have been some changes since then, of course: the wolf and bear have gone, as has the beaver, which has left just a memory of its presence in the name of Beverley and a few other town names. The wildcat has left England for Scotland, but the **pine marten** is holding its own, thanks to the massive spread of conifer plantations.

There have been changes of habitat too: the **red deer**, for example, forced out of the woodlands by coppicing, is now found wild on open upland such as the Lake District, the herds seen in forests and parks being semi-domesticated. The **fallow deer** was brought over by the Romans and became a favourite target for the baronial hunt. The native **roe deer**, hunted almost to extinction two hundred years ago, was reintroduced, and is now the deer most often seen in the open countryside, although like all deer species they are shy and usually active only around dawn and dusk. **Sika deer**, rather smaller than red deer, were introduced in the seventeenth century, while the pig-like **muntjac** and small **Chinese water deer** are more recent arrivals, descended from wildlife park escapees. Other mammalian oddities are the goats living wild in the Lake District, the semi-wild ponies of the New Forest and Dartmoor and the wallabies that bounce around the Peak District.

Badgers link the woodlands and more open terrain, preferring to dig their burrows (or setts) among trees, though their foraging trails run out into the fields where they dig for young rabbits and earthworms. The sett entrance is a wide, clean hole – if you see a sizeable burrow littered with food remnants, the odds are that you're looking at a **fox**'s "earth". Badgers and foxes are associated with darkness, but it's likely their nocturnal activities are a human-influenced modification – foxes are often active during daylight hours in areas where they feel safe (you can even see them in suburban gardens), and badgers forage by day in quiet places such as remote coastal valleys. However, the **dormouse** – a species recognized by its squirrel-like tail – is a truly nocturnal animal, and one of the few true indigenous hibernators. It is typical of hazel coppice, building its nest from the bark of the honeysuckle that is usually found growing here – peeled stems can be the clue to its presence.

The **grey squirrel**, one of the most familiar English "wild" animals, is an introduction from North America that has virtually ousted the native red squirrel – though there's evidence that a strain of super-resilient red is fighting back in the Merseyside area. **Hares** are native – the brown hare found in the lowlands, the grey in some Pennine areas – but the **rabbit** was introduced in Norman times to be raised for its meat and fur. Having escaped and bred relentlessly, the rabbit has for centuries been a natural lawnmower, helping to create the fine sward of the chalk downlands and other grasslands.

Rabbits are preyed on by **stoats** and **weasels**, which also prey on **mice**, **voles** and **shrews**. These similar small species may share some larders, but generally do not compete with each other for food: bank voles for example, eat seeds, field voles eat grass, and the sharp-nosed shrew has a mainly insect diet and is almost ceaselessly active, needing to eat its own weight every day. Like the blue cornflower, the **harvest mouse** has fled the modern arable fields, now making its nest high amongst the reedbeds of waterways. Of the purely wetland species, the **water rat** (in fact a vole) is widespread and the **otter** is making a comeback in a few areas, despite water pollution and disturbance to its nesting "holts". The otter also has a serious competitor in the **mink**, a species escaped from fur farms but well equipped to survive in the wild, being capable of swimming after fish and climbing up to birds' nests.

On the coast, **common seals** haul out on the mud flats of the Wash to give birth in June, whereas **grey seals** are more common on rocky coasts, where they give birth in noisy "rookeries" in December. Only decades ago, almost every seaside resort used to boast its "own" **porpoises** or **dolphins**; such semi-resident animals have largely disappeared from the

bays, although visitors are sometimes seen, and the occasional whale might swim up one of the larger estuaries.

In built-up areas, in addition to foxes and hedgehogs, **bats** are a familiar sight at dusk. Contrary to myth, they rarely nest in belfries (with their sensitive hearing, the bells would drive them demented), preferring the warm roof-spaces and cladding of modern houses.

REPTILES, FISH AND INSECTS

For the **adder** (England's only venomous species) and **grass snake**, deserted railway cuttings offer a palatable replacement for more natural habitats – the latter is especially fond of wet places. Things are more difficult for the **smooth snake**, which is totally reliant on fragmented heathland and is therefore now comparatively rare – the same is true of the **sand lizard**. The **common lizard** has fared better. The clearance of field ponds means that springtime frogspawn is harder to find – the modern **frog** stronghold is in fact the garden pond. **Common toads** rely more on ancestral breeding ponds, to which they travel miles: some local conservation groups even organize toad patrols at key road crossings. The scuttling **natterjack toad** is also rare, restricted to a few sand dunes and similar sites. **Newts** are most obvious in spring – like the other amphibians they tend to spend most of the year hidden away on land.

The most natural of the fish populations are those of the classic game fish, the native **brown trout** and **salmon**, the first still plentiful in the downland streams of the south and the mountain streams of the north, the latter migratory and nowadays only common in the tumbling northern rivers. England's coarse fish – all freshwater species unrelated to the salmon family – have widely interbred with specimens raised in reservoirs and farms for sport; similarly the American rainbow trout, once found only in commercial pens, has escaped to breed wild in some areas. That other famed migrator, the **eel**, is still caught in numbers in the Somerset levels and in the East Anglian fens.

There are over three thousand different species of beetle in England – but few are noticed apart from the sizeable **maybug** and **stag beetle**, both most common near old semi-natural oak woods in the south. Bees, flies, gnats and wasps are of course very widespread, as are the dazzling **mayflies** and **dragonflies**, to be found on England's cleaner bodies of water. Many species of **butterfly** are fairly widespread in scrubby places, with the gorgeous **peacock butterfly** often seen in gardens. Deserted railway cuttings are a stronghold of some of the commoner **browns** and **skippers**. Generally, though, butterflies are choosy about the plants on which they lay their eggs, which means that many species are closely linked with very specific habitats. The **Adonis** and **chalkhill blues** need the low-growing horseshoe vetch of old downland, while the **fritillaries** need the violets of old oak woodland and the most exotic of all, the **swallowtail**, relies on a relative of cow parsley that grows in the Norfolk Broads, and is thus rarely seen elsewhere. However, some swallowtails may fly in from France during the summer, when the migrant **clouded yellow** often arrives in large numbers along the south coast.

BOOKS

Most of the books listed below are in print and in paperback – those that are out of print (o/p) should be easy to track down in second-hand book shops. Publishers are detailed with the British publisher first, separated by an oblique slash from the US publisher, where both exist. Where books are published in only one of these countries, UK or US precedes the publisher's name; where the book is published by the same company in both countries, the name of the company appears just once.

TRAVEL AND JOURNALS

Bill Bryson, *Notes from a Small Island* (Black Swan/Avon). Bryson's best-selling amd highly amusing account of his farewell journey round Britain.

Nick Danziger, *Danziger's Britain* (Flamingo/Trafalgar Square). A well-timed journey through the "other Britain" of council estates and poverty. Captures the mood of the underclass created by Thatcher and sets a tall order for the present Blairite administration.

Daniel Defoe, *Tour through the Whole Island of Great Britain* (Penguin). Classic travelogue, opening a window onto Britain in the 1720s.

Charles Jennings, *Up North* (UK Abacus: Little, Brown). A provocative, but very readable account of a journey round the north of England, by a self-confessed southerner.

H.V. Morton, *In Search of London* (UK Methuen). Snapshots of London life in the 1920s.

Samuel Pepys, *The Diary of Samuel Pepys* (UK Fontana). Pepys kept a voluminous diary from 1660 until 1669, recording the fall of the Commonwealth, the Restoration, the Great Plague and the Great Fire, as well as describing the daily life of the nation's capital. The unabridged version is published in eleven weighty tomes; Fontana has published an abridged version.

J.B. Priestley, *English Journey* (o/p). Quirky account of Bradford-born author's travels around England in the 1930s.

Jonathan Raban, *Coasting* (UK Picador). Trip around the coast of England, with the occasional trip ashore in order to make supercilious remarks about the locals.

Paul Theroux, *The Kingdom by the Sea* (Penguin). Thoroughly bad-tempered critique of a depressed and drizzly nation.

Dorothy Wordsworth, *The Grasmere Journals* (Oxford University Press). Engaging diaries of William's sister, with whom he shared Dove Cottage in the Lake District.

HISTORY, SOCIETY AND POLITICS

Julian Barnes, *Letters from London (1990–1995)* (Picador/Vintage). Social and cultural commentary from *New Yorker* column covering fall of Thatcher and emergence of Blair.

Venerable Bede, *Ecclesiastical History of the English People* (Penguin). First-ever English history, written in seventh-century Northumbria.

Asa Briggs, *Social History of England* (Penguin/Random House). Immensely accessible overview of English life from Roman times to the 1980s.

Beatrix Campbell, *Diana Princess of Wales: How sexual politics shook the monarchy* (UK Women's Press). A little hastily written perhaps, but still the most penetrating insight into the life and times of Diana – and the appalling callousness of her in-laws. Read this and you'll never want Charles to be king (if you ever wanted a king at all).

Alan Clark, *Diaries* (UK Phoenix). Candid, conceited and often cutting insight into the heart of Thatcher's government by controversial former minister. Easily the most interesting of the barrow loads of political memoirs churned out in the 1980s and 1990s.

Friedrich Engels, *The Condition of the Working Class in England* (Penguin). Portrait of life in England's hellish industrial towns, written in 1844 when Engels was only 24.

Gretchen Gerzina, *Black England* (UK Allison & Busby). An interesting study of the role of Black people in Britain's history.

Mark Girouard, *Life in the English Country House* (Yale University Press). Fascinating documentation of day-to-day existence with the landed gentry; packed with the sort of facts that get left out by tour guides.

Stuart Hall, **Martin Jacques and others**, *The Politics of Thatcherism* (UK Lawrence & Wishart). A collection of essays on the impact of Thatcherism by leading left-wing academics of the 1980s.

Christopher Hill, *The English Revolution* (UK Penguin); *The World Turned Upside-Down* (UK Penguin). Britain's foremost Marxist historian, Hill is without doubt the most interesting writer on the Civil War and Commonwealth period.

Eric Hobsbawm *The Age of Revolution (1789–1848)*; *The Age of Capital (1848-1875)*; *The Age of Empire (1875-1914)*; and *The Age of Extremes (1914-1991)* (all Abacus: Little, Brown/Vintage). A series of four books dealing with the development of Europe since the French Revolution.

W.G. Hoskins, *The Making of the English Landscape* (UK Penguin). Absorbing account of the changing English countryside from pre-Roman times to the present day.

Arthur Marwick, *British Society since 1945* (UK Penguin). Readable social history, taking you up to the late 1980s.

Brian Moynahan, *The British Century* (UK Seven Dials). A lavish coffee-table book telling the story of the twentieth century in black-and-white photographs.

George Orwell, *The Road to Wigan Pier*, *Down and Out in Paris and London* (both Penguin/Harcourt Brace). *Wigan Pier* depicts the effects of the Great Depression on the industrial communities of Lancashire and Yorkshire; *Down and Out* is Orwell's tramp's-eye view of the world, written with first-hand experience – the London section is particularly harrowing.

Sheila Rowbotham, *Hidden from History* (Pluto). An uncompromising account of the last 300 years of women's oppression in Britain.

W.A. Speck, *A Concise History of Britain* (Cambridge University Press). Straightforward political history from 1707 to 1975.

A.J.P. Taylor, *English History 1914–45* (UK Oxford University Press). Thought-provoking survey from Britain's finest populist historian.

E.P. Thompson, *The Making of the English Working Class* (Penguin/Random House). A seminal text – essential reading for anyone who wants to understand the fabric of British society.

G.M. Trevelyan, *English Social History* (UK Penguin). A "history of people with the politics left out" in Trevelyan's own words – liberal social history from Chaucer to 1901.

REGIONAL GUIDES

Paul Bailey (ed), *Oxford Book of London* (OUP). Typically authoritative Oxford anthology of writings, observations and opinions about the capital.

Christopher Hibbert (ed), *Pimlico County History Guides* (o/p). An informative series giving a detailed history of selected English counties. Counties covered include Bedfordshire, Cambridgeshire, Dorset, Lincolnshire, Norfolk, Oxfordshire, Somerset (with Bath and Bristol), Suffolk and Sussex.

Daphne du Maurier, *Vanishing Cornwall* (UK Penguin). Good overall account of Cornwall from an author who lived most of her life there.

Jan Morris ed. *Oxford Book of Oxford* (OUP). Adulatory but inspiring collection on Oxford by the famous travel writer and city-phile.

Alan Myers, *Myers' Literary Guide: The North East* (UK Carcanet). Exhaustive account of the Northeast's literary heritage, including details of any writer who ever spent any time in the region.

A. Wainwright *A Coast to Coast Walk* (Michael Joseph/Mermaid). Beautiful palm-sized guide book by acclaimed English hiker and Lake District expert. Printed from his handwritten notes and sketched maps. Also in the series are seven authoritative books covering a variety of walks and climbs in the Lake District. Not all are available in the US.

Ben Weinreb and Christopher Hibbert, *The London Encyclopaedia* (o/p). More than 1000 pages of concisely presented and well-illustrated information on London past and present – the most fascinating single book on the capital.

Gilbert White, *Natural History of Selborne* (Penguin). Masterpiece of nature writing, observing the seasons in a Hampshire village.

Ordnance Survey Walks (UK OS and Jerrold). Series of practical guides with maps and route descriptions to popular outdoor spots such as the Yorkshire Dales, Chilterns, Cornwall and Cotswolds. Also useful are spiral-bound series of Cycles (UK Hamlyn) describing routes in such places as Cumbria and the Lakes, Dorset, Hampshire and the Isle of Wight.

ART, ARCHITECTURE AND ARCHEOLOGY

Nicholas Best and Jason Hawkes *Historic Britain from the Air* (UK Orion). Beautiful aerial photos illustrate this geographical overview of Britain from Roman times to the aftermath of the Blitz.

Richard Bisgrove, *The National Trust Book of the English Garden* (o/p). Excellent socio-cultural-botanical history, making the best introduction to the subject.

Robert Harbison, *Shell Guide to English Parish Churches* (UK Deutsch). Refreshingly opinionated and lushly illustrated survey of some of England's finest buildings.

Samantha Hardingham, *England: a guide to recent architecture* (Ellipsis/Knickerbocker). A handy pocket-sized book detailing the best of England's modern buildings.

Andrew Hayes, *Archaeology of the British Isles* (St Martin's Press). Useful introduction to the subject from Stone Age caves to early medieval settlements.

Thomas Packenham, *Meetings With Remarkable Trees* (Orion/Random). Unusual but intriguing large-format picture book about the author's favourite sixty trees, delving into their character as much as the botany.

Nikolaus Pevsner, *The Englishness of English Art* (UK Penguin). Wide-ranging romp through English art concentrating on Hogarth, Reynolds, Blake and Constable, including a section on the Perpendicular style and landscape gardening.

Pevsner and others, *The Buildings of England* (UK Penguin). Magisterial series, at least one volume per county, covering just about every inhabitable structure in the country. This project was initially a one-man show, but later authors have revised Pevsner's text, inserting newer buildings but generally respecting the founder's personal tone.

T.W. Potter and Catherine Johns, *Roman Britain* (British Museum Press/Harvard University Press). Generously illustrated account of Roman occupation written by the British Museum's own curators.

LITERATURE CLASSICS

Jane Austen, *Pride and Prejudice; Sense and Sensibility; Emma* and *Persuasion* (all Penguin). All-time classics on manners, society and the pursuit of the happy ever after; all laced with bathos and ironic plot twists.

R.D. Blackmore, *Lorna Doone* (Penguin/Oxford University Press). Blackmore's swashbuckling, melodramatic romance, set on Exmoor, has done more for West Country tourism than anything else since.

James Boswell, *Life of Samuel Johnson* (Penguin). England's most famous man of letters and pioneer dictionary-maker has his engagingly low-life Scottish biographer to thank for the longevity of his reputation.

Charlotte Brontë, *Jane Eyre* (Penguin). Deep and harrowing and quietly feminist story of a much put-upon governess.

Emily Brontë, *Wuthering Heights* (Penguin). The ultimate bodice-ripper, complete with volcanic passions, craggy landscapes, ghostly presences and gloomy Calvinist villagers.

John Bunyan, *Pilgrim's Progress* (Penguin/Oxford University Press). Simple, allegorical tale of hero Christian's struggle to achieve salvation; a staple read for the masses until the onset of agnosticism this century.

Samuel Butler, *The Way of All Flesh* (Penguin). Popular Edwardian novel debunking orthodox Victorian pieties, partly set in Nottinghamshire.

Geoffrey Chaucer, *Canterbury Tales* (Penguin/Bantam). Fourteenth-century collection of bawdy verse tales told during a pilgrimage to Becket's shrine at Canterbury and translated into modern English blank verse.

Daniel Defoe, *Journal of a Plague Year* (Oxford University Press). An account of the Great Plague seen through the eyes of an East End saddler and written some sixty years after the event.

Charles Dickens, *Bleak House; David Copperfield; Little Dorrit; Oliver Twist; Hard Times* (all Penguin). Many of Dickens's novels are set in London, including *Bleak House, Oliver Twist* and *Little Dorrit*, which contain some of his most trenchant pieces of social analysis; *Hard Times*, however, is set in a Lancashire mill town, while *David Copperfield* draws on Dickens's own unhappy experiences as a boy, with much of the action taking place in Kent and Norfolk.

George Eliot, *Scenes of Clerical Life; Middlemarch* (both Penguin); *Mill on the Floss* (Penguin/Oxford University Press). Eliot (real name Mary Ann Evans) wrote mostly about the county of her birth, Warwickshire, setting for the three depressing tales from her fictional debut,

Scenes of Clerical Life. Middlemarch is a gargantuan portrayal of English provincial life prior to the Reform Act of 1832, while *Mill on the Floss* is based on her own childhood experiences.

Henry Fielding, *Tom Jones* (Penguin). Mock-epic comic novel detailing the exploits of its lusty orphan-hero, set in Somerset and London.

Elizabeth Gaskell, *Sylvia's Lovers; Mary Barton* (Penguin). *Sylvia's Lovers* is set in a Whitby (Monkshaven in the novel) beset by press-gangs, while *Mary Barton* takes place in Manchester and has strong Chartist undertones.

Thomas Hardy, *Far from the Madding Crowd; The Mayor of Casterbridge; Tess of the D'Urbervilles; Jude the Obscure* (all Penguin). Hardy's novels contain some famously evocative descriptions of his native Dorset, but at the time of their publication it was Hardy's defiance of conventional pieties that attracted most attention: *Tess*, in which the heroine has a baby out of wedlock and commits murder, shocked his contemporaries, while his bleakest novel, the Oxford-set *Jude the Obscure*, provoked such a violent response that Hardy gave up novel-writing altogether.

Jerome K. Jerome, *Three Men in a Boat* (Penguin). Light-hearted accident-prone paddle on the River Thames.

Rudyard Kipling, *Stalky & Co* (Oxford University Press). Nine stories about a mischievous trio of schoolboys, drawn from Kipling's experiences of public school in Devon.

Sir Thomas Malory, *La Morte d'Arthur* (Penguin/Northwestern University Press). Fifteenth-century tales of King Arthur and the Knights of the Round Table, written while the author was in London's Newgate Prison.

Thomas De Quincey, *Confessions of an English Opium Eater* (UK Penguin). Tripping out with the most famous literary drug-taker after Coleridge – *Fear and Loathing in Las Vegas* it isn't, but neither is this a simple cautionary tale.

William Shakespeare, *Complete Works* (Oxford University Press). The entire output at a bargain price. For individual plays, you can't beat the Arden Shakespeare series, each volume containing illuminating notes and good introductory essays.

Lawrence Sterne, *Tristram Shandy* (Oxford University Press/Penguin). Anarchic, picaresque eighteenth-century ramblings based on life in a small English village, and full of bizarre textual devices – like an all-black page in mourning for one of the characters.

William Makepeace Thackeray, *Vanity Fair* (Penguin). A sceptical but compassionate overview of English capitalist society by one of the leading realists of the mid-nineteenth century.

Anthony Trollope, *Barchester Towers* (Penguin). The "Barsetshire" novels, of which *Barchester Towers* is the best known, are set in and around a fictional version of Salisbury. John Major's favourite author.

Izaak Walton, *Compleat Angler* (Oxford University Press). Light-hearted seventeenth-century fishing guide set on London's River Lea, sprinkled with poems and songs, which has gone through more reprints than any other comparable book in the English language.

TWENTIETH-CENTURY WORKS

Kate Atkinson, *Behind the Scenes At the Museum* (Black Swan/Picador). Amusing, lucid, highly engaging saga about an extended Yorkshire family.

Peter Ackroyd, *English Music* (UK Penguin). A typical Ackroyd novel, constructing parallels between interwar London and distant epochs to conjure a kaleidoscopic vision of English culture. His other novels, such as *Chatterton*, *Hawksmoor* and *The House of Doctor Dee*, are variations on his preoccupation with the English psyche's darker depths.

Kingsley Amis, *Lucky Jim* (Penguin). Difficult to believe that an establishment figure like Amis was once one of the "Angry Young Men" of the 1950s. *Lucky Jim*, the novel that made him famous, is hilariously funny in the opinion of many.

Martin Amis, *London Fields* (UK Vintage). "Ferociously witty, scabrously scatological and balefully satirical" observation of low-life London, or pretentious drivel from literary London's favourite bad boy, depending on your viewpoint.

Arnold Bennett, *Anna of the Five Towns; Clayhanger* trilogy (Penguin/Everyman). Bennett's first novel, *Anna*, is the story of a miser's daughter and like the later *Clayhanger* trilogy is set in the Potteries.

Joseph Conrad, *The Secret Agent* (Penguin/Modern). Spy story based on the 1906 anarchist bombing of Greenwich Observatory, exposing the hypocrisies of both the police and anarchists.

Ford Madox Ford, *Parade's End* (UK Carcanet). Ford's tetralogy, one of the great unread masterpieces of English literature, is an unsurpassed evocation of the passing of old Tory England in the aftermath of World War I.

E.M. Forster, *Howard's End* (Penguin/Signet). Bourgeois angst in Hertfordshire and Shropshire; the best book by one of the country's best-loved modern novelists.

John Fowles, *The Collector* (Vintage/Abacus: Little, Brown); *The French Lieutenant's Woman*, *Daniel Martin* (Vintage/Back Bay). *The Collector*, Fowles' first, is a psychological thriller in which the heroine is kidnapped by a psychotic pools-winner, the story being told once by each protagonist. *The French Lieutenant's Woman*, set in Lyme Regis on the Dorset coast, is a tricksy neo-Victorian novel with a famous DIY ending. *Daniel Martin* is a dense, realistic novel set in postwar Britain.

Stella Gibbons, *Cold Comfort Farm* (Penguin). Merciless parody of primitivist rural fiction of the type popularized by the likes of Mary Webb.

William Golding, *The Spire* (Faber/Harcourt Brace). Atmospheric novel centred on the building of a cathedral spire, taking place in a thinly disguised medieval Salisbury.

Robert Graves, *Goodbye to All That* (Penguin/Anchor). Horrific and wryly humorous memoirs of boarding school and World War I trenches, followed by postwar trauma and life in Wales, Oxford and Egypt.

Graham Greene, *Brighton Rock*, *The Human Factor*, and *Heart of the Matter* (all Penguin). Three of the best from the prolific Greene: *Brighton Rock* is a melancholic thriller with heavy Catholic overtones, set in the criminal underworld of a seaside resort; *The Human Factor*, written some 40 years later, probes the underworld of London's spies; while the *Heart of the Matter* (Penguin) is a searching and very English novel that noses round the Anglo-Catholic mind.

A.E. Housman, *A Shropshire Lad* (Penguin/Dover). Collection of bucolic and love poems, popular for their lyrical gloom and idealized vision of the English countryside.

D.H. Lawrence, *Sons and Lovers*; *The Rainbow*, *Women in Love* (all Penguin); *Selected Short Stories* (Penguin). Before he got his funny ideas about sex and became all messianic, Lawrence wrote magnificent prose on daily working-class life in Nottinghamshire's pit villages – or rather his vision of it. His interpretation never went down well with the locals and even now his name can raise a snarl or two. Lawrence's early short stories contain some of his finest writing, as does the early *Sons and Lovers*, a fraught, autobiographical novel. With *The Rainbow* and *Women in Love*, his other two major novels, the loopy sub-Nietzschean theorizing slowly gains the upper hand.

Laurie Lee, *Cider with Rosie* (UK Penguin). Reminiscences of adolescent bucolic frolics in the Cotswolds during the 1920s.

Somerset Maugham, *Liza of Lambeth* (o/p); *Of Human Bondage* (o/p). Maugham rated himself a "second-rater" but these books are packed with vivid local colour: *Liza of Lambeth* is a depiction of Cockney low-life; *Of Human Bondage* is set in Whitstable and Canterbury and based on Maugham's own experiences as an orphan.

Daphne du Maurier, *Frenchman's Creek* (UK Arrow); *Jamaica Inn* (Arrow/Avon); *Rebecca* (Arrow/Avon). Nail-biting, swashbuckling romantic novels set in the author's adopted home of Cornwall.

Alan Sillitoe, *Saturday Night, Sunday Morning* (Flamingo/Plumsock Mesoamerican). Gritty account of factory life and sexual shenanigans in Nottingham in the late 1950s.

Iain Sinclair, *Down River* (o/p). A rambling, fictional journey through contemporary London.

David Storey, *This Sporting Life* (UK Methuen); *Saville* (UK Vintage). Storey's first novel, *This Sporting Life*, is a grimly realistic portrayal of a Rugby League player in the north of England. *Saville*, which won him the Booker Prize, revolves around his favourite themes of mid-life crisis and loss of class identity.

Graham Swift, *Waterland* and *Last Orders* (Picador/Vintage). *Waterland* is a family saga set in East Anglia's fenlands – excellent on the history and appeal of this superficially drab landscape. Booker-Prize-winning *Last Orders* reminisces with four old folk on a trip to the south coast to scatter a friend's ashes.

Adam Thorpe, *Ulverton* (UK Vintage). Imaginative re-creation of life in a small town in southwest England over the course of three centuries.

Evelyn Waugh, *Sword of Honour* trilogy (Penguin/Knopf); *Brideshead Revisited* (Penguin/Abacus: Little, Brown). The trilogy is essentially a lightweight remake of Ford's *Parade's*

End (see p.946), albeit laced with some of Waugh's funniest set-pieces. The best-selling *Brideshead Revisited* is possibly his worst book, rank with snobbery, nostalgia and money-worship.

Virginia Woolf, *Orlando* (Penguin/Harcourt Brace); *Mrs Dalloway* (Penguin/Harcourt Brace). Woolf's lover, Vita Sackville-West, is the model for *Orlando*, whose life spans four centuries and both genders. *Mrs Dalloway*, which relates the thoughts of a London society hostess and a shell-shocked war veteran, sees Woolf's "stream of consciousness" style in full flow.

ANTHOLOGIES

English Mystery Plays, (Penguin). These simple Christian tales were produced annually in Chester, York, Wakefield and other great English towns, and are often revived even now.

English Verse, ed. J. Hayward (Penguin). Overview from Sir Thomas Wyatt to Auden, Spender and MacNiece.

Four English Comedies, (Penguin). Laugh a minute from Congreve, Jonson, Goldsmith and Sheridan.

Landmarks of Modern British Drama, (o/p). The 1960s volume features plays by Wesker, Osborne, Pinter and Orton; the 1970s volume covers the likes of Ayckbourn, Brenton, Stoppard and Caryl Churchill.

Literature of Renaissance England, ed. Hollander & Kermode (Oxford University Press). Spenser's *Faerie Queene*, a bit of Marlowe, Shakespeare's Sonnets, Donne, Jonson and Milton.

Modern British Literature, ed. Hollander & Kermode (Oxford University Press). Weighted towards the classic writers of the earlier part of the century – Hardy, Conrad, Lawrence etc.

The New Poetry, ed. Hulse, Kennedy & Morley (UK Bloodaxe). Over 50 poets, all born since World War II.

The Restoration and the Eighteenth Century, ed. Price (Oxford University Press). From Dryden, Swift and Pope to Sterne.

Victorian Prose and Poetry, ed. Trilling & Bloom (Oxford University Press). Carlyle, Ruskin, Tennyson, Rossetti and Wilde's *Ballad of Reading Gaol*.

GLOSSARIES

ARCHITECTURAL TERMS

Aedicule Small decorative niche formed by two columns or pilasters supporting a gable.

Aisle Clear spaces parallel to the nave, usually with lower ceiling than the nave.

Altar Table at which the Eucharist is celebrated, at the east end of the church. (When church is not aligned to the geographical east, the altar end is still referred to as the "east" end.)

Ambulatory Passage behind the chancel.

Apse The curved or polygonal east end of a church.

Arcade Row of arches on top of columns or piers, supporting a wall.

Ashlar Dressed building stone worked to a smooth finish.

Bailey Area enclosed by castle walls.

Baldachin Canopy over an altar.

Barbican Defensive structure built in front of main gate.

Barrel vault Continuous rounded vault, like a semi-cylinder.

Boss A decorative carving at the meeting point of the lines of a vault.

Box pew Form of church seating in which each row is enclosed by high, thin wooden panels.

Broach spire Octagonal spire rising straight out of a square tower.

Buttress Stone support for a wall; some buttresses are wholly attached to the wall, others take the form of a tower with a connecting arch, known as a "flying buttress".

Capital Upper section of a column, usually carved.

Chancel Section of the church where the altar is located.

Chantry Small chapel in which masses were said for the soul of the person who financed its construction; none built after the reign of Henry VIII.

Choir Area in which the church service is conducted; next to or same as chancel.

Clerestory Upper storey of nave, containing a line of windows.

Coffering Regular recessed spaces set into a ceiling.

Corbel Jutting stone support, often carved.

Crenellations Battlements with square indentations.

Crossing The intersection of the nave and the transepts.

Decorated Middle Gothic style; about 1280–1380.

Dogtooth Form of early Gothic decorative stonework, looking like raised "X"s.

Dormer Window raised above the main roof.

Early English First phase of Gothic architecture in England, about 1150–1280.

Fan vault Late Gothic form of vaulting, in which the area between walls and ceiling is covered with stone ribs in the shape of an open fan.

Finial Any decorated tip of an architectural feature.

Flushwork Kind of surface decoration in which tablets of white stone alternate with pieces of flint; very common in East Anglia.

Gallery A raised passageway.

Gargoyle Grotesque exterior carving, usually decorative form of water spout.

Hammer beam Type of ceiling in which horizontal beams support vertical pieces that connect to the roof timbers.

Keep Main structure of a castle.

Lady Chapel Chapel dedicated to the Virgin, often found at the east end of major churches.

Lancet Tall, narrow and plain window.

Lantern Upper part of a dome or tower, often glazed.

Lunette Window or panel shaped like a half-moon.

Misericord Carved ledge below a tip-up seat, usually in choir stalls.

Motte Mound on which a castle keep stands.

Mullion Vertical strip between the panes of a window.

Nave The main part of the church to the west of the crossing.

Ogee Double curve; distinctive feature of Decorated style.

Oriel Projecting window.

Palladian Eighteenth-century classical style adhering to the principles of Andrea Palladio.

Pediment Triangular space above a window or doorway.

Perpendicular Late Gothic style, about 1380–1550.

Pier Massive column, often consisting of several fused smaller columns.

Pilaster Flat column set against a wall.

Reredos Painted or carved panel behind an altar.

Rood screen Wooden screen supporting a crucifix (or rood), separating the choir from the nave; few survived the Reformation.

Rose window Large circular window, divided into vaguely petal-shaped sections.

Sedilia Seats for the participants in the church service, usually on south side of the choir.

Stalls Seating for clergy in the choir area of a church.

Tracery Pattern formed by narrow bands of stone in a window or on a wall surface.

Transept Sections of the main body of the church at right angles to the choir and nave.

Tympanum Panel over a doorway, often carved in medieval churches.

Vault Arched ceiling.

ANGLO-AMERICAN TERMS

Bill Restaurant check.

Biscuit Cookie or a cracker.

Bonnet Car hood.

Boot Car trunk.

Caravan Trailer.

Car park Parking lot.

Cheap Inexpensive.

Chemist Pharmacist.

Chips French fries.

Coach Bus.

Crisps Potato chips.

Dual Carriageway Divided highway.

Dustbin Trash can.

First floor Second floor.

Flat Apartment.

Fortnight Two weeks.

Ground floor First floor.

Hire Rent.

High Street Main Street.

Jam Jelly.

Jelly Jell-O.

Jumble sale Yard sale.

Jumper Sweater.

Lay-by Road shoulder.

Leaflet Pamphlet.

Lift Elevator.

Lorry Truck.

Motorway Highway.

Off-licence Liquor store.

Pants Underwear.

Petrol Gasoline.

Pudding Dessert.

Queue Line.

Return ticket Round-trip ticket.

Roundabout Rotary interchange.

Single carriageway Non-divided highway.

Single ticket One-way ticket.

Stalls Orchestra seats.

Stone Fourteen pounds (weight).

Subway Pedestrian passageway.

Sweets Candy.

Tights Pantyhose.

Torch Flashlight.

Trainers Sneakers.

Trousers Pants.

Vest Undershirt.

INDEX

Stay in touch with us!

ROUGH*NEWS* **is Rough Guides' free newsletter.
In four issues a year we give you news, travel
issues, music reviews, readers' letters and the
latest dispatches from authors on the road.**

I would like to receive ROUGH*NEWS*: please put me on your free mailing list.

NAME . . . .

ADDRESS . . . .

Please clip or photocopy and send to: Rough Guides, 62–70 Shorts Gardens, London WC2H 9AB,
England or Rough Guides, 375 Hudson Street, New York, NY 10014, USA.

ROUGH GUIDES: Travel

Amsterdam
Andalucia
Australia

Austria
Bali & Lombok
Barcelona
Belgium &
  Luxembourg
Belize
Berlin
Brazil
Britain
Brittany &
  Normandy
Bulgaria
California
Canada
Central America
Chile
China
Corfu & the
  Ionian Islands
Corsica
Costa Rica
Crete
Cuba
Cyprus
Czech & Slovak
  Republics

Dodecanese
Dominican
  Republic
Egypt
England
Europe
Florida
France
French Hotels &
  Restaurants 1999
Germany
Goa
Greece
Greek Islands
Guatemala
Hawaii
Holland
Hong Kong
  & Macau
Hungary
India
Indonesia
Ireland
Israel & the
  Palestinian
  Territories
Italy
Jamaica
Japan
Jordan

Kenya
Laos
London
London
  Restaurants
Los Angeles
Malaysia,
  Singapore &
  Brunei
Mallorca &
  Menorca
Maya World
Mexico
Morocco
Moscow
Nepal
New England
New York
New Zealand
Norway
Pacific Northwest
Paris
Peru
Poland
Portugal
Prague
Provence & the
  Côte d'Azur
The Pyrenees
Romania

St Petersburg
San Francisco
Sardinia
Scandinavia
Scotland
Scottish Highlands
  & Islands
Sicily
Singapore

South Africa
Southern India
Southwest USA
Spain
Sweden
Syria
Thailand
Trinidad & Tobago
Tunisia
Turkey
Tuscany & Umbria
USA
Venice
Vienna
Vietnam
Wales
Washington DC
West Africa
Zimbabwe &
  Botswana

AVAILABLE AT ALL GOOD BOOKSHOPS

ROUGH GUIDES: Mini Guides, Travel Specials and Phrasebooks

MINI GUIDES

Antigua
Bangkok
Barbados
Big Island of
  Hawaii
Boston
Brussels
Budapest

Sydney
Tokyo
Toronto

Dublin
Edinburgh
Florence
Honolulu
Jerusalem
Lisbon
London
  Restaurants
Madrid
Maui
Melbourne
New Orleans
Seattle
St Lucia

TRAVEL SPECIALS

First-Time Asia
First-Time
  Europe
Women Travel

PHRASEBOOKS

Czech
Dutch

Egyptian Arabic
European
French
German
Greek
Hindi & Urdu
Hungarian
Indonesian
Italian
Japanese

Mandarin
  Chinese
Mexican
  Spanish
Polish
Portuguese
Russian
Spanish
Swahili
Thai
Turkish
Vietnamese

ROUGH GUIDES:
Reference and Music CDs

REFERENCE
Classical Music
Classical:
  100 Essential CDs
Drum'n'bass
House Music
Jazz
Music USA

Opera
Opera:
  100 Essential CDs
Reggae
Reggae:
  100 Essential CDs
Rock
Rock:
  100 Essential CDs
Techno
World Music
World Music:
  100 Essential CDs
English Football
European Football

Internet
Millennium

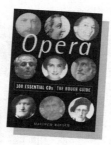

ROUGH GUIDE MUSIC CDs
Music of the
  Andes
Australian
  Aboriginal
Brazilian Music
Cajun & Zydeco

Classic Jazz
Music of
  Colombia
Cuban Music
Eastern Europe

Music of Egypt
English Roots
  Music
Flamenco
India & Pakistan
Irish Music
Music of Japan
Kenya & Tanzania
Native American
North African
Music of Portugal

Reggae
Salsa
Scottish Music
South African
  Music
Music of Spain
Tango
Tex-Mex
West African
  Music
World Music
World Music Vol 2
Music of
  Zimbabwe

the perfect getaway vehicle

low-price holiday car rental.

rent a car from holiday autos and you'll give yourself real freedom to explore your holiday destination. with great-value, fully-inclusive rates in over 4,000 locations worldwide, wherever you're escaping to, we're there to make sure you get excellent prices and superb service.

what's more, you can book now with complete confidence. our £5 undercut* ensures that you are guaranteed the best value for money in holiday destinations right around the globe.

drive away with a great deal, call holiday autos now on **0990 300 400** and quote ref RG.

holiday autos miles ahead

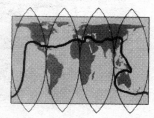